TAXATION OF
INDIVIDUAL
INCOME

TAXATION OF INDIVIDUAL INCOME

Eleventh Edition

J. Martin Burke
Professor of Law Emeritus
University of Montana
School of Law

Michael K. Friel
Professor of Law and Director
Graduate Tax Program
University of Florida
College of Law

Casebook ISBN: 978-1-6328-2442-4
Looseleaf ISBN: 978-1-6328-2444-8

Library of Congress Cataloging-in-Publication Data

Burke, J. Martin, author.
    Taxation of individual income / J. Martin Burke, Professor of Law University of Montana School of Law; Michael K. Friel, Professor of Law and Director, Graduate Tax Program University of Florida College of Law.—Eleventh Edition.
    pages cm
    ISBN 978-1-63282-442-4 (hardbound)
    1. Income tax—Law and legislation—United States—Cases. I. Friel, Michael K., author. II. Title.
KF6369.B87 2015
343.7305'2—dc23

2015014304

NOTE TO USERS

To ensure that you are using the latest materials available in this area, please be sure to periodically check the LexisNexis Law School web site for downloadable updates and supplements at www.lexisnexis.com/lawschool.

Editorial Offices
630 Central Ave., New Providence, NJ 07974 (908) 464-6800
201 Mission St., San Francisco, CA 94105-1831 (415) 908-3200
www.lexisnexis.com

MATTHEW◊BENDER

Dedication

To Jackie and Jonathan
and My Mother and Father — MKF

To My Mother and Father
and My Eleven Brothers and Sisters — JMB

Preface

Strange as it may sound, this preface is intended to be read by the students who use this text. We are, however, not unmindful of the temptation to turn past any preface — so we will keep it short:

If you are like many beginning tax students, you have no tax background and you approach the basic course somewhat warily, with a vague sense that the course is important and an accompanying concern that its complexities may be overwhelming. You shall find, we trust, that the complexities are manageable. But the course is indeed an important one. Tax issues pervade the practice of law. Lawyers need not be tax specialists, of course, but it seems fair to expect that a lawyer will have a working knowledge of the underlying principles and special vocabulary of the tax law so as to be able to recognize and discuss fact patterns raising common tax problems and thus avoid misdirecting a client.

This text approaches the study of individual income taxation through the problem method. We have chosen to use the problem method for specific reasons. It requires students to engage in an exacting analysis of facts and to synthesize rules and concepts. Students must work with facts over and over again, without the analysis of those facts being provided by someone else; and students must determine on their own the relative importance of facts given — and not given — rather than be told what is important. Issues are not framed by someone else, but must instead be extracted from the information presented. The problem method, in effect, encourages the development of problem solving skills. And problem solving is what lawyers ought to do and ought to do well. In sum, the text employs the problem method because we believe it to be the most effective, challenging and satisfying way to study the federal income taxation of individuals. We also believe the framework surrounding the problems themselves is critical, and with this in mind, the text has been designed as a series of self-contained chapters. We recommend the following approach to the study of each chapter.

Each chapter begins with a set of problems. Begin your study of the chapter by reading the problems carefully. Do not attempt to solve the problems at this point, but think about them as you read through the rest of the chapter; use the problems as a focus for your study of the materials that follow. After reading the problems, read the next two sections of the Chapter, which set forth the "objectives" and "vocabulary" for the chapter. The objectives will serve as a guide to the chapter and (following completion of the problems) they will also serve as a means of testing your comprehension of the principles, rules and techniques covered in the chapter. The vocabulary section highlights the significant terms and phrases introduced in the chapter. Tax law has its own vocabulary, and one of the fundamentals in problem solving is the ability to understand and apply the relevant terminology. The vocabulary section provides no definitions; rather, as with the objectives, it is intended that you will return to this section following completion of the problems to test your ability to define, in your own words, the listed terms.

Following this initial reading of the problems, objectives and vocabulary, read the assigned sections of the Internal Revenue Code and Treasury Regulations. Read them, it scarcely needs saying, with particular care. Then proceed to the narrative "overview" of the topics covered in the chapter. This overview is intended to provide not an exhaustive

Preface

analysis of the subject at hand but a perspective and a foundation for your study of the materials covered in the chapter. The overview is ordinarily followed by selected cases, administrative rulings or legislative history excerpts, which conclude the chapter.

After reading the Code and regulations, the overview and the other assigned materials, return to the problems and proceed to work them through. After completing the problems, return to the objectives and vocabulary sections and conclude your preparation of the chapter by making the self-assessment these sections provide. We wish you well as you commence what we hope will be a most rewarding course of study.

J. Martin Burke
Michael K. Friel

Acknowledgements

Since the Tenth Edition of this casebook was published in August 2012, Congress has made numerous changes to the Internal Revenue Code. Those changes, combined with new court and administrative materials, have necessitated a new edition. As in the past, we have used the preparation of this new edition as an opportunity to revise many of our problem sets, to prune away outdated materials, and to take advantage of helpful suggestions from our tax colleagues throughout the nation and our students at the University of Florida College of Law and the University of Montana School of Law. We are most grateful to them. We are also indebted to Linda Kirby of the University of Florida College of Law and to Elisabeth Ebben, our LexisNexis editor. Their assistance and support in the preparation of the manuscript for the Eleventh Edition were indispensable, and for that we are most appreciative.

Table of Contents

Table of Contents

Table of Contents

Table of Contents

Table of Contents

Table of Contents

Table of Contents

Table of Contents

Table of Contents

Table of Contents

Table of Contents

Table of Contents

Table of Contents

Table of Contents

Table of Contents

Table of Contents

Table of Contents

Table of Contents

Table of Contents

Table of Contents

Table of Contents

Table of Contents

Table of Contents

Chapter 1

INTRODUCTION TO FEDERAL INCOME TAXATION

I. PROBLEM

Caroline Taxpayer, a business consultant who owns and operates her own unincorporated business, uses the cash method of accounting and reports her income on a calendar year basis. She has provided you with the following information concerning her financial affairs during the current calendar year and asks you to compute her tax liability:

1. With regard to her consulting business:

   (a) She received $275,000 in fees through a combination of cash and checks from clients;

   (b) She provided $10,000 in consulting services to one client, a landscaping company, in exchange for $10,000 in landscaping services the client provided, at Caroline's request, for Caroline's mother;

   (c) Clients still owed her $30,000 for services she provided during the year;

   (d) She paid an employee $60,000 in wages during the year;

   (e) She paid $20,000 for building maintenance, utilities, and office supplies during the year; and

   (f) She purchased an office building for $500,000 which she expects to use in her business for the next 30 years.

2. Caroline incurred $5,000 in commuting costs in traveling from her home to work during the year.

3. Caroline received $19,000 in interest income this year from an investment account managed by her bank. She paid the bank $1,000 for its management services.

4. Caroline owns her home, on which she made mortgage payments in the amount of $24,000 during the year. Included in the $24,000 were $18,000 in interest payments and $6,000 in principal payments.

5. Two years ago, Caroline purchased 100 shares of stock in ABC corporation for $15,000. At the end of last year, the stock had a fair market value of $25,000. This year she received $1,000 in dividends on the stock. She sold the stock at year-end for $30,000.

6. Caroline contributed $9,000 in cash during the year to the church she attends.

7. Caroline paid state and local general sales taxes of $3,000 on the purchase of various items for personal use or consumption. She paid real property taxes of $5,000 on her home. She also paid $14,000 in estimated state income taxes and $40,000 in estimated federal income taxes with respect to her business.

Assignment for Chapter 1:

Read the "Analysis of Tax Liability of Caroline Taxpayer" included in the materials. In conjunction with your reading of the analysis, skim the sections of the Internal Revenue Code and the Regulations cited in the "Analysis." The "Analysis" assumes that Caroline files a return for the current year as an unmarried individual who is not a head of household or surviving spouse. The purpose of the "Analysis" is to provide you with an overview of the computation of individual income tax liability under the Internal Revenue Code.

Materials: Overview of the Federal Tax Law
               Analysis of Computation of Tax Liability of Caroline Taxpayer

II. VOCABULARY

By the end of this chapter, you should be able to explain the following terms:

gross income
adjusted gross income
above-the-line deductions
below-the-line deductions
standard deduction
personal exemption
taxable income
tax credit
rate schedule
joint return
tax bracket
marginal rate
timing
withholding tax
tax base
imputed income

III. OBJECTIVES

1. To list and explain fundamental questions our income tax system must address.
2. To identify receipts and expenditures likely to have tax significance.
3. To recall the formula for determining an individual's tax liability.
4. To explain the significance of adjusted gross income.
5. To explain the significance of the standard deduction.

6. To recognize there are some deductions taken into account in determining adjusted gross income ("above-the-line deductions") and some deductions which taxpayers may only claim if they elect to itemize their deductions. (These latter deductions are referred to as "below-the-line deductions.")

7. To distinguish a tax credit from a deduction.

8. To explain the differing tax savings produced by tax credits and deductions depending on a person's tax bracket.

9. To describe the general organization of the Internal Revenue Code with respect to income, exclusions, deductions and credits.

IV. OVERVIEW

A. A Brief History of Federal Income Tax

The federal income tax had its beginning with the ratification of the 16th Amendment to the U.S. Constitution in 1913. The amendment provides:

> The Congress shall have the power to lay and collect taxes on incomes, from whatever source derived, without apportionment among the several states and without regard to any census or enumeration.

This amendment set the stage for the 1913 Income Tax Act, an act imposing a very low rate of taxes. Given the high exemption levels established in that act, only a small fraction of the American public paid income taxes. In 1920, for example, there were only about five and one-half million taxable individual income tax returns filed, although 62,667,000 Americans were 20 years of age or older! In 1920, a family earning $10,000 a year (quite a sum for that time) would have paid only $558 in income tax. By 1928, the family earning $10,000 would pay only $40 in federal income tax.

While initially only the well-to-do were subject to income taxes, the pool of taxpayers radically increased in the 1940s primarily as a result of the government's need for additional revenues to fund the American war effort in World War II. Thus, while only 14.7 million individual income tax returns were filed in 1940, 49.8 million individual income tax returns were filed in 1945. Today, the great majority of adult Americans are required to file individual income tax returns, with approximately 145 million individual income tax returns being filed each year.

Needless to say, the almost overnight movement from a system which taxed relatively few people to a mass tax system created serious administrative problems. To alleviate some of the collection difficulties and to assure taxpayer compliance, the modern tax withholding system was created. Under that system, employers are required to withhold from their employees' compensation a sum, determined by reference to a specially formulated schedule, which approximates the federal income taxes an employee will owe. Amounts withheld by employers are periodically remitted to the Treasury. The success of our federal income tax system is largely attributable to the withholding system.

Our federal income tax system serves a number of functions apart from raising revenues to operate the government. The tax system also allocates the cost of public goods and services among Americans on an ability-to-pay basis. It accomplishes this through a progressive rate structure whereby high income taxpayers generally pay a larger percentage of their income in taxes than low income taxpayers. Exactly how progressive our system is and ought to be are topics of ongoing debate. Changes in deductions, exclusions and credits, as well as changes in tax rates and tax brackets, all affect the progressivity of the system.

In addition, Congress uses the federal income tax as a tool of social policy. Throughout the course, you will examine various Internal Revenue Code provisions reflecting social concerns of the Congress. For example, § 163 of the Code allows taxpayers to deduct home mortgage interest. Congress' stated purpose in allowing the deduction of such a personal expense is to encourage home ownership. Section 121, providing a substantial exclusion for gain on the sale of a principal residence, not only encourages home ownership, but minimizes tax as a factor in deciding whether to sell one's home. Another familiar example of the use of tax as a tool of social policy is § 170, the charitable deduction provision. By providing a deduction for charitable contributions, the government indirectly subsidizes various social programs benefitting large segments of our population.

Finally, Congress often uses the federal income tax to implement economic policy. For example, the accelerated cost recovery system of § 168 stimulates the economy by allowing businesses to depreciate certain tangible property rapidly, thereby encouraging businesses to invest in new equipment. Similarly, Congress occasionally enacts provisions intended to stimulate investment in particular activities, industries, or businesses, or in particular geographic areas or localities.

Is it proper to use the tax system to influence an individual's economic or personal decisions? Undoubtedly, many people significantly alter their economic behavior to take advantage of tax breaks. For example, significant tax advantages, e.g., a deduction for qualified residence interest, may encourage individuals to purchase homes rather than renting.

When one views the entire body of tax law, the purposes and effects of which go far beyond the mere collection of revenues, its study becomes more interesting. Indeed, tax is not just a sterile game of questions and answers involving only arithmetic. Rather, it is a study in governmental policy.

As you consider various aspects of the tax system during this course, ask yourself whether the provisions you are studying make sense not only from a revenue standpoint but also from an economic and social point of view. Begin evaluating the strengths and weaknesses of our tax system. Consider the administrability of the Code's provisions. In addition, ask yourself what regulatory effect, if any, a provision has — does it discourage or encourage a certain course of conduct?

B.   The Tax Practice

And now for a few words about the tax practice. One would be very short-sighted to believe tax work is relegated to a very small part of the practicing bar. As a practical matter, almost every practitioner will encounter clients with tax problems. As a result, attorneys must understand the general principles of the tax law so that they can assist their clients in making business and personal planning decisions.

Tax practice involves not only applying tax principles to past events or transactions but, more importantly, advising clients regarding the tax implications of actions they are about to undertake. For example, in representing a client in a divorce action, attorneys advise clients on numerous matters having significant tax consequences, *e.g.*, property settlement, child support and alimony. While the tax tail should not wag the dog, the attorney nonetheless should carefully evaluate and explain to a client the tax consequences of any proposed settlement or arrangement.

To advise a client and to predict the tax consequences of a particular course of action, one must have an understanding of the structure of our income tax law. Knowledge of the sources of the tax law is critical. Appendix 1 at the end of this book contains a section entitled "Sources of Tax Law." Read the brief discussion of tax sources carefully and make an effort during the course to locate and examine the research sources described.

C. Resolution of Tax Issues Through the Judicial Process

1. Trial Courts

If the Commissioner of the Internal Revenue Service asserts a deficiency in income tax, *i.e.*, claims that the taxpayer has failed to pay all that is owed, the taxpayer may:

    (a) refuse to pay the tax and petition the Tax Court for a redetermination of the deficiency; or

    (b) pay the deficiency, file an administrative claim for refund, and upon denial of the claim, sue for refund in federal district court or the United States Court of Federal Claims.

Three courts have original jurisdiction in federal tax cases: the Tax Court, the United States District Courts and the United States Court of Federal Claims.

a. The Tax Court

Of the three courts having original jurisdiction in tax cases, the Tax Court is the most important. The Tax Court has often been referred to as the "poor person's court" because the taxpayer commences an action in that court for redetermination of a deficiency *without first paying the asserted deficiency.* In contrast, actions for refund in the federal district courts and the Court of Federal Claims are, as the nature of the action indicates, commenced only after an asserted deficiency has been paid.

Because the Tax Court hears only tax cases, it is the most sophisticated trial court from the standpoint of tax expertise. The Tax Court has 19 members. The Tax Court, known as the Board of Tax Appeals until 1943, was established in 1924. Prior to the Tax Reform Act of 1969, the Tax Court was technically an independent agency of the executive branch of the federal government. The 1969 Act renamed the court the "United States Tax Court" and gave it "constitutional status" under Article 1, Section 8, Clause 9 of the Constitution, so that it is now part of the judicial branch. The change to constitutional status gives the Tax Court the power to punish for contempt and to issue writs to enforce its decisions.

Although the Tax Court has its headquarters in Washington, D.C., it regularly holds hearings in principal cities throughout the United States. Cases are tried without a jury by one judge, who submits an opinion to the chief judge for consideration. The chief judge will either allow the decision to stand or refer it to the full court for review. Reviewed opinions of the Tax Court are likely to be accorded greater weight. Published opinions of the Tax Court always indicate whether the opinion has been reviewed. Dissenting opinions are published.

b. Federal District Courts

The United States District Courts have jurisdiction in any tax case against the United States seeking a refund of tax, regardless of the amount involved. Unlike actions before the Tax Court, suits in the federal district courts may be tried before juries. The taxpayer must bring tax actions against the United States in the district in which the taxpayer resides, or, in the case of a corporation, in the district in which it has its principal place of business. As indicated above, a taxpayer cannot litigate a tax action in the federal district courts without first paying the amount in dispute and then commencing a refund action.

c. The United States Court of Federal Claims

The United States Court of Federal Claims was created by the Federal Courts Improvement Act of 1982. The court inherited substantially all of the jurisdiction formerly exercised by the United States Court of Claims. The Court of Federal Claims has jurisdiction over all tax suits against the United States regardless of amount. Jury trial is not available in the Court of Federal Claims. The jurisdiction of the court extends throughout the United States. Where one resides makes no difference. The principal office of the Court of Federal Claims is in the District of Columbia, but the court may hold hearings at such times and in such places as it may fix by rule of the court. Like the federal district courts, the Court of Federal Claims has no jurisdiction to hear deficiency cases. The taxpayer must pay the deficiency, thus converting the suit into a refund suit, before bringing an action before the court.

2. Appellate Courts

Appeals from the Tax Court are heard as a matter of right by the Federal Courts of Appeals of the United States. Jurisdiction is in the court for the circuit in which the taxpayer resides. Prior to its decision in *Golsen v. Commissioner*, 54 T.C. 742 (1970), the Tax Court did not regard itself as bound by the decisions of any particular federal court of appeals, even the court which would hear the case in question on appeal. In *Golsen*, the Tax Court reversed itself and announced it would follow a decision of the federal court to which an appeal from a Tax Court decision would be made, if the federal appeals court decision were squarely on point.

Prior to 1982, decisions of the Court of Claims were reviewed by the Supreme Court under the certiorari procedure. The 1982 Court Improvement Act created the United States Court of Appeals for the Federal Circuit, which has exclusive jurisdiction of an appeal from a final decision of the United States Court of Federal Claims. Decisions of the Court of Appeals for the Federal Circuit are reviewable by the Supreme Court.

Decisions of the federal district courts may, as a matter of right, be appealed to the appropriate federal court of appeals.

3.   Selection of Forum

As the above brief description of the various trial courts indicates, the taxpayer aggrieved by a decision of the Internal Revenue Service has a choice regarding the forum in which resolution of the tax issue may be sought. As a practical matter, one's finances may prove controlling in choosing a court. Thus, because a taxpayer is not entitled to sue in federal district court or the United States Court of Federal Claims unless a deficiency is paid and a refund claim pursued, the Tax Court will often be the favored forum, since one may commence an action there without having paid the asserted deficiency. Other factors likely to influence taxpayers and their advisors in choosing a forum will be the desire for a jury trial, the expertise of the Tax Court judges, and the past record of the particular court on a given issue. For example, if a taxpayer's claim for refund raises an issue on which the Court of Federal Claims has ruled favorably for other taxpayers, a taxpayer could be expected to bring a refund action in that court.

V.   ANALYSIS OF THE COMPUTATION OF TAX LIABILITY OF CAROLINE TAXPAYER

Chapter 1 is intended as an overview of individual income taxation. The problem presented requires you to think about the kinds of issues our tax system must address. It also introduces you to the method for computing an individual's income tax liability. During the rest of the course, you will be studying the details of the outline presented in this problem. If you are feeling a little uncomfortable after wrestling with the problem in this Chapter, don't despair. This problem and its analysis will make far more sense to you as you work through the materials in this casebook.

A.   Basic Questions Addressed by an Income Tax System

As the problem demonstrates, there are a number of questions our tax law must answer:

First, *what* items of economic income or gain will be includable in gross income?

Second, *what* costs will be allowable as deductions?

Third, *when* is an amount included in income? *When* is the taxpayer entitled to claim a deduction for an amount that is deductible?

Fourth, *who* is the taxpayer — *who* is going to be taxed on items of income?

Fifth, what is the *character* of the items of income or the deductions?

B.   Evaluating the Taxpayers' Tax Liability

To determine the tax liability of Caroline Taxpayer, you will need to answer two questions:

(a)   What is the applicable tax rate?

(b)   What is the tax rate applied to — that is, what is the tax base?

The answer to the first of these two questions is relatively simple. Internal Revenue Code § 1(c) provides the rates for unmarried individuals (other than surviving spouses and heads of household). Caroline will use these tax rates. Tax rates have varied considerably over the years. For example, a major change in the rates occurred as part of the Tax Reform Act of 1986, when tax rates were significantly reduced — immediately prior to 1986 the maximum individual income tax rate was 50%; and five years prior to that, the top rate was as high as 70%. Under current law, the maximum rate for individuals in 2015 is 39.6%, although there is a 28% maximum rate on "net capital gain" income and a 20% cap on "adjusted net capital gain." § 1(a), (h), (i). Note that the income levels at which the higher rates apply vary according to the taxpayer's filing status. Review the various subsections of § 1.

As you read the subsections of § 1, you will find that the appropriate tax rate is applied to the "taxable income" of the taxpayer. In calculating a taxpayer's taxable income, the five questions discussed above become important. Section § 63(b) provides that, for individuals who do not itemize their deductions, the term "taxable income" means "adjusted gross income minus (1) the standard deduction, and (2) the deduction for personal exemptions provided in section 151." For all other taxpayers, "taxable income" means "gross income minus the deductions allowed by this chapter [Chapter 1 of Subtitle A of the Internal Revenue Code] (other than the standard deduction)." § 63(a).

1. Gross Income

In computing taxable income, the first order of business is to determine gross income. "Gross income" is defined in § 61: "Except as otherwise provided in this subtitle, gross income means all income from whatever source derived, including (but not limited to) the following items:" A list of 15 items follows.

What does § 61 mean when it refers to "this subtitle"? The reference is to Subtitle A of Title 26 of the United States Code. Subtitle A includes all income tax provisions beginning with § 1 and ending with § 1563. Note that "gross income" is defined as "all income." Thus, the definition really does not help us very much. As you might expect, there are numerous cases in which the courts have struggled with the meaning of the term "gross income." Generally, courts have been expansive in their definition of income.

Let us turn now to the problem and determine Caroline's gross income. First, the $275,000 in cash and checks she receives in her consulting business constitute gross income.

The $10,000 value of the landscaping services rendered to her mother presents a tougher question. Caroline rendered consulting services and received in exchange landscaping work she requested be done for her mother. The form of compensation one receives generally makes no difference in determining what constitutes gross income. Regulation § 1.61-1(a) specifically says gross income includes income realized in any form whether in money, property or services. Regulation § 1.61-2(d)(1) provides that "if services are paid for in exchange for other services, the fair market value of such other services taken in payment must be included in income as compensation. . . . " These rules regarding form of compensation are obviously very important in our tax system. But for these rules, taxpayers would be encouraged to barter for goods and services they need.

Although it was Caroline's mother rather than Caroline who received the landscaping services, Caroline will nonetheless have to include the value of these services in her gross income. Otherwise, taxpayers in high tax brackets would constantly shift their income to related taxpayers in a lower bracket. The courts have fashioned the "assignment of income" doctrine to prevent income shifting, and numerous statutory provisions reflect congressional application of that doctrine. Thus, Caroline is considered to have $285,000 in gross income.

Can Caroline's business expenses noted above be deducted from the $285,000 in arriving at her gross income figure? The answer is "No" — § 61 says nothing about net income. As you will see, however, the Code specifically authorizes deductions for expenses incurred in one's trade or business.

Clients owed Caroline $30,000 for consulting work performed during the current year. Is any of this amount includable in her gross income for the year? The answer is "No." She is a "cash method" taxpayer. She did not *actually* or *constructively* receive any of the $30,000. Caroline therefore is not required to include any of the $30,000 in her gross income. As you will study later in the course, a cash method taxpayer includes income only when it is *actually* or *constructively* received. *See* § 451(a); Reg. § 1.446-1(c)(1)(i).

Caroline received $19,000 in interest income this year. This amount clearly constitutes gross income under § 61(a)(4). May the $1,000 management fee be deducted in arriving at gross income? As before, the answer is "No." Instead, the $1,000 fee will be considered when Caroline computes her deductions.

Caroline sold her stock in ABC Corporation for $15,000 more than she paid for it. This $15,000 gain must be included in her gross income under § 61(a)(3) as gain derived from dealing in property. Because she had held the stock as a capital asset for more than one year, the $15,000 gain will be characterized as long-term capital gain. That characterization will not affect the dollar amount of gross income. Note, however, that the maximum rate on "net capital gain" — a necessary component of which is long-term capital gain — is less than the maximum rate on ordinary income. § 1(h). Thus, the long-term capital gain characterization may ultimately prove beneficial for that reason. In addition, as we shall see in studying character-ization in detail in Chapter 31, capital gain characterization can also be significant when a taxpayer has recognized capital losses. § 1211(b). Finally, Caroline also received $1,000 in dividend income from the ABC stock. Dividends are included in income under § 61(a)(7). However, dividends are included in the computation of net capital gain and thus are taxed at the preferential rate accorded net capital gain, rather than at ordinary income rates as high as 39.6%. § 1(h)(11).

An additional point should be considered at this time. By the end of last year, the stock had appreciated in value by $10,000. Was Caroline required to include any of that $10,000 in her gross income for last year? Is it appropriate to permit her to exclude from last year's income an amount which is clearly an economic gain? Assume she could have sold the stock and collected $10,000 of gain on December 31 last year. Alternatively, consider the administrative problems involved, and the forced sales that might result if taxpayers were required to account for the appreciation and the depreciation in assets during the year. Congress, the courts and the Service all agree no inclusion is required in these circumstances. The $10,000 appreciation in their stock is not considered to have been "realized" by Caroline. Until such time as the appreciation is realized, *e.g.*, the stock is sold, there will be no inclusion.

2.   Adjusted Gross Income

Caroline had no other income in the current year. Thus, her gross income is $320,000 (consisting of the $275,000 in cash and checks received in the consulting business; the $10,000 value of the landscaping services; $20,000 in interest and dividends; and the $15,000 gain on the stock sale). Having determined her gross income, you should now determine her adjusted gross income. Section § 62 defines adjusted gross income as gross income less certain deductions. Note that § 62 merely defines adjusted gross income; *it is not a deduction granting provision! In general, only those deductions listed in § 62 are taken into account in computing adjusted gross income.* Thus, there are two categories of deductions. The first category is comprised of deductions a taxpayer may consider in determining his or her adjusted gross income; these are referred to as *"above-the-line"* deductions. The second category of deductions consists of those deductions a taxpayer may take into account only after the adjusted gross income has been determined; these are referred to as *"below-the-line"* deductions.

A few comments on adjusted gross income (AGI) are necessary at this point. Adjusted gross income may be viewed as an interim measure of taxable income. Prior to 1944, taxpayers simply itemized all of their deductions. Whatever business deductions they had and whatever personal deductions, *e.g.*, charitable deductions and home mortgage interest deductions, they were allowed, all had to be listed separately on the return. In the early years of our modern tax history, this itemization was manageable from an administrative standpoint because relatively few people were required to file returns. However, in the early 1940s when ours became a mass system of taxation, this itemization was viewed as extremely burdensome not only for the taxpayer attempting to complete a tax return, but also for the Internal Revenue Service in reviewing the tax returns filed.

In 1944, as part of a tax simplification act, Congress decided that, in lieu of itemizing their *personal deductions*, taxpayers should be given the right to elect a "standard deduction." If a taxpayer elected to use the standard deduction rather than itemizing all of her personal deductions, the taxpayer would be entitled to deduct the amount specified by Congress regardless of what deductible personal expenses the taxpayer had actually incurred. If, in the aggregate, a taxpayer's personal deductions exceeded the standard deduction, the taxpayer would not elect the standard deduction but would instead itemize her personal deductions. Regardless of whether a taxpayer elected the standard deduction, a taxpayer would be allowed to deduct her trade or business expenses. Thus, the standard deduction eliminates the need for taxpayers with relatively small amounts of personal deductions to itemize those deductions and maintain records substantiating those deductions. Today, approximately two-thirds of filers take advantage of the standard deduction.

In 1944, Congress provided the standard deduction would be a percentage of the taxable income determined after taking into account trade or business expenses but before taking into account deductible personal expenses. There was not in existence, however, any interim measure of gross income less business expenses to which the standard deduction percentage could be applied. Congress therefore created an interim measure known as "adjusted gross income." Beginning with the 1944 Act, a taxpayer would compute taxable income by deducting business expenses from gross income. This figure was the taxpayer's adjusted gross income. The taxpayer would then elect either to itemize other deductions or to take the standard deduction. Disregarding the personal exemptions available, the taxpayer's taxable income then equaled the difference between the adjusted gross income and either the taxpayer's itemized deductions or the standard deduction.

Note the standard deduction under current law is a set dollar amount that is adjusted annually for inflation, rather than a percentage of adjusted gross income.[1]

Adjusted gross income continues to serve as a dividing line between those deductions allowed to all taxpayers regardless of whether they itemize (the "above-the-line" deductions) and those deductions which may be taken only if the taxpayer itemizes (the "below-the-line" deductions). *See* § 63(e). AGI is also important because it is used to limit certain personal expenses (for example, the charitable deduction is limited to a percentage of AGI) and is used as a basis in calculating various other "tax-related" amounts.

3. Deductions

The deduction provisions of the Code begin with § 161. Most deductions reflect the notion that our tax system permits a deduction for the costs incurred in producing income. As discussed previously, however, a number of deduction provisions are not integral to our tax system and exist only because of certain economic and social policies Congress seeks to implement. As you begin considering the deduction provisions, keep in mind that while gross income is given a very expansive definition, the courts consider deductions as a matter of "legislative grace." Deduction provisions are, therefore, narrowly construed.

When one thinks of deductions, one usually thinks in terms of some expenditure. Some expenditures are generally currently deductible. One example would be the wages an employer pays to an employee. Other expenditures are never deductible. Personal expenses, for example, are generally not deductible. § 262. Some expenditures are deductible, but not all at once; rather, they are deducted (accounted for) over a period of time. For example, if one purchases a building for use in one's business, the cost of the building will not be deductible in the year of purchase but rather will be deductible during the life of the building. One final point must be emphasized regarding deductions. *Every time you have an expense you believe is deductible, you must find a specific Code section authorizing the deduction.*

---

[1] For example, the "basic standard deduction" for calendar year 2015 has risen to $12,600 on a joint return and $6,300 on the return of an unmarried individual (not a surviving spouse or head of household) on account of inflation adjustments. *See* § 63(c)(2)(A), (4), (7); Rev. Proc. 2014-61, 2014-47 I.R.B. 860.

With that background, consider what expenditures of Caroline Taxpayer are deductible.

Caroline paid $60,000 in wages and $20,000 for various business-related expenses. Section 162(a) provides that these amounts will be deductible as trade or business expenses. As such, they are above-the-line deductions according to § 62(a)(1).

Caroline purchased a building during the current year costing $500,000. The building will provide a benefit to her business over many years. To permit a current deduction for the entire $500,000 would cause some distortion because the cost of the building is associated not only with producing income this year but also with producing income in subsequent years. Appropriately, § 263 requires the cost of the building to be capitalized. The building cost represents a capital expenditure according to Reg. § 1.263(a)-2(d)(1). Section 168, which you will study in some detail later in this course, specifically allows the building to be depreciated. Depreciation represents an allowance for the reasonable exhaustion, wear, and tear of property used in a trade or business or property held for production of income. *See* § 167(a). Section 168 provides a spreading technique for recovering the cost of tangible property used in business or for the production of income. For purposes of your computation, assume that the depreciation deduction allowed this year with respect to the building will be $10,000. In other words, on her tax return Caroline will be allowed to deduct $10,000 of the $500,000 building cost this year and will deduct the remaining $490,000 in future years pursuant to § 168.

The § 168 deduction represents a business expense and therefore is properly taken into account in computing adjusted gross income; it is an above-the-line deduction. § 62(a)(1).

Caroline incurred $5,000 in expenses in commuting to and from work each day. This amount is not deductible. Rather, it is viewed as a nondeductible personal expense. Reg. § 1.162-2(e) and § 1.262-1(b)(5). The theory underlying denial of a deduction in this case is that where one lives is a matter of personal preference. Hence, a person choosing to live miles away from his or her business should not be permitted to claim a deduction for commuting expenses.

The bank's fee for managing Caroline's investment account was $1,000. Does § 162(a) authorize a deduction for this expense? No. Investing in stocks and bonds and otherwise managing one's investments has been held not to constitute a trade or business within the meaning of § 162. *Higgins v. Commissioner*, 312 U.S. 212 (1941) (included in the materials in Chapter 12). This result seemed unfair since the dividends and interest produced by the stocks and bonds were taxable income. Congress, therefore, in response to *Higgins*, enacted § 212 which specifically provides a deduction for expenses paid or incurred during the taxable year "for the production or collection of income." Thus, the management fee will be deductible as an investment activity expense under § 212.

Is the management fee deductible above the line? No. Under § 62, only limited types of § 212 expenses are deductible above the line and the management fee is not one of them. This is a curious result because it seems taxpayers should always be allowed to deduct expenses incurred in the production of taxable income. There is no good policy reason to deny above-the-line treatment to this expense, and yet Congress has done so. Thus, the expense will be significant only if the taxpayer has below-the-line expenses greater than the standard deduction. By contrast, were the management fee a business expense, it would be deductible above the line and would not be subject to the potential wastage or disallowance that below-the-line deductions face. *See* § 62(a)(1).

Caroline made mortgage payments in the amount of $24,000 — $6,000 of which represented principal payments. Are the principal payments deductible? No. Mortgage payments on one's personal residence represent a personal expenditure. Generally, as noted, personal expenditures are not deductible. § 262. (For similar reasons, no depreciation deduction is allowed with respect to the residence.)

Is the $18,000 interest portion of the mortgage payment deductible? Surely this is a personal expense just as a principal payment is a personal expense. Section 163(a), however, specifically allows a deduction for "all interest paid or accrued within the taxable year on indebtedness." Section 163(h) qualifies this general rule by providing that personal interest is generally not deductible. Personal interest, however, does not include so-called "qualified residence interest." As you will study later in this course, home mortgage interest such as Caroline paid in this problem may be "qualified residence interest" and thus be deductible. For purposes of this problem, we will assume that the interest is deductible under § 163. To the extent § 163(a) permits Caroline to deduct interest on personal debt such as a home mortgage, it represents an exception to the general rule that personal expenditures are not deductible. Indeed, this section provides one of the significant tax breaks enjoyed by homeowners. Certainly, this deduction is not one mandated by a system which seeks to tax net income.

Having determined that the $18,000 interest payment is deductible, the next question is whether the deduction is above or below the line. Recall that § 62 lists the above-the-line deductions. While interest expense may be an above-the-line deduction if it is incurred in a trade or business, per § 62(a)(1), interest expense incurred with respect to a personal debt is not listed as an above-the-line deduction. Thus, the $18,000 interest deduction may not be used in computing adjusted gross income. In this problem, it will be taken into account in computing Caroline's taxable income.

Caroline paid real property taxes of $5,000 on her home. This represents a personal expense, and thus one might conclude it is nondeductible under § 262. Congress, however, authorizes in § 164 a deduction for certain taxes even though they are personal in nature. Among those taxes are real property taxes. *See* § 164(a)(1). The deduction is taken below the line.

May Caroline deduct the state and local general sales tax and the state income tax she paid this year? Section 164(a)(3) allows a deduction for state income tax. Section 164(b)(5), however, puts to Caroline an election: deduct either state and local incomes taxes or state and local general sales taxes. Because the total estimated state income taxes paid ($14,000) are a greater amount, that is the deduction Caroline will take.² No deduction may be taken for federal income tax paid. As noted below, however, Caroline will be given credit for any federal income taxes paid. The state income tax deduction is a below-the-line deduction. The question remains: Since these taxes are personal in nature, should they be deductible at all?

Caroline contributed $9,000 to her church. Section 170 provides a deduction for charitable contributions. There are limits, however, on charitable deductions. In this case, § 170(b)(1)(A) limits the Taxpayers' deduction to 50% of her "contribution base." Section 170(b)(1)(F) provides that "contribution base" means "adjusted gross income." Thus, so long as Caroline has an adjusted gross income of at least $18,000, she will be entitled to a full $9,000 deduction for the charitable contribution. The charitable contribution deduction, as you might expect, is a below-the-line deduction.

4.   Calculating Adjusted Gross Income

Caroline is thus "allowed" the following deductions:

above-the-line deductions:

wages	$60,000
office supplies, etc.	20,000
depreciation	10,000
TOTAL	$90,000

below-the-line deductions:

management fee	$1,000
interest	18,000
state income tax	14,000
real property taxes	5,000
charitable contributions	9,000
TOTAL	$47,000

Returning to the definition of adjusted gross income in § 62(a):

AGI = Gross income less the above-the-line deductions

Thus, AGI = $320,000 − $90,000 = $230,000

5.   Taxable Income

Itemize or Use Standard Deduction? Next, you must determine Caroline's taxable income. As noted earlier, the formula for computing taxable income depends on whether the taxpayer itemizes deductions, *i.e.*, elects to claim below-the-line deductions rather than taking the standard deduction. If the taxpayer does not itemize deductions, the taxpayer is entitled only to the standard deduction in lieu of

---

² This election has been available only since 2004. Congress made general sales taxes nondeductible in 1986 and they remained so until 2004. Since 2004, Congress has extended § 164(b)(5) on a temporary basis several times. Recently, it extended § 164(b)(5) through 2015 and will likely extend it thereafter on a year-to-year basis or make it permanent.

any below-the-line deductions (other than the personal exemption, discussed *infra*). Note the definition for itemized deductions in § 63(d). Clearly, if a taxpayer's below-the-line deductions exceed the standard deduction, as will be the case with Caroline, the taxpayer should be advised to itemize.

If she elects to itemize, Caroline will determine her taxable income by subtracting from her gross income of $320,000 all of her allowable deductions. § 63(a). For taxpayers itemizing deductions, the computation of adjusted gross income is not specifically required by § 63(b); however, for taxpayers who have made charitable contributions or have other expenses, the deductibility of which depend on the amount of the adjusted gross income, their adjusted gross income must be determined. Having already computed Caroline's adjusted gross income, the only deductions which remain to be taken in computing her taxable income are the below-the-line deductions and the personal exemption.

Section 67: the 2% Floor on Miscellaneous Itemized Deductions. Section 67 provides certain itemized deductions may not be deducted except to the extent that, in the aggregate, such deductions exceed 2% of the taxpayer's adjusted gross income. This 2% floor on itemized deductions not only reduces the tax benefits of certain deductions, but also the number of taxpayers claiming the deductions. The floor relieves taxpayers of the burden of record keeping with respect to certain expenditures unless they expect that, in the aggregate, the expenditures will exceed the floor. In turn, the Internal Revenue Service's work in auditing returns is reduced. With respect to each deduction studied in this course, ask yourself whether the deduction is subject to this 2% floor. Note that, under § 67(b), Caroline's deductions for home mortgage interest, state income tax, real property tax, and charitable contributions are not subject to the 2% rule of § 67(a). The bank management fee of $1,000, however, is subject to the rule. It is clear this $1,000 expense does not exceed 2% of Caroline's adjusted gross income of $230,000; therefore, it will not be deductible. Thus, Caroline's itemized deductions are cut back from $47,000 to $46,000 by § 67.

The § 68 Overall Limitation on Itemized Deductions. There is, however, yet another hurdle itemized deductions must surmount. Section 68 provides that otherwise allowable itemized deductions are reduced by 3% of the amount by which the taxpayer's adjusted gross income exceeds and inflation-adjusted "applicable amount" (or, if lesser, the reduction is 80% of otherwise allowable itemized deductions). § 68(a). As a result, a taxpayer will not be subject to the § 68 cutback unless the taxpayer's adjusted gross income exceeds the "applicable amount." In the Taxpayer Relief Act of 2012, Congress set the "applicable amount" for a taxpayer (like Caroline Taxpayer), who is not married and who is not a surviving spouse or head of household, at $250,000. That amount, however, is adjusted for inflation.[3] Assume the "applicable amount" for the current year is $258,250. Because Caroline's adjusted gross income of $230,000 does not exceed the "applicable amount," her allowable itemized deductions will not be reduced by § 68.

---

[3] For 2015, the applicable amount for an unmarried taxpayer who is not married and who is not a surviving spouse or head of household is $258,250. Rev. Proc. 2014-61, *supra*.

Personal Exemptions. Next, it is necessary to determine the deduction for the personal exemption. Section 151(a) provides that there will be a deduction for personal exemptions. Section 151(d)(1) sets the exemption amount, in general, at $2,000, adjusted for inflation after 1989 as set forth in § 151(d)(4).[4] In addition, Congress has added a provision under which the exemption amount may be reduced, and potentially eliminated, for high-income taxpayers. Under § 151(d)(3), the exemption amount is reduced by two percentage points for each $2,500 (or fraction thereof) by which the taxpayer's adjusted gross income exceeds the inflation-adjusted "applicable amount" in effect under § 68(b). As noted above, we are assuming the "applicable amount" under § 68(b) for Caroline Taxpayer's purposes is $258,250 (the 2015 "applicable amount" for an unmarried individual who is not a surviving spouse or head of household). Because Caroline's adjusted gross income of $230,000 does not exceed the "applicable amount," any personal exemptions to which Caroline is entitled will not be subject to reduction under § 151(d)(3).

Caroline may claim one personal exemption. In the case of married taxpayers filing a joint return, there are two taxpayers, and therefore, as the applicable Treasury regulation provides, there will be two personal exemptions. Reg. § 1.151-1(b). In addition to the exemptions provided for the taxpayer, there are additional exemptions for each dependent who meets the requirements set out in § 152. Here, we assume Caroline has no dependents. Taxpayers who have minor children will typically be able to claim an exemption for each child under § 152 and the "qualifying child" provisions of § 152(c). Assume the current inflation-adjusted exemption amount is $4,000. With one exemption on her return, Caroline will claim a total deduction of $4,000. Even if Caroline did not elect to itemize, § 63(b) makes it clear that she is entitled to claim personal exemptions in addition to the standard deduction.

The personal exemption and the standard deduction provide a floor assuring that taxpayers will not be taxed unless they have income greater than the combined amount of the personal exemptions allowed and the standard deduction. As noted in the legislative history of the 1986 Tax Reform Act, "[a]n overriding goal of the Committee is to relieve families with the lowest incomes from Federal income tax liability. Consequently, the Bill increases the amounts of both the personal exemption and the standard deduction . . . so that the income level at which individuals begin to have tax liability (the tax threshold) will be raised sufficiently to free millions of poverty-level individuals from Federal income tax liability."[5]

Calculating Taxable Income. Caroline's taxable income therefore is:

Adjusted Gross Income			$230,000
less:	itemized deductions	− 46,000	
	personal exemptions	− 4,000	50,000
Taxable Income			$180,000

---

[4] For 2015, the inflation-adjusted personal exemption is $4,000. Rev. Proc. 2014-61, *supra.*

[5] H.R. 99-426 p. 82 (1985); Senate Rep. 99-313 p. 31, 32 (1986). *See also* General Explanation of the Tax Reform Act of 1986 prepared by the Staff of the Joint Committee on Taxation, p. 15.

6. Tax Rates

Next, you must apply the appropriate tax rate under § 1. Sections 1(c) and 1(i) list seven different rates, or brackets: 10%, 15%, 25%, 28%, 33%, 35% and 39.6%. The income level at which the higher rates begin to apply depends on one's filing status. In addition, the statutory brackets themselves are to be adjusted for inflation. § 1(f). Under the tax rate tables of § 1(c), for 2015,[6] the tax on a return with taxable income of $180,000 is $18,481.25 on the first $90,750, plus 28% of the excess over $90,750. Thus computed, Caroline's *preliminary* § 1(c) tax liability is $43,471.25. This liability is preliminary because it can be affected by the maximum capital gains rate provision of § 1(h).

Section 1(h) will apply when, as here, the taxpayer has a net capital gain. The purpose of § 1(h) is to provide preferential tax rates for net capital gain. The preferential rates may vary based on the taxpayer's bracket and on the components of the net capital gain. Section 1(h) is remarkably complex and will be studied in detail in Chapter 31. It must suffice at this point to simply note: (1) Since Caroline has $1,000 in dividend income, a $15,000 long term capital gain from the sale of the ABC stock, and no other capital gains or capital losses, her net capital gain is $16,000. §§ 1(h)(ii), 1222(11). (2) Under the facts of this problem, all of the net capital gain will be taxed at a 15% tax rate. § 1(h)(1)(C). Accordingly, under 1(h), Caroline's § 1 tax liability is limited to the sum of two amounts:

(1) the regular § 1(c) tax on $164,000, which is $38,991.25 (the $164,000 figure represents the previously-determined taxable income of $180,000, less the net capital gain of $16,000 — which would otherwise be taxed at 25% or 28%); plus

(2) the special § 1(h) tax rate of 15% on the $16,000 net capital gain, which equals $2,400. But for § 1(h), this $16,000 would be taxed at the higher rates of § 1(c) and (i).[7] With § 1(h), the § 1 liability is thus $41,391.25.

Credits. Are the computations finished? Not yet. Next, you must determine whether any credits may be taken against the tax. The Code sections providing tax credits are generally §§ 21–53. The most common credit is found in § 31 — the credit for withholding taxes paid through the year by employers on behalf of the employees. Allowance of this credit makes sense since, in effect, employees are prepaying their income taxes via the payment of the withholding tax.

Caroline is not subject to withholding tax because she is self-employed. She would, however, be required to make advance payments on the tax on her self-employment income. Here Caroline paid $40,000. This type of advance payment is referred to as an estimated tax payment. Caroline paid $40,000 estimated tax and that amount would also be deducted from Caroline's tax liability figure. As a result of these credits for withholding and estimated tax payments, she will owe the U.S. Treasury $1,391.25 ($41,391.25 minus $40,000).

---

[6] The tax rate tables for 2015 are in Rev. Proc. 2014-61, *supra.*

[7] It is assumed Caroline's limitation will be determined under § 1(h)(1)(A)(i). An alternative § 1(h) limit can apply in some circumstances. *See* § 1(h)(1)(A)(ii). The alternative limitation is designed simply to ensure the 15% tax bracket is fully utilized before the higher capital gains rates are applied.

At this point, you should consider the difference between a deduction and a credit. A credit reduces one's tax on a dollar for dollar basis, whereas a deduction reduces taxable income, thus providing a reduction in tax that is dependent on the tax bracket of the individual. For example, a $1,000 deduction results in a $350 tax savings for a person in a 35% tax bracket, but only a $150 tax savings for a person in a 15% tax bracket. By contrast, a $1,000 tax credit saves a person $1,000 in taxes regardless of a person's tax bracket.

Conclusion

This chapter has provided you with the big picture.[8] Now you will begin studying the details of the individual income tax system. You should return to this chapter throughout the course to refresh your memory on just how each specific detail fits into the overall picture.

---

[8] Actually, for many taxpayers, an additional chore remains — namely determining whether additional tax will be imposed by the "alternative minimum tax" of § 55. The alternative minimum tax is considered in detail in Chapter 45; to introduce its complexities at this point would be premature.

Chapter 2

GROSS INCOME: CONCEPTS AND LIMITATIONS

I. PROBLEMS

1. Marcella, a recent law school graduate, is an associate with a large law firm. Which, if any, of the following items must Marcella report as gross income?

    (a) Her salary of $75,000 per year. Marcella's take-home pay was only $50,000, however, as the firm withheld $15,000 for federal income taxes, $5,500 in Social Security taxes (employee's share of Social Security and Medicare) and $4,500 for state income taxes.

    (b) A year-end bonus of $5,000 received from the law firm in recognition of the quality of her work.

    (c) A walnut bookcase Marcella purchased from the firm for $150. The bookcase was in excellent condition and had a fair market value of $400. It was one of fifteen bookcases the firm sold when it eliminated a large part of its law library. The other bookcases were sold for the same price to other lawyers and legal assistants of the firm.

    (d) A firm retreat at a popular ski resort in the Rocky Mountains. The firm scheduled the three-day retreat as an opportunity for all of the partners and associates in the firm's various offices around the country to come together to meet each other. Firm meetings during the retreat were scheduled in the afternoon to enable firm members to ski during the morning hours. The firm paid all of Marcella's transportation, meals and lodging expenses. Her expenses amounted to approximately $2,500. All firm partners and associates were required to attend the retreat.

    (e) A small greenhouse worth $2,500 constructed on Marcella's property by her brother, Bill. Bill insisted on building the greenhouse for Marcella as a way of thanking her for the legal work she had done for him at no charge. Bill did not charge Marcella for either his labor or the materials he purchased to construct the greenhouse.

    (f) Marcella found a purse containing substantial cash and valuable jewelry in the back seat of a taxi. She located identifying information in the purse and returned it to the grateful owner, who gave Marcella $2,000.

    (g) Marcella represented herself in a lawsuit regarding certain real property she owned. Had Marcella hired an attorney to represent her, she would have paid approximately $10,000 in legal fees.

2. Mitch purchases stock in XYZ Corporation in Year 1 for $1,000. At the end of Year 1, the stock is worth $1,500. In Year 2 when the stock is worth $2,000, Albert offers to buy the stock for $2,000, but Mitch declines. In Year 3, when the stock is worth $2,500, Mitch borrows $2,000 from Bank, pledging the stock as security for the loan. In Year 4, Mitch repays the $2,000 he borrowed. In Year 5, when the stock is worth $3,000, Mitch gives it to Creditor to satisfy a $3,000 debt owed to Creditor. Does Mitch have any gross income? When?

Assignment for Chapter 2:

Complete the problems.

Read: Internal Revenue Code: § 61; merely skim §§ 31, 85, 86.
        Treasury Regulations: §§ 1.61-1, 1.61-2(a)(1), (d)(1), (2)(i), 1.61-8(a), 1.61-9(a), 1.61-11(a), 1.61-14(a).

        Materials: Overview
                     Commissioner v. Glenshaw Glass
                     Cesarini v. United States
                     Old Colony Trust Company v. Commissioner
                     Revenue Ruling 79-24
                     McCann v. United States
                     Pellar v. Commissioner
                     Roco v. Commissioner

II. VOCABULARY

accession to wealth
appreciation
bargain purchase
barter
exclusion
fair market value
gross income
imputed income
realization

III. OBJECTIVES

1. To explain the characteristics of gross income.
2. To contrast the *Eisner v. Macomber* definition of "income" with the discussion of "income" in *Glenshaw Glass*.
3. To recall that *Glenshaw Glass* provides that accessions to wealth generally constitute gross income.
4. To predict whether an item received by a taxpayer will be characterized as gross income.
5. To describe several forms, other than cash, in which income may be realized.

6.   To recognize barter transactions.

7.   To reconstruct multiple-party barter arrangements by providing cash payments in lieu of the bartering.

8.   To generalize regarding circumstances in which valuation will be difficult or uncertain.

9.   To distinguish issues involving whether income has been realized from issues involving the form and amount of income.

10.   To provide examples of realization events.

11.   To provide examples of imputed income.

12.   To provide examples of bargain purchases.

13.   To distinguish a non-compensatory bargain purchase from a compensatory one.

IV. OVERVIEW

What does the term "income" mean to you? Can you list characteristics of "income"? Can the receipt of something other than cash constitute "income"? Is "income" limited to compensation for services or property or are all receipts "income"? Do receipts have to be recurrent to be "income"? Is the value which we add to property by means of our work "income"?

Certainly, the most basic question confronted in our federal income tax system is "What is income"? The answer to that question is not simple. One cannot merely rely on common usage, nor will one find much solace in the definitions of economists. Rather, the answer is found in an examination of the interplay of congressional purpose, administrative goals, accounting concepts and public policy as defined by the Congress, the courts and the Treasury. This Chapter and the next several Chapters will address the what-is-income question and provide some answers.

A. The Search for a Definition of Income

Modern federal income tax originated with the Sixteenth Amendment to the U.S. Constitution, adopted in 1913, which provides:

> The Congress shall have the power to lay and collect taxes on incomes, *from whatever source derived*, without apportionment among the several states and without regard to any census or enumeration. (Emphasis added.)

This amendment set the stage for the 1913 Tax Act's definition of net income:

> The net income of a taxable person shall include *gains, profits, and income* derived from salaries, wages, or compensation for personal services of whatever kind and in whatever form paid, or from professions, vocations, businesses, trade, commerce, or sales, or dealings in property, whether real or personal, growing out of the ownership or use of or interest in real or personal property; and also from interest, rent, dividends, securities, or the transaction of any lawful business carried on for gain or profit, or *gains or profits and income derived from any source whatever*.

Tax Law of October 3, 1913. H.R. 3321, II, sub.B (emphasis added).

Compare the above definition with the current definition of "gross income" in § 61(a) of the Internal Revenue Code of 1986. Note the breadth of both provisions: the 1913 Act provided that income includes "gains or profits and income derived from any source," while the § 61(a) definition is simpler — gross income is "all income from whatever source derived." Both definitions enumerate items constituting gross income. Note, for example, the listing of such common forms of income as wages and salaries, rents, dividends and interest. The list provided in current § 61(a), however, is much broader and includes items one might not otherwise consider income, *e.g.*, fringe benefits, cancellation of indebtedness, and alimony and separate maintenance payments.

Neither the 1913 definition nor the current definition of income provides any concise, all-encompassing standard for determining income. As the history of judicial and administrative rulings suggests, however, Congress cannot be faulted for failing to provide such a standard. Arguably, both § 61(a) and its 1913 predecessor were never intended to be the exclusive definition of income, but, rather, were little more than descriptions of a necessary step in a mathematical formula for computing "taxable income." Thus, in defining "gross income" in § 61, Congress was merely describing the first step in the calculation of "adjusted gross income" and "taxable income."

More important, as the Supreme Court noted in *Glenshaw Glass*, a case included in this Chapter, Congress, in defining "gross income," intended to exert "the full measure of its taxing power." As soon became apparent, the early judicial efforts to express the concept of income in some simply stated standard were unsatisfactory. In *Eisner v. Macomber*, 252 U.S. 189, 206–207 (1920), the Court described "income" as: "[T]he gain derived from capital, from labor, or from both combined, provided it be understood to include profit gained through a sale or conversion of capital assets. . . . "

Reread the definition of "net income" in the 1913 Tax Act. The *Eisner v. Macomber* standard embodied many of the notions contained in that act. Nonetheless, the definition was incomplete. The Board of Tax Appeals so indicated in *Hawkins v. Commissioner*, 6 BTA 1023, 1024 (1927), when it noted:

> [I]t is conceivable that since the income tax is primarily an application of the idea of measuring taxes by financial ability to pay, as indicated by the accretion to one's economic wealth during the year, there may be cases in which taxable income will be judicially found although outside the precise scope of the description already given.

The words of the Board of Tax Appeals were prophetic. Eleven years after its decision in *Eisner v. Macomber*, the Supreme Court, in *U.S. v. Kirby Lumber Co.*, 284 U.S. 1 (1931), considered whether the discharge of a corporate debt for an amount less than the face of the debt resulted in income to the debtor. The Court ruled that it did. Obviously, the *Eisner v. Macomber* definition of income would not have readily accommodated discharge of debt, and yet the taxpayer had clearly benefitted economically from the discharge. Although not citing the *Macomber* definition, the Court, in an apparent reference to it, commented that it saw "nothing to be gained by the discussion of judicial definitions."

Lest there should be any question regarding the continued viability of the *Eisner v. Macomber* definition of income, the Supreme Court, in *Glenshaw Glass*, emphasized the *Macomber* definition "was not meant to provide a touchstone to all future gross income questions." Read *Glenshaw Glass* carefully. What characteristics of punitive damages did the Supreme Court emphasize as its basis for concluding such damages constitute gross income? What guidance, if any, does *Glenshaw Glass* provide for evaluating whether an item should be treated as gross income?

In *Roco v. Commissioner*, included in the materials, the Tax Court applied *Glenshaw Glass* in concluding that qui tam payments under the federal False Claims Act constituted income. In its decision, the Tax Court specifically rejected the taxpayer's reliance on *Eisner v. Macomber*, noting "the Supreme Court has limited *Eisner v. Macomber* chiefly to the taxability of stock dividends."

While the many court decisions addressing the question of "What is gross income?" may not have resulted in a simple definition, the decisions are nonetheless instructive. Decisions like *Glenshaw Glass*, *Cesarini*, and *Roco*, which follow this Overview, emphasize that the concept of "income" developed by the Congress, the courts and the Treasury is both widely inclusive and elastic.

Congress has done much to resolve any questions regarding whether an item is income. Not only has Congress expanded the list of items specifically included in "gross income" under § 61, it has also added a number of sections which expressly characterize certain receipts as income. In almost every case, in expanding the scope of gross income, Congress has been motivated by a desire to clarify the law, to make the tax laws more equitable, or to expand the tax base. For example, § 86 provides that taxpayers with income over a certain level must report part of their Social Security payments as gross income. This extension of the income concept reflects a concern for equity, since Social Security payments can appropriately be viewed as merely deferred compensation. Likewise, § 61(a)(1) provides that fringe benefits not specifically excluded are includable in gross income. Section 85 requires the inclusion of unemployment benefits in gross income regardless of a recipient's income level, reflecting the view that unemployment compensation constitutes wage replacement payments and should not receive more favorable tax treatment than wages.

For a variety of policy reasons, Congress has specifically excluded certain items from gross income. One of the most important provisions is § 102 excluding gifts and bequests. The importance of the exclusion provisions to one's understanding of gross income cannot be overstated. Several subsequent Chapters address the more important statutory exclusions.

In sum, § 61 and its enumeration of specific items of gross income, together with the other statutory provisions characterizing certain items as gross income, describe most of the items constituting income. Items not specifically addressed by the statute should be evaluated by reference to those that are. It will be seen that income generally includes items that add to the taxpayer's net worth. The statutory exclusions referred to previously as well as certain limited judicial and administrative exclusions discussed in later Chapters limit the scope of gross income and must always be considered when determining whether an item is includable in gross income.

B. Income Realized in Any Form

The regulations explicitly provide that gross income may be realized in any form, whether money, property or services. Reg. § 1.61-1(a). If services are paid for in property, the fair market value of the property is the measure of compensation; if paid for in the form of services, the value of the services received is the amount of compensation. Reg. § 1.61-2(d)(1). Fair market value is generally defined as the price a willing buyer would pay a willing seller, with neither under a compulsion to buy or sell, and both having reasonable knowledge of relevant facts. Reg. § 20.2031-1(b). It seems obvious that a tax system cannot depend on the taxpayer's receipt of cash as the *sine qua non* of income. Although most taxpayers presumably cannot dictate the form of payments they receive and have to accept cash, some taxpayers occasionally or routinely receive payment in services or property, and, to that extent, would receive an unwarranted tax advantage were gross income limited to cash receipts. For example, if Lawyer prepares a will for Plumber, it would be anomalous to charge Lawyer with $100 of income when Lawyer receives $100 cash from Plumber and then hires Plumber to do $100 worth of plumbing work, but to charge Lawyer with no income when the cash is dispensed with and Plumber does the plumbing in exchange for the will. Suppose Lawyer owes Accountant $100. Does Lawyer avoid income on the will preparation by directing Plumber to pay $100 to Accountant, or by directing Plumber to provide $100 in plumbing services to Accountant in discharge of Lawyer's obligation to Accountant? Surely it cannot reasonably be argued that Lawyer has not received anything for the preparation of the will.

Cash payment, of course, serves as a very convenient measure of the amount of Lawyer's income; measurement may be much less certain when valuation of goods or services is necessary, but the difficulty of measurement should not obscure the fact of payment. Nonetheless, you might begin to consider how far we are willing to take the principle that the form of income is irrelevant. Should non-cash receipts of minor value be disregarded due to problems in administration and enforcement by the Internal Revenue Service, and record-keeping or valuation problems for taxpayers? How minor is minor? If hard-to-value property is received, should taxation await its disposition by the taxpayer when valuation will presumably be ascertainable? Should enforcement be particularly vigorous — or relatively relaxed — if taxpayers believe no one really reports all non-cash income? Different situations, and different administrators, can lead to different answers.

Consider one example that touches on these questions. Employers sometimes permit employees who travel at company expense on company business to retain for later personal use the frequent flyer miles earned by the business travel. In theory, retention and use of the frequent flyer miles for personal travel is a form of compensation. Nonetheless, as a result of the valuation, timing, and administrative problems presented, the Service in Announcement 2002-18, 2002-1 C.B. 621 stated "[it would] not assert that any taxpayer has understated his federal tax liability by reason of the receipt or personal use of frequent flyer miles . . . attributable to the taxpayer's business or official travel. Any future guidance on the taxability of these benefits will be applied prospectively." Thus, a taxpayer, who accumulates frequent flyer miles as a result of business travel paid for by her employer, is not required to report any gross income as a result of the receipt of the frequent flyer miles or her use of those miles for personal travel.

C. Realization, Imputed Income and Bargain Purchases

Does gross income encompass all "accessions to wealth"? Clearly not! We now consider some very real limits on the meaning of gross income, limits no less real for the fact that they are not explicitly expressed in any provision of the Internal Revenue Code.

The Realization Requirement. Assume Emily bought 100 shares of stock in Organic Foods, Inc. early this year for $100 per share, its value at the time. The stock is now worth $150 per share. Given low or moderate rates of inflation, it seems clear that by any common understanding of the term — and by economic definitions as well — Emily is wealthier now than she was when she bought the stock. Do we therefore tax her on this increased wealth, on the "income" reflected in the increased value of the share of stock? The instinctive answer one gives is that we do not tax mere appreciation in value of property. That is the correct answer under our income tax system, as well. The technical reason for this non-taxation is that the appreciation has not been "realized"; Emily will not be charged with income until such realization occurs. The most obvious of "realization events" would be Emily's sale of the stock for cash, but, as was emphasized earlier, income is not found in cash alone. Similarly, realization events are not limited to cash sales. For example, Treasury regulations speak of gain or loss as being realized "from the conversion of property into cash or from the exchange of property for other property differing materially either in kind or in extent." Reg. § 1.1001-1(a). The Code itself refers to an amount "realized" on the "sale or other disposition" of property. § 1001(b). In any case, although it is clear that the mere appreciation in value of Emily's stock is not realization of income, it should be equally clear that Emily is wealthier, and a system that taxed all accessions to wealth would tax that increase.

One of the early important tax cases is *Eisner v. Macomber*, introduced to you above for purposes of its definition of income, and mentioned again here as we consider the realization requirement. Mrs. Macomber owned stock in Standard Oil of California. She and the other shareholders received a 50% stock dividend — that is, a dividend in the form of additional corporate stock rather than a cash dividend. Under the Revenue Act of 1916, the stock dividend was taxable, but the Supreme Court held (5-4) that no gain and no income had been realized by reason of the stock dividend and Congress had no power to tax it under the Constitution. The majority opinion suggested realization is a constitutional requirement, i.e., Congress could not constitutionally tax unrealized gain. In that sense, *Macomber* was the high-water mark of the realization requirement. By the time of *Helvering v. Horst*, 311 U.S. 112 (1940), however, the Supreme Court was suggesting in dicta that the realization requirement was merely a rule of "administrative convenience," a far cry from the heady days of *Macomber.* Today, there appears to be a broad consensus that realization is not a constitutionally-required prerequisite to taxation. In the Supreme Court's 1991 decision in *Cottage Savings Association v. Commissioner*, 499 U.S. 554, the issue presented was whether a savings and loan association "realized" losses on the exchange of its interests in one group of home mortgage loans for interests in a different group of home mortgage loans. The Court began by affirming "the concept of realization is 'founded on administrative convenience.'" 499 U.S. at 559. The Court concluded the losses had in fact been realized because, based on the regulations under § 1001,

> an exchange of property gives rise to a realization event so long as the exchanged properties are "materially different" — that is, so long as they embody legally distinct entitlements. Cottage Savings' transactions at issue here easily satisfy this test. Because the participation interests exchanged . . . derived from loans that were made to different obligors and secured by different homes, the exchanged interests did embody legally distinct

entitlements. Consequently, we conclude that Cottage Savings realized its losses at the point of the exchange.

Cottage Savings Association v. Commissioner, 499 U.S. at 566.

To suggest Congress could tax unrealized gain is not to suggest Congress intends to do so. The realization requirement is a pervasive, popularly-supported aspect of our tax system, and there is no indication Congress is about to reverse course in this regard. Assuming Congress could tax "mere appreciation," consider the policy reasons for and against doing so. On the one hand, taxing each year's appreciation would more nearly match tax income and economic income; it would thus tend to place on the same tax footing persons who are economically similarly situated. One might also argue the tax laws should not discourage the sale of property, and that the realization requirement does so by permitting each year's unrealized appreciation to go untaxed, thus levying the entire tax in the year of disposition. On the other hand, and without attempting a complete cataloging, two major reasons are typically offered in support of the present system. First, measuring the appreciation (and, presumably, depreciation) in all of the property of every taxpayer every year would present enormous administrative problems for taxpayers and the Internal Revenue Service. How are assets having no established market to be accurately and easily valued? How much time, cost, and complexity can reasonably be imposed on the average taxpayer? Can the Service be expected to scrutinize every valuation? It might be suggested, however, that such administrative problems would be adequately resolved by a more limited change in the rule. Perhaps the realization requirement would be discarded only with respect to particularly liquid assets, such as publicly traded stock, or with respect to investments of such a type or magnitude — real estate investments of a certain size, for example — that we presume the taxpayer has ready access to reliable valuation assistance. Or would the line be simply too difficult to draw, or too arbitrary to accept? Second, it is often claimed that it would be fundamentally unfair to treat unrealized gains as income because taxpayers might well lack the cash to pay resulting taxes and might thus be forced to sell assets — perhaps at artificially low prices, given the need for cash — to pay the tax. Might this problem be sufficiently ameliorated by limiting the scope of any rule dispensing with the realization requirement?

In the end, whatever your views on the merits of the realization requirement, consider what is at stake. To return to the example with which we began this section, does Emily go forever untaxed on her economic gain? Indeed not. When Emily "realizes" the gain, it will be taxed. Realization is fundamentally a matter of timing. The unrealized total gain, of course, may fluctuate from time to time as the property's value changes, but that total will be treated as income only on realization. To describe realization as a matter of timing should, nonetheless, not be seen as a dismissive comment. In taxes, as in life, timing can be everything — a proposition we explore in some detail in chapters to come.

Imputed Income. The concept of imputed income is often difficult to grasp. How can it be argued that one has "income" from self-help activities, such as mowing the lawn, shaving, or repairing a leaky pipe, and from the use of one's own property, such as the homeowner's occupancy of a home? Let us promptly confirm that imputed income is not taxed, even though the Internal Revenue Code contains no specific exclusion to that effect. The exclusion is rather a matter of administrative practice, but no less firmly established for that reason. It may be helpful to divide imputed income into two categories, imputed income from services and imputed income from property, and, in order to appreciate the economic benefit involved, to approach the topic by way of example.

Imputed income from owning and using one's own property is typically illustrated by a homeowner-versus-renter example. Assume John and Mary each have $250,000 to invest. John uses his $250,000 to buy a house he lives in, and which has a rental value of $25,000 per year. Mary invests her $250,000 in an investment paying 10% — $25,000 — per year. Mary rents a house identical to John's for $25,000 per year. Ignoring homeowner's or renter's costs, consider their situations: each has a $250,000 asset, each derives a $25,000 per year benefit from that asset — John in the form of the $25,000 rental value of his home, Mary in the form of $25,000 cash — but Mary's return on her investment is taxed, while John's equivalent return is nontaxable. Their economic positions and income are identical, but their tax positions are not. Similar, though less significant or dramatic, examples could be developed with respect to ownership and use of other property, from automobiles, boats and washing machines, to pencil sharpeners, bottle cap openers and steak knives, and everything in between. Should such economic benefits be taxed? How would the value of the benefit be determined? In general, the administrative nightmare summoned forth is so powerful that even theorists limit their tax proposals to such big-ticket items as houses. The problem of determining rental value, it is suggested, may be overcome by applying a uniform percentage to the house's value as determined for local property tax purposes. The resulting amount would then be the rental value for federal income tax purposes. Would you agree with such proposals? Are your objections conceptual or administrative ones? If rental value were taxed, would a deduction for "rental expenses" be appropriate? Consider some of the implications of the existing system. Does it favor home ownership over renting, even leaving aside such matters as the tax deduction for mortgage interest (§ 163) and real property taxes (§ 164) and the exclusion of gain on a sale (§ 121)? Should renters be able to exclude from income the money they apply to rent (or, to approach it differently, be given a deduction for rent paid)? Are there aspects of home ownership that justify the difference in treatment?

Imputed income is also present — but again, not treated as income and not taxed — in the economic benefit arising from self-help, i.e., from performing services for oneself, one's family or others. Assume, for example, that the going rate for mowing lawns is $24. Assuming a 20% tax rate, if you choose to hire someone to mow your lawn, you will have to earn $30, paying tax of $6, to have $24 left over for the lawn mowing. Alternately, however, you can stay home, mow the lawn yourself, and have no income and pay no taxes on the value of your time or the benefit your services produced. Are the results consistent? Consider another example. What are the tax consequences if (ignoring any gift possibilities) you and your neighbor mow each other's identical lawns? Recall the discussion on income realized in any form. What are the tax consequences if each of you mows your own lawn instead — should the tax results be any different? Finally, consider a somewhat different example. Assume Doctor A and Doctor B have each been earning $200,000 a year from practicing medicine. Doctor A decides to spend most of her time treating the poor for free and reduces her paid practice to $40,000 per year. Should we tax A on the value of the free services she renders? Or may a taxpayer simply waive payment without being charged with income? Doesn't this happen, in a sense, whenever we assist others without expecting or seeking compensation? Suppose Doctor B, on the other hand, continues to earn $200,000 annually, but gives away $160,000 of it to various poor people so that they can pay for needed medical services. What is B's gross income? Should A and B be treated any differently?

The list of self-help activities that produce some economic benefit is endless, from relatively marketable activities such as lawyers drafting their own wills and doctors diagnosing their own ailments, to the most trivial, mundane and nonmarketable of activities. It is not seriously proposed that they be taxed. One special type of service, however, raises serious tax policy questions. The value of full-time household services — taking care of the house, taking care of children and family — performed by homemakers is obviously substantial. Assume, for purposes of illustration, a value of $40,000 per year on these services and a 20% tax rate; contrast the family with a full-time homemaker spouse with the family where the parents work outside the home and hire homemaker services. The former receives, in effect, $40,000 of economic benefits tax-free; the latter obtains the benefits only after earning $50,000 and paying $10,000 in taxes. To put it another way, if the employer pays the housekeeper $40,000 per year, the housekeeper pays $8,000 to the government, and the employer-housekeeper unit thus has $8,000 less than it had at the outset. But if employer and housekeeper marry, with the housekeeping services performed as before, that same $8,000 stays within the two-person unit. What should the appropriate federal tax policy in this area be?

The tax questions related to imputed income that tend to arise in practice are those associated with self-employment or employment activities. In *Morris v. Commissioner*, 9 B.T.A. 1273, 1278 (1928) (acq.), the Board of Tax Appeals stated the value of farm products consumed by the owner was not income.

> If products of a farm consumed thereon are income to the producer, it would seem to follow that the rental value of the farmer's home, the gratuitous services of his wife and children, and the value of the power derived from draft animals owned by the farmer and used without cost should also be so considered. It is obvious that such items are comparable to the rental value of a private residence, which has never been regarded as income or as a factor in the determination of tax liability.

A number of cases have been litigated involving commissions paid to salespersons purchasing for their own account. The taxpayers claim the transaction should be viewed as a reduction in purchase price, a bargain purchase, in effect. (Bargain purchases are discussed below.) In *Commissioner v. Daehler*, 281 F.2d 823 (5th Cir. 1960), the taxpayer, a real estate salesman, purchased property listed with a broker who was not his employer. That broker divided the commission with the taxpayer's employer-broker, who in turn paid a commission to taxpayer. The Fifth Circuit, reversing the Tax Court, held that the taxpayer's commission was income to him, not a reduction in purchase price. Earlier, in *Commissioner v. Minzner*, 279 F.2d 338 (5th Cir. 1960), also reversing the Tax Court, the Fifth Circuit held an insurance agent could be taxed on the commissions he received on life insurance he purchased on his own life.

Bargain Purchases. We conclude this Overview with some brief comments on bargain purchases, but the brevity should not be considered a measure of the topic's significance. Assume you purchase an asset at a bargain price — that is, assume the fair market value of the asset is greater than the price you paid for it. Is it not fair and accurate to say you have had an accession to wealth? Should that increase in your wealth be taxed as income? The Tax Court, in *Pellar v. Commissioner*, included in the materials, confirmed that bargain purchases generally do not constitute gross income. The reasons for such a rule are not hard to discern. It would presumably be administratively unworkable to require taxpayers and the Service to look behind every acquisition to determine whether one of the participants received a taxable bargain, and if so, in what amount. It makes obvious good sense to assume no bargain element is present in the vast bulk of arm's length transactions, and, if one is, it is too speculative to measure or is minimal enough to ignore. The occasional, obvious and measurable bargain purchase can thus perhaps be tolerated for the sake of the basic rule.

Should the same rule apply where the transaction is not at arm's length? Recall the most common, fundamental type of gross income — compensation for services. Can we ignore the "bargain purchase" when it occurs in an employment setting? Obviously not, and the regulations are quite explicit on this point. If property is transferred as compensation for services in an amount less than its fair market value, the difference between the fair market value and the amount paid is gross income. Reg. § 1.61-2(d)(2)(i). Suppose, for example, that Ed's employer sells the employer's car, worth $15,000, to Ed for only $10,000. Is the sale compensatory in nature? If so, Ed has income of $5,000, the difference between the value of the car and the amount Ed paid. But if the sale is noncompensatory, i.e., if Ed simply makes a bargain purchase of a car his employer wanted to sell quickly to anyone prepared to pay at least $10,000, then we presumably conclude that Ed has no income. But how does Ed establish the noncompensatory nature of the sale if that is indeed the case? The rule that a bargain purchase itself is not income is thus easy to state, but determining whether a bargain element is present or whether it represents compensation for services is, on occasion, somewhat more difficult. (Even when there is no doubt about the presence of a bargain and its relationship to employment, we might, as a matter of policy, choose to exclude the bargain element, within limits, from income. See § 132, excluding certain fringe benefits from income. We shall postpone examination of § 132 until a later chapter).

One final point. Be careful not to misapply the realization requirement in connection with a compensatory bargain purchase that constitutes gross income. Assume, for example, an employer transfers to an employee, as compensation, stock worth $500 in return for payment of $100. Regulation § 1.61-2(d)(2)(i) provides the employee has gross income of $400. It would be incorrect to argue the employee had no income because the $400 gain had not been realized and would not be realized until the employee disposed of the stock. The $400 difference does not constitute appreciation in the stock's value while in the hands of the employee. The property was given to the employee as compensation and it is the fair market value of that property that must be used to measure the compensatory element in the transaction.

COMMISSIONER v. GLENSHAW GLASS CO.
United States Supreme Court
348 U.S. 426 (1955)

MR. CHIEF JUSTICE WARREN delivered the opinion of the Court.

. . . .

The question is whether money received as exemplary damages for fraud or as the punitive two-thirds portion of a treble-damage antitrust recovery must be reported by a taxpayer as gross income under Section 22(a) of the Internal Revenue Code of 1939 [predecessor to I.R.C. § 61 of the Internal Revenue Code of 1986]. The Court of Appeals affirmed the Tax Court's ruling in favor of the taxpayers. Because of the frequent recurrence of the question and differing interpretations by the lower courts of this Court's decisions bearing upon the problem, we granted the Commissioner of Internal Revenue's ensuing petition for certiorari.

The facts of the case were largely stipulated and are not in dispute. So far as pertinent they are as follows: . . . The Glenshaw Glass Company, a Pennsylvania corporation, manufactures glass bottles and containers. It was engaged in protracted litigation with the Hartford-Empire Company, which manufactures machinery of a character used by Glenshaw. Among the claims advanced by Glenshaw were demands for exemplary damages for fraud and treble damages for injury to its business by reason of Hartford's violation of the federal antitrust laws. In December, 1947, the parties concluded a settlement of all pending litigation, by which Hartford paid Glenshaw approximately $800,000. Through a method of allocation which was approved by the Tax Court and which is no longer in issue, it was ultimately determined that, of the total settlement, $324,529.94 represented payment of punitive damages for fraud and antitrust violations. Glenshaw did not report this portion of the settlement as income for the tax year involved. The Commissioner determined a deficiency claiming as taxable the entire sum less only deductible legal fees. As previously noted, the Tax Court and the Court of Appeals upheld the taxpayer.

It is conceded by the respondents that there is no constitutional barrier to the imposition of a tax on punitive damages. Our question is one of statutory construction: are these payments comprehended by Section 22(a)?

The sweeping scope of the controverted statute is readily apparent:

SEC. 22. GROSS INCOME.

(a) GENERAL DEFINITION. — "Gross income" includes gains, profits, and income derived from salaries, wages, or compensation for personal service . . . of whatever kind and in whatever form paid, or from professions, vocations, trades, businesses, commerce, or sales, or dealings in property, whether real or personal, growing out of the ownership or use of or interest in such property; also from interest, rent, dividends, securities, or the transaction of any business carried on for gain or profit, *or gains or profits and income derived from any source whatever. . . .* (Emphasis added.)

This Court has frequently stated that this language was used by Congress to exert in this field "the full measure of its taxing power." *Helvering v. Clifford,* 309 U.S. 331, 334; *Irwin v. Gavit,* 268 U.S. 161, 166. Respondents contend that punitive damages, characterized as "windfalls" flowing from the culpable conduct of third parties, are not within the scope of the section. But Congress applied no limitations as to the source of taxable receipts, nor restrictive labels as to their nature. And the Court has given a liberal construction to this broad phraseology in recognition of the intention of Congress to tax all gains except those specifically exempted. Thus, the fortuitous gain accruing to a lessor by reason of the forfeiture of a lessee's improvements on the rented property was taxed in *Helvering v. Bruun,* 309 U.S. 461. Such decisions demonstrate that we cannot but ascribe content to the catchall provision of Section 22(a), "gains or profits and income derived from any source whatever." The importance of that phrase has been too frequently recognized since its first appearance in the Revenue Act of 1913 to say now that it adds nothing to the meaning of "gross income."

Nor can we accept respondents' contention that a narrower reading of Section 22(a) is required by the Court's characterization of income in *Eisner v. Macomber,* 252 U.S. 189, 207, as "the gain derived from capital, from labor, or from both combined." The Court was there endeavoring to determine whether the distribution of a corporate stock dividend constituted a realized gain to the shareholder, or changed "only the form, not the essence," of his capital investment. It was held that the taxpayer had "received nothing out of the company's assets for his separate use and benefit." The distribution, therefore, was held not a taxable event. In that context — distinguishing gain from capital — the definition served a useful purpose. But it was not meant to provide a touchstone to all future gross income questions.

Here we have instances of undeniable accessions to wealth, clearly realized, and over which the taxpayers have complete dominion. The mere fact that the payments were extracted from the wrongdoers as punishment for unlawful conduct cannot detract from their character as taxable income to the recipients. Respondents concede, as they must, that the recoveries are taxable to the extent that they compensate for damages actually incurred. It would be an anomaly that could not be justified in the absence of clear congressional intent to say that a recovery for actual damages is taxable but not the additional amount extracted as punishment for the same conduct which caused the injury. And we find no such evidence of intent to exempt these payments.[1]

Nor does the 1954 Code's legislative history, with its reiteration of the proposition that statutory gross income is "all-inclusive," give support to respondent's

---

[1] The long history of departmental rulings holding personal injury recoveries nontaxable on the theory that they roughly correspond to a return of capital cannot support exemption of punitive damages following injury to property. . . . Damages for personal injury are by definition compensatory only. Punitive damages, on the other hand, cannot be considered a restoration of capital for taxation purposes.

position. The definition of gross income has been simplified, but no effect upon its present broad scope was intended.[2] Certainly punitive damages cannot reasonably be classified as gifts, . . . nor do they come under any other exemption provision in the Code. We would do violence to the plain meaning of the statute and restrict a clear legislative attempt to bring the taxing power to bear upon all receipts constitutionally taxable were we to say that the payments in question here are not gross income. . . .

Reversed.

MR. JUSTICE DOUGLAS dissents.

CESARINI v. UNITED STATES
United States District Court, Northern District of Ohio
296 F. Supp. 3 (1969),
aff'd, 482 F.2d 812 (6th Cir. 1970)

YOUNG, DISTRICT JUDGE:

This is an action by the plaintiffs as taxpayers for the recovery of income tax payments made in the calendar year 1964. Plaintiffs contend that the amount of $836.51 was erroneously overpaid by them in 1964, and that they are entitled to a refund in that amount. . . .

Plaintiffs are husband and wife. . . . In 1957, the plaintiffs purchased a used piano at an auction sale for approximately $15.00, and the piano was used by their daughter for piano lessons. In 1964, while cleaning the piano, plaintiffs discovered the sum of $4,467.00 in old currency, and since have retained the piano instead of discarding it as previously planned. Being unable to ascertain who put the money there, plaintiffs exchanged the old currency for new at a bank, and reported the sum of $4,467.00 on their 1964 joint income tax return as ordinary income from other sources. On October 18, 1965, plaintiffs filed an amended return with the District Director of Internal Revenue in Cleveland, Ohio, this second return eliminating the sum of $4,467.00 from the gross income computation and requesting a refund in the amount of $836.51, the amount allegedly overpaid as a result of the former inclusion of $4,467.00 in the original return for the calendar year of 1964. On January 18, 1966, the Commissioner of Internal Revenue rejected taxpayers' refund claim in its entirety, and plaintiffs filed the instant action in March of 1967. . . .

The starting point in determining whether an item is to be included in gross income is, of course, Section 61(a) of Title 26 U.S.C., and that section provides in part:

---

[2] In discussing Section 61(a) of the 1954 Code, the House Report states: "This section corresponds to section 22(a) of the 1939 Code." While the language in existing section 22(a) has been simplified, the all-inclusive nature of statutory gross income has not been affected thereby. Section 61(a) is as broad in scope as section 22(a). Section 61(a) provides that gross income includes "all income from whatever source derived." This definition is based upon the 16th Amendment and the word " 'income' is used in its constitutional sense." H.R. Rep. No. 1337, *supra*, note 10, at A18.

Except as otherwise provided in this sub-title, *gross income means all income from whatever source derived*, including (but not limited to) the following items: . . . . (Emphasis added.)

Subsections (1) through (15) of Section 61(a) then go on to list fifteen items specifically included in the computation of the taxpayer's gross income, and Part II of Subchapter B of the 1954 Code (Sections 71 *et seq.*) deals with other items expressly included in gross income. While neither of these listings expressly includes the type of income which is at issue in the case at bar, Part III of Subchapter B (Sections 101 *et seq.*) deals with items specifically excluded from gross income, and found money is not listed in those sections either. This absence of express mention in any of the code sections necessitates a return to the "all income from whatever source" language of Section 61(a) of the code, and the express statement there that gross income is "not limited to" the following fifteen examples. Section 1.61-1(a) of the Treasury Regulations, the corresponding section to Section 61(a) in the 1954 Code, reiterates this broad construction of gross income, providing in part:

Gross income means all income from whatever source derived, unless excluded by law. *Gross income includes income realized in any form*, whether in money, property, or services. . . . (Emphasis added.)

The decisions of the United States Supreme Court have frequently stated that this broad all-inclusive language was used by Congress to exert the full measure of its taxing power under the Sixteenth Amendment to the United States Constitution. *Commissioner v. Glenshaw Glass Co.*, 348 U.S. 426 (1955).

In addition, the Government in the instant case cites and relies upon an I.R.S. Revenue Ruling which is undeniably on point:

The finder of treasure-trove is in receipt of taxable income, for Federal income tax purposes, to the extent of its value in United States currency, for the taxable year in which it is reduced to undisputed possession. Rev. Rul. 61, 1953-1 C.B. 17.

The plaintiffs argue that the above ruling does not control this case for two reasons. The first is that subsequent to the Ruling's pronouncement in 1953, Congress enacted Sections 74 and 102 of the 1954 Code, Section 74 expressly including the value of prizes and awards in gross income in most cases, and Section 102 specifically exempting the value of gifts received from gross income. From this, it is argued that Section 74 was added because prizes might otherwise be construed as non-taxable gifts, and since no such section was passed expressly taxing treasure-trove, it is therefore a gift which is non-taxable under Section 102. This line of reasoning overlooks the statutory scheme previously alluded to, whereby income from all sources is taxed unless the taxpayer can point to an express exemption. Not only have the taxpayers failed to list a specific exclusion in the instant case, but also the Government has pointed to express language covering the found money, even though it would not be required to do so under the broad language of Section 61(a) and the foregoing Supreme Court decisions interpreting it.

In partial summary, then, the arguments of the taxpayers which attempt to avoid the application of Rev. Rul. 61, 1953-1 are not well taken. . . . While it is generally true that revenue rulings may be disregarded by the courts if in conflict with the code and the regulations, or with other judicial decisions, plaintiffs in the instant case have been unable to point to any inconsistency between the gross income sections of the code, the interpretation of them by the regulations and the courts, and the revenue ruling which they herein attack as inapplicable. On the other hand, the United States has shown a consistency in letter and spirit between the ruling and the code, regulations, and court decisions.

Although not cited by either party, and noticeably absent from the Government's brief, the following Treasury Regulation appears in the 1964 Regulations, the year of the return in dispute:

Section 1.61-14 Miscellaneous items of gross income.

(a) In general. In addition to the items enumerated in section 61(a), there are many other kinds of gross income. . . . *Treasure trove, to the extent of its value in United States currency, constitutes gross income for the taxable year in which it is reduced to undisputed possession.* (Emphasis added.)

Identical language appears in the 1968 Treasury Regulations, and is found in all previous years back to 1958. This language is the same in all material respects as that found in Rev. Rul. 61, 1953-1 C.B. 17, and is undoubtedly an attempt to codify that ruling into the Regulations which apply to the 1954 Code. This Court is of the opinion that Treas. Reg. Section 1.61-14(a) is dispositive of the major issue in this case if the $4,467.00 found in the piano was "reduced to undisputed possession" in the year petitioners reported it, for this Regulation was applicable to returns filed in the calendar year of 1964.

This brings the Court to the second contention of the plaintiffs: that if any tax was due, it was in 1957 when the piano was purchased, and by 1964 the Government was blocked from collecting it by reason of the statute of limitations. [See I.R.C. § 6501(a) which generally establishes a 3-year statute of limitations.] Without reaching the question of whether the voluntary payment in 1964 constituted a waiver on the part of the taxpayers, this Court finds that the $4,467.00 sum was properly included in gross income for the calendar year of 1964. Problems of when title vests, or when possession is complete in the field of federal taxation, in the absence of definitive federal legislation on the subject, are ordinarily determined by reference to the law of the state in which the taxpayer resides, or where the property around which the dispute centers is located. Since both the taxpayers and the property in question are found within the State of Ohio, Ohio law must govern as to when the found money was "reduced to undisputed possession" within the meaning of Treas. Reg. Section 1.61-14 and Rev. Rul. 61, 1953-1 C.B. 17.

In Ohio, there is no statute specifically dealing with the rights of owners and finders of treasure trove, and in the absence of such a statute the common-law rule of England applies, so that "title belongs to the finder as against all the world except the true owner." *Niederlehner v. Weatherly,* 78 Ohio App. 263, 69 N.E.2d 787 (1946), appeal dismissed, 146 Ohio St. 697 67 N.E.2d 713 (1946). The *Niederlehner* case held, *inter alia,* that the owner of real estate upon which money is found does not have title as against the finder. Therefore, in the instant case if plaintiffs had resold the piano in 1958, not knowing of the money within it, they later would not be able to succeed in an action against the purchaser who did discover it. Under Ohio law, the plaintiffs must have actually found the money to have superior title over all but the true owner, and they did not discover the old currency until 1964. Unless there is present a specific state statute to the contrary, . . . the majority of jurisdictions are in accord with the Ohio rule. . . . Therefore, this Court finds that the $4,467.00 in old currency was not "reduced to undisputed possession" until its actual discovery in 1964, and thus the United States was not barred by the statute of limitations from collecting the $836.51 in tax during that year.

OLD COLONY TRUST COMPANY v. COMMISSIONER
United States Supreme Court
279 U.S. 716 (1929)

Mr. Chief Justice Taft delivered the opinion of the Court.

. . . The petitioners are the executors of the will of William M. Wood, deceased. On June 27, 1925, before Mr. Wood's death, the Commissioner of Internal Revenue notified him by registered mail of the determination of a deficiency in income tax against him for the years 1919 and 1920, under the Revenue Act of 1918. An appeal was taken to the Board of Appeals. The Board approved the action of the Commissioner and found a deficiency in the federal income tax return of Mr. Wood for the year 1919 of $708,781.93, and for the year 1920 of $350,837.14. . . .

The facts certified to us are substantially as follows:

William M. Wood was president of the American Woolen Company during the years 1918, 1919, and 1920. In 1918 he received as salary and commissions from the company $978,725, which he included in his federal income tax return for 1918. In 1919 he received as salary and commissions from the company $548,132.27, which he included in his return for 1919.

August 3, 1916, the American Woolen Company had adopted the following resolution, which was in effect in 1919 and 1920:

Voted: That this company pay any and all income taxes, State and Federal, that may hereafter become due and payable upon the salaries of all the officers of the company, including the president, William M. Wood; the comptroller, Parry C. Wiggin; the auditor, George R. Lawton; and the following members of the staff, to-wit: Frank H. Carpenter, Edwin L. Heath, Samuel R. Haines, and William M. Lasbury, to the end that said persons and officers shall receive their salaries or other compensation in full without deduction on account of income taxes, State or Federal, which taxes are to be paid out of the treasury of this corporation.

This resolution was amended on March 25, 1918, as follows:

Voted: That, in referring to the vote passed by this board on August 3, 1916, in reference to income taxes, State and Federal, payable upon the salaries or compensation of the officers and certain employees of this company, the method of computing said taxes shall be as follows, viz:

> The difference between what the total amount of his tax would be, including his income from all sources, and the amount of his tax when computed upon his income excluding such compensation or salaries paid by this company.

Pursuant to these resolutions, the American Woolen Company paid to the collector of internal revenue Mr. Wood's federal income and surtaxes due to salary and commissions paid to him by the company, as follows:

Taxes for 1918 paid in 1919 . . . . $681,169.88

Taxes for 1919 paid in 1920 . . . . $351,179.27

The decision of the Board of Tax Appeals here sought to be reviewed was that the income taxes of $681,169.88 and $351,179.27 paid by American Woolen Company for Mr. Wood were additional income to him for the years 1919 and 1920.

The question certified by the Circuit Court of Appeals for answer by this Court is:

> Did the payment by the employer of the income taxes assessable against the employee constitute additional taxable income to such employee?

Coming now to the merits of this case, we think the question presented is whether a taxpayer, having induced a third person to pay his income tax or having acquiesced in such payment as made in discharge of an obligation to him, may avoid the making of a return thereof and the payment of a corresponding tax. We think he may not do so. The payment of the tax by the employers was in consideration of the services rendered by the employee and was a gain derived by the employee from his labor. The form of the payment is expressly declared to make no difference. It is therefore immaterial that the taxes were directly paid to the Government. The discharge by a third person of an obligation to him is equivalent to receipt by the person taxed. The certificate shows that the taxes were imposed upon the employee, that the taxes were actually paid by the employer and that the employee entered upon his duties in the years in question under the express agreement that his income taxes would be paid by his employer. This is evidenced by the terms of the resolution passed August 3, 1916, more than one year prior to the year in which the taxes were imposed. The taxes were paid upon a valuable consideration, namely, the services rendered by the employee and as part of the compensation therefor. We think therefore that the payment constituted income to the employee.

Nor can it be argued that the payment of the tax . . . was a gift. The payment for services, even though entirely voluntary, was nevertheless compensation within the statute. This is shown by the case of *Noel v. Parrott*, 15 F.2d 669. There it was resolved that a gratuitous appropriation equal in amount of $3 per share on the outstanding stock of the company be set aside out of the assets for distribution to certain officers and employees of the company and that the executive committee be authorized to make such distribution as they deemed wise and proper. The executive committee gave $35,000 to the plaintiff taxpayer. The court said,

In no view of the evidence, therefore, can the $35,000 be regarded as a gift. It was either compensation for services rendered, or a gain or profit derived from the sale of the stock of the corporation, or both; and, in any view, it was taxable as income.

It was next argued against the payment of this tax that if these payments by the employer constitute income to the employee, the employer will be called upon to pay the tax imposed upon this additional income, and that the payment of the additional tax will create further income which will in turn be subject to tax, with the result that there would be a tax upon a tax. This it is urged is the result of the Government's theory, when carried to its logical conclusion, and results in an absurdity which Congress could not have contemplated.

In the first place, no attempt has been made by the Treasury to collect further taxes, upon the theory that the payment of the additional taxes creates further income, and the question of a tax upon a tax was not before the Circuit Court of Appeals and has not been certified to this Court. We can settle questions of that sort when an attempt to impose a tax upon a tax is undertaken, but not now. . . . It is not, therefore, necessary to answer the argument based upon an algebraic formula to reach the amount of taxes due. The question in this case is, "Did the payment by the employer of the income taxes assessable against the employee constitute additional taxable income to such employee?" The answer must be "Yes."

AUTHORS' NOTE

Because the Service did not attempt to impose a "tax upon a tax" in *Old Colony Trust Company*, the Supreme Court did not rule on "the validity of the imposition of such a tax." It is now clear, however, that courts will uphold the pyramiding of tax liability in appropriate cases. *Safe Harbor Water Power Co. v. U.S.*, 303 F.2d 928 (Ct. Cl. 1962).

REVENUE RULING 79-24
1979-1 C.B. 60

FACTS

Situation 1. In return for personal legal services performed by a lawyer for a housepainter, the housepainter painted the lawyer's personal residence. Both the lawyer and the housepainter are members of a barter club, an organization that annually furnishes its members a directory of members and the services they provide. All the members of the club are professional or trades persons. Members contact other members directly and negotiate the value of the services to be performed.

Situation 2. An individual who owned an apartment building received a work of art created by a professional artist in return for the rent-free use of an apartment for six months by the artist.

LAW

The applicable sections of the Internal Revenue Code of 1954 and the Income Tax Regulations thereunder are 61(a) and 1.61-2, relating to compensation for services.

Section 1.61-2(d)(1) of the regulations provides that if services are paid for other than in money, the fair market value of the property or services taken in payment must be included in income. If the services were rendered at a stipulated price, such price will be presumed to be the fair market value of the compensation received in the absence of evidence to the contrary.

HOLDINGS

Situation 1. The fair market value of the services received by the lawyer and the housepainter are includible in their gross incomes under section 61 of the Code.

Situation 2. The fair market value of the work of art and the six months fair rental value of the apartment are includible in the gross incomes of the apartment-owner and the artist under section 61 of the Code.

McCANN v. UNITED STATES
United States Court of Claims
81-2 U.S.T.C. § 9689 (Ct. Cl. 1981),
aff'd, 696 F.2d 1386 (Fed. Cir. 1983)

WHITE, SENIOR TRIAL JUDGE:

The plaintiffs in these cases, which were consolidated for trial purposes, sue for refunds of income taxes (and interest thereon) which the plaintiffs were required to pay pursuant to deficiency notices issued by the Internal Revenue Service.

The *McCann* case had its inception when Elvia R. McCann and Mrs. Leone A. McCann, who are husband and wife and residents of Shreveport, Louisiana, made a round trip between Shreveport and Las Vegas, Nevada, in 1973 for the purpose of attending a seminar (the term used by the witnesses) that was conducted in Las Vegas by Mrs. McCann's employer, Security Industrial Insurance Company (Security). All the traveling and other expenses of Mr. and Mrs. McCann in connection with attendance at the Las Vegas seminar were paid by Security.

In filing their joint income tax return for 1973, the McCanns did not include in their gross income any amount reflecting the cost to Security of paying the McCanns' expenses on the Las Vegas trip.

The Internal Revenue Service, upon auditing the McCanns' 1973 income tax return, decided that the fair market value of the Las Vegas trip should have been included in the McCanns' gross income, determined the amount of the fair market value of the trip, and issued a deficiency notice.

Mr. and Mrs. McCann paid the deficiency, amounting to $199.16, plus accrued interest of $64.97.

Thereafter, the McCanns filed a claim for refund; and, when relief from the

Internal Revenue Service was not forthcoming, the McCanns instituted the present litigation.

Security is engaged in the sale of life, burial, and accident insurance. Security's best-selling policy is a burial policy with a face amount of $600, which provides merchandise and services necessary for a complete funeral at one of the several funeral homes with which Security has contractual relationships. Many of Security's policy-holders are religious people who live in rural areas of Louisiana.

Security's sales organization consists of a home office in Donaldsonville, Louisiana, and 26 district offices located in other parts of Louisiana.

Ever since 1950, Security has sponsored what is commonly referred to as an annual sales seminar at some place outside the State of Louisiana. These seminars have been held in (among other places): Biloxi, Mississippi; Miami Beach, Florida; Washington, D.C.; New York, New York; San Francisco, California; Houston, Texas; Atlanta, Georgia; Las Vegas, Nevada; and Mexico City, Mexico. The purpose and format of the seminars have been the same through the years.

An agent qualifies to attend a seminar if he or she achieved a specified net increase in sales during the preceding calendar year.

Each agent, staff manager, or district manager who qualifies to attend a seminar is entitled to take along his or her spouse, or another family member. . . . All travel and other expenses of employees and their guests attending seminars are paid by Security.

However, agents and other employees who qualify for seminars are not required to attend; and their promotional opportunities are not adversely affected if they fail to attend.

Security emphasizes the pleasure aspects of seminars. The company schedules sightseeing tours; furnishes participants with lists of tennis courts and golf courses at, and descriptive travel brochures concerning, seminar sites; and chooses locations which (in the opinion of the company) will have "excitement" and "charisma" for qualifying employees. New Orleans, Louisiana, has never been chosen as a seminar site because of the familiarity of company personnel with New Orleans.

The *McCann* case involves the seminar which Security held in Las Vegas, at the Caesar's Palace Hotel, from June 17 through June 20, 1973. A total of 74 of Security's employees qualified to attend the seminar in Las Vegas. This total included 47 agents, or 11.7 percent of the 400 agents employed by the company in 1973. A total of 66 employees, out of the 74 who qualified, actually attended the seminar in Las Vegas; and, the number attending included 40 agents, out of the 47 who qualified.

The total cost to Security of the Las Vegas seminar amounted to $68,116.96. This amount included all the expenses (airfare, lodging, meals, cocktail parties, sightseeing tours, shows, local transportation, and gratuities) of each individual who attended the seminar.

As previously indicated, Mr. and Mrs. McCann attended the Las Vegas seminar in 1973. Mrs. McCann qualified for attendance by achieving the required net increase in sales during the calendar year 1972; and Mr. McCann went along as her guest in accordance with Security's policy of permitting a qualifying employee to take along a spouse or other family member. All the travel and other expenses of Mr. and Mrs. McCann were paid by Security.

As the program for the seminar in Las Vegas was typical of the programs at other seminars sponsored by Security, it will be outlined in some detail.

The official program for the Las Vegas seminar began with a cocktail party at 5:00 p.m. on June 17, 1973. Senior officers of Security and their spouses greeted the other participants at the door. The cocktail party was followed by a dinner of prime ribs, served with wine. E.J. Ourso, president and chief executive officer of Security, delivered a welcoming address; and housekeeping announcements were made. The dinner was followed by a show at the Circus Maximus, featuring singer Diana Ross and "topless" dancers. The remainder of the evening was free time. Some of the participants went to a second show, but the younger participants spent the free time in dancing, drinking, and carousing.

On June 18, there was a group breakfast at 8:00 a.m. There was no formal program at the breakfast; and only housekeeping announcements (such as those relating to lost baggage, the location of certain rooms, and the agenda for the day) were made. The breakfast was followed by a business meeting from 9 to 11 a.m. This meeting featured a panel discussion, the panel being composed of leading agents and one spouse and being moderated by a district manager. The panel discussion was followed by a question-and-answer session and concluding remarks by Mr. Ourso. Employees of Security, but not their guests, were required to attend the business meeting. The business meeting was followed by lunch and a trip to Boulder Dam in the afternoon. At 5:30 p.m. there was a cocktail party and group meeting at the Dunes, followed by dinner and a stage show, "Casino de Paris," which featured "topless" dancers. Alcoholic beverages were served at the dinner and show.

On June 19, there was a group meeting and breakfast at 9:00 a.m.; and this was followed by free time until 11:00 a.m. (the program suggested that the free time be spent "sunning in the Garden of the Gods, playing tennis, or just relaxing"). Lunch was held from 11:00 a.m. to 12:00 noon. There was no formal program at either breakfast or lunch; and only housekeeping announcements were made. Lunch was followed by a tour of the Mint Hotel beginning at 2:00 p.m. At 6:00 p.m., there was a "Farewell to Las Vegas" cocktail party and group meeting. There was no formal program at this function. A banquet was held beginning at 7:00 p.m., and wine was served with the dinner. Mr. Ourso made a speech, reviewing the activities of the company during the preceding year, and then he bestowed an award on each agent, staff manager, and district manager in attendance. The banquet concluded with a guest speaker, an attorney for Security, who spoke of his pride in being associated with the company.

The first question to be decided in the *McCann* case is whether, as determined by the Internal Revenue Service, the McCanns should have included in their 1973 income tax return, as part of their gross income, an amount based upon the cost to Security of defraying their travel and other expenses on the trip to Las Vegas.

In this connection, the Internal Revenue Code of 1954 defines gross income as meaning "all income from whatever source derived" . . . (26 U.S.C. § 61(a)). The Supreme Court has said that Congress intended by this statutory provision to tax *all* gains, except those specifically exempted (*Commissioner v. Glenshaw Glass Co.*, 348 U.S. 426, 430 (1955)), and that the term "income" includes any economic or financial benefit conferred as compensation, however accomplished (*Commissioner v. Smith*, 324 U.S. 177, 181 (1945)).

An implementing regulation declares that gross income may include money, property, services, meals, accommodations, or stock, or may be in any other form. Treas. Reg. § 1.61-1(a). Thus, in a situation where an employer pays an employee's expenses on a trip that is a reward for services rendered by the employee, the value of the reward must be regarded as income to the employee. . . .

The all-expenses trip to Las Vegas — with its airfare, lodging, meals, cocktails, sightseeing tours, shows, local transportation, and gratuities — which Mr. and Mrs. McCann received from Security was obviously an economic benefit to them. Moreover, they received this benefit as a reward for Mrs. McCann's good work in increasing her net sales by a specified amount during the preceding calendar year (1972). Only 47 agents, out of 400 agents employed by Security, qualified for the 1973 seminar in Las Vegas by achieving the required net increase in sales during 1972. The 47 agents (or so many of them as wished to make the trip) were rewarded by receiving from Security the all-expenses trip to Las Vegas for themselves and their spouses, or other family members. The 353 agents who failed to achieve the specified net increase in sales during 1972 did not receive the reward.

Therefore, the reward to Mrs. McCann, although not in the form of money, was clearly compensation to her for the services that she had rendered to Security during 1972, and was within the meaning of income, as that term is used in 26 U.S.C. § 61(a). *Commissioner v. Lo Bue*, 351 U.S. 243, 247 (1956).

When services are paid for in a form other than in money, it is necessary to determine the fair market value of the thing received. Treas. Reg. § 1.61-2(d)(1).

In the present case, the Internal Revenue Service decided that the fair market value of the Las Vegas trip which Mr. and Mrs. McCann received from Security was equivalent to the cost of the trip to Security. At the trial, the plaintiff did not introduce any evidence challenging the correctness of the administrative determination on this point. Accordingly, in view of the presumption of legality which supports official administrative actions, the determination of the Internal Revenue Service concerning the fair market value of the Las Vegas trip which Mr. and Mrs. McCann received from Security will be accepted by the court as correct.

PELLAR v. COMMISSIONER
United States Tax Court
25 T.C. 299 (1955), acq. 1956-2 C.B. 7

[Petitioners entered into an agreement with a construction company for the erection of a dwelling on land previously purchased by petitioners. The actual cost of construction was substantially in excess of the price fixed in the agreement, the excess being in part due to "extras" requested by petitioners, and in part to increased labor costs and errors in construction work on the part of contractor. The fair market value of the dwelling (exclusive of the value of the land) at the time of completion was materially in excess of the price fixed in the agreement, but was materially less than the actual cost of construction. The contractor had never expected to make a profit on the construction work and was satisfied to take a small loss. This was because Sam Briskin, father of Rosalie Pellar, one of the petitioners, had an interest in several corporations which had employed the contractor for construction work in amounts totaling in excess of a million dollars, and Briskin had likewise, at various times, recommended the contractor to others. The contractor agreed to do the work for petitioners at the arranged price to keep Briskin's goodwill in the hope of future business from the Briskin interests and from others to whom the contractor might be recommended by Briskin.]

. . . .

The only issue for decision is whether or not petitioners received income by virtue of the construction of a residence for them where the cost of construction and the fair market value of the residence materially exceeded the agreed price paid to the contractor for such construction.

OPINION

FISHER, JUDGE: Respondent appears to have based his statutory notice of deficiency upon the theory that petitioners received income by virtue of the construction of their home in an amount measured by the excess of the total cost to Ragnar Benson, Inc., for constructing the dwelling over the amount paid by the Pellars. . . . For practical purposes, and as background for our discussion, we think we need only discuss whether or not the excess of the fair market value of the property (excluding land) over cost constituted income to the Pellars. We have found as an ultimate fact, upon consideration of the entire record, that such fair market value, on completion, was $70,000. The agreed price paid by the Pellars to Ragnar Benson, Inc., was $40,000. The Pellars likewise paid $23,466.94 in purchasing the ground, completing the house, and landscaping and improving the grounds. Eliminating $8,500 paid for the land, we have the net sum of $14,966.94, which, when added to the $40,000 paid to Ragnar Benson, Inc., gives a total of approximately $55,000 paid by the Pellars for a house worth $70,000.

The substantial issue is, therefore, whether the differential of approximately $15,000 was income to the Pellars. . . .

For the purpose of our discussion, therefore, we limit the issue to the question of whether the fact that . . . petitioners got $15,000 more house than they paid for, resulted in the realization by petitioners of taxable income.

We think there can be no doubt that the general rule is that the purchase of property for less than its value does not, of itself, give rise to the realization of taxable income. Such realization normally arises, and is taxed, upon sale or other disposition.

In *Palmer v. Commissioner*, 302 U.S. 63 (1937), the Supreme Court said (pp. 68, 69):

In Sections 111, 112 and 113 of the Revenue Act of 1928, [26 U.S.C.A. Pars. 111, 112 and notes, 113 note], profits derived from the purchase of property, as distinguished from exchanges of property, are ascertained and taxed as of the date of its sale or other disposition by the purchaser. Profit, if any, accrues to him only upon sale or disposition, and the taxable income is the difference between the amount thus realized and its cost, less allowed deductions. It follows that one does not subject himself to income tax by the mere purchase of property, even if at less than its true value, and that taxable gain does not accrue to him before he sells or otherwise disposes of it. Specific provisions establishing this basis for the taxation of gains derived from purchased property were included in the 1916 and each subsequent revenue act and accompanying regulations.

In 1 Mertens, Law of Federal Income Taxation, page 227, paragraph 5.25, we find the following:

5.25. Income Realized Through Purchase. No taxable income results from the purchase of property assuming that the transaction is one at arm's length and that the relationship of the parties does not introduce into the transaction other elements indicating that the transaction is not simply a purchase but involves an exchange of other considerations. It requires strong evidence to rebut the presumption that what appears in good faith to be a purchase is not such. The fact that the property may be acquired at a bargain price or one below its "fair market value" does not require a departure from this rule.

Taxable gain does not accrue to the purchaser of property until he sells or otherwise disposes of it. This concept is specifically incorporated in the statute in the provisions providing for the recognition of gain or loss on the sale or other disposition of property.

As indicated above, acquisitions of property may result in taxable income where they do not represent purchases or where some other purpose is consummated by the acquisition of the property. There are many instances where this is true. For example, property acquired in connection with a "bargain purchase" may represent compensation where the seller and the purchaser bear the relationship of employer and employee, or a dividend distribution, or a gift. The purchase by a corporation of its own bonds at a price below their issuing price is another frequent example of a purchase giving rise to taxable income.

While the facts before us are obviously unusual, we fail to find any circumstances on the basis of which we may determine that petitioners realized taxable income upon the principles announced by the authorities cited above. In the instant case, there was no employer-employee relationship from which we might infer that the $15,000 differential was compensatory. It is clear, likewise, that the elements of a dividend are not present. Nor is there any other theory brought to our attention from which we may hold that income was realized.

The Pellars did receive more value than that paid for. This opportunity was afforded them because Ragnar Benson wanted Briskin's goodwill, any future business controlled by Briskin, and a continuation in the future of Briskin's favorable recommendations. Nevertheless, there was no obligation for Briskin (or petitioners) to favor Benson, in the future, in any of such respects.

We add that we do not think Benson himself had any idea, when he agreed to build the house, that his voluntary investment in goodwill would be so costly. Once the project was in motion, however, he adhered to his agreement as a matter of policy. We need not consider whether it was enforceable. Whether he will gain or lose in the end is no more before us than the question of petitioners' ultimate realization of gain upon future sale or exchange of the property.

We think that Benson's actions were akin to lavish expenditures for presents or entertaining. We think no more was intended by him, and that, in all events, petitioners were not obligated, in any legal sense, for services rendered or other affirmative response.

Respondent's substantial reliance is upon *Commissioner v. Glenshaw Glass Co.*, 348 U.S. 425, 75 S. Ct. 473 (1955). It is necessary only to point out, in distinguishing the *Glenshaw* case, that it involved the taxation of exemplary damages for fraud and punitive treble damages for antitrust violations.

We hold, upon the foregoing discussion, that petitioners, under the circumstances discussed, realized no taxable income.

Decision will be entered for petitioners.

AUTHORS' NOTE

As noted in the opinion, Ragnar Benson, the contractor, agreed to build the Pellar's home at the arranged price to keep the goodwill of Rosalie Pellar's father, Sam Briskin, whose corporations had provided the contractor with millions of dollars in construction contracts. Query: Should the focus of the Service have been Sam Briskin rather than Rosalie Pellar, i.e., should the Service have argued that Sam Briskin had compensation income as a result of the "bargain element" in the home constructed for his daughter? If the Service had focused on the relationship between Sam Briskin and Ragnar Benson, the Service could have had argued that the relationship between Benson and Briskin introduced into the transaction "other elements indicating that the transaction [was] not simply a purchase but [involved] an exchange of other considerations." See the quote from 1 Mertens, Law of Federal Income Taxation, in the opinion.

ROCO v. COMMISSIONER
United States Tax Court
121 T.C. 160 (2003)

Opinion: COLVIN, JUDGE.

Respondent determined a deficiency in petitioner's 1997 Federal income tax of $610,446 and an accuracy-related penalty under section 6662(a) of $122,093.

Petitioner sued the New York University Medical Center (NYUMC) in a qui tam action under the False Claims Act (FCA). In the qui tam action, petitioner claimed that NYUMC had submitted false information to the United States which resulted in a substantial overpayment of Federal funds to NYUMC. NYUMC agreed to pay $15,500,000 to the United States in settlement of the case. The United States paid petitioner $1,568,087 in 1997 as his share of the settlement proceeds.

The issues for decision are:

1. Whether the $1,568,087 payment that petitioner received from the United States in 1997 is includable in gross income. We hold that it is.

2. Whether petitioner is liable for the accuracy-related penalty under section 6662(a) for 1997. We hold that he is. [This portion of the opinion is omitted.]

FINDINGS OF FACT

Some of the facts have been stipulated and are so found.

A. Petitioner and His Spouse

Petitioner and his wife, Milagros Roco (Mrs. Roco), have been married since January 24, 1971. Both petitioner and Mrs. Roco are accountants and have accounting degrees from the University of the East, Manila, the Philippines. Petitioner was employed as an accountant by NYUMC in New York, from 1974 to 1992. Mrs. Roco has worked as an income tax auditor for the State of New York Department of Taxation and Finance since 1977. She began training others to do tax audits in 1988.

B. Qui Tam Actions

Congress enacted the FCA in 1863. . . . Under the FCA, either the United States or a private person (the relator) may bring an action, known as a qui tam action, against any person who knowingly presents to the Government a false or fraudulent claim for payment. The relator in a qui tam action is the agent of the United States, in whose name the suit is brought. The relator may recover attorney's fees and a share of the Government's recovery if the claim is successful.

C. Petitioner's Lawsuit Against NYUMC

Petitioner was fired by NYUMC in 1992 after he told his superiors that he believed NYUMC had substantially overcharged the United States. In 1993, petitioner, acting as the relator, filed a qui tam action against NYUMC in the U.S. District Court for the Southern District of New York. In that case, petitioner alleged that, from 1984 to 1993, NYUMC submitted false information and overcharged the United States for costs associated with federally sponsored research grants and Medicaid, Medicare, and Blue Cross/Blue Shield reimbursements. Petitioner researched the law concerning qui tam actions, drafted the complaint, and appeared pro se in the qui tam proceeding.

The U.S. Attorney for the Southern District of New York intervened in the case.

The case was settled in April 1997. Under the settlement, NYUMC agreed to pay the United States $15,500,000, and the United States paid petitioner $1,568,087 on May 13, 1997. Petitioner, NYUMC, and the United States stipulated:

> The United States agrees to pay the Relator $1,568,087 within a reasonable time following receipt of the full settlement amount from defendant as described in paragraph 2. . . . This Stipulation does not in any manner affect any Claims the United States has or may have against the Relator arising under title 26 of the United States Code ("Internal Revenue Code") and the regulations promulgated thereunder, or from any obligations created by this Stipulation.

Petitioner asked Deborah Pugh (Pugh), the Department of Justice attorney who handled the qui tam case, whether the qui tam payment was includable in gross income for Federal income tax purposes. She told him she did not know and recommended that he consult an attorney. Petitioner asked Pugh to omit the paragraph quoted above, but she declined to do so. The Department of Justice issued to petitioner a Form 1099-MISC, Miscellaneous Income, showing that it had paid him $1,568,087 in 1997.

D. Petitioner's Efforts to Determine the Tax Treatment of the Qui Tam Payment

Petitioner and Mrs. Roco believed that their accounting and tax backgrounds were sufficient to enable them to correctly determine whether the qui tam payment was includable in gross income for Federal income tax purposes. Petitioner and Mrs. Roco researched tax cases, the Internal Revenue Code, Internal Revenue Service (IRS) regulations, tax publications, and tax treatises. Petitioner and Mrs. Roco correctly concluded that none of those authorities discuss whether payments to a relator in a qui tam case are includable in the relator's gross income. Mrs. Roco told petitioner that she thought the qui tam payment was probably not includable in gross income.

After he received the Form 1099-MISC, petitioner requested a private letter ruling from the IRS on July 23, 1997, as to the income tax consequences of the qui tam payment he received. Petitioner's request was assigned to Sheldon Iskow (Iskow). In August 1997, Iskow told petitioner that there were no court cases holding that qui tam payments are includable in gross income. Iskow also told petitioner that he believed a qui tam payment is taxable because it is analogous to a reward, and that the IRS would rule that the qui tam payment was taxable unless petitioner provided legal authorities for his position or withdrew his request for a ruling. Petitioner withdrew the letter ruling request.

E. Petitioner's 1997 Tax Returns

Petitioner made no estimated tax payments to the United States in 1997 relating to the qui tam payment, but he did make an estimated tax payment of $80,500 to the State of New York. Mrs. Roco helped petitioner prepare and file his Form 1040, Individual Income Tax Return, for 1997. Petitioner did not report the qui tam payment on his State and Federal returns for 1997.

Petitioner and Mrs. Roco filed joint Federal returns for 1995, 1996, 1998, 2000, and 2001, but they filed separate returns for 1997. They expected respondent to discover that petitioner had not reported the $1,568,087 payment by matching the Form 1099-MISC with his 1997 return, and that respondent would decide to audit petitioner's 1997 return. Mrs. Roco believed she might lose her job if she owed substantial tax for failing to report the qui tam payment.

The IRS began the examination of petitioner's 1997 income tax return in 1999.

OPINION

Whether the $1,568,087 Qui Tam Payment Is Includable in Income

. . . .

The qui tam payment to petitioner was the equivalent of a reward for petitioner's efforts to obtain repayment to the United States of overcharges by NYUMC. Rewards are generally includable in gross income. Sec. 1.61-2(a), Income Tax Regs.

Petitioner contends that, if qui tam payments are includable in gross income, taxpayers will be discouraged from bringing actions under the FCA. We disagree that this possibility justifies holding for petitioner. Petitioner's point could also be made with respect to taxing any reward, but rewards are clearly includable in gross income under section 1.61-2(a)(1), Income Tax Regs.

Petitioner contends that the $1,568,087 qui tam payment is not includable in gross income because it is not gain derived from capital or labor. *See Eisner v. Macomber*, 252 U.S. 189, 207 (1920). We disagree. Gross income includes all income from whatever source derived unless excluded by law. Sec. 61; *Commissioner v. Glenshaw Glass Co.*, 348 U.S. 426, 430 (1955). The Internal Revenue code provides no exclusion from gross income for proceeds received by a relator in a qui tam proceeding. In *Eisner v. Macomber, supra*, the Supreme Court decided that a shareholder-taxpayer did not realize gain on the receipt of a stock dividend. The Supreme Court said that income is " 'gain derived from capital, from labor, or from both combined,' " but it does not include "enrichment through increase in value of capital investment."

. . . .

Neither qui tam payments nor punitive damages are intended to compensate the recipient for actual damages. Punitive damages are includable in gross income. . . . In *Commissioner v. Glenshaw Glass Co.*, the Supreme Court said that gross income includes all accessions to wealth and that the definition of income in *Eisner v. Macomber, supra*, "was not meant to provide a touchstone to all future gross income questions." *Commissioner v. Glenshaw Glass Co., supra* at 431. [Later in its *Roco* opinion, the Tax Court said that "The Supreme Court has limited *Eisner v. Macomber* chiefly to the taxability of stock dividends."] The payment to a relator in a qui tam action is not a penalty imposed on the wrongdoer; instead, it is a financial incentive for a private person to provide information and prosecute claims relating to fraudulent activity.

We conclude that the $1,568,087 qui tam payment that petitioner received in 1997 is includable in gross income.

. . . .

To reflect the foregoing,

Decision will be entered for respondent.

Chapter 3

THE EFFECT OF AN OBLIGATION TO REPAY

I. PROBLEMS

1. Since January of Year 1, Jack has been employed as a sales representative for a company selling home security systems. In addition to a base salary of $5,000 per month, Jack is entitled to a commission on every security system he sells. Jack's employer pays him commissions on a semi-annual basis on November 1 and May 1 each year. In November of Year 5, Jack received a commission check for $25,000. One month later, Jack's employer advised him he had mistakenly been credited with commissions on two sales that had been rescinded by the purchasers. According to the employer, Jack's November commission check should have been $21,000. The company demanded that Jack repay immediately the $4,000 difference. Jack refused, arguing the two sales were rescinded only because his employer had failed to meet its obligations under the sales contracts. The dispute between Jack and his employer continued until February, Year 6 when Jack and his employer reached an agreement whereby Jack repaid the employer $2,000. For tax purposes, how should Jack treat the $25,000 commission check received in November of Year 5 and the repayment of $2,000 in Year 6?

2. Rocky, who is in the business of providing financial management services, convinced an elderly client to give him $100,000 to invest in the stock market. Instead of investing the funds as the client expected, Rocky used the funds to gamble. He thought he could double the money the client had given him and thus be in a position to fulfill his obligation to his client while at the same time making a substantial sum of money for himself. Unfortunately, Rocky's hopes were not realized. He lost all $100,000. Rocky waited for months before advising the client he had lost the client's money gambling. Rocky promised to repay the client the full $100,000 over the next 18 months. Hoping to recover his money, the client agreed to this arrangement and never reported Rocky to the authorities. As he promised, Rocky repaid the client the $100,000. Advise Rocky regarding the tax consequence, if any, of the receipt and repayment of the $100,000.

3. Mark owns a private garbage collection service. Mark sends bills to his customers on the first of every month. If Mark has not received payment within 20 days of the mailing of a bill, Mark sends a second billing statement to the customer. By the time some customers receive the second billing statement, they have already mailed their monthly payment to Mark. Some of these customers mistakenly send another check upon

receipt of the second billing statement, resulting in double payment for the same bill. When that occurs, Mark, consistent with general business practice, shows a credit balance on the customer's account and applies that credit balance to the customer's bill for the following month. If a customer who has overpaid requests a refund of the overpayment, Mark always issues the refund. Typically, however, customers who overpay don't request refunds as they know they will be credited for the overpayment on their subsequent bill. At the end of December of the current year, Mark holds a total of $5,000 in customer overpayments which he has credited to customer accounts. Should Mark report the overpayments this year or next year, when he anticipates actually earning the overpayments?

4. Kevin owns a number of homes he rents to university students. Kevin requires the students to pay a security deposit in the amount of one month's rent. The rental agreement used by Kevin specifically provides that security deposits will be applied (a) to compensate Kevin for any property damage or (b) to cover any unpaid rent. If the tenant complies with all terms of the agreement, Kevin must return the security deposit. Kevin neither maintains a separate account for nor pays interest on the security deposits. Whenever a tenant damages the property, Kevin bills the tenant for the full amount of the damages without deducting the security deposit. Typically, Kevin's tenants either ask that the security deposit be applied to the last month's rent or fail to pay the last month's rent. In any event, Kevin rarely returns a security deposit to a tenant. How would you advise Kevin to treat the security deposits for tax purposes?

5. Karen is a fitness consultant and personal trainer. She charges her clients $2,000, payable in advance, for a month-long diet and exercise regimen designed to lose a pre-determined amount of weight. Karen promises to refund the $2,000 fee to anyone who follows the diet and exercise regimen but fails to lose the specified amount of weight. Karen estimates that she refunds about 5% of the fees on this basis. At the end of December she holds $20,000 in fees from clients whose month-long regimens end in January. When must Karen report these fees?

Assignment for Chapter 3:

Complete the problems.

Read: Internal Revenue Code: § 61(a). Merely skim § 1341(a).
        Treasury Regulations: §§ 1.61-8(b), -14(a).

        Materials: Overview
                     North American Oil Consolidated v. Burnet
                     James v. United States
                     Commissioner v. Indianapolis Power & Light Co.

II.   VOCABULARY

claim of right doctrine

III. OBJECTIVES

1. To explain the rationale for excluding borrowed money from income.

2. To explain the rationale for including illegal payments as income.

3. To apply the claim of right doctrine to a given set of facts.

4. To distinguish a security deposit from an advance payment.

5. To distinguish among funds received under a claim of right, illegal payments, and loans or deposits.

6. To recall that advance payments are includible as gross income upon receipt as are payments received under a claim of right.

IV. OVERVIEW

A. Loans

Do loan proceeds constitute gross income? In some cases, a loan may make a borrower feel wealthier. Perhaps the money may be spent in whatever manner the borrower wishes, and investment or consumption opportunities previously unattainable may now be seized. Nonetheless, what is intuitive to the layman will be confirmed by the tax expert and the economist: Loans are not gross income. No code provision or regulation announces this rule, but the rule is absolutely clear and fixed, and the rationale for it is straightforward. A loan does not represent an "accession to wealth" or increase the taxpayer's net worth because the loan proceeds are accompanied by an equal and offsetting liability: the borrower has an obligation to repay the loan, and it is this repayment obligation that negates treatment of a loan as income. See *Commissioner v. Tufts*, 461 U.S. 300, 307 (1983), included in Chapter 37.

As a corollary to this rule, it logically follows that repayment of a loan does not reduce gross income — or, to put it in terms we will use when we study the topic of deductions, repayment is not a deductible expense. You might also recall a lender has no income when a loan is repaid. The lender has no deduction when the loan is made; the repayment is merely a recovery of capital for him. An aside: we could design an internally consistent tax system that reversed these rules. For example, the borrower's loan proceeds could be subject to tax and loan repayments could then be deductible. Proposals for a so-called consumption tax incorporate such provisions. Loan proceeds available for consumption purposes would be subject to the consumption tax. Loan repayments, which effectively reduce the amount available for consumption, would reduce the consumption tax base and hence the consumption tax. We, however, are studying a federal tax system based on one's income, not one's consumption, and loans and repayments do not enter or reduce the income tax base.

It is, of course, true that not every loan is fully repaid by its borrower. Since our rationale for not treating the loan as income was the taxpayer's offsetting obligation to repay the loan, it is not surprising that a failure to repay may generate tax consequences. Suppose, for example, a third party repays the loan on behalf of the borrower. Recall *Old Colony Trust* and the compensatory payment of the employee's tax liability by his employer; payment of one's liabilities by another may thus give rise to gross income. (Obviously, not every payment of another's liability is compensatory in nature. For example, the payment could in some circumstances represent a gift to the borrower.) Suppose, alternatively, all or part of the debt is forgiven by the lender. Isn't this functionally equivalent to the lender making payment (to the lender) on behalf of the borrower to the extent of the amount forgiven? If the lender is also the employer, is there any reason why the principles of *Old Colony Trust* should not apply and the employee/borrower be treated as having received compensation? We will study these and related questions in some detail when we consider the case of *Kirby Lumber* and the topic of discharge-of-indebtedness income in Chapter 9. Suffice it to say at this point that our tax system does not take advantage of hindsight, return to the original loan transaction and recast it as income from the outset. The loan remains a loan; it is the forgiveness that may constitute income. For the time being, however, let us assume we live in a world where borrowers always repay their loans.

Let us also pass over a number of other loan-related issues that are more appropriately covered later in the course, such as the deductibility of interest, the proper timing of interest income to the lender and interest expense to the borrower, the tax treatment of loans made at below-market interest rates, and other matters. The proper foundations for these topics have not yet been laid, and our discussions will be more profitable, and we hope less taxing, when they have been.

It may not always be obvious whether a disbursement constitutes a loan or a taxable payment. For example, suppose a corporation makes substantial cash disbursements to a shareholder, permits the shareholder to use the corporation's credit card for personal purposes, and pays federal and state tax liabilities owed by the shareholder. In *Morrison v. Commissioner*, T.C. Memo. 2005-53, the Commissioner argued the payments and disbursements constituted taxable constructive dividends to the shareholder. Despite the absence of a note or other written instrument, an examination of the totality of the circumstances led the Tax Court to conclude the payments and disbursements were loans: the court found the corporation had enough funds to make the loans, the shareholder had enough income to repay the loans, and there was evidence the shareholder had in fact made loan repayments, including interest.

The Tax Court, summarizing its own position and that of other courts, has noted:

> . . . the determination of whether a transfer of funds constitutes a loan is a question of fact. . . . In order for a transfer of funds to constitute a loan, at the time the funds are transferred there must be an unconditional obligation (*i.e.*, an obligation that is not subject to a condition precedent) on the part of the transferee to repay, and an unconditional intention on the part of the transferor to secure repayment, of such funds. . . . Whether a transfer of funds constitutes a loan may be inferred from objective characteristics surrounding the transfer, including the presence or absence of a debt instrument, collateral securing the purported loan, interest accruing on the purported loan, repayments of the transferred funds, and any attributes indicative of an enforceable obligation on the part of the transferee to repay the funds transferred.

Karns Prime & Fancy Food, Ltd. v. Commissioner, T.C. Memo 2005-233, *aff'd*, 494 F.3d 404 (3d Cir. 2007). As recently noted by the Tax Court: "A bona fide loan requires both parties to have an actual, good-faith intent to establish a debtor-creditor relationship when the funds are advanced. An intent to establish a debtor-creditor relationship exists if the debtor intends to repay the loan and the creditor intends to enforce the repayment." *Fisher v. Commissioner*, T.C. Memo 2014-219.

B. Claim of Right

Assume you find a wallet containing $1,000. After unsuccessfully seeking to locate the owner, you decide to keep the money. Suppose, however, local law provides that, if the person who lost the wallet returns and claims the money at any time within the next two years, you must return the money to him. In these circumstances, is the found money income to you? To recast the question in terms we used in discussing loans: if the proceeds of a loan are not income because the borrower is subject to an unconditional obligation to make repayment, what is the proper tax treatment of money (or other property) received subject to a *contingent* repayment obligation?

In addressing this issue, the United States Supreme Court, in *North American Oil Consolidated v. Burnet*, reproduced in the materials, enunciated the following standard commonly known as the "claim of right doctrine":

> If a taxpayer receives earnings under a claim of right and without restriction as to its disposition, he has received income which he is required to return [that is, to report on his tax return], even though it may still be claimed that he is not entitled to retain the money, and even though he may still be adjudged liable to restore its equivalent.

As we shall see when we study timing aspects of deductions, a taxpayer who properly reports income under the claim of right doctrine is entitled to a deduction (or possibly a reduction in taxes under § 1341) if subsequently required to refund the money. But the taxpayer may never be required to return the money, and under the claim of right doctrine we do not await the resolution of a contingency to decide whether or not the receipt of the money was income. Money received under a claim of right, without restriction as to disposition, is income; the contingent repayment obligation does not allow the receipt to be treated as a loan.

The boundaries of the claim of right doctrine are less easy to state than the rule itself. What degree of restriction, for example, negates its application? Suppose the taxpayer sets aside the amounts received, retains control over them, and elects not to use them pending resolution of the dispute. *Commissioner v. Alamitos Land Co.*, 112 F.2d 648 (9th Cir. 1940), applies the claim of right doctrine in a case of such self-imposed, voluntary restraint, as does Revenue Ruling 55-137, 1955-1 C.B. 215, to possible excess revenues collected by a utility company and then placed in a bank account (jointly controlled by the utility and its bonding company) so as to be available for repayment if required on ultimate settlement of the dispute. By contrast, where the taxpayer, under court order, was required to deposit with the clerk of the court possible excess commissions collected, the amounts so deposited were not income. Rev. Rul. 69-642, 1969-2 C.B. 9. Similarly, if an attorney is required by a state's code of professional responsibility to deposit money advanced by clients in a special segregated account, the attorney is not in receipt of income when the advance is received. *Miele v. Commissioner*, 72 T.C. 284 (1979).

Funds over which the taxpayer acts only as a conduit are not received under a claim of right. As the Tax Court has stated: "We accept as sound law the rule that a taxpayer need not treat as income money which he did not receive under a claim of right, which was not his to keep, and which he was required to transmit to someone else as a mere conduit." *Diamond v. Commissioner*, 56 T.C. 530, 541 (1971), *aff'd*, 492 F.2d 286 (7th Cir. 1974). For example, in a case where a city employee received what the government characterized as bribes, but promptly passed all the funds on to another official, the employee was held to be merely a conduit for the flow of funds, and thus not taxable on the funds. *Pierson v. Commissioner*, T.C. Memo. 1976-281. In *Ford Dealers Advertising Fund v. Commissioner*, 55 T.C. 761 (1971), *aff'd*, 456 F.2d 255 (5th Cir. 1972), a nonprofit corporation received funds that were to be utilized solely for its nonprofit purposes. The court held the funds were received "in trust," destined for a specific use, with no gain accruing to the taxpayer, and thus not includable in gross income.

C. Illegal Income

The tax treatment of illegal payments has been marked by uncertainty and course reversal. It was long clear that gains from an illegal business may be taxed. *See United States v. Sullivan*, 274 U.S. 259 (1927), and the discussion in *James v. United States* in the materials. But should an embezzler's gain be taxable? Such illegally seized money can be analogized to a loan in the sense that the wrongdoer's receipts are subject to an offsetting absolute, unconditional obligation to make repayment. The embezzler does not have even a semblance of a claim of right to the funds, and hence the application of claim of right notions seems untenable. By contrast, it may seem troubling or intolerable to some for an embezzler to be legally entitled to tax-free treatment on his illegally acquired funds, precisely because of their illegal provenance. To make crime a tax shelter and vice its own reward may not be a completely satisfactory tax policy.

The Supreme Court's 1961 decision in *James v. United States*, included in the materials, holds embezzled funds constitute gross income, and is the rule today. Previously, in *Commissioner v. Wilcox*, 327 U.S. 404 (1946), the Court had held embezzled funds are not includable in gross income because of the embezzler's obligation to repay. Subsequently, in *Rutkin v. United States*, 343 U.S. 130 (1952), the Court distinguished between embezzlement and extortion, and held extorted funds constituted income, reasoning that the extortioner's victim is considerably less likely than the embezzler's victim to demand repayment. Several years later, *James* eliminated this nice distinction and overruled *Wilcox*.

Although *James* appears to stand for the proposition that all illegal receipts are within gross income, questions may arise on the margins. In *Gilbert v. Commissioner*, 552 F.2d 478 (2d Cir. 1971), the taxpayer made unauthorized withdrawals of corporate funds and subsequently pleaded guilty to state and federal charges of having unlawfully withdrawn the funds. He had, however, promptly informed several of the corporate officers and directors of the withdrawals, and apparently believed he was acting in the best interests of the corporation as well as his own in withdrawing the funds to meet a "margin call" on stock he had purchased. The Second Circuit concluded a taxpayer did not realize income under the *James* test on funds withdrawn from a corporation where the taxpayer fully intended to repay them, expected with a reasonable certainty to be able to repay them, believed the withdrawals would be approved by the corporation, and made a prompt assignment of assets sufficient to secure the amount owed. The corporation was not able to recover fully the amounts withdrawn, but in these circumstances both the taxpayer and the Second Circuit regarded the transaction as being in the nature of a loan.

As *James* suggests, and the Service concedes, repayment of illegal income entitles the taxpayer to a deduction. Rev. Rul. 65-254, 1965-2 C.B. 50. Suppose that, in the same year the embezzlement occurs, the embezzler is caught, promises to make repayment, and executes a confession of judgment in favor of the victim. Does the embezzlement still constitute gross income? The Second Circuit said "yes" in *Buff v. Commissioner*, 496 F.2d 847 (1974), reversing the Tax Court, and rejecting the argument that the "consensual recognition" of indebtedness within the same tax year transformed the transaction into a loan; it also noted no payment had actually been made on the judgment. Suppose an embezzler's victim, however, explicitly agrees to transform the embezzlement into a loan retroactively. Should that make a difference?

In any event, will it always be easy to distinguish loans and illegal income, or to differentiate the swindler from the failed, but legitimate promoter who has lost the funds loaned to or invested in his enterprise? The taxpayers in *Kreimer v. Commissioner*, T.C. Memo 1983-672, had been convicted of obtaining loans under false pretenses amounting to fraud. The Commissioner sought to tax the funds received by the taxpayers as income. Despite the taxpayers' misrepresentations, the Tax Court nevertheless concluded the transactions constituted loans since the taxpayers had always regarded and treated the obligations as bona fide debt they intended to repay. By contrast, where a consistent pattern of fraudulent dealing demonstrates an absence of an intent to repay, merely labelling the funds obtained as "loans" will not avoid gross income. *United States v. Rochelle*, 384 F.2d 748 (5th Cir. 1967); *United States v. Rosenthal*, 470 F.2d 837 (2d Cir. 1972).

The receipt of illegal income may raise significant Fifth Amendment questions. May a taxpayer successfully assert his constitutional rights against compulsory self-incrimination, and decline on that basis to report his illegal income? The boundaries of the Fifth Amendment protections are not completely clear in regard to tax returns and proceedings, but you might note the Supreme Court has stated:

> If the form of return provided called for answers that the defendant was privileged from making, he could have raised the objection on the return, but could not on that account refuse to make any return at all. . . . It would be an extreme if not an extravagant application of the Fifth Amendment to say that it authorized a man to refuse to state the amount of his income because it had been made in crime. But if the defendant desired to test that or any other point, he should have tested it in the return so that it would be passed upon. He could not draw a conjurer's circle around the whole matter by his own deduction that to write any word upon the government blank would bring him into danger of the law.

United States v. Sullivan, 274 U.S. 259, 263–64 (1927).

D. Deposits

The regulations explicitly provide that rent paid in advance generally constitutes gross income in the year it is received regardless of the period covered or the taxpayer's method of accounting. Reg. § 1.61-8(b). An advance payment of income is still income. By contrast, a loan is not income because there is an offsetting obligation of repayment. How should "deposits" be treated? Are they properly analogous to loans under the duty-to-repay rationale — thus nontaxable — or are they more like advance payments of income and properly taxable on receipt? The answer, of course, is: "It depends." The question arises most frequently with respect to "security deposits" in connection with landlord-tenant leases, although as *Indianapolis Power & Light Company* in the materials illustrates, utility company deposit cases have presented the issue as well. Suppose a landlord receives what is labelled a security deposit, but there is no duty to segregate the deposit or pay interest on it, and the landlord may keep the deposit and apply it to the last month's rent. Should the label be controlling? Is such a deposit any different from advance payment of the last month's rent?

In *Indianapolis Power & Light*, the Supreme Court held that control over the conditions of refund is the determinative factor in deciding whether a "deposit" will be taxable as an advance or nontaxable. The Tax Court in a later case summarized the Supreme Court's holding in *Indianapolis Power & Light* as follows: "[I]f the payor controls the conditions under which the money will be repaid or refunded, generally, the payment is not income to the recipient. By contrast, if the recipient of the payment controls the conditions under which the payment will be repaid or refunded, . . . the recipient has some guaranty that it will be allowed to keep the money, and hence, the recipient enjoys complete dominion over the payment." *Herbel v. Commissioner*, 106 T.C. 392, 413–14 (1996). In other words, as indicated by the Supreme Court in *Indianapolis Power & Light*, the mere fact of refundability is not in itself sufficient for identifying nontaxable deposits; refundability must be within the buyer's control.

The "complete dominion" or "control" standard of *Indianapolis Power & Light* was applied in the rental context in *Highland Farms, Inc. v. Commissioner*, 106 T.C. 237 (1996). In that case, the taxpayer operated a residential retirement community that provided several types of accommodations, among which were rentals of apartments and a lodge. Residents of the apartments and the lodge were required to pay an "entry fee" prior to occupancy and monthly rentals thereafter. The taxpayer treated the entry fees, which were not placed in escrow, as "earned out" on a pro rata basis over five years (in the case of apartments) or over 20 years (with respect to the lodge). At the end of these periods, the entry fee was fully nonrefundable, but prior thereto a tenant who terminated occupancy was entitled to a pro rata refund of the entry fee. For tax purposes, the taxpayer treated the entry fee as constituting income only to the extent it became nonrefundable and nonforfeitable within a tax year. The Tax Court, relying upon *Indianapolis Power & Light*, held for the taxpayer:

> In the instant case, the residents of the apartment and the lodge, if they decided to move out of their units, had a right to a refund of a portion of their entry fees in accordance with the schedules stated in their respective

rental contracts. The refunds were within the residents' control, and petitioner had "no unfettered 'dominion' over the money at the time of receipt." At the time the entry fees were paid, the only amounts petitioner was guaranteed to be allowed to keep were the nonrefundable portions. Thus, we hold that the refundable portions were not advance payments for services or prepaid rent. . . . Petitioner included in income for a specific taxable year those portions of the entry fees for the apartments and the lodge that became nonrefundable or nonforfeitable within that tax year. This method of accounting for the entry fees clearly reflects income. . . .

Id. at 252.

Similarly, in *Perry Funeral Home, Inc. v. Commissioner*, T.C. Memo 2003-340, the Tax Court, relying on the "complete dominion" or "control" rationale of *Indianapolis Power & Light*, concluded amounts received by the taxpayer funeral home pursuant to so-called "preneed funeral contracts" constituted nontaxable deposits and therefore would be includable in the taxpayer's income only upon the taxpayer's actual provision of goods and services pursuant to the contract. Under the preneed funeral contract, a buyer prepaid the taxpayer for certain goods and services to be provided by the taxpayer upon the buyer's death. State regulations, however, specifically provided preneed funeral contracts could be cancelled by the buyer or the buyer's legal representative at any time prior to the actual provision of the goods and services by the taxpayer. Taxpayer's records indicated that, during the period from approximately 1997 through the time of trial in 2003, only six preneed contracts were canceled.

The Tax Court rejected the Service's argument that prepayments under the preneed contracts were not the equivalent of a refundable security deposit or loan and, hence, were not controlled by the standards set forth in *Indianapolis Power & Light*. The Tax Court emphasized that, just as in *Indianapolis Power & Light*, the buyer of the preneed contract or the buyer's legal representative controlled the conditions under which money paid to the taxpayer would be refunded. As a result, the taxpayer had no guaranty it could keep the money received and therefore did not have "unfettered dominion" over the money. As in *Indianapolis Power & Light*, the Tax Court noted that, while factors such as the taxpayer's control over deposits (*i.e.*, absence of a trust fund), unrestricted use, nonpayment of interest, and later application of the moneys to goods and services may be probative, they are not dispositive in evaluating whether the taxpayer had the level of dominion necessary to treat a prepayment as gross income upon receipt. The Tax Court also rejected the Service's argument that the taxpayer's historical percentage of cancellations was so low that the cancellation right should be disregarded. According to the court, "it is the bona fide existence of such a right, not the exercise or frequency of exercise, which controls. . . . [W]e would be hard pressed to say that the right here was illusory when cancellations did occur, and corresponding refunds were given, in the course of [taxpayer's] business."

The Tax Court in *Perry Funeral Home* also noted that, to the extent *Indianapolis Power & Light* identifies an advance payment as one which protects against the risk that the buyer will back out before the taxpayer has a chance to perform, the preneed contracts and payments fail to serve that function because of the open-ended nature of the cancellation right. The taxpayer's opportunity to provide the designated goods and services and thereby earn the prepaid funds (thereby eliminating the cancellation right) was contingent upon the later choice of the buyer's legal representatives to call upon petitioner to act under the contract.

NORTH AMERICAN OIL CONSOLIDATED v. BURNET
United States Supreme Court
286 U.S. 417 (1932)

MR. JUSTICE BRANDEIS delivered the opinion of the Court.

The question for decision is whether the sum of $171,979.22 received by the North American Oil Consolidated in 1917, was taxable to it as income of that year.

The money was paid to the company under the following circumstances. Among many properties operated by it in 1916 was a section of oil land, the legal title to which stood in the name of the United States. Prior to that year, the Government, claiming also the beneficial ownership, had instituted a suit to oust the company from possession; and on February 2, 1916, it secured the appointment of a receiver to operate the property, or supervise its operations, and to hold the net income thereof. The money paid to the company in 1917 represented the net profits which had been earned from that property in 1916 during the receivership. The money was paid to the receiver as earned. After entry by the District Court in 1917 of the final decree dismissing the bill, the money was paid, in that year, by the receiver to the company. The Government took an appeal . . . to the Circuit Court of Appeals. In 1920, that Court affirmed the decree. . . . In 1922, a further appeal to this Court was dismissed by stipulation. . . .

The income earned from the property in 1916 had been entered on the books of the company as its income. It had not been included in its original return of income for 1916; but it was included in an amended return for that year which was filed in 1918. Upon auditing the company's income and profits tax returns for 1917, the Commissioner of Internal Revenue determined a deficiency based on other items. The company appealed to the Board of Tax Appeals. There, in 1927 the Commissioner prayed that the deficiency already claimed should be increased so as to include a tax on the amount paid by the receiver to the company in 1917. The Board held that the profits were taxable to the receiver as income of 1916; and hence made no finding whether the company's accounts were kept on the cash receipts and disbursements basis or on the accrual basis. The Circuit Court of Appeals held that the profits were taxable to the company as income of 1917, regardless of whether the company's returns were made on the cash or on the accrual basis. . . . This Court granted a writ of certiorari.

It is conceded that the net profits earned by the property during the receivership constituted income. The company contends that they should have been reported by the receiver for taxation in 1916; that if not returnable by him, they should have been returned by the company for 1916, because they constitute income of the company accrued in that year; and that if not taxable as income of the company for

1916, they were taxable to it as income for 1922, since the litigation was not finally terminated in its favor until 1922.

First. The income earned in 1916 and impounded by the receiver in that year was not taxable to him, because he was the receiver of only a part of the properties operated by the company. . . . The Regulations of the Treasury Department have consistently construed these statutes [requiring receivers to file tax returns] as applying only to receivers in charge of the entire property or business of a corporation. . . .

Second. The net profits were not taxable to the company as income of 1916. For the company was not required in 1916 to report as income an amount which it might never receive. There was no constructive receipt of the profits by the company in that year, because at no time during the year was there a right in the company to demand that the receiver pay over the money. Throughout 1916 it was uncertain who would be declared entitled to the profits. It was not until 1917, when the District Court entered a final decree vacating the receivership and dismissing the bill, that the company became entitled to receive the money. Nor is it material, for the purposes of this case, whether the company's return was filed on the cash receipts and disbursements basis, or on the accrual basis. In neither event was it taxable in 1916 on account of income which it had not yet received and which it might never receive.

Third. The net profits earned by the property in 1916 were not income of the year 1922 — the year in which the litigation with the Government was finally terminated. They became income of the company in 1917, when it first became entitled to them and when it actually received them. If a taxpayer receives earnings under a claim of right and without restriction as to its disposition, he has received income that he is required to return even though it may still be claimed that he is not entitled to retain the money, and even though he may still be adjudged liable to restore its equivalent. . . . If in 1922 the Government had prevailed, and the company had been obliged to refund the profits received in 1917, it would have been entitled to a deduction from the profits of 1922, not from those of any earlier year. . . .

Affirmed.

JAMES v. UNITED STATES
United States Supreme Court
366 U.S. 213 (1961)

Mr. Chief Justice Warren announced the judgment of the Court and an opinion in which Mr. Justice Brennan, and Mr. Justice Stewart concurred.

The issue before us in this case is whether embezzled funds are to be included in the "gross income" of the embezzler in the year in which the funds are misappropriated under . . . § 61(a) of the Internal Revenue Code of 1954.

The facts are not in dispute. The petitioner is a union official who, with another person, embezzled in excess of $738,000 during the years 1951 through 1954 from his employer union and from an insurance company with which the union was doing business. Petitioner failed to report these amounts in his gross income in those years and was convicted for willfully attempting to evade the federal income tax due for each of the years 1951 through 1954. . . .

In *Wilcox*, the Court held that embezzled money does not constitute taxable income to the embezzler in the year of the embezzlement under § 22 of the Internal Revenue Code of 1939 [predecessor to current § 61]. Six years later, this Court held, in *Rutkin v. United States*, 343 U.S. 130, that extorted money does constitute taxable income to the extortionist in the year that the money is received under § 22(a) of the Internal Revenue Code of 1939.

Since Wilcox embezzled the money, held it "without any semblance of a bona fide claim of right," and therefore "was at all times under an unqualified duty and obligation to repay the money to his employer," the Court found that the money embezzled was not includable within "gross income." But, Rutkin's legal claim was no greater than that of Wilcox. It was specifically found "that petitioner had no basis for his claim . . . and that he obtained it by extortion." Both Wilcox and Rutkin obtained the money by means of a criminal act; neither had a bona fide claim of right to the funds. Nor was Rutkin's obligation to repay the extorted money to the victim any less than that of Wilcox. The victim of an extortion, like the victim of an embezzlement, has a right to restitution. Furthermore, it is inconsequential that an embezzler may lack title to the sums he appropriates while an extortionist may gain a voidable title. Questions of federal income taxation are not determined by such "attenuated subtleties." Thus, the fact that Rutkin secured the money with the consent of his victim is irrelevant. Likewise unimportant is the fact that the sufferer of an extortion is less likely to seek restitution than one whose funds are embezzled. What is important is that the right to recoupment exists in both situations.

It had been a well-established principle, long before either *Rutkin* or *Wilcox*, that unlawful, as well as lawful, gains are comprehended within the term "gross income." Section II B of the Income Tax Act of 1913 provided that "the net income of a taxable person shall include gains, profits, and income . . . from . . . the transaction of any *lawful* business carried on for gain or profit, or gains or profits and income derived from any source whatever. . . . " (Emphasis supplied.) When the statute was amended in 1916, the one word "lawful" was omitted. This revealed, we think, the obvious intent of that Congress to tax income derived from both legal and illegal sources, to remove the incongruity of having the gains of the honest laborer taxed and the gains of the dishonest immune. Thereafter, the Court held that gains from illicit traffic in liquor are includable within "gross income." And, the Court has pointed out, with approval, that there "has been a widespread and settled administrative and judicial recognition of the taxability of unlawful gains of many kinds." These include protection payments made to racketeers, ransom payments paid to kidnappers, bribes, money derived from the sale of unlawful insurance policies, graft, black market gains, funds obtained from the operation of lotteries, income from race track bookmaking and illegal prize fight pictures.

The starting point in all cases dealing with the question of the scope of what is included in "gross income" begins with the basic premise that the purpose of Congress was "to use the full measure of its taxing power." *Helvering v. Clifford*, 309 U.S. 331, 334. And the Court has given a liberal construction to the broad phraseology of the "gross income" definition statutes in recognition of the intention of Congress to tax all gains except those specifically exempted. The language of § 22(a) of the 1939 Code, "gains or profits and income derived from any source whatever," and the more simplified language of § 61(a) of the 1954 Code, "all income from whatever source derived," have been held to encompass all "accessions to wealth, clearly realized, and over which the taxpayers have complete dominion." *Commissioner of Internal Revenue v. Glenshaw Glass Co.*, 348 U.S. 426, 431. A gain "constitutes taxable income when its recipient has such control over it that, as a practical matter, he derives readily realizable economic value from it." Under these broad principles, we believe that petitioner's contention, that all unlawful gains are taxable except those resulting from embezzlement, should fail.

When a taxpayer acquires earnings, lawfully or unlawfully, without the consensual recognition, express or implied, of an obligation to repay and without restriction as to their disposition, "he has received income which he is required to return, even though it may still be claimed that he is not entitled to retain the money, and even though he may still be adjudged liable to restore its equivalent." *North American Oil Consolidated v. Burnet, supra*, 286 U.S. at page 424. In such case, the taxpayer has "actual command over the property taxed — the actual benefit for which the tax is paid." This standard brings wrongful appropriations within the broad sweep of "gross income"; it excludes loans. When a law-abiding taxpayer mistakenly receives income in one year, which receipt is assailed and found to be invalid in a subsequent year, the taxpayer must nonetheless report the amount as "gross income" in the year received. We do not believe that Congress intended to treat a law-breaking taxpayer differently. Just as the honest taxpayer may deduct any amount repaid in the year in which the repayment is made, the Government points out that, "If, when, and to the extent that the victim recovers back the misappropriated funds, there is of course a reduction in the embezzler's income."

We believe that *Wilcox* was wrongly decided and we find nothing in congressional history since then to persuade us that Congress intended to legislate the rule. . . .

But, we are dealing here with a felony conviction under statutes which apply to any person who "willfully" fails to account for his tax or who "willfully" attempts to evade his obligation. . . .

We believe that the element of willfulness could not be proven in a criminal prosecution for failing to include embezzled funds in gross income in the year of misappropriation so long as the statute contained the gloss placed upon it by *Wilcox* at the time the alleged crime was committed. Therefore, we feel that petitioner's conviction may not stand and that the indictment against him must be dismissed.

Accordingly, the judgment of the Court of Appeals is reversed and the case is remanded to the District Court with directions to dismiss the indictment.

Mr. Justice Black, whom Mr. Justice Douglas joins, concurring in part and dissenting in part.

II.

We think *Wilcox* was right when it was decided and is right now. It announced no new, novel doctrine. One need only look at the Government's briefs in this Court in the *Wilcox* case to see just how little past judicial support could then be mustered had the Government sought to send *Wilcox* to jail for his embezzlement under the guise of a tax evasion prosecution. The Government did cite many cases from many courts saying that under the federal income tax law gains are no less taxable because they have been acquired by illegal methods. This Court had properly held long before *Wilcox* that there is no "reason why the fact that a business is unlawful should exempt it from paying the taxes that if lawful it would have to pay. . . . "

The whole basis of the *Wilcox* opinion was that an embezzlement is not in itself "gain" or "income" to the embezzler within the tax sense, for the obvious reason that the embezzled property still belongs, and is known to belong, to the rightful owner. It is thus a mistake to argue that petitioner's contention is "that all unlawful gains are taxable except those resulting from embezzlement."

The whole picture can best be obtained from the court's opinion in *McKnight v. Commissioner*, 127 F.2d 572, written by Judge Sibley, one of the ablest circuit judges of his time. He recognized that the taxpayer could not rely upon the unlawfulness of his business to defeat taxation if he had made a "gain" in that business. He pointed out, however, that the ordinary embezzler "got no title, void or voidable, to what he took. He was still in possession as he was before, but with a changed purpose. He still had no right nor color of right. He claimed none." Judge Sibley's opinion went on to point out that the "first takings [of an embezzler] are, indeed, nearly always with the intention of repaying, a sort of unauthorized borrowing. It must be conceded that no gain is realized by borrowing, because of the offsetting obligation." Approaching the matter from a practical standpoint, Judge Sibley also explained that subjecting the embezzled funds to a tax would amount to allowing the United States "a preferential claim for part of the dishonest gain, to the direct loss and detriment of those to whom it ought to be restored." He was not willing to put the owner of funds that had been stolen in competition with the United States Treasury Department as to which one should have a preference to get those funds.

It seems to us that Judge Sibley's argument was then and is now unanswerable.

An illustration of what this could mean to a defrauded employer is shown in this very case by the employer's loss of some $700,000, upon which the Government claims a tax of $559,000.

It seems to be implied that one reason for overruling *Wilcox* is that a failure to hold embezzled funds taxable would somehow work havoc with the public revenue or discriminate against "honest" taxpayers and force them to pay more taxes. We believe it would be impossible to substantiate either claim. Embezzlers ordinarily are not rich people against whom judgments, even federal tax judgments, can be enforced.

It follows that, except for the possible adverse effect on rightful owners, the only substantial result that one can foresee from today's holding is that the Federal Government will, under the guise of a tax evasion charge, prosecute people for a single embezzlement. But the Constitution grants power to Congress to get revenue not to prosecute local crimes. And if there is any offense which under our dual system of government is a purely local one which the States should handle, it is embezzlement or theft.

COMMISSIONER v. INDIANAPOLIS POWER & LIGHT COMPANY
United States Supreme Court
493 U.S. 203 (1990)

JUSTICE BLACKMUN delivered the opinion of the Court.

Respondent Indianapolis Power & Light Company (IPL) requires certain customers to make deposits with it to assure payment of future bills for electric service. Petitioner, Commissioner of Internal Revenue, contends that these deposits are advance payments for electricity and therefore constitute taxable income to IPL upon receipt. IPL contends otherwise.

I.

IPL is a regulated Indiana corporation that generates and sells electricity in Indianapolis and its environs. It keeps its books on the accrual and calendar year basis. During the years 1974 through 1977, approximately 5% of IPL's residential and commercial customers were required to make deposits "to insure prompt payment," as the customers' receipts stated, of future utility bills. These customers were selected because their credit was suspect. Prior to March 10, 1976, the deposit requirement was imposed on a case-by-case basis. IPL relied on a credit test but employed no fixed formula. The amount of the required deposit ordinarily was twice the customer's estimated monthly bill. IPL paid 3% interest on a deposit held for six months or more. A customer could obtain a refund of the deposit prior to termination of service by requesting a review and demonstrating acceptable credit. The refund usually was made in cash or by check, but the customer could choose to have the amount applied against future bills.

In March 1976, IPL amended its rules governing the deposit program. See Title 170, Ind. Admin. Code § 4-1-15 (1988). Under the amended rules, the residential customers from whom deposits were required were selected on the basis of a fixed formula. The interest rate was raised to 6% but was payable only on deposits held for 12 months or more. A deposit was refunded when the customer made timely payments for either nine consecutive months, or for 10 out of 12 consecutive months so long as the two delinquent months were not themselves consecutive. A customer could obtain a refund prior to that time by satisfying the credit test. As under the previous rules, the refund would be made in cash or by check, or, at the customer's option, applied against future bills. Any deposit unclaimed after seven years was to escheat to the State. See Ind. Code § 32-9-1-6(a) (1988).

IPL did not treat these deposits as income at the time of receipt. Rather, as required by state administrative regulations, the deposits were carried on its books as current liabilities. Under its accounting system, IPL recognized income when it mailed a monthly bill. If the deposit was used to offset a customer's bill, the utility made the necessary accounting adjustments. Customer deposits were not physically segregated in any way from the company's general funds. They were commingled with other receipts and at all times were subject to IPL's unfettered use and control. It is undisputed that IPL's treatment of the deposits was consistent with accepted accounting practice and applicable state regulations.

Upon audit of respondent's returns for the calendar years 1974 through 1977, the Commissioner asserted deficiencies. The Commissioner took the position that the deposits were advance payments for electricity and therefore were taxable to IPL in the year of receipt. He contended that the increase or decrease in customer deposits outstanding at the end of each year represented an increase or decrease in IPL's income for the year. IPL disagreed and filed a petition in the United States Tax Court for redetermination of the asserted deficiencies.

In a reviewed decision, with one judge not participating, a unanimous Tax Court ruled in favor of IPL. The court followed the approach it had adopted in *City Gas Co. of Florida v. Commissioner of Internal Revenue*, 74 T.C. 386 (1980), *rev'd*, 689 F.2d 943 (CA 11 1982). It found it necessary to "continue to examine all of the circumstances," and relied on several factors in concluding that the deposits in question were properly excluded from gross income. It noted, among other things, that only 5% of IPL's customers were required to make deposits; that the customer rather than the utility controlled the ultimate disposition of a deposit; and that IPL consistently treated the deposits as belonging to the customers, both by listing them as current liabilities for accounting purposes and by paying interest.

The United States Court of Appeals for the Seventh Circuit affirmed the Tax Court's decision. The court stated that "the proper approach to determining the appropriate tax treatment of a customer deposit is to look at the primary purpose of the deposit based on all the facts and circumstances. . . . " The court appeared to place primary reliance, however, on IPL's obligation to pay interest on the deposits. It asserted that "as the interest rate paid on a deposit to secure income begins to approximate the return that the recipient would be expected to make from 'the use' of the deposit amount, the deposit begins to serve purposes that comport more squarely with a security deposit." *Id.*, at 1169. Noting that IPL paid interest on the customer deposits throughout the period in question, the court upheld, as not clearly erroneous, the Tax Court's determination that the principal purpose of these deposits was to serve as security rather than as prepayment of income.

Because the Seventh Circuit was in specific disagreement with the Eleventh Circuit's ruling in *City Gas Co. of Florida, supra,* we granted certiorari to resolve the conflict.

II.

We begin with the common ground. IPL acknowledges that these customer deposits are taxable as income upon receipt if they constitute advance payments for electricity to be supplied. The Commissioner, on his part, concedes that customer deposits that secure the performance of nonincome-producing covenants — such as a utility customer's obligation to ensure that meters will not be damaged — are not taxable income. And it is settled that receipt of a loan is not income to the borrower. IPL, stressing its obligation to refund the deposits with interest, asserts that the payments are similar to loans. The Commissioner, however, contends that a deposit which serves to secure the payment of future income is properly analogized to an advance payment for goods or services. See Rev. Rul. 72-519, 1972-2 Cum. Bull. 32, 33 ("[W]hen the purpose of the deposit is to guarantee the customer's payment of amounts owed to the creditor, such a deposit is treated as an advance payment, but when the purpose of the deposit is to secure a property interest of the taxpayer, the deposit is regarded as a true security deposit").

In economic terms, to be sure, the distinction between a loan and an advance payment is one of degree rather than of kind. A commercial loan, like an advance payment, confers an economic benefit on the recipient: a business presumably does not borrow money unless it believes that the income it can earn from its use of the borrowed funds will be greater than its interest obligation. Even though receipt of the money is subject to a duty to repay, the borrower must regard itself as better off after the loan than it was before. The economic benefit of a loan, however, consists entirely of the opportunity to earn income on the use of the money prior to the time the loan must be repaid. And in that context our system is content to tax these earnings as they are realized. The recipient of an advance payment, in contrast, gains both immediate use of the money (with the chance to realize earnings thereon) and the opportunity to make a profit by providing goods or services at a cost lower than the amount of the payment.

The question, therefore, cannot be resolved simply by noting that respondent derives some economic benefit from receipt of these deposits.[1] Rather, the issue turns upon the nature of the rights and obligations that IPL assumed when the deposits were made. In determining what sort of economic benefits qualify as income, this Court has invoked various formulations. It has referred, for example, to "undeniable accessions to wealth, clearly realized, and over which the taxpayers have complete dominion." *Commissioner v. Glenshaw Glass Co.*, 348 U.S. 426, 431, 75 S. Ct. 473, 477, 99 L. Ed. 483 (1955). It also has stated: "When a taxpayer acquires earnings, lawfully or unlawfully, without the consensual recognition, express or implied, of an obligation to repay and without restriction as to their disposition, he has received income. . . . " *James v. United States*, 366 U.S., at 219, 81 S. Ct., at 1055. IPL hardly enjoyed "complete dominion" over the customer deposits entrusted to it. Rather, these deposits were acquired subject to an express "obligation to repay," either at the time service was terminated or at the time a customer established good credit. So long as the customer fulfills his legal obligation to make timely payments, his deposit ultimately is to be refunded, and both the timing and method of that refund are largely within the control of the customer.

---

[1] See *Illinois Power Co.*, 792 F.2d, at 690. See also Burke & Friel, *Recent Developments in the Income Taxation of Individuals, Tax-Free Security: Reflections on Indianapolis Power & Light*, 12 Rev. of Taxation of Individuals 157, 174 (1988) (arguing that economic-benefit approach is superior in theory, but acknowledging that "an economic-benefit test has not been adopted, and it is unlikely that such an approach will be pursued by the Service or the courts").

The Commissioner stresses the fact that these deposits were not placed in escrow or segregated from IPL's other funds, and that IPL therefore enjoyed unrestricted use of the money. That circumstance, however, cannot be dispositive. After all, the same might be said of a commercial loan; yet the Commissioner does not suggest that a loan is taxable upon receipt simply because the borrower is free to use the funds in whatever fashion he chooses until the time of repayment. In determining whether a taxpayer enjoys "complete dominion" over a given sum, the crucial point is not whether his use of the funds is unconstrained during some interim period. The key is whether the taxpayer has some guarantee that he will be allowed to keep the money. IPL's receipt of these deposits was accompanied by no such guarantee.

Nor is it especially significant that these deposits could be expected to generate income greater than the modest interest IPL was required to pay. Again, the same could be said of a commercial loan, since, as has been noted, a business is unlikely to borrow unless it believes that it can realize benefits that exceed the cost of servicing the debt. A bank could hardly operate profitably if its earnings on deposits did not surpass its interest obligations; but the deposits themselves are not treated as income. Any income that the utility may earn through use of the deposit money of course is taxable, but the prospect that income will be generated provides no ground for taxing the principal.

The Commissioner's advance payment analogy seems to us to rest upon a misconception of the value of an advance payment to its recipient. An advance payment, like the deposits at issue here, concededly protects the seller against the risk that it would be unable to collect money owed it after it has furnished goods or services. But an advance payment does much more: it protects against the risk that the purchaser will back out of the deal before the seller performs. From the moment an advance payment is made, the seller is assured that, so long as it fulfills its contractual obligation, the money is its to keep. Here, in contrast, a customer submitting a deposit made no commitment to purchase a specified quantity of electricity, or indeed to purchase any electricity at all.[2] IPL's right to keep the money depends upon the customer's purchase of electricity, and upon his later decision to have the deposit applied to future bills, not merely upon the utility's adherence to its contractual duties. Under these circumstances, IPL's dominion over the fund is far less complete than is ordinarily the case in an advance-payment situation.

The Commissioner emphasizes that these deposits frequently will be used to pay for electricity, either because the customer defaults on his obligation or because the customer, having established credit, chooses to apply the deposit to future bills rather than to accept a refund. When this occurs, the Commissioner argues, the transaction, from a cash-flow standpoint, is equivalent to an advance payment. In his

---

[2] A customer, for example, might terminate service the day after making the deposit. Also, IPL's dominion over a deposit remains incomplete even after the customer begins buying electricity. As has been noted, the deposit typically is set at twice the customer's estimated monthly bill. So long as the customer pays his bills in a timely fashion, the money he owes the utility (for electricity used but not yet paid for) almost always will be less than the amount of the deposit. If this were not the case, the deposit would provide inadequate protection. Thus, throughout the period the deposit is held, at least a portion is likely to be money that IPL has no real assurance of ever retaining.

view this economic equivalence mandates identical tax treatment.

Whether these payments constitute income when received, however, depends upon the parties' rights and obligations at the time the payments are made. The problem with petitioner's argument perhaps can best be understood if we imagine a loan between parties involved in an ongoing commercial relationship. At the time the loan falls due, the lender may decide to apply the money owed him to the purchase of goods or services rather than to accept repayment in cash. But this decision does not mean that the loan, when made, was an advance payment after all. The lender in effect has taken repayment of his money (as was his contractual right) and has chosen to use the proceeds for the purchase of goods or services from the borrower. Although, for the sake of convenience, the parties may combine the two steps, that decision does not blind us to the fact that in substance two transactions are involved.[3] It is this element of choice that distinguishes an advance payment from a loan. Whether these customer deposits are the economic equivalents of advance payments, and therefore taxable upon receipt, must be determined by examining the relationship between the parties at the time of the deposit. The individual who makes an advance payment retains no right to insist upon the return of the funds; so long as the recipient fulfills the terms of the bargain, the money is its to keep. The customer who submits a deposit to the utility, like the lender in the previous hypothetical, retains the right to insist upon repayment in cash; he may choose to apply the money to the purchase of electricity, but he assumes no obligation to do so, and the utility therefore acquires no unfettered "dominion" over the money at the time of receipt.

When the Commissioner examines privately structured transactions, the true understanding of the parties, of course, may not be apparent. It may be that a transfer of funds, though nominally a loan, may conceal an unstated agreement that the money is to be applied to the purchase of goods or services. We need not, and do not, attempt to devise a test for addressing those situations where the nature of the parties' bargain is legitimately in dispute. This particular respondent, however, conducts its business in a heavily regulated environment; its rights and obligations vis-a-vis its customers are largely determined by law and regulation rather than by private negotiation. That the utility's customers, when they qualify for refunds of deposits, frequently choose to apply those refunds to future bills rather than taking repayment in cash does not mean that any customer has made an unspoken commitment to do so.

Our decision is also consistent with the Tax Court's long-standing treatment of lease deposits — perhaps the closest analogy to the present situation. The Tax Court traditionally has distinguished between a sum designed as a prepayment of rent — which is taxable upon receipt — and a sum deposited to secure the tenant's performance of a lease agreement. *See, e.g., J. & E. Enterprises, Inc. v. Commissioner,* 26 T.C.M. 944 (1967).[4] In fact, the customer deposits at issue here are less

---

[3] The Commissioner contends that a customer's decision to take his refund while making a separate payment for services, rather than applying the deposit to his bill, would amount to nothing more than an economically meaningless "exchange of checks." But in our view the "exchange of checks," while less convenient, more accurately reflects the economic substance of the transactions.

[4] In *J. & E. Enterprises* the Tax Court stated: "If a sum is received by a lessor at the beginning of

plausibly regarded as income than lease deposits would be. The typical lease deposit secures the tenant's fulfillment of a contractual obligation to pay a specified rent throughout the term of the lease. The utility customer, however, makes no commitment to purchase any services at all at the time he tenders the deposit.

We recognize that IPL derives an economic benefit from these deposits. But a taxpayer does not realize taxable income from every event that improves his economic condition. A customer who makes this deposit reflects no commitment to purchase services, and IPL's right to retain the money is contingent upon events outside its control. We hold that such dominion as IPL has over these customer deposits is insufficient for the deposits to qualify as taxable income at the time they are made.

The judgment of the Court of Appeals is affirmed.

It is so ordered.

---

a lease, is subject to his unfettered control, and is to be applied as rent for a subsequent period during the term of the lease, such sum is income in the year of receipt even though in certain circumstances a refund thereof may be required. . . . If, on the other hand, a sum is deposited to secure the lessee's performance under a lease, and is to be returned at the expiration thereof, it is not taxable income even though the fund is deposited with the lessor instead of in escrow and the lessor has temporary use of the money. . . . In this situation the acknowledged liability of the lessor to account for the deposited sum on the lessee's performance of the lease covenants prevents the sum from being taxable in the year of receipt." 26 TCM, at 945–946.

In Rev. Rul. 72-519, 1972-2 Cum. Bull. 32, the Commissioner relied in part on *J. & E. Enterprises* as authority for the proposition that deposits intended to secure income-producing covenants are advance payments taxable as income upon receipt, while deposits intended to secure nonincome-producing covenants are not. *Id.*, at 33. In our view, neither *J. & E. Enterprises* nor the other cases cited in the Revenue Ruling support that distinction. *See Hirsch Improvement Co. v. Commissioner of Internal Revenue*, 143 F.2d 912 (CA2), *cert. denied*, 323 U.S. 750, 65 S. Ct. 84, 89, L. Ed. 601 (1944); *Mantell v. Commissioner*, 17 T.C. 1143 (1952); *Gilken Corp. v. Commissioner*, 10 T.C. 445 (1948), *aff'd*, 176 F.2d 141 (CA 6 1949). These cases all distinguish between advance payments and security deposits, not between deposits that do and do not secure income-producing covenants.

Chapter 4

GAINS DERIVED FROM DEALINGS IN PROPERTY

I. PROBLEMS

1. Speculator purchased a 5-acre tract of land ten years ago for $100,000. He sold the entire tract of land this year for $300,000. How much income must Speculator report? What result if he subdivides the tract into five 1-acre parcels and sells each parcel for $75,000?

2. Maggie purchased a summer home for $500,000. In purchasing the home, she used $100,000 of her own funds and borrowed the other $400,000 of the purchase price from a local bank, giving the bank a mortgage on the home.

   (a) What basis will Maggie have in the summer home? Would your answer change if Maggie had purchased the summer home under a contract whereby she paid the seller $100,000 down and agreed to pay the balance of $400,000 (plus interest on the unpaid balance) over the next ten years?

   (b) Assume, during the five years following the purchase of the home, Maggie paid $100,000 on the principal balance owing the bank under the original mortgage. She thus reduced the amount of the mortgage to $300,000. How, if at all, will the $100,000 in principal payments affect Maggie's basis in the summer home?

   (c) Assume that having reduced the mortgage balance to $200,000, Maggie refinanced the property to secure a lower interest rate and to take advantage of the significant equity she had in the home as a result of an increase in property values. As part of the refinancing of the home, Maggie borrowed an additional $250,000 from the bank, thus increasing her mortgage to $450,000. Maggie used the refinancing proceeds as follows: $75,000 to remodel the summer home; $125,000 to purchase a tract of land she will hold for investment; and $50,000 to pay for a European vacation for her family. What impact will the refinancing have on Maggie's basis in the summer home? What basis will Maggie have in the tract of land she purchased for investment?

   (d) Two years after remodeling the summer home, Maggie, who had never used the home as her principal residence, sold it. The purchaser paid Maggie $300,000 in cash and assumed the balance of $400,000 which Maggie then owed on the mortgage encumbering the home. How much gain, if any, will Maggie realize on the sale of the home? What basis will the purchaser take in the home?

3. Clare, a collector of modern art, owes Liz $6,000 in legal fees. Liz purchases one of Clare's paintings for $6,000. Clare then uses the $6,000 to pay the legal fees owed to Liz. Five years later when the painting has significantly increased in value, Liz sells the painting for $10,000. What tax consequences to Liz from the foregoing events? Alternatively, assume that Liz, instead of paying Clare $6,000 for the painting, agrees to accept it as payment in full of the legal fees. Assume, as before, that Liz sells the painting for $10,000 five years later. What are the tax consequences to Liz of the receipt and eventual sale of the painting?

4. Katie owns an undeveloped five-acre tract of land in Phoenix, Arizona. Katie's Phoenix land has a fair market value of $750,000 and her adjusted basis in the land is $450,000. Katie transfers her Phoenix land to Patrick in exchange for a tract of undeveloped lakefront property Patrick owns at Lake Tahoe. Katie plans to build a home for herself on the Lake Tahoe property she acquires from Patrick. Assume Patrick's Lake Tahoe property also has a fair market value of $750,000 and he has an adjusted basis of $100,000 in the property. Patrick, who was recently employed in Phoenix, plans to use the Phoenix land he acquires from Katie to build a home for his family.

    (a) What are the tax consequences to Katie and Patrick on the exchange, *i.e.*, what gain, if any, will each recognize and what basis will each take in the property received in the exchange?

    (b) How would your answers to (a) change if, instead of a fair market value of $750,000, Katie's Phoenix land had a fair market value of $800,000 and Patrick transferred to Katie his Lake Tahoe property plus $50,000 in cash in exchange for her land?

    (c) Assume the facts of (b) above except that instead of giving Katie $50,000 in cash, Patrick assumed a $50,000 mortgage encumbering Katie's Phoenix land. Assume also that, during the following year, after Patrick paid $10,000 on the mortgage, he abandoned the idea of building his family home on the Phoenix land and, instead, sold the land for $900,000. The purchaser paid Patrick $860,000 in cash and assumed the $40,000 balance that was then owing on the mortgage encumbering the land. What are the tax consequences to Patrick on the sale of the Phoenix land? What basis will Katie have in the Lake Tahoe property acquired in the exchange?

    (d) Assume Katie's Phoenix land has a fair market value of $800,000, an adjusted basis of $450,000, and is encumbered by a $300,000 mortgage; and assume Patrick's Lake Tahoe land has a fair market value of $750,000, an adjusted basis of $100,000, and is encumbered by a mortgage of $200,000. What are the tax consequences to Katie and Patrick if they exchange properties, with each assuming the mortgage encumbering the property being acquired, and with Katie also transferring $50,000 in cash to Patrick to equalize the exchange?

Assignment for Chapter 4:

Complete the problems.

Read: Internal Revenue Code: §§ 61(a)(3), 1001(a), (b) and (c); 1011(a); 1012. Skim
        §§ 1016(a)(1), (2); 1031(a)(1).
        Treasury Regulations: §§ 1.61-6(a); 1.1001-1(a); 1.1001-2(a)(1), (3) and (4)(i),
        (ii).

        Materials: Overview
                     Philadelphia Park Amusement Co. v. U.S.

II.   VOCABULARY

amount realized
basis
adjusted basis
cost basis
tax cost basis
gain
recovery of capital
nonrecourse debt
recourse debt
taxable exchange

III.   OBJECTIVES

1. To explain in your own words the relationship between recovery of capital
    and gain.

2. To explain generally the relationship between "adjusted basis" and "basis."

3. To explain the relationship between adjusted basis and gain; to explain the
    relationship between amount realized and gain.

4. To recall § 1001 provides the formula for computing gain and loss.

5. To recall § 1012 provides that basis is generally the taxpayer's cost.

6. To recall § 61(a)(3) provides that "gains derived from dealings in property"
    constitute gross income.

7. To explain the relationship between basis and recourse liabilities incurred
    or assumed in acquiring property.

8. To explain the relationship between amount realized and recourse liabili-
    ties assumed by the purchaser.

9. To identify circumstances in which a taxpayer has a "tax cost" basis in
    property.

10. To determine the taxpayer's basis when the taxpayer either (1) uses her
    own money to purchase property or (2) borrows money on a recourse basis
    to purchase property.

11. To determine the amount of gain which a taxpayer realizes on the sale or
    exchange of property (1) when the property sold is not encumbered by

liabilities; and (2) when it is encumbered by liabilities.

12. To explain why the cost basis of property received in a taxable exchange will always be the fair market value of the property received in the exchange.

IV.   OVERVIEW

"Recovery of Capital." "Basis." "Adjusted Basis." "Amount Realized." These related terms are terms of art to the tax practitioner. An understanding of their meaning is essential to your understanding of the tax treatment of even the most common property transactions. At this juncture of the course, these terms are critical to your understanding of § 61(a)(3), which specifies that gross income includes "gains derived from dealings in property."

Let's use a simple example for purposes of considering the gain-as-income concept:

> Melissa purchased a share of stock in XYZ Corporation for $80 last year. During the next 12 months, the stock increased at the rate of $10 per month. Melissa sold the stock this year for $200. How much income must Melissa report?

Having previously studied the "realization" concept, you should understand that, during the period she owned the stock, Melissa was not required to report the appreciation on the stock as gross income. Thus, although the stock may be publicly traded and its increasing value documented daily in the reports of the New York Stock Exchange, Melissa "realized" no income so long as she owned the stock. The sale of the stock, however, was a realization event. Did Melissa realize *gain* from the sale of the stock? If so, how much? $200? $120? What does § 61(a)(3) mean by "*gain derived from dealings in property*"?

When in doubt about the meaning of a statutory provision like § 61(a)(3), where should you turn first? The applicable Treasury regulation, of course! Regulation § 1.61-6(a) is very helpful in this regard. It provides "gain is the excess of the amount realized over the unrecovered cost or other basis for the property sold or exchanged." In addition, it notes "[t]he specific rules for computing the amount of gain or loss are contained in Section 1001 and the regulations thereunder."

Section 1001 contains a definition of gain comparable to that in Reg. § 1.61-6(a) with one exception — instead of "unrecovered cost" § 1001(a) speaks of "adjusted basis." You will find that "unrecovered cost" is often a helpful way to think of adjusted basis. More on that later.

Section 1001(b) provides that the "amount realized" on the sale or other disposition of property equals the money received plus the fair market value of any other property received. Melissa's amount realized is thus $200.

What is her adjusted basis in the stock? Thinking in terms of "unrecovered cost," one might conclude it is $80, *i.e.*, the amount Melissa paid for the stock. Indeed, that is her adjusted basis. Consider how one would arrive at that conclusion statutorily. Section 1001(a) directs the taxpayer to § 1011 for a definition of adjusted basis. Section 1011(a) provides that adjusted basis is equal to the basis as determined under § 1012 (or other appropriate section) adjusted as provided in § 1016. While numerous provisions in the Code address basis, the most significant provision is § 1012. According to § 1012, basis equals cost "except as otherwise provided. . . . " In subsequent Chapters you will consider other basis provisions which give meaning to the "except-as-otherwise-provided" language. In Melissa's case, her basis is her "cost." "Cost" is a term of art. Its commonly understood definition, *i.e.*, an amount paid for an item, will suffice in most cases, including Melissa's. Thus, Melissa's basis in the stock is $80.

Determination of adjusted basis requires a consideration of § 1016, a detailed analysis of which at this time would be premature. Suffice it to say, however, that § 1016 requires a taxpayer to adjust her basis in property to reflect any recovery of her investment or any additional investment made in the property. In other words, adjusted basis reflects the impact events occurring subsequent to one's acquisition of property may have on the amount of one's investment in the property. Two brief examples will demonstrate the necessity of adjustments to basis:

> **Example 1:** Jackie purchased a home for $250,000 and subsequently added a room to the home at a cost of $50,000. Although Jackie's original basis in the home was $250,000, she must adjust the basis in her home to reflect the additional investment associated with the new room. Therefore, Jackie's adjusted basis in the home (or unrecovered cost) is $300,000.

> **Example 2:** Assume the same facts as Example 1. Assume also that a greenhouse attached to Jackie's home was completely destroyed in a hail storm and Jackie recovered $10,000 from her insurance company as a result. Instead of investing the $10,000 in repairing the greenhouse, she used it for a family vacation. Because the insurance proceeds represent a partial recovery of Jackie's investment in the home, she must adjust her basis to reflect that recovery. Her adjusted basis (or unrecovered cost) in the home is therefore $290,000, *i.e.*, $300,000 less the $10,000 recovery.

Unlike the taxpayer in either of the above examples, Melissa has neither invested more in the XYZ company nor recovered any of her cost. Therefore, no adjustments may be made to Melissa's basis. Her adjusted basis is the same as her original basis, *i.e.*, $80.

Now that the amount realized and adjusted basis are known, the amount of Melissa's gain, and therefore her income, from the sale of the stock is readily computed. The amount realized of $200 less the adjusted basis of $80 equals $120 of gain which constitutes gross income under § 61(a)(3).

This example demonstrates a fundamental principle in our income tax system — a taxpayer may recover tax-free her investment (capital) in property before being charged with income from a disposition of the property. Having paid $80 for the stock, Melissa was entitled to recover $80 from the sale of the stock tax-free. Had Melissa sold the stock for only $80, she would have had no gain and thus no income. Had she sold the stock for less than $80, she would have had a loss. Only the excess of the amount realized over her investment of $80 constituted income. Thus, as noted, Melissa would only report $120 of gain on the sale of the XYZ stock. The concept demonstrated by this example is often referred to as the "recovery of capital" or "return of capital" concept. "Basis" and "adjusted basis" implement the recovery of capital concept by providing a measure of the capital (or investment) the taxpayer is entitled to recover tax-free. Simply stated, they prevent previously taxed dollars from being taxed a second time.

That the recovery of capital concept is implicit in the notion of "income" was recognized by the Supreme Court in *Doyle v. Mitchell Bros. Co.*, 247 U.S. 179 (1918), a case interpreting the Corporation Excise Tax Act of 1909. The issue in *Doyle* was whether under this 1909 act gross receipts from the conversion of assets constituted gross income. Concluding that a business, in computing its gross income, may deduct its cost in the assets sold from its gross receipts, the Court noted:

> [W]e think, that by the true intent and meaning of the act, the entire proceeds of a mere conversion of capital assets were not to be treated as income. Whatever difficulty there may be about a precise and scientific definition of "income," it imports . . . something entirely distinct from principal or capital either as a subject of taxation or as a measure of the tax; conveying rather the idea of gain or increase. . . . Understanding the term in this natural and obvious sense, it cannot be said that a conversion of capital assets invariably produces income. If sold at less than cost, it produces rather loss or outgo. Nevertheless, in many if not in most cases there results a gain that properly may be accounted as a part of the "gross income" received "from all sources"; and by applying to this the authorized deductions we arrive at "net income." In order to determine whether there has been gain or loss, and the amount of the gain if any, we must withdraw from the gross proceeds an amount sufficient to restore the capital value that existed at the commencement of the period under consideration.

Id. at 184, 185.

As demonstrated above, §§ 61(a)(3) and 1001 reflect the very standard discussed by the Court in *Doyle*. With respect to income from a business, read the first sentence of Reg. § 1.61-3, which specifically adopts the recovery of capital concept of *Doyle*.

Let us return to Melissa's stock sale to consider one other issue. Assume, prior to selling the stock, Melissa had received a $10 dividend from XYZ Company. How would that receipt be treated? Would it, like the insurance proceeds in the greenhouse example above, constitute a tax-free return of capital requiring a downward adjustment of Melissa's basis in the stock, thereby increasing her gain when she sold the stock for $200? Or would the dividend constitute profit from Melissa's investment in XYZ that should be treated as income? Pursuant to § 61(a)(7), the dividend constitutes gross income. To be sure, Congress could have provided that dividends paid by corporations to their shareholders are tax free until a shareholder has recovered her basis (investment) in the stock, but it chose not to do so. Instead, a dividend is viewed as earnings on or profit from one's investment, much the way rent represents earnings on one's property or interest represents earnings on one's money. Just as rents (§ 61(a)(5)) and interest (§ 61(a)(4)) are gross income, so too are dividends. Because Melissa must report the $10 dividend as gross income, she is not treated as having recovered any of her investment in the stock, and her basis in the stock is not adjusted to reflect the receipt of the dividend.

The recovery of capital concept is applicable in contexts other than dispositions of property. The concept is commonly applied in the borrowing context. Assume Sondra lends Daniel $1,000. When Daniel repays the $1,000, does Sondra have income? Surely not! Sondra has no "accession to wealth" within the meaning of

Glenshaw Glass. Rather, she has merely recovered the amount loaned to Daniel, and is thus restored to the position she was in immediately prior to making the loan. For Sondra, the repayment of the loan principal represented merely a recovery of capital. Other examples of the application of the concept will be considered in later chapters in this text.

A. Tax Cost Basis

Assume Lawyer received a parcel of land from Client in lieu of cash compensation for the legal services Lawyer had rendered Client. The land had a fair market value of $50,000 — exactly equal to the fee Client owed Lawyer. Because the form of income makes no difference, Lawyer has $50,000 of income. Reg. § 1.61-1(a). Assume Lawyer subsequently sells the land for $60,000. How much gain, if any, must Lawyer report? Lawyer's amount realized is clearly $60,000. What is Lawyer's adjusted basis? Section 1012 defines "basis" as "cost." Here, Lawyer paid nothing out-of-pocket to Client for the land. Does that mean Lawyer's basis is $0? If so, upon selling the land for $60,000, Lawyer would have $60,000 of gain, all of which would constitute gross income under § 61(a)(3). Since Lawyer had already reported $50,000 of income upon receipt of the land from Client, would it make sense to require lawyer to report another $60,000 of gain upon the sale of the land? In other words, will Lawyer have to report a total of $110,000 of gross income as a result of the receipt of the land and its subsequent sale?

Certainly not! Had Client paid Lawyer $50,000 in cash which Lawyer immediately used to purchase the land from Client, Lawyer's basis in the land would have been $50,000 and Lawyer's gain on the subsequent sale of the land would have been only $10,000. Thus, the total income reported by Lawyer would have been $60,000, *i.e.*, the $50,000 of cash compensation received plus the $10,000 of gain on the sale of the land. That result is more reasonable than the one first suggested. Where Lawyer receives the land in lieu of $50,000 cash and then sells it for $10,000 more than its value when received, Lawyer's total income should not exceed $60,000. In the real world of tax, it doesn't! Having reported $50,000 of compensation income upon receipt of the land from Client, Lawyer is appropriately treated as having a basis in the land of $50,000. This basis is commonly referred to as a "tax cost basis." Read Regulation § 1.61-2(d)(2)(i) carefully. When Lawyer subsequently sells the land for $60,000, Lawyer's gain is only $10,000. The total income from the receipt and sale of the land is thus $60,000, just as though Lawyer first received $50,000 in cash, purchased the land for that amount, and sold the land for $60,000.

Let's consider a slight variation of the above facts. Assume the fair market value of the land was $60,000 and Lawyer paid Client $10,000 for the land. While one might be tempted to conclude that Lawyer has simply made a bargain purchase and therefore need not report any income, the nature of the relationship of the parties and the circumstances of the land transfer (*i.e.*, the intention of Client to compensate Lawyer for services rendered) establishes that what one might view as the $50,000 "bargain element" is merely Client's means of paying Lawyer's fee. As in the prior example, Lawyer should report $50,000 of gross income. What will

Lawyer's basis be in the land? Regulation § 1.61-2(d)(2)(i) indicates that Lawyer's basis will be the sum of the $10,000 Lawyer paid for the land plus the $50,000 difference between the fair market value of the land at the time of the transfer and the amount Lawyer paid for the land. Lawyer's basis in the land will therefore be $60,000. If, for example, Lawyer sells the land for $65,000, Lawyer would report only $5,000 of gain.

We might take the latter hypothetical a step further and inquire as to the tax consequences to Client. Assume that Client had an adjusted basis of $30,000 in the land Client transferred to Lawyer. Client should be required to report gain in the amount of the difference between Client's amount realized of $60,000 (*i.e.*, the $50,000 value of services rendered by Lawyer plus the $10,000 cash paid by Lawyer) and Client's adjusted basis of $30,000. Client therefore has $30,000 of gain. In other words, it is just as though Client sold the land to Lawyer for $60,000 in cash and then took $50,000 of the sale proceeds and paid that amount to Lawyer for the legal services Lawyer had rendered Client. In addition, as will be discussed in Chapter 12, Client may be entitled to deduct the legal fees paid to Lawyer.

B.   Impact of Liabilities

1.   Impact on Basis

The amount of a taxpayer's initial basis or investment in property is clear when no liabilities encumber the property and the taxpayer pays cash for the property. Computation of the taxpayer's basis is complicated, however, if the taxpayer/purchaser remains obligated to the seller for part of the purchase price, assumes a liability of the seller, takes the property subject to the liability, or borrows money from a third party to pay the purchase price. Consider the following examples:

> **Example 1:** Last month, Julie purchased a tract of unimproved land from Paul for $100,000 and borrowed the full $100,000 from the Last National Bank. Assume Julie gave the bank a promissory note for $100,000, secured by a mortgage on the land. The note is a recourse note, *i.e.*, if Julie fails to make loan payments as required, the Bank can look not only to the land for purposes of repayment but also to all of Julie's other property. What basis does Julie have in the land? In borrowing the funds to purchase the land, Julie incurred an obligation to repay the Last National Bank. Presumably, she will repay the loan and thus ultimately make a $100,000 investment in the land. Therefore, isn't her cost (and therefore her basis) really $100,000? The courts long ago concluded it is. The Supreme Court noted in *Commissioner v. Tufts*, 461 U.S. 300, 307 (1983), that when a taxpayer receives a loan and applies the loan proceeds to the purchase price of property used to secure the loan, "[b]ecause of the obligation to repay, the taxpayer is entitled to include the amount of the loan in computing his basis in the property; the loan under Section 1012 is part of the taxpayer's cost of the property. . . . [The] resultant benefits to the taxpayer are predicated on the assumption that the mortgage will be repaid in full." Thus, whether the funds Julie used to purchase the land are borrowed or were from her savings, her basis in the land is the same — $100,000.

Example 2: Assume the same facts as in Example 1 except Julie borrowed the $100,000 from Paul instead of the Last National Bank, *i.e.*, Paul sold the land to Julie under a contract requiring Julie to pay him the purchase price over a period of time. Does it make any difference that the "lender" is also the seller? The answer is "No." Julie's basis in the property is $100,000, the same basis as in Example 1.

Example 3: Assume the same facts as in Example 2 except Julie is not personally liable for repayment of the borrowed funds. Thus, if she should default on the contract, her property, other than the land, would not be subject to Paul's claims. Where no personal liability is associated with borrowing, the borrowing is considered "nonrecourse." Does the nonrecourse nature of the loan change the taxpayer's basis? The Commissioner in *Crane v. Commissioner*, 331 U.S. 1 (1947), argued nonrecourse and recourse debt should be accorded the same treatment; the Supreme Court agreed. In Chapter 38, we will consider the *Crane* rationale and the special problems associated with nonrecourse liabilities. This chapter focuses on the impact of recourse liabilities on basis and amount realized.

By reflecting in basis the debt incurred by a taxpayer in acquiring property, the tax system gives credit to a taxpayer for an investment the taxpayer has yet to make. Because depreciation deductions are computed with reference to one's basis in property, this treatment of debt can be very beneficial to a taxpayer acquiring depreciable assets. See Chapter 14 for a detailed discussion of depreciation. Having received advance credit for making the investment, however, the taxpayer may not increase her basis when the debt is paid. Thus, in Example 1 above, if Julie makes a principal payment of $5,000 to Last National Bank on her loan, that payment does not affect her basis in the land; her basis remains $100,000.

2. Impact on Amount Realized

Determination of the amount realized by a seller is likewise not straightforward when the property sold is encumbered by liabilities for which the purchaser directly or indirectly becomes responsible. Consider the following facts:

> Assume Daniel purchased a home for $300,000. Daniel borrowed $250,000 of the purchase price and gave the lender a recourse note secured by a mortgage on the property. The other $50,000 of the purchase price was paid from Daniel's savings. Three years later, when Daniel still owed $230,000 to the lender, Daniel sold the property to Michael for $325,000. Michael paid Daniel $95,000 cash (Daniel's equity in the home) and assumed the $230,000 liability encumbering the home.

What is Daniel's amount realized? $95,000 or $325,000? Section 1001(b) provides in relevant part that the "amount realized from the sale of property is the sum of any money received plus the fair market value of the property (other than money) received. . . . " Note the Code provision makes no mention of liability relief. If one considered Daniel's amount realized to be only the $95,000 of cash he actually received, a very strange result would follow. Daniel's basis (adjusted basis) in the home is $300,000. (See the previous discussion of the impact of liabilities on basis. Note that in paying $20,000 on his mortgage, Daniel did not increase his basis in the home. As explained previously, he had already received advance credit for making that payment.) If Daniel's amount realized is only $95,000, Daniel has sustained a $205,000 loss. That, of course, can't be right. The home appreciated $25,000 in value after Daniel purchased it. Therefore, rather than a loss, Daniel should have a gain of $25,000. By contrast, if the liability assumed by Michael is included in Daniel's amount realized, the correct result is reached: Daniel will realize $25,000 of gain, *i.e.*, the difference between his amount realized of $325,000 ($95,000 cash plus $230,000 liability assumed) and the adjusted basis of the home ($300,000). Thus, a necessary corollary to the inclusion of liabilities in basis is the inclusion in amount realized of those liabilities of the taxpayer assumed by the purchaser. Reg. § 1.1001-2(a)(1) and (4)(i), (ii) reflect this principle. Read those regulation provisions carefully. After studying *Old Colony Trust Company v. Commissioner*, you should not be surprised by this result. See also *Commissioner v. Tufts*, 461 U.S. 300, 309–310 (1983), included in Chapter 38.

At this juncture, you should understand two general rules: (1) recourse liabilities incurred by a taxpayer in the acquisition of property are included in the taxpayer's basis in that property; and (2) recourse liabilities of a seller, assumed by a purchaser, are included in the seller's amount realized. (We shall see in Chapter 38 that similar rules apply to nonrecourse liabilities.)

C.   Basis of Property Acquired in Taxable Exchange

Assume Henri owns a bottle of very rare French red wine, which he purchased for $5,000 and is now worth $10,000. Assume Denise owns an 18th-century American colonial desk, purchased for $12,500 but now worth only $10,000. If Henri and Denise exchange the wine and desk, what basis will each of them have in the property acquired? Applying § 1012, we would expect both of them to have a basis equal to the "cost" of the acquired property. But what is the cost of property acquired in an exchange — the value of the property relinquished or the value of the property acquired? In this example, the values of the exchanged properties are identical and whichever we look to we get the same answer: the basis of the acquired property is $10,000.

Because the value of property relinquished in an exchange generally equals the value of property received, one may generally assume it does not matter whether one looks to the value of the relinquished property or acquired property to determine basis. That assumption, unfortunately, will not always be correct. Assume, when Henri and Denise actually exchanged properties, the value of Denise's desk had fallen from $10,000 to $9,000 while Henri's wine retained its $10,000 value. Will Henri's basis in the desk received from Denise equal the $10,000 value of the wine he transferred to Denise in the exchange? Assuming this is the case, let's consider Henri's situation. Henri's amount realized on the exchange of his wine is $9,000, the fair market value of the desk received from Denise. Henri's adjusted basis in the wine was $5,000. Therefore, Henri's gain under § 1001(a) is $4,000. If Henri's basis in the desk received from Denise were $10,000, the value of the wine he gave to Denise in the exchange, there would be a $1,000 loss inherent in the desk since that property has a fair market value of only $9,000. Were Henri to sell the desk for its fair market value of $9,000 the day after the exchange, Henri would recognize the $1,000 loss. Combining the gain realized by Henri on the exchange ($4,000) with the loss (of $1,000) on the hypothetical sale, Henri would have realized a net gain of $3,000. But if Henri had merely sold his wine for $9,000 to some third party, because he had contractually obligated himself to do so (just as he had contractually obligated himself to exchange the wine for a $9,000 desk), Henri would have recognized $4,000 of gain. Clearly, the result should be no different where there is first an exchange for the desk and then a conversion to cash. And yet, if we conclude Henri's basis in the desk is $10,000, there will be a difference, *i.e.*, Henri's gain will be understated. That obviously does not make sense.

Consider Denise's situation. She exchanged a desk that had declined in value to $9,000 for wine worth $10,000. Is her basis in the wine equal to the $9,000 value of the desk she transferred? Her amount realized is $10,000, the value of the wine received. Her adjusted basis in the desk was $12,500. Therefore, her § 1001(a) loss on the exchange is $2,500. If, as suggested, her basis in the $10,000 of newly acquired wine is $9,000, the fair market value of the desk she gave to Henri in the exchange, she will have a potential gain of $1,000. Were she to sell the wine the next day for $10,000, Denise would recognize this $1,000 gain. Combining the exchange and sale, Denise's net loss would only be $1,500. Again, if one were to eliminate the exchange and assume Denise merely sold the desk for $10,000 cash — that is, if we assume a third party was contractually obligated to pay $10,000 for the desk, as Henri had been contractually obligated to transfer $10,000 worth of wine for the desk, her loss would be $2,500. Thus, to treat Denise's basis in the wine received from Henri as equaling the value of the desk she gave to Henri is to understate her loss. Again, we reach a nonsensical result.

The dilemma raised by the above example was considered by the Court of Claims (now the United States Court of Federal Claims) in *Philadelphia Park Amusement Co. v. U.S.*, 126 F. Supp. 184 (Ct. Cl. 1954), included in the materials. The taxpayer in that case operated an amusement park in Philadelphia. Under the circumstances presented, the Court of Claims rejected the view that the § 1012 cost basis of property received in a taxable exchange is the fair market value of the property *relinquished* in the exchange. Rather, the court held "the cost basis of the property received in a taxable exchange is the fair market value of the property *received* in the exchange" (emphasis added). The court's rationale is expressed in terms of the inappropriateness of allowing a "stepped-up basis, without paying a tax therefor" or, alternatively, the inappropriateness of having the taxpayer "subjected to a double tax."

As demonstrated in *Philadelphia Park* and in the Henri-Denise example, gain and loss may be distorted if the cost basis of property received in a taxable exchange is considered to be equal to the fair market value of property given in the exchange. In effect, when that standard was applied to Henri in the above example, he took a stepped-up basis in the desk, which resulted in a reduction of the net gain he ultimately had to report. By contrast, Denise was subject to a double tax in that the amount of loss she actually sustained on the transaction was understated. Applying instead the standard established by the Court of Claims, these distortions are eliminated, *i.e.*, Henri's basis in the desk will be $9,000 rather than $10,000; Denise's basis in the wine will be $10,000 rather than $9,000. The standard enunciated in *Philadelphia Park* has specific application to those exchanges where the properties exchanged differ in value as in the above example. If the properties exchanged do not differ in value, one can confidently determine the basis in the property received by reference to the value of the property relinquished, but only because the values do not differ.

If the basis of property received in a taxable exchange is equal to the amount realized on the exchange, that is, equal to the value of the property received on the exchange, how does one compute basis where the value of the property received, and hence the amount realized, cannot be determined with reasonable accuracy? See the guidance the court in *Philadelphia Park* provides in these circumstances: first, where at least the property relinquished may be valued and second, where neither the property received nor the property relinquished may be valued with reasonable accuracy.

PHILADELPHIA PARK AMUSEMENT CO. v. UNITED STATES
United States Court of Claims
126 F. Supp. 184 (1954)

[Authors' Synopsis of the Facts: The taxpayer owned a 50-year franchise from the City of Philadelphia to operate a railroad to serve an amusement park. In conjunction with the exercise of its rights under this franchise, the taxpayer constructed the Strawberry Bridge across a river. Some years later, the taxpayer exchanged the bridge with the City of Philadelphia for a 10-year extension of the taxpayer's railroad franchise. The taxpayer later abandoned its railroad franchise and arranged for a bus company to give passenger service to the amusement park. The taxpayer claimed a deduction for the unrecovered cost of the franchise and contended that unrecovered cost had to be measured by reference to the undepreciated cost of the bridge which it had given in exchange for the extension of the franchise.]

This brings us to the question of what is the cost basis of the 10-year extension of taxpayer's franchise. Although defendant contends that Strawberry Bridge was either worthless or not "exchanged" for the 10-year extension of the franchise, we believe that the bridge had some value, and that the contract under which the bridge was transferred to the City clearly indicates that the one was given in consideration of the other. The taxpayer, however, has failed to show that the exchange was one that falls within the nonrecognition provisions of . . . the Code and, therefore, it was a taxable exchange. . . .

The gain or loss, whichever the case may have been, should have been recognized, and the cost basis under section [1012] of the Code, of the 10-year extension of the franchise was the cost to the taxpayer. The succinct statement in section [1012] that "the basis of property shall be the cost of such property" although clear in principle, is frequently difficult in application. One view is that the cost basis of property received in a taxable exchange is the fair market value of the property given in the exchange. The other view is that the cost basis of property received in a taxable exchange is the fair market value of the property received in the exchange. As will be seen from the cases and some of the Commissioner's rulings the Commissioner's position has not been altogether consistent on this question. The view that "cost" is the fair market value of the property given is predicated on the theory that the cost to the taxpayer is the economic value relinquished. The view that "cost" is the fair market value of the property received is based upon the theory that the term "cost" is a tax concept and must be considered in the light of the designed interrelationship of [the gain and loss and basis provisions of the Code] and the prime role that the basis of property plays in determining tax liability. We believe that when the question is considered in the latter context that the cost basis of the property received in a taxable exchange is the fair market value of the property received in the exchange.

When property is exchanged for property in a taxable exchange the taxpayer is taxed on the difference between the adjusted basis of the property given in exchange and the fair market value of the property received in exchange. For purposes of determining gain or loss, the fair market value of the property received is treated as cash and taxed accordingly. To maintain harmony with the fundamental purpose of these sections, it is necessary to consider the fair market value of the property received as the cost basis to the taxpayer. The failure to do so would result in allowing the taxpayer a stepped-up basis, without paying a tax therefor, if the fair market value of the property received is less than the fair market value of the property given, and the taxpayer would be subjected to a double tax if the fair market value of the property received is more than the fair market value of the property given. By holding that the fair market value of the property received in a taxable exchange is the cost basis, the above discrepancy is avoided and the basis of the property received will equal the adjusted basis of the property given plus any gain recognized, or that should have been recognized, or minus any loss recognized, or that should have been recognized.

Therefore, the cost basis of the 10-year extension of the franchise was its fair market value on August 3, 1934, the date of the exchange. The determination of whether the cost basis of the property received is its fair market value or the fair market value of the property given in exchange therefor, although necessary to the decision of the case, is generally not of great practical significance because the value of the two properties exchanged in an arms-length transaction are either equal in fact, or are presumed to be equal. The record in this case indicates that the 1934 exchange was an arms-length transaction and, therefore, if the value of the extended franchise cannot be determined with reasonable accuracy, it would be reasonable and fair to assume that the value of Strawberry Bridge was equal to the 10-year extension of the franchise. The fair market value of the 10-year extension of the franchise should be established but, if that value cannot be determined with reasonable certainty, the fair market value of Strawberry Bridge should be established and that will be presumed to be the value of the extended franchise. This value cannot be determined from the facts now before us since the case was prosecuted on a different theory.

The taxpayer contends that the market value of the extended franchise or Strawberry Bridge could not be ascertained and, therefore, it should be entitled to carry over the undepreciated cost basis of the bridge as the cost of the extended franchise. . . . If the value of the extended franchise or bridge cannot be ascertained with a reasonable degree of accuracy, the taxpayer is entitled to carry over the undepreciated cost of the bridge as the cost basis of the extended franchise. . . . However, it is only in rare and extraordinary cases that the value of the property exchanged cannot be ascertained with reasonable accuracy. We are presently of the opinion that either the value of the extended franchise or the bridge can be determined with a reasonable degree of accuracy. Although the value of the extended franchise may be difficult or impossible to ascertain because of the nebulous and intangible characteristics inherent in such property, the value of the bridge is subject to more exact measurement. Consideration may be given to expert testimony on the value of comparable bridges, Strawberry Bridge's reproduction cost and its undepreciated cost, as well as other relevant factors.

Therefore, because we deem it equitable, judgment should be suspended and the question of the value of the extended franchise on August 3, 1934, should be remanded to the Commissioner of this court for the taking of evidence and the filing of a report thereon.

The failure of taxpayer to properly record the transaction in 1934 and thereafter does not prevent the correction of the error, especially under the circumstances of this case. . . . The taxpayer has lost not only the depreciation deductions for the years 1935 to 1944 of the cost of its original franchise, but also the benefit of the depreciation deduction for the cost of the extended franchise, even though the basis of the former was and the latter will be reduced by the amount of depreciation that should have been taken for this period.

We, therefore, conclude that the 1934 exchange was a taxable exchange and that the taxpayer is entitled to use as the cost basis of the 10-year extension of its franchise its fair market value on August 3, 1934, for purposes of determining depreciation and loss due to abandonment, as indicated in this opinion.

Chapter 5

GIFTS, BEQUESTS AND INHERITANCE

I. PROBLEMS

1. Elizabeth, who has a solo law practice, is a community activist. She serves as chairwoman of the board of a major nonprofit organization in her community and is also chairwoman of a state political party. During the holiday season, Elizabeth received a number of presents from various organizations and individuals, including:

   (a) a $10,000 Rolex watch from a major corporate client together with a note stating: "Happy Holidays! We want you to have this small token of our appreciation for your commitment to the rule of law";

   (b) a $100 holiday gift basket of fruit, cheeses, and crackers from the CEO of the nonprofit organization noted above; and

   (c) a $50 gift certificate to an organic food store from a voter who noted that Elizabeth's thoughtful advocacy of bi-partisanship during the midterm election had inspired her.

   Explain the tax consequences, if any, to Elizabeth with respect to each of the above presents.

2. At the request of her frail, elderly father, Lawrence, Maria moved out of her rental apartment to live with and care for him in his home for the last few years of his life. At the time he made the request, Lawrence indicated he would devise his home to Maria if she agreed to the arrangement. Maria said there was no need for him to do so, noting she was single and lived nearby whereas Lawrence's two other children were married with families and lived more than 1,000 miles away. Maria lived with and cared for Lawrence during the last three years of his life. At his death, his will devised the home to Maria, noting the devise was made in gratitude for her care, and devised the balance of his estate in equal shares to Maria and her two siblings. What tax consequences to Maria as a result of the devise of the home? *want it to be inheritance*

3. Years ago, Dan purchased for investment purposes a tract of undeveloped land for $100,000. This year, Dan deeded the land to his son, Will, as a gift. The land had a $250,000 fair market value at the time of the gift and an adjusted basis to Dan of $100,000.

   (a) Will either Dan or Will recognize income on the transfer? What basis does Will take in the land?

(b) How, if at all, would your answers to (a) change, if Dan is also Will's employer?

(c) How would your answers to (a) change if, instead of giving the land to Will, Dan sold it to Will for $50,000? For $200,000?

(d) How would your answers to (a) change if Dan's land were encumbered by a mortgage in the amount of $125,000 and Will agreed to assume the mortgage?

(e) Assume in part (a) Dan's land was worth only $90,000 when he made the gift of the land to Will. What tax consequences to Will when he subsequently sells the land for $90,000? For $80,000? For 95,000? For 110,000?

(f) Assume Dan devised the land to Will and the land had a fair market value of $250,000 at the time of Dan's death. What tax consequences to Will? What basis does Will take in the land?

(g) How would your answers to (f) change if the land had a fair market value of $75,000 at the time of Dan's death?

(h) Assume Dan gives the land to his father, George, when the land has a fair market value of $250,000. George dies two months later and devises the land, still worth $250,000, to Dan's son, Will. What basis does Will take in the land?

Assignment for Chapter 5:

Complete the problems.

Read: Internal Revenue Code: §§ 102; 274(b)(1); 1014(a)(1), (b)(1), (b)(6); 1014(e); 1015(a); skim §§ 1015(d)(1)(A) and (6), and 1041.
Treasury Regulations: §§ 1.102-1(a)–(c); 1.1001-1(e); 1.1001-2(a)(1), (4)(ii) and (iii); 1.1014-2(a)(1) and (5); 1.1015-1(a); 1.1015-4; Prop. Reg. § 1.102-1(f).

Materials: Overview
Commissioner v. Duberstein
Wolder v. Commissioner
Olk v. United States
Goodwin v. United States

II. VOCABULARY

gift
bequest
devise
inheritance
part-gift, part-sale
exclusion
stepped-up basis
stepped-down basis
carryover basis
basis for purposes of computing loss

III.   OBJECTIVES

1. To distinguish gifts and bequests from compensation and other taxable receipts.

2. To recall the *Duberstein* definition of the term "gift" as used in § 102.

3. To explain in your own words the statutory limitations on the exclusion of gifts, bequests, etc.

4. To recall that § 102 excludes gifts, bequests, devises and inheritances.

5. To recall that the disposition of appreciated property by gift generally does not constitute a realization event for the donor.

6. To apply the basis rules of § 1015 to situations in which gifts are made of appreciated and depreciated property.

7. To compute the tax consequences to a donor who makes a transfer that is in part a gift and in part a sale.

8. To apply the § 1014 basis rule and to contrast it to the basis rule in § 1015.

9. To explain the tax consequences to a donor who gives property encumbered by liabilities for which the donee assumes responsibility.

IV. OVERVIEW

Gifts — we give and receive them on a variety of occasions. But have we ever given much (any) consideration to the tax consequences of them? *Glenshaw Glass* teaches us that accessions to wealth generally constitute income. Is a gift an accession to wealth? Clearly so, if it is in the form of cash or other tangible or intangible property. Does it constitute income? No! In each income tax act since 1913, Congress has specifically excluded gifts from income.

The continued exclusion of gifts can be justified for both public policy and administrative reasons. Most gifts occur within the family unit. Indeed, the sharing of goods and services is common in any household. Sometimes that sharing manifests itself in a formal way through a gift from one family member to another on a special occasion, *e.g.*, a birthday; at other times the sharing is informal, such as daily meals shared by members of the same household, cars and other equipment used in common by family members, etc. Such formal and informal sharing arrangements are natural and important aspects of family life and should not be burdened with tax considerations. Furthermore, administratively it would be impossible to enforce a rule that such sharing arrangements give rise to gross income.

The exclusion for gifts, however, is not limited to intrafamily wealth transfers. Friends exchange gifts and gifts even occur in the employment setting between employers and employees. Certainly, the further a transfer is removed from the family context, the more strained becomes the justification for a gift exclusion and the more likely the Service and the courts are to question whether the transfer really rises to the level of a gift. Furthermore, because substantial gifts even in the family context clearly enrich one economically, perhaps the Code should provide that any gift in excess of $10,000 (or some other appropriate figure) constitutes gross income. Do you agree?

A. What Is Excluded by Section 102?

1. The Nature of a Gift

Section 102 excludes gifts as well as property acquired from a decedent through bequest, devise or inheritance. Thus, property we receive as a result of the generosity of a person either during his lifetime or at his death is excluded from income. The law seems so simple. Its application has proven otherwise.

A threshold question under § 102 is whether what is received can be characterized as a gift, bequest, devise or inheritance. If it cannot be so characterized, then the § 102 exclusion obviously is inapplicable. Identifying excludable gifts is generally no problem when transfers are between family members or close friends. By contrast, gifts made in a commercial or business setting raise troubling characterization questions. Taxpayers receiving "gifts" in those settings have, as a matter of course, claimed the shelter of § 102, thus placing considerable strain on that section and forcing the courts to attempt to define its scope.

The motive of the donor is critical in characterizing receipts as gifts under § 102. The Supreme Court in *Commissioner v. Duberstein*, included in the materials, stated, "[a] gift in the statutory sense . . . proceeds from a 'detached and disinterested generosity . . . out of affection, respect, admiration, charity or like impulses.' . . . And in this regard, the most critical consideration . . . is the transferor's 'intention.' " This language has been repeatedly cited by the courts as establishing the criteria for evaluating whether the receipt of property constitutes a gift. Did the Supreme Court intend by this language to establish a standard? Apparently not. The Court specifically states in *Duberstein:* "Decision of the issue presented in these cases must be based ultimately on the application of the fact-finding tribunal's experience with the mainsprings of human conduct to the totality of the facts of each case." In commercial and business settings, this application has proven a challenge and, not surprisingly, has produced inconsistent results.

Recognizing the difficulties associated with distinguishing gifts from compensation, Congress has imposed statutory limitations on gifts. Perhaps the most significant limitation denies a § 102(a) exclusion for amounts transferred by an employer to, or for the benefit of, an employee. See § 102(c)(1), enacted in 1986.[1]

In 1962, Congress added another provision designed to limit significantly the number of gifts made by businesses. Section 274(b) disallows a deduction for gifts to individuals in excess of $25. Thus, a business making "gifts" is faced with a choice: on the one hand, it can transfer property to an individual and characterize the transfer as compensation and presumably entitle itself to a business deduction. Considering the emphasis placed by *Duberstein* on the "donor's" motive, the effect of such characterization by the business is almost assuredly a denial of a § 102 exclusion to the recipient. By contrast, the business can support the recipient's characterization of the transfer as an excludable gift, thereby losing the right to claim a deduction. In any event, one must keep in mind § 102(c)(1) negates gift status for transfers from employers to employees. Such transfers, as a result, do not implicate § 274(b) which applies only to items excludable as gifts under § 102.

2. The Nature of a Bequest or Inheritance

With respect to cash or other property received as the result of another's death, *i.e*, bequests, devises, and inheritance, a threshold question similar to that in the gift context is raised: is the cash or property received a bequest, devise or inheritance, or is it compensation or some other form of taxable income? For example, it is not uncommon for the validity of a will to be challenged by heirs of the estate. The Supreme Court, in *Lyeth v. Hoey*, 305 U.S. 188 (1938), considered "[w]hether property received by an heir from the estate of his ancestor is acquired by

---

[1] At the same time Congress enacted § 102(c)(1), it enacted § 74(c), discussed in Chapter 7, which placed explicit limitations and conditions on the exclusion from income of "employee achievement awards" given by employers. By expressly providing that employer-employee transfers do not constitute excludable gifts, Congress prevents evasion of the § 74(c) limitations by means of labeling the transfer as a gift. Furthermore, as will be discussed in Chapter 11, § 132 provides an exclusion for certain fringe benefits including so-called "de minimis" fringe benefits. The legislative history to § 102(c)(1) specifically notes "the rule under present law whereby de minimis fringe benefits may be deductible by the employer but are not taxable to the employee can apply to employee awards of low value, including traditional awards (such as a gold watch) upon retirement after lengthy service for an employer." (H.R. Rep. 99-426, 99th Cong. 1st Sess., p. 105.)

inheritance, when it is distributed under an agreement settling a contest by the heir of the validity of the decedent's will. . . . " While acknowledging that state law is determinative on matters such as the validity of the will or the identification of the heirs of a decedent, the Court emphasized that characterization of a distribution from the estate is a federal question. According to the Court, Congress, in enacting § 102, intended to impose a uniform rule. Through the use of the language "bequest, devise, or inheritance" in § 102, "Congress used comprehensive terms embracing all acquisitions in the devolution of a decedent's estate." The Court therefore concluded the amounts received through the settlement agreement were excludable.

The *Wolder* decision in the materials presents another character question similar to that in *Duberstein*: Were the amounts received by an attorney under the terms of a client's will compensation for services rendered by the attorney during the lifetime of the client, or did they constitute a bequest? The same analysis used in *Duberstein* is applicable. *Wolder*, in addition to raising a characterization question, raises a professional responsibility question. To what extent should an attorney assist a client in the preparation of the will when the attorney is a legatee or devisee under the will?[2]

In summary, the language of § 102(a) is deceptively simple. A case-by-case approach to characterization is necessary. As you solve the gift problems presented at the beginning of this chapter, we urge you to apply your "experience with the mainsprings of human conduct" to the facts presented. Through your reading of the materials included in this chapter and through the problems presented, you will discover the truth in the Supreme Court's statement that its definition of excludable gift does not "satisfy an academic desire for tidiness, symmetry and precision."

3. Statutory Limitations on the Exclusion — Section 102(b)

As is so often the case in the tax law, Congress gives and Congress takes away; an exclusion is provided and then the exclusion is limited. Section 102 reflects such a give and take arrangement. Specifically, § 102(b) provides two limitations on the exclusion. First, the income from property excluded as a gift, bequest, devise, and inheritance is not excluded. § 102(b)(1). Thus, if X gives Y a share of IBM stock, the value of the stock is excluded from Y's income but the dividends which IBM distributes to Y are not. Obviously, if an exclusion were permitted for the income from property gifted, inherited or devised, the income tax base would be radically narrowed. Those living on income from inherited wealth would never pay tax.

A second limitation provided by § 102(b)(2) denies an exclusion for gifts, whether made during life or at death, of income from property. Consider the following

---

[2] Rule 1.8(c) of the ABA Model Rules of Professional Conduct provides:

A lawyer shall not solicit any substantial gift from a client, including a testamentary gift, or prepare on behalf of a client an instrument giving the lawyer or a person related to the lawyer any substantial gift unless the lawyer or other recipient of the gift is related to the client. For purposes of this paragraph, related persons include a spouse, child, grandchild, parent, grandparent or other relative or individual with whom the lawyer or the client maintains a close, familial relationship.

common example: Mother dies leaving a portfolio of stocks and bonds in trust for the benefit of her son and her grandchildren. The trust provides Trust Company will manage the portfolio and will distribute all income from the stocks and bonds annually to the son. When the son dies, the trust will terminate and all of the trust property will be distributed in equal shares to the grandchildren who are then alive. Students who have recently completed a property course will recognize the son has an equitable life estate, while the grandchildren have a contingent remainder interest. The son and the grandchildren have both received as "gifts" an interest in the same property. Will these "gifts" be excluded from income?

From § 102(b)(1), we know if Mother had merely given the stocks and bonds outright to her son, the son could have excluded the value of the stocks and bonds, but not the income from them. By merely dividing the ownership in the stocks and bonds between an income beneficiary, the son, and remainderpersons, the grandchildren, should Mother be able to avoid § 102(b)(1) and thus assure the exclusion of the income from the stocks and bonds? The Supreme Court answered "No" to that question in *Irwin v. Gavit*, 268 U.S. 161 (1925), which presented a fact pattern similar to that in the preceding paragraph. Examining the applicable provisions of the Code, the Court noted:

> [The statute provides that net income includes] "gains or profits and income derived from any source whatever, including the income from but not the value of property acquired by gift, bequest, devise or descent." The language quoted leaves no doubt in our minds that if a fund were given to trustees for A for life with remainder over, the income received by the trustees and paid over to A would be income of A under the statute. It seems to us hardly less clear that even if there were a specific provision that A should have no interest in the corpus, the payments would be income none the less. . . . In the first case, it is true that the bequest might be said to be of the corpus for life, in the second it might be said to be of the income. But we think that the provision of the act that exempts bequests assumes the gift of a corpus and contrasts it with income arising from it, but was not intended to exempt income properly so-called simply because of a severance between it and the principal fund.

Id. at 166–67.

Section 102(b)(2) merely codifies the holding of *Irwin v. Gavit*. So who gets the benefit of the exclusion in our hypothetical — the son or the grandchildren? The answer is clearly the grandchildren. Is this result appropriate? As an alternative, the exclusion could be divided between the son and the grandchildren in proportion to the property interest which each received. Thus, assume the portfolio had a value of $100,000 at the date of Mother's death and, actuarially, the son's income interest was worth 60% of the value of the portfolio and the grandchildren's remainder interest only 40%. The alternative could exclude from the son's income the first $60,000 of income he receives from the trust and exclude from the grandchildren's income $40,000 of the trust property they ultimately receive. Section 102(b)(2) implicitly rejects the alternative; the entire $100,000 exclusion flows to the grandchildren.

B. Basis of Property Received by Gift, Bequest, or Inheritance

1. Gifts of Appreciated Property

As should be clear from Chapter 4, the taxpayer's basis in property is critical in determining the gain or loss realized by the taxpayer upon disposition of the property. We therefore need to be concerned about basis when gifts excludable under § 102(a) are made. Consider the following example. Claude purchases a share of XYZ stock for $200 and gives the stock to Mary when the stock is worth $500 per share. Has Claude realized $300 of gain that he should be required to recognize? What basis does Mary have in the stock?

The two questions are related. There is gain potential of $300 in Claude's stock that should not disappear merely because Claude gives the stock to Mary. Perhaps Claude should be treated as having realized and recognized the gain when he gives Mary the stock. If so, then the basis Mary takes in the stock upon receiving it should reflect the fact that the $300 of gain inherent in the stock has been reported by Claude. In other words, Mary's basis should be $500. Thus, if she were to sell the stock for $500, no gain would be realized. But should the disposition of property by gift be treated as a realization event? Wouldn't that discourage gifts as well as create valuation problems? Assuming the making of a gift is not considered a realization event, how can the $300 gain potential be preserved? One method, of course, would be to require Mary to retain the same basis in the stock that Claude had. Thus, if Mary were to sell the stock for its fair market value of $500, there would be $300 of gain. Who would report that gain? Claude? Mary? Is it consistent with the exclusion of § 102(a) to make Mary report gain inherent in the stock at the time it was given to her?

These questions have been answered by Congress and by the courts. Read § 1015(a) carefully. You will note that, applied to the facts of our hypothetical, this section provides Mary's basis will be the same as Claude's.[3] In Chapter 4 you were introduced to the cost basis rule of § 1012. Section 1015 provides a different basis rule in the case of gifts. Mary's basis is referred to as a "substituted basis" or a "transferred basis." § 7701(a)(42), (43).

The transferred basis rule assures the $300 of gain inherent in the stock when the gift was made remains subject to taxation. As you may already have surmised, the transferred basis rule shifts the tax burden associated with the appreciated value of the stock from Claude to Mary. In *Taft v. Bowers*, 278 U.S. 470 (1929), the Supreme Court rejected a donee's challenge to the constitutionality of such a shift. In that case the taxpayer received a gift of appreciated stock from her father. The taxpayer subsequently sold the stock. She conceded she was taxable on any appreciation in the stock occurring while she owned the stock, but argued she was not taxable on appreciation that occurred during the period her father owned the stock. The Supreme Court disagreed:

---

[3] To the extent Claude paid any gift tax attributable to the appreciation in the stock, § 1015(d)(1) and (d)(6) would increase Mary's basis by that amount.

If, instead of giving the stock to petitioner, the donor had sold it at market value, the excess over the capital he invested (cost) would have been income therefrom and subject to taxation under the Sixteenth Amendment. He would have been obliged to share the realized gain with the United States. He held the stock — the investment — subject to the right of the sovereign to take part of any increase in its value when separated through sale or conversion and reduced to his possession. Could he, contrary to the express will of Congress, by mere gift enable another to hold this stock free from such right, deprive the sovereign of the possibility of taxing the appreciation when actually severed, and convert the entire property into a capital asset of the donee, who invested nothing, as though the latter had purchased at the market price? And after a still further enhancement of the property, could the donee make a second gift with like effect, etc.? We think not.

In truth the stock represented only a single investment of capital — that made by the donor. And when through sale or conversion the increase was separated therefrom, it came income from that investment in the hands of the recipient subject to taxation according to the very words of the Sixteenth Amendment. By requiring the recipient of the entire increase to pay a part into the public treasury, Congress deprived her of no right and subjected her to no hardship. She accepted the gift with knowledge of the statute and, as to the property received, voluntarily assumed the position of her donor. When she sold the stock she actually got the original sum invested, plus the entire appreciation; and out of the latter only was she called on to pay the tax demanded. . . .

There is nothing in the Constitution which lends support to the theory that gain actually resulting from the increased value of capital can be treated as taxable income in the hands of the recipient only so far as the increase occurred while he owned the property. . . .

Id. at 482–84.

In effect, *Taft v. Bowers* confirms that another limitation exists with respect to the general exclusion rule for gifts, *i.e.*, the appreciation inherent in gifts may ultimately be taxed to the donee.

2.   Gifts of Property — Basis in Excess of Fair Market Value

As you will discover in Chapter 34, our tax law generally prohibits the shifting of income from one taxpayer to another. Nevertheless, as demonstrated above, the transferred basis rule of § 1015(a) and the rule of *Taft v. Bowers* together enable a donor to shift potential gain (income) to a donee. Considering the progressive rate structure of § 1, a taxpayer in a high bracket may be encouraged to make gifts of appreciated property to a related taxpayer in a lower tax bracket so that the gain, when ultimately realized, will be taxed at the lowest possible rates. May a donor likewise shift potential losses to a donee?

For example, assume Claude in the above example was in a 10% income tax bracket while Mary was in a 30% bracket. Assume also that Claude's stock purchased for $200 was only worth $50. If Claude gives the stock to Mary, will Mary's basis be $200, thus enabling her to claim a $150 loss deduction when the stock is sold? A $150 loss deduction would only be worth $15 to Claude (*i.e.*, 10% × $150) whereas the deduction is worth $45 to Mary (*i.e.*, 30% × $150). Curiously, while permitting the use of gifts to shift income, Congress has prohibited the shifting of losses. Read § 1015(a) again and explain how it accomplishes that goal. Given the special loss rule of § 1015(a), if Mary were to sell the stock for $50, no loss would be realized and the $150 loss inherent in the stock while Claude held it would simply disappear. *See* Reg. § 1.1015-1(a)(2). Knowing this, you might advise Claude to sell the stock himself and give the proceeds to Mary, thus enabling him to make a $50 gift and also assuring deductibility of the $150 loss.

3.   Basis of Property Received by Bequest or Inheritance

To your expanding list of basis provisions, one more must be added. Section 1014 has historically governed the determination of basis of property received by bequest, devise or inheritance. This provision generally "steps-up" (or "steps-down") the basis of property acquired from a decedent to the fair market value of the property at the time of the decedent's death. § 1014(a)(1).[4]

As noted above, § 1014 provides that property acquired from a decedent generally takes a basis equal to the fair market value of the property at the date of the decedent's death. Thus, in the case of appreciated property, § 1014 provides tax amnesty for the gain inherent in the property at the time of a person's death. The devisee or heir receiving the "stepped-up basis" can sell the property for its value as of the decedent's death and not realize any gain. Only that appreciation occurring after the decedent's death will be subject to tax. By contrast, if property decreased in value during the lifetime of the decedent so the decedent's basis exceeded the value of the property, § 1014(a) will negate the loss inherent in the property.

Section 1014(a) applies not only to property owned by the decedent at the time of his death which is transferred by the decedent's will or pursuant to the intestate succession laws of a jurisdiction, but also to property acquired through other means, *e.g.*, joint tenancy or community property. *See* § 1014(b). Particular attention should be paid to § 1014(b)(6), which makes § 1014 applicable to a surviving spouse's one-half share of community property "if at least one-half of the whole of the community interest in such property was includable in determining the value of the decedent's gross estate" for federal estate tax purposes.

Considering the potentially significant tax breaks associated with § 1014(a), is there anything to prevent a taxpayer from getting a tax windfall by giving highly appreciated properties to a terminally ill relative, knowing the taxpayer will soon receive the properties back by way of devise or inheritance? Assuming the size of the relative's taxable estate is such that there would probably be no federal estate tax generated by the property, the taxpayer would thus receive the benefits of a stepped-up basis tax-free. Read § 1014(e). Note its scope and limitations and

---

[4] Section 1014(a)(2)–(4) provides alternate basis rules applicable in special circumstances.

consider whether it is adequate to prevent such game-playing.

C. Part-Gift, Part-Sale

Assume Sally sold a lake-front lot to her favorite grandchild, Erin, for $50,000. Sally's adjusted basis in the lot was $75,000 and the lot had a value of $250,000 at the time of the sale to Erin. What basis would Erin take in the lot? $50,000 via § 1012? $75,000 via § 1015(a)? What tax consequences, if any, are there to Sally? May Sally claim a loss deduction since she sold the lot for an amount less than her adjusted basis?

The sale of property for less than fair market value is common between family members and even close friends. Substantively, the transaction involves a sale in part and a gift in part. Recognizing the potential for confusion that such a mixed transaction provides, the Treasury has promulgated regulations resolving the questions raised above. Regulation § 1.1001-1(e) states that the seller-donor has gain to the extent that the amount realized exceeds the adjusted basis of the property. The same regulation also appropriately provides that no loss is recognized on such a transaction. Thus, in our hypothetical, Sally would have no gain or loss. The examples provided by this regulation are helpful and should be carefully read.[5]

Regulation § 1.1015-4 addresses the question regarding Erin's basis raised above. The regulation provides that the donee's basis will be the greater of the amount the donee paid for the property or the adjusted basis of the donor. Note that, consistent with § 1015(a), a special rule limits the donee's basis, for purposes of computing loss, to the fair market value of the property at the time of the transfer to the donee. Thus, Erin's basis in the lot will be $75,000, i.e., the greater of the amount she paid Sally ($50,000) or Sally's adjusted basis ($75,000).

Suppose Sally's lot was subject to a liability of $50,000, and Erin, in lieu of paying Sally $50,000 in cash, assumes the liability. The same result obtains: the transaction is still in part a gift and in part a sale. Since a liability assumed or taken subject to by a donee is treated as an amount paid, Sally's amount realized is still $50,000. Reg. § 1.1001-2(a)(1), (4)(ii). Neither gain nor loss is recognized on the transaction. Furthermore, Erin takes a $75,000 basis in the lot just as before. Note, however, that gain can be recognized on a part-gift, part-sale if the liability assumed exceeds the seller-donor's basis in the property. For example, if the liability assumed by Erin were $90,000 (and Sally's basis remained $75,000), the amount realized would be $90,000, and gain of $15,000 would be realized and recognized on the part-gift, part-sale. *See also Diedrich v. Commissioner*, 457 U.S. 191 (1982). Under these circumstances, Erin's basis in the lot would be $90,000. Reg. § 1.1015-4(b) Ex. 2.

---

[5] Different rules exist in the case of a part-gift, part-sale to charity. *See* § 1011(b) discussed in Chapter 26.

COMMISSIONER v. DUBERSTEIN
United States Supreme Court
363 U.S. 278 (1960)

MR. JUSTICE BRENNAN delivered the opinion of the Court.

The taxpayer, Duberstein, was president of the Duberstein Iron & Metal Company, a corporation with headquarters in Dayton, Ohio. For some years the taxpayer's company had done business with Mohawk Metal Corporation, whose headquarters were in New York City. The president of Mohawk was one Berman. The taxpayer and Berman had generally used the telephone to transact their companies' business with each other, which consisted of buying and selling metals. The taxpayer testified, without elaboration, that he knew Berman "personally" and had known him for about seven years. From time to time in their telephone conversations, Berman would ask Duberstein whether the latter knew of potential customers for some of Mohawk's products in which Duberstein's company itself was not interested. Duberstein provided the names of potential customers for these items.

One day in 1951 Berman telephoned Duberstein and said that the information Duberstein had given him had proved so helpful that he wanted to give the latter a present. Duberstein stated that Berman owed him nothing. Berman said that he had a Cadillac as a gift for Duberstein, and that the latter should send to New York for it; Berman insisted that Duberstein accept the car, and the latter finally did so, protesting however that he had not intended to be compensated for the information. At the time Duberstein already had a Cadillac and an Oldsmobile, and felt that he did not need another car. Duberstein testified that he did not think Berman would have sent him the Cadillac if he had not furnished him with information about the customers. It appeared that Mohawk later deducted the value of the Cadillac as a business expense on its corporate income tax return.

Duberstein did not include the value of the Cadillac in gross income for 1951, deeming it a gift. The Commissioner asserted a deficiency for the car's value against him, and in proceedings to review the deficiency the Tax Court affirmed the Commissioner's determination. It said that "The record is significantly barren of evidence revealing any intention on the part of the payor to make a gift. . . . The only justifiable inference is that the automobile was intended by the payor to be remuneration for services rendered to it by Duberstein." The Court of Appeals for the Sixth Circuit reversed. 265 F.2d 28.

The exclusion of property acquired by gift from gross income under the federal income tax laws was made in the first income tax statute passed under the authority of the Sixteenth Amendment, and has been a feature of the income tax statutes ever since. The meaning of the term "gift" as applied to particular transfers has always been a matter of contention. Specific and illuminating legislative history on the point does not appear to exist. Analogies and inferences drawn from other revenue provisions, such as the estate and gift taxes, are dubious. . . . The meaning of the statutory term has been shaped largely by the decisional law. With this, we turn to the contentions made by the Government in these cases.

First. The Government suggests that we promulgate a new "test" in this area to serve as a standard to be applied by the lower courts and by the Tax Court in dealing with the numerous cases that arise.[6] We reject this invitation. We are of opinion that the governing principles are necessarily general and have already been spelled out in the opinions of this Court, and that the problem is one which, under the present statutory framework, does not lend itself to any more definitive statement that would produce a talisman for the solution of concrete cases. The cases at bar are fair examples of the settings in which the problem usually arises. They present situations in which payments have been made in a context with business overtones . . . a businessman giving something of value to another businessman who has been of advantage to him in his business. In this context, we review the law as established by the prior cases here.

The course of decision here makes it plain that the statute does not use the term "gift" in the common-law sense, but in a more colloquial sense. This Court has indicated that a voluntary executed transfer of his property by one to another, without any consideration or compensation therefor, though a common-law gift, is not necessarily a "gift" within the meaning of the statute. For the Court has shown that the mere absence of a legal or moral obligation to make such a payment does not establish that it is a gift. *Old Colony Trust Co. v. Commissioner*, 279 U.S. 716, 730. And, importantly, if the payment proceeds primarily from "the constraining force of any moral or legal duty," or from "the incentive of anticipated benefit" of an economic nature, *Bogardus v. Commissioner*, 302 U.S. 34, 41, it is not a gift. And, conversely, "[w]here the payment is in return for services rendered, it is irrelevant that the donor derives no economic benefit from it." *Robertson v. United States*, 343 U.S. 711, 714. A gift in the statutory sense, on the other hand, proceeds from a "detached and disinterested generosity," *Commissioner v. Lo Bue*, 351 U.S. 243, 246; "out of affection, respect, admiration, charity or like impulses." *Robertson v. United States, supra,* at 714. And in this regard, the most critical consideration, as the Court was agreed in the leading case here, is the transferor's "intention." *Bogardus v. Commissioner*, 302 U.S. 34, 43. "What controls is the intention with which payment, however voluntary, has been made." *Id.*, at 45 (dissenting opinion).

The Government says that this "intention" of the transferor cannot mean what the cases on the common-law concept of gift call "donative intent." With that we are in agreement, for our decisions fully support this. Moreover, the *Bogardus* case itself makes it plain that the donor's characterization of his action is not determinative — that there must be an objective inquiry as to whether what is called a gift amounts to it in reality. . . . It scarcely needs adding that the parties' expectations or hopes as to the tax treatment of their conduct in themselves have nothing to do with the matter.

It is suggested that the *Bogardus* criterion would be more apt if rephrased in terms of "motive" rather than "intention." We must confess to some skepticism as to whether such a verbal mutation would be of any practical consequence. We take it that the proper criterion, established by decision here, is one that inquires what the basic reason for his conduct was in fact — the dominant reason that explains his

---

[6] The Government's proposed test is stated: "Gifts should be defined as transfers of property made for personal as distinguished from business reasons."

action in making the transfer. Further than that we do not think it profitable to go.

Second. The Government's proposed "test," while apparently simple and precise in its formulation, depends frankly on a set of "principles" or "presumptions" derived from the decided cases, and concededly subject to various exceptions; and it involves various corollaries, which add to its detail. Were we to promulgate this test as a matter of law, and accept with it its various presuppositions and stated consequences, we would be passing far beyond the requirements of the cases before us, and would be painting on a large canvas with indeed a broad brush. The Government derives its test from such propositions as the following: That payments by an employer to an employee, even though voluntary, ought, by and large, to be taxable; that the concept of a gift is inconsistent with a payment's being a deductible business expense; that a gift involves "personal" elements; that a business corporation cannot properly make a gift of its assets. The Government admits that there are exceptions and qualifications to these propositions. We think, to the extent they are correct, that these propositions are not principles of law but rather maxims of experience that the tribunals which have tried the facts of cases in this area have enunciated in explaining their factual determinations. Some of them simply represent truisms: it doubtless is, statistically speaking, the exceptional payment by an employer to an employee that amounts to a gift. Others are overstatements of possible evidentiary inferences relevant to a factual determination on the totality of circumstances in the case: it is doubtless relevant to the over-all inference that the transferor treats a payment as a business deduction, or that the transferor is a corporate entity. But these inferences cannot be stated in absolute terms. Neither factor is a shibboleth. The taxing statute does not make nondeductibility by the transferor a condition on the "gift" exclusion; nor does it draw any distinction, in terms, between transfers by corporations and individuals, as to the availability of the "gift" exclusion to the transferee. The conclusion whether a transfer amounts to a "gift" is one that must be reached on consideration of all the factors.

Third. Decision of the issue presented in these cases must be based ultimately on the application of the fact-finding tribunal's experience with the mainsprings of human conduct to the totality of the facts of each case. The nontechnical nature of the statutory standard, the close relationship of it to the data of practical human experience, and the multiplicity of relevant factual elements, with their various combinations, creating the necessity of ascribing the proper force to each, confirm us in our conclusion that primary weight in this area must be given to the conclusions of the trier of fact.

This conclusion may not satisfy an academic desire for tidiness, symmetry and precision in this area, any more than a system based on the determinations of various fact-finders ordinarily does. But we see it as implicit in the present statutory treatment of the exclusion for gifts, and in the variety of forums in which federal income tax cases can be tried. If there is fear of undue uncertainty or overmuch litigation, Congress may make more precise its treatment of the matter by singling out certain factors and making them determinative of the matter, as it has done in one field of the "gift" exclusion's former application, that of prizes and awards. . . .

Fourth. A majority of the Court is in accord with the principles just outlined. And, applying them to the *Duberstein* case, we are in agreement, on the evidence we have set forth, that it cannot be said that the conclusion of the Tax Court was "clearly erroneous." It seems to us plain that as trier of the facts it was warranted in concluding that despite the characterization of the transfer of the Cadillac by the parties and the absence of any obligation, even of a moral nature, to make it, it was at bottom a recompense for Duberstein's past services, or an inducement for him to be of further service in the future. We cannot say with the Court of Appeals that such a conclusion was "mere suspicion" on the Tax Court's part. To us it appears based in the court of informed experience with human affairs that fact-finding tribunals should bring to this task.

Accordingly, . . . the judgment of this Court is that the judgment of the Court of Appeals is reversed. . . .

It is so ordered.

WOLDER v. COMMISSIONER
United States Court of Appeals, Second Circuit
493 F.2d 608 (1974)

OAKES, CIRCUIT JUDGE:

[This case] essentially turn[s] on one question: whether an attorney contracting to and performing lifetime legal services for a client receives income when the client, pursuant to the contract, bequeaths a substantial sum to the attorney in lieu of the payment of fees during the client's lifetime. . . . [T]he Tax Court held that the fair market value of the stock and cash received under the client's will constituted taxable income under Section 61, Int. Rev. Code of 1954, and was not exempt from taxation as a bequest under Section 102 of the Code. From this ruling the . . . taxpayers, Victor R. Wolder, the attorney, and his wife, who signed joint returns, appeal. . . .

      . . . .

There is no basic disagreement as to the facts. On or about October 3, 1947, Victor R. Wolder, as attorney, and Marguerite K. Boyce, as client, entered into a written agreement which, after reciting Mr. Wolder's past services on her behalf in an action against her ex-husband for which he had made no charge, consisted of mutual promises, first on the part of Wolder to render to Mrs. Boyce "such legal services as she shall in her opinion personally require from time to time as long as both . . . shall live and not to bill her for such services," and second on the part of Mrs. Boyce to make a codicil to her last will and testament giving and bequeathing to Mr. Wolder or to his estate "my 500 shares of Class B common stock of White Laboratories, Inc.," or "such other . . . securities" as might go to her in the event of a merger or consolidation of White Laboratories. Subsequently, in 1957, White Laboratories did merge into Schering Corp. and Mrs. Boyce received 750 shares of Schering common and 500 shares of Schering convertible preferred. In 1964 the convertible preferred was redeemed for $15,845. In a revised will dated April 23, 1965, Mrs. Boyce, true to the agreement with Mr. Wolder, bequeathed to him or his estate the sum of $15,845 and the 750 shares of common stock of Schering Corp. There is no dispute but that Victor R. Wolder had rendered legal services to Mrs.

Boyce over her lifetime (though apparently these consisted largely of revising her will) and had not billed her therefor so that he was entitled to performance by her under the agreement, on which she had had a measure of independent legal advice. At least the New York Surrogate's Court (DiFalco, J.) ultimately so found in contested proceedings in which Mrs. Boyce's residuary legatees contended that the will merely provided for payment of a debt and took the position that Wolder was not entitled to payment until he proved the debt in accordance with Section 212, New York Surrogate's Court Act. The Surrogate Court proceedings on the part of the residuary legatees were not instituted until the latter part of February, 1966, and the surrogate's decision thereon was not handed down until September, 1966.

Wolder argues that the legacy he received under Mrs. Boyce's will is specifically excluded from income by virtue of Section 102(a), Int. Rev. Code of 1954, which provides that "Gross Income does not include the value of property acquired by gift, bequest, devise or inheritance. . . . "

. . . [H]ere there is no dispute but that the parties did contract for services and — while the services were limited in nature — there was also no question but that they were actually rendered. Thus the provisions of Mrs. Boyce's will, at least for federal tax purposes, went to satisfy her obligation under the contract. The contract in effect was one for the postponed payment of legal services, *i.e.*, by a legacy under the will for services rendered during the decedent's life.

[In interpreting Section 102(a) with respect to gifts, the Supreme Court held in *Commissioner v. Duberstein*] that the true test is whether in actuality the gift is a bona fide gift or simply a method for paying compensation. This question is resolved by an examination of the intent of the parties, the reasons for the transfer, and the parties' performance in accordance with their intentions — "what the basic reason for [the donor's] conduct was in fact — the dominant reason that explains his action in making the transfer." 363 U.S. at 286. . . .

Indeed, it is to be recollected that Section 102 is, after all, an exception to the basic provision in Section 61(a) that "Except as otherwise provided in this subtitle, gross income means all income from whatever source derived, including . . . (1) Compensation for services, including fees, commissions and similar items. . . . " The congressional purpose is to tax income comprehensively. *Commissioner v. Jacobson*, 336 U.S. 28, 49, 69 S. Ct. 358, 93 L. Ed. 477 (1949). A transfer in the form of a bequest was the method that the parties chose to compensate Mr. Wolder for his legal services, and that transfer is therefore subject to taxation, whatever its label whether by federal or by local law may be. . . .

Taxpayer's argument that he received the stock and cash as a "bequest" under New York law and the decisions of the surrogates is thus beside the point. New York law does, of course, control as to the extent of the taxpayer's legal rights to the property in question, but it does not control as to the characterization of the property for federal income tax purposes. . . . New York law cannot be decisive on the question whether any given transfer is income under Section 61(a) or is exempt under Section 102(a) of the Code. We repeat, we see no difference between the transfer here made in the form of a bequest and the transfer under *Commissioner v. Duberstein, supra*, which was made without consideration, with no legal or moral obligation, and which was indeed a "common-law gift," but which was nevertheless held not to be a gift excludable under Section 102(a).

Judgment in the appeal of Victor R. Wolder and Marjorie Wolder affirmed. . . .

OLK v. UNITED STATES
United States Court of Appeals, Ninth Circuit
536 F.2d 876 (1976)

SNEED, CIRCUIT JUDGE:

This is a suit to obtain a refund of federal income taxes. The issue is whether monies, called "tokes" in the relevant trade, received by the taxpayer, a craps dealer employed by Las Vegas casinos, constitute taxable income or gifts within the meaning of section 102(a), Int. Rev. Code of 1954. The taxpayer insists "tokes" are non-taxable gifts. If he is right, he is entitled to the refund for which this suit was brought. The trial court in a trial without a jury held that "tokes" were gifts. The Government appealed and we reverse and hold that "tokes" are taxable income.

I. *The Facts*

There is no dispute about the basic facts which explain the setting in which "tokes" are paid and received. The district court's finding with respect to such facts which we accept are, in part, as follows:

> In 1971 plaintiff was employed as a craps dealer in two Las Vegas gambling casinos, the Horseshoe Club and the Sahara Hotel. The basic services performed by plaintiff and other dealers were described at trial. There are four persons involved in the operation of the game, a boxman and three dealers. One of the three dealers, the stickman, calls the roll of the dice and then collects them for the next shooter. The other two dealers collect losing bets and pay off winning bets under the supervision of the boxman. The boxman is the casino employee charged with direct supervision of the dealers and the play at one particular table. He in turn is supervised by the pit boss who is responsible for several tables. The dealers also make change, advise the boxman when a "player would like a drink and answer basic questions about the game for the players."

> Dealers are forbidden to fraternize or engage in unnecessary conversation with the casino patrons, and must remain in separate areas while on their breaks. Dealers must treat all patrons equally, and any attempt to provide special service to a patron is grounds for termination.

> At times, players will give money to the dealers or place bets for them. The witnesses testified that most casinos do not allow boxmen to receive money from patrons because of their supervisory positions, although some do permit this. The pit bosses are not permitted to receive anything from patrons because they are in a position in which they can insure that a patron receives some special service or treatment.

The money or tokes are combined by the four dealers and split equally at the end of each shift so that a dealer will get his share of the tokes received even while he is taking his break. Uncontradicted testimony indicated that a dealer would be terminated if he kept a toke rather than placed it in the common fund.

Casino management either required the dealers to pool and divide tokes or encouraged them to do so. Although the practice is tolerated by management, it is not encouraged since tokes represent money that players are not wagering and thus cannot be won by the casino. Plaintiff received about $10 per day as his share of tokes at the Horseshoe Club and an average of $20 per day in tokes at the Sahara.

Additional findings of fact by the district court are that the taxpayer worked as a stickman and dealer and at all times was under the supervision of the boxman who in turn was supervised by the pit boss. Also the district court found that patrons sometimes give money to dealers, other players or mere spectators at the game, but that between 90–95% of the patrons give nothing to a dealer. No obligation on the part of the patron exists to give to a dealer and "dealers perform no service for patrons which a patron would normally find compensable." Another finding is that there exists "no direct relation between services performed for management by a dealer and benefit or detriment to the patron."

There then follows two final "findings of fact" which taken together constitute the heart of the controversy before us. These are as follows:

17. The tokes are given to dealers as a result of impulsive generosity or superstition on the part of players, and not as a form of compensation for services.

18. Tokes are the result of detached and disinterested generosity on the part of a small number of patrons.

These two findings, together with the others set out above, bear the unmistakable imprint of *Commissioner v. Duberstein*, 363 U.S. 278 (1959). . . .

II. *Finding Number 18 Is a Conclusion of Law*

The position of the taxpayer is simple. The above findings conform to the meaning of gifts as used in section 102 of the Code. *Duberstein* further teaches, the taxpayer asserts, that whether a receipt qualified as a non-taxable gift is "basically one of fact," *id.* at 290, 80 S. Ct. at 1199, 4 L. Ed. 2d at 1228 and appellate review of such findings is restricted to determining whether they are clearly erroneous. Because none of the recited findings are clearly erroneous, concludes the taxpayer, the judgment of the trial court must be affirmed.

We could not escape this logic were we prepared to accept as a "finding of fact" the trial court's characterization. The conclusion that tokes "are the result of detached and disinterested generosity" on the part of those patrons who engage in the practice of toking is a conclusion of law, not a finding of fact. Finding number 17, on the other hand, which establishes that tokes are given as the result of impulsive generosity or superstition on the part of the players is a finding of fact to which we are bound unless it is "clearly erroneous" which it is not.

III. *Finding Number 18 and Other Conclusions of Law Based Thereon Are Erroneous*

Freed of the restraint of the "clearly erroneous" standard, we are convinced that finding number 18 and all derivative conclusions of law are wrong. "Impulsive generosity or superstition on the part of the players" we accept as the dominant motive. In the context of gambling in casinos open to the public such a motive is quite understandable. However, our understanding also requires us to acknowledge that payments so motivated are not acts of "detached or disinterested generosity." Quite the opposite is true. Tribute to the gods of fortune which it is hoped will be returned bounteously soon can only be described as an "involved and intensely interested" act.

Moreover, in applying the statute to the findings of fact, we are not permitted to ignore those findings which strongly suggest that tokes in the hands of the ultimate recipients are viewed as a receipt indistinguishable, except for erroneously anticipated tax differences, from wages. The regularity of the flow, the equal division of the receipts, and the daily amount received indicate that a dealer acting reasonably would come to regard such receipts as a form of compensation for his services. The manner in which a dealer may regard tokes is, of course, not the touchstone for determining whether the receipt is excludable from gross income. It is, however, a reasonable and relevant inference well-grounded in the findings of fact.

Our view of the law is consistent with the trend of authorities in the area of commercial gratuities as well as with the only decision squarely in point, *Lawrence E. Bevers*, 26 T.C. 1218 (1956), and this Circuit's view of tips as revealed in *Roberts v. Commissioner*, 176 F.2d 221 (9th Cir. 1949). Generalizations are treacherous but not without utility. One such is that receipts by taxpayers engaged in rendering services contributed by those with whom the taxpayers have some personal or functional contact in the course of the performance of the services are taxable income when in conformity with the practices of the area and easily valued. Tokes, like tips, meet these conditions. That is enough.

The taxpayer is not entitled to the refund he seeks.

Reversed.

GOODWIN v. UNITED STATES
United States Court of Appeals, Eighth Circuit
67 F.3d 149 (1995)

LOKEN, CIRCUIT JUDGE:

The Reverend and Mrs. Lloyd L. Goodwin appeal the denial of a refund of income taxes they paid on substantial payments received from members of Reverend Goodwin's congregation. The district court upheld the Commissioner of Internal Revenue's decision that the payments were taxable income, not excludable gifts. We reject the government's proposed standard for resolving this question but nonetheless affirm the district court's decision.

When Reverend Goodwin became pastor of the Gospel Assembly Church in Des Moines, Iowa (the "Church"), in 1963, it had a modest congregation of twenty-five members. Under Goodwin's stewardship, the congregation has grown to nearly four hundred persons. During the three tax years at issue, 1987 through 1989, Goodwin's annual salary from the Church was $7,800, $14,566 and $16,835; he also received a Church parsonage valued at $6,000 per year. The Goodwins reported these amounts on their joint income tax returns.

In 1966, members of the Church congregation began making "gifts" to the Goodwins, initially at Christmas and later on three "special occasion" days each year. At first, the contributors purchased items such as furniture and works of art. But after five years, they began to give cash. By 1987, the congregation had developed a regular procedure for making special occasion gifts. Approximately two weeks before each special occasion day, the associate pastor announced — before Church services — when the Goodwins were not present — that those who wish to contribute to the special occasion gift may do so. Only cash was accepted to preserve anonymity. Contributors placed the cash in envelopes and gave it to the associate pastor or a Church deacon. The associate pastor then gathered the cash and delivered it to the Goodwins. The Church did not keep a record of the amount given nor who contributed to each gift. The Goodwins did not report the special occasion gifts as taxable income. For the tax years 1987–1989, the Commissioner estimated that the Goodwins received $15,000 in "special occasion gifts" each year. The Commissioner assessed deficiencies for the 1987–1989 tax years based upon the estimated unreported special occasion gifts. The Goodwins paid the deficiencies and filed this refund suit in district court. . . . The parties filed cross-motions for summary judgment and a lengthy stipulation that included the following agreed facts:

1. There is no formal written policy or requirement that anyone contribute to the "special occasion gift."

2. No Church member is counseled to give, or encouraged to give specific amounts.

3. All members of the Church deposed or interviewed maintain that the "special occasion gifts" are gifts given to the [Goodwins] out of love, respect, admiration and like impulses and are not given out of any sense of obligation or any sense of fear that [Reverend Goodwin] will leave their parish if he is not compensated beyond his yearly salary.

4. Church members who were deposed or interviewed . . . did not deduct the money they gave the [Goodwins] as a charitable contribution to the Church.

5. The Church trustees, who set [Goodwin's] annual compensation, will testify that they do not know the amount of the "special occasion gifts" received and do not consider those "gifts" in setting his annual compensation.

The district court granted summary judgment in favor of the government, concluding that the special occasion gifts are taxable income to the Goodwins. . . .

. . . [T]he government urges that we adopt the following test to govern whether transfers from church members to their minister are gifts:

> The feelings of love, admiration and respect that professedly motivated the parishioners to participate in the special occasion offerings arose from and were directly attributable to the services that taxpayer performed for them as pastor of the church. Since the transfers were tied to the performance of services by taxpayer, they were, as a matter of law, compensation.

We reject that test as far too broad. For example, it would include as taxable income every twenty dollar gift spontaneously given by a church member after an inspiring sermon, simply because the urge to give was "tied to" the minister's services. It would also include a departing church member's individual, unsolicited five hundred dollar gift to a long-tenured, highly respected priest, rabbi, or minister, a result that is totally at odds with the opinions of all nine Justices in *Bogardus v. Commissioner*:

> Has [the payment] been made with the intention that services rendered in the past shall be requited more completely, though full acquittance has been given? If so, it bears a tax. Has it been made to show good will, esteem, or kindliness toward persons who happen to have served, but who are paid without thought to make requital for the service? If so, it is exempt.

302 U.S. 34, 45 (1937) (Brandeis, J., dissenting from the Court's decision that unsolicited transfers by shareholders to former employees after a company was sold were gifts) (emphasis added). We thus turn to the facts of this case, applying *Duberstein's* objective, no-talisman approach to evaluating transferor intent.[7]

The Goodwins argue that they must prevail as a matter of law, or at a minimum that the district court erred in granting summary judgment for the government, because it is stipulated that the Church members made the special occasion gifts out of love, admiration, and respect, not out of a sense of obligation or fear that Goodwin might otherwise leave. We disagree.

From an objective perspective, the critical fact in this case is that the special occasion gifts were made by the congregation as a whole, rather than by individual Church members. The cash payments were gathered by congregation leaders in a routinized, highly structured program. Individual Church members contributed anonymously, and the regularly-scheduled payments were made to Reverend Goodwin on behalf of the entire congregation.

Viewing the question of transferor intent from this perspective makes it clear that the payments were taxable income to the Goodwins. The congregation funds the Church, including Reverend Goodwin's salary. The special occasion gifts were

---

[7] Many courts nevertheless give talismanic weight to a phrase used more casually in the *Duberstein* opinion — that a transfer to be a gift must be the product of "detached and disinterested generosity," 363 U.S. at 285. It is the rare donor who is completely "detached and disinterested." To decide close cases using this phrase requires careful analysis of what detached and disinterested means in different contexts. Thus, the phrase is more sound bite than talisman.

substantial compared to Goodwin's annual salary. The congregation, collectively, knew that without these substantial, on-going cash payments, the Church likely could not retain the services of a popular and successful minister at the relatively low salary it was paying. In other words, the congregation knew that its special occasion gifts enabled the Church to pay a $15,000 salary for $30,000 worth of work. Regular, sizable payments made by persons to whom the taxpayer provides services are customarily regarded as a form of compensation and may therefore by treated as taxable income. See, *e.g.*, *Olk v. United States*, 536 F.2d 876, 879 (9th Cir.), cert. denied, 429 U.S. 920.

. . . The stipulated facts of this case demonstrate that the congregation as a whole made special occasion gifts on account of Reverend Goodwin's on-going services as pastor of the Church. Therefore, no reasonable jury could conclude that these payments were excludable from the Goodwins' taxable income, and summary judgment was appropriate.[8]

The judgment of the district court is affirmed.

---

[8] In the district court, both parties ignored the fact that Congress amended the governing statute in 1986. Section 102(c)(1) of the Code now provides that § 102(a) "shall not exclude from gross income any amount transferred by or for an employer to, or for the benefit of, an employee." Although the legislative history suggests that § 102(c)(1) was enacted to address other fact situations, its plain meaning may not be ignored in this case. That meaning seems far from plain, however. The Church members are not Rev. Goodwin's "employer," and the question whether their payments to Goodwin were made "for" his employer seems little different than the traditional gift inquiry under *Duberstein* and *Bogardus*. We therefore decline the government's belated suggestion that we affirm on the alternative ground of § 102(c)(1).

Chapter 6

SALE OF A PRINCIPAL RESIDENCE

I. PROBLEMS

1. Susan is the western regional manager for a large national corporation. Her job requires that she travel away from her Los Angeles office two weeks per month. On January 1, 2013, she purchased and moved into a home in Los Angeles. On September 1, 2014, the corporation transferred her to its New York City office headquarters for a temporary four-month assignment, from September 1 to December 31, 2014, to develop a new training program for district supervisors. During those four months, Susan lived in a New York hotel. Susan was very pleased with the assignment because her parents and siblings all live in the New York City area. At the end of the four-month period, Susan agreed to return to New York every other month to supervise the training program she had developed. At that point she decided to buy a New York City condominium and, for the first eight months of 2015, she alternated living in her Los Angeles home and her New York City condominium. At the end of the eight months, Susan decided to sell her Los Angeles home and rent an apartment instead. She sold the Los Angeles home at a substantial gain on September 1, 2015.

   (a) Did Susan own and use her Los Angeles home as her principal residence for the requisite time for § 121 purposes?

   (b) Assume Susan's Los Angeles home was situated on two city lots. Her house was on one of the lots. She used the other lot for her vegetable and flower gardens. Assume for purposes of this question that the Los Angeles home constituted her principal residence. On September 1, 2015, Susan sold the house and the lot on which it was located to Abby. On the same day, she sold the other lot to Emily. Susan realized $125,000 gain on each sale. May she take advantage of § 121 with respect to each sale?

2. Brian and Jennifer, husband and wife, purchased a home in Seattle in 2006 for $350,000 and held title to the home as joint tenants with right of survivorship. The home was their principal residence until May 2014 when they moved to a town in northern Idaho where they purchased a home for $250,000. In January of 2015, Brian and Jennifer finally sold their Seattle home. The purchaser paid Brian and Jennifer $750,000 in cash and assumed a $250,000 mortgage encumbering the property. Brian and Jennifer added an additional room to the Seattle home and, as a result, had an adjusted basis in that home of $400,000.

    (a)   Explain the tax consequences to Brian and Jennifer on the sale of their Seattle home. Assume Brian and Jennifer file a joint tax return for the year and they had never previously taken advantage of § 121.

    (b)   Would your answer to (a) change if the title to the Seattle home was held by Jennifer in her name alone?

3.   On May 1, 2015, Tom and Chris married and moved into a new home they purchased in Miami, Florida. Prior to their marriage, Tom owned his own home in Fort Lauderdale, Florida; Chris owned her own home in Miami. They each sold their separate homes in 2015. Tom sold his Fort Lauderdale home on March 1, 2015 for $550,000. Tom had owned and used that home as his principal residence since 2005. He had an adjusted basis in the home of $400,000. Chris never lived in Tom's Fort Lauderdale home. Chris sold her Miami home in December 2015. She had owned and used the Miami home as her principal residence since 2002. She had a $300,000 adjusted basis in the home and sold it for $800,000. Tom never lived in Chris' Miami home. Neither Tom nor Chris had ever taken advantage of Section 121. Assume Tom and Chris file a joint return for 2015, how much gain, if any, must they report as gross income on their joint return for 2015 assuming they take full advantage of the § 121 exclusion? Had Tom and Chris consulted you before they sold their respective homes, what advice might you have given them regarding a way to maximize the benefits provided by § 121?

4.   Andrew is not married but has a domestic partner, Tim. Andrew purchased a new home in Minneapolis on January 1, 2014 and took title to the home in his name alone. After Andrew and Tim had used the Minneapolis home as their principal residence for exactly 18 months, they moved to Washington, D.C. because of a job promotion Andrew received. Andrew sold the Minneapolis home on September 1, 2015 and realized $150,000 of gain on the sale. Assume that 12 months prior to the sale of the Minneapolis home, Andrew had used Section 121 to exclude gain from the sale of a home he had used as his principal residence when he lived in Ann Arbor, Michigan.

    (a)   How much of the realized gain, if any, on the Minneapolis home may Andrew exclude under § 121?

    (b)   Assume the above facts except that it was Andrew's domestic partner, Tim, who had to relocate from Minneapolis to Washington, D.C. as a result of a job promotion. Andrew quit his job, sold the Minneapolis home and moved to Washington, D.C. to be with Tim. How much of the realized gain, if any, on the Minneapolis home may Andrew exclude under § 121?

5.   Abby, who is single, worked in New York City where, until her retirement in August 2011, she lived in a rented apartment. On January 1, 2006, Abby purchased a home in East Hampton which, prior to her retirement, she used only on weekends. On January 1, 2012, Abby gave up her New York City apartment and made the East Hampton home her principal residence until January 1, 2015 when she moved out and put the East Hampton home on the market. She sold the East Hampton home on January 1, 2016 and

realized $300,000 of gain on the sale. Assuming Abby has never previously taken advantage of § 121, how much of the $300,000 of realized gain may she exclude under § 121?

Assignment for Chapter 6:

Complete the problems.

Read: Internal Revenue Code: § 121(a), (b), (c), (d)(1)–(3), (6), (7), and (11), (f).
Regulations: §§ 1.121-1(a), (b)(1), (2), 3(i)–(ii)(A), (4) Ex. 1 and 2, (c)(1), (2)(i), (4); 1.121-2(a)(4) Ex. 3 and 4; 1.121-3(b), (c)(1) and (2), (d)(1) and (2), (e)(1) and (2), (f), (g); 1.121-4(a), (b), (g).

Materials: Overview
Guinan v. United States
Gates v. Commissioner

II. VOCABULARY

principal residence

III. OBJECTIVES

1. To explain in your own words the policy underlying § 121.

2. To recall § 121 is an exclusion provision.

3. To list factors which would be relevant in determining under what circumstances a residence is a taxpayer's principal residence.

4. To explain the maximum amount of gain excludable under § 121.

5. To explain the ownership and use requirements that generally must be satisfied to qualify for the § 121 exclusion.

6. To recall § 121 provides a special exception to the ownership and use requirements when a sale of a residence results from a change in the place of employment, health, or certain unforseen circumstances.

7. To explain the safe harbors provided by the regulations with respect to a sale of a principal residence resulting from a change in the place of employment, health, or unforseen circumstances.

8. To explain the computation of the reduced maximum exclusion under § 121.

9. To explain the special rules attributing the ownership and/or use of a residence by a spouse to another spouse or former spouse.

IV. OVERVIEW

The Internal Revenue Code encourages home ownership. Chapter 22 considers the popular deduction for home mortgage interest; Chapter 23 addresses the deduction for property taxes. This Chapter focuses on perhaps the most significant tax benefit enjoyed by homeowners — the exclusion available under § 121 for gains realized on the sale or exchange of one's principal residence.

Prior to 1997 taxpayers were able to avoid recognition of gain on the sale of their home so long as they "bought up", *i.e.*, purchased a new home costing at least as much as the sale price of the old home. Any gain realized but not recognized on the sale of the old residence was preserved in the basis of the new residence. The amount of gain that could thus be "rolled over" into the basis of the new home was not limited but, except as described below, was merely deferred, not excluded.

Pre-1997 law, however, provided a special rule under which taxpayers age 55 or older could exclude up to $125,000 of gain on the sale of their principal residence. This special rule, however, was only a once-in-a-lifetime benefit: once a taxpayer or taxpayer's spouse had taken advantage of the exclusion, it was never again available.

In 1997, Congress repealed the provision permitting "rollover" of gain on the sale of a principal residence, but it dramatically expanded the provision permitting exclusion of gain. As a result, § 121 now provides a very substantial exclusion for gains from the sale of a residence the taxpayer has owned and used as her principal residence for periods aggregating two years or more during the five year period ending on the date of the sale or exchange.

A. Ownership and Use Requirements of Section 121

Under current § 121, taxpayers may exclude up to $250,000 ($500,000 with respect to certain joint returns) of the gain on the sale or exchange of a qualifying principal residence. Like its predecessor, current § 121 does not require that the residence sold be one's principal residence at the time of the sale or exchange. Rather, the statute requires only that the taxpayer have owned and used the property as a principal residence "for periods aggregating 2 years or more" during the five year period.[1]

Consider the following examples:

Example 1: Erik and Liz purchased a home in Seattle in 2008 and made that home their principal residence until March 1, 2012, when Liz's work required her to move to Portland. Although the condominium they rented in Portland became their principal residence and they intended to live in Portland permanently, they kept the Seattle home so that their daughter Emily, a second year law student, would have a place to live until she graduated. Erik and Liz sold their Seattle home on December 1, 2014, realizing a very substantial gain on the sale. Although Erik and Liz were not using the Seattle home as their principal residence at the time of the sale, they had used the home as such during more than two of the five years

---

[1] I.R.C. § 121(a).

before the sale. Assuming all other requirements of § 121 are satisfied, Erik and Liz would be entitled to exclude their gain up to the statutory limits. Note, under prior law, unless Erik and Liz were 55 years of age or older, no exclusion would have been available. Furthermore, under prior law, no § 1034 rollover of gain would have been possible since Erik and Liz did not purchase a new home.

Example 2: Assume the same facts as in Example 1 except that Erik and Liz did not sell the Seattle home in 2014, but instead, on March 1, 2015, after living in Portland three years, moved back to Seattle and again made the Seattle home their principal residence. They lived there until March 1, 2016, when they sold the home at a substantial gain. Under these circumstances, they would be eligible for the § 121 exclusion because the home was their principal residence for periods aggregating two years (March 1, 2011 through February 28, 2014, and March 1, 2015 through February 28, 2016) or more during the five year period before the sale (that is, during March 1, 2011 through February 28, 2016). Note the statute does not require two years of continuous occupancy of a home as one's principal residence, but only periods of such occupancy totaling two years during the five year period.

The ownership and use requirements may be satisfied during nonconcurrent periods so long as the taxpayer satisfies each of them within the five year period ending on the date of the sale or exchange.[2]

Example 3: Assume the facts of Example 1 except Erik and Liz rented the Seattle home in 2008 instead of purchasing it. Assume also that in March 2012, when they moved to Portland, they purchased the home so their daughter Emily would have a place to live while she attended law school in Seattle. As in Example 1, Erik and Liz sold the Seattle home on December 1, 2014. The § 121 exclusion will apply to the sale of the Seattle home because Erik and Liz owned the home for at least two years out of the five years preceding the sale (March 2012 until December 1, 2014) and they used the Seattle home as their principal residence for at least two years during the five year period preceding the sale (from December 1, 2009, until March 1, 2012).[3]

Regulation § 1.121-1(c)(2) defines "use" as requiring occupancy. Short temporary absences, such as absences because of vacations or seasonal absence (even if accompanied by rental of the residence), will be counted as periods of use.

Example 4: Pat, a college professor, purchased a home on February 2, 2013 for use as his principal residence. During 2013 and 2014, Pat traveled to Italy each summer for two months to teach in a summer program. Pat sold the home on March 2, 2015. Although in the five year period preceding the date of the sale Pat used the residence for a total of less than two years (21 months), the Section 121 exclusion will apply to the gain from the sale of the

---

[2] Reg. § 1.121-1(c).

[3] Reg. § 1.121-1(c)(4) Ex. 3.

residence because the two-month periods during which Pat was in Italy each summer are short temporary absences and are counted as periods of use in determining whether Pat used the residence for the requisite period.[4] By contrast, if Pat, instead of spending two months each summer in Italy, were to spend his sabbatical, lasting from September 1, 2013 until August 30, 2014 in Italy, Pat's absence would not be considered a short temporary absence and could not be counted towards Pat's use of the property. As a result, Pat would not be eligible for the Section 121 exclusion.[5]

Section 121 contains a number of special rules related to the ownership and use requirements of § 121(a). If an unmarried individual sells or exchanges property subsequent to the death of his or her spouse, the individual's use and ownership periods for purposes of Section 121(a) will include the period the deceased spouse owned and used the property. § 121(d)(2).

Example 5: Martha has owned and used a house as her principal residence since July 1, 1997. Martha and Bill marry on July 1, 2013, and from that date they use Martha's house as their principal residence. The title to the house remains in Martha's name alone. Martha dies on August 15, 2015. Bill inherits the house and continues to use it as his principal residence. Bill, who had not remarried, sells the house on June 1, 2016. Although Bill has owned the house for less than two years, Bill will be considered to have satisfied the ownership requirements of Section 121 because Bill's period of ownership includes the period that Martha owned and used the property before her death.[6]

If an individual receives property in a transaction described in § 1041 (*i.e.*, a transfer of property between spouses or former spouses), that individual's ownership period for purposes of § 121(a) will include the ownership period of the transferor. § 121(d)(3)(A); Reg. § 1.121-4(b)(1).

Example 6: Anna and Bob divorce. Under the terms of a property settlement, Anna transfers title to a home she owned to Bob. Although Bob never had any previous ownership interest in the home, for purposes of § 121(a), Bob will be considered to have owned the home for the period that Anna owned the home.

Likewise, if an individual continues to have an ownership interest in a residence but is not living in the residence because the individual's spouse or former spouse is granted use of the residence under a divorce or separation instrument, the individual will nonetheless be deemed to use the property during the period her spouse or former spouse is granted the use of the property. § 121(d)(3)(B); Reg. § 1.121-4(b)(2).

Example 7: Mary and Pat divorce. Under the divorce decree, Mary is required to move out of the family home but will continue to have an

---

[4] Reg. § 1.121-1(c)(4) Ex. 5.

[5] Reg. § 1.121-1(c)(4) Ex. 4.

[6] This example is based on the example provided in Reg. § 1.121-4(a)(2).

ownership interest in it. The divorce decree provides that Pat may continue to live in the home until the couple's child (who will be living with Pat) attains the age of 18. The home is then to be sold and the proceeds are to be divided equally between Mary and Pat. Assume the couple's child attains the age of 18 five years later and the home is then sold at a significant gain. Although Mary has not used the home as her principal residence during the five year period before the sale, she will be deemed to have so used it during that period as a result of the application of § 121(d)(3)(B).

If an individual becomes physically or mentally incapable of self-care, the use rules are modified. If the individual owns and uses the residence for one year in the five year period, the individual will be treated as using the property for any period during the five year period in which the individual, while owning the property, resides in a facility satisfying certain requirements. § 121(d)(7).

In 2007, Congress added § 121(b)(4) to address a situation of considerable concern to some individuals selling a home not long after the death of a spouse. Consider the following example:

> **Example 8:** Bill's wife, Martha, died September 1, 2006. On December 31, 2006, Bill sold the home he and Martha had jointly owned and lived in for almost fifty years. Bill realized $450,000 of gain on the sale of the home. [Note: Bill would have been entitled to a stepped-up basis for Martha's one-half of the home under § 1014(b)(9).] Pursuant to § 6013, Bill was allowed to file a joint return for Martha and himself for 2006, the year of Martha's death. He could not, however, file a joint return thereafter unless he remarried. Because Bill was entitled to file a joint return for 2006, all $450,000 of the gain from the sale of the home may be excluded under § 121(b)(2). In the alternative, assume Bill sold the home two days later — on January 2, 2007. Bill obviously may not file a joint return with Martha for 2007. As a result, Bill could only exclude $250,000 of the gain on the sale of the home.

As the above example illustrates, when a taxpayer decides to sell the family home after the death of a spouse, the timing of the sale could make a huge difference in terms of the amount of the exclusion available. To prevent a widowed spouse from having to rush to complete a sale within the same year as the death of a spouse, Congress enacted § 121(b)(4) effective for sales or exchanges after December 31, 2007. This provision allows a widowed taxpayer who has not remarried to sell or exchange his principal residence and claim an exclusion of up to $500,000 if the sale or exchange occurs not later than two years after the date of death of the taxpayer's spouse and the requirements of § 121(b)(2)(A) were met immediately before the date of the spouse's death. Thus, in the above example, if Bill's sale of the home occurred on January 2, 2008 (or for that matter, any time before September 1, 2008), Bill would have the benefit of an exclusion of up to $500,000.

In 2008, Congress added § 121(b)(5) providing that the § 121 exclusion shall not apply to the gain allocated to periods of "nonqualified use." In effect, Congress determined the gain warranting exclusion was the gain that accrued during the time the residence served as the taxpayer's principal residence, not the gain that accrued during the time the taxpayer owned the property but was not using it as a principal residence — for example, during the time the property was business or rental property, not the taxpayer's principal residence. To avoid the daunting administrative complexities, costs, and uncertainties that would be involved in re-valuing the property each time it acquired or lost principal residence status, Congress adopted a simplified method for allocating accrued gain between periods of qualified use and nonqualified use. The gain allocation is based on the ratio which aggregate periods of nonqualified use during the taxpayer's ownership of the property bear to the period the taxpayer owned the property. Generally speaking, a period of nonqualified use is a period (after 2008) during which the property was not used as the taxpayer's principal residence (or the principal residence of the taxpayer's spouse or former spouse). § 121(b)(5)(C)(i). However, there are three exceptions, including an exception for any portion of the 5-year period in § 121(a) which is after the last date the property was used as a principal residence by the taxpayer or taxpayer's spouse. § 121(b)(5)(C)(ii)(I).

> **Example 9:** Mary owned her home from January 1, 2011 to December 31, 2016, when she sold it at a gain of $150,000. Mary occupied her home as her principal residence for the period from January 1, 2011 through December 31, 2014. Thereafter, she rented the home from January 1, 2015 to December 31, 2016, the date of the sale. At first glance, it appears that, during the 6-year period of Mary's ownership (January 2011 through December 2016), there were two years of nonqualified use (January 2015 through December 2016). If so, this would mean that 33% of the gain (2 years out of 6 years), or $50,000, was allocated to a period of nonqualified use and was not excludable under § 121. However, under the exception noted above, a period of nonqualified use does not include any portion of the § 121(a) 5-year period which is after the last date the property was used as the taxpayer's principal residence. As a result, there is no period of nonqualified use in this example, and the entire $150,000 gain is excludable.

> **Example 10:** Given the strong rental market, Alexis purchased a residence on January 1, 2011 with the intent of holding the residence as a rental property. Alexis paid $200,000 for the residence. Alexis rented the residence to university students for the first two years she owned it, i.e., from January 1, 2011 through December 31, 2012. On January 1, 2013, Alexis moved into the residence and made it her principal residence until January 1, 2015 when she moved out of the residence and put it up for sale. She sold the residence on January 1, 2016 for $500,000. Assume that Alexis' adjusted basis in the residence was still $200,000. (For purposes of this example, we will ignore the depreciation deductions Alexis would be allowed with respect to the residence during the period she rented the residence. We will discuss depreciation in Chapter 14.) Assume the only reason Alexis sold the home was that she wanted a larger home. Assume also that Alexis has never taken advantage of § 121. Under these circumstances, Alexis has two years of nonqualified use (specifically, the years 2011 and 2012) during the five years she owned the property. As a result, 2/5 or 40% of her $300,000 of realized gain on the sale of the home is not eligible for exclusion under § 121. The remaining 3/5 of the gain, or $180,000 of gain, will be eligible for exclusion under § 121.

Note that, to the extent the taxpayer was allowed depreciation deductions during the rental period, the gain allocable to the depreciation is not excluded. § 121(d)(6). Section 121(b)(5)(D) provides that the nonqualified use rule is to be applied after § 121(d)(6), and that the allocation of gain to a period of nonqualified use is made without regard to § 121(d)(6).

B.   Amounts Excludable Under Section 121

As a general rule, § 121 allows a taxpayer to exclude up to $250,000 of gain on the sale of a principal residence. The exclusion applies to only one sale or exchange every two years. § 121(b)(3). Note the special exception to this rule under § 121(c). If taxpayers file a joint return, the taxpayers may exclude up to $500,000 of the gain if certain requirements are met. Those requirements are: (1) one of the spouses must satisfy the ownership requirement; (2) both spouses must satisfy the use requirement; and (3) neither spouse has used the exclusion within the past two years. Consider the following examples:

> **Example 1:** Rob and Misti have resided in the same home throughout their 15-year marriage. Title to their suburban home, however, is in Rob's name alone. Rob and Misti, desiring to live in a downtown location, sold their home this year at a gain of $400,000 and rented a large apartment in the downtown. They file a joint return. Under § 121, Rob and Misti will be entitled to exclude all $400,000 of the gain on their home as a result of the application of § 121(b)(2), which eliminates the need for Misti to meet the ownership requirement if a joint return is filed. This special rule reflects congressional recognition that it is not uncommon for title to property to be in the name of just one spouse. For example, title may be in the name of only one spouse because that spouse owned the home prior to the marriage and the title was never changed into both spouses' names.

> **Example 2:** Allen purchased a home three years ago. Two years ago, Barbara moved in with him, and they were married six months ago. Allen and Barbara sold the home this year at a significant gain. Allen and Barbara file a joint tax return for the year of sale. As in Example 1, Barbara has no ownership interest as such in the home. Again, it suffices that Allen satisfies the ownership requirement. Even though they were not married throughout the two years they lived together in the home, both Allen and Barbara satisfy the use requirement. Assuming neither Allen or Barbara had used the § 121 exclusion in the past two years, they would be entitled to exclude up to $500,000 of the gain on the sale of the home.

Other circumstances also enable a married couple to claim exclusions totaling up to $500,000 on the sale of homes without satisfying the specific requirements of § 121(b)(2)(A). For example, assume a husband and wife each owned their own home before they married and they sold both of the homes shortly after they married. If the other requirements of § 121 are satisfied, the husband and the wife will each be entitled to exclude up to $250,000 of gain from his or her sale. (Note the use by one spouse of the exclusion within the past two years will not prevent the other spouse from claiming an exclusion of up to $250,000 on the sale of her principal residence.) Similarly, a husband and wife working in different parts of the country and having separate principal residences would be entitled to exclude up to $250,000 of the gain on the sale of each of the residences. Note, however, if the gain on the husband's residence were $200,000 and the gain on the wife's residence were $300,000, the couple could only exclude a total of $450,000 of gain on their joint return, *i.e.*, the husband could exclude $200,000 and the wife could exclude only $250,000. The wife may not use her husband's unused exclusion of $50,000 to exclude the gain in excess of her $250,000 exclusion limit. The couple would therefore have to report $50,000 of the $500,000 of gain.[7]

Under § 121, two people who are not married but who jointly owned and used the same home as their principal residence would each be eligible to exclude up to $250,000 of their respective gain, assuming that all other requirements of § 121 were satisfied.

> **Example 3:** Scott and Rusty purchased a home as tenants-in-common with each owning one-half of the value of the home. They used the home as their principal residence for five years and then sold it at a significant gain. The gain would be split evenly between Scott and Rusty and each of them could exclude up to $250,000 of the gain.

If a sale or exchange occurs because of "a change in place of employment, health, or . . . [certain] unforseen circumstances," and a taxpayer consequently fails to meet the ownership and use requirements of § 121(a) or the once-every-two-year rule of § 121(b)(3), § 121(c) provides that some or all of the gain may still be excluded. The maximum excludable amount of gain will be a fraction of the $250,000 ($500,000 in the case of a joint return where the requirements of § 121(b)(2) are met) limit. Read § 121(c)(1) carefully and consider its application in the following examples:

> **Example 4:** Sean purchases a home and lives in it for a year and then is transferred by his employer to a different city. Sean sells the home and realizes a gain of $300,000. Sean had never previously used the § 121 exclusion. Because of the circumstances, Sean's failure to satisfy the two year ownership and use requirement will not negate the availability of an exclusion. Under the formula in § 121(c)(1), the exclusion will be limited to a fraction of the $250,000 exclusion which otherwise would have been available. That fraction will have as its numerator the length of time Sean owned and used the home as his principal residence (here 1 year) and the denominator will be 2 years. Thus, the fraction is ½. Sean therefore will be entitled to exclude up to $125,000 of gain. Here, the gain was $300,000. Sean will thus be required to recognize $175,000 of gain.

> **Example 5:** Sean owned a home he had used as his principal residence since 2006. On July 1, 2014, Sean married Trish. The couple made Sean's home their principal residence. On July 1, 2015, Sean and Trish sell that home (which had remained titled in Sean's name alone) because of a change in the location of both of their jobs. Neither Sean nor Trish had used the § 121 exclusion previously. The gain on the sale of the home was $500,000. Sean and Trish file a joint return. Because Sean and Trish have not both

---

[7] Reg. § 1.121-2(a)(4) Ex. 3.

used the home as their principal residence for at least two years during the five year period preceding the sale of the home, the maximum dollar limitation amount that may be claimed by Sean and Trish will not be $500,000, but rather will be the sum of each spouse's limitation amount determined as if they had not been married. Sean is eligible to exclude up to $250,000 of gain because he meets the requirements of § 121. Trish is not eligible to exclude the maximum dollar limitation amount. Instead, she is eligible to claim a reduced exclusion. Because the sale of the home is due to a change in place of employment, Trish is eligible to exclude a fraction of the $250,000 exclusion otherwise available to her. That fraction will have as its numerator the length of time Trish used the home as her principal residence (here 1 year) and the denominator will be 2 years. Thus, the fraction is ½. Trish will be entitled to exclude up to $125,000 of gain. Therefore, Sean and Trish will be eligible to exclude $375,000 of the $500,000 of gain on the sale of the home.

Example 6: Ron owned a home he had used as his principal residence since 2006. On July 1, 2014, Ron's longtime companion Sally moved into Ron's home and, on the same day, Ron transferred a one-half interest in the home to Sally as a tenant-in-common. On December 1, 2014, Sally gave birth to Mark, Ron's and Sally's first child. Sally resigned from her position as comptroller of a company so that she could be at home to take care of Mark. On July 1, 2015, Ron and Sally sold their home because Ron's employer transferred him to the employer's main office located hundreds of miles away in another state. The gain on the sale of their home was $500,000. Ron and Sally purchased a new home near the place of Ron's new employment. Sally did not seek employment in the new location. Neither Ron nor Sally had previously taken advantage of § 121. Ron and Sally are not married and therefore are not eligible to file a joint return. Ron's share of the gain on the sale of the home is $250,000. Because he owned and used the home as his principal residence for at least two years prior to the sale, Ron is entitled to exclude the entire $250,000 of gain allocable to him. Sally, by contrast, is not eligible to exclude all $250,000 of her gain, since she had owned and used the home for only one year. Instead, she is eligible to claim a reduced exclusion because the sale of the home was due to a change in her co-owner's place of employment. Regulation § 1.121-3(c)(1) provides that a sale will be treated as a sale by reason of a change in place of employment if the primary reason for the sale is a change in the location of a "qualified" individual's employment. A "qualified individual" is defined in Regulation § 1.121-3(f)(3) to include the co-owner of the taxpayer's residence. Sally will be entitled to an exclusion equal to a fraction of the maximum exclusion ($250,000) which would otherwise be available to her. As in Example 5, that fraction will have as its numerator the length of time Sally owned and used the home as her principal residence (here 1 year) and the denominator will be 2 years. The fraction is ½ (one-half) thus allowing Sally to exclude up to $125,000 of gain.

Note that "qualified individuals," for purposes of the reduced maximum exclusion, include not only the co-owner of the taxpayer's residence, as in the above example, but also the taxpayer, the taxpayer's spouse, and persons who have the same principal place of abode as the taxpayer. (The list is further expanded where the change if residence is by reason of health.) Reg. § 1.121-3(f).

Also note the guidance provided in the Regulation § 1.121-3 regarding the reduced maximum exclusion. These regulations provide so-called "safe harbors" relating to sales or exchanges by reason of change in (1) employment — requiring in part that the new place of employment be at least 50 miles farther from the old residence than was the former place of employment (or if there was no former place of employment, a distance of at least 50 miles between the new employment and the old residence); (2) health — requiring a physician recommend a change of residence for reasons of health (as defined therein); or (3) unforseen circumstances. In this regard, consider specifically the various safe harbors provided under Regulation § 1.121-3(e)(2) regarding sales or exchanges by reason of unforseen circumstances. Regulation § 1.121-3(e)(3) authorizes the Commissioner of the Internal Revenue Service to designate other events or situations as "unforseen circumstances." Pursuant to that authority, the Service has issued numerous rulings finding that certain situations constituted unforseen circumstances, *e.g.*, an unexpected adoption; criminal activity in the neighborhood; or other danger to the taxpayer from others' knowledge of his place of residence.[8]

Finally, with respect to the exclusion amount, consider the fact that the $250,000/$500,000 maximums discussed above are not subject to inflation or cost-of-living adjustments. Should they be?

C. Principal Residence

Section 121 requires that a residence be "used by the taxpayer as a principal residence for periods aggregating two years." There are two prongs to this requirement. First, the residence must be the taxpayer's principal residence. Second, once the principal residence is determined, one must determine whether the property was used (occupied) as the taxpayer's principal residence for the requisite period. PLR 200645001. See Section IV.A., *supra*, for discussion of "use" of a residence as a principal residence.

Under the regulations interpreting § 121, if a taxpayer alternates between two residences, the residence the taxpayer uses a majority of the time during the year will ordinarily be considered the taxpayer's principal residence for the year. Reg. § 1.121-1(b)(2).

---

[8] Although it is premature to discuss depreciation (a topic covered in detail in Chapter 14), § 121(d)(6) provides the exclusion shall not apply to the gain realized on a sale of one's principal residence to the extent that the taxpayer claimed depreciation deductions with respect to that residence at any time after May 6, 1997. This provision is commonly applicable when the taxpayer has claimed depreciation deductions as a result of a home office. Assume after May 6, 1997, the taxpayer had properly claimed a total of $15,000 in depreciation deductions with respect to her home office. The taxpayer sold the home and realized $75,000 in gain. Under § 121(d)(6), only $60,000 of that gain would be subject to exclusion under § 121(a). The $15,000 balance would be subject to capital gains tax, discussed in Chapter 31. Assume the same facts except that the taxpayer had realized $300,000 of gain. The exclusion would not apply to $15,000 of the gain since that was the amount of depreciation claimed. It would apply to the remaining $285,000 of gain but only up to the $250,000 limit. Thus, the taxpayer could exclude $250,000 of gain, assuming all requirements of § 121 were satisfied.

Example: During a five year period, Taxpayer spends five months per year at Taxpayer's home on the coast and seven months each year at her home in the city. Taxpayer sells the home on the coast. Although Taxpayer has owned and used the home on the coast as her residence for periods aggregating more than 2 years during the five year period prior to sale, the home on the coast will ordinarily not be considered her principal residence.

This majority-of-the-time test, however, is not dispositive. The final regulations, relying on cases decided under old §§ 121 and 1034, also include a nonexclusive list of factors relevant in identifying a property as a taxpayer's principal residence: (i) taxpayer's place of employment; (ii) the principal place of abode of family members; (iii) the address listed on the taxpayer's federal and state tax returns, driver's license, automobile registration, and voter registration card; (iv) the taxpayer's mailing address for bills and correspondence; (v) the location of the taxpayer's banks; and (vi) the location of religious organizations and recreational clubs with which the taxpayer is affiliated. Reg. § 1.121-1(b)(2). Note how the district court in *Guinan v. United States*, included in the materials, applied the regulations to a case involving a taxpayer owning more than two residences.

An important issue related to the determination of "principal residence" is the extent to which the property owned in conjunction with the dwelling place may be considered to be part of the principal residence. In *Bogley v. Commissioner*, 263 F.2d 746 (4th Cir. 1959), the taxpayer's home was on a thirteen-acre tract of land. The taxpayer unsuccessfully sought to sell as a unit his home and the thirteen acres on which it was situated. He finally subdivided the property and sold the house together with three acres of land. Thereafter, within the year, the taxpayer sold the remaining land as two five-acre tracts. The purchaser of the taxpayer's house bought one of the five-acre tracts. The taxpayer, claiming the house and all thirteen acres constituted his principal residence, argued that the gain from the sale of each part of the property should be treated as gain from the sale of a principal residence. The Fourth Circuit concluded that the two five-acre tracts had been used as part of the principal residence of the taxpayer and had never been converted to any other use. Therefore, these tracts retained their character as part of the principal residence even after the house and the three acres were sold. Regulation § 121-1(b)(3)(i) follows *Bogley* and provides specific requirements for the exclusion of gain from the sale of vacant land used as part of the taxpayer's principal residence. How much land surrounding a home can be considered part of the principal residence? That determination will obviously depend on all of the facts and circumstances.

Vacation homes are typically located in recreational areas where property values often increase rapidly. The ability to exclude large amounts of gain associated with the sale of such homes will tempt taxpayers to convert their vacation homes into principal residences for the requisite two-year period prior to selling the vacation home.

Example 1: Assume Maurice owns a highly appreciated summer home located on a lake 60 miles from the city in which Maurice lives and works. If Maurice moves to the lake home and lives there for two calendar years, commuting each day to work, will Maurice be entitled to claim the benefit of § 121 when he sells the lake home? In other words, will the lake home have been converted to Maurice's principal residence for a two year period? Because of the weight accorded the amount of time spent using a property as one's residence, Maurice appears to have a strong argument that the lake home qualifies as Maurice's principal residence. It is not uncommon for individuals to commute significant distances to work each day. Thus, for example, an individual may live on Long Island and spend hours commuting by train to New York City to work each day. The individual's Long Island home will be considered to be that individual's principal residence. Maurice should be treated no differently. See, however, Regulation § 1.121-1(b)(2) for a list of other factors relevant to the determination of Maurice's principal residence.

Example 2: Assume the facts of Example 1, except Maurice lives at the lake for a total of 24 months during the five years before he sells the lake home and commutes to work during those months. Will Maurice be eligible for § 121 on the basis that he has used the lake home as his principal residence for periods aggregating two years or more during the five year period before the sale? Based upon the language of Reg. §§ 1.121-1(b)(2) and 1.121-1(b)(4) Ex. 1 and, depending on the circumstances, Maurice's lake home may not be considered Maurice's principal residence in some or any of the five years. For example, if Maurice lived in the lake home for eight months in Year 1, but only four months in each of Years 2–5, the lake home might be his principal residence in Year 1, but not in any other year. In any year that the lake home is not considered Maurice's principal residence, the time spent at the lake home that year will not be counted in determining whether Maurice satisfies the use requirement. Thus, Maurice may not be eligible for the exclusion. This result, however, is not entirely free from doubt, considering that the regulations do not make the majority-of-the-time-during-the-year test dispositive. One suspects the Service and the courts will spend considerable time in the coming years evaluating whether a residence of the taxpayer constitutes that taxpayer's principal residence.

In summary, the 1997 expansion of the § 121 exclusion provided an enormous benefit to homeowners. Although some taxpayers will realize gain on the sale of their homes in excess of the § 121 limits, § 121 will exclude the gain from most home sales in this country.

GUINAN v. UNITED STATES
United States District Court, District of Arizona
2003-1 U.S.T.C. (CCH) P50,475 (2003)

This is an action by the plaintiffs seeking a refund of $45,009.00 for income taxes they paid in the 1998 tax year on the gain realized from the sale of their residence in Wisconsin. The plaintiffs filed an amended income tax return in January 2001 in which they excluded that gain pursuant to 26 U.S.C. § 121; the Internal Revenue Service disallowed the requested refund in December 2001. The issue before the Court is whether the plaintiffs' Wisconsin residence was their principal residence for purposes of 26 U.S.C. § 121(a), which, as amended by the Taxpayer Relief Act of

1997, provides in relevant part that "gross income shall not include gain from the sale . . . of property if, during the 5-year period ending on the date of sale . . . , such property has been owned and used by the taxpayer as the taxpayer's principal residence for periods aggregating 2 years or more."

The plaintiffs purchased their Wisconsin residence in March 1993 and sold it on September 15, 1998. During the five-year period prior to the sale of the Wisconsin residence the plaintiffs, who are retired, also owned homes in Georgia and Arizona. Their Georgia residence, which they owned when they purchased the Wisconsin residence, was sold in 1996, at which time they purchased a home in Arizona. The plaintiffs generally resided at their Wisconsin home during the warmer months and at their Georgia or Arizona homes during the rest of the year. According to the plaintiffs' affidavit, which the United States does not dispute, during the five-year period from September 15, 1993 through September 15, 1998 the plaintiffs occupied their Wisconsin residence for 847 days, their Georgia residence for 563 days, and their Arizona residence for 375 days.

The plaintiffs, as the taxpayers claiming a refund due to an exclusion from income, bear the burden of proving that their Wisconsin residence was their principal residence during the relevant time period. The Court concludes as a matter of law that they have not met that burden.

The United States concedes that the plaintiffs owned and used their Wisconsin residence for the duration required by § 121(a) during the relevant five year period. *See* Treasury Regulation § 1.121-1(c). Since what remains disputed is whether the plaintiffs used the Wisconsin residence as their principal residence during that time period, the Court looks to Treasury Regulation § 1.121-1(b)(2) for guidance. . . .

The Court concurs with the United States that the fact that the plaintiffs utilized the Wisconsin residence on more days in total during the relevant five year period than either the Georgia residence or the Arizona residence is not determinative for purposes of § 121(a) since the governing regulation refers to the time spent in a residence during a single tax year. *See* § 1.121-1(b)(2). ("The property that the taxpayer uses a majority of the time *during the year* ordinarily will be considered the taxpayer's principal residence." (Emphasis added). The plaintiffs' own undisputed figures fail to establish that the Wisconsin house was their principal residence inasmuch as they show that the plaintiffs spent more time in the Wisconsin house only during the first year of the five-year period (1993–1994), and that for each of the other four years they spent the majority of each year either at the Georgia house (1994–1995 and 1995–1996), or the Arizona house (1996–1997 and 1997–1998); their figures also show that for the entirety of the five-year period they spent more time in the Georgia and Arizona houses combined than they did in the Wisconsin house (52.5% versus 47.5%, respectively).

The Court also concurs with the United States that while time spent in a residence is a major factor, if not the most important factor, in determining whether it is the principal residence, other factors are also relevant, *See* § 1.121-1(b)(2), and in this case those other factors, taken as a whole, do not establish that the Wisconsin house was the plaintiffs' principal residence during the relevant time period.

First, a majority of the relevant factors do not actually favor any one of the residences as being the principal residence: the location of the plaintiffs' recreational and other activities do not favor Wisconsin since the evidence reflects activities in both Wisconsin and Georgia, e.g., while Mr. Guinan served on the board of their Wisconsin homeowners' association and the plaintiffs returned to Wisconsin during the winter months for major holidays and to attend Green Bay Packers games, both of the plaintiffs were actively involved in tennis activities in Georgia and Mr. Guinan lectured at local Georgia colleges; the location of the principal abodes of the plaintiffs' children do not favor any of the residences since none of the children then lived in Wisconsin, Georgia, or Arizona; the location where the plaintiffs received their mail and did their banking does not favor Wisconsin since the plaintiffs received mail and had bank accounts at each residence; and the location where the plaintiffs registered their vehicles does not favor Wisconsin since while the plaintiffs kept one car and two boats in Wisconsin, they kept two cars at their Georgia house and then at their Arizona house.

Second, other important factors, however, definitely point to the Wisconsin residence as not being the plaintiffs' principal residence in that, during the relevant time period, neither plaintiff filed any Wisconsin state tax return but did file Georgia and/or Arizona state returns, neither plaintiff was registered to vote in Wisconsin but both were registered in Georgia and then in Arizona, neither plaintiff had a Wisconsin driver's license but both had a Georgia license and then an Arizona license, and the plaintiffs treated their Arizona house as their principal residence for the 1999 tax year for purposes of the now-repealed 26 U.S.C. § 1034(a).

Third, the one relevant factor decidedly favoring Wisconsin as the principal residence, i.e., the imposing size of the Wisconsin house, is insufficient as a matter of law to overcome the facts and circumstances establishing that Wisconsin was not the plaintiffs' principal residence for purposes of § 121(a).

GATES v. COMMISSIONER
United States Tax Court
135 T.C. 1 (2010)

MARVEL, JUDGE:

[The taxpayers used a house on Summit Road as their principal residence for a period of at least two years from August 1996 to August 1998. The taxpayers decided to enlarge and remodel the original house, and they hired an architect. The architect advised petitioners that more stringent building and permit restrictions had been enacted since the original house was built. As a result of the architect's advice, the taxpayers determined they would demolish the house and construct a new three-bedroom home on the property. The new house they constructed had a very different shape from that of the original house, and was apparently two to three times larger than the footprint of the original house. Only about one-half of the land area of the original house overlapped with the land area covered by the new house, and no part of the original foundation perimeter corresponded to the foundation perimeter of the new house.

Taxpayers never resided in the new house. On April 7, 2000, they sold the new house for $1,100,000. The sale resulted in a $591,406 gain to petitioners. In the case before the Tax Court, the taxpayers challenged an IRS determination that the gain on the home was not eligible to be excluded under § 121.]

The issue presented arises from the fact that section 121(a) does not define two critical terms — "property" and "principal residence." Section 121(a) simply provides that gross income does not include gain from the sale or exchange of property if "such property" has been owned and used by the taxpayer "as the taxpayer's principal residence" for the required statutory period.

Respondent contends that petitioners did not sell property they had owned and used as their principal residence for the required statutory period because they never occupied the new house as their principal residence before they sold it. Respondent's argument interprets the term "property" to mean, or at least include, a dwelling that was owned and occupied by the taxpayer as his "principal residence" for at least 2 of the 5 years immediately preceding the sale. Respondent urges this Court to conclude that a qualifying sale under section 121(a) is one that includes the sale of a dwelling used by the taxpayer as his principal residence. Because petitioners never resided in the new house before its sale in 2000, respondent maintains that the new house was never petitioners' principal residence.

Predictably, petitioners disagree. Petitioners argue that any analysis of section 121(a) must recognize that the exclusion thereunder applies to the gain on the sale of *property* that was used as the taxpayer's principal residence. Petitioners' argument focuses on two facts — petitioners used the original house as their principal residence for the period required by section 121(a) and they sold the land on which the original house had been situated. Petitioners contend that the term "property" includes not only the dwelling but also the land on which the dwelling is situated. Petitioners seem to argue that the requirements of section 121(a) are satisfied if a taxpayer lived in any dwelling on the property for the required 2-year period even if that dwelling is not the dwelling that is sold. Petitioners contend that because they used the original house and the land on which it was situated as their principal residence for the required term, the Summit Road property qualifies as their principal residence and $500,000 of the gain generated by the sale of the property is excluded under section 121.

Because section 121 does not define the terms "property" and "principal residence," we must apply accepted principles of statutory construction to ascertain Congress' intent. It is a well-established rule of construction that if a statute does not define a term, the term is given its ordinary meaning. . . .

[After consulting various dictionaries for the meaning of "property" and "principal residence," the Tax Court noted] [b]ecause there is more than one possible meaning for both the term "property" and the term "principal residence," we cannot conclude that the meaning of section 121(a) is clear and unambiguous. Section 121(a) is not explicit as to whether Congress intended section 121 to apply to a sale of property when the property sold does not include the dwelling that the taxpayer used as a principal residence for the period that section 121(a) requires. Because section 121(a) is ambiguous, we may examine the legislative history of section 121 and its predecessor provisions to ascertain Congress' intent regarding the proper tax treatment of principal residence sales.

[The Tax Court then reviewed the legislative history of Section 1034 (now repealed) and old Section 121.]

The legislative history demonstrates that Congress intended the term "principal residence" to mean the primary dwelling or house that a taxpayer occupied as his principal residence. Nothing in the legislative history indicates that Congress intended section 121 to exclude gain on the sale of property that does not include a house or other structure used by the taxpayer as his principal place of abode. Although a principal residence may include land surrounding the dwelling, the legislative history supports a conclusion that Congress intended the section 121 exclusion to apply only if the dwelling the taxpayer sells was actually used as his principal residence for the period required by section 121(a).

The conclusion that we reach from an examination of the legislative history surrounding the enactment of section 121 is bolstered by and is consistent with regulations promulgated under the predecessor provisions of section 121. Section 1.121-3(a), Income Tax Regs., under former section 121, provided that the term "principal residence" has the same meaning as in section 1034 and the regulations thereunder. Section 1.1034-1(c)(3)(i), Income Tax Regs., under former section 1034 (section 1034 regulations), provided that whether property was used by the taxpayer as his principal residence depended on all the facts and circumstances in each case, including the good faith of the taxpayer. The section 1034 regulations further provided that property used by the taxpayer as his principal residence may include a houseboat, a house trailer, or stock held by a tenant-stockholder in a cooperative housing corporation, if the dwelling which the taxpayer is entitled to occupy as such stockholder is used by him as his principal residence. The focal point of the section 1034 regulations was the dwelling unit a taxpayer uses as his principal residence. The section 1034 regulations reinforce our conclusion that to obtain the benefits of former section 1034, a taxpayer who sells a dwelling must have actually used it as his principal residence.

Our conclusion regarding the meaning that Congress attaches to the terms "property" and "principal residence" in section 121(a) is also consistent with caselaw interpreting former section 1034, as in effect before its repeal . . . .

Regulations under amended sec. 121, as currently in effect, provide that if a taxpayer meets certain requirements, gain from the sale of land alone may qualify for the sec. 121 exclusion. Sec. 1.121-1(b)(3), Income Tax Regs. However, to qualify under this provision of the regulations, the taxpayer must still sell a "dwelling unit" that meets the requirements under sec. 121 within 2 years before or after the sale of the land . . . .

Although we recognize that petitioners would have satisfied the requirements under section 121 had they sold or exchanged the original house instead of tearing it down, we must apply the statute as written by Congress. Rules of statutory construction require that we narrowly construe exclusions from income. Under section 121(a) and its legislative history, we cannot conclude on the facts of this case that petitioners sold their principal residence. Accordingly, we hold that petitioners may not exclude from income under section 121(a) the gain realized on the sale of the Summit Road property.

To reflect the foregoing,

Decision will be entered for respondent.

Reviewed by the Court.

COLVIN, COHEN, GALE, THORNTON, WHERRY, GUSTAFSON, PARIS, and MORRISON, JJ., agree with this majority opinion.

HALPERN, J., dissenting:

There is adequate ground for the majority's conclusion that, to qualify for the section 121 exclusion, the taxpayer must sell not only the land on which her principal residence is located but also the principal residence itself. Nevertheless, I think that there is also adequate ground for concluding that petitioners' sale of the new house qualified for that exclusion.

Interpretation Contrary to the Remedial Intent of Section 121(a)

The gain exclusion rule of section 121(a) applies if three conditions are met: (1) There must be a sale or exchange (without distinction, sale); (2) the sale must be of "property * * * owned and used by the taxpayer as the taxpayer's principal residence" (the property use condition), and (3) the property use condition must be satisfied for 2 out of the 5 years ending on the date of sale of the property (the temporal condition). The majority focuses on the second condition (the property use condition) and interprets the condition as being satisfied only if the property sold constitutes, at least in part, "a house or other structure used by the taxpayer as his principal place of abode. . . . "

While the majority is correct that the Supreme Court has said that exclusions from income are to be narrowly construed, . . . the Supreme Court has also said that, if the meaning of a tax provision liberalizing the law from motives of public policy is doubtful, then it should not be narrowly construed. . . .

With that latter rule of construction in mind, consider a taxpayer whose longtime home is demolished by a natural disaster (a hurricane). The taxpayer lacks insurance. Nevertheless, she rebuilds on the same land (perhaps a bit further from the ocean) and lives in the rebuilt house for 18 months, and then she sells the house and land at a gain. Although the taxpayer satisfies the property use condition, I assume that, nevertheless, under the majority's analysis, she gets no exclusion because she fails the temporal condition; i.e., she has not lived in the rebuilt house for 2 or more of the last 5 years. I assume further that, if her house had been only damaged (and not demolished), and she repaired it, she would get an exclusion. That seems like an untenable distinction to me.

Difficult Interpretative Questions

The majority's interpretation of the property use condition naturally suggests that there is some recognizable difference between remodeling a house and demolishing and rebuilding the house. I assume the majority does not mean to suggest that any remodeling of a home (1) terminates the use of that home as the taxpayer's principal residence and (2) resets the temporal clock to zero time elapsed. If not, then is there some level of remodeling that does (1) terminate the use of the home as the taxpayer's principal residence and (2) set the temporal clock to zero? What about a taxpayer who, wanting a bigger house, demolishes the old house (but not the foundation) and constructs a larger (taller) house using the old foundation? Is that remodeling or rebuilding? What about keeping part of the foundation, and expanding horizontally? If that is remodeling, then there may be an easy way for the Court to reach a similar result in the case before us. The parties have stipulated an exhibit, a blueprint, that shows footprints of both the old and the new house. I have examined the exhibit, and the footprints overlap. Might we not conclude that part of the foundation of the old house was incorporated into the new, thus making the case a remodeling case and not a rebuilding case?

The majority's report will undoubtedly raise the kind of remodeling versus rebuilding questions that I have raised. I think that the better course would be to avoid provoking those questions.

. . . .

Conclusion

I would treat the demolition and reconstruction of petitioners' house no differently from a renovation. . . .

WELLS, GOEKE, KROUPA, and HOLMES, JJ., agree with this dissent.

Chapter 7

SCHOLARSHIPS AND PRIZES

I. PROBLEMS

1. Joan won a computer programming competition for high school students. The competition was sponsored by the Computer Store, which awarded computers to Joan and her teacher, Ted. The Computer Store, which purchased the computers for $900 each, lists such computers for sale at $2,000, although it occasionally sells them at reduced prices as low as $1,600. Ted had a comparable computer already, so he promptly sold the computer he received to a fellow teacher for $1,200. What tax consequences to Ted and to Joan?

2. In honor of her twentieth anniversary of teaching high school mathematics, the school district gave Mary a computer worth $1,200, which cost the district $1,000. What possible tax consequences to Mary? Does your answer change if the computer was worth $2,000?

3. The tuition at State Law School is $20,000 per year for state residents and $40,000 per year for nonresidents. The law school waives the out-of-state differential for Nancy, a nonresident, who is serving as an unpaid research assistant to Professor Jones on preparation of a new book. Nancy will work about 200 hours for Professor Jones, and will receive 3 hours of academic credit for her research work. All students must study legal research, either by taking the regular classroom course or by arranging an individual program with one of the professors. In addition, a number of students also do paid research work with professors for $10 an hour. Does Nancy have any income?

4. Al Athlete is an outstanding high school basketball player. Private University awards a basketball scholarship to him covering tuition and fees ($30,000) and room and board ($10,000). Private U. obviously expects Al to be a star on its team. Any income?

5. The law firm of Bigger and Bigger awards Betty a $10,000 tuition scholarship for earning the highest grades through 2 years of law school, and simultaneously offers her a job as an associate with the firm following her graduation next year. Betty accepts the scholarship and the job. Is the scholarship taxable?

Assignment for Chapter 7:

Complete the problems.

Read: Internal Revenue Code: §§ 74; 274(j)(2), (3); 102(c); 117(a)–(c). Skim

§§ 117(d); 127(a), (c)(1); 132(a)(3), (e)(1).
Treasury Regulations: §§ 1.74-1(a); 1.102-1; Prop. Reg. §§ 1.74-2; 1.117-6(b), (c)(1)–(3)(i), (d)(1)–(3), (e).

Materials: Overview
             McCoy v. Commissioner
             Bingler v. Johnson

II.   VOCABULARY

scholarship
fellowship grant
qualified scholarship
employee achievement award

III.   OBJECTIVES

1. To distinguish among prizes, scholarships and gifts.

2. To recall that prizes are generally included in income.

3. To recognize factors that may be applied in determining the fair market value of a prize in-kind.

4. To recall and apply the special exclusion for employee achievement awards and the limitation on the amount excludable.

5. To recall that non-degree candidates receive no exclusion for qualified scholarships.

6. To recall the purposes for which qualified scholarships may be used.

7. To distinguish between scholarships and disguised compensation.

IV. OVERVIEW

Prior to 1954, no statute explicitly addressed the taxability of prizes and awards and scholarships. As a result, they were excluded from income only if they qualified as "gifts" under the forerunner of present § 102. As enacted in 1954, § 74 generally included prizes and awards in gross income, but made a major exception for awards based on "religious, charitable, scientific, educational, artistic, literary, or civic achievement," provided the recipient was selected without action on his part to enter the contest, and also was not required to render substantial future services. § 74(b)(1), (2). Section 117, also first enacted in 1954, excluded "scholarships and fellowships" from gross income for both degree candidates and non-degree candidates, subject to certain dollar and other limitations in the case of non-degree candidates. The exclusionary provisions of both statutes, however, were significantly narrowed in 1986.

A. Prizes and Awards

Prizes and awards are generally taxable. The pre-1986 exception applicable to recipients of "meritorious achievement" awards had often been criticized on policy grounds. Prizes and awards represent a clear accession to wealth, it was argued, and ought to be taxed, particularly since the value of the exclusion increases with the tax bracket of the recipient, and since the presence of the exclusion may provide a temptation to disguise taxable compensation as a tax-exempt prize. This argument prevailed, § 74(b)(3) was added to the Code, and the meritorious achievement exception now applies only if the recipient gives up the prize. Specifically, in addition to meeting the pre-1986 requirements — religious, charitable, etc. achievement, no action to enter, no substantial future services — to qualify for the exclusion, the recipient must also designate a governmental unit or qualifying charity to which the payor transfers the prize. § 74(b)(3). A timely designation must be made and carried out before the award is used. Prop. Reg. §§ 1.74-1(c)(1), (d), (e)(2). Since the recipient of such a prize or award could presumably avoid gross income by simply rejecting the award (see, e.g., Rev. Rul. 57-374, 1957-2 C.B. 69), the statutory scheme, in a sense, broadens the right to reject: in addition to outright rejection, a qualifying designation and transfer also avoids gross income. Since no gross income is generated, no charitable deduction is allowed either. Prop. Reg. § 1.74-1(f). Does the provision serve any purpose? If the recipient accepted the prize (receiving gross income) and then transferred it to a qualifying charity (receiving a charitable deduction), would the net tax result be the same? In many cases, the answer is "Yes." Suppose, however, by way of example, the taxpayer's itemized deductions were less than the standard deduction or the taxpayer's charitable contributions for the year exceeded the § 170(b) limitations. The transfer-to-charity rule may thus be useful in some circumstances.

The principal exclusion now in § 74 is for "employee achievement awards." §§ 74(c), 274(j). The exclusion for employee achievement awards constitutes congressional approval and encouragement of "double" tax benefits — that is, a deduction for the employer and an exclusion for the employee — in certain restricted circumstances. The statutory scheme requires, in part, that the award consist of tangible personal property, given in recognition of a qualifying length of service or safety achievement. A "qualified plan award" is an employee achievement award under a written plan that does not discriminate in favor of highly compensated employees, provided the average annual cost for all employee achievement awards does not exceed $400. § 274(j)(3)(B). The employer's deduction for the cost of employee achievement awards is limited to $400 per year for each employee, except the limit may increase to a maximum of $1,600 with respect to qualified plan awards. § 274(j)(2). If the cost of the award is fully deductible to the employer, the employee may exclude the award from income. If the cost is not fully deductible, the award constitutes gross income to the extent its value or cost (whichever is greater) exceeds the deduction limit. (The "excess cost" amount, however, cannot be greater than the value of the award itself.) Thus, assume an employee achievement award (not a qualified plan award) cost the employer $500 and had a value of $600. The employer's deduction is limited to $400 under § 274(j)(2)(A). Since the greater of cost or value exceeds the deduction limit by $200, the employee must report gross income of $200, but the remaining portion of the value ($400) is excluded. § 74(c)(2). This statutory exclusion is complemented by the congressional determination that employee awards should generally not be classified as gifts, and that § 102 should not apply to transfers from employer to employee. §§ 102(c)(1) and 274(b). In addition to the provisions of § 74(c), an independent basis for excluding certain employee awards may be found in the *de minimis* fringe benefit provisions. *See* § 132(e)(1); Prop. Reg. § 1.74-2(e). The fringe benefit rules are studied in detail in Chapter 11.

The fact prizes and awards are generally taxable means difficult valuation issues may be presented when an award is not in cash. The regulations state the measure of income is fair market value. Reg. § 1.74-1(a)(2). Consider in this regard *McCoy v. Commissioner*, included in the materials.

B. Qualified Scholarships

The exclusion for scholarships and fellowships is limited to "qualified scholarships" received by degree-seeking students at qualifying educational institutions. § 117(a). There is no exclusion for scholarships or fellowships received by those who are not candidates for degrees. (However, educational costs that qualify as trade or business expenses are deductible. *See* Reg. § 1.162-5. The deductibility of educational expenses is examined in Chapter 18. In addition, a limited amount of postsecondary educational expenses may qualify for a tax credit under § 25A. *See* Chapter 18.) The term "candidate for a degree" includes students attending a primary or secondary school, and undergraduate or graduate students pursuing an academic or professional degree at a college or university. It also includes students pursuing, at educational institutions, certain qualifying employment-training programs or programs acceptable for full credit towards a bachelor or higher degree. Prop. Reg. § 1.117-6(c)(4).

Prior to 1986, there was no limit on the statutory exclusion for amounts received by degree candidates as scholarships, and the exclusion thus extended to amounts used to cover ordinary living expenses, including meals and lodging. In 1986, Congress limited the exclusion under § 117(a) to "qualified scholarships." A "qualified scholarship" is limited to that portion of a scholarship or fellowship used for "qualified tuition and related expenses," a term that encompasses required tuition, fees, books, supplies, and equipment. § 117(b)(2). Although the statute requires the scholarship be used for required tuition and related expenses in accordance with the conditions of the grant, actual "tracing" of funds is not required. Prop. Reg. § 1.117-6(e). The student is entitled to exclude an otherwise qualifying scholarship up to the aggregate amount incurred for qualified tuition and course-related expenses; no exclusion is allowed for scholarship amounts earmarked for nonqualifying purposes, such as room and board, travel, and incidental living expenses. Prop. Reg. § 1.117-6(c)(1). In addition, no exclusion is allowed for scholarship amounts that represent payment for services. § 117(c)(1). The 1986 statutory change thus eliminates the perceived inequity of allowing a tax benefit for personal living expenses to scholarship recipients, while denying it to non-scholarship students and to non-students generally. The exclusion, of course, still provides a tax benefit to scholarship students with respect to tuition and fees; apart from the limited credit allowed by § 25A, non-scholarship students must still fund these costs from after-tax dollars. Is even this disparity in treatment warranted?

There has been considerable litigation as to whether payments made in an educational setting constituted an excluded scholarship or fellowship, or compensation for services. See Prop. Reg. § 1.117-6(d) and *Bingler v. Johnson* in the materials. Particularly litigious, and particularly likely to lose, have been medical interns and residents trying to cast their remuneration as a fellowship grant. *See, e.g., U.S. v. Detroit Medical Center,* 557 F.3d 412 (6th Cir. 2009); *U.S. v. Memorial Sloan-Kettering Cancer Center,* 563 F.3d 19 (9th Cir. 2009). Graduate teaching and research assistants have also litigated frequently, losing where it was found they were primarily being paid to teach rather than paid to study. *See, e.g., Farmer v. Commissioner,* T.C. Memo 1990-199; *Meehan v. Commissioner,* 66 T.C. 794 (1976). In the case of employer-employee scholarships generally, it is difficult, as one might expect, to avoid application of the "quid pro quo" reasoning of *Bingler v. Johnson* that holds the "scholarship" to be taxable compensation.

Although employer-employee scholarships may be unlikely to qualify under § 117(a), some employer-provided educational benefits are nonetheless tax-free. "Qualified tuition reduction" programs, essentially a special fringe benefit for employees of educational organizations and their family members, are non-taxable, provided they do not discriminate in favor of highly compensated employees, even though the programs are clearly compensatory in nature and of potentially great value. The exclusion is limited to tuition reduction for education below the graduate level, although this limitation does not apply to tuition reduction for graduate students engaged in teaching or research for the institution. See § 117(d), and note the restriction in § 117(c)(1). Is this exclusion justifiable? Education-related fringe benefits of more general applicability are the educational assistance programs described in § 127. Employer payments for educational assistance to the employee are excluded from gross income, up to a maximum of $5,250 per year. The program cannot discriminate in favor of highly compensated employees and is subject to various other requirements. Educational assistance includes tuition and course-related expenses, but payments for meals, lodging, transportation and certain other expenditures do not qualify. § 127(c)(1). There is no requirement the education be job-related or part of a degree program, and purely personal educational benefits may thus be obtained on a tax-free basis. Reg. § 1.127-2(c)(4). Is this exclusion warranted? In a related vein, suppose a corporation establishes a private foundation to provide scholarships to children of employees, or to employees themselves. Does *Bingler v. Johnson* apply? The Service has announced scholarship treatment obtains if the grants are controlled and limited by substantial non-employment-related factors so the employment relationship is no more than an initial qualifying condition. Rev. Proc. 76-47, 1976-2 C.B. 670.

Finally, consider the relationship between § 117 and the provisions dealing with prizes and awards and with gifts. Are scholarships and fellowships, by virtue of § 74(a), automatically included in gross income if they do not constitute qualified scholarships? May they qualify as gifts? See Prop. Reg. § 1.117-6(b)(1), stating that non-qualifying scholarships and fellowships are generally includable in income, and holding the § 102 exclusion inapplicable. Also see the Reg. § 1.102-1(a) regulations stating § 102 does not apply to prizes and awards or to scholarships and fellowships.

McCOY v. COMMISSIONER
United States Tax Court
38 T.C. 841 (1962), *acq.* 1963-2 C.B. 5

During 1956 petitioner was employed by the Hotpoint Appliance Sales Co., a division of the General Electric Company. During that year and for several years prior thereto, the Hotpoint Company sponsored an annual sales contest and distributed awards to the winners. As a result of the 1956 contest, petitioner received as an award from General Electric, a new 1957 Lincoln Capri two-door coupe automobile equipped with radio, heater, power steering, power brakes, and white sidewall tires. The award was presented to petitioner at a banquet held in Jacksonville, Florida, on November 5, 1956. At the time of the award, the 1957 Lincoln models had been on the market about 1 month. The cost of the automobile to General Electric Company was $4,452.54.

After receiving the automobile, the petitioner drove it from Jacksonville, Florida, to his then home in Knoxville, Tennessee. On the advice of a representative of his employer he went to an authorized Lincoln-Mercury dealer in that city to get an appraisal of the automobile, the result of which is not disclosed by the record. Within 10 days after receiving the Lincoln car, petitioner traded it to a dealer for $1,000 in cash and a 1957 Ford Country Squire station wagon with power equipment, having a dealer's price of $2,600. Petitioner included in his adjusted gross income for the year 1956 the amount of $3,600 as the value of the Lincoln automobile.

For the year 1956 General Electric Company submitted to the respondent an information return . . . in which it reported the payment of additional compensation to petitioner in the amount of $4,452.54, which was the cost to it of the Lincoln automobile.

OPINION

Section 74(a) of the Internal Revenue Code of 1954 provides, with exceptions not here material, for the inclusion in gross income of amounts received as prizes and awards. Section 1.74-1(a)(2) of the Income Tax Regulations, promulgated pursuant to that section, provides that if the award is not made in money but is made in goods or services then the fair market value of such goods or services is the amount to be included in income.

The petitioner does not deny that there should be included in his taxable income the fair market value of the Lincoln automobile, and indeed he included the amount of $3,600 in his income tax return for 1956 on account thereof. He contends that the $3,600 represents the fair market value of the automobile in his hands since that was the amount which he realized when he traded it in, 10 days later, for a Ford station wagon, the dealer's price of which was $2,600, and boot of $1,000.

The petitioner recognizes that his employer paid $4,452.54 for the automobile, but contends that this does not represent its fair market value to him, arguing that if the employer had attempted to sell the automobile, rather than give it to him, the car would have brought a much lesser price than the amount originally paid for it.

The respondent contends that the fair market value of this automobile was $4,452.54, the amount which the petitioner's employer had paid for it. He points to the fact that after receiving the automobile, the petitioner owned it for 10 days and drove it from Jacksonville, Florida, to Knoxville, Tennessee, and contends that this use depreciated the value of the car below its value at the time of its receipt by petitioner.

The evidence does not show precisely when the petitioner's employer purchased the automobile, but it was within a month prior to the time it was given to the petitioner. When the car was received by the petitioner it was a new car in the sense that it had not been actually used. However, we think it is common knowledge of which we may take notice, that when an automobile has been purchased from a dealer the purchaser cannot, on a sale of the car, normally realize the price which he paid for the car, even though it has not been actually used. We think that a substantial part of the reduction in value of the car in question is attributable to this fact. On the other hand, we cannot conclude that the full reduction in value to $3,600 was attributable to this factor. It is also a matter of which we may take notice that the value of an automobile is reduced as a result of use. We think the fair market value of the car was reduced to a substantial extent as a result of the petitioner's having owned and used it for 10 days and having driven it from Jacksonville, Florida, to his home in Knoxville, Tennessee.

Thus, in our opinion, neither the price paid by the employer nor the price received by the petitioner establishes the fair market value of the car in the petitioner's hands at the time he received it. The evidence adduced does not permit of an exact determination of such fair market value. Under the circumstances, we have exercised our best judgment and have concluded and found as a fact that the value of the Lincoln automobile had a fair market value of $3,900 at the time it was received by the petitioner. *Cf. Cohan v. Commissioner*, 39 F.2d 540. That amount should be included in the petitioner's taxable income instead of the $3,600 reported by the petitioner in his return.

Decision will be entered under Rule 50.

BINGLER v. JOHNSON
United States Supreme Court
394 U.S. 741 (1969)

MR. JUSTICE STEWART delivered the opinion of the Court.

We are called upon in this case to examine for the first time Section 117 of the Internal Revenue Code of 1954, which excludes from a taxpayer's gross income amounts received as "scholarships" and "fellowships." The question before us concerns the tax treatment of payments received by the respondents from their employer, the Westinghouse Electric Corporation, while they were on "educational leave" from their jobs with Westinghouse.

During the period here in question the respondents held engineering positions at the Bettis Atomic Power Laboratory in Pittsburgh, Pennsylvania, which Westinghouse operates under a "cost-plus" contract with the Atomic Energy Commission. Their employment status enabled them to participate in what is known as the Westinghouse Bettis Fellowship and Doctoral Program. That program, designed both to attract new employees seeking further education and to give advanced training to persons already employed at Bettis, offers a two-phase schedule of subsidized postgraduate study in engineering, physics, or mathematics.

Under the first, or "work-study," phase, a participating employee holds a regular job with Westinghouse and in addition pursues a course of study at either the University of Pittsburgh or Carnegie-Mellon University. The employee is paid for a 40-hour work week, but may receive up to eight hours of "release time" per week for the purpose of attending classes. "Tuition remuneration," as well as reimbursement for various incidental academic expenses, is provided by the company.

When an employee has completed all preliminary requirements for his doctorate, he may apply for an educational leave of absence, which constitutes the second phase of the Fellowship Program. He must submit a proposed dissertation topic for approval by Westinghouse and the AEC. Approval is based, *inter alia*, on a determination that the topic has at least some general relevance to the work done at Bettis. If the leave of absence is secured, the employee devotes his full attention, for a period of at least several months, to fulfilling his dissertation requirement. During this period he receives a "stipend" from Westinghouse, in an amount based on a specified percentage (ranging from 70% to 90%) of his prior salary plus "adders," depending upon the size of his family. He also retains his seniority status and receives all employee benefits, such as insurance and stock option privileges. In return he not only must submit periodic progress reports, but under the written agreement that all participants in the program must sign, also is obligated to return to the employ of Westinghouse for a period of at least two years following completion of his leave. Upon return he is, according to the agreement, to "assume duties commensurate with his education and experience," at a salary "commensurate with the duties assigned."

The respondents all took leaves under the Fellowship Program at varying times during the period 1960–1962, and eventually received their doctoral degrees in engineering. Respondents Johnson and Pomerantz took leaves of nine months and were paid $5,670 each, representing 80% of their prior salaries at Westinghouse. Respondent Wolfe, whose leave lasted for a year, received $9,698.90, or 90% of his previous salary. Each returned to Westinghouse for the required period of time following his educational leave.

Westinghouse, which under its own accounting system listed the amounts paid to the respondents as "indirect labor" expenses, withheld federal income tax from those amounts. The respondents filed claims for refund, contending that the payments they had received were "scholarships," and hence were excludable from income under Section 117 of the Code, which provides in pertinent part:

(a) General rule.

In the case of an individual, gross income does not include—

(1) any amount received—

(A) As a scholarship at an educational institution (as defined in section 151(e)(4)), or

(B) as a fellowship grant. . . .

When those claims were rejected, the respondents instituted this suit in the District Court for the Western District of Pennsylvania, against the District Director of Internal Revenue. After the basically undisputed evidence regarding the Bettis Program had been presented, the trial judge instructed the jury in accordance with Treas. Reg. on Income Tax (1954 Code) Section 1.117-4(c), 26 CFR Section 1.117-4(c), which provides that amounts representing "compensation for past, present, or future employment services," and amounts "paid . . . to . . . an individual to enable him to pursue studies or research primarily for the benefit of the grantor," are not excludable as scholarships. The jury found that the amounts received by the respondents were taxable income. Respondents then sought review in the Court of Appeals for the Third Circuit, and that court reversed, holding that the Regulation referred to was invalid, that the jury instructions were therefore improper, and that on the essentially undisputed facts it was clear as a matter of law that the amounts received by the respondents were "scholarships" excludable under Section 117. 396 F.2d 258.

The holding of the Court of Appeals with respect to Treas. Reg. Section 1.117-4(c) was contrary to the decisions of several other circuits — most notably, that of the Fifth Circuit in *Ussery v. United States*, 296 F.2d 582, which explicitly sustained the Regulation against attack and held amounts received under an arrangement quite similar to the Bettis Program to be taxable income. Accordingly, upon the District Director's petition, we granted certiorari to resolve the conflict and to determine the proper scope of Section 117 and Treas. Reg. Section 1.117-4(c) with respect to payments such as those involved here. 393 U.S. 949.

In holding invalid the Regulation that limits the definitions of "scholarship" and "fellowship" so as to exclude amounts received as "compensation," the Court of Appeals emphasized that the statute itself expressly adverts to certain situations in which funds received by students may be thought of as remuneration. After the basic rule excluding scholarship funds from gross income is set out in Section 117(a), for instance, subsection (b)(1) stipulates:

> In the case of an individual who is a candidate for a degree at an educational institution . . . , subsection (a) shall not apply to that portion of any amount received which represents payment for teaching, research, or other services in the nature of part-time employment required as a condition to receiving the scholarship or the fellowship grant.

In addition, subsection (b)(2) limits the exclusion from income with regard to nondegree candidates in two respects: first, the grantor must be a governmental agency, an international organization, or an organization exempt from tax under Section 501(a), (c)(3) of the Code; and second, the maximum exclusion from income available to a nondegree candidate is $300 per month for not more than 36 months. Since these exceptions are expressly set out in the statute, the Court of Appeals, relying on the canon of construction that *expressio unius est exclusio alterius*, concluded that no additional restrictions may be put on the basic exclusion from income granted by subsection (a) — a conclusion forcefully pressed upon us by the respondents.

Congress' express reference to the limitations just referred to concededly lends some support to the respondents' position. The difficulty with that position, however, lies in its implicit assumption that those limitations are limitations on an exclusion of all funds received by students to support them during the course of their education. Section 117 provides, however, only that amounts received as "scholarships" or "fellowships" shall be excludable. And Congress never defined what it meant by the quoted terms. As the Tax Court has observed:

> [A] proper reading of the statute requires that before the exclusion comes into play there must be a determination that the payment sought to be excluded has the normal characteristics associated with the term "scholarship."

Reese v. Commissioner, 45 T.C. 407, *aff'd*, 373 F.2d 742. The regulation here in question represents an effort by the Commissioner to supply the definitions that Congress omitted. And it is fundamental, of course, that as "contemporaneous constructions by those charged with administration of" the Code, the Regulations "must be sustained unless unreasonable and plainly inconsistent with the revenue statutes," and "should not be *overruled*, except for weighty reasons." *Commissioner v. South Texas Lumber Co.*, 333 U.S. 496, 501. In this respect our statement last term in *United States v. Correll*, 389 U.S. 299, bears emphasis:

> [W]e do not sit as a committee of revision to perfect the administration of the tax laws. Congress has delegated to the Commissioner, not to the courts, the task of prescribing "all needful rules and regulations for the enforcement" of the Internal Revenue Code. 26 U.S.C. Section 7805(a). In this area of limitless factual variations, "it is the province of Congress and

the Commissioner, not the courts, to make the appropriate adjustments."

Id., at 306–307. Here, the definitions supplied by the Regulation clearly are *prima facie* proper, comporting as they do with the ordinary understanding of "scholarships" and "fellowships" as relatively disinterested, "no-strings" educational grants, with no requirement of any substantial quid pro quo from the recipients.

The implication of the respondents' *expressio unius* reasoning is that any amount paid for the purpose of supporting one pursuing a program of study or scholarly research should be excludable from gross income as a "scholarship" so long as it does not fall within the specific limitations of Section 117(b). Pay received by a $30,000 per year engineer or executive on a leave of absence would, according to that reasoning, be excludable as long as the leave was granted so that the individual could perform work required for a doctoral degree. This result presumably would not be altered by the fact that the employee might be performing, in satisfaction of his degree requirements, precisely the same work which he was doing for his employer prior to his leave and which he would be doing after his return to "employment" — or by the fact that the fruits of that work were made directly available to and exploited by the employer. Such a result would be anomalous indeed, especially in view of the fact that under Section 117 the comparatively modest sums received by part-time teaching assistants are clearly subject to taxation. Particularly in light of the principle that exemptions from taxation are to be construed narrowly, we decline to assume that Congress intended to sanction — indeed, as the respondents would have it, to compel — such an inequitable situation.

The legislative history underlying Section 117 is, as the Court of Appeals recognized, "far from clear." We do not believe, however, that it precludes, as "plainly inconsistent" with the statute, a definition of "scholarship" that excludes from the reach of that term amounts received as compensation for services performed. The 1939 Internal Revenue Code, like predecessor Codes, contained no specific provision dealing with scholarship grants. Whether such grants were includable in gross income depended simply upon whether they fell within the broad provision excluding from income amounts received as "gifts." Thus case-by-case determinations regarding grantors' motives were necessary. The cases decided under this approach prior to 1954 generally involved two types of financial assistance: grants to research or teaching assistants — graduate students who perform research or teaching services in return for their stipends — and foundation grants to post-doctoral researchers. In cases decided shortly before the 1954 Code was enacted, the Tax Court, relying on the "gift" approach to scholarships and fellowships, held that amounts received by a research assistant were taxable income, but reached divergent results in situations involving grants to post-doctoral researchers.

In enacting Section 117 of the 1954 Code, Congress indicated that it wished to eliminate the necessity for reliance on "case-by-case" determinations with respect to whether "scholarships" and "fellowships" were excludable as "gifts." Upon this premise the respondents hinge their argument that Congress laid down a standard under which all case-by-case determinations — such as those that may be made under Treas. Reg. § 1.117-4(c) — are unnecessary and improper. We have already indicated, however, our reluctance to believe that Section 117 was designed to exclude from taxation all amounts, no matter how large or from what source, that are given for the support of one who happens to be a student. The sounder inference is that Congress was merely "recogni[zing] that scholarships and fellowships are sufficiently unique . . . to merit [tax] treatment separate from that accorded gifts," and attempting to provide that grants falling within those categories should be treated consistently — as in some instances, under the generic provisions of the 1939 Code, they arguably had not been. Delineation of the precise contours of those categories was left to the Commissioner.

Furthermore, a congressional intention that not all grants received by students were necessarily to be "scholarships" may reasonably be inferred from the legislative history. In explaining the basis for its version of Section 117-(b)(2), the House Ways and Means Committee stated that its purpose was to "tax those grants which are in effect merely payments of a salary during a period while the recipient is on leave from his regular job." This comment related, it is true, to a specific exception to the exclusion from income set out in subsection (a). But, in view of the fact that the statute left open the definitions of "scholarship" and "fellowship," it is not unreasonable to conclude that in adding subsection (b) to the statute Congress was merely dealing explicitly with those problems that had come explicitly to its attention — viz., those involving research and teaching assistantships and post-doctoral research grants — without intending to forbid application to similar situations of the general principle underlying its treatment of those problems. One may justifiably suppose that the Congress that taxed funds received by "part-time" teaching assistants, presumably on the ground that the amounts received by such persons really represented compensation for services performed, would also deem proper a definition of "scholarship" under which comparable sorts of compensation — which often, as in the present case, are significantly greater in amount — are likewise taxable. In providing such a definition, the Commissioner has permissibly implemented an underlying congressional concern. We cannot say that the provision of Treas. Reg. Section 1.117-4(c) that taxes amounts received as "compensation" is "unreasonable or plainly inconsistent with the . . . statut[e]."

Under that provision, as set out in the trial court's instructions, the jury here properly found that the amounts received by the respondents were taxable "compensation" rather than excludable "scholarships." The employer-employee relationship involved is immediately suggestive, of course, as is the close relation between the respondents' prior salaries and the amount of their "stipends." In addition, employee benefits were continued. Topics were required to relate at least generally to the work of the Bettis Laboratory. Periodic work reports were to be submitted. And, most importantly, Westinghouse unquestionably extracted a *quid pro quo*. The respondents not only were required to hold positions with Westinghouse throughout the "work-study" phase of the program, but also were obligated to return to Westinghouse's employ for a substantial period of time after completion of their leave. The thrust of the provision dealing with compensation is that bargained-for payments, given only as a "quo" in return for the quid of services rendered — whether past, present, or future — should not be excludable from income as "scholarship" funds. That provision clearly covers this case.

Accordingly, the judgment of the Court of Appeals is reversed, and that of the District Court reinstated.

It is so ordered.

Chapter 8

LIFE INSURANCE AND ANNUITIES

Part A:
Life Insurance

I. PROBLEMS

1. When Paula bought her home, she also purchased a term insurance policy on her life in the face amount of her home mortgage, $100,000. The insurance policy was a decreasing term insurance policy, *i.e.*, the amount of the insurance protection decreased as the balance owing on the mortgage decreased. Paula died ten years after purchasing the home and after she had paid $5,000 in insurance premiums. She devised the home to her husband, Andrew. The insurance proceeds amounted to $85,000 and were payable to Andrew, who used the proceeds to prepay the entire mortgage on the home. What tax consequences to Andrew as a result of the receipt and use of the insurance proceeds? What tax consequences, if any, to Andrew and the mortgagee if, under the terms of the insurance contract, the proceeds are payable to the mortgagee, which is the bank that lent Paula the money to purchase the home?

   Should be included

2. When he was 45 years old, Rick purchased an ordinary life insurance policy in the face amount of $40,000, naming his wife Mary as beneficiary. Rick paid an annual premium of $1,200 on the policy. At the time of Rick's death, the policy had a cash surrender value of $14,000. The insurance company paid Mary the $40,000 face amount. Rick had paid a total of $18,000 in premiums prior to his death. Had Rick purchased $40,000 of term insurance rather than whole life insurance, his total premium payments over the same period would have amounted to $6,000. What are the tax consequences to Mary upon receipt of the insurance proceeds? Explain the difference, if any, between the tax treatment of ordinary life insurance in this case and term insurance. *tax-free*

   $12,000 = excess
   2,000 = interest
   6,000 = term
   $16,000 = mortality gain

3. Assume the ordinary life insurance policy in Problem 2 had provided that the insurance proceeds of $40,000 would not be paid upon death. Instead, the insurance company would hold the proceeds for 18 months following the insured's death and then pay to the beneficiary a total of $47,500. What tax consequences to Mary when she receives the $47,500? *taxed*

4. John is a key employee of Closely Held, Inc. When he retired, John purchased from Closely Held an insurance policy Closely Held owned on his life. The face amount of the policy was $250,000. Closely Held had paid

   §101a2B

147

not taxed bc transferred to the insured

total premiums of $75,000 on the policy. At the time of John's retirement, the policy had a cash surrender value of $60,000 and Closely Held sold it to John for that amount. John thereafter made all premium payments when they were due. What are the tax consequences, if any, when John dies 10 years later and his son, Philip, the beneficiary, receives the $250,000 in insurance proceeds? How would your answer change if Closely Held sold the policy to Philip for $60,000, rather than selling the policy to John, and Philip made all premium payments until the time of his father's death?

Assignment for Chapter 8, Part A: Life Insurance:

Complete the problems.

Read: Internal Revenue Code: § 101(a), (c), (d); Skim §§ 79, 101(g), 101(j) and 7702
        Treasury Regulations: § 1.101-1(a)(1), -1(b)
        Materials: Overview

II.   VOCABULARY

term insurance
cash value
inside build-up
mortality gains and losses

III.   OBJECTIVES

1. To recall § 101 excludes insurance proceeds paid by reason of the death of the insured.

2. To recall risk-shifting and risk distribution are essential elements of insurance.

3. To determine the tax consequences, given sufficient facts, of life insurance proceeds paid on an installment basis.

4. To construct an example that applies the transfer-for-value rules involving life insurance contracts.

IV. OVERVIEW

A full account of the tax treatment of life insurance would be complex and technical. This overview will instead concentrate on some fundamental rules and leave exploration of the intricacies to other times and places.

With respect to life insurance, the basic rule is clear: life insurance proceeds paid "by reason of the death of the insured" are excluded from gross income. § 101(a)(1). To grasp the full significance of this exclusion, it is helpful to distinguish between the "risk element" and the "savings element" in life insurance. That portion of an insurance premium that purchases insurance against the risk of dying at a given time represents the risk element; that portion, if any, that exceeds the actuarial cost of pure risk insurance represents the savings element.[1] Consider an example of "term insurance." Assume Taxpayer pays a $100 premium for a $50,000 one-year term life insurance policy on his life. If Taxpayer dies during that one-year period, the insurance company pays $50,000 to Taxpayer's beneficiary. If Taxpayer does not die during the one-year period, Taxpayer receives nothing when the year is up, and has no coverage unless the insurance is renewed. In a real sense, of course, it is incorrect to say Taxpayer receives nothing for his $100 premium, since Taxpayer has in fact received the insurance coverage, and the security and peace of mind that come with it. The tax consequences of Taxpayer's dying, or not dying, during the one-year period are straightforward. If Taxpayer dies, his beneficiary receives $50,000 on Taxpayer's $100 "investment," but this $49,900 "mortality gain" is tax-free under § 101(a)(1). Conversely, if Taxpayer survives the period, he has "lost" his $100 bet with the insurance company; and he has a "mortality loss." Taxpayer is ordinarily not entitled to any tax deduction for the premium. It is typically a nondeductible personal expense. § 262.[2] The insurance company, of course, is insuring a great many other taxpayers, and it has set its premium on an actuarially sound basis, so that in the aggregate the premiums collected, and any earnings on them, will not only cover the payments that must be made for taxpayers who "win" their gambles, but pay the company's expenses and provide a profit as well.

Why do the mortality gains for the "winning" taxpayers receive tax-free treatment? A number of reasons could be advanced. Life insurance proceeds might be viewed as somewhat equivalent to gifts and bequests, which are excluded from gross income under § 102. The exclusion of the increase in the "value" of the policy (in our example, from $100 at the time of purchase to $50,000 at death) is similar to the exclusion provided by the basis step-up rules of § 1014 for property passing at death. In addition, by providing tax-free treatment to life insurance proceeds under § 101, and nondeductibility of their premiums under § 262, the whole matter can be

---

[1] An insurance premium also contains a "loading component" that reflects the insurance company's expenses and profit margin. For ease of illustration, we will regard the loading component as simply absorbed within the risk and savings elements of a premium.

[2] In some instances, payment of a premium on life insurance may constitute a deductible expense, as when an employer pays the premium on an employee's life insurance as a form of compensation to the employee. It is assumed in the Overview, however, that the life insurance under discussion is purchased for personal purposes, and that the premiums are nondeductible under § 262. (Even where § 262 is not applicable, deduction of premiums may be disallowed by other provisions. *See, e.g.*, §§ 263(a), 264, 265(a)(1).)

seen, in the aggregate at least, as roughly a wash from the standpoint of the government. Assuming that taxation of the proceeds would entail allowing a deduction for premiums, or for recovery of basis in some fashion, the present system may be viewed as the simplest and most efficient way of addressing the issue. Moreover, we may simply want to use the tax system to encourage people to provide some protection against sudden loss of family earnings. Finally, of course, the circumstances in which life insurance proceeds are received — upon the death of the insured, who may perhaps be the family breadwinner — may obviously be regarded as a particularly inappropriate time to tax the beneficiary.

We have thus far discussed term insurance with a one-year term. Assume Taxpayer, having survived Year 1, wants to take out a $50,000 policy for another year. In that event, all else being equal, Taxpayer's Year 2 premium will be greater than $100 for the simple reason that being one year older has, statistically speaking, increased Taxpayer's risk of dying. Thus, as each year passes, the premium for a one-year term policy on Taxpayer's life will increase. Suppose Taxpayer wishes to buy term insurance for a five-year period, but pay the same premium each year. Since Taxpayer's risk factor increases each year, a level premium means that in the first year the premium must be set at a level that is greater than the actuarial cost of pure risk insurance for that year; the excess portion of the premium, and earnings on it, in effect supplement the later years' premiums which in themselves do not cover the actuarial costs for those years.

The savings element of life insurance is certainly present in the multi-year, level-premium term insurance just discussed. But term insurance builds up no cash value. Other types of life insurance — such as "ordinary life insurance," "whole life insurance," "variable life insurance," "universal life insurance," and numerous variations — are designed to do more than provide risk insurance over a period of time; they also act as investment vehicles. Consider ordinary life insurance in which a constant level premium is paid to provide a given amount of insurance over the life of the insured. The premium paid is necessarily greater than it would be for the same amount of term insurance. Only part of the premium insures the taxpayer against the risk of dying; the remainder is in effect invested by the insurance company on behalf of Taxpayer, and over the years a "cash value" builds up, reflecting not only the excess portions of the premiums, but also the earnings on them. The later the insured's death occurs, the greater is the amount of the insurance proceeds that consists of the cash value build-up. The owner of the policy may typically borrow against the cash value, or obtain it outright by termination of the policy by surrendering it. However, under current law, neither the Taxpayer nor the insurance company is taxed on this "inside build-up" while it accumulates. This tax deferral is a central advantage of savings via life insurance. Suppose, for example, the Taxpayer purchased term insurance, and placed the "excess" portion of the ordinary life insurance premium in the bank to draw interest. The interest on bank savings is taxable, so the bank savings would grow more slowly than the untaxed "savings" invested in life insurance.

Let us test our understanding of the interaction of the risk element and savings element and the § 101(a)(1) exclusion. Assume Taxpayer has owned for 15 years an ordinary life policy with a face value of $50,000, and has paid $1,200 per year, or a total of $18,000, in premiums. Also assume pure risk insurance would have cost only

$10,000, and the insurance company has earned $4,000 for Taxpayer on the "excess" $8,000 in premiums; the cash value is thus $12,000. Taxpayer dies, and his beneficiary receives the $50,000. The tax consequences are clear: the entire $50,000 is tax-free under § 101(a)(1). But what does that $50,000 really consist of?

(1) $8,000:   return of the "excess" portion of the premium;
(2) $4,000:   interest earned by the "excess" amount;
(3) $10,000: return of the term portion of premium;
(4) $28,000: the net mortality gain. (Recall the policy had a cash value of $12,000. Thus, $38,000 of the proceeds are properly allocable to term insurance. Since the actuarial cost of that insurance, on our facts, was $10,000, the net mortality gain was $28,000.)

As noted, mortality gains on life insurance are untaxed. The return of the savings element, the "excess" portion of the premium, is also properly tax-free under normal return-of-capital principles. But why should the *interest* earned on the savings element be tax-exempt rather than merely tax-deferred? Tax reform proposals have often attacked this element of life insurance taxation, and argued no policy justification exists for giving favored treatment to savings in the form of life insurance. It is thus often proposed this *"inside build-up"* in life insurance be currently taxed.

A few additional comments on the scope and operation of the § 101 exclusion are in order. The exclusion applies to the proceeds of "life insurance contracts," a term defined in § 7702. The essential elements of insurance generally are the shifting of risk from policyholder to insurer and the distribution of risk among the policyholders. The purpose of the statutory definition is to permit the full tax advantages associated with life insurance to be available only to those contracts where the risk element is real and substantial, and not to permit what are basically investment programs with a minor life insurance element to qualify as life insurance for tax purposes. Thus, if the contract in question is a life insurance contract under local law, but does not meet the requirements of § 7702, mortality gains are excluded from income, but the interest earnings on the investment portion of the contract are taxed currently to the policyholder; tax-free inside build-up is lost. In this chapter, we will not examine the technical requirements of the definition, but instead shall assume that what is labeled a life insurance contract satisfies § 7702.

Even though the contract in question is a life insurance contract, it is necessary that the proceeds be payable "by reason of the death of the insured" to qualify for the § 101 exclusion. This requirement typically poses no problem. However, suppose a seller of property on the installment basis takes out insurance on the life of the purchaser in an amount equal to the unpaid balance of the purchase price. The Service has ruled such insurance proceeds do not qualify under § 101(a) since they are paid not "by reason of the death of the insured," but rather, in effect, by reason of the unpaid debt; they are instead collections of the unpaid purchase price. Rev. Rul. 70-254, 1970-1 C.B. 31.

Another issue concerns insurance contracts designed to provide, in addition to death benefits, so-called "living benefits" as well. One type of living benefit is an "accelerated death benefit," pursuant to which payment on a policy insuring a terminally ill individual may be "accelerated" — that is, paid prior to death, in recognition of the substantial medical and other expenses that are not infrequently encountered in protracted terminal illnesses. Similar benefits may also be provided to severely disabled chronically ill individuals who may, for example, require long term nursing care or hospitalization. Furthermore, even if such benefits are not available under the terms of the life insurance contract, it may be possible to sell or assign the death benefit under the contract to a third party. Are such pre-death payments or proceeds excludable under § 101(a) as "paid by reason of the death of the insured"? Section 101(g) provides detailed special rules under which the answer is "Yes" for qualifying amounts under a life insurance contract on the life of an insured who is a terminally ill or chronically ill individual. Such amounts will be excluded from income as an amount paid by reason of the death of the insured under § 101(a).

Suppose the insured, who is neither terminally nor chronically ill, surrenders an ordinary life insurance policy for its cash value. It is obvious the proceeds are not payable by reason of death, and § 101 does not apply. What applies instead are the rules of § 72(e), and those rules extend an additional tax advantage to life insurance because they provide the proceeds are taxable only to the extent they exceed the total consideration paid for the policy (*i.e.*, the insured's basis in the policy). § 72(e)(6). In effect, the taxpayer is permitted to deduct otherwise nondeductible premiums! An example: Suppose a taxpayer received $10,000 on the surrender of her ordinary life policy after having paid total premiums over the years equal to $9,000. Assume only $4,000 of the premiums represented the actuarial cost of term insurance. In reality, it is the remaining $5,000 in "savings" that has produced the $10,000 return; thus the return-of-capital amount should be $5,000 and the income reported $5,000. However, by permitting the risk portion of the premium also to offset the $10,000 received, taxable income is only $1,000. The normally nondeductible "mortality loss" of $4,000 is made deductible. By way of contrast, had the taxpayer paid $4,000 for term insurance (and survived) and also paid $5,000 for an investment that grew to $10,000 over the years — and this is the functional equivalent of our example — the reported income would be $5,000 and the cost of term insurance would be nondeductible under § 262.

Life insurance proceeds on account of the insured's death may be paid either in a lump-sum or in installments. Section 101(a)(1) applies to both cases. However, the exclusion is not intended to cover post-death earnings on the proceeds. Thus, interest payments on amounts withheld by the insurer under an agreement to pay interest are taxable. § 101(c). For example, assume life insurance proceeds are $100,000, to be paid to Beneficiary two years after Taxpayer's death. In the interim, Beneficiary receives $6,000 per year interest. The interest payments are taxable; the $100,000 paid two years hence is not. Alternatively, assume life insurance proceeds of $100,000 are to be paid in five annual installments of $25,000 each. In this case, plainly an interest component is built into the installments to compensate for the delayed payment of the death benefits. In effect, § 101(d) here provides that the principal portion of each installment shall be tax-free, and the interest portion taxable. The excluded amount, the "amount held by the insurer" in the statutory phrase, is to be prorated equally over the installments if the installments are for a fixed number of years; the proration will be over the beneficiary's life expectancy (in accordance with the insurer's mortality table) if the installments are to be paid for the life of the beneficiary. Payments in excess of the prorated portions are taxable. Reg. § 1.101-4(a)–(c). This mechanism for distinguishing the taxable portion of a payment from the nontaxable portion is similar to that used with regard to annuities under § 72, and is discussed at greater length below.

To this point, we have assumed Taxpayer was the insured and the owner of the insurance policy. Section 101(a)(1), however, does not require the insured be the owner of the policy, nor does it prohibit the owner of a policy from also being the beneficiary of insurance on the life of another. Thus, if A has an insurable interest in the life of B, A may take out a policy in which B is the insured and A is the beneficiary; the proceeds A receives by reason of B's death will be within the § 101(a)(1) exclusion.[3]

Suppose, however, B subsequently purchased the policy from A. We now must cope with the transfer for value rules of § 101(a)(2). Unless one of the exceptions applies — and you are urged to take a careful look at the exceptions — the exclusion will be limited to the consideration B paid A plus any premiums or other amounts subsequently paid by B. Insurance proceeds in excess of these payments will be taxable. The policy reasons for the transfer-for-value provisions are not completely clear. Legislative history suggests Congress found the prospect of speculating in life insurance sufficiently distasteful to warrant denial of tax free treatment in profitable transactions. Section 101(a)(2), however, applies not just to arm's length commercial transactions, but to intra-family purchases as well. Note that B may avoid the unfavorable tax results of § 101(a)(2) by simply purchasing a new policy directly from the insurer.

Finally, this is an appropriate point to call § 79 to your attention. Congress has encouraged employers to provide group-term life insurance for their employees by treating the employer-paid cost of providing up to $50,000 of such insurance as a tax-free fringe benefit. The employer's cost for insurance in excess of the $50,000 level is taxable compensation. Special rules apply to employee benefit plans that discriminate in favor of so-called "key employees." § 79(d).

---

[3] Note, however, § 101(j), which generally provides that, in the case of employer-owned life insurance contracts, the amount excluded as a death benefit by the applicable policyholder (as defined by § 101(j)(3)(B)) cannot exceed an amount equal to the sum of the premiums and other amounts paid by the policyholder for the contract.

Part B:
Annuities

I. PROBLEMS

1. George Smith pays Friendly Life Insurance $5,000 on January 1 of this year, George's 55th birthday. Friendly agrees to pay George (or his estate) $1,000 a year for ten years. How will the first $1,000 payment be taxed?

2. Suppose, alternatively, George pays Friendly $10,000, and Friendly agrees to pay George $1,000 a year for the rest of George's life. How will the first $1,000 payment be taxed?

3. What tax consequences in Problem 2 if George dies after three payments have been made by Friendly?

4. Assume the facts of Problem 2 and that George is still living 30 years from now. How will the next $1,000 payment he receives be taxed?

5. Suppose George on his 60th birthday pays Friendly $15,000, and Friendly agrees to pay $1,000 a year to George and his wife Susan, or the survivor, for as long as either of them is living. Susan, whose birthday was the day before George's, is 53 years old. How will the first $1,000 payment be taxed?

Assignment for Chapter 8, Part B: Annuities:

Complete the problems.

Read: Internal Revenue Code: § 72(a), (b), (c), (e)(1)–(4); skim § 7520
         Treasury Regulations: § 1.72-1(b), -4(a), -5(a), -6(a), -9 Tables V, VI as necessary
         Materials: Overview

II. VOCABULARY

annuity
exclusion ratio
investment in the contract
expected return
joint and survivor annuity
private annuity

III. OBJECTIVES

1. To give examples of annuities for a fixed term, and of annuities based on life expectancies.

2. To explain the tax treatment of mortality gains and losses under annuity contracts.

3. Given sufficient facts, to determine the exclusion ratio for an annuity and apply that ratio to the payment.

4. To determine the expected return multiple that is applicable to a one-life annuity (Table V) or a joint and survivor annuity (Table VI) using any given ages.

5. To distinguish among the tax treatment of interest on a bank account, interest on a deferred payment annuity, and interest on the savings element in a life insurance policy.

IV. OVERVIEW

An annuity may be defined as a series of payments over a period of time. For tax purposes, the regulations under § 72 describe "amounts received as an annuity" as amounts payable at regular intervals over more than a year, provided the time period or the total amount payable is determinable on the date payments are deemed to begin. Reg. § 1.72-1(b). For example, an annuity might consist of monthly payments for ten years, or for the life of the annuitant. Suppose Taxpayer purchases an annuity for $10,000 from an insurance company. In return, the company agrees to pay Taxpayer $1,000 a year for the next 25 years. Taxpayer will thus receive a total of $25,000 which in substance consists of: (1) a $10,000 return of her investment, which under return-of-capital principles should be tax-free; and (2) a $15,000 profit on her investment, which is the functional equivalent of interest on the $10,000 and properly taxable. The tax question is not whether to tax $15,000 as income; that is a given. The question is really one of timing. Taxpayer will receive $1,000 a year — how should each $1,000 payment be taxed? We could permit the first 10 payments to be received tax-free, and tax fully each of the last 15 payments. In other words, we could permit basis to be recovered first, before imposing any tax. The taxpayer would clearly prefer this approach. We could provide for basis recovery to be last — the revenue collector's choice. Thus, the first 15 payments would be fully taxed as income, and the last 10 payments would be the nontaxable return of basis. We could also choose an in-between method, and prorate the income over the term of the payments. This is the approach taken by § 72. Thus, with a $10,000 investment and $25,000 in total payments, 10/25 (40%) of each payment is nontaxable return of basis. The $15,000 of income is 60% (15/25) of the $25,000 total, so 60% of each payment is income. As a result, $600 of each $1,000 payment is gross income and $400 is nontaxable. At the end of 25 years, Taxpayer will have received $10,000 tax-free ($400 x 25) and been taxed on $15,000 ($600 x 25).

The statutory language that accomplishes this result is in the "exclusion ratio" of § 72(b)(1). It directs us to construct a fraction (the exclusion ratio) in which the numerator is the "investment in the contract" and the denominator is the "expected return" under the contract. These terms, defined in § 72(c)(1) and (c)(3), are $10,000 and $25,000, respectively, in our example. The fraction or exclusion ratio is $10,000/$25,000, or 40%. Section 72(b)(1) provides "that part" (*i.e.*, 40%) of the "amount received as an annuity" (each $1,000 payment) is not gross income. The non-excluded portion is included in gross income pursuant to § 72(a)(1). To summarize, the excluded portion is:

$$\text{Amount received as an annuity} \times \frac{\text{Investment in the Contract}}{\text{Expected Return}} = \text{Amount Excluded}$$

or

$$\$1,000 \times \frac{\$10,000}{\$25,000} = \$400$$

Although this method of spreading income over the term of the payments may seem simple enough, one might, nonetheless, object that it does not really make economic sense: rather than spreading the $15,000 "interest" element evenly over the payments, it would be economically far more realistic to recognize that interest will be greatest in the first year (when the principal sum held by the insurer is greatest) and will decrease thereafter as the remaining principal balance decreases by reason of the $1,000 payments.

The example previously given involved payments over a stated number of years. Suppose, as is commonly the case, the annuity was to be paid for as long as Taxpayer lived. Although we do not know in advance how many years Taxpayer will live, by consulting mortality tables we can determine how many years Taxpayer is actuarially "expected" to live, and can compute an "expected return" under the annuity contract. § 72(c)(3)(A). For example, if we assume Taxpayer is 59 years old on the annuity starting date — See § 72(c)(4) — her "expected return multiple" is 25, and therefore we expect her to receive 25 payments of $1,000, or $25,000. Reg. § 1.72-9, Table V. The exclusion ratio under § 72(b)(1) would be 40%, just as before, and $400 of each $1,000 payment she received would be excluded from income.

Suppose, as is likely to be the case, that Taxpayer lives for something more or less than 25 years. Living more than 25 years will result in a "mortality gain" for Taxpayer — more than the expected 25 payments; living less than 25 years will cause a "mortality loss" to Taxpayer. (Thus, with life insurance Taxpayer bets on an early death; with a lifetime annuity Taxpayer gambles on a long life). How should the matter of mortality gains and losses on annuities be treated for tax purposes?

Given the uncertainty, it might be tempting to levy no tax at all until Taxpayer had recovered her investment. This is how annuities were taxed before there was any annuity provision in the Code. In 1934, however, Congress chose to tax annuities by treating as income that portion of each annuity payment that equalled 3% of the consideration paid for the annuity; the excess portion of each payment was tax-free until the consideration was recovered, and then the payment was entirely taxable. In 1954, Congress adopted the exclusion ratio mechanism described above and set forth in present § 72(b)(1). Prior to 1986, however, mortality gains and losses under annuity contracts were effectively ignored — that is, a taxpayer who died before having fully recovered her investment in the contract received no deduction for the unrecovered basis; conversely, a taxpayer who outlived her life expectancy, and had fully recovered her investment, was nonetheless permitted to continue to apply the exclusion ratio to subsequent payments — in other words, to recover more than her investment tax-free. Congress changed these rules on mortality gains and losses in 1986 to provide that, once investment in the annuity contract is fully recovered, further payments are fully taxable. § 72(b)(2). If a taxpayer dies before fully recovering her investment, the unrecovered investment is deductible for her last tax year. § 72(b)(3). In our example, if Taxpayer survives 25 years, the full $1,000 will be taxable starting with the 26th payment. On the other hand, if Taxpayer dies after receiving 20 payments, her recovered amount is only $8,000 ($400 x 20); the unrecovered investment of $2,000 will be deductible for her last taxable year.

A few additional points. Many annuities are two-life joint and survivor annuities — that is, payable for the life of the survivor of two persons. Table VI in the regulations tells us what the expected return multiples are in that case. For example, if an annuity is payable for the life of the survivor of Taxpayer and

Spouse, and if on the annuity starting date, Taxpayer is 58 and Spouse is 54, the multiple is 33.6 (or in our $1,000 annual payment example, there is an expected return of $33,600).

We have also to this point assumed our lifetime annuities have no "refund feature." For example, if Taxpayer pays $10,000 for a lifetime annuity of $1,000 per year, but dies after receiving only one payment, we have assumed Taxpayer in effect simply "loses" $9,000. It is far more likely that the annuity contract contains a refund feature of some sort. For example, the insurer may guarantee payments for a certain number of years, or guarantee that, if the consideration paid exceeds the amounts paid out up to death, the excess will be paid to the annuitant's estate or beneficiary. The presence of a refund feature requires that the "investment in the contract" (used in computing the exclusion ratio) be decreased. § 72(c)(2)(A). Decreasing the investment in the contract reduces the exclusion ratio fraction, and thus reduces the amount of each annuity payment excluded from income.

Annuities provide excellent tax advantages. Annuities are typically deferred payment annuities; premiums are paid in for a number of years before payment commences. During those "pay in" years the premiums are earning investment income free of tax, and the earnings are not taxed until the annuity starting date. At one time, funds withdrawn before the annuity starting date were simply treated as tax-free returns-of-capital up to the amount of the taxpayer's investment. This was perceived as an abuse of the annuity rules, and now such withdrawals (including loans) are taxable to the extent of earnings on the investment. § 72(e)(2), (3), (4). Moreover, premature distributions from an annuity contract may also be subject to a 10% penalty tax. § 72(q). Nonetheless, the tax-deferral on annuity earnings prior to payment makes annuities an attractive long-term investment. Employer pension plans, for example, are often funded by means of annuity contracts. So-called "qualified" pension plans enjoy favored tax treatment, but they must comply with a great number of special requirements. *See* § 401. To make it less attractive to employers to use deferred annuity contracts as a way to fund nonqualified pensions for the benefit of highly compensated employees — and thus avoid the requirements and limitations of qualified pension plans, while still obtaining the tax deferral benefits of such annuities — Congress enacted § 72(u). Under that provision, subject to some exceptions, investment earnings are subject to tax on a current basis if the annuity contract is not held by a natural person — if, for example, it is held by a corporation.

Annuities are ordinarily issued by commercial insurers, but § 72 and its fundamental tax rules apply to so-called private annuities as well. However, private annuities may raise some additional tax issues. For example, when one person transfers money or property to another in return for an annuity, the parties may not be dealing at arm's length, and the money or property transferred may be worth more or less than the annuity received; the question thus arises as to how the differential is characterized for tax purposes. Is it a gift, dividend, compensation, etc.?

Part C:
Individual Retirement Accounts

I. PROBLEMS

1. Ron (age 52) and Mary (age 48) filed a joint return and had an adjusted gross income for IRA purposes of $155,000. Ron, an active participant in a pension plan, had gross income from compensation of $80,000; Mary's gross income from compensation was $70,000. She was not an active participant in a pension plan. How much may each of them contribute, alternatively, to a deductible IRA, a nondeductible IRA, and a Roth IRA?

2. Grace receives a distribution of $20,000 from her IRA. Prior to the distribution, her account balance in the IRA was $100,000, consisting of her contributions over the years, totaling $60,000, and the earnings thereon, totaling $40,000. Assume this is her only IRA, and that her account balance at the end of the year is $80,000. How will the $20,000 distribution be taxed? Assume, alternatively, that (1) the distribution is a qualified distribution from a Roth IRA; (2) the distribution is from a deductible IRA — *i.e.*, all contributions to the IRA were deductible; and (3) the distribution is from a nondeductible IRA — *i.e.*, the IRA is not a Roth IRA and all contributions to the IRA were nondeductible.

3. How would your answer to Problem (2) change if the distribution were a nonqualified distribution (with respect to the Roth IRA) or if the "early distribution" penalty of § 72(t) applied (with respect to the deductible IRA and the nondeductible IRA)?

Assignment for Chapter 8, Part C: Individual Retirement Accounts

Complete the Problems.

Read: Internal Revenue Code: §§ 219(a), (b)(1), (b)(5), (c), (d)(1), (e)(1), (g); 408(a), (b), (d)(1), (2), (e)(1), (o); 408A(a), (b), (c)(1)–(5), (d)(1), (2); 72(t)(1), (2), (10); 7701(a)(37).
Review as necessary § 72(a)–(c), (e).
Materials: Overview

II. VOCABULARY

deductible IRA

nondeductible IRA

Roth IRA

III. OBJECTIVES

1. To determine the maximum contribution an individual may make to a deductible IRA, a nondeductible IRA and a Roth IRA.

2. To determine an individual's eligibility to contribute to a deductible IRA or a Roth IRA.

3. To describe the tax treatment of contributions to, and distributions from, a deductible IRA, a nondeductible IRA and a Roth IRA.

IV. OVERVIEW

As an encouragement to savings and investment, principally for retirement purposes, Congress has authorized tax-favored devices commonly known as "IRAs" (individual retirement accounts or annuities) to which taxpayers may make annual above-the-line contributions of up to $5,000, with adjustments for inflation. § 219(b)(1), (5)(A), (5)(C).[4] There are various types of IRAs, with differing tax attributes. All IRAs share with annuities the tax advantage that funds invested in an IRA grow on a tax-free basis until distributed. In this Overview we consider the deductible IRA, the nondeductible IRA and the Roth IRA.[5]

Deductible IRAs. Section 219 authorizes an annual deduction of up to $5,000 adjusted for inflation for qualifying cash contributions to an IRA.[6] The deduction, however, is phased out where the taxpayer, or the taxpayer's spouse, is an active participant in certain pension plans and has a specially computed adjusted gross income in excess of a specified dollar amount. § 219(g). For example, for 2007 and thereafter, and as adjusted for inflation, the "applicable dollar amount" for a taxpayer who is an active participant and is filing a joint return is $80,000. At that level, the § 219 deduction limit of $5,000 starts to phase out, and is reduced to zero when adjusted gross income exceeds the applicable dollar amount by $20,000. (Note that a separate, much higher, inflation-adjusted applicable dollar amount of $150,000 applies to a taxpayer who is not an active participant and is filing a joint return. § 219(g)(7), (8).) No deduction is allowed for contributions once the taxpayer reaches age 70½. § 219(d). The amount allowable as a deduction cannot in any event exceed the taxpayer's compensation income. § 219(b)(1). However, for married persons filing a joint return the compensation of the taxpayer's spouse is taken into account in determining compensation. § 219(c). In effect, a homemaker spouse with no employment income is thus allowed to contribute up to an inflation-adjusted $5,000 per year to an IRA.

The deductible limit noted in the previous paragraph is increased for taxpayers age 50 or older by $1,000. § 219(b)(5)(B). Thus, the $5,000 limit becomes a $6,000 limit for an individual 50 or older.

The individual retirement accounts themselves are subject to the rules of § 408. Under § 408(e)(1), the accounts are exempt from taxation. The accrued income in an IRA is not taxed until distributed. Distributions from IRAs are includable in gross income under the annuity rules of § 72. § 408(d)(1). (There are provisions, however, not discussed here, under which distributions may be "rolled over" to other IRAs or other qualified retirement plans on a tax-free basis.) Thus, where the contributions to an IRA are deductible, and the income accrued by the IRA has not been taxed, all distributions from the IRA will be fully taxable. The investment- for-retirement

---

[4] Section 7701(a)(37) defines the term "individual retirement plan" to include individual retirement accounts, described in § 408(a), and individual retirement annuities, described in § 408(b). For convenience, we will simply refer to them as IRAs.

[5] So-called "Coverdell Education Savings Accounts," authorized by § 530, will be summarized in Chapter 18. These are tax-favored vehicles to pay for higher education expenses. Their provisions are not coordinated with those of the IRAs discussed in this Overview.

[6] A limited credit for IRA contributions is also available for lower-income taxpayers whose adjusted gross incomes do not exceed specified limits. § 25B(a), (b).

purpose of the IRA is effectuated in two ways. Distributions from an IRA must commence by April 1 of the year following the year the taxpayer reaches age 70½. §§ 401(a)(9)(C), 408(a)(6), (b)(3); Reg. § 1.408-8 Q&A 3. There is, conversely, a 10% penalty tax on "early distributions" from an IRA. §§ 72(t), 4974(c). The penalty, which applies only to the income portion of the distribution, does not apply to distributions after age 59½, or on retirement after reaching age 55, or in certain other enumerated circumstances. § 72(t)(2). Recall that a similar penalty tax applies to early distributions from an annuity that is not an IRA. *See* § 72(q).

Nondeductible IRAs. Active participants in certain pension plans, with adjusted gross incomes greater than the phase-out limits, cannot make deductible contributions to IRAs. Such taxpayers are, however, permitted to make nondeductible contributions to an IRA. *See* § 408(o). Total annual contributions, deductible and nondeductible, which a taxpayer makes to one or more IRAs cannot exceed $5,000, as adjusted for inflation. § 408(o)(2). The increased limit for those 50 or older, noted above, applies here as well. As is the case with deductible contributions, nondeductible contributions cannot be made once the taxpayer reaches age 70½. Although contributions to a nondeductible IRA do not have the benefit of deductibility, they at least enjoy the advantage of tax-deferral: the income earned by the IRA is not currently taxed and thus grows tax-free until distribution. Under the annuity rules of § 72, pursuant to § 408(d)(1), distributions attributable to nondeductible contributions are prorated between the contributions and the income earned on them, and such distributions are thus taxable only to the extent of the income portion. "Early distributions" are subject to the 10% penalty tax noted above with respect to the income portion of a distribution, and mandatory distributions must commence by April 1 of the year following the year the taxpayer reaches age 70½.

Roth IRAs. The 1997 Tax Act created a new type of IRA known as a "Roth IRA." A Roth IRA must be so designated when it is established. § 408A(b). Contributions to Roth IRAs are nondeductible. § 408A(c)(1). However, the distinguishing feature of a Roth IRA is that qualifying distributions from a Roth IRA are completely tax-free.

Contributions to all of one's IRAs — deductible, nondeductible, Roth — cannot exceed the contribution limits noted above. (The special increase limit for individuals 50 or over, noted previously, applies to Roth IRAs). *See* § 408A(c)(2). Contributions to a Roth IRA are further limited based on the taxpayer's modified adjusted gross income. In the case of a joint return, for example, the maximum contribution is phased out to zero for an inflation-adjusted modified adjusted gross income between $150,000 and $160,000. § 408A(c)(3). ("Rollovers" to a Roth IRA from another IRA are not subject to the contribution limitations based on modified adjusted gross income.)

"Qualified distributions" from a Roth IRA are excluded from income. § 408A(d)(1)(A). In general, qualified distributions are those that meet two conditions: (1) They satisfy a 5-year holding period, *i.e.*, they do not take place within the 5-tax-year period that begins with the first tax year for which a contribution is made to a Roth IRA; and (2) they are made after the taxpayer attains age 59½, dies, or is disabled. § 408A(d)(2). (Under an additional exception, distributions to pay for "qualified first-time homebuyer expenses," as defined in § 72(t)(2)(F), may also constitute qualified distributions. § 408A(d)(2)(A)(iv), 408A(d)(5).) Furthermore, unlike the deductible and nondeductible IRAs, contributions may be made to a Roth IRA after age 70½, and there is no requirement that distributions from a Roth IRA commence once the taxpayer reaches 70½. § 408A(c)(4), (5). These features somewhat undercut the retirement-income purpose of an IRA.

Because of the rules relating to income limits and to active-participant status, some taxpayers will not be able in a given year to make a contribution either to a deductible IRA or to a Roth IRA. For those taxpayers, only the nondeductible IRA will be available that year. Other taxpayers may be eligible to make a contribution to a Roth IRA, but not to a deductible IRA; given the potential tax-exempt treatment of the earnings, such taxpayers may choose to make a contribution to a Roth IRA rather than to a traditional nondeductible IRA. Similarly, those taxpayers eligible to make contributions to a deductible IRA because they are not active participants, but ineligible to contribute to a Roth IRA because of their income levels, would presumably choose the deductible rather than the nondeductible IRA. Finally, some taxpayers may have the choice between contribution to a deductible IRA or to a Roth IRA. Assuming full funding, identical investment results and unchanging tax rates, a present value analysis indicates that they will achieve identical economic results. However, given such factors as the unpredictability of future tax rates and each individual taxpayer's interest or lack of interest in an immediate deduction, one can anticipate that different taxpayers will make different choices.

Chapter 9

DISCHARGE OF INDEBTEDNESS

I. PROBLEMS

1. Donald borrowed $5,000 three years ago to assist his daughter who had incurred significant legal fees in a divorce battle. After repaying $3,000 of the loan, Donald was forced to resign from his job for health reasons and, although he was not technically insolvent, Donald was unable to continue to make payments on the loan. Under the circumstances, the lender forgave the balance of the loan. What tax consequences to Donald if the lender were: (a) a local bank; (b) Donald's employer; or (c) Donald's brother?

2. Kevin received a bill for $10,000 for landscaping work done on his personal residence. Kevin, who was unhappy with the quality of the work, refused to pay the $10,000. The landscaper reduced the bill to $6,000 and Kevin paid that amount.

   (a) Assuming Kevin is solvent, does Kevin have discharge of indebtedness income under these circumstances?

   (b) How would your answer to (a) change, if at all, if the landscaper first succeeded in getting a judgment against Kevin for the full $10,000 and only thereafter agreed to the $6,000 payment in settlement of the dispute when Kevin threatened to appeal the judgment?

   (c) How would your answer to (a) change, if at all, if the landscaping work had been done on Kevin's business premises, Kevin did not dispute the amount owed but the landscaper, because of Kevin's cash flow problems, was willing to accept a $6,000 payment in satisfaction of the $10,000 bill. Assume Kevin would be entitled to deduct the cost of the landscaping work as a business expense.

3. In connection with her business, Samantha borrowed $50,000 from Lender last year, giving Lender an unsecured note in that amount. This year, because of a deteriorating economic climate, Lender agreed to accept $25,000 in cash from Samantha in full settlement of the note on which Samantha still owed $45,000.

   (a) Assume Samantha is solvent. Does she have discharge of indebtedness income?

   (b) Would your answer change if, instead of Samantha paying Lender $25,000, Samantha's parents purchased Samantha's note from Lender for $25,000 and then promptly forgave Samantha the amount owing under the note?

4. Allison, whose principal residence is New York City, purchased from Anthony a two-bedroom condominium in East Hampton, New York, which Allison uses on weekends and holidays during the year. The purchase price of the East Hampton condominium was $1,000,000. Allison paid Anthony $100,000 as a downpayment on the condominium and agreed to pay him the $900,000 balance over the next 15 years together with a market rate of interest on the unpaid balance. This year, when the principal balance owing on the condominium was $750,000, the fair market value of the condominium fell to $650,000 because of a dramatic downturn in the economy. As a result, Allison was prepared to default on her contract with Anthony. To prevent a default, Anthony agreed to forgive $100,000 of the balance owing by Allison on the contract and to recalculate Allison's monthly payments accordingly. Assume Allison is solvent. What are the tax consequences, if any, to Allison as a result of the $100,000 of debt forgiveness?

5. When housing prices were high, Roger purchased a home in Seattle for $900,000, making that home his principal residence. Roger paid $150,000 of his own money as a downpayment on the home, borrowed the other $750,000 of the purchase price from a Seattle bank, and gave the bank a mortgage on the Seattle home. Three years later, as a result of a decline in the Seattle housing market when a major employer left the area, Roger's home has a fair market value of only $600,000. Roger still owes $700,000 on the bank loan he used to acquire the home. Concerned the Seattle housing market would only continue to deteriorate, Roger ceased making payments on the bank loan. The bank foreclosed on the loan. At the foreclosure sale, the bank sold the home for $550,000. The bank forgave the remaining $150,000 Roger owed it.

   (a) What are the tax consequences, if any, to Roger on the forgiveness of $150,000 of his indebtedness to the Seattle bank?

   (b) How would your answers to (a) change, if at all, if, instead of foreclosing on the loan, the Seattle bank restructured the loan, forgiving $150,000 of the $700,000 balance owing by Roger?

6. Bill borrowed $200,000 from Judy and later, when Bill was insolvent, Judy accepted a tract of unimproved land from Bill in satisfaction of the debt. The land, which Bill had purchased as an investment for $50,000, had an appraised fair market value of $150,000 at the time Judy received it. Immediately prior to the transaction, Bill's liabilities included the $200,000 debt to Judy and $50,000 of indebtedness to other parties. In addition, however, Bill had guaranteed repayment of a $25,000 bank loan his son had taken out. The loan comes due in the near future, and the son estimates there is a "50/50 chance" he can repay it. Other than the tract of land Bill transferred to Judy, Bill's only other assets are his personal property including his cars and household furnishings, which have a total value of $75,000. As a result of Judy's acceptance of the land in satisfaction of the debt, these items of personal property are now Bill's only assets. He continues to owe $50,000 to third parties and to be the guarantor of his son's $25,000 loan.

    (a) How much discharge of indebtedness income, if any, must Bill report as a result of the settlement of the debt owed to Judy? Does he have any other income?

    (b) What basis will Judy take in the land she received from Bill?

7. Lloyd is a professional actor. At a time when his liabilities exceeded the fair market value of his assets, Lloyd received $10,000 for his appearance in a toothpaste commercial Even after receiving this money, Lloyd remained insolvent. What are the tax consequences to Lloyd of receiving the $10,000? Does your answer change if Lloyd owed $10,000 to the producer of the commercial and the producer canceled this debt in lieu of paying $10,000 to Lloyd?

Assignment for Chapter 9:

Complete the problems.

Read: Internal Revenue Code: §§ 61(a)(12); 102(a); 108(a), (d)(1)–(3), (d)(9), (e)(1), (2), (4) and (5), (f)(1)–(3), (h); skim §§ 108(b)(1), (2), (3)(A), (c), (i)(1), (3)–(5)(A), (B); 1017(a), (b)(1), (b)(2), (b)(3)(A) and (B).
Treasury Regulations: § 1.61-12(a); § 1.108-2(a), (b); § 1.1001-2(a)(1)–(4)(iii), -(2)(c) Ex. 8; skim § 1.1017-1(a)(1), (2).

    Materials: Overview
             United States v. Kirby Lumber Co.
             Revenue Ruling 84-176
             Gehl v. Commissioner

II. VOCABULARY

insolvency
income from the discharge of indebtedness

III. OBJECTIVES

1. To recall that § 61(a)(12) specifically includes in gross income "income from the discharge of indebtedness."

2. To explain why the forgiveness of debt may constitute income.

3. To explain the reasoning of the Supreme Court in *Kirby Lumber Co.* and *Kerbaugh-Empire* and to evaluate the soundness of that reasoning.

4. To distinguish situations in which the cancellation of indebtedness should be held to constitute a gift or compensation from situations in which it should be treated as income from the discharge of indebtedness under § 61(a)(12).

5. To explain and apply the insolvency exclusion of § 108(a).

6. To explain and apply the retroactive purchase price reduction exception of § 108(e)(5).

7. To explain and apply the exception for deductible items provided in § 108(e)(2).

8. To explain and apply the related party rules of § 108(e)(4).

9. To explain and apply the special rule of § 108(h) relating to qualified principal residence indebtedness.

10. To explain and apply the rule of § 108(f) as it relates to the discharge of certain student loans.

IV.   OVERVIEW

As you learned in Chapter 3, loan proceeds do not constitute gross income nor is a deduction allowed when loans are repaid. Raised but unanswered by that chapter was an important question: does the forgiveness of all or part of the loan generate income? If asked the question now, you would likely answer that one who borrows more than he is required to pay back has obviously been enriched and therefore must report income. In support of your answer, you might cite *Glenshaw Glass*. Although your answer is reasonable, it is not completely accurate.

The history of the legislative, judicial and administrative treatment of the forgiveness of debt is rife with confusion and inconsistency. The courts have been ambivalent regarding the proper treatment of debt forgiveness. A brief review of the pertinent case law is revealing.

In its 1926 decision in *Bowers v. Kerbaugh-Empire Co.*, 271 U.S. 170, the Supreme Court considered whether a taxpayer who borrowed money repayable in German marks realized income when the taxpayer repaid the loan with greatly devalued marks. Stated another way, did the taxpayer have income because it required far fewer dollars to repay the loan than the dollar equivalent of the original loan proceeds? The Court ruled for the taxpayer. It reasoned that because the borrowed money was entirely lost in a business venture, repayment of the loan with devalued marks only reduced the taxpayer's loss. The Court concluded "the mere diminution of loss is not gain, profit or income."

On the bare facts of *Kerbaugh-Empire*, one may have concluded that no income should be realized if the taxpayer borrowed X marks and repaid X marks. Note, however, in finding for the taxpayer, the Court did not adopt that simple rationale. Why? Because our tax system computes gain, loss, and income in terms of dollars — not foreign currency. Thus, in *Kerbaugh-Empire*, the taxpayer was deemed to have borrowed X dollars but to have repaid only Y dollars. It is the excess of the X dollars deemed borrowed over the Y dollars deemed repaid that concerned the Commissioner and was addressed by the Court. Query: Would there be any income tax issue if the taxpayer had actually borrowed dollars and repaid the same amount of dollars but, because of inflation, the dollars used to repay the loan had a purchasing power equal to less than half of the purchasing power of the dollars borrowed? Does the Internal Revenue Code pervasively address distortions created by inflation?[1]

Consider the emphasis the Court in *Kerbaugh-Empire* placed on the fact the borrowed funds were lost in an unsuccessful enterprise. Should the success of a venture to which borrowed funds are applied be relevant to a determination of whether income is triggered when one repays less than the amount borrowed? Theoretically, it should not. The exclusion of loan proceeds from income is based on the existence of an offsetting obligation to repay the loan. If the loan is not repaid in full, then the taxpayer-debtor should be required to report the excess of the loan proceeds over the amount repaid as income.

---

[1] See M. Chirelstein, Federal Income Taxation, Sec. 3.01 (Current Edition), for an enlightening discussion of that issue.

In *U.S. v. Kirby Lumber Co.*, included in the materials, the Supreme Court had an opportunity to reconsider the *Kerbaugh-Empire* treatment of debt repayment. Instead, the Court chose to distinguish that case, thus assuring its continued viability. In cursory fashion, the Court in *Kirby Lumber* held the repayment of a corporate debt at less than its face amount constituted income. Read the opinion carefully. Can you explain the reasoning of the Court? Note Reg. § 1.61-12(a).

While the Court's reasoning in *Kirby Lumber* is not entirely clear, the Court's holding emphasizes that the taxpayer was solvent at all relevant times and that the balance sheet of the taxpayer reflected an increased net worth (or a "clear gain" in the Court's words) as a result of the reduction of liabilities without a dollar-for-dollar reduction of assets. As noted by the Ninth Circuit in *Merkel v. Commissioner*, 192 F.3d 844, 849 (9th Cir. 1999): "The reasoning in *Kirby Lumber* has been called the 'freeing-of-assets' theory. Under this theory, a taxpayer realizes gain when a debt is discharged because after the discharge the taxpayer has fewer liabilities to offset her assets. The taxpayer's existing assets, which otherwise would have gone toward repaying the debt, are freed." As with *Kerbaugh-Empire*, one may ask why the "freeing of assets" should be significant in determining whether income is realized when one repays less than one has borrowed. Conceptually, the "freeing of assets" should not make a difference. But *Kirby Lumber* teaches that it does and its "freeing-of-assets" rationale has proven a lasting and, arguably, an unfortunate legacy.

In adding § 61(a)(12), providing "income from discharge of indebtedness" constitutes income, Congress in 1954 did not alter the effect of either *Kirby Lumber* or *Kerbaugh-Empire*. Rather, Congress merely codified the notion that under some circumstances the discharge of indebtedness constitutes income. Congress made no effort to identify those circumstances, apparently assuming the courts and the Treasury would hammer out that detail. They have, and *Kirby Lumber* and *Kerbaugh-Empire* are part of the detail. Congress, however, re-entered the picture in 1980 by enacting § 108 providing an exclusion from gross income when discharge of indebtedness occurs in certain listed circumstances, including bankruptcy or insolvency.

A. Specific Rules Governing Exclusion

1. Discharge of Indebtedness When Taxpayer Is Insolvent

Assume A, who leases a commercial building from B, has fallen substantially behind in his lease payments. Assume also, at the beginning of this year, A is insolvent and A and B negotiate a settlement whereby A agrees to pay B 25% of the lease payments in arrears and B, hoping to keep A occupying the building, agrees to cancel the balance of the delinquent payments and to reduce A's rent in the future. Even after the cancellation, however, A remains insolvent. Does A have income as a result of this cancellation of debt? Is this a *Kirby Lumber* case or is it closer to *Kerbaugh-Empire*?

In the example, A has had the beneficial use of B's property, but, considering the cancellation, is not returning to B equal value. On similar facts, the Commissioner in *Dallas Transfer and Terminal Warehouse v. Commissioner*, 70 F.2d 95 (5th Cir.

1934), argued a lessee-taxpayer had income. Rejecting the Commissioner's argument, the Fifth Circuit compared the situation to a bankruptcy proceeding where a debtor surrenders property to pay part of his debts and the remainder of the debts are discharged. Citing *Eisner v. Macomber*, the court reasoned the discharge of debt "did not result in the debtor acquiring something of exchangeable value in addition to what he had before. There is a reduction or extinguishment of liabilities without any increase of assets. There is an absence of such gain or profit as is required to come within the accepted definition of income." The Fifth Circuit, distinguishing *Kirby Lumber*, noted that Kirby Lumber's "assets having been increased by the cash received for the bonds, by the repurchase of some of those bonds at less than par, the taxpayer, to the extent of the difference between what it received for those bonds and what it paid in repurchasing them, had an asset which had ceased to be offset by any liability, with a result that after that transaction *the taxpayer had greater assets than it had before.*" (Emphasis added). *Id.* at 96.

Cases like *Dallas Transfer & Terminal Warehouse Co.* established that, if a taxpayer were insolvent both before and after the discharge or cancellation of a debt, no income resulted.[2] While it might be viewed as mean-spirited for the courts to find income when debt is discharged in such insolvency circumstances, isn't that the theoretically correct result?

Let's modify the above example slightly and assume, as a result of the discharge, A is again solvent. Now is there income and, if so, how much? In *Lakeland Grocery Co. v. Commissioner*, 36 B.T.A. 289 (1937), the United States Board of Tax Appeals held a debtor realized income to the extent that the discharge of indebtedness made the debtor solvent. In *Lakeland Grocery*, the creditors seeking to permit the taxpayer to remain in business agreed to a plan resulting in the forgiveness of approximately $90,000 of debt. As a result, the taxpayer-debtor became solvent to the extent of almost $40,000. Relying on *Kirby Lumber Co.*, the Board of Tax Appeals concluded the taxpayer had realized approximately $40,000 of gain when "it obtained assets clear of liabilities." Thus, synthesizing the *Dallas Transfer & Terminal Warehouse Co.* and the *Lakeland Grocery* line of cases, one could define the judicially developed "insolvency exception" as follows: "No income arises from discharge of indebtedness if the debtor is insolvent both before and after the transaction; and if the transaction leaves the debtor with assets whose value exceeds remaining liabilities, income is realized only to that extent."[3]

In 1980, Congress specifically addressed the discharge of indebtedness of bankrupt or insolvent taxpayers by enacting § 108. That section not only codifies the judicial and administrative exclusions discussed previously, but literally replaces them. Thus, except as provided in § 108, there is "no insolvency exception from the general rule that gross income includes income from the discharge of indebtedness." § 108(e)(1).

---

[2] *See Main Properties, Inc.*, 4 T.C. 364 (1944); *Highland Farms Corporation*, 42 B.T.A. 1314 (1940); *see also* I.T. 1564, II-1 C.B. 59 (1923) (holding that "a taxpayer receives no income by virtue of a discharge of indebtedness resulting from an adjudication in bankruptcy"). While the ruling was later declared obsolete, it demonstrates the longstanding recognition of an insolvency exception.

[3] S. Rpt. 96-1035, 1980-2 C.B. at 623.

Section 108(a)(1) specifically provides the discharge of indebtedness will not generate gross income if "the discharge occurs in a title 11 [bankruptcy] case" or if "the discharge occurs when the taxpayer is insolvent." Note that § 108(a)(3), like *Lakeland Grocery*, limits the insolvency exclusion to "the amount by which the taxpayer is insolvent." Section 108(d)(3) defines "insolvent" to mean "the excess of liabilities over the fair market value of assets." The determination of this excess is "determined on the basis of the taxpayer's assets and liabilities immediately before the discharge."

In *Merkel v. Commissioner*, 109 T.C. 463 (1997), *aff'd* 192 F.3d 844 (9th Cir. 1999), the Tax Court provided the following example: Assume a debtor has indebtedness of $100 owed to C, assets of $130, and another liability of $100. Assume C discharges the debtor of the indebtedness for payment of $20. The statutory insolvency calculation would provide the debtor is insolvent by $70 ($200 − $130) and the amount of the exclusion under § 108(a)(1)(B) would be limited to that amount pursuant to § 108(a)(3); the debtor under § 61(a)(12) realizes $80 ($100 − $20) of income and excludes $70 of that amount under § 108(a)(1)(B) for net income recognition of $10.

Merkel v. Commissioner is a case of first impression addressing the issue of whether contingent liabilities, *e.g.*, the potential liability a taxpayer may have as a result of personally guaranteeing another person's loan, should be treated as "liabilities" for purposes of applying the insolvency exception under § 108(a)(1)(B). The Ninth Circuit affirmed the Tax Court determination that, to claim the benefit of the insolvency exclusion, the taxpayer must prove "with respect to any obligation claimed to be a liability, that, as of the [insolvency] calculation date, it is more probable than not that he will be called upon to pay that obligation in the amount claimed." The Ninth Circuit noted:

> The origins of § 108(a)(1)(B) demonstrate that Congress intended for only those liabilities in the amount that actually offset assets to be considered in calculating insolvency for purposes of the income tax exclusion. We agree with the Tax Court's conclusion that "an indiscriminate inclusion of obligations to pay . . . in the statutory insolvency calculation . . . without any consideration of how speculative those obligations may be, would render meaningless any inquiry into whether assets are freed upon the discharge of indebtedness." We also agree, based on Congress' purpose of not burdening an insolvent debtor with an immediate tax liability, that Congress considered a debtor's ability to pay an immediate tax on discharge of indebtedness income the "controlling factor" in determining whether the § 108(a)(1)(B) exception applies. Accordingly, a taxpayer claiming to be insolvent for purposes of § 108(a)(1)(B) and challenging the Commissioner's determination of deficiency must prove by a preponderance of the evidence that he or she will be called upon to pay an obligation claimed to be a liability and that the total amount of liabilities so proved exceed the fair market value of his or her assets.[4]

---

[4] 192 F.3d at 850.

The relief afforded debtors by § 108(a), however, is not without its costs. Specifically, § 108(b) requires certain tax attributes of the taxpayer-debtor be reduced. While the reduction rules are complex and the detail is beyond the scope of this course, you should note that among the tax attributes subject to reduction is the taxpayer's basis in property. § 108(b)(2)(E). (For provisions governing the reduction of basis, see § 1017.) The effect of reducing a taxpayer's basis in property is, of course, either to increase the gain realized or decrease the loss realized when taxpayer sells, exchanges or otherwise disposes of the property. In addition, if the property is depreciable property, reduction in basis will decrease the total amount of depreciation deductions allowable. We will study depreciation in detail in Chapter 14. Thus, § 108, rather than always providing a permanent exclusion for income, typically merely defers reporting of income and may reduce other tax benefits such as depreciation deductions.[5]

Consider the following example. Kevin borrowed $150,000 from Bill. Later, when Kevin was insolvent, Bill accepted $75,000 from Kevin in satisfaction of the debt. Immediately prior to Kevin's payment to Bill, Kevin's assets consisted of $100,000 in cash and business equipment worth $40,000 with an adjusted basis of $60,000. Thus, Kevin's assets totaled $140,000 and his liability to Bill was $150,000, leaving Kevin insolvent to the extent of $10,000. As a result of Bill's forgiveness of $75,000 of the debt, Kevin is solvent to the extent of $65,000, *i.e.*, Kevin has $25,000 of cash and business equipment worth $40,000. Under these circumstances, § 108(a)(3) will exclude only $10,000 of the $75,000 of canceled debt. Kevin will thus have $65,000 of cancellation of indebtedness income. As a result of the operation of § 108(b)(2)(E) and § 1017(b)(2), Kevin's adjusted basis in the equipment will be reduced to $50,000. Thus, although Kevin has avoided recognition of $10,000 in income, there is a price to be paid, *i.e.*, the reduction in the basis of the equipment. As a result of that reduction, Kevin will ultimately lose $10,000 in depreciation deductions, *i.e.*, he will only be allowed $50,000 in depreciation deductions instead of $60,000 with respect to the property. Alternatively, if Kevin were to sell the equipment the following year for its fair market value of $40,000, he would report a $10,000 loss (amount realized of $40,000 less adjusted basis of $50,000) rather than a $20,000 loss (amount realized of $40,000 less adjusted basis of $60,000).

2.   Disputed or Contested Debts

If the amount of a debt is disputed, settlement of the amount does not constitute a discharge of indebtedness. As noted by the Tenth Circuit in *Preslar v. Commissioner*,[6]

The "contested liability" or, as it is occasionally known, "disputed debt" doctrine rests on the premise that if a taxpayer disputes the original

---

[5] Section 108(b)(2)(E) cross references the basis adjustment rules of § 1017, which authorize regulations that determine the properties subject to basis reduction. § 1017(b)(1); Reg. § 1.1017-1. Section 1017 also provides a special rule in bankruptcy or insolvency cases that generally limits the required basis reduction to the excess of the taxpayer's aggregate property bases over the taxpayer's aggregate liabilities. § 1017(b)(2). In effect, to the extent this special rule is applicable, the taxpayer is able to exclude debt discharge from income without making a corresponding basis reduction.

[6] 167 F.3d 1323, 1327–28 (10th Cir. 1999).

amount of a debt in good faith, a subsequent settlement of that dispute is "treated as the amount of debt cognizable for tax purposes." In other words, the "excess of the original debt over the amount determined to have been due" may be disregarded in calculating gross income.

According to the Tenth Circuit in *Preslar*, "to implicate the contested liability doctrine, the original amount of the debt must be unliquidated"[7] — that is, the amount of the debt must be disputed.

The Tenth Circuit was critical of the Third Circuit's 1990 decision in *Zarin v. Commissioner* which concluded that a liquidated debt, if unenforceable, would implicate the contested liability doctrine.[8] In *Zarin*, the taxpayer incurred a $3,435,000 gambling debt which he disputed on the basis that the debt was unenforceable under state law. Ultimately, the taxpayer and the casino settled the dispute for $500,000. The Third Circuit, relying on the contested liability doctrine, rejected the Commissioner's argument that the taxpayer had discharge of indebtedness income equal to the difference between the gambling debt and the $500,000. The Commissioner argued the contested liability doctrine was inapplicable because the debt was liquidated, *i.e.*, Zarin did not contest the amount of the debt but rather based his contest on the unenforceability of the debt. According to the Commissioner, the contested liability doctrine is only applicable when there is an unliquidated debt. The Third Circuit rejected this rationale, emphasizing that, when a debt is unenforceable, the amount of the debt is in dispute. According to the court, the settlement of the debt for $500,000 fixed the amount of the debt cognizable for tax purposes. Because Zarin paid the $500,000, the court concluded there could be no discharge of indebtedness income.

In criticizing *Zarin*, the Tenth Circuit in *Preslar* noted:

> The whole theory behind requiring that the amount of a debt be disputed before the contested liability exception can be triggered is that only in the context of disputed debts is the IRS unaware of the exact consideration initially exchanged in a transaction. The mere fact that a taxpayer challenges the enforceability of a debt in good faith does not necessarily mean he or she is shielded from discharge-of-indebtedness income upon resolution of the dispute. . . . A total denial of liability is not a dispute touching upon the amount of the underlying debt. . . . "If the parties initially treated the transaction as a loan when the loan proceeds were received, thereby not declaring the receipt as income, then the transaction should be treated consistently when the loan is discharged and income should be declared in the amount of the discharge." . . . A holding to the contrary would strain IRS treatment of unenforceable debts and, in large part, disavow the Supreme Court's mandate that the phrase "gross income" be interpreted as broadly as the Constitution permits.[9]

---

[7] *Id.* at 1328.

[8] 916 F.2d 110.

[9] 167 F.3d at 1328.

The Tax Court in *Earnshaw v. Commissioner*, T.C. Memo 2002-191, followed *Preslar* in concluding that a taxpayer who settled a credit card dispute with the issuing bank had discharge of indebtedness income. The court emphasized a significant part of the debt owed by the taxpayer was uncontested and liquidated. Discharge of liability for any of such debt therefore constituted discharge of indebtedness income.

3. Purchase-Money Debt Reduction for Solvent Debtors

Section 108(e)(5) codifies another judicial exclusion related to the discharge of debt. Assume a taxpayer purchases property agreeing to pay the purchase price to the seller over a period of time. Subsequent to the purchase, the taxpayer refuses to pay the entire balance of the purchase price because of irregularities associated with the sale or because of defects in the property. The parties resolve their dispute by agreeing to a reduction in the balance of the purchase price. While it is true that the debt of the taxpayer has been canceled in part, the courts considering such circumstances held no income resulted but rather merely a retroactive reduction in the purchase price.[10] As a result, the basis of the taxpayer in the property was correspondingly reduced.[11] Section 108(e)(5) codifies this exception. Note, however, that § 108(e)(5) extends the exception beyond the dispute settlement area. Consider whether the statutory exclusion is justifiable.[12]

4. Acquisition of Indebtedness by Person Related to Debtor

For purposes of determining how much income a taxpayer has from the discharge of indebtedness, § 108(e)(4) specifically provides that, if a person related to a debtor acquires the indebtedness, the acquisition shall be treated as an acquisition by the debtor. For example, assume Donna owns more than 50% of the stock in XYZ Corporation and is therefore "related" to XYZ within the meaning of § 108(e)(4). XYZ issues its own bonds for which it receives par value. Subsequently, Donna repurchases the bonds on the open market for an amount considerably less than par. Under the rationale of *Kirby Lumber*, does XYZ have discharge of indebtedness income? Considering Donna, and not XYZ, repurchased the bonds, one might conclude XYZ has no discharge of indebtedness income. Section 108(e)(4), however, attributes Donna's acquisition of the bonds to XYZ and thus prevents XYZ from avoiding discharge of indebtedness income. In Revenue Ruling 91-47, 1991-2 C.B. 16, taxpayer sought to avoid discharge of indebtedness income and § 108(e)(4) by arranging for an unrelated person to form a corporation for the purpose of acquiring the taxpayer's indebtedness. Shortly after the corporation was

---

[10] *Hirsch v. Commissioner*, 115 F.2d 656 (7th Cir. 1940); *Helvering v. A.L. Killian Co.*, 128 F.2d 433 (8th Cir. 1948); *Gehring Publishing Co., Inc. v. Commissioner*, 1 T.C. 345 (1942).

[11] *Commissioner v. Sherman*, 135 F.2d 68 (6th Cir. 1943).

[12] The taxpayers in *Payne v. Commissioner*, T.C. Memo. 2002-191, argued their settlement of indebtedness with a credit card issuer represented a retroactive reduction in the rate of interest charged by the issuer and thus a reduction of the "purchase price" of the loans under § 108(e)(5). But the Tax Court held § 108(e)(5) does not apply where the only relationship between the parties is that of debtor and creditor.

formed and the indebtedness acquired, the taxpayer purchased all of the stock in the corporation. The Service ruled that to permit the taxpayer to avoid discharge of indebtedness under these circumstances would elevate form over substance and would frustrate the policy underlying § 108(e)(4). *See* Reg. § 1.108-2(c)(1).

5. Discharge of Deductible Debt

Recall the example earlier in this Overview involving the landlord who canceled rent payments owed by an insolvent commercial tenant. The example illustrated the judicial development of the insolvency exception to cancellation of indebtedness income. Suppose, however, the commercial tenant was not insolvent when the past due rent was forgiven. Income to the tenant? No! Section 108(e)(2) provides that forgiveness of a debt does not generate income if the payment of the debt would have been deductible. The rationale for this provision is that, if discharge of indebtedness income were to be imputed to the tenant, the tenant would be entitled to a deduction for the past due rent which would completely offset the discharge of indebtedness income.

6. Discharge of Certain Student Loans

To encourage students to engage in public service in occupations or areas with unmet needs, *e.g.*, encouraging doctors or teachers to work in rural or low-income areas, Congress enacted § 108(f)(1) excluding from gross income amounts otherwise includable in gross income by reason of the discharge (in whole or in part) of any student loan. The discharge must be pursuant to a provision of such loan under which all or part of the indebtedness of the individual would be discharged "if the individual worked for a certain period of time in certain professions for any of a broad class of employers." Unlike the other provisions of § 108, § 108(f) excludes discharge of debt from gross income without requiring any reduction in the taxpayer's other tax attributes.

For purposes of § 108(f), a "student loan" includes any loan made by qualified lenders to an individual to assist the individual in attending an educational institution maintaining a regular faculty and curriculum having a regularly enrolled student body. § 108(f)(2). Qualified lenders include (1) the United States, or an instrumentality or agency thereof, (2) a State, territory, or possession of the United States, or the District of Columbia, or any political subdivision thereof, (3) certain tax-exempt public benefit corporations, or (4) the educational organization itself under certain conditions specified in § 108(f)(2)(D).

Section 108(f)(2) (flush language) provides the term "student loan" also includes any loan made by a qualifying educational institution to refinance student loans that assisted an individual in attending the educational institution but only if the refinancing loan is pursuant to a program designed to encourage students to engage in public service. For example, in Revenue Ruling 2008-34, 2008-2 C.B. 76, the Service concluded that the § 108(f) exclusion applied to the discharge of loans made under a law school's Loan Repayment Assistance Program (LRAP). The ruling described the LRAP as follows:

Under the LRAP, the law school makes loans that refinance the graduates' original student loan(s). To qualify for an LRAP loan, a graduate must work in a law-related public service position for, or under the direction of, a tax-exempt charitable organization or a governmental unit, including a position in (1) a public interest or community service organization, (2) a legal aid office or clinic, (3) a prosecutor's office, (4) a public defender's office, or (5) a state, local, or federal government office. The amount of the LRAP loan is based on the graduate's outstanding student loan debt and annual income. After the graduate works for the required period in a qualifying position, the law school will forgive all or part of the graduate's LRAP loan.

7.   Discharge of Qualified Principal Residence Indebtedness

As a result of the subprime mortgage crisis, home foreclosure sales have become common. In many cases, because of a slump in housing prices, the proceeds of a foreclosure sale are inadequate to cover the balance of the outstanding mortgage on the foreclosed home. Given the financial condition of the borrower, lenders often simply forgive the remaining indebtedness. For the unfortunate borrower/taxpayer who lost her home another problem loomed: the amount of forgiven indebtedness would normally constitute discharge of indebtedness income under § 61(a)(12). In response to this foreclosure problem, Congress enacted § 108(a)(1)(E) and (h), providing an exclusion for "qualified principal residence indebtedness" discharged on or after January 1, 2007 and before January 1, 2015. Note these provisions are not limited to foreclosure sales but rather are applicable to the discharge of any qualified principal residence indebtedness so long as the discharge is directly related to a decline in the value of the residence or to the financial condition of the taxpayer. § 108(h)(3). "Qualified principal residence indebtedness" is defined as up to $2 million of indebtedness secured by the taxpayer's principal residence so long as the indebtedness is acquisition indebtedness, *i.e.,* indebtedness incurred in constructing, acquiring or substantially improving the residence. § 108(h)(2), (3). Section 108(h)(5) provides the term "principal residence" shall have the same meaning as it does for purposes of the § 121 exclusion. (*See* Chapter 6.) The new exclusion provision takes precedence over the insolvency exclusion unless the taxpayer otherwise elects. § 108(a)(2)(C).

A taxpayer taking advantage of the exclusion under § 108(a)(1)(E) must reduce (but not below zero) her basis in her principal residence by the amount excluded. § 108(h)(1). In this regard, assume a situation where the lender does not foreclose but the lender and borrower renegotiate the loan terms, including monthly payments and the amount of the loan. Although excluded by § 108(a)(1)(E), the amount of indebtedness discharged as a result of the renegotiation will reduce the borrower's/taxpayer's basis in her principal residence. Consequently, on a subsequent sale of the residence, the borrower/taxpayer will realize a greater gain (or smaller loss). Of course, in the case of a subsequent sale, the § 121 exclusion is available to the taxpayer if she satisfies the ownership, use and other requirements of that provision.

8. Other Exclusion Provisions

In addition to the provisions specifically described above, § 108 provides special exclusion provisions related to the discharge of qualified farm indebtedness (§ 108(a)(1)(C) and (g)) and qualified real property business indebtedness (§ 108(a)(1)(D) and (c)). The qualified farm indebtedness discharge rule essentially permits certain solvent as well as insolvent farmers to exclude from gross income the discharge of farm debt up to the combined amount of certain tax attributes and the basis of qualifying property. Under § 108(a)(1)(D) and (c), a noncorporate taxpayer can avoid gross income where, as a result of the decline in the value of business property, there is a discharge of acquisition indebtedness with respect to that property; the taxpayer, however, must reduce the basis of the business property. The details of both of these special exclusion rules are beyond the scope of this casebook.

B. Discharge of Indebtedness as Gift, Compensation, Etc.

Kirby Lumber did not mark the end of the Supreme Court's consideration of debt repayment issues. In *Commissioner v. Jacobson*, 336 U.S. 28 (1949), the Court considered whether a discharge of indebtedness could be considered an excludable gift under § 102(a) and its predecessors. The Court, faced with a fact pattern similar to *Kirby Lumber*, concluded the gift exclusion was not applicable where a debtor purchased his own obligations at a discount. The Court noted the sellers in *Jacobson* sought to minimize their loss by getting as high a price as possible for the bonds; the taxpayer (maker of the bonds), by contrast, sought to reduce his obligation by purchasing the bonds as cheaply as possible. According to the Court, there was no evidence of any intent on the part of the bondholders to make a gift to the taxpayer, an intent that would indeed be extraordinary in a commercial context. In light of *Jacobson*, it is doubtful any taxpayer will be successful in arguing the discharge of indebtedness in a commercial context constitutes an excludable gift. In this regard, review the Court's later landmark decision in *Commissioner v. Duberstein* studied in Chapter 5.

Notwithstanding *Jacobson*, however, in certain contexts the cancellation of indebtedness can be an excludable gift. Thus, if a parent lends money to a child and subsequently forgives the debt, the forgiveness of the debt would likely be considered a gift excludable under § 102(a).

Likewise, the cancellation of indebtedness under some circumstances may represent a form of compensation or some other form of payment which should not be considered "income from the discharge of indebtedness" within the meaning of § 61(a)(12). Revenue Ruling 84-176 reproduced in the materials is instructive in this regard and emphasizes the importance of careful factual analysis. Similarly, some transactions, like that described in *Gehl v. Commissioner* in the materials, may generate both discharge of indebtedness income excludable in part or in whole under Section 108 and income, *e.g.*, gain, which is not excludable under Section 108.

UNITED STATES v. KIRBY LUMBER CO.
United States Supreme Court
284 U.S. 1 (1931)

Mr. Justice Holmes delivered the opinion of the Court.

In July, 1923, the plaintiff, the Kirby Lumber Company, issued its own bonds for $12,126,800 for which it received their par value. Later in the same year it purchased in the open market some of the same bonds at less than par, the difference of price being $137,521.30. The question is whether this difference is a taxable gain or income of the plaintiff for the year 1923. By the Revenue Act of (November 23,) 1921, gross income includes "gains or profits and income derived from any source whatever," and by the Treasury Regulations that have been in force through repeated reenactments, "If the corporation purchases and retires any of such bonds at a price less than the issuing price or face value, the excess of the issuing price or face value over the purchase price is gain or income for the taxable year." We see no reason why the Regulations should not be accepted as a correct statement of the law.

In *Bowers v. Kerbaugh-Empire Co.*, 271 U.S. 170, the defendant in error owned the stock of another company that had borrowed money repayable in marks or their equivalent for an enterprise that failed. At the time of payment the marks had fallen in value, which so far as it went was a gain for the defendant in error, and it was contended by the plaintiff in error that the gain was taxable income. But the transaction as a whole was a loss, and the contention was denied. Here there was no shrinkage of assets and the taxpayer made a clear gain. As a result of its dealings it made available $137,521.30 in assets previously offset by the obligation of bonds now extinct. We see nothing to be gained by the discussion of judicial definitions. The defendant in error has realized within the year an accession to income, if we take words in their plain popular meaning, as they should be taken here.

Judgment reversed.

REVENUE RULING 84-176
1984-2 C.B. 34

ISSUE

Is the amount owed by a taxpayer, that is forgiven by a seller in return for a release of a contract counterclaim, income from discharge of indebtedness pursuant to § 61(a)(12) of the Internal Revenue Code and thereby subject to exclusion under § 108?

FACTS

The taxpayer, a domestic corporation, is a wholesale distributor. In 1981, it entered into two contracts with an unrelated seller under which the taxpayer agreed to purchase various quantities of goods. The goods were to be shipped in six lots between March and August, 1982. The seller subsequently shipped all of lot 1 and part of lot 2, and then refused to ship the rest of the order. At the time of this refusal, the taxpayer had an outstanding account payable to the seller of 1,000x dollars for goods actually shipped.

After the seller failed to ship the remaining goods, the taxpayer refused to pay the 1,000x dollars already owed. The seller then filed suit against the taxpayer in U.S. District Court for such payment. The taxpayer later filed a counterclaim for breach of contract, claiming damages for lost profits.

In December, 1982, the parties settled the suit. The taxpayer agreed to pay the seller 500x dollars of the 1,000x dollars outstanding indebtedness. The remaining 500x dollars was "forgiven" by the seller in return for executing a release of the breach of contract counterclaim.

LAW AND ANALYSIS

Section 61(a) of the Code provides that gross income means gross income from whatever source derived. Section 61(a)(12) provides that gross income includes income from discharge of indebtedness. Section 1.61-12(a) of the Income Tax Regulations provides that a taxpayer may realize income by the payment of obligations at less than their face value.

The Supreme Court in *United States v. Kirby Lumber Co.*, 284 U.S. 1 (1931), established the principle that the gain or saving that is realized by a debtor upon the reduction or cancellation of the debtor's outstanding indebtedness for less than the amount due may be "income" for federal tax purposes. The taxpayer-corporation in *Kirby Lumber* had purchased its own bonds at a discount in the open market. Holding that the difference between the issue price and the price at which the bonds were subsequently acquired represented taxable income to the corporation, the Court said that as a result of these purchases, the taxpayer made available $137,521.30 of assets previously offset by the obligation of bonds now extinct. The taxpayer had realized within the year an accession to income.

Not every indebtedness that is canceled results in gross income being realized by the debtor "by reason of" discharge of indebtedness within the meaning of § 108 of the Code. If a cancellation of indebtedness is simply the medium for payment of some other form of income, § 108 does not apply. For example, if an employee owes his employer $100 and renders $100 worth of services to the employer in return for cancellation of the debt, the employee has received personal services income, rather than income from cancellation for indebtedness within the meaning of § 108. In such a case, the full amount of the indebtedness is satisfied by the performance of services having a value equal to the debt. Since the debt cancellation is only the medium of paying the personal services income, § 108 is inapplicable. *See Spartan Petroleum Co. v. United States*, 437 F. Supp. 733 (D.S.C. 1977). (Citations omitted.)

The Senate Finance Committee Report regarding the amending of § 108 of the Code in the Bankruptcy Tax Act of 1980, discusses the exceptions to the general rule of income realization when indebtedness is forgiven or otherwise canceled. That report acknowledges the proposition set forth in *Spartan Petroleum* that income from cancellation of indebtedness does not automatically fall within the scope of the debt discharge rules. It states in a footnote that debt discharge that is only a medium for some other form of payment, such as a gift or salary, is treated as that form of payment rather than under the debt discharge rules. Footnote 6, S. Rep. No. 1035, 96th Cong., 2d Sess. 8 (1980), 1980-2 C.B. 624.

In this situation, the settlement should be analyzed as if the taxpayer actually received compensation for damages arising out of the seller's breach of contract and then paid the full amount of the account payable. There is no requirement that money be actually exchanged in order for taxation to result. The amount received by the taxpayer for the breach of contract is ordinary income because the facts demonstrate that the taxpayer was reimbursed for lost profits and income. Therefore, the 500x dollars not paid by the taxpayer to the seller was the medium through which income from the damages for breach of contract arose. This amount is to be treated as a payment for lost profits rather than a discharge of indebtedness.

HOLDING

The amount owed by the taxpayer that is forgiven by the seller in return for a release of a contract counterclaim is not income from discharge of indebtedness under § 61(a)(12) of the Code. . . .

GEHL v. COMMISSIONER
United States Court of Appeals, Eighth Circuit
50 F.3d 12 (1995)

Bogue, Senior District Judge:

Background

Prior to the events in issue, the taxpayers borrowed money from the Production Credit Association of the Midlands (PCA). Mortgages on a 218 acre family farm were given to the PCA to secure the recourse loan. As of December 30, 1988, the taxpayers were insolvent and unable to make the payments on the loan, which had an outstanding balance of $152,260. The transactions resolving the situation between the PCA and the taxpayers form the basis of the current dispute.

Pursuant to a restructuring agreement, taxpayers, by deed in lieu of foreclosure, conveyed 60 acres of the farm land to the PCA on December 30, 1988, in partial satisfaction of the debt. The taxpayers' basis in the 60 acres was $14,384 and they were credited with $39,000 towards their loan, the fair market value of the land. On January 4, 1989, taxpayers conveyed, also by deed in lieu of foreclosure, an additional 141 acres of the mortgaged farm land to the PCA in partial satisfaction of the debt. Taxpayers' basis in the 141 acres was $32,000 and the land had a fair market value of $77,725. Taxpayers also paid $6,123 in cash to the PCA to be applied to their loan. The PCA thereupon forgave the remaining balance of the taxpayers' loan, $29,412. Taxpayers were not debtors under the Bankruptcy Code during 1988 or 1989, but were insolvent both before and after the transfers and discharge of indebtedness.

After an audit, the Commissioner of Revenue (Commissioner) determined tax deficiencies of $6,887 for 1988 and $13,643 for 1989 on the theory that the taxpayers had realized a gain on the disposition of their farmland in the amount by which the fair market value of the land exceeded their basis in the same at the time of the transfer (gains of $24,616 on the 60 acre conveyance and $45,645 on the conveyance of the 141 acre conveyance). The taxpayers petitioned the Tax Court for redetermination of their tax liability for the years in question contending that any gain they realized upon the transfer of their property should not be treated as income because they remained insolvent after the transactions.

The Tax Court found in favor of the Commissioner. In doing so, the court "bifurcated" its analysis of the transactions, considering the transfers of land and the discharge of the remaining debt separately. The taxpayers argued that the entire set of transactions should be considered together and treated as income from the discharge of indebtedness. As such, any income derived would be excluded as the taxpayers remained insolvent throughout the process. . . . As to the discharge of indebtedness, the court determined that because the taxpayers remained insolvent after their debt was discharged, no income would be attributable to that portion of the restructuring agreement.

On the other hand, the court found the taxpayers to have received a gain includable as gross income from the transfers of the farm land (determined by the excess of the respective fair market values over the respective basises). This gain was found to exist despite the continued insolvency in that the gain from the sale or disposition of land is not income from the discharge of indebtedness. The taxpayers appealed.

Discussion

We review the Tax Court's interpretation of law de novo. . . . Discussion of this case properly begins with an examination of I.R.C. Section 61 which defines gross income under the Code. In order to satisfy their obligation to the PCA, the taxpayers agreed to participate in an arrangement which could potentially give rise to gross income in two distinct ways. I.R.C. Section 61(a)(3) provides that for tax purposes, gross income includes "gains derived from dealings in property." Likewise, income is realized pursuant to I.R.C. Section 61(a)(12) for "income from discharge of indebtedness."

There can be little dispute with respect to Tax Court's treatment of the $29,412 portion of the debt forgiven subsequent to the transfers of land and cash. The Commissioner stipulated that under I.R.C. Section 108(a)(1)(B), the so-called "insolvency exception," the taxpayers did not have to include as income any part of the indebtedness that the PCA forgave. The $29,412 represented the amount by which the land and cash transfers fell short of satisfying the outstanding debt. The Tax Court properly found this amount to be excluded.

Further, the Tax Court's treatment of the land transfers, irrespective of other portions of the restructuring agreement, cannot be criticized. Section 1001 governs the determination of gains and losses on the sale or exchange of property. Section 1001(a) provides that "[t]he gain from the sale or other disposition of property shall be the excess of the amount realized therefrom over the adjusted basis. . . . " The taxpayers contend that because the disposition of their land was compulsory and that they had no discretion with respect to the proceeds, the deeds in lieu of foreclosure are not "sales" for the purposes of section 1001. We disagree. A transfer of property by deed in lieu of foreclosure constitutes a "sale or exchange" for federal income tax purposes. *Allan v. Commissioner of Revenue*, 86 T.C. 655, 659–60, *affd.* 856 F.2d 1169, 1172 (8th Cir. 1988). The taxpayers' transfers by deeds in lieu of foreclosure of their land to the PCA in partial satisfaction of the recourse debt were properly considered sales or exchanges for purposes of section 1001.

Taxpayers also appear to contend that under their circumstances, there was no "amount realized" under I.R.C. Sections 1001(a–b) and thus, no "gain" from the land transfers as the term is used in I.R.C. Section 61(a)(3). Again, we must disagree. The amount realized from a sale or other disposition of property includes the amount of liabilities from which the transferor is discharged as a result of the sale or disposition. Treas. Reg. Section 1.1001-2(a)(1). Simply because the taxpayers did not actually receive any cash proceeds from the land transfers does not mean there was no amount realized. Via the land transfers, they were given credit toward an outstanding recourse loan to the extent of the land's fair market value. This loan had to be paid back. It is clear that the transfers of land employed to satisfy that end must be treated the same as receiving money from a sale. In this case the land transfers were properly considered "gains derived from dealings in property" to the extent the fair market value in the land exceeded the taxpayers' basis in said land. I.R.C. Sections 61(a)(3), 1001(a).

The taxpayers' primary and fundamental argument in this case is the Tax Court's refusal to treat the entire settlement of their loan, including the land transfers, as coming within the scope of I.R.C. Section 108. As previously stated, Section 108 and attending Treasury Regulations act to exclude income from the discharge of indebtedness where the taxpayer thereafter remains insolvent. The taxpayers take issue with the bifurcated analysis conducted by the Tax Court and contend that, because of their continued insolvency, Section 108 acts to exclude any income derived from the various transactions absolving their debt to the PCA.

As an initial consideration, the taxpayers read the insolvency exception of Section 108 too broadly. I.R.C. Section 61 provides a nonexclusive list of fifteen items which give rise to income for tax purposes, including income from discharge of indebtedness. Of the numerous potential sources of income, Section 108 grants an exclusion to insolvent taxpayers only as to income from the discharge of indebtedness. It does not preclude the realization of income from other activities or sources.

While Section 108 clearly applied to a portion of the taxpayers' loan restructuring agreement, the land transfers were outside the section's scope and were properly treated independently. . . .

There is ample authority to support Tax Court's bifurcated analysis and substantive decision rendered with respect to the present land transfers. The Commissioner relies heavily on Treas. Reg. Section 1.1001-2 and example 8 contained therein, which provides:

. . . The amount realized on a sale or other disposition of property that secures a recourse liability does not include amounts that are (or would be if realized and recognized) income from the discharge of indebtedness under section 61(a)(12). . . .

(c) Examples . . .

Example (8). In 1980, F transfers to a creditor an asset with a fair market value of $6,000 and the creditor discharges $7,500 of indebtedness for which F is personally liable. The amount realized on the disposition of the asset is its fair market value ($6,000). In addition, F has income from the discharge of indebtedness of $1,500 ($7,500 − $6,000).

We believe the regulation is controlling and serves . . . to provide support for the decision rendered by the Tax Court.

Conclusion

For the reasons stated, we affirm the decision of the Tax Court.

Chapter 10

COMPENSATION FOR PERSONAL INJURY AND SICKNESS

I. PROBLEMS

1. The building in which Emily conducted her travel agency was damaged by a large truck that struck the building at high speed when its driver lost control of the vehicle. Emily had to suspend her business operations for two months while repairs were made to the building. In the negligence action she brought against the driver, Emily recovered $75,000 for the cost *→ non-tax* of repairs to the building and $50,000 in lost profits. What are the tax *↳ tax* consequences to Emily?

2. Lance is a karate instructor who charges $500 per day for providing karate instruction to students of various ages and skill levels. On many occasions, Lance has sustained visible bruises caused, unintentionally of course, by blows struck by students he is instructing. May Lance exclude all or part of the $500 payment he receives on days he sustains such injuries? *no*

3. Tom, a self-employed landscape architect, was injured last year in an accident in which he was struck by a car driven by a drunk driver. Tom filed a negligence suit against the driver, seeking over $2 million in compensatory and punitive damages. This year, the parties to the action settled the suit out of court for $900,000, which the parties agreed to allocate as follows:

Payment for pain and suffering:	$500,000	*T*
Reimbursed medical expenses:	$100,000	*NT*
Future medical expenses:	$50,000	*NT*
Lost income:	$100,000	*T*
Punitive damages:	$150,000	*T*

Tom paid the medical expenses of $100,000 last year from his own funds and was allowed a medical expense deduction of $70,000 under § 213.

(a) What are the tax consequences to Tom as a result of this settlement? In answering the question, consider each item to which the settlement was allocated.

(b) Assume Tom insisted that the entire $900,000 settlement be allocated to pain and suffering even though in his lawsuit he had sought recovery for the items listed in the settlement described above. Desiring to settle the lawsuit, the defendants agree to the allocation.

What are the tax consequences to Tom of this settlement?

(c)   What are the tax consequences to Tom's wife Phyllis if she recovers $100,000 from the defendants for loss of consortium due to the injuries suffered by her spouse? How would your answer change, if at all, if Phyllis accepts the offer of defendants to pay her a total of $150,000 if she will agree to payment of that amount over a five year period in equal annual installments of $30,000 each? *taxable*

4.   Martha, a business graduate of a major university and a C.P.A., accepted a position with a prominent accounting firm. Shortly after beginning employment, Martha began to be sexually harassed by her supervisor at the firm. The harassment involved not only verbal statements and gestures by the supervisor, but also unwelcome physical contact, including embraces and kisses, and in one instance, the bruising of her arm when she tried to break away when the supervisor grabbed her arm. Two months after Martha complained to the managing partner of the firm that she was being sexually harassed by the supervisor, she was fired. In its notice of dismissal, the firm indicated Martha's performance did not reflect the level of competence expected of new associates. As a result of the sexual harassment and her discharge, Martha suffered severe emotional distress which exacerbated a pre-existing ulcer condition and ultimately resulted in her hospitalization for bleeding ulcers. In addition, Martha has suffered depression and is being treated by a psychologist. Martha has been unable to locate suitable new employment. In full settlement of all claims which Martha may have against them, including wrongful discharge and sexual harassment claims, the firm offers Martha $500,000. In assessing whether to accept the settlement, Martha asks your advice regarding the potential tax consequences of the settlement. What advice would you give?

5.   Susan was injured in an accident and lost the sight in one eye. She incurred $30,000 in medical expenses. She had an accident and health policy she had purchased with her own funds that paid her $15,000 for medical expenses, $10,000 for lost wages, and $25,000 for the loss of sight. What tax consequences from her receipt of these payments? Alternatively, assume that her only policy was an accident and health policy provided by her employer which paid her $20,000 for medical expenses, $12,000 for lost wages, and $20,000 for the loss of sight. What tax consequences from her receipt of these payments? Finally, assume that Susan had both the policy she purchased and the policy her employer provided and that the two policies paid the amounts described above. What tax results?

Assignment for Chapter 10:

Complete the problems.

Read: Internal Revenue Code: §§ 104(a) and (c); 105(a)–(c), (e); 106(a).
         Treasury Regulations: §§ 1.104-1(a)–(d); 1.105-1(a), -2, -3; 1.213-1(g); Reg. § 1.104-1(c).

Materials: Overview
             Commissioner v. Schleier

Domeny v. Commissioner
Perez v. Commissioner

II. VOCABULARY

damages
personal physical injury
punitive damages

III. OBJECTIVES

1. To recall amounts received on account of personal physical injuries or sickness, including periodic payments, are excluded from income.

2. To explain what constitutes a "personal physical injury" within the meaning of § 104(a)(2).

3. To explain the significance of the phrase "on account of" in § 104(a)(2).

4. To distinguish between damages received for personal physical injuries and damages received for nonphysical personal injuries or for business or property injuries.

5. To explain the tax treatment of damages awarded on account of lost wages in cases involving personal physical injuries and cases not involving personal physical injuries.

6. To explain the tax treatment of punitive damages.

7. To apply § 104(a)(2) to common fact patterns.

8. To determine when medical expense reimbursements are included in income.

9. To recall workers' compensation payments are excluded from income.

10. To distinguish between self-financed and employer-financed accident and health insurance plans in terms of the tax treatment of payments thereunder.

11. To evaluate the policy justifying the exclusion of personal physical injury awards.

IV. OVERVIEW

Sections 104 and 105 exclude from gross income certain amounts received on account of personal physical injury or sickness. These provisions, which are complemented by the § 106(a) exclusion from income of employer-provided coverage under health and accident plans, are now commonly regarded as an expression of congressional compassion for those who suffer personal physical injury or illness. The tax collector is, in effect, barred from inflicting on these victims the further pain of tax liability for the compensation they may receive. (One may, of course, ask whether taxing such payments would ultimately lead to an increase in payments sufficient to cover the tax; if so, consider who is the beneficiary of the present exclusionary rules.) The predecessor of the current provisions dates back to the Revenue Act of 1918, at which time there was considerable doubt as to whether personal injury payments or accident insurance proceeds constituted income in a constitutional sense, or instead represented a type of nontaxable conversion of capital lost through the injury or illness. The 1918 Act resolved these doubts in favor of income exclusion. Although most agree such payments are within the reach of the congressional taxing power, the exclusion has persisted, albeit with a number of alterations enacted over the intervening years.

A. Damages

1. Business or Property Damages

With respect to business or property damages, the leading case of *Raytheon Products Corp. v. Commissioner*, 144 F.2d 110, 113 (1st Cir. 1944), instructs that we ask "in lieu of what were the damages awarded." For example, unless there is a specific rule to the contrary, damages awarded on account of lost profits would be taxable; a recovery for property damage would be measured against the basis of the property to determine the taxpayer's realized gain or loss. In *Raytheon*, a corporate taxpayer, settled its suit for damages under the antitrust laws and claimed it was entitled to exclude from income as a nontaxable return of capital most of the proceeds it received. The First Circuit disagreed:

> Damages recovered in an antitrust action are not necessarily nontaxable as a return of capital. As in other types of tort damage suits, recoveries which represent a reimbursement for lost profits are income. . . . The reasoning is that since the profits would be taxable income, the proceeds of litigation which are their substitute are taxable in like manner.
>
> Damages for violation of antitrust acts are treated as ordinary income where they represent compensation for loss of profits. . . .
>
> The test is not whether the action was one in tort or contract but rather the question to be asked is, "In lieu of what were the damages awarded?". . . . Where the suit is not to recover lost profits but is for injury to good will, the recovery represents a return of capital and, with certain limitations to be set forth below, is not taxable.
>
> But, to say that the recovery represents a return of capital in that it takes the place of the business good will is not to conclude that it may not

contain a taxable benefit. Although the injured party may not be deriving a profit as a result of the damage suit itself, the conversion thereby of his property into cash is a realization of any gain made over the cost or other basis of the good will prior to the legal interference. Thus A buys Blackacre for $5,000. It appreciates in value to $50,000. B tortiously destroys it by fire. A sues and recovers $50,000 tort damages from B. Although no gain was derived by A from the suit, his prior gain due to the appreciation in value of Blackacre is realized when it is turned into cash by the money damages.

Compensation for the loss of Raytheon's good will in excess of its cost is gross income. . . .

Id. at 113, 114.

2. Exclusion for Damages Received on Account of Personal Physical Injuries or Physical Sickness: History

Section 104(a)(2) excludes from income any damages received, whether by suit or agreement, as a lump-sum or periodic payment, on account of personal physical injuries or physical sickness. Note that § 104(a)(2) distinguishes between personal physical injuries and all other injuries, including non-physical injuries and injuries to one's business or property.

The policy justification for the § 104(a)(2) exclusion has never been articulated by Congress. The exclusion is often presumed to rest on compassion, but it has also been suggested damages for personal injury do not constitute income because they do not add to wealth but merely restore a loss of capital. *See Starrels v. Commissioner*, 304 F.2d 574 (9th Cir. 1962), *aff'g* 35 T.C. 646 (1961). Is the lost capital analysis theoretically sound? Does the taxpayer have a tax basis in his or her injured person? Might the exclusion be justified in part because of the involuntary nature of the "conversion of capital" that occurred?

Early judicial and administrative decisions excluding personal injury recoveries from income did not rely on the statutory predecessor to § 104(a)(2), but instead found — wholly apart from the statutory exclusion — such recoveries simply did not constitute gross income within the meaning of the forerunner of present § 61. A 1922 administrative ruling held that there was "no gain, and therefore no income" derived from damages received for alienation of affection or for defamation of personal character. Solicitor's Opinion 132, I-1 C.B. 92 (1922). An early Tax Court decision similarly held that payment received for injury to personal reputation was nontaxable because it "in no event involves income. . . . [The] compensation . . . adds nothing to the individual. . . . It is an attempt to make the plaintiff whole as before the injury." *Hawkins v. Commissioner*, 6 B.T.A. 1023, 1025 (1927). Even after the *Eisner v. Macomber* characterization of income (income is the gain derived from capital, from labor, or from both combined . . .) had been supplanted by broader income notions, *e.g.*, *Glenshaw Glass*, the practice of excluding damages from income on nonstatutory grounds persisted. Revenue Ruling 56-518, 1956-2 C.B. 25, for example, held that certain damages received on account of wartime persecution were "in the nature of reimbursement for the deprivation of civil and personal rights and [did] not constitute taxable income." As late as 1974, the Service, without mentioning § 104(a)(2), held that amounts received on account of alienation of affection or in consideration of surrendering custody of a minor child were not income; the ruling held that Solicitor's Opinion 132 was superseded since its position — that the damages were excluded because they did not constitute income, not because they came within the terms of the statutory exclusion — was also set forth under the current statute and regulations. Rev. Rul. 74-77, 1974-1 C.B. 33. The revenue rulings just cited have since been declared obsolete by the Service[1] and the cases and rulings now generally look to § 104(a)(2) as the basis for holding damages nontaxable.

In enacting the predecessor to § 104(a)(2), Congress likely intended to exclude only those damages received on account of physical injuries. Nonetheless, the courts and even the Service prior to a legislative amendment in 1996 did not distinguish between physical and nonphysical injuries. For example, the Tax Court held damages for defamation of personal reputation were excludable under the statute. *Seay v. Commissioner*, 58 T.C. 32 (1972) (Acq.). Historically, the dividing line between excludable and nonexcludable damages under § 104(a)(2) was between personal and non-personal injuries. Because neither the statute nor the regulation interpreting it defined "personal injury," it fell to the courts to determine what injuries would be considered "personal." In an important decision excluding damages received on account of injuries to a taxpayer's professional reputation, the Tax Court in *Threlkeld v. Commissioner*, 87 T.C. 1294 (1986), *aff'd*, 848 F.2d 81 (6th Cir. (1988), held that "personal injury" for purposes of § 104(a)(2) referred to "any invasion of the rights that an individual is granted by virtue of being a person in the sight of the law." This definition easily encompassed not only traditional non-physical injuries such as defamation but a broad array of newly-minted, and generally employment-related, actions for non-physical injuries. For example, damages awarded under 42 U.S.C. 1983 for violation of free speech rights were held nontaxable in *Bent v. Commissioner*, 87 T.C. 236, *aff'd*, 835 F.2d 67 (1987), as were damages on account of discrimination on the basis of sex and national origin in *Metzger v. Commissioner*, 88 T.C. 834, *aff'd*, 845 F.2d 1013 (1988).

In addition to providing an expansive definition to the term "personal injury" as used in § 104(a)(2), *Threlkeld* also emphasized that the exclusion could not properly be limited only to those components of an award that compensate for non-economic losses; economic losses were also excludable:

> [w]hether the damages received are paid on account of "personal injuries" should be the beginning and the end of the inquiry. To determine whether the injury complained of is personal, we must look to the origin and character of the claim . . . and not to the consequences that result from the injury.

87 T.C. at 1299. As a result, prior to the 1996 amendments, employees recovering awards for wrongful discharge, sex discrimination or any other employment-related claim constituting a "personal injury" within the *Threlkeld* definition could exclude

---

[1] Revenue Ruling 56-518 was declared obsolete by Revenue Ruling 2007-14, 2007-1 C.B. 747, and Revenue Ruling 74-77 was declared obsolete by Revenue Ruling 98-37, 1998-2 C.B. 133.

not only the damages received on account of emotional distress or other psychological injuries suffered, but also lost wages.

Although § 104(a)(2) was enacted in 1918, Treasury did not promulgate regulations interpreting that provision until 1960. The 1960 regulations, which, as discussed *infra*, were substantially amended in 2012 to reflect the impact of congressional and judicial developments, provided that § 104(a)(2) excluded only those amounts received through the prosecution or settlement of claims "based on tort or tort type rights."

3.   Supreme Court Limitations on Section 104(a)(2)

The first significant limitations on the increasingly broad scope of § 104(a)(2) were to be found in two U.S. Supreme Court decisions, *Burke v. U.S.*, 504 U.S. 229 (1992), and *Commissioner v. Schleier*, 515 U.S. 323 (1995). *Burke* was the first Supreme Court decision to interpret § 104(a)(2). In *Burke*, employees of the Tennessee Valley Authority (TVA) brought, and ultimately settled, an action against TVA under Title VII of the Civil Rights Act of 1964, alleging the TVA had engaged in illegal sex discrimination. In reversing the lower court's decision holding the settlement amount excludable, the Supreme Court emphasized that the then-applicable regulation interpreting § 104(a)(2), as noted above, linked "personal injury" with tort principles by defining "damages received" as an amount received through prosecution or settlement of a claim "based on tort or tort type rights." Upon finding that the statute in question provided a narrow range of remedies and thus did not create a claim based on tort-type rights, the Court concluded the amounts received were not excluded by § 104(a)(2). As discussed *infra*, the tort-type requirement was eliminated by regulations issued in 2012.

Commissioner v. Schleier, included in the materials, addressed the excludability of awards for back pay and liquidated damages under the Age Discrimination in Employment Act (ADEA). In *Schleier*, the Court shifted the focus to the statutory language, emphasizing that the key question to be asked in applying § 104(a)(2) is whether the damages received were "on account of," *i.e.*, actually compensated for, personal injury. *Schleier* indicates that damages are "on account of" personal injuries for § 104(a)(2) purposes only if they bear a close nexus to the personal injury, *i.e.*, "the injury justifies [the] damages" or the damages are intended to compensate the taxpayer for the personal injury and the consequences causally linked to the injury. If that relationship between the damages and personal injuries does not exist, no exclusion is available. For example, in *Schleier*, because the Court concluded the liquidated damages were not intended to compensate the taxpayer for any personal injuries, *e.g.*, psychological harm, but rather were intended to punish the wrongdoer, no exclusion for the liquidated damages was appropriate. Similarly, the backpay was not excludable because the necessary nexus between the backpay and a personal injury did not exist, *i.e.*, regardless of whether the taxpayer suffered any personal injury as a result of his discharge from employment at age 60, he was still entitled to the backpay under the ADEA. In other words, the backpay was not intended to compensate the taxpayer for a personal injury or its consequences but rather to ensure that the taxpayer received those wages the taxpayer would have earned had the taxpayer not been illegally discharged. Thus, under § 104(a)(2), as amended in 1996, backpay that is "completely independent" of a personal physical injury is not received "on account of" the personal physical injury and cannot be excluded under § 104(a)(2). *See* Rev. Rul. 96-65, 1996-2 C.B. 6.

In some respects, the standard adopted by the *Schleier* Court is identical to the historic "in lieu of what" test of *Raytheon Products Corp. v. Commissioner* discussed previously. That test arguably provides the narrowest interpretation of the "on account of" language, ensuring that only those damages for personal injury are excludable. Strictly applied, however, the "in lieu of what" test would result in backpay, lost wages and other damages for nonpersonal harms never being excluded unless it could be established they were intended as a measure of the personal injury. Doesn't *Schleier*, at least in its car accident hypothetical, suggest a more generous test regarding economic losses? In this regard, note specifically the Court's conclusion in the hypothetical that the recovery for lost wages would be excludable "as long as the lost wages resulted from time in which the taxpayer was out of work as a result of her injuries." In a private letter ruling, PLR 200041022, discussed herein, the Service has indicated its agreement with the Court's application of the "on account of" language of § 104(a)(2) to lost wages.

4.   Restricting the Exclusion to Physical Injury or Physical Sickness

Despite the Supreme Court's limitations on the scope of § 104(a)(2), Congress nonetheless viewed § 104(a)(2) as too broad in scope, allowing taxpayers, particularly those who were victims of employment discrimination, to exclude awards which were primarily intended to compensate them for lost wages or lost profits. Congress therefore chose in 1996 to limit the exclusion by restricting it to those damages received on account of "physical" injuries or "physical" sickness.[2] In addition, Congress specifically provided that "emotional distress" is not to be treated — save only for related medical care expenses — as a physical injury or physical sickness. *See* Reg. § 1.104-1(c). Thus, as a result of the 1996 amendments limiting § 104(a)(2) to physical injuries or physical sickness, damages from a range of personal injury actions which had historically been excludable, e.g., libel, slander, wrongful discharge, and employment discrimination, became taxable.

For purposes of determining excludability under § 104(a)(2), the legislative history of the 1996 act amending that provision relies on an "origin-of-the-claim" standard. Thus, the House Committee Report states: "if an action has its origin in a physical injury or physical sickness, then all damages (other than punitive damages) that flow therefrom are treated as payments received on account of physical injury or physical sickness. . . . " The legislative history thus suggests congressional adoption of the *Schleier* standard, i.e., that § 104(a)(2) excludes all

---

[2] As a result of the taxation after 1996 of damages received on account of *non-physical* personal injuries, a question arose in a number of lower court cases involving taxable personal injury awards: whether the portion of the award paid to plaintiff's attorney under a contingent fee agreement was income to the plaintiff. The Supreme Court held in *Commissioner v. Banks*, 543 U.S. 426 (2005), that, as a general rule the plaintiff's income included the contingent fee paid to the attorney. See Chapter 34, Assignment of Income, for a discussion of the anticipatory assignment of income. However, see also § 62(a)(20), enacted in 2004, allowing an above-the-line deduction for certain attorney fees and court costs and providing very significant relief from the holding in *Banks*.

damages intended to compensate a taxpayer for a physical injury or physical sickness and the consequences, including economic consequences, e.g., lost wages or income, resulting from that injury or sickness. Consider whether it is appropriate to exclude economic damages such as lost wages even if a causal connection exists between those damages and a physical injury or physical sickness.

As you consider Problem 4, evaluate whether the dichotomy between physical and non-physical injuries is justifiable as a matter of policy. The Sixth Circuit rejected a Fifth Amendment Equal Protection challenge to amended § 104(a)(2), finding the distinction between physical and non-physical injury to be rationally related to articulated government purposes, i.e., the establishment of a uniform policy regarding taxation of damage awards and the reduction of litigation. *Young v. U.S.*, 332 F.3d 893 (6th Cir. 2003).[3] What impact, if any, would you expect the amendments to § 104(a)(2) to have upon the settlement of employment discrimination cases? The Sixth Circuit suggests that the amendments were intended to reduce litigation. A review of the post-1996 Act case law suggests Congress may have failed in that regard.

a.   Personal Physical Injury or Physical Sickness

Section 104(a)(2) does not define "physical injury" or "physical sickness." Likewise, there is no regulation defining these terms. The Service issued a private letter ruling in 2000 that provides some limited guidance. PLR 200041022 states "direct unwanted or uninvited physical contacts resulting in *observable bodily harms* such as bruises, cuts, swelling, and bleeding are personal physical injuries under § 104(a)(2)" (emphasis added). In this ruling, the Service refused to issue a ruling regarding the application of the § 104(a)(2) exclusion to damages on account of a "pain incident" where the physical contact did not manifest itself in the form of a cut, bruise or other similar bodily harm. The Service, noting general rules regarding issuance of letter rulings, stated "a letter ruling will not ordinarily be issued because of the factual nature of the problem. Because the perception of pain is essentially subjective, it is a factual matter."

Since the issuance of the private letter ruling, there has been some additional guidance provided by the Service and courts regarding the interpretation to be given "personal physical injury and physical sickness." Thus, in PLR 200121031, the Service recognized that a sheetrocker who had contracted and suffered asbestos-related lung cancer and other asbestos related diseases as a result his long exposure to asbestos in his work had suffered a "physical injury" within the meaning of that term in § 104(a)(2). In *Domeny v. Commissioner*, included in the materials, the flare-up of the taxpayer's multiple sclerosis condition caused by a hostile workplace was held to constitute a physical injury or physical sickness. Likewise, in *Parkinson v. Commissioner*, T.C. Memo 2010-142, the court held that a heart attack and its physical aftereffects suffered by a taxpayer as a result of

---

[3] Taxation of damages awarded on account of non-physical injuries has been held to be both constitutional and within the scope of § 61. *See Murphy v. IRS*, 493 F.3d 170 (D.C. Cir. 2007); *Stadnyk v. Commissioner*, T.C. Memo 2008-289, *aff'd in unpublished opinion*, 2010 U.S. App. Lexis 4209 (6th Cir. Feb. 26, 2010).

emotional distress inflicted upon the taxpayer in his workplace constituted a "physical injury or physical sickness" for § 104(a)(2) purposes.

While the Service in PLR 200041022 indicated its refusal to issue a ruling regarding whether pain unaccompanied by a cut or bruise constituted a "physical injury," the Tax Court in *Amos v. Commissioner*, T.C. Memo 2003-329, concluded that some of the damages awarded a taxpayer were excludable under § 104(a)(2) apparently without a showing of bruises, cuts or other observable bodily harms. *Amos v. Commissioner* involved former professional basketball player Dennis Rodman. In a 1997 game pitting Rodman's Chicago Bulls against the Minnesota Timberwolves, Rodman twisted his ankle when he fell into a group of photographers, including the taxpayer Amos. Rodman kicked Amos in the groin. Amos was taken by ambulance to a hospital where he complained he had experienced considerable pain. Hospital personnel observed that Amos was able to walk, but that he was limping and complained of pain. There apparently was no observable swelling or bruising in the groin area. Amos immediately retained a lawyer and shortly afterwards the matter was settled by Rodman's payment of $200,000 to Amos. The settlement agreement provided, without allocation, that the settlement covered not only any physical injuries Amos suffered but also Amos' agreement not to defame Rodman, disclose the existence or terms of the agreement, or assist in any criminal prosecution against Rodman with respect to the matter. The court concluded that a significant part of the settlement was intended to compensate Amos for a personal physical injury within the meaning of § 104(a)(2) and held that $120,000 of the settlement was excludable under that provision. *Amos* appears to indicate that some physical contacts, e.g., a kick in the groin, constitute a personal physical injury even though there is no cut, bruise or other observable bodily harm.

Does false imprisonment constitute a personal physical injury? In view of the fact that states and the federal government often provide compensation to individuals who have been wrongly incarcerated, the question is anything but academic. Authority on the issue is limited. In *Stadnyk v. Commissioner*, T. C. Memo 2008-289, *aff'd in an unpublished opinion*, 2010 U.S. App. LEXIS 4209 (6th Cir. Feb. 26, 2010), the court rejected taxpayer's argument that "physical restraint and detention and the resulting deprivation of personal liberty is [itself] a physical injury." In that case, the taxpayer was wrongfully detained for only about eight hours. In a deposition, the taxpayer had indicated she had not suffered any physical injury as a result of her arrest and detention, i.e., in arresting and detaining her no one had "put their hands on her, grabbed her, jerked her around, bruised her or hurt her." Nonetheless, the taxpayer argued the physical loss of her freedom constituted a "personal physical injury" within the meaning of § 104(a)(2). The Sixth Circuit, affirming the Tax Court, stated that taxpayer sought "to create a per se rule that every false imprisonment claim necessarily involves a physical injury, even though physical injury is not a required element of false imprisonment under [applicable state law]." The court conceded that false imprisonment might result in a physical injury, such as an injured wrist as a result of being handcuffed. "But the mere fact that false imprisonment involves a physical act — restraining the victim's freedom — does not mean that the victim is *necessarily* physically injured *as a result* of that physical act." What difference, if any, would or should it make if, instead of being wrongly detained for a matter of hours, a taxpayer were wrongly imprisoned for years?

b.   Emotional Distress

As noted, § 104(a)(2) specifically provides that "emotional distress shall not be treated as a physical injury or physical sickness." Just as the statute and regulations do not define "personal physical injury or physical sickness" for purposes of § 104(a)(2), they do not define "emotional distress." The House Committee report for the 1996 Act, however, does note "the term emotional distress includes physical symptoms (e.g., insomnia, headaches, and stomach disorders) which may result from such emotional distress." House Committee Report on Small Business Job Protection Act of 1996 (H.R. 3448) at 142–43, n.24. The Report notes that, since emotional distress is not a physical injury or physical sickness, "[t]he exclusion from gross income does not apply to any damages received (other than for medical expenses . . .) based on a claim of employment discrimination or injury to reputation accompanied by a claim for emotional distress." *Id.* at 143. If, however, the claim had its origin in a personal physical injury, a recovery for emotional distress may be excludable. In this regard, the Report states: "[T]he exclusion . . . applies to any damages received based on a claim of emotional distress that is attributable to a physical injury or physical sickness." Incorporating this statutory change, the amended regulation § 1.104-1(c) promulgated in 2012 and discussed *infra* specifically provides: "Emotional distress is not considered a physical injury or physical sickness. However, damages for emotional distress attributable to a physical injury or physical sickness are excluded from income under section 104(a)(2)." Reg. § 1.104-1(c)(1).

What constitutes a "symptom" of emotional distress? As noted above, the legislative history provides three examples, insomnia, headaches, and stomach disorders. Since the 1996 amendments to § 104(a)(2), courts have identified other symptoms of emotional distress including loss of appetite, emotional instability, anxiety, and depression. In *Parkinson v. Commissioner*, noted above, the Tax Court concluded that a taxpayer who suffered a heart attack as a result of the emotional distress he experienced in the workplace had suffered a physical injury within the meaning of § 104(a)(2). In rejecting the Commissioner's argument that the settlement in that case was entirely for emotional distress, the Court noted:

> In a medical context, a "symptom" is "subjective evidence of disease or of a patient's condition, i.e., such evidence as perceived by the patient." The Sloane-Dorland Annotated Medical-Legal Dictionary, 496 (Supp. 1992). A "symptom" is distinguished from a "sign", defined as "any objective evidence of a disease, i.e., such evidence as is perceptible to the examining physician, as opposed to the subjective sensations (symptoms) of the patient. . . .

> It would seem self-evident that a heart attack and its physical afteref- fects constitute physical injury or sickness rather than mere subjective sensations or symptoms of emotional distress. . . .

> Insofar as respondent means to suggest that claims of physical injury or sickness are not compensable in a cause of action for intentional infliction

of emotional distress, respondent is mistaken. When it first recognized the tort of intentional infliction of emotional distress, the Court of Appeals of Maryland in *Harris v. Jones*, 281 Md. 560, 380 A.2d 611, 613 (1977), looked to the Restatement, Torts 2d, Sec. 46(1) (1965), which states:

> One, who by extreme and outrageous conduct intentionally or recklessly causes severe emotional distress to another, is subject to liability for such emotional distress, and *if bodily harm to the other results from it, for such bodily harm.* [Emphasis added.]

In *Blackwood v. Commissioner*, T.C. Memo. 2012-190, the taxpayer, who suffered from depression, was fired by her employer, and, as a result of the termination, her "depression relapsed, causing her to suffer symptoms such as insomnia, sleeping too much, migraines, nausea, vomiting, weight gain, acne and pain in her back, shoulder and neck." The taxpayer sought to exclude under § 104(a)(2) the amount of the settlement she negotiated with her employer. In holding for the Commissioner that the damages were for emotional distress and not for personal physical injury or physical sickness, the Tax Court distinguished *Domeny*, noted above and included in the materials, on the grounds that the taxpayer in *Blackwood* "did not provide evidence that [her] physical symptoms of depression were severe enough to rise to the level of physical injury or physical sickness" or that she had been medically determined to be "too ill to work."

The provision in the 1996 Act negating emotional distress as a physical injury or physical sickness has generated considerable controversy. In her 2009 report to Congress, the National Taxpayer Advocate noted:

> Although the medical community increasingly believes that mental illness is caused by physical/chemical abnormalities or changes in the body and may produce physical symptoms as well — effectively blurring the line between physical suffering and mental suffering — the tax code continues to treat taxpayers differently according to their illnesses. Under current law, if a taxpayer is awarded compensation for depression or anxiety resulting from sexual harassment in the workplace, for example, the award would be includible in gross income because current law provides an exclusion only for awards received on account of physical injury or sickness. The National Taxpayer Advocate recommends that Congress amend IRC Section 104(a)(2) to exclude from gross income any payments received as a settlement or judgment for mental anguish, emotional distress and pain and suffering.

National Taxpayer Advocate's 2009 Annual Report to Congress (Dec. 31, 2009), IRS Publication 2104C (Rev. 12-2009), at 31. Do you agree?

c. Recoveries by Individuals Other than Individual Suffering Physical Injury or Sickness

The legislative history of the 1996 Act is clear that, if a claim has its origin in a physical injury or physical sickness, it is not necessary that the recipient of damages be the individual who suffered the physical injury or sickness. The House Report states: "if an action has its origin in a physical injury or physical sickness, then all damages (other than punitive damages) that flow therefrom are treated as payments received on account of physical injury or physical sickness whether or not the recipient of the damages is the injured party." The Report provides the following example: "damages (other than punitive damages) received by an individual on account of a claim for loss of consortium due to the physical injury or physical sickness of such individual's spouse are excludable from gross income." House Report on Small Business Job Protection Act of 1996 (H.R. 3448) at 143. Thus, in PLR 200121031 addressing damages received by a taxpayer for the asbestos-related lung cancer and other asbestos related diseases that killed her husband, a sheetrocker, the Service noted:

> Husband contracted physical diseases from exposure to asbestos. These diseases were the proximate cause of the circumstances giving rise to Taxpayer's loss of consortium claim, survival action and wrongful death action. Because there exists a direct link between the physical injury suffered and the damages recovered, Taxpayer may exclude from gross income any economic damages compensating for such injury. These would include damages received for the survival action, loss of consortium and wrongful death of Taxpayer's spouse.

5.   The Current Regulations and the Definition of "Damages"

Prior to its amendment in 2012, Regulation § 1.104-1(c) required payments excluded under § 104(a)(2) to be received "through prosecution of a legal suit or action based upon tort or tort-type rights, or through a settlement agreement entered into in lieu of such prosecution." Based upon that language, courts denied exclusion for amounts received pursuant to contracts permitting others to take actions which, but for the contract, would have been tortious. For example, in *United States v. Garber*, 589 F.2d 843 (5th Cir. 1979), the § 104(a)(2) exclusion was not allowed to a taxpayer who periodically sold her blood plasma, and who contended the payment received constituted damages for the personal injury she sustained each time she gave blood. According to the Fifth Circuit, the statutory exclusion necessitates some sort of claim against the payor, and the mere fact the taxpayer experienced pain and discomfort in giving blood did not make the purchaser's actions tortious.

In view of the Supreme Court's decision in *Commissioner v. Schleier*, included in the materials, and the congressional amendment of § 104(a)(2) in 1996, discussed *supra*, Treasury in 2012 amended Regulation § 1.104-1(c). The amended regulations eliminated the need to establish that an action or settlement was based on tort or tort-type rights. In its preamble to the amended regulation, Treasury noted:

> Before the 1996 amendment, the section 104(a)(2) exclusion was not limited to damages for physical injuries or sickness. The tort-type rights test was intended to distinguish damages for personal injuries from, for example, damages for breach of contract. Since that time, however, *Commissioner v. Schleier*, 515 U.S. 323, 115 S. Ct. 2159, 132 L. Ed. 2d 294 (1995), has interpreted the statutory "on account of" test to exclude only damages directly linked to "personal" injuries or sickness. Furthermore, under the

1996 Act, only damages for personal physical injuries or physical sickness are excludable. These legislative and judicial developments have eliminated the need to base the section 104(a)(2) exclusion on tort cause of action and remedy concepts. [T.D. 9573, 77 F.R. 3107.]

The 2012 regulations thus reverse the result in *Burke*, discussed *supra*, by providing the § 104(a)(2) exclusion is applicable "to damages recovered for a personal physical injury or physical sickness under a statute, *even if that statute does not provide for a broad range of remedies. The injury need not be defined as a tort under state or common law.*" (Emphasis added.)

With the elimination of the "tort or tort-type" requirement, the amended regulations define "damages" simply as "an amount received (other than workers' compensation) through prosecution of a legal suit or action, or through a settlement agreement entered into in lieu of prosecution." In *Perez v. Commissioner*, 144 T.C. No. 4 (2015), included in the materials, a case addressing the tax consequences of amounts the taxpayer received under contracts whereby the taxpayer "donated" her eggs to an infertile couple, the Tax Court considered whether the Secretary of the Treasury could "implicitly require a lawsuit or threat of one as a condition of excluding 'damages' from taxable income." *Id.* Holding the regulation definition of "damages" valid, the court concluded that the amounts received by the taxpayer constituted compensation for services rather than "damages" excludable under § 104(a)(2).

6.   Punitive Damages

The excludability of punitive damages under § 104(a)(2) has been the subject of numerous conflicting court decisions and administrative rulings. In 1989, Congress, in an effort to clarify the law in this regard, amended § 104(a)(2) to provide the statutory exclusion did not apply "to any punitive damages in connection with a case not involving physical injury or sickness." To be sure, all this amendment did was specify that no exclusion was available for punitive damages arising out of non-physical personal injuries. The statute failed to address the tax status of punitive damages arising out of physical personal injuries or sickness. In *O'Gilvie v. U.S.*, 519 U.S. 79 (1996), the Supreme Court held § 104(a)(2) (prior to the 1996 amendments) did not exclude punitive damages. Relying specifically on the interpretation it had given in *Schleier* to the "on account of" language of § 104(a)(2), the Supreme Court reasoned that "punitive damages are not covered [by § 104(a)(2)] because they are an element of damages not designed to compensate victims, rather they are punitive in nature." The 1996 amendments to § 104(a)(2) clarify that the statutory exclusion does not apply to punitive damages.[4]

---

[4] However, § 104(c) provides that prior law continues to apply to a limited category of punitive damages, namely to punitive damages received in a wrongful death action if the "applicable State law (as in effect on September 13, 1995 and without regard to any modification after such date) provides . . . that only punitive damages may be awarded in such an action." Apparently, Congress concluded it would be unfair to make the exclusion of wrongful death damages to depend upon whether a state's law characterized wrongful death damages as compensatory or punitive in nature.

7. Allocation of Awards

Because punitive damages are not excludable, a taxpayer negotiating the settlement of a case involving a physical personal injury may be tempted to insist that the entire settlement amount be allocated to the physical injury even though the taxpayer's pleadings requested both compensatory and punitive damages.[5] The tortfeasor/payor may be indifferent to the characterization of the settlement and agree to the proposed allocation. Will the settlement agreement's characterization of the entire award as compensation for the physical injuries be respected? The answer is not completely clear. The Service, however, is likely to scrutinize settlements carefully and to challenge allocations resulting from settlement negotiations which it does not consider to be arms-length. See *Robinson v. Commissioner*, 102 T.C. 116 (1994), *aff'd in part*, 70 F.3d 34 (5th Cir. 1995), in which the Tax Court held it was not bound by a state court judgment allocating 95% of certain settlement proceeds to tort-like personal injuries. In that case, the taxpayers, following a jury verdict which awarded the taxpayers amounts for lost business profits and personal injuries as well as $50 million in punitive damages, entered into an agreement with the defendant settling their lawsuit for a specific sum considerably less than the verdict amount. The taxpayers unilaterally prepared a final judgment making the allocation in question. The defendant bank, apparently anxious to settle the suit and recognizing the taxpayers' desire to avoid tax, acquiesced in the allocation. The presiding judge, without reviewing the allocation, signed the judgment. The Tax Court, emphasizing that it could make its own determination of the proper allocation of the settlement proceeds, ultimately held the taxpayers could exclude 37.3% of the settlement under § 104(a)(2), with the balance being includable in gross income.

Similarly, in *Bagley v. Commissioner*, 105 T.C. 396 (1995), the court agreed the Service should not be bound by a settlement agreement allocating all of the $1.5 million settlement to personal injuries. A jury had previously awarded the taxpayer $1,000,000 for personal injuries and $5,000,000 in punitive damages. The court emphasized that the critical question in determining the tax status of settlement amounts was "in lieu of what" was the settlement amount paid. The court concluded that, under the facts of the case, the taxpayer could not expect to recover more than $1,000,000 for the personal injuries; the balance of $500,000 of the settlement proceeds therefore represented a payment in lieu of punitive damages.

Contrast *Bagley* and *Robinson* with *McKay v. Commissioner*, 102 T.C. 465 (1994) (*vacated on other grounds*, 84 F.3d 433 (5th Cir. 1996)), in which the Tax Court respected an allocation in the settlement agreement of approximately three-fourths of the settlement award to personal injury claims and one-fourth to taxpayer's contract claims. In *McKay*, a jury had awarded taxpayer over $1.6 million for lost compensation and over $12.8 million for "future damages" as a result

---

[5] A related issue can arise with respect to the allocation of expenses incurred in pursuing personal injury claims. In general, expenses otherwise deductible will not be allowed if they are allocated to tax-exempt income. *See* § 265. Consider, therefore, the taxpayer who pays attorney fees to obtain a personal injury award, where some portion of the award is excludable under § 104(a)(2), but the remainder is taxable. To the extent the attorney fees are properly allocable to the tax-exempt income, they will be nondeductible. *See* Chapters 12 and 27.

of taxpayer's wrongful discharge. These damages were then trebled to over $43 million for the employer's violation of the Racketeer Influenced and Corrupt Organizations Act (RICO). Following the jury verdict, the parties engaged in negotiations resulting in a $16 million settlement most of which was allocated to the taxpayer's wrongful discharge tort claim. Upholding the allocation, the Tax Court emphasized the adversarial nature of the negotiations leading to the allocation of the award. Specifically, the court stressed that the tortfeasor in *McKay* had insisted that none of the settlement be allocated to the RICO violations or punitive damages.

8. Periodic Payments

Periodic payments are excludable under § 104(a)(2). A simple example illustrates the exclusion of periodic payments. Assume Victor sues George in a personal physical injury action. Pursuant to a settlement agreement, George agrees to pay Victor $3,000 per month for the next ten years. Under the statute, Victor will be entitled to exclude the entire amount he receives over the next 10 years, even though a significant portion of the payments in effect constitutes interest income. Contrast that situation to one in which Victor receives a lump sum payment, and invests in an annuity which pays exactly $3,000 per month for the next ten years. In that situation, Victor would be entitled to exclude the lump sum received, but would have to report a portion of each year's annuity payments as income pursuant to § 72. Section 104(a)(2) thus encourages injured taxpayers to structure their settlement awards so as to exclude the interest component of periodic payments. (Section 130 of the Code addresses the tax treatment of amounts paid to so-called "structured settlement companies." Such companies accept assignments of obligations to make periodic payments from those who are actually liable to pay the damages.)

B. Accident and Health Insurance

It is appropriate to consider together the provisions of §§ 104(a)(3) and 105. Under § 104(a)(3), payments received through accident or health insurance policies are excluded from gross income, provided the policy was not financed by the taxpayer's employer or by employer contributions not includable in the taxpayer's income. In effect, if the taxpayer is willing to finance his own accident and health insurance with after-tax dollars, payments thereunder will be tax-free.

Such is not the case with employer-financed plans. Payments made by employer-financed accident and health plans are not exempt under § 104(a)(3), but instead are governed by § 105. Section 105(a) generally includes these payments in the employee's gross income. The Code, however, provides exceptions for medical expense reimbursements and certain payments for permanent bodily injury or disfigurement. §§ 105(b) and (c). For example, "sick pay" or wage continuation payments are taxable under employer-financed insurance; similar payments are nontaxable under a self-financed plan.

One may similarly contrast the tax treatment of medical expense payments under self-financed and employer-financed insurance plans. The § 105(b) exclusion for medical care for the taxpayer, spouse and dependents is limited to the actual medical expenses incurred; under § 104(a)(3), however, payments that exceed the medical expenses incurred remain tax-free. Revenue Ruling 69-154, 1969-1 C.B. 46, illustrates the difference: If the taxpayer has two self-financed health insurance policies that in combination make medical payments totaling $1,200 when actual medical expenses are only $900, all of the payments (including the excess $300) are nontaxable. If both policies are employer-financed, then the $300 excess reimbursement would be includable in gross income. If one policy is employer-financed and the other is self-financed, then the excess reimbursement is allocated in proportion to the relative payments made by each policy. For example, if 70%, or $840, of the total payments of $1,200 were made by the employer-financed policy, then 70%, or $210, of the excess reimbursement of $300 would be attributed to that policy and included in income. The remaining 30% ($90) of the excess reimbursement would be allocated to the self-financed policy and excluded from income under § 104(a)(3).

Suppose, however, a single policy is financed by both taxpayer and employer. Payment under such a policy is treated as self-financed in proportion to that part of the total premium paid by the taxpayer. Assume the employer policy in the previous example was financed half by employer contributions and half by after-tax employee contributions. Again, since that policy made 70% of the total payments, 70%, or $210, of the excess reimbursement is attributable to it. However, since the employer made only half of the contributions to the total premium, only half of the excess reimbursement ($105) is attributable to the employer's contribution, and thus only $105 is includable in gross income.

Recall at this point the § 106(a) exclusion for employer-provided coverage under accident and health plans. In summary, § 106(a) permits employer contributions to accident and health plans to be made on a tax-free basis to the employee, but § 105(a) makes payments under such employer-financed plans taxable, except to the extent §§ 105(b) or (c) applies.

As noted previously, payments under employer-financed plans are excluded to the extent they compensate for permanent bodily injury or disfigurement of the taxpayer, spouse, or dependents, provided the payments are computed with reference to the nature of the injury and not the period of absence from work. Section 105(c). If such amounts are paid under a workers' compensation act, they are excluded by § 104(a)(1). Reg. § 1.105-3. Section 105(c), however, could apply to, and exclude, any amounts paid in excess of the applicable workers' compensation act, since such excess amounts would not be excludable under § 104(a)(1).

C. Previously Deducted Medical Expenses

Section 213 permits a deduction for unreimbursed medical expenses in excess of a floor based on the taxpayer's adjusted gross income. Medical expenses incurred on account of a personal physical injury, unreimbursed and thus deducted in the year paid, may be reimbursed in a later year as part of a claim for damages on account of personal physical injury. Nonetheless, despite the nexus of the reimbursed expenses to the injury, amounts attributable to previously deducted medical expenses are not excluded from income. §§ 104(a), 105(b). The reason is an obvious one: to allow an expenditure to be deducted from income, and then to allow the reimbursement of the expense to be excluded from income would constitute a double tax benefit for the same amount, and the Code properly prohibits that.

Reimbursements for nondeductible medical expenses, however, are excluded from income under §§ 104 and 105. *See* Reg. § 1.213-1(g). Is this exclusion at variance with the § 262 general principle of nondeductibility of personal expenditures and the § 213 limited deductibility of extraordinary medical expenses?

In some instances, a payment for personal injury or sickness, based in part on the taxpayer's medical expenses, may be made in the form of an undifferentiated lump sum. In Revenue Ruling 75-230, 1975-1 C.B. 93, the Service required that a lump sum award in a personal injury suit settled out of court be allocated between medical expenses and other components of the award. According to the ruling, the Service will respect an allocation made by the parties unless the allocation is unreasonable; where no allocation is made, the settlement will be presumed to be attributable first to medical expenses previously deducted, and thus includable in income to the extent of the prior medical expense deduction allowed. Awards for future medical expenses were addressed by Revenue Ruling 75-232, 1975-1 C.B. 94. Such awards may be excluded from income, but to the extent of the allocations to future medical expenses, the taxpayer may not deduct those future medical expenses under § 213 when they are incurred.

D. Workers' Compensation

Section 104(a)(1) excludes from income amounts received under workers' compensation acts as compensation for personal injuries or sickness. The regulations provide the exclusion also extends to payments under a statute "in the nature of a workmen's compensation act," but not to retirement payments to the extent based on age, length of service, or employee contributions, even where retirement is caused by occupational injury or illness. Reg. § 1.104-1(b). Conversely, compensation for nonoccupational injury or illness is not within § 104(a)(1), even if the label of workers' compensation is placed upon the payment.

E. Certain Disability Pensions

Military disability pensions and certain other government disability pensions are excluded from income under § 104(a)(4). Except for certain grandfathered pensions, this exclusion is now sharply limited, however, by § 104(b) to persons receiving compensation for combat-related injuries and to those who would on application receive disability compensation from the Veterans' Administration. A special provision also provides an exclusion for disability income attributable to injuries suffered in a terrorist attack upon an employee of the United States engaged in performance of official duties outside the United States. § 104(a)(5).

COMMISSIONER v. SCHLEIER
United States Supreme Court
515 U.S. 323 (1995)

JUSTICE STEVENS delivered the opinion of the Court.

The question presented is whether § 104(a)(2) of the Internal Revenue Code authorizes a taxpayer to exclude from his gross income the amount received in settlement of a claim for backpay and liquidated damages under the Age Discrimination in Employment Act of 1967 (ADEA). . . .

II

Section 61(a) of the Internal Revenue Code provides a broad definition of "gross income": "Except as otherwise provided in this subtitle, gross income means all income from whatever source derived." 26 U.S.C. § 61(a). We have repeatedly emphasized the "sweeping scope" of this section and its statutory predecessors. *Commissioner v. Glenshaw Glass Co.*, 348 U.S. 426, 429, 75 S. Ct. 473, 99 L. Ed. 483 (1955). *See also United States v. Burke*, 504 U.S. at 233. We have also emphasized the corollary to § 61(a)'s broad construction, namely the "default rule of statutory interpretation that exclusions from income must be narrowly construed." *United States v. Burke*, 504 U.S. at 248 (Souter, J., concurring in judgment) . . . .

Respondent recognizes § 61(a)'s "sweeping" definition and concedes that his settlement constitutes gross income unless it is expressly excepted by another provision in the Code. Respondent claims, however, that his settlement proceeds are excluded from § 61(a)'s reach by 26 U.S.C. § 104(a). § 104(a) provides an exclusion for five categories of "compensation for personal injuries or sickness." Respondent argues that his settlement award falls within the second of those categories, which excludes from gross income "the amount of any damages received . . . on account of personal injuries or sickness." § 104(a)(2). . . .

In our view, the plain language of the statute undermines respondent's contention. Consideration of a typical recovery in a personal injury case illustrates the usual meaning of "on account of personal injuries." Assume that a taxpayer is in an automobile accident, is injured, and as a result of that injury suffers (a) medical expenses, (b) lost wages, and (c) pain, suffering, and emotional distress that cannot be measured with precision. If the taxpayer settles a resulting lawsuit for $30,000 (and if the taxpayer has not previously deducted her medical expenses, see § 104(a)), the entire $30,000 would be excludable under § 104(a)(2). The medical expenses for injuries arising out of the accident clearly constitute damages received "on account of personal injuries." Similarly, the portion of the settlement intended to compensate for pain and suffering constitutes damages "on account of personal injury." Finally, the recovery for lost wages is also excludable as being "on account of personal injuries," as long as the lost wages resulted from time in which the taxpayer was out of work as a result of her injuries. *See, e.g., Threlkeld v. Commissioner*, 87 T.C. 1294, 1300 (1986) (hypothetical surgeon who loses finger through tortious conduct may exclude any recovery for lost wages because "this injury . . . will also undoubtedly cause special damages including loss of future income"), aff'd, 848 F.2d 81 (C.A.6 1988). The critical point this hypothetical illustrates is that each element of the settlement is recoverable not simply because the taxpayer received a tort settlement, but rather because each element of the settlement satisfies the requirement set forth in § 104(a)(2) (and in all of the other subsections of § 104(a)) that the damages were received "on account of personal injuries or sickness." In contrast, no part of respondent's ADEA settlement is excludable under the plain language of § 104(a)(2). Respondent's recovery of back wages, though at first glance comparable to our hypothetical accident victim's recovery of lost wages, does not fall within § 104(a)(2)'s exclusion because it does not satisfy the critical requirement of being "on account of personal injury or sickness." Whether one treats respondent's attaining the age of 60 or his being laid off on account of his age as the proximate cause of respondent's loss of income, neither the birthday nor the discharge can fairly be described as a "personal injury" or "sickness." Moreover, though respondent's unlawful termination may have caused some psychological or "personal" injury comparable to the intangible pain and suffering caused by an automobile accident, it is clear that no part of respondent's recovery of back wages is attributable to that injury. Thus, in our automobile hypothetical, the accident causes a personal injury which in turn causes a loss of wages. In age discrimination, the discrimination causes both personal injury and loss of wages, but neither is linked to the other. The amount of back wages recovered is completely independent of the existence or extent of any personal injury. In short, § 104(a)(2) does not permit the exclusion of respondent's back wages because the recovery of back wages was not "on account of" any personal injury and because no personal injury affected the amount of back wages recovered.

Respondent suggests, nonetheless, that the liquidated damages portion of his settlement fits comfortably within the plain language of § 104(a)(2)'s exclusion. . . .

We agree with respondent that if Congress had intended the ADEA's liquidated damages to compensate plaintiffs for personal injuries, those damages might well come within § 104(a)(2)'s exclusion. There are, however, two weaknesses in respondent's argument. First, even if we assume that Congress was aware of the Court's observation [in *Overnight Motor Transportation Co. v. Missel*, 316 U.S. 572 (1942)] that the liquidated damages authorized by the FLSA [Fair Labor Standards Act] might provide compensation for some "obscure" injuries, it does not necessarily follow that Congress would have understood that observation as referring to injuries that were personal rather than economic. Second, and more importantly, we have previously rejected respondent's argument: We have already concluded that the liquidated damages provisions of the ADEA were a significant departure from those in the FLSA, see *Lorillard v. Pons*, 434 U.S. at 581; *Trans World Airlines, Inc. v. Thurston*, 469 U.S. at 126, and we explicitly held in *Thurston*: "Congress intended for liquidated damages to be punitive in nature." *Id.*, at 125.

Our holding in *Thurston* disposes of respondent's argument and requires the conclusion that liquidated damages under the ADEA, like back wages under the ADEA, are not received "on account of personal injury or sickness."[6]

---

[6] We find odd the dissent's suggestion . . . that our holding today assumes that the intangible harms of discrimination do not constitute personal injuries. We of course have no doubt that the intangible harms of discrimination can constitute personal injury, and that compensation for such harms may be

. . . .

In sum, the plain language of § 104(a)(2) [establishes a requirement] that a taxpayer must meet before a recovery may be excluded under § 104(a)(2). . . . [T]he taxpayer must show that the damages were received "on account of personal injuries or sickness." For the reasons discussed above, we believe that respondent has failed to satisfy [this] requirement, and thus no part of his settlement is excludable under § 104(a)(2).

The judgment is reversed.

It is so ordered.

[JUSTICE SCALIA concurred in the judgment. JUSTICES O'CONNOR, THOMAS and SOUTER dissented.]

DOMENY v. COMMISSIONER
United States Tax Court
T.C. Memo 2010-9

Petitioner resided in California at the time her petition was filed. After completing high school petitioner obtained a degree in visual merchandising, cost, and design. She worked in theater and visual merchandising for approximately 20 years in the San Francisco area. Following those positions, petitioner became involved in professional fundraising for nonprofit organizations. After approximately 2 1/2 years as a professional fundraiser petitioner was employed by the Pacific Autism Center for Education (PACE) in 2000.

During 1996 before her employment with PACE petitioner was diagnosed with multiple sclerosis (MS). At the onset of her MS she experienced numbness from the waist down. The numbness receded to her feet, leaving them numb. She also experienced fatigue, lightheadedness, vertigo, and sometimes a burning sensation behind her eyes. Petitioner found the prescribed treatment (which did not ameliorate the symptoms of her condition) more profoundly troublesome than her symptoms, so she chose to "manage" her symptoms without medication. She left her position as a professional fundraiser before being hired by PACE, because she was seeking a job situation were she would not have to spend as much time on her feet.

Petitioner's duties with PACE included community development, fundraising, and writing grants. Petitioner enjoyed her work with PACE, and she was motivated by the children and parents who were involved with PACE's autism program. The fact that petitioner was ill with MS motivated her involvement with the cause of autism and the underlying fundraising activities.

After a while PACE appointed a new executive director who was to be petitioner's supervisor. The new executive director did not want petitioner to socialize or be

---

excludable under § 104(a)(2). However, to acknowledge that discrimination may cause intangible harms is not to say that the ADEA compensates for such harms, or that any of the damages received were on account of those harms.

involved with parents of autistic children, although she was required to somehow approach them for fundraising purposes. Petitioner had a strained relationship with her supervisor, who restricted her duties. By 2004 these concerns and conditions in petitioner's workplace caused her MS symptoms to flare up. In November 2004 it came to petitioner's attention that the director was embezzling funds from PACE's students' personal accounts. Petitioner went to PACE's board members with this information, and she was told that they would take care of the situation. Petitioner felt tension concerning her supervisor's alleged embezzlement. In particular she was upset that PACE sent her out to raise funds from parents, knowing that funds were being embezzled by her supervisor. Petitioner advised her superiors on several occasions of her unhealthful work environment, including her stress from the embezzlement and PACE's failure to take any action. The series of events involving the embezzlement and resulting severance of the residential director caused petitioner much distress, and during that time her MS symptoms intensified.

Petitioner's symptoms continued to worsen, and on March 7, 2005, she left work. On the next day she visited her primary care physician, Dr. Chris E. Chung. At that time Dr. Chung determined that petitioner was too ill, because of her MS symptoms, to return to work and that she should not return to work until after March 21, 2005. Petitioner's March 7, 2005, symptoms from MS included: Vertigo, shooting pain in both legs, difficulty walking due to numbness in both feet, a burning sensation behind her eyes, and extreme fatigue. On or about March 8, 2005, petitioner notified PACE by facsimile of Dr. Chung's diagnosis and of the doctor's instructions that she not return to work until after March 21, 2005. After sending the facsimile on March 8, 2005, petitioner received a telephone call from PACE's executive director, who notified her that her employment would be terminated effective March 15, 2005. After that telephone conversation petitioner's physical MS symptoms were "spiking", including shooting pain up her legs, fatigue, burning eyes, spinning head, vertigo, and lightheadedness. During the taxable year 2005 petitioner was employed by PACE from January 1 through March 15.

Because of these circumstances, petitioner contacted a lawyer to seek redress from PACE. She explained the circumstances of her employment, illness, and dismissal to the lawyer, who agreed that she had a cause of action, and petitioner retained the lawyer to pursue PACE. Petitioner's lawyer negotiated with PACE lawyers, and a settlement was reached. The settlement agreement was entitled "Severance Agreement and Release of Claims" (the agreement). In the agreement petitioner released [PACE from a list of possible causes of action based on federal, state and common law].

Under the agreement $33,308 was the total amount PACE agreed to pay. Of the $33,308, $8,187.50 was compensation due to petitioner, which PACE agreed to send directly to petitioner's attorney. Petitioner reported the $8,187.50 on her 2005 Federal income tax return as wage compensation. Another $8,187.50 was sent directly to petitioner's attorney, and petitioner was not issued a Form 1099-MISC, Miscellaneous Income, or Form W-2, Wage and Tax Statement, by PACE for that amount. PACE paid the remaining $16,933 to petitioner without withholding deductions and issued a Form 1099-MISC reflecting that the amount was "Non-employee compensation."

Discussion

The sole question to be considered is whether the $16,933 settlement amount petitioner received is excludable from her gross income under section 104(a)(2). More specifically, the parties disagree about whether petitioner received the settlement for her physical condition.

To prevail, petitioner must show that her claim against PACE was based on tort or tort type rights [Regulation § 1.104-1(c), effective January 23, 2012, has eliminated this requirement] and that the damages were received on account of physical injuries or sickness. *Commissioner v. Schleier*, 515 U.S. 323, 337 (1995); see also *Commissioner v. Banks*, 543 U.S. 426 (2005). The agreement, pursuant to which the $16,933 was paid, contains a list of numerous possible causes of action or rights that petitioner was releasing in exchange for the payment. In all respects, the settlement agreement is ambiguous regarding any specific reason for the payment. Respondent relies on that ambiguity as showing that PACE had no specific intent when making the settlement payment. When a settlement agreement lacks express language stating the specific purpose of the settlement payment, the most important factor for courts to consider is the intent of the payor. Accordingly, we must decide the reason or intent for the payment. This is a purely factual inquiry.

There can be no doubt that petitioner's claim against PACE was based on tort or tort type rights. . . . The focus of the parties' arguments is on the second requirement of the *Schleier* test, that the damages be received on account of physical injury or sickness. It has been held that the second test "can only be satisfied if there is 'a direct causal link' between the damages and the personal injuries sustained." *Banaitis v. Commissioner*, 340 F.3d 1074, 1080 (9th Cir. 2003) . . . .

When damages are paid in connection with a settlement agreement, we first look to the underlying agreement to determine whether it expressly states that the damages compensate for "personal physical injuries or physical sickness" under sec. 104(a)(2). If the agreement is ambiguous or lacks express language specifying the purpose of the compensation, courts then proceed to examine the intent of the payor. The payor's intent can be "based on all the facts and circumstances of the case, including the complaint that was filed and the details surrounding the litigation." [The Tax Court noted that Petitioner's failure to bring suit or make formal allegations against PACE "is not necessarily detrimental to * * * [her] efforts to establish the existence of an underlying tort-type cause of action . . . ."] Petitioner's exposure to a hostile and stressful work environment exacerbated her MS symptoms to a point where she was unable to work. This fact was confirmed by her doctor, who prescribed 2 weeks off. Petitioner notified her employer of her condition and faxed to her employer her doctor's diagnosis together with his instructions that she take time off from work because of illness. A short time later the executive director advised petitioner by telephone that her employment would be terminated effective March 15, 2009.

Petitioner obtained the services of an attorney and explained (in greater detail) the circumstances of her employment, illness, and termination from employment. The attorney met with petitioner's employer's attorney and worked out a settlement of petitioner's claim against her employer. The agreement contained a blanket release from any and all claims that petitioner might have had, but had no specific or express statement of the payor's intent.

An inference can be drawn, however, from the terms of the settlement agreement. The manner in which PACE agreed to pay out the settlement compensation reveals some recognition of petitioner's claim and condition. The $33,308 settlement was segregated into three separate and distinct payments. One amount ($8,187.50) was reflected as employee compensation due to petitioner which PACE agreed to pay directly to petitioner's attorney. Petitioner reported that $8,187.50 on her 2005 Federal income tax return as wage compensation. Another $8,187.50 was sent directly to petitioner's attorney, and no Form 1099-MISC or Form W-2 was issued to petitioner by PACE for that amount. The remaining $16,933 was paid by PACE to petitioner, and the payment was not reduced by withholding. PACE issued a Form 1099-MISC reflecting that the $16,933 was "Nonemployee compensation."

The differing tax and reporting treatments used for the three payments show that PACE was aware that at least part of petitioner's recovery may not have been subject to tax; i.e., was due to physical illness. Coupled with that inference is the fact that petitioner advised PACE of her illness before her employment was terminated and the likelihood that her attorney represented petitioner's circumstances to PACE in the course of the settlement negotiations. Petitioner made no other claim. We find that PACE intended to compensate petitioner for her acute physical illness caused by her hostile and stressful work environment.

In summary, petitioner has shown that her work environment exacerbated her existing physical illness. [The Tax Court noted "It is of no consequence that petitioner had the MS condition before the flareup caused by her hostile work environment."] Petitioner's condition and her MS flareup caused by her working conditions was intense and long lasting. Petitioner was physically unable to work until sometime in 2006, more than 1 year following her termination. She has shown that the only reason for the $16,933 payment was to compensate her for her physical injuries.

To reflect the foregoing and to account for concessions of the parties, Decision will be entered under Rule 155.

PEREZ v. COMMISSIONER
144 T.C. No. 4 (2015)

HOLMES, JUDGE

Nichelle Perez received $20,000 under contracts that she signed with a clinic before she underwent a prolonged series of painful injections and operations to retrieve her unfertilized eggs for transfer to infertile couples. The contracts said that she was being paid in compensation for her pain and suffering. The Code says that *damages* for pain and suffering are not taxable. Was the $20,000 Perez received "damages"?

FINDINGS OF FACT

Perez is a 29-year-old single woman from Orange County, California. She is a high-school graduate and worked as a full-time sales associate for Sprint. In her early 20s Perez learned about egg donation. Her Internet search soon led her to the website of the Donor Source International, LLC — an egg-donation agency in Orange County that matches egg donors with women and couples struggling to conceive on their own.

A. The Donor Source

The Donor Source is a for-profit California company that has been in business since 2003. It is one of approximately 30 donor agencies in California and in 2009 supervised roughly 250 egg-donation cycles for its customers. . . .

The Donor Source fixes the fee for first-time egg donors based on where the donor lives. For Southern California women, first-time donors are promised $5,500 — and the price goes up with each subsequent donation. The Donor Source is registered with the American Society for Reproductive Medicine, which caps the compensation for egg donors at $5,000 to $10,000. The Donor Source also promises to reimburse its suppliers for their expenses in traveling to and from their medical appointments.

B. The Contracts

But such promises of future payments all depend on prospective parents' picking a particular donor. Once they do, the donor signs two contracts — one with the Donor Source and one with the anonymous intended parents. . . .

Perez signed one contract with the Donor Source in February 2009. It promised her money:

> Donor Fee: Donor and Intended Parents will agree upon a Donor Fee for Donor's time, effort, inconvenience, pain, and suffering in donating her eggs. This fee is for Donor's good faith and full compliance with the donor egg procedure, not in exchange for or purchase of eggs and the quantity or quality of eggs retrieved will not affect the Donor Fee.

> > This meant that if Perez kept her side of the deal, but produced unusable eggs or no eggs at all, she would still be paid the contract price. The contract plainly provides that it is not for the sale of body parts . . . .

> > The contract between Perez and the intended parents is in all ways consistent with the contract with the Donor Source. It provides that Perez's payment is "in consideration for all of her pain, suffering, time, inconvenience, and efforts." The contract waives any and all parental or custodial rights Perez may have over the donated eggs. Once the eggs are removed, they immediately become the property of the intended parents and are fertilized almost immediately. It also states:

This Agreement does not instruct any of the Parties on the issue of taxation of any payment made or received pursuant to this Agreement or to any agreement with The Donor Source.

After signing the contracts, the Donor Source told Perez to take birth control pills for approximately a month to synch her menstrual cycle with that of the intended mother. Then, up until March 27, 2009 — the egg-retrieval date — Perez underwent a series of intrusive physical examinations. . . . She had to self-administer hormonal injections using a one-inch needle. Perez injected herself with 10 units of Lupron each morning from March 7 to March 11, and she had to take the shots right into her stomach, which often bruised and hurt her. With complete credibility Perez said that these procedures were "actually very painful * * * it was burning the entire time you were injecting it."

As the retrieval date approached, the injection schedule increased. Between March 16 and 25, she had to self-administer anywhere from one to three daily injections of Lupron, Follistim, and Menopur. She made around 22 injections into her stomach during this period. Every time she had to administer another dose of the hormones, she had to search for a part of her stomach not already covered in bruises.

Then on March 25 Perez administered to herself — under the observation of a professional at a fertility clinic — the final "trigger shot" of hCG. This is an intramuscular injection in the lower hip that goes through a two-inch needle. The shots caused Perez significant physical pain deep in her muscles as well as extreme abdominal bloating.

On the retrieval date, Perez was required to undergo anesthesia for the procedure. Doctors informed her that anesthesia carries with it a risk of possible death, and so she had to sign another liability waiver just before she went under. . . . After it was over, Perez felt cramped and bloated; she had mood swings, headaches, nausea, and fatigue.

But she'd kept the promises she made and got a check for $10,000. [During the same year, Perez went through a second round of egg donation, entering into agreements identical to the first set she had signed. Again, she received a check for $10,000.]

The Donor Source sent a Form 1099 to Perez for $20,000 for tax year 2009. After consulting other egg donors online, Perez concluded that the money was not taxable because it compensated her only for pain and suffering; therefore, she left it off her tax return. The Commissioner disagreed and sent her a notice of deficiency. Perez timely filed a petition, and we tried the case in California, where Perez still lives.

OPINION

We acknowledge that this case has received some publicity in tax and nontax publications, which is why it is important to state clearly what it does not concern. It does not require us to decide whether human eggs are capital assets. It does not require us to figure out how to allocate basis in the human body, or the holding period for human-body parts, or the character of the gain from the sale of those parts.

A. Nature of the Compensation

So what is this case about? Both parties agree that payments Perez received were not for the sale of her eggs. Perez argues that they were in exchange for the pain, suffering, and physical injuries she endured as part of the egg-retrieval process; the Commissioner, on the other hand, argues Perez was simply compensated for services rendered. The only two cases we have found that are anywhere near this issue are Green v. Commissioner, 74 T.C. 1229 (1980) and United States v. Garber, 607 F.2d 92 (5th Cir. 1979). Both involved the exchange of blood plasma for compensation. In Green, the taxpayer was paid by the pint, and we found her to be engaged in the sale of tangible property rather than the performance of services. Green, 74 T.C. at 1234. In Garber, the Fifth Circuit suggested the taxpayer might be engaged in the sale of property because the extent of her compensation was directly related to the concentration of antibodies in the plasma she produced. Garber, 607 F.2d at 97. It also noted that Garber had to undergo uncomfortable — and possibly dangerous — artificial stimulation and plasmapharesis to produce her plasma. This, the court observed, weighed in favor of finding that she was engaged in the performance of services. But because the appeal was from a criminal conviction, the court concluded that it didn't have to solve this puzzle, and could instead decide the case on the ground that a criminal prosecution for tax evasion was "an inappropriate vehicle for pioneering interpretations of tax law."

Both of Perez's 2009 contracts with the Donor Source specify that her compensation is in exchange for her "good faith and compliance with the donor egg procedure." Unlike the taxpayers in Green and Garber, who were paid by the quantity and the quality of plasma produced, Perez's compensation depended on neither the quantity nor the quality of the eggs retrieved, but solely on how far into the egg-retrieval process she went. On this key point, the testimony of both parties to the contracts agrees with the contract language. We have to find that Perez was compensated for services rendered and not for the sale of property.

And, as we know, "gross income means all income from whatever source derived, including * * * compensation for services." Sec. 61(a)(1). But this general rule of inclusion has many exceptions, and the one that Perez points us to is section 104(a)(2). Thus the only issue we address is whether a taxpayer who suffers physical pain or injury while performing a contract for personal services may exclude the amounts paid under that service contract as "damages * * * received * * * on account of personal physical injuries or physical sickness" even though the taxpayer knew that such injury or sickness might occur and consented to it in advance. Sec. 104(a)(2).

Before the regulations were amended, section 1.104-1(c) used to require payments excluded under section 104(a)(2) be "received * * * through prosecution of a legal suit or action based upon tort or tort type rights, or through a settlement agreement entered into in lieu of such prosecution." Sec. 1.104-1(c), Income Tax Regs. (former regulations), amended by T.D. 9573, 77 Fed. Reg. 3106-01, 3107 (Jan. 23, 2012). There were thus two separate requirements for a taxpayer to exclude income under section 104(a)(2): (1) the underlying cause of action giving rise to the recovery had to be based on tort or tort-type rights; and (2) the taxpayer had to receive the payment on account of his or her personal injuries or sickness. Commissioner v. Schleier, 515 U.S. 323, 333–34 (1995). . . .

But the Secretary has amended these regulations and abandoned the Schleier language requiring a "tort or tort-type right." . . . The regulation now states:

Section 104(a)(2) excludes from gross income the amount of any damages (other than punitive damages) received (whether by suit or agreement and whether as lump sums or as periodic payments) on account of personal physical injuries or physical sickness.

Despite the change in the language, the new requirements look a lot like the old ones: (1) damages received (2) on account of personal physical injuries or physical sickness.

B. Damages Requirement

The regulations define the term "damages" as "an amount received (other than workers' compensation) through prosecution of a legal suit or action, or through a settlement agreement entered into in lieu of prosecution." Sec. 1.104-1(c)(1), Income Tax Regs. Perez questions whether the Secretary's regulatory interpretation of "damages" is permissible — whether the word "damages" in the Code allows the Secretary to implicitly require a lawsuit or threat of one as a condition of excluding "damages" from taxable income. This is an argument that the regulation is invalid, which means we must pull into the Chevron station. See Chevron, U.S.A., Inc. v. Natural Res. Def. Council, Inc., 467 U.S. 837, 843–44 (1984) . . . .

We first ask if Congress has spoken directly to the question at issue. If not, we consider instead whether the Commissioner's regulation is a "reasonable interpretation" of Congress's intent. The Code doesn't define "damages", and so we can swiftly hop up onto Chevron's step two.

On this step, we find a regulation invalid only if it is "arbitrary or capricious in substance or manifestly contrary to the statute." . . . Perez argues that the definition of "damages" in the regulation is invalid because it requires prosecution (or threat of prosecution) of a legal suit as a prerequisite for a payment's exclusion from income. A walk through the regulation's history seems in order here.

From the beginning of tax time, awards or settlement proceeds for personal injuries have been excluded from taxation. The first section 104 regulations, enacted in 1960, required damages to be linked to a tort or tort-type right. And this "tort or tort-type right" was the focus of the regulations for half a century but, as Perez correctly points out, it is no longer. Perez cites several cases in support of her argument that we should interpret "damages" in section 104(a)(2) broadly to mean compensation in money received for a loss regardless of any legal suit or action.

. . . .

In Starrels v. Commissioner, 35 T.C. 646 (1961), aff'd, 304 F.2d 574 (9th Cir. 1962), we held that amounts contracted in advance for a consent to an invasion of privacy were taxable income and weren't excluded by section 104(a)(2). The Ninth Circuit agreed with us, and held that the section "reads most naturally in terms of payment for injuries sustained *prior to* a suit or settlement agreement." The court went on to note that these types of payments for personal injuries are excluded from gross income "because they make the taxpayer whole from a previous loss of personal rights." . . .

Again in Roosevelt v. Commissioner, 43 T.C. 77 (1964), we held that amounts FDR Jr. received for his share of the proceeds from a play about the life of his father were not excluded by section 104(a)(2). We reasoned that "moneys paid to any taxpayer as compensation for an *advance* waiver of possible future damages for personal injuries, would constitute taxable income to him under section 61 of the 1954 Code; and would not be excludable from his gross income under section 104(a)(2) of said Code." . . .

Perez very clearly has a legally recognized interest against bodily invasion. But we must hold that when she forgoes that interest — and consents to such intimate invasion for payment — any amount she receives must be included in her taxable income. Had the Donor Source or the clinic exceeded the scope of Perez's consent, Perez may have had a claim for damages. But the injury here, as painful as it was to Perez, was exactly within the scope of the medical procedures to which she contractually consented. Twice. Her physical pain was a byproduct of performing a service contract, and we find that the payments were made not to compensate her for some unwanted invasion against her bodily integrity but to compensate her for services rendered.

But what is one to make of the regulation's amendment to remove the "tort and tort-type right" requirement? One should always pause before holding that an amendment didn't change anything. But here the reason is clear — the amendment *did* change the law — it just didn't change the law for people like Perez. In 1992 the Supreme Court decided United States v. Burke, 504 U.S. 229 (1992). It held that title VII backpay settlement awards were not excludable from income under section 104(a)(2). At the time the statute read "damages received * * * on account of personal injuries," and the taxpayer pounced on the argument that her settlement with the Tennessee Valley Authority for unlawfully discriminating against her because she was a woman fit that requirement. Not so, said the Supreme Court. The Court emphasized that since the 1960s the Commissioner has formally linked the section 104(a)(2) exclusion to "tort or tort-type rights." It pronounced:

> "The essential element of an exclusion under section 104(a)(2) is that the income involved must derive from some sort of tort claim against the payor. . . . As a result, common law tort concepts are helpful in deciding whether a taxpayer is being compensated for a 'personal injury' " * * *

Id. (quoting Threlkeld v. Commissioner, 87 T.C. 1294, 1305 (1986)). A few years later, in Schleier, the Supreme Court reinforced the tort or tort-type right standard when it held that payments received in an Age Discrimination in Employment Act settlement were not excludable under section 104(a)(2). Schleier, 515 U.S. at 337. The remedial scheme there also did not comport with traditional tort-type remedies, because the Act did not provide for compensation keyed to actual harm suffered.

Shortly after the restrictive decisions in Burke and Schleier, Congress amended the Code and the Secretary in 2009 rewrote his regulations. This amended Code section and regulation let taxpayers who recovered under no-fault statutes exclude the "damages" that they received, even if they did not receive them for a "tort-type" claim. As we said in Simpson, the effect of removing the tort requirement from the regulation was to reverse the result in Burke and allow the exclusion for damages awarded under no-fault statutes. See Simpson, 141 T.C. at 346.

In 2012 the Commissioner officially explained that the "tort-type rights test was intended to distinguish damages for personal injuries from, for example, damages for breach of contract." T.D. 9573. The change in the section 104 regulation reflected a profusion of remedies for persons who are physically injured and recover under no-fault statutes, so that they are treated like those who are physically injured and recover through more traditional actions in tort. But that regulation still addresses situations where a taxpayer settles a claim for physical injuries or physical sickness before — or at least in lieu of — seeing litigation through to its conclusion.

This small change just helped tax regulation keep up with a bit of a shift in American law toward administrative or statutory remedies and away from common-law tort for some kinds of personal injuries. It is not at all arbitrary, capricious, or manifestly contrary to the Code. But it also doesn't help Perez. We completely believe Perez's utterly sincere and credible testimony that the series of medical procedures that culminated in the retrieval of her eggs was painful and dangerous to her present and future health. But what matters is that she voluntarily signed a contract to be paid to endure them. This means that the money she received was not "damages".

We conclude by noting that the result we reach today by taking a close look at the language and history of section 104 is also a reasonable one. We see no limit on the mischief that ruling in Perez's favor might cause: A professional boxer could argue that some part of the payments he received for his latest fight is excludable because they are payments for his bruises, cuts, and nosebleeds. A hockey player could argue that a portion of his million-dollar salary is allocable to the chipped teeth he invariably suffers during his career. And the same would go for the brain injuries suffered by football players and the less-noticed bodily damage daily endured by working men and women on farms and ranches, in mines, or on fishing boats. We don't doubt that some portion of the compensation paid all these people reflects the risk that they will feel pain and suffering, but it's a risk of pain and suffering that they agree to before they begin their work. And that makes it taxable compensation and not excludable damages. Because Perez's compensation was not "damages" under section 104(a)(2), we must rule against her on the main issue in the case.

Decision will be entered for respondent.

Chapter 11

FRINGE BENEFITS

I. PROBLEMS

1. Lenora manages a flower shop in a small town. Florence, the owner of the shop, pays Lenora a salary of $2,500 per month and permits Lenora to live rent-free in one of the apartments Florence owns in the town. Lenora, however, is required to pay all utilities associated with the apartment. Lenora's use of the apartment bears no relationship to her management of the flower shop. The apartment has a fair market rental value of $800 per month. Based on these facts, may Lenora treat the value of the apartment as an excludable fringe benefit?

2. William is president of a prestigious midwestern university. In addition to his salary, William and his family have the rent-free use of a large historic home located near the center of the university campus. It has long been the university's tradition that its president and the president's family occupy the home commonly referred to as "the president's mansion." The home is equipped with a commercial kitchen and has large drawing rooms enabling the president to entertain university alumni and donors, hold gala university dinners for visiting dignitaries, and to meet with groups of university administrators, faculty, staff, and students. William estimates he hosts a university-related gathering at least three times a week in the home, which has a fair market rental value of $5,500 per month. One could easily rent for $3,000 per month any number of very nice homes in the community which would be suitable for the day-to-day needs of William's family.

   (a) Does William have any gross income as a result of the rent-free use of the president's mansion?

   (b) How would your answer to (a) change, if at all, if the president's mansion were located ten blocks from the university campus?

   (c) Assume the university maintained a two-bedroom apartment in Washington, D.C. primarily for business use by the president and other university officials who often travel to D.C. to meet with members of Congress and directors of different government agencies. The university's board of trustees has authorized William and his family to use the apartment for personal purposes so long as the apartment has not otherwise been scheduled for university business purposes. Every spring William takes his family on a week-long vacation to D.C. to enjoy the cherry blossoms and the many other attractions of the city. They always use the university's apartment on these trips. Does William have any gross income as a result of the rent-free use of the

D.C. apartment on these family trips?

3. The Anytown Post gave Lawrence a free one-month subscription to the newspaper. After receiving the Anytown Post for the month, Lawrence was under no obligation to subscribe. If he did subscribe, however, Anytown Post offered to give him 50% off the normal annual subscription rate of $240. Lawrence enjoyed reading the paper, and after the one-month free subscription expired, he took advantage of the one-year subscription rate. Does Lawrence have any income as a result of the free one-month subscription or the special one-year subscription rate?

4. Ron is employed as a lawyer in the corporate headquarters of National Airlines in Washington, D.C. National employees and their families (defined by National as spouse or domestic partner, children, and parents of employees) receive free travel on a standby basis on National flights and 50% discounts on reserved seats. National employees also receive 50% discounts on personal lodging at the New York City Grand Hotel owned by National. What are the tax consequences in the following circumstances?

    (a) On a vacation trip to New York, Ron and his wife Susan flew without charge on a standby basis; their adult daughter Donna received a 50% discount on her reserved seat. All seats on the flight normally cost $500.

    (b) While in New York, Ron and Susan received a 50% discount on their hotel bill of $2,000, as did Donna on her $2,000 bill.

    (c) How do your answers to (a) and (b) change if Susan instead was Steven, Ron's domestic partner, and if Donna instead was Mary, Ron's mother?

    (d) Assume the 50% discount at the New York City Grand Hotel also applies to purchases in the hotel gift shop. Ron bought a gold bracelet in the gift shop for $1,000 as a gift for his mother. The cost of the bracelet to the gift shop was $1,000, and without the discount, the bracelet would have sold for $2,000.

    (e) In addition to the discounts listed previously, National also provides Ron with (1) free parking in a private garage across the street from National's headquarters, for which National pays $350 per month to the owner of the garage; (2) a public transit pass, for which National pays the transit company $100 per month; (3) office decor of Ron's choice, including furniture, artwork, and antiques; (4) free limousine service, in company vehicles, for business and personal travel within the metropolitan area; and (5) free use of a cell phone owned by National and provided to Ron for business use, although personal use is also permitted, with all charges paid by National.

Assignment for Chapter 11:

Complete the problems.

Read: Internal Revenue Code: §§ 61(a); 119(a), (b); 132(a)–(j)(1). Skim §§ 79(a); 106; 125(a), (d)(1), (f); 127(a); 129(a).

Treasury Regulations: §§ 1.61-21(a)(1)–(4), (b)(1) and (2); 1.119-1(a), (b), (c)(1), (e); 1.132-2(a)(1), (2), (3), (5), (b), (c); 1.132-3(a)(1)–(4), (b)(1), (c)(1)(i) and (ii), (e); 1.132-4(a)(1)(iii), (iv); 1.132-5(a)(1)(iii), (v), (2); 1.132-6(a), (b), (c), (d)(2)(i) and (ii), (4), (e); 1.132-7(a)(1)(i), (2), (4); 1.132-8(a)(1).

Materials: Overview
              Benaglia v. Commissioner
              United States v. Gotcher
              Statement by Donald C. Lubick on Fringe Benefits
              Excerpt from Examination of President Nixon's Tax Returns
              for 1969–1972

II. VOCABULARY

fringe benefit
statutory fringe benefits
cafeteria plan
no-additional-cost service
qualified employee discount
working condition fringe
de minimis fringe
qualified transportation fringe
convenience of employer
line of business

III. OBJECTIVES

1. To explain the convenience of the employer doctrine and to identify circumstances when it may apply.

2. To recall that § 119 excludes employer-provided meals and lodging under certain conditions.

3. To explain the requirements of § 119.

4. To predict whether employer-provided meals or lodging will be excluded in a given situation.

5. To recall that § 132 excludes an array of common fringe benefits.

6. To apply the exclusion for no additional-cost service.

7. To apply the exclusion for qualified employee discount.

8. To apply the exclusion for *de minimis* fringe benefits.

9. To apply the exclusion for working condition fringe benefits.

10. To apply the exclusion for qualified transportation fringe benefits.

11. To explain the valuation of fringe benefits which are not excluded from gross income.

12. To evaluate whether exclusions for the fringe benefits listed in § 132 and § 119 are appropriate, and to evaluate whether those provisions are administrable.

IV. OVERVIEW

Consider the following story: You are a third year associate for a large law firm who has worked long hours for the past few years and has now received an offer you can't refuse to join the legal department of A.B., Inc., a Fortune 500 company. Your salary and bonus schedule at A.B. will be competitive with that offered to senior associates at leading law firms. However, what enticed you to join A.B. were the "perks" — an excellent health, accident and life insurance program, unrestricted use by you and your family of a new company-owned recreational center, including a swimming pool, gym, tennis courts, running track, weight room, etc., a parking spot in a garage located less than a block from your office, substantial discounts on the products sold by A.B., Inc., an attractively furnished office with spectacular views of the city, free breakfasts and lunches in an elegant restaurant located in the A.B. office complex, use of company cars and occasionally company planes, as well as other amenities to make your professional life pleasant.

While celebrating your success, one of your friends half-jokingly asked if you could afford to pay the taxes on all of these "perks." What a silly question! You informed him that by their very nature, "perks" were nontaxable. Your friend muttered something about *Glenshaw Glass* and economic benefit and you changed the subject. But later, while working online, you started thinking about "perks" and taxes and decided a little tax research would not be harmful to your health. You immediately discovered a few bits of authority which shook your belief in the inherent nontaxability of "perks." For starters, § 61(a)(1) provides that, among other things, gross income includes "fringe benefits." Regulation § 1.61-1(a) provides the form of receipt doesn't matter and "income may be realized . . . in the form of services, meals, accommodations, stock or other property, as well as in cash." And lest there should be any doubt, even the Supreme Court noted that the concept of gross income is intended "to include in taxable income any economic or financial benefit conferred on the employee as compensation, whatever the form or mode in which it is effected." *Commissioner v. Smith*, 324 U.S. 177, 181 (1945).

This superficial survey left you uneasy and so you continued your research and found the following instructive discussion of fringe benefits:

FRINGE BENEFITS

Without giving much thought to the matter, one might assume any benefit accorded an employee in connection with his employment constitutes compensation. That standard would surely be overly broad. It may, however, be preferable to the treatment of fringe benefits actually employed by the Service, the courts and the Congress during the last 90 years. As a result of such treatment, the law regarding the tax treatment of fringe benefits is to be found in a patchwork of legislative, judicial and administrative rules.

A. Meals and Lodging

The uncertain and piecemeal tax treatment of fringe benefits is perhaps best exemplified in the historic treatment of meals and lodging provided by an employer to an employee. The earliest rulings of the Service established the excludability of meals and lodging provided to employees. For example, the Service, in a 1919 ruling, excluded the room and board furnished seamen aboard a ship. O.D. 265, 1 C.B. 71 (1919). A 1920 ruling exempted " 'supper money' paid by an employer to an employee, who voluntarily performs extra labor for his employer after regular business hours." O.D. 514, 2 C.B. 90 (1920). These and similar meals and lodging exclusions were premised on the notion that the benefits given employees were for the convenience of the employer. This so-called "convenience of employer doctrine" soon was adopted by the Treasury and the courts as providing the standard for determining whether employer-provided meals and lodging were excludable. The convenience of employer doctrine required taxpayers to establish that benefits accorded them as employees were grounded in business necessity. For example, in O.D. 915, 4 C.B. 85–86 (1921), the Service held:

> [W]here the employees of a hospital are subject to immediate service on demand at any time during the twenty-four hours of the day and on that account are required to accept quarters and meals at the hospital, the value of such quarters and meals may be considered as being furnished for the convenience of the hospital and does not represent additional compensation to the employees. On the other hand, where the employees . . . could, if they so desired, obtain meals and lodging elsewhere than in the hospital and yet perform the duties required of them by such hospital, the ratable value of the board and lodging furnished is considered additional compensation.

Similarly, in the *Benaglia* decision, included in the materials, the fact that the taxpayer's presence in the hotel was necessary justified excluding from income the meals and lodging provided him.

But the convenience of employer doctrine was not a tidy one and the Service and the courts were inconsistent in their treatment of employer-provided meals and lodging. In 1950, the Service took the position that, if the employer characterized a benefit as compensation, the benefit would be treated as income regardless of the fact that the benefit was provided for the convenience of the employer. Some courts rejected this position while others embraced it. As a result, similarly situated taxpayers were treated differently depending on which standard was used.

To resolve the confusion, Congress added § 119 in 1954. Read § 119 carefully. How does § 119(b)(1) resolve the employer-characterization issue? Note particularly the retention of the convenience of employer doctrine. Is the convenience of the employer requirement in § 119(a) necessary, given that meals and lodging must be furnished on the business premises and, in the case of lodging, the employee must accept it as a condition of his employment? Regulation § 1.119-1(b)(3) provides: "condition of employment means that [the employee] be required to accept the lodging in order to enable him properly to perform the duties of his employment. Lodging will be regarded as furnished to enable the employee properly to perform the duties of his employment when, for example, the lodging is furnished because the employee is required to be available for duty at all times or because the employee could not perform the services required of him unless he is furnished such lodging." Isn't that regulation merely an application of the convenience of the employer standard as developed in the early rulings?

Having examined the administrative, judicial and legislative underpinnings of the exclusion for meals and lodging, one should now consider whether the exclusion is justifiable. Although the provision of meals or lodging may be for the convenience of the employer, the fact remains that personal needs of the employee are satisfied. As suggested by the dissent in *Benaglia*, perhaps the value of the benefit to the employee should be treated as income. In that case, there was evidence the taxpayer would have incurred expense of $3,600 per year if he lived elsewhere. Conceding that the greater value of the accommodations at the Royal Hawaiian Hotel should not be taxed to him, why shouldn't Benaglia have been required to report as income the $3,600 per year he saved? Justifying the exclusion of benefits provided for the convenience of the employer, the Tax Court, in *Van Rosen v. Commissioner*, 17 T.C. 834 (1951), reasoned: "[t]hough there was an element of gain to the employee, in that he received subsistence and quarters which otherwise he would have had to supply for himself, he had nothing he could take, appropriate, use and expend according to his own dictates, but rather, the ends of the employer's business dominated and controlled, just as in the furnishing of a place to work and in the supplying of the tools and machinery with which to work. The fact that certain personal wants and needs of the employee were satisfied was plainly secondary and incidental to the employment." 17 T.C. at 838. Does this reasoning convince you that the entire value of the meals and lodging should be excluded?

In addition to providing meals and lodging to employees, employers, as in *Benaglia*, often provide meals and lodging to the employee's family. Section 119 initially did not address this matter. In 1959, the Service issued Revenue Ruling 59-409, which would have triggered additional income to an employee for the value of benefits provided to members of his family. This ruling was withdrawn without comment the following year, and in 1978, Congress amended § 119 to exclude meals and lodging provided to an employee's spouse and dependents. How can the spouse and dependents of an employee satisfy the convenience of the employer requirement? Shouldn't the value of benefits provided to members of the employee's family be taxed to the employee?

Not surprisingly, the enactment of § 119 did not end disputes between taxpayers and the Service regarding the exclusion of meals and lodging. Rather, it focused attention on the "business premises," "condition of employment" and "convenience of employer" requirements. For example, in *Caratan v. Commissioner*, 442 F.2d 606 (9th Cir. 1971), the Service contended that owner-employees of a farming corporation could not exclude the value of the living accommodations provided them because they had failed to establish that they were required to accept the lodging as a condition of their employment. The Tax Court agreed, noting that, since there was available housing in a residential area ten minutes from the farm, it was not necessary to the performance of their duties that the taxpayers live in the housing provided by their corporation. The Ninth Circuit, in reversing, relied on Reg. § 1.119-1(b)(3), *supra*. The court stressed that, pursuant to the regulation, it was enough for the taxpayer to establish he was required to be available for duty at all times. "It is not necessary to show that the duties would be impossible to perform without such lodging being available." The availability of nearby housing was therefore irrelevant.

In *Commissioner v. Kowalski*, 434 U.S. 77 (1977), the Supreme Court considered whether cash payments made to state police troopers as meal allowances were excudable under § 119. The Court concluded that cash payments were not excludable under that section which, according to the Court, excluded only meals in kind. According to the Court, the taxpayer's reliance on the general convenience of employer doctrine developed in the case law was misplaced because § 119 places specific limitations on the exclusion for meals and lodging. As will be discussed below, occasional supper money is excludable as a *de minimis* fringe benefit under § 132(a)(4). That provision and the regulations interpreting it, however, would not be applicable to the meal allowance provided to the state troopers in *Kowalski* because it was regularly paid and thus could not be considered "occasional."

The convenience of employer doctrine, utilized first by the Service to exclude meals and lodging, has been codified in § 119. The doctrine, however, has an existence beyond § 119 as is demonstrated by the 1968 decision in *U.S. v. Gotcher*, included in the materials, and to some extent by § 132 discussed below. After reading *Gotcher*, ask yourself whether an employer/employee relationship is necessary for the application of the convenience of employer doctrine. Should free samples we receive from businesses seeking to advertise their products or services be excluded on a theory comparable to the convenience of employer doctrine?

In sum, the treatment of employer-provided meals and lodging over the years reflects the difficulty the courts, the Service, and the Congress have had in establishing exclusions and defining their limits, and reflects as well their lenient attitude regarding the taxation of employer-provided benefits.

B. Fringe Benefits and Section 132

Congress' piecemeal approach with respect to fringe benefits is reflected in a number of other exclusion provisions. A non-exhaustive list of so-called "statutory fringe benefits" would include employee group term life insurance under $50,000 (§ 79); employer-provided accident and health benefits (§§ 105, 100(a)); and dependent care assistance programs (§ 129). Qualified retirement plans (§ 401 *et seq.*) constitute a particularly significant fringe benefit for many employees.

In addition to statutory fringe benefits, a host of non-statutory employer-provided fringe benefits existed, but generally were ignored by the Service or treated as nontaxable. For example, in 1921, the Service ruled that "personal transportation passes issued by a railroad company to its employees and their families . . . are considered gifts and the value does not constitute taxable income to the employees." O.D. 946, 4 C.B. 110 (1920). In light of your study of *Duberstein*, do you agree?

The Service's hands-off approach to non-statutory fringe benefits invited employers and employees to negotiate compensation packages laden with "nontaxable" fringe benefits. Both the employer and the employee benefitted from such arrangements — on the one hand, it was typically cheaper for the employer to provide fringe benefits than to increase employee's salaries; on the other hand, the employee receiving fringe benefits was able to satisfy certain personal needs or desires without any tax cost. The only loser was the federal fisc. Yet, it was not until the early 1970s that Treasury finally moved to address the tax status of many common fringe benefits. By that time, the notion that most nonstatutory fringe benefits were nontaxable was firmly entrenched. The Treasury's regulatory efforts were sufficiently controversial that they were blocked by a congressional moratorium on fringe benefit regulations. It was not until 1984 that Congress enacted the first comprehensive treatment of fringe benefits.

The centerpiece of the fringe benefit legislation of 1984 is § 132. Initially recognizing four categories of excludable fringe benefits, § 132 today lists eight categories of excludable benefits:[1] (1) no-additional-cost service; (2) qualified employee discount; (3) working condition fringe; (4) *de minimis* fringe; (5) qualified transportation fringe; (6) qualified moving expense reimbursement; (7) qualified retirement planning services; and (8) qualified military base realignment and closure fringe.[2]

1. No-Additional-Cost Service

Congress recognized that companies engaged in the airline, railroad, or hotel businesses often have excess capacity (*e.g.*, extra seats on a scheduled airline flight) which will remain unused for lack of paying customers. As a result, such businesses commonly make this excess capacity available free of charge to employees and their families. Because there is essentially no cost incurred by the employer in allowing an employee to occupy an otherwise empty seat on a company aircraft or an empty room in a hotel, Congress opted to exclude from income the entire value of such services, subject to a number of restrictions.

First, the service must be one offered for sale to customers in the ordinary course of business. § 132(b)(1). For example, if an employee of a corporation has personal business in Emerald City and the company allows the employee to occupy an otherwise empty seat on the corporate jet which is being flown to Emerald City for business reasons, the benefit enjoyed by the employee fails the "for sale to customers" standard. Considering no additional cost is incurred by the corporation in allowing the employee to occupy an otherwise empty seat, is this requirement justified? Consider how the benefit should be valued for tax purposes, and see the valuation discussion *infra*.

A second requirement contained in § 132(b)(1) is that the service be offered in the line of business of the employer in which the employee is performing services. This line of business requirement is best explained by the following excerpt from the legislative history:

---

[1] An additional category of excludable fringe benefits, qualified tuition reductions, was added by the 1984 legislation and is included in § 117(d). *See* Chapter 7.

[2] Qualified moving expense reimbursement is discussed in Chapter 19, Part A: Moving Expenses. It will therefore not be discussed in this chapter. Qualified retirement planning services and qualified military base realignment and closure fringe will not be discussed in this text.

Under this limitation, for example, an employer which provides airline services and hotel services to the general public is considered to consist of two separate lines of business. As a consequence, the employees of the airline business of the employer may not exclude the value of free hotel rooms provided by the hotel business of the employer and vice versa. The purpose of the line of business limitation is to avoid, to the extent possible, the competitive imbalances and inequities which would result from giving the employees of a conglomerate or other large employer with several lines of business a greater variety of tax free benefits than could be given to the employees of a small employer with only one line of business. Thus, small businesses will not be disadvantaged in their ability to compete with large businesses providing the same goods or services. . . .

H.R. Rep. 98-432, 98th Cong., 2d Sess., p. 1594–95 (1984).

While the line of business requirement is easily applied to the employees of the airline business in the legislative history example, how does one apply it to the accountant who does all of the accounting work for both the airline and the hotel divisions of the company? See Reg. § 1.132-4(a)(1)(iv), providing that the performance of substantial services directly benefiting more than one line of business is treated as the performance of substantial services in all such lines of business.

Section 132(b)(2) provides a third requirement, *i.e.*, that the employer incur no substantial additional cost (including forgone revenue). Reg. § 1.132-2(a)(5) provides "for purposes of determining whether any revenue is forgone, it is assumed that the employee would not have purchased the service unless it were available to the employee at the actual price charged to the employee." Reg. § 1.132-2(c) states that permitting airline employees to take personal flights at no charge and to receive reserved seats results in forgone revenue and therefore employees receiving the free flights are not eligible for the no-additional-cost exclusion. Section 132(b)(2) also provides that whether an employer incurs any substantial additional cost be determined without regard to any amount which an employee might be required to pay. Thus, employee payment does not serve to transform an employer-provided service into a "no-additional-cost" service, although such payment may obviously be quite relevant in measuring the income, if any, the employee receives from the employer's provision of the service. Finally, the statute refers to "substantial" additional costs. For example, are the housekeeping costs associated with maintenance of hotel rooms "substantial" additional costs to the owner of a hotel chain who permits employees to use rooms which otherwise would remain vacant? See Reg. § 1.132-2(a)(5)(ii), to the effect that the cost of services "merely incidental" to the primary service rendered are generally not "substantial."

It is also worth noting the regulations, after listing several "excess capacity services" that qualify as no-additional-cost services, specifically state that non-excess capacity services, which do not so qualify, may nonetheless be fully or partially excluded from income under the "qualified employee discount" rules discussed below. Reg. § 1.132-2(a)(2).

A fourth requirement is contained in § 132(j)(1) which prohibits discrimination in favor of highly compensated employees, a term which, as defined in § 414(q), can include officers and owners. *See* Reg. § 1.132-8(a)(1). If the nondiscrimination rule is violated, Reg. § 1.132-8(a)(2) provides only the members of the highly compensated group, rather than all employees receiving benefits, will be subject to tax.

Section 132(i) provides a special rule authorizing reciprocal agreements between employers in the same line of business, thus enabling the employers to provide tax-free benefits to one another's employees. Such reciprocal agreements must be in writing and the employers may not incur any substantial additional costs (including forgone revenues) in providing such services. This rule resulted in part from the lobbying efforts of airline flight attendants who had come to depend on interline passes which enable many attendants to "commute" by air to their jobs.

The exclusion of no-additional-cost services is limited to services provided "employees." Section 132(h) defines employee to include one's spouse and dependent children as well as certain retired and disabled employees and the surviving spouse of a deceased employee. Section 132(h)(3) provides a special rule treating the use of air transportation by the parent of an employee as use by the employee. See also § 132(j)(5) which provides favorable treatment for affiliates of airlines.

In *Charley v. Commissioner*, 91 F.3d 72 (9th Cir. 1996), the taxpayer argued § 132(a)(1) excluded from income amounts he received for frequent flyer miles which he converted to cash. Taxpayer was president of a company engaged in a business which investigated the causes of industrial accidents. The taxpayer and his wife owned a majority of the shares in the company. In his capacity as an employee of the company, the taxpayer travelled to various accident sites to inspect machinery. The company had an "unwritten policy" that frequent flyer miles earned by an employee as a result of travel for the company became the sole property of the employee.

When a client's work required the taxpayer to travel by air, the company charged the client for a round-trip, first class ticket. The taxpayer would instruct the company's travel agent to arrange round-trip coach service to the destination but to charge the company for first class travel. The taxpayer would then use his frequent flyer miles, most of which were earned on company travel, to upgrade the coach ticket to first class. The taxpayer would instruct the travel agent to transfer funds to his personal travel account in an amount equal to the difference between the coach ticket and the amount the company was charged for the round-trip first class ticket. The Service argued the funds credited to the taxpayer's personal travel account constituted taxable income.

Rejecting the taxpayer's novel argument that the amounts credited represented a "no-additional-cost service," excludable under § 132(a)(1), the court noted that the taxpayer's company did not offer frequent flyer miles for sale to customers in the ordinary course of its business. (The court specifically refused to reach the issue of whether the frequent flyer miles the company allowed the taxpayer to keep constituted additional compensation to the taxpayer.) Instead, the court concluded that either the travel credit arrangement represented additional compensation to the taxpayer from his company or the taxpayer had simply sold his frequent flyer miles in which he had a zero basis. Under either analysis, the amount credited to his personal travel fund constituted gross income.

The Service has subsequently announced that:

> Consistent with prior practice, the IRS will not assert that any taxpayer has understated his federal tax liability by reason of the receipt of personal use of frequent flyer miles or other in-kind promotion benefits attributable to the taxpayer's business or official travel. Any future guidance on the taxability of these benefits will be applied prospectively.

Announcement 2002-18, 2002-10 I.R.B. 621. The announcement, however, goes on to say that this relief does not apply to benefits that are converted to cash, or to compensation paid in the form of such benefits, or to benefits used for tax avoidance purposes.

2.   Qualified Employee Discount

The exclusion for qualified employee discounts reflects congressional recognition of the long-standing practice of businesses to provide discounts to their employees on the same goods and services they sell to the general public. Retailers appeared before the congressional subcommittee considering the fringe benefit legislation and argued for continuation of the exclusion of discounts on goods and services employees enjoyed. The following excerpt suggests the kind of concerns Congress addressed in enacting the legislation:

> Providing discounts stimulates a company's sales to a natural group of customers who might not otherwise buy as much of the company's merchandise. Since the discounted price generally is higher than the employer's cost, by offering employees a discount, a company can increase overall sales as well as profits. . . .
>
> Providing discounts to employees serves another important interest of the employer — namely the stimulation of sales to the general public. By encouraging employees to purchase the employer's merchandise, employee discounts help the employer to educate his employees about the merchandise he sells. Employees who have had personal experience with the store's merchandise make more effective sales persons; their morale is higher, and they are often more loyal advocates of their employer and his goods. . . . In addition, providing employee discounts is an effective means to advertise a store's merchandise. Seeing a salesperson wearing apparel and accessories sold at the store may encourage customers to try on and purchase similar goods. Finally, providing employee discounts causes an effective stimulus to sales by a "multiplier effect." This effect results from employees being accompanied on shopping trips by others who become customers as a result of the trip.
>
> Employee discounts have not been taxed since the income tax was enacted in 1913. Unlike wages which compensate employees for services rendered, employee discounts bear no relationship to job performance. The value of the discount to any individual employee depends not on the quality of his or her job performance but on the quantity of his or her purchase. Accordingly, employee discounts do not constitute compensation and should not be treated as such for tax purposes.

. . . Moreover, a change in policy to impose a tax on employee discounts would also raise a difficult question of valuation. . . . [F]air market value is fraught with numerous deficiencies. It is not always readily or clearly determinable. The objective dollar value of a discount simply does not accurately measure its real value. For example, comparable merchandise may be available at a promotional sale or at a nearby store at the same or even a lower net price than the employee pays with the discount. If store X's $100 item is regularly available in store Y for $75, why should an employee recognize income if X permits him or her to buy the item for $75 (a 25% discount). It is difficult in a case such as this to identify the value that is being taxed.[3]

Section 132(c) limits the amount of discount which will be excludable and provides separate limitations for property and for services. The exclusion for employee discounts on services is limited to 20% of the price at which the services are being offered by the employer to customers. By contrast, the exclusion for employee discounts on property is limited to the employer's gross profit percentage, which is the excess of the aggregate sales price for the property sold by the employer over the aggregate cost of such property to the employer, divided by the aggregate sales price. Consider the following example provided by the legislative history:

> [I]f total sales of . . . merchandise during a year were $1,000,000 and the employer's cost for the merchandise was $600,000, then the gross profit percentage for the year is 40% [$1,000,000 minus $600,000 equals $400,000 which is 40% of $1,000,000]. Thus, an employee discount with respect to such merchandise is excluded from income to the extent it does not exceed 40% of the selling price of the merchandise to nonemployee customers. If in this case the discount allowed to the employee exceeds 40% (for example, 50%), the excess discount on a purchase (10% in the example) is included in the employee's gross income.[4]

Is the distinction between services and property justifiable?

Section 132(c)(4) defines "qualified property or services." The definition contains the same "for sale to customers" and "line of business" requirements of § 132(b). In addition, note that real property and personal property held for investment do not qualify for the § 132(c) exclusion. For example, the exclusion would not apply to employee purchases of stocks or bonds, gold coins or residential and commercial real estate. In imposing this limitation, Congress was concerned that such property could typically be sold by employees "at close to the same price at which the employer sells the property to its nonemployee customers."[5]

---

[3] Testimony of Mr. Dexter Tight, Senior Vice President and General Counsel of the GAP Stores, Inc. on Behalf of the National Retail Merchants Association on H.R. 3525, "Permanent Tax Treatment of Fringe Benefits Act," Before the Ways and Means Subcommittee on Select Revenue Measures (August 1, 1983).

[4] H.R. 98-432, p. 1599, 98th Cong. 2d Sess.

[5] *Id.* at 1597.

The scope of the term "employee" as used in § 132(c) is the same as that in § 132(b), and the anti-discrimination rules applicable to the no-additional-cost service exclusion are also applicable to the qualified employee discount exclusion. *See* § 132(j)(1).[6] Note, however, that the reciprocal agreement rules of § 132(i) are not applicable to qualified employee discounts.

3.   Working Condition Fringe Benefits

Employers typically provide employees with all of the tools, office space, and supplies an employee needs. In addition, the employer may provide necessary transportation, subscriptions to current literature in the employee's particular field, and other property or services to facilitate the employee's work. Such property and services are so closely connected to job performance that were the employee, rather than the employer, to pay for them, the employee would be entitled to deduct their cost as a business expense. Thus, when they are provided by the employer, they should not be considered compensation to the employee. Congress in § 132(a)(3) has excluded these so-called "working condition fringe benefits." See the definition in § 132(d). Do the anti-discrimination rules apply to working condition fringe benefits? Should they?

Cash payments to an employee do not qualify as working condition fringes unless the employee is required to use the payments for expenses incurred in a specific or pre-arranged qualifying activity, verify such use, and return any excess to the employer. Reg. § 1.132-5(a)(1)(v). Rules are also provided for determining the working condition fringe portion of vehicle usage, where an employee uses an employer-provided vehicle for both business and personal purposes. Reg. § 1.132-5(b). Consumer product testing — that is, the use by employees of employer-manufactured consumer goods, such as automobiles, for testing and evaluation outside the employer's office — was an area of some particular concern to Congress, and the regulations, drawing on legislative history to § 132, delineate the requirements for such employee use to qualify as a working condition fringe benefit. Reg. § 1.132-5(n).

In Rev. Rul. 92-69, 1992-2 C.B. 51, the Service concluded employer-provided outplacement services were excludable by employees as working condition fringe benefits. According to the ruling, "if [an] employer . . . derives a substantial business benefit from the provision of such outplacement services that is distinct from the benefit it would derive from the mere payment of additional compensation, such as promoting a positive corporate image, maintaining employee morale, and avoiding wrongful termination suits, the service may generally be treated as a working condition fringe." *Id.* at 53.

In *Townsend Industries v. United States*, 342 F.3d 890 (8th Cir. 2003), the court held the per-employee cost of the taxpayer's annual fishing trip constituted a working condition fringe benefit excludable from employee income and deductible to the employer as a business expense. Following its annual two-day meeting, the

---

[6] A special rule treats the leased section of a department store as part of the line of business of the person operating the department store and treats employees in the leased section as employees of that person. § 132(j)(2).

taxpayer sponsored a four-day, expense-paid fishing trip to a resort in Canada. The testimony indicated that, although the trips were voluntary, "nearly all employees felt an obligation to attend." There was also considerable testimony regarding the business discussions that took place among those attending. The court concluded that "Townsend had a realistic expectation to gain concrete future benefits from the trip based on its knowledge of its own small company, its knowledge of the utility of interpersonal interactions that probably would not occur but for the trip, and its knowledge of its own past experience."

In Notice 2011-72, 2011-2 C. B. 407, the Service addressed the treatment of employer-provided cell phones. According to the Service, if an employer provides an employee a cell phone primarily for noncompensatory reasons, e.g., the employer needs to be able to contact the employee at all times regarding work-related emergencies or the employee needs to be available to clients when the employee is not in her office, the use of the cell phone by the employee for business purposes will be considered an excludable working condition fringe. Under these circumstances, the value of any use by the employee of the cell phone for personal purposes will be considered an excludable *de minimis* fringe benefit.

4. *De Minimis* Fringe Benefits

Reflecting a congressional desire for administrative convenience, § 132(a)(4) excludes "*de minimis* fringe benefits," defined in § 132(e)(1).

Note the emphasis placed on "frequency" as a factor for determining whether a benefit is *de minimis*. Note also that, unlike the no-additional-cost service, qualified employee discount, and working condition fringe benefit rules, the *de minimis* exception does not necessitate an employer-employee relationship between the provider and recipient. Thus, for example, benefits received by a director of a corporation may constitute excludable *de minimis* fringe benefits.

The regulations provide special rules for excluding meals, occasional meal money, and the value of meals provided in an employer-operated eating facility as *de minimis* fringe benefits. Reg. §§ 1.132-6(d)(2), 1.132-7. The regulations also list a variety of common benefits that do or do not qualify as *de minimis*. Reg. § 1.132-6(e). *De minimis* fringe benefit status is explicitly denied to any cash or cash equivalent benefits, other than those allowed by the special rules. Reg. § 1.132-6(c). Note that the anti-discrimination rules do not apply to *de minimis* fringe benefits. Should they?

5. Qualified Transportation Fringe Benefits

Section 132(a)(5) excludes from gross income "qualified transportation fringe" benefits. Qualified transportation fringe benefits include parking, transit passes, vanpool benefits and bicycle commuting reimbursement benefits. Note the specific dollar limitations under § 132(f)(2) and (5)(F)(ii) for excludable amounts. These limitations are adjusted for inflation. § 132(f)(6). Section 132(f)(3) provides that "qualified transportation fringe" includes a cash reimbursement by an employer to an employee although it imposes a special limitation in this regard with respect to transit passes. The modest exclusion for bicycle commuting reimbursement benefits was added in 2008. Evaluate the exclusion for qualified transportation fringe benefits from a public policy perspective.

C. Valuation

Fringe benefits not excluded from income under § 132 or another section of the Code are, of course, subject to tax pursuant to § 61(a)(1). ~~The regulations make clear the measure of income is the fair market value of the fringe benefit, less any excludable portion of the fringe benefit and any amount paid by the recipi~~ent. Reg. § 1.61-21(b)(1). Special, and extensive, valuation rules are provided, however, with respect to employer-provided vehicles, chauffeur services, commercial and non-commercial air travel, and eating facilities. The regulations explicitly tax the value of the fringe benefit to the employee, even though the benefit may actually be received by someone else. Reg. § 1.61-21(a)(4).

Postscript: Review the list of "perks" A.B., Inc., will be providing you. Are they taxable?

BENAGLIA v. COMMISSIONER
United States Board of Tax Appeals
36 B.T.A. 838 (1937)

Findings of Fact

The petitioners are husband and wife, residing in Honolulu, Hawaii. . . . The petitioner has, since 1926 and including the tax years in question, been employed as the manager in full charge of the several hotels in Honolulu owned and operated by Hawaiian Hotels, Ltd., a corporation of Hawaii, consisting of the Royal Hawaiian, the Moana and bungalows, and the Waialae Golf Club. These are large resort hotels, operating on the American plan. Petitioner was constantly on duty, and, for the proper performance of his duties and entirely for the convenience of his employer, he and his wife occupied a suite of rooms in the Royal Hawaiian Hotel and received their meals at and from the hotel.

Petitioner's salary has varied in different years, being in one year $25,000. In 1933 it was $9,625, and in 1934 it was $11,041.67. These amounts were fixed without reference to his meals and lodging, and neither petitioner nor his employer ever regarded the meals and lodging as part of his compensation or accounted for them.

Opinion

STERNHAGEN:

The Commissioner has added $7,845 each year to the petitioner's gross income as "compensation received from Hawaiian Hotels, Ltd.", holding that this is "the fair market value of rooms and meals furnished by the employer. . . . " The deficiency notice seems to hold that the rooms and meals were not in fact supplied "merely as a convenience to the hotels" of the employer.

From the evidence, there remains no room for doubt that the petitioner's residence at the hotel was not by way of compensation for his services, not for his personal convenience, comfort or pleasure, but solely because he could not otherwise perform the services required of him. The evidence of both the employer and employee shows in detail what petitioner's duties were and why his residence in the hotel was necessary. His duty was continuous and required his presence at a moment's call. He had a lifelong experience in hotel management and operation in the United States, Canada, and elsewhere, and testified that the functions of the manager could not have been performed by one living outside the hotel, especially a resort hotel such as this. The demands and requirements of guests are numerous, various, and unpredictable, and affect the meals, the rooms, the entertainment, and everything else about the hotel. The manager must be alert to all these things day and night. He would not consider undertaking the job and the owners of the hotel would not consider employing a manager unless he lived there. This was implicit throughout his employment, and when his compensation was changed from time to time no mention was ever made of it. Both took it for granted. The corporation's books carried no accounting for the petitioner's meals, rooms, or service.

Under such circumstances, the value of meals and lodging is not income to the employee, even though it may relieve him of an expense which he would otherwise bear. In *Jones v. United States*, . . . the subject was fully considered in determining that neither the value of quarters nor the amount received as commutation of quarters by an Army officer is included within this taxable income. There is also a full discussion in the English case of *Tennant v. Smith*, H.L. (1892) App. Cas. 150, III British Tax Cases 158. A bank employee was required to live in quarters located in the bank building, and it was held that the value of such lodging was not taxable income. The advantage to him was merely an incident of the performance of his duty, but its character for tax purposes was controlled by the dominant fact that the occupation of the premises was imposed upon him for the convenience of the employer. The Bureau of Internal Revenue has almost consistently applied the same doctrine in its published rulings.

. . . Of course it cannot be said as a categorical proposition of law that, where an employee is fed and lodged by his employer, no part of the value of such perquisite is income. If the Commissioner finds that it was received as compensation and holds it to be taxable income, the taxpayer contesting this before the Board must prove by evidence that it is not income. . . . The determination of the Commissioner on the point in issue is reversed.

Reviewed by the Board.

ARNOLD, dissenting:

Conceding that petitioner was required to live at the hotel and that his living there was solely for the convenience of the employer, it does not follow that he was not benefitted thereby to the extent of what such accommodations were reasonably worth to him. His employment was a matter of private contract. He was careful to specify in his letter accepting the employment that he was to be furnished with living quarters, meals, etc., for himself and wife, together with the cash salary, as compensation for his employment. Living quarters and meals are necessities which he would otherwise have had to procure at his own expense. His contract of employment relieved him to that extent. He has been enriched to the extent of what they are reasonably worth.

The majority opinion is based on the finding that petitioner's residence at the hotel was solely for the convenience of the employer and, therefore, not income. While it is no doubt convenient to have the manager reside in the hotel, I do not think the question here is one of convenience or of benefit to the employer. What the tax law is concerned with is whether or not petitioner was financially benefited by having living quarters furnished to himself and his wife. He may have preferred to live elsewhere, but we are dealing with the financial aspect of petitioner's relation to his employer, not his preference. He says it would cost him $3,600 per year to live elsewhere.

At most the arrangement as to living quarters and meals was of mutual benefit, and to the extent it benefitted petitioner it was compensation in addition to his cash salary, and taxable to him as income.

UNITED STATES v. GOTCHER
United States Court of Appeals, Fifth Circuit
401 F.2d 118 (1968)

THORNBERRY, CIRCUIT JUDGE:

In 1960, Mr. and Mrs. Gotcher took a twelve-day expense-paid trip to Germany to tour the Volkswagen facilities there. The trip cost $1,372.30. His employer, Economy Motors, paid $348.73, and Volkswagen of Germany and Volkswagen of America shared the remaining $1,023.53. Upon returning, Mr. Gotcher bought a twenty-five percent interest in Economy Motors, the Sherman, Texas Volkswagen dealership, that had been offered to him before he left. Today he is President of Economy Motors in Sherman and owns fifty percent of the dealership. Mr. and Mrs. Gotcher did not include any part of the $1,372.30 in their 1960 income. The Commissioner determined that the taxpayers had realized income to the extent of the $1,372.30 for the expense-paid trip and asserted a tax deficiency of $356.79, plus interest. Taxpayers paid the deficiency, plus $89.29 in interest, and thereafter timely filed suit for a refund. The district court held that the cost of the trip was not income or, in the alternative, was income and deductible as an ordinary and necessary business expense. . . . We affirm the district court's determination that the cost of the trip was not income to Mr. Gotcher ($686.15); however, Mrs. Gotcher's expenses ($686.15) constituted income and were not deductible.

Section 61 of the Internal Revenue Code of 1954 defines gross income as income from whatever source derived and specifically includes fifteen items within this definition. The court below reasoned that the cost of the trip to the Gotchers was not income because an economic or financial benefit does not constitute income under section 61 unless it is conferred as compensation for services rendered. This conception of gross income is too restrictive since it is well settled that section 61 should be broadly interpreted and that many items, including noncompensatory gains, constitute gross income.

Sections 101-23 specifically exclude certain items from gross income. Appellant argues that the cost of the trip should be included in income since it is not specifically excluded by sections 101-23, reasoning that section 61 was drafted broadly to subject all economic gains to tax and any exclusions from gross income are limited to the enumerated exclusions. . . .

In determining whether the expense-paid trip was income within section 61, we must look to the tests that have been developed under this section. The concept of economic gain to the taxpayer is the key to section 61. . . . This concept contains two distinct requirements: There must be an economic gain, and this gain must primarily benefit the taxpayer personally. In some cases, as in the case of an expense-paid trip, there is no direct economic gain, but there is an indirect economic gain inasmuch as a benefit has been received without a corresponding diminution in wealth. Yet even if expense-paid items, as meals and lodging, are received by the taxpayer, the value of these items will not be gross income, even though the employee receives some incidental benefit, if the meals and lodging are primarily for the convenience of the employer. See Int. Rev. Code of 1954, § 119.

The trip was made in 1959 when VW was attempting to expand its local dealerships in the United States. The "Buy American" campaign and the fact that the VW people felt they had a "very ugly product" prompted them to offer these tours of Germany to prospective dealers. The VW story was related by Mr. Horton, who is Manager of Special Events for VW of America. His testimony was uncontradicted and unimpeached. He stated that VW operations were at first so speculative that cars had to be consigned with a repurchase guarantee. In 1959, when VW began to push for its share of the American market, its officials determined that the best way to remove the apprehension about this foreign product was to take the dealer to Germany and have him see his investment first-hand. It was believed that once the dealer saw the manufacturing facilities and the stability of the "new Germany" he would be convinced that VW was for him. Furthermore, VW considered the expenditure justified because the dealer was being asked to make a substantial investment of his time and money in a comparatively new product. Indeed, after taking the trip, VW required him to acquire first-class facilities. It was also hoped that this would be accomplished by following the international architectural plans that VW had for its dealerships. It was also hoped that the dealer would adopt VW's international plan for the sales and services department. Mr. Horton testified that VW could not have asked that this upgrading be done unless it convinced the dealer that VW was here to stay. Apparently these trips have paid off since VW's sales have skyrocketed and the dealers have made their facilities top-rate operations under the VW requirements for a standard dealership.

The activities in Germany support the conclusion that the trip was oriented to business. The Government makes much of the fact that the travel brochure allocated only two of the twelve days to the touring of VW factories. This argument ignores the uncontradicted fact that not all of the planned activities were in the brochure. There is ample support for the trial judge's finding that a substantial amount of time was spent touring VW facilities and visiting local dealerships. VW had set up these tours with local dealers so that the travelers could discuss how the facilities were operated in Germany. Mr. Gotcher took full advantage of this opportunity and even used some of his "free time" to visit various local dealerships. Moreover, at almost all of the evening meals VW officials gave talks about the organization and passed out literature and brochures on the VW story.

Some of the days were not related to touring VW facilities, but that fact alone cannot be decisive. The dominant purpose of the trip is the critical inquiry and some pleasurable features will not negate the finding of an overall business purpose. *See Patterson v. Thomas* [289 F.2d 108 (5th Cir. 1961)]. Since we are convinced that the agenda related primarily to business and that Mr. Gotcher's attendance was prompted by business considerations, the so-called sightseeing complained of by the Government is inconsequential. . . . Indeed, the district court found that even this touring of the countryside had an indirect relation to business since the tours were not typical sight-seeing excursions but were connected to the desire of VW that the dealers be persuaded that the German economy was stable enough to justify investment in a German product. We cannot say that this conclusion is clearly erroneous. Nor can we say that the enthusiastic literary style of the brochures negates a dominant business purpose. It is the business reality of the total situation, not the colorful expressions in the literature, that controls. Considering the record, the circumstances prompting the trip, and the objective achieved, we conclude that the primary purpose of the trip was to induce Mr. Gotcher to take out a VW dealership interest.

The question, therefore, is what tax consequences should follow from an expense-paid trip that primarily benefits the party paying for the trip. In several analogous situations the value of items received by employees has been excluded from gross income when these items were primarily for the benefit of the employer. Even before these items were excluded by the 1954 Code, the Treasury and the courts recognized that they should be excluded from gross income. Thus it appears that the value of any trip that is paid by the employer or by a businessman primarily for his own benefit should be excluded from gross income of the payee on similar reasoning. . . .

In the recent case of *Allen J. McDonell*, 26 T.C.M. 115, Tax Ct. Mem. 1967-18, a sales supervisor and his wife were chosen by lot to accompany a group of contest winners on an expense-paid trip to Hawaii. In holding that the taxpayer had received no income, the Tax Court noted that he was required by his employer to go and that he was serving a legitimate business purpose though he enjoyed the trip. The decision suggests that in analyzing the tax consequences of an expense-paid trip one important factor is whether the traveler had any choice but to go. Here, although taxpayer was not forced to go, there is no doubt that in the reality of the business world he had no real choice. The trial judge reached the same conclusion. He found that the invitation did not specifically order the dealers to go, but that as a practical matter it was an order or directive that if a person was going to be a VW dealer, sound business judgment necessitated his accepting the offer of corporate hospitality. So far as Economy Motors was concerned, Mr. Gotcher knew that if he was going to be a part-owner of the dealership, he had better do all that was required to foster good business relations with VW. Besides having no choice but to go, he had no control over the schedule or the money spent. VW did all the planning. In cases involving noncompensatory economic gains, courts have emphasized that the taxpayer still had complete dominion and control over the money to use it as he wished to satisfy personal desires or needs. Indeed, the Supreme Court has defined income as accessions of wealth over which the taxpayer has complete control. *Commissioner v. Glenshaw Glass Co.* [348 U.S. 426 (1955)]. Clearly, the lack of control works in taxpayer's favor here.

McDonell also suggests that one does not realize taxable income when he is serving a legitimate business purpose of the party paying the expenses. . . . Since this is a matter of proof, the resolution of the tax question really depends on whether Gotcher showed that his presence served a legitimate corporate purpose and that no appreciable amount of time was spent for his personal benefit and enjoyment.

Examination of the record convinces us that the personal benefit to Gotcher was clearly subordinate to the concrete benefits to VW. The purpose of the trip was to push VW in America and to get the dealers to invest more money and time in their dealerships. Thus, although Gotcher got some ideas that helped him become a better dealer, there is no evidence that this was the primary purpose of the trip. Put another way, this trip was not given as a pleasurable excursion through Germany or as a means of teaching taxpayer the skills of selling. He had been selling cars since 1949. The personal benefits and pleasure were incidental to the dominant purpose of improving VW's position on the American market and getting people to invest money.

As for Mrs. Gotcher, the trip was primarily a vacation. She did not make the tours with her husband to see the local dealers or attend discussions about the VW organization. This being so, the primary benefit of the expense-paid trip for the wife went to Mr. Gotcher in that he was relieved of her expenses. He should therefore be taxed on the expenses attributable to his wife. Nor are the expenses deductible since the wife's presence served no bona fide business purpose for her husband. Only when the wife's presence is necessary to the conduct of the husband's business are her expenses deductible under section 162. Also, it must be shown that the wife made the trip only to assist her husband in his business. A single trip by a wife with her husband to Europe has been specifically rejected as not being the exceptional type of case justifying a deduction. *Warwick v. United States*, E. D. Va. 1964, 236 F. Supp. 761.

Affirmed in part; Reversed in part.

Statement by Donald C. Lubick, Assistant Secretary of Treasury for Tax Policy to House Ways and Means Committee Task Force on Fringe Benefits
Hearing of Aug. 14, 1978

INEQUITY AND ECONOMIC INEFFICIENCY CAUSED BY EXEMPTING FRINGE BENEFITS FROM TAX

Fringe benefits come in a wide variety of shapes and sizes. They also vary widely in their patterns of distribution.

As the Commissioner has pointed out, the nature and extent of fringe benefits vary from industry to industry, from employer to employer within industries, and from employee to employee in the case of a single employer. For these reasons, exempting fringe benefits from tax or valuing them at less than real value creates substantial tax inequities among employees.

Fairness requires that taxpayers with equal incomes be treated equally for income tax purposes. Compensation received in kind may be just as valuable as compensation received in cash. When fringe benefits are exempted from tax, taxpayers with equal incomes pay unequal taxes.

Exempting fringe benefits from tax produces unfairness not only among employees at the same income level, but also among employees at different income levels. When a fringe benefit is exempted from tax, the exemption is of greater value to a high-income taxpayer than to a low-income taxpayer.

When a fringe benefit is exempted from tax, the resulting tax savings to the employee makes the fringe benefit worth more than cash compensation of equal value. Suppose, for example, that an employee in the 50 percent tax bracket receives as a fringe benefit an item worth $100.

In order to purchase that tax benefit out of after-tax dollars, the employee would have to earn $200 in wages, pay tax on the wages, and then use the remainder to purchase the item. It is true that the item may not be worth $100 to the employee; that is, the employee may only be willing to pay $80 in after-tax wages for the item.

Still, since that would require $160 in before-tax wages, the employee would prefer the $100 fringe benefit to any amount of wages up to $160. Thus, exempting fringe benefits from tax creates a strong incentive to convert cash compensation into tax-free fringe benefits.

This incentive to provide tax-free fringe benefits instead of cash has unfortunate effects.

First, it is likely to result in significant erosion of the tax base. This, in turn, would make it necessary to increase tax rates for items of income which are not exempt fringe benefits in the first place.

As taxpayers perceive themselves as being treated unfairly in comparison to other taxpayers, they may begin to lose confidence in the income tax system and in government. In a tax system that is dependent upon self-reporting, such a decline in confidence may lead to a decline in compliance.

Second, an incentive to provide tax-free fringe benefits instead of cash reduces economic efficiency. When fringe benefits are exempted from tax, employees demand and employers provide more compensation in the form of those benefits than they would if the benefits were taxed. This shift in demand causes a distortion in the economy. The tax law is interfering with free choice in the allocation of economic resources.

Third, exempting fringe benefits from tax leads to distortions in labor markets and creates inequities among employers. Employees accept less total compensation if a portion is in tax-free fringe benefits than if the entire compensation is in cash.

In the example I gave before, an employer offering less than $160 in wages could not compete with an employer offering the $100 fringe benefit.

Thus, employers who are able to provide compensation in the form of tax-free fringe benefits are given a competitive advantage over employers who are not. When fringe benefits are exempted from tax, employees shift to the tax-preferred industries.

In sum, exempting fringe benefits from tax leads to inequalities among employees and employers and distortions in demand and labor markets. These inequities and distortions imply added complexity in the economy and loss of welfare to individuals.

Staff of the Joint Committee on Internal Revenue Taxation, Examination of President Nixon's Tax Returns for 1969–72
93d Cong., 2d Sess. (1974)

PERSONAL USE OF GOVERNMENT AIRCRAFT BY THE PRESIDENT'S FAMILY AND FRIENDS

1. Scope of Examination

Since the President took office in 1969, members of his family and their friends, unaccompanied by him in many instances, have traveled extensively in the United States Government aircraft. It appears that some of these flights were in connection with the performance of official duties, such as standing in for the President in his absence. This seems to be particularly true for many of the trips by Mrs. Nixon.

A question has been raised whether, for flights which were not primarily official business and, therefore, personal, the cost of such unreimbursed Government-furnished transportation should be considered additional income to the President.

Flights that appear to be personal are particularly those taken by Julie and Tricia to join either David Eisenhower or Edward Cox while the latter were either students or stationed in various cities other than Washington, D.C. On several occasions both Edward Cox and David Eisenhower joined Julie and Tricia on flights to and from these same cities and to and from the President's homes in either Key Biscayne, Florida, or San Clemente, California. Occasionally, members of the

President's family took along friends or guests on these flights.

2. Analysis of Tax Treatment

Economic Benefit to the President

This aspect of the examination involves two basic questions. The first is whether the free use of Government transportation by the President's family and friends created income subject to Federal tax. If the answer to the first question is in the affirmative, it is necessary to determine to whom the income should properly be taxed.

Under section 61 of the Internal Revenue Code of 1954, gross income is defined as "all income from whatever source derived" unless excluded by other provisions of the Internal Revenue Code. The statute specifically enumerates 15 items included within the definition, but carefully provides that gross income is not limited to these 15 items. In providing this all-inclusive language, it is clear that Congress intended that the term "gross income" be given a broad interpretation.[7] In discussing section 61 of the 1954 Code, the Committee Reports note that the new section corresponds to section 22(a) of the 1939 Code and states that "[w]hile the language in existing section 22(a) has been simplified, the all-inclusive nature of statutory gross income has not been affected thereby."

Amounts received by an employee from his employer are generally taxed to the employee as compensation because of the existing employment relationship. This does not mean that an expenditure by the employer is income only if it is intended to be conferred as actual compensation for services rendered. Such a concept of gross income is too restrictive. Further, items of gross income need not be in the form of cash; it is sufficient that an item can be valued in terms of money. . . .

The issues presented here are to an extent unique, since there is no public record of prior determination of tax consequences in a situation of this type. It is possible however to approach these questions in light of the employment relationship which exists between the U.S. Government and the President and to examine the authorities in the general area of benefits flowing between the employer and employee. The staff also considers the many decisions involving the corporation-shareholder relationship to have an application to this area of the examination.

[T]he . . . Internal Revenue Service has contended successfully that a share-holder's use of a wide range of corporate assets resulted in income to the shareholder. The courts have held that constructive dividends were realized from the shareholder's personal use of a corporate owned yacht, an automobile, supplies and materials, and a lake house. Constructive dividends have also been found to result to the shareholder by corporation payments of the shareholder's home expenses, club expenses, life insurance policy premiums, and travel expenses.

The court decisions have not been confined to constructive dividend results, but have also found that compensation income resulted from the personal use of

---

[7] *Commissioner v. Glenshaw Glass Co.*, 348 U.S. 426, 432 (1955).

corporate facilities or from corporate payments for personal purposes of the individual taxpayer. . . .

There is also the question of whether taxable income can be attributed to an employee for the use of the employer's facilities or services by his friends or family members. This question in a sense involves the doctrine of constructive receipt, but not in the traditional sense, since we are not concerned with the question of when income is taxable, but with the question of who should be taxed on the economic benefit.

With respect to this issue, the authorities recognize it is not necessary that the individual taxpayer himself receive the direct benefit of the use of the facility or the payment of the expenses by the employer.

In *United States v. Gotcher*, 68-2 U.S.T.C. 9546, 401 F.2d 118 (5th Cir. 1968), the taxpayer was held to have realized income through a supplier's payment of his wife's travel expenses on a trip to tour the supplier's plant. The basis for the attribution of income to the taxpayer was that the supplier's payments had relieved him of financial responsibility for the wife's expenses.

It is, of course, obvious that if a taxpayer entertains or benefits his friends by use of his employer's property, this does not change the result that the use is income to the taxpayer, any more than the taxpayer would be entitled to a deduction if he took part of his salary and rented comparable facilities for the benefit of his friends.

It is apparent that Mrs. Nixon, the President's daughters, and the friends of the Nixon family have enjoyed the personal use of the Presidential aircraft only because of the employment relationship between the President and the United States. It is, therefore, the belief of the staff that the President has realized taxable income where members of his family or his friends had free use of Government transportation for personal excursions or where it has not been established that they were on Government business. The staff also considers this to be equally applicable where the President's family and/or friends accompanied him on trips which for him were in the performance of the official duties of the President, but for which there is no evidence that the family and/or friends performed any official functions.

Measure of Income

Where it is determined that an employee has received compensation other than in money, "the fair market value of the property or services taken in payment must be included in income." Regs. Sec. 1.61-2(d). Generally, where compensation is paid by allowing the taxpayer to enjoy the use of property, courts look to the rental value of the property to determine the amount of the compensation. . . .

It is the staff's belief, however, that in order to reach a reasonable and equitable measure of the benefit to the President, it is necessary to consider the reason Government aircraft were used to transport the President's family and friends. Because of security precautions, such as the risk of hijacking, the Secret Service recommends that these individuals not travel on commercial scheduled airlines. But for these considerations the family and friends could have traveled on commercial airlines. In recognition of these circumstances, the staff believes that the appropriate measure of the President's economic benefit is the cost of first class commercial fares for the trips provided by Government aircraft, rather than charter rates or the costs of the use of the aircraft.

STAFF CONCLUSION

The staff believes that the personal use of Government airplanes by the President's family and friends should be classified as income to him for income tax purposes. . . .

One question involves the issue of whether there should be an inclusion in income of any amount with respect to the President's own use of Government aircraft. Some of his use could be classified as primarily personal since the flights take him to locations where he spends a significant part of his time on vacation. However, it is also pointed out that the President, by the nature of his office, must hold himself available for work at virtually any time. In part because of this characteristic of the Presidency and in part because of the uncertain status of such items in the past, the staff is not recommending that any amounts be included in income with respect to personal transportation of the President. In making this recommendation, the staff is not suggesting this be foreclosed as a possible issue in the future.

NOTE ON MISCELLANEOUS EXCLUSIONS

Tax-Exempt Interest:

Interest on state and local bonds is excluded from gross income under § 103(a). The exclusion has been part of the income tax law since its inception in 1913. Although the primary justification for the original provision was a concern about the constitutionality of federal taxation of state and local obligations, most scholars today believe there is little doubt it would be constitutional to impose a federal tax on such interest income.

Determining whether one should invest in a tax-exempt bond calls for a review of the tax bracket of the taxpayer in question and the rate of return on comparable taxable investments. Thus, for example, assume an investor has a choice of two bonds: a taxable corporate bond paying 10% interest and a tax-free municipal bond paying 8% interest. If the investor is in the 15% marginal tax bracket, the after-tax return on the corporate bond exceeds 8%, and it is therefore preferable. For the investor in a marginal tax bracket that exceeds 20%, the after-tax return on the corporate bond is less than 8%, and the municipal bond is the better choice. (Note, however, that interest on certain types of state and local bonds may be subject to the "alternative minimum tax" of § 55, a provision studied later in the course, and a matter to consider in making the comparison of after-tax returns.) As the example demonstrates, the exclusion is worth more to taxpayers in higher tax brackets and it has often been criticized on that account.

Section 103(a) makes it possible for state and local governments to sell their bonds at lower interest rates than would be the case if the bonds were taxable. The exclusion is therefore justified by some as a form of federal assistance to local government, a type of revenue sharing in which the federal government forgoes tax revenues in order to reduce local government expenses. It has often been pointed out, however, that, if a subsidy is intended, the subsidy is an inefficient one when an investor's marginal tax bracket exceeds the spread between otherwise comparable taxable and non-taxable bonds. The federal tax revenue forgone in these cases does not fully translate into state and local savings realized. For example, if an investor in the 35% bracket purchases a $10,000, 8% municipal bond rather than a comparable 10% corporate bond, the investor saves $350 in federal taxes, but the municipality saves — and the investor forgoes — only $200 worth of interest. Historically, the interest rates on tax-free bonds, as a percentage of the interest rate on taxable bonds, has been such that taxpayers in higher brackets can generally effect such net gains by investing in municipal bonds.

The § 103(a) exclusion, as might be expected, has been exploited by local governments to such a degree that Congress, concerned with abuse, has imposed various restrictions on the basic exclusion. *See* § 103(b). By way of a brief summary, and without making any attempt to explore the details, one may divide state and local bonds into three categories. In the first category are "governmental bonds," which are bonds issued to finance general governmental operations and facilities such as schools, roads, government buildings, water and sewer facilities and the like. Governmental bonds are tax-exempt, and free of most of the restrictions imposed on non-governmental bonds. The second category consists of "private activity bonds" — bonds issued to finance the activities of non-governmental persons. Local governments have often used the § 103(a) exclusion to issue bonds that financed the development of private businesses and industries, and other activities that were private or only semi-public in nature. The general rule adopted by Congress is that interest on private activity bonds is taxable in the absence of a specific exception to the contrary. A number of exceptions have been provided, and, subject to various restrictions, including an annual volume limitation for most private activity bonds, interest on such "qualified" private activity bonds is tax-exempt. The third category consists of arbitrage bonds. State and local governments are treated by the Treasury as tax-exempt entities under the Internal Revenue Code. It could thus be quite profitable for them to take advantage of their tax-exempt status, and the relatively low interest expense § 103(a) makes possible, by investing the proceeds of a bond issue — pending disbursement for its given purposes — at a rate of return in excess of the interest rate payable on the bonds. The congressional response, in general terms, is that such "arbitrage profits" belong to the federal government. Thus, all tax-exempt bonds — governmental or private activity — are subject to various arbitrage restrictions, and to a requirement that certain arbitrage profits be rebated to the federal treasury.

The significance of the exceptions notwithstanding, keep in mind the general rule expressed in § 103(a). Consider also a question to which we will return at various times later in the course: If a particular receipt is excluded from gross income — interest on municipal bonds, for example — should the expenses incurred in earning that income be deductible? Do you understand why, as a matter of policy, the answer should be "no"? In this regard, see § 265, a provision we study directly in Chapter 27.

Sections 109 and 1019:

Congress enacted §§ 109 and 1019 in 1942 to overturn the Supreme Court's decision in *Helvering v. Bruun*, 309 U.S. 461 (1940), holding that a lessor was taxable, on forfeiture of a leasehold, on the value of a building erected by the tenant on the lessor's premises. Section 109 excludes from the income of a lessor on termination of a lease the value of improvements made to the property by the lessee (other than as rent). However, since the special basis rule of § 1019 denies any basis adjustment on account of such exempt income, the gain the lessor realizes is really tax-deferred rather than permanently excluded. Since basis is not adjusted, no increase in depreciation deductions occurs by reason of the improvement. The tax-deferred gain will be accounted for upon the lessor's sale or other disposition of the property. Consider whether as a matter of policy §§ 109 and 1019 are an appropriate response to the *Helvering v. Bruun* problem.

The parenthetical clause of § 109 provides that the exclusion does not apply to rent. The regulations at § 1.61-8(c) provide that improvements by a lessee which are a "substitute for rent" constitute gross income to the lessor, and further state that whether an improvement is a rental substitute depends on the intention of the parties, as indicated by the terms of the lease or surrounding circumstances. The distinction § 109 requires — between improvements that are rental substitutes and those that are not — may obviously be a difficult one to make in a given set of circumstances.

Credit for adoption expenses and exclusion for adoption payments made by employer:

Section 23 provides taxpayers with a maximum credit against income tax liability of $10,000 (adjusted for inflation) for qualified adoption expenses paid or incurred by the taxpayer. Section 23(d) defines "qualified adoption expenses" to include reasonable and necessary adoption fees, courts costs, attorney fees and other expenses directly related to the adoption of an "eligible child" (other than the child of the taxpayer's spouse). An "eligible child" means an individual who has not attained the age of 18 or who is physically or mentally incapable of caring for himself. § 23(d)(2). There are special provisions for children with "special needs." With respect to the adoption of a child who is not a citizen or resident of the United States, § 23(e) provides the credit will not be available until the adoption is finalized. The credit is phased out ratably for taxpayers whose adjusted gross income (as specially modified) exceeds $150,000 (adjusted for inflation) and is fully phased out when the adjusted gross income exceeds the phase-out threshold by $40,000.

Section 137 authorizes an employee to exclude from gross income amounts paid or expenses incurred by an employer for qualified adoption expenses in connection with the employee's adoption of a child. The amount of the exclusion cannot exceed $10,000 (adjusted for inflation). Like the credit, the exclusion is phased out once employee's specially modified adjusted gross income exceeds $150,000 (adjusted for inflation). "Qualified adoption expenses" has the same meaning as that term is used in Section 23.

Government Welfare Payments:

Without relying on any explicit statutory authority, the Service has held a variety of government benefits to be excluded from gross income. Recall, however, from Chapter 2, that unemployment benefits, once treated as non-taxable by the Service, are now fully included in income, and that Social Security benefits, also formerly tax-free in full, are now partially taxable. Taxing these benefits may stem from viewing unemployment compensation as a wage replacement program, and from viewing Social Security as, at least in part, a program of deferred compensation. Welfare-type benefits, by contrast, tend to lack the nexus to compensation, are seemingly more in the nature of charitable gifts, and thus are excludable from gross income on that basis. Moreover, to the extent benefits are based on need, treating them as income would, in any event, likely generate little or no taxable income in the great majority of cases. Thus, government disbursements in the nature of welfare payments are held to be tax-free; see, for example, Revenue Ruling 98-19, 1998-1 C.B. 840, excluding relocation payments authorized by a federal act and made to an individual moving from a flood-damaged residence to another residence; also see Revenue Ruling 76-144, 1976-1 C.B. 17, excluding disaster relief grants from income. However, government transfer payments made without regard to need are likely to be taxed; see, for example, Revenue Ruling 85-39, 1985-1 C.B. 21, *amplified by* Revenue Ruling 90-56, 1990-2 C.B. 102, holding that "dividend payments" made by Alaska to its adult residents were taxable because they were not general welfare program payments, not restricted to those in need, and not characterized as gifts. In addition, payments made by nongovernmental entities are not considered payments for the general welfare and are therefore not excluded from the recipient's gross income under the general welfare exclusion. However, these payments may be excluded as gifts under § 102. See, for example, Revenue Ruling 99-44, 1999-2 C.B. 549, holding that payments made by a charity to an individual that responds to the individual's needs and do not proceed from any moral or legal duty are motivated by detached and disinterested generosity, and therefore are excludable from the individual's gross income under § 102.

Section 139: Disaster Relief Payments

The Victims of Terrorism Tax Relief Act of 2001 added § 139 to the Code. Section 139(a) provides that gross income does not include any amount received by an individual as a qualified disaster relief payment. Section 139(b) provides, in part, that the term "qualified disaster relief payment" means any amount paid to or for the benefit of an individual:

(1) to reimburse or pay reasonable and necessary personal, family, living, or funeral expenses incurred as a result of a qualified disaster (§ 139(b)(1));

(2) to reimburse or pay reasonable and necessary expenses incurred for the repair or rehabilitation of a personal residence or repair or replacement of its contents to the extent that the need for such repair, rehabilitation, or replacement is attributable to a qualified disaster (§ 139(b)(2));

(3) by a person furnishing or selling transportation as a common carrier by reason of the death or personal physical injury incurred as a result of a qualified disaster; or

(4) by a Federal, State, or local government, or agency or instrumentality thereof, in connection with a qualified disaster in order to promote the general welfare (§ 139(b)(4)).

"Qualified disaster" is defined in § 139(c) to mean:

(1) a disaster that results from a terroristic or military action as defined in § 692(c)(2);

(2) a federally declared disaster as defined in § 165(h)(3)(C)(i);

(3) a disaster resulting from an accident involving a common carrier, or from any other event that the Secretary determines to be of a catastrophic nature; or

(4) with respect to amounts described in § 139(b)(4), a disaster that is determined by any applicable Federal, State, or local authority to warrant assistance from the Federal, State, or local government or an agency or instrumentality thereof.

As noted in Revenue Ruling 2003-12, 2003-1 C.B. 283, § 139 codifies in part but does not supplant the administrative general welfare exclusion with respect to certain disaster relief payments to individuals. Revenue Ruling 2003-12 provides examples of payments made by (a) government, (b) charitable organizations, and (c) employers to pay or reimburse certain reasonable and necessary medical, temporary housing, or transportation expenses incurred by individuals as a result of a flood. The ruling demonstrates how the payments may be excludable under the general welfare exclusion, § 139, or § 102.

Educational Savings Bonds:

Section 135, enacted in 1988 to encourage savings for higher education, excludes from income interest on "qualified U.S. savings bonds" used to pay higher education expenses of the taxpayer, spouse or dependent. § 135(a), (c). The exemption is subject to an inflation-adjusted phase-out based on the taxpayer's modified adjusted gross income. § 135(b)(2). The exemption is also limited where the redemption proceeds for the year from qualifying bonds exceed the higher education expenses paid during the year. § 135(b)(1). Qualifying higher education expenses include tuition and required fees at eligible institutions, reduced by certain scholarships and benefits received with respect to the student. § 135(c)(2), (d)(1).

Foreign Earned Income:

In what is likely to be our only venture into the specialized world of foreign or international tax, note § 911 excludes, from the gross income of United States citizens or residents living abroad, provided certain requirements are met, up to $80,000 per year (adjusted for inflation) of foreign-earned income, plus an additional "housing cost amount." Congress has justified this substantial exclusion as encouraging Americans to work abroad in order to help promote the export of American goods and services, and make American business more competitive in foreign markets.

Foster Care Payments:

To provide a tax encouragement to foster care, certain foster care payments are excluded from income by § 131. Provided various requirements are met, the exclusion applies to amounts paid as reimbursement for expenses and also to "difficulty of care" payments as well — that is, payments in the nature of compensation for caring for a physically, mentally, or emotionally handicapped individual.

Section 126 Payments:

Section 126 excludes from income certain federal or state payments under a variety of conservation, environmental, forestry and wildlife programs. No basis adjustment is permitted on account of the exclusion with respect to property acquired or improved with the payment — a provision reminiscent of § 1019 in connection with the § 109 exclusion. Disposition of "§ 126 property" is subject to § 1255.

Certain Living Expenses:

Section 123 excludes from gross income insurance payments received as reimbursement or compensation for the increase in living expenses incurred on account of casualty to a principal residence. For guidance in determining the scope of the § 123 exclusion, see the regulations thereunder. For examples applying the exclusion where insurance payments and increased living expenses are spread over a multi-year period, see Revenue Ruling 93-43, 1993-2 C.B. 69.

Chapter 12

BUSINESS AND PROFIT SEEKING EXPENSES

I. PROBLEMS

1. Casey owns an executive placement agency that he operates as a sole proprietorship. Earlier this year, Casey hired his daughter, Brennan, as a placement advisor. Brennan, who recently earned her MBA, is one of three placement advisors working for Casey; the other two placement advisors have college degrees but neither has an MBA. Casey hired Brennan at a salary equal to that he paid the other placement advisors even though they had far more experience. Given the profitability of his agency, Casey gave each of the three placement advisors a substantial bonus at year end. Brennan received a bonus of $25,000; the other placement advisors received a bonus of $10,000.

    (a) May Casey deduct the salary and bonus he paid to Brennan?

    (b) If the bonus paid to Brennan was deemed excessive given the nature of Brennan's work, her experience, and the salaries paid to individuals performing comparable work, how would the bonus be treated for tax purposes?

    (c) How would your analysis in (b) change, if at all, if Casey's business were incorporated? In answering this question, assume Casey is the sole shareholder of the corporation.

2. Finn is a self-employed certified financial planner in Palm Desert, California. Determine which, if any, of the following costs incurred by Finn during the year are deductible:

    (a) Finn advised a client to invest $50,000 in a company that was manufacturing a low-cost but high-tech mousetrap. Finn's enthusiasm for the company's product was not shared by the public generally and the stock became worthless. Wishing to avoid hard feelings, Finn paid $25,000 to the client.

    (b) Finn paid $25,000 per year to an agency that provides chauffeur service. Under his contract with the agency, Finn is entitled to up to 8 hours of chauffeur service per week. Finn usually takes advantage of this service a couple of times each week when he makes house calls to some of his wealthy clients. Finn tells you: "The chauffeur service enables me to forget the problems of the world while I ride in luxury. My clients are impressed when they see me arrive in a chauffeured limousine. They assume that I must know what I'm doing."

3. Abby, the long-time chief financial officer for a hospital in Indiana, became disgruntled with her employment because of the tremendous stress associated with her job. She hired an executive placement agency in Chicago to assist her in locating a position that would use her abilities and experience but not involve working in health care. During the past year, Abby incurred a range of expenses associated with the job hunt, including trips to Chicago to meet with the placement agency as well as trips to various locations in the country to interview for positions. Abby, with the help of the placement agency, finally found and accepted a position in Seattle. Abby's new position is that of chief financial officer for a start-up technology company. Abby is particularly pleased with the new job because, unlike her old position, this position requires considerable travel, including foreign travel. May Abby deduct the cost of the trips to Chicago and other locations associated with her job search? How would your answer change, if at all, if Abby, having been offered the job in Seattle, decided to keep her job in Indiana when the hospital offered her a substantial salary increase?

4. Mark is a 35 year-old local television newscaster. His television work requires "appropriate" dress, and accordingly, he maintains, as his employer expects, an extensive wardrobe of expensive suits, shirts and ties which he uses for his twice-nightly newscasts. In off-duty hours, Mark never wears the clothes worn at work but, like his friends, prefers to wear very casual attire. Are the acquisition costs of Mark's television garb deductible?

5. Phil, bored with his lucrative tax practice, decides to enter the fast-food business. He buys the Burt's Burgers franchise for his area for $500,000. Rather than purchasing a building for the business, Phil decides to rent commercial space and spends $5,000 in advertising for such space. After finally renting a well-located commercial building, Phil spent two months remodeling the building. During this period prior to opening, Phil also paid $5,000 in building rent, $3,000 for employee training sessions at the headquarters of Burt's Burgers, and $6,000 in wages to the employees who were being trained. May Phil deduct the advertising, rental, employee training and wage expenses he incurred prior to opening the business?

6. Vic has a portfolio of stocks and bonds worth about $300,000. This year he pays $200 for a subscription to the Wall Street Journal, $25 for a copy of "A Guide to Tax-Free Bonds," and $500 for a newsletter and investment advice from a financial planner. Vic pays $200 for a one-year rental of a safe deposit box to hold his stock certificates and bonds and other important papers, and he also pays his accountant $400 to prepare his tax return. Finally, Vic pays you, his lawyer, $250 to tell him whether all these expenses, including your fee, are deductible. What's your answer?

Assignment for Chapter 12:

Complete the problems.

Read: Internal Revenue Code: §§ 162(a), (c), 195, 212 and 262.
         Treasury Regulations: §§ 1.162-1(a), 1.162-2(a) and (b), 1.162-8, 1.162-9,

1.212-1(a), (b), (d), (e), (f), (g), (h), (l), (o), (p); 1.262-1(b)(3), (4), (5), (8).

Materials: Overview
            Welch v. Helvering
            Higgins v. Commissioner
            Commissioner v. Groetzinger
            Revenue Ruling 75-120
            Pevsner v. Commissioner

II. VOCABULARY

deduction
ordinary
necessary
trade or business
capital expenditure
amortization
start-up expense

III. OBJECTIVES

1. To recall § 162 is the primary business deduction provision in the Code.

2. To list factors relevant in determining whether an expense is "ordinary and necessary."

3. To predict whether a given expense is "ordinary and necessary."

4. To list the characteristics of a "trade or business."

5. To distinguish between pre-operating expenses and operating expenses.

6. To identify factors relevant in determining whether compensation is reasonable.

7. To predict, in a given situation, whether compensation will be deemed reasonable.

8. To predict in a given situation whether the cost and maintenance of clothing will be deductible as a business expense.

9. To explain the significance of the "carrying on" requirement in § 162(a).

10. To predict in any given fact pattern whether employment-seeking expenses will be deductible.

11. To recall § 195 permits a current deduction and/or the amortization of start-up expenditures, and to apply that provision to a given fact pattern.

12. To recall § 212 allows the deduction of certain non-trade or business expenses, and to apply § 212 to given fact patterns.

13. To recall § 212 allows the deduction of costs incurred in connection with the determination, collection or refund of any tax.

IV. OVERVIEW

With this chapter, we begin the study of deductions. The business deduction of § 162 and the "profit-seeking" deduction of § 212 reflect the principle that "net income," rather than gross income, should be subject to tax. As a result, expenses necessary to the earning of items of gross income ought to be allowed as deductions. Two related points should be noted now. First, "personal" expenses — those expenses not within the business or profit-seeking classification — generally will not be deductible in determining the net income subject to tax. Section 262(a) expresses this point in broad language. Second, some expenditures are regarded as "capital expenditures" because they were made to obtain an asset lasting for some substantial or indefinite period of time. For that reason, capital expenditures of the business or profit-seeking type generally may not be deducted in full at the time of the expenditure. Instead, they must be deducted in increments over some period, or perhaps deducted, in effect, only on disposition of the asset. Capital expenditures are studied in the next Chapter in some detail. For now, you should begin to appreciate an important and difficult part of tax law: the need to draw lines between business or profit-seeking expenses and personal expenses.

A. Business Deductions — Section 162

Consider the following hypothetical: Seeking to secure its large inventory of stock from loss should the death of the President of the United States occasion a fall in stock prices, a New York securities firm purchases a term insurance policy on the life of the President. The firm deducts the insurance premiums as a business expense. The Service challenges the deduction. What result? The answer requires consideration of deductions in general and business deductions specifically.

While courts have historically viewed deductions as a matter of legislative grace,[1] Congress has authorized deductions for most expenses incurred in producing income. The Internal Revene Code taxes gain, profit or net income — not gross receipts. For example, if a retailer pays $10,000 for inventory she sells to the public for $20,000, her gross income is not $20,000, but $10,000. Regulation § 1.61-3(a) interprets the § 61(a)(2) language "gross income derived from business" to mean "the total sales, less the cost of goods sold." Similarly, if a house painter is paid $25,000 for his services during the year but pays $5,000 for the paint he uses, he will be taxed on $20,000 and not $25,000.

Which provision supports the painter's deduction for the $5,000 in paint costs? Which provision would the securities firm rely on in deducting the premium on the policy insuring the life of the President? Section 162 is the obvious candidate. Section 162 is the business deduction workhorse of the Code; more dollars are deducted on the authority of this provision than any other in the Internal Revenue Code. Revisit Problem 1 in Chapter 1. The expenses Caroline Taxpayer incurred in that problem for wages and supplies are classic examples of deductible business expenses.

---

[1] *See, e.g., Interstate Transit Lines v. Commissioner*, 319 U.S. 590 (1943).

The first 27 words of § 162(a) establish a number of significant requirements for the deduction of costs associated with a business: (1) the cost must be an "expense"; (2) the expense must be "ordinary"; (3) it must be "necessary"; (4) it must be "paid or incurred during the taxable year"; and (5) it must be paid or incurred in "carrying on" a "trade or business." Whether a cost constitutes an "expense" will be considered in the next Chapter. Requirement (4) relates to timing and will be discussed in Chapters 28 and 29. The "ordinary and necessary" and "carrying on a trade or business" requirements will be considered in detail in this Chapter.

1. The Expense Must Be "Ordinary and Necessary"

a. Is the Expense "Ordinary"?

In *Welch v. Helvering*, included in the materials, the Supreme Court, assessing the deductibility of payments made by a taxpayer to the creditors of his bankrupt employer, considered the meaning of the term "ordinary" as used in the predecessor to § 162. According to the Court, the term "ordinary" requires that a cost be customary or expected in the life of a business. What is customary or expected in a business? "Life in all its fullness must supply the answer. . . . " While the Court found that the fullness of life indicated business people did not "ordinarily" make payments such as those in question, the Court's decision raises more questions than it answers. Can *Welch v. Helvering* be viewed merely as a failure of proof case, or is the Court suggesting a taxpayer may not deduct payments she is not legally obligated to pay?

In *Jenkins v. Commissioner*, T.C. Memo. 1983-667, the court allowed country songwriter and singer, Harold L. Jenkins, whose stage name was Conway Twitty, to deduct as a business expense amounts he repaid to investors in his defunct fast food venture, Twitty Burger, Inc. Consider the following excerpt from this well-known case:

> The question presented is whether one person (Conway Twitty) may deduct the expenses of another person (Twitty Burger). In order to determine whether the disallowed expenditures are deductible by petitioner under section 162 we must (1) ascertain the purpose or motive of the taxpayer in making the payments and (2) determine whether there is a sufficient connection between the expenditures and the taxpayer's trade or business. . . .
>
> Respondent argues that the payments Conway Twitty made to the investors in Twitty Burger are not deductible by him as ordinary and necessary business expenses under section 162 because there was no business purpose for the payments and, additionally, there was no relationship between his involvement in Twitty Burger and his business of being a country music entertainer. Respondent argues that the payments in question here were made by Conway Twitty gratuitously in that petitioner had no personal liability to the holders of the debentures and made the payments merely out of a sense of moral obligation. Relying on *Welch v. Helvering* . . . respondent concludes that while it was "very nice" of

petitioner to reimburse the investors in Twitty Burger, the required nexus between the expenditures and Conway Twitty's career as a country music entertainer does not exist and therefore the payments were not "ordinary and necessary" within the meaning of section 162.

Petitioner argues that the rule of *Welch v. Helvering* is not applicable to the case at bar because petitioner made the payments in question to protect his reputation and earning capacity in his ongoing business of being a country music entertainer whereas in *Welch* the Supreme Court held that the payments made there were capital expenditures of the taxpayer's new business. Petitioner maintains that . . . the ~~expenditures in issue here are deductible under section 162 if the payments were made primarily with a business motive and if there is a sufficient connection between the payments and the taxpayer's trade or business.~~

The question presented for our resolution is purely one of fact. While previously decided cases dealing with this issue are somewhat helpful there is, quite understandably, no case directly on point with the facts before us. As the Supreme Court recognized in *Welch v. Helvering*, many cases in the federal courts deal with phases of the problem presented in the case at bar. To attempt to harmonize them would be a futile task. They involve the appreciation of particular situations, at times with border-line conclusions.

There is no suggestion in the record that any of the payments were made in order to protect petitioner's investment in Twitty Burger or to revitalize the corporation. It is petitioner's contention that Conway Twitty repaid the investors in Twitty Burger from his personal funds in order to protect his personal business reputation. While it is clear from the facts that Conway was under no legal obligation to make such payments, (at least in the sense that the corporate debentures were not personally guaranteed by him), the law is clear that the absence of such an obligation is not in itself a bar to the deduction of such expenditures under section 162. In addition, the fact that the petitioner also felt a moral obligation to the people who had entrusted him with their funds does not preclude the deductibility of the payments so long as the satisfaction of the moral obligation was not the primary motivation for the expenditures.

After a thorough consideration of the record we are convinced that petitioner Conway Twitty repaid the investors in Twitty Burger with the primary motive of protecting his personal business reputation. There was the obvious similarity of the name of the corporation and petitioner's stage name. There is no doubt that the corporation's name was chosen with the idea of capitalizing on Conway Twitty's fame as a country music performer. Additionally, many of the investors were connected with the country music industry. While there is no doubt that part of petitioner's motivation for making the payments involved his personal sense of morality, we do not believe that this ethical consideration was paramount.

Petitioner testified as follows concerning his motivations for repaying the Twitty Burger investors:

I'm 99 percent entertainer. That's just about all I know. The name Conway Twitty, and the image that I work so hard for since 1955 and '56 is the foundation that I, my family, and the 30 some odd people that work for me stand on. They depend on it, and they can depend on it. . . .

I handled it that way because of that. Because of the image. And second and very close to it, I handled it that way because I think it is morally right, and if you owe a man something, you pay him.

When we got the letter from Walter Beach and from [Merle] Haggard's lawyer . . . my people said, hey, you know, we've got some letters from people saying they are going to sue you, and that you might have done something wrong as far as securities and all that stuff goes. It just scares you to death.

I mean it did me. And it would most people. I know it would. And so you — you don't want any part of that. A law suit like that with — say if Merle Haggard sued Conway Twitty or if Walter Beach sued Conway Twitty and you're in court, and they are saying it's fraud and something to do with the securities thing, and, you know, all the years I've worked for are gone. If my fans didn't give up on me, it would warp me psychologically. I couldn't function anymore because I'm the type of person I am. . . .

The country music fan is different than the people I had dealt with back in the '50's and the kids. They will stay right with you as long as you stay within certain boundaries. They expect a lot out of you because you — a country singer deals with . . . feelings and things inside of people — you know — you can listen to the words in a country song, and you're dealing with emotions and feelings. . . .

Petitioner presented the expert testimony of William Ivey, the Director of Country Music Foundation in Nashville, Tennessee. In his report . . . he stated as follows:

Country entertainers go to great lengths to protect their images, for they correctly realize that both business associates and fans judge their artistic efforts in the light of perceptions of the artist's personality, professional conduct, and moral character. The business side of country music is a highly personal activity which depends heavily upon knowledge of reputation and past performance. . . .

Reputation can have an even greater effect upon an entertainer as it influences fans. Virtually every article written about Conway Twitty stresses the effort he makes to meet his fans. . . . Devotion to fans is a crucial part of Conway's great success, and his scrupulously maintained reputation is one element in maintaining his intense popularity. . . .

Stories abound of the problems encountered by artists who have not followed Conway's example. George Jones, Waylon Jennings, and

Johnny Paycheck are all great entertainers, but each has been plagued by personal problems which have limited the extent of their success. Had, in the matter before this court, Conway Twitty allowed investors to be left dangling with heavy losses following the collapse of the Twitty Burger chain, the multiple lawsuits, unfavorable news stories and disgruntled investors would have all damaged that very reputation which was a key element in Conway's image as an artist. Though he would have continued to perform and record, there exists serious doubt that he would have achieved the unparalleled success he enjoyed during the 1970's had his reputation been so injured. . . . Had he allowed investors to suffer as a result of Twitty Burger's failure, both his reputation and his career would thus have been damaged.

We conclude that there was a proximate relationship between the payments made to the holders of Twitty Burger debentures and petitioner's trade or business as a country music entertainer so as to render those payments an ordinary and necessary expense of that business. Although, as respondent argues, the chances of a successful lawsuit against Conway Twitty by any of the investors or the Securities and Exchange Commission was remote, we agree with petitioner that the possibility of extensive adverse publicity concerning petitioner's involvement with the defunct corporation and the consequent loss of the investors' funds was very real. We do not believe it is necessary for us to find that adverse publicity emanating from Conway Twitty's failure to repay the investors in Twitty Burger would have ruined his career as a country music singer. Rather, we need only find that a proximate relationship existed between the payments and petitioner's business. We find that such relationship exists. It is not necessary that the taxpayer's trade or business be of the same type as that engaged in by the person on whose behalf the payments are made. . . .

In making these payments petitioner was furthering his business as a country music artist and protecting his business reputation for integrity. The mere fact that they were voluntary does not deprive them of their character as ordinary and necessary business expenses.[2]

---

[2] Judge Irwin closed his opinion in *Jenkins* with the following "Ode to Conway Twitty":

Twitty Burger went belly up
But Conway remained true
He repaid his investors, one and all
It was the moral thing to do.
His fans would not have liked it
It could have hurt his fame
Had any investors sued him
Like Merle Haggard or Sonny James.
When it was time to file taxes
Conway thought what he would do
Was deduct those payments as a business expense
Under section one-sixty-two.
In order to allow these deductions
Goes the argument of the Commissioner

In *Deputy v. Dupont*, 308 U.S. 488, 495–496 (1940), decided subsequent to *Welch v. Helvering*, the Supreme Court's discussion of "ordinary" was somewhat more illuminating:

> Ordinary has the connotation of normal, usual or customary. To be sure, an expense may be ordinary though it happens but once in the taxpayer's lifetime. . . . Yet the transaction which gives rise to it must be of common or frequent occurrence in the type of business involved. . . . Hence, the fact that a particular expense would be an ordinary or common one in the course of one business and so deductible . . . does not necessarily make it such in connection with another business. . . . As stated in *Welch v. Helvering*, "[w]hat is ordinary, though there must always be a strain of constancy within it, is nonetheless a variable affected by time and place and circumstance." One of the extremely relevant circumstances is the nature and scope of the particular business out of which the expense in question accrued. The fact that an obligation to pay has arisen is not sufficient. It is the kind of transaction out of which the obligation arose and its normalcy in the particular business which are crucial and controlling.

A quarter of a century later, in *Commissioner v. Tellier*, 383 U.S. 687 (1966), the Court, in allowing a deduction for legal expenses incurred by a taxpayer in defending himself in a criminal business action, noted:

The payments must be ordinary and necessary
To a business of the petitioner.
Had Conway not repaid the investors
His career would have been under cloud,
Under the unique facts of this case
Held: The deductions are allowed.

In a poetic reprise, the Service responded to the opinion with the following "Ode to Conway Twitty: A Reprise":

Harold Jenkins and Conway Twitty
They are both the same
But one was born
The other achieved fame.
The man is talented
And has many a friend
They opened a restaurant
His name he did lend.
They are two different things
Making burgers and song
The business went sour
It didn't take long.
He repaid his friends
Why did he act
Was it business or friendship
Which is fact?
Business the court held
It's deductible they feel
We disagree with the answer
But let's not appeal.
Recommendation: Nonacquiescence.

AOD 1984-022.

The principal function of the term "ordinary" in § 162(a) is to clarify the distinction, often difficult, between those expenses that are currently deductible and those that are in the nature of capital expenditures, which, if deductible at all, must be amortized over the useful life of the asset. . . . The legal expenses deducted by the respondent were not capital expenditures. They were incurred in his defense against charges of past criminal conduct, not in the acquisition of a capital asset. Our decisions establish that counsel fees comparable to those here involved are ordinary business expenses, even though a "lawsuit affecting the safety of a business may happen once in a lifetime."

While it is generally easy to determine whether costs incurred in the day-to-day conduct of a business are "ordinary," the courts and the Service nonetheless regularly encounter cases demanding careful consideration. For example, the issue presented in the hypothetical at the outset of this overview was the subject of *Goedel v. Commissioner*, 29 B.T.A. 1 (1939). The Board of Tax Appeals concluded the premiums paid by a securities firm on a life insurance policy covering President Roosevelt were not deductible. The court doubted that other businesses "accustomed to buying insurance in connection with their business" would use funds to purchase an insurance policy of the nature acquired by the firm. If a securities firm presented you with the same case today, would you advise the firm on the authority of *Goedel* that it could never deduct the premium? Is the fact an expenditure is unprecedented in a business reason enough to find it is not "ordinary" and therefore not deductible under § 162?

In *Gilliam v. Commissioner*, T.C. Memo 1986-81, the taxpayer, an artist with a history of mental and emotional problems, created a major disturbance on an airline while flying to Memphis to lecture and teach. The taxpayer, who was indicted for violating certain federal criminal statutes and sued by a passenger whom he injured, sought to deduct as business expenses (1) the legal fees incurred in defending the criminal action and (2) the settlement paid to the injured passenger. Disallowing the claimed deductions, the Tax Court reasoned that artists and teachers while travelling on business do not generally engage in conduct like the taxpayer's; the costs incurred were not part of the taxpayer's transportation costs and his actions aboard the aircraft did not further his trade or business. In short, the taxpayer's costs were not "ordinary" within the meaning of § 162.

The Tax Court in *Gilliam* distinguished *Dancer v. Commissioner*, 73 T.C. 1103 (1980), where the court allowed a deduction for the costs a taxpayer incurred in settling a negligence action arising from an automobile accident which occurred while he was travelling on business. The *Dancer* court noted:

It is true that the expenditure in the instant case did not further petitioner's business in any economic sense; nor is it, we hope, the type of expenditure that many businesses are called upon to pay. Nevertheless, neither factor lessens the direct relationship between the expenditure and the business. Automobile travel by petitioner was an integral part of this business. As rising insurance rates suggest, the cost of fuel and routine servicing are not the only costs one can expect in operating a car. As unfortunate as it may be, lapses by drivers seem to be an inseparable

incident of driving a car. . . . Costs incurred as a result of such an incident
are just as much a part of overall business expenses as the cost of fuel.

Id. at 1108–09. By contrast, Gilliam, while a passenger on a plane, committed acts
which, but for his successful temporary insanity defense, would have been criminal.
Such acts cannot be said to be "inseparable incidents" of travelling on an airplane.
The Tax Court in *Gilliam* emphasized the taxpayer's "activities were not directly in
the conduct of his trades or businesses," but "merely occurred in the course of
transportation connected with Gilliam's trades or businesses." Quoting from
Dancer, the Tax Court noted "in cases like this where the cost is an adjunct of and
not a direct cost of transporting an individual, we have not felt obliged to routinely
allow the expenditure as a transportation costs deduction." T.C. Memo 1986-81.
Should it make any difference that Gilliam's conduct occurred while he was
travelling rather than, for example, while Gilliam was attending an opening of a
show of his new works?

To this point our focus has been on the Supreme Court's suggestion in *Welch v.
Helvering* that an "ordinary" expense is a customary or expected expense. But note
that the Court also appeared in *Welch* to give a second meaning to that term —
namely, that "ordinary" expenses are apparently to be distinguished from capital
expenditures such as reputation (goodwill) or learning. After completing the next
Chapter, relating to capital expenditures, ask if *Welch* could (or should) have been
decided on the basis that the costs in question were capital expenditures in the
nature of goodwill. Problem 1 in this Chapter provides an opportunity to reflect on
the meaning of *Welch* and the scope of its application.

b. Is the Expense "Necessary"?

In *Welch*, the Court interpreted the term "necessary" to mean "appropriate and
helpful" and indicated it would be slow to "override" the judgment of a business
person regarding the necessity of any costs incurred. Given *Welch*'s interpretation
of the "necessary" standard, it is not surprising that few cases have focused on the
determination of whether a cost is "necessary." In *Palo Alto Town & Country
Village, Inc. v. Commissioner*, 565 F.2d 1388 (9th Cir. 1977), the Ninth Circuit
reversed a Tax Court decision holding that costs incurred in maintaining an
airplane on a standby basis were not ordinary and necessary. The Tax Court found
the evidence the taxpayers offered regarding the need for a plane on a standby
basis to be inconsistent with the business the taxpayer actually conducted. The
court concluded the taxpayers "did not use the airplane with sufficient frequency to
justify the expense of maintaining it on a permanent standby basis as ordinary and
necessary for the conduct of [their] business." T.C. Memo 1973-223. The Ninth
Circuit, however, noted "the Tax Court didn't deny that on one occasion the
immediate availability of the plane, arising from its standby status, led to a saving
of almost $1,000,000 in interest on a loan, or that not having the plane on standby
would result in delays in getting Palo Alto personnel back home from their
business trips, or that chartering a plane and keeping it on standby would be much
more expensive than taxpayers' standby arrangement." 565 F.2d at 1390. According
to the Ninth Circuit, the facts indicated having a plane "on a standby basis was
certainly appropriate and helpful to the business, and it was a response one would
normally expect a business in taxpayers' circumstances to make." 565 F.2d at 1391.

The expense was thus both ordinary and necessary. As the case suggests, the determination of whether an expense is "necessary" is a factual determination.

Contrast Palo Alto Town & Country Village, Inc. with Henry v. Commissioner, 36 T.C. 879 (1961). In *Henry*, the taxpayer, a tax lawyer and accountant, purchased a yacht on which he flew a red, white and blue pennant with the numerals "1040" on it. The taxpayer claimed his use of the yacht served to promote his business by providing the taxpayer contacts in the yachting circles, thereby potentially increasing his client base. Among other things, the taxpayer claimed the unusual pennant on the yacht generated inquiries from other people with yachts and provided the taxpayer and his family with opportunities to discuss the nature of the taxpayer's business. The Tax Court rejected taxpayer's claim that, under the circumstances, he was entitled to deduct the costs of insuring and maintaining the yacht. The court specifically concluded the taxpayer had not established the yacht was "necessary" for taxpayer's trade or business. The court noted "in determining that which is 'necessary' to a taxpayer's trade or business, the taxpayer is ordinarily the best judge on the matter and we would hesitate to substitute our own discretion for his with regard to whether an expenditure is 'appropriate and helpful' in the purposes of his business. But where, as in this case, the expenditures may well have been made to further ends which are primarily personal, this ordinary constraint does not prevail; petitioner must show affirmatively that his expenses were 'necessary' to the conduct of his professions." 36 T.C. at 884. The court examined the facts and concluded the taxpayer had not established he had taken up boating "solely or even primarily to serve the needs of his practice or that he would not have operated [the yacht] regardless of whatever business advantages he hoped to derive from this sport. . . . [T]he claimed expenses, when considered in relation to the fees which petitioner attributes to yachting, are inordinate and do not indicate the requisite proximate relationship between his sporting activities and his business. . . . The pennant may have some relationship to the conduct of taxpayer's business. But the evidence does not show how any specific fee resulted from his operating a yacht." 36 T.C. at 885.

Similarly, in *Dobbe v. Commissioner*, T.C. Memo 2000-330, *aff'd*, 2003 U.S. App. LEXIS 5419 (9th Cir. Mar. 19, 2003), the Tax Court rejected a corporation's attempt to deduct the cost of landscaping around the personal residence of its sole shareholders (Bernardus and Klazina Dobbe). The corporation (Holland America) engaged in the business of importing and growing flower bulbs, which it sold to cut flower producers. The corporation's principal place of business was located on a farm the Dobbes owned and leased to their corporation. The Tax Court, however, found the corporation did not lease the Dobbes' residence located on the farm. The corporation

> argued that the entire landscaping expense, incurred primarily to install landscaping near and surrounding Mr. and Mrs. Dobbe's residence, was properly deducted under section 162. According to petitioners, the new landscaping was necessary to improve the "first impression" of Holland America's business and allowed Holland America to display and promote its products to the public. Respondent contends the majority of the landscaping was done to improve the grounds surrounding Mr. and Mrs. Dobbe's residence, including the front, side, and back yards and the area near the

outdoor swimming pool; therefore, the improvements made to property owned by Mr. and Mrs. Dobbe primarily benefited Mr. and Mrs. Dobbe personally and are not deductible as a business expense.

Under appropriate circumstances, landscaping expenses may be deductible when the expenses legitimately are connected to the taxpayer's trade or business and the requirements for deductibility otherwise are met. When, however, a corporation makes an expenditure that primarily benefits the corporation's shareholders and only tangentially benefits the corporation's business, the amount of the expenditure may be taxed to the shareholder as a constructive dividend and is not deductible under section 162.

[Authors' Note: It is not uncommon for a closely-held corporation to incur expenditures which the corporation seeks to deduct, but which primarily benefit the corporation's shareholders or members of the shareholders' family. Such expenditures are treated as disguised or constructive dividends, which are includable in gross income under § 61(a)(7) by the shareholders and are not deductible by the corporation.]

We accept, for the sake of argument, that the appearance of a business and its grounds can contribute to the success of the business. We also acknowledge that Holland America's clients visited the farm regularly. Most, if not all, of the landscaping improvements, however, were installed near and surrounding Mr. and Mrs. Dobbe's residence. Although some of the improvements could be seen by Holland America's customers who visited the farm for business purposes, the incidental benefit to the corporation does not trump the primarily personal benefit to Mr. and Mrs. Dobbe.

[P]etitioners offered little evidence that the landscaping improvements were appropriate or necessary to the maintenance and development of Holland America's business. Drive-by customers accounted for a very small percentage of Holland America's sales, and there is no evidence in the record demonstrating that sales to Holland America's regular customers increased in any material way as a result of the improvements. We hold that petitioners have not proven that the landscaping expenses were ordinary and necessary business expenses deductible by Holland America under section 162. [The Tax Court also held that the Dobbes had received a constructive dividend in the amount of the fair market value of the landscaping.]

In contrast, the costs associated with taxpayer's equestrian-related activities in *Topping v. Commissioner*, T.C. Memo 2007-92, were held to be ordinary and necessary expenses of her business of designing horse barns and homes. The Tax Court found that taxpayer's "business methodology" involved entering in and attending horse shows where she made contacts with prospective clients. The taxpayer relied on her exposure and reputation as a highly-skilled amateur horse rider and owner, believing that, if she sold her horses or gave up riding, potential clients would think she had failed financially and would not rely on her as a designer of their horse barns or homes. Taxpayer did not advertise her business through traditional advertising media such as equestrian magazines, websites, or newspapers as she believed her clientele would perceive that kind of advertising as "tacky or gauche." The Service argued that the equestrian expenses were not ordinary and necessary expenses of her design business, but were personal expenditures instead, and relied upon the *Henry* case, discussed above, in support of its argument. In rejecting the Commissioner's position, the court noted that the taxpayer in *Henry* failed to show that his boating activities produced a single client or that it was ordinary in his profession to incur such expenses.

> While we are mindful that expenses for personal pursuits do not become deductible expenses simply because they afford contacts with possible future clients, the situation in this case is entirely different from the facts in *Henry*. Petitioner has proven that her equestrian activities are necessary to her success as an interior designer. The unique nature of petitioner's design business made it an ordinary expense to partake in equestrian-related activities to achieve the peer acceptance to attract clients. We have found that petitioner's design and equestrian activity is part of an integrated business plan and that petitioner's clientele is almost exclusively derived from her equestrian contacts. Petitioner also offered corroborating testimony that . . . conventional advertising [would] evoke a negative reaction from [prospective clients]. Respondent's arguments focus on petitioner's means to an end, but neglect the most important fact of all — petitioner's plan worked. Her startup business was a success from the beginning and continues to be successful. . . . Petitioner has credibly demonstrated that the measures she takes to build her client base are both ordinary and necessary.

> The evidence does not establish and respondent has not argued convincingly that any particular expense was unnecessary or excessive. Obviously, keeping and maintaining horses is expensive. Petitioner demonstrated that she has done what she can to keep costs down. . . . Respondent offers numerous ratios of the expenses associated with the equestrian activities to the profit from [her business]. Petitioner does what is necessary to maintain her reputation in the equestrian world, and we find that she does not do so in an extravagant manner. The fact remains that petitioner's design business depends heavily on her equestrian-related activities for its success. We therefore find and hold that not only are petitioner's equestrian expenses ordinary and necessary, but that they are reasonable in amount.

Topping, T.C. Memo 2007-92.

"Reasonable" salaries. Salaries and other compensation are among the most common expenses incurred by any business. Section 162(a)(1) specifically addresses salaries and provides only reasonable salaries may be deducted. Does this "reasonableness" requirement add anything to the "ordinary and necessary" standard? Likely not. The element of reasonableness is inherent in the phrase "ordinary and necessary." An unreasonably large salary is not an ordinary and necessary expense of a business.[3] So why would any business choose to pay an

---

[3] In 1993, Congress enacted a provision, § 162(m), disallowing the deduction of certain employee

unreasonably large salary? The answer is that, where parties are related, shifting income from one party to the other may be advantageous.

The best example of this is found in the context of closely held corporations where the owners of the corporation are also likely to be corporate employees. Although the corporation may be owned by one or two people, the corporation is nevertheless a separate taxable entity, thus affording both the possibility and the desirability of income shifting. Profits generated by the corporation are taxed to it, and, if those profits are then distributed as dividends by the corporation to its shareholders, those profits are taxed again to the shareholders. This double tax can be eliminated if the corporation can successfully characterize its distributions to shareholders or their family members as deductible salaries or compensation; hence, the temptation to disguise dividends as deductible wages. Through the use of large salaries, a successful corporation can reduce its own tax and at the same time distribute profits to its owners. If the owners of the business determine that the corporation should distribute the profits rather than accumulate them, the corporation can save taxes by characterizing the distributions as deductible salaries rather than nondeductible dividends.[4] The reasonableness standard is the primary obstacle to this strategy.

While that standard is easy to understand, its application is often difficult. In *Elliotts, Inc. v. Commissioner*, 716 F.2d 1241 (9th Cir. 1983), the Ninth Circuit suggested that the reasonableness of compensation paid to a shareholder-employee, particularly a sole shareholder, should be evaluated from the perspective of a hypothetical independent investor:

> A relevant inquiry is whether an inactive, independent investor would be willing to compensate the employee as he was compensated. The nature and quality of the services should be considered, as well as the effect of those services on the return the investor is seeing on his investment. The corporation's rate of return on equity would be relevant to the independent investor in assessing the reasonableness of compensation in a small corporation where excessive compensation would noticeably decrease the rate of return.

Id. at 1245. Against this background, the court identified a number of factors that its prior cases had identified as relevant to determining whether the compensation at issue was attributable to the taxpayer's employment relationship with the corporation or to the taxpayer's role as sole shareholder: (a) the employee's role in the company, including hours and duties and importance to the success of the

---

compensation in excess of $1,000,000. This limitation is applicable to the chief executive officers of publicly held corporations or an employee of such corporation whose compensation must be reported to shareholders under the Securities Exchange Act of 1934 "by reason of such employee being among the 4 highest compensated officers for the taxable year (other than the chief executive officer)." § 162(m)(2), (3). Note § 162(m)(4)(B) and (C) providing some important and perhaps very major exceptions to the $1,000,000 limit.

[4] The 2003 Tax Act added § 1(h)(11), taxing dividends at preferential rates. As a result, the corporation's incentive to characterize corporate distributions as deductible compensation may be in tension with the desire of a shareholder-employee to receive preferentially-taxed dividends rather than additional compensation, which, of course enjoys no tax preference. The tax brackets of the corporation and the shareholder-employee can play large roles in resolving this tension.

company; (b) a comparison of the employee's salary to salaries paid by similar companies for similar services; (c) the size and complexity of the company and general economic conditions; (d) the existence of a relationship between company and employee which would permit nondeductible corporate dividends to be disguised as deductible compensation; and (e) whether the compensation at issue stems from a compensation program that itself is reasonable, longstanding, and consistently applied. The court emphasized that no single factor is determinative but, rather, the employment situation must be viewed as a whole, and it repeatedly invoked as a touchstone whether the compensation formula would allow a reasonable return on equity to an independent investor.

The "independent investor test" suggested by the Ninth Circuit has been adopted by other courts, including the Seventh Circuit in *Exacto Spring Corporation v. Commissioner*, 196 F.3d 833 (7th Cir. 1999). According to Judge Posner, who wrote the Seventh Circuit's opinion, a multi-factor test is vague and nondirective and "invites [a court] to set itself up as a superpersonnel department for closely held corporations, a role unsuitable for courts. . . . The judges of the Tax Court are not equipped by training or experience to determine the salaries of corporate officers. No judges are." *Id.* at 835. With respect to the independent investor test, Judge Posner added:

> There is, fortunately, an indirect market test, as recognized by the Internal Revenue Service's expert witness. A corporation can be conceptualized as a contract in which the owner of assets hires a person to manage them. The owner pays the manager a salary and in exchange the manager works to increase the value of the assets that have been entrusted to his management; that increase can be expressed as a rate of return to the owner's investment. The higher the rate of return (adjusted for risk) that a manager can generate, the greater the salary he can command. If the rate of return is extremely high, it will be difficult to prove that the manager is being overpaid, for it will be implausible that if he quit if his salary was cut, and he was replaced by a lower-paid manager, the owner would be better off; it would be killing the goose that lays the golden egg. The Service's expert believed that investors in a firm like Exacto would expect a 13 percent return on their investment. Presumably they would be delighted with more. They would be *overjoyed* to receive a return more than 50 percent greater than they expected — and 20 percent, the return that the Tax Court found that investors in Exacto had obtained, is more than 50 percent greater than the benchmark return of 13 percent.

Id. at 838–39 (emphasis in original).

In *Menard, Inc. v. Commissioner*, T.C. Memo 2004-207, the Service argued that the $20.6 million compensation paid by the taxpayer to its chief executive officer and majority shareholder in 1998 was not reasonable and it therefore disallowed part of the deduction claimed by the company under § 162. The Tax Court concluded that, under the independent investor test articulated in *Exacto Spring*, the compensation paid the CEO would be presumed to be reasonable in view of the rate of return on investment generated by the taxpayer, but that this presumption of reasonableness was rebutted when one considered the amount paid to CEOs by other comparable publicly traded companies. In this regard, the Tax Court relied on Reg. § 1.162-7(b)(3) providing that reasonable compensation "is only such amount as would ordinarily be paid for like services by like enterprises under like circumstances" and it concluded that the compensation paid to taxpayer's CEO was reasonable only to the extent of approximately $7 million, with the balance constituting a nondeductible constructive dividend.

The Tax Court decision in *Menard* was reversed by the Seventh Circuit. *Menard, Inc. v. Commissioner*, 560 F.3d 620 (7th Cir. 2009). The appellate court concluded that the Tax Court erred in disallowing a deduction for the compensation in excess of $7 million, reasoning, in an opinion written by Judge Posner, that:

> All businesses are different, all CEOs are different, and all compensation packages for CEOs are different. . . . The main focus of the Tax Court's decision . . . was on whether Menard's compensation exceeded that of comparable CEOs in 1998 — that is, whether it was objectively excessive. . . . The CEO of Home Depot was paid that year only $2.8 million, though it is a much larger company that Menards; and the CEO of Lowe's, also a larger company, was paid $6.1 million. But salary is just the beginning of a meaningful comparison, because it is only one element of a compensation package. Of particular importance to this case is the amount of risk in the compensation structure. . . . A risky compensation structure implies that the executive's salary is likely to vary substantially from year to year — high when the company has a good year, low when it has a bad one. [Indeed, in Menard's case, the bulk of the compensation came from a 5% bonus program established 25 years earlier.] Mr. Menard's average annual income may thus have been considerably less than $20 million — a possibility the Tax Court ignored. Had the corporation lost money in 1998, Menard's total compensation would have been only $157,500 — less than the salary of a federal judge — even if the loss had not been his fault. . . . Nor did the Tax Court consider the severance packages, retirement plans, or perks of the CEOs with whom it compared Menard (though it did take account of their stock options), even though such differences can make an enormous difference to an executive's compensation. . . . [The adjustment the Tax Court made to arrive at its conclusion that the compensation in excess of $7.1 million was nondeductible] disregarded differences in the full compensation packages of the three executives being compared, differences in whatever challenges faced the companies in 1998, and differences in the responsibilities and performance of the three CEOs.
>
> We have discussed risk; with regard to responsibilities there is incomplete information about the compensation paid other senior management besides Mr. Menard himself, and no information about the compensation paid the senior management of Home Depot and Lowe's other than those companies CEOs. The relevance of such information is that it might show that Menard was doing work that in other companies is delegated to staff, or conversely that staff was doing all the work and Menard was, in substance though not in form, clipping coupons. The former inference is far more likely, given the undisputed evidence of Menard's workaholic, micromanaging ways and the fact the Menard's board of directors is a tiny

dependency of Mr. Menard. He does the work that in publicly held companies like Home Depot and Lowe's is done by boards that have more than two directors besides the CEO. Of course they are larger companies — Home Depot's revenues were seven times as great as Menard's in 1998 — so we would expect them to have more staff. But we are given no information on how much more staff they had. We know that, besides Menard himself, Menards — already a $3.4 billion company in 1998 — had only three corporate officers. The Tax Court thought it suspicious that they were modestly compensated. . . . The Tax Court did not consider the possibility, which the evidence supports, that Menard really does do it all himself. . . . We conclude that in ruling that Menard's compensation was excessive in 1998, the Tax Court committed clear error, and its decision is therefore reversed.

Menard, at 623, 626–28.

Clothing. As noted in *Bernardo v. Commissioner,* T.C. Memo 2004-199, "[g]enerally, the cost of a business wardrobe required as a condition of employment is considered a nondeductible personal expense within the meaning of section 262 if the purchased clothing is suitable for general or personal wear." In this regard, the Tax Court has required that a taxpayer, seeking to deduct clothing costs, satisfy a three-part standard. Specifically, under the Tax Court standard, the taxpayer must establish that (1) the clothing is required or essential in the taxpayer's employment; (2) the clothing is not, in fact, used for taxpayer's general or personal wear; and (3) the clothing is not suitable for general or personal wear. But the Tax Court has held that such suitability is determined by reference to the lifestyle of the taxpayer in question, an inherently subjective test. *Id.* By contrast, the IRS disavows the use of the subjective test and utilizes as its standard an objective test, i.e., the clothing is not adaptable to general usage as ordinary clothing, based upon generally accepted standards for ordinary wear. The Service's position was endorsed by the Fifth Circuit in *Pevsner,* included in the materials.

In some cases, because of the taxpayer's inability to satisfy the burden of the Tax Court's subjective test, the Tax Court test and the objective test of *Pevsner* may actually produce the same results. In this regard, consider the facts of *Bernardo v. Commissioner.* There, the taxpayer, in her position as district manager for Mervyn's, was required by her employer to wear black or white dresses or suits while on the job. To acquire the clothing necessary for her position, the taxpayer had no need to go to "specialized" stores. Furthermore, there was no company logo required to be on taxpayer's clothing. Taxpayer contended that she owned no black or white dresses or suits and thus was required to purchase a new wardrobe, the cost of which she sought to deduct. Rejecting the taxpayer's position, the Tax Court noted that she did not satisfy two of its three tests: she failed the Tax Court's subjective test as she provided no evidence that the clothing was unsuitable, in terms of price, quality, or style for her personal wear, and she also failed to provide evidence that she never wore the clothing away from work. Thus, the Tax Court reached the same result, i.e., denial of deduction, that would have been reached by a court employing the *Pevsner* objective test.

In Revenue Ruling 70-474, 1970-2 C.B. 34, 35, the Service ruled deductible the uniform acquisition and maintenance costs for police officers, firemen, letter carriers, nurses, bus drivers and railway men "required to wear distinctive types of uniforms while at work . . . which are not suitable for ordinary wear." See also Reg. § 1.262-1(b)(8) relating to "equipment" of members of the armed services and the uniforms of reservists. In Revenue Ruling 67-115, 1967-1 C.B. 30, the cost of required military fatigue uniforms, the off-duty wearing of which was prohibited, was held deductible. However, when work clothing may be worn off-duty, who decides upon its "suitability" for such wear?

Public Policy Considerations. May a deduction be denied on the grounds that its allowance would frustrate public policy? The Supreme Court, in *Tank Truck Rentals v. Commissioner*, 356 U.S. 30 (1958), disallowed a truck company's deduction of fines paid for violation of state maximum weight laws, concluding such costs could not be considered necessary "if allowance of the deduction would frustrate sharply defined national or state policies proscribing particular types of conduct, evidenced by some governmental declaration thereof." According to the Court, "the test of nondeductibility always is the severity and immediacy of the frustration resulting from the allowance of the deduction. The flexibility of such standard is necessary if we are to accommodate both the congressional intent to tax only net income, and the presumption against congressional intent to encourage violation of declared public policy." 356 U.S. at 33–35. The Court concluded that to permit deduction of the fines imposed by the state would only encourage noncompliance by taking the "sting" out of the penalty.

The same day it decided *Tank Trunk Rentals*, the Court concluded, in *Commissioner v. Sullivan*, 356 U.S. 27 (1958), that rent and wage expenses incurred in operating an illegal bookmaking establishment were deductible. According to the Court, if it denied the deduction, it "would come close to making [such a gambling enterprise] taxable on the basis of its gross receipts, while all other business would be taxable on the basis of net income. If that choice is to be made, Congress should do it." 356 U.S. at 29. The Court distinguished *Tank Trunk Rentals*, noting that allowance of a deduction for the fines would have been a device for avoiding the consequences of violating the state maximum weight limits.

Recognizing the difficulty in determining what constitutes "sharply defined national or state policies" and in applying the "severity and immediacy" test of *Tank Trunk Rentals*, Congress in 1969 and 1971 amended § 162, adding provisions disallowing deductions for certain fines, penalties, bribes and antitrust payments. § 162(c), (f), (g).[5] The 1969 Senate Finance Committee report stated: "The provision for the denial of deductions for payments in [the situations covered by the 1969 legislation] is intended to be all inclusive. Public policy, in other circumstances, generally is not sufficiently clearly defined to justify the disallowance of deductions."[6] Explaining the 1971 legislation, the Senate report noted: "The Committee continues to believe that the determination of when a deduction should be denied

---

[5] Section 280E disallows a deduction or credit for costs incurred in a trade or business which consists of "trafficking in controlled substances . . . which is prohibited by Federal law or the law of any State in which such trade or business is conducted."

[6] S. Rpt. No. 91-552, 91st Cong. 1st Sess (1969), 1969-3 C.B. 597.

should remain under the control of Congress."[7]

2.   "Carrying On a Trade or Business"

a.   What Constitutes a "Trade or a Business"?

The existence of a trade or business is key to deductions under § 162. And yet, as the Supreme Court in *Commissioner v. Groetzinger*, included in the materials, indicated, neither the Code nor the regulations contain a definition of "trade or business." Nevertheless, only on rare occasions since 1913 have the courts considered the meaning of "trade or business." Both *Groetzinger* and *Higgins v. Commissioner*, also included in this chapter, represent such occasions. As in its 1941 decision in *Higgins*, the Court in *Groetzinger* some 45 years later concluded that the status of an enterprise as a trade or business depends on the facts. The Court, however, provided some guidance. Specifically, the Court rejected the formulation of Justice Frankfurter that "carrying on any trade or business involves holding one's self out to others as engaged in the selling of goods or services." In a more positive vein, the Court in *Groetzinger* stated: "We accept the fact that to be engaged in a trade or business, the taxpayer must be involved in the activity with continuity and regularity and the taxpayer's primary purpose for engaging in the activity must be for income or profit. A sporadic activity, a hobby, or an amusement diversion does not qualify."

Whether the taxpayer has a bona fide objective of making a profit must be determined each year by considering all the facts and circumstances related to the activity during the year. Reg. § 1.183-2(a) lists the following factors for determining whether an activity is engaged in for profit: (1) the manner in which the taxpayer carries on the trade or business; (2) the expertise of the taxpayer or his or her advisers; (3) the time and effort expended by the taxpayer in carrying on the activity; (4) the expectation that assets used in the activity may appreciate in value; (5) the success of the taxpayer in carrying on other similar or dissimilar activities; (6) the taxpayer's history of income or losses with respect to the activity; (7) the amount of occasional profits, if any, which are earned; (8) the financial status of the taxpayer; and (9) elements of personal pleasure or recreation. Although this regulation interprets § 183 addressing so-called "hobby losses," the factors listed in

---

[7] S. Rpt. No. 92-437, 92nd Cong. 1st Sess. (1971), 1972-1 C.B. 599. While Congress may have preempted the courts from using public policy as a basis for denying deductions for trade or business expenses otherwise deductible under § 162, the courts and the Service continue to use the public policy rationale as a basis for denying deductions under § 165. Thus, in Revenue Ruling 81-24, 1981-1 C.B. 79, the Service, relying on public policy grounds, denied a loss deduction to a taxpayer for the destruction of a building as a result of arson committed by him. *See also Holt v. Commissioner*, 69 T.C. 75 (1977).

An example of a congressional policy change came about in 1993 when Congress reversed 30-year old legislation allowing the deduction of lobbying expenses. As amended, § 162(e) disallows any deduction for amounts paid or incurred in connection with (1) influencing legislation or (2) any direct communication with a covered executive branch official in an attempt to influence official actions or positions of the official. § 162(e)(1)(A), (D). The disallowance rule for influencing legislation does not apply to "legislation of any local council or similar governing body." § 162(e)(2). Considering businesses commonly incur expenses in lobbying state legislatures and Congress, what is the justification for disallowing lobbying expenses? Should the exception for local governments exist? Does § 162(e) disallow costs which a business may incur, for example, in merely monitoring legislation during sessions of a state legislature?

the regulation are equally applicable to the trade or business determination that is made for § 162 purposes. *See, e.g., Keanini v. Commissioner*, 94 T.C. 41 (1990). See also *Storey v. Commissioner*, T.C. Memo. 2012-115. No one factor listed in the regulation is determinative and whether the taxpayer is engaged in the activity for profit does not depend upon merely counting those factors suggesting the presence of a profit motive and comparing the number to those factors indicating the opposite. Reg. § 1.183-2(b).

Contrast *Groetzinger* and *Higgins* and consider whether the distinction drawn in *Higgins* is justifiable. While the Court in *Higgins* determined that the management of one's own investments is not a trade or business, other courts have nevertheless distinguished so-called "traders" from "investors." A "trader" is considered to be engaged in a trade or business; while an "investor" like Mr. Higgins is not. A "trader's" activities are directed toward short-term trading with income being derived principally from the sale of securities rather than from the dividends and interest which "investors" typically seek. Thus, a taxpayer's investment intent, the nature of the income to be derived from the activity, and the extent and regularity of the taxpayer's securities transactions will be relevant in determining whether the taxpayer is to be deemed a "trader" engaged in a trade or business, or an "investor" who is not. *Moller v. U.S.*, 721 F.2d 810 (Fed. Cir. 1983); *Purvis v. Commissioner*, 530 F.2d 1332 (9th Cir. 1976).

b.   The "Carrying On" Requirement

The development of a new business ordinarily involves two stages before the trade or business becomes operational. First, in the investigatory stage, a person may review various kinds of business before deciding to acquire or to enter into a specific business. The leading case, *Frank v. Commissioner*, 20 T.C. 511 (1953), involved a taxpayer who sought to purchase and operate a newspaper or radio station. The taxpayer, who ultimately purchased a newspaper, made trips to numerous cities to investigate possible purchases, incurring various travel expenses and legal fees in connection with the investigations. The Tax Court denied a deduction:

> The travel expenses and legal fees spent in searching for a newspaper business with a view to purchasing the same cannot be deducted under the provisions of section [162], Internal Revenue Code. The petitioners were not engaged in any trade or business at the time the expenses were incurred. The trips made by the taxpayers were not related to the conduct of the business that they were then engaged in but were preparatory to locating a business venture of their own. The expense of investigating and looking for a new business and trips preparatory to entering a business are not deductible as an ordinary and necessary business expense incurred in carrying on a trade or business. . . . The word "pursuit" in the statutory phrase "in pursuit of a trade or business" is not used in the sense of "searching for" or "following after," but in the sense of "in connection with" or "in the course of" a trade or business. It presupposes an existing business with which petitioner is connected.

Id. at 513, 14. The legislative history of § 195, addressing so-called "start-up" expenses discussed below, reinforces the point.

> Business investigatory expenses generally are nondeductible regardless of whether they are incurred by an existing business in relation to another business or by a taxpayer who is not in any business. However, taxpayers may be able to deduct a loss for business investigatory expenses incurred in an unsuccessful attempt to acquire a specific business. Nevertheless, business investigatory expenses of a general nature normally are viewed as being either nondeductible personal expenses or as not being ordinary and necessary trade or business expenses, viz., because no business exists, within the meaning of section 162 of the Code.

H. Rept. No. 96-1278, 96th Cong. 2d Sess. (1980) p. 9.

The second stage in the development of a business occurs after the taxpayer has decided to acquire or establish a specific business and commences preparations for its operation. In *Richmond Television Corporation v. U.S.*, 345 F.2d 901, *rev'd and remanded on another issue*, 382 U.S. 68 (1965), the taxpayer sought to deduct certain personnel training expenses incurred prior to receiving the Federal Communications Commission license necessary to operate. The Fourth Circuit, considering the deductibility of these expenses, held "[e]ven though a taxpayer has made a firm decision to enter into business and over a considerable period of time spent money in preparation for entering that business, he still has not engaged in carrying on any trade or business within the intendment of Section 162(a) until such time as the business has begun to function as a going concern and performed those activities for which it was organized." 345 F.2d at 907. The taxpayer was required to treat these pre-operating expenses as capital expenditures.

The "carrying on" requirement, resulting in a distinction between pre-opening or start-up costs and operating costs of a business, can be justified on the ground that costs incurred in investigating a business, training personnel, lining-up distributors, suppliers, or potential customers, setting up books and records, and otherwise placing a new business in an operational posture, provide benefits long beyond the current tax year and therefore should not be currently deductible. Such expenses are analogous to the costs incurred in acquiring an existing business, or buildings and equipment for an existing business. As you will study in detail in the next Chapter, those acquisition costs generally cannot be currently deducted, but must be capitalized.

The "carrying on" requirement also assists in preventing the taxpayer from deducting personal expenses. The excerpt from the legislative history to § 195 above suggests that investigation expenses may actually be personal expenses which should not be deductible. As this and subsequent Chapters indicate, drawing the line between nondeductible personal expenses and deductible business expenses has been an enormously difficult job for Congress, the Service and the courts. The "carrying on" requirement forces the taxpayer to establish that expenses are actually associated with the *operation* of a trade or business, making it more likely that the expenses are genuinely business-related, as opposed to being merely personal expenses.

c.   Section 195 and the Amortization of Certain Pre-Operational or Start-Up Costs

In many cases, drawing the line between pre-operating and operating expenses is not as easy as in *Richmond Television*, where the date of the issuance of the FCC license provided a bright dividing line. Considerable controversy developed in the courts regarding the characterization of expenses as either start-up or operating expenses. To reduce the controversy and litigation in this area and to encourage the formation of new businesses, Congress in 1979 added § 195 to the Code authorizing the amortization of start-up expenses. As the House Report to § 195 explained:

> [E]xpenditures eligible for amortization must satisfy two requirements. First, the expenditure must be paid or incurred in connection with creating, or investigating the creation or acquisition of, a trade or business *entered into by the taxpayer.* Second, the expenditure involved must be one which would be allowable as a deduction for the taxable year in which it is paid or incurred if it were paid or incurred in connection with the expansion of an existing trade or business in the same field as that entered into by the taxpayer. Under the provision, eligible expenses consist of *investigatory costs* incurred in reviewing a prospective business prior to reaching a final decision to acquire or to enter that business. These costs include expenses incurred for the analysis or survey of potential markets, products, labor supply, transportation facilities, etc. Eligible expenses also include *startup costs* which are incurred subsequent to a decision to establish a particular business and prior to the time when the business begins."

H.R. Rep. No. 96-1278, 96th Cong. 2d Sess. (1980), p. 10 (emphasis added).

As originally enacted, § 195 permitted the taxpayer to elect to amortize (*i.e.* to pro-rate at an even level) business start-up expenditures over a period of not less than 60 months. Legislation in 2004 amended § 195 to allow a taxpayer to deduct up to $5,000 of start-up expenditures in the taxable year in which the active trade or business begins. However, the $5,000 amount is reduced (but not below zero) by the amount the start-up expenditures exceed $50,000. Thus, if start-up expenditures are $5,000 or less, they are currently deductible in full. If they are $55,000 or more, the $5,000 current deduction is completely eliminated. If the start-up expenditures are between $5,000 and $50,000, the current deduction is $5,000 and the remaining start-up expenditures are amortized over 180 months. If the start-up expenditures are between $50,000 and $55,000, the $5,000 current deduction is reduced, dollar for dollar, by the start-up expenditures in excess of $50,000. The remainder of the start-up expenditures, that is, the portion of the start-up expenditures that cannot be currently deducted, are amortized over a 180-month period (or the same 15-year amortization period used for § 197 intangibles as discussed in Chapter 42) beginning with the month in which the active trade or business begins. For example, assume the start-up expenditures were $52,000. Since $52,000 is $2,000 in excess of $50,000, the $5,000 current deduction limit is reduced to $3,000, which is the amount that can be currently deducted. The remaining $49,000 of start-up expenditures must be amortized over 180 months. Note one must actually engage in the trade or business to deduct or amortize start-up expenditures under § 195. Why is there such a requirement?

d. Application of the "Carrying On" Requirement to Employees

As demonstrated in Revenue Ruling 75-120 in the materials, the pre-operating/operating distinction reflected in *Frank* and *Richmond Television* has carried over into the employment-seeking context. The courts and the Service agree that a taxpayer may be in the trade or business of being an employee. *Primuth v. Commissioner*, 54 T.C. 374 (1970). Furthermore, an employee can have more than one trade or business. For example, a person who works full time as a tax specialist with an accounting firm and also regularly teaches tax as an adjunct professor at a local college will be deemed engaged in two businesses: tax accounting and teaching. If an employee incurs costs in seeking a job with a new employer, may the employee deduct those costs as trade or business expenses under § 162? The answer turns on whether the employee can establish that the costs were incurred in "carrying on" a trade or business. If the expenses were incurred in an effort to commence a new trade or business, they will not satisfy the "carrying on" requirement and, like the pre-operating expenses in *Richmond Television*, will be treated as capital expenditures. By contrast, if the expenses were incurred by an employee in finding work in the same trade or business, the "carrying on" requirement would be satisfied and the costs (e.g., resume costs, postage, etc.) would be deductible. Deductible employee business expenses, however, are generally deductible below the line and are subject to the 2% floor imposed by § 67.

The scope of an employee's current trade or business is obviously critical in evaluating the deductibility of costs incurred in seeking new employment. Determining the scope of an employee's trade or business has proven difficult. In *Primuth v. Commissioner*, the taxpayer was the secretary-treasurer for a small corporation. He paid a fee to an employment agency to assist him in securing new employment and obtained a new job with increased responsibilities as secretary-controller with a larger corporation. The Tax Court found the taxpayer was carrying on the trade or business of being a "corporate executive" and concluded the employment agency expense was deductible since it was incurred "to permit [the taxpayer] to continue to carry on that very trade or business — albeit with a different corporate employer." 54 T.C. at 379. Judge Tannenwald, concurring in *Primuth*, suggested that whether the employment-seeking expenses were incurred in the employee's current trade or business or a new trade or business could be determined by "comparing the position which the taxpayer occupied before and after the change [of employment]. Perhaps the categorization of corporate executive will not always be applicable, but, in this case, petitioner was at all times a financial corporate executive." 54 T.C. at 382.

The courts subsequently extended the *Primuth* principle to other contexts involving payment of employment counseling fees. In *Cremona v. Commissioner*, 58 T.C. 219 (1972), for example, the taxpayer-employee was held to be in the trade or business of being an "administrator," and job counseling fees he incurred to improve his job opportunities in that business were deductible even though the taxpayer did not succeed in obtaining new employment. The Tax Court in *Cremona* rejected the Commissioner's argument that employment-seeking costs were only deductible if new employment was actually secured. The Service advocated this seeking/securing standard presumably to assure the employment-seeking expenses were business related. Read Revenue Ruling 75-120 carefully and note how it preserves the pre-operating/operating notion while at the same time eliminating the seeking/securing standard. It should be noted that nothing in the legislative history of § 195 indicates Congress intended employment seeking expenses to be amortizable investigation costs under § 195.

Will the Service require inclusion in gross income of travel reimbursements received by students from prospective employers who invite students for interviews? In a revenue ruling pre-dating Revenue Ruling 75-120, the Service, without indicating whether the interviewee was engaged in a trade or business, held the reimbursement received by an interviewee was not gross income. Revenue Ruling 63-77, 1963-1 C.B. 177. Assuming a law student is invited to interview with a law firm and incurs travel expenses, may the student exclude the travel reimbursement received from the firm based on this ruling and, perhaps, the *Gotcher* "convenience of employer" doctrine discussed in Chapter 11?

In *Rockefeller v. Commissioner*, 762 F.2d 264 (1985), the Second Circuit addressed pre-operating/operating notions as they apply to employment-seeking expenses. In that case, counsel for Rockefeller's estate sought to establish that Nelson Rockefeller, in seeking the Vice Presidency of the United States following the resignation of President Nixon in the summer of 1974, was merely continuing to engage in the same trade or business in which he had been involved for years. Rockefeller had previously held various federal and state positions, including the governorship New York. In view of his longtime work in government, counsel for his estate characterized him as being engaged in the trade or business of being "an executive in federal and state governments," "an executive in public office," "a governmental executive," or "an executive in public service." Having characterized Rockefeller's trade or business broadly, counsel for his estate asserted the Vice Presidency was simply a continuation of that business which justified a deduction for the costs incurred by Rockefeller in seeking the Vice Presidency. Despite the estate's arguments to the contrary, the Second Circuit concluded, as did the Tax Court, that Rockefeller's tasks and activities as Vice President were not the same as those associated with the other positions he had held. The costs he incurred in seeking the Vice Presidency were therefore not deductible.

A final issue arising in the employment setting is how long a taxpayer may be unemployed and still be considered to be in the trade or business of his former employment. In *Furner v. Commissioner*, 393 F.2d 292 (7th Cir. 1968), *rev'g*, 47 T.C. 165 (1966), a teacher who took a leave from teaching for a year to obtain a master's degree in her field was held to be "carrying on" her trade or business for the year, thus allowing her educational expenses to be deducted. The "obvious principle," according to *Primuth*, "is that it is possible for an employee to retain, at least temporarily, his status of carrying on his own trade or business independent of receiving any compensation from a particular employer." 54 T.C. at 378. Equally obvious, however, is the fact that a prolonged period of unemployment will terminate one's status as being engaged in a trade or business. According to the Second Circuit in *Estate of Rockefeller v. Commissioner*, to take advantage of this "hiatus principle," a taxpayer must establish that during the hiatus he intended to resume the same trade or business. What remains uncertain is how long a person can be unemployed without losing her trade or business status. The Service appears to have embraced a one-year period as a standard. See Rev. Rul. 68-591, 1968-2 C.B. 73, reprinted in Chapter 18.

B. Section 212 Deductions

Congress enacted the forerunner of § 212 in 1942 in response to the Supreme Court's decision in *Higgins v. Commissioner.* Section 212, sometimes referred to as the non-trade-or-business analog to § 162, allows a deduction for the "ordinary and necessary" expenses of producing or collecting income, maintaining property held for the production of income, or determining, collecting or refunding any tax. Thus, with the enactment of § 212, the expenses incurred by an investor like Mr. Higgins, *e.g.*, secretarial assistance and the assistance of accountants, financial advisors and lawyers, would be deductible even though the investor would not be deemed to carry on a trade or business.[8] See Chapter 19 for a discussion of the application of §§ 162, 212, and 262 to legal expenses.

The regulations provide some delineation and elaboration and a variety of examples of expenditures falling within or without the statutory provisions. Reg. § 1.212-1. Note that § 212 deductions are treated as miscellaneous itemized deductions. According to Revenue Ruling 92-29, 1992-1 C.B. 20, expenses for tax return preparation related to one's business are above-the-line deductions, while other tax return preparation expenses are below-the-line deductions. No deduction, however, is allowable for expenditures allocable to tax-exempt income. Reg. § 1.212-1(e). For example, to the extent attorney fees are incurred to prosecute and collect a tax-exempt injury claim (*see* Chapter 10), the fees will be nondeductible. Recall that the taxpayers in *Frank v. Commissioner*, who sought to enter the newspaper business, could not deduct the costs of investigating the purchase of a newspaper as a business expense under § 162. Could they deduct the costs under § 212 instead, in effect making an end run around the "carrying on a

---

[8] As noted previously, the difference between § 162 deductions and § 212 deductions is significant since the former are deductible in computing adjusted gross income (above-the-line deductions) under § 62 whereas the latter generally must instead be claimed as itemized deductions (below-the-line deductions) subject as well to the § 67 cutback as miscellaneous itemized deductions. Given this difference, it is not surprising the tax law acknowledges that not all taxpayers who buy and sell securities should be treated as investors like Mr. Higgins and denied the advantages of deductions under § 162. "[F]or Federal tax purposes, a person who purchases and sells securities falls into one of three distinct categories, dealer, trader or investor." Endicott v. Commissioner, T.C. Memo. 2013-199. Both dealers and traders are deemed to be in a trade or business and may deduct expenses under § 162. Investors, like Mr. Higgins, are not and cannot. Dealers have been characterized as "middlemen" performing the usual services of retailers or wholesalers of goods. But how are traders distinguished from investors? "For a taxpayer to be a trader, the trading activity must be substantial, regular and continuous enough to constitute a trade or business. . . . [T]o constitute a trade or business, (1) the trading activity [must be] substantial, and (2) the taxpayer [must seek] to catch the swings in the daily market movements and to profit from these short-term changes . . . ." *Endicott.* In contrast, an investor typically seeks capital appreciation and income from the investments, without regard to the short-term changes.

trade or business" requirement of § 162? The Tax Court said "No":

> Neither are the travel and legal expenses incurred by the petitioners in
> their attempt to find and purchase a business deductible under section
> [212], Internal Revenue Code, which allows the deduction of expenses
> incurred in the production or collection of income or in the management,
> conservation, or maintenance of property held for the production of income.
> There is a basic distinction between allowing deductions for the expense of
> producing or collecting income, in which one has an existent interest or
> right, and expenses incurred in an attempt to obtain income by the creation
> of some new interest. . . . The expenses here involved are of the latter
> classification. The traveling costs were incurred in an endeavor to acquire
> a business which might, in the future, prove productive of income. It might
> reasonably be said that petitioners were engaged in the active search of
> employment as newspaper owners, but that cannot be regarded as a
> business. It is much like the situation . . . found in *McDonald v. Commis-
> sioner*, 323 U.S. 57, where it was held that a Pennsylvania court of common
> pleas judge seeking reelection could not deduct under section [212]
> expenses of such campaign. The Supreme Court said "his campaign
> contributions were not expenses incurred in being a judge but in trying to
> be a judge for the next ten years."

Frank, 20 T.C. at 514.

WELCH v. HELVERING
United States Supreme Court
290 U.S. 111 (1933)

MR. JUSTICE CARDOZO delivered the opinion of the Court.

The question to be determined is whether payments by a taxpayer, who is in business as a commission agent, are allowable deductions in the computation of his income if made to the creditors of a bankrupt corporation in an endeavor to strengthen his own standing and credit.

In 1922 petitioner was the secretary of the E. L. Welch Company, a Minnesota corporation, engaged in the grain business. The company was adjudged an involuntary bankrupt, and had a discharge from its debts. Thereafter the petitioner made a contract with the Kellogg Company to purchase grain for it on a commission. In order to reestablish his relations with customers whom he had known when acting for the Welch Company and to solidify his credit and standing, he decided to pay the debts of the Welch business so far as he was able. In fulfillment of that resolve, he made payments of substantial amounts during five successive years. . . . The Commissioner ruled that these payments were not deductible from income as ordinary and necessary expenses, but were rather in the nature of capital expenditures, an outlay for the development of reputation and good will. The Board of Tax Appeals sustained the action of the Commissioner . . . and the Court of Appeals for the Eighth Circuit affirmed. . . . The case is here on certiorari.

> In computing net income there shall be allowed as deductions . . . all the ordinary and necessary expenses paid or incurred during the taxable year in carrying on any trade or business. . . .

We may assume that the payments to creditors of the Welch Company were necessary for the development of the petitioner's business, at least in the sense that they were appropriate and helpful. *McCulloch v. Maryland*, 4 Wheat 316. He certainly thought they were, and we should be slow to override his judgment. But the problem is not solved when the payments are characterized as necessary. Many necessary payments are charges upon capital. There is need to determine whether they are both necessary and ordinary. Now, what is ordinary, though there must always be a strain of constancy within it, is none the less a variable affected by time and place and circumstance. Ordinary in this context does not mean that the payments must be habitual or normal in the sense that the same taxpayer will have to make them often. A lawsuit affecting the safety of a business may happen once in a lifetime. The counsel fees may be so heavy that repetition is unlikely. None the less, the expense is an ordinary one because we know from experience that payments for such a purpose, whether the amount is large or small, are the common and accepted means of defense against attack. *Cf. Kornhauser v. United States*, 276 U.S. 145. The situation is unique in the life of the individual affected, but not in the life of the group, the community, of which he is a part. At such times there are norms of conduct that help to stabilize our judgment, and make it certain and objective. The instance is not erratic, but is brought within a known type.

The line of demarcation is now visible between the case that is here and the one supposed for illustration. We try to classify this act as ordinary or the opposite, and the norms of conduct fail us. No longer can we have recourse to any fund for business experience, to any known business practice. Men do at times pay the debts of others without legal obligation or the lighter obligation imposed by the usages of trade or by neighborly amenities, but they do not do so ordinarily, not even though the result might be to heighten their reputation for generosity and opulence. Indeed, if language is to be read in its natural and common meaning . . . , we should have to say that payment in such circumstances, instead of being ordinary is in a high degree extraordinary. There is nothing ordinary in the stimulus evoking it, and none in the response. Here, indeed, as so often in other branches of the law, the decisive distinctions are those of degree and not of kind. One struggles in vain for any verbal formula that will supply a ready touchstone. The standard set up by the statute is not a rule of law; it is rather a way of life. Life in all its fullness must supply the answer to the riddle.

The Commissioner of Internal Revenue resorted to that standard in assessing the petitioner's income, and found that the payments in controversy came closer to capital outlays than to ordinary and necessary expenses in the operation of a business. His ruling has the support of a presumption of correctness, and the petitioner has the burden of proving it to be wrong. . . . Unless we can say from facts within our knowledge that these are ordinary and necessary expenses according to the ways of conduct and the forms of speech prevailing in the business world, the tax must be confirmed. But nothing told us by this record or within the sphere of our judicial notice permits us to give that extension to what is ordinary and necessary. Indeed, to do so would open the door to many bizarre analogies. One man has a family name that is clouded by thefts committed by an ancestor. To add to his own standing he repays the stolen money, wiping off, it may be, his income for the year. The payments figure in his tax return as ordinary expenses. Another man conceives the notion that he will be able to practice his vocation with greater ease and profit if he has an opportunity to enrich his culture. Forthwith the price of his education becomes an expense of the business reducing the income subject to taxation. There is little difference between these expenses and those in controversy here. Reputation and learning are akin to capital assets, like the good will of an old partnership. . . . For many, they are the only tools with which to hew a pathway to success. The money spent in acquiring them is well and wisely spent. It is not an ordinary expense of the operation of a business.

The decree should be Affirmed.

HIGGINS v. COMMISSIONER
United States Supreme Court
312 U.S. 212 (1941)

Mr. Justice Reed delivered the opinion of the Court.

Petitioner, the taxpayer, with extensive investments in real estate, bonds and stocks, devoted a considerable portion of his time to the oversight of his interests and hired others to assist him in offices rented for that purpose. For the tax years in question, 1932 and 1933, he claimed the salaries and expenses incident to looking after his properties were deductible under Sec. 23 (a) of the Revenue Act of 1932. The Commissioner refused the deductions.

Petitioner's financial affairs were conducted through his New York office pursuant to his personal detailed instructions. His residence was in Paris, France, where he had a second office. By cable, telephone and mail, petitioner kept a watchful eye over his securities. While he sought permanent investments, changes, redemptions, maturities and accumulations caused limited shiftings in his portfolio. These were made under his own orders. The offices kept records, received securities, interest and dividend checks, made deposits, forwarded weekly and annual reports and undertook generally the care of the investments as instructed by the owner. Purchases were made by a financial institution. Petitioner did not participate directly or indirectly in the management of the corporations in which he held stock or bonds. The method of handling his affairs under examination had been employed by petitioner for more than thirty years. No objection to the deductions had previously been made by the Government.

The Board of Tax Appeals held that these activities did not constitute carrying on a business. . . . The Circuit Court of Appeals affirmed, and we granted certiorari because of conflict.

Petitioner urges that the "elements of continuity, constant repetition, regularity and extent" differentiate his activities from the occasional like actions of the small investor. His activity is and the occasional action is not "carrying on business." On the other hand, the respondent urges that "mere personal investment activities never constitute carrying on a trade or business, no matter how much of one's time or of one's employees' time they may occupy."

Since the first income tax act, the provisions authorizing business deductions have varied only slightly. The Revenue Act of 1913 allowed as a deduction "the necessary expenses actually paid in carrying on any business." By 1918 the present form was fixed and has so continued. No regulation has ever been promulgated which interprets the meaning of "carrying on a business," nor any rulings approved by the Secretary of the Treasury, *i.e.*, Treasury Decisions.

. . . .

To determine whether the activities of a taxpayer are "carrying on a business" requires an examination of the facts in each case. As the Circuit Court of Appeals observed, all expenses of every business transaction are not deductible. Only those are deductible which relate to carrying on a business. The Bureau of Internal Revenue has this duty of determining what is carrying on a business, subject to reexamination of the facts by the Board of Tax Appeals and ultimately to review on the law by the courts on which jurisdiction is conferred. The Commissioner and the Board appraised the evidence here as insufficient to establish petitioner's activities as those of carrying on a business. The petitioner merely kept records and collected interest and dividends from his securities, through managerial attention for his investments. No matter how large the estate or how continuous or extended the work required may be, such facts are not sufficient as a matter of law to permit the courts to reverse the decision of the Board. Its conclusion is adequately supported by this record, and rests upon a conception of carrying on business similar to that expressed by this Court for an antecedent section. [§ 214(a)(1)].

Affirmed.

COMMISSIONER v. GROETZINGER
United States Supreme Court
480 U.S. 23 (1987)

[From the syllabus: For most of 1978, respondent devoted 60 to 80 hours per week to parimutuel wagering on dog races with a view to earning a living from such activity, had no other employment, and gambled solely for his own account. His efforts generated gross winnings of $70,000 on bets of $72,032, for a net gambling loss for the year of $2,032. Although he reported this loss on his 1978 tax return, he did not utilize it in computing his adjusted gross income or claim it as a deduction. Upon audit, the Commissioner of Internal Revenue determined that, under the Internal Revenue Code of 1954 (Code) as it existed in 1978, respondent was subject to the Alternative Minimum Tax because part of the gambling loss deduction to which he was entitled was an "ite[m] of tax preference." Under the Code, such items could be lessened by certain deductions that were "attributable to a trade or business carried on by the taxpayer." In redetermining respondent's tax deficiency, the Tax Court held that he was in the "trade or business" of gambling, so that no part of his gambling losses were an item of tax preference subjecting him to the

Alternative Minimum Tax for 1978. The Seventh Circuit Court of Appeals affirmed.]

BLACKMUN, J.:

. . .

The phrase "trade or business" has been in § 162(a) and in that section's predecessors for many years. Indeed, the phrase is common in the Code, for it appears in over 50 sections and 800 subsections and in hundreds of places in proposed and final income tax regulations. The slightly longer phrases, "carrying on a trade or business," and "engaging in a trade or business," themselves are used no less than 60 times in the Code. The concept thus has a well-known and almost constant presence on our tax-law terrain. Despite this, the Code has never contained a definition of the words "trade or business" for general application, and no regulation has been issued expounding its meaning for all purposes. Neither has a broadly applicable authoritative judicial definition emerged. Our task in this case is to ascertain the meaning of the phrase as it appears in the sections of the Code with which we are here concerned. . . .

In *Deputy v. DuPont*, 308 U.S. 488 (1940), the Court was concerned with what were "ordinary and necessary" expenses of a taxpayer's trade or business, within the meaning of § 23(a) of the Revenue Act of 1928, 45 Stat. 799. In ascertaining whether carrying charges on short sales of stock were deductible as ordinary and necessary expenses of the taxpayer's business, the Court *assumed* that the activities of the taxpayer in conserving and enhancing his estate constituted a trade or business, but nevertheless disallowed the claimed deductions because they were not "ordinary" or "necessary." 308 U.S., at 493–497. Justice Frankfurter, in a concurring opinion joined by Justice Reed, did not join the majority. He took the position that whether the taxpayer's activities constituted a trade or business was "open for determination," *id.*, at 499, and observed:

> " '. . . carrying on any trade or business,' within the contemplation of § 23(a), involves holding one's self out to others as engaged in the selling of goods or services. This the taxpayer did not do. . . . "

Next came *Higgins v. Commissioner*, 312 U.S. 212 (1941). There the Court, in a bare and brief unanimous opinion, ruled that salaries and other expenses incident to looking after one's own investments in bonds and stocks were not deductible under § 23(a) of the Revenue Act of 1932, 47 Stat. 179, as expenses paid or incurred in carrying on a trade or business. [T]he Court seemed to do little more than announce that the facts in each case must be examined; that not all expenses of every business transaction are deductible; and that "[n]o matter how large the estate or how continuous or extended the work required may be, such facts are not sufficient as a matter of law to permit the courts to reverse the decision of the Board." 312 U.S., at 215–18. The opinion, therefore, — although devoid of analysis and not setting forth what elements, if any, in addition to profit motive and regularity, were required to render an activity a trade or business — must stand for the propositions that full-time market activity in managing and preserving one's own estate is not embraced within the phrase "carrying on a business," and that salaries and other expenses incident to the operation are not deductible as having been paid or incurred in a trade or business. . . . [T]he Court in that case did not even cite *DuPont* and thus paid no heed whatsoever to the content of Justice Frankfurter's pronouncement in his concurring opinion. Adoption of the Frankfurter gloss obviously would have disposed of the case in the Commissioner's favor handily and automatically, but that easy route was not followed. . . .

From these observations and decisions, we conclude (1) that, to be sure, the statutory words are broad and comprehensive; (2) that, however, expenses incident to caring for one's own investments, even though that endeavor is full-time, are not deductible as paid or incurred in carrying on a trade or business; (3) that the opposite conclusion may follow for an active trader; (4) that Justice Frankfurter's attempted gloss upon the decision in *DuPont* was not adopted by the Court in that case; (5) that the Court, indeed, later characterized it as an "adumbration"; and (6) that the Frankfurter observation, specifically or by implication, never has been accepted as law by a majority opinion of the Court, and more than once has been totally ignored. We must regard the Frankfurter gloss merely as a two-Justice pronouncement in a passing moment, and, while entitled to respect, as never having achieved the status of a Court ruling. One also must acknowledge that *Higgins*, with its stress on examining the facts in each case, affords no readily helpful standard, in the usual sense, with which to decide the present case and others similar to it. The Court's cases, thus, give us results, but little general guidance. . . .

If a taxpayer, as Groetzinger is stipulated to have done in 1978, devotes his full-time activity to gambling, and it is his intended livelihood source, it would seem that basic concepts of fairness (if there be much of that in the income tax law) demand that his activity be regarded as a trade or business just as any other readily accepted activity, such as being a retail store proprietor or, to come closer categorically, as being a casino operator or as being an active trader on the exchanges.

It is argued, however, that a full-time gambler is not offering goods or his services, within the line of demarcation that Justice Frankfurter would have drawn in *DuPont*. Respondent replies that he indeed is supplying goods and services, not only to himself but, as well, to the gambling market; thus, he says, he comes within the Frankfurter test even if that were to be imposed as the proper measure. "It takes two to gamble," Brief for Respondent 3. Surely, one who clearly satisfies the Frankfurter adumbration usually is in a trade or business. But does it necessarily follow that one who does not satisfy the Frankfurter adumbration is not in a trade or business? One might well feel that a full-time gambler ought to qualify as much as a full-time trader,[9] as courts have held. The Commissioner, indeed, accepts the trader result. Tr. of Oral Arg. 17. In any event, while the offering of goods and services usually would qualify the activity as a trade or business, this factor, it seems to us, is not an absolute prerequisite.

We are not satisfied that the Frankfurter gloss would add any helpful dimension to the resolution of cases such as this one, or that it provides a "sensible test," as the Commissioner urges. See Brief for Petitioner 36. It might assist now and then,

---

[9] "It takes a buyer to make a seller and it takes an opposing gambler to make a bet." Boyle, *What is a Trade or Business?*, 39 Tax Lawyer 737, 768 (1985).

when the answer is obvious and positive, but it surely is capable of breeding litigation over the meaning of "goods," the meaning of "services," or the meaning of "holding one's self out." And we suspect that — apart from gambling — almost every activity would satisfy the gloss. A test that everyone passes is not a test at all. We therefore now formally reject the Frankfurter gloss which the Court has never adopted anyway.

Of course, not every income-producing and profit-making endeavor constitutes a trade or business. . . . We accept the fact that to be engaged in a trade or business, the taxpayer must be involved in the activity with continuity and regularity and that the taxpayer's primary purpose for engaging in the activity must be for income or profit. A sporadic activity, a hobby, or an amusement diversion does not qualify.

It is suggested that we should defer to the position taken by the Commissioner and by the Solicitor General, but, in the absence of guidance, for over several decades now, through the medium of definitive statutes or regulations, we see little reason to do so. We should defer, instead, to the Code's normal focus on what we regard as a common-sense concept of what is a trade or business. Otherwise, as here, in the context of a minimum tax, it is not too extreme to say that the taxpayer is being taxed on his gambling losses,[10] a result distinctly out of line with the Code's focus on income.

We do not overrule or cut back on the Court's holding in *Higgins* when we conclude that if one's gambling activity is pursued full time, in good faith, and with regularity, to the production of income for a livelihood, and is not a mere hobby, it is a trade or business within the meaning of the statutes with which we are here concerned. Respondent Groetzinger satisfied that test in 1978. Constant and large-scale effort on his part was made. Skill was required and was applied. He did what he did for a livelihood, though with a less than successful result. This was not a hobby or a passing fancy or an occasional bet for amusement.

We therefore adhere to the general position of the *Higgins* Court, taken 45 years ago, that resolution of this issue "requires an examination of the facts in each case." 312 U.S., at 217. This may be thought by some to be a less-than-satisfactory solution, for facts vary. (Citations omitted.) But the difficulty rests in the Code's wide utilization in various contexts of the term "trade or business," in the absence of an all-purpose definition by statute or regulation, and in our concern that an attempt judicially to formulate and impose a test for all situations would be counterproductive, unhelpful, and even somewhat precarious for the overall integrity of the Code. We leave repair or revision, if any be needed, which we doubt, to the Congress where we feel, at this late date, the ultimate responsibility rests.

The judgment of the Court of Appeals is affirmed.

---

[10] "The more he lost, the more minimum tax he has to pay." Boyle, 39 Tax Lawyer at 754.

REVENUE RULING 75-120
1975-1 C.B. 55

The Internal Revenue Service has reconsidered its position whether amounts paid by an employee in seeking new employment are deductible under section 162 or 212 of the Internal Revenue Code of 1954.

[T]he longstanding position of the Service has been that expenses incurred by employees in seeking and actually securing new employment are deductible as ordinary and necessary business expenses, but that expenses incurred in seeking but not securing new employment are not deductible. (Emphasis added)

This distinction between expenses for unsuccessfully and successfully seeking new employment has been rejected by the United States Tax Court.

See for example, *Leonard F. Cremona,* 58 T.C. 219 (1972); *David J. Primuth,* 54 T.C. 374 (1970). The *Primuth* opinion concluded that an employee is engaged in the trade or business of performing services as an employee separate and apart from the performance of those services for his existing employer. The court held in *Cremona* that expenses incurred in seeking new employment in the employee's present trade or business are deductible under section 162 of the Code even though new employment was not secured.

In view of the above, *it is now the position of the Service that expenses incurred in seeking new employment in the same trade or business are deductible under section 162 of the Code if directly connected with such trade or business as determined by all the objectives facts and circumstances.* [Emphasis added]

However, such expenses are not deductible if an individual is seeking employment in a new trade or business even if employment is secured. If the individual is presently unemployed, his trade or business would consist of the services previously performed for his past employer if no substantial lack of continuity occurred between the time of the past employment and the seeking of the new employment. Such expenses are not deductible by an individual where there is a substantial lack of continuity between the time of his past employment and the seeking of the new employment, or by an individual seeking employment for the first time. Such expenses are not deductible under section 212(1) of the Code which applies only to expenses incurred with respect to an existing profit-seeking endeavor not qualifying as a trade or business.

If a taxpayer travels to a destination and while at such destination seeks new employment in his present trade or business and also engages in personal activities, traveling expenses to and from such destination are deductible only if the trip is related primarily to seeking such new employment. The amount of time during the period of the trip that is spent on personal activity compared to the amount of time spent on seeking such new employment is important in determining whether the trip is primarily personal. Section 1.162-2(b) of the regulations. *See Patterson v. Thomas,* 289 F.2d 108 (5th Cir. 1961).

Expenses while at the destination that are properly allocable to seeking new employment in the taxpayer's present trade or business are deductible even though the traveling expenses to and from the destination are not deductible. Section 1.162-2(b)(1) of the regulations.

PEVSNER v. COMMISSIONER
United States Court of Appeals, Fifth Circuit
628 F.2d 467 (1980)

JOHNSON, CIRCUIT JUDGE:

This is an appeal by the Commissioner of Internal Revenue from a decision of the United States Tax Court. The Tax Court upheld taxpayer's business expense deduction for clothing expenditures in the amount of $1,621.91 for the taxable year 1975. We reverse.

Since June 1973 Sandra J. Pevsner, taxpayer, has been employed as the manager of the Sakowitz Yves St. Laurent Rive Gauche Boutique located in Dallas, Texas. The boutique sells only women's clothes and accessories designed by Yves St. Laurent (YSL), one of the leading designers of women's apparel. Although the clothing is ready to wear, it is highly fashionable and expensively priced. Some customers of the boutique purchase and wear the YSL apparel for their daily activities and spend as much as $20,000 per year for such apparel.

As manager of the boutique, the taxpayer is expected by her employer to wear YSL clothes while at work. In her appearance, she is expected to project the image of an exclusive lifestyle and to demonstrate to her customers that she is aware of the YSL current fashion trends as well as trends generally. Because the boutique sells YSL clothes exclusively, taxpayer must be able, when a customer compliments her on her clothes, to say that they are designed by YSL. In addition to wearing YSL apparel while at the boutique, she wears them while commuting to and from work, to fashion shows sponsored by the boutique, and to business luncheons at which she represents the boutique. During 1975, the taxpayer bought, at an employee's discount, the following items: four blouses, three skirts, one pair of slacks, one trench coat, two sweaters, one jacket, one tunic, five scarves, six belts, two pairs of shoes and four necklaces. The total cost of this apparel was $1,381.91. In addition, the sum of $240 was expended for maintenance of these items. Although the clothing and accessories purchased by the taxpayer were the type used for general purposes by the regular customers of the boutique, the taxpayer is not a normal purchaser of these clothes. The taxpayer and her husband, who is partially disabled because of a severe heart attack suffered in 1971, lead a simple life and their social activities are very limited and informal. Although taxpayer's employer has no objection to her wearing the apparel away from work, taxpayer stated that she did not wear the clothes during off-work hours because she felt that they were too expensive for her simple everyday lifestyle. Another reason why she did not wear the YSL clothes apart from work was to make them last longer. Taxpayer did admit at trial, however, that a number of the articles were things she could have worn off the job and in which she would have looked "nice."

On her joint federal income tax return for 1975, taxpayer deducted $990 as an ordinary and necessary business expense with respect to her purchase of the YSL clothing and accessories. However, in the Tax Court, taxpayer claimed a deduction for the full $1,381.91 cost of the apparel and for the $240 cost of maintaining the apparel. The Tax Court allowed the taxpayer to deduct both expenses in the total amount of $1,621.91. The Tax Court reasoned that the apparel was not suitable to the private lifestyle maintained by the taxpayer. This appeal by the Commissioner followed.

The principal issue on appeal is whether the taxpayer is entitled to deduct as an ordinary and necessary business expense the cost of purchasing and maintaining the YSL clothes and accessories worn by the taxpayer in her employment as the manager of the boutique. This determination requires an examination of the relationship between Section 162(a) of the Internal Revenue Code of 1954, which allows a deduction for ordinary and necessary expenses incurred in the conduct of a trade or business, and Section 262 of the Code, which bars a deduction for all "personal, living, or family expenses." Although many expenses are helpful or essential to one's business activities — such as commuting expenses and the cost of meals while at work — these expenditures are considered inherently personal and are disallowed under Section 262.

The generally accepted rule governing the deductibility of clothing expenses is that the cost of clothing is deductible as a business expense only if: (1) the clothing is of a type specifically required as a condition of employment, (2) it is not adaptable to general usage as ordinary clothing, and (3) it is not so worn. *Donnelly v. Commissioner*, 262 F.2d 411, 412 (2d Cir. 1959).[11]

In the present case, the Commissioner stipulated that the taxpayer was required by her employer to wear YSL clothing and that she did not wear such apparel apart from work. The Commissioner maintained, however, that a deduction should be denied because the YSL clothes and accessories purchased by the taxpayer were adaptable for general usage as ordinary clothing and she was not prohibited from using them as such. The Tax Court, in rejecting the Commissioner's argument for the application of an objective test, recognized that the test for deductibility was whether the clothing was "suitable for general or personal wear" but determined that the matter of suitability was to be judged subjectively, in light of the taxpayer's lifestyle. Although the court recognized that the YSL apparel "might be used by some members of society for general purposes," it felt that because the "wearing of YSL apparel outside work would be inconsistent with . . . (taxpayer's) lifestyle," sufficient reason was shown for allowing a deduction for the clothing expenditures.

In reaching its decision, the Tax Court relied heavily upon *Yeomans v. Commissioner*, 30 T.C. 757 (1958). In *Yeomans*, the taxpayer was employed as fashion coordinator for a shoe manufacturing company. Her employment necessitated her attendance at meetings of fashion experts and at fashion shows sponsored by her employer. On these occasions, she was expected to wear clothing that was new, highly styled, and such as "might be sought after and worn for personal use by women who make it a practice to dress according to the most advanced or extreme

---

[11] When the taxpayer is prohibited from wearing the clothing away from work a deduction is normally allowed. *See Harsaghy v. Commissioner*, 2 T.C. 484 (1943). However, in the present case no such restriction was placed upon the taxpayer's use of the clothing.

fashions." 30 T.C. at 768. However, for her personal wear, Ms. Yeomans preferred a plainer and more conservative style of dress. As a consequence, some of the items she purchased were not suitable for her private and personal wear and were not so worn. The Tax Court allowed a deduction for the cost of the items that were not suitable for her personal wear. Although the basis for the decision in *Yeomans* is not clearly stated, the Tax Court in the case *sub judice* determined that

> [a] careful reading of *Yeomans* shows that, without a doubt, the Court based its decision on a determination of Ms. Yeomans' lifestyle and that the clothes were not suitable for her use in such lifestyle. Furthermore, the Court recognized that the clothes Ms. Yeomans purchased were suitable for wear by women who customarily wore such highly styled apparel, but such fact did not cause the court to decide the issue against her. Thus, *Yeomans* clearly decides the issue before us in favor of the petitioner.

T.C. Memo 1979-311 at 9–10.

Notwithstanding the Tax Court's decision in *Yeomans*, the Circuits that have addressed the issue have taken an objective, rather than subjective, approach. *Stiner v. United States*, 524 F.2d 640, 641 (10th Cir. 1975); *Donnelly v. Commissioner*, 262 F.2d 411, 412 (2d Cir. 1959). An objective approach was also taken by the Tax Court in *Drill v. Commissioner*, 8 T.C. 902 (1947). Under an objective test, no reference is made to the individual taxpayer's lifestyle or personal taste. Instead, adaptability for personal or general use depends upon what is generally accepted for ordinary street wear. The principal argument in support of an objective test is, of course, administrative necessity. The Commissioner argues that, as a practical matter, it is virtually impossible to determine at what point either price or style makes clothing inconsistent with or inappropriate to a taxpayer's lifestyle. Moreover, the Commissioner argues that the price one pays and the styles one selects are inherently personal choices governed by taste, fashion, and other unmeasurable values. Indeed, the Tax Court has rejected the argument that a taxpayer's personal taste can dictate whether clothing is appropriate for general use. See *Drill v. Commissioner*, 8 T.C. 902 (1947). An objective test, although not perfect, provides a practical administrative approach that allows a taxpayer or revenue agent to look only to objective facts in determining whether clothing required as a condition of employment is adaptable to general use as ordinary streetwear. Conversely, the Tax Court's reliance on subjective factors provides no concrete guidelines in determining the deductibility of clothing purchased as a condition of employment.

In addition to achieving a practical administrative result, an objective test also tends to promote substantial fairness among the greatest number of taxpayers. As the Commissioner suggests, it apparently would be the Tax Court's position that two similarly situated YSL boutique managers with identical wardrobes would be subject to disparate tax consequences depending upon the particular manager's lifestyle and "socio-economic level." This result, however, is not consonant with a reasonable interpretation of Sections 162 and 262.

For the reasons stated above, the decision of the Tax Court upholding the deduction for taxpayer's purchase of YSL clothing is reversed. Consequently, the portion of the Tax Court's decision upholding the deduction for maintenance costs for the clothing is also.

Reversed.

Chapter 13

CAPITAL EXPENDITURES

I. PROBLEMS

1. Dorothy paid the following amounts this year with respect to a successful retail clothing store she has operated as a sole proprietor in a 50-year-old building she has owned for a number of years. Discuss whether each of the expenditures is currently deductible under § 162 or must be capitalized under § 263.

   (a) $50,000 to replace the entire roof of the building after a roof inspection indicated the rafters and the roof decking had rotted, creating the potential for the entire roof to collapse.

   (b) $40,000 to upgrade the entire electrical system of the building to provide expanded lighting possibilities and greatly increase the power available throughout the building.

   (c) $20,000 to repaint the interior of the building with a new color scheme and replace some broken floor tiles near the entrance. Would your answer change if Dorothy arranged for the repainting of the interior of the building and the replacing of the broken floor tiles to take place at the same time as the roof replacement in (a)?

   (d) $75,000 to convert a large shed adjacent to the building into a shop where Dorothy's customers can purchase damaged and clearance items from her business. Dorothy had been using the shed strictly for storage purposes.

   (e) $26,000 to purchase a set of display cases specially designed for Dorothy's business. What if, instead, Dorothy leased the set of display cases under a three-year lease agreement whereby Dorothy agreed to make lease payments of $9,000 each year during the three-year lease term. Assume the lease agreement provided that, at the end of the three-year lease, Dorothy had the option to purchase the display cases for $750.

   (f) $2,000 to purchase cleaning supplies for which Dorothy keeps no records of consumption. Assume it is likely that the supplies will be enough to satisfy the needs of Dorothy's business for the current year and part of the following year.

   (g) $30,000 to design a user-friendly website for Dorothy's business; $5,000 to develop a two-year advertising campaign; $3,000 to prepare the advertising content for the business' website this year; $10,000 to run radio and newspaper advertisements as part of the new two-year advertising campaign; and $15,000 to purchase and install a new neon sign for her building.

(h) $5,000 paid on February 1 to purchase fire, theft, and liability insurance covering the 12-month period beginning February 1 of this year. What difference, if any, would it make if Dorothy paid the $5,000 insurance premium in advance on December 31 of last year?

(i) $15,000 in legal fees to clear a cloud on Dorothy's title to the land on which the building is situated. Assume the cloud has existed on Dorothy's title since she purchased the property. Would your answer be different if the fees were paid to remove a lien on the land that was illegally placed on it last year by a person who was trying to defraud Dorothy?

(j) $50,000 to acquire a five-year lease on the vacant lot adjacent to Dorothy's building to be used for customer parking. Dorothy paid a $1,000 bonus to her assistant for successfully negotiating the lease. She also paid $5,000 in wages to a handyman employed by her business to construct a fence around the leased lot.

2. Dorothy would like to open a second business (modeled on the first) in the metropolitan area, provided there is enough demand and provided she can find the right location. She hires a business consulting firm to assist her. The consultants conduct market surveys and other research to determine demand and to investigate potential locations for the second business. Dorothy pays the consulting firm a fee of $50,000. To what extent is the fee deductible, if at all? Would the answer be different if Dorothy, instead of opening a second retail clothing business, had been interested in the possibility of owning a women's health and fitness center and had hired the consultants to carry out the same research activities with respect to a health and fitness center?

Assignment for Chapter 13:

Complete the problems.

Read: Internal Revenue Code: §§ 263(a); 161; 162(a). Review § 195. Skim §§ 263A(a), (b), (g), (h); 174(a);

Treasury Regulations: §§ 1.162-3(a)(1), (2), (c)(1); 1.162-4(a); 1.162-11; 1.263(a)-1(a)–(e); 1.263(a)-2(a), (c), (d)(1), (e), (f)(1)–(3)(i), (f)(4) Ex. 1, 2, 5, and 10, (g) and (h)(1); 1.263(a)-3(d), (e)(1), (2)(i) and (ii), (3)(i), (g)(1), (2)(i), (i)(1), (3), (6) Ex. 1 and 2, (j)(1), (2), (3) Ex. 6, 7, 8, 12, 13, and 23, (k)(1), (6), (7) Ex. 10, 11, 14, 15, 22 and 23, (l)(1), (o) and (p); 1.263(a)-4(a), (b)(1), (3), (c)(1)(vi), (xiv), (d)(1), (2)(i)(A), (B), (2), (5), (6)(i), (vii) Ex. 1, 8, (9)(i), (e)(1)(i), (4), (5), (f)(1), (8) Ex. 1, 2, (g)(1). Skim §§ 1.263(a)-1(f); 1.263(a)-3(h); 1.263(a)-3(n); 1.263(a)-5(a), (b)(1), (d)(1), (2), (3)(i), (e); 1.461-1(a)(1), (2).

Materials: Overview
           Commissioner v. Idaho Power Co.
           Midland Empire Packing Co. v. Commissioner
           Mt. Morris Drive-In Theatre Co. v. Commissioner
           Revenue Ruling 2001-4

II. VOCABULARY

capital expenditure
improvement
repair
capitalize
acquisition cost
betterment
restoration

III. OBJECTIVES

1. To distinguish between repairs and improvements.

2. To describe the purpose of the rule prohibiting deduction of capital expenditures.

3. To describe the origin-of-the-claim test.

4. To recall that expenditures to defend or protect title are capital expenditures.

5. To describe the tax treatment of costs incurred to acquire or produce property.

6. To explain the "12 month rule" as a means of distinguishing a capital expenditure from a currently deductible expense.

7. To describe when prepaid expenses will not be deductible currently.

8. To explain the treatment of transaction costs with regard to the acquisition of both tangible and intangible property.

9. To explain what constitute a unit of property for purposes of § 263 and Reg. §§ 1.263(a)-1, 1.263(a)-2, 1.263(a)-3 and 1.162-3.

10. To explain the safe harbor for routine maintenance.

11. To explain what amounts are treated as paid for betterments or for restorations.

12. To recall the amounts paid to acquire or create intangibles must be capitalized.

13. To recall the tax treatment of advertising expenses and expansion costs.

14. To distinguish between purchase and lease of property.

15. To explain the relationship between capitalization of an expenditure and basis.

IV. OVERVIEW

A. Deductible Expense or Capital Expenditure?

Assume a successful entrepreneur, after an extensive search, identifies a downtown restaurant available for purchase, pays a lawyer to prepare a contract of sale and various other documents necessary for the purchase, and then buys the restaurant. After operating the restaurant for two years, he spends a considerable sum expanding the restaurant, and, at the same time, buys new fixtures, furniture, and multi-year liability insurance policies. May he deduct the various costs he has incurred? Because our tax system taxes net income, taxpayers are generally allowed to deduct their business expenses from their business income. If we looked solely to § 162, we would probably conclude the taxpayer's costs were properly deductible under that section. But, as § 161 warns us, § 162 deductions are subject to exceptions. The most important exception is found in § 263, denying deductions for capital expenditures. Specifically, § 263 denies a deduction for the cost of new buildings or for permanent improvements or betterments increasing the value of the property, and for restoration costs for which an allowance is made. The regulations list examples of capital expenditures, including the cost of acquisition or production or improvement of real or personal tangible property and the cost of acquisition or creation of intangible property. Reg. § 1.263(a)-1(d).

The above example demonstrates the rationale for the prohibition on deduction of capital expenditures. A capital expenditure provides a benefit that persists, that contributes to generating income over a period of years; its value is not consumed or dissipated within the current year. Since a capital expenditure incurred by a business contributes to income over a period of years, a deduction for its cost in the current year will generally not be permitted; to do so would result in excessive mismatching of business income and the expenses that produced that income. Indeed, it is the matching of current expenditures with future income that is at the heart of the capitalization requirement. This is not to say, however, the cost of a capital expenditure can never be recovered. The regulations provide that capitalized costs will be recovered "through depreciation, cost of goods sold, or by an adjustment to basis at the time the property is placed in service, sold, used, or otherwise disposed of by the taxpayer." Reg. §§ 1.263(a)-2(h), 1.263(a)-3(p), and 1.263(a)-4(g)(1).

We will postpone to the next chapter the study of the recovery of capital expenditures; let us begin here to learn to identify the creature. But let us also begin to appreciate that what is typically at stake in distinguishing capital expenditures from current deductions is timing. Is the expense fully recoverable — *i.e.*, deductible — now? Is it instead recoverable bit by bit over a number of years? Or, worse yet for the taxpayer, is it recoverable only when the property in question is disposed of? Depending on the time and the money involved, the answer to the timing question can be expensive. By contrast, where the amounts and time periods involved are minimal, might it not make sense for administrative reasons to permit current deductions even for expenses that arguably produce some hard-to-measure benefit in future years? See, for example, Reg. § 1.162-3(a)(2) (authorizing the deduction of the amount paid for "incidental" materials and supplies during the year, where no records of consumption or inventories are kept and where taxable income is clearly reflected).[1]

B. Defining Capital Expenditure — *INDOPCO*

Distinguishing capital expenditures from currently deductible expenses is sometimes difficult. As the Supreme Court reiterated in *INDOPCO, Inc. v. Commissioner*, 503 U.S. 79, 86 (1992), "the 'decisive distinctions' between current expenses and capital expenditures 'are those of degree and not of kind.' " (Quoting from *Welch v. Helvering*, 290 U.S. 111, 114 (1933)). Commenting on the relationship between deductions and capital expenditures, the Court added:

> The notion that deductions are exceptions to the norm of capitalization finds support in various aspects of the Code. Deductions are specifically enumerated and thus are subject to disallowance in favor of capitalization. *See* §§ 161, 261. Nondeductible capital expenditures, by contrast, are not exhaustively enumerated in the Code; rather than providing a "complete list of nondeductible expenditures," . . . § 263 serves as a general means of distinguishing capital expenditures from current expenses. . . . For these reasons, deductions are strictly construed and allowed only "as there is a clear provision therefor."

503 U.S. at 84.

In *INDOPCO*, the Court affirmed the Third Circuit's decision in *National Starch and Chemical Corporation v. Commissioner*, 918 F.2d 426 (1990), holding that consulting and legal fees incurred by a company in deciding whether to accept another company's friendly takeover bid provided a long term benefit and therefore had to be capitalized. On appeal, the taxpayer argued that, contrary to the Third Circuit's decision, the longevity of the benefits derived from an expenditure was irrelevant in determining current deductibility. According to the taxpayer, the Supreme Court's decision in *Lincoln Savings & Loan Ass'n*, 403 U.S. 345 (1971), had established a new test — the "separate and distinct asset" test — for determining whether expenditures had to be capitalized. In *Lincoln Savings & Loan Ass'n*, the Court required the taxpayer to capitalize the "additional premium," which it and other state savings and loan associations were required to pay to the Federal Savings and Loan Insurance Corporation for the purpose of insuring their deposits, because the "additional premium" created a "separate and distinct asset."

Rejecting the INDOPCO taxpayer's argument, the Supreme Court noted:

> *Lincoln Savings* stands for the simple proposition that a taxpayer's expenditure that "serves to create or enhance . . . a separate and distinct" asset should be capitalized under § 263. It by no means follows, however, that *only* expenditures that create or enhance separate and distinct assets are to be capitalized under § 263. . . . In short, *Lincoln Savings* holds that the creation of a separate and distinct asset well may be a sufficient but not a necessary condition to classification as a capital expenditure. . . .

[1] In the same vein, see Reg. § 1.162-12, allowing farmers to deduct the cost of "ordinary tools of short life or small cost, such as hand tools, including shovels, rakes, etc. . . . "

Nor does our statement in *Lincoln Savings* . . . that "the presence of an ensuing benefit that may have some future aspect is not controlling" prohibit reliance on future benefit as a means of distinguishing an ordinary business expense from a capital expenditure. Although the mere presence of an incidental future benefit . . . may not warrant capitalization, a taxpayer's realization of benefits beyond the year in which the expenditure is incurred is undeniably important in determining whether the appropriate tax treatment is immediate deduction or capitalization. . . . Indeed, the text of the Code's capitalization provision, § 263(a)(1), which refers to "permanent improvements or betterments," itself envisions an inquiry into the duration and extent of the benefits realized by the taxpayer.

503 U.S. at 86, 87.

Focusing on the facts of the case, the Supreme Court concluded the taxpayer had failed to carry its burden of establishing that the expenses were "ordinary and necessary" within the meaning of § 162(a). Rather, the facts indicated "the transaction produced significant benefits to National Starch that extended beyond the tax year in question." *Id.* at 88. Among other benefits, the Court noted that, as a result of the takeover, the taxpayer would benefit from the enormous resources, especially basic technology, of the acquiring company. National Starch also "obtained benefits through its transformation from a publicly held, freestanding corporation into a wholly owned subsidiary of Unilever." *Id.* The Court emphasized its decision was consistent with other decisions holding expenses "incurred for the purpose of changing the corporate structure for the benefit of future operations are not ordinary and necessary expenses." *Id.* The *INDOPCO* decision thus appeared to focus, in deciding capitalization questions, on whether the expenditure at issue generated future benefits and whether those benefits were significant.

The guidance *INDOPCO* provides certainly leaves room for ambiguity and disagreement. In that regard, it may be useful to bear in mind it is the concern with matching income and related expenses that underlies the capitalization requirement. Such matching ought therefore ordinarily be carried out, and capitalization imposed, at least in the absence of administrative or compliance burdens that are such as to make matching impractical or unwarranted. Consider in this regard the following excerpt from the decision by the Seventh Circuit Court of Appeals in *US Freightways Corp. v. Commissioner*, 270 F.3d 1137 (2001):

Freightways is a long-haul freight trucking company that operates throughout the continental United States. . . . Every year it is required to purchase a large number of permits and licenses and to pay significant fees and insurance premiums in order legally to operate its fleet of vehicles. . . . None of the licenses and permits at issue was valid for more than twelve months, nor did the benefits of any of the fees and insurance premiums paid extend beyond a year from the time the expense was incurred. . . . After auditing Freightways' tax return, the Commissioner concluded that Freightways should have capitalized its 1993 . . . expenses and deducted them ratably over the 1993 and 1994 tax years. . . .

We turn . . . to the central reason the Commissioner, as affirmed by the Tax Court, gave: that no matter what other characteristics an expenditure has, if it is made in one tax year and its useful life extends "substantially" (an undefined term) beyond the close of that year, then it must be capitalized. Perhaps this rule works in some simple cases. It relies on an implicit spectrum between things that are consumed immediately and those that last well beyond a year. . . . The problem is that many things fall somewhere in the middle of this hypothetical spectrum. . . .

Even the Commissioner concedes the ordinariness of Freightways' . . . expenses for companies in the trucking business. Not only are they ordinary, but as Freightways, points out, they recur, with clockwork regularity, every year. Both this court and the IRS have recognized this type of regularity as something that tends to support a finding of deductibility. . . .

The Commissioner responds that some distortion remains as long as the expenses are not capitalized. . . . In his appellate brief, the Commissioner asserts that expensing was allowing Freightways in a sense to borrow deductions from later years and thus to lower its tax burdens year after year: . . . We agree with him that the mere fact that certain expenditures recur does not negate the distorting effect of expensing that predictably occurred here — the interest-free government loan that comes from the deduction remains the same regardless of whether the . . . expenses are unchanged throughout the corporate life of Freightways.

But perfection is a lot to ask for, even in the administration of the tax laws. . . .

Freightways' final point is that perfection in temporal matching comes at too high a price for these kinds of expenses. At some point the "administrative costs and conceptual rigor" of achieving a more perfect match become too great. . . . Here, there is a considerable administrative burden that Freightways and any similarly situated taxpayer will bear if it must always allocate one-year expenses to two tax years, year in and year out. It argues that the gain in precision for the taxing authorities is far outweighed by the administrative burden it will bear in performing this task. . . .

We conclude that, for the particular kind of expenses at issue in this case fixed, one-year items where the benefit will never extend beyond that term, that are ordinary, necessary, and recurring expenses for the business in question the balance of factors under the statute and regulations cuts in favor of treating them as deductible expenses under I.R.C. § 162(a). We therefore reverse the Tax Court's ruling to the contrary.

Id. at 1139–47. See the discussion, *infra*, regarding the 12-month rule now part of the regulations governing the capitalization of intangibles.

C. Administrative Guidance: the Capital Expenditures Regulations

As emphasized by the Supreme Court in *INDOPCO* and as demonstrated by the facts of that case, the requirement that certain expenditures be capitalized is fundamental and pervasive in the tax law and manifests itself in many guises. Given the importance of the capitalization requirement and the uncertainty regarding its application, Treasury over the last decade has provided considerable guidance by means of extensive regulations addressing particular categories of capital expenditures. What follows is an overview of important sets of regulations interpreting § 263 and specifically addressing (a) amounts paid to acquire or produce tangible property; (b) amounts paid to improve tangible property; (c) amounts paid to acquire or create intangibles; and (d) amounts paid or incurred to acquire a trade or business.

1. Amounts Paid to Acquire or Produce Tangible Property

Regulations finalized in September 2013 explicitly state that, as a general rule, amounts a taxpayer pays to acquire or produce a "unit of real or personal property,"[2] including leasehold improvements, land and land improvements, building, machinery and equipment, and furniture and fixtures must be capitalized and will result in the taxpayer taking a basis in the property equal to the amount capitalized. Reg. §§ 1.263(a)-2(d)(1), 1.263(a)-2(f)(3)(i), and 1.263(a)-2(g).[3] Such amounts include the invoice price, transaction costs, and costs for work performed prior to the date the unit of property is placed in service by the taxpayer. *Id.*

Under the regulations, "transaction costs" are amounts paid to facilitate acquisition of real or personal property and include, among other items, amounts paid for (1) "negotiating the terms or structure of the acquisition and obtaining tax advice on the acquisition"; (2) "preparing and reviewing the documents effectuating the acquisition of property (for example, preparing the bid, offer, sales contract, or purchase agreement); (3) "examining and evaluating the title of property"; (4) "conveying property between the parties. . . . "; and (5) "finders' fees or brokers' commissions." Reg. § 1.263(a)-2(f)(1) and (2)(ii). Compensation paid to employees and overhead, however, are not treated as amounts that facilitate the acquisition of

---

[2] Because the term "unit of real or personal property" is defined in the regulations addressing the capitalization of amounts paid to improve tangible property, it will be discussed in the part of this Overview focusing on improvements made to tangible property.

[3] In the case of property that is inventory in the hands of the taxpayer, capitalized amounts are included in inventory costs. Regulation § 1.263(a)-1(f)(1) provides a *de minimis* rule whereby taxpayers may *elect* to deduct certain amounts paid to acquire tangible property. For example, taxpayers who have "applicable financial statements" and who have accounting procedures which treat as an expense for non-tax purposes amounts paid for property costing less than a specified dollar amount or property with an economic useful life of 12 months or less, may deduct amounts for the property not exceeding "$5,000 per invoice (or per item as substantiated by the invoice or other amount as identified in published guidance in the Federal Register or in the Internal Revenue Bulletin.)" Taxpayers without applicable financial statements are limited to deducting $500 per invoice (or per item as substantiated by the invoice) or other amount as provided in published guidance. . . . " The *de minimis* rule does not apply to amounts paid for land. Reg. § 1.263(a)-1(f)(2).

real or personal property. Taxpayers, nonetheless, may elect to capitalize even those amounts. Reg. § 1.263(a)-2(f)(2)(iv).

> **Example 1**: Elizabeth purchases a building to house her law practice. She paid $500,000 for the building and incurred transaction costs within the meaning of Reg. § 1.263(a)-2(f)(1) and (2), brokerage fees, etc., amounting to $25,000. Elizabeth will be required to capitalize the purchase price of the land as well the transaction costs incurred in acquiring the building. In turn, the purchase price of the building together with the transaction costs will become Elizabeth's initial basis in the building. Thus, Elizabeth's initial basis for the building will be $525,000. If, two years later, Elizabeth were to spend $300,000 to expand the building, the expansion cost would likewise be a capitalizable acquisition cost and would result in an upward adjustment of her basis in the building under § 1016(a)(1).

> **Example 2:** Bill purchases for $100,000 a piece of heavy equipment for use in his construction business. Bill will be required to capitalize the $100,000 cost of the equipment and will, as a result, take a basis of $100,000 in that equipment.

While the regulations make clear that, as a general rule, the costs incurred in acquiring an asset must be capitalized, determining whether a particular cost is properly classifiable as an acquisition cost, can be controversial. Notwithstanding the recently finalized regulations, case law long predating those regulations continues to be important in classifying costs as acquisition costs or otherwise. In *Woodward v. Commissioner*, 397 U.S. 572 (1970), and its companion case, *United States v. Hilton Hotels Corp.*, 397 U.S. 580 (1970), the issue was the deductibility of appraisal and litigation costs the taxpayers incurred in determining the price of stock they were required to purchase from dissenting shareholders under applicable state law. Noting that the title to the stock was not at issue, the taxpayers argued the primary purpose of the litigation was the determination of the stock's value. Given valuation as the "primary purpose" of the litigation, they argued the litigation costs were not acquisition costs. The Supreme Court, however, rejected the taxpayer's "primary purpose" standard, and held, instead, the proper inquiry was whether the "origin of the claim" litigated was in the acquisition of the stock; if so, as it was in these cases, the costs were capital expenditures.

Amounts paid to defend or perfect title to real or personal property are deemed to be amounts paid to acquire or produce property and must therefore be capitalized. Reg. § 1.263(a)-2(e)(1). Under the regulations, it is not merely the costs incurred in perfecting a recently-acquired title, but also those incurred in the defense of a pre-existing one that must be capitalized. Where, however, a dispute does not relate to the title to property but rather the income from it, courts have held the costs incurred to be deductible. See, for example, *Southland Royalty Co. v. United States*, 582 F.2d 604 (Ct. Cl. 1978), allowing a deduction for costs incurred in an action to recover additional royalty payments but disallowing a current deduction and, instead, requiring capitalization for costs incurred in a suit to determine the longevity of an intervening leasehold interest.

Another aspect of the capitalization-of-acquisition-costs rule is presented in *Commissioner v. Idaho Power*, a case reprinted in the materials. *Idaho Power* addresses the question of how a taxpayer should treat the costs of constructing an asset having a useful life extending substantially beyond the taxable year. Costs ordinarily regarded as currently deductible, e.g., wages or rent, take on a different status when they are part of the "acquisition cost" of constructed property. *Idaho Power* principles were applied by the Seventh Circuit in *Encyclopaedia Britannica v. United States*, 685 F.2d 212 (7th Cir. 1982). In that case, Encyclopaedia Britannica sought to deduct currently amounts it had agreed to pay another publishing company for researching, preparing, editing, and arranging a manuscript for a book to be called *The Dictionary of Natural Sciences*. The Seventh Circuit disagreed with Encyclopaedia Britannica's characterization of the payments as payment for services and, instead, concluded the payments were for the acquisition of an asset, a book that would yield income to Encyclopaedia Britannica over a period of years. As the court noted: "From the publisher's standpoint, a book is just another rental property; and just as the expenditures in putting a building into shape to be rented must be capitalized, so, logically at least, must the expenditures used to create a book. . . . *Id.* at 214. If you hire a carpenter to build a tree house that you plan to rent out, his wage is a capital expenditure to you. *See Commissioner of Internal Revenue v. Idaho Power Co.* . . . ."

Congress, in 1986, enacted § 263A, which incorporate the principles of *Idaho Power* and requires capitalization of direct and indirect costs — including certain interest costs — incurred by taxpayers who manufacture, construct, or produce real or tangible personal property, or who acquire or hold inventory property for resale. *See* § 263A(a), (b), (f), and (g). Voluminous regulations have been issued to implement the statutory directive. As noted above, the capitalization of costs creates or increases basis depending on the circumstances.

2. Amounts Paid to Improve Tangible Property

a. Improvements: Historic Rules

It has long been axiomatic that expenditures for repairs or maintenance, which do not materially add to value or appreciably prolong useful life, are deductible. By contrast, improvements or replacements are not deductible but must be capitalized (and thus added to the taxpayer's basis in the property). As reflected in the two Tax Court decisions, *Midland Empire Packing Co. v. Commissioner* and *Mt. Morris Drive-In Theatre v. Commissioner*, included in the materials, distinguishing a repair from an improvement has generated considerable controversy. The following excerpt from Revenue Ruling 2001-4, 2001-1 C.B. 295 which addressed the tax treatment of costs incurred in performing work on aircraft as part of an aircraft maintenance program summarizes well the historic distinctions the courts and the Service drew between repairs and improvements. In many respects, this ruling set the stage for the 2013 regulations discussed below with regard to the capitalization of amounts paid for the improvement of tangible property.

> Any properly performed repair, no matter how routine, could be considered to prolong the useful life and increase the value of the property if it is compared with the situation existing immediately prior to that repair. Consequently, courts have articulated a number of ways to distinguish

between deductible repairs and non-deductible capital improvements. For example, in *Illinois Merchants Trust Co. v. Commissioner*, 4 B.T.A. 103, 106 (1926), *acq.*, V-2 C.B. 2, the court explained that repair and maintenance expenses are incurred for the purpose of keeping the property in an ordinarily efficient operating condition over its probable useful life for the uses for which the property was acquired. Capital expenditures, in contrast, are for replacements, alterations, improvements, or additions that appreciably prolong the life of the property, materially increase its value, or make it adaptable to a different use. In *Estate of Walling v. Commissioner*, . . . the court explained that the relevant distinction between capital improvements and repairs is whether the expenditures were made to "put" or "keep" property in ordinary efficient operating condition. In *Plainfield-Union Water Co. v. Commissioner*, . . . the court stated that if the expenditure merely restores the property to the state it was in before the situation prompting the expenditure arose and does not make the property more valuable, more useful, or longer-lived, then such an expenditure is usually considered a deductible repair. In contrast, a capital expenditure is generally considered to be a more permanent increment in the longevity, utility, or worth of the property. The Supreme Court's decision in *INDOPCO Inc. v. Commissioner*, 503 U.S. 79 (1992) does not affect these general principles. *See* Rev. Rul. 94-12, 1994-1 C.B. 36 . . . .

Even if the expenditures include the replacement of numerous parts of an asset, if the replacements are a relatively minor portion of the physical structure of the asset, or of any of its major parts, such that the asset as whole has not gained materially in value or useful life, then the costs incurred may be deducted as incidental repairs or maintenance expenses. *See Buckland v. United States*, 66 F. Supp. 681, 683 (D. Conn. 1946) (costs to replace all window sills in factory building were deductible repairs). *See also, e.g., Libby & Blouin Ltd. v. Commissioner*, 4 B.T.A. 910 (1926) (costs to replace all the tubing in sugar evaporator, which were small parts in a large machine, were deductible repairs). The same conclusion is true even if such minor portion of the asset is replaced with new and improved materials. *See, e.g. Badger Pipeline v. Commissioner*, T.C.M. 1997-457 (costs to replace 1,000 feet of pipeline in a 25-mile section of pipeline were deductible repairs, regardless of whether the new pipe was of better quality or has a longer life).

If, however, a major component or a substantial structural part of the asset is replaced and, as a result, the asset as a whole has increased in value, life expectancy, or use, then the costs of the replacement must be capitalized. *See, e.g., Denver & Rio Grande Western R.R. Co. v. Commissioner*, 279 F.2d 368 (10th Cir. 1960) (costs to replace major portion of a viaduct — all of the floor planks and 85–90% of the stringers — were capital expenditures); *P. Dougherty Co. v. Commissioner*, 159 F.2d 269, 272 (4th Cir. 1946) (costs to replace entire stern section of barge with new materials were capital expenditures); *Vanalco Inc. v. Commissioner*, T.C.M. 1999-265 (cost to replace the cell lining, an essential and substantial component of the cell, was required to be capitalized); *Stark v. Commissioner*, T.C.M.

1999-1 (costs to replace building roof were capital expenditures). . . .

In addition, although the high cost of the work performed may be considered in determining whether an expenditure is capital in nature, cost alone is not dispositive. *Compare R.R. Hensler, Inc. v. Commissioner*, 73 T.C. 168, 177 (1979), *acq. in result, 1980-2 C.B. 1* (the fact that taxpayer's expense was large does not change its character as ordinary); *Buckland* at 683 (replacements of relatively minor proportions of the entire physical asset constitute repairs even where high in cost); and *American Bemberg*, 10 T.C. 361 (1948) (deduction allowed for drilling and grouting to prevent cave-ins even though the total cost of the expenditures exceeded $1.1 million), *with Wolfsen Land & Cattle Co. v. Commissioner*, 72 T.C. 1, 17 (1979) (costs to dragline an irrigation ditch were capital expenditures, in part, because they could be as high as the cost to construct a new ditch); and *Stoeltzing v. Commissioner*, 266 F.2d 374, 376 (3d Cir. 1959) (expenditures could not be incidental repairs because they exceeded by almost 200% the cost of the building).

Similarly, the fact that a taxpayer is required by a regulatory authority to make certain repairs or to perform certain maintenance on an asset in order to continue operating the asset in its business does not mean that the work performed materially increases the value of such asset, substantially prolongs its useful life, or adapts it to a new use. *See, e.g., Midland Empire Packing Co. v. Commissioner*, 14 T.C. 635 (1950), *acq.*, 1950-2 C.B. 3 . . . *L&L Marine Service Inc. v. Commissioner*, T.C.M. 1987-428 (work performed on barges that was necessary to enable the barges to continue to qualify for sea duty was a deductible repair).

The materials include an additional excerpt from Revenue Ruling 2001-4 reflecting the kind of work done as part of a "heavy maintenance visit" required periodically by an aircraft's maintenance manual. The analysis of Situation 1 in the Revenue Ruling would appear to apply today even after the promulgation of the final regulations discussed below. *See* Reg. § 1.263(a)-3(i)(6) Ex. 1 and 2. As a result, the excerpt provides helpful guidance in determining today what costs will be deemed repair costs and what costs must be capitalized.

b.   Improvements: The Final Regulations

For some time, the Service recognized the need to provide further clarification with regard to the deduction-versus-capitalization rules relating to the repair or improvement of tangible property. To that end, the Service, in 2004, announced its intent to propose regulations providing "clear, consistent and administrable rules that will reduce the uncertainty and controversy in this area, while also preventing the distortion of income." Notice 2004-6, 2004-1 C.B. 308. The effort to provide guidance proved daunting. Treasury originally issued proposed regulations under § 263(a) in 2006. Those regulations were withdrawn and new proposed regulations were issued in 2008. Finally, at the end of 2011, temporary regulations were issued. Treasury issued final regulations in September of 2013.

The final regulations provide considerable guidance. Unlike earlier regulations which, among other matters, focused on whether expenditures materially increased the value of property, the final regulations steer clear of focusing on value in addressing the capitalization of amounts paid to improve tangible property. The final regulations provide general rules for determining the appropriate unit of property to which the regulations apply and specifically require capitalization of amounts paid to bring about: (1) a betterment to a unit of property; (2) the restoration of a unit of property; or (3) the adaption of a unit of property to a new or different use. Reg. § 1.263(a)-3(d).[4]

Determining the Unit of Property. Determination of the appropriate unit of property is critical in the application of the regulations addressing amounts paid to improve tangible property. For example, to decide whether a cost associated with property is to be treated as a deductible repair cost or a capitalizable improvement cost, one must first identify the unit of property that will be the focus of the repair/improvement analysis. The prior regulations did not provide rules for identifying a unit of property, thus leaving it to the courts to make the determination of the unit of property to be considered in applying the repair/improvement analysis. For example, in *FedEx Corporation v. United States*, 291 F. Supp. 2d 699 (W.D. Tenn. 2003), *aff'd*, 412 F. Supp. 3d 617 (6th Cir. 2005), the court, in determining whether the taxpayer could deduct currently the costs associated with maintenance of its jet aircraft engines and auxiliary power units, noted that, in applying the repair regulations, it first had to decide whether the aircraft themselves, rather than the engines or power units, were the appropriate units of property to which to apply the regulations. Applying factors similar to those discussed below and included in the final regulations, the court determined the aircraft themselves were the appropriate units of property for purposes of applying the repair regulations and thus concluded the maintenance performed on the engines and power units preserved, but did not prolong, the life of the aircraft. Obviously, had the engines themselves been the units of property to be analyzed, the court would likely have reached a different conclusion.

The final regulations provide, in general, the unit-of-property determination will be made using a functional interdependence standard. For property other than buildings, "all components that are functionally interdependent comprise a single unit of property. Components of property are functionally interdependent if the placing in service of one component by the taxpayer is dependent on the placing in service of the other component by the taxpayer." Reg. § 1.263(a)-3(e)(3)(i). In one example, the regulations conclude a laptop computer and a printer used in providing legal services constitute separate units of property because they are not functionally interdependent components, i.e., the placing in service of the computer is not dependent on the placing in service of the printer. Reg. § 1.263(a)-3(e)(6) Ex. 9.

The regulations contain a special rule for buildings whereby a building and its structural components are generally treated as a single unit of property. Reg. § 1.263(a)-3(e)(2)(i). Note, however, certain structural components of a building

---

[4] Regulation § 1.263(a)-3(h) creates a safe harbor for "small taxpayers," i.e., taxpayers whose average annual gross receipts for the three preceding table years is less than or equal to $10,000,000. Under this safe harbor, the taxpayer may generally elect not to apply the improvement rules to certain building property.

constitute "building systems" deemed to be separate from the building structure. As a result, the improvement rules of the regulations must be applied to each "building system." Reg. § 1.263(a)-3(e)(2)(ii)(B).

The Routine Maintenance Safe Harbor. The final regulations create a safe harbor whereby amounts paid for routine maintenance on a unit of property will be deemed *not* to improve that unit of property, thus enabling a current deduction of the cost of such maintenance. Reg. § 1.263(a)-3(i)(1). With regard to a building unit, the recurring activities a taxpayer expects to perform to keep the building in its "ordinarily efficient operating condition" constitute routine maintenance. Such activities include "the inspection, cleaning, and testing of the building structure or each building system, and the replacement of damaged or worn parts with comparable and commercially available replacement parts." Reg. § 1.263(a)-3(i)(1)(i). For activities to be routine, however, the taxpayer must "reasonably expect" to perform them more than once during the 10-year period after the building or building system is placed in service by the taxpayer. *Id.* A similar safe harbor rule is applicable to routine maintenance with regard to other property except that, instead of the 10-year period noted above, the property's class life is utilized. Reg. § 1.263(a)-3(i)(1)(ii). With regard to buildings or other property, factors such as industry practice and manufacturers' recommendations are considered in determining whether the maintenance is routine.

Routine maintenance, however, does not include amounts paid for a betterment to a unit of property, amounts paid for certain replacement of components of a unit of property, amounts paid to adapt a unit of property to a new or different use, and amounts paid for certain other work. Reg. § 1.263(a)-3(i)(3).

The regulations provide two example of a taxpayer operating a commercial airline engaged in the business of transporting passengers and freight throughout the United States and abroad. The airline is required by the aircraft maintenance manual (designed by the manufacturer and approved by the Federal Aviation Administration) to conduct certain "engine shop visits" every four years requiring the aircraft engines to be removed from the aircraft and shipped to an outside vendor who performs a range of activities on the engines, e.g., disassembly, cleaning, inspection, repair or replacement of parts that aren't in conformity with certain specifications, and testing. Under the circumstances, the regulation examples conclude the amounts paid for the engine shop visits are within the routine maintenance safe harbor and need not be capitalized. Reg. § 1.263(a)-3(i)(6) Ex. 1 and 2. Thus, the costs incurred in the "engine shop visits" would be deductible as repair costs. Note these regulation examples essentially reflect the position the Service took in Situation 1 presented in Rev. Rul. 2001-4, included in the materials.

Prior to the promulgation of the final regulations, the courts had developed a plan of rehabilitation doctrine requiring taxpayers to capitalize otherwise deductible repair or maintenance costs incurred as a part of a general plan of rehabilitation. *See, e.g., United States v. Wehrli*, 400 F.2d 686 (10th Cir. 1968). Under this doctrine, an item which is part of a "general plan of rehabilitation, modernization, and improvement of the property, must be capitalized, even though standing alone the item may appropriately be classified as one of repair." *Id.* The final regulations do not include the court-created plan of rehabilitation doctrine but, instead, provide that:

> A taxpayer must capitalize all the direct costs of an improvement and all the indirect costs (including, for example otherwise deductible repair costs) that directly benefit or are incurred by reason of an improvement. Indirect costs [such as repair and maintenance costs] arising from activities that do not directly benefit and are not incurred by reason of an improvement are not required to be capitalized under § 263(a) regardless of whether the activities are performed at the same time as an improvement.

Reg. § 1.263(a)-3(g)(1)(i). Thus, the plan of rehabilitation doctrine has been obsoleted to the extent the doctrine provides a different standard. In this regard, consider two examples:

> **Example 1:** Assume a taxpayer pays for a significant upgrade of the electrical system in its building. To accomplish the work of adding wiring, outlets, etc. throughout the electrical system, a contractor hired by the taxpayer had to make holes in a number of walls in the building. As a result, the taxpayer also incurred costs in patching these holes and repainting the walls. As is discussed in the material that follows, the upgrade of the electrical system constitutes an improvement in the nature of a betterment. Under Reg. § 1.263(a)-3(g)(1)(i), even though the patching and repainting of walls would normally be considered deductible repairs under Reg. § 1.162-4, because these costs directly benefit and are incurred by reason of the improvement to the taxpayer's building, they, together with all the upgrade costs, must also be capitalized. [This example is based on Reg. § 1.263(a)-3(j)(3) Ex. 23.]

> **Example 2:** Assume the same facts as in Example 1 except, in addition, the contractor repaired a broken door handle on one of the doors in the building. The amounts paid for the repair of the door handle do not directly benefit and were not incurred by reason of the upgrade of the electrical system and the related patching and repainting of the walls. Pursuant to Reg. § 1.263(a)-3(g)(1)(i), therefore, the costs incurred in repairing the door handle are deductible repair costs even though the door handle repair occurred at the same time as an improvement. *See* Reg. § 1.263(a)-3(k)(7) Ex. 11.

Betterments. Under Reg. § 1.263(a)-3(j)(1), an amount paid results in the betterment of property only if it "(i) ameliorates a material condition or defect that . . . existed prior to the taxpayer's acquisition of the unit of property . . . ; (ii) results in a material addition . . . to the unit of property; or (iii) results in a material increase in capacity, . . . productivity, efficiency, strength, quality or output of the unit of property. . . . " The regulations provide examples of amounts that must be capitalized because they constitute a "betterment" since they ameliorate a pre-existing material condition, e.g., to prevent further leakage of gasoline and resultant soil contamination, a purchaser of land removes the underground storage tanks left by the prior occupant. Reg. § 1.263(a)-3(j)(3) Ex. 1. By contrast, under a fact pattern identical to that of *Midland Empire Packing Co.*, included in the materials, the regulations find no betterment as a result of the addition of a concrete liner to the walls of a meat processing plant. Reg. § 1.263(a)-3(j)(3) Ex. 12.

The regulations provide a helpful example of a "building refresh" that is not deemed to constitute a betterment. The building refresh consists of "cosmetic and layout changes to the store's interiors and general repairs and maintenance to the store building to modernize the store buildings and reorganize the merchandise displays. The work at each store consists of replacing and reconfiguring display tables and racks to provide better exposure of the merchandise, making corresponding lighting relocations and flooring repairs, moving one wall to accommodate the reconfiguration of tables and racks, patching holes in walls, repainting the interior structure with a new color scheme to coordinate with new signage, replacing damaged ceiling tiles, cleaning and repairing wood flooring throughout the store building, and power washing building exteriors." Reg. § 1.263(a)-3(j)(3) Ex. 6. This regulation example is helpful in identifying the kinds of work and combinations of work that may be viewed as repairs which are immediately deductible.

Restoration. The regulations identify a range of situations in which an amount will be treated as being paid to restore a unit of property, including (1) if it returns the unit of property to its ordinarily efficient operating condition after the property has deteriorated to a state of disrepair and is no longer functional for its intended use; (2) if it results in the rebuilding of the unit of property to a like-new condition after the end of the economic useful life of the property; and (3) if it is for the replacement of a major component or a substantial structural part of the unit of property. Reg. § 1.263(a)-3(k)(1). Significantly, these regulations provide that the replacement of a major component or substantial structural part requires consideration of "all the facts and circumstances . . . [including] the quantitative or qualitative significance of the part or combination of parts in relation to the unit of property. A major component is a part or combination of parts that performs a discrete and critical function in the operation of a unit of property. . . . A substantial structural part is a part or combination of parts that comprises a large portion of the physical structure of the unit of property." Reg. § 1.263(a)-3(k)(6)(i). In this regard, the regulations provide an example wherein an entirely new roof of a business building is treated as a major component or substantial part of the building. Reg. § 1.263(a)-3(k)(7) Ex. 14.

Adaptation of Property to a New or Different Use. The regulations indicate an amount will be treated as paid to adapt a unit of property to a new or different use "if the adaptation is not consistent with the taxpayer's intended ordinary use of the unit of property at the time the property was originally placed in service by the taxpayer." Reg. § 1.263(a)-3(l)(1). As an example of such an adaptation, the regulations identify a situation in which a manufacturing facility is converted to a showroom. Reg. § 1.263(a)-3(l)(3) Ex. 1.

3. Amounts Paid to Acquire or Create Intangibles

Sustained uncertainties and disagreements as to the application of *INDOPCO* led the Service in 2002 to issue proposed regulations relating to the capitalization of intangibles. The preamble to the proposed regulations described the approach the Service was taking with respect to *INDOPCO*:

A fundamental purpose of section 263(a) is to prevent the distortion of taxable income through current deduction of expenditures relating to the production of income of future years. Thus, in determining whether an expenditure should be capitalized, the Supreme Court has considered whether the expenditure produces a significant future benefit. *INDOPCO, Inc. v. Commissioner*, 503 U.S. 79 (1992). A "significant future benefit" standard, however, does not provide the certainty and clarity necessary for compliance with, and sound administration of, the law. Consequently, the IRS and Treasury Department believe that simply restating the significant future benefit test, without more, would lead to continued uncertainty on the part of taxpayers and continued controversy between taxpayers and the IRS. Accordingly, the IRS and Treasury Department have initially defined the exclusive scope of the significant future benefit test through the specific categories of intangible assets for which capitalization is required in the proposed regulations. The future benefit standard underlies many of those categories. . . . [However, if] an expenditure is not described in one of the categories in the proposed regulations or in subsequent future guidance, taxpayers and IRS field personnel need not determine whether that expenditure produces a significant future benefit.

The preamble to the final regulations promulgated in 2004 adopted the same approach:

As in the proposed regulations, the final regulations provide that an amount paid to acquire or create an intangible not otherwise required to be capitalized by the regulations is not required to be capitalized on the ground that it produces significant future benefits for the taxpayer, unless the IRS publishes guidance requiring capitalization of the expenditure.

The general rule of the regulations requires the capitalization of amounts paid to acquire or create an intangible, to "facilitate" the acquisition or creation of an intangible, or to create or enhance a separate and distinct asset. Reg. § 1.263(a)-4(b)(1).

Among the examples given of "acquired intangibles" are ownership interests in corporations, partnerships or other entities; debt instruments; options to provide or acquire property; leases; patents or copyrights; and franchises or trademarks. Reg. § 1.263(a)-4(c)(1). The cost of acquiring such intangibles must be capitalized.

"Created intangibles" include financial interests (which in turn include ownership interests in corporations, partnerships or other entities; debt instruments; and options to provide or acquire property); prepaid expenses; certain membership fees; amounts paid to create (or terminate) certain contracts for property or services; and amounts paid to defend title to intangible property. Reg. § 1.263(a)-4(d)(2) through (9). Again, the costs of creating the intangibles must be capitalized. Reg. § 1.263(a)-4(d)(1).

It is hardly surprising capitalization is required for such intangibles. The Service has, for example, taken the position for many years that prepaid expenses must generally be capitalized, pointing to the First Circuit opinion in *Commissioner v.*

Boylston Market Association, which, in requiring the capitalization of the purchase of three years' fire insurance, stated:

> Advance rentals, payments of bonuses for acquisition and cancellation of leases, and commissions for negotiating leases are all matters which the taxpayer amortizes over the life of the lease. . . . [T]he payments are prorated primarily because the life of the asset extends beyond the taxable year. To permit the taxpayer to take a full deduction in the year of payment would distort his income. Prepaid insurance presents the same problem and should be solved in the same way.

131 F.2d 966, 968 (1942).

The regulations also provide for capitalizing amounts paid to "facilitate" the acquisition or creation of an intangible — or in the language of the regulations, to facilitate a "transaction." The rule of the regulations is that an amount facilitates a transaction, and thus must be capitalized, if the amount is "paid in the process of investigating or otherwise pursuing the transaction." Reg. § 1.263(a)-4(e)(1)(i). There are, however, significant simplifying conventions under which (1) employee compensation and overhead, and (2) de minimis costs (amounts not in excess of $5,000) are treated as amounts that do not facilitate the acquisition or creation of intangibles, and thus need not be capitalized. Reg. § 1.263(a)-4(e)(4). In effect, the regulations opt for ease of administration and record-keeping over the more accurate measurement of income that would in theory emerge from precise allocations of employee time, overhead and minor costs to each of the taxpayer's transactions.

Another significant simplification provision is a "12-month rule," under which capitalization is not required for amounts paid for a right or benefit that does not extend beyond the earlier of (1) 12 months from first realizing the right or benefit, or (2) the end of the tax year following the year of payment. Reg. § 1.263(a)-4(f)(1). Assume, for example, a 12-month license is purchased on June 15, Year 1, where the license period runs from July 1, Year 1, to June 30, Year 2. Because the right or benefit does not extend more than 12 months beyond July 1, the date it is first realized, and because the right or benefit does not extend beyond Year 2 (the end of the year following the year of payment), the payment need not be capitalized. Is there an echo of the *US Freightways* reasoning in the 12-month rule? Note that renewal rights may need to be taken into account in determining compliance with the rule. Reg. § 1.263(a)-4(f)(5). For applications of the 12-month rule to prepaid expenses, see Reg. § 1.263(a)-4(f)(8), Examples (1) and (2).

Amounts paid to facilitate the acquisition of a trade or business or to change the business' capital structure must also be capitalized. Reg.§ 1.263(a)-5(a). The simplifying conventions relating to employee compensation and overhead and to de minimis costs also apply here. Reg. § 1.263(a)-5(d). The regulations also identify, with respect to certain common types of business acquisitions, "inherently facilitative" amounts that must always be capitalized (such as the cost of appraisals, of preparation and review of purchase agreements, and of property transfers between parties to the transaction); otherwise, amounts paid to investigate and pursue the transaction, but which are not inherently facilitative, are deemed to facilitate the transaction (and thus require capitalization) only with respect to activities performed after a letter of intent has been executed or the material terms of the transaction have been approved by the governing authority of the taxpayer. Reg. § 1.263(a)-5(e). Costs incurred, prior to those trigger events, to investigate and otherwise pursue an acquisition are not subject to this capitalization requirement.[5]

4. Amounts Paid with Regard to the Sale, Removal, or Retirement of an Asset

Amounts paid to sell tangible or intangible property are not currently deductible under §§ 162 or 212 but must, instead, be capitalized. Reg. § 1.263(a)-1(e). As noted in the regulations, the practical consequence is that, on the sale of the property, the gain is reduced or the loss is increased by treating the disposition costs as a reduction in the amount realized.

If, however, the asset in question is simply retired and discarded, the cost is ordinarily deductible. For example, in Revenue Ruling 2000-7, 2001-1 C.B. 712, the taxpayer removed and discarded telephone poles and installed new ones. The ruling notes the "costs of removing an asset have been historically allocable to the removed asset and, thus, generally deductible when the asset is retired and the costs are incurred." The removal costs in question were properly allocable to the retired poles and were not required to be capitalized. The fact their retirement might be part of a project that replaced them with new poles did not change the result, since the

---

[5] In a case that arose prior to the promulgation of the intangibles regulations and that reflects the requirement that the acquisition costs subject to capitalization include contingent liabilites assumed in connection with the acquisition, *Illinois Tool Works v. Commissioner*, 355 F.3d 997 (7th Cir. 2004), the taxpayer purchased a company and agreed to assume certain liabilities of the seller including a patent infringement suit pending against it. As part of its due diligence in acquiring the company, the taxpayer reviewed the patent infringement lawsuit and determined it was meritless and that the worst-case scenario suggested an exposure of $1–$3 million. The purchase price was adjusted accordingly. After the taxpayer had purchased the company, the plaintiff in the patent infringement lawsuit offered to settle the case for $1 million; the taxpayer refused the offer. Following a jury trial, the plaintiff ultimately received a $17 million judgment that was upheld on appeal. The taxpayer sought to deduct $16 million of the judgment, contending that only $1 million ought to be capitalized. Generally, when an obligation is assumed in connection with the purchase of capital assets, payments satisfying the obligation are nondeductible capital expenditures. Nonetheless, the taxpayer argued that it should have to capitalize only $1 million of the judgment because, had the taxpayer not mishandled the lawsuit after acquiring the company, the taxpayer would have settled the lawsuit for $1 million.

The Seventh Circuit, affirming the Tax Court decision, disagreed with the taxpayer's position, noting that the taxpayer had agreed to pay a contingent liability as part of its consideration for the purchase of the company. 117 T.C. 39 (2001). Under the circumstances, the court concluded that because the acquisition of the company was meant to benefit the taxpayer into the future, the expense of acquisition must be capitalized. According to the court, the fact that a contingent liability, once fixed, ultimately exceeded the parties' expectations does not render it any less a part of the purchase price. In this case, the court noted, "protection from an aberrant jury verdict needed to be sought during contract formation, not after the fact in the form of an immediate tax deduction." The Seventh Circuit also rejected the taxpayer's argument that its earlier decision in *Staley Mfg. Co. v. Commissioner*, 119 F.3d 482 (7th Cir. 1997), directed a different outcome. The taxpayer suggested that the opinion in *Staley* required a pragmatic approach to allocating the $17 million between those amounts that should be capitalized and those that should be currently deductible. The taxpayer's theory was that it had mishandled the lawsuit subsequent to acquiring the company. The Seventh Circuit disagreed. It concluded that the lawsuit had been mishandled from the outset, "arriving in [taxpayer's] hands fully formed."

removal costs were held to be related to the retired poles, not to assets with a useful life substantially beyond the current year (the new poles). The final regulations regarding amounts paid to improve tangible property confirm the continued application of the rule articulated in Revenue Ruling 200-7. Reg. § 1.263(a)-3(g)(2)(i).

Another "retirement" issue arose in *Steger v. Commissioner*, 113 T.C. 227 (1999). In *Stegar*, the taxpayer was a lawyer who, upon retirement from law practice, purchased a nonpracticing malpractice insurance policy, the purpose of which was to provide insurance coverage for an indefinite period of time for any malpractice the taxpayer may have committed prior to the retirement (but of which no claim had arisen as of retirement). The cost of the policy was held deductible. The court noted "it is a longstanding rule of law that if a taxpayer incurs a business expense but is unable to deduct the cost . . . either as a current expense or through yearly depreciation deductions, the taxpayer is allowed to deduct the expense for the year in which the business ceases to operate." *Id.* at 230. Thus, the Tax court held that, even if the insurance policy constituted an asset with a useful life extending substantially beyond the taxable year, its cost was nonetheless deductible because the taxpayer purchased it in the year the business ceased.

D. Miscellaneous Items

1. Expansion Costs

Consider a related topic. How should expenditures incurred to expand an existing business be treated? As was seen in the previous chapter, expenses incurred prior to "carrying on a trade or business" are not currently deductible. Does a taxpayer engaged in expansion activities incur currently deductible expenses, analogous to "maintenance" of property?

In *Briarcliff Candy Corp. v. Commissioner*, 475 F.2d 775 (2d Cir. 1973), a pre-*INDOPCO* case, the taxpayer's costs in establishing a "franchise" division to promote sales in new retail outlets were held to be deductible. The *Briarcliff* court found the facts there brought the case "squarely within the long recognized principle that expenditures for the protection of an income from loss or diminution" are currently deductible and not capital in nature. The *Briarcliff* court noted the organizational changes which the taxpayers had made in that case in order to spread its sales into a new territory "were not comparable to the acquisition of a new additional branch or division to make and sell a new and different product." 475 F.2d at 787. Similarly, in *Colorado Springs National Bank v. U.S.*, 505 F.2d 1185 (10th Cir. 1974), the issue was whether costs incurred by a bank in creating credit card services for customers were currently deductible or had to be capitalized. The Tenth Circuit found that credit cards represented merely a new method for banks to provide letters of credit to their customers. Relying on *Briarcliff*, the court held the bank had no property interest in the credit card procedures. Under these circumstances, the costs it incurred in establishing the credit card operation were currently deductible.

Clearly the costs of entering a new line of business ought not be currently deductible, but in light of *INDOPCO*, the question arises as to whether even the expansion costs of an existing business must be capitalized on the grounds they are necessarily productive of significant future benefits. The Service appears not to take this position. In Revenue Ruling 2000-4, 2000-1 C.B. 331, the Service seemingly re-affirmed the *Briarcliff* holding of deductibility. The issue in that ruling was whether the taxpayer could deduct the costs incurred in obtaining, maintaining and renewing certifications of compliance with certain international quality standards, known as "ISO 9000," intended to ensure the provision of quality services or products. In the course of holding the ISO 9000 certification costs to be deductible because, under *INDOPCO*, they did not result in future benefits that were more than incidental, the Service specifically cited *Briarcliff* in support of the statement that "even if ISO 9000 certification facilitates the expansion of the taxpayer's existing business, the mere ability to sell in new markets and to new customers, without more, does not result in significant future benefits." The 2004 intangibles regulations do not appear to run counter to this position.

2. Business Downsizing Cost

Costs associated with business "down-sizing," the converse of expansion, can also raise capitalization questions. In Revenue Ruling 94-77, 1994-2 C.B. 19, the Service considered whether severance payments made by a taxpayer to its employees were deductible as business expenses or, in view of *INDOPCO*, had to be capitalized. Concluding the severance payments did not have to be capitalized but could be deducted currently, the Service stated: "although severance payments made by a taxpayer to its employees in connection with a business down-sizing may produce some future benefits, such as reducing operating costs and increasing operating efficiencies, these payments principally relate to previously rendered services of those employees. Therefore, such severance payments are generally deductible as business expenses."

3. Employee Training Costs

Expenditures for employee training also raise capitalization issues. Should the costs of maintaining the quality of a business' workforce be viewed as comparable to incidental repairs and therefore be currently deductible, or are they costs which provide longterm benefits and thus constitute capital expenditures? Historically, training costs, including the costs of trainers and expenses incurred in updating training manuals, have been deemed currently deductible expenses. Does *IN-DOPCO* change that result? The answer, according to Revenue Ruling 96-62, 1996-2 C.B. 9, is "No." While acknowledging there may be some future benefits to be derived from employee training, the ruling nonetheless states that training costs will generally be deductible business expenses. The ruling cites examples of costs associated with training employees to operate new equipment, and training new employees of an ongoing business. According to the ruling, training costs must be capitalized only in unusual circumstances where the training provides benefits significantly beyond those traditionally associated with training in the ordinary course of business. The ruling addresses only those employee training costs incurred while a taxpayer is actually carrying on a trade or business and does not apply to start-up costs.

4. Advertising Expenses

Advertising expenses may often provide benefits that continue well beyond the current taxable year. A case could presumably be made for capitalizing all advertising costs except to the extent the taxpayer can demonstrate their benefits are sufficiently short-lived. Nonetheless, the long-standing administrative practice is generally to treat advertising expenses as currently deductible. In the aftermath of *INDOPCO*, the Service, in Revenue Ruling 92-80, 1992-2 C.B. 57, reaffirmed the deductibility of advertising expenses: "The *INDOPCO* decision does not affect the treatment of advertising costs under section 162(a) of the Code. These costs are generally deductible under that section even though advertising may have some future effect on business activities, as in the case of institutional or goodwill advertising. *See* section 1.162-1(a) and section 1.162-20(a)(2) of the regulations."

In *RJR Nabisco Inc. v. Commissioner*, T.C. Memo. 1998-252, the Commissioner sought to distinguish between the costs of developing advertising campaigns and the costs of executing or carrying out those campaigns arguing that advertising execution expenditures generate principally short-term benefits and are thus currently deductible, whereas advertising campaign expenditures provide only long-term benefits and ought to be capitalized. The Tax Court rejected the distinction:

> Although the case law admits the possibility of allocation between the short-and long-term benefits of advertising expenditures and, thus, would provide a basis for the Commissioner to insist that a taxpayer prove the portion of his advertising expenditures allocable to current benefits, the authorities previously cited, section 1.162-20(a)(2), Income Tax Regs., and Rev. Rul. 92-80, *supra*, establish that the Secretary and the Commissioner, respectively, have eschewed that approach with respect to ordinary business advertising, even if long-term benefits (*e.g.*, goodwill) are the taxpayer's primary objective. . . . The result, as a practical matter, is that, notwithstanding certain long-term benefits, expenditures for ordinary business advertising are ordinary business expenses if the taxpayer can show a sufficient connection between the expenditure and the taxpayer's business. . . . Generally, [however,] expenditures for billboards, signs, and other tangible assets associated with advertising remain subject to the usual rules regarding capitalization. . . . *Alabama Coca-Cola Bottling Co. v. Commissioner*, T.C. Memo 1969–123 (cost of signs, clock, and scoreboards having a useful life of 5 years not deductible). . . .

The regulations appear to follow this approach. See, for example, Reg. § 1.263(a)-4(l) Ex. 7, which concludes that capitalization is not required for "product launch costs" that include payments "to develop and implement a marketing strategy and an advertising campaign to raise consumer awareness" for a new pharmaceutical product.[6]

---

[6] The example notes that the payments are not amounts paid (1) to acquire or create, or facilitate the acquisition or creation of, one of the specified self-created intangibles subject to capitalization; or (2) to create a separate and distinct intangible asset.

E. Purchase or Lease

Section 162(a)(3) specifically authorizes the deduction of rental payments with respect to property used in a trade or business but only if the taxpayer does not take title and has no equity in the property. The line between a lease and a purchase agreement may in some cases be very thin, causing the Service to question the deductibility of "rent" the taxpayer is paying. Are the rental payments being made by the taxpayer really disguised acquisition costs, routinely capital in nature, or are they what they purport to be, rental payments applicable to the current year and routinely deductible? Why might a taxpayer prefer to characterize as a lease an arrangement that is, in substance, an arrangement to acquire actual ownership of the property? *See* Problem 1(d).

COMMISSIONER v. IDAHO POWER CO.
United States Supreme Court
418 U.S. 1 (1974)

Mr. Justice Blackmun delivered the opinion of the Court.

This case presents the sole issue whether, for federal income tax purposes, a taxpayer is entitled to a deduction from gross income, under Sec. 167(a), for depreciation on equipment the taxpayer owns and uses in the construction of its own capital facilities, or whether the capitalization provision of Sec. 263(a)(1) of the Code, 26 U.S.C. Sec. 263(a)(1), bars the deduction.

I.

Nearly all the relevant facts are stipulated. The taxpayer-respondent, Idaho Power Company, is a Maine corporation organized in 1915, with its principal place of business at Boise, Idaho. It is a public utility engaged in the production, transmission, distribution, and sale of electric energy. The taxpayer keeps its books and files its federal income tax returns on the calendar year accrual basis. The tax years at issue are 1962 and 1963.

For many years, the taxpayer has used its own equipment and employees in the construction of improvements and additions to its capital facilities. The major work has consisted of transmission lines, transmission switching stations, distribution lines, distribution stations, and connecting facilities.

During 1962 and 1963, the tax years in question, taxpayer owned and used in its business a wide variety of automotive transportation equipment, including passenger cars, trucks of all descriptions, power-operated equipment, and trailers. Radio communication devices were affixed to the equipment and were used in its daily operations. The transportation equipment was used in part for operation and maintenance and in part for the construction of capital facilities having a useful life of more than one year.

On its books, the taxpayer used various methods of charging costs incurred in connection with its transportation equipment either to current expense or to capital accounts. To the extent the equipment was used in construction, the taxpayer charged depreciation of the equipment, as well as all operating and maintenance costs (other than pension contributions and social security and motor vehicle taxes) to the capital assets so constructed. This was done either directly or through clearing accounts in accordance with procedures prescribed by the Federal Power Commission and adopted by the Idaho Public Utilities Commission.

For federal income tax purposes, however, the taxpayer treated the depreciation on transportation equipment differently. It claimed as a deduction from gross income all the year's depreciation on such equipment, including that portion attributable to its use in constructing capital facilities. The depreciation was computed on a composite life of 10 years and under straight-line and declining-balance methods. The other operating and maintenance costs the taxpayer had charged on its books to capital were not claimed as current expenses and were not deducted.

To summarize: On its books, in accordance with Federal Power Commission-Idaho Public Utilities Commission prescribed methods, the taxpayer capitalized the construction-related depreciation, but for income tax purposes that depreciation increment was claimed as a deduction under Sec. 167(a).

Upon audit, the Commissioner of Internal Revenue disallowed the deduction for the construction-related depreciation. He ruled that depreciation was a non-deductible capital expenditure to which Sec. 263(a)(1) had application. He added the amount of the depreciation so disallowed to the taxpayer's adjusted basis in its capital facilities, and then allowed a deduction for an appropriate amount of depreciation on the addition, computed over the useful life (30 years or more) of the property constructed. A deduction for depreciation of the transportation equipment to the extent of its use in day-to-day operation and maintenance was also allowed. The result of these adjustments was the disallowance of depreciation, as claimed by the taxpayer on its returns, in the net amounts of $140,429.75 and $96,811.95 for 1962 and 1963, respectively. This gave rise to asserted deficiencies in taxpayer's income taxes for those two years of $73,023.47 and $50,342.21.

The taxpayer asserts that its transportation equipment is used in its "trade or business" and that depreciation thereon is therefore deductible under Sec. 167(a)(1) of the Code. The Commissioner concedes that Sec. 167 may be said to have a literal application to depreciation on equipment used in capital construction, Brief for Petitioner 16, but contends that the provision must be read in light of Sec. 263(a)(1) which specifically disallows any deduction for an amount "paid out for new buildings or for permanent improvements or betterments." He argues that Sec. 263 takes precedence over Sec. 167 by virtue of what he calls the "priority-ordering" terms (and what the taxpayer describes as "housekeeping" provisions) of Sec. 161 of the Code, 26 U.S.C. Sec. 161, and that sound principles of accounting and taxation mandate the capitalization of this depreciation.

It is worth noting the various items that are not at issue here. The mathematics, as such, is not in dispute. The taxpayer has capitalized, as part of its cost of acquisition of capital assets, the operating and maintenance costs (other than depreciation, pension contributions, and social security and motor vehicle taxes) of the transportation equipment attributable to construction. This is not contested. The Commissioner does not dispute that the portion of the transportation equipment's depreciation allocable to operation and maintenance of facilities, in contrast with construction thereof, qualifies as a deduction from gross income. There is no disagreement as to the allocation of depreciation between construction and maintenance. The issue, thus, comes down primarily to a question of timing, as the Court of Appeals recognized, 477 F.2d, at 692, that is, whether the construction-related depreciation is to be amortized and deducted over the *shorter* life of the equipment or, instead, is to be amortized and deducted over the *longer* life of the capital facilities constructed.

II.

Our primary concern is with the necessity to treat construction-related depreciation in a manner that comports with accounting and taxation realities. Over a period of time a capital asset is consumed and, correspondingly over that period, its theoretical value and utility are thereby reduced. Depreciation is an accounting device which recognizes that the physical consumption of a capital asset is a true cost, since the asset is being depleted.[7] As the process of consumption continues, and depreciation is claimed and allowed, the asset's adjusted income tax basis is reduced to reflect the distribution of its cost over the accounting periods affected. The Court stated in *Hertz Corp. v. United States*, 364 U.S. 122, 126 (1960): "[T]he purpose of depreciation accounting is to allocate the expense of using an asset to the various periods which are benefitted by that asset". . . . When the asset is used to further the taxpayer's day-to-day business operations, the periods of benefit usually correlate with the production of income. Thus, to the extent that equipment is used in such operations, a current depreciation deduction is an appropriate offset to gross income currently produced. It is clear, however, that different principles are implicated when the consumption of the asset takes place in the construction of other assets that, in the future, will produce income themselves. In this latter situation, the cost represented by depreciation does not correlate with production of current income. Rather the cost, although certainly presently incurred, is related to the future and is appropriately allocated as part of the cost of acquiring an income-producing capital asset.

The Court of Appeals opined that the purpose of the depreciation allowance under the Code was to provide a means of cost recovery, *Knoxville v. Knoxville Water Co.*, 212 U.S. 1, 13–14 (1909), and that this Court's decisions, *e.g., Detroit*

---

[7] The Committee on Terminology of the American Institute of Certified Public Accountants has discussed various definitions of depreciation and concluded that:

> These definitions view depreciation, broadly speaking, as describing not downward changes of value regardless of their causes but a money cost incident to exhaustion of usefulness. The term is sometimes applied to the exhaustion itself, but the committee considers it desirable to emphasize the cost concept as the primary if not the sole accounting meaning of the term: thus, *depreciation* means the cost of such exhaustion, as *wages* means the cost of labor.

2 APB Accounting Principles, Accounting Terminology Bulletin No. 1 — Review and Resume 48, p. 9512 (1973) (emphasis in original).

Edison Co. v. Commissioner, 319 U.S. 98, 101 (1943), endorse a theory of replacement through "a fund to restore the property." 477 F.2d, at 691. Although tax-free replacement of a depreciating investment is one purpose of depreciation accounting, it alone does not require the result claimed by the taxpayer here. Only last Term, in *United States v. Chicago, B. & Q.R. Co.*, 412 U.S. 401 (1973), we rejected replacement as the strict and sole purpose of depreciation:

> Whatever may be the desirability of creating a depreciation reserve under these circumstances, as a matter of good business and accounting practice, the answer is . . . [d]epreciation reflects the cost of an existing capital asset, not the cost of a potential replacement.

Id., at 415. Even were we to look to replacement, it is the replacement of the constructed facilities, not the equipment used to build them, with which we would be concerned. If the taxpayer now were to decide not to construct any more capital facilities with its own equipment and employees, it, in theory, would have no occasion to replace its equipment to the extent that it was consumed in prior construction.

Accepted accounting practice and established tax principles require the capitalization of the cost of acquiring a capital asset. In *Woodward v. Commissioner*, 397 U.S. 572, 575 (1970), the Court observed: "It has long been recognized, as a general matter, that costs incurred in the acquisition . . . of a capital asset are to be treated as capital expenditures." This principle has obvious application to the acquisition of a capital asset by purchase, but it has been applied, as well, to the costs incurred in a taxpayer's construction of capital facilities.

There can be little question that other construction-related expense items, such as tools, materials, and wages paid construction workers, are to be treated as part of the cost of acquisition of a capital asset. The taxpayer does not dispute this. Of course, reasonable wages paid in the carrying on of a trade or business qualify as a deduction from gross income. Sec. 162(a)(1) of the 1954 Code, 26 U.S.C. Sec. 162(a)(1). But when wages are paid in connection with the construction or acquisition of a capital asset, they must be capitalized and are then entitled to be amortized over the life of the capital asset so acquired. . . .

Construction-related depreciation is not unlike expenditures for wages for construction workers. The significant fact is that the exhaustion of construction equipment does not represent the final disposition of the taxpayer's investment in that equipment; rather, the investment in the equipment is assimilated into the cost of the capital asset construction. Construction-related depreciation on the equipment is not an expense to the taxpayer of its day-to-day business. It is, however, appropriately recognized as a part of the taxpayer's cost or investment in the capital asset. The taxpayer's own accounting procedure reflects this treatment, for on its books the construction-related depreciation was capitalized by a credit to the equipment account and a debit to the capital facility account. By the same token, this capitalization prevents the distortion of income that would otherwise occur if depreciation properly allocable to asset acquisition were deducted from gross income currently realized. . . .

An additional pertinent factor is that capitalization of construction-related depreciation by the taxpayer who does its own construction work maintains tax parity with the taxpayer who has its construction work done by an independent contractor. The depreciation on the contractor's equipment incurred during the performance of the job will be an element of cost charged by the contractor for his construction services, and the entire cost, of course, must be capitalized by the taxpayer having the construction work performed. The Court of Appeals' holding would lead to disparate treatment among taxpayers because it would allow the firm with sufficient resources to construct its own facilities and to obtain a current deduction, whereas another firm without such resources would be required to capitalize its entire cost including depreciation charged to it by the contractor.

The presence of Sec. 263(a)(1) in the Code is of significance. Its literal language denies a deduction for "[a]ny amount paid out" for construction or permanent improvement of facilities. The taxpayer contends, and the Court of Appeals held, that depreciation of construction equipment represents merely a decrease in value and is not an amount "paid out," within the meaning of Sec. 263(a)(1). We disagree.

The purpose of Sec. 263 is to reflect the basic principle that a capital expenditure may not be deducted from current income. It serves to prevent a taxpayer from utilizing currently a deduction properly attributable, through amortization, to later tax years when the capital asset becomes income producing. The regulations state that the capital expenditures to which Sec. 263(a) extends include the "cost of acquisition, construction, or erection of buildings." Treas. Reg. Sec. 1.263(a)-2(a). This manifests an administrative understanding that for purposes of Sec. 263(a)(1), "amount paid out" equates with "cost incurred." The Internal Revenue Service for some time has taken the position that construction-related depreciation is to be capitalized. Rev. Rul. 59-380, 1959-2 Cum. Bull. 87; Rev. Rul. 55-252, 1955-1 Cum. Bull. 319.

There is no question that the cost of the transportation equipment was "paid out" in the same manner as the cost of supplies, materials, and other equipment, and the wages of construction workers. The taxpayer does not question the capitalization of these other items as elements of the cost of acquiring a capital asset. We see no reason to treat construction-related depreciation differently. In acquiring the transportation equipment, taxpayer "paid out" the equipment's purchase price; depreciation is simply the means of allocating the payment over the various accounting periods affected. As the Tax Court stated in *Brooks v. Commissioner*, 50 T.C., at 935, "depreciation — inasmuch as it represents a using up of capital — is as much an 'expenditure' as the using up of labor or other items of direct cost."

Finally, the priority-ordering directive of Sec. 161 — or, for that matter, Sec. 261 of the Code, 26 U.S.C. Sec. 261 — requires that the capitalization provision of Sec. 263(a) take precedence, on the facts here, over Sec. 167(a). Section 161 provides that deductions specified in Part VI of Subchapter B of the Income Tax Subtitle of the Code are "subject to the exceptions provided in part IX." Part VI includes Sec. 167 and Part IX includes Sec. 263. The clear import of Sec. 161 is that, with stated exceptions set forth either in Sec. 263 itself or provided for elsewhere (as, for example, in Sec. 404 relating to pension contributions), none of which is applicable here, an expenditure incurred in acquiring capital assets must be capitalized even when the expenditure otherwise might be deemed deductible under Part VI.

We hold that the equipment depreciation allocable to taxpayer's construction of capital facilities is to be capitalized.

The judgment of the Court of Appeals is reversed.

It is so ordered.

MIDLAND EMPIRE PACKING COMPANY v. COMMISSIONER
United States Tax Court
14 T.C. 635 (1950)

ARUNDELL, JUDGE:

The issue in this case is whether an expenditure for a concrete lining in petitioner's basement to oilproof it against an oil nuisance created by a neighboring refinery is deductible as an ordinary and necessary expense under section 23(a) of the Internal Revenue Code, on the theory it was an expenditure for a repair . . . .

The respondent has contended, in part, that the expenditure is for a capital improvement and should be recovered through depreciation charges and is, therefore, not deductible as an ordinary and necessary business expense . . . .

It is none too easy to determine on which side of the line certain expenditures fall so that they may be accorded their proper treatment for tax purposes. In *Illinois Merchants Trust Co., Executor*, 4 B.T.A. 103, at page 106, we discussed this subject in some detail and in our opinion said:

> . . . In determining whether an expenditure is a capital one or is chargeable against operating income, it is necessary to bear in mind the purpose for which the expenditure was made. To repair is to restore to a sound state or to mend, while a replacement connotes a substitution. A repair is an expenditure for the purpose of keeping the property in an ordinarily efficient operating condition. It does not add to the value of the property, nor does it appreciably prolong its life. It merely keeps the property in an operating condition over its probable useful life for the uses for which it was acquired. Expenditures for that purpose are distinguishable from those for replacements, alterations, improvements, or additions which prolong the life of the property, increase its value, or make it adaptable to a different use. The one is a maintenance charge, while the others are additions to capital investment which should not be applied against current earnings.

It will be seen from our findings of fact that for some 25 years prior to the taxable year petitioner had used the basement rooms of its plant as a place for the curing of hams and bacon and for the storage of meat and hides. The basement had been entirely satisfactory for this purpose over the entire period in spite of the fact that there was some seepage of water into the rooms from time to time. In the taxable year it was found that not only water, but oil, was seeping through the concrete walls of the basement of the packing plant and, while the water would soon drain out, the oil would not, and there was left on the basement floor a thick scum of oil which gave off a strong odor that permeated the air of the entire plant, and the fumes from the oil created a fire hazard. It appears that the oil which came from a nearby refinery had also gotten into the water wells which served to furnish water for petitioner's plant, and as a result of this whole condition the Federal meat inspectors advised petitioner that it must discontinue the use of the water from the wells and oilproof the basement, or else shut down its plant.

To meet this situation, petitioner during the taxable year undertook steps to oilproof the basement by adding a concrete lining to the walls from the floor to a height of about four feet and also added concrete to the floor of the basement. It is the cost of this work which it seeks to deduct as a repair. The basement was not enlarged by this work, nor did the oilproofing serve to make it more desirable for the purpose for which it had been used through the years prior to the time that the oil nuisance had occurred. The evidence is that the expenditure did not add to the value or prolong the expected life of the property over what they were before the event occurred which made the repairs necessary. It is true that after the work was done the seepage of water, as well as oil, was stopped, but, as already stated, the presence of the water had never been found objectionable. The repairs merely served to keep the property in an operating condition over its probable useful life for the purpose for which it was used.

While it is conceded on brief that the expenditure was "necessary," respondent contends that the encroachment of the oil nuisance on petitioner's property was not an "ordinary" expense in petitioner's particular business. But the fact that petitioner had not theretofore been called upon to make a similar expenditure to prevent damage and disaster to its property does not remove that expense from the classification of "ordinary" for, as stated in *Welch v. Helvering*, 290 U.S. 111, "ordinary in this context does not mean that the payments must be habitual or normal in the sense that the same taxpayer will have to make them often . . . the expense is an ordinary one because we know from experience that payments for such a purpose, whether the amount is large or small, are the common and accepted means of defense against attack. *Cf. Kornhauser v. United States*, 276 U.S. 145. The situation is unique in the life of the individual affected, but not in the life of the group, the community, of which he is a part." Steps to protect a business building from the seepage of oil from a nearby refinery, which had been erected long subsequent to the time petitioner started to operate its plant, would seem to us to be a normal thing to do, and in certain sections of the country it must be a common experience to protect one's property from the seepage of oil. Expenditures to accomplish this result are likewise normal.

In *American Bemberg Corporation*, 10 T.C. 361, we allowed as deductions, on the ground that they were ordinary and necessary expenses, extensive expenditures made to prevent disaster, although the repairs were of a type which had never been needed before and were unlikely to recur. In that case the taxpayer, to stop cave-ins of soil which were threatening destruction of its manufacturing plant, hired an engineering firm which drilled to the bedrock and injected grout to fill the cavities where practicable, and made incidental replacements and repairs, including tightening of the fluid carriers. In two successive years the taxpayer expended $734,316.76 and $199,154.33, respectively, for such drilling and grouting and $153,474.20 and $79,687.29, respectively, for capital replacements. We found that the cost (other than replacement) of this program did not make good the depreciation previously allowed, and stated in our opinion:

> In connection with the purpose of the work, the Proctor program was intended to avert a plant-wide disaster and avoid forced abandonment of the plant. The purpose was not to improve, better, extend, or increase the original plant, nor to prolong its original useful life. Its continued operation was endangered; the purpose of the expenditures was to enable petitioner to continue the plant in operation not on any new or better scale, but on the same scale and, so far as possible, as efficiently as it had operated before. The purpose was not to rebuild or replace the plant in whole or in part, but to keep the same plant as it was and where it was.

The petitioner here made the repairs in question in order that it might continue to operate its plant. Not only was there danger of fire from the oil and fumes, but the presence of the oil led the Federal meat inspectors to declare the basement an unsuitable place for the purpose for which it had been used for a quarter of a century. After the expenditures were made, the plant did not operate on a changed or larger scale, nor was it thereafter suitable for new or additional uses. The expenditure served only to permit petitioner to continue the use of the plant, and particularly the basement for its normal operations.

In our opinion, the expenditure of $4,868.81 for lining the basement walls and floor was essentially a repair and, as such, it is deductible as an ordinary and necessary business expense.

Decision will be entered under Rule 50.

MT. MORRIS DRIVE-IN THEATRE CO. v. COMMISSIONER
United States Tax Court
25 T.C. 272 (1955)

The only issue for decision is whether the amount of $8,224 spent by the petitioner in 1950 to construct a drainage system was deductible either as an ordinary and necessary business expense or as a loss, as contended by the petitioner, or whether it was a nondepreciable capital expenditure, as determined by the Commissioner.

FINDINGS OF FACT

In 1947 petitioner purchased 13 acres of farm land located on the outskirts of Flint, Michigan, upon which it proceeded to construct a drive-in or outdoor theatre. Prior to its purchase by the petitioner the land on which the theatre was built was farm land and contained vegetation. The slope of the land was such that the natural drainage of water was from the southerly line to the northerly boundary of the property and thence onto the adjacent land, owned by David and Mary D. Nickola, which was used both for farming and as a trailer park. The petitioner's land sloped sharply from south to north and also sloped from the east downward towards the west so that most of the drainage from the petitioner's property was onto the southwest corner of the Nickolas' land. The topography of the land purchased by petitioner was well known to petitioner at the time it was purchased and developed. The petitioner did not change the general slope of its land in constructing the drive-in theatre, but it removed the covering vegetation from the land, slightly increased the grade, and built aisles or ramps which were covered with gravel and were somewhat raised so that the passengers in the automobiles would be able to view the picture on the large outdoor screen.

As a result of petitioner's construction on and use of this land, rain water falling upon it drained with an increased flow into and upon the adjacent property of the Nickolas. This result should reasonably have been anticipated by petitioner at the time when the construction work was done.

The Nickolas complained to the petitioner at various times after petitioner began the construction of the theatre that the work resulted in an acceleration and concentration of the flow of water which drained from the petitioner's property onto the Nickolas' land causing damage to their crops and roadways. On or about October 11, 1948, the Nickolas filed a suit against the petitioner in the Circuit Court for the County of Genesee, State of Michigan, asking for an award for damages done to their property by the accelerated and concentrated drainage of the water and for a permanent injunction restraining the defendant from permitting such drainage to continue. Following the filing of an answer by the petitioner and of a reply thereto by the Nickolas, the suit was settled by an agreement dated June 27, 1950. This agreement provided for the construction by the petitioner of a drainage system to carry water from its northern boundary across the Nickolas' property and thence to a public drain. The cost of maintaining the system was to be shared by the petitioner and the Nickolas, and the latter granted the petitioner and its successors an easement across their land for the purpose of constructing and maintaining the drainage system. The construction of the drain was completed in October 1950 under the supervision of engineers employed by the petitioner and the Nickolas at a cost to the petitioner of $8,224, which amount was paid by it in November 1950. The performance by the petitioner on its part of the agreement to construct the drainage system and to maintain the portion for which it was responsible constituted a full release of the Nickolas' claims against it. The petitioner chose to settle the dispute by constructing the drainage system because it did not wish to risk the possibility that continued litigation might result in a permanent injunction against its use of the drive-in theatre and because it wished to eliminate the cause of the friction between it and the adjacent landowners, who were in a position to seriously interfere with the petitioner's use of its property for outdoor theatre purposes. A settlement based on a monetary payment for past damages, the petitioner believed, would not remove the threat of claims for future damages.

On its 1950 income and excess profits tax return the petitioner claimed a deduction of $822.40 for depreciation of the drainage system for the period July 1, 1950, to December 31, 1950. The Commissioner disallowed without itemization $5,514.60 of a total depreciation expense deduction of $19,326.41 claimed by the petitioner. In its petition the petitioner asserted that the entire amount spent to construct the drainage system was fully deductible in 1950 as an ordinary and necessary business expense incurred in the settlement of a lawsuit, or, in the alternative, as a loss, and claimed a refund of part of the $10,591.56 of income and excess profits tax paid by it for that year.

The drainage system was a permanent improvement to the petitioner's property, and the cost thereof constituted a capital expenditure.

The stipulation of facts and the exhibits annexed thereto are incorporated herein by this reference.

OPINION

KERN, JUDGE:

When petitioner purchased, in 1947, the land which it intended to use for a drive-in theatre, its president was thoroughly familiar with the topography of this land which was such that when the covering vegetation was removed and graveled ramps were constructed and used by its patrons, the flow of natural precipitation on the lands of abutting property owners would be materially accelerated. Some provision should have been made to solve this drainage problem in order to avoid annoyance and harassment to its neighbors. If petitioner had included in its original construction plans an expenditure for a proper drainage system no one could doubt that such an expenditure would have been capital in nature.

Within a year after petitioner had finished its inadequate construction of the drive-in theatre, the need of a proper drainage system was forcibly called to its attention by one of the neighboring property owners, and under the threat of a lawsuit filed approximately a year after the theatre was constructed, the drainage system was built by petitioner who now seeks to deduct its cost as an ordinary and necessary business expense, or as a loss.

We agree with respondent that the cost to petitioner of acquiring and constructing a drainage system in connection with its drive-in theatre was a capital expenditure.

There was no sudden catastrophic loss caused by a "physical fault" undetected by the taxpayer in spite of due precautions taken by it at the time of its original construction work as in *American Bemberg Corporation*, 10 T.C. 361; no unforeseeable external factor as in *Midland Empire Packing Co.*, 14 T.C. 635; and no change in the cultivation of farm property caused by improvements in technique and made many years after the property in question was put to productive use as in *J. H. Collingwood*, 20 T.C. 937. In the instant case, it was obvious at the time when the drive-in theatre was constructed, that a drainage system would be required to properly dispose of the natural precipitation normally to be expected, and that until this was accomplished, petitioner's capital investment was incomplete. In addition, it should be emphasized that here there was no mere restoration or rearrangement of the original capital asset, but there was the acquisition and construction of a capital asset which petitioner had not previously had, namely, a new drainage system.

That this drainage system was acquired and constructed and that payments therefor were made in compromise of a lawsuit is not determinative of whether such payments were ordinary and necessary business expenses or capital expenditures. "The decisive test is still the character of the transaction which gives rise to the payment." *Hales-Mullaly v. Commissioner*, 131 F.2d 509, 511, 512.

In our opinion the character of the transaction in the instant case indicates that the transaction was a capital expenditure.

Reviewed by the Court.

Decision will be entered for the respondent.

RAUM, J., concurring:

The expenditure herein was plainly capital in nature, and, as the majority opinion points out, if provision had been made in the original plans for the construction of a drainage system there could hardly be any question that its cost would have been treated as a capital outlay. The character of the expenditure is not changed merely because it is made at a subsequent time, and I think it wholly irrelevant whether the necessity for the drainage system could have been foreseen, or whether the payment therefor was made as a result of the pressure of a law suit.

FISHER, J., agrees with this concurring opinion.

RICE, J., dissenting:

It seems to me that *J. H. Collingwood*, 20 T.C. 937 (1953), *Midland Empire Packing Co.*, 14 T.C. 635 (1950), *American Bemberg Corporation*, 10 T.C. 361 (1948), *aff'd*, 177 F.2d 200 (C.A. 1949), and *Illinois Merchants Trust Co., Executor*, 4 B.T.A. 103 (1926), are ample authority for the conclusion that the expenditure which petitioner made was an ordinary and necessary business expense, which did not improve, better, extend, increase, or prolong the useful life of its property. The expenditure did not cure the original geological defect of the natural drainage onto the Nickolas' land, but only dealt with the intermediate consequence thereof. The majority opinion does not distinguish those cases adequately. And since those cases and the result reached herein do not seem to me to be able to "live together," I cannot agree with the majority that the expenditure here was capital in nature.

OPPER, JOHNSON, BRUCE and MULRONEY, J.J. agree with this dissent.

REVENUE RULING 2001-4
2001-1 C.B. 295

FACTS

X is a commercial airline engaged in the business of transporting passengers and freight throughout the United States and abroad. To conduct its business, *X* owns or leases various types of aircraft. As a condition of maintaining its operating license and airworthiness certification for these aircraft, *X* is required by the Federal Aviation Administration "FAA" to establish and adhere to a continuous maintenance program for each aircraft within its fleet. These programs, which are designed by X and the aircraft's manufacturer and approved by the FAA, are incorporated into each aircraft's maintenance manual. The maintenance manuals require a variety of periodic maintenance visits at various intervals during the operating lives of each aircraft. The most extensive of these for X is termed a "heavy maintenance visit" (also known in the industry as a "D check," "heavy C check," or "overhaul"), which is required to be performed by X approximately every eight years of aircraft operation. The purpose of a heavy maintenance visit, according to X's maintenance manual, is to prevent deterioration of the inherent safety and reliability levels of the aircraft equipment and, if such deterioration occurs, to restore the equipment to their inherent levels.

In [Situation 1], X reasonably anticipated at the time the aircraft was placed in service that the aircraft would be useful in its trade or business for up to 25 years, taking into account the repairs and maintenance necessary to keep the aircraft in an ordinarily efficient operating condition. In addition, . . . the aircraft . . . is fully depreciated for federal income tax purposes at the time of the heavy maintenance visit.

Situation 1

In 2000, X incurred $2 million for the labor and materials necessary to perform a heavy maintenance visit on the airframe of Aircraft 1, which X acquired in 1984 for $15 million (excluding the cost of engines). To perform the heavy maintenance visit, X extensively disassembled the airframe, removing items such as its engines, landing gear, cabin and passenger compartment seats, side and ceiling panels, baggage stowage bins, galleys, lavatories, floor boards, cargo loading systems, and flight control surfaces. As specified by X's maintenance manual for Aircraft 1, X then performed certain tasks on the disassembled airframe for the purpose of preventing deterioration of the inherent safety and reliability levels of the airframe. These tasks included lubrication and service; operational and visual checks; inspection and functional checks; restoration of minor parts and components; and removal, discard, and replacement of certain life-limited single cell parts, such as cartridges, canisters, cylinders, and disks.

Whenever the execution of a task revealed cracks, corrosion, excessive wear, or dysfunctional operation, X was required by the maintenance manual to restore the airframe to an acceptable condition. This restoration involved burnishing corrosion; repairing cracks, dents, gouges, punctures, or scratches by burnishing, blending, stop-drilling, or applying skin patches or doublers over the affected area; tightening or replacing loose or missing fasteners, rivets, screws, bolts, nuts, or clamps; repairing or replacing torn or damaged seals, gaskets, or valves; repairing or replacing damaged or missing placards, decals, labels, or stencils; additional cleaning, lubricating, or painting; further inspecting or testing, including the use of sophisticated non-destructive inspection methods; repairing fiberglass or laminated parts; replacing bushings, bearings, hinges, handles, switches, gauges, or indicators; repairing chaffed or damaged wiring; repairing or adjusting various landing gear or flight surface control cables; replacing light bulbs, window panes, lenses, or shields; replacing anti-skid materials and stops on floors, pedals, and stairways;

replacing floor boards; and performing minor repairs on ribs, spars, frames, longerons, stringers, beams, and supports.

In addition to the tasks described above, X also performed additional work as part of the heavy maintenance visit for Aircraft 1. This work included applying corrosion prevention and control compounds; stripping and repainting the aircraft exterior; and cleaning, repairing, and painting airframe interior items such as seats, carpets, baggage stowage bins, ceiling and sidewall panels, lavatories, galleys, and passenger service units. Other additional work included implementing certain outstanding service bulletins ("SBs") issued by the aircraft manufacturer and airworthiness directives ("ADs") issued by the FAA. Implementing these SBs and ADs involved inspecting specific skin locations and applying doublers over the areas where cracks were found; inspecting bolts or fasteners at specific locations, and replacing those found to be broken, worn, or missing; and installing structural reinforcements between body frames in a small area in the lower aft fuselage to reduce skin wrinkling and replacing a small number of the wrinkled skin panels in this area with stronger skin panels.

None of the work performed by X as part of the heavy maintenance visit (including the execution of SBs and ADs) for Aircraft 1 resulted in a material upgrade or addition to its airframe or involved the replacement of any (or a significant portion of any) major component or substantial structural part of the air-frame. This work maintained the relative value of the aircraft. The value of the aircraft declines as it ages even if the heavy maintenance work is performed.

After 45 days, the heavy maintenance visit was completed, and Aircraft 1 was reassembled, tested, and returned to X's fleet. X then continued to use Aircraft 1 for the same purposes and in the same manner that it did prior to the performance of the heavy maintenance visit. The performance of the heavy maintenance visit did not extend the useful life of the airframe beyond the 25-year useful life that X anticipated when it acquired the airframe.

ANALYSIS

In *Situation 1*, the heavy maintenance visit on Aircraft 1 primarily involved inspecting, testing, servicing, repairing, reconditioning, cleaning, stripping, and repainting numerous airframe parts and components. The heavy maintenance visit did not involve replacements, alterations, improvements, or additions to the airframe that appreciably prolonged its useful life, materially increased its value, or adapted it to a new or different use. Rather, the heavy maintenance visit merely kept the airframe in an ordinarily efficient operating condition over its anticipated useful life for the uses for which the property was acquired. *See Illinois Merchant Trust Co. at 106*; *Estate of Walling at 192–193*; Ingram Industries, Inc. at 538–539. The fact that the taxpayer was required to perform the heavy maintenance visit to maintain its airworthiness certificate does not affect this determination. *See Midland Empire Packing at 642.*

Although the heavy maintenance visit did involve the replacement of numerous airframe parts with new parts, none of these replacements required the substitution of any (or a significant portion of any) major components or substantial structural parts of the airframe so that the airframe as a whole increased in value, life expectancy, or use. . . . Thus, the facts in *Situation I* are distinguishable from those in *Rev. Rul. 88-57* in which all of the structural components of a railroad freight car were either reconditioned or replaced so that the car was restored to a "like new" condition with a new, additional service life of 12 to 14 years. Moreover, the heavy maintenance visit also did not restore the airframe, or make good exhaustion for which an allowance had been made within the meaning of § 263 (a) (2). In order to have a restoration under § 263 (a) (2), much more extensive work would have to be done so as to substantially prolong the useful life of the airframe. Thus, the costs of the heavy maintenance visit constitute expenses for incidental repairs and maintenance under § 1.162-4.

. . . Accordingly, the costs incurred by *X* for the heavy maintenance visit in *Situation 1* may be deducted as ordinary and necessary business expenses under § 162.

Chapter 14

DEPRECIATION

I. PROBLEMS

1. With respect to each of the following assets associated with a new luxury hotel, explain whether the asset is depreciable or nondepreciable.

   (a) The tract of land on which the hotel is constructed.

   (b) Fences, concrete sidewalks, and driveways on the grounds of the hotel.

   (c) Valuable antique furnishings and carpets that are part of the decor of the public spaces throughout the hotel.

   (d) The furnishings in the guest rooms.

2. Liz owns an engineering business. She consults you regarding the deductibility of a sophisticated piece of new equipment she purchased for use in her business on January 19, Year 1. The purchase price for the equipment was $1,000,000. Liz used $200,000 of her own money and borrowed the other $800,000 from a local bank to purchase the equipment. The equipment, which is 5-year property under § 168, is the only depreciable property she placed in service during the year. Liz's taxable income from her engineering business in Year 1 was $1,500,000, computed without regard to any deductions allowable with respect to the new equipment.

   (a) Disregarding any application of § 179 and § 168(k), how much depreciation may Liz claim with respect to the piece of new equipment in Year 1? In Year 2? What is the equipment's adjusted basis at the beginning of Year 3?

   (b) What will the equipment's adjusted basis be at the beginning of Year 7 assuming Liz continues to own and use the piece of equipment in her engineering business?

   (c) How much depreciation may Liz claim with respect to the equipment in Year 3 if she sells it on December 31 of that year? What will her adjusted basis be in the equipment for purposes of computing the gain or loss on the sale of the equipment?

   (d) How would your answers to (a), (b), and (c) change, if at all, if Liz had purchased the new equipment on December 19, Year 1, instead of January 19, Year 1?

   (e) How would your answer to part (a) change if Liz elects under § 179 to deduct the maximum allowable, which you should assume to be $500,000, under that provision?

    (f) What is the total amount Liz may deduct with respect to the equipment in Year 1, assuming a $500,000 limit under § 179 and also assuming the applicability of § 168(k)(1) to the property?

3. On March 30 of the current year, Pete purchased and placed in service an office building for $1,500,000. Of that amount, $500,000 was allocated to the land on which the building was situated and $1,000,000 to the building itself. Pete paid $500,000 down on the property and agreed to pay the balance in installments over the next 20 years.

    (a) May Pete claim a § 179 deduction or § 168(k)(1) additional depreciation with respect to the purchase of the office building?

    (b) How much depreciation may Pete claim on the office building in the year of purchase? How much depreciation may he claim the following year?

Assignment for Chapter 14:

Complete the problems.

Read: Internal Revenue Code: §§ 167(a), (b), (c)(1), (e)(1), (f)(1); 168 (a)–(f)(1), (i)(1), (i)(2), (i)(6), (i)(12); 168(k)(1), (2)(A), (D)(iii); 179(a), (b), (c), (d)(1), (d)(10). Skim § 197.
Treasury Regulations: §§ 1.167(a)-1(a); 1.167(a)-2; 1.167(a)-3; 1.167(a)-10(a); 1.167(g)-1; 1.168(a)-1; 1.179-1(b), (c), (f)(1).

    Materials: Overview
        Revenue Ruling 68-232
        Simon v. Commissioner
        Liddle v. Commissioner
        Revenue Procedure 87-56
        Revenue Procedure 87-57
        IRS Publication 946 — Table A-7a — Depreciation Table for Nonresidential Real Property

II. VOCABULARY

depreciation
amortization
depreciable property
3-year property
5-year property
7-year property
nonresidential real property
residential rental property
Section 179 property
useful life
asset depreciation range (ADR)
class life
recovery period
straight line depreciation
double declining balance method

salvage value
half-year convention
mid-quarter convention
mid-month convention

III. OBJECTIVES

1. To explain in your own words the purpose of depreciation and amortization deductions.

2. To explain in your own words the different methods for computing depreciation under § 168.

3. To explain what continuing significance § 167 has, given the existence of § 168.

4. To identify depreciable and nondepreciable assets.

5. To explain the relationship between depreciation deductions and adjusted basis.

6. To compute the adjusted basis of a depreciable asset after depreciation deductions have been claimed.

7. To explain the significance of depreciation deductions which are allowable but which the taxpayer fails to claim.

8. To identify Section 179 property.

9. To explain the relationship between § 179 and § 168.

10. To compute the adjusted basis in Section 179 property after the taxpayer has elected to expense part of the cost of the property.

11. To explain the impact the borrowing of funds to purchase an asset has on the computation of depreciation deductions and the § 179 deduction.

IV. OVERVIEW

A. Depreciation

Assume you are a successful plaintiffs' attorney who maintains a solo practice in Seattle. For twenty years, you practiced from a rented suite of offices in a downtown Seattle bank building. You decide to build your own office building in the suburbs. You purchase a tract of land for $1,000,000 and construct an office complex on the property at a cost of $2,000,000. You intend to use half of the building for your law practice and the remainder of the building will be leased to an accounting firm. Assuming you could pay all of the above costs in a single year, may you deduct $3,000,000 on that year's tax return? If you answered "Yes," return to the previous Chapter and give additional thought to § 263. If you concluded there would be no current deduction because both the land and the building represent capital expenditures, you may proceed.

Clear reflection of income is a general goal of the Internal Revenue Code. Because our tax system taxes only net income, those costs incurred in producing income are generally deductible. Considering that the land and building will generate income to you over a number of years, deduction of the entire cost of the land and building in the year of purchase would radically distort the computation of your taxable income, not only for the year of purchase, but also for each of the years during which you held the property for use in your trade or business or for the production of income. Likewise, if the costs incurred in purchasing the land and in building the office structure could only be deducted when you sold or otherwise disposed of the property, income would be distorted during all of the years in which the property was used. In effect, your acquisition and building expenditures represent costs incurred in producing income both in the current year and in years to come. If you are entitled to deduct the costs of the land and building, you should be required to deduct those costs as income is earned. In other words, your costs should be spread over time.

How much should you be entitled to deduct in any given year and for how many years should you be entitled to a deduction? If we were to assume the building and the land would never wear out or become obsolete, we might reasonably conclude no deduction should be granted. Under those circumstances, you should be entitled to recover your investment only when you dispose of the property. As noted in Chapter 4, the § 1001 formula for computing gain and loss enables a taxpayer to recover any unrecovered cost (adjusted basis) in the property.

Focusing our attention on the building, however, it is obvious that the building will not be useful forever. Like computers and vehicles, buildings ultimately wear out or become obsolete. There is thus a cost associated with the use of the building, *i.e.*, the cost of the wear, tear and obsolescence of the building in any given tax year. If we want an accurate measure of the annual cost of using the office building, we should measure the value of the building at the beginning of the tax year and the value at the end of the tax year. The decrease, if any, in the building's value during that year should be a deductible cost of producing income from your law business and from rent during that year.

How long would you be entitled to claim such deductions? In theory, you would expect to claim deductions for so long as you used the building in your trade or business or for investment. Of course, you would not be permitted to deduct an amount in excess of your cost. The impracticality of such annual measurement both from the standpoint of the Service and the taxpayer should be obvious.

To enable taxpayers to deduct the costs associated with the use of business or investment property, Congress developed a cost recovery system allowing taxpayers to write off or deduct their capital investment (or cost) over a specified period of time — the recovery period. The Supreme Court in *Idaho Power* (reprinted in Chapter 13) explained depreciation as follows:

> Depreciation is an accounting device which recognizes that the physical consumption of a capital asset is a true cost, since the asset is being depleted. As the process of consumption continues, and depreciation is claimed and allowed, the asset's adjusted income tax basis is reduced to reflect the distribution of its cost over the accounting periods affected. . . . "The purpose of depreciation accounting is to allocate the expense of using an asset to the various periods which are benefited by that asset. . . . " When the asset is used to further the taxpayer's day-to-day business operations, the periods of benefit usually correlate with the production of income.

418 U.S. 1, 10–11 (1974).

Certain fundamental questions must be addressed by any depreciation system: What property is subject to depreciation? Over what period may one's costs be recovered through depreciation deductions? What method will be used for computing the amount of the depreciation deductions?

1. Depreciable Property

Section 167, the principal depreciation provision, defines "depreciation deduction" as "a reasonable allowance for the exhaustion, wear and tear (including a reasonable allowance for obsolescence) — (1) of property used in the trade or business, or (2) of property held for the production of income." Because ours is a tax system taxing net income and because generally no deduction is allowed for personal expenses, it is appropriate that the trade, business, or investment limitation be imposed. As a result, one may not depreciate a personal residence. See, however, Chapter 21, addressing home office deductions. Although one's home has a limited useful life, the wear and tear on it is a nondeductible personal expense. Note that a taxpayer is not permitted to depreciate property that is held as inventory or is held primarily for sale to customers. *See* Reg. § 1.167(a)-2; Rev. Rul. 89-25, 1989-1 C.B. 79.

Not only must the property be used in one's trade, business, or for investment, it must also be "subject to wear and tear, decay or decline from natural causes, exhaustion, or obsolescence. Land, . . . stock, and other assets that . . . do not decline in value predictably [are] not depreciable."[1] In the past, some taxpayers sought to render land depreciable by carving out term interests in land with the remainder interest being held by a related person. For example, assume Dan is interested in purchasing a tract of farmland. Rather than purchasing a fee simple interest in the land, Dan purchases a 25-year term interest in the land and Dan's daughter, Cathy, purchases the remainder. Because a term interest has a limited life, Dan expects to be able to write off the cost of the interest by means of depreciation-type deductions. Congress enacted § 167(e), however, to prevent taxpayers like Dan from claiming such deductions.

Will a taxpayer ever recover the cost of assets that are not depreciable because they are not wasting assets, *e.g.*, land or stock, or are not used in the taxpayer's trade or business, *e.g.*, one's home? The answer is "It depends." Recall in Chapter 4 the formula for computing gain, *i.e.*, amount realized less adjusted basis. § 1001(a). Recall also that basis represents one's cost; and "adjusted basis," as the term suggests, merely refers to the basis adjusted to reflect certain tax significant items, *e.g.*, depreciation deductions, which affect basis. If one disposes of property in a taxable transaction, one will recognize gain only to the extent that the amount realized on the transfer exceeds one's adjusted basis. For example, if Taxpayer purchases a lake cabin for $100,000, uses it during summers for a number of years, and then sells it for $175,000, Taxpayer will realize $75,000 of gain. Given the formula for computing gain, Taxpayer has been allowed to recover his capital investment (or cost) of $100,000 before any gain is realized. By contrast, if Taxpayer were to sell the cabin for $90,000, there would be a $10,000 loss, but Taxpayer would not be allowed a $10,000 loss deduction because the loss represents a personal expense. See §§ 165 and 262, discussed in Chapter 15. Thus, for tax purposes, Taxpayer is not allowed to recover his full capital investment, *i.e.*, basis, but only $90,000 of it.

Contrast the personal residence in the above example with the purchase and sale of stock. Because stock is not subject to wear and tear, it is not depreciable property. Regulation § 1.167(a)-3. If, for example, Taxpayer purchased 100 shares of stock for $10,000, Taxpayer could not claim depreciation deductions with respect to the stock even though the stock decreases in value. Taxpayer will, however, be entitled to recover the full basis of the stock upon its disposition. If Taxpayer sells the stock for $12,000, Taxpayer will only report $2,000 of gain; the other $10,000 of the sales price merely represents a recovery of Taxpayer's basis. By contrast, if Taxpayer sells the stock for $7,000, Taxpayer will be entitled to claim a $3,000 loss deduction pursuant to § 165(c)(2), which will be addressed in Chapter 15. He will, thereby, have accounted for his full basis of $10,000, *i.e.*, $7,000 of his basis offset the $7,000 of the amount realized, and the remaining $3,000 of basis gave rise to a $3,000 loss deduction.

---

[1] *General Explanation of the Economic Recovery Tax Act of 1981*, Staff of the Joint Committee on Taxation, H. Rep. 4242, 97th Cong., p. 67.

2.   Recovery Period — The Useful Life Concept

As noted previously, if the most accurate measurement of the cost of producing income is sought, depreciation deductions should be taken throughout the period an asset is used in the production of income. Of course, we don't know at the time an asset is acquired exactly how many years the taxpayer will use the asset in a trade or business or for investment. We can, however, estimate how long a particular asset can be expected to be useful in an income-producing activity. An asset's useful life is not necessarily coextensive with its actual physical life. The regulations at § 1.167(a)-1(b) describe the useful life as the period over which the asset may reasonably be expected to be useful to the taxpayer in the taxpayer's business or other income-producing activity. For example, a car may be in running condition for twenty or thirty years; its usefulness in a particular business, however, may be limited to only a few years. The determination of useful life thus requires an asset-by-asset determination.

A direct correlation exists between the useful life of an asset and the size of the annual depreciation deduction. The longer the useful life, the smaller the annual deduction. Early in our tax history, the taxpayer had the burden of establishing the useful life of an asset. Considering the speculative nature of this determination, considerable controversy ensued between the Service and taxpayers regarding useful lives. To alleviate some of the problems, the Treasury has provided guidelines prescribing useful lives for specific assets and classes of assets.

Congress in 1971 enacted § 167(m) which authorized Treasury to create an Asset Depreciation Range (ADR) providing an industry-wide set of useful lives for classes of assets. Taxpayers could select useful lives 20% longer or shorter than the so-called midpoint life. Not only did ADR reduce disputes regarding the useful lives of assets, it also permitted taxpayers to write off the cost of acquiring assets over a much shorter period. See the excerpt in the materials from Revenue Procedure 87-56, which provides the Asset Depreciation Range. With certain exceptions, however, the ADR system did not prescribe useful lives for real property. The depreciation of real property continued to be governed by earlier guidelines which provided useful lives ranging from 40 years for apartment buildings to 60 years for warehouses.

Notwithstanding the shorter useful lives authorized by the 1971 ADR system, some correlation continued to exist between the prescribed useful lives and the actual economic lives of assets. Any such correlation, however, was negated in 1981 when Congress, both as a simplification measure and as a stimulant to the economy, provided a new system for depreciating tangible property. The Accelerated Cost Recovery System, known as ACRS, significantly de-emphasized the useful life concept by assigning all tangible property to one of five recovery periods based on the asset's "class life" as defined in § 168(i)(1).

Under the Accelerated Cost Recovery System enacted in 1981 and applicable to tangible depreciable property placed in service after December 31, 1981, most real property was classified as 15-year property, meaning the cost of buildings such as the office complex in our example could be written off over a 15-year period. In addition, most tangible personal property was classified as 3-year property or 5-year property and could be written off over three or five years. Property with no assigned class life, *e.g.*, the 19th-century violin bows in the *Simon* case, included in the materials, under ACRS was treated as 5-year property. These shortened useful lives, combined with accelerated methods of computing depreciation, enabled taxpayers to write off the cost of newly acquired property far more rapidly than before.

Congress, however, subsequently amended ACRS, creating the current depreciation system, the so-called Modified Accelerated Cost Recovery System (MACRS), which is applicable to tangible depreciable property placed in service after December 31, 1986. This modified system, by comparison to ACRS, expands the number of recovery periods and lengthens the recovery period of real property and, to some extent, certain tangible personal property. For example, under current law "nonresidential real property," like our office complex, is depreciated over 39 years and "residential rental property" is depreciated over 27.5 years. Property other than "nonresidential real property" and "residential rental property" must generally be classified within one of six recovery periods — three, five, seven, ten, fifteen, and twenty years. The most important of these categories are the 3-year, 5-year and 7-year classes. Section 168(e)(1) defines each of these classes by reference to the "class life" of assets. The "class life" of an asset is its midpoint life in the Asset Depreciation Range (ADR) discussed previously. See the excerpt from Revenue Procedure 87-56, included in the materials, for special class life rules. Section 168(e)(3)(B)(i) provides that 5-year property includes, among other items, automobiles or light general-purpose trucks, despite the fact that these assets technically have the same class life as 3-year property. In addition, 5-year property includes computers, copying equipment, and heavy general purpose trucks. The 7-year property class is now the catchall class and includes all personal property with no assigned class life under ADR.

As previously noted, Congress in enacting ACRS and the current MACRS significantly de-emphasized the useful life concept. Historically, only assets with a determinable useful life were depreciable. Thus, as noted in Revenue Ruling 68-232, included in the materials, a valuable art piece was not considered depreciable property because it did not have a determinable useful life. A question which has sparked considerable disagreement between the courts and the Service is whether, in view of the changes wrought by ACRS and MACRS, a taxpayer must still establish that an asset has a determinable useful life for the asset to be depreciable. In this regard, consider carefully the excerpts in the materials from the Tax Court decisions in *Simon v. Commissioner* (allowing professional violinists to depreciate their 19th-century violin bows) and *Liddle v. Commissioner* (allowing a professional musician to depreciate a 17th-century bass viol).

In *Selig v. Commissioner*, T.C. Memo. 1995-519, *Simon* and *Liddle* were followed and the taxpayer was allowed depreciation deductions on "exotic automobiles" he owned and exhibited for a fee at car shows. The question, according to the Tax Court, was whether a depreciation deduction was allowable for automobiles held in a "pristine condition" and exhibited for a fee in the taxpayer's trade or business:

> The long and the short of it is yes, provided the automobiles are subject to obsolescence. We have found that the exotic automobiles were state-of-the-art, high technology vehicles with unique design features or equipment.

We have no doubt that, over time, the exotic automobiles would, because of just those factors, become obsolete in petitioner's business. *The fact that petitioners have failed to show the useful lives of the exotic automobiles is irrelevant.*

Id. (emphasis added). Although there was no evidence that the automobiles were subject to wear and tear, the court was nonetheless convinced they "had a useful life as show cars shorter than their ordinary useful life and, thus, suffered obsolescence" and also that they "were not museum pieces of indeterminable useful life." *Id.*

3. Depreciation Methods

Just as Congress has manipulated the useful life concept to increase or decrease depreciation rates, it has also varied the methods used to compute depreciation. Depreciation methods may be separated into two categories: straight line depreciation and accelerated depreciation. Currently, the Code utilizes both depreciation methods. The straight line method is the simplest. In general, under the straight line method, one merely divides the cost of the asset by the number of years in the recovery period to determine the depreciation allowance for the given year. For example, assume Taxpayer builds an apartment building that costs $275,000 and qualifies as residential rental property with a useful life of 27.5 years. Assume the salvage value, *i.e.*, remaining value at the end of the 27.5-year period, is $0. In theory, the taxpayer should be entitled to deduct 3.6% (*i.e.*, 100%/27.5) of the $275,000 cost or $10,000 per year, so that after 27.5 years, the taxpayer would have deducted the full $275,000 cost of the building. The 3.6% is the straight line rate of depreciation. Regulation § 1.167(b)-1 provides: "Under the straight line method the cost or other basis of the property less its estimated salvage value is deductible in equal annual amounts over the period of the estimated useful life of the property." If there were a salvage value to the property at the end of the 27.5 years, the annual depreciation deductions would be computed by subtracting the salvage value from the $275,000 cost and dividing the balance by 27.5. Section 168(b)(4), however, provides that salvage value is treated as zero, thereby allowing a taxpayer to recover the entire cost of property during the recovery period.

Acknowledging that property does not wear out at an even rate and desiring to stimulate the economy by authorizing more rapid depreciation, Congress authorized accelerated methods of recovery. The effect of these methods is to permit larger depreciation deductions in the early years of the recovery period than in the later years, *i.e.*, the depreciation deductions are "front-loaded." One such accelerated method is known as the declining balance method. It differs from the straight line method in that a greater fixed rate is used and applied, not to the total cost of property each year as in the straight line example above, but to the cost less the depreciation deductions claimed for prior years (*i.e.*, the adjusted basis). See the definition of declining balance method in Reg. § 1.167(b)-2(a). The most common declining balance methods are the so-called 200% or double declining balance method and the 150% declining balance method.

Consider the following example which demonstrates the double or 200% declining balance method: Taxpayer purchases for $30,000 a machine for business use.

The machine has a useful life of 5 years. The straight line rate of depreciation would be 20%, *i.e.*, 100% divided by 5. As its name suggests, the double declining balance method authorizes Taxpayer to use a depreciation rate twice that of straight line, or, in this example, 40%. Note the difference between the depreciation Taxpayer may claim under the straight line and double declining balance methods:

	straight line	double declining balance
Year 1	$6,000	$12,000 (40% x $30,000)
Year 2	$6,000	$7,200 (40% x $18,000)
Year 3	$6,000	$4,320 (40% x $10,800)
Year 4	$6,000	$2,592 (40% x $6,480)
Year 5	$6,000	$1,555 (40% x $3,888)[2]

The front-loading effect of the double-declining balance should be obvious from this example.

Section 168(b)(1) provides that, with respect to 3-year, 5-year and 7-year property, the 200% declining balance method shall be used, but the taxpayer shall shift to the straight line method in the year that method, if applied to the adjusted basis at the beginning of such year, would produce the larger deduction. Note §§ 168(g)(2) and 168(g)(7) authorize taxpayers to elect an alternative depreciation system, allowing the taxpayer to depreciate property over a longer time period using the straight line method. Presumably, taxpayers would seldom elect to use this system.

Section 168(b)(3) requires taxpayers to use the straight line method to depreciate residential rental property and nonresidential real property. The alternative depreciation method provided by § 168(g)(2) may be elected by a taxpayer with respect to real property and will have the effect of lengthening the period over which depreciation deductions are claimed. For example, a taxpayer may elect to depreciate residential rental property over a 40-year period rather than a 27.5-year period.

4. Conventions

The applicable recovery period during which depreciation may be claimed begins when the property is placed in service. Regulation § 1.46-3(d)(1)(ii) defines "placed in service" to mean "placed in a condition or state of readiness and availability for the specifically assigned function." To avoid difficulties associated with computing depreciation for fractions of a year, Congress has adopted a number of conventions. Residential rental property and nonresidential real property placed in service during any month are deemed placed in service on the mid-point of such month. §§ 168(d)(2), (4)(B). The depreciation amount for the full year is then prorated according to the number of months during which the property was in service for the particular year. For example, if a calendar year taxpayer places residential rental property in service on the last day of January, the property will be deemed to have

---

[2] The declining balance method always leaves a balance at the end of the asset's useful life (*i.e.*, $2,333 in the example). *See* Reg. §§ 1.167(b)-2(a), (b).

been placed in service at the middle of the month. The depreciation amount for the first year will equal 11.5/12 or 23/24 of the annual depreciation amount. In the year of disposition, the taxpayer will likewise pro-rate the annual depreciation deduction over the number of months the property was in service during that year and will take the mid-month convention into account. For example, if a taxpayer sells residential real property on June 2, the taxpayer will be deemed to have sold the property at the midpoint of the month and will be entitled to claim 5 1/2 months of depreciation. No depreciation deduction is allowed for property placed in service and disposed of during the same taxable year. § 1.168(d)-1(b)(3)(ii).

All other classes of property are generally subject to a half-year convention, *i.e.*, any property placed in service during the tax year (or disposed of during any taxable year) is deemed placed in service (or disposed of) on the mid-point of the tax year. §§ 168(d)(1), (4)(A). For example, a calendar year taxpayer who purchases a piece of business equipment for business use on December 1 will ordinarily be deemed to have placed the equipment in service on July 1, and will therefore be entitled to one-half year's depreciation on it. In the year in which the equipment is disposed of, the taxpayer will generally compute the depreciation deduction, if any, for the year on the assumption that the equipment was sold on July 1 of that year. However, to prevent taxpayers from taking undue advantage of this half-year convention, Congress has provided that, if the properties placed in service (other than nonresidential real and residential rental property) during the last three months of the year have aggregate bases greater than 40% of the aggregate bases of all properties placed in service that year, a mid-quarter convention will apply instead of the half-year convention. § 168(d)(3).[3]

The Treasury has published Revenue Procedure 87-57, included in part in the materials, which sets forth tables incorporating the various conventions, enabling depreciation deductions to be computed quickly. In the year of disposition, the taxpayer is entitled to claim depreciation, again using the above conventions.

As previously noted, § 168 is generally applicable to tangible depreciable property placed in service after 1986. Intangible property, *e.g.*, patents and copyrights, continues to be subject to the depreciation rules of § 167 unless otherwise treated under § 197 discussed *infra*. Under § 167(f)(1), computer software is depreciable over a 36-month period using the straight line method. As suggested by the discussion of the development of the law, *supra*, depending on when property was placed in service, it may be subject to any one of a number of different depreciation schemes.

---

[3] Under the mid-quarter convention, property placed in service during any calendar quarter of a taxable year (or disposed of during any quarter of a taxable year) is treated as placed in service (or disposed of) on the mid-point of such calendar quarter. Section 168(d)(3)(B) also provides that any property placed in service and disposed of during the same taxable year will likewise not be considered in determining whether the mid-quarter convention is applicable.

B. Computing the Depreciation Deduction

Section 168(a) provides the depreciation deduction for tangible property shall be determined by using: "(1) the applicable depreciation method; (2) the applicable recovery period; and (3) the applicable convention." In computing the depreciation deductions authorized by the Code, one should begin with the adjusted basis of the property. Reg. § 1.167(g)-1. In the case of purchased property, that figure will generally be its cost. For example,[4] assume that in January, Year 1, a taxpayer purchases for $100,000 a piece of equipment with a 6-year class life for business use. Assume the equipment is the only depreciable property the taxpayer placed in service during the year. The depreciation for the first year will be computed with reference to the $100,000 purchase price, *i.e.*, the equipment's basis. We must now determine the appropriate recovery period. Section 168(e)(1) classifies property with a class life that is more than four years but less than 10 years as 5-year property; § 168(c)(1) provides that the applicable recovery period for 5-year property is 5 years. Therefore, the recovery period for the equipment is 5 years. Next, we must determine the applicable depreciation method. Section 168(b)(1) provides that the 200% declining balance method (switching to straight line) is the appropriate method for 5-year property. Finally, we must determine the applicable convention. Generally, the applicable convention for 5-year property is the half-year convention and that is the convention applicable to the equipment. (The mid-quarter convention is inapplicable because the equipment was purchased early in the year and is the only depreciable property placed in service during the year.) § 168(d)(1). With this information, we should then locate the appropriate table in Revenue Procedure 87-57, included in the materials. Table 1 in that Revenue Procedure matches our needs. According to that table, the depreciation rate for Year 1 will be 20%. Applying that rate to the "unadjusted basis"[5] of the equipment, the taxpayer will be entitled to claim a depreciation deduction of $20,000 in Year 1 (*i.e.*, $100,000 × .20 = $20,000). In Year 2, the depreciation rate will be 32%, yielding a depreciation deduction of $32,000 (*i.e.*, $100,000 × .32 = $32,000). Using this same method of computation, the depreciation in Years 3 through 6 will be $19,200, $11,520, $11,520, and $5,760. Note, because of the half-year convention, the recovery period for 5-year property will actually extend over 6 calendar years.

In sum, using Table 1 of Revenue Procedure 87-57, the depreciation schedule for the equipment is as follows:

Recovery Year	"Unadjusted Basis"	Depreciation Rate	Depreciation
1	$100,000	20%	$20,000
2	$100,000	32%	$32,000

---

[4] In this example, we disregard any application of §§ 179 or 168(k).

[5] The tables set forth in this Revenue Procedure provide the appropriate depreciation rate to be applied to the "unadjusted basis" of the property in each year of the recovery period. Simply stated, the term "unadjusted basis" means the adjusted basis of the property, disregarding any depreciation deductions claimed by the taxpayer. Thus, the unadjusted basis of the equipment is $100,000 in each of the six years of the recovery period. See the depreciation schedule for the equipment provided in the text.

Recovery Year	"Unadjusted Basis"	Depreciation Rate	Depreciation
3	$100,000	19.20%	$19,200
4	$100,000	11.52%	$11,520
5	$100,000	11.52%	$11,520
6	$100,000	5.76%	$5,760
TOTALS		100%	$100,000

The taxpayer will thus claim depreciation deductions totaling $100,000 (the full cost of the equipment) over six calendar years.

Students are often dismayed when they read the language of § 168(b)(1) and then look at the depreciation tables provided in the Revenue Procedure. Most students expect to see a depreciation rate which is consistent with their understanding of the 200% declining balance method. Thus, students expect the depreciation rate in Year 1 will be 20%, *i.e.*, one-half of the double declining balance rate of 40% (see prior discussions regarding the double declining balance method and the half-year convention). Table 1 does not disappoint the students in this regard. But, in Year 2, students expect the depreciation rate will be 40%, *i.e.*, twice the straight line rate of 20%. Instead, Table 1 provides a depreciation rate of 32%. Furthermore, students expect in Year 2 the depreciation rate of 40% will be applied against an adjusted basis of $80,000 (*i.e.*, $100,000 less Year 1 depreciation of $20,000). Rather, as indicated in the depreciation schedule above, the depreciation rate is applied to the full $100,000 cost (*i.e.*, the unadjusted basis) of the equipment. Despite these apparent discrepancies, Table 1 actually does incorporate the Congressional directive in § 168(b)(1); it merely does so in a fashion that makes computation of depreciation simpler for taxpayers. If you use the purist's approach and carefully compute the depreciation for each year according to the formula set out in the statute and without the aid of the Treasury's tables, you will discover your results are identical to the results we reached using Table 1.[6]

The same approach used above to compute depreciation deductions for tangible personal property should be used for computing depreciation deductions for nonresidential real property or residential rental property. In the case of such real property, however, the straight line method will be used together with the mid-month convention.

Finally, it is appropriate to note a significant, but seemingly temporary, modification to the foregoing discussion on computing the depreciation deduction under § 168. Section 168(k)(1) authorizes an additional first-year depreciation

---

[6] For example, the adjusted basis of the equipment after Year 1 is $80,000. Applying the 40% Year 2 depreciation rate to $80,000 produces a $32,000 deduction — exactly equivalent to 32% of the unadjusted basis of $100,000. Students wishing to pursue this matter further should locate the complete text of Revenue Procedure 87-57 and read the detailed discussion regarding the computation of depreciation provided therein. Invariably, students using Table 1 in Revenue Procedure 87-57 are puzzled by the method it employs to apply the statutory requirement that one shift to the straight line method when that method will produce the greater deduction. The full text of Revenue Procedure 87-57 provides a detailed discussion of that requirement and its application.

deduction in the amount of 50% of the cost of "qualified property" in the year it is placed in service. Qualifying property includes tangible depreciable property with a recovery period of 20 years or less — a limitation which generally excludes depreciable real property — and certain other limited categories of property. § 168(k)(2). A critical requirement is that the property must be new property — that is, its original use must commence with the taxpayer. § 168(k)(2)(A)(ii). This requirement reflects its origins at a time Congress was interested in stimulating an economy teetering on recession. The provision initially applied only to 2008 and 2009, but multiple extensions followed, the last of which applied § 168(k)(1) through 2014. Extension beyond 2014, even if retroactive, is likely. Unlike § 179, there is no dollar limit on the use of § 168(k)(1). A taxpayer may elect out of § 168(k) with respect to any class of property for any tax year, in which case the election out applies to all property in that class placed in service that year. § 168(k)(2)(D)(iii).

The following quote from the legislative history to the 2010 Act (*Joint Committee Technical Explanation*, JCX-55-10) describes the operation of § 168(k):

> The provision (§ 168(k)) allows an additional first-year depreciation deduction equal to 50 percent of the adjusted basis of qualified property. . . . The basis of the property and the depreciation allowances in the year the property is placed in service and later years are appropriately adjusted to reflect the additional first-year depreciation deduction. . . . The taxpayer may elect out of additional first-year depreciation for any class of property for any taxable year.

> The interaction of the additional first-year depreciation allowance with the otherwise applicable depreciation allowance may be illustrated as follows. Assume that in 2009, a taxpayer purchases new depreciable property and places it in service. The property's cost is $1,000, and it is five-year property subject to the half-year convention. The amount of additional first-year depreciation allowed under the provision is $500. The remaining $500 of the cost of the property is deductible under the rules applicable to five-year property. Thus, 20 percent, or $100, is also allowed as a depreciation deduction in 2009. The total depreciation deduction with respect to the property for 2009 is $600. The remaining $400 cost of the property is recovered under otherwise applicable rules for computing depreciation.

> Property qualifying for the additional first-year depreciation deduction must meet all of the following requirements. First, the property must be . . . property to which the Modified Accelerated Cost Recovery System (MACRS) applies with an applicable recovery period of 20 years or less. . . . Second, the original use of the property must commence with the taxpayer after December 31, 2007. Third, the taxpayer must purchase the property within the applicable time period. . . .

C. Amortization of Intangibles — Section 197

In 1993, Congress added § 197 allowing taxpayers to amortize certain intangibles ratably over a 15-year period. Section 197 should, in large part, negate the kinds of disputes which previously arose between the Service and taxpayers regarding whether an intangible has a limited useful life which can be estimated with reasonable accuracy. Most notably, § 197 allows the amortization of purchased goodwill and going concern value. Because of its importance in the sale and purchase of a business, we will defer detailed examination of § 197 until Chapter 42.

D. Relationship Between Basis and Depreciation

As noted at the outset of this Overview, depreciation is the means whereby a taxpayer recovers the cost of depreciable property used in a trade or business or investment activity. Recall that when a taxpayer is required to capitalize the cost of depreciable property, that is, when the taxpayer is not permitted to deduct the cost currently, the taxpayer gets a basis in the property equal to the cost. With respect to depreciable property, it is basis that the taxpayer recovers through depreciation deductions. Since the adjusted basis reflects the unrecovered cost of property, it is appropriate to adjust the basis of property for depreciation deductions allowable. Read § 1016(a)(2), which provides for the adjustment of basis for amounts allowable for depreciation. A taxpayer must reduce her basis in a depreciable asset by the depreciation claimed "but not less than the amount allowable." This requirement prevents a taxpayer from choosing when depreciation will be deducted. Thus, a taxpayer failing to claim an allowable depreciation deduction with respect to an asset must still reduce the basis of the asset by the allowable depreciation amount.

Consider the following example: Marcella purchases a commercial building for $1,000,000, uses it in her business during a 10-year period, and then sells it for $800,000. Assume the depreciation allowable during the years Marcella owned the building equalled $250,000. Marcella's adjusted basis in the building would therefore be $750,000 ($1,000,000 − $250,000). Marcella's gain on the sale of the building would be computed using the § 1001 formula: amount realized less adjusted basis equals gain realized. Marcella's gain would be $50,000 (*i.e.*, $800,000 − $750,000).

E. Section 179 — Expensing Tangible Personal Property

While costs incurred in acquiring an asset with a useful life extending substantially beyond the tax year are generally not deductible, § 179 allows taxpayers to expense (*i.e.*, to deduct currently) the cost of acquisition of certain depreciable business assets. This provision is applicable only to "Section 179 property," *i.e.*, generally tangible personal property acquired by purchase for use in the active conduct of a trade or business. Section 179 is elective. *See* § 179(c).

Section 179(b)(1) generally limits to $500,000 the amount that can be expensed under § 179 with respect to qualifying property placed in service during a year. Section 179(b)(2) reduces the $500,000 limitation on a dollar for dollar basis to the extent the cost of section 179 property placed in service by a taxpayer during the taxable year exceeds $2,000,000.[7] These limitations suggest that Congress intended

---

[7] The $500,000 and $2,000,000 limitations, strictly speaking, apply only to the years 2010 through

§ 179 as a break for small businesses. Section 179(b)(3) further limits the § 179 deduction to the amount of income from the taxpayer's trade or business during the year; the taxpayer, however, may carryover any amount of the deduction which would otherwise be allowable. § 179(b)(3)(A).[8]

For example, if Judy purchased and placed in service a $750,000 piece of used equipment for use in her business in a year when the $500,000 limit was in effect, Judy could expense, *i.e.*, deduct currently, $500,000 of the purchase price under § 179(b)(1). Furthermore, the amount eligible to be expensed by Judy would be reduced by $1 for every dollar by which the aggregate cost of qualifying property placed in service during the year by Judy exceeded $2,000,000. § 179(b)(2). A third limitation would prevent Judy from expensing an amount greater than the taxable income she derived from business during the year. § 179(b)(3)(A). As suggested in the examples at the end of this section, the balance of the purchase price would have to be recovered over time by way of depreciation deductions under § 168.

Over the years, the § 179 limitations were increased several times before reaching the $500,000 level. Legislative history to 2003 tax legislation, which increased the limits under § 179(b)(1) and (2), contains the following instructive comments regarding the congressional policy underlying the increase:

> The [House Ways and Means] Committee believes that section 179 expensing provides two important benefits for small businesses. First, it lowers the cost of capital for tangible property used in a trade or business. With a lower cost of capital, the Committee believes small businesses will invest in more equipment and employ more workers. Second, it eliminates depreciation record keeping requirements with respect to expensed property.

How does the § 179 election affect the basis the taxpayer has in Section 179 property? Obviously, § 179 is merely a means of recovering one's cost in property. Therefore, an adjustment must be made to the basis of Section 179 property placed in service during the year to the extent that a § 179 deduction with respect to that property was claimed. *See* Reg. § 1.179-1(f).

> **Example 1:** Assume the § 179(b)(1) limitation this year is $500,000. Also assume the taxpayer has sufficient business income this year so that the § 179 deduction is not limited by § 179(b)(3). The taxpayer purchases a piece of equipment for business use at a cost of $400,000 in June this year. It is the taxpayer's only purchase of depreciable property for the year. Accordingly, if the taxpayer so elects, the taxpayer may expense, that is, currently deduct, the entire $400,000 cost under § 179 this year. The taxpayer's adjusted basis in the equipment will then be zero.

2014. The limitations for 2015 and later years, at the time this edition goes to press, are only $25,000 under § 179(b)(1) and $200,000 under § 179(b)(2). Congress has chosen to extend the $500,000 and $2,000,000 limits on a one-year or two-year basis several times in recent years. It is widely expected to do so again for 2015 and later years, even if retroactively.

[8] For purposes of this rule, taxable income from the conduct of an active trade or business is computed without regard to the cost of the expensed property. § 179(b)(3)(C).

Example 2: Assume the facts of Example 1, except that the cost of the equipment is $600,000. The taxpayer may elect to expense up to $500,000 of the cost under § 179. If the taxpayer so elects, may the taxpayer also claim a depreciation deduction for this year with respect to the equipment? The answer is "Yes." Assuming that the equipment is 5-year property, the taxpayer will, pursuant to the half-year convention, claim one-half year's depreciation. To what extent, if any, will the § 179 deduction affect the depreciation computation? Before computing the depreciation deduction, the basis in the equipment must be adjusted to reflect the § 179 deduction claimed. Thus, the adjusted basis to which the depreciation percentage will be applied will be $100,000 rather than $600,000. If no adjustment were made to the basis for the § 179 deduction, the taxpayer, through the combination of the § 179 deduction plus the deductions under § 168 (and disregarding § 168(k)), would ultimately deduct more than 100% of the cost of the equipment — clearly an improper result. The taxpayer will be entitled to $20,000 of depreciation (that is, 20% of $100,000) under § 168(a) in addition to the $500,000 of § 179 deduction. At the beginning of the next year, the taxpayer's adjusted basis in the property will be $80,000.

Example 3: Assume the facts of Example 2 and also assume that the taxpayer is allowed a 50% additional first year depreciation deduction under § 168(k)(1). First, one must reduce the taxpayer's basis by the $500,000 taxpayer expensed under § 179. The taxpayer's adjusted basis for purposes of § 168(k) is thus $100,000 as in Example 2. Under § 168(k), the taxpayer will be allowed additional first year depreciation equal to 50% of the $100,000 adjusted basis or a $50,000 deduction. The taxpayer's unadjusted basis for purposes of the general rules of § 168 will be $50,000 and taxpayer will be entitled to a depreciation deduction equal to 20% of the $50,000 or $10,000. Thus, the taxpayer will deduct a total of $560,000 of the $600,000 cost this year.

Example 4: Assume the facts of Example 1, except that the taxpayer purchases two pieces of equipment for business use, each one costing $300,000. The taxpayer may divide the $500,000 limitation in any proportion she wishes between the two pieces of equipment. For example, the taxpayer could expense the entire cost of one piece, reducing the adjusted basis to zero, and apply the remaining $200,000 limitation amount to the second piece, reducing its adjusted basis to $100,000, to be recovered by a § 168 deduction as indicated in Examples 2 and 3. The taxpayer could alternatively spread the $500,000 limitation equally between the two pieces, or in any other proportion. The remaining adjusted basis on each piece would then be recovered under § 168, as in Examples 2 and 3.

F.   The Relationship of Debt to Depreciation

As you learned in Chapter 4, a taxpayer who borrows money to purchase property is considered to have a basis in the property equal to the cost of the property, even though that cost has been financed initially by another. That basis is used for purposes of computing the depreciation deduction. For example, if a taxpayer borrows $1,000,000 to purchase a $1,000,000 piece of heavy equipment for use in a business, the taxpayer will be entitled to depreciate the equipment using $1,000,000 as the basis for depreciation. Likewise, § 179 is applicable regardless of whether the taxpayer used her own funds or borrowed funds to purchase the property. It makes no difference whether the taxpayer borrowed the money from a third person or borrowed the money from the party selling the equipment. The possible advantages to the taxpayer under these circumstances should be obvious — the taxpayer has not yet incurred any out-of-pocket expense but nonetheless is permitted to claim depreciation deductions. As you will learn in Chapter 44, taxpayers have availed themselves of the tax breaks associated with this relationship between debt and depreciation. Congress, however, has enacted legislation which significantly reduces the tax shelter opportunities previously available. *See* Chapter 44.

G. Conclusion

Returning to the hypothetical at the outset of this chapter, you should now understand that the land which you purchased is not depreciable and that its cost will be recovered only upon the sale or exchange of the property. By contrast, the office complex is depreciable and its cost may be recovered over a 39-year period under the rules for nonresidential real property in § 168.

REVENUE RULING 68-232
1968-1 C.B. 79

A valuable and treasured art piece does not have a determinable useful life. While the actual physical condition of the property may influence the value placed on the object, it will not ordinarily limit or determine the useful life. Accordingly, depreciation of works of art generally is not allowable.

A.R.R. 4530, C.B. II-2,145 (1923), is superseded since the position set forth therein is restated under current law in this Revenue Ruling.

AUTHORS' NOTE

A.R.R. 4530, which was superseded by Revenue Ruling 68-232 above, provided in pertinent part:

> It appears that A, being a man of artistic temperament, has furnished his office with furniture, etc., not of a style usually found in business offices; that such furnishings are of a very expensive type and among them are works of art and curios; it is claimed that the furnishings are only such as are proper in the office of a man following A's profession (motion-picture director). While it is not believed that anyone may for tax purposes be limited as to the amount he is to expend for office furniture, it is the opinion of the committee that works of art and curios are not, in A's case, properly to be classed as business assets, and that such articles are not subject to such depreciation as is allowable as a deduction from gross income for

income tax purposes, the value and desirability of such articles, as a general rule, increasing with age. . . .

SIMON v. COMMISSIONER
United States Tax Court
103 T.C. 247 (1994), *aff'd*, 68 F.3d 41 (2d Cir. 1995)

LARO, JUDGE:

Due to concessions by the parties, the sole issue for decision is whether petitioners are entitled to deduct depreciation claimed under the accelerated cost recovery system (ACRS) for the year in issue. Petitioners claimed depreciation on two 19th-century violin bows that they used in their trade or business as full-time professional violinists. As discussed below, we hold that petitioners may depreciate their violin bows during the year in issue.

FINDINGS OF FACT

Richard Simon started playing and studying the violin in 1943, at the age of 7. In 1945, he was awarded a full scholarship to the Manhattan School of Music. He studied the violin there through college and received a bachelor of music degree in 1956. Following his graduation, Richard Simon pursued a master's degree in music by taking additional courses at the Manhattan School of Music and Columbia University. Throughout his education, Richard Simon studied the violin under many renowned musicians.

In 1965, Richard Simon joined the New York Philharmonic Orchestra (Orchestra) and began playing in its first violin section. In 1981, he joined and began playing with the New York Philharmonic Ensembles (Ensembles) (hereinafter, the Orchestra and the Ensembles are collectively referred to as the Philharmonic). Since 1965, Richard Simon has maintained two careers, one as a player with the Orchestra (and later with the Philharmonic) and the second as a soloist, chamber music player, and teacher.

Fiona Simon began playing and studying the violin at the age of 4. Her musical studies included courses at Purcell School in London from 1963-71 and at the Guildhall School of Music from 1971-73. Throughout her career, Fiona Simon studied the violin with renowned musicians.

In 1985, Fiona Simon joined the Philharmonic and began playing in its first violin section. Since 1985, Fiona Simon has maintained two careers, one as a full-time player with the Philharmonic and a second as a soloist, chamber music player, teacher, and free-lance performer.

During the year in issue, petitioners were both full-time performers with the Philharmonic, playing locally, nationally, and internationally in the finest concert halls in the world. In 1989, petitioners performed four concerts per week with the Philharmonic, playing over 200 different works, and attended many rehearsals with the Philharmonic that were more demanding and more time-consuming than the concerts. Petitioners also carried out the busy schedules connected with their second careers.

Construction of a Violin Bow

A violin bow consists of a flexible wooden stick, horsehair, a frog, and a ferrule (screw). The stick, which varies in thickness, weight, and balance, is the working part of the bow and is an integral part in the production of sound through vibration. It is designed so that horsehair can be stretched between its ends.

The horsehair is a group of single strands of hair that come from the tails of Siberian horses. A hatchet-shaped head holds one end of the horsehair, and the other end is attached to a frog. The frog, which is inserted into the stick, is a movable hollow piece by which the bow is held. The frog has an eyepiece on the end that catches the screw. The screw is the small knob at the end of the bow that is adjusted to tighten or loosen the horsehair in order to change the tension on the horsehair. The horsehair is the part of the bow that touches the violin strings. Rosin is applied to the horsehair to supply the frictional element that is necessary to make the violin strings vibrate.

Old violins played with old bows produce exceptional sounds that are superior to sounds produced by newer violins played with newer bows. The two violin bows in issue were made in the 19th century by Francois Xavier Tourte (1747–1835). Francois Tourte is considered the premier violin bow maker. In particular, he is renowned for improving the bow's design. (Hereinafter, the two bows in issue are separately referred to as Bow 1 and Bow 2, and are collectively referred to as the Tourte bows.)

Purchase of the Tourte Bows

On November 13, 1985, petitioners purchased Bow 1 for $30,000; the bow was purchased from Moes & Moes, Ltd., a dealer and restorer of violins and violin bows. On December 3, 1985, petitioners purchased Bow 2 from this dealer for $21,500. The sticks, frogs, and screws were originals of Francois Tourte at the time of each purchase. No cracks or other defects were apparent in the sticks at the time of each purchase. The frogs and screws, however, were not in playable condition. Therefore, petitioners replaced them.

Petitioners acquired the Tourte bows for regular use in their full-time professional employment as violinists. Petitioners purchased the Tourte bows for their tonal quality, not for their monetary value. In the year of acquisition, petitioners began using the Tourte bows with the original sticks in their trade or business as full-time professional violinists. Petitioners continued to use the Tourte bows with the original sticks during the year in issue.

Depreciation Deductions Claimed for the Tourte Bows

On their 1989 Form 1040, petitioners claimed a depreciation deduction of $6,300 with respect to Bow 1 and $4,515 with respect to Bow 2; these amounts were in accordance with the appropriate ACRS provisions that applied to 5-year property.

See sec. 168(b)(1). [Authors' note: The 5-year classification was the catchall class under ACRS. Thus, tangible personal property, like the bows, which did not have a class life was assigned to this class.] Respondent disallowed petitioners' depreciation deduction in full and reflected her disallowance in the notice of deficiency at issue here.

Conditions Affecting the Wear and Tear of Violin Bows

Playing with a bow adversely affects the bow's condition; when a musician plays with a bow, the bow vibrates up, down, sideways, and at different angles. In addition, perspiration from a player's hands enters the wood of a bow and ultimately destroys the bow's utility for playing. Cracks and heavy-handed bearing down while playing certain pieces of music also create wear and tear to a bow. A player who has a heavy hand may cause the stick to press against the horsehair; in turn, this may cause the bow to curve and warp. . . . Petitioners' use of the Tourte bows during the year in issue subjected the bows to substantial wear and tear.

Frequent use of a violin bow will cause it to be "played out," meaning that the wood loses its ability to vibrate and produce quality sound from the instrument. From the point of view of a professional musician, a "played out" bow is inferior and of limited use. The Tourte bows were purchased by petitioners, and were playable by them during the year in issue, only because the Tourte bows were relatively unused prior to petitioners' purchase of them; the Tourte bows had been preserved in pristine condition in collections. At the time of trial, the condition of the Tourte bows had deteriorated since the dates of their purchase. Among other things, the sticks on the Tourte bows were worn down.

Value of the Tourte Bows

On November 21, 1985, Bow 1 was appraised for insurance purposes as having a fair market value of $35,000. On December 3, 1985, Bow 2 was appraised for insurance purposes as having a fair market value of $25,000. Petitioners obtained both appraisals from Moes & Moes, Ltd.

In 1994, at the time of trial, the Tourte bows were insured with the Philharmonic for $45,000 and $35,000, respectively. These amounts are based on an appraisal dated May 14, 1990, from Yung Chin Bowmaker, a restorer and dealer of fine bows. The record does not indicate whether these appraised amounts were the fair market values of the Tourte bows or were their replacement values.

An independent market exists for the Tourte bows and other antique bows. Numerous antique bows (including bows made by Francois Tourte) are regularly bought and sold in this market. The Tourte bows are unadorned; they are not as lavish or decorative as some other bows (including other bows made by Francois Tourte) that are sold in the independent market. Adornments on other bows include engravings, gold, silver, ivory, and mother of pearl.

One factor that adds value to the Tourte bows is the fact that Pernambuco wood, the wood that was used to make the sticks, is now very scarce. The wood that is currently used to make the sticks of violin bows is inferior to Pernambuco wood.

OPINION

. . . The issue that we must decide is whether petitioners are entitled to deduct depreciation under ACRS with respect to the Tourte bows.

Taxpayers have long been allowed asset depreciation deductions in order to allow them to allocate their expense of using an income-producing asset to the periods that are benefited by that asset. The primary purpose of allocating depreciation to more than 1 year is to provide a more meaningful matching of the cost of an income-producing asset with the income resulting therefrom; this meaningful match, in turn, bolsters the accounting integrity for tax purposes of the taxpayer's periodic income statements. . . . Such a system of accounting for depreciation for Federal income tax purposes has been recognized with the approval of the Supreme Court for over 65 years; as the Court observed in 1927: "The theory underlying this allowance for depreciation is that by using up the plant, a gradual sale is made of it." *United States v. Ludey*, 274 U.S. 295, 301 (1927). . . . In this sense, an allocation of depreciation to a given year represents that year's reduction of the underlying asset through wear and tear. . . . Depreciation allocations also represent a return to the taxpayer of his or her investment in the income-producing property over the years in which depreciation is allowed.

Prior to the Economic Recovery Tax Act of 1981 (ERTA), Pub.L. 97-34, 95 Stat. 172, personal property was depreciated pursuant to section 167 of the Internal Revenue Code of 1954 (1954 Code). Section 167(a) provided:

> SEC. 167(a). General Rule. — There shall be allowed as a depreciation deduction a reasonable allowance for the exhaustion, wear and tear (including a reasonable allowance for obsolescence)—
>
> (1) of property used in the trade or business, or
>
> (2) of property held for the production of income.

The regulations under this section expanded on the text of section 167 by providing that personal property was only depreciable before ERTA if the taxpayer established the useful life of the property. See sec. 1.167(a)-1(a) and (b), Income Tax Regs.

The "useful life" of property under pre-ERTA law was the period over which the asset could reasonably be expected to be useful to the taxpayer in his or her trade or business, or in the production of his or her income. . . . This useful life period was not always the physical life or maximum useful life inherent in the asset. . . . A primary factor to consider in determining an asset's useful life was any "wear and tear and decay or decline from natural causes" that was inflicted upon the asset. Sec. 1.167(a)-1(b), Income Tax Regs.

Before ERTA, the primary method that was utilized to ascertain the useful life for personal property was the asset depreciation range (ADR) system. Under the ADR system, which was generally effective for assets placed in service after 1970 and before 1981, property was grouped into broad classes of industry assets, and each class was assigned a guideline life. A range of years, *i.e.*, the ADR, was then provided for each class of personal property; the ADR extended from 20 percent below to 20 percent above the guideline class life. For each asset account in the class, the taxpayer selected either a class life or an ADR that was utilized as the useful life for computing depreciation. If an asset was not . . . eligible for ADR treatment, or if the taxpayer did not elect to use the ADR system, the useful life of that asset was generally determined based on either the particular facts and circumstances that applied thereto, or by agreement between the taxpayer and the Commissioner. . . .

In enacting ERTA, the Congress found that the pre-ERTA rules for determining depreciation allowances were unnecessarily complicated and did not generate the investment incentive that was critical for economic expansion. The Congress believed that the high inflation rates prevailing at that time undervalued the true worth of depreciation deductions and, hence, discouraged investment and economic competition. The Congress also believed that the determination of useful lives was "complex" and "inherently uncertain," and "frequently [resulted] in unproductive disagreements between taxpayers and the Internal Revenue Service." S.Rept. 97-144, at 47 (1981), 1981-2 C.B. 412, 425. Accordingly, the Congress decided that a new capital cost recovery system would have to be structured which, among other things, lessened the importance of the concept of useful life for depreciation purposes. . . . This new system is ACRS. ACRS is mandatory and applies to most tangible depreciable assets placed in service after 1980 and before 1987.

The rules implementing ACRS were prescribed in section 168. [Authors' note: the court then sets forth the relevant statutory provisions of ACRS, focusing specifically on the assignment of recovery periods to different classes of property, *e.g.*, 3-year and 5-year property.]

Thus, through ERTA, the Congress minimized the importance of useful life by: (1) Reducing the number of periods of years over which a taxpayer could depreciate his or her property from the multitudinous far-reaching periods of time listed for the ADR system to the four short periods of time listed in ERTA (*i.e.*, the 3-year, 5-year, 10-year, and 15-year ACRS periods), and (2) basing depreciation on an arbitrary statutory period of years that was unrelated to, and shorter than, an asset's estimated useful life. This minimization of the useful life concept through a deemed useful life was in spirit with the two main issues that ERTA was designed to address, namely: (1) Alleviating the income tax problems that resulted mainly from complex depreciation computations and useful life litigation, and (2) responding to economic policy concerns that the pre-ERTA depreciation systems spread the depreciation deductions over such a long period of time that investment in income-producing assets was discouraged through the income tax system. S.Rept. 97-144, *supra* at 47, 1981-2 C.B. at 425. See generally 1981 Bluebook, at 75.

With respect to the pre-ERTA requirement of useful life, the Commissioner had initially taken the position that a taxpayer generally could not deduct depreciation on expensive works of art and curios that he purchased as office furniture. See A.R.R. 4530, II-2 C.B. 145 (1923). This position was superseded by a similar position that was reflected in Rev.Rul. 68-232, 1968-1 C.B. 79.

In the instant case, respondent determined that petitioners were not entitled to deduct depreciation for the Tourte bows. On brief, respondent supports her disallowance with two primary arguments. First, respondent argues that the useful lives of the Tourte bows are indeterminable because the bows are treasured works of art for which it is impossible to determine useful lives. According to respondent, the Tourte bows are works of art because the Tourte bows have existed for more than 100 years and have increased in value overthat time; the presence of an independent market for the Tourte bows also gives them a value independent of their capacity to be used to play music, and serves to extend their useful lives indefinitely.

As an alternative to this first argument, respondent argues that the Tourte bows are depreciable under section 168 only if petitioners first prove that each bow has a determinable useful life within the meaning of section 167. In this regard, respondent contends that petitioners must prove a specific or reasonable estimate of the number of years that the Tourte bows will be useful in order to depreciate them under ACRS. Given that the Tourte bows have existed for more than 100 years, respondent concludes, petitioners may not depreciate the Tourte bows because petitioners cannot determine the number of remaining years during which the Tourte bows will continue to be useful.

Petitioners' argument is more straightforward. According to petitioners, they may claim depreciation on the Tourte bows because the Tourte bows: (1) Were necessary to their profession as full-time professional violinists, and (2) suffered wear and tear attributable to their use in that profession. In this regard, petitioners contend, the Tourte bows can be used to produce beautiful sounds superior to those produced by any newer bow, and the Tourte bows harmonize this beautiful music with the reputation of the Philharmonic as one of the most prestigious orchestras in the world.

We agree with petitioners that they may depreciate the Tourte Bows under ACRS. ERTA was enacted partially to address and eliminate the issue that we are faced with today, namely, a disagreement between taxpayers and the Commissioner over the useful life of assets that were used in taxpayers' trades or businesses. With this "elimination of disagreements" purpose in mind, the Congress defined five broad classes of "recovery property," and provided the periods of years over which taxpayers could recover their costs of this "recovery property." Two of these classes, the 3-year and 5-year classes, applied only to personal property; the 3-year class included certain short-lived assets such as automobiles and light-duty trucks, and the 5-year class included all other tangible personal property that was not within the 3-year class. H. Conf. Rept. 97-215, at 206–208 (1981), 1981-2 C.B. 481, 487–488. Thus, under section 168 as added to the 1954 Code by ERTA, personal property that is "recovery property" must be either 3-year or 5-year class property. Sec. 168(c)(2) as added to the 1954 Code by ERTA ("Each item of recovery property shall be assigned to one of the following classes of property"). Although "3-year property" requires a taxpayer to determine whether the property had a class life under ADR of 4 years or less, the term "5-year property" is appropriately designed to include all other section 1245 class property.

Inasmuch as section 168(a) allows a taxpayer to deduct depreciation with respect to "recovery property," petitioners may deduct depreciation on the Tourte bows if the bows fall within the meaning of that term. The term "recovery property" is defined broadly under ERTA to mean tangible property of a character subject to the allowance for depreciation and placed in service after 1980. Accordingly, property is "recovery property" if it is: (1) tangible, (2) placed in service after 1980, (3) of a character subject to the allowance for depreciation, and (4) used in the trade or business, or held for the production of income.

The Tourte bows fit snugly within the definition of recovery property. First, it is indisputable that the Tourte bows are tangible property, and that they were placed in service after 1980. Thus, the first two prerequisites for ACRS depreciation are met. Second, petitioners regularly used the Tourte bows in their trade or business as professional violinists during the year in issue. Accordingly, we conclude that petitioners have also met this prerequisite for depreciating the Tourte bows.

The last prerequisite for depreciating personal property under section 168 is that the property must be "of a character subject to the allowance for depreciation." The term "of a character subject to the allowance for depreciation" is undefined in the 1954 Code. Comparing the language that the Congress used in section 167(a) of the 1954 Code immediately before its amendment by ERTA, with the language that it used in section 168(a) and (c)(1) as added to the 1954 Code by ERTA, we believe that the Congress used the term "depreciation" in section 168(c)(1), to refer to the term "exhaustion, wear and tear (including a reasonable allowance for obsolescence)" that is contained in section 167(a). Accordingly, we conclude that the term "of a character subject to the allowance for depreciation" means that property must suffer exhaustion, wear and tear, or obsolescence in order to be depreciated. Accordingly, petitioners will meet the final requirement under section 168 if the Tourte bows are subject to exhaustion, wear and tear, or obsolescence.

We are convinced that petitioners' frequent use of the Tourte bows subjected them to substantial wear and tear during the year in issue. Petitioners actively played their violins using the Tourte bows, and this active use resulted in substantial wear and tear to the bows. Indeed, respondent's expert witness even acknowledged at trial that the Tourte bows suffered wear and tear stemming from petitioners' business; the witness testified that the Tourte bows had eroded since he had examined them 3 years before, and that wood had come off them. Thus, we conclude that petitioners have satisfied the final prerequisite for depreciating personal property under section 168, and, accordingly, hold that petitioners may depreciate the Tourte bows during the year in issue. Allowing petitioners to depreciate the Tourte bows comports with the text of section 168, and enables them to match their costs for the Tourte bows with the income generated therefrom. Refusing to allow petitioners to deduct depreciation on the Tourte bows, on the other hand, would contradict section 168 and vitiate the accounting principle that allows taxpayers to write off income-producing assets against the income produced by those assets.

With respect to respondent's arguments in support of a contrary holding, we believe that respondent places too much reliance on the fact that the Tourte bows are old and have appreciated in value since petitioners acquired them. Indeed, respondent believes that this appreciation, in and of itself, serves to prevent petitioners from claiming any depreciation on the Tourte bows. We disagree; section 168 does not support her proposition that a taxpayer may not depreciate a business asset due to its age, or due to the fact that the asset may have appreciated in value over time. . . . Moreover, we find merit in petitioners' claim that they should be able to depreciate an asset that receives substantial wear and tear through frequent use in their trade or business. Simply stated, the concept of depreciation is appropriately designed to allow taxpayers to recover the cost or other basis of a business asset through annual depreciation deductions.

We also reject respondent's contention that the Tourte bows are nondepreciable because they have value as collectibles independent of their use in playing musical instruments, and that this value prolongs the Tourte bows' useful life forever. First, it is firmly established that the term "useful life" under pre-ERTA law refers to the period of time in which a particular asset is useful to the taxpayer in his or her trade or business. Thus, the fact that an asset such as the Tourte bows may outlive a taxpayer is not dispositive of the issue of whether that asset has a useful life for depreciation purposes under pre-ERTA law. Second, the same argument concerning a separate, nonbusiness value can be made of many other assets. Such types of assets could include, for example, automobiles, patented property, highly sophisticated machinery, and real property. For the Court to delve into the determination of whether a particular asset has a separate, nonbusiness value would make the concept of depreciation a subjective issue and would be contrary to the Congress' intent to simplify the concept and computation of depreciation.

With respect to respondent's contention that petitioners must prove a definite useful life of the Tourte bows, we acknowledge that the concept of useful life was critical under pre-ERTA law. Indeed, the concept of useful life was necessary and indispensable to the computation of depreciation because taxpayers were required to recover their investments in personal property over the estimated useful life of the property. Sec. 1.167(a)-1(a), Income Tax Regs. However, the Congress enacted ERTA, in part, to avoid constant disagreements over the useful lives of assets, to shorten the writeoff periods for assets, and to encourage investment by providing for accelerated cost recovery through the tax law. S.Rept. 97-144, at 47 (1981), 1981-2 C.B. 412, 425. To these ends, the Congress created two short periods of years over which taxpayers would depreciate tangible personal property used in trade or business; the 3-year and 5-year recovery periods, respectively, are the deemed useful life of personal property. After the taxpayer has written off his or her asset over this 3-year or 5-year period, the taxpayer's basis in that asset will be zero; thus, the taxpayer will need to purchase a new asset in order to receive a future tax deduction with respect thereto. Respondent's argument that a taxpayer must first prove the useful life of personal property before he or she may depreciate it over the 3-year or 5-year period would bring the Court back to pre-ERTA law and reintroduce the disagreements that the Congress intended to eliminate by its enactment of ERTA. This the Court will not do.

Determinable means "that can be determined." Webster's New World Dictionary 375 (3d coll. ed. 1988). Accordingly, once a taxpayer establishes that an asset is subject to exhaustion, wear and tear, or obsolescence, we can determine whether its useful life is 3-year or 5-year class property under ACRS. As coherently and succinctly stated by this Court in a Court-reviewed opinion:

> Availability of deductions for depreciation on tangible property in this case is dependent solely upon compliance with section 168, which has only two requirements for deduction of depreciation. First, the asset (tangible) must be of a type which is subject to wear and tear, decay, decline, or

exhaustion. . . . Second, the property must be used in the taxpayer's trade or business or held for the production of income. . . . The language of the section is unequivocal. [*Noyce v. Commissioner*, 97 T.C. at 689.]

We have considered all other arguments made by respondent and find them to be without merit.

Ruwe, Judge, concurring:

In this case, section 168 is being applied to violin bows used by professional violinists. Everyone would ordinarily agree that such an asset is the "type" of asset that would be subject to an allowance for depreciation.

Under section 167, depreciation was allowed over the useful life of the asset in order to allow taxpayers to deduct the anticipated loss in value attributable to wear and tear. This, in turn, required the often difficult task of proving the useful life and salvage or residual value of the asset. In a significant step in the direction of tax simplification, both of these requirements were eliminated by section 168, which specifies the number of years over which the cost of certain types of assets may be deducted and eliminates the need to calculate salvage or residual value in order to determine the expected economic loss.

Everyone seems to favor tax simplification until the simplified law is actually applied to a real set of facts and produces a less-than-perfect result. The dissenting opinions would resurrect the obligation to establish an asset's actual expected useful life and the actual expected decrease in value over that life, in order to qualify for a section 168 deduction. It is unclear whether the dissenters intend to limit their analyses to assets that are "works of art," whatever that term may mean. However, their legal theories would seem to apply to any case where the Commissioner raises the useful life and value issues.

I can understand the dissenters' concern that section 168 might allow an asset to be written off over a period much shorter than its actual useful life and that the entire cost might be deducted despite the fact that there might be no actual economic decrease in value. However, that is the price of the tax simplification implicit in section 168.

LIDDLE v. COMMISSIONER
United States Tax Court
103 T.C. 285 (1994), *aff'd*, 65 F.3d 329 (3d Cir. 1995)

[Authors' note: The sole issue for decision in this case was whether the taxpayer was entitled to the 1987 depreciation deduction that he claimed under the Accelerated Cost Recovery System (ACRS) on a 17th-century Ruggeri bass viol (Viol) that petitioner used in his trade or business as a full-time professional musician. During the relevant time period, the taxpayer used the Viol as his primary instrument in his full-time professional work as a musician. As the majority noted: "he used it for practice, auditions, rehearsals, and performances with symphony orchestras. Petitioner's use of the Viol subjected it to wear and tear that did not reduce its economic value." Applying the same analysis as that used in *Simon*, the majority opinion concluded that the taxpayer was entitled to the depreciation deduction claimed. The dissenting opinion of Judge Halpern is included below for your careful consideration.]

HALPERN, JUDGE, dissenting:

Section 168(a) allows a deduction with respect to recovery property. For purposes of section 168(a), property is recovery property if, among other things, it is tangible property of a character subject to the allowance for depreciation. Sec. 168(c)(1). Petitioners bear the burden of proving that the Viol is recovery property. The majority has found that "Petitioner's use of the Viol subjected it to wear and tear that did not reduce its economic value." The majority has also found that, with regard to valuable instruments such as the Viol, "there is no evidence that such wear and tear [as is suffered by musical instruments in general] exhausts the utility and value of the instruments over definite time periods." Based on those two findings, I would conclude that petitioners have failed to carry their burden of proving that the Viol is recovery property, because they have failed to prove that it is of a character subject to the allowance for depreciation. Accordingly, I would hold for respondent that petitioners are not entitled to a deduction under section 168 with respect to the Viol.

Relationship Between Sections 167 and 168

Section 167(a) provides that a reasonable allowance for the exhaustion, wear and tear, and obsolescence of property used in the trade or business or of property held by the taxpayer for the production of income shall be allowed as a depreciation deduction. In the case of recovery property within the meaning of section 168, the deduction allowable under section 168 is, with certain exceptions, deemed to constitute the reasonable allowance provided for by section 167. If not clear from the face of the statute, pertinent legislative history makes clear that no property for which a depreciation deduction would be unavailable under section 167 can qualify for a deduction under section 168. Indeed, section 1.168-3(a)(1)(ii), Proposed Income Tax Regs. states: "Property is considered recovery property only if such property would have been depreciable under section 167."

The Relationship of Wear and Tear to Useful Life

Under section 167, it is necessary to establish the useful life of property in order to determine the year's allowance for exhaustion, wear and tear, and obsolescence. Section 1.167(a)-1(a), Income Tax Regs., provides, in part:

> The allowance is that amount which should be set aside for the taxable year in accordance with a reasonably consistent plan (not necessarily at a uniform rate), so that the aggregate of the amounts set aside, plus the salvage value, will, at the end of the estimated useful life of the depreciable property, equal the cost or other basis of the property as provided in section 167(g) and 1.167(g)-1. . . .

It is beyond dispute that no deduction is allowable under section 167 with respect to property that does not have a determinable useful life (*i.e.*, a useful life capable of being settled, fixed, or determined). Wear and tear clearly are factors to be considered in fixing or determining the useful life of property. See sec. 1.167(a)-1(b), Income Tax Regs. Nevertheless, the useful life of property may remain undetermined (*i.e.*, undeterminable) despite a showing of wear and tear. As Professors Bittker and Lokken have put it: "the taxpayer must be able to show that the property is subject to exhaustion, wear and tear, or obsolescence during a period whose duration can be estimated with reasonable accuracy." Bittker & Lokken, Federal Taxation of Income, Estates and Gifts, par. 23.2.4, at 23–32 (2d ed. 1989); see sec. 1.167(a)-3, Income Tax Regs. (depreciation allowed for intangibles reasonably shown to be of use for only a limited period). Thus, for instance, if regular maintenance would prevent or restore the loss in utility occasioned by wear and tear (such that, on account of such maintenance, the property will not wear out), the expectation of wear and tear alone is an insufficient basis upon which to claim a deduction for depreciation.

Majority's Findings

The majority finds that the wear and tear suffered by the Viol is not of a kind that would force the Viol to be retired from service after a determinable period. Indeed, it appears that, with regular maintenance, the Viol has remained playable for over 200 years. Simply put, the Viol is not property subject to wear and tear that, in a tax sense, limits its life and entitles the owner to a deduction for depreciation.

Majority's Failing

The majority has failed to discriminate between property with a useful life that, although undetermined, is determinable and property with a useful life that is indeterminable. The majority's failure results from its misidentification of "property of a character subject to the allowance for depreciation." See sec. 168(c)(1). By focusing only on wear and tear, and ignoring altogether whether the useful life of the property is determinable, the majority has identified, and allowed a deduction for, a class of property that contains property for which no deduction is allowable under section 167: viz, property with an indeterminable useful life. Section 168 indicates plainly enough that Congress wished to eliminate some disputes over useful life. Nothing indicates, however, that Congress intended to allow a deduction for property of a type that, previously, had been nondepreciable on account of the taxpayer's inability to establish a useful life. Section 168 (as here in issue) was added to the Code by section 201(a) of the Economic Recovery Tax Act of 1981 (ERTA), Pub.L. 97-34, 95 Stat. 172, 203. H. Conf. Rept. 97-215 (1981), 1981-2 C.B. 481, accompanied the conference agreement with respect to H.R. 4242, 97th Cong., 1st Sess. (1981), which was enacted as ERTA. The portion of the Joint Explanatory Statement of the Committee of Conference relevant to section 201(a) of ERTA contains the following:

> House bill. — Under present law, assets used in a trade or business or for the production of income are depreciable if they are subject to wear and tear, decay or decline from natural causes or obsolescence. Assets that do not decline in value on a predictable basis or that do not have a determin-

able useful life, such as land, goodwill, and stock are not depreciable.

> Under the House bill, most tangible depreciable property (real and personal) is covered by the accelerated cost recovery system (ACRS). However, ACRS does not apply to (1) property not depreciated in terms of years . . . and (2) property amortized. . . .

H. Conf. Rept. 97-215, *supra*, 1981-2 C.B. at 487. It is difficult, if not impossible, to read that language in light of the conference agreement and believe that the conferees intended property with an indeterminable useful life to be eligible for ACRS.

Difficulties Faced by the Majority

The majority's interpretation presents it with clear difficulties. The majority acknowledges that "works of art" remain nondepreciable, and, thus, outside of section 168. Traditionally, of course, that is because works of art generally lack a determinable useful life. See, *e.g., Clinger v. Commissioner*, T.C. Memo. 1990-459 (petitioner failed to establish that painting had determinable useful life); Rev. Rul. 68-232, 1968-1 C.B. 79. The majority, however, distinguishes nondepreciable works of art on the ground that they are not used "actively, regularly, and routinely" to produce income in a trade or business. The statutory source of that test is unidentified. Perhaps the majority is simply indulging in the presumption that, for want of active, regular, and routine use, works of art have an indefinite useful life. If so, then I fail to see why useful life (*i.e.*, the determinability thereof) is not a question of fact here to be proven by petitioners.

Not a Clean Slate

Congress did not write on a clean slate when it added section 168 to the Code. The slate already contained section 167, which, with respect to the aspect at issue, Congress left unmodified. In effect, Congress added section 168 on top of section 167. If active, regular, and routine use are to replace determinable useful life as the touchstone for depreciability, then I believe that the majority has opened a loophole that it is inconceivable Congress intended. What is to stop wealthy taxpayers from stuffing (indeed, overstuffing) their offices with valuable antique furniture that they may write off over the 7-year recovery period now applicable to office furniture? In *Noyce v. Commissioner*, 97 T.C. 670, 688 (1991), we rejected the notion that depreciation deductions must be reasonable in amount. Now, as long as the property is regularly (and actively) used for business purposes, we decide to turn a blind eye to its utility as a (valuable) collectible. It seems to me that we — and not Congress — have declared a field day for purveyors of fine antique furniture and other dual-purpose collectibles. It is our job to interpret the statutes as Congress wrote them and not to interpret them as if we had written them. The latter is what I fear the majority has done, and I cannot join that effort. For that reason, I dissent.

REVENUE PROCEDURE 87-56 (Excerpt)
1987-2 C.B. 674

SECTION 1. PURPOSE

The purpose of this revenue procedure is to set forth the class lives of property that are necessary to compute the depreciation allowances available under section 168 of the Internal Revenue Code, as amended by section 201(a) of the Tax Reform Act of 1986 (Act), 1986-3 (Vol. 1) C.B. 38. Rev. Proc. 87-57, page 17, this Bulletin, describes the applicable depreciation methods, applicable recovery periods, and applicable conventions that must be used in computing depreciation allowances under section 168.

SEC. 2. GENERAL RULES OF APPLICATION

.01 In general. This revenue procedure specifies class lives and recovery periods for property subject to depreciation under the general depreciation system provided in section 168(a) of the Code or the alternative depreciation system provided in section 168(g).

.02 Definition of Class Life. Except with respect to certain assigned property described in section 3 of this revenue procedure, for purposes of both the general depreciation system and the alternative depreciation system, the term "class life" means the class life that would be applicable for any property as of January 1, 1986, under section 167(m) of the Code (determined without regard to paragraph 4 thereof and determined as if the taxpayer had made an election under section 167(m)). The class life that would be applicable for any property as of January 1, 1986, under section 167(m), is the asset guideline period (midpoint class life) for the asset guideline class in which such property is classified under Rev. Proc. 83-35, 1983-1 C.B. 745. However, for purposes of the alternative depreciation system, section 168(g)(3)(B) assigns a class life to certain property that is taken into account under section 168 rather than the class life that would be applicable as of January 1, 1986. The class life of property that is either determined as of January 1, 1986, under Rev. Proc. 83-35 or assigned under section 168(g)(3)(B) may be modified by the Secretary pursuant to authority granted under section 168(i)(1). See section 4 of this revenue procedure.

.03 Rev. Proc. 83-35. Rev. Proc. 83-35 sets out the asset guideline classes, asset guideline periods and ranges, and annual asset guideline repair allowance percentages for the Class Life Asset Depreciation Range System. The asset guideline periods (midpoint class lives) set out in Rev. Proc. 83-35 are also used in defining the classes of recovery property under the Accelerated Cost Recovery System (that is, section 168 of the Code as in effect prior to amendment by section 201 of the Act). Rev. Proc. 83-35 remains effective for property subject to depreciation under those systems. Rev. Proc. 83-35 does not apply to property subject to depreciation under section 168, other than as a basis for determining the class lives of such property under section 2.02 of this revenue procedure.

.04 Property with no class life. Property that is neither described in an asset guideline class listed in section 5 of this revenue procedure nor assigned a class life under section 168(g)(3)(B) of the Code is treated as property having no class life for purposes of section 168 unless and until a class life is prescribed by the Secretary pursuant to the authority granted under section 168(i)(1). See section 4 of this revenue procedure. The general and alternative depreciation systems contain separate rules for classifying property that does not have a class life.

SEC. 4. PRESCRIPTION AND MODIFICATION OF CLASS LIVES

.01 Section 168(i)(1)(B) of the Code provides that the Secretary, through an office established in the Treasury, shall monitor and analyze actual experience with respect to all depreciable assets. Except in the case of section 1250 property that is residential rental property or nonresidential real property, the Secretary, through that office, (i) may prescribe a new class life for any property, (ii) in the case of assigned property, may modify any assigned item, or (iii) may prescribe a class life for any property that does not have a class life within the meaning of section 2.02 of this revenue procedure. Any class life or assigned item that is prescribed or modified pursuant to this authority shall be used for all purposes in determining depreciation allowances under the general depreciation system and the alternative depreciation system. In the case of assigned property as defined in section 168(i)(1)(E), no class life set forth in this revenue procedure nor any other assigned item may be modified, unless such modification reflects a shortening of such class life, for property placed in service prior to January 1, 1992.

.02 Prescription or modification of class lives under the authority granted in section 168(i)(1)(B) of the Code shall reflect the anticipated useful lives, and the anticipated decline in value over time (that is, economic depreciation) of an asset to the industry or other group. Rules and practices governing prescription and modification of class lives pursuant to the authority granted in section 168(i)(1)(B) shall be announced through the office referred to in section 4.01 of this revenue procedure.

SEC. 5. TABLES OF CLASS LIVES AND RECOVERY PERIODS

.01 Except for property described in section 5.02, below, the class lives (if any) and recovery periods for property subject to depreciation under section 168 of the Code appear in the tables below. These tables are based on the definition of class life in section 2.02 of this revenue procedure and the assigned items described in section 3 of this revenue procedure.

.02 For purposes of depreciation under the general depreciation system, residential rental property has a recovery period of 27.5 years and nonresidential real property has a recovery period of 31.5 years. For purposes of the alternative depreciation system, residential rental and non-residential real property each has a recovery period of 40 years. . . .

Asset class	Description of assets included	Class Life (in years)	Recovery Periods (in years)	
			General Depreciation System	Alternative Depreciation System
00.11	**Office Furniture, Fixtures, and Equipment:** Includes furniture and fixtures that are not a structural component of a building. Includes such assets as desks, files, safes, and communications equipment. Does not include communications equipment that is included in other classes.	10	7	10
00.12	**Information Systems:** Includes computers and their peripheral equipment used in administering normal business transactions and the maintenance of business records, their retrieval and analysis. . . . Also, does not include equipment of a kind used primarily for amusement or entertainment of the user	6	5	5
00.13	**Data Handling Equipment, except Computers:** Includes only typewriters, calculators, adding and accounting machines, copiers, and duplicating equipment	6	5	6
00.21	**Airplanes (airframes and engines), except those used in commercial or contract carrying of passengers or freight, and all helicopters (airframes and engines)**	6	5	6
00.22	**Automobiles, Taxis**	3	5	5
00.23	**Buses**	9	5	9
00.241	**Light General Purpose Trucks:** Includes trucks for use over the road (actual unloaded weight less than 13,000 pounds)	4	5	5

Asset class	Description of assets included	Class Life (in years)	Recovery Periods (in years)	
			General Depreciation System	Alternative Depreciation System
00.242	**Heavy General Purpose Trucks:** Includes heavy general purpose trucks, concrete ready mix-truckers, and ore trucks, for use over the road (actual unloaded weight 13,000 pounds or more)	6	5	6
00.003	**Land Improvements:** Includes improvements directly to or added to land . . . provided such improvements are depreciable. Examples of such assets might include sidewalks, roads, canals, . . . fences, landscaping, shrubbery. . . .	20	15	20

REVENUE PROCEDURE 87-57 (Excerpt)
1987-2 C.B. 687

Table 1.   **General Depreciation System**
Applicable Depreciation Method: 200 or 150 Percent
Declining Balance Switching to Straight Line
Applicable Recovery Periods: 3, 5, 7, 10, 15, 20
years
Applicable Convention: Half-year

If the Recovery Year is:	and the Recovery Period is:					
	3-year	5-year	7-year	10-year	15-year*	20-year*
	the Depreciation Rate is:					
1	33.33	20.00	14.29	10.00	5.00	3.750
2	44.45	32.00	24.49	18.00	9.50	7.219
3	14.81	19.20	17.49	14.40	8.55	6.677
4	7.41	11.52	12.49	11.52	7.70	6.177
5		11.52	8.93	9.22	6.93	5.713
6		5.76	8.92	7.37	6.23	5.285
7			8.93	6.55	5.90	4.888
8			4.46	6.55	5.90	4.522
9				6.56	5.91	4.462
10				6.55	5.90	4.461
11				3.28	5.91	4.462
12					5.90	4.461
13					5.91	4.462
14					5.90	4.461
15					5.91	4.462
16					2.95	4.461
17						4.462
18						4.461
19						4.462
20						4.461
21						2.231

*Authors' Note: Under § 168(b)(2), 15-year and 20-year property are subject to depreciation under the 150 percent declining balance method.

Table 2.   General Depreciation System
              Applicable Depreciation Method: 200 or 150 Percent
              Declining Balance Switching to Straight Line
              Applicable Recovery Periods: 3, 5, 7, 10, 15, 20
                years
              Applicable Convention: Mid-quarter (property placed
                in service in first quarter)

If the Recovery Year is:	and the Recovery Period is:					
	3-year	5-year	7-year	10-year	15-year	20-year
	the Depreciation Rate is:					
1	58.33	35.00	25.00	17.50	8.75	6.563
2	27.78	26.00	21.43	16.50	9.13	7.000
3	12.35	15.60	15.31	13.20	8.21	6.482
4	1.54	11.01	10.93	10.56	7.39	5.996
5		11.01	8.75	8.45	6.65	5.546
6		1.38	8.74	6.76	5.99	5.130
7			8.75	6.55	5.90	4.746
8			1.09	6.55	5.91	4.459
9				6.56	5.90	4.459
10				6.55	5.91	4.459
11				0.82	5.90	4.459
12					5.91	4.460
13					5.90	4.459
14					5.91	4.460
15					5.90	4.459
16					0.74	4.460
17						4.459
18						4.460
19						4.459
20						4.460
21						0.557

Table 3.   General Depreciation System
               Applicable Depreciation Method: 200 or 150 Percent
               Declining Balance Switching to Straight Line
               Applicable Recovery Periods: 3, 5, 7, 10, 15, 20
                  years
               Applicable Convention: Mid-quarter (property placed
                  in service in second quarter)

If the Recovery Year is:	and the Recovery Period is:					
	3-year	5-year	7-year	10-year	15-year	20-year
	the Depreciation Rate is:					
1	41.67	25.00	17.85	12.50	6.25	4.688
2	38.89	30.00	23.47	17.50	9.38	7.148
3	14.14	18.00	16.76	14.00	8.44	6.612
4	5.30	11.37	11.97	11.20	7.59	6.116
5		11.37	8.87	8.96	6.83	5.658
6		4.26	8.87	7.17	6.15	5.233
7			8.87	6.55	5.91	4.841
8			3.33	6.55	5.90	4.478
9				6.56	5.91	4.463
10				6.55	5.90	4.463
11				2.46	5.91	4.463
12					5.90	4.463
13					5.91	4.463
14					5.90	4.463
15					5.91	4.462
16					2.21	4.463
17						4.462
18						4.463
19						4.462
20						4.463
21						1.673

Table 4.   General Depreciation System
           Applicable Depreciation Method: 200 or 150 Percent
           Declining Balance Switching to Straight Line
           Applicable Recovery Periods: 3, 5, 7, 10, 15, 20
             years
           Applicable Convention: Mid-quarter (property placed
             in service in third quarter)

If the Recovery Year is:	and the Recovery Period is:					
	3-year	5-year	7-year	10-year	15-year	20-year
	the Depreciation Rate is:					
1	25.00	15.00	10.71	7.50	3.75	2.813
2	50.00	34.00	25.51	18.50	9.63	7.289
3	16.67	20.40	18.22	14.80	8.66	6.742
4	8.33	12.24	13.02	11.84	7.80	6.237
5		11.30	9.30	9.47	7.02	5.769
6		7.06	8.85	7.58	6.31	5.336
7			8.86	6.55	5.90	4.936
8			5.53	6.55	5.90	4.566
9				6.56	5.91	4.460
10				6.55	5.90	4.460
11				4.10	5.91	4.460
12					5.90	4.460
13					5.91	4.461
14					5.90	4.460
15					5.91	4.461
16					3.69	4.460
17						4.461
18						4.460
19						4.461
20						4.460
21						2.788

Table 5.   General Depreciation System
           'Applicable Depreciation Method: 200 or 150 Percent
           Declining Balance Switching to Straight Line
           Applicable Recovery Periods: 3, 5, 7, 10, 15, 20
              years
           Applicable Convention: Mid-quarter (property placed
              in service in fourth quarter)

If the Recovery Year is:	and the Recovery Period is:					
	3-year	5-year	7-year	10-year	15-year	20-year
	the Depreciation Rate is:					
1	8.33	5.00	3.57	2.50	1.25	0.938
2	61.11	38.00	27.55	19.50	9.88	7.430
3	20.37	22.80	19.68	15.60	8.89	6.872
4	10.19	13.68	14.06	12.48	8.00	6.357
5		10.94	10.04	9.98	7.20	5.880
6		9.58	8.73	7.99	6.48	5.439
7			8.73	6.55	5.90	5.031
8			7.64	6.55	5.90	4.654
9				6.56	5.90	4.458
10				6.55	5.91	4.458
11				5.74	5.90	4.458
12					5.91	4.458
13					5.90	4.458
14					5.91	4.458
15					5.90	4.458
16					5.17	4.458
17						4.458
18						4.459
19						4.458
20						4.459
21						3.901

Table 6. General Depreciation System
Applicable Depreciation Method: Straight Line
Applicable Recovery Period: 27.5 years
Applicable Convention: Mid-month

If the Recovery Year is:

And the Month in the First Recovery Year the Property is Placed in Service is:
the Depreciation Rate is:

Recovery Year	1	2	3	4	5	6	7	8	9	10	11	12
1	3.485	3.182	2.879	2.576	2.273	1.970	1.667	1.364	1.061	0.758	0.455	0.152
2	3.636	3.636	3.636	3.636	3.636	3.636	3.636	3.636	3.636	3.636	3.636	3.636
3	3.636	3.636	3.636	3.636	3.636	3.636	3.636	3.636	3.636	3.636	3.636	3.636
4	3.636	3.636	3.636	3.636	3.636	3.636	3.636	3.636	3.636	3.636	3.636	3.636
5	3.636	3.636	3.636	3.636	3.636	3.636	3.636	3.636	3.636	3.636	3.636	3.636
6	3.636	3.636	3.636	3.636	3.636	3.636	3.636	3.636	3.636	3.636	3.636	3.636
7	3.636	3.636	3.636	3.636	3.636	3.636	3.636	3.636	3.636	3.636	3.636	3.636
8	3.636	3.636	3.636	3.636	3.636	3.636	3.636	3.636	3.636	3.636	3.636	3.636
9	3.636	3.636	3.636	3.636	3.636	3.636	3.636	3.636	3.636	3.636	3.636	3.636
10	3.637	3.637	3.637	3.637	3.637	3.637	3.636	3.636	3.636	3.636	3.636	3.636
11	3.636	3.636	3.636	3.636	3.636	3.636	3.637	3.637	3.637	3.637	3.637	3.637
12	3.637	3.637	3.637	3.637	3.637	3.637	3.636	3.636	3.636	3.636	3.636	3.636
13	3.636	3.636	3.636	3.636	3.636	3.636	3.637	3.637	3.637	3.637	3.637	3.637
14	3.637	3.637	3.637	3.637	3.637	3.637	3.636	3.636	3.636	3.636	3.636	3.636
15	3.636	3.636	3.636	3.636	3.636	3.636	3.637	3.637	3.637	3.637	3.637	3.637
16	3.637	3.637	3.637	3.637	3.637	3.637	3.636	3.636	3.636	3.636	3.636	3.636
17	3.636	3.636	3.636	3.636	3.636	3.636	3.637	3.637	3.637	3.637	3.637	3.637
18	3.637	3.637	3.637	3.637	3.637	3.637	3.636	3.636	3.636	3.636	3.636	3.636
19	3.636	3.636	3.636	3.636	3.636	3.636	3.637	3.637	3.637	3.637	3.637	3.637
20	3.637	3.637	3.637	3.637	3.637	3.637	3.636	3.636	3.636	3.636	3.636	3.636
21	3.636	3.636	3.636	3.636	3.636	3.636	3.637	3.637	3.637	3.637	3.637	3.637
22	3.637	3.637	3.637	3.637	3.637	3.637	3.636	3.636	3.636	3.636	3.636	3.636
23	3.636	3.636	3.636	3.636	3.636	3.636	3.637	3.637	3.637	3.637	3.637	3.637
24	3.637	3.637	3.637	3.637	3.637	3.637	3.636	3.636	3.636	3.636	3.636	3.636
25	3.636	3.636	3.636	3.636	3.636	3.636	3.637	3.637	3.637	3.637	3.637	3.637
26	3.637	3.637	3.637	3.637	3.637	3.637	3.636	3.636	3.636	3.636	3.636	3.636
27	3.636	3.636	3.636	3.636	3.636	3.636	3.637	3.637	3.637	3.637	3.637	3.637
28	1.970	2.273	2.576	2.879	3.182	3.485	3.636	3.636	3.636	3.636	3.636	3.636
29	0.000	0.000	0.000	0.000	0.000	0.000	0.152	0.455	0.758	1.061	1.364	1.667

IRS Publication 946
— Table A-7a —
Depreciation Table for Nonresidential Real Property

The following table, from IRS Publication 946, "How to Depreciate Property" (2005), p. 72, provides depreciation rates for nonresidential rental property subject to the 39-year recovery period under the Revenue Reconciliation Act of 1993:

Table A–7a. Nonresidential Real Property
Mid-Month Convention
Straight Line — 39 Years

Month property placed in service

Year	1	2	3	4	5	6	7	8	9	10	11	12
1	2.461%	2.247%	2.033%	1.819%	1.605%	1.391%	1.177%	0.963%	0.749%	0.535%	0.321%	0.107%
2-39	2.564	2.564	2.564	2.564	2.564	2.564	2.564	2.564	2.564	2.564	2.564	2.564
40	0.107	0.321	0.535	0.749	0.963	1.177	1.391	1.605	1.819	2.033	2.247	2.461

Chapter 15

LOSSES AND BAD DEBTS

I. PROBLEMS

1. Dan owns a delivery business serving the Rocky Mountain states. In March of last year Dan purchased for $60,000 a new truck for use in his business. Dan sold the truck in September of this year for $35,000 to an unrelated person. The truck's appraised fair market value was $40,000 at the time of the sale. Dan's adjusted basis in the truck was $38,400 at the time of the sale.

    (a) May Dan deduct the loss he incurred on the sale? If so, how much loss may he deduct?

    (b) What result to Dan if he did not use the truck in his business but rather used it as his personal vehicle? Assume the truck's adjusted basis was $60,000 at the time of the sale.

    (c) What result to Dan in part (a) above if, instead of selling the truck this year, the truck was stolen and never recovered. Assume Dan had no insurance on the truck.

    (d) Assume that, instead of Dan selling the truck, the truck was totaled in an accident caused by the negligence of another person. Dan brought an action against that individual seeking reimbursement for the full fair market value of the truck. The action was finally settled out of court 18 months later. In the settlement, Dan received $35,000 for the destruction of his truck. When may Dan claim a loss deduction and in what amount?

2. Brittnie purchased on the open market 100 shares of Hi-Tech, Inc. stock three years ago for $15,000. Almost immediately after Brittnie purchased the stock, the stock fell in value to $5,000.

    (a) Brittnie believes the decline in the value of her Hi-Tech stock was a function of the fraudulent activity of various corporate officers of Hi-Tech. May she claim a loss deduction for the decline in value of her stock? Evaluate Brittnie's position.

    (b) Assume instead of purchasing the Hi-Tech stock, Brittnie opened an investment account with M, an investment advisor and securities broker. She invested $15,000 in the account and authorized M to make purchases, sales, and reinvestments of securities on her behalf. Over the past five years since she opened the account with M, on the basis of the monthly and annual statements issued to her by M, Brittnie reported a total of $10,000 of net investment gains on her federal income tax returns. She, however, never requested or received any distributions from her investment account. This year, Brittnie learned that she and others had been victims of a Ponzi scheme developed by M and that her stated investment account of $25,000 was actually worthless. Will Brittnie be entitled to claim a loss deduction and, if so, in what amount?

3. Ten years ago, Calvin's solely-owned corporation, which owns and operates a number of retail shoe stores, purchased lakefront land for $500,000. The intent was to build a cabin on the property for use by Calvin's family and friends. Because of a marital problem, however, Calvin never developed the property. He did occasionally use the property for picnics, camping, and boating purposes. This year, Calvin's corporation sold the property for $450,000. May the corporation deduct the loss on the property? Any tax consequences to Calvin?

4. Mary purchased an apartment in New York City for $1.2 million and made the apartment her principal residence for five years. Because of a job transfer, Mary moved to Seattle. At the time Mary moved, the apartment had an appraised fair market value of $1 million although her adjusted basis in the apartment was still $1.2 million. For almost two years, Mary tried unsuccessfully to sell the apartment. During that period, the apartment remained vacant and Mary made no effort to rent it. She finally found a buyer this year and sold the apartment for $950,000.

   (a) May Mary claim deductions for depreciation and maintenance expenses with respect to the apartment for the period during which she attempted to sell it? May she claim a loss on the sale of the apartment?

   (b) What difference, if any, would it make in your answer to (a) if Mary had offered the apartment for rent following her move to Seattle but, because of the large number of apartments available for rent, was unable to rent the apartment?

   (c) What difference, if any, would it make in your answer to (a) if Mary did not offer the apartment for sale because she was convinced New York real estate prices would rise significantly in the next few years? Assume that, at the same time, she was unwilling to offer the apartment for rent because she was concerned that renters could seriously damage it.

   (d) Assume that, after moving to Seattle, Mary rented the apartment for two years. When it became clear she would not be returning to New York, she sold the apartment. Assume Mary had been allowed depreciation deductions totaling $70,000 up to the time of the sale. What are the tax consequences to Mary if she sold the apartment for $900,000? $950,000?

5. Aunt Mabel devised her home to her favorite nephew, Harry. Her adjusted basis in her home was $100,000, but it was worth $300,000 at her death. Harry, in desperate need of cash, promptly sold the home for $250,000. What are the tax consequences to Harry?

6. Peter, an orthopedic surgeon, agreed to loan his brother Paul $200,000 so that Paul could start his own business. Paul signed a promissory note, agreeing to repay Peter $200,000 together with a market rate of interest on the unpaid balance. As a result of the failure of his business two years later, Paul did not repay Peter. One of the reasons Paul's business failed was that his primary customer declared bankruptcy and was unable to pay Paul the $250,000 he owed him. Paul is currently insolvent. Any deduction for Peter? Under what circumstances, if any, could Paul claim a deduction for the amount of the debt owed him by his customer?

7. Gloria was a reporter for a local newspaper owed by her family's corporation. Gloria owned 5% of the corporation's stock and her parents owned the remaining 95%. To keep the newspaper alive, Gloria loaned $100,000 to the corporation, which had been losing money for years. One year later, however, the newspaper failed. The following year, the corporation liquidated and Gloria received nothing. May Gloria deduct the $100,000 loan she will never be repaid? If so, what is the character of her loss? May Gloria deduct the loss on her stock? If so, what is the character of her loss?

Assignment for Chapter 15:

Complete the problems.

Read: Internal Revenue Code: §§ 165(a)–(f), (g)(1), (g)(2); 166. See also § 6511(d)(1).

Treasury Regulations: §§ 1.165-1; 1.165-4(a); 1.165-7(a), (b)(1); 1.165-8; 1.165-9; 1.166-1(a), (b), (c), (d)(1), (e); 1.166-2(a), (b), (c); 1.166-5(b), (d); 1.167(g)-1. Skim also §§ 1.165-2(a); 1.167(a)-8(a)(4).

Materials: Overview
             Cowles v. Commissioner
             United States v. Generes
             Revenue Ruling 2009-9

II. VOCABULARY

business bad debt
nonbusiness bad debt

III. OBJECTIVES

1. To distinguish between a realized loss and a mere decline in value.

2. To recall the limit on the amount deductible under both § 165 and § 166.

3. To compute the amount of loss recognized by a taxpayer in a given factual setting.

4. To describe circumstances in which a personal residence will be deemed to have been converted to income-producing property.

5. To explain the "lesser of" rule applicable to losses on property converted from personal to income-producing purposes.

6. To explain the timing of deductions allowed under § 165 or § 166.

7. To recall that § 166 controls when both § 165 and § 166 are nominally applicable.

8. To distinguish bad debts from gifts, compensation, or other transactions that do not give rise to bad debts.

9. To recall the distinction drawn between individual and non-individual losses in § 166.

10. To distinguish a business debt from a nonbusiness debt.

11. To recall the differing tax treatment given business and nonbusiness bad debts in § 166.

12. To give an example of when § 165 treatment is preferable to § 166 treatment, and vice versa.

IV. OVERVIEW

In Chapter 14, we studied the depreciation deduction as a method by which a taxpayer is permitted to recover capitalized costs. This chapter focuses on the deductions allowed by §§ 165 and 166 for losses and bad debts. Although at first glance these deductions may seem to have nothing in common with depreciation, they, too, may be regarded as statutory mechanisms providing for cost recovery in qualifying circumstances. For example, business equipment purchased for $1,000 will have an adjusted basis of zero after depreciation deductions totally $1,000 have been taken. Alternatively, suppose that after $600 of depreciation deductions have been taken, reducing the adjusted basis to $400, the equipment is sold for $100, resulting in an allowable loss of $300. The loss of $300 allows the taxpayer to recover the part of its $1,000 investment that had not been recovered through depreciation deductions ($600) and the proceeds of the sale ($100).

A. Losses

Section 165(a) authorizes a deduction for any uncompensated loss sustained during the year. Section 165(c), however, restricts the loss deduction for individuals to trade or business losses, losses in profit-seeking transactions, and casualty or theft losses. What does this suggest about losses sustained by corporations? The deduction allowed by § 165(c)(3) for personal losses resulting from a casualty or theft is considered in detail in Chapter 24 in conjunction with other deductions allowed for personal expenditures. Note, however, that a casualty or theft involving the taxpayer's business or investment property is governed by § 165(c)(1) or (c)(2), and not by (c)(3). Thus, for example, assume Taxpayer's uninsured business vehicle is destroyed by fire. Despite the casualty nature of the resulting loss, the loss is within § 165(c)(1) and is not subject to § 165(c)(3) and the limitations imposed by § 165(h), as would have been the case had the destruction occurred to Taxpayer's personal vehicle.

1. The Business or Profit Requirement for Individuals

Consistent with the principle that personal expenditures are generally nondeductible, § 165(c)(1) and (c)(2) require an individual's losses to be incurred in a business or profit-seeking transaction if they are to be deductible. This same requirement applies to the depreciation deduction. To permit the deduction of a personal loss is functionally equivalent to permitting depreciation of personal-use property or authorizing a deduction for personal expenses. Section 165(c)(1) and (c)(2) are thus appropriate restrictions on the sweeping language of § 165(a).

Section 165(c)(1) echoes the "trade or business" language of § 162(a); activities that constitute a trade or business for § 162 purposes should also qualify as a trade or business when the focus shifts to § 165. See Chapter 12 with respect to what constitutes a trade or business. In many cases, an individual will be indifferent as to whether a deductible loss falls within § 165(c)(1) or (c)(2), but in some circumstances it matters. For example, business losses may be deducted above the line — see § 62(a)(1) — while losses on profit-seeking transactions are below-the-line deductions unless they result from the sale or exchange or property. § 62(a)(3). Similarly, the net operating loss rules of § 172 also favor business losses over investment or other nonbusiness losses in the computation of net operating loss carrybacks and carryforwards.

More frequently, however, the dividing line at issue in § 165(c) litigation is not the line between business and profit-seeking activities, but the line between such activities, on the one side, and personal activities on the other. The language of § 165(c)(2) recalls that of § 212 and can be understood as part of the congressional response to the *Higgins* decision studied in Chapter 12. For example, if an expense with respect to property is deductible under § 212, a loss on that property is generally allowed under § 165(c)(2). Perhaps the most common example of a § 165(c)(2) loss is the loss an investor incurs upon selling stock for less than he paid for it. It is, nonetheless, worth stressing the specific language of § 165(c)(2).

Suppose, for example, Taxpayer buys her personal residence for $500,000 and some years later, when it is still her residence, sells it for $450,000. Is the $50,000 loss allowed? Instinctively, one responds that the loss is personal and nondeductible. But suppose Taxpayer insists that, at the time she offered the home for sale, she was hoping to make a profit, and she is thus in the same position as the unfortunate stock investor. Is the loss now deductible? The regulations, of course, answer this specific question negatively. Reg. § 1.165-9(a). But the principle extends beyond personal residences. Section 165(c)(2) speaks of a "transaction entered into for profit"; surely it cannot be enough that at the time of sale a taxpayer was hoping to make a profit since such a rule invites the virtual elimination of taxable income. The unlucky stock investor presumably had the requisite profit motive when he "entered into" the purchase of stock, and this is what distinguishes his situation from that of the residential homeowner. The fact that, prior to disposition, a loss was inevitable does not preclude finding that the transaction was entered into for profit.

Under the regulations, however, personal-use property may be converted into income-producing property so as to qualify for a § 165(c)(2) deduction on disposition. *See* Reg. § 1.165-9(b)(1). The question of whether a conversion has occurred is most apt to arise with regard to residences. See *Cowles v. Commissioner* in the materials, denying a loss where a former residence was offered for rent, but never actually rented, prior to sale.

Although the Service denied a loss deduction under the circumstances in *Cowles*, the Service nevertheless conceded that an offer to rent was sufficient to satisfy the "held for the production of income" standard of §§ 167 and 212. In *Newcombe v. Commissioner*, 54 T.C. 1298 (1970), cited in *Cowles*, §§ 167 and 212 deductions (depreciation and maintenance) were denied where the taxpayers offered their former residence for sale but not for rent. According to the Tax Court, however, an offer for sale could have effected conversion of the former residence to "property held for the production of income" if the taxpayer had established that he was seeking to realize "postconversion appreciation" in the value of the property. Where the profit sought by the taxpayer represents only the appreciation which took place during the period the taxpayer occupied the property, the property will not be deemed to have been "held for the production of income." 54 T.C. at 1303. "The placing of the property on the market for immediate sale, at or shortly after the time of its abandonment as a residence, will ordinarily be strong evidence that a taxpayer is not holding the property for postconversion appreciation in value. . . .

[I]f a taxpayer believes that the value of the property may appreciate and decides to hold it for some period in order to realize upon such anticipated appreciation, as well as any excess over his investment, it can be said that the property is being 'held for the production of income.' And this would be true regardless of whether his expectation of gain was reasonable." *Id.* at 1302-1303. Do the various distinctions made in *Cowles* and *Newcombe* make sense? Should the language "transaction entered into for profit" in § 165(c)(2) be interpreted differently than the language "held for the production of income" in § 167(a) and § 212?

A taxpayer may claim that personal-use property, such as a residence, has been purchased not only for personal purposes, but with the hope of making a profit on ultimate disposition. The taxpayer's primary purpose, however, will be controlling. See *Austin v. Commissioner*, 298 F.2d 583, 584 (2d Cir. 1962), stating that the "position for which petitioners contend [that simply having a profit motive satisfies the statute] would not provide a workable interpretation of § 165. . . . The logical interrelation of § 165 and § 262 requires a decision as to which of the two motives was dominant, so that one or the other section can be applied." It is exceedingly doubtful the profit-motive will be considered dominant when a taxpayer is making personal use of residential property. For example, in *Gevirtz v. Commissioner*, 123 F.2d 707 (2d Cir. 1941), the taxpayer bought land intending to build an apartment house on it, but instead (because other apartments were being built in the area) built and occupied a large residence, capable of conversion to apartments. Some years later, she vacated the property and thereafter tried unsuccessfully to rent or sell it. Ultimately, surrendering it to the mortgagee, she claimed a loss deduction. The court denied the deduction, holding she had abandoned her original profit motive and that the possibility of future business use was "clearly subsidiary" to her personal use.

Where property, however, is actually used at times for personal purposes and at other times for business or profit-seeking purposes, allocation of a loss between the (nondeductible) personal use and (deductible) business or profit-seeking use is allowable. See, for example, Revenue Ruling 72-111, 1972-1 C.B. 56, making such an allocation with respect to a loss realized on selling an automobile used partly for business and partly for personal purposes. A similar allocation is necessary when a loss is realized on property converted from personal to business or profit-seeking purposes. The loss attributable to the period of personal use is nondeductible, consistent with the general principle expressed in § 262. The subsequent business or profit-seeking loss is allowable. *See* Reg. §§ 1.165-9(b)(2), 1.165-9(c).

Under § 165(b), a taxpayer is not allowed a loss deduction in excess of the taxpayer's basis. Note the "lesser of" rule provided in the regulations: basis is limited, for loss purposes, to the lesser of fair market value or basis at the time of conversion adjusted for items, *e.g.*, depreciation, for the period subsequent to the conversion of the property to income-producing purposes. Any loss associated with personal use of the property prior to its conversion thus remains nondeductible. For example, if a car was purchased for $30,000 and used solely for personal purposes, no adjustment to its original basis of $30,000 would be made for depreciation since the car was not depreciable property within the meaning of §§ 167 and 168. Under the "lesser of" rule, if the car is later converted to business use when its value is only $15,000, a subsequent loss under § 165 cannot exceed $15,000 without rendering deductible the decline in value during the period of personal use. Consider, however, a conversion in the opposite direction. Suppose business property is converted to personal use, and a loss is thereafter realized. No deduction is allowable under §§ 165(c)(1) or (c)(2). Is this result appropriate? Should a loss be allowed on conversion?

As previously noted, in the case of personal-use property, *e.g.*, one's home, which is converted to income producing purposes, Regulation § 1.165-9(a)(2) requires that the taxpayer's basis for computing loss on that property, as determined under the "lesser of" rule, be adjusted for items such as depreciation for the period following the conversion. How is depreciation computed with respect to property converted to business or investment use? Regulation § 1.167(g)-1 states "the fair market value on the date of such conversion, if less than the adjusted basis of the property at that time, is the basis for computing depreciation." Consider the above example regarding the car converted to business use. The fair market value of the car at the time of the conversion was $15,000 while the taxpayer's adjusted basis in the car was the $30,000 taxpayer initially paid for the car. Taxpayer's depreciation deductions will thus be computed with reference to the $15,000 value and not the $30,000 adjusted basis of the taxpayer. Assuming the taxpayer thereafter uses the car solely for business purposes, the total depreciation deductions allowable with respect to the car over its remaining life will equal $15,000. Regulation § 1.167(g)-1 thus prevents the taxpayer from deducting the decline in the car's value attributable to the period of personal use.

Assume the taxpayer, after claiming $5,400 in depreciation deductions on the car following its conversion to business use, sells the car. The taxpayer's adjusted basis for computing loss under Regulation § 1.165-9(a)(2) will be $9,600 (*i.e.*, $15,000 less the $5,400 in depreciation deductions allowed). If the taxpayer sells the car for anything less than $9,600, the taxpayer will be entitled to a loss. What if the taxpayer sells the car for $10,000? Obviously, if for loss purposes the taxpayer's basis is $9,600, the taxpayer will not have a loss. Will the taxpayer have any gain? The answer is "No." *The "lesser of" rule of Regulation § 1.165-9(a)(2) relates only to the computation of loss!* For gain purposes, the taxpayer's adjusted basis will be taxpayer's original basis of $30,000 (what taxpayer paid for the car) less the $5,400 in depreciation deductions allowed to the taxpayer with respect to the car. Taxpayer's unrecovered cost in the car (or adjusted basis for computing gain on the sale of the car) is $24,600. Thus, the taxpayer will only recognize gain if the taxpayer sells the car for more than $24,600.[1] A sale price between $9,600 and $24,600 will produce neither gain nor loss.

Consider the situation where an individual, who owned a home and used it solely as a personal residence, dies and devises the home to another. If the home had been sold during the decedent's lifetime, no loss would have been allowed. What are the tax consequences, however, to the devisee if the devisee, upon receipt of title to the property, immediately sells it at a loss without ever having made any personal use

---

[1] This makes sense since a taxpayer should not be required to report gain on the sale of an asset unless the taxpayer receives more than the taxpayer's unrecovered cost in the asset. Here, the taxpayer paid $30,000 for the car and recovered $5,4000 by way of depreciation deductions. Appropriately, taxpayer's adjusted basis for computing gain is $24,600.

of the property? Will the loss be deductible under § 165(c)(2) or will the loss be disallowed on the theory that the property's tax status as personal-use property had been established by the decedent? The courts have allowed a deduction under these circumstances holding "the tax status of the property became neutral at the moment of death and the use the devisee thereafter made of the property determined its future tax status." *Campbell v. Commissioner*, 5 T.C. 272 (1945); *Estate of Miller v. Commissioner*, T.C. Memo 1967-44. The decision of the devisee to sell the property immediately will, in effect, convert the property into investment property, and any loss on its sale will be deemed a loss incurred in a "transaction entered into for profit" within the meaning of § 165(c)(2). *Id.*

2.   When Is a Loss Sustained?

As noted above, § 165 provides that, for a loss to be deductible, the loss must be "sustained during the taxable year." The regulations elaborate on that requirement providing "a loss shall be treated as sustained during the taxable year in which the loss occurs as evidenced by closed and completed transactions and as fixed by identifiable events occurring in such taxable year." Reg. § 1.165-1(d)(1). *See also* Reg. § 1.165-1(b). A sale or exchange of property typically "fixes" the loss under § 165, but, just as mere appreciation in value does not constitute gross income, a mere decline in value is not a loss "sustained." Revenue Ruling 84-145, 1984-2 C.B. 47, for example, held an air carrier did not sustain a deductible loss when its route authorities, as a result of airline deregulation, declined substantially in value but were not sold or abandoned as worthless.

A loss is, however, allowed for "securities," as defined by § 165(g)(2), when they become "worthless." The regulations note that even an "extensive" shrinkage of value is not sufficient for this purpose. Reg. § 1.165-4(a). Determining worthlessness can obviously be a difficult matter; the Supreme Court has said that worthlessness is determined not by the taxpayer's good faith subjective belief, but by an examination of all the facts and circumstances. *Boehm v. Commissioner*, 326 U.S. 287 (1945). Disputes are bound to result, not only as to the fact of worthlessness, but as to when it occurred. If worthlessness actually occurred in a year for which a refund claim is barred by the statute of limitations, the consequences are harsh. This problem, at least, has been eased considerably by § 6511(d), which extends the normal three-year statute of limitations to seven years for refund claims based on § 165(g).

The obsolescence or permanent abandonment of property may also give rise to a loss deduction. See Reg. § 1.165-2 relating to obsolete nondepreciable property, and Reg. § 1.167(a)-8(a)(4) relating to abandonment of depreciable property. Note that theft losses are treated as sustained in the year the theft loss is discovered. § 165(e); Reg. § 1.165-1(d)(3). See Revenue Ruling 2009-9, included in the materials.

3.   Not Compensated for by Insurance or Otherwise: Existence of a Claim for Reimbursement

In addition to the requirement that a loss be "sustained during the taxable year," § 165(a) also requires that the loss "not be compensated for by insurance or otherwise." In other words, to the extent a taxpayer receives reimbursement for a loss, the taxpayer has not actually sustained a loss allowable for tax purposes. Reflecting this standard, Reg. § 1.165-1(d)(2) and (3) in effect provide that, if an event resulting in a loss occurs and the taxpayer has a claim for reimbursement for which there is a "reasonable prospect of recovery," no deduction shall be allowed until the taxable year in which it can be ascertained with "reasonable certainty" whether such reimbursement will be received. As noted by the Tax Court in *Urtis v. Commissioner*, T.C. Memo 2013-66:

> A reasonable prospect of recovery exists when the taxpayer has a bona fide claim for recoupment from third parties or otherwise, and when there is a substantial possibility that such claims will be decided in the taxpayer's favor. . . . However, claims with only remote or nebulous potential for success will not postpone the deduction. . . .

> Whether a reasonable prospect of recovery exists is a question of fact, determined by examining all facts and circumstances. . . . The standard to be applied is primarily objective, but the taxpayer's subjective attitude and beliefs are not to be ignored. . . .

> One of the relevant factors in considering whether a reasonable prospect of recovery exists is whether the taxpayer has filed a lawsuit to recoup the loss. . . . Unless litigation is speculative or without merit, where the taxpayer deems the chance of recovery sufficiently probable to warrant bringing a lawsuit and pursuing it with reasonable diligence to a conclusion, the taxpayer should postpone the loss deduction until the litigation is terminated.

4. Amount of the Deduction

Section 165(b) limits the amount of the loss deduction to the adjusted basis of the property in question. This limitation is appropriate because the taxpayer suffering a loss on property is not required to treat as income the excess of the property's fair market value over its adjusted basis. For example, if a taxpayer sustains an uninsured loss on the destruction of business or investment property having a value of $100 and an adjusted basis of only $10, the deductible loss is only $10. Because $90 in lost value was not included in taxpayer's income, to allow a loss for the $90 would amount to a double tax benefit. Note in Revenue Ruling 2009-9 that the amount of theft loss from a fraudulent investment arrangement will, under the right circumstances, include not only the amount the taxpayer initially invested but also the amount of income the taxpayer reported on the investment. Of course, to the extent a taxpayer receives insurance or other compensation, the loss is offset and the deduction reduced. § 165(a).

5. Disallowed Losses

Losses otherwise allowable under § 165 may be disallowed by other provisions of the Code. See, for example, § 267(a)(1) disallowing losses on "related party" sales or exchanges; and § 1091, denying losses on "wash sales" of stock or securities. These provisions are considered in Chapter 27.

B.   Bad Debts

Section 166 allows a deduction for debts becoming worthless within the taxable year. Unlike § 165(c), which provides special rules for losses sustained by individuals, § 166 does not draw a distinction between corporate and individual taxpayers. It does, however, draw a line between business and nonbusiness bad debts, a matter addressed below. Although a bad debt is simply one type of loss, Congress has provided rules for bad debts that differ from the rules of § 165. Where a debt is evidenced by a "security," the rules of § 165 govern, and § 166 does not apply. § 166(e).

1.   Bona Fide Debt Requirement

The provisions of § 166 are applicable only if a "bona fide debt" exists. There must be a debtor-creditor relationship based on a valid, enforceable obligation to pay a fixed or determinable sum of money. Reg. § 1.166-1(c). A gift is not a debt. Not surprisingly, the Service will carefully scrutinize family or related-party advances to determine whether a bona fide debt was created. Where the relationship is a close one, it will be presumed, subject to rebuttal, that a gift and not a loan was intended.

2.   Worthlessness

The debt must be a "bad" debt for a deduction to be allowable. For example, even when bona fide debt is present, forgiveness or cancellation of the debt may constitute a gift rather than evidence of worthlessness, and no deduction will be allowable. In some cases, of course, a debt may be canceled for business reasons. Again, no deduction will be allowed by § 166 if the debt was not worthless, but, if the provisions of § 162 are otherwise satisfied, a deduction will be allowable under that section.

The regulations require consideration of "all pertinent evidence" with regard to the determination of worthlessness. Although factual disputes are inevitable, the regulations do not require a taxpayer to pursue legal action to establish worthlessness. Reg. §§ 1.166-2(a), (b). Given the potential difficulty in determining when worthlessness occurs, § 6511(d) provides a seven-year statute of limitation for refund claims under § 166. Thus, even where the taxpayer has mistakenly determined the year of worthlessness, there will ordinarily still be time to file a refund claim for the proper year.

3.   Business or Nonbusiness Debts

Section 166(d) distinguishes between business and nonbusiness debts. Business debts are deductible under § 166(a)(1) in the year they become wholly worthless. Moreover, partially worthless business debts are also deductible, under § 166(a)(2), up to the amount charged off within the year. The business bad debt rules do not distinguish between individuals and corporations.

By contrast, nonbusiness bad debts are deductible only upon becoming wholly worthless. The court in *Buchanan v. U.S.*, 87 F.3d 197, 199 (7th Cir. 1996), emphasized the importance of such total worthlessness, noting "if even a modest fraction of the [nonbusiness] debt can be recovered," the debt is not worthless for purposes of § 166 and no deduction is available. According to the court, bifurcating the debt into recoverable and nonrecoverable portions and allowing a deduction for the nonrecoverable portion would be inconsistent with the § 166(d)(1)(B) requirement that the debt be completely worthless.

Nonbusiness debts, even if completely worthless, are deductible only as short term capital losses, rather than as ordinary losses as is the case with business bad debts. § 166(d)(1). Capital loss characterization is relatively disadvantageous because, under § 1211, the deduction of capital losses is limited. In the case of an individual, capital losses in a given year are deductible only to the extent of the individual's capital gains plus an additional $3,000. In other words, although a taxpayer with capital gains can deduct capital losses up to the amount of his capital gains, capital losses are thereafter deductible only at the rate of $3,000 a year, and, thus, from a timing standpoint, the characterization rule of § 166(d) can be quite harsh in some circumstances. See Chapter 31 for a full discussion of capital gains and losses. The legislative history of the predecessor of § 166(d), enacted in 1942, suggests Congress was concerned with the potential for abuse:

> The present law gives the same treatment to bad debts incurred in nonbusiness transactions as it allows to business bad debts. An example of a nonbusiness bad debt would be an unrepaid loan to a friend or relative. . . . This liberal allowance for nonbusiness bad debts has suffered considerable abuse through taxpayers making loans which they do not expect to be repaid.

H. Rep. No. 2333, 77th Cong. 1st Sess. (1942), 1942-2 C.B. 372, 408. This legislative history indicates the congressional purpose behind § 166(d) was to effect a compromise between outright disallowance and equal treatment with business debts. The Supreme Court has found the provision was intended to place "nonbusiness investments in the form of loans on a footing with other nonbusiness investments." *Putnam v. Commissioner*, 352 U.S. 82, 92 (1956).

Section 166(d)(2) defines a nonbusiness debt as "a debt other than a debt created or acquired in connection with the taxpayer's business, or a debt the loss from the worthlessness of which is incurred in the taxpayer's business." A context in which disputes commonly arise is that of the shareholder-employee who has made unrepaid advances to a closely held corporation. Is such a loan a business debt or a nonbusiness debt? In a leading case in this area, *Whipple v. Commissioner*, 373 U.S. 193 (1963), the Supreme Court held that a controlling shareholder's organizational, promotional and managerial services to a corporation did not cause loans to the corporation to be classified as business debts:

> Petitioner must demonstrate that he is engaged in a trade or business, and lying at the heart of his claim is the issue upon which the lower courts have divided and which brought the case here: That where a taxpayer furnishes regular services to one or many corporations, an independent trade or business of the taxpayer has been shown. But . . . petitioner's claim must be rejected.

Devoting one's time and energies to the affairs of a corporation is not of itself, and without more, a trade or business of the person so engaged. Though such activities may produce income, profit or gain in the form of dividends or enhancement in the value of an investment, this return is distinctive to the process of investing and is generated by the successful operation of the corporation's business as distinguished from the trade or business of the taxpayer himself. When the only return is that of an investor, the taxpayer has not satisfied his burden of demonstrating that he is engaged in a trade or business since investing is not a trade or business and the return to the taxpayer, though substantially the product of his services, legally arises not from his own trade or business but from that of the corporation. Even if the taxpayer demonstrates an independent trade or business of his own, care must be taken to distinguish bad debt losses arising from his own business and those actually arising from activities peculiar to an investor concerned with, and participating in, the conduct of the corporate business.

If full-time service to one corporation does not alone amount to a trade or business, which it does not, it is difficult to understand how the same service to many corporations would suffice. To be sure, the presence of more than one corporation might lend support to a finding that the taxpayer was engaged in a regular course of promoting corporations for a fee or commission, . . . or for a profit on their sale, . . . but in such cases there is compensation other than the normal investor's return, income received directly for his own services rather than indirectly through the corporate enterprise, ... On the other hand, since the Tax Court found, and the petitioner does not dispute, that there was no intention here of developing the corporations as going businesses for sale to customers in the ordinary course, the case before us inexorably rests upon the claim that one who actively engages in serving his own corporations for the purpose of creating future income through those enterprises is in a trade or business. That argument is untenable . . . and we reject it. Absent substantial additional evidence, furnishing management and other services to corporations for a reward not different from that flowing to an investor in those corporations is not a trade or business. . . .

373 U.S. at 201–203. An employee, however, is engaged in business as an employee. *See* § 62(a)(1); *Primuth v. Commissioner*, 54 T.C. 374 (1970). If an employee can demonstrate that a loan to one's employer is in effect required to insure continued employment, the loan is a business debt arising out of the trade or business of being an employee. *See Trent v. Commissioner*, 291 F.2d 669 (2d Cir. 1961). According to the regulations, the loan must bear a proximate relationship to the taxpayer's trade or business. Reg. § 1.166-5(b). When a loan is prompted by both investment and business reasons, as is often the case when the taxpayer is both shareholder and employee, the Supreme Court has held the business motive must be dominant for the debt to be characterized as a business debt. See *United States v. Generes* in the materials.

4. Amount Deductible

The amount of a bad debt deduction is the debt's adjusted basis. § 166(b). This rule is self-evident in situations where the taxpayer has loaned money to the debtor. Suppose, however, a cash basis creditor cannot collect wages, rents, or other receivables owed to him. The regulations provide that no bad debt deduction is allowed unless such amounts have been included in income, which would not be the case with the cash method taxpayer. Reg. § 1.166-1(e). In performing services without compensation, the taxpayer's net worth is unchanged; if no income was recognized, no loss is appropriate. If income was recognized, as in the case of an accrual method taxpayer, a deduction is allowed. Alternatively, suppose court-ordered child support payments are not paid to the taxpayer, who then expends her own funds to support the children. Is the taxpayer entitled to a bad debt deduction? Revenue Ruling 93-27, 1993-1 C.B. 32, says "No," on the grounds that the taxpayer does not have any basis in the obligation imposed on another to make the support payments. Taxpayer's own expenditures did not create or affect the other person's obligation to make the payments. Thus, those expenditures could not create a basis in the obligation.

5. Guarantees

Losses arising out of loan guarantees are treated as losses from bad debts, and are classified as business or nonbusiness debts based on their connection with the taxpayer's trade or business. Reg. § 1.166-9.

C. Bad Debts and Losses: The Interplay Between Sections 166 and 165

Depending on the circumstances, taxpayers may seek to characterize a loss under § 165 rather than under § 166, and vice versa. Investment-related losses, for example, are subject to capital loss treatment if they fall under § 166; this is not necessarily the case under § 165. By contrast, if the loss in question is a personal one, § 165 denies a deduction (except for casualty and theft losses), where § 166 at least allows a short-term capital loss. With respect to this latter point, the distinction § 166 draws is between business and nonbusiness debts; although some commentators express varying degrees of reservation, the prevailing view is that personal bad debts are deductible, assuming the debt is bona fide, despite the absence of any business or profit-seeking motivation on the part of the lender. Is this consistent with the treatment of personal expenditures generally?

According to the Supreme Court, §§ 165 and 166 are mutually exclusive, and, where both provisions are applicable in a given situation, § 166 governs. *Spring City Foundry Co. v. Commissioner*, 292 U.S. 182 (1934).

COWLES v. COMMISSIONER
United States Tax Court
T.C. Memo 1970-198 (1970)

TANNENWALD, JUDGE:

FINDINGS OF FACT

In 1958, petitioners acquired real property located in Bellevue, Washington, which they used as a residence from 1958 until June 1964. During that time, petitioner Theodore Cowles, Jr. (hereinafter Theodore) was employed by the General Electric Company as Operating Manager, Northwest. In 1964, he was transferred to Barrington, Illinois.

On March 8, 1964, petitioners contracted with real estate brokers for their services in selling their Bellevue residence. On July 28, 1964, petitioners contracted with other real estate brokers for their services in renting as well as selling the residence. The property remained on the market until October 11, 1966. During the intervening period, two offers for rental were received. The first was rejected because it was too low. The second was withdrawn when the prospective tenant decided instead to purchase another house. On October 11, 1966, petitioners sold the Bellevue residence for $26,000.

Petitioners' cost basis at the time of both the first and second listing with the real estate brokers was $34,745. The fair market value of the property at those times was $34,500. The property was originally offered for sale at $35,500.

OPINION

. . . [T]he sole issue remaining for decision is the deductibility of a loss suffered by petitioners on the sale of property which had been their personal residence. Upon Theodore's transfer of employment in 1964, petitioners ceased to occupy the property and offered it for rent or for sale for $35,500. Petitioners' cost basis and the fair market value of the property at the time it was so offered was $34,745 and $34,500, respectively. The property was never rented (although two offers for rent were received) and it was finally sold for $26,000 in 1966.

The question before us is whether the loss which petitioners suffered was sustained in a "transaction entered into for profit" within the meaning of section 165(c)(2). Petitioners contend that the fact that the property was offered for rent as well as for sale is sufficient to bring the loss within the ambit of that section. Respondent concedes that offers to rent furnish a sufficient basis to entitle petitioners to certain deductions with respect to "property held for the production of income" under Sections 212 and 167. *Compare Frank A. Newcombe*, 54 T.C. 1278 (1970). He nevertheless contends that mere offers to rent or sell are insufficient to meet the statutory requirement of a "transaction entered into for profit." In so doing, he argues that the property was not "prior to its sale, rented or otherwise appropriated to income-producing purposes." See Section 1.165-9, Income Tax Regs.

It is important to note that we do not have before us a situation where there has been an actual rental of residential property. *Cf. Heiner v. Tindle*, 276 U.S. 582 (1928); *Leland Hazard*, 7 T.C. 372 (1946). Nor do we have a situation where the taxpayer has so dealt with the property, or the arrangements with respect to its use or disposition, that he might be said to have "otherwise appropriated (it) to income-producing purposes." See *Rumsey v. Commissioner*, 82 F.2d 158, 160 (C.A. 2, 1936). . . .

Concededly this case reflects some conceptual difficulties. It is not readily apparent how a mere offer to rent property is sufficient to justify a holding that it is "held for the production of income" within the meaning of Sections 212 and 167 but not sufficient to permit a holding that it is "otherwise appropriated to income-producing purposes" within the meaning of Section 1.165-9, Income Tax Regs. But such a distinction has long been established in the decided cases. . . . Perhaps if we were writing on a clean slate, we would be inclined to re-examine this distinction. But, in light of the foregoing decisions, as well as those hereinafter cited, we are unwilling to chart a new course. . . . Nor does the fact that the sale of the property was incident to Theodore's transfer of employment support a conclusion in petitioners' favor. . . .

We hold that mere offers to sell or rent are insufficient to provide the necessary foundation for the deduction of a loss incurred in a "transaction entered into for profit," as required by section 165(c)(2). . . .

REVENUE RULING 2009-9
2009-1 C.B. 735

ISSUES:

(1) Is a loss from criminal fraud or embezzlement in a transaction entered into for profit a theft loss or a capital loss under § 165 of the Internal Revenue Code?

(2) Is such a loss subject to either the personal loss limits in § 165(h) or the limits on itemized deductions in §§ 67 and 68?

(3) In what year is such a loss deductible?

(4) How is the amount of such a loss determined?

. . . .

FACTS

A is an individual who uses the cash receipts and disbursements method of accounting and files federal income tax returns on a calendar year basis. B holds himself out to the public as an investment advisor and securities broker.

In Year 1, A, in a transaction entered into for profit, opened an investment account with B, contributed $100x to the account, and provided B with power of attorney to use the $100x to purchase and sell securities on A's behalf. A instructed B to reinvest any income and gains earned on the investments. In Year 3, A contributed an additional $20x to the account.

B periodically issued account statements to A that reported the securities purchases and sales that B purportedly made in A's investment account and the balance of the account. B also issued tax reporting statements to A and to the Internal Revenue Service that reflected purported gains and losses on A's investment account. B also reported to A that no income was earned in Year 1 and that for each of the Years 2 through 7 the investments earned $10x of income (interest, dividends, and capital gains), which A included in gross income on A's federal income tax returns.

At all times prior to Year 8 and part way through Year 8, B was able to make distributions to investors who requested them. A took a single distribution of $30x from the account in Year 7.

In Year 8, it was discovered that B's purported investment advisory and brokerage activity was in fact a fraudulent investment arrangement known as a "Ponzi" scheme. Under this scheme, B purported to invest cash or property on behalf of each investor, including A, in an account in the investor's name. For each investor's account, B reported investment activities and resulting income amounts that were partially or wholly fictitious. In some cases, in response to requests for withdrawal, B made payments of purported income or principal to investors. These payments were made, at least in part, from amounts that other investors had invested in the fraudulent arrangement.

When B's fraud was discovered in Year 8, B had only a small fraction of the funds that B reported on the account statements that B issued to A and other investors. A did not receive any reimbursement or other recovery for the loss in Year 8. The period of limitation on filing a claim for refund under § 6511 has not yet expired for Years 5 through 7, but has expired for Years 1 through 4.

B's actions constituted criminal fraud or embezzlement under the law of the jurisdiction in which the transactions occurred. At no time prior to the discovery did A know that B's activities were a fraudulent scheme.

LAW AND ANALYSIS

Issue 1. Theft loss.

Section 165(a) allows a deduction for losses sustained during the taxable year and not compensated by insurance or otherwise. For individuals, § 165(c)(2) allows a deduction for losses incurred in a transaction entered into for profit, and § 165(c)(3) allows a deduction for certain losses not connected to a transaction entered into for profit, including theft losses. Under § 165(e), a theft loss is sustained in the taxable year the taxpayer discovers the loss. Section 165(f) permits a deduction for capital losses only to the extent allowed in §§ 1211 and 1212. . . . [Capital gains and losses are discussed in detail in Chapter 31. As suggested in the Overview, taxpayers would typically prefer a loss to be characterized as an "ordinary loss" rather than a "capital loss" because of the significant limitation on the deductibility of capital losses.]

For federal income tax purposes, "theft" is a word of general and broad connotation, covering any criminal appropriation of another's property to the use of the taker, including theft by swindling, false pretenses and any other form of guile. . . . A taxpayer claiming a theft loss must prove that the loss resulted from a taking of property that was illegal under the law of the jurisdiction in which it occurred and was done with criminal intent. . . . However, a taxpayer need not show a conviction for theft. . . .

The character of an investor's loss related to fraudulent activity depends, in part, on the nature of the investment. For example, a loss that is sustained on the worthlessness or disposition of stock acquired on the open market for investment is a capital loss, even if the decline in the value of the stock is attributable to fraudulent activities of the corporation's officers or directors, because the officers or directors did not have the specific intent to deprive the shareholder of money or property. . . .

In the present situation, . . . B specifically intended to, and did, deprive A of money by criminal acts. B's actions constituted a theft from A, as theft is defined for § 165 purposes. Accordingly, A's loss is a theft loss, not a capital loss.

Issue 2. Deduction limitations.

Section 165(h) imposes two limitations on casualty loss deductions, including theft loss deductions, for property not connected either with a trade or business or with a transaction entered into for profit. [The Service, after analyzing the theft losses under the facts set forth above, concluded that, in opening an investment account with B, A entered into a transaction for profit. A's theft loss therefore is deductible under § 165(c)(2) and is not subject to the § 165(h) limitations. The Service further concluded that the theft loss, although an itemized deduction, was not subject to § 67 which provides that miscellaneous itemized deductions may be deducted only to the extent their aggregate amount exceeds two percent of adjusted gross income.]

Issue 3. Year of deduction.

Section 165(e) provides that any loss arising from theft is treated as sustained during the taxable year in which the taxpayer discovers the loss. Under §§ 1.165-8(a)(2) and 1.165-1(d), however, if, in the year of discovery, there exists a claim for reimbursement with respect to which there is a reasonable prospect of recovery, no portion of the loss for which reimbursement may be received is sustained until the taxable year in which it can be ascertained with reasonable certainty whether or not the reimbursement will be received, for example, by a settlement, adjudication, or abandonment of the claim. Whether a reasonable prospect of recovery exists is a question of fact to be determined upon examination of all facts and circumstances.

A may deduct the theft loss in Year 8, the year the theft loss is discovered, provided that the loss is not covered by a claim for reimbursement or other recovery as to which A has a reasonable prospect of recovery. To the extent that A's deduction is reduced by such a claim, recoveries on the claim in a later taxable year are not includible in A's gross income. If A recovers a greater amount in a later year, or an amount that initially was not covered by a claim as to which there was a reasonable prospect of recovery, the recovery is includible in A's gross income in the later year under the tax benefit rule, to the extent the earlier deduction reduced A's income tax. See § 111; § 1.165-1(d)(2)(iii). Finally, if A recovers less than the amount that was covered by a claim as to which there was a reasonable prospect of recovery that reduced the deduction for theft in Year 8, an additional deduction is allowed in the year the amount of recovery is ascertained with reasonable certainty.

Issue 4. Amount of deduction.

Section 1.165-8(c) provides that the amount deductible in the case of a theft loss is determined consistently with the manner described in § 1.165-7 for determining the amount of a casualty loss, considering the fair market value of the property immediately after the theft to be zero. Under these provisions, the amount of an investment theft loss is the basis of the property (or the amount of money) that was lost, less any reimbursement or other compensation.

The amount of a theft loss resulting from a fraudulent investment arrangement is generally the initial amount invested in the arrangement, plus any additional investments, less amounts withdrawn, if any, reduced by reimbursements or other recoveries and reduced by claims as to which there is a reasonable prospect of recovery. If an amount is reported to the investor as income in years prior to the year of discovery of the theft, the investor includes the amount in gross income, and the investor reinvests the amount in the arrangement, this amount increases the deductible theft loss.

Accordingly, the amount of A's theft loss for purposes of § 165 includes A's original Year 1 investment ($100x) and additional Year 3 investment ($20x). A's loss also includes the amounts that A reported as gross income on A's federal income tax returns for Years 2 through 7 ($60x). A's loss is reduced by the amount of money distributed to A in Year 7 ($30x). If A has a claim for reimbursement with respect to which there is a reasonable prospect of recovery, A may not deduct in Year 8 the portion of the loss that is covered by the claim.

UNITED STATES v. GENERES
United States Supreme Court
405 U.S. 93 (1971)

Mr. Justice Blackmun delivered the opinion of the Court.

A debt a closely held corporation owed to an indemnifying shareholder-employee became worthless in 1962. The issue in this federal income tax refund suit is whether, for the shareholder-employee, that worthless obligation was a business or a nonbusiness bad debt within the meaning and reach of Sections 166(a) and (d) of the Internal Revenue Code of 1954, as amended, 26 U.S.C. Sections 166(a) and (d), and of the implementing Regulations Section 1.166-5.

The issue's resolution is important for the taxpayer. If the obligation was a business debt, he may use it to offset ordinary income and for carryback purposes under Sec. 172 of the Code, 26 U.S.C. Sec. 172. On the other hand, if the obligation is a nonbusiness debt, it is to be treated as a short-term capital loss subject to the restrictions imposed on such losses by Sec. 166(d)(1)(B) and Sections 1211 and 1212, and its use for carryback purposes is restricted by Sec. 172(d)(4). The debt is one or the other in its entirety, for the Code does not provide for its allocation in part to business and in part to nonbusiness.

In determining whether a bad debt is a business or a nonbusiness obligation, the Regulations focus on the relation the loss bears to the taxpayer's business. If, at the time of worthlessness, that relation is a "proximate" one, the debt qualifies as a business bad debt and the aforementioned desirable tax consequences then ensue.

The present case turns on the proper measure of the required proximate relation. Does this necessitate a "dominant" business motivation on the part of the taxpayer or is a "significant" motivation sufficient?

Tax in an amount somewhat in excess of $40,000 is involved. The taxpayer, Allen H. Generes, prevailed in a jury trial in the District Court. On the Government's appeal, the Fifth Circuit affirmed by a divided vote. Certiorari was granted to resolve a conflict among the circuits.

I.

The taxpayer as a young man in 1909 began work in the construction business. His son-in-law, William F. Kelly, later engaged independently in similar work. During World War II the two men formed a partnership in which their participation was equal. The enterprise proved successful. In 1954 Kelly-Generes Construction Co., Inc., was organized as the corporate successor to the partnership. It engaged in the heavy-construction business, primarily on public works projects.

The taxpayer and Kelly each owned 44% of the corporation's outstanding capital stock. The taxpayer's original investment in his shares was $38,900. The remaining 12% of the stock was owned by a son of the taxpayer and by another son-in-law. Mr. Generes was president of the corporation and received from it an annual salary of $12,000. Mr. Kelly was executive vice-president and received an annual salary of $15,000.

The taxpayer and Mr. Kelly performed different services for the corporation. Kelly worked full time in the field and was in charge of the day-to-day construction operations. Generes, on the other hand, devoted no more than six to eight hours a week to the enterprise. He reviewed bids and jobs, made cost estimates, sought and obtained bank financing, and assisted in securing the bid and performance bonds that are an essential part of the public-project construction business. Mr. Generes, in addition to being president of the corporation, held a full-time position as president of a savings and loan association he had founded in 1937. He received from the association an annual salary of $19,000. The taxpayer also had other sources of income. His gross income averaged about $40,000 a year during 1959–1962.

Taxpayer Generes from time to time advanced personal funds to the corporation to enable it to complete construction jobs. He also guaranteed loans made to the corporation by banks for the purchase of construction machinery and other equipment. In addition, his presence with respect to the bid and performance bonds is of particular significance. Most of these were obtained from Maryland Casualty Co. That underwriter required the taxpayer and Kelly to sign an indemnity agreement for each bond it issued for the corporation. In 1958, however, in order to eliminate the need for individual indemnity contracts, taxpayer and Kelly signed a blanket agreement with Maryland whereby they agreed to indemnify it, up to a designated amount, for any loss it suffered as surety for the corporation. Maryland then increased its line of surety credit to $2,000,000. The corporation had over $14,000,000 gross business for the period 1954 through 1962.

In 1962 the corporation seriously underbid two projects and defaulted in its performance of the project contracts. It proved necessary for Maryland to complete the work. Maryland then sought indemnity from Generes and Kelly. The taxpayer indemnified Maryland to the extent of $162,104.57. In the same year he also loaned $158,814.49 to the corporation to assist it in its financial difficulties. The corporation subsequently went into receivership and the taxpayer was unable to obtain reimbursement from it.

In his federal income tax return for 1962 the taxpayer took his loss on his direct loans to the corporation as a nonbusiness bad debt. He claimed the indemnification loss as a business bad debt and deducted it against ordinary income. Later he filed claims for refund for 1959–1961, asserting net operating loss carrybacks under Sec. 172 to those years for the portion, unused in 1962, of the claimed business bad debt deduction.

In due course the claims were made the subject of the jury trial refund suit in the United States District Court of the Eastern District of Louisiana. At the trial Mr. Generes testified that his sole motive in signing the indemnity agreement was to protect his $12,000-a-year employment with the corporation. The jury, by special interrogatory, was asked to determine whether taxpayer's signing of the indemnity agreement with Maryland "was proximately related to his trade or business of being an employee" of the corporation. The District Court charged the jury, over the Government's objection, that significant motivation satisfies the Regulations' requirement of proximate relationship. The court refused the Government's request for an instruction that the applicable standard was that of dominant rather than significant motivation.

After twice returning to the court for clarification of the instruction given, the jury found that the taxpayer's signing of the indemnity agreement was proximately related to his trade or business of being an employee of the corporation. Judgment on this verdict was then entered for the taxpayer.

The Fifth Circuit majority approved the significant-motivation standard so specified and agreed with a Second Circuit majority in *Weddle v. Commissioner*, 325 F.2d 849, 851 (1963), in finding comfort for so doing in the tort law's concept of proximate cause. Judge Simpson dissented. 427 F.2d, at 284. He agreed with the holding of the Seventh Circuit in *Niblock v. Commissioner*, 417 F.2d 1185 (1969), and with Chief Judge Lumbard, separately concurring in *Weddle*, 325 F.2d, at 852, that dominant and primary motivation is the standard to be applied.

II.

A. The fact responsible for the litigation is the taxpayer's dual status relative to the corporation. Generes was both a shareholder and an employee. These interests are not the same, and their differences occasion different tax consequences. In tax jargon, Generes' status as a shareholder was a nonbusiness interest. It was capital in nature and it was composed initially of tax-paid dollars. Its rewards were expectative and would flow, not from personal effort, but from investment earnings and appreciation. On the other hand, Generes' status as an employee was a business interest. Its nature centered in personal effort and labor, and salary for that endeavor would be received. The salary would consist of pre-tax dollars.

Thus, for tax purposes it becomes important and, indeed, necessary to determine the character of the debt that went bad and became uncollectible. Did the debt center on the taxpayer's business interest in the corporation or on his nonbusiness interest? If it was the former, the taxpayer deserves to prevail here. *Trent v. Commissioner*, 291 F.2d 669 (CA2 1961). . . .

B. Although arising in somewhat different contexts, two tax cases decided by the Court in recent years merit initial mention. In each of these cases a major shareholder paid out money to or on behalf of his corporation and then was unable to obtain reimbursement from it. In each he claimed a deduction assertable against ordinary income. In each he was unsuccessful in this quest:

1. In *Putnam v. Commissioner*, 352 U.S. 82 (1956), the taxpayer was a practicing lawyer who had guaranteed obligations of a labor newspaper corporation in which he owned stock. He claimed his loss as fully deductible in 1948 under Sec. 23(e)(2) of the 1939 Code. The standard prescribed by that statute was incurrence of the loss "in any transaction entered into for profit, though not connected with the trade or business." The Court rejected this approach and held that the loss was a nonbusiness bad debt subject to short-term capital loss treatment under Sec. 23(k)(4). The loss was deductible as a bad debt or not at all. See Rev. Rul. 60-48, 1960-1 Cum. Bull. 112.

2. In *Whipple v. Commissioner*, 373 U.S. 193 (1963), the taxpayer had provided organizational, promotional, and managerial services to a corporation in which he owned approximately an 80% stock interest. He claimed that this constituted a trade or business and, hence, that debts owing him by the corporation were business bad debts when they became worthless in 1953. The Court also rejected that contention and held that Whipple's investing was not a trade or business, that is, that "[d]evoting one's time and energies to the affairs of corporation is not of itself, and without more, a trade or business of the person so engaged." 373 U.S., at 202. The rationale was that a contrary conclusion would be inconsistent with the principle that a corporation has a personality separate from its shareholders and that its business is not necessarily their business. The Court indicated its approval of the Regulations' proximate-relation test:

Moreover, there is no proof (which might be difficult to furnish where the taxpayer is the sole or dominant stockholder) that the loan was necessary to keep his job or was otherwise proximately related to maintaining his trade or business as an employee. *Compare Trent v. Commissioner*, [291 F.2d 669 (CA2 1961)].

373 U.S. at 204. The Court also carefully noted the distinction between the business and the nonbusiness bad debt for one who is both an employee and a shareholder.[2]

These two cases approach, but do not govern, the present one. They indicate, however, a cautious and not a free-wheeling approach to the business bad debt. Obviously, taxpayer Generes endeavored to frame his case to bring it within the area indicated in the above quotation from *Whipple v. Commissioner.*

III.

We conclude that in determining whether a bad debt has a "proximate" relation to the taxpayer's trade or business, as the Regulations specify, and thus qualifies as a business bad debt, the proper measure is that of dominant motivation, and that only significant motivation is not sufficient. We reach this conclusion for a number of reasons:

A. The Code itself carefully distinguishes between business and nonbusiness items. It does so, for example, in Sec. 165 with respect to losses, in Sec. 166 with respect to bad debts, and in Sec. 162 with respect to expenses. It gives particular tax benefits to business losses, business bad debts, and business expenses, and gives lesser benefits, or none at all, to nonbusiness losses, nonbusiness bad debts, and nonbusiness expenses. It does this despite the fact that the latter are just as adverse in financial consequence to the taxpayer as are the former. But this distinction has been a policy of the income tax structure ever since the Revenue Act of 1916, Sec. 5(a), 39 Stat. 759, provided differently for trade or business losses than it did for losses sustained in another transaction entered into for profit. And it has been the specific policy with respect to bad debts since the Revenue Act of 1942 incorporated into Sec. 23(k) of the 1939 Code the distinction between business and nonbusiness bad debts. 56 Stat. 820.

The point, however, is that the tax statutes have made the distinction that the Congress therefore intended it to be a meaningful one, and that the distinction is not to be obliterated or blunted by an interpretation that tends to equate the business bad debt with the nonbusiness bad debt. We think that emphasis upon the significant rather than upon the dominant would have a tendency to do just that.

B. Application of the significant-motivation standard would also tend to undermine and circumscribe the Court's holding in *Whipple* and the emphasis there that a shareholder's mere activity in a corporation's affairs is not a trade or business. As Chief Judge Lumbard pointed out in his separate and disagreeing concurrence in *Weddle, supra*, 325 F.2d, at 852–853, both motives — that of protecting the investment and that of protecting the salary — are inevitably involved, and an

---

[2] "Even if the taxpayer demonstrates an independent trade or business of his own, care must be taken to distinguish bad debt losses arising from his own business and those actually arising from activities peculiar to an investor concerned with, and participating in, the conduct of the corporate business." 373 U.S., at 202.

inquiry whether employee status provides a significant motivation will always produce an affirmative answer and result in a judgment for the taxpayer.

C. The dominant-motivation standard has the attribute of workability. It provides a guideline of certainty for the trier of fact. The trier then may compare the risk against the potential reward and give proper emphasis to the objective rather than to the subjective. As has just been noted, an employee-shareholder, in making or guaranteeing a loan to his corporation, usually acts with two motivations, the one to protect his investment and the other to protect his employment. By making the dominant motivation the measure, the logical tax consequence ensues and prevents the mere presence of a business motive, however small and however insignificant, from controlling the tax result at the taxpayer's convenience. This is of particular importance in a tax system that is so largely dependent on voluntary compliance.

D. The dominant-motivation test strengthens and is consistent with the mandate of Sec. 262 of the Code, 26 U.S.C. Sec. 262, that "no deduction shall be allowed for personal, living, or family expenses" except as otherwise provided. It prevents personal considerations from circumventing this provision.

G. The Regulations' use of the word "proximate" perhaps is not the most fortunate, for it naturally tempts one to think in tort terms. The temptation, however, is best rejected, and we reject it here. In tort law factors of duty, of foreseeability, of secondary cause, and of plural liability are under consideration, and the concept of proximate cause has been developed as an appropriate application and measure of these factors. It has little place in tax law where plural aspects are not usual, where an item either is or is not a deduction, or either is or is not a business bad debt, and where certainty is desirable.

IV.

The conclusion we have reached means that the District Court's instructions, based on a standard of significant rather than dominant motivation, are erroneous and that, at least, a new trial is required. We have examined the record, however, and find nothing that would support a jury verdict in this taxpayer's favor had the dominant-motivation standard been embodied in the instructions. Judgment *n.o.v.* for the United States, therefore, must be ordered. *See Neely v. Eby Construction Co.*, 386 U.S. 317 (1967).

As Judge Simpson pointed out in his dissent . . . the only real evidence offered by the taxpayer bearing upon motivation was his own testimony that he signed the indemnity agreement "to protect my job," that "I figured in three years' time I would get my money out," and that "I never once gave it [his investment in the corporation] a thought."

The statements obviously are self-serving. In addition, standing alone, they do not bear the light of analysis. What the taxpayer was purporting to say was that his $12,000 annual salary was his sole motivation, and that his $38,900 original investment, the actual value of which prior to the misfortunes of 1962 we do not know, plus his loans to the corporation, plus his personal interest in the integrity of the corporation as a source of living for his son-in-law and as an investment for his son and his other son-in-law, were of no consequence whatever in his thinking. The comparison is strained all the more by the fact that the salary is pre-tax and the investment is taxpaid. With his total annual income about $40,000, Mr. Generes may well have reached a federal income tax bracket of 40% or more for a joint return in 1958–1962. The $12,000 salary thus would produce for him only about $7,000 net after federal tax and before any state income tax. This is the figure, and not $12,000, that has any possible significance for motivation purposes, and it is less than 1/5 of the original stock investment.

We conclude on these facts that the taxpayer's explanation falls of its own weight, and that reasonable minds could not ascribe, on this record, a dominant motivation directed to the preservation of the taxpayer's salary as president of Kelly-Generes Construction Co., Inc.

The judgment is reversed and the case is remanded with direction that judgment be entered for the United States.

It is so ordered.

Chapter 16

TRAVEL EXPENSES

I. PROBLEMS

1. Dick, an insurance broker, owns and operates an independent home and auto insurance agency located in Suburbia. Dick works out of a small office located in downtown Suburbia. The office is about three miles from Dick's home. While Dick does about 60% of his work at the office, he spends considerable time out of the office visiting homeowners regarding their home insurance needs and assessing their property for purposes of the various insurance companies he represents. Dick's market area includes Suburbia as well as a number of smaller towns within a 100 mile radius of Suburbia.

   (a) May Dick deduct his transportation costs in going from his residence to his office each morning? *no, commuters fares non-deductible*

   (b) May Dick deduct his transportation costs in driving from his office to visit clients either in Suburbia or the surrounding towns? *yes bc large % of job*

   (c) If, instead of stopping at his office some mornings, Dick drives directly from his residence to the home of a client in either Suburbia or another town, may Dick deduct his transportation costs? Would your answer be different if Dick's office were in his home rather than being located elsewhere? *yes* *we would still have to look at the purpose*

   (d) At the end of some workdays, Dick, without returning to his office, drives directly to his residence from wherever he met his last clients. May Dick deduct the costs he incurs in driving home? *no bc it'd count as commuting*

   (e) Dick typically eats lunch each workday at a small café located on the same block as his insurance agency. When visiting clients outside of Suburbia, Dick will often eat lunch in the town he is visiting. May Dick deduct any of these meal expenses? *it can be considered incident*

2. Elaine, a professor at State University, often travels on behalf of the University. The costs of her transportation, meals and lodging are reimbursed by the University. Elaine recently attended a conference in another part of the country. She incurred $600 in transportation costs, $750 for three nights lodging, and $150 for meals. Upon her return, she filed an expense statement together with receipts for the transportation, meals and lodging costs. The University reimbursed Elaine the full $1,500 cost of her trip. How should Elaine report the costs of the trip and the subsequent reimbursement from the University? *the costs would be deductible the reimbursement wouldn't*

3. Alexis, a highly regarded tax lawyer, maintains a solo law practice in Seattle. As an active member of the Tax Section of the American Bar Association, Alexis attends meetings of the section throughout the country. This year, the Tax Section held a summer meeting at a resort near Glacier National Park, Montana. Alexis and her spouse planned their family's summer vacation to coincide with the meeting. The family drove 600 miles from their home in Seattle to the resort where the three day meeting was being held. The family rented a two bedroom cabin at the resort for a week. During the three-day meeting, Alexis' spouse took care of their two children, taking them on short hikes and boat rides. He accompanied Alexis to all of the social gatherings associated with the meeting. While Alexis was attending the meeting, he also took messages for her from her secretary in Seattle. Once the meeting had concluded, Alexis and her family spent the rest of their time enjoying Glacier Park. In general, describe the expenses, if any, which Alexis may deduct as a result of her attendance at the Tax Section meeting.

4. When he entered law school, Dan purchased a house in Blackstone, the town where the law school is located. He lived in the house throughout the three years of law school. Upon completion of his degree, Dan accepted a job in a city located about 500 miles from Blackstone. Dan decided to keep his house in Blackstone and rented the house for $900 per month to some law students. Twice a year Dan returns to Blackstone to check on his rental property. He usually spends the weekend in Blackstone and incurs transportation, meals and lodging expense. Invariably, Dan chooses weekends to travel to Blackstone when there is an important football game or some major law school event. May Dan deduct any of the expenses he incurs in traveling to and from Blackstone?

5. Marco, who is 22, dreams of becoming one of the best golfers in the world. His golf game has developed to the point where he now enters golf tournaments throughout the country. Apart from income he receives from a trust which his parents have established for his benefit, Marco's sole source of income is from his golfing activities. He periodically wins modest sums of money in tournaments he enters; in addition, he receives payments for golf lessons he gives novice golfers at various courses around the country. He, however, has never earned more than $20,000 per year in his golfing activities. Marco, who spends most of his time traveling the golf circuit, considers his home to be the one bedroom apartment over the garage attached to his parent's home. He receives all of his mail at his parents' home and always lists their home as his permanent address. After golfing trips, he always returns there. In exchange for the right to use the apartment, Marco pays his parents $50 per month and, when he is at home, does the yard work and repair work around the house. While Marco sometimes practices his golf game on a course in the town where he and his parents live, all of his money-making activities associated with golf occur in other locations around the country. Although Marco usually stays with friends and acquaintances while traveling, he nonetheless incurs significant transportation expenses and some meals and lodging expenses. May Marco deduct these expenses?

Assignment for Chapter 16:

Complete the problems.

Read: Internal Revenue Code: §§ 62(a)(1), (2)(A); 162(a); 212; 274(c), (d), (h), (m), (n).
        Treasury Regulations §§ 1.62-2(c)–(f); 1.162-2; 1.262-1(b)(5); skim §§ 1.132-5(t); 1.62-2(c)(2)(i), (d)(1), (e)(1), (f).

Materials: Overview
             United States v. Correll
             Revenue Ruling 99-7
             Henderson v. Commissioner
             Bogue v. Commissioner

II.   VOCABULARY

tax home
overnight rule
temporary employment
indefinite employment
"lavish or extravagant"

III.   OBJECTIVES

1.   To identify deductible transportation expenses.

2.   To recall commuting expenses are nondeductible personal expenses.

3.   To identify transportation expenses that should be characterized as commuting expenses and to distinguish these from deductible transportation expenses.

4.   To apply the primary purpose test of Reg. § 1.162-2(b)(2).

5.   To apply the overnight rule.

6.   To recall meal expenses are generally subject to the 50% rule.

7.   To explain and to apply the temporary employment doctrine relating to the deduction of meals and lodging.

8.   To recall the limited circumstances in which the taxpayer may deduct the travel expenses of his spouse.

9.   To explain the extent to which travel expenses may be deducted under § 212.

10. To recall specific limitations exist with respect to expenses incurred in attending conventions outside of North America or on cruise ships.

11. To determine the tax consequences of reimbursed employee expenses.

IV. OVERVIEW

Rules, rules and more rules! Few areas of the tax law contain as many rules as are to be found with respect to the deduction of meals, lodging and transportation expenses. Because these expenses often have a significant personal expense flavor, the Congress, Service and the courts have engaged in a variety of line-drawing exercises intended to assure that only expenses predominantly business in nature are deducted. The result is a plethora of sometimes inconsistent rulings and decisions which often create arbitrary distinctions.

A. Commuting

While your office is in the center of the business district of a large city, you live in a quiet residential area one hour's drive from the city. Sometimes you use public transportation to go to and from the office; at other times you drive to your office and incur both highway tolls and parking fees. May you deduct these transportation costs? Are they deductible under § 162 as "ordinary and necessary" business expenses or do they represent nondeductible personal expenses?

The choice of where one lives is generally personal. If you chose to do so, you could live nearer your workplace and avoid the costs associated with your daily commute. Commuting costs are therefore appropriately viewed as personal in nature and nondeductible under § 262. *See* Reg. § 1.262-1(b)(5). In *Commissioner v. Flowers*, 326 U.S. 465 (1946), the Supreme Court denied a deduction for travel expenses to a taxpayer who lived in Jackson, Mississippi, but whose principal place of employment was in Mobile, Alabama. The taxpayer was able to do much of his work at an office in Jackson and so spent most of his time there by his own choice. He did need to spend some time in Mobile, however, and sought to deduct the cost of trips from Jackson to Mobile and the cost of meals and lodging in Mobile. In denying the deduction, the Supreme Court stated that, to be deductible, a travel expense must satisfy three elements: it must be reasonable and necessary; it must be incurred away from home; and

> the expense must be incurred in pursuit of business. This means that there must be a direct connection between the expenditure and the carrying on of the trade or business of the taxpayer or of his employer. Moreover, such an expenditure must be necessary or appropriate to the development and pursuit of the business or trade.

> The facts demonstrate clearly that the expenses were not incurred in the pursuit of the business of the taxpayer's employer, the railroad. Jackson was his regular home. Had his post of duty been in that city, the cost of maintaining his home there and of commuting or driving to work concededly would be non-deductible living and personal expenses lacking the necessary direct relation to the prosecution of the business. The character of such expenses is unaltered by the circumstance that the taxpayer's post of duty was in Mobile, thereby increasing the costs of transportation, food, and lodging. Whether he maintained one abode or two, whether he traveled three blocks or three hundred miles to work, the nature of these expenditures remained the same.

The added costs in issue, moreover, were as unnecessary and inappropriate to the development of the railroad's business as were his personal and living costs in Jackson. They were incurred solely as the result of the taxpayer's desire to maintain a home in Jackson while working in Mobile, a factor irrelevant to the maintenance and prosecution of the railroad's legal business. The fact that he traveled frequently between the two cities and incurred extra living expenses in Mobile, while doing much of his work in Jackson, was occasioned solely by his personal propensities. The railroad gained nothing from his arrangement except the personal satisfaction of the taxpayer.

The exigencies of business rather than the personal conveniences and necessities of the traveler must be the motivating factors. Such was not the case here.

Id. at 470–74. Would the following statement adequately address the issue raised in *Flowers:* the taxpayer's expenses in traveling to and from Mobile constituted nondeductible commuting expenses?

A recent application of the *Flowers* rule involved the taxpayer in *Wilbert v. Commissioner,* 553 F. 3d 544 (7th Cir. 2009), who worked for Northwest Airlines, and owned and maintained a home in Wisconsin close to his work in Minneapolis. To avoid being laid off, he exercised his contractual "bumping" rights, based on seniority, to obtain work assignments in various cities other than Minneapolis. (He did not have the option to continue working for the airline in Minneapolis.) Rather than move his family, he continued to maintain the family home in Wisconsin. As a result, he incurred significant additional living expenses in connection with the short-term assignments in other cities, expenses he sought to deduct. The deduction, however, was denied, even though the court acknowledged "it would hardly have been realistic to expect him to pull up stakes and move to Anchorage and then to Chicago and then to New York and then back to Anchorage." Nonetheless, according to the court:

> The problem with a test that focuses on the reasonableness of the taxpayer's decision not to move is that it is bound to prove nebulous in application . . . We are sympathetic to Wilbert's plight and recognize the artificiality of supposing that, as the government argues, he made merely a personal choice to "commute" from Minneapolis to Anchorage, and Chicago, and New York, as if Minneapolis were a suburb of those cities. But the statutory language, the precedents, and the considerations of administrability that we have emphasized persuade us to reject the test of reasonableness. . . . [W]e fall back on the rule of *Flowers,* . . . that unless the taxpayer has a business rather than a personal reason to be living in two places, he cannot deduct his traveling expenses if he decides not to move.

Wilbert, at 548, 549.

Should a taxpayer who works at a nuclear power plant be entitled to deduct part or all of her commuting costs if state or federal law prohibits residences within a ten mile radius around the power plant? In *Sanders v. Commissioner,* 439 F.2d 296 (9th Cir. 1971), *cert. denied,* 404 U.S. 864, the court disallowed deductions claimed by taxpayers for travel expenses between their work place at Vandenberg Air Force Base and the nearest community surrounding it where civilians such as the taxpayers could live. Civilians could not reside on the Air Force base. The Ninth Circuit quoted with approval the reasoning of the Tax Court: "There is no convincing way to distinguish the expenses here from those of suburban commuters. Petitioner's hardships are no different than those confronting the many taxpayers who cannot find suitable housing close to their urban place of employment and must daily commute to work. We see no reason why petitioners in the case at bar should receive more favored tax treatment than their urban counterparts who also cannot live near their worksites." 439 F.2d at 299; 52 T.C. 964, 970 (1969). Do you agree?

Consider the following positions the Service has taken regarding transportation to and from one's workplace:

(a) A taxpayer who works in two different locations on the same day for the same employer may deduct the cost of travelling from one work location to the other. "If at the end of his workday he goes home directly from his second place of employment, his trip would ordinarily be regarded as commuting and his transportation expenses would be nondeductible, at least in those situations where his transportation expenses in going from that location to his home do not exceed those from his headquarters office to his home." Rev. Rul. 55-109, 1955-1 C.B. 261, 263.

(b) "Where an employee having two separate employers is required to work on the same day at a different location within the same city for each of his employers, it is recognized that his transportation expenses in going from his first to his second place of employment are not incurred in discharging the duties of either job or in carrying on the business of either employer. . . . However, since both such positions constitute part of the employee's trade or business, local transportation expenses in getting from one place of employment to another constitute ordinary and necessary expenses incurred in carrying on his combined trade or business and in discharging his duties at both obligations during the same day." Rev. Rul. 55-109, 1955-1 C.B. at 263.

In addition, review Revenue Ruling 99-7 in the materials for the Services's position regarding transportation to temporary work locations. Is this position consistent with the Service's longstanding rule that commuting expenses are not deductible? The Tax Court's decision in *Bogue v. Commissioner*, included in the materials, provides a thoughtful discussion of Revenue Ruling 99-7 and caselaw applicable to commuting.

Is a taxpayer who performs work-related tasks while traveling from his residence to his principal place of work engaged in non-deductible commuting or deductible § 162(a) travel? Consider *Pollei v. Commissioner*, 877 F.2d 838 (10th Cir. 1989), where two police captains were permitted to deduct the maintenance and operating costs of driving their personal cars between their homes and police headquarters, based on their being in an "on duty" status at such times. The Salt Lake City Police Department had ordered command-level officers, including the two captains in *Pollei*, to provide their own transportation during their tours of duty:

By that same order, petitioners' tours of duty were extended to begin and end when the officers left for work or arrived home in their cars, rather than when they actually arrived at or left from police headquarters. [The Police Department] provided and installed necessary equipment in each officer's privately-owned vehicle to enable its use as an unmarked police car. Officers were required to notify the police dispatcher before leaving, and on arriving home, and were "on call" during their travel time to and from headquarters. While en route to headquarters or their homes, petitioners were expected to monitor the radio channels to be aware of the ongoing police activities, observe their subordinate officers in the field, patrol the streets, and respond to dispatcher calls for assistance. Petitioners were also required to call in any time they used the unmarked cars, whether they were on or off duty at the time.

. . . .

The Tax Court concluded that petitioners' responsibilities were no greater when in transit to and from headquarters than when petitioners used their unmarked vehicles for personal errands. However, the Tax Court's conclusion fails to acknowledge petitioners' supervisory roles and the [Police Department's] reliance on their daily drive to and from headquarters. By requiring petitioners' tour of duty to begin with their departure from and end upon their arrival at home, the [Department] was provided with a regular addition to the number of commanders supervising police activities. Petitioners' occasional or happenstance use of their unmarked cars on personal business while off-duty could not provide the [Department] with a similar expectation of a regular increment in its supervisory staff.

The IRS argues that allowing petitioners to claim these expenses will result in a deluge of claims for similar exceptions from taxpayers who may routinely or even occasionally perform work-related tasks during their commute to work. It fears, for example, that an employee using a portable dictaphone or a car telephone while driving to work could claim deductions for commuting expenses under section 162(a). We view the facts and circumstances in this case as sufficiently unique to preclude that fear from becoming reality.

We think it unlikely that most employees could justifiably claim their performance of work-related tasks during their commute to their jobs as a condition of their employment. Rather, it is more likely that most employees perform these tasks voluntarily, perhaps for their convenience or to enhance their work record. Petitioners' performance of supervisory and patrol responsibilities as they drove to headquarters was mandated by the [Department] order, and petitioners were subject to discipline if they did not carry out those responsibilities. Petitioners had no other option but to drive their unmarked cars between their homes and headquarters. Use of public transportation was not a viable alternative for petitioners, who testified that they could not thereby monitor the police radio and respond to emergencies or dispatcher calls while traveling to and from headquarters. Petitioners' situation thus can be distinguished from cases in which a commuter's choice of residence location or personal convenience were cited as reasons for the disallowance of commuting expenses. . . .

When conditions of employment restrict an employee's discretion in typically personal choices such as meals eaten during working hours or mode of commuting to work, "that which may be a personal expense under some circumstances can when prescribed by company regulations, directives and conditions, lose its character as a personal expense and take on the color of a business expense."

Other factors limiting the potential number of successful claims under our holding today are the public service and safety aspects of petitioners' employment, factors reflected in the [Department's] orders directing petitioners' mode of daily travel to and from headquarters. Most employees cannot legitimately claim a similar public service or safety component to their jobs, and so will be unable to justify the deduction of commuting expenses in reliance on our decision here.

Id. at 839–42.

Are you persuaded by the *Pollei* court's assurances that the taxpayers' situation is sufficiently unique to preclude numerous other exceptions?

B. Other Transportation Expenses

Assume you fly to another city to take a deposition or to argue a case. May you deduct your transportation expenses? The answer is clearly "Yes." Such expenses are ordinary and necessary; they are solely business-related. Likewise, if it is necessary during your workday to take a taxi or to drive your own car across town to visit a client, the expense incurred is deductible. A taxpayer whose principal place of business is located in his own residence may deduct the entire amount of transportation expenses incurred in driving from his home to meet clients or to engage in other business activity. In none of these situations is it necessary for the taxpayer to consider the "away from home" requirement of § 162(a)(2) with respect to such expenses; the general rule of § 162(a) is sufficient.[1]

Often, however, the characterization of one's transportation expenses is not so simple. Assume you live in Hawaii and travel to New York to take a deposition. Following the deposition, you spend three additional days in New York attending

---

[1] Generally, travel outside of the United States is subject to the same standards as domestic travel. For example, an American entrepreneur engaged in international business is entitled to deduct the travel expenses incurred in traveling to foreign countries if the travel is primarily related to his business. Where, however, the taxpayer travels outside the North American area to attend a business convention, seminar or similar meeting, Congress has imposed certain limitations. Specifically, Congress lists in § 274(h)(1) certain factors which must be considered in determining whether it is reasonable for the convention, seminar or meeting to be held outside the North American area. No deduction is allowed for costs incurred in attending conventions, seminars or meetings on cruise ships which have ports of call outside of the U.S or its possessions; and a limitation of $2,000 per year is placed on deductions for expenses of conventions held on cruise ships which meet the requirements of imposed by § 274(h)(2). Note the definition of North American area in § 274(h)(3)(A) and the specific reporting requirements of § 274(h)(5).

opera and theater, enjoying art in SoHo, and visiting your favorite museums. May you still deduct the roundtrip airfare incurred in traveling to New York? May you deduct only a part of it? If your primary purpose for the travel is business, you will be entitled to deduct the transportation costs which are business related. By contrast, if the trip is primarily personal in nature, transportation expenses (and other traveling expenses) are not deductible, although any expenses incurred while at the destination and allocable to your business are deductible. Read Reg. § 1.162-2(b)(1) carefully.

The concern that transportation expenses often are heavily tainted with a personal flavor caused Congress to limit the amount taxpayers could deduct when the mode of transportation is a cruise ship or some other form of luxury water transportation. *See* § 274(m)(1). As noted by the Staff of the Joint Committee on Taxation, "[t]axpayers who engage in luxury water travel ostensibly for business purposes may have chosen this means of travel for personal enjoyment over other reasonable alternatives that may better serve business purposes by being faster and less expensive. Also, the costs of luxury water travel may include elements of entertainment and meals (not separately charged) that are not present in other transportation."[2]

In addition to the limitation on luxury water transportation, Congress also added § 274(m)(2), denying a deduction for expenses for travel as a form of education. For example, a high school Latin teacher who spends the summer in Rome will no longer be permitted to deduct the travel expenses as § 162 educational expenses.

C.   Expenses for Meals and Lodging While in Travel Status

Congress added the statutory predecessor to § 162(a)(2) in 1921 to permit the entire amount of meal and lodging expenses to be deducted when taxpayer is "away from home." (As discussed in Chapter 17, § 274(n) now limits the deduction of meals to 50% of their cost.) Prior to this congressional action, meals and lodging expenses incurred by a taxpayer while on a business trip were deductible only to the extent they exceeded the amount required for such purposes while the taxpayer was home.[3] In claiming deductions for meals and lodging under the law prior to the 1921 enactment, taxpayers were required to provide a statement showing among other items: (1) the "number of members in taxpayer's family dependent upon him for support"; and (2) the "average monthly expense incident to meals and lodging for the entire family, including the taxpayer himself when at home." Given the difficulty of administering an "excess cost" standard such as that contained in the prior law, the Treasury Department itself asked Congress to amend § 162 to allow taxpayers to deduct the entire amount of their meal and lodging expenses while traveling away from home on business.

With respect to meals, the Service long ago developed the so-called "overnight rule" or "sleep or rest rule" addressed in the *Correll* decision included in the materials. The Service, in Revenue Ruling 75-170, 1975-1 C.B. 60, ruled that

---

[2]   Staff of the Joint Committee on Taxation, General Explanation of the Tax Reform Act of 1986, p.62.

[3]   T.D. 3101, 3 C.B. 191.

railroad employees who have been authorized to stop performing their regular duties to get substantial sleep or rest prior to returning to their home terminals may deduct the costs of their meals and lodging. In that ruling, the Service clarified the meaning of the "overnight rule" noting:

> such absence need not be an entire 24-hour day or throughout the hours from dusk until dawn, but it must be of such duration or nature that the taxpayers cannot reasonably be expected to complete the round trip without being released from duty, or otherwise stopping . . . the performance of their regular duties, for sufficient time to obtain substantial sleep or rest.

> However, the Service does not consider the brief interval during which employees may stop, or be released from duty, for sufficient time to eat, but not to obtain substantial sleep or rest, as being an adequate rest period to satisfy the requirement for deducting the cost of meals on business trips completed within one day. Thus, amounts incurred and paid for such meals are not deductible.

Id. at 61.

The deduction for lodging recognizes that a taxpayer on a business trip incurs duplicate expenses in maintaining an apartment or home at his principal place of work and incurring additional expense in securing lodging in some other city while on business. In the run of the mill business travel case, the deduction for lodging generally is appropriate. A more difficult question regarding deductions for lodging can arise in cases where the taxpayer works in more than one place and doesn't incur duplicate lodging expenses. In *Glazer v. Commissioner*, T.C. Memo. 1990-645, the taxpayer worked for his employer in Albany, New York, each year from January through June, then moved from Albany to New York City where he would work in another office of his employer from July through December, and then he would move back to Albany. When Glazer moved to New York City, he vacated his Albany apartment, taking all his personal possessions with him. He claimed Albany as his home and sought to deduct his New York City living expenses under § 162(a)(2). The Tax Court said "No": "In the context of section 162(a)(2), the taxpayer must incur substantial continuing living expenses at a permanent place of residence. . . . Such requirement is in accord with the purpose underlying section 162(a)(2), *i.e.*, to ease the burden which falls upon the taxpayer who, because of the exigencies of his trade or business, must maintain two places of abode and thereby incur additional and duplicative living expenses." T.C. Memo. 1990-645. Denying the deduction, the Tax Court concluded that New York City was his tax home during the time he lived there. Consider in this regard both the majority and dissenting opinions in *Henderson v. Commissioner*, included in the materials. Should duplication of housing expenses be a prerequisite for claiming a deduction for lodging?

D. "Away from Home"

Surprisingly, the phrase "away from home" has never been interpreted by the Supreme Court, although the Court has had ample opportunity to consider it. The courts and the Service have not agreed upon the phrase's meaning. The longstanding position of the Internal Revenue Service is that "home," within the meaning of § 162(a)(2), is the taxpayer's principal place of business. If the taxpayer has more than one employer or works in more than one location, the principal place of business is a factual determination. *See* Rev. Rul. 75-432, 1975-2 C.B. 60. Facts such as the amount of time the taxpayer spends working in a location and the amount of business activity generated in a given location are relevant to the determination.

The Fifth Circuit in *Robertson v. Commissioner*, 190 F.3d 392 (5th Cir. 1999) provides a good example of the application of the Service's position. Judge Robertson was a professor of law at the University of Mississippi in Oxford when he was appointed to the Mississippi Supreme Court, located in Jackson, Mississippi. Following his appointment, he continued to live in Oxford and taught one course each semester at the law school. He spent four days each work week in Jackson, although he was only required to be in Jackson two days a week for court business. The judge did much of his judicial work at the law school library in Oxford. For his judicial service, Robertson received $75,000 per year as compared to the $15,000 per year he received for teaching at the law school.

On these facts, the Fifth Circuit affirmed the Tax Court's decision holding that Jackson was Robertson's tax home and, therefore, his travel expenses associated with his judicial work in Jackson would not be deductible. With reference to the word "home" in § 162, the Fifth Circuit stated:

> The word "home" for purposes of § 162 does not have its usual and ordinary meaning. This court has repeatedly recognized that the term "home" means the vicinity of the taxpayer's principal place of business and not where his personal residence is located. Thus a taxpayer's "home" for purposes of § 162 is that place where he performs his most important functions or spends most of his working time. If the taxpayer has two places of business or employment separated by considerable distances, the court applies an objective test [by which] it considers the length of time spent at each location, the degree of activity at each location and the relative proportion of the taxpayer's income derived from each location.

Id. at 395.

Contrast the position of the Fifth Circuit with that of the Second Circuit. The Second Circuit, in *Rosenspan v. U.S.*, 438 F.2d 905 (2d Cir. 1971), *cert. denied*, 404 U.S. 864, considering the meaning of "home" in § 162(a)(2), noted: "When Congress uses such a nontechnical word in a tax statute, presumably it wants administrators and courts to read it in the way that ordinary people would understand, and not 'to draw on some unexpressed spirit outside the bounds of the normal meaning of word. . . . ' The construction which the Commissioner has long advocated not only violates this principle but is unnecessary for the protection of the revenue that he seeks. That purpose is served, without any distortion of language, by the third condition laid down in *Flowers*, 326 U.S. at 470, namely, 'that there must be a direct connection between the expenditure and the carrying on of the trade or business of the taxpayer or of his employer' and that 'such an expenditure must be necessary or appropriate to the development and pursuit of the business or trade.' " 438 F.2d at 911. The Second Circuit's determination that "home" means "home" has the effect of placing an emphasis on the business necessity of incurring travel expenses.

As even the Second Circuit would apparently admit, the Fifth Circuit's and the Service's definition of home and the Second Circuit's definition will likely produce the same results in almost all cases. *Rosenspan* may perhaps represent the exception. There, the taxpayer, a traveling jewelry salesman, had no permanent residence, although he stored some of his personal belongings at his brother's home in Brooklyn and used his brother's address for purposes of voter registration, vehicle licensing and filing of tax returns. The taxpayer periodically visited the headquarters of the company in New York. Relying on the Service's historic position that "home" means principal place of business, the taxpayer argued the company's headquarters in New York was his tax home and therefore all of his sales trips were deductible. The Service, however, abandoned its historic definition of "home," and argued the taxpayer's travel expenses during the year were not deductible because the taxpayer had no "home" to be "away from." The Second Circuit, applying its definition of "home," agreed and found for the Service.[4] Compare *Rosenspan* with *Henderson*, which is included in the materials.

Special treatment is accorded taxpayers engaged in temporary jobs. Generally, such a taxpayer will be considered to be in "travel status" and travel expenses paid or incurred in connection with the temporary assignment away from home are deductible. *Peurifoy v. Commissioner*, 358 U.S. 59 (1958). In characterizing an assignment as "temporary" for purposes of this rule, the Service historically employed the so-called "one-year presumption." Under this presumption, assignments away from home of one year or less were generally considered temporary; assignments of over one year were presumed indefinite and thus not subject to the above deduction rule regarding temporary employment. The one-year presumption could be overcome if a taxpayer could demonstrate he realistically expected the job to last less than two years and expected to return to his home when the job ended. *See, e.g., Blankenship v. Commissioner*, T.C. Memo 1979-366.

In 1992, Congress amended § 162(a) to provide a "taxpayer shall not be treated as temporarily away from home during any period of employment if such period exceeds one year." Revenue Ruling 93-86, 1993-2 C.B. 71, addresses the application of amended § 162(a) in common fact scenarios. The ruling holds:

> if employment away from home in a single location is realistically expected to last (and does in fact last for 1 year or less), the employment is temporary in the absence of facts and circumstances indicating otherwise. If employment away from home in a single location is realistically expected to last for more than 1 year or there is no realistic expectation that the

---

[4] Consistent with *Rosenspan*, the Tax Court in *Christy v. Commissioner*, T.C. Memo. 1993-156, held that a taxpayer who was a caddie for professional golfers and travelled to tournaments throughout the U.S. was an itinerant worker without a tax home. Although the taxpayer maintained a room in his brother's condominium, he did not pay rent but paid only his share of utilities, phone bills and food. The Tax Court noted that, despite the taxpayer's personal ties to the area where his brother lived, the "majority of [his] living expenses . . . were incurred and paid where the [taxpayer] was physically present. The ratio of expenses paid on the road to the amounts paid to [taxpayer's] brother in a best case scenario is 30:1. [Taxpayer] has not proved that he incurred substantial living expenses at his alleged permanent place of residence."

employment will last for 1 year or less, the employment is indefinite, regardless of whether it actually exceeds 1 year. If employment away from home in a single location initially is realistically expected to last for 1 year or less, but at some later date the employment is realistically expected to exceed 1 year, that employment will be treated as temporary (in the absence of facts and circumstances indicating otherwise) until the date that the taxpayer's realistic expectation changes.

With respect to the last part of the holding, the Service provided the following example. A taxpayer regularly employed in one location was assigned to a location some 250 miles away. The taxpayer reasonably expected the assignment away from home would last only nine months, after which time she would return home. After eight months, however, she was asked to remain for seven more months (for a total stay of 15 months). The Service concluded that taxpayer's employment away from home would be treated as "temporary" for the first eight months and as "indefinite" for the remaining seven months.

Ordinarily, seasonal employment is another form of temporary employment. Suppose, however, an employee has two or more seasonal jobs on an ongoing basis:

> A seasonal job to which an employee regularly returns, year after year, is regarded as being permanent rather than temporary employment. For example, a railroad employee might habitually work eight or nine months each year transporting ore from the same terminal, maintaining a residence of the employee's family at or near such work location. During the winter, when the ore-hauling service is suspended, the same employee might also be employed for three or four months each year at another regular seasonal post of duty, taking up residence at or near such employment. The ordinary rule is that when an employee leaves one permanent job to accept another permanent job, such employee is regarded as abandoning the first job for the second, and the principal post of duty shifts for the old to the new place of employment. The employee in the above example, however, is not regarded as having abandoned the ore-hauling assignment during the period in which that service is suspended since the employee reasonably expects to return to it during the appropriate following season. The employee is conducting a trade or business each year at the same two recurring, seasonal places of employment, and under these circumstances the tax home does not shift during alternate seasons from one business location to the other, but remains stationary at the principal post of duty throughout the taxable year. In each case of this nature, a factual determination must be made in order to establish which of the seasonal posts of duty is the principal post of duty. Of course, the employee may only deduct the cost of the meals and lodging at the minor place of employment while duties there require such employee to remain away from the principal post of duty.

Rev. Rul. 75-432, 1975-2 C.B. 60, 62. Consider in this regard the situation of the taxpayer in *Andrews v. Commissioner*, 931 F.2d 132 (1st Cir. 1991) who engaged in a seasonal business in the Boston area. During the off-season, the taxpayer bred and raced horses in central Florida. Taxpayer owned homes in both Boston and

Florida and worked approximately six months in each location. Taxpayer sought to deduct his travel expenses, including meals and lodging, associated with his Florida business. The Commissioner argued Andrews had two tax homes and as a result was never "away from home" within the meaning of § 162(a)(2). The First Circuit concluded otherwise, holding a taxpayer could only have one "home" for purposes of § 162(a)(2) and that duplicate living expenses while on business at the other home ("the minor post of duty") were a cost of producing income and therefore deductible. The court in *Andrews* remanded the case for determination of which of the two homes constituted the taxpayer's home. As noted by the court, in determining which home constituted the taxpayer's "home" for purposes of § 162(a)(2), "the guiding policy must be that the taxpayer is reasonably expected to locate his home, for tax purposes, at his 'major post of duty' so as to minimize the amount of business travel away from home that is required. . . . "

E. Travel Expenses of Spouse

Historically, a taxpayer could deduct the travel expenses of her spouse who accompanied her on a business trip if she could establish a bona fide business reason for his presence. Reg. § 1.162-2(c). The expenses of a spouse had to be ordinary and necessary in connection with the business of the taxpayer. In 1993, however, Congress added § 274(m)(3), severely restricting deductions for the travel expenses of a spouse, dependent or other person who accompanies a taxpayer on a business trip. Under this provision, a taxpayer may not deduct such expenses unless (1) the spouse, dependent, or other individual accompanying the taxpayer is a bona fide employee of the taxpayer; (2) the travel of the spouse, dependent or other individual is for a bona fide business purpose; and (3) the spouse, dependent or other individual could otherwise deduct the expense. Does § 274(m)(3) represent good tax policy? Note that employer-paid expenses for spousal travel, otherwise nondeductible to the employer under § 274(m)(3), may be treated by the employer as deductible compensation to the employee pursuant to § 274(e)(2); if not so treated, a nondeductible employer-paid expense is presumably a fringe benefit, the tax treatment of which to the employee is subject to the working condition fringe benefit rules of § 132. *See* Reg. § 1.132-5(t)(1).

F. Reimbursed Employee Expenses

Employees commonly reimburse their employees for travel expenses incurred for business purposes. What are the tax consequences to the employee of the expense and the reimbursement? The answer is best approached by recalling that an employee may claim a deduction under § 162 for ordinary and necessary expenses, including travel expenses, incurred in his trade or business as an employee. However, such expenses may be deducted above the line only if they are reimbursed expenses satisfying the special rule of § 62(c). § 62(a)(2)(A), (c). Unreimbursed employee expenses, or reimbursed expenses not satisfying the § 62(c) rules are below the line deductions, subject to reduction under the 2%-floor rule of § 67, and useful in any event only for taxpayers who itemize rather than take the standard deduction.

Qualifying reimbursement arrangements are labeled "accountable plans" by the regulations. Amounts paid to an employee under an accountable plan are excluded from gross income. Reg. § 1.62-2(c)(4). Since the reimbursement does not constitute income, the expense is not deductible; the result is a wash from the employee's standpoint. (For federal income tax purposes, this is identical to including the reimbursement in income and permitting an above-the-line deduction for the expense. The approach of the regulations, however, makes things much simpler for the employee.) By contrast, amounts paid to an employee under a "nonaccountable plan" are included in income, and the expense is deductible only as a below-the-line, miscellaneous itemized deduction. Reg. § 1.62-2(c)(5).

The regulations require an accountable plan to satisfy a three-part test. Reg. § 1.62-2(c)(2)(i). First, the reimbursement arrangement must provide reimbursements, advances or allowances only for deductible business expenses — the so-called "business connection" requirement. Reg. § 1.62-2(d)(1). Second, the expense must be properly substantiated. Reg. § 1.62-2(e)(1). "For example, with respect to travel away from home, [the regulation] requires that information sufficient to substantiate the amount, time, place and business purpose of the expense must be submitted to the payor." Reg. § 1.62-2(e)(2). The regulations, however, provide that qualifying arrangements for per diem allowances or mileage allowances for travel away from home may be deemed to satisfy the substantiation requirement. *See* Reg. §§ 1.62-2(e)(2), 1.274-5T(g), (j). Third, the reimbursement arrangement must require the employee to return any amount in excess of the substantiated expenses within a reasonable time. Reg. § 1.62-2(f)(1). (If the employee fails to do so, the excess amount is treated as paid under a nonaccountable plan and is thus includable in income. Reg. § 1.62-2(c)(2), (3).) Again, special rules are provided by which arrangements for per diem allowances and mileage allowances for travel away from home may be deemed to satisfy this requirement. Reg. § 1.62-2(f)(2).

G.   Business-Related Meals

Meals may still be deductible as ordinary and necessary business expenses under § 162(a) even when the taxpayer is not away from home. In such cases, the express provisions of § 162(a)(2) and the other sections are inapplicable. Reg. § 1.262-1(b)(5). If a taxpayer takes a client to lunch, the cost of the client's lunch is generally deductible as a business expense. But may the taxpayer in such a situation also deduct her own lunch? These questions are considered in detail in Chapter 17 addressing entertainment and business meals. As discussed in more detail in Chapter 17, the Code specifically: imposes stiff substantiation requirements for the deduction of meal expenses, § 274(a); requires the taxpayer to be present at a meal for which an expense deduction is sought, § 274(k); and limits the meal expense deduction to 50% of its cost, § 274(n).

H.   Relationship to Section 212

Travel expenses and meal expenses may be incurred in an income-producing activity which does not rise to the level of a trade or business. Are such expenses deductible under § 212? While § 212 and the regulations thereunder are silent, it is clear from other provisions such as § 274(c) and (d) that Congress intended such meals and lodging expenses to be deductible under § 212 subject to the same rules as meals and lodging expenses under § 162. For example, in *Harris v. Commissioner*, T.C. Memo. 1978-332, the court allowed a § 212 deduction for travel expenses (including airplane fare, meals and lodging, local transportation costs and airport parking expenses) the taxpayer incurred in travelling from St. Louis to Charlotte, North Carolina, to maintain certain lots he was holding for investment.

Even though deductibility may be available under § 212, recall that, whereas § 162 expenses are generally allowable in computing adjusted gross income (§ 62(a)(1)), most § 212 expenses are deductible only as itemized deductions and, even then, as miscellaneous itemized deductions, are subject to the 2% floor of § 67. One of the recurring difficult tax questions involving rental real estate is whether the expenses attributable to a relatively low level of rental activity constitute § 162 business expenses or, instead, are § 212 expenses related to property held for production of income. At least in the case of rental expenses, the deduction is above the line under § 62, whether part of a business (§ 62(a)(1)) or, instead, a § 212 non-business activity for the production of income (§ 62(a)(4)).

Finally, note § 274(h)(7), denying a deduction under § 212 for expenses allocable to a convention, seminar, or similar meeting. Congress' specific concern was that taxpayers were using § 212 to deduct expenses of investment seminars and tax shelter seminars held in locations (including overseas locations) ideal for vacations and structured to provide time for extensive leisure activity. Travel expenses associated with business conventions and seminars, however, remain deductible under § 162 subject to the specific rules discussed previously.

I. Substantiation Requirements

In addition to the specific requirements of §§ 162 and 212, taxpayers seeking to deduct transportation, meals, lodging or other travel and entertainment expenses must meet the substantiation requirements imposed by § 274(d), which are considered in Chapter 17.

UNITED STATES v. CORRELL
United States Supreme Court
389 U.S. 299 (1967)

MR. JUSTICE STEWART delivered the opinion of the Court.

The Commissioner of Internal Revenue has long maintained that a taxpayer traveling on business may deduct the cost of his meals only if his trip requires him to stop for sleep or rest. The question presented here is the validity of that rule.

The respondent in this case was a traveling salesman for a wholesale grocery company in Tennessee. He customarily left home early in the morning, had breakfast and lunch on the road, and returned home in time for dinner. In his income tax returns for 1960 and 1961, he deducted the cost of his morning and noon meals and "traveling expenses" incurred in the pursuit of his business "while away from home" under Sec. 162(a)(2) of the Internal Revenue Code of 1954. Because the respondent's daily trips required neither sleep nor rest, the Commissioner disallowed the deductions, ruling that the cost of the respondent's meals was a "personal living" expense under sec. 262 rather than a travel expense under sec. 162(a)(2). The respondent paid the tax, sued for a refund in the District Court, and there received a favorable jury verdict. The Court of Appeals for the Sixth Circuit affirmed, holding that the Commissioner's sleep or rest rule is not "a valid regulation under the present statute." 369 F.2d 87, 90. In order to resolve a conflict among the circuits on this recurring question of federal income tax administration, we granted certiorari. 388 U.S. 905.

Under sec. 162(a)(2), taxpayers "traveling . . . away from home in the pursuit of a trade or business" may deduct the total amount "expended for meals and lodging." As a result, even the taxpayer who incurs substantial hotel and restaurant expenses because of the special demands of business travel receives something of a windfall, for at least part of what he spends on meals represents a personal living expense that other taxpayers must bear without receiving any deduction at all.[5] Not surprisingly, therefore, Congress did not extend the special benefits of sec. 162(a)(2) to every conceivable situation involving business travel. It made the total cost of meals and lodging deductible only if incurred in the course of travel that takes the taxpayer "away from home." The problem before us involves the meaning of that limiting phrase.

In resolving that problem, the Commissioner has avoided the wasteful litigation and continuing uncertainty that would inevitably accompany any purely case-by-case approach to the question of whether a particular taxpayer was "away from home" on a particular day. Rather than requiring "every meal-purchasing taxpayer to take pot luck in the courts," the Commissioner has consistently construed travel "away from home" to exclude all trips requiring neither sleep nor rest, regardless of how many cities a given trip may have touched, how many miles it may have covered, or how many hours it may have consumed. By so interpreting the statutory phrase, the Commissioner has achieved not only ease and certainty of application but also substantial fairness, for the sleep or rest rule places all one-day travelers on a similar tax footing, rather than discriminating against intracity travelers and commuters, who of course cannot deduct the cost of the meals they eat on the road. See *Commissioner v. Flowers*, 326 U.S. 465.

Any rule in this area must make some rather arbitrary distinctions,[6] but at least

---

[5] Because sec. 262 makes "personal, living, or family expenses" nondeductible, the taxpayer whose business requires no travel cannot ordinarily deduct the cost of the lunch he eats away from home. But the taxpayer who can bring himself within the reach of sec. 162(a)(2) may deduct what he spends on his noon-time meal although it costs him no more, and relates no more closely to his business, than does the lunch consumed by his less mobile counterpart.

[6] The rules proposed by the respondent and by the two *amici curiae* filing briefs on his behalf are not exceptional in this regard. Thus, for example, the respondent suggests that sec. 162(a)(2) be construed to cover those taxpayers who travel outside their "own home town," or outside "the greater . . . metropolitan area" where they reside. One *amicus* stresses the number of "hours spent and miles traveled away from the taxpayer's principal post of duty," suggesting that some emphasis should also be placed upon the number of meals consumed by the taxpayer "outside the general area of his home."

the sleep or rest rule avoids the obvious inequity of permitting the New Yorker who makes a quick trip to Washington and back, missing neither his breakfast nor his dinner at home, to deduct the cost of his lunch merely because he covers more miles than the salesman who travels locally and must finance all his meals without the help of the Federal Treasury. And the Commissioner's rule surely makes more sense than one which would allow the respondent in this case to deduct the cost of his breakfast and lunch simply because he spends a greater percentage of his time at the wheel than the commuter who eats breakfast on his way to work and lunch a block from his office.

The Court of Appeals nonetheless found in the "plain language of the statute" an insuperable obstacle to the Commissioner's construction. We disagree. The language of the statute — "meals and lodging . . . away from home" — is obviously not self-defining.[7] And to the extent that the words chosen by Congress cut in either direction, they tend to support rather than defeat the Commissioner's position, for the statute speaks of "meals and lodging" as a unit, suggesting — at least arguably — that Congress contemplated a deduction for the cost of meals only where the travel in question involves lodging as well. Ordinarily, at least, only the taxpayer who finds it necessary to stop for sleep or rest incurs significantly higher living expenses as a direct result of his business travel,[8] and Congress might well have thought that only taxpayers in that category should be permitted to deduct their living expenses while on the road.[9] In any event, Congress certainly recognized, when it promulgated sec. 162(a)(2), that the Commissioner had so understood its statutory predecessor. This case thus comes within the settled principle that

[7] The statute applies to the meal and lodging expenses of taxpayers "traveling . . . away from home." The very concept of "traveling" obviously requires a physical separation from one's house. To read the phrase "away from home" as broadly as a completely literal approach might permit would thus render the phrase completely redundant. But of course the words of the statute have never been so woodenly construed. The commuter, for example, has never been regarded as "away from home" within the meaning of sec. 162(a)(2) simply because he has traveled from his residence to his place of business. See *Commissioner v. Flowers*, 326 U.S. 465, 473. More than a dictionary is thus required to understand the provision here involved, and no appeal to the "plain language" of the section can obviate the need for further statutory construction.

[8] The taxpayer must ordinarily "maintain a home for his family at his own expense even when he is absent on business," *Barnhill v. Commissioner*, 148 F.2d 913, 917, and if he is required to stop for sleep or rest, "continuing costs incurred at the permanent place of abode are duplicated." *James v. United States*, 308 F 2d 204, 206. The same taxpayer, however, is unlikely to incur substantially increased living expenses as a result of business travel, however far he may go, so long as he does not find it necessary to stop for lodging. One *amicus curiae* brief filed in this case asserts that "those who travel considerable distance such as (on) a one-day jet trip between New York City and Chicago" spend more for "comparable meals (than) those who remain at their home base" and urges that all who travel "substantial distances" should therefore be permitted to deduct the entire cost of their meals. It may be that eating at a restaurant costs more than eating at home, but it cannot seriously be suggested that a taxpayer's bill at a restaurant mysteriously reflects the distance he has traveled to get there.

[9] The court below thought that "[i]n an era of supersonic travel, the time factor is hardly relevant to the question of whether or not . . . meal expenses are related to the taxpayer's business. . . . " 369 F.2d 87, 89–90. But that completely misses the point. The benefits of sec. 162(a)(2) are limited to business travel "away from home," and *all* meal expenses incurred in the course of such travel are deductible, however unrelated they may be to the taxpayer's income-producing activity. To ask that the definition of "away from home" be responsive to the business necessity of the taxpayer's meals is to demand the impossible.

"Treasury regulations and interpretations long continued without substantial change, applying to unamended or substantially reenacted statutes, are deemed to have received congressional approval and have the effect of law." *Helvering v. Winmill*, 305 U.S. 79, 83; *Fribourg Nav. Co. v. Commissioner*, 383 U.S. 272, 283.

Alternatives to the Commissioner's sleep or rest rule are of course available. Improvements might be imagined. But we do not sit as a committee of revision to perfect the administration of the tax laws. Congress has delegated to the Commissioner, not to the courts, the task of prescribing "all needful rules and regulations for the enforcement" of the Internal Revenue Code. 26 U.S.C. sec. 7805(a). In this area of limitless factual variations, "it is the province of Congress and Commissioner, not the courts, to make the appropriate adjustments." *Commissioner v. Stidger*, 386 U.S. 287, 296. The role of the judiciary in cases of this sort begins and ends with assuring that the Commissioner's regulations fall within his authority to implement the congressional mandate in some reasonable manner. Because the rule challenged here has not been shown deficient on that score, the Court of Appeals should have sustained its validity. The judgment is therefore

Reversed.

AUTHORS' NOTE

In *Christey v. U.S.*, 841 F.2d 809 (8th Cir.), *cert. denied*, 489 U.S. 1016 (1988), the Eighth Circuit considered whether members of the Minnesota Highway Patrol could deduct as ordinary and necessary business expenses under § 162 the cost of meals which they ate in restaurants while on duty. The Eighth Circuit specifically distinguished *Commissioner v. Kowalski*, 434 U.S. 77 (1977), as a § 119 exclusion case and held that the meal costs were deductible. The court stated:

> The district court . . . reasoned that the number of duty related restrictions and requirements concerning their meals "effectively extended the performance of the troopers' duties from patrol cars on highways to tables in restaurants." . . . The restrictions here and their cumulative effect are substantial. The troopers must eat at certain times and places. The troopers remain on duty throughout their meals. They may not bring a meal from home or return home to eat their meal. As part of their job the troopers are required during their meal break to be available to the public not only to respond to emergencies but to provide any information the public may seek. Thus, they are frequently interrupted during meals and are subject to being called away from a meal for an emergency, whether they have eaten what they have paid for or not.

> In light of the circumstances of this case, we believe the district court's conclusion that the meal expenses which the taxpayers incurred while on duty . . . were deductible as ordinary and necessary expenses under Section 162(a) is not clearly erroneous.

841 F.2d at 812–13. A dissenting opinion noted:

> [I]f the general provisions of Section 162(a) were available to render job-related-meal expenses deductible, it is difficult to see why the Supreme

Court in *United States v. Correll* needed to concern itself with whether they were travelling expenses under Section 162(a)(2). Rather, in *United States v. Correll* the Supreme Court recognized that in general, a taxpayer's meal expenses are personal and nondeductible under Section 262, and that the court needed to concern itself only with the special benefits of Section 162(a)(2) which . . . gives the business traveler "something of a windfall, for at least part of what he spends on meals represents a personal living expenses that other taxpayers must bear without receiving any deduction at all. . . . " The district court here did not, in its discussion of the deductibility of taxpayers' meal expenses, take Section 262 into account. The court was legally obligated to apply Section 262, however, and in disregarding this provision of the Internal Revenue Code, plainly erred. In addition, the court never made the proper analysis to determine whether an expense is personal or business. It failed, as the majority does now, to recognize that meal expenses are personal and would be incurred whether or not a taxpayer engaged in business activity. Hence, its decision is incorrect.

Id. at 815–16.

REVENUE RULING 99-7
1999-1 C.B. 361

ISSUE

Under what circumstances are daily transportation expenses incurred by a taxpayer in going between the taxpayer's residence and a work location deductible under § 162(a) of the Internal Revenue Code?

LAW AND ANALYSIS

Section 162(a) allows a deduction for all the ordinary and necessary expenses paid or incurred during the taxable year in carrying on any trade or business. Section 262, however, provides that no deduction is allowed for personal, living, or family expenses.

A taxpayer's costs of commuting between the taxpayer's residence and the taxpayer's place of business or employment generally are nondeductible personal expenses under §§ 1.162-2(e) and 1.262-1(b)(5) of the Income Tax Regulations. However, the costs of going between one business location and another business location generally are deductible under § 162(a). Rev. Rul. 55-109, 1955-1 C.B. 261.

Section 280A(c)(1)(A) (as amended by § 932 of the Taxpayer Relief Act of 1997, Pub. L. No. 105-34, 111 Stat. 881, effective for taxable years beginning after December 31, 1998) provides, in part, that a taxpayer may deduct expenses for the business use of the portion of the taxpayer's personal residence that is exclusively used on a regular basis as the principal place of business for any trade or business of the taxpayer. (In the case of an employee, however, such expenses are deductible only if the exclusive and regular use of the portion of the residence is for the convenience of the employer.) In *Curphey v. Commissioner*, 73 T.C. 766 (1980), the Tax Court held that daily transportation expenses incurred in going between an office in a taxpayer's residence and other work locations were deductible where the home office was the taxpayer's principal place of business within the meaning of § 280A(c)(1)(A) for the trade or business conducted by the taxpayer at those other work locations. The court stated that "[w]e see no reason why the rule that local transportation expenses incurred in travel between one business location and another are deductible should not be equally applicable where the taxpayer's principal place of business with respect to the activities involved is his residence." 73 T.C. at 777–778 (emphasis in original). Implicit in the court's analysis in Curphey is that the deductibility of daily transportation expenses is determined on a business-by-business basis.

Rev. Rul. 190, 1953-2 C.B. 303, provides a limited exception to the general rule that the expenses of going between a taxpayer's residence and a work location are nondeductible commuting expenses. Rev. Rul. 190 deals with a taxpayer who lives and ordinarily works in a particular metropolitan area but who is not regularly employed at any specific work location. In such a case, the general rule is that daily transportation expenses are not deductible when paid or incurred by the taxpayer in going between the taxpayer's residence and a temporary work site inside that metropolitan area because that area is considered the taxpayer's regular place of business. However, Rev. Rul. 190 holds that daily transportation expenses are deductible business expenses when paid or incurred in going between the taxpayer's residence and a temporary work site outside that metropolitan area.

Rev. Rul. 90-23, 1990-1 C.B. 28, distinguishes Rev. Rul. 190 and holds, in part, that, for a taxpayer who has one or more regular places of business, daily transportation expenses paid or incurred in going between the taxpayer's residence and temporary work locations are deductible business expenses under § 162(a), regardless of the distance.

Rev. Rul. 94-2, 1994-1 C.B. 311, amplifies and clarifies Rev. Rul. 190 and Rev. Rul. 90-23, and provides several rules for determining whether daily transportation expenses are deductible business expenses under § 62(a). Under Rev. Rul. 94-47 a taxpayer generally may not deduct daily transportation expenses incurred in going between the taxpayer's residence and a work location. A taxpayer, however, may deduct daily transportation expenses incurred in going between the taxpayer's residence and a temporary work location outside the metropolitan area where the taxpayer lives and normally works. In addition, Rev. Rul. 94-47 clarifies Rev. Rul. 90-23 to provide that a taxpayer must have at least one regular place of business located "away from the taxpayer's residence" in order to deduct daily transportation expenses incurred in going between the taxpayer's residence and a temporary work location in the same trade or business, regardless of the distance. In this regard, Rev. Rul. 94-47 also states that the Service will not follow the decision in *Walker v. Commissioner*, 101 T.C. 537 (1993). Finally, Rev. Rul. 94-47 amplifies Rev. Rul. 190 and Rev. Rul. 90-23 to provide that, if the taxpayer's residence is the taxpayer's principal place of business within the meaning of § 280A(c)(1)(A), the taxpayer may deduct daily transportation expenses incurred in going between the taxpayer's residence and another work location in the same trade or business, regardless of whether the other work location is regular or temporary and regardless of the distance.

For purposes of both Rev. Rul. 90-23 and Rev. Rul. 94-47, a temporary work location is defined as any location at which the taxpayer performs services on an irregular or short-term (*i.e.*, generally a matter of days or weeks) basis. However, for purposes of determining whether daily transportation expense allowances and per diem travel allowances for meal and lodging expenses are subject to income tax withholding under § 3402, Rev. Rul. 59-371, 1959 — C.B. 236, provides a 1-year standard to determine whether a work location is temporary. Similarly, for purposes of determining the deductibility of travel away-from-home expenses under § 162(a)(2), Rev. Rul. 93-86, 1993 — C.B. 71, generally provides a 1-year standard to determine whether a work location will be treated as temporary.

The Service has reconsidered the definition of a temporary work location in Rev. Rul. 90-23 and Rev. Rul. 94-47, and will replace the "irregular or short-term (*i.e.*, generally a matter of days or weeks) basis" standard in those rulings with a 1-year standard similar to the rules set forth in Rev. Rul. 59-371 and Rev. Rul. 93-86.

If an office in the taxpayer's residence satisfies the principal place of business requirements of § 280A(c)(1)(A), then the residence is considered a business location for purposes of Rev. Rul. 90-23 or Rev. Rul. 94-47. In these circumstances, the daily transportation expenses incurred in going between the residence and other work locations in the same trade or business are ordinary and necessary business expenses (deductible under § 162(a)). In contrast, if an office in the taxpayer's residence does not satisfy the principal place of business requirements of § 280A(c)(1)(A), then the business activity there (if any) is not sufficient to overcome the inherently personal nature of the residence and the daily transportation expenses incurred in going between the residence and regular work locations. In these circumstances, the residence is not considered a business location for purposes of Rev. Rul. 90-23 or Rev. Rul. 94-47, and the daily transportation expenses incurred in going between the residence and regular work locations are personal expenses (nondeductible under §§ 1.162-2(e) and 1.262-1(b)(5)).

For purposes of determining the deductibility of travel-away-from-home expenses under § 162(a)(2), Rev. Rul. 93-86 defines "home" as the "taxpayer's regular or principal (if more than one regular) place of business."

HOLDING

In general, daily transportation expenses incurred in going between a taxpayer's residence and a work location are nondeductible commuting expenses. However, such expenses are deductible under the circumstances described in paragraph (1), (2), or (3) below.

(1) A taxpayer may deduct daily transportation expenses incurred in going between the taxpayer's residence and a temporary work location outside the metropolitan area where the taxpayer lives and normally works. However, unless paragraph (2) or (3) below applies, daily transportation expenses incurred in going between the taxpayer's residence and a

temporary work location within that metropolitan area are nondeductible commuting expenses.

(2) If a taxpayer has one or more regular work locations away from the taxpayer's residence, the taxpayer may deduct daily transportation expenses incurred in going between the taxpayer's residence and a temporary work location in the same trade or business, regardless of the distance. (The Service will continue not to follow the Walker decision.)

(3) If a taxpayer's residence is the taxpayer's principal place of business within the meaning of § 280A(c)(1)(A), the taxpayer may deduct daily transportation expenses incurred in going between the residence and another work location in the same trade or business, regardless of whether the other work location is regular or temporary and regardless of the distance.

For purposes of paragraphs (1), (2), and (3), the following rules apply in determining whether a work location is temporary. If employment at a work location is realistically expected to last (and does in fact last) for 1 year or less, the employment is temporary in the absence of facts and circumstances indicating otherwise. If employment at a work location is realistically expected to last for more than 1 year or there is no realistic expectation that the employment will last for 1 year or less, the employment is not temporary, regardless of whether it actually exceeds 1 year. If employment at a work location initially is realistically expected to last for 1 year or less, but at some later date the employment is realistically expected to exceed 1 year, that employment will be treated as temporary (in the absence of facts and circumstances indicating otherwise) until the date that the taxpayer's realistic expectation changes, and will be treated as not temporary after that date.

The determination that a taxpayer's residence is the taxpayer's principal place of business within the meaning of § 280A(c)(1)(A) is not necessarily determinative of whether the residence is the taxpayer's tax home for other purposes, including the travel-away-from-home deduction under § 162(a)(2).

EFFECT ON OTHER DOCUMENTS

Rev. Rul. 190 and Rev. Rul. 59-371 are obsoleted. Rev. Rul. 90-23 and Rev. Rul 94-47 are modified (regarding the definition of temporary work location) and superseded.

HENDERSON v. COMMISSIONER
United States Court of Appeals, Ninth Circuit
143 F.3d 497 (1998)

Opinion of the Court

WIGGINS, CIRCUIT JUDGE:

We must decide whether a taxpayer may claim Boise, Idaho as his "tax home" for the 1990 tax year even though virtually all of his work that year was for a traveling ice show. James Henderson claimed deductions under Internal Revenue Code § 162(a)(2) for living expenses incurred "away from home" while on the tours. The Commissioner disallowed the deductions, concluding that Henderson had no legal tax home for purposes of § 162(a)(2) because he lacked the requisite business reasons for living in Boise between ice show tours. As a result of the disallowance, Henderson had a deficiency in his 1990 federal income tax of $1,791. The Tax Court upheld the Commissioner's decision. We have jurisdiction under 26 U.S.C. § 7482(a), and we affirm.

Henderson's parents lived in Boise, where they had reared him. Even after graduating from the University of Idaho in 1989, he maintained many personal contacts with Boise. For instance, he received mail at his parents' residence, lived there between work assignments, and kept many belongings and his dog there. He also was registered to vote in Idaho, paid Idaho state income tax, maintained an Idaho driver's license, and maintained his bank account in Idaho. During 1990, he spent about two to three months in Boise, staying at his parents' residence. While he was there, he performed a few minor jobs to maintain or improve the family residence.

In 1990, Henderson worked as a stage hand for Walt Disney's World of Ice, a traveling show. His employers' corporate offices were in Vienna, Virginia. Henderson was employed on a tour by tour basis. He testified that at the end of one tour, he would be contacted about participating in the next one. Following the completion of a tour, he returned to his parents' home in Boise.

He worked on three different Disney tours that year. The first lasted from January 1 to May 13, the second from July to November, and the third from December 5 to December 31. He traveled on tour to thirteen states and Japan. The tours stopped in each city for a few days or weeks. While traveling, he received $30 per day to cover expenses. Henderson claims that he looked periodically for employment in Boise between the tours, but the evidence showed that he worked as a stage hand only for a single ZZ Top concert. The Tax Court found that while he returned to Boise in his "idle time," his source of employment during the tax year had no connection to Boise. On appeal, Henderson contends that his 1990 tax home was Boise, primarily based on his extensive personal contacts there.

Internal Revenue Code § 162(a)(2) allows a deduction for all ordinary and necessary "traveling expenses . . . while away from home in the pursuit of a trade or business." 26 U.S.C. § 162(a)(2). This section embodies "a fundamental principle of taxation" — that the cost of producing income is deductible from a person's taxable income. *Hantzis v. Commissioner*, 638 F.2d 248, 249 (1st Cir. 1981). To qualify for the "away from home" deduction, the Supreme Court has held that the taxpayer's expenses must (1) be reasonable and necessary expenses, (2) be incurred while away from home, and (3) be incurred while in the pursuit of a trade or business. *Commissioner v. Flowers*, 326 U.S. 465, 470 (1946).

The first and third criteria are not at issue. The subject of this appeal is whether the expenses Henderson claims as deductions were incurred while "away from home." If Henderson establishes that his home was Boise, his reasonable traveling expenses on the Disney tours are deductible. The Tax Court concluded that Boise was not Henderson's tax home because his choice to live there had nothing to do with the needs of his work; thus, the Tax Court held that Henderson could not claim the deduction for traveling expenses incurred while away from Boise. It held that Henderson had no tax home because he continuously traveled for work. We agree.

Henderson builds a strong case that he treated Boise as his home in the usual sense of the word, but "for purposes of [section] 162, 'home' does not have its usual and ordinary meaning." *Putnam v. United States*, 32 F.3d 911, 917 (5th Cir. 1994) ("In fact, 'home' — in the usual case — means 'work.' "). We have held that the term "home" means "the taxpayer's abode at his or her principal place of employment." *Folkman v. United States*, 615 F.2d 493, 495 (9th Cir. 1980); see also *Coombs v. Commissioner*, 608 F.2d 1269, 1275 (9th Cir. 1979) (stating that "tax home" is generally, but not always, exact locale of principal place of employment). If a taxpayer has no regular or principal place of business, he may be able to claim his place of abode as his tax home. A taxpayer may have no tax home, however, if he continuously travels and thus does not duplicate substantial, continuous living expenses for a permanent home maintained for some business reason. *James v. United States*, 308 F.2d 204, 207 (9th Cir. 1962). . . .

Clearly, if a taxpayer has no "home" for tax purposes, then he cannot deduct under § 162(a)(2) for expenses incurred "away from home." This is for good reason. In James, we examined the statutory precursor to the present version of § 162(a) and explained that the deduction was designed to mitigate the burden on taxpayers who travel on business. 308 F.2d at 207. The burden exists "only when the taxpayer has a 'home,' the maintenance of which involves substantial continuing expenses which will be duplicated by the expenditures which the taxpayer must make when required to travel elsewhere for business purposes." Id.; see also *Andrews*, 931 F.2d at 135 (emphasizing that the deduction's purpose was to mitigate duplicative expenses); *Hantzis*, 638 F.2d at 253. Thus, a taxpayer only has a tax home-and can claim a deduction for being away from that home-when it appears that he or she incurs substantial, continuous living expenses at a permanent place of residence. *James*, 308 F.2d at 207-08.

Revenue Ruling 73-539, 1973-2 C.B. 37, outlines three factors to consider in determining whether a taxpayer has a tax home or is an itinerant. Essentially, they are (i) the business connection to the locale of the claimed home; (ii) the duplicative nature of the taxpayer's living expenses while traveling and at the claimed home; and (iii) personal attachments to the claimed home. While subjective intent can be considered in determining whether he has a tax home, objective financial criteria are usually more significant. Barone, 85 T.C. at 465.

The location of Henderson's tax home is a determination of fact reviewed for clear error. *Frank v. United States*, 577 F.2d 93, 97 (9th Cir. 1978). Similarly, we believe the determination of whether a taxpayer has a tax home or is an itinerant depends on the facts of each case and should be reviewed for clear error. Considering these factors, the Tax Court did not clearly err when it concluded that Henderson is an itinerant taxpayer. First, Henderson had virtually no business reason for his tax home to be in any location — he constantly traveled in 1990 as part of his work with the World on Ice tours. His personal choice to return to Boise was not dictated by business reasons. Except for brief intervals, he was employed for the tours. He worked only one night in Boise. While he testified he looked for other work in Boise between tours, he also testified that at the end of each tour he would have a contract talk with the company manager about the next tour. The Tax Court determined that Henderson merely returned to Boise during his "idle time" between tours. While his reasons for returning may be entirely understandable, we cannot say the Tax Court clearly erred in concluding they were personal, not business, reasons. His minimal employment efforts in Boise do not change this analysis. The importance of the business reason for residing in a certain place is illustrated in *Hantzis*. In that case, the First Circuit disallowed the "away from home" deduction for a law student from Boston who took a summer job in New York. The court held that she did not have a tax home in Boston, even though her husband lived in Boston and she lived there during the school year, because she had no business reason to maintain a home in Boston during the summer while she worked in New York. The court explained why the deduction did not apply in those circumstances:

> Only a taxpayer who lives one place, works another and has business ties to both is in the ambiguous situation that the temporary employment doctrine is designed to resolve. . . . [A] taxpayer who pursues temporary employment away from the location of his usual residence, but has no business connection with that location, is not "away from home" for purposes of section 162(a)(2).

Hantzis, 638 F.2d at 255.

Second, Henderson did not have substantial, continuing living expenses in Boise that were duplicated by his expenses on the road. The evidence showed that he lived with his parents when he stayed in Boise. The Tax Court found that he paid no rent and had no ownership interest in his parents' home. His financial contributions in Boise were limited. He contributed some labor to maintenance and improvement of the home while he was there, and he paid about $500 for supplies. While his parents may have expended money that benefitted Henderson as well — *i.e.*, maintaining a mortgage, paying utilities, and so forth — this is not a substantial living expense incurred by Henderson. Further, any minor expense he may have incurred while living with his parents was not continuing during the periods while he traveled on tour. That is, there is no evidence he had any expenses in Boise while he traveled on the Disney tours.

The fact that Henderson may have incurred higher expenses while traveling with Disney than he would have if he had obtained a full-time job in Boise is not dispositive. The issue presented is whether his claimed expenses were incurred while he was away from his tax home. To assume that Henderson is entitled to the deduction simply because Henderson incurred higher expenses than he would have had he worked in Boise ignores the important question of whether Boise was his tax home at all. Only if Boise is his tax home can Henderson claim deductions for expenses incurred while away from Boise.

Because these two factors weigh against finding that he had a tax home in Boise, the Tax Court did not clearly err when it discounted his evidence on the third factor: personal attachment to Boise. Henderson cites cases, *e.g. Horton v. Commissioner*, 86 T.C. 589, 593, (1986), which hold that a taxpayer may treat a personal residence as his tax home even if it is not the same as the place of his temporary employment with a certain employer. This principle does not help Henderson, however, because he cannot establish any (non-de minimis) business connection to Boise to justify the position that it was his permanent tax home. See *Hantzis*, 638 F.2d at 254–55. Thus, travel away from Boise while on tour with Disney was not travel "away from home" as that term is understood for income tax purposes.

KOZINSKI, CIRCUIT JUDGE, dissenting.

The Tax Code provides that travel expenses are fully deductible, so long as they are incurred while "away from home" in the pursuit of business. I.R.C. § 162(a)(2). Henderson fits comfortably within this language. He lived with his parents in Boise, which made their home his home under any reasonable definition of the term. And he incurred travel expenses in pursuing a job that moved from town to town. Given the itinerant nature of his employment, Henderson could not have avoided these travel expenses by moving his home closer to work. He is thus easily distinguished from the taxpayer in *Hantzis v. Commissioner*, 638 F.2d 248 (1st Cir. 1981), who could have avoided the travel expenses altogether by moving closer to her work. *Hantzis*'s extra-statutory requirement that a home is not a "tax home" unless dictated by business necessity has no application when the job itself has no fixed location.

The other reasons offered by the IRS for denying Henderson his traveling expense deduction are not supported by the Code or the regulations, nor do they make any sense. That Henderson's parents did not charge him room and board is of no consequence. Neither the Code nor common experience requires that a taxpayer pay for his home, else all minors and many in-laws would be deemed homeless. "Home" is not a term of art; it is a common English word meaning a permanent place where a person lives, keeps his belongings, receives his mail, houses his dog — just as Henderson did. Indeed, a grown son living in his parents' house is said to be living "at home." Whether he compensates his parents in cash, by doing chores or through filial affection is none of the Commissioner's business. What matters is that, by going on the road in pursuit of his job, Henderson had to pay for food and lodging that he would not have had to buy had he stayed home. *James v. United States*, 308 F.2d 204 (9th Cir. 1962), cuts against the government. Despite some imprecise language in the opinion, the facts there were very different. George James was on the road 365 days a year and had no permanent home; he spent his entire life traveling from hotel to motel. Wherever a weekend or holiday found him, he would stay there until it came time to go to his next location. James thus was, indeed, a tax turtle — someone with no fixed residence. Henderson is very different: He had a home in Boise, a place where he returned when he wasn't working. He was no more a tax turtle than anyone else who travels a lot for business. That his home happens to be owned by his parents makes it no less his home.[10]

Fast planes and automobiles have turned us into a nation of itinerants. The

---

[10]   James's emphasis on duplication of expenses is unnecessary to the holding, and mistaken to boot. Duplication is one possible method of sifting out business expenses from personal ones, but not the method chosen by Congress. Section 162(a)(2) requires only that the taxpayer be away from home in pursuit of business; meals, for example, are fully deductible even though the expense is not duplicated back at home.

tradition of families living together in one city, even under one roof, is sadly disappearing. Yet there is virtue in keeping families together, in parents who welcome their adult children under their roof. Leave it to the IRS to turn a family reunion into a taxable event. Henderson is being hit with extra taxes because his lifestyle doesn't conform to the IRS's idea of normalcy. But why should the government get extra money because the Hendersons chose to let their son live at home? Had they given him $600 a month to rent an apartment next door, Henderson surely would have gotten the travel deduction. I see no reason why the Henderson family ought to be penalized because the parents gave their son a gift of housing rather than cash — or why the Commissioner should be the beneficiary of this parental generosity.

If Congress had said it must be so, I would bow to its wisdom. But Congress said no such thing and I do not feel bound to give the same deference to the Commissioner's litigating position. Given the dearth of authority or common sense supporting the Commissioner's view, we are free to encourage happy family arrangements like those between Henderson and his mom and dad. In the name of family values, I respectfully dissent.

BOGUE v. COMMISSIONER
United States Tax Court
T.C. Memo 2011-164

[T]he issue we must decide [is] . . . [w]hether petitioner is entitled to deduct certain transportation expenses for travel between his residence and worksites during the years in issue . . . .

FINDINGS OF FACT

Petitioner is an independent contractor based in Cherry Hill, New Jersey. During the years in issue, petitioner lived in a house owned by his fiancé, Janis Pannepacker (Ms. Pannepacker) (we sometimes also refer to Ms. Pannepacker's house as petitioner's residence). During the years in issue, petitioner was building an addition to Ms. Pannepacker's house in his spare time.

During the years in issue, petitioner worked with Raymond J. Mancino (Mr. Mancino) to renovate residential properties. During his 2005 tax year, petitioner worked on properties at the following locations: East Upsal Street, Philadelphia, Pennsylvania; Wissahickon Avenue, Philadelphia, Pennsylvania; and Seminole Avenue, Melrose Park, Pennsylvania. During his 2006 tax year, petitioner worked on properties at the following locations: Seminole Avenue, Melrose Park, Pennsylvania; Albright Avenue, Elkins Parks, Pennsylvania; and Coles Mills Road, Haddonfield, New Jersey. Those five work locations (hereinafter sometimes referred to as worksites) were 20.1, 15.7, 15.0, 14.7, and 4.0 miles, respectively, from petitioner's residence. He worked at each of the worksites for a number of months and then, when the project at that worksite was finished, he moved to another worksite. Petitioner also received some income from his work as a track team coach. . . .

On his returns for the years in issue, petitioner claimed deductions for a variety of expenses related to his transportation between his residence and the worksites.

He claimed deductions for car and truck expenses of $9,232 and $9,657.50 on Schedules C, Profit or Loss from Business, attached to his tax returns for 2005 and 2006, respectively. In addition to car and truck expenses, petitioner deducted as part of his "Other Expenses" on his Schedules C amounts for tolls that he paid on the way to worksites. He claimed deductions of $660 and $400 for those tolls during 2005 and 2006, respectively. As part of the insurance expenses he reported on his Schedules C, petitioner deducted auto insurance expenses of $2,028 and $1,866 for 2005 and 2006, respectively. Petitioner also deducted $650 in car rental expenses for the period during 2005 when he was renting a car after the 1991 Ford Explorer became inoperable. . . .

OPINION

A. Commuting Expenses

Respondent contends that many of petitioner's expenses, including the amounts petitioner claimed for car and truck expenses, tolls, auto insurance, and car rental expenses, are not deductible because they are commuting expenses. As a general rule, expenses for traveling between one's home and one's place of business or employment constitute commuting expenses and, consequently, are nondeductible personal expenses. See sec. 262(a); *Commissioner v. Flowers*, 326 U.S. 465 (1946). . . .

As the Supreme Court explained in *Commissioner v. Flowers*, the core reason commuting expenses are not deductible is that the taxpayer makes a personal choice about where to live. In *Flowers*, the taxpayer was a longtime resident of Jackson, Mississippi, who accepted a job that required him to spend most of his time in Mobile, Alabama. For personal reasons, the taxpayer decided to continue to maintain a home in Jackson and made repeated trips between Jackson and Mobile. The Supreme Court held that the taxpayer was not entitled to deduct the costs of traveling from Jackson to Mobile, despite the substantial distance, because those costs were incurred for personal reasons and not in the pursuit of the business of his employer. The Supreme Court explained:

> The facts demonstrate clearly that the expenses were not incurred in the pursuit of the business of the taxpayer's employer, the railroad. Jackson was his regular home. Had his post of duty been in that city the cost of maintaining his home there and of commuting or driving to work concededly would be non-deductible living and personal expenses lacking the necessary direct relation to the prosecution of the business. The character of such expenses is unaltered by the circumstance that the taxpayer's post of duty was in Mobile, thereby increasing the costs of transportation, food and lodging. Whether he maintained one abode or two, whether he traveled three blocks or three hundred miles to work, the nature of these expenditures remained the same.

> The added costs in issue, moreover, were as unnecessary and inappropriate to the development of the railroad's business as were his personal and living costs in Jackson. They were incurred solely as the result of the taxpayer's

desire to maintain a home in Jackson while working in Mobile, a factor irrelevant to the maintenance and prosecution of the railroad's legal business. * * * The fact that he traveled frequently between the two cities and incurred extra living expenses in Mobile, while doing much of his work in Jackson, was occasioned solely by his personal propensities. * * *

By holding that commuting expenses are personal, the Supreme Court placed those expenses in the category of nondeductible expenses now governed by section 262(a). Such personal expenses contrast with trade or business expenses, which are deductible provided they satisfy the requirements of section 162. Section 162(a) provides that a deduction is allowed for "all the ordinary and necessary expenses paid or incurred during the taxable year in carrying on a trade or business".

Three exceptions to the general rule that commuting expenses are nondeductible have evolved since the Supreme Court decided *Flowers*. The first exception is that expenses incurred traveling between a taxpayer's residence and a place of business are deductible if the residence is the taxpayer's principal place of business (home office exception). The second exception is that travel expenses between a taxpayer's residence and temporary work locations outside of the metropolitan area where the taxpayer lives and normally works are deductible (temporary distant worksite exception). The third exception is that travel expenses between a taxpayer's residence and temporary work locations, regardless of the distance, are deductible if the taxpayer also has one or more regular work locations away from the taxpayer's residence (regular work location exception). Petitioner contends that his transportation expenses driving between his residence and worksites qualify under all three exceptions; we will consider each exception in turn.

1. The Home Office Exception

[Authors' note: The court found that taxpayer did not come within this exception. See Chapter 21 for a discussion of the home office rules of I.R.C. § 280A.]

2. The Temporary Distant Worksite Exception

The temporary distant worksite exception is also rooted in caselaw. In *Schurer v. Commissioner*, 3 T.C. 544 (1944), we held that the taxpayer was entitled to deduct travel and lodging expenses stemming from a series of temporary worksites at which the taxpayer worked during the year, all of which were distant from the taxpayer's residence. Our decision in that case was based, in part, on the fact that the taxpayer had no principal place of business during the tax year. The IRS acquiesced to our decision in *Schurer* and later issued Rev. Rul. 190, 1953-2 C.B. 303, which stated that when an employee "is employed for a strictly temporary (as distinguished from an indefinite) period on a construction project situated at a distance from the metropolitan area in which he is regularly employed, he may deduct * * * his actual expenses incurred for daily transportation between his principal or regular place of employment and such job".

Originally, when courts decided whether transportation expenses were nondeductible commuting expenses, they focused only on the nature of the job: whether it was of temporary or indefinite duration. In *Peurifoy v. Commissioner*, 358 U.S.

59, 60, 79 S. Ct. 104, 3 L. Ed. 2d 30, 1958-2 C.B. 916 (1958), the Supreme Court summarized the law as follows:

> Generally, a taxpayer is entitled to deduct unreimbursed travel expenses under this subsection only when they are required by "the exigencies of business." * * *

> To this rule, however, the Tax Court has engrafted an exception which allows a deduction for expenditures of the type made in this case when the taxpayer's employment is "temporary" as contrasted with "indefinite" or "indeterminate." * * *

However, over the years, a number of courts added an additional requirement that the temporary worksite had to be distant from the area where the taxpayer lives and normally works. See *Dahood v. United States*, 747 F.2d 46, 48 (1st Cir. 1984) . . . . The Court of Appeals for the First Circuit explained the reasoning underlying the temporary distant worksite exception as follows:

> A judicial exception has been carved out of this general rule [that commuting expenses are nondeductible] to cover instances when people commute long distances to their workplaces for business, rather than personal, reasons. This exception permits taxpayers to deduct commuting expenses to a job that is temporary, as opposed to indefinite, in duration. The exception has been deemed necessary because "it is not reasonable to expect people to move to a distant location when a job is foreseeably of limited duration." Implicit in this exception is the requirement that the taxpayer commute to a worksite distant from his or her residence. Without such a requirement, the absurd result would obtain of permitting a taxpayer, who commuted to a succession of temporary jobs, to deduct commuting expenses, no matter how close these jobs were to his residence.

Dahood v. United States, supra at 48.

Consistent with the holdings of similar cases, the IRS has memorialized the temporary distant worksite exception in Rev. Rul. 99-7, 1999-1 C.B. at 361, which states: "A taxpayer * * * may deduct daily transportation expenses incurred in going between the taxpayer's residence and a temporary work location outside the metropolitan area where the taxpayer lives and normally works." The revenue ruling defines a temporary work location as one that "is realistically expected to last (and does in fact last) for 1 year or less". Neither Rev. Rul. 99-7, *supra*, nor any of its predecessors defines the term "metropolitan area". The revenue ruling does not explain the rationale for the temporary distant worksite exception. However, as we read the revenue ruling, on the basis of the caselaw cited above, the revenue ruling recognizes that taxpayers whose work consists of many temporary worksites might not always have a choice about the location of those worksites. Although the taxpayer's choices about where to live and where to "normally work" are personal and it is assumed the taxpayer will live near the place of employment, it is unreasonable to expect that a taxpayer will move to a distant location for a temporary job. The taxpayer's choice to take a temporary job at a remote location is therefore dictated by business needs more than personal preference.

Petitioner contends that because he lived in Cherry Hill, New Jersey, and most of his worksites were across the State line in Pennsylvania, those worksites were temporary work locations not within his "metropolitan area". Because "metropolitan area" is not defined in any revenue ruling, petitioner argues that we should refer to the Office of Management and Budget (OMB) for a definition of "metropolitan", which petitioner contends is an urban area with more than 50,000 people. However, petitioner is mistaken about how the OMB defines "metropolitan area". The OMB defines a "metropolitan statistical area" or a "micropolitan statistical area" as "an area containing a recognized population nucleus and adjacent communities that have a high degree of integration with that nucleus." Standards for Defining Metropolitan and Micropolitan Statistical Areas, 65 Fed. Reg. 82,228 (Dec. 27, 2000). A metropolitan statistical area is distinguished from a micropolitan statistical area by having a population core of at least 50,000. However, petitioner's reference to the definitions used by the OMB does not support his contention because, as defined by the OMB, petitioner's residence in Cherry Hill, New Jersey, and all of his temporary worksites are part of the Philadelphia-Camden-Wilmington Metropolitan Statistical Area. See Office of Mgmt. & Budget, Exec. Office of the President, OMB Bull. No. 06-01, Update of Statistical Area Definitions and Guidance on Their Uses (2005).

Nonetheless, we decline to adopt any such rigid definition for deciding when a taxpayer's temporary worksites take him "outside the metropolitan area where the taxpayer lives and normally works." Adopting such a rigid definition would inevitably lead to some absurd results. In some situations, a rigid definition would disallow the deduction of travel expenses that should be permitted. The metropolitan statistical areas (MSAs) defined by the OMB are often quite large, such as the Philadelphia-Camden-Wilmington MSA. A taxpayer who lives and normally works near the outskirts of one MSA may normally drive only 5 miles to and from worksites. However, if that taxpayer accepts work at a temporary worksite on the opposite end of the MSA, but still within the MSA, the taxpayer could end up driving as much as 100 miles each way yet not be able to deduct such transportation expenses because the worksite is still within the MSA.

In other situations, such a rigid definition would allow commuting expense deductions that should not be permitted. For instance, a taxpayer may live on the border of two MSAs. If that taxpayer normally has worksites in one MSA and only occasionally has worksites in the other MSA, the taxpayer would be permitted to deduct the expenses incurred in traveling to the worksites in the second MSA even if the distance traveled were no greater than that normally traveled when working at worksites in the first MSA. Accordingly, employing rigid definitions would frustrate the intent of the primary principle that commuting expenses are nondeductible.

Indeed, we conclude that respondent's use of the term "metropolitan area" is not helpful for answering the question of whether petitioner's travel expenses are deductible under the temporary distant worksite exception. Instead, we will evaluate the facts and circumstances to decide whether the travel expenses in question were incurred in traveling to a worksite unusually distant from the area where petitioner lives and normally works. Such an approach is consistent with the approach historically taken by a number of other courts. See *Ellwein v. United States*, 778 F.2d 506, 511 (8th Cir. 1985) (holding that it was necessary to consider whether the taxpayer's temporary worksites were within the "work area" of the city that was the taxpayer's tax home); *Dahood v. United States*, 747 F.2d at 48 (for commuting expenses to a temporary worksite to be deductible, that temporary worksite must be "distant from * * * [the taxpayer's] residence"); *Frederick v. United States*, 603 F.2d 1292, 1295 (8th Cir. 1979) (commuting expenses to a temporary worksite "a considerable distance" from the taxpayer's residence were deductible).

As the maps introduced by respondent at trial show, petitioner's residence in Cherry Hill, New Jersey, is approximately 10 miles east of Philadelphia. Most of petitioner's worksites during the years in issue were in Philadelphia or its suburbs to the north. Petitioner had five worksites that were 20.1, 15.7, 15.0, 14.7, and 4.0 miles from his residence. Consequently, it was petitioner's normal practice during the years in issue to travel about 15 miles from his residence to a worksite. There was nothing unusual about those trips. Even the worksite that was farthest from petitioner's residence was still within the city limits of Philadelphia. Given that four out of five of petitioner's worksites during the years in issue were in either Philadelphia or its suburbs to the north, we conclude that those areas are the areas where petitioner normally worked. Accordingly, we hold that he was not entitled to deduct travel expenses incurred in driving between his residence and those worksites. Consequently, we conclude that petitioner is not eligible to deduct his commuting expenses under the temporary distant worksite exception.

3. The Regular Work Location Exception

Unlike the first two exceptions, the regular work location exception is not rooted in caselaw. Rather, the regular work location exception was originally articulated by the Commissioner in Rev. Rul. 90-23, *supra*. The current version of the regular work location exception is found in Rev. Rul. 99-7, 1999-1 C.B. at 362, which states: "If a taxpayer has one or more regular work locations away from the taxpayer's residence, the taxpayer may deduct daily transportation expenses incurred in going between the taxpayer's residence and a temporary work location in the same trade or business, regardless of the distance." Rev. Rul. 99-7, *supra*, does not define "regular work location". However, Rev. Rul. 90-23, 1990-1 C.B. at 28, defines "regular place of business" as "any location at which the taxpayer works or performs services on a regular basis." We infer that the same definition should apply to "regular work location" under Rev. Rul. 99-7, supra, except that a "regular work location" may not include the taxpayer's residence. We also infer that, because "regular work location" is contrasted with "temporary work location", the two are mutually exclusive.

Rev. Rul. 90-23, 1990-1 C.B. at 29, explains the rationale for the regular work location exception by analogy to Rev. Rul. 190, *supra*:

> A taxpayer who pays or incurs daily transportation expenses on trips between the taxpayer's residence and one or more regular places of business is like the taxpayer described in Rev. Rul. 190 who pays or incurs daily transportation expenses on trips between the taxpayer's residence and temporary work sites within the metropolitan area that is considered the taxpayer's regular place of business. Such daily transportation ex-

penses are nondeductible commuting expenses. On the other hand, a taxpayer who has one or more regular places of business and who pays or incurs daily transportation expenses for trips between the taxpayer's residence and temporary work locations is like the taxpayer described in Rev. Rul. 190 who pays or incurs deductible daily transportation expenses for trips between the taxpayer's residence and temporary work sites outside the metropolitan area that is considered the taxpayer's regular place of business. Thus, for a taxpayer who has one or more regular places of business, daily transportation expenses paid or incurred in going between the taxpayer's residence and temporary work locations are deductible business expenses under section 162(a) of the Code regardless of the distance.

We do not follow the Commissioner's reasoning. It is unclear why the Commissioner considers analogous the situation where a taxpayer travels between the taxpayer's residence and a distant temporary work location and the situation where the taxpayer has one or more regular work locations and travels between the taxpayer's residence and a nearby temporary work location. The exception would be logical if it were limited to distant temporary work locations. However, as it stands, the regular work location exception reaches a result similar to what the Court of Appeals for the First Circuit labeled "absurd" when it held that there was an implicit requirement that, in order for travel expenses between a taxpayer's residence and a temporary work location to be deductible, the temporary work location must be distant from the taxpayer's residence. See *Dahood v. United States, supra* at 48. Nonetheless, we will treat the regular work location exception as a concession by the Commissioner.

In the instant case, petitioner's only work locations during the years in issues were worksites where he performed renovations. All of those worksites were temporary as defined in Rev. Rul. 99-7, *supra*, and petitioner has not shown that he had other, regular work locations. Accordingly, petitioner has not established facts that would qualify him for respondent's concession. Consequently, we conclude that petitioner is not entitled to deduct his commuting expenses under the regular work location exception.

Because petitioner has failed to qualify under any of the three exceptions, we hold that his expenses in traveling between his worksites and his residence were nondeductible commuting expenses.

Chapter 17

ENTERTAINMENT AND BUSINESS MEALS

I. PROBLEMS

1. Pat Pending is a patent attorney who is an associate in a 20-person law firm; he also teaches a course on patent law on a part-time basis at the local law school. On Monday, he and the three other patent lawyers in the firm have their weekly luncheon to discuss their cases, a practice strongly encouraged by the firm's senior partners; each lawyer pays for his or her own lunch. On Tuesday, Pat buys dinner for himself and three of his patent students following the afternoon class. On Wednesday, Pat buys lunch for himself and his friend Larry, a stockbroker (every other Wednesday, Larry buys lunch); Pat and Larry always discuss a number of topics, but they make it a point to include a discussion about Pat's stock portfolio. On Thursday, Pat has lunch on his own at a favorite, quiet restaurant, where he can review his notes for a deposition scheduled immediately after lunch. On Friday, Pat has lunch with the president of the local Inventors Society and her husband, so that Pat may get better acquainted with her; the lunches are at Pat's expense. What meal expenditures may Pat deduct? Assume Pat receives no reimbursement for any of the above costs.

2. Your client, Mary Johnson, is the owner of a New York gallery. Mary's wealthy college friend, Joyce Smith, and Joyce's husband, Jim, arrived in town on Wednesday. Mary and her husband took the Smiths out to dinner that night at a cost of $500; in the cab ride to the restaurant, Mary described her gallery's recent acquisitions and suggested that Joyce come to the gallery the next day. No business was discussed at dinner. After dinner, Mary gave the Smiths two $150 theatre tickets for that evening, and Mary and her husband returned home. The next morning, Joyce stopped by the gallery, met with Mary, viewed the collection and left without buying anything. Mary asks you whether the dinner and the theatre tickets are deductible. If so, how does she substantiate the expenses?

3. Tom Dooley, a life insurance agent, is a member of the Deluxe Country and Tennis Club. He pays annual dues of $5,000 plus additional charges for meals. Most of his use of the Club is for business lunches or dinners with clients and prospective clients. Tom also pays $1,000 per year for use of the Club's tennis courts once a week. On 20 days this year Tom plays tennis with local lawyers from whom he hopes to obtain referrals. On 20 other days he invites present clients to play tennis and have dinner at the Club to review their insurance coverage. On another 10 days this year Tom plays tennis at the Club with his children. May Tom deduct any of the

expenditures noted? What, if any, additional information would be helpful in determining the deductibility of Tom's expenditures?

Assignment for Chapter 17:

Complete the problems.

Read: Internal Revenue Code: §§ 274(a), (d), (e), (h), (k), (l), (n); 262; 162(a). Review § 274(b) and skim remaining subsections of § 274.
Treasury Regulations: §§ 1.262-1(b)(5); 1.274-1; 1.274-2; 1.274-5T. See also § 1.162-17.

Materials: Overview
Walliser v. Commissioner
Moss v. Commissioner
Churchill Downs, Inc. v. Commissioner

II. VOCABULARY

Cohan rule
Sutter rule

III. OBJECTIVES

1. To distinguish the alternative standards for the deductibility of entertainment activities.

2. To provide an example of a deductible entertainment expense under the "directly related to" standard.

3. To provide an example of a deductible entertainment expense under the "associated with" standard.

4. To recall the expenditures to which the 50% limitation rule applies.

5. To recall the rule regarding deductions in connection with entertainment facilities.

6. To describe the substantiation requirements and expenditures to which they apply.

7. To determine whether or not the cost of a taxpayer's own business meal is likely to be deductible.

IV. OVERVIEW

A. Business or Pleasure?

The problem of drawing the boundary line between business and personal expenses is a persistent, pervasive one in our tax system. The problem becomes particularly acute with regard to business-related entertainment expenses. It seems undeniable that, at least in some circumstances, entertainment activities provide a necessary "social lubricant" — to borrow an expression from the Seventh Circuit's opinion in *Moss v. Commissioner*, reprinted below — and can be shown to be directly productive of business orders and profits. Section 162, it would seem, authorizes a deduction for such ordinary and necessary business expenses. But § 262 denies a deduction for personal expenses, and most entertainment expenses, however intimate their connection to the taxpayer's business, also seem inherently personal and, well, just too much fun to trust fully the taxpayer's assertion of business purpose. Perhaps, if customary business entertaining consisted of a visit to the dentist, the pure business motivation behind an ostensibly personal expenditure would be more readily apparent. But business entertainment is more apt to consist of restaurant dining, parties, theatre, ball games, cruises and the like, and most of the time there is indeed likely to be some plausible business connection to the expenditures involved. When, and to what extent, should § 162 prevail over § 262? As a practical matter, of course, Congress is not likely to answer the question on a purely theoretical level. Practical considerations intrude, not to mention fairness and equity; expense-account living, and deductible wining and dining, for example, are practiced far more often by the highly-paid executive than the minimum wage worker. By contrast, many businesses argue their very survival depends on the deductibility of a significant portion of their goods or services, and that business failure and unemployment is too high a price to pay for ending all entertainment-related deductions.

Prior to 1962, the deduction of entertainment expenses was governed by the ordinary and necessary standard of § 162, and under that standard it was relatively easy to deduct such expenses, even where the personal element appeared to loom quite large. In one well-known case, *Sanitary Farms Dairy, Inc. v. Commissioner*, 25 T.C. 463 (1955), the cost to a dairy of sending its president and controlling shareholder and his wife, both experienced hunters, on an African big game hunt was held to be an ordinary and necessary business expense, since the hunt was intended to, and did in fact provide "extremely good advertising [for the dairy] at a relatively low cost"; the court noted there was extensive newspaper coverage of the trip, films of the hunt were shown back home, and trophies from the hunt were displayed in the dairy's museum. Moreover, the ease with which entertainment expenses could be deducted was exacerbated by the so-called "*Cohan* rule." In *Cohan v. Commissioner*, 39 F.2d 540 (2d Cir. 1930), Judge Learned Hand held that where the taxpayer, the theatrical manager and producer George M. Cohan, had spent substantial sums on tax-deductible entertaining, but kept no account of them, it was error for the Board of Tax Appeals to allow no deduction at all; rather, the Board was directed to make on remand "as close an approximation as it can, bearing heavily if it chooses upon the taxpayer whose inexactitude is of his own making." *Id.* at 544. The *Cohan* rule thus inhibited administrative policing of entertainment expenses; it undoubtedly encouraged many taxpayers to inflate their expenses and to include quite marginal ones on their returns, trusting that approximation would produce acceptable results if they were audited, and reaping windfalls if they were not.

The perception that abuse was widespread and deep, that personal expenses with little business connection were routinely being deducted, led President Kennedy, in 1961, to propose the complete disallowance of entertainment expenses. The congressional response, in the Revenue Act of 1962, was something considerably less. Section 274, enacted that year, did impose, in § 274(a), requirements for entertainment expenses supplementing the ordinary and necessary rules of § 162; it also established, in § 274(d), substantiation requirements intended to overturn the *Cohan* rule in this area. Nonetheless, the substantiation requirements were not a problem for those willing to keep records, and the § 274(a) requirements were easy to meet. In 1978, the perception of abuse led to further congressional action, with the amendment of § 274(a) to deny any deduction for most entertainment facilities.

Further restrictions to § 274 were added in 1986; the congressional concern with the personal element in business entertainment, and the 1986 response to it are described in the following excerpt:

> In general, prior law required some heightened showing of a business purpose for travel and entertainment costs, as well as stricter substantiation requirements than those applying generally to all business deductions; this approach is retained under the [1986] Act. However, the prior-law approach failed to address a basic issue inherent in allowing deductions for many travel and entertainment expenditures — the fact that, even if reported accurately and having some connection with the taxpayer's business, such expenditures also convey substantial personal benefits to the recipients.
>
> The Congress believed that prior law, by not focusing sufficiently on the personal-consumption element of deductible meal and entertainment expenses, unfairly permitted taxpayers who could arrange business settings for personal consumption to receive, in effect, a Federal tax subsidy for such consumption that was not available to other taxpayers. The taxpayers who benefit from deductibility tend to have relatively high incomes, and in some cases the consumption may bear only a loose relationship to business necessity. For example, when executives have dinner at an expensive restaurant following business discussions and then deduct the cost of the meal, the fact that there may be some bona fide business connection does not alter the imbalance between the treatment of those persons, who have effectively transferred a portion of the cost of their meal to the Federal Government, and other individuals, who cannot deduct the cost of their meals.
>
> The significance of this imbalance is heightened by the fact that business travel and entertainment often may be more lavish than comparable activities in a nonbusiness setting. For example, meals at expensive restaurants and the most desirable tickets at sports events and the theatre

are purchased to a significant degree by taxpayers who claim business deductions for these expenses. This disparity is highly visible, and has contributed to public perceptions that the tax system under prior law was unfair. Polls indicated that the public identified the full deductibility of normal personal expenses such as meals and entertainment tickets to be one of the most significant elements of disrespect for and dissatisfaction with the tax system.

General Explanation to the Tax Reform Act of 1986, Jt. Comm. on Taxation, 99th Cong., 2d Sess., pp. 60–61.

To reflect this personal element, and in lieu of including it in income, Congress has now generally limited the deduction for business meals and entertainment to 50% of the otherwise allowable amount. § 274(n)(1). *Churchill Downs, Inc. v. Commissioner*, included in the materials, provides an excellent example of the application of the 50% limitation of § 274(n) and the test for determining whether an activity constitutes entertainment. For an alternative approach to the problems associated with entertainment and meal expenses, see § 274(b). Should its rule be applied to entertainment expenses generally?

B.   Entertainment Activities

Section 274(a)(l) disallows any deduction for an activity "of a type generally considered to constitute entertainment, amusement, or recreation" unless (in addition to meeting the usual requirements for either a business deduction, or — per § 274(a)(2)(B) — a § 212 deduction) the taxpayer satisfies one of two tests: The expenditure must be either (l) "directly related to" the active conduct of the trade or business; or (2) "associated with" the active conduct of the trade or business and directly preceded or followed by a substantial and bona fide business discussion. The regulations flesh all this out in considerable detail.

Satisfaction of the "directly related to" standard requires entertainment that does more than merely promote goodwill. *See* Reg. § l.274-2(c)(3). Thus, in general, the "directly related to" standard requires that the taxpayer (1) reasonably anticipate some income or specific business benefit from the expense, (2) actively engage in a business discussion, (3) be motivated principally by the business aspect of the business-entertainment combination, and (4) establish the expenditure is allocable to the taxpayer and persons with whom the taxpayer is engaged in the active conduct of trade or business. However, it is not necessary that more time be spent on business than on entertainment. Alternative ways of satisfying the "directly related to" standard are also provided; see, for example, the "clear business setting" test of Reg. § l.274-2(c)(4). But note that, if the taxpayers are not present or there are "substantial distractions," such as at nightclubs, theatres, sporting events, and cocktail parties, the expenditure is generally considered not to be directly related to the taxpayer's business. Reg. § l.274-2(c)(7).

The strictures of the "directly related to" statute are loosened considerably by the "associated with" standard. Under the latter, the taxpayer must have a "clear business purpose" for making the expenditure, but an intent to maintain business goodwill or obtain new business satisfies this requirement. Reg. § 1.274-2(d)(2). The substantial, bona fide business discussion that precedes or follows the entertainment must be for the purpose of obtaining income or other specific business benefit, and the business aspect must be the principal aspect of the combined business and entertainment; but it is not necessary that more time be spent on business than entertainment, nor must the business and entertainment necessarily take place on the same day. There is, of course, no requirement that any business be conducted during entertainment that is "associated with" the taxpayer's business. Moreover, as respects the entertainment expenses for spouses, see Reg. § 1.274-2(d)(4). In sum, the path to deductibility of entertainment activity expenses — albeit at the now reduced rate of 50% — seems not too excessively narrowed by § 274.[1]

As noted previously, § 274(n) generally limits the deduction for "any" food or beverage expense or entertainment expense to 50% of the otherwise allowable amount. Also note the special rules for business meals in § 274(k)(1) — no deduction is allowed unless the meal is not lavish or extravagant, and the taxpayer or the taxpayer's employee is present; note the face-value limitation on most entertainment tickets in § 274(l)(1). Since the 50% rule of § 274(n) applies to the otherwise allowable expenses, other limitations should be applied first. For example, if under § 274(k) a $150 meal is lavish or extravagant to the extent of $50, only $100 is otherwise allowable, and the 50% limitation would result in a $50 deduction. (Taxes and tips relating to a meal or entertainment activity are included as part of its cost for purposes of applying the 50% limitations; transportation cost

---

[1] One of our favorite Section 274 decisions is *Sullivan v. Commissioner*, T.C. Memo 1982-150. Edward Sullivan, the taxpayer, operated a service station known as Sully's DX Station in Chickasha, Oklahoma. Sully initially gave S&H Green Stamps to his customers but then decided he would attract more business by offering customers, many of whom were oil field workers, free beer. The beer "was kept in an old Coca Cola vending machine [Sully] had purchased and from which he removed the coin mechanism. . . . Usually the customer would park his car in a gas stall, and, while the vehicle was being filled with gasoline or serviced, the customer was offered and allowed to drink beer in the station. Customers normally had one or two beers. . . . [Sully's] business increased after he began offering free beer to his customers." The issue, of course, was the deductibility of the beer in light of Section 274. Could Sully satisfy the rules for the deduction of entertainment expenses? According to the Tax Court he did. Footnote 4 of the Tax Court decision is a memorable one:

Petitioner's points are succinctly stated in his brief as follows:

When I first opened my station business was very slow, as usual with a new business. Next I started using S&H Green Stamps to boost my sales. The majority of oil field workers (my customers) were single men who didn't have much time for licking stamps. I began giving beer. I know from past experience that "oilers" would much rather drink ice cold beer than lick stamps after a long hot day in the oil fields. . . . If I were to continue with Green Stamps I would have never increased my business. In 1977 my business was really strong until I got sick and had to sell out. I still feel good about it and I still have every receipt from every beer purchase as well as every Green Stamp purchase I ever made. Sir I really don't feel in my heart how a small business man can be put down because he had an idea and made it work. . . .

The force and truth of these statements are self-evident. We have no doubt that an oil worker, after a long, hard day in the field would much prefer to stop by Sully's Service Station for gas and a cold beer rather than go home licking S&H Green Stamps. Unlike the complex rule in *Shelly's* case — that nemesis of all first year law students of real property — the rule in Sully's case is simply that a small businessman who wants to obtain customers and sell more of his products can offer free beer to beer lovers. Stated differently, in exchange for purchasing gas, oil and other services, Sully said to his customers "This Bud's for you."

to or from a business meal, however, is not subject to the reduction.) In addition, the 50% limitation does not apply to employees who receive reimbursement from their employers, provided the employee accounts to the employer as required by § 274(d). § 274(n)(2)(A), (e)(3). It is the employer who is then subject to the 50% limitation of § 274(n).

C.   Entertainment Facilities

Congress decided in the Revenue Act of 1978 that, with respect to entertainment facilities, the potential for abuse was simply too great to continue allowing their use on a tax-deductible basis. Section 274 therefore generally denies any deductions for entertainment facilities. § 274(a)(1)(B). Examples of possible entertainment facilities, as listed by the regulations, include hunting lodges, swimming pools, airplanes and vacation homes. Reg. § 1.274-2(e)(2). There is an exception to nondeductibility where the facility is used "primarily" for business purposes, *e.g.*, more than 50% business use. *See* § 274(a)(2)(C); Reg. § 1.274-2(e)(4)(iii).

Under Regulation § 1.274-2(e)(4)(iii)(b), a taxpayer will establish that a facility was used primarily for the furtherance of his trade or business "if he establishes that more than 50% of the total calendar days of use of the facility by . . . the taxpayer during the taxable year were days of business use." Under that regulation, if, on a calendar day, a taxpayer makes any use of a facility and if taxpayer's primary use of the facility on that day is ordinary and necessary within the meaning of §§ 162 or 212, that day will constitute a "day of business use." A facility is deemed to have been primarily used for business use if it was used for the conduct of a substantial and bona fide business discussion. Even if the taxpayer satisfies the "primarily for" test, only that portion of the item "directly related to" the active conduct of the taxpayer's trade or business is allowed. § 274(a)(2)(C). Thus, for example, even though the taxpayer's use of a facility on a given day may count towards satisfying the "primarily for" test because the use is ordinary and necessary under §§ 162 or 212, the use may not meet the "directly related to" test and therefore expenditures associated with that day's use will not be deductible. In any event, no deduction is allowed for club dues, regardless of the taxpayer's satisfaction of the primary use test. § 274(a)(3).

It is clear that otherwise allowable expenses for entertainment activities are not denied simply by reason of their association with an entertainment facility:

> For example, if a salesman took a customer hunting for a day at a commercial shooting preserve, the expenses of the hunt, such as hunting rights, dogs, a guide, etc., would be deductible provided that the current law requirements of substantiation, adequate records, ordinary and necessary, directly related, etc. are met. However, if the hunters stayed overnight at a hunting lodge on the shooting preserve, the cost attributable to the lodging would be nondeductible but expenses for any meals would be deductible if they satisfied the requirements of current law. The shooting preserve should provide the taxpayer with an allocation of charges attributable to the overnight lodging for the taxpayer and guests.

General Explanation of the Revenue Act of 1978, Jt. Comm. on Taxation, 95th Cong. 2d. Sess., 207. It is sometimes difficult to distinguish between a deductible entertainment activity and the nondeductible use of an entertainment facility. In *Harrigan Lumber Co. Inc., v. Commissioner*, 88 T.C. 1562 (1987), *aff'd*, 851 F.2d 362 (11th Cir. 1988), the Tax Court denied a deduction for annual lease payments for exclusive hunting rights on a ten-acre tract of land. The taxpayer used the hunting area, and a hunting lodge it built on the land, to entertain its business suppliers and customers. The Tax Court held the hunting area was a "facility" and the lease payments were "items with respect to a facility," although it conceded:

> The distinction drawn by the Conference Report [to the Revenue Act of 1978] between entertainment activities within the meaning of section 274(a)(1)(A) and entertainment facilities within the meaning of section 274(a)(1)(B) is fuzzy at best. We discern from the examples and discussion in the legislative history, however, that a material difference between an entertainment activity that includes the use of real or personal property and an entertainment facility is whether the property used for the entertainment is occupied exclusively by the taxpayer for or during the recreation or entertainment. For example, use of a skybox at the stadium would not constitute exclusive occupancy of the sports stadium where the entertainment takes place.

> In this case, petitioner has exclusive right to use the hunting area for hunting, fishing and other recreation. Petitioner's exclusive lease of the hunting rights grants to petitioner, on prior notice, unfettered access to the hunting area. The hunting area is where the recreation takes place. During petitioner's recreation in the hunting area, petitioner has exclusive occupancy of the hunting area. Therefore, the hunting area is a facility used in connection with entertainment within the meaning of section 274(a)(1)(B).

> Petitioner argues, however, that the lease payments are expenditures for an intangible property right which is separate and apart from the real property to which the hunting rights are attached, and therefore, such expenditures are out-of-pocket expenses, which are deductible pursuant to section 1.274-2(e)(3)(iii)(a), Income Tax Regs. Petitioner argues further [based on the example from legislative history, quoted above, dealing with deductible hunting expenses] that hunting rights were considered specifically by Congress which decided that they were expenses of an activity and not expenses "with respect to" a facility.

> In the above example the expenditures for the hunting rights, which are considered to be part of an activity and not "with respect to" a facility, are for the non-exclusive use of a commercial hunting preserve for one day. The taxpayer [in the example] has no control over the use of the property by others, no exclusive occupancy of the preserve for hunting and no right to access the property beyond the limited time permitted. The expenditure thus viewed relates more to the entertainment activity than to the entertainment facility. Where the taxpayer is, however, granted exclusive use of and unfettered access to the property, the character of the expenditure changes. Instead of being an expense incurred solely in

connection with the particular activity, it becomes an expense for the continuing enjoyment of the property itself for the specified recreational purposes. In this case, petitioner's payments gave it continuing, unfettered access to the property and exclusive occupancy in order to hunt, fish and cook out. Moreover, these rights are meaningless apart from the hunting area to which they attach. Petitioner's payments were not made simply to acquire and hold "rights" but were made to enjoy the use of the property. Therefore, we reject petitioner's argument. The lease payments are an item "with respect to" a facility used in connection with entertainment within the meaning of section 274(a)(1)(B).

Id., at 1566–68.

Two concurring opinions declined to adopt the majority's formulation, but nonetheless held for the Commissioner, relying in whole or in part on the long-term nature of the lease. *Harrigan Lumber* was followed in *On Shore Quality Control Specialist, Inc. v. Commissioner*, T.C. Memo. 1996-95, where the Tax Court disallowed the deduction of lease payments for use of a ranch for hunting purposes on the ground that the ranch was an entertainment facility. Under the taxpayer's lease arrangements, some friends and business acquaintances of the owner were also allowed to hunt on the ranch. The taxpayer thus argued the ranch, under *Harrigan Lumber*, was not a "facility" with respect to the taxpayer because the lease was not an exclusive one. The *On Shore* court, however, concluded that the exclusivity language in *Harrigan Lumber* referred to the right of the lessee to bar the general public from participation, not a limited number of persons covered by the lease, and it held that where the taxpayer "dominates" the hunting rights as in *On Shore*, the rights should be treated as exclusive ones, and the lease payments should be disallowed.

D.   Substantiation Requirements

Section 274(d) imposes special substantiation requirements on entertainment expenses, travel expenses, and other listed expenses. By the terms of the statute, the taxpayer is required to substantiate either by "adequate records" or "by sufficient evidence corroborating his own statement" the following: (1) the amount of the expense; (2) the time and place it was incurred; (3) the business purpose for the expense; and (4) the business relationship to the taxpayer of the persons entertained. The clear purpose of § 274(d) is to reverse the *Cohan* rule with regard to the listed types of expense. If substantiation is not provided, the deduction is disallowed even though it is otherwise properly deductible.

The "adequate records" requirement generally involves maintaining an account book, diary or similar records with entries made at or near the time of the expense, together with documentary evidence (bills and receipts) in support of the entries. Reg. § 1.274-5T (c)(2). However, documentary evidence is generally not required for expenditures of less than $75. Reg § 1.274-5(c)(2). If the "adequate records" requirement is not met, the taxpayer must establish substantiation by his own statement, together with sufficient corroborative evidence; an uncorroborated statement will not support the deduction. Reg. § 1.274-5T(c)(3).

The regulations provide exceptions to the general substantiation requirement in certain circumstances. Note, for example, an employee "incurring" reimbursed expenses does not have to report the reimbursement or the expenses, if he makes an "adequate accounting" to the employer. Reg. § 1.274-5T(f)(2). No substantiation is required for certain per diem and mileage allowances. *See* Reg. § 1.274-5(g). In any case, however, excess reimbursements are reportable as income.

E.   Exceptions

Section 274(e) provides a number of exceptions to the basic rule of § 274(a). Section 274(e)(2)(A), for example, indicates the disallowance rule does not apply to the extent the taxpayer's payment of an expense is treated as compensation to the recipient. Note, however, that substantiation is nonetheless required for § 274(d) expenses, except to the extent waived by the § 274(d) regulations themselves.

F.   Business Meals

As discussed in previous chapters, § 162(a)(2) allows a deduction for one's own meals while away from home on business; § 119 excludes from income meals furnished for the convenience of the employer; and § 132 excludes occasional supper money from income. Nonetheless, outside of safe harbors such as these, the proper tax treatment of one's own business meals remains somewhat controversial and uncertain; the matter is by no means squarely addressed by § 274, despite the restrictions it places on meal expenditures generally.

The seminal case on the deductibility of one's own business meals is *Sutter v. Commissioner*, 21 T.C. 170 (1953). Sutter, an industrial surgeon, sought to deduct, among other items, the cost of his own lunches at meetings of the local Chamber of Commerce and Hospital Council as well as a variety of business entertainment expenses. The Tax Court concluded that, despite the business context, the "cost of meals, entertainment, and similar items for one's self and one's dependents" (at least while not "away from home") is a personal expense and presumptively nondeductible. The presumption of nondeductibility, however, could be overcome by "clear and detailed evidence . . . that the expenditure in question was different from or in excess of that which would have been made for the taxpayer's personal purposes." 21 T.C. at 173. Despite the burden the *Sutter* rule places on the taxpayer, the Service recognized the administrative problems (for questionable amounts of revenue) its vigorous enforcement would entail, and long ago announced a more liberal policy. In Revenue Ruling 63-144, 1963-2 C.B. 129, 135, which consists of a series of questions and answers on the deductibility of business expenditures for entertainment, travel, and gifts under § 274, the Service posed and answered the following question:

Personal Portion of Business Meals

31. Question: Several of these questions and answers refer to the cost of the taxpayer entertaining a business customer at lunch or dinner. To what extent is the cost of the taxpayer's own meal deductible?

Answer: Judicial decisions under established law, applying the statutory rules that deductions are not allowed for personal expenses, hold that a taxpayer cannot obtain a deduction for the portion of his meal cost which does not exceed an amount he would normally spend on himself. The Service practice has been to apply this rule largely to abuse cases where taxpayers claim deductions for substantial amounts of personal living expenses. The Service does not intend to depart from this practice.

The right to deduct the cost of one's own business meal may be particularly questioned when the meal involves only co-workers, partners, or other such colleagues, as opposed to meals involving entertainment of customers or clients. In other words, if co-workers talk business over lunch, may each of them deduct the lunch expense? Consider in this regard the case of *Moss v. Commissioner*, which follows below. On what does the Seventh Circuit focus in denying the deduction?

Moss v. Commissioner is not the only case that has presented the question of deducting meals involving only co-workers. In *Sibla v. Commissioner* and *Cooper v. Commissioner*, both at 611 F.2d 1260 (9th Cir. 1980), firemen were allowed to deduct their contributions, required by law, to a fund for daily meals at the fire station, a contribution required whether or not they were able to eat the meal or be present at the station. However, in other cases, the taxpayer has not fared so well. For example, in *Wells v. Commissioner*, T.C. Memo 1977-419, the Tax Court denied a deduction to a county public defender for the costs of taking several staff members to lunch once a month, and of periodically taking two or three members and guests to dinner. In dictum, the court stated that occasional lunch meetings of a law firm of comparable size (over 33 attorneys) would be deductible; however, it held the costs to be not ordinary and necessary for the usual civil servant, such as the county public defender.

In *Fenstermaker v. Commissioner*, T.C. Memo 1978-210, several executives of a company were reimbursed for up to 144 lunches per year, most of which were with fellow employees, though some were with outside consultants. Although company business was discussed at each meal, the reimbursements were included in income; no deduction was allowed for the expenditures on the ground that no showing had been made that the expenses exceeded what would have been incurred for personal purposes, and that only such excess would be deductible. Compare *Moss v. Commissioner* on this point. Is it appropriate that the deductibility of a meal turn on the taxpayer's personal lunch standards? Should one's own meals ever be deductible? Should different rules exist when entertaining clients and when lunching with co-workers?

In another case, an employee sought to deduct the unreimbursed costs of (1) taking her employer's business customers to lunch and (2) providing periodic meals and parties to employees under her supervision so they would have higher morale. The Tax Court held that to deduct business entertainment or meals under §§ 162 and 274 an employee "must show that the employer required or expected her to incur and to bear the expenses without reimbursement." See *Dunkelberger v. Commissioner*, T.C. Memo 1992-723, where the taxpayer satisfied this requirement as to the business customers, but not with respect to the co-workers.

WALLISER v. COMMISSIONER
United States Tax Court
72 T.C. 433 (1974)

TANNENWALD, JUDGE:

During the taxable years 1973 and 1974, [petitioner] James [Walliser] was vice president and branch manager of the First Federal Savings & Loan Association (First Federal) of Dallas, Tex., Richardson branch office. . . .

During the taxable years at issue, petitioners [James and Carol Walliser] traveled abroad in tour groups organized primarily for people involved in the building industry. In 1973, petitioners took two such trips. The first was to Rio de Janeiro and was sponsored by General Electric Co. (General Electric). It began on March 23, 1973, and ended on March 31, 1973. Their second trip, to London and Copenhagen, was sponsored by Fedders Co. (Fedders) and ran from October 3, 1973, to October 15, 1973.

In 1974, petitioners went to Santo Domingo on a tour organized by Fedders which began on September 27, 1974, and ended on October 4, 1974.

The builders' tours were arranged as guided vacation trips, with sightseeing and other recreational activities. Petitioners, however, went on the tours because James found that they provided an unusual opportunity to associate with many potential and actual customers and believed that the tours would generate business, thereby helping him to meet his loan production quotas and obtain salary raises. . . .

Because James spent so much time with actual or potential customers, petitioners found the tours to be strenuous, and Carol, in particular, did not enjoy them. Petitioners took vacations with their family in the vicinity of Austin, Tex., in 1973 and in Puerto Vallarta, Mexico, in 1974.

On their 1973 and 1974 tax returns, petitioners deducted, as employee business expenses, one-half of the price of each of the tours (the portion attributable to James' travel). . . .

OPINION

Initially, we must determine whether petitioners are entitled, under section 162, to deduct as employee business expenses costs incurred by James in connection with his travel on tours for builders organized by General Electric and Fedders. If we hold that the requirements of that section are satisfied, then we must face the further question as to the extent to which the limitations of section 274 apply.

Section 162(a)(2) allows a deduction for all ordinary and necessary expenses paid or incurred during the taxable year in carrying on any trade or business, including traveling expenses incurred while away from home in the pursuit of a trade or business. The question is essentially one of fact. *Commissioner v. Heininger*, 320 U.S. 467, 475 (1943); *Henry v. Commissioner*, 36 T.C. 879, 883 (1961). Petitioners must show that the expenses were incurred primarily for business rather than social reasons and that there was a proximate relation between the cost of the builders' tours and James' business as an officer of First Federal. *Henry v. Commissioner, supra* at 884; *Larrabee v. Commissioner*, 33 T.C. 838, 841 (1960).

James' primary responsibility as an officer of First Federal was marketing loans. He was assigned loan production quotas and considered yearly increases in his salary to be contingent upon meeting those quotas. The participants in the General Electric and Fedders tours were not a random group of Texas vacationers. On the contrary, they were largely builders and developers from Texas, the area in which First Federal operated. Thus, the tours were a useful means of maintaining relations with existing customers of First Federal and reaching prospective customers. Indeed, the record indicated that some of the participants considered the social relationships with James, including their association with him on the tours, as an influencing factor in their decisions to seek loans from First Federal.

The fact that, during the years at issue, First Federal did not reimburse James for the costs of his travel does not render his expenses nondeductible. Where a corporate officer personally incurs expenditures which enable him to better perform his duties to the corporation and which have a direct bearing on the amount of his compensation or his chances for advancement, unreimbursed expenses may be deductible under § 162.[2] *Heidt v. Commissioner*, 274 F.2d 25, 27–28 (7th Cir. 1959), *aff'd*, T.C. Memo. 1959-31; *Schmidlapp v. Commissioner*, 96 F.2d 680, 681–682 (2d Cir. 1938); *Christensen v. Commissioner*, 17 T.C. 1456 (1952); *Abraham v. Commissioner*, 9 T.C. 222, 228 (1947) (see endnote). First Federal expected its officers in charge of marketing activities to participate in public or social functions without reimbursement and examined their performance in this regard when evaluating their compensation and overall value to the company. *Compare Tyler v. Commissioner*, 13 T.C. 186, 192 (1949). James met his loan quotas in 1973 and 1974 and received raises in his salary at the end of those years. In a later year, he became head of First Federal's interim loan department.

Moreover, the evidence tends to show that First Federal considered the trips valuable in generating goodwill. Although First Federal, which was in the midst of a program of budget cutbacks in 1973 and 1974, did not reimburse James for the tours as it had done in prior years, it continued to grant him additional leave with pay for the time he was on the tours.

Finally, the testimony of petitioners, and particularly of Carol, which we found straightforward and credible, tended to show that the tours were strenuous, and not particularly enjoyable, experiences because of the amount of time expended in cultivating business and, therefore, that petitioners did not undertake the tours for primarily personal reasons.

We conclude that, under the circumstances of this case, the requisite proximate relation has been shown to constitute James' travel expenses as "ordinary and necessary" business expenses within the meaning of section 162(a)(2).

We now turn our attention to the applicability of section 274, the issue on which

---

[2] The rule is otherwise where the corporate employee is entitled to, but does not seek, reimbursement from the corporation. *Stolk v. Commissioner*, 40 T.C. 345, 357 (1963), *aff'd per curiam*, 326 F.2d 760 (2d Cir. 1964); *Coplon v. Commissioner*, T.C. Memo. 1959-34, *aff'd per curiam*, 277 F.2d 534 (6th Cir. 1960).

respondent has concentrated most of his fire. That section disallows a deduction in certain instances for expenses which would otherwise be deductible under section 162. Respondent argues that the requirements of section 274 are applicable here and have not been satisfied in that petitioners have failed: (1) To show that James' trips were "directly related" to the active conduct of his business (sec. 274(a)); (2) to substantiate the business purpose of his expenditures (sec. 274(d)); and (3) to allocate his time spent in foreign travel between personal and business activities (sec. 274(c)). . . .

Petitioners urge that the "directly related" test of section 274(a) is not applicable because the expenditures at issue were incurred for travel, not entertainment. We disagree.

Section 274(a) relates to activities of a type generally considered to constitute "entertainment, amusement, or recreation." Section 1.274-2(b), Income Tax Regs., defines "entertainment, amusement, or recreation" as follows:

> (b) *Definitions — (1) Entertainment defined — (i) In general. For purposes of this section, the term "entertainment" means any activity which is of a type generally considered to constitute entertainment, amusement, or recreation, such as* entertaining at night clubs, cocktail lounges, theaters, country clubs, golf and athletic clubs, sporting events, and on hunting, fishing, *vacation and similar trips, including such activity relating solely to the taxpayer* or the taxpayer's family. . . .
>
> (ii) *Objective test. An objective test shall be used to determine whether an activity is of a type generally considered to constitute entertainment.* Thus, if an activity is generally considered to be entertainment, it will constitute entertainment for purposes of this section and section 274(a) regardless of whether the expenditure can also be described otherwise, and even though the expenditure relates to the taxpayer alone. This objective test precludes arguments such as that "entertainment" means only entertainment of others or that an expenditure for entertainment should be characterized as an expenditure for advertising or public relations. [Emphasis added.]

This regulation is squarely based on the language of the legislative history of section 274 and we find it to be valid as it relates to the issue herein.

This regulation and the Congressional committee reports from which it is derived leave no doubt that the deductibility of an expenditure for travel, on what would objectively be considered a vacation trip, is subject to the limitations of subsection 274(a), even where the expenditure relates solely to the taxpayer himself. *See* H. Rep. 1447, 87th Cong., 2d Sess. (1962), 1962-3 C.B. 405, 424; S. Rept. 1881, 87th Cong., 2d Sess. (1962), 1962-3 C.B. 707, 734. Furthermore, section 1.274-2(b)(1)(iii), Income Tax Regs., provides that "any expenditure which might generally be considered . . . either for travel or entertainment, shall be considered an expenditure for entertainment rather than for . . . travel." This regulation too has a solid foundation in the statute, which provides, in section 274(h), authority for the promulgation of regulations necessary to carry out the purpose of section 274 and in the committee reports, which provide that rules be prescribed for determining whether section 274(a) should govern where another section is also applicable. H. Rept. 1447, *supra*, 1962-3 C.B. at 534; S. Rept. 1881, *supra*, 1962-3 C.B. at 882.

Although the participants in the tours that petitioners took were drawn, for the most part, from the building industry, their activities — sightseeing, shopping, dining — were the same as those of other tourists. Fedders presented some awards to persons considered outstanding in its sales or promotional programs on the tours but did not conduct any business meetings. Nor is there any evidence that any business meetings were conducted on the 1973 General Electric tour; on the itinerary for the 1974 tour, for which petitioners canceled their reservation, only 1 hour out of 10 days of guided tours, dinners, and cocktail parties, was set aside for a business meeting. Under the objective test set forth in the regulations, it is irrelevant that petitioners did not regard the trips as vacations or did not find them relaxing. Clearly, the tours were of a type generally considered vacation trips and, thus, under the objective test, constituted entertainment for the purposes of section 274(a). Therefore, the requirements of that section must be satisfied.

For a deduction to be allowed for any item under section 274(a)(1)(A), the taxpayer must establish that the item was directly related to the active conduct of the taxpayer's trade or business or, in the case of an item directly preceding or following a substantial and bona fide business discussion, that such item was associated with the active conduct of the taxpayer's trade or business.

The "directly related" test requires that a taxpayer show a greater degree of proximate relationship between an expenditure and the taxpayer's trade or business than that required by section 162. H. Rept. 1447, *supra*, 1962-3 C.B. at 424; Conf. Rept. 2508, 87th Cong., 2d Sess. (1962), 1962-3 C.B. 1129, 1143–1144. Section 1.274-2(c)(3), Income Tax Regs., provides that, for an expenditure to be directly related to the active conduct of the taxpayer's trade or business, it must be shown that the taxpayer had more than a general expectation of deriving some income or business benefit from the expenditure, other than the goodwill of the person or persons entertained. While the language of this regulation is awkward and not completely apt in a situation where the entertainment expenditure relates to the taxpayer alone, it is clear, nevertheless, that more than a general expectation of deriving some income at some indefinite future time is necessary for an expenditure to be deductible under section 274(a). H. Rept. 1447, *supra*, 1962-3 C.B. at 424; Conf. Rept. 2508, *supra*.

The record shows that petitioners participated in the builders' tours because they provided an opportunity for James to meet new people who might be interested in the services he, and First Federal, had to offer and to maintain good personal relations with people already using those services. While James discussed business continually during the tours, his wife testified that this was typical of his behavior during all social activities. He engaged in general discussions about business conditions and the services he could provide to a builder but did not engage in business meetings or negotiations on the tours. James could not directly connect particular business transactions with specific discussions which occurred during the trips. In short, petitioners' purpose in taking the trips was to create or maintain goodwill for James and First Federal, his employer, in order to generate some future business. Although the evidence tends to indicate that the trips did, in fact, enhance goodwill and contribute to James' success in loan production and otherwise constituted ordinary and necessary business expenses deductible under section 162, we hold, nevertheless, that Congress intended, by means of the more stringent standard of the "directly related" test in section 274(a), to disallow deductions for this type of activity, which involves merely the promotion of goodwill in a social setting. See *St. Petersburg Bank & Trust Co. v. United States*, 362 F. Supp. 674, 680 (M.D. Fla. 1973), *aff'd in an unpublished order*, 503 F.2d 1402 (5th Cir. 1974).

We also hold that the petitioners' trips do not qualify as entertainment "associated with" the active conduct of a trade or business. To be deductible, entertainment "associated with" the active conduct of a trade or business must directly precede or follow a substantial business discussion. In *St. Petersburg Bank & Trust Co. v. United States, supra*, a decision affirmed by the Fifth Circuit, the District Court concluded that the phrase "directly preceding or following" in section 274(a)(1)(A) should be read restrictively in cases in which entertainment expenditures are related to the taxpayer's trade or business only in that they promote goodwill. In view of the legislative history, which reveals that the "associated with" test is an exception to the general rule intended to limit deductions for entertainment which has as its sole business purpose the promotion of goodwill, we agree with the District Court's conclusion. Accordingly, we do not consider the costs of the vacation trips to be deductible under section 274(a)(1)(A) as entertainment directly preceded or followed by a substantial and bona fide business discussion merely because James had general discussions of a business nature intended to promote goodwill during the course of the trips. See *St. Petersburg Bank & Trust Co. v. United States, supra* at 681.

We conclude that section 274(a) bars a deduction for the costs of James' trips. Because of this conclusion, we do not consider whether those costs were substantiated in accordance with the requirements of section 274(d) or properly allocated between personal and business activities under section 274(c).

Decision will be entered for the respondent.

MOSS v. COMMISSIONER
United States Court of Appeals, Seventh Circuit
758 F.2d 211 (1985)

POSNER, CIRCUIT JUDGE:

The taxpayers, a lawyer named Moss and his wife, appeal from a decision of the Tax Court disallowing federal income tax deductions of a little more than $1,000 in each of two years, representing Moss's share of his law firm's lunch expense at the Cafe Angelo in Chicago. 80 T.C. 1073 (1983). The Tax Court's decision in this case has attracted some attention in tax circles because of its implications for the general problem of the deductibility of business meals. . . .

Moss was a partner in a small trial firm specializing in defense work, mostly for one insurance company. Each of the firm's lawyers carried a tremendous litigation caseload, averaging more than 300 cases, and spent most of every working day in courts in Chicago and its suburbs. The members of the firm met for lunch daily at the Cafe Angelo near their office. At lunch the lawyers would discuss their cases with the head of the firm, whose approval was required for most settlements, and they would decide which lawyer would meet which court call that afternoon or the next morning. Lunchtime was chosen for the daily meeting because the courts were in recess then. The alternatives were to meet at 7:00 a.m. or 6:00 p.m., and these were less convenient times. There is no suggestion that the lawyers dawdled over lunch, or that the Cafe Angelo is luxurious.

The framework of statutes and regulations for deciding this case is simple, but not clear. Section 262 of the Internal Revenue Code (Title 26) disallows, "except as otherwise expressly provided in this chapter," the deduction of "personal, family, or living expenses." Section 119 excludes from income the value of meals provided by an employer to his employees for his convenience, but only if they are provided on the employer's premises; and section 162(a) allows the deduction of "all the ordinary and necessary expenses paid or incurred during the taxable year in carrying on any trade or business, including — . . . (2) traveling expenses (including amounts expended for meals . . .) while away from home. . . . " Since Moss was not an employee but a partner in a partnership not taxed as an entity, since the meals were not served on the employer's premises, and since he was not away from home (that is, on an overnight trip away from his place of work, see *United States v. Correll*, 389 U.S. 299, 88 S. Ct. 445, 19 L. Ed. 2d 537 (1967)), neither section 119 nor section 162(a)(2) applies to this case. The Internal Revenue Service concedes, however, that meals are deductible under section 162(a) when they are ordinary and necessary business expenses (provided the expense is substantiated with adequate records, see section 274(d)) even if they are not within the express permission of any other provision and even though the expense of commuting to and from work, a traveling expense but not one incurred away from home, is not deductible. Treasury Regulations on Income Tax § 1.262-1(b)(5); *Fausner v. Commissioner*, 413 U.S. 838, 93 S. Ct. 2820, 37 L. Ed. 2d 996 (1973) (per curiam).

The problem is that many expenses are simultaneously business expenses in the sense that they conduce to the production of business income and personal expenses in the sense that they raise personal welfare. This is plain enough with regard to lunch; most people would eat lunch even if they didn't work. Commuting may seem a pure business expense, but is not; it reflects the choice of where to live, as well as where to work. Read literally, section 262 would make irrelevant whether a business expense is also a personal expense; so long as it is ordinary and necessary in the taxpayer's business, thus bringing section 162(a) into play, an expense is (the statute seems to say) deductible from his income tax. But the statute has not been read literally. There is a natural reluctance, most clearly manifested in the regulation disallowing deduction of the expense of commuting, to lighten the tax burden of people who have the good fortune to interweave work with consumption. To allow a deduction for commuting would confer a windfall on people who live in the suburbs and commute to work in the cities; to allow a deduction for all business-related meals would confer a windfall on people who can arrange their work schedules so they do some of their work at lunch.

Although an argument can thus be made for disallowing any deduction for business meals, on the theory that people have to eat whether they work or not, the result would be excessive taxation of people who spend more money on business meals because they are business meals than they would spend on their meals if they were not working. Suppose a theatrical agent takes his clients out to lunch at the expensive restaurants that the clients demand. Of course he can deduct the expense of their meals, from which he derives no pleasure or sustenance, but can he also deduct the expense of his own? He can, because he cannot eat more cheaply; he cannot munch surreptitiously on a peanut butter and jelly sandwich brought from home while his client is wolfing down tournedos Rossini followed by souffle au grand marnier. No doubt our theatrical agent, unless concerned for his longevity, derives personal utility from his fancy meal, but probably less than the price of the meal. He would not pay for it if it were not for the business benefit; he would get more value from using the same money to buy something else; hence the meal confers on him less utility than the cash equivalent would. The law could require him to pay tax on the fair value of the meal to him; this would be (were it not for costs of administration) the economically correct solution. But the government does not attempt this difficult measurement; it once did, but gave up the attempt as not worth the cost, see *United States v. Correll, supra*, 389 U.S. at 301 n. 6, 88 S. Ct. at 446 n. 6. The taxpayer is permitted to deduct the whole price, provided the expense is "different from or in excess of that which would have been made for the taxpayer's personal purposes." *Sutter v. Commissioner*, 21 T.C. 170, 173 (1953).

Because the law allows this generous deduction, which tempts people to have more (and costlier) business meals than are necessary, the Internal Revenue Service has every right to insist that the meal be shown to be a real business necessity. This condition is most easily satisfied when a client or customer or supplier or other outsider to the business is a guest. Even if Sydney Smith was wrong that "soup and fish explain half the emotions of life," it is undeniable that eating together fosters camaraderie and makes business dealings friendlier and easier. It thus reduces the costs of transacting business, for these costs include the frictions and the failures of communication that are produced by suspicion and mutual misunderstanding, by differences in tastes and manners, and by lack of rapport. A meeting with a client or customer in an office is therefore not a perfect substitute for a lunch with him in a restaurant. But it is different when all the participants in the meal are coworkers, as essentially was the case here (clients occasionally were invited to the firm's daily luncheon, but Moss has made no attempt to identify the occasions). They know each other well already; they don't need the social lubrication that a meal with an outsider provides — at least don't need it daily. If a large firm had a monthly lunch to allow partners to get to know associates, the expense of the meal might well be necessary, and would be allowed by the Internal Revenue Service. See *Wells v. Commissioner*, 36 T.C.M. 1698, 1699 (1977), *aff'd without opinion*, 626 F.2d 868 (9th Cir. 1980). But Moss's firm never had more than eight lawyers (partners and associates), and did not need a daily lunch to cement relationships among them.

It is all a matter of degree and circumstance (the expense of a testimonial dinner, for example, would be deductible on a morale-building rationale); and particularly of frequency. Daily — for a full year — is too often, perhaps even for entertainment of clients, as implied by *Hankenson v. Commissioner*, 47 T.C.M. 1567, 1569 (1984), where the Tax Court held nondeductible the cost of lunches consumed three or four days a week, 52 weeks a year, by a doctor who entertained other doctors who he hoped would refer patients to him, and other medical personnel.

We may assume it was necessary for Moss's firm to meet daily to coordinate the work of the firm, and also, as the Tax Court found, that lunch was the most convenient time. But it does not follow that the expense of the lunch was a necessary business expense. The members of the firm had to eat somewhere, and the Cafe Angelo was both convenient and not too expensive. They do not claim to have incurred a greater daily lunch expense than they would have incurred if there had been no lunch meetings. Although it saved time to combine lunch with work, the meal itself was not an organic part of the meeting, as in the examples we gave earlier where the business objective, to be fully achieved, required sharing a meal.

The case might be different if the location of the courts required the firm's members to eat each day either in a disagreeable restaurant, so that they derived less value from the meal than it cost them to buy it, *cf. Sibla v. Commissioner*, 611 F.2d 1260, 1262 (9th Cir. 1980); or in a restaurant too expensive for their personal tastes, so that, again, they would have gotten less value than the cash equivalent. But so far as appears, they picked the restaurant they liked most. Although it must be pretty monotonous to eat lunch the same place every working day of the year, not all the lawyers attended all the lunch meetings and there was nothing to stop the firm from meeting occasionally at another restaurant proximate to their office in downtown Chicago; there are hundreds.

An argument can be made that the price of lunch at the Cafe Angelo included rental of the space that the lawyers used for what was a meeting as well as a meal. There was evidence that the firm's conference room was otherwise occupied throughout the working day, so as a matter of logic Moss might be able to claim a part of the price of lunch as an ordinary and necessary expense for work space. But this is cutting things awfully fine; in any event Moss made no effort to apportion his lunch expense in this way.

Affirmed.

CHURCHILL DOWNS, INC. v. COMMISSIONER
United States Court of Appeals, Sixth Circuit
307 F.3d 423 (2002)

Siler, Circuit Judge.

Petitioner Churchill Downs, Incorporated appeals the United States Tax Court's judgment that they were entitled to deduct only 50% of certain expenses they incurred in 1994 and 1995 because the expenses qualified as "entertainment" for purposes of Internal Revenue Code ("I.R.C.") § 274(n)(1)(B). For the reasons stated below, we affirm.

The facts of this case are not in dispute. Churchill Downs owns and operates the Churchill Downs race track in Louisville, Kentucky, and three other race tracks. Churchill Downs conducts horse races at these tracks, and earns revenues from wagering, admissions and seating charges, concession commissions, sponsorship revenues, licensing rights, and broadcast fees. Although Churchill Downs does not compete directly with other race tracks due to differences in the timing of race events, it competes for patrons with other sports, entertainment, and gaming operations.

Churchill Downs' biggest race is the Kentucky Derby, held each year on the first Saturday in May. Churchill Downs host the following events in connection with the race: (1) a "Sport of Kings" gala, (2) a brunch following the post position drawing for the race, (3) a week-long hospitality tent offering coffee, juice, and donuts to the press, and (4) the Kentucky Derby Winner's Party. The Sport of Kings Gala includes a press reception/cocktail party, dinner, and entertainment. . . .

In 1994, Churchill Downs also agreed to host another race, the Breeder's Cup, at the Churchill Downs racetrack. Its contract with Breeders' Cup Limited ("BCL") obligated it to host certain promotional events designed to enhance the significance of the Breeders' Cup races as a national and international horse racing event. These events included: (1) a press reception cocktail party and dinner, (2) a brunch, and (3) a press breakfast. . . .

Finally, Churchill Downs hosted a number of miscellaneous dinners, receptions, cocktail parties and other events indirectly associated with one or both of these races. . . .

Churchill Downs deducted the full amount of these Kentucky Derby and Breeders' Cup expenses on its 1994 and 1995 federal income tax returns as "ordinary and necessary business expenses" pursuant to I.R.C. § 162, 26 U.S.C. § 162(a). In a notice of tax deficiency, Respondent, the Commissioner of Internal Revenue ("Commissioner"), rejected this treatment and concluded that Churchill Downs was entitled to deduct only 50% of these expenses. The Tax Court agreed with the Commissioner, and Churchill Downs now appeals the Tax Court's rejection of its petition for a redetermination of the deficiency.

I.R.C. § 162(a) allows a taxpayer to deduct "all the ordinary and necessary expenses paid or incurred during the taxable year in carrying on any trade or business." 26 U.S.C. § 162(a). I.R.C. § 274(a) disallows certain deductions otherwise permitted by § 162. . . . I.R.C. § 274(n)(1) further limits deductions for entertainment expenses, providing that: "The amount allowable as a deduction for (A) any expense for food or beverages, and (B) any item with respect to an activity which is of a type generally considered to constitute entertainment, amusement, or recreation, or with respect to a facility used in connection with such activity, shall not exceed 50 percent of the amount of such expense or item which would (but for this paragraph) be allowable as a deduction under this Chapter."

The Commissioner does not dispute that all of the expenses at issue qualify as "ordinary and necessary" business expenses "directly related" to the "active conduct" of Churchill Downs' business, and thus that some deduction of these expenses is allowed. However, he argues that § 274(n)(1) applies to limit deduction of these expenses because they qualify as items associated with activity generally considered entertainment.

[The Court then quotes Reg. § 1.274-2(b)(1)(ii).] Each party relies on [the regulation] language as support for its position. Churchill Downs argues that the Derby and Breeders' Cup expenses at issue should not be considered entertainment expenses because these pre- and post-race events "showcased" its "entertainment product." Specifically, it contends that the Sport of Kings Gala and the other invitation-only events generated publicity and media attention which introduced its races to the public in the same manner that a dress designer's fashion show introduces its product to clothing buyers. In response, the Commissioner relies on § 1.274-2(b)(1)(ii)'s statement that an item generally considered to be entertainment is subject to the 50% limitation even where it may be otherwise characterized as an advertising or public relations expense. The Commissioner argues that the brunches, dinners, galas, and parties at issue qualify on their face as items "generally considered entertainment" and, following § 1.274-2(b)(1)(ii), that they are not saved from this classification by the fact that these amounts were spent to publicize Churchill Downs' racing events.

These arguments expose an inherent tension in § 1.274-2(b)(1)(ii). On the one hand, § 1.274-2(b)(1)(ii) states that an item generally considered to be entertainment is subject to the 50% limitation even if it may be described otherwise, in particular as advertising or public relations. At the same time, the regulation suggests that certain expenses generally considered entertainment but somehow instrumental to the conduct of a taxpayer's business do not qualify as "entertainment" for purposes of § 274(n). The regulation draws the line between pure publicity and entertainment events integral to the conduct of the taxpayer's business by providing the contrasting examples of a fashion show offered by a dress designer to store buyers (not entertainment) and a fashion show offered by an appliance manufacturer to the spouses of its buyers (entertainment). See 26 C.F.R. § 1.274-2(b)(1)(ii). In the first example, the event is attended by the taxpayer's primary customers, and the taxpayer's product is present at the event and is the focus of it. In contrast, the second example reflects a purely social event focused on something unrelated to the taxpayer's product, held to generate good will among selected third parties with the expectation that they will influence the taxpayer's primary customers into buying its product.

Here, as the Tax Court found, Churchill Downs is in the business of staging horse races and makes its money primarily from selling admission to the races and accepting wagers on them. However, no horse racing was conducted at the dinners and other events at issue. Nor did the events, held away from the track at rented facilities, provide attendees with an opportunity to learn more about the races — for example, the horses that would appear, the odds associated with each horse, the types of wagers available, track conditions, etc. — similar to the product information store buyers might acquire at a fashion show. Rather, Churchill Downs concedes that the events were planned simply as social occasions. Nor were the events open to the gaming public that attends Churchill Downs races and wagers on them. Instead, Churchill Downs invited selected dignitaries and members of the media to these private receptions, not with the expectation that they would later consume significant amounts of its product, but rather in the hopes that they would influence its primary customer base, the general public, to do so, either through the example of their attendance or through favorable reporting. As Churchill Downs explained, the attendance of the celebrities at these pre-race events was "essential" because "the presence of those individuals in Louisville for two or more days before the races gave rise to related publicity and media attention that helped sustain and advance the glamour and prestige of the races." In other words, the purpose of the galas and dinners was not to make Churchill Downs' product directly available to its customers or to provide them with specific information about it, but rather to create an aura of glamour in connection with the upcoming races and generally to arouse public interest in them. In this regard, the dinners, brunches, and receptions at issue most closely resemble the example given above of a fashion show held for the wives of appliance retailers, and are best characterized not as a product introduction event used to conduct the taxpayer's business, but as pure advertising or public relations expenses. Accordingly, we conclude that the Kentucky Derby and Breeder's Cup expenses at issue qualify as "entertainment" under § 1.274-2(b)(1)(ii)'s objective standard.

As an alternative argument, Churchill Downs contends that, under the objective test, an event generally considered entertainment should not be deemed "entertainment" for purposes of § 274 where the event itself is the product the taxpayer is selling. In support of this position, it relies on a statement in the legislative history of § 274(n)(1) that:

> The trade or business of the taxpayer will determine whether an activity is of the type generally considered to constitute entertainment. . . . For example, with respect to a taxpayer who is a professional hunter, a hunting trip would not generally be considered a recreation-type activity.

S. Rep. No. 87-1881 (1962). Churchill Downs argues that its entertainment products, the Kentucky Derby and the Breeders' Cup, necessarily include the Sport of Kings Gala and the other brunches, dinners and receptions at issue as integral parts of a unified entertainment experience.

We disagree. Unlike the hunter in the example above, who earns his money by hosting recreational hunting trips, Churchill Downs did not make any money from hosting the Sport of Kings Gala or the other events for which it seeks a deduction. Indeed, these events are easily separable from Churchill Downs' business because its primary customers, the gaming public, were not permitted to attend them, either by purchasing tickets or otherwise. Instead, Churchill Downs offered the tickets free of charge to a select few it describes as "members of the media, members of the horse industry, dignitaries, and celebrities" in order to raise public awareness of a later event (the races) which the public could attend and from which Churchill Downs made its money. Although Churchill Downs argues, as any business that depends on advertising may, that it made money as a result of these publicity events, this does not change their nature as something distinct from what was actually sold. The Commissioner puts it succinctly: "taxpayers were in the horse racing business, not the business of throwing parties." Accordingly, it is inappropriate to characterize these non-race events as Churchill Downs' "product." Thus, even if § 274(n)(1)'s limitation could be read not to apply where an entertainment event is itself the product sold by the taxpayer, there is no reason to apply such an exception here. We therefore reject Churchill Downs' "entertainment product" argument.

[I.R.C. § 274(a)] shall not apply to—

(7) *Items available to public.* — Expenses for goods, services, and facilities made available by the taxpayer to the general public.

(8) *Entertainment sold to customers.* — Expenses for goods or services (including the use of facilities) which are sold by the taxpayer in a bona fide transaction for an adequate and full consideration in money or money's worth.

26 U.S.C. § 274(e) (emphasis in original). Churchill Downs argues that the Gala expenses and other items at issue are exempt from § 274(a) pursuant to this section either because these events were available to the general public or because they qualify as entertainment sold to customers.

Churchill Downs does not dispute that these events were by invitation only, or that such invitations were offered only to a small number of individuals. However, it argues that amounts spent on these events meet the requirements of § 274(e)(7) because the expenditures were incurred to promote other events, the Kentucky Derby and Breeders' Cup races, which were open to the general public. We reject this argument. Regardless of whether Churchill Downs incurred these expenses in order to promote an upcoming event open to the public, the goods and services purchased with these expenditures were not "made available" to the general public, as § 274(e)(7) requires, but rather only to a few invited guests at pre- and post-race dining events and the Sport of Kings Gala.

Churchill Downs also relies on an Internal Revenue Service ("IRS") technical advice memorandum holding that food, beverages, lodging, and entertainment offered free by a casino to "high rollers" qualified as "items available to the public" for purposes of I.R.C. § 274(e)(7). See Tech. Advice Mem. 9641005 (July 27, 1996) ("TAM"). The IRS reasoned that all of the benefits provided were items the casino routinely offered to the paying public as part of its stock in trade. As such, the IRS concluded, this practice of "comping" favored customers was akin to providing free product samples, a practice Congress previously had characterized as making goods available to the general public. The agency also concluded that the fact that a customer was required to engage in some amount of gaming activity in order to receive this benefit did not prevent it from being "available to the public" for purposes of § 274(e)(7). However, the IRS concluded that "outside comps" — benefits offered to customers but products by third parties and provided outside the taxpayer's premises — did not fall within this product sample rationale, and were not exempt under § 274(e)(7). Here Churchill Downs argues that invitations to the Sport of Kings Gala and the other non-race events were akin to the "comps" provided to favored customers at a casino.

We reject this argument. As an initial matter, written determinations like the TAM have no procedural value to parties other than the taxpayer they are issued to, and I.R.C. § 6110(k)(3) prohibits taxpayers from relying on them in proceedings before the agency. See 26 U.S.C. § 6110(k)(3); see also *Liberty Nat'l Bank & Trust Co. v. United States*, 867 F.2d 302, 304–05 (6th Cir. 1989) (disallowing reliance on private letter rulings). Furthermore, unlike the "comps" offered to casino patrons, the dinners and galas at issue here are not the products that members of the general public routinely purchase from Churchill Downs, namely, admission to horse races or wagers. Indeed, Churchill Downs does not sell admission to these non-race dining events at all. Nor does the provision of these benefits appear to have been based on the recipient's attendance at the races, or as an inducement for future attendance. Rather, Churchill Downs acknowledges that the recipients were selectively chosen based on their ability to generate publicity for its races. Finally, as the Commissioner points out, the food, drink, and entertainment appear to have been provided largely by third parties at offsite locations, and thus more closely resemble the "outside comping" example which the agency concluded fell outside of § 274(e)(7). For all these reasons, the TAM does not support Churchill Downs' argument that these items should be exempted under § 274(e)(7) as "items available to the public."

In regards to its "entertainment sold to customers" argument, Churchill Downs concedes that those invited to the Sport of Kings Gala and the other occasions did not pay for the privilege of attending these events. Nevertheless Churchill Downs once again argues that these dinners and brunches were integral parts of an encompassing entertainment event — the races — which members of the public did in fact pay to attend. For the reasons already discussed above, this argument is unpersuasive.

As a final matter, it would seem that, even if these events were deemed not to constitute "entertainment" for purposes of §§ 274(a) and (n)(1)(B), § 274(n)(1)(A) would preclude full deduction of many of the expenses at issue here. See 26 U.S.C. § 274(n)(1)(A). That section, read in conjunction with the rest of § 274(n)(1), provides that "the amount allowable as a deduction under this chapter for . . . any expense for food or beverages . . . shall not exceed 50 percent of the amount of such expense or item which would (but for this paragraph) be allowable as a deduction under this chapter." *Id.* This limitation does not appear to be contingent on a classification of the expenses as "entertainment." Given that the events at issue are mainly dinners, brunches, breakfast, and receptions, it seems likely that a significant portions of the expenses for which Churchill Downs seeks deduction are for food and beverages. However, we need not resolve this issue, which the parties have not briefed, because we conclude that the expenses associated with these events already are subject to the 50% limitation as items "generally considered entertainment."

Affirmed.

Chapter 18

EDUCATION EXPENSES

I. PROBLEMS

1. Mark is a lawyer in San Diego whose practice is limited to representing clients in estate planning and taxation matters. He traveled to New York City this year to take an intensive one-week course entitled "Spanish for Beginners." Mark remained in New York for a second week for sightseeing and visiting friends from law school. While in New York, he stayed in a hotel and ate his meals in restaurants. The company that provides the Spanish course offered the same course in San Diego earlier in the year, but Mark preferred to take the course offered in New York instead. May Mark deduct the cost of the course and the transportation, meals, and lodging associated with the trip to New York?

2. After Susan graduated from college, she began working as a teller at a local bank. Ten months after she began working at the bank, she enrolled in a two-year part-time MBA program that allowed her to keep working at the bank and offered the MBA degree with a specialization in financial management. May she deduct the tuition for the MBA program?

3. George is a paralegal at a downtown law firm. George became so interested in the law that he decided to enroll in an evening and weekend law school program at a local law school. Because the program is part-time, it will take George four years to earn his J.D. George finds the formal instruction he is receiving in law school assists him in his paralegal work with the firm.

    (a) To what extent, if any, may George deduct the costs (including interest costs on education loans) he is incurring in the law school program?

    (b) What tax results to George if the law firm pays George's law school expenses?

    (c) What results to George if the law firm pays the cost incurred by George in taking a writing course at a local college? The law firm is interested in George improving his writing skills so that he can more effectively edit briefs, motions and other documents produced by the attorneys at the firm.

    (d) What result to George if the law firm pays for up to six credit hours per year of undergraduate or graduate course work by firm employees? George takes advantage of the program and takes graduate courses in history at a local college.

4. Margaret is a part-time athletics instructor at a private high school. In an effort to improve her chances for full-time employment at the high school

447

(and at other schools as well), Margaret volunteers to help in the school's counseling center by counseling students on university opportunities and post-high-school employment. She takes a course at the local community college entitled "Career Counseling." Is the tuition for the course deductible?

Assignment for Chapter 18:

Complete the problems.

Read: Internal Revenue Code §§ 162(a); 274(m)(2).
            Treasury Regulations: § 1.162-5(a)–(c), (e).

            Materials: Overview
                              Takahashi v. Commissioner
                              Wassenaar v. Commissioner
                              Furner v. Commissioner
                              Revenue Ruling 68-591
                              Sharon v. Commissioner
                              Note: Education Tax Incentives

II.   VOCABULARY

skill-maintenance and employer-requirement tests
minimum-educational-requirements and new-trade-or-business tests

III.   OBJECTIVES

1.   To identify educational expenses that satisfy the skill-maintenance test and educational expenses that satisfy the employer-requirement test.

2.   To identify educational expenses nondeductible under the minimum-educational-requirements test, and educational expenses nondeductible under the new-trade-or-business test.

3.   To distinguish between temporary and indefinite suspensions in carrying on a trade or business.

4.   To summarize the rules regarding the deductibility of travel expenses related to education.

5.   To determine when an educational activity is sufficiently related to job skills to satisfy the skill-maintenance test.

6.   To distinguish a new trade or business from a mere change in duties.

7.   To recall the regulations provide that all teaching and related duties shall be considered to involve the same kind of work.

8.   To determine when a taxpayer has commenced "carrying on" a trade or business.

IV. OVERVIEW

In the early years of the Internal Revenue Code, the Service opposed allowance of a deduction for an individual's education expenses as it regarded them as inherently personal in nature. *Hill v. Commissioner*, 181 F.2d 906 (4th Cir. 1950), which allowed a teacher a deduction for summer school expenses, was the first case holding educational expenses deductible. The area continued to be governed by case law and rulings until 1958, when a comprehensive set of regulations was issued under § 162. The 1958 regulations placed great emphasis on the "primary purpose" of the individual in incurring the expenses. These regulations ultimately proved unsatisfactory and were replaced in 1967 by the current regulations, which, in general, seek to rely on more objective criteria. This Chapter will focus in part on the eligibility of certain educational costs for deduction as business expenses under § 162. In addition, the Chapter will provide an overview of a variety of tax incentives for non-business education expenses, including tax credits for higher education costs.

A. Deductibility of Educational Expenses Under Section 162

The deductibility of an educational expense may to some extent be seen as a matter of determining in which of three pigeonholes it properly belongs. An individual's educational expense may be purely personal — a lover of fine foods taking a course in gourmet cooking offered by a local restaurant, perhaps — in which case it is surely and properly nondeductible under § 162. *See* § 262. The expense, alternatively, may be indubitably business-related — suppose, for example, our student of gourmet cooking is the owner of a small restaurant, taking the class to maintain his skills, perhaps to expand his repertoire modestly; in these circumstances, the expense seems ordinary and necessary under § 162(a). Finally, the expense, although business-related, may be capital in nature and therefore nondeductible under § 162: our student might be a frustrated lawyer, taking the gourmet cooking class as one of a series of classes in a course of study leading to a certificate as a master chef, and an entree to a new career.

The utility of this personal-business-capital approach to educational expenses has its limits. For one thing, many educational expenses do not fit neatly within a single category, but have characteristics that overlap the boundary lines. For another, cases and rulings on occasion describe as "personal" what is more accurately labeled a capital expenditure. Furthermore, given the range of new educational incentives in the Code, some educational costs which might historically have been characterized as non-deductible capital expenditures are deductible today at least in part (or give rise to a credit) because of § 222 (or § 25A.) For example, a law school education may have its moments, but its cost is hardly a "personal" expenditure equivalent to food, clothing, shelter, recreation and the like. In addition, the regulations under § 162 permit deductions for educational expenses that "improve" skills as well as merely "maintain" them; this, of course, may simply be a bow to the inevitable, considering the daunting practical difficulties in trying to distinguish between maintenance and improvement in this context. Most importantly, however, one should understand that historically an individual's educational expenses in the nature of capital expenditures were treated quite differently from the typical business-related capital expenditures. Instead of permitting the cost to be depreciated or amortized over time, or allowing the cost to be recovered on disposition or retirement, the expense was simply disallowed. Thus, for example, ignoring any application of § 222, the cost of a law school education cannot be deducted over the life expectancy or working-life expectancy of the lawyer, nor is the cost allowed as a deduction upon the retirement or death of the lawyer. It is difficult to find a satisfactory theoretical justification for this result. The regulations under § 162 apparently take the position that such costs "constitute an inseparable aggregate of personal and capital expenditures." Reg. § 1.162-5(b)(1). Undoubtedly, such a rule eases the administration of educational expenses. Without it, for example, would lawyers argue for amortization of college expenses because a bachelor's degree is a prerequisite for admission to law school?

The regulations under § 162 dealing with educational expenses establish these rules: An individual may deduct educational expenses that either (1) maintain or improve skills required in his employment or trade or business, or (2) meet the express requirements of his employer, or applicable law, necessary to retain his established employment relationship, status, or rate of compensation. Reg. § 1.162-5(a). However, an expense is nondeductible under § 162 (even though it may satisfy the skill-maintenance or employer-requirement test) if it either (1) meets the minimum educational requirements for qualification in the taxpayer's employment or trade or business, or (2) qualifies the taxpayer for a new trade or business. Reg. § 1.162-5(b)(2). The taxpayer is thus required to avoid both of the two latter tests, while at the same time satisfying one of the two former tests.

B.   The Skill-Maintenance or Employer-Requirement Tests of Regulation Section 1.162-5(a)

Assuming the expense is not disallowed under the minimum-educational-requirements or new-trade-or-business tests, an individual may deduct educational expenses that maintain or improve skills required in his employment or trade or business. Under the regulations, "refresher courses or courses dealing with current developments as well as academic or vocational courses" fall within this category. Reg. § 1.162-5(c)(1). Thus, the skills maintenance test allows professionals to deduct the expenses associated with attendance at update seminars pertinent to their work. An early example, prior to the issuance of the regulations, is found in *Coughlin v. Commissioner*, 203 F.2d 307 (2d Cir. 1953), allowing a deduction to a practicing tax attorney for the cost of attending the annual New York University Institute on Federal Taxation.

By contrast, a Chicago police detective was not permitted to deduct the cost of college studies consisting of a major in philosophy. *Carroll v. Commissioner*, 418 F.2d 91 (7th Cir. 1969). Although the police department "encouraged policemen to attend colleges and universities," and although a college education may "improve the job skills of all who avail themselves of it," the taxpayer failed to demonstrate a sufficient relationship between the education and the particular job skills required by a policeman so as to remove the expense from the realm of disallowed personal expenses. College courses are not necessarily classified as nondeductible, but these courses were "general and basically unrelated" to the taxpayer's duties as a policeman. *Id.* at 95. Similarly, in *Takahashi v. Commissioner*, a case included in the materials, educational expenses related to a Hawaiian seminar were also held nondeductible for want of sufficient "connection" or "germaneness" to the taxpayer's job skills.

Another issue that may arise in conjunction with the skill maintenance test is whether the taxpayer is carrying on a trade or business at the time the educational expense in question is incurred. In *Wassenaar v. Commissioner*, a case in the materials, a taxpayer who had not practiced law as an attorney was not allowed to deduct the cost of his master of laws degree in taxation. (Note the taxpayer's attempt to define his trade or business in a way that avoided the "carrying on" problem, and also note the Tax Court's response.) In *Link v. Commissioner*, 90 T.C. 460 (1988), the taxpayer lost his attempt to deduct the expenses incurred to obtain a master's degree in business administration (MBA). The taxpayer had commenced the two-year MBA program following graduation from college with a degree in operations research and three months' employment with Xerox Corporation as a market research analyst. The Tax Court's analysis was as follows:

> Implicit in both section 162 and the regulations is that the taxpayer must be established in a trade or business before any expenses are deductible. The question of whether petitioner was established in a trade or business is one of fact which we must discern from the evidence in this record.
>
> . . . .
>
> There are a number of factors indicating that petitioner's employment at Xerox was merely a temporary hiatus in a continuing series of academic endeavors. [Among them] is the period of time of employment, both in absolute and relative terms. Petitioner worked only 3 months at Xerox before leaving to attend graduate school. While we decline to set a minimum period of time that one must be employed, such a short period of time is relevant evidence. In addition, viewing petitioner's post-high school activities as a continuum, he was employed in his field only 3 months out of a total of 6 years. Moreover, he effectively ceased employment when he returned to school. [During the two-year program, the taxpayer held part-time work at the university as a student research assistant and also held summer work and part-time work as a corporate intern, a job available only to MBA students.] The job at Xerox was but another summer position in an otherwise continuous pattern of schooling which petitioner decided he needed prior to establishing himself in a trade or business.

Id. at 463–64.

A question related to those raised in *Wassenaar* and *Link* is whether a taxpayer, having clearly at one time carried on a trade or business, has abandoned or withdrawn from that trade or business when the educational expenses are incurred. The issue may arise when the taxpayer ceases working full-time in order to undertake full-time schooling. See the *Furner* case in the materials. The position of the Internal Revenue Service, as reflected in Revenue Ruling 68-591 in the materials, is that a suspension of employment for a year or less will ordinarily be considered temporary. The Tax Court, however, in approving as temporary a two-year suspension to attend business school commented "There is no magic in a one-year limit. . . . " (*Sherman v. Commissioner*, T.C. Memo. 1977-301), and the courts look at all the facts and circumstances in determining whether the suspension is temporary.

As an alternative to the skill-maintenance test, the taxpayer may deduct educational expenses that meet the express requirements of his employer or applicable law imposed as a condition to retention of his established employment relationship, status, or rate of compensation. Reg. § 1.162-5(c)(2). The employer-requirement test thus applies only with respect to "express requirements," and the regulations go on to impose additional limitations. The requirements must be imposed for a "bona fide business purpose." Moreover, only the "minimum education necessary" to retention of job, status, or pay will qualify; education beyond the minimum may, however, satisfy the skill maintenance test. A case noted earlier, *Hill v. Commissioner*, 181 F.2d 906 (4th Cir. 1950), which predates the regulations, exemplifies satisfaction of the employer-requirement test. In order to renew her teaching certificate, a public school teacher was required by state regulation either to take college courses or pass an examination; she chose the former, and the cost of attending summer school to acquire the college credits was held deductible as an ordinary and necessary business expense. Public school teachers are among the main beneficiaries of the employer-requirement test, but other professions, such as law and medicine, are increasingly adopting mandatory continuing education requirements as a condition to retention of a license to practice. Note, however, that the public school teachers in *Takahashi v. Commissioner* conceded the inapplicability of the employer-requirement test to their Hawaiian seminar expenses. Footnote 2 of the opinion explains why they did so.

C. The Minimum-Educational-Requirements and New-Trade-or-Business Tests of Regulation Section 1.162-5(b)

An individual may not deduct educational expenses required to meet the minimum educational requirements for qualification in his employment or trade or business. Reg. § 1.162-5(b)(2). However, once an individual has met those requirements, the expenses incurred to satisfy a subsequent change in the requirements will be deductible. The regulations point out that actually performing particular job duties does not establish that one has met the minimum educational requirements for qualification. Details are provided on the applicability of the minimum-education rule to educational institutions, and the rule is illustrated by examples involving secondary and university teachers, and a law student hired by a law firm. Reg. § 1.162-5(b)(2)(iii).

An individual is also prohibited from deducting educational expenses "part of a program of study . . . which will lead to qualifying him in a new trade or business." Reg. § 1.162-5(b)(3)(i). Note that this is an objective test. The fact that an individual may not intend to pursue the new trade or business, but may simply wish to improve his skills in his present employment, does not make the expenses deductible. If the education qualifies the individual in a new trade or business, no deduction is allowed.

In a recent case denying an educational deduction to a 62-year-old Methodist minister who took courses at a local Catholic university and ultimately earned a bachelor's degree, the Tax Court reiterated its view that "it may be all but impossible for a taxpayer to establish that a bachelor's degree program does not qualify the taxpayer in a new trade or business." *Warren v. Commissioner*, T.C. Memo. 2003-175. In *Warren*, the taxpayer took courses he deemed relevant to his ministry, including Introduction to Counseling, Internship in Ministry Practice, Death and Dying as a Life Cycle, Modern Social Problems, The Family, Community, Ethics in Human Services, Symphonic Choir, Basic Writing, and Writing Strategies. Applying the objective test of the regulations, the Tax Court, concluding that the degree program qualified the taxpayer for a new trade or business, stated "[t]he courses taken by the taxpayer provided him with a background in a variety of social issues that could have prepared him for employment with several public agencies and private non-profit organizations outside of the ministry. Whether or not petitioner remains in the ministry is irrelevant."

Likewise, it appears clear that obtaining a law degree qualifies an individual for a new trade or business. An engineer or accountant cannot deduct the cost of obtaining a law degree, even if the study is mandated by his employer, and he intends to continue his nonlegal profession. Reg. § 1.162-5(b)(3)(ii), Ex. (2). Similarly, in *Galligan v. Commissioner*, T.C. Memo. 2002-150, *aff'd*, 2003-1 U.S. Tax Cas. (CCH) P50,381 (8th Cir. 2003), the court held a law librarian could not deduct the expenses of a law school education, although the court conceded that the legal education would be helpful to her in her work as a law librarian. As the Tax Court noted: "by attending law school and obtaining her degree, Ms. Galligan became entitled to seek admission to the bar, as she did, and to enter the practice of law if she should choose. . . . [She apparently indicated that she did not intend to practice law.] Ms. Galligan's law school education was part of a program which qualified her for a new trade or business."

By contrast, the regulations provide that a mere "change of duties" is not equivalent to a new trade or business if the new duties involve "the same general type of work" as the present employment. The issue is thus to draw the line where the "new duties" move beyond the same general type of work to become a new trade or business. The line-drawing is done in a quite generous way for teachers; the regulations provide that all teaching and related duties involve the same general type of work. For example, not only is there no new trade or business involved in a teacher who moves from elementary to secondary school, or from one subject matter to another, but, somewhat remarkably, a change from teacher to guidance counselor or to principal also involves no new trade or business. Reg. § 1.162-5(b)(3)(i). For non-teachers, the regulations illustrate the distinction between the same general type of work and a new trade or business by providing that the cost to a psychiatrist of study and training in psychoanalysis is deductible. Reg. § 1.162-5(b)(3)(ii), Ex. (4).

The Tax Court has applied what it described in *Glenn v. Commissioner*, 62 T.C. 270, 275 (1974), as a "commonsense approach" to determining when new titles or abilities constitute a new trade or business:

[A] comparison [is] made between the types of tasks and activities which the taxpayer was qualified to perform before the acquisition of a particular title or degree, and those which he is qualified to perform afterwards. . . . Where we have found such activities and abilities to be significantly different, we have disallowed an educational expense deduction, based on our finding that there had been qualifications for a new trade or business.

By way of examples, public accountants and certified public accountants were held in *Glenn v. Commissioner* to be in separate trades or businesses, as were fixed-wing airline pilots and helicopter pilots in *Lee v. Commissioner*, T.C. Memo. 1981-26. See the case of *Sharon v. Commissioner* in the materials, where the Tax Court, in a decision affirmed by the Ninth Circuit, cited other cases applying the common sense approach and found that a licensed New York attorney qualified for a new trade or business on obtaining his California license to practice law. The *Sharon* case involves other issues as well. Note the distinction drawn between expenses held to constitute nondeductible personal expenditures and licensing fees held amortizable over the taxpayer's life expectancy. Compare in this regard the regulations at § 1.212-1(f).

In contrast to cases involving the denial of deductions for educational expenses leading to a new trade or business, the Tax Court, in *Allemeier v. Commissioner*, T.C. Memo. 2005-207 (2005), allowed a taxpayer to deduct his MBA tuition because the MBA did not qualify the taxpayer for a new trade or business. In reaching its conclusion, the Tax Court applied the "commonsense approach" of *Glenn v. Commissioner*, noted above, and compared the types of activities the taxpayer was qualified to perform before acquiring the MBA with those he was qualified to perform afterwards. Based on that comparison, the Tax Court found that the taxpayer's business did not change significantly after the taxpayer enrolled in the MBA program. (Compare *Allemeier* with *Link v. Commissioner*, discussed previously.) In addition, the Tax Court concluded that, because the MBA did not qualify Allemeier for a professional certification or license, his case was distinguishable from cases involving taxpayers embarking on a course of study that qualified them for a professional certification or license, *e.g.*, cases involving law study leading to a law degree where the taxpayer performed many of the same activities following the law degree that taxpayer had performed before earning the degree. See Reg. § 1.162-5(b)(3)(ii), Ex. 2 and *Galligan v. Commissioner*, noted previously.

Consistent with its decision in *Allemeier v. Commissioner*, the Tax Court in *Singleton-Clarke v. Commissioner*, T.C. Summary Op. 2009-182, held that a registered nurse who earned her MBA with a specialization in health care management could deduct the cost of the MBA education as she was already performing the tasks and activities of her trade or business before commencing the MBA program. Prior to pursuing the MBA, taxpayer had served for a number of years as a quality control coordinator at acute care hospitals and medical centers. After earning the degree, she was hired by another hospital as a performance management coordinator, a position comparable to the positions she had held prior to pursuing the MBA. The court, in finding for the taxpayer, noted:

> An MBA degree is different from a degree that serves as foundational qualification to attain a professional license. . . . An MBA is a more

general course of study that does not lead to a professional license or certification. *Allemeier v. Commissioner*, T.C. Memo. 2005-207. This Court has had differing outcomes when deciding whether a taxpayer may deduct education expenses related to pursing an MBA, depending on the facts and circumstances of each case. *The decisive factor generally is whether the taxpayer was already established in their trade or business.* [Emphasis added.]

Foster v. Commissioner, T.C. Summ. Op. 2008-22, illustrates the fact that the deductibility of MBA expenses turns on the taxpayer's circumstances. The taxpayer, who had been a project manager for an engineering consulting company before entering the MBA program, accepted a position of vice president of marketing with a different company after the program. In holding the MBA expenses nondeductible, the court said:

> [P]etitioner has not demonstrated her involvement in nonengineering management before receiving her MBA; rather, her MBA qualifies her for the trade or business of business management. Likewise, petitioner has not proven that her engineering roles included marketing duties; yet, her position as vice president of marketing indicates that she was so qualified after the MBA.

D.   Travel Expenses

Section 274(m)(2) disallows any deduction for travel as a form of education. The legislative history to this provision suggests the skepticism Congress had concerning the educational travel deductions claimed by teachers and other taxpayers:

> The committee is concerned about deductions claimed for travel as a form of "education." The committee believes that any business purpose served by traveling for general educational purposes, in the absence of a specific need such as engaging in research which can only be performed at a particular facility, is at most indirect and insubstantial. By contrast, travel as a form of education may provide substantial personal benefits by permitting some individuals in particular professions to deduct the cost of a vacation, while most individuals must pay for vacation trips out of after-tax dollars, no matter how educationally stimulating the travel may be. Accordingly, the committee bill disallows deductions for travel that can be claimed only on the ground that the travel itself is "educational," but permits deductions for travel that is a necessary adjunct to engaging in an activity that gives rise to a business deduction relating to education.

H.R. Rep. 99-426, 99th Cong., 1st Sess. (1985), p. 122.

As the legislative history indicates, travel expenses, meals and lodging remain deductible where an individual travels away from home "primarily" to obtain education, the expenses of which are deductible. *See* Reg. § 1.162-5(e)(1). The regulations employ a facts and circumstances test for determining the primary purpose of a trip, citing as an important factor the relative amounts of time spent in personal and educational activities. The regulations and the examples thereunder also provide that even when the trip is not primarily personal, expenses properly allocable to personal activities may not be deducted; conversely, when the trip is primarily personal, the transportation costs are nondeductible, but meals and lodging allocable to the educational activity may still be deducted.

TAKAHASHI v. COMMISSIONER
United States Tax Court
87 T.C. 126 (1986)

NIMS, JUDGE:

After concessions, [one issue is:] Whether petitioners are entitled to deduct certain expenses which they incurred to attend a seminar in Hawaii as education expenses under section 162(a). . . .

During the years in issue, petitioners were employed as science teachers by the Los Angeles Unified School District. Approximately 25 percent of Mrs. Takahashi's students were minorities while almost all of Mr. Takahashi's students were minorities. Most of the minority students taught by petitioners were Hispanic.

Pursuant to article 3.3 of the California State Education Code, a teacher employed by the Los Angeles Unified School District must complete a minimum of two semester units in a course of study dealing with multicultural societies to receive promotions and salary increases. During 1981, petitioners attended a seminar held in Hawaii entitled "The Hawaiian Cultural Transition in a Diverse Society" which satisfied the requirements of article 3.3.

Petitioners, together with their 2½ year-old son, spent 10 days in Hawaii. Petitioners attended the seminar on 9 out of the 10 days during which they were in Hawaii. The seminar program lasted from 1 to 6 hours each day and consisted of classroom instruction as well as tours of Polynesian cultural attractions and visits to the homes of local natives. When petitioners were not participating in the seminar they would take their son sightseeing or spend time relaxing at the beach.

Petitioners incurred expenses totaling $2,373 in connection with their trip to Hawaii. A portion of these expenses were incurred for their son's travel and meals as well as for personal activities engaged in by petitioners which were unrelated to the seminar.

On Form 2106 (Employee Business Expenses) attached to their 1981 Form 1040, petitioners claimed the expenses they incurred in connection with their Hawaiian trip as an education expense under Section 162(a). In the notice of deficiency, respondent disallowed this deduction in full with the explanation that petitioners had not established that the expenses were paid or incurred during the taxable year or that the expenses were ordinary and necessary to their business.

Under Section 1.162-5(a), Income Tax Regs., education expenses are deductible as ordinary and necessary business expenses if the education (1) maintains or improves skills required by the individual in his employment or other trade or business, or (2) meets the express requirements of the individual's employer. If a taxpayer incurs education expenses while traveling away from home which satisfy one or both of these tests, his expenditures for travel, meals, and lodging incurred while away from home are deductible only if the individual travels away from home primarily for educational reasons. Only expenditures incurred for meals and lodging during the time actually spent participating in deductible education pursuits are allowable. Sec. 1.162-5(e)(1), Income Tax Regs.

Petitioners do not contend nor does the record contain any evidence that petitioners' attendance at the seminar was required by their employer.[1] Rather, petitioners contend that because the seminar on "Hawaiian Cultural Transition in a Diverse Society" enabled them to better understand their minority students, the seminar maintained or improved skills required by them to teach science to minority students. Petitioners further contend that they traveled to Hawaii primarily to attend the seminar. Petitioners therefore conclude that the expenses they incurred in connection with the seminar, including travel, meals, and lodging, are fully deductible as education expenses under Section 162(a).

Respondent contends that petitioners have not established that the seminar maintained or improved skills required by them to perform their jobs as science teachers, and, therefore, that none of the expenses petitioners incurred in connection with their trip to Hawaii are deductible. Respondent further contends that even if the seminar maintained or improved petitioner's teaching skills, petitioners' education expense deduction should not be allowed because petitioners traveled to Hawaii primarily for a vacation rather than to obtain education. Finally, respondent contends that even if petitioners traveled to Hawaii primarily to obtain education, they have provided no records or credible testimony upon which to allocate the cost of their Hawaiian trip between deductible business expenses and nondeductible personal expenses.

On the record before us, we do not think that petitioners' participation in the seminar maintained or improved skills required by them to perform their jobs as science teachers, and petitioners have conceded that their attendance was not required by their employer. Consequently, since petitioners fail to satisfy the threshold tests of section 1.162-5(a) of the regulations, we need not consider whether petitioners have satisfied the travel provisions of section 162-5(e) of the regulations.

When a taxpayer claims, pursuant to the first of the tests contained in section 1.162-5(a) of the regulations, that an education expense was incurred in order to maintain or improve his existing skills, he must demonstrate a connection between the course of the study and his particular job skills. *Schwartz v. Commissioner*, 69 T.C. 877, 889 (1978), citing *Baker v. Commissioner*, 51 T.C. 243 (1968). We do not

---

[1] Sec. 1.162-5(c)(2), Income Tax Regs., provides in pertinent part that "Only the minimum education necessary to the retention by the individual of his established employment relationship, status, or rate of compensation may be considered as undertaken to meet the express requirements of the taxpayer's employer." The seminar attended by petitioners satisfied the requirements of art. 3.3 of the California State Education Code and therefore made petitioners eligible for promotions and salary increases. Petitioner's participation in this seminar in no way affected the retention of their current employment relationship, status, or rate of compensation.

think petitioners have demonstrated this connection. Although Mrs. Takahashi cited "greater rapport" and "better understanding of people," she could point to "no real tangible thing" to connect the Hawaiian multicultural course which she took with the skills required of a science teacher. Similarly, with respect to Mr. Takahashi, the record shows no evidence that the course which he attended in Hawaii had any nexus with his teaching of science. Mr. Takahashi did not testify at the trial.

Petitioners cite *Hilt v. Commissioner*, T.C. Memo. 1981-672, as illustrating a situation where the education-travel deduction was disallowed only because the taxpayers "did not engage in any specific course of study or spend any time acquiring information from individuals specifically knowledgeable in the areas of Hawaiian culture or history." 42 T.C.M. 1718, at 1721–1722. As in the case before us, *Hilt* involved California teachers who traveled to Hawaii with a child and claimed section 162(a) education expense deductions. The deductions claimed in *Hilt* were based in some part at least upon taxpayers' obtaining "professional growth units" under California law which, when obtained, would have increased taxpayers' salary levels.

Petitioners apparently wish us to infer from the above-quoted language in *Hilt* that any expenditures incurred for general cultural enrichment, if duly substantiated, will be allowable as education expense deductions. However, in the context of petitioners' professional duties as science teachers, the Hawaiian Cultural Transition course does not in our judgment fall within the category of a "refresher," "current developments," or "academic or vocational" course required by the regulations. Sec. 1.162-5(c)(1), Income Tax Regs. The Hawaiian Cultural Transition course is simply not sufficiently germane to the teaching of science to bring the course within the category of expenditures for education which maintains or improves skills required by the individual in his employment. Sec. 1.162-5(a)(1), Income Tax Regs. We accordingly hold for respondent on this issue.

WASSENAAR v. COMMISSIONER
United States Tax Court
72 T.C. 1195 (1979)

FINDINGS OF FACT

The petitioner graduated from Wayne State University Law School (Wayne State) in Detroit, Mich., in June 1972. He served on law review while at Wayne State in both 1971 and 1972, and although he was a member of the board of editors, his services were no different from those of any other law review member. His duties included editing legal material, checking sources of legal articles, and writing legal articles. He received compensation for such services from Wayne State in the amounts of $845 in 1971 and $1,314 in 1972.

From June to September 1971, the petitioner worked for the law firm of Warner, Norcross & Judd (Warner firm). He prepared legal memorandums, drafted legal documents, and consulted with clients in the presence of an attorney from the firm. He received $2,920 from the Warner firm as compensation for his services that summer.

The petitioner was not employed during the summer following his graduation from law school; instead, he prepared for the Michigan bar, which he took in July 1972. However, he continued to search for employment with a law firm during such period. In October 1972, he passed the bar exam, but he was not formally admitted to the Michigan bar until May of 1973.

In September 1972, the petitioner began courses in the graduate law program in taxation at New York University (NYU), and he graduated with a masters degree in taxation in May 1973. During 1973, he incurred the following expenses in connection with his studies at NYU:

Travel	$96
Meals and lodging	1,085
Auto expense	64
Tuition and books	1,450
Miscellaneous expenses	96
Total	$2,781

The petitioner's principal residence was Holland, Mich., while he lived in New York to attend NYU during the year in issue. Following his graduation from NYU, the petitioner returned to Detroit to commence employment with the law firm of Miller, Canfield, Paddock & Stone (Miller firm).

From 1963 until his beginning law school at Wayne State, the petitioner held numerous positions and worked for numerous employers. In 1965, he was employed by the Sunday School Guide Publishing Co., the city of Holland, Mich., the Capital Park Motel in Lansing, Mich., and the Motor Wheel Corp. in Lansing, Mich. He worked for the city of Holland, Fleetwood Furniture, and H. J. Heinz Co. in 1966. The petitioner was employed by three employers in 1967 — the Klaasen Printing Co, Fleetwood Furniture, and Wiersma Construction Co. In 1968, he worked for General Electric Co., and he worked for Lear Siglar Co. in 1969.

On his Federal income tax return for 1973, the petitioner deducted the expenses he incurred while attending NYU as an employee business expense. In his notice of deficiency, the Commissioner disallowed the deduction on the ground that such expenses were not ordinary and necessary expenses paid or incurred in connection with any trade or business.

OPINION

The first issue for decision is whether the petitioner may deduct as an ordinary and necessary expense incurred in his trade or business the expense for tuition, books, meals, lodging, and other miscellaneous items paid by him while he obtained his masters degree in taxation.

The petitioner contends that for more than 10 years prior to 1973, he was in a trade or business of "rendering his services to employers for compensation." He contends that he was engaged in the trade or business of "analyzing and solving legal problems for compensation" while he worked on the law review at Wayne State, while he worked for the Warner firm, and later while he worked for the Miller firm. He maintains that the graduate courses in taxation helped maintain and improve his skills in that work. On the other hand, the Commissioner takes the position that the petitioner never began the practice of law until the summer of 1973 and that his attendance at NYU was merely the completion of his program of education preparatory to the practice of law. In the alternative, the Commissioner argues that the petitioner's expenses for travel and meals and lodging are not deductible since he was not "away from home" while attending NYU.

The petitioner artfully attempts to characterize his trade or business as "analyzing and solving legal problems for compensation," and he received compensation for the performance of such services. Nevertheless, it is clear that the petitioner's intended trade or business at the time he attended NYU was that of an attorney, with an emphasis on the law of taxation. We observe that he enrolled in the masters in taxation program at NYU directly from law school, and there was thus an uninterrupted continuity in his legal education. . . . Although the work the petitioner performed before his graduation from law school and NYU was admittedly of a legal nature, such work in no way constituted his being engaged in the practice of law. Before his admission to the bar in May of 1973, he was not authorized to practice law as an attorney. Therefore, his expenses at NYU were not incident to the trade or business of practicing law, and thus, he was not maintaining or improving the skills of that profession within the purview of section 1.162-5(a)(1), Income Tax Regs. See, *e.g.*, *Fielding v. Commissioner*, 57 T.C. 761 (1972) (medical school graduate was denied a business expense deduction for tuition cost of his residency since expenses were not incident to any profession that he previously practiced); *Horodysky v. Commissioner*, 54 T.C. 490 (1970) (taxpayer who had been a lawyer in Poland was denied a business expense for cost of obtaining an American law school degree since he had no previous employment as a lawyer in this country).

Moreover, although the petitioner completed the requirements for admission to the bar in 1972, he was not formally admitted until May of 1973, and until that time, he could not engage in the practice of law. It is a well-established principle that being a member in good standing of a profession is not tantamount to carrying on that profession for the purpose of section 162(a). . . .

Because the petitioner had not practiced law as an attorney before his attendance at NYU, his situation is not analogous to that of other professionals who have been allowed educational expense deductions under section 162(a). In such cases, the taxpayer was already firmly established in his profession and was truly taking courses or attending a seminar for the purpose of maintaining or improving the skills of his profession. See *Coughlin v. Commissioner*, 203 F.2d 307 (2d Cir. 1953), rev'g and remanding 18 T.C. 528 (1952) (attorney allowed business deduction for expenses incurred in attending NYU Tax Institute seminar). . . .

In addition, the petitioner is also denied a deduction for his expenses at NYU by section 1.162-5(b)(3), Income Tax Regs., which provides that educational expenses are not deductible if the education "is part of a program of study being pursued by him which will lead to qualifying him in a new trade or business." The petitioner's attendance at NYU was a part of his "program of study" of becoming a lawyer, a trade or business in which he was not previously engaged before his attendance there. After his admission to the bar in May of 1973 and his completion of the program at NYU, he was authorized to and began the practice of law, a wholly different trade or business from any in which he had been previously engaged. *Cf. Diaz v. Commissioner*, 70 T.C. 1067 (1978), *aff'd*, 607 F.2d 995 (2d Cir. 1979).

The petitioner is also not entitled to an educational expense deduction on the theory that he was engaged in the trade or business of "rendering his services to employers for compensation." It is a well-established principle that educational expenses must bear a direct and proximate relation to the taxpayer's trade or business. In *Carroll v. Commissioner*, 51 T.C. at 215, this Court stated that it is not sufficient that "the petitioner's education is helpful to him in the performance of his employment." The education must be more than tenuously related to the skills required in the taxpayer's occupation; it must be proximately related to such skills. We cannot accept the petitioner's argument that courses in the more advanced fields of tax law have any proximate relation to his past employment with the Sunday School Guide Publishing Co., Fleetwood Furniture, or the Capital Park Motel — some of his employers as many as 7 years before his attendance at NYU.

In support of his position, the petitioner cites the case of *Primuth v. Commissioner*, 54 T.C. 374, 377 (1970), in which this Court recognized "that a taxpayer may be in the trade or business of being an employee." However, *Primuth* simply held that a fee expended to secure employment is deductible as a business expense under Section 162. The case did not involve a claim for an educational deduction, and thus, it offers no support for the petitioner's position. Accordingly, we must hold that the petitioner's expenses in obtaining a masters of law degree in taxation are not deductible as an ordinary and necessary business expense of being an attorney at the time such expenses were incurred and since, therefore, he was not maintaining or improving the skills of such trade or business. Such expenses are nondeductible personal expenses. (Sec. 262.) Therefore, it is unnecessary to consider the Commissioner's alternative argument that the petitioner's expenses for travel and meals and lodging are not deductible since he was not "away from home" while attending NYU.

The second issue for consideration is whether the petitioner's expenses of attending NYU are deductible under Section 212 as:

ordinary and necessary expenses paid or incurred during the taxable year. . . .

(3) in connection with the determination, collection, or refund of any tax.

The petitioner contends that the expenses he incurred at NYU in obtaining a masters degree in taxation are deductible under such section because the courses he took assisted him in preparing his Federal income tax return. Although the Commissioner admits that the petitioner's courses in taxation at NYU assisted him in preparing his tax return and determining the amount due, he contends that the petitioner's expenses in this regard were not "ordinary and necessary." We must agree with the Commissioner.

To be deductible under Section 212, any expenses must meet the ordinary and necessary test. (Sec. 1.212-1(d), Income Tax Regs.) Thus, the expenses "must be reasonable in amount and must bear a reasonable and proximate relation" to the purpose for the expenditure. Sec. 1.212-1(d), Income Tax Regs.; see, *e.g.*, *Commis-*

sioner v. Flowers, 326 U.S. 465 (1946); *Limericks, Inc. v. Commissioner*,165 F.2d 483,484 (5th Cir. 1948), aff'g 7 T.C. 1129 (1946). It strains our credulity to conclude that the petitioner's total expenses of $2,781 incurred while attending NYU are reasonable in amount or bear any reasonable relationship to the preparation of his tax return. Moreover, Section 1.212-1(f), Income Tax Regs., provides: "Among expenditures not allowable as deductions under section 212 are the following: . . . expenses of taking special courses or training." The petitioner's expenditures at NYU clearly constitute "special courses" and are non-deductible pursuant to Section 1.212-1(f), Income Tax Regs., as well. Accordingly, we hold that the petitioner's educational expenses are not deductible under Section 212(3).

In conclusion, we hold that the petitioner's educational expenses are not deductible under Section 162 since he was not engaged in a trade or business of being an attorney at the time he incurred such expenses, that his educational expenses are not deductible under Section 212(3) since such expenses were not reasonable in amount and did not bear a reasonable relationship to the alleged purpose for the expenditure. . . .

Decision will be entered for the respondent.

FURNER v. COMMISSIONER
United States Court of Appeals, Seventh Circuit
393 F.2d 292 (1968)

FAIRCHILD, CIRCUIT JUDGE:

Petitioner Mary O. Furner is a junior high teacher who devoted the school year 1960-1 to full time graduate study and claimed the expenses as deductions from income for those years. The commissioner disallowed the deductions and the tax court, in a reviewed opinion, with two judges dissenting, upheld the commissioner. . . .

Petitioner majored in social studies at a teachers' college, and received her bachelor's degree in 1957. She taught at Argyle, Minnesota in grades 7–12 during the school year, 1957-8. In the school years 1958-9 and 1959-60 she taught social studies (primarily history) at eighth grade level at Crookston, Minnesota.

Petitioner believed that her teaching required greater depth of subject matter than she possessed. Because it would be difficult to obtain the course work she wanted in history on a part time basis, she arranged to attend Northwestern University as a full time graduate student during the school year 1960-1. The Crookston school system does not customarily grant leaves of absence and she resigned in June, 1960.

She taught at a reading camp during the summer of 1960, and attended Northwestern from September, 1960 until she received a master of arts degree in August, 1961. She performed no teaching duties during that period.

In April, 1961, petitioner signed a contract to teach in a junior high school in DeKalb, Illinois, beginning in September, 1961. In DeKalb she has taught two history courses, regarded as "social studies."

The tax court found as ultimate facts (1) that petitioner was not engaged in carrying on a trade or business of teaching during the time she was attending Northwestern University and (2) that she took the graduate work primarily for the purpose of obtaining a new position or substantial advancement in position or for meeting the minimum qualifications of certain schools for a teacher of social studies at the junior high school level. The tax court held that each of those facts made the expenses nondeductible.

The commissioner concedes on the review that ultimate fact (2) is no longer relevant, even if correctly determined. His counsel tells us that

> new Treasury Regulations were promulgated on May 1, 1967, by T.D. 6918, 1967-21 Int. Rev. Bull. 8 (amending Section 1.162-5, Treasury Regulations on Income Tax (1954 Code)), and these Regulations are to be applied retroactively. They supply more objective criteria for determining if educational expenditures are properly deductible as business expenses than was the case under the pre-existing Regulations which emphasized the taxpayer's subjective intent. For example, they provide that educational expenses will be nondeductible if they relate to training for a "new trade or business," but treat all teaching and related duties as involving the same general type of work. (Sec. 1.162-5(b)(3).) They do not use the "new position" test, and we therefore do not propose to argue here that taxpayer was undertaking her graduate training in order to obtain such a "new position." Further, it appears that the Commissioner did not assert the "minimum requirements" argument in the Tax Court, and the taxpayer's discussion of the record evidence relating to this point . . . has merit. We therefore do not propose to raise the "minimum requirements" theory in this Court.

Thus we are concerned solely with the tax court's determination, whether it be finding of fact or conclusion of law, that petitioner was not carrying on a trade or business of teaching while a graduate student under these circumstances.

The fact that petitioner was not on leave from a school system employer while studying during a normal school year seems to have been deemed critical. If the petitioner had been on leave from Crookston without pay, all other facts being identical, the commissioner's present position, though his counsel tells us that he is reconsidering it, would have led him to allow the deduction.

We gather that the tax court would reach the same conclusion. The tax court said:

> In the instant case since petitioner was not employed or otherwise actively engaged in teaching or on a leave of absence from any teaching position or actively seeking to uninterruptedly continue in a teaching position by obtaining such a position to commence prior to the completion of her graduate studies, we conclude that at the time the expenditures here involved were made, petitioner, though still a member of the teaching profession, was not engaged in the practice of that profession so as to be "carrying on" a trade or business.

Apparently the commissioner and the tax court accord controlling importance to whether a teacher's period of study (expenses for which would otherwise qualify for deduction) interrupts the regularity of the teacher's employment as a teacher during successive school years, following the traditional pattern. Enrollment for study is not deemed to interrupt regularity (1) if undertaken during traditional vacation periods, (2) if the study is part-time during a school year while the teacher is also performing teaching duties, or (3) if the study is full-time during a school year, but an employment relationship technically continues by virtue of leave, granted by the employing school.

The governing statute is the very general provision allowing deduction of "all the ordinary and necessary expenses paid or incurred . . . in carrying on any trade or business. . . . " The commissioner and tax court put too much emphasis, we think, on whether the course of study displaces performance of teaching activity during the period of the year, when it is traditional for teachers to teach, and give insufficient consideration to the broader question whether the relationship of the course of study to intended future performance as a teacher is such that the expenses thereof can reasonably be considered ordinary and necessary in carrying on the business of teaching. Factors which make it advantageous to undertake the course of study in a single year rather than to spread it out over several summers are surely relevant.

Expert testimony in the record before the tax court leads to two conclusions, nowhere rebutted. One is that it is not unusual, and is becoming more usual, for teachers to enroll in full time graduate study for an academic year in order to keep up with expanding knowledge and improve their understanding of the subjects they teach. It also appears, as is common knowledge, that many school systems require teachers to earn additional academic credits from time to time.

An amicus brief filed by an attorney for the National Education Association suggests that graduate courses in education can be obtained conveniently in summer sessions and evening extension classes, but that the full range of courses in liberal arts and sciences is usually available only during the academic year with reduced offerings in summer sessions.

Given these facts, a year of graduate study under the circumstances disclosed here is as much a normal incident of carrying on the business of teaching as study during vacation periods.

The record also indicates that it was not common in 1960 for schools to grant leaves of absence; that in some systems where leave is granted a teacher receives reduced compensation and agrees to return after the leave, but that most leave is unpaid, there is no agreement to return, and most teachers do not return.

Our second conclusion is that leave status seems to have little meaning as a criterion of whether or not a teacher's graduate study is a normal incident of carrying on the business of teaching. In petitioner's case, where her school employer did not grant leaves, it can not, in our opinion, be a reasonable basis for finding that her study was not such an incident.

The tax court's finding, based as it was, on the fact that petitioner was not on leave, is clearly erroneous. The present record, moreover, would not support a finding that petitioner did not reasonably expect to return to teaching activity after her year of study, nor a finding on any other basis that her graduate study was not a normal incident of her carrying on the business of teaching.

The commissioner and the tax court rely upon *Canter v. United States* [354 F.2d 352 (Ct. Cl. 1965)], holding that expenses incurred by a nurse for professional education, after leave from her previous nursing job had expired, were not deductible. The majority opinion in that case does, indeed, support the idea that being on leave status is critical. Approval was given to "the proposition that, before a person can qualify for a deduction under section 162, he must either be engaged in remunerative activity or have a definite connection, such as leave of absence, with a position." We respectfully disagree with the breadth of that statement, excluding, as it does, consideration of the relationship of the education with intended future resumption of business activity.

We point out, however, that the facts in *Canter* were quite different from those before us. Mrs. Canter ceased active performance of her nursing duties February 1, 1958, and obtained an educational leave of absence until November 1, 1958. She was enrolled in a university from February 1, 1958 to June 1960 when she was awarded a bachelor's degree. She pursued graduate study from September, 1960 to June, 1962 when she received a master's degree. She then again became employed. The deductions claimed were for 1960, part for undergraduate and part for graduate study. It does not appear what if any demonstration was made to the court that undergraduate and graduate study for a period of over four years was a normal incident of carrying on the business of nursing.

The decisions of the tax court will be reversed.

REVENUE RULING 68-591
1968-2 C.B. 73

The Internal Revenue Service will follow, to the extent stated below, the decision of the United States Court of Appeals for the Seventh Circuit in the case of *Mary O. Furner v. Commissioner*, 393 F.2d 292 (1968), *rev'g* 47 T.C. 165 (1966).

In this case, the appellate court held that amounts spent by a teacher who left her position to pursue a full-time graduate course for one academic year were deductible as educational expenses under section 1.162-5 of the Income Tax Regulations, even though she was not on leave status from the school system and, upon graduation, accepted a teaching position different from her previous job.

The Service will follow the *Furner* decision in cases where the requirements of section 162 of the Code and the regulations thereunder are satisfied, and where the facts are substantially the same as those in the *Furner* case, that is, where a taxpayer, in order to undertake education or training to maintain or improve skills required in his employment or other trade or business, temporarily ceases to engage actively in employment or other trade or business. Ordinarily, a suspension for a period of a year or less, after which the taxpayer resumes the same employment or trade or business, will be considered temporary.

However, the Service does not agree with any construction of the *Furner* opinion under which an expense could be considered incurred while carrying on a trade or business within the meaning of section 162 of the Code (although in fact such trade or business is not being carried on) merely because (1) the study might be a "normal incident" of carrying on a trade or business and (2) the taxpayer subjectively intends to resume that trade or business at some indefinite future date.

SHARON v. COMMISSIONER
United States Tax Court
66 T.C. 515 (1976),
aff'd, 591 F.2d 1273 (9th Cir. 1978)

SIMPSON, JUDGE:

The Commissioner determined deficiencies in the petitioners' Federal income tax in the amounts of $235.56 for 1969 and $653.70 for 1970. Due to concessions, the following issues remain for decision: . . . (2) whether the petitioners are entitled to amortization deductions under section 167(a)(1) with respect to certain educational and other expenses incurred to enable the petitioner Joel A. Sharon to obtain a license to practice law in the State of New York; (3) whether the petitioners may deduct or amortize costs incurred by the petitioner Joel A. Sharon in taking the California bar examination and miscellaneous expenses incurred in obtaining admissions to courts in that State; (4) whether the petitioners may deduct under section 162, or amortize pursuant to section 167, the cost of petitioner Joel A. Sharon's admission to the Supreme Court of the United States.

FINDINGS OF FACT

Bar Admission Expenses

The petitioner attended Brandeis University from September 1957 to June 1961 and received a bachelor of arts degree upon his graduation.

After graduation from Brandeis University, the petitioner entered Columbia University School of Law, receiving a bachelor of laws degree in June 1964.

In order to be eligible to take the New York bar examination, the petitioner was required to graduate from a fully accredited 4-year undergraduate institution and give evidence of his successful completion of 3 years of study at an accredited law school. The petitioner expended a total of $210.20 in gaining admission to practice law in the State of New York. This amount included $175.20 for bar review courses and materials related thereto and a New York State bar examination fee of $25.

The petitioner was admitted to practice law in the State of New York on December 22, 1964. Thereafter, he was employed as an attorney by a law firm in New York City until 1967, when he accepted a position in the Office of Regional Counsel, Internal Revenue Service, and moved to California.

Although not required by his employer to be a member of the California bar, the petitioner decided to become a member of that State's bar after moving there. However, he found that the study of California law, which he undertook in preparation for the California bar examination, was helpful in his practice of law as an attorney in the Regional Counsel's office. The petitioner spent the following amounts in order to gain membership in the California bar:

Registration as law student in California	$20
California bar review course	230
General bar examination fee	150
Attorney's bar examination fee	375
Admittance fee	26
Total	$801

In 1969, the petitioner also spent a total of $11 in order to be admitted to practice before the U.S. District Court for the Northern District of California and the U.S. Court of Appeals for the Ninth Circuit. The petitioner's employer required only that he be admitted to practice before the U.S. Tax Court.

In 1970, the petitioner incurred the following expenses in connection with his admission to the U.S. Supreme Court:

Round trip air fare, San Francisco to New York	$238.35
Round trip rail fare, New York to Washington, and miscellaneous expenses..	75.00
Total	$313.35

The petitioner's employer did not require that he be admitted to practice before the U.S. Supreme Court but did assist him in this matter. The Chief Counsel of the IRS personally moved the admission of a group of IRS attorneys, including the petitioner. Furthermore, two of his supervisors signed his application as personal references.

During 1970, the U.S. Supreme Court rules required a personal appearance before it in Washington, D.C., to be admitted to practice.

On their return for 1969, the petitioners claimed a deduction for "Dues and Professional Expenses" of $492. The Commissioner disallowed $385 of such deduction on the grounds that the disallowed portion was not a deductible business expense, but was a nondeductible capital expenditure. On their return for 1970, the petitioners claimed a deduction for $313.35 for the cost of petitioner Joel A. Sharon's admission to practice before the U.S. Supreme Court. The Commissioner also disallowed such deduction. In addition to challenging the disallowed deductions, the petitioners alleged in their petition that they were entitled to amortize or depreciate the cost of petitioner Joel A. Sharon's education. The Commissioner denied this allegation in his answer.

OPINION

. . . .

2. Amortization of License to Practice Law in New York

The next issue to be decided is whether the petitioner may amortize the cost of obtaining his license to practice law in New York. The petitioner contends that he is entitled under Section 167 to amortize the cost of such license over the period from the date of his admission to the bar to the date on which he reaches age 65, when he expects to retire. In his cost basis of this "intangible asset," he included the costs of obtaining his college degree ($11,125), obtaining his law degree ($6,910), a bar review course and related materials ($175.20), and the New York State bar examination fee ($25). As justification for including these education expenses in the cost of his license, he points out that, in order to take the New York bar examination, he was required to have graduated from college and an accredited law school.

The petitioners rely upon Section 1.167(a)-3 of the Income Tax Regulations, which provides in part:

> If an intangible asset is known from experience or other factors to be of use in the business or in the production of income for only a limited period, the length of which can be estimated with reasonable accuracy, such an intangible asset may be the subject of a depreciation allowance. . . .

There is no merit in the petitioner's claim to an amortization deduction for the cost of his education and related expenses in qualifying himself for the legal profession. His college and law school expenses provided him with a general education which will be beneficial to him in a wide variety of ways. The costs and responsibility for obtaining such education are personal. Section 1.262-1(b)(9) of the Income Tax Regulations provides that expenditures for education are deductible only if they qualify under Section 162 and Section 1.162-5 of the regulations. In the words of Section 1.162-5(b), all costs of "minimum educational requirements for qualification in . . . 'employment' are personal expenditures or constitute an inseparable aggregate of personal and capital expenditures.' " There is no "rational" or workable basis for any allocation of this inseparable aggregate between the nondeductible personal component and a deductible component of the total expense. *Fausner v. Commissioner*, 413 U.S. 838, 839 (1973). Such expenses are not made any less personal or any more separable from the aggregate by attempting to capitalize them for amortization purposes. Since the inseparable aggregate includes personal expenditures, the preeminence of Section 262 over section 167 precludes any amortization deduction. The same reasoning applies to the costs of review courses and related expenses taken to qualify for the practice of a profession. *William D. Glenn*, 62 T.C. 270, 274–276 (1974).

In his brief, the petitioner attempts to distinguish our opinion in *Denmann* by asserting that he is not attempting to capitalize his educational costs, but rather, the cost of his license to practice law. Despite the label which the petitioner would apply to such costs, they nonetheless constitute the costs of his education, which are personal and nondeductible. Moreover, in his petition, he alleged that the capital asset he was seeking to amortize was his education.

There remains the $25 fee paid for the petitioner's license to practice in New York. This was not an educational expense but was a fee paid for the privilege of practicing law in New York, a nontransferable license which has value beyond the taxable years, and such fee is a capital expenditure. The Commissioner has limited his argument to the educational expenses and apparently concedes that the fee may be amortized. Since the amount of the fee is small, the petitioner might, ordinarily, be allowed to elect to deduct the full amount of the fee in the year of payment, despite its capital nature. *Cf.* Sec. 1.162-12(a), Income Tax Regs., with respect to the treatment of inexpensive tools. However, since the fee was paid prior to the years in issue, we cannot allow a current deduction in this case. Therefore, in view of the Commissioner's concession and our conclusion with respect to the third and fourth issues, a proportionate part of such fee may be added to the amounts to be amortized in accordance with our resolution of the third issue.

3. License to Practice Law in California

The next issue to be decided is whether the petitioner may deduct or amortize the expenses he incurred in gaining admission to practice before the State and Federal courts of California. The Commissioner disallowed the amounts paid in 1969 to take the attorney's bar examination in California and the amounts paid for admission to the bar of the U.S. District Court for the Northern District of California and for admission to the U.S. Court of Appeals for the Ninth Circuit. He determined that such expenses were capital expenditures. In his brief, the petitioner argues for a current deduction only if the costs of his license to practice in California are not amortizable.

It is clear that the petitioner may not deduct under Section 162(a) the fees paid to take the California attorney's bar examination and to gain admission to practice before two Federal courts in California. In *Arthur E. Ryman, Jr., supra,* an associate professor of law sought to deduct as an ordinary business expense the cost of his admission to the bar of the State in which he resided. We held that since the taxpayer could reasonably expect the useful life of his license to extend beyond 1 year, the cost of such license was a capital expenditure and not a currently deductible business expense. Unlike the small fee paid to New York, the aggregate amount of such payments in 1969 is too large to disregard their capital nature and allow the petitioners to deduct them currently.

In connection with his alternative claim that he be allowed to amortize the costs of acquiring his license to practice law in California, the petitioner asserts that such costs total $801. Such amount includes the cost of a California bar review course, registration fees, and other items specified in our Findings of Fact. However, the petitioner is in error in including the cost of his bar review course, $230, in the capital cost of his license to practice in California.

It is clear that the amount the petitioner paid for the bar review course was an expenditure "made by an individual for education" within the meaning of section 1.162-5(a) of the Income Tax Regulations. See *William D. Glenn,* 62 T.C. 270, 273–274 (1974); sec. 1.162-5(b)(2)(iii), example (3), Income Tax Regs. Although the petitioner was authorized to practice law in some jurisdictions when he took the California bar review course such course was nevertheless educational in the same sense as the first bar review course.

Nor may the petitioner treat the payment for the California bar review course as part of the costs of acquiring his license to practice in California. Educational expenses which are incurred to meet the minimum educational requirements for qualification in a taxpayer's trade or business or which qualify him for a new trade or business are "personal expenditures or constitute an inseparable aggregate of personal and capital expenditures." Sec. 1.162-5(b), Income Tax Regs. We find that the bar review course helped to qualify the petitioner for a new trade or business so that its costs were personal expenses.

We have previously adopted a "commonsense approach" in determining whether an educational expenditure qualifies a taxpayer for a "new trade or business." *Kenneth C. Davis*, 65 T.C. 1014, 1019 (1976); *William D. Glenn*, 62 T.C. at 275; *Ronald F. Weiszmann*, 52 T.C. 1106, 1110 (1969), *aff'd*, 443 F.2d 29 (9th Cir. 1971). If the education qualifies the taxpayer to perform significantly different tasks and activities than he could perform prior to the education, then the education qualifies him for a new trade or business. *William D. Glenn, supra*; *Ronald F. Weiszmann, supra*. Thus, we have held that a professor of social work is in a different trade or business than a social caseworker. *Kenneth C. Davis, supra*. A licensed public accountant is in a different trade or business than a certified public accountant. *William D. Glenn, supra*. A registered pharmacist is in a different trade or business than an intern pharmacist, even though an intern performs many of the same tasks as a registered pharmacist, but under supervision. *Gary Antzoulatos*, T.C. Memo. 1975-327.

Before taking the bar review course and passing the attorney's bar examination, the petitioner was an attorney licensed to practice law in New York. As an attorney for the Regional Counsel, he could represent the Commissioner in this Court. However, he could not appear in either the State courts of California, the Federal District Courts located there, nor otherwise act as an attorney outside the scope of his employment with the IRS. If he had done so, he would have been guilty of a misdemeanor. Yet, after receiving his license to practice law in California, he became a member of the State bar with all its accompanying privileges and obligations. He could appear and represent clients in all the courts of California. By comparing the tasks and activities that the petitioner was qualified to perform prior to receiving his license to practice in California with the tasks and activities he was able to perform after receiving such license, it is clear that he has qualified for a new trade or business. Consequently, the expenses of his bar review course were personal and are not includable in the cost of his license to practice law in California.

It is true that even before he became a member of the bar of California, the petitioner was engaged in the business of practicing law. . . . However, in applying the provisions of Section 1.162-5 of the regulations to determine whether educational expenses are personal or business in nature, it is not enough to find that the petitioner was already engaged in some business — we must ascertain the particular business in which he was previously engaged and whether the education qualified him to engaged in a different business. Before taking the bar review course and becoming a member of the bar of California, the petitioner could not generally engage in the practice of law in that State, but the bar review course helped to qualify him to engage in such business.

The Commissioner does not argue that the capital expenditures incurred in obtaining his license to practice law in California may not be amortized. In a series of cases, the courts have held that the fees paid by physicians to acquire hospital privileges are not current business expenses but are capital expenditures amortizable over the doctor's life expectancy. We hold that the petitioner may treat the costs of acquiring his license to practice in California in a similar manner. Such costs include:

Registration Fee	$20
General bar exam fee	150
Attorney's bar exam fee	350
Admittance fee	26
U.S. District Court fee	6
U.S. Court of Appeals fee	5
Total	$582

Although the petitioner testified that he would retire at age 65 if he were financially able to do so, such testimony is not sufficient to establish the shorter useful life for which he argues.

4. Supreme Court Admission

The fourth issue to be decided is whether the petitioner may either deduct or amortize the cost of gaining admission to practice before the U.S. Supreme Court. The petitioner deducted the travel costs he incurred in 1970 in traveling to Washington, D.C., to be personally present for the Supreme Court admission, as required by that Court's rules. The Commissioner disallowed the deduction and argued in his brief that such expenditures were capital in nature since the petitioner acquired an asset with a useful life beyond 1 year.

In his brief, the petitioner concedes that he may not deduct the costs he incurred if we find that his license to practice before the Supreme Court is an intangible asset with a useful life of more than 1 year. For the same reasons that we have concluded the petitioner's New York and California licenses were intangible assets with a useful life of more than 1 year, we also hold that his Supreme Court license is an intangible asset with a useful life exceeding 1 year. Thus, the petitioner may not deduct under section the cost of obtaining such license.

In order for such license to be amortizable pursuant to section 167, the petitioner must show that it was property used in his trade or business. There is little evidence concerning the petitioner's "use" in 1970 of his license to practice before the Supreme Court. However, he did testify that the admission to various bars was a factor used in evaluating attorneys for promotion by his employer, and the Commissioner never disputed such testimony. Furthermore, it is altogether appropriate for any attorney-at-law to become a member of the bar of the Supreme Court whenever it is convenient for him to do so. No one can know when the membership in such bar may be useful to him in the practice of law — it may bring tangible benefits today, tomorrow, or never; yet, if one holds himself out to practice law, there is ample reason for him to acquire membership in the bar of the Supreme Court. Under these circumstances, we find that the intangible asset acquired by becoming a member of such bar was used by the petitioner in 1970 and hold that he may amortize the costs of acquiring such asset over his life expectancy.

To reflect the foregoing,

Decisions will be entered under Rule 155.

Scott, J., dissenting:

I respectfully disagree with the conclusion of the majority that the $25 license fee paid by petitioner to New York, the $571 paid to take the California bar examination, the $11 for admission to practice before two Federal courts in California, and the $313.35 paid for travel to Washington, via New York, to practice before the United States Supreme Court are properly amortizable over petitioner's life expectancy. I agree that these expenditures, except for transportation to Washington, via New York, the place of the home of petitioner's family, are capital expenditures. However there is nothing in this record to show the reasonable useful life of these expenditures. How long petitioner will practice law and where are so conjectural as to cause there to be no way to ascertain the reasonable useful life of the asset petitioner acquired through his capital expenditures. Although respondent apparently makes no contention that the trip to Washington, via New York, when petitioner was admitted to practice before the Supreme Court was personal, the clear inference from the fact that he did go to New York where his family lived before coming to Washington and returned there after he came to Washington is that petitioner went to New York to visit his family and incidentally came to Washington to be admitted to practice before the Supreme Court. However, if the view of the majority, that the cost of travel to Washington, via New York, was properly part of the cost of petitioner's admission to practice before the Supreme Court, were proper, then this, as the other capital expenditures, should not be amortizable since the useful life of the asset acquired is not reasonably ascertainable.

Sterrett, J., agrees with this dissent.

Irwin, J., dissenting:

I disagree with that portion of the majority opinion which holds that petitioner may not treat the payment for the California bar review course as a part of the cost of acquiring his license to practice law in California. In the past, we have indeed adopted a "commonsense approach" in determining whether an educational expenditure qualifies a taxpayer for a "new trade or business." However, I think we depart from that approach when we hold that an attorney, licensed to practice law in New York, qualifies for a new trade or business when he obtains a license to practice law in California. In *William D. Glenn, supra* at 275, we stated:

We have not found a substantial case law suggesting criteria for determining when the acquisition for new titles or abilities constitutes the entry into a new trade or business for purposes of section 1.162-5(c)(1), Income Tax Regs. What has been suggested, and we uphold such suggestion as the only commonsense approach to a classification, is that a comparison be made between the *types of tasks and activities which the taxpayer was qualified to perform before the acquisition of a particular title to degree, and those which he is qualified to perform afterwards.* *Ronald F. Weiszmann,* 52 T.C. 1106, 1110 (1969), *aff'd,* 443 F.2d 29 (9th Cir. 1971). Where we have found such activities and abilities to be significantly different, we have disallowed an educational expense deduction, based on our finding that there had been qualification for a new trade or business. *Ronald F. Weiszmann, supra.* [Emphasis supplied.]

In my view there is no difference in the *types* of tasks and activities which petitioner was qualified to perform before and after he acquired his California license. By virtue of being licensed to practice in California, petitioner could perform the same types of tasks and activities in that state as he was already qualified to perform in New York. In this regard, respondent takes the position that once an individual is qualified to teach in State A, a college course taken in order to qualify for a teaching position in State B is neither a minimum educational requirement of his trade or business nor education qualifying him for a new trade or business. Rev. Rul. 71-58, 1971-1 C.B. 55. I would similarly conclude that once an individual is qualified to practice law in one State, a bar review course taken in preparation for the bar exam of another State is not education leading to qualification for a new trade or business.

NOTE: EDUCATION TAX INCENTIVES

The cost of education, particularly higher education, has skyrocketed in recent years. Significant increases in tuition have not been limited to private institutions; state institutions, like their private counterparts, regularly raise tuition to account for the lack of adequate state support. Parents today must begin saving for their children's college education when their children are quite young and, even then, students and their parents will likely find themselves borrowing substantial sums of money to pay for education expenses. Prior to 1996, Congress had generally failed to provide tax incentives or tax relief to parents or students with respect to education costs.

In response to intense political pressure, Congress has created a host of tax incentives principally for higher education. These incentives now include tax credits, and deductions and exclusions from income, and, in general, are aimed at higher education expenses that would not be deductible as business expenses under § 162. They represent, in other words, a deliberate policy determination to provide tax incentives for expenditures that would typically be regarded, under the regulations, as "personal expenditures or . . . an inseparable aggregate of personal and capital expenditures." Reg. § 1.162-5(b)(1). Several of the more prominent incentives are described below.

1. *Education Credits*

Hope Scholarship Credit. The Hope Scholarship Credit is a tax credit of up to $1,500 per student (plus inflation adjustments) for a maximum of two years, for the qualified tuition and related expenses of higher education. § 25A(b). The credit, which consists of 100% of the first $1,000 of qualifying expenses plus 50% of the next $1,000 of qualifying expenses, may be claimed for the qualifying expenses of the taxpayer, the taxpayer's spouse, and dependents. Among the restrictions and limitations on the Hope Credit are the following:

(a) Qualifying expenses are essentially tuition and required fees, except for nonacademic fees. § 25A(f).

(b) Eligible students are only those who are enrolled at least half-time in one of the first two years of postsecondary education in a program leading to a degree, certificate, or other recognized educational credential. Note that the credit is allowed for a maximum of two years, and not for years that begin after the student has completed the first two years of postsecondary education. § 25A(b)(2).

(c) The credit is phased out for taxpayers with modified gross incomes between $40,000 and $50,000 (between $80,000 and $100,000 on joint returns.) § 25A(b)(1), (d). The credit and the modified adjusted gross income limitations are inflation-adjusted. § 25A(h).

However, for 2009 through 2017, the Hope Credit (known for this purpose as the American Opportunity Tax Credit) is increased to a maximum of $2,500; is available for the first four years of post-secondary education, not two; has increased adjusted gross income limits and a broadened definition of qualifying expenses; and is partially refundable. § 25A(i).

Lifetime Learning Credit. The Lifetime Learning Credit is a tax credit of up to $2,000 per taxpayer for the qualified tuition and related expenses of higher education. § 25A(c)(1). The credit, which amounts to 20% of no more than $10,000 of qualifying expenses, may be claimed for the qualifying expenses of the taxpayer, the taxpayer's spouse, and dependents. The same phase-out rules, based on modified adjusted gross income, that apply to the Hope Credit also apply to the Lifetime Learning Credit. § 25A(d). (However, the increased income limits for the Hope Credit for 2009 through 2017, noted above, do not apply to the Lifetime Learning Credit.) The two credits are coordinated by a rule that prohibits taking both credits for the same student in the same year: the qualifying expense of a student for whom a Hope Credit is allowed may not be taken into account for purposes of the Lifetime Learning Credit. § 25A(c)(2)(A). For example, assume a student qualifies for both credits and the student's qualifying educational expenses amount to $5,000. If the taxpayer claims the Hope Scholarship Credit based on the first $2,000 of the student's qualifying expenses, the taxpayer may not claim any Lifetime Learning Credit with respect to the student. In other words, a choice must be made between the two credits with respect to a given student's qualified education expenses. It is, however, permissible to claim a Hope Credit on account of one student's qualifying expenses, and to claim a Lifetime Learning Credit on account of another student's qualifying expenses. (The two credits share a common definition of qualifying expenses. § 25A(f)(1), (i)(3).)

Aside from the amount of the credit, the Lifetime Learning Credit differs from the Hope Credit in several respects. First, as its name indicates, the Lifetime Learning Credit is not limited to a maximum number of years or to a specified number of years of higher education. Graduate-level education, for example, may qualify for the credit. Second, there is no requirement under the Lifetime Learning Credit that a student be enrolled at least on a half-time basis in a degree-granting program; a single course at an eligible educational institution will suffice. Third, the Lifetime Learning Credit is calculated on a per taxpayer basis rather than on a per student basis, as with the Hope Credit. No matter how many eligible students there may be among the taxpayer and the taxpayer's spouse and dependents, the maximum credit remains $2,000. (Note that married taxpayers must file jointly to claim the credit.) § 25A(g)(6). In any case, neither the Hope Credit nor the Lifetime Learning Credit may be allowed for any expense for which a deduction is allowed.

2. Education Deductions

Deduction for Qualified Tuition and Related Expenses. In 2001, Congress added a new tax incentive for educational expenses, an above-the-line deduction for qualified higher education expenses. §§ 62(a)(18) and 222. Congress added this deduction in recognition of the fact that in some cases a deduction may provide greater relief than the credits that are available. In the case of a taxpayer whose adjusted gross income does not exceed $65,000 ($130,000 in the case of a joint return), up to $4,000 of qualified tuition and related expenses (essentially tuition and required academic fees, *see* §§ 25A(f), 222(d)) may be deducted. If the taxpayer's adjusted gross income exceeds $65,000 but does not exceed $80,000 (in the case of joint returns, if adjusted gross income exceeds $130,000 but does not exceed $160,000), the qualified tuition and expenses of up to $2,000 can be deducted. Other taxpayers get no deduction. § 222(b)(2). The deduction cannot be taken in the same year for the same student for whom a Hope Credit or Lifetime Learning Credit is claimed. § 222(c)(2). The § 222 deduction expired at the end of 2014 but is expected to be reinstated.

Interest Deduction for Interest on Qualified Education Loans. Section 221(a) authorizes an above-the-line deduction for interest paid by a taxpayer on any qualified education loan. § 62(a)(17). The maximum deduction is $2,500. The deduction is phased out for a taxpayer with modified adjusted gross income between $50,000 and $65,000 (between $100,000 and $130,000 on joint returns), as adjusted for inflation. § 221(f). The deduction is available with respect to loans incurred by the taxpayer to pay for the cost of attendance for the taxpayer, taxpayer's spouse, and taxpayer's dependents at institutions of higher education while enrolled at least half-time in a program leading to a degree or other recognized educational credential. *See* § 221(d). Interest deductions generally are discussed further in Chapter 22.

3. Education Exclusions from Income

Coverdell Education Savings Accounts. Coverdell Education Savings Accounts are trust accounts that may be created for any child under the age of 18 for the purpose of paying the child's qualified higher education expenses or qualified elementary and secondary education expenses. § 530(b)(1) and (2). The total contributions to one or more Education Savings Accounts for the benefit of any given child may not exceed $2,000 per year. § 530(b)(1). (Query: Considering the enormous costs of higher education, is the ceiling of $2,000 per year for a maximum of approximately 18 years too low?) The balances in a Coverdell Education Savings Account must be distributed to a beneficiary no later than 30 days after the beneficiary attains age 30.[2]

Qualified education expenses include: expenses for tuition, fees, academic tutoring, special needs services in the case of special needs beneficiaries, books, supplies, computer equipment and other equipment; and expenses for room, board, uniforms and transportation. § 530(b)(2), (3).

Any individual can contribute to a child's Education Savings Account, up to the $2,000 maximum, except that for individuals with modified adjusted gross income between $95,000 and $110,000 (between $190,000 and $220,000 on joint return), the $2,000 maximum is phased out. § 530(c)(1). Thus, an individual with income above the upper limit cannot contribute to an Education Savings Account.

Although contributions to Education Savings Accounts are nondeductible, the accounts grow tax-free until withdrawal, and any withdrawal will be tax-free to the extent it does not exceed the child's qualified higher education expenses for the year of withdrawal. § 530(d)(2). (Withdrawals that exceed such expenses are generally subject to taxation, plus a 10% penalty tax on that portion of the excess withdrawal that represents earnings on the contributions. § 530(d)(4)). Unused portions of Education Savings Accounts may be rolled over to other Education Savings Accounts of the child or members of the child's family.) § 530(d)(5). Amounts distributed from an Education Savings Account will be excluded even though a taxpayer takes advantage of the Hope or Lifetime Learning Credit in the same year so long as the amounts distributed from the Education Savings Account are not used for the same qualified expenses for which either a Hope or Lifetime Learning Credit is claimed. § 530(d)(2)(C).

Section 529 Qualified Tuition Programs. In 1996, Congress enacted § 529, providing for deferral of income earned on amounts placed in qualified state-authorized pre-paid tuition plans or college savings accounts to meet qualified higher education expenses. Unlike the Coverdell Education Savings Accounts, Section 529 Qualified Tuition Plans were not limited to those taxpayers whose modified adjusted gross incomes were within a certain dollar amount. "Qualified higher education expenses," like the definition given that term for purposes of the Coverdell Education Savings Accounts, includes expenses for tuition, fees, books,

---

[2] I.R.C. § 530(b)(1). The age limitations in § 530(b)(1) will not apply to "special needs children" (individuals who "because of physical, mental or emotional condition [including learning disability] require additional time to complete his or her education."

supplies and equipment as well as certain room and board expenses. § 529(e)(3).

In 2001, Congress (a) extended the benefits of § 529 to cover pre-paid tuition plans of private post-secondary institutions (§ 529(b)(1)); (b) provided that distributions from qualifying state Section 529 plans for payment of qualified higher education expenses would be excluded from gross income (§ 529(c)(1), (3)(B)(i) and (ii)); (c) provided that distributions after 2003 from qualifying tuition programs established by private institutions (*i.e.*, an entity other than a state or state agency) will be excluded from gross income (§ 529(c)(1), (3)(B)(i)–(iii)); and (d) imposed an additional 10% tax on the amount of a distribution from a qualified tuition plan that is includible in gross income (§ 529(c)(6)). In addition, Congress authorized taxpayers to claim a Hope Credit or Lifetime Learning Credit and at the same time claim the benefits of the exclusion under § 529 for distributions from a qualified tuition plan to the same student so long as the distribution from the qualified tuition plan is not used for the same expenses for which either the Hope Credit or Lifetime Learning Credit is claimed. § 529(c)(3)(B)(v).

Educational Assistance Programs. As noted in Chapter 7 in connection with scholarships, employer payments for educational assistance to an employee are excluded from the employee's gross income and wages up to a maximum of $5,250 per year. § 127(a). Educational assistance includes tuition and course-related expense, but payments for meals, lodging, transportation and certain other expenditures do not qualify. § 127(c)(1). There is no requirement that the education be job-related or part of a degree program. Purely personal educational benefits may thus be obtained on a tax-free basis. [Note that education expenses will also be excludable if they qualify as a working condition fringe benefit under § 132. *See* Chapter 11.] In 2001, § 127 was extended to include educational assistance for graduate education.

Income From U.S. Savings Bonds to Pay Higher Education Expenses. As discussed briefly in the Note on Miscellaneous Exclusions following Chapter 11, § 135 excludes from income the redemption proceeds of "qualified U.S. savings bonds" in the case of an individual who pays "qualified higher education expenses" during the taxable year. Limitations, however, exist based on the amount of qualified higher education expenses paid during one year and on the taxpayer's modified adjusted gross income (as adjusted for inflation) § 135(a), (b)(1), (2), and (c).

Chapter 19

MOVING EXPENSES, CHILD CARE, LEGAL EXPENSES

Part A:
Moving Expenses

I. PROBLEMS

1. Susan Martin, a sole practitioner, lives in Ames, 15 miles from her place of work in Barrow. Assume she accepts a job teaching at a law school located in Connors, and she will move to Dover. What time and distance requirements must Susan satisfy to deduct her moving expenses?

2. Assume Susan satisfies the time and distance requirements, and her moving expenses are as follows:

   (a) $10,000 to move her household belongings to Dover.

   (b) $800, including $200 in meals and $300 in lodging, for Susan to drive to Eaton to visit her mother and then drive on to Dover.

   (c) $1,000 for Susan's husband, Tom, and their six-year old child to fly to Dover.

   (d) $5,000 to stay in a motel in Dover for two months while waiting to move into a new house.

   (e) $750 in transportation, meals, and lodging for Susan and Tom's trip to Dover to investigate housing there after Susan accepted the new job.

   The law school reimburses Susan $12,000 for her moving expenses. What are the tax consequences to Susan as a result of the move?

Assignment for Chapter 19, Part A: Moving Expenses:

Complete the problems.

Read: Internal Revenue Code: §§ 217(a)–(d), (f); 82; 132(a)(6), (g); 62(a)(15).
   Treasury Regulations: § 1.217–2(a), (b)(2), (3), (4), (8), (d)(1)–(3).
   Materials: Overview

II.   VOCABULARY

allowable moving expenses
qualified moving expense reimbursement

III. OBJECTIVES

1. To summarize the time and distance tests for the moving expense deduction.

2. To summarize the definition of the term "moving expenses."

3. To recall that qualified moving expense reimbursements are excluded from income.

4. To recall that moving expense reimbursements, other than qualified ones, constitute income.

5. To distinguish §§ 162 and 217 in terms of eligibility for deductions under each section.

IV. OVERVIEW

Prior to 1964, no deduction was allowed for employment-related moving expenses. Reimbursement for moving expenses incurred by an employee's relocation to a new job with the same employer was treated as nontaxable on the ground that the expenses were incurred primarily for the benefit of the employer. In 1964, Congress enacted both §§ 217 and 82, the former providing a deduction for certain moving expenses, and the latter requiring the inclusion in income of all reimbursements for moving expenses. Significant statutory changes, however, were made in 1993. First, the category of allowable moving expenses, described below, was narrowed considerably. In addition, an employer's payment or reimbursement of otherwise-deductible moving expenses — known as a "qualified moving expense reimbursement" — was made an excludable fringe benefit under § 132. *See* § 132(a)(6), (g). Finally, § 82 was amended to require inclusion in income of all reimbursements for moving expenses, except to the extent excluded by § 132. Section 82, however, continues to operate independently of § 217 to a considerable degree; a reimbursement is taxable, unless it constitutes a qualified moving expense reimbursement, regardless of whether a deduction for the expense is allowable under § 217.

The legislative policy behind § 217 has been expressed as follows:

> The mobility of labor is an important and necessary part of the nation's economy, since it reduces unemployment and increases productive capacity. It has been estimated that approximately one-half million employees are requested by their employers to move to new job locations each year. In addition, self-employed individuals relocate to find more attractive or useful employment. Substantial moving expenses often are incurred by taxpayers in connection with employment-related relocation, and these expenses may be regarded as a cost of earning income.

General Explanation of the Tax Reform Act of 1969, Jt. Comm. on Taxation, 91st Cong., 2d Sess., 101 (1970). Section 217 applies to the self-employed as well as to employees; it applies not only to those changing jobs with the same employer, but to persons entering the work force for the first time, to employees beginning work for a new employer, and to self-employed persons entering a new trade or business or moving to a new location. Reg. § 1.217-2(a)(3)(i). Compare § 217 in this respect to § 162.

The preliminary requirement for a deductible moving expense is that it be incurred "in connection with the commencement of work." § 217(a). Under the regulations at § 1.217-2(a)(3)(i), the move must bear "a reasonable proximity both in time and place" to the new principal place of work, although the taxpayer need not have made arrangements for work prior to the move. The reasonable-proximity-in-time requirement is met if the moving expenses are incurred within one year of the commencement of work; those incurred after that one-year period may be held to lack the requisite proximity in time, depending on the circumstances of the case.

The statute also imposes two substantive, but mechanical, requirements, one relating to minimum distance, and the other involving a minimum period of employment in the new location. First, the taxpayer's new principal place of work must be at least 50 miles farther from his former residence than was his former principal place of work. § 217(c)(1). In other words, if his commute to work would have increased at least 50 miles had he remained in his old residence, the distance test is met. Second, the taxpayer must be a full-time employee in the general location of the new principal place of work (though not necessarily with only one employer) for at least 39 weeks during the 12-month period immediately following the move. (Self-employed individuals, as well as employees who do not meet the 39-week, 12-month rule, must satisfy a full-time work test of 78 weeks within the 24-month period after the move, with 39 of the weeks in the first 12 months.) § 217(c)(2). The full-time employment requirement is waived in case of death, disability and certain involuntary separations from work. § 217(d)(1). The requirements, and their component parts, are detailed in the regulations. In general, what policy is served by these 50-mile and 39-week requirements?

The allowable moving expenses are set forth in § 217(b): A deduction is allowed for the cost of transporting the taxpayer, other household members, and household belongings from the old residence to the new one, as well as for the reasonable cost of lodging en route. § 217(b)(1)(A), (b)(1)(B). Meal costs, however, do not qualify as moving expenses. All moving expenses are subject to a reasonableness requirement. § 217(a); Reg. § 1.217-2(b)(2).

Allowable moving expenses may be deducted to the extent they are not paid for or reimbursed by the taxpayer's employer. (Recall that such payments or reimbursements are excluded from the employee's income as qualified moving expense reimbursements. § 132(a)(6). If an employee deducts an allowable expense in one year, employer reimbursement received in a subsequent year is not excluded from income. § 132(g).) Moving expenses are deductible for the year in which they are paid or incurred (in accordance with the taxpayer's accounting method), rather than in the year in which the minimum period of employment requirement is satisfied. The taxpayer may elect to claim the deduction on the tax return for the year the expense was paid or incurred, provided it is possible to satisfy the employment requirement; if the requirement is, in fact, not met, the deducted amount constitutes income for the first year the requirement cannot be met. § 217(d)(2), (d)(3). (Similarly, it seems clear that an employer reimbursement initially excluded from income under § 132(a)(6) would also constitute § 82 income in the first year the employment requirement cannot be met.) Alternatively, the taxpayer who has not yet satisfied the employment requirement can instead forego taking the deduction in the original return, and file an amended return or claim for refund if the requirement is subsequently met. Reg. § 1.217-2(d)(2)(ii). The § 217 deduction is an above-the-line deduction, thus placing on the same tax footing those individuals who are reimbursed by employers and those who are not. § 62(a)(15).

Note a taxpayer takes inconsistent positions in claiming a deduction under § 162 for travel expenses incurred away from home at a new principal place of work and in also claiming a deduction under § 217 for moving expenses in connection with the commencement of work there. Which section actually governs depends on the facts and circumstances involved. Reg. § 1.217-2(c)(3)(iii). See also Reg. § 1.217-2(a)(1). For § 217 purposes, employment at the new principal place of work must be permanent or indefinite, rather than merely temporary, as is the case under § 162(a)(2). Schweighardt v. Commissioner, 54 T.C. 1273 (1970). See also Goldman *v. Commissioner*, 497 F.2d 382 (6th Cir. 1974), disallowing a § 217 deduction for the costs of moving taxpayer and his family back to their previous home, following a one-year temporary job elsewhere, in connection with which taxpayer had been allowed travel expenses under § 162.

Part B:
Child Care Expenses

I. PROBLEM

Doris Jones, who has an adjusted gross income of $34,000 a year, is a single parent with three children, 17-year-old Adam, 11-year-old Brian, and 9-year-old Cathy. Doris, who works five days a week from 9:00 a.m. to 6:00 p.m. at a local store, paid a friend $75 a week during the school year (40 weeks) to come to her house three days a week after school to watch the children, do household work, and prepare dinner. Adam does these chores twice a week, but cannot to do it more often than that. Without her friend's assistance, Doris would have to negotiate a reduced workday with her employer or find a new job that would enable her to be home when the children were not in school. During the summer, Doris paid the same friend $150 a week for 10 weeks to do the same tasks for extended hours. In addition, there was one week during which Brian went on a wilderness outing at a cost of $400; Doris' parents gave her the money, as a gift, to pay for the outing. Doris' friend charged only $100 for her services that week. Finally, there was one additional week during which both Brian and Cathy went with Doris' sister and her sister's children on a visit to see various distant relatives. Doris paid her sister $100 and did not hire her friend's services for that week. What child care credit is Doris entitled to claim? In answering this question, assume the earned income limitation of § 21(d) does not apply.

Assignment for Chapter 19, Part B: Child Care Expenses

Complete the problem.

Read: Internal Revenue Code: § 21; skim § 129.

Materials: Overview

II. VOCABULARY

employment-related expenses
qualifying individual

III. OBJECTIVES

1. To summarize the requirements for an employee-related expense for purposes of the child care credit.

2. To provide an example of when the child care credit would be more advantageous to the taxpayer than the exclusion relating to dependent care assistance programs.

IV. OVERVIEW

In *Smith v. Commissioner*, 40 B.T.A. 1038 (1939), the Board of Tax Appeals determined that child care expenditures, in the absence of specific legislative authority, were personal in nature and could not be deducted even when incurred to enable parents to work. Although acknowledging that "certain disbursements normally personal may become deductible by reason of their intimate connection with an occupation carried on for profit," and that child care expenses "may in some indirect and tenuous degree relate to the circumstances of a profitable occupation," the Board was "not prepared to say that the care of children, like similar aspects of family and household life, is other than a personal concern." *Id.* at 1039.

Specific legislative authority for a child care deduction was first enacted in 1954; the deduction, which was always limited in amount, although the limits were increased over the years, was repealed in 1976 in favor of the limited child care credit now found in § 21.

Section 21 applies only if there are "employment-related expenses" and one or more "qualifying individuals." § 21(a)(1). Employment-related expenses generally are expenses for household services and for the care of a qualifying individual, incurred to enable the taxpayer to be gainfully employed when there are one or more qualifying individuals with respect to the taxpayer. § 21(b)(2)(A). A qualifying individual is (1) a dependent of the taxpayer under the age of 13 for whom the taxpayer is eligible to claim a dependency exemption, (2) a dependent of the taxpayer who is physically or mentally incapable of caring for himself or herself, and who has the same home as the taxpayer, or (3) the spouse of the taxpayer if the spouse is physically or mentally incapable of caring for himself or herself, and who has the same home as the taxpayer. § 21(b)(1).

The cost of qualifying services is limited to the taxpayer's earned income (and for a married couple, to the lesser of their two earned incomes), and in any case, such cost cannot exceed $6,000 (or $3,000, if there is only one qualifying individual involved). § 21(c), (d)(1). The tax credit allowed is 35% of this amount if the taxpayer's adjusted gross income is $15,000 or less; the credit declines to 20% as adjusted gross income increases. § 21(a)(2). Specifically, § 21(a)(2) provides that the 35% credit percentage is reduced, but not below 20%, by 1 percentage point for each $2,000 (or fraction thereof) of the adjusted gross income above $15,000. Therefore, the credit percentage is reduced to 20% for taxpayers with adjusted gross income over $43,000. The maximum allowable credit is thus $1,050 for one dependent ($3,000 × 35%) and $2,100 for two or more ($6,000 × 35%). The credit is not refundable; thus, if the credit exceeds the tax liability, the excess credit is not allowed. The credit is not allowable with respect to payments to certain related individuals. § 21(e)(6).

An example of the issues that have arisen in determining what constitutes employment-related expenses is found in *Zoltan v. Commissioner*, 79 T.C. 490 (1982), where the Tax Court held summer camp expenses and a portion of the cost of a trip to Washington, D.C., incurred to assure the well-being and protection of a child while the taxpayer was gainfully employed, qualified for the credit. (Section 21 was amended in 1987, in response to cases like *Zoltan*, to provide overnight camp expenses will not qualify as employment-related expenses.) The *Zoltan* decision was

486 MOVING EXPENSES, CHILD CARE, LEGAL EXPENSES   CH. 19

distinguished in *Perry v. Commissioner*, 92 T.C. 470 (1989), where a child care credit was denied for the cost of air travel for children to stay with their grandparents for school holidays, even though the cost of a babysitter for the holidays would have been greater. *Perry* noted the bus transportation to Washington in *Zoltan* was held to be part of the child care. By contrast, the air travel in *Perry* was found to be preliminary to the care the grandparents were to provide, and thus constituted transportation expenses rather than child care.

Section 129 excludes from the gross income of an employee amounts paid or incurred by an employer pursuant to a dependent care assistance program. The exclusion cannot exceed $5,000. § 129(a)(2)(A). Section 129(e)(7) disallows a deduction or credit under any other Code section for any amount excluded from income by § 129. The applicable dollar limit under § 21 is reduced by the aggregate amount excluded under § 129. § 21(c). For example, a taxpayer with one qualifying individual who has $3,000 in otherwise eligible employment-related expenses but who excludes $1,000 of dependent care assistance under § 129 must reduce the dollar limit of eligible employment-related expenses for the § 21 credit by the amount excluded under § 129. Therefore, in the example, the dollar limit is reduced to $2,000 ($3,000 − $1,000 = $2,000). Assume your child care expenses are $5,000. Given a choice between an additional $5,000 in taxable salary or $5,000 through a dependent care assistance program, which would you prefer?

Part C:
Legal Expenses

I. PROBLEM

George Harris operates Tri-City Package Delivery Service as a sole proprietor. His son Junior sometimes borrows one of the Tri-City delivery trucks when he goes out with friends in the evening. On one of these occasions, Junior is involved in an accident with the truck, and both George and Junior are sued for damages as a result. George retains the Tri-City lawyer to defend them, and incurs $25,000 in legal fees in a successful defense. Are the fees deductible? Is your answer the same if Tri-City is a corporation, and it is sued along with George and Junior? Does it matter if the case is settled or lost by George, Junior or Tri-City Corp.?

Assignment for Chapter 19, Part C: Legal Expenses

Complete the problem.

Read: Internal Revenue Code: §§ 162(a), 212, 262.
       Treasury Regulations: § 1.212-1(l), § 1.262-1(b)(7).
       Materials: Overview
       United States v. Gilmore (reprinted in Chapter 37)

II. VOCABULARY

origin of the claim test

III. OBJECTIVES

1. To apply the origin of the claim test to a given set of facts.

2. To distinguish the origin of the claim test and the rules relating to capital expenditures.

IV. OVERVIEW

To distinguish between deductible and nondeductible legal expenses, the Supreme Court has applied an "origin-of-the-claim" test. If the origin of the claim litigated lies in a personal, as opposed to a business or profit-seeking transaction, the expenses are nondeductible.

> [T]he characterization, as "business" or "personal," of the litigation costs of resisting a claim depends on whether or not the claim *arises in connection with* the taxpayer's profit-seeking activities. It does not depend on the *consequences* that might result to a taxpayer's income-producing property from a failure to defeat the claim. . . .

United States v. Gilmore, 372 U.S. 39, 48 (1963). In *Gilmore*, the taxpayer's legal expenses in connection with a divorce were held nondeductible on the ground that the wife's claims to his income-producing property stemmed entirely from the marital relationship. The origin-of-the-claim test was also applied in a companion case to *Gilmore, United States v. Patrick*, 372 U.S. 53 (1963), to deny a deduction for legal fees incident to a property settlement agreement involving transfers of stock, lease of real property, and creation of a trust for the benefit of the taxpayer's wife and children. Regulation § 1.262-1(b)(7) permits a deduction for fees and costs properly attributable to the production or collection of alimony, which is gross taxable income under § 71. Consider whether you find the origin-of-the-claim test, which has now been applied in many contexts, fully satisfactory. Will a claim's "origin" be readily determinable? Would you propose a different test?

Legal expenses, even if business-related, are subject to the capital expenditures rule of § 263, discussed in Chapter 13. See, for example, the *Woodward* case, discussed in Chapter 13. In both the *Gilmore* and *Patrick* cases, the Supreme Court found it unnecessary to consider the Government's alternative arguments that the legal fees were capital expenditures. In subsequent litigation, however, the taxpayer in *Gilmore* was permitted to add the legal expenses incurred in the divorce to the basis of the property in question, on the theory that "defense of title" litigation expenses are capital expenditures, regardless of whether the litigation is primarily business or personal in character. *Gilmore v. United States*, 245 F. Supp. 383 (N.D. Cal. 1965). Is this result an appropriate one? Is it inconsistent with the Supreme Court's decision in *Gilmore*?

Gilmore notes "expenses of contesting tax liabilities" were made deductible by the addition of § 212(3) to the Code. 372 U.S. at 48, n. 16. See the language of that section and of the regulations thereunder at § 1.212-1(l). Does § 212(3) apply only where there are contested tax liabilities? It is now generally accepted that § 212(3) allows a deduction for tax planning advice as well. See *Merians v. Commissioner*, 60 T.C. 187 (1973), where a divided Tax Court allowed a deduction for the portion of an estate planning fee it found allocable to tax advice. Also see Revenue Ruling 72-545, 1972-2 C.B. 179, where the Service allowed deductions for tax advice in various situations incident to divorce, and Revenue Ruling 89-68, 1989-1 C.B. 82, allowing a deduction for legal fees incurred to obtain a ruling from the Service on the deductibility of certain medical expenses.

If a deduction is available for a portion of a legal fee, it is obviously incumbent upon a lawyer to provide the client with a statement allocating the fee between the deductible and nondeductible portions. As a practical matter, the allocation the lawyer makes is likely to be determinative in the ordinary case. Consider then the ethical issues that may arise when such an allocation is necessary and the lawyer's client is anxious to see the allocation weighted towards deductibility to the maximum extent possible.

Chapter 20

HOBBY LOSSES

I. PROBLEMS

1. Mark grew up on a farm, where he worked evenings and weekends until age 17, when he went away to college. He has always remained interested in farming. After graduating from college 25 years ago he embarked on a career in advertising. Mark's wife, Nancy, is a schoolteacher and their combined income is $150,000 per year. Mark and Nancy, who have two teenage children and live in Chicago, have talked for several years about finding an alternative source of income, both now and for the future. Four years ago they decided dairy farming was their best choice, and they investigated available farms in neighboring states. In December, Year 1, after two years of searching, they found and purchased an 80-acre farm for $160,000. The farm had not been run as a dairy farm for eight years prior to the purchase, and all farming equipment had been removed. All farm buildings were obsolete or in need of considerable repair work. Mark promptly leased the farm land to a tenant farmer for Years 2 through 6 for $50 per acre per year; this rent represented the farm's only income. During Years 2 through 6, Mark visited the farm (a five-hour drive from Chicago) almost every weekend during the growing season and twice a month otherwise. (Nancy and the children visited the farm on an average of once every five or six weeks.) During the visits Mark primarily spent his time restoring the farmhouse and an abandoned orchard, but he also worked on neighboring farms as a way of learning the dairy farming business. He also subscribed to dairy farming journals and spoke on several occasions with the local agricultural extension agent. Through Year 6, Mark and Nancy have purchased no farming equipment or livestock. They have also kept no formal books of account with respect to the farm, but they do keep receipts and canceled checks relating to farm expenditures. The farm contains no recreational facilities and is not used for entertaining, nor used as a residence. During visits to the farm, Mark and Nancy stay with Mark's sister and her family, who live in a town about thirty miles south of the farm. The farm's expenses to date have averaged about $20,000 per year. Mark expects the farm to be profitable by Year 10 or Year 11; he has hired a contractor to remodel the farm house, and work will commence on the other structures once that remodeling is complete. Are Mark and Nancy's farm losses during Years 2 through 6 subject to the limitations of § 183?

2. Assume Mark and Nancy's farm activity is subject to § 183. The gross income from operating the farm was $300 in Year 8, $27,000 in Year 9, $24,000 in Year 10, and $31,000 in Year 11. Assume that the farm is not used

as Mark and Nancy's residence during any of the years. Their expenses during these years were:

	Year 8	Year 9	Year 10	Year 11
Travel	$500	$4,000	$4,000	$4,000
Depreciation	250	6,000	6,000	5,000
Taxes	500	3,000	3,000	3,000
Repairs	–	2,000	2,000	3,000
Employee Wages	–	6,000	6,000	6,000
Mortgage Interest	250	4,000	4,000	3,000
Supplies	–	5,500	6,500	5,500
Advertising		500	500	500
Total	$1,500	$31,000	$32,000	$30,000

What expenses may Mark and Nancy deduct during Years 8–11? Assume Mark and Nancy's combined income from their other work (advertising and school teaching) remains $150,000 per year.

Assignment for Chapter 20:

Complete the problems.

Read: Internal Revenue Code: §§ 183(a)–(d); 280A(f)(3).
Treasury Regulations: §§ 1.183-1(a), (b)(1) and (2), (c)(1), (d)(1) and (2), (e); 1.183-2.

> Materials: Overview
> *Dreicer v. Commissioner*
> *Remuzzi v. Commissioner*

II.   VOCABULARY

hobby loss
activity not engaged in for profit

III.   OBJECTIVES

1. To distinguish activities not engaged in for profit from those that are engaged in for profit.

2. To determine when the § 183(d) presumption applies.

3. To determine what deductions are allowable, in what order and to what extent, in respect to an activity not engaged in for profit.

IV. OVERVIEW

Losses incurred in carrying on personal hobbies clearly should not be, and are not, deductible. Losses incurred in carrying on a trade, business or in other profit-seeking activities are generally taken into account in determining a taxpayer's overall net income on which tax liability is based. The temptation to characterize a personal hobby and its associated expenses as business or profit-related is an obvious one. To prevent taxpayers from using a personal hobby as a tax shelter, Congress enacted § 183 of the Code, which limits deductions attributable to activities "not engaged in for profit."

A. Historical Development

Prior to the enactment of § 183 in 1969, the Code had contained a "hobby loss" provision (repealed as part of the 1969 changes) that limited to $50,000 per year the business losses that an individual could use to offset other income; the limitation applied, however, only where the business losses exceeded $50,000 a year for 5 consecutive years. This original hobby loss provision proved to have such limited applicability that Congress came to regard it as unsatisfactory. In fashioning a new hobby loss provision in 1969, Congress therefore took a different tack:

> In addition to the [pre-1969] hobby loss provision, some court cases have provided another basis on which the loss can be denied; namely, that the activity carried on by the taxpayer from which the loss results is not a business but is merely a hobby. . . . [T]his basic principle provides a more effective and reasonable basis for distinguishing situations where taxpayers are not carrying on a business to realize a profit, but rather are merely attempting to utilize the losses from the operation to offset their other income.

S. Rep. No. 91-552, p. 103.

In the form proposed by the House of Representatives, § 183 would have barred the deduction of losses resulting from activities carried on without a "reasonable expectation" of profit. The Senate, however, objected to this standard for distinguishing hobbies from business or profit-seeking activities:

> [R]equiring a taxpayer to have a reasonable expectation of profit may cause losses to be disallowed in situations where an activity is being carried on as a business rather than as a hobby. Accordingly, [in the Senate bill] . . . the focus is to be on whether the activity is engaged in for profit rather than whether it is carried on with a reasonable expectation of profit. This will prevent the rule from being applicable to situations where many would consider that it is not reasonable to expect an activity to result in a profit even though the evidence available indicates that the activity actually is engaged in for profit. For example, it might be argued that there was not a "reasonable" expectation of profit in the case of a bona fide inventor or a person who invests in a wildcat oil well. A similar argument might be made in the case of a poor person engaged in what appears to be an inefficient farming operation. . . . [T]his provision should not apply to these situations . . . if the activity actually is engaged in for profit.

[I]n making the determination of whether an activity is not engaged in for profit, . . . an objective rather that a subjective approach is to be employed. Thus, although a reasonable expectation of profit is not to be required, the facts and circumstances (without regard to the taxpayer's subjective intent) would have to indicate that the taxpayer entered the activity with the objective of making a profit. As previously indicated, a taxpayer who engaged in an activity in which there was a small chance of a large profit, such as a person who invested in a wildcat oil well or an inventor, could qualify under this test even though the expectation of profit might be considered unreasonable.

Id. at 103–04.

The Senate's objections prevailed in the enactment of § 183, and the regulations under the section clearly echo parts of the legislative history. *See* Reg. § 1.183-2(a).

B.   Section 183 Activities

The rules of § 183 apply to an "activity not engaged in for profit." As a preliminary matter, it may be necessary to determine whether a given set of undertakings or transactions constitutes only one, or more than one, activity. In the latter case, income and expenses must be allocated among activities. *See generally* Reg. § 1.183-1(d). Each activity must be tested separately as to whether it is an "activity not engaged in for profit." This critical phrase is central to the statute, and is defined by § 183(c) to mean those activities which do not qualify for deductions under either §§ 162 or 212(1) or (2). In an effort to flesh out this statutory definition, the regulations provide a list of nine relevant factors, drawn from the case law on hobby losses, that "should normally be taken into account" in determining whether an activity *is* engaged in for profit:

(1) The manner in which the taxpayer carries on the activity;

(2) The expertise of the taxpayer or his advisors;

(3) The time and effort expended by the taxpayer in carrying on the activity;

(4) The expectation that assets used in the activity may appreciate in value;

(5) The success of the taxpayer in carrying on other similar or dissimilar activities;

(6) The taxpayer's history of income or losses with respect to the activity;

(7) The amount of occasional profits, if any, which are earned;

(8) The financial status of the taxpayer; and

(9) The elements of personal pleasure or recreation.

Reg. § 1.183-2(b). No one factor or number of factors is determinative, nor are the nine listed factors necessarily the only ones to be considered. Rather, the regulations employ an all-the-facts-and-circumstances test, with "greater weight . . . given to objective facts than to the taxpayer's mere statement of his intent." Reg. § 1.183-2(a). For example, in *Antonides v. Commissioner*, 893 F.2d 656 (4th Cir. 1990), the court determined a yacht chartering venture was an activity not engaged in for profit under § 183. The court noted that based on a financial analysis of the cash flow from the yacht chartering venture, the taxpayer could not have anticipated making a profit on the operation within the foreseeable future, if ever. Nor could the taxpayer reasonably expect to make a profit as a result of the appreciation of the yacht. Although the taxpayers would have liked to have made a profit, the court concluded that, given all of the facts, the taxpayers were not actually motivated by the prospect of profit in acquiring the yacht.

Similarly, in *Nissley v. Commissioner*, T.C. Memo. 2000-178, the Tax Court concluded that the taxpayers were not engaged for profit in operating an Amway distributorship. (Amway is a supplier of household and personal use products. An Amway distributor makes money, in part, by selling the products to customers, but principally by recruiting others as distributors and receiving a bonus based on their sales and the sales of the distributors they in turn recruit.) The Tax Court noted that the distributorship generated consistent and substantial losses; the taxpayers failed to maintain a written business plan, budget, monthly expense report or break-even analysis; they lacked prior Amway-type experience, but had substantial income from other sources; and they derived personal pleasure from the Amway activities, including the opportunity to purchase at a discount Amway products for their personal use. Based on these factors, the court concluded the taxpayers had not engaged in the Amway activity for profit.

By contrast, in *Weller v. Commissioner*, T.C. Memo 2011-224, the court, applying the nine nonexclusive factors of Reg. § 1.183-2(b) noted above, concluded that a former Boeing employee who created a limited liability company providing private glider flight instruction and glider plane rides was engaged in the glider activities for profit. The taxpayer in *Weller* purchased a high-performance glider with inherited money and secured the appropriate licenses and training to satisfy FAA requirements to operate as a glider flight instructor. He conducted the glider activities primarily on weekends from March through November, generally devoting all of his weekends during that period to glider activities. Taxpayer advertised his services through flyers placed in airports and aviation-related businesses as well advertisements placed in a flying publication. The Tax Court downplayed the significance of the fact taxpayer did not maintain thorough books and records for his glider activities beyond his flight logs. According to the court, the taxpayer's failure in this regard did not conclusively establish the lack of profit objective. "The purpose of maintaining books and records is more than to memorialize for tax purposes the existence of the subject transactions; it is to facilitate a means of periodically determining profitability and analyzing expenses such that proper cost saving measures might be implemented in a timely and efficient manner." In this regard, the court noted the taxpayer did review the expenses of his company and made adjustments to reduce expenses. Likewise the court rejected the notion that the taxpayer's enjoyment of flying demonstrated that the taxpayer's glider activity was not engaged in for profit. Citing one of its earlier decisions, the Tax Court stated, "a business will not be turned into a hobby merely because the owner finds it pleasurable; suffering has never been a prerequisite to deductibility." *Jackson v. Commissioner*, 59 T.C. 312, 317 (1972). *See also* Reg. § 1.183-2(b)(9).

It is not unusual for the judicial weighing process associated with § 183 to include a reference to the taxpayer's "predominant purpose" with respect to the activity. In one case, the Fourth Circuit commented:

> We note that the Tax Court [in the opinion below] required of the taxpayers a "predominant purpose and intention" of making a profit. The regulations provide that an activity will not be treated as not engaged in for profit merely because the taxpayer has purposes or motivation other than solely to make a profit, . . . § 1.183-2(b)(9), but that deductions are not allowable under sections 162 or 212 for activities carried on primarily as a sport or hobby, or for recreation . . . § 1.183-2(a). . . . Our cases under section 162 have required only "the purpose of making a profit". . . . We find nothing in section 183 or its legislative history changing this analysis or requiring this purpose to be predominant. . . . Section 183 requires simply that an activity be "engaged in for profit." The Senate report indicates only that under section 183 a taxpayer must have entered or continued an activity with "the objective of making a profit." We recognize, however, that under a related provision, I.R.C. § 166, the Supreme Court has required that a taxpayer have a "dominant business motivation" to avoid the less favorable tax treatment of nonbusiness bad debts, *United States v. Generes*, 405 U.S. 93,103 (1972), and that other courts have required under sections 162 and 183 that a taxpayer have the "primary purpose" of making a profit. Whether or not a taxpayer must have the "primary" or "predominant" purpose of making a profit under sections 162, 183, or 212, we need not and do not decide [in the instant case.]

Faulconer v. Commissioner, 748 F.2d 890, 895–6 n. 10 (4th Cir. 1984).

Does the Supreme Court decision in *Commissioner v. Groetzinger* (the "gambler case"), in Chapter 12, have any bearing on this issue?

Note that § 183(d) creates a rebuttable presumption that the activity was engaged in for profit, with respect to a given year, if the activity was profitable (that is, if gross income exceeded deductions) for three years in the five-year period ending with the year in question. No inference to the contrary arises from a failure to establish the presumption. Reg. § 1.183-1(c)(1). If the presumption is not applicable, then the matter proceeds under the normal rule that the assessment of the Commissioner is presumptively correct and the taxpayer carries the burden of proving the assessment incorrect.

Also note that § 280A of the Code provides special rules for deductions relating to a "dwelling unit used by the taxpayer as a residence." We postpone the study of § 280A to the next chapter, where we deal with "dual-use" property generally. However, it is worth pointing out here that, in order to avoid potential overlap problems, § 183 does not apply to any dwelling unit for any year (or portion thereof) to which § 280A applies, although such year nevertheless counts for purposes of the § 183(d) presumption. § 280A(f)(3).

Section 183 applies to individuals, "S corporations" (electing small business corporations; see § 1361), estates and trusts. Reg. § 1.183-1(a). Case law has extended § 183 to partnership activities as well. *See, e.g., Brannen v. Commissioner*, 78 T.C. 471 (1982), *aff'd*, 722 F.2d 695 (11th Cir. 1984). With respect to corporations other than S corporations, the regulations provide that no inference is to be drawn from § 183 that any corporate activity is or is not a business or engaged in for profit. Reg. § 1.183-1(a).

C. Deductions Allowable Under Section 183

Although sometimes described as a disallowance provision, § 183 is actually a deduction-granting provision rather than a disallowance provision. If the activity in question constitutes a trade or business, or one engaged in for the production or collection of income or for the management, conservation or maintenance of property held for the production of income, deductions are allowable under §§ 162 or 212(1) or (2); in that case, § 183 is simply not applicable. If, however, the taxpayer is engaged in an activity in which deductions are not allowed under §§ 162 or 212, then § 183 allows deductions as set forth in § 183(b).

Section 183(b) establishes three categories of permitted deductions. Category 1 deductions are those, such as home mortgage interest under § 163(h)(3) and state and local property taxes under § 164, which are allowed to a taxpayer whether or not an activity is engaged in for profit. They are allowed, pursuant to § 183(b)(1), without regard to the income of the activity. Deductions that are attributable to the activity but do not come within this first category are allowed only to the extent the gross income from the activity exceeds the total Category 1 deductions. § 183(b)(2). For example, assume that an activity not engaged in for profit generates gross income of $1000, and has Category 1 deductions of $1,100. Although § 183(b)(1) allows all $1,100 to be deducted, no other deductions attributable to the activity, outside Category 1, could be taken. If, however, Category 1 deductions were only $700, then up to $300 in additional deductions would be allowable under § 183(b)(2). Section 183 thus adopts as a basic policy that deductions attributable to a not-engaged-in-for-profit activity should always be allowable at least to the extent of the income from the activity. Does § 183, in this regard, merely codify a pre-existing general tax principle? Or would deductions outside Category 1 always be denied but for § 183?

The § 183 regulations divide into two separate, additional categories those deductions that do not fall within Category 1. Reg. § 1.183-1(b)(1)(ii), (iii). Category 2 deductions are those that do not result in a basis adjustment and that would otherwise be allowed if the activity were engaged in for profit; garden-variety §§ 162 or 212 expenses would fit in Category 2. Category 3 deductions are those, such as depreciation, that result in basis adjustments and that would be allowed if the activity were engaged in for profit. Category 2 deductions must be taken prior to Category 3 deductions. Category 3 deductions are thus allowed only to the extent the gross income from the activity exceeds the combined total of Category 1 and Category 2 deductions. For example, assume an activity not engaged in for profit generates $1,000 of gross income, and has expenses attributable to the activity of $500 for local property taxes, $400 for current wages paid, and $300 for depreciation. Under § 183(b) and the regulations, deductions would be allowed for the full amount of the property taxes (as a Category 1 item), the full amount of the wages (a Category 2 item, allowed in full because Category 1 and 2 items do not exceed gross income from the activity), and for $100 of depreciation (a Category 3 item, limited to $100 so as not to exceed the gross income ceiling). Note that in the event the activity used more than one depreciable asset, the regulations provide a formula for allocating the limited basis adjustment among multiple depreciable assets. Reg. § 1.183-1(b)(2). Are the deductions allowable under § 183 subject to the § 67 2% floor?

DREICER v. COMMISSIONER
United States Tax Court
78 T.C. 642 (1982)

[The factual background to this case was summarized as follows by the Court of Appeals for the District of Columbia, when it reversed and remanded the first Tax Court decision on this matter:

"Dreicer, a citizen of the United States, maintains his residence in the Canary Islands, Spain, and engages heavily in global travel. He derives a substantial income as beneficiary of a family trust, and in the early 1950s, Dreicer began to focus his professional attention on the fields of tourism and dining. In 1955, he published *The Diner's Companion*, a compilation of his opinions on dining and on various restaurants throughout the world, but the book was a commercial failure. Undaunted, Dreicer conceived the idea of some day writing another book, this one to enshrine his reminiscence on a life dedicated to epicurism and travel. In preparation for this sybaritic swan song, he spent the next twenty years traveling about the world, staying in some of the finest hotels and dining in some of the best restaurants. The material he gathered was also to be utilized in lectures before travel organizations and public appearances on radio and television. By the mid-1970s, Dreicer had completed a rough draft of the second book — parts of which originally had appeared in *The Diner's Companion* — and titled it *My 27 Year Search for the Perfect Steak — Still Looking*. Two publishing houses to which he submitted the manuscript, however, returned it, and seemingly he abandoned all hope of publishing.

"When Dreicer filed his federal income tax returns for 1972 and 1973, he claimed deductible losses of $21,795.76 and $28,022.05, respectively, for travel and other related business expenses. The Commissioner of Internal Revenue thereafter issued a notice of deficiency, disallowing the deductions on the ground that the losses arose from activities not pursued for profit, and the Tax Court agreed. The court disputed Dreicer's characterization of his professional self as a multi-media personality, finding instead that he was a writer-lecturer on tourism and dining. Having so defined his activity for Section 183 analysis, the court concluded that he had not entertained a bona fide expectation of profit for writing and lecturing, and on that account denied the deductions." 665 F.2d 1292, 1294–5 (D.C. Cir. 1981.)

The Circuit Court also noted that the claimed expenses had exceeded, on the average, $25,000 per year since 1956. The Tax Court opinion on remand follows.]

OPINION

SIMPSON, JUDGE:

In *Dreicer v. Commissioner*, T.C. Memo, 1979-395, we sustained the Commissioner's determination that, based on all of the facts and circumstances of that case, Mr. Dreicer's activities as a writer and lecturer were not engaged in for profit within the meaning of section 183, Internal Revenue Code of 1954. Mr. Dreicer appealed such decision to the Court of Appeals for the District of Columbia Circuit. That court, although it sustained our factual findings, reversed such decision on the ground that we had applied an erroneous legal standard in determining whether Mr. Dreicer's activities were engaged in for profit and remanded the case to us to reconsider our decision in light of what it determined was the correct legal standard under section 183. *Dreicer v. Commissioner*, 665 F.2d 1292 (D.C. Cir. 1981).

In our prior opinion, we stated that the standard for determining whether an individual is carrying on a trade or business so that his expenses are deductible under section 162 is:

> [w]hether the individual's primary purpose and intention in engaging in the activity is to make a profit. . . . The taxpayer's expectation of profit need not be a reasonable one; it is sufficient if the taxpayer has a bona fide expectation of realizing a profit, regardless of the reasonableness of such expectation. . . . The issue of whether a taxpayer engages in an activity with the requisite intention of making a profit is one of fact to be resolved on the basis of all the surrounding facts and circumstances of the case . . . and the burden of proving the requisite intention is on the petitioner. . . .

We then proceeded to apply such standard to the facts and circumstances of that case, using the relevant factors outlined in section 1.183-2(b), Income Tax Regs. Based on such analysis, we concluded that Mr. Dreicer's activities were not engaged in for profit within the meaning of section 183 "since he did not have a bona fide expectation of profit."

On appeal, Mr. Dreicer argued that we had applied an incorrect legal standard, in that we predicated our decision on his profit expectation rather than his profit objective. 665 F.2d at 1297. The Court of Appeals examined the legislative history of section 183 and determined that the proper standard was whether the taxpayer engaged in the activity with the objective of making a profit, not whether he had a reasonable expectation of making a profit. 665 F.2d at 1298–1299. The proper standard was expressed by that court as "when profit is actually and honestly his objective though the prospect of achieving it may seem dim." 665 F.2d at 1294. The Court of Appeals found that rather than focusing our analysis on whether Mr. Dreicer had an objective of making a profit, we focused on whether he had "a bona fide expectation of profit." The court apparently feared that we were equating a bona fide expectation of profit with a reasonable expectation of profit. 665 F.2d at 1299. Thus, it held that we had applied an erroneous legal standard in determining whether Mr. Dreicer's activities were engaged in for profit.

The purpose of the standard adopted by the Court of Appeals is to allow deductions where the evidence indicates that the activity is actually engaged in for profit even though it might be argued that there is not a reasonable expectation of profit. See S. Rep. 91-552 (1969), 1969-3 C.B. 423, 489–490. We are in total agreement with the Court of Appeals that this is the proper legal standard under section 183. However, a taxpayer's declaration of his motive to make a profit is not controlling. His motive is the ultimate question; yet, it must be determined by a careful analysis of all the surrounding objective facts, and greater weight is given to such facts than to his mere statement of intent. Sec. 1.183-2(a) and (b), Income Tax Regs. Thus, although a reasonable expectation of profit is not required, the facts and circumstances must indicate that the taxpayer entered into the activity, or continued the activity, with the actual and honest objective of making a profit. 665 F.2d at 1294. See sec. 1.183-2(a), Income Tax Regs.

Although the courts sometimes use different language to describe the test, the courts have universally sought to ascertain the taxpayer's true intent. For example, in *Blake v. Commissioner*, T.C. Memo. 1981-579, we used the terms "bona fide expectation of realizing a profit," "profit motive or objective," "view toward realization of a profit" and "profit oriented venture" to refer to the same thought, namely, an objective of making a profit. It was in this sense that we used the term "bona fide expectation of profit" in our prior opinion, and we intended that such language have the same meaning as an actual and honest profit objective. Nevertheless, in view of the difficulties generated by our use of such language, which resulted in the remand by the Court of Appeals, we have undertaken to re-examine the record with a view to determining whether the required actual and honest profit objective was present in this case.

Mr. Dreicer would have us find that he was like the wildcat driller or the inventor (see sec. 1.183-2(c), Exs. 5 and 6, Income Tax Regs.), continuing his endeavors in the face of adverse results in the hope of one day reaping a large profit. However, such statement of intent is not supported by the objective facts of this case. For many years, he sustained large losses; there was no realistic possibility that he could ever earn sufficient income from his activity to offset such losses (sec. 1.183-2(b)(6) and (7), Income Tax Regs.); he was able to continue to bear such losses only because of his large resources (sec. 1.183-2(b)(8), Income Tax Regs.); a review of the entire record fails to convince us that Mr. Dreicer conducted his activities in a businesslike manner calculated to earn a profit (sec. 1.183-2(b)(1), (2), (5), (6), Income Tax Regs.); rather, there is a strong indication that he enjoyed his life of travel. Sec. 1.183-2(b)(8) and (9), Income Tax Regs. In conclusion, we find and hold that Mr. Dreicer failed to meet his burden of proving that in carrying on his activity as a writer and lecturer, he had an actual and honest objective of making a profit.

Our prior decision will be re-entered.

REMUZZI v. COMMISSIONER
United States Tax Court
T.C. Memo. 1988-8

KORNER, JUDGE:

Findings of Fact

Petitioner Robert Remuzzi ("Dr. Remuzzi") is an orthopedic surgeon. His wife Rachael Remuzzi ("Mrs. Remuzzi") is a housewife. They and their five children live in Leesburg, Virginia, on a 74 acre farm that Mrs. Remuzzi named Fairleigh Farm.

Dr. Remuzzi was born in New York City and attended college and medical school at Georgetown University in Washington, D.C. Mrs. Remuzzi was raised on a farm in Australia. Dr. and Mrs. Remuzzi were married in the early 1970s and moved to Leesburg. Petitioners lived with their children in a home located in a housing development on a half acre lot. They quickly became interested in moving out of the development and onto a farm.

In early 1976, Dr. Remuzzi began to treat Llewellyn Payne ("Payne"), who was then a tenant on a farm near Middleburg, Virginia. Dr. Remuzzi told Payne of his desire to buy a farm and discussed the possibility of Payne's being a tenant on the farm. Dr. Remuzzi loaned Payne $15,000 and Payne agreed to become a tenant on Dr. Remuzzi's farm if Remuzzi purchased a suitable property.

Dr. Remuzzi found a suitable property and purchased it in May of 1978. The property consisted of about 35 acres of pasture and 40 acres of woods. A main house, tenant house, and various farm buildings were situated on five acres. The property was in complete disrepair, and had not been operated as a farm for about ten years. Payne agreed to move to the property, repair it, and maintain it, in return for the right to live in the tenant house rent free and the right to graze his small herd of cattle on the property. Payne was to repay his loan from Dr. Remuzzi by giving Dr. Remuzzi half of the calves born to the herd until the fair market value of the calves equaled the amount of the loan. Thereafter Payne was to split his profits from raising cattle with Dr. Remuzzi.

Petitioners moved to the property in August of 1978. Payne and his family moved into the tenant house located on the property in November of 1978. Payne brought to the property his cattle herd, which numbered thirty head, and his farm equipment, which consisted of a tractor, a bushhog, and a small combine. During the winter of 1978–79, Payne repaired fences and bushhogged pasture land. At the end of the summer of 1979, Payne removed his herd from the property because there was not enough fenced land with pasturage on the property to support the herd. Payne brought the herd back to the property in the fall of 1979 after additional fences were repaired.

Payne's behavior and work habits began deteriorating in the winter of 1979–80, and continued to deteriorate during the spring and summer of 1980. As his behavior deteriorated, he performed less and less farm work.

As Payne was no longer living up to his agreement to maintain the property, Dr. Remuzzi required him to begin paying rent on the tenant house and, on July 1, 1980, had him sign a note for the $15,000 loan. By the fall of 1980, Payne became mentally unable to function and the local sheriff began repossessing his property, including his cattle. In the spring of 1981 Payne's wife had him committed. After Payne was committed, Dr. Remuzzi obtained a default judgment against him for the $13,800 balance of the loan. Dr. Remuzzi was unable to satisfy the judgment.

As Payne began neglecting his duties, petitioners were forced to make other arrangements to have farm work done. Petitioners' oldest son, who was ten at the time, assumed responsibility for feeding the few cattle that petitioners owned. Petitioners hired college students to perform other necessary maintenance work.

Dr. Remuzzi separated his expenses for the property from his family's general living expenses by maintaining a separate checking account for the property and by saving bills that related to it. He kept no other records of the property's finances, however. Petitioners reported their revenues and expenses from the property as farm income and expenses on their joint Federal income tax returns for 1978, 1979, 1980, 1981, and 1982. The results reported were as follows:

| | | Expenses | | | Net Income |
Year	Receipts	Interest	Taxes	Other	(Loss)
1978	$1,200.00	$8,192.20	$—	$8,713.18	($15,705.38)
1979	260.00	14,837.00	705.00	22,597.00	(38,239.00)
1980	1,200.00	15,363.00	508.00	20,416.00	(35,087.00)
1981	2,715.00	15,095.00	156.00	34,275.00	(46,811.00)
1982	360.00	11,216.15	2,212.43	10,196.16	(23,264.14)
Totals	$5,735.60	$64,703.35	$3,581.43	$96,557.34	($159,106.52)

Year	Rent from Tenant House	Timber	Fire Wood	Cattle	Hay & Other	Total
1978	$1,200.00	$—	$—	$—	$—	$1,200.00
1979	—	260.00	—	—	—	260.00
1980	1,200.00	—	—	—	—	1,200.00
1981	1,800.00	—	50.00	865.00	—	2,715.00
1982	—	—	—	—	360.60	360.60
Totals	$4,200.00	$260.00	50.00	$865.00	360.60	$5,735.60

The receipts reported by petitioners from the property consist of the following items:

The $865.00 of revenue from cattle sales resulted from the sales of two sides of beef, one of which was purchased by petitioners themselves, and one of which was purchased by their friends.

The $34,275 of "other expenses" for 1981 includes petitioners' $13,800 bad debt from Payne.

Dr. Remuzzi reported the following earnings from his medical practice for the years 1978 through 1982:

Year	Earnings
1978	$124,368.49
1979	138,889.00
1980	160,156.00
1981	190,661.00
1982	218,272.29

Petitioners enjoy living on their property. They take walks through the woods; their son has a pony.

Respondent audited petitioners' returns for the years at issue and determined that their farm losses were incurred in an activity not entered into for profit. He accordingly disallowed the following claimed losses relating to petitioners' farm activity:

		1980	1981
Schedule F Loss		$35,087	$46,811
Less:	Interest	(14,163)	(12,380)
	Real Estate Taxes	(508)	(156)
Net Amount Disallowed		$20,416	$34,275

OPINION

Farm

The first issue for decision is whether petitioners operated Fairleigh Farm for profit. If Fairleigh Farm was not engaged in for profit, expenses related to its operation are deductible only as allowed by section 183. Whether Fairleigh Farm was engaged in for profit turns on whether petitioners had a bona fide objective of making a profit when entering into and continuing the activity. Petitioners' objective is a question of fact to be determined from all the facts and circumstances. The burden of proof is on petitioners.[1] Greater weight is given to the objective facts than

---

[1] Sec. 183(d) provides that if gross income exceeds deductions attributable to an activity for two (now three) or more of the taxable years in the five consecutive years ending with the taxable year at issue, there is a presumption that the activity was engaged in for profit. As petitioners had not yet operated Fairleigh Farm for five years at the close of the years at issue, sec. 183(e) allows them to elect to have the determination of whether the presumption applies be made at the close of the fourth taxable year following the taxable year in which they first engaged in the activity. Sec. 183(e)(3) requires the election under sec. 183(e) to be made at such time as the Secretary prescribes. Sec. 12.9(c)(2), Temp. Income Tax Regs., 39 Fed. Reg. 9947 (March 15, 1974), requires the election to be made no later than sixty days after the taxpayer receives written notice proposing to disallow deductions attributable to an activity not engaged in for profit under sec. 183.

Although the record does not establish whether petitioners timely made a sec. 183(e) election, it does

to statements of intent. . . .

The regulations under section 183 list nine factors that should normally be taken into account in determining whether an activity is engaged in for profit: (1) The manner in which the taxpayer carries on the activity; (2) the expertise of the taxpayer or his advisors; (3) The time and effort expended by the taxpayer in carrying on the activity; (4) the expectation that the assets used in the activity may appreciate in value; (5) the success of the taxpayer in carrying on other similar or dissimilar activities; (6) the taxpayer's history of income or losses with respect to the activity; (7) the amount of occasional profits, if any, that are earned; (8) the financial status of the taxpayer; and (9) the elements of personal pleasure or recreation involved in the activity. See Sec. 1.183-2(b). . . . These factors are not exclusive and are to be applied according to the unique facts of each case. Sec. 1.183-2(b), Income Tax Regs. Accordingly, no one factor, nor a majority of the nine factors, need be considered determinative.

In determining whether an activity is engaged in for profit, we are guided also by the Congressional purpose in enacting section 183:

The legislative history surrounding section 183 indicates that one of the prime motivating factors behind its passage was Congress' desire to create an objective standard to determine whether a taxpayer was carrying on a business for the purpose of realizing a profit or was instead merely attempting to create and utilize losses to offset other income. [Citation omitted; *Jasionowski v. Commissioner*, 66 T.C. 312, 321 (1976)]. Congressional concern stemmed from a recognition that, "Wealthy individuals have invested in certain aspects of farm operations solely to obtain 'tax losses' — largely bookkeeping losses — for use to reduce their tax on other income. . . . One of the remarkable aspects of the problem is pointed up by the fact that persons with large non-farm income have a remarkable propensity to lose money in the farm business." S. Rept. 91-552 (1969), 1969-3 C.B. 423, 635 (Individual Views of Senator Albert Gore). With this background in mind we turn to the facts before us.

A review of the entire record in this case convinces us that petitioners have not proven that Fairleigh Farm was an activity engaged in for profit. The record instead indicates that petitioners, who had substantial nonfarm income in each of the years at issue, simply preferred to live on a farm and attempted to deduct their personal expenses of maintaining and improving their domicile as business expenses.

Financial Status of Petitioners

Section 1.183-2(b)(8), Income Tax Regs., provides, in relevant part, that "substantial income from sources other than the activity (particularly if the losses from the activity generate substantial tax benefits) may indicate that the activity is not engaged in for profit. . . . " This factor indicates that petitioners did not operate

---

establish that they would not be entitled to the presumption provided by sec. 183(d) even if they had made such an election. Fairleigh Farm was unprofitable in each of its first five years of operation, 1978 through 1982. This case is therefore distinguishable from *Faulconer v. Commissioner*, 748 F.2d 890 (4th Cir. 1984), rev'g T.C. Memo. 1983-165, in which a taxpayer had placed the burden of proof on respondent under sec. 183(d) by proving that an activity was profitable for two out of five consecutive years.

Fairleigh Farm for profit. They had substantial income from Dr. Remuzzi's medical practice. The losses from Fairleigh Farm offset that income and substantially reduced their tax liability.

Manner in which Petitioners Carried on Fairleigh Farm

Section 1.183-2(b)(1), Income Tax Regs., provides that the manner in which taxpayers carry on an activity is normally a factor that should be taken into account in determining whether an activity is engaged in for profit. The manner in which petitioners carried on Fairleigh Farm indicates that it was not engaged in for profit. To begin with, there is no evidence that petitioners performed any analysis before purchasing the property of the expenses that would be necessary to restore the property to operating condition. Dr. Remuzzi testified that the property had not been operated as a farm for ten years and was in a state of utter disrepair. Had he truly been approaching the purchase of the property with a view toward earning a profit by operating it as a farm, it is inconceivable to us that he would not have at least estimated the expenses of repairing the property.

Once they purchased the farm, there is no evidence that petitioners made any efforts to monitor its profitability or significantly reduce its expenses, which dwarfed its income during the years at issue. We believe they would have done so if they were sincerely interested in operating it profitably. Although Dr. Remuzzi testified that he planned to increase the size of his cattle herd, there is no evidence that he estimated the revenues and expenses that the property could expect to achieve with more cattle to determine whether it could then be operated profitably. We view the financial records petitioners did maintain for the property as the minimum necessary to support their deductions for tax purposes. In short, the manner in which the Remuzzis became involved in Fairleigh Farm and the manner in which it was operated evidence a disregard for its profitability.

History of Losses

Considering the manner in which petitioners engaged in Fairleigh Farm, it is not surprising that they suffered large and consistent losses. The revenues that petitioners received from the property were regularly dwarfed by the expenses they incurred. Sections 1.183-2(b)(6) and (7), Income Tax Regs., provide that the amount of losses suffered by an activity are factors that should normally be taken into account in determining whether an activity is engaged in for profit. Petitioners' large and consistent losses indicate that Fairleigh Farm was not engaged in for profit.[2]

Petitioners blame their losses on Payne's disability, and argue that the disability was an unforeseen circumstance that was beyond their control. See sec. 1.183-2(b)(6), Income Tax Regs. Even assuming, *arguendo*, that their losses were due to Payne's disability, which is doubtful considering the fact that the losses began well

---

[2] Cattle farming is not a highly speculative activity such as horse racing in which taxpayers have an opportunity to earn substantial profits in one year to offset losses suffered in others. *Cf. Faulconer v. Commissioner, supra.*

before the disability manifested itself and continued after he left, we do not consider the loss of an employee to be the type of unforeseen or fortuitous circumstance contemplated by the regulations as beyond the control of a taxpayer. The loss of an employee, whether through resignation, dismissal, or incapacitation, is a common event in the life of a business and is an occurrence that profit oriented businessmen take into account before entering businesses.

Petitioners' Business Experience

Section 1.183-2(b)(2), Income Tax Regs., provides that the expertise of the taxpayer or his advisors is a factor that should normally be considered in determining whether an activity is engaged in for profit. Neither of petitioners had ever before operated a farm. Dr. Remuzzi had no farming background or expertise. Although Dr. Remuzzi testified that his wife had grown up on a farm and had once raised a cow when she was a member of the Australian equivalent of the 4-H Club, there is no evidence that she was so involved in the activities of the farm that she developed an expertise in cattle raising. Dr. Remuzzi's testimony that she was only occasionally involved in the operation of petitioners' farm suggests that she in fact had no special expertise. Although petitioners' farm tenant Payne had served as a tenant on another farm and owned a small herd of cattle, there is no evidence that he had the experience and expertise required to operate petitioners' farm profitably. In sum, the experience of petitioners and Payne does not support their argument that they engaged in Fairleigh Farm for profit.

Time and Effort Expended by Petitioners

Section 1.183-2(b)(3), Income Tax Regs., states that the time and effort expended by taxpayers in carrying on an activity is normally a factor to be considered in determining whether the activity is engaged in for profit. This factor does not support petitioners' argument that Fairleigh Farm was operated for profit. Dr. Remuzzi was an active surgeon during the years at issue and had little time to devote to farm operations. There is no evidence that Mrs. Remuzzi or the Remuzzis' young children devoted significant time and effort to farm work. Although section 1.183-2(b)(3), Income Tax Regs., provides that "the fact that the taxpayer devotes a limited amount of time to an activity does not necessarily indicate a lack of profit motive where the taxpayer employs competent and qualified persons to carry on such activity," the evidence fails to establish that petitioners did so. Petitioners concededly employed Payne to perform day to day farm work but, as was discussed *supra*, there is no evidence that, even before he was disabled by Alzheimer's disease, he was qualified to operate Fairleigh Farm profitably. After Payne became disabled in 1980, petitioners employed only college students to perform maintenance work. There is no evidence that the students were competent and qualified to operate the farm profitably.

Expectation that Assets Used In Activity May Appreciate In Value

Section 1.183-2(b)(4), Income Tax Regs., provide that a taxpayer may intend to realize profit from the appreciation of the value of assets used in an activity. We accord this factor little weight in our analysis. Although petitioner did testify that Fairleigh Farm had appreciated in value, there was no evidence presented that petitioners purchased the farm expecting to profit from appreciation in its value. The evidence instead suggests that petitioners purchased Fairleigh Farm for personal reasons. *Cf. Roberts v. Commissioner*, T.C. Memo. 1987-182.

Elements of Personal Pleasure or Recreation

Section 1.183-2(b)(9), Income Tax Regs., provides in relevant part, that "The presence of personal motives in [the] carrying on of an activity may indicate that the activity is not engaged in for profit, especially where there are recreational or personal elements involved." This factor indicates that petitioners did not engage in Fairleigh Farm for profit and explains why petitioners operated the property as they did. The evidence indicates that petitioners moved to Fairleigh Farm for personal reasons. Dr. Remuzzi's testimony established that he had decided to purchase a farm before he met Payne. It was only after he met Payne, however, that he decided to raise cattle on the farm. The fact that Dr. Remuzzi had decided to purchase a farm before he decided what farm activity to engage in suggests that farming was not the reason he decided to move to a farm. Other aspects of Dr. Remuzzi's testimony suggest that petitioners moved to the farm for personal reasons. He testified that his wife had been raised on a farm and it is reasonable to presume that petitioners' move to a farm was prompted by her desire to raise the family in a similar environment. He also admitted that his family enjoyed taking walks through the woods and that his son owned a pony.

Having applied the nine factors listed under section 183 to the facts of this case, we conclude that they fail to support petitioners' position that they operated Fairleigh Farm for profit. We accordingly hold that petitioners have failed to prove that Fairleigh Farm was an activity engaged in for profit.

Bad Debt

Having concluded that petitioners have failed to prove that Fairleigh Farm was an activity engaged in for profit, we must next decide whether their $13,800 bad debt from Payne was a business bad debt as they argue or whether it was instead a nonbusiness bad debt as respondent determined. Petitioners have the burden of proving that the debt was a business bad debt as respondent determined in his notice of deficiency that it was a nonbusiness bad debt. . . .

A nonbusiness bad debt is defined in section 166(d)(2) as:

. . . a debt other than—

(A) a debt created or acquired (as the case may be) in connection with a trade or business of the taxpayer; or

(B) a debt the loss from the worthlessness of which is incurred in the taxpayer's trade or business.

To establish that their loss qualifies as a business bad debt, petitioners must prove that the loan to Payne was proximately related to a trade or business engaged in by them. . . . Petitioners argue that their bad debt was a business bad debt because it resulted from a loan made in connection with their operation of Fairleigh Farm. We disagree.

Petitioners' argument assumes that Fairleigh Farm was a trade or business. To qualify as a trade or business, a taxpayer's primary purpose for engaging in the activity must be for income or profit. *Commissioner v. Groetzinger*, 480 U.S. 23, 107 S. Ct. 980 (1987). We have already held that petitioners have failed to prove that Fairleigh Farm was an activity engaged in for profit. We accordingly hold that they have failed to prove that the bad debt that resulted from their loan to Payne was a business bad debt.

To reflect the foregoing,

Decision will be entered for respondent.

Chapter 21

HOME OFFICES, VACATION HOMES, AND OTHER DUAL USE PROPERTY

I. PROBLEMS

1. David is a math teacher at Trinity High School, a privately owned and operated school. In addition to teaching several math classes as an employee of Trinity, David runs his own math tutoring business, providing private math instruction after normal school hours to Trinity students and to students from other high schools. Trinity permits David to use one of its classrooms for all his tutoring sessions and for some administrative work in connection with the tutoring. However, David conducts the majority of his administrative work and all his preparation work for the tutoring at his home office, which he uses exclusively for tutoring-related activities. He never meets with students at his home office. On average, David spends 24 hours a week on his private tutoring business, 8 hours at Trinity and 16 hours at his home office.

   (a) May he deduct the expenses of his home office?

   (b) If so, may he deduct transportation costs between his home and Trinity?

   (c) Would the answer to question (a) change if David paid one of the secretaries at Trinity to handle all the administrative work for the tutoring business, and David spent all 16 hours per week at the home office on preparation for the tutoring?

   (d) Would the answer to question (a) change if David also used the home office for 10 hours per week for class-preparation connected to his math teaching responsibilities at Trinity, in addition to the 16 hours per week on tutoring-connected activities?

   (e) Would the answer to question (a) change if David were an employee of Trinity for purposes of both the tutoring activities and the several math classes he teaches?

2. Cathy, an accountant for XYZ Corporation, works 40 hours a week and is paid a salary of $60,000 per year. To supplement her income, Cathy maintains a part-time accounting practice in her home. She uses one of the rooms in her home as her office and meets clients there. The room represents approximately 15% of the living space in Cathy's home. The room is furnished with a desk, a bookcase, a filing cabinet, a telephone and telephone answering machine, computer, a couch and a couple of chairs. Cathy has a separate telephone line for her accounting business and for

Internet use. During the current year, Cathy had gross income of $10,000 from her private accounting practice. She had the following expenses: supplies — $600; advertising — $1,500; office telephone service, including Internet connection — $900. With respect to her home, Cathy incurred the following expenses: real estate taxes — $6,000; interest on the mortgage on her home — $24,000; fire and casualty insurance premiums — $4,000; maintenance of the yard — $600; and total utility charges (other than telephone) — $3,000. Assume the adjusted basis of Cathy's home is $400,000 and that, if the home were depreciable, the depreciation deduction for the entire home for the current year would have been $16,000. Assuming her home office is Cathy's principal place of business for her private accounting practice, how much of these expenses associated with her home may Cathy deduct? What tax consequences would any current depreciation deductions have in the event Cathy subsequently sold her home at a gain?

3. Cathy owns a lakeside cabin. During the current year, she spent 20 days at the cabin and rented the cabin at $225 per day (fair rental value) for 100 days. Cathy incurred the following expenses during the year with respect to the cabin:

Real estate taxes	$1,500
Maintenance expenses	$750
Realtor's fee for managing the property	$2,250
Utilities	$750
Fire Insurance	$750

Annual depreciation on the cabin (computed pursuant to § 168) would amount to $1,500 for the current year. How much, if any, of the above expenses may Cathy deduct for the current year?

4. In January of Year 1 Cathy purchased a laptop computer for $2,000 for use in her private accounting practice. Because she prefers it to the computer XYZ provides, she often brings the computer with her to use in her office at XYZ. Cathy, a calendar year taxpayer, estimates that in Year 1 25% of the computer's use was related to her work at XYZ and the balance was related to her work in her private accounting practice.

(a) Disregarding any application of § 168(k), explain how Cathy will compute depreciation deductions on the computer for Year 1. May Cathy elect to expense part or all of the computer using § 179? Will the § 168 (or § 179) deductions claimed by Cathy impact Cathy's home office deductions in Problem 2? Explain.

(b) What result if in Year 2 Cathy discontinues using the computer in conjunction with her work at XYZ, uses the computer 40% of the time in her private accounting practice, and uses it 60% of the time for personal purposes?

Assignment for Chapter 21:

Complete the problems.

Read: Internal Revenue Code: §§ 168(k)(1), (2)(A), (D), and (F)(i); 280A(a), (b), (c)(1)–(c)(3), (c)(5), (d)(1), (d)(2), (e), (f)(1), (f)(3), (f)(4), (g); 280F(a), (b), (d)(1), (d)(2), (d)(4), (d)(5), (d)(6)(A) and (B). Review § 121(d)(6); Skim § 280F(d)(7).
Proposed Treasury Regulations: §§ 1.280A-2(a)–(d), (g), (h), (i); 1.280A-3(a)–(d).

Materials: Overview
                  Popov v. Commissioner

II.   VOCABULARY

home office
vacation home
listed property
recapture

III.   OBJECTIVES

1. To explain generally the congressional intent underlying §§ 280A and 280F.

2. To recall that § 280A limits home office and vacation home deductions.

3. To recall that § 280F limits deductions for passenger automobiles and other listed property.

4. To explain the relationship between §§ 280A and 183.

5. To compute the deductions which a taxpayer may claim with respect to a home office.

6. To compute the depreciation deductions a taxpayer may claim with respect to a passenger automobile.

7. To compute the depreciation deductions a taxpayer may claim with respect to a home computer or other listed property.

IV. OVERVIEW

We are told America's favorite sport is baseball. After studying the last few chapters, however, you may begin to suspect that, at least for many taxpayers, baseball has been superseded by a sport which almost anyone, at any age and regardless of physical condition, may play — the conversion of nondeductible personal expenses into deductible business or investment expenses. The rules of the game, however, are not as clear as those used in baseball, and the umpires — Congress, the courts and the Commissioner — are regularly forced to make some close calls.

The home office, the vacation home, the home computer and the business car all share in common the possibility of being used for both personal and business purposes. Separating the business or investment element from the personal element is challenging. In the context of mixed-use property, the umpires have developed different rules to guide their decision-making.

A. Home Office Deductions

Congress in 1976 added § 280A to provide objective criteria by which deductions for home offices (and vacation homes) could be evaluated. Section 280A(a) generally disallows deductions with respect to dwelling units used by the taxpayer during the taxable year as a residence.

Section 280A is best understood by considering the state of the law prior to 1976, as reflected in the story of Stephen Bodzin, an attorney-adviser in the Office of the Chief Counsel of the Internal Revenue Service. *See Bodzin v. Commissioner*, 60 T.C. 820 (1973). Bodzin's duties included working on public and private tax rulings as well as internal opinions addressing a variety of tax problems. The normal working hours for his job were 9:00 a.m. to 5:30 p.m. Bodzin, however, was a conscientious professional and often brought work home with him to the rented apartment in which he lived with his wife and child. Bodzin's apartment included a study he used as his home office. The study, an 8' by 12' room, contained bookshelves with not only an assortment of tax publications but also the personal libraries of both Bodzin and his wife. The room was furnished with a desk, chair, cabinets and lamps. Bodzin used the room to work on matters assigned him, read about current tax developments, work on the first draft of tax memoranda, prepare for conferences associated with his work, pay bills, reconcile his monthly bank statement, and work on his stamp collection. While Bodzin was provided an office by the Government, he found that, given the distance between his apartment and place of work and his desire to spend time with his family, it was more convenient for him to work at home in the evenings and on weekends rather than return to his office.

Bodzin paid $2,100 to rent the apartment in 1967. He claimed that $100 of that amount was attributable to the use of his study as a home office and deducted it as a business expense under § 162. The Commissioner disallowed the deduction; Bodzin petitioned the Tax Court for a redetermination of his tax. While $100 is not a significant amount, the Commissioner obviously regarded the matter, as did Judge Quealy, one of three dissenting Tax Court judges in the ensuing case,

Bodzin v. Commissioner, as "the nose of the camel." 60 T.C. at 828. Judge Quealy summarized the Commissioner's view of the matter when he noted: "It is common practice for lawyers, doctors, engineers, and other professionals who have any interest in attaining excellence in their profession, to read up on technical publications and other informative materials outside of their normal working hours. Such a practice hardly justifies claiming some part of the cost of the residence as a trade or business expense within the meaning of Section 162." *Id.*

The Commissioner's arguments were two: (a) an employee could not claim a home office deduction unless the home office were a condition of employment enabling the employee to perform his employment duties; and (b) "where the work was done at home only as a matter of convenience in spite of adequate office facilities, the deduction is properly disallowed." *Id.* at 825.

The Tax Court majority rejected these standards, holding "the applicable test for judging the deductibility of home office expenses is whether, like any other business expense, the maintenance of an office in the home is appropriate and helpful under all the circumstances." *Id.* The existence of employer-provided office space was not determinative of whether the home office was "appropriate and helpful." Applying the standard, the Tax Court majority concluded the § 162 deduction was appropriate, noting: "It makes no difference that the petitioner was not required to maintain a home office, that he wanted merely to do a good job, and that he liked his work. The expenses were 'necessary' because they were appropriate and helpful in the conduct of his business. They enabled him to keep a facility in his home wherein he could, and did, work. . . . They were 'ordinary,' and not capital, in nature." *Id.* at 826.

In his dissent, Judge Scott noted:

> Under the holding of the majority opinion, there would certainly be no professional person, and very few, if any, business people, who would not be entitled to deduct as a business expense some portion of the cost of rental of a home or the maintenance of a house since the great majority of such persons do professional reading and written work for themselves or their employers in their homes. In fact, this is probably true of the work they do unless their work is purely mechanical in nature. In my view it was never the intent of section 162 to change the personal expenditure of a taxpayer for a home for himself and his family into a business merely because the taxpayer is sufficiently interested in the work in which he engages to do some work in his home.

Id. at 827.

Echoing the same thoughts was Judge Featherston, who in his dissent stressed that the issue is whether the rental expenses were incurred in carrying on the taxpayer's trade or business. As he noted, nothing in the record indicated Bodzin would not have incurred the same rental expense even if he had done his overtime work at the office. This comment mirrored Judge Quealy's position that, at a minimum, the taxpayer should be required to establish "that the space claimed to have been devoted to this purpose in the residence of the taxpayer would not have been acquired except for such purpose." *Id.* at 829. Judge Featherston drew the following analogy:

> Surely the Commissioner would not be heard to claim petitioner received additional taxable income if he used his Internal Revenue Service office for such personal purposes as storing his golf clubs, keeping his umbrella or raincoat available for a rainy day, eating his lunch, taking personal telephone calls, etc. Such uses are merely incidental to the business use of the office. Similarly, petitioner's use of a room in his apartment for a few hours of overtime work each week is merely incidental to the purely personal purpose for which the rent was expended.

Id. at 827, 828.

The Bodzin story, however, did not end in the Tax Court. The Fourth Circuit, in a brief opinion, reversed the Tax Court, noting "Bodzin did not use any part of his apartment as his place of business; like most lawyers and judges, he sometimes, by choice, did some of his reading and writing at home." 509 F.2d 679, 681 (4th Cir. 1975). According to the court, the deduction claimed by Bodzin was subject to the following language from Reg. § 1.262-1(b)(3):

> Expenses of maintaining a household, including amounts paid for rent, water, utilities, domestic service, and the like, are not deductible. A taxpayer who rents a property for residential purposes, but incidentally conducts business there (his place of business being elsewhere) shall not deduct any part of the rent. If, however, he uses part of the house as his place of business, such portion of the rent and other similar expenses as is properly attributable to such place of business is deductible as a business expense.

Considering no part of the apartment was used as Bodzin's place of business, the Fourth Circuit held it was unnecessary to decide whether the taxpayer's home office was "appropriate and helpful" in carrying on his business. Thus, it was unclear whether the Fourth Circuit in a dual use case would use the "appropriate and helpful" standard.

The Tax Court majority and dissenting opinions and the Fourth Circuit decision in *Bodzin* reflect well the differing views regarding the appropriate standard for home office deductions. To resolve the confusion in this area, Congress in the 1976 legislation rejected the "appropriate and helpful" standard and replaced it with more objective criteria. As noted by the Senate Finance Committee:

> With respect to the "appropriate and helpful" standard employed in the court decisions, the determination of the allowance of a deduction for these expenses is necessarily a subjective determination. In the absence of definitive controlling standards, the "appropriate and helpful" test increases the inherent administrative problems because both business and personal uses of the residence are involved and substantiation of the time used for each of these activities is clearly a subjective determination. In many cases the application of the appropriate and helpful test would appear to result in treating personal living, and family expenses which are directly attributable to the home (and therefore not deductible) as ordinary and

necessary business expenses, even though those expenses did not result in additional or incremental costs incurred as a result of the business use of the home.

With the enactment of § 280A, taxpayers like Bodzin can avoid the disallowance of their home office expenses only if they meet the § 280A(c)(1) requirements. Specifically, under § 280A(c)(1), they must satisfy the exclusivity and regular use standards, one of the standards under § 280A(c)(1)(A)–(C), and a "convenience of employer" standard. Had § 280A existed at the time *Bodzin* was decided, the matter would have been easily resolved, *i.e.*, Bodzin could not meet any of these standards.

But this is not to say § 280A led to the easy resolution of all home office expense issues. The main occasion for litigation was the § 280A(c)(1)(A) standard that the home office constitute the taxpayer's "principal place of business." In 1993, the Supreme Court, addressing conflicting standards in the lower courts, held the principal place of business was the "most important or significant" place for the business, as determined by two primary considerations: "the relative importance of the activities performed at each business location and the time spent at each place." *Soliman v. Commissioner*, 506 U.S. 168 (1993). Applying this test to Dr. Soliman, a self-employed anesthesiologist who spent most of his working time performing medical services at three hospitals, the Court held his home office was not the principal place of business, despite the fact it was his only office and was essential to carrying on his medical practice. [Dr. Soliman maintained his billing and patient logs in his home office and used the office to contact patients and surgeons and read medical journals.] Rather, the actual treatment Dr. Soliman provided at the hospitals was "the essence of the professional service . . . , the most significant event in the professional transaction," thus rendering the home office less important than the hospitals from the standpoint of his business. That Dr. Soliman spent more time at the hospitals than at his home office further supported the determination his home office was not his principal place of business.

As reflected by the last sentence of § 280A(c)(1), Congress has reversed the result in *Soliman*. Pursuant to that sentence, a home office can be a "principal place of business" if it is used for "administrative or management activities . . . , [and] if there is no other fixed location of such trade or business where the taxpayer conducts substantial administrative or management activities. . . . " Of course, to the extent this legislative definition of principal place of business does not apply in a given situation, the *Soliman* test will presumably continue to control.

Employees seeking to deduct home office expenses must also satisfy the "convenience of the employer" standard of § 280A(c)(1), an issue the Supreme Court did not need to address with the self-employed taxpayer in *Soliman*. In an earlier case, *Weissman v. Commissioner*, 751 F.2d 512 (2d Cir. 1984), the Second Circuit held a college professor was entitled to deduct the expenses of his home office he used for the scholarly research and writing required as a condition of his employment. The only office space provided by his employer was an office shared with several other professors. After holding that the home office, where he spent 80% of his working week, constituted the taxpayer's principal place of business, the court considered the convenience-of-the-employer requirement:

[I]t becomes clear that Professor Weissman has also satisfied the convenience-of-the-employer test. The cost of maintaining his home office was almost entirely additional to nondeductible personal living expenses because it was used exclusively for employment-related activities and because such use was necessary as a practical matter if Professor Weissman was faithfully to perform his employment duties. This practical necessity negates any claim that the office was used as a matter of personal convenience rather than for the convenience of the employer. . . . [H]ere the employer provided some space, *i.e.*, a shared office at the library. . . . [H]owever, . . . the relevant fact is that the employer provided no *suitable* space for engaging in necessary employment-related activities. Although City College has provided some space to Professor Weissman, it has not provided space in which he can effectively carry out his employment duties. The maintenance of a home office was not a personal preference of the employee; it spared the employer the cost of providing a suitable private office and thereby served the convenience of the employer.

Id. at 516–17. Query: Would Professor Weissman satisfy the principal place of business test enunciated in *Soliman*?

Even if a taxpayer satisfies the business use requirements of § 280A(c)(1), the amount of the deductions allowed for a home office is severely limited by § 280A(c)(5). The gross income from the use of the residence for trade or business purposes is the ceiling for deductions.[1] This ceiling is reduced by (1) those deductions the taxpayer could claim regardless of whether the home office were used for trade or business purposes (*e.g.*, the portion of real estate taxes or mortgage interest allocable to the home office);[2] and (2) those deductions attributable to the trade or business activity but not allocable to the dwelling unit itself (*e.g.*, secretarial expense, supplies, business telephone). Expenditures not related to the use of the dwelling unit for business purposes, (*e.g.*, expenditures for lawn care), are not taken into account in computing deductions allowable under § 280A. The typical home office expenses are rent expense (as in *Bodzin*), depreciation, insurance, mortgage interest, property taxes, and utilities.

Study the following example based on an example provided in Proposed Regulation § 1.280A-2(i)(7):

Clare, a self-employed individual, uses an office in her home on a regular basis as a place of business for meeting with clients of her consulting service. She makes no other use of the office during the taxable year and uses no other premises for the consulting activity. Clare has a special telephone line for the office and occasionally employs secretarial assistance. She also has a gardener care for the lawn around her home during the year. According to Clare, 10% of the general expenses for the dwelling unit are allocable to the office. On the basis of the following figures, she

---

[1] The taxpayer may engage in business not only in his home office but at another location as well. For purposes of the § 280A(c)(5) limitation, the taxpayer will be required to allocate the gross income between the different business locations. All relevant facts, *e.g.*, the time the taxpayer engages in business at each location, must be taken into consideration in making the allocation. *See* Prop. Reg. § 1.280A-2(i)(2)(ii).

[2] *See* §§ 163(a), 164(a)(1), 280A(b).

determines that the sum of the allowable business deductions for the use of the office is $1,050 ($1,900 of gross income less $850 of expenditures not allocable to use of the unit):

Gross income from consulting services $1,900

less:

(a) *expenditures not allocable to use of unit* (§ 280A(c)(5)(B)(ii))

Secretarial expenses	$500	
Business telephone	150	
Supplies	200	
Total	$850	

(b) *always allowable deductions* (§ 280A(c)(5)(B)(i))

	Total	Allocable to Office
Mortgage interest	$5,000	$500[3]
Real estate taxes	2,000	200
Total Allocable to Office		$700
Sum of (a) and (b)		$1,550

Section 280A(c)(5) limit on further deductions:

Gross income of $1,900 less $1,550 . . . . $350

Thus, only $350 of Clare's other expenses may be deducted under § 280A(c)(5). Assume the share of the other expenses allocable to her home office was as follows:

	Total	Allocable to Office
Insurance	$600	$60
Utilities (other than residential telephone)	900	90
Lawn Care	500	0
Depreciation	3,200	320
Total Allocable to Office		$470

---

[3] Prop. Reg. § 1.280A-2(i)(3) provides that "the taxpayer may determine the expenses allocable to the portion of the unit used for business purposes by any method that is reasonable under the circumstances. If the rooms in the dwelling unit are of approximately equal size, the taxpayer may ordinarily allocate the general expenses for the unit according to the number of rooms used for the business purpose. The taxpayer may also allocate general expenses according to the percentage of the total floor space in the unit that is used for the business purpose. Expenses which are attributable only to certain portions of the unit, *e.g.*, repairs to kitchen fixtures, shall be allocated in full to those portions of the unit. Expenses which are not related to the use of the unit for business purposes, *e.g.*, expenditures for lawn care, are not taken into account for the purposes of Section 280A."

The amount of other deductions allocable to the unit exceeds the $350 limit. Prop. Reg. § 1.280A-2(i)(5) provides an ordering rule for claiming deductions and requires that those deductions which do not cause an adjustment to basis be claimed first. Thus, the insurance and utility charges totalling $150 would be deductible first, leaving only $200 of the depreciation which may be deducted. The $120 of depreciation allocable to use of the unit which may not be deducted may be carried over to the succeeding tax year. § 280A(c)(5). Based on your study of the above example, consider how § 280A prevents taxpayers from converting personal expenses into deductible business expenses.

Recognizing "the calculation, allocation, and substantiation of allowable deductions attributable to the use of a portion of the taxpayer's residence for business purposes can be complex and burdensome for small business owners," the Service issued Revenue Procedure 2013-13, 2013-1 C.B. 478, providing an optional safe harbor method for determining the allowable deduction for certain business uses of a residence under § 280A. Under the safe harbor method (which the taxpayer can elect on an annual basis), the taxpayer multiplies the allowable square footage for a home office by a prescribed rate. The allowable square footage is the portion of a home "used in a qualified business use of the home," but not to exceed 300 square feet, and the prescribed rate is $5.00. Thus, the maximum yearly deduction under the safe harbor method is $1,500, an amount that, in many cases, will be much lower than the deduction amount computed under the traditional method noted above. Taxpayers using the safe harbor method must continue to satisfy all requirements of § 280A for determining their eligibility to claim a deduction. Taxpayers using the safe harbor method may continue to deduct, to the extent allowed by the Code, any expense related to the home that is deductible without regard to whether there is a qualified business use of the home for that taxable year, e.g., qualified residence interest, property taxes, etc.

B. Vacation Home Deductions

In 1976 Congress also addressed deductions taxpayers claimed for expenses associated with the rental of their vacation homes. Consider the situation where taxpayer purchases a summer home on a lake. The taxpayer rents the home for one month each summer and personally uses the home for the remainder of the summer. Should the taxpayer be allowed to claim deductions such as depreciation, maintenance and insurance deductions with respect to the vacation home on the basis that the rental of the home is a business or investment activity? Should it make a difference if the expenses attributable to the rental, including depreciation, exceed the rental income? The likelihood is that the taxpayer is not really concerned about making an economic profit from the rental, but instead wishes to minimize the expense of owning recreational property.

Prior to the 1976 legislation, one might have argued the vacation home expenses were subject to the hobby loss rules of § 183, limiting deductions for activities not entered into for profit. Section 183, enacted in 1969, provides that, if a taxpayer engages in an activity not intended to produce a profit, the taxpayer may, to a limited extent, deduct expenses which would have been deductible if the activity were engaged in for profit. The taxpayer may deduct expenses only to the extent of the gross income from the activity, less deductions for items like taxes and home mortgage interest which would have been deductible in any event. If the activity is for profit, the taxpayer is not subject to this limitation on deductions. A fact and circumstances test is applied to determine whether a particular activity constitutes a not-for-profit activity. For a detailed discussion of § 183, see Chapter 20.

Section 183 and its regulations, however, provide no definitive rules for determining how much personal use of a vacation home would render the rental of such a home an activity not engaged in for profit, and therefore subject to the § 183 limitations. Furthermore, the determination of whether a taxpayer rents property for the purpose of making a profit involves an examination of taxpayer's motive and the primary purpose for which the vacation home is held. Such a determination is largely subjective and extremely difficult to make. As in the case of home office deductions, Congress sought in § 280A to provide objective criteria by which the status of the rental of vacation homes could be determined and, in appropriate circumstances, deductions could be limited.

Section 280A limits the deductions a taxpayer may claim with respect to the rental of a dwelling unit if the taxpayer uses the dwelling unit for personal purposes for a period that exceeds the greater of 14 days or 10% of the number of the days during the year for which the vacation home is rented at a fair rental. *See* § 280A(d)(1). Note the rules of § 280A(d)(2) defining what constitutes personal use of a unit.

> **Example 1:** A taxpayer rents a dwelling for 60 days and uses that unit for personal purposes on 14 or fewer days. The dwelling unit will not be deemed to be "used as a residence." By contrast, if the taxpayer used the dwelling for personal purposes for more than 14 days, § 280A(a) would be applicable.

> **Example 2:** A taxpayer rents a dwelling unit for 180 days and uses that unit for personal purposes for 18 or fewer days. Under these circumstances, the dwelling unit will not be deemed to be "used as a residence." As a result, § 280A(a) would not be applicable. By contrast, § 280A would be applicable if the taxpayer had used the residence for more than 18 days for personal purposes.

Under the limitation imposed by § 280A(c)(5), deductions attributable to the rental may not be claimed in excess of the amount by which the gross income derived from the rental activity exceeds the deductions otherwise allowable without regard to such rental activity, *e.g.*, mortgage interest and real estate taxes. In *Bolton v. Commissioner*, 694 F.2d 556 (9th Cir. 1982), the court held these "otherwise allowable expenses" must be ratably allocated to each day of the tax year, regardless of the use of the unit on any given day.[4] *See* § 280A(e)(2). By contrast, § 280A(e)(1) provides that the portion of expenses (insurance, depreciation, utilities, etc.) allocable to rental activities is limited to an amount determined

---

[4] The Commissioner's interpretation of § 280A(e)(2) was based on Prop. Reg. § 1.280A-3(d). Insofar as the regulations deal with allocation of mortgage interest and real property taxes to rental use, the Court rejected the Commissioner's interpretation as unreasonable.

on the basis of the ratio of time the home is actually rented for a fair rental to the total time the vacation home is used during the taxable year for all purposes, including rental. Any rental expenses not deductible as a result of this limit may be carried forward to the succeeding taxable year. § 280A(c)(5).[5]

If a taxpayer limits to less than 15 days the rental of a dwelling unit she uses during the year as a residence, § 280A(g) provides that, "notwithstanding any other provision of § 280A or § 183," the taxpayer will not be allowed any deduction otherwise allowable because of the rental use of the dwelling unit and *the income derived from the rental use will not be included in the taxpayer's gross income.*

> **Example:** Alice rents her five-bedroom home in East Hampton, New York for two weeks each summer, charging $15,000 per week. Alice uses the home as her principal residence during the rest of the year. As a result of the *de minimis* rule of Section 280A(g), Alice is not required to include the $30,000 of rental income in her gross income. She may not deduct, however, any expenses associated with the rental but may deduct her property taxes, home mortgage interest, and other expenses that are deductible regardless of whether the property is rented.

C. Other Dual Use Property

1. Computers and Other "Listed Property"

The home computer has become a household item for many Americans. Recognizing taxpayers often use computers for both personal and business reasons and might seek to convert nondeductible personal expenses into deductible business expenses, Congress in 1984 imposed limitations on deductions for computers (and other "listed property").[6] See the definition of "listed property" in § 280F(d)(4)(A). Unless the business use percentage for the taxable year exceeds 50%, the taxpayer is required to use the alternative depreciation system of § 168(g), and is thus limited to straight line depreciation on the property. § 280F(b)(1), (3). This cap on allowable depreciation, together with the § 280F(d)(1) rule treating any deduction allowable as a result of a § 179 election as a § 168 depreciation deduction, negates the use of § 179 by taxpayers failing to meet the 50% standard. For example, if a taxpayer purchases an $8,000 computer and uses it over 50% of the time for personal purposes, the taxpayer must use the alternative depreciation system and may not deduct any depreciation amount (including a § 179 amount) in excess of the amount determined under § 168(g).

In addition, Congress has provided a special recapture rule in § 280F(b)(2) to address situations where, in a year following the year the "listed property" is placed

---

[5] In addition to the business use and rental use exceptions, § 280A(c) lists other exceptions to the general disallowance rule of § 280A(a). Special rules exist for space used for the storage of business inventory or product samples (§ 280A(c)(2)) and for a dwelling unit used regularly in a day care business (§ 280A(c)(4)).

[6] A computer (and peripheral equipment) used exclusively at a regular business establishment and owned or leased by the person operating such establishment does not constitute "listed property" and therefore is not subject to the limitations of § 280F(b).

in service, the taxpayer fails to meet the 50% use standard. The necessity for this recapture rule is explained as follows by the Staff of the Joint Committee on Taxation:

> Congress was also concerned that some taxpayers acquired automobiles and other property very late in the taxable year and claimed a very high percentage of business use for that portion of the year. Business use in subsequent years would often be minimal. Taxpayers could nonetheless claim full ACRS deductions for that first year and not be subject to recapture by reason of greatly diminished business use in the subsequent years.

General Explanation of the Revenue Provisions of the Tax Reform Act of 1984, Staff of the Joint Committee on Taxation, H.R. 4170, 98th Cong., p. 560.

Section 280F(d)(3) significantly limits the ability of employees to claim depreciation deductions on home computers. If the employee uses his own computer (or other "listed property") in connection with his employment, no depreciation deduction is available to the employee unless he can establish the use of the computer is "for the convenience of the employer and is required as a condition of his employment." As noted in the Conference Report:

> [T]he terms "convenience of the employer" and "condition of employment" [are intended] to have the same meaning [in § 280F(d)(3)] as [they do] with respect to the exclusion from gross income for lodging furnished to an employee. In order to satisfy the condition of employment requirement, the property must be required in order for the employee to properly perform the duties of his employment. This requirement is not satisfied merely by an employer's statement that the property is required as a condition of employment.

H. Rep. No. 98-861, p. 1027. An employee will thus find it difficult to claim a depreciation deduction with respect to a home computer or other "listed property" used in connection with his employment.

2. Passenger Automobiles

Passenger automobiles are also treated as "listed property," and are therefore subject to the depreciation limitations described above. Thus, unless a taxpayer uses a passenger automobile[7] more than 50% of the time for trade or business purposes, the taxpayer may not use the accelerated depreciation percentages provided by § 168. Instead, the straight line method of depreciation, computed over a five-year period, must be used[8] and no § 179 election is available.

---

[7] The limitations are applicable to "passenger automobiles," defined in § 280F(d)(5) as any 4-wheeled vehicle manufactured primarily for use on streets, roads, and highways and rated at 6,000 pounds unloaded gross vehicle weight or less.

[8] Use of the passenger car for the production of income but not in a trade or business does not count for purposes of meeting the 50% floor. However, production of income use is considered in computing the amount of depreciation which may be claimed. The Conference Report provides the following instructive example: "[I]f a specified asset is used 30 percent in a trade or business and 30 percent in the production of income, the taxpayer may not claim . . . ACRS and must instead compute depreciation under the

But Congress did not stop there. As reflected in the following passage from the General Explanation of the Tax Reform Act of 1984 prepared by the Staff of the Joint Committee on Taxation, Congress had a special concern for tax abuse potential it perceived to be associated with passenger automobiles:[9]

> Congress believed that the investment incentives afforded by investment tax credit and accelerated cost recovery should be directed to encourage capital formation, rather than to subsidize the element of personal consumption associated with the use of very expensive automobiles. . . . To the extent an automobile is required for [necessary business] transportation, the generally allowable tax benefits should be available. Beyond that point, however, the extra expense of a luxury automobile provides, in effect, a tax-free personal emolument which Congress believed should not qualify for tax credits or acceleration of depreciation deductions because such expenditures do not add significantly to the productivity which these incentives were designed to encourage.

> In addition, Congress was concerned . . . that some taxpayers had attempted to convert personal use to business use through a variety of arguments, such as . . . that signs, special paint, personalized license plates, or unique hood ornaments made the car a constant advertisement so that all use was business-related.[10]

To prevent, or at least reduce, this abuse, Congress has limited the depreciation allowable with respect to a passenger automobile in the year it is placed in service and succeeding years, as follows:

Tax Year	Maximum Depreciation Allowed
First	$2,560
Second	$4,100
Third	$2,450
Each Succeeding Year	$1,475

§ 280F(a)(1)(A). These limits are adjusted for inflation for automobiles placed in service after 1988.[11]

[straight line method]. If, however, any asset is used 70 percent in a trade or business and 20 percent for the production of income, the taxpayer may claim . . . ACRS based on 90 percent business use." H. Rep. No. 98-861, p. 1026.

[9] H.R. 4170, 98th Cong., p. 559.

[10] The Conference Report makes the following comment:

> Commuting is not business use, regardless of whether work is performed during the trip. Thus, for example, a business telephone call made on a telephone installed in an automobile while the taxpayer is commuting to work does not transform the character of the trip from commuting to business. This is also true for a business meeting held in a car while the taxpayer is commuting to work. Similarly, a business telephone call made on an otherwise personal trip does not transform the character of the trip from personal to business. In a likewise manner, the fact that an automobile is used to display material that advertises the owner's or user's trade or business does not convert an otherwise personal use into business use.

H. Rep. No. 98-861, p. 1028.

[11] I.R.C. § 280F(d)(7). Note for passenger automobiles placed in service after 2007 and before 2015,

The applicable limitation is applied after depreciation is computed under § 168 and before the depreciation amount is reduced to reflect the portion of the automobile's use that is personal use. *See* § 280F(a)(2). The depreciation deduction determined after applying the statutory limitations is then further reduced by the proportion of the total use during that year that is personal use.[12] Consider the following examples:

Example 1: On July 1, Year 1, Marilyn purchases for $30,000 and places in service a passenger automobile which is 5-year recovery property under § 168. The automobile is used exclusively in her business. Marilyn plans to use the accelerated depreciation percentages under § 168. In Year 1, without the § 280F(a)(1) limitation, her depreciation deduction under the half-year convention would be 20% of $30,000 or $6,000. Given § 280F(a)(2), and disregarding inflation adjustments to the § 280F(a)(1) limits and any application of § 168(k), however, Marilyn is only allowed a depreciation deduction of $2,560.[13] If she continues to use the car exclusively in business during Years 2–5, her depreciation deductions will be $4,100, $2,450, $1,475, and $1,475, respectively. Marilyn will obviously not have recovered the entire cost of the car during the recovery period. How does the Code treat the balance of the unrecovered cost? *See* § 280F(a)(1)(B).

Example 2: Assume the same facts as in Example 1 except Marilyn uses the automobile only 25% of the time in her business and 75% of the time for personal purposes. Because the business use does not exceed 50%, she may not use the accelerated depreciation percentages and is limited by § 280F(b)(2) to the straight line method. Again disregarding inflation adjustments, Marilyn's maximum depreciation deduction for the year the property is placed in service is still $2,560 (§ 280F(a)(2)(A)(i)) which is less than the maximum depreciation computed using § 168(g), *i.e.*, 10% of $30,000 or $3,000 (note the use of the half-year convention). This maximum depreciation amount of $2,560 must now be allocated between the personal use and business use. Only 25% of $2,560 or $640 is deductible in the year

---

§ 168(k)(2)(F)(i) increased the first year depreciation allowable under § 280F(a)(1)(A) by $8,000 for automobiles to which the 50% additional first year depreciation rules of § 168(k)(1)(A) applied. Thus, for example, to the inflation adjusted § 280F limit of $3,160 for passenger automobiles placed in service in 2014, one would add $8,000 thereby enabling a taxpayer to deduct up to $11,160 of depreciation with regard to any qualified passenger automobile. (At the time this casebook went to press, Congress had not extended the application of § 168(k) beyond 2014.) When § 280F was enacted in 1984, its limitation on depreciation deductions was directed at so-called luxury cars. Today, many medium-priced (non-luxury) cars are subject to the § 280F depreciation limitations.

[12] General Explanation of the Revenue Provisions of the Tax Reform Act of 1984 prepared by the Staff of the Joint Committee on Taxation, p. 561.

[13] Note that because § 179 deductions are considered depreciation deductions under § 168, the taxpayer in Example 1 would not be entitled to elect to take a § 179 deduction. Under § 280F the use of the § 179 election is available only under the following circumstances:

a. In the case of a passenger automobile, only if the 50% business use standard is satisfied and the amount of the § 168 depreciation deduction is less than the cap imposed by § 280F(a)(2). Considering how low that cap is, it is doubtful that taxpayers will benefit much from § 179 with respect to passenger automobiles which they purchase.

b. In the case of other listed property, only if the 50% business use standard is satisfied.

the automobile is placed in service. Note, however, for the purpose of computing depreciation deductions in subsequent years, Marilyn is treated as having been allowed a depreciation deduction in the prior year equal to the amount she would have been allowed if she had used the automobile exclusively for business purposes in the prior year. Of course, the § 280F(a)(1) limitation must be taken into consideration. Thus, for purposes of computing depreciation in subsequent years, Marilyn will be deemed to have been allowed $2,560 in depreciation in the year that the automobile was placed in service, rather than just the $640 actually allowed. *See* § 280F(d)(2); Temp. Reg. § 1.280F-4T(a)(1) and (2).

In sum, Congress, by means of §§ 280A and 280F, has attempted to prevent taxpayers in certain contexts from converting nondeductible personal expenses into deductible business or investment expenses. Such policing of the business/personal expense borders, however, has been accomplished only by adding considerable complexity to an already complex Code. Can you think of any simpler way to police this area?

POPOV v. COMMISSIONER
United States Court of Appeals, Ninth Circuit
246 F.3d 1190 (2001)

HAWKINS, CIRCUIT JUDGE:

This case concerns the continuing problem of the home office deduction. We conclude, on the facts of this case, that a professional musician is entitled to deduct the expenses from the portion of her home used exclusively for musical practice.

Facts and Procedural Background

Katia Popov is a professional violinist who performs regularly with the Los Angeles Chamber Orchestra and the Long Beach Symphony. She also contracts with various studios to record music for the motion picture industry. In 1993, she worked for twenty-four such contractors and recorded in thirty-eight different locations. These recording sessions required that Popov be able to read scores quickly. The musicians did not receive the sheet music in advance of the recording sessions; instead, they were presented with their parts when they arrived at the studio, and recording would begin shortly thereafter. None of Popov's twenty-six employers provided her with a place to practice.

Popov lived with her husband Peter, an attorney, and their four-year-old daughter Irina, in a one-bedroom apartment in Los Angeles, California. The apartment's living room served as Popov's home office. The only furniture in the living room consisted of shelves with recording equipment, a small table, a bureau for storing sheet music, and a chair. Popov used this area to practice the violin and to make recordings, which she used for practice purposes and as demonstration tapes for orchestras. No one slept in the living room, and the Popovs' daughter was not allowed to play there. Popov spent four to five hours a day practicing in the living room.

In their 1993 tax returns, the Popovs claimed a home office deduction for the living room and deducted forty percent of their annual rent and twenty percent of their annual electricity bill. The Internal Revenue Service ("the Service") disallowed these deductions, and the Popovs filed a petition for redetermination in the Tax Court.

The Tax Court concluded that the Popovs were not entitled to a home office deduction. Although "practicing at home was a very important component to [Popov's] success as a musician," the court found that her living room was not her "principal place of business." In the court's view, her principal places of business were the studios and concert halls where she recorded and performed, because it was her performances in these places that earned her income.

Analysis

The Internal Revenue Code allows a deduction for a home office that is exclusively used as "the principal place of business for any trade or business of the taxpayer." 26 U.S.C. § 280A(c)(1)(A). The Code does not define the phrase "principal place of business."

A. The *Soliman* Tests

Our inquiry is governed by *Commissioner v. Soliman*, 506 U.S. 168, 113 S. Ct. 701, 121 L. Ed. 2d 634 (1993), the Supreme Court's most recent treatment of the home office deduction. In *Soliman*, the taxpayer was an anesthesiologist who spent thirty to thirty-five hours per week with patients at three different hospitals. None of the hospitals provided Soliman with an office, so he used a spare bedroom for contacting patients and surgeons, maintaining billing records and patient logs, preparing for treatments, and reading medical journals.

The Supreme Court denied Soliman a deduction for his home office, holding that the "statute does not allow for a deduction whenever a home office may be characterized as legitimate." *Id.* at 174. Instead, courts must determine whether the home office is the taxpayer's principal place of business. Although the Court could not "develop an objective formula that yields a clear answer in every case," the Court stressed two primary considerations: "the relative importance of the activities performed at each business location and the time spent at each place." *Id.* at 174–75. We address each in turn.

1. The Relative Importance

The importance of daily practice to Popov's profession cannot be denied. Regular practice is essential to playing a musical instrument at a high level of ability, and it is this level of commitment that distinguishes the professional from the amateur.[14]

---

[14] One who doubts this might consult George Bernard Shaw's observation that "hell is full of

Without daily practice, Popov would be unable to perform in professional orchestras. She would also be unequipped for the peculiar demands of studio recording: The ability to read and perform scores on sight requires an acute musical intelligence that must be constantly developed and honed. In short, Popov's four to five hours of daily practice lay at the very heart of her career as a professional violinist.

Of course, the concert halls and recording studios are also important to Popov's profession. Without them, she would have no place in which to perform. Audiences and motion picture companies are unlikely to flock to her one-bedroom apartment. In *Soliman*, the Supreme Court stated that, although "no one test is determinative in every case," "the point where goods and services are delivered must be given great weight in determining the place where the most important functions are performed." *Id.* at 175. The Service places great weight on this statement, contending that Popov's performances should be analogized to the "service" of delivering anesthesia that was at issue in *Soliman*; these "services" are delivered in concert halls and studios, not in her apartment.

We agree with Popov that musical performance is not so easily captured under a "goods and services" rubric. The German poet Heinrich Heine observed that music stands "halfway between thought and phenomenon, between spirit and matter, a sort of nebulous mediator, like and unlike each of the things it mediates — spirit that requires manifestation in time, and matter that can do without space."[15] Heinrich Heine, Letters on the French Stage (1837), quoted in Words about Music: A Treasury of Writings 2 (John Amis & Michael Rose eds., 1989). Or as Harry Ellis Dickson of the Boston Symphony Orchestra explained more concretely:

> A musician's life is different from that of most people. We don't go to an office every day, or to a factory, or to a bank. We go to an empty hall. We don't deal in anything tangible, nor do we produce anything except sounds. We saw away, or blow, or pound for a few hours and then we go home. It is a strange way to make a living!

Harry Ellis Dickson, Gentlemen, More Dolce Please (1969), quoted in Drucker v. Comm'r, 715 F.2d 67, 68–69 (2d Cir. 1983).

It is possible, of course, to wrench musical performance into a "delivery of services" framework, but we see little value in such a wooden and unblinking application of the tax laws. *Soliman* itself recognized that in this area of law "variations are inevitable in case-by-case determinations." 506 U.S. at 175. We believe this to be such a case. We simply do not find the "delivery of services" framework to be helpful in analyzing this particular problem. Taken to extremes, the Service's argument would seem to generate odd results in a variety of other areas as well. We doubt, for example, that an appellate advocate's primary place of business is the podium from which he delivers his oral argument, or that a professor's primary place of business is the classroom, rather than the office in which he prepares his lectures.

---

musical amateurs." George Bernard Shaw, Man and Superman, act 3 (1903).

[15] Although not, perhaps, without practice space.

We therefore conclude that the "relative importance" test yields no definitive answer in this case, and we accordingly turn to the second prong of the *Soliman* inquiry.

2. Amount of Time

Under *Soliman*, "the decisionmaker should . . . compare the amount of time spent at home with the time spent at other places where business activities occur." *Id.* at 177. "This factor assumes particular significance when," as in this case, "comparison of the importance of the functions performed at various places yields no definitive answer to the principal place of business inquiry." *Id.*[16] In *Soliman*, the taxpayer spent significantly more time in the hospitals than he did in his home office. In this case, Popov spent significantly more time practicing the violin at home than she did performing or recording.[17]

This second factor tips the balance in the Popovs' favor. They are accordingly entitled to a home office deduction for Katia Popov's practice space, because it was exclusively used as her principal place of business.

AUTHORS' NOTE:

The court never had to consider the exclusivity requirement of § 280A(c)(1) as that requirement was conceded before trial.

---

[16] Justices Thomas and Scalia concurred in *Soliman*, but noted that the Court provided no guidance if the taxpayer "spent 30 to 35 hours at his home office and only 10 hours" at the hospitals. 506 U.S. at 184 (Thomas, J., concurring) (Which factor would take precedence? The importance of the activities undertaken at home . . . ? The number of hours spent at each location? I am at a loss, and I am afraid the taxpayer, his attorney, and a lower court would be as well." *Id.*

[17] The Service argues that the evidence is unclear as to "how much time Mrs. Popov spent practicing at home as opposed to the time she spent performing outside of the home." It is true that the evidence is not perfectly clear and that the Tax Court made no specific comparative findings. However, the Tax Court found that she practiced four to five hours a day in her apartment. If we read this finding in the light most generous to the Service and assume that she only practiced four hours a day 300 days a year, Popov would still have practiced 1200 hours in a year. She testified that she performed with two orchestras for a total of 120–140 hours. If she spent a similar amount of time recording, she would still be spending about five hours practicing for every hour of performance or recording. The only plausible reading of the evidence is that Popov spent substantially more time practicing than she did performing or recording.

Chapter 22

THE INTEREST DEDUCTION

I. PROBLEMS

1. To what extent, if any, may the taxpayers in (a)–(e) below deduct the interest payments made during the taxable year?

    (a) Kevin paid $5,000 in interest on a bank loan used to pay operating expenses of his retail shoe business.

    (b) Abigail paid $1,500 in interest on a loan she obtained to purchase a car for her personal use and $1,000 in interest on credit cards used to make personal purchases.

    (c) Jackson, who recently graduated from law school, paid $3,000 in interest on loans from his aunt he used to pay his undergraduate and law school tuition.

    (d) Megan, a cash method taxpayer who operates her own piano studio where she provides private piano lessons, prepaid the interest for the next three years on a bank loan she used to purchase a grand piano for her business.

    (e) Evan paid $2,500 in interest on a loan he used to purchase stock. The corporation issuing the stock has not typically paid dividends to its shareholders. Evan, however, purchased the stock for its growth potential. During the current year, Evan received $500 in interest income and $1,500 in dividends on other stock he owns and paid an investment advisor $600 for advising him on the sale and purchase of stocks and bonds.

2. Braedon purchased a home for $2,000,000, paying $600,000 down and borrowing the remaining $1,400,000 from a bank to which he gave a mortgage on the home. Braedon will use the home as his principal residence.

    (a) Of the $1,400,000 bank loan, how much constitutes "acquisition indebtedness" within the meaning of § 163(h)(3)(B)? How much, if any, of the loan constitutes "home equity indebtedness" within the meaning of § 163(h)(3)(C)?

    (b) How do the answers to (a) change if Braedon and Chris, an unmarried couple, jointly purchased the home, paying down $300,000 each and incurring joint and several liability for the $1,400,000 mortgage? Assume each uses the home as a principal residence.

(c)   How do the answers to (a) change if Braedon is married to Chris, who also uses the home as a principal residence, but only Braedon owns the home and is liable on the $1,400,000 mortgage? Assume that Braedon and Chris file a joint return, or alternatively, separate returns.

3.   In January of Year 1, Patrick bought a home for $600,000 by paying $100,000 from his own funds and borrowing the remaining $500,000 from Home Town Bank. The bank loan was secured by a mortgage on the home. At the time Patrick borrowed the money to purchase the home, it was customary for lenders to charge a borrower points on the amount borrowed. Patrick paid the bank $10,000 in points and $50,000 in interest during Year 1.

(a)   May Patrick deduct the Year 1 points and the interest?

(b)   In January of Year 8, when Patrick's home had a value of $800,000 and the balance on his mortgage was $400,000, Patrick refinanced the property to take advantage of a low interest rate offered by XYZ Mortgage Company. Patrick borrowed $600,000 from XYZ, using $400,000 of the loan proceeds to pay in full the balance owing to Home Town Bank on the original mortgage. Patrick used $140,000 of the loan proceeds to add a room to the home and the balance of $60,000 of the proceeds to pay his car loans and credit card balances. In Year 8, Patrick paid a total of $39,000 in interest to XYZ. How much, if any, of that interest will be deductible?

(c)   Assume the facts of (b). Assume also that in Year 8 Patrick entered into a fifteen year installment contract to purchase a lake cottage which Patrick intends to use as his summer home. Patrick agreed to pay $500,000 for the home. Patrick's obligation to the seller under the contract was secured by a mortgage on the cottage. Assume Patrick paid $40,000 down and the first principal payment on the $460,000 owed to the seller was not due under the contract until Year 9. In Year 8, however, Patrick was required to pay the interest that accrued during that year on the unpaid principal balance. The interest for Year 8 amounted to $35,000 which Patrick paid on December 31, Year 8. May Patrick deduct the $35,000 interest?

(d)   Assume the facts of (a). In Year 5, when the balance owing to Home Town Bank on his home mortgage was $440,000, Patrick refinanced the home with Home Town Bank solely to take advantage of a significant decrease in home mortgage interest rates. At the time of the refinancing, Patrick owed Home Town Bank $10,000 in interest on the original mortgage. Under the terms of the refinancing arrangement, Patrick borrowed $450,000 from Home Town Bank but did not receive any of the loan proceeds. Instead, Home Town Bank withheld $440,000 of the proceeds as payment of the $440,000 principal balance owing on the original mortgage and withheld the remaining $10,000 as payment for the $10,000 in interest which Patrick owed the bank on that mortgage. May Patrick deduct the $10,000 in interest that was deemed to be paid as a result of the bank's withholding of $10,000 from the refinancing proceeds?

Assignment for Chapter 22:

Complete the problems.

Read: Internal Revenue Code: §§ 1(h)(2); 163(a), (d)(1)–(3)(B)(i), (4)(A)–(C), (5)(A)(i), (B), (h)(1), (2), (3)(A)–(C), (4)(A)(i); 221; 461(g); Skim §§ 263A(a), (b); 265(a)(2); 103(a).
Treasury Regulations: Skim § 1.163-8T(a)(1), (3), (c)(1), (m)(3); 1.163-9T(a), (b)(1), (b)(2)(A).

Materials: Overview
Revenue Ruling 2010-25
Sophy v. Commissioner
Bronstein v. Commissioner
Davison v. Commissioner

II. VOCABULARY

interest
points
qualified residence interest
investment interest
acquisition indebtedness
home equity indebtedness
qualified education loan

III. OBJECTIVES

1. To distinguish interest payments from other payments.

2. To recall the limitations on the deduction of personal interest.

3. To determine the amount of personal interest which may be deducted as "qualified residence interest."

4. To explain generally the limitation on the deduction of investment interest.

5. To recall interest paid or incurred in a trade or business is deductible, except to the extent it must be capitalized.

6. To recall a cash method taxpayer may not deduct current interest payments related to a subsequent tax year.

7. To explain and apply the limits on the use of borrowed funds to pay interest.

8. To recall the payment of a deductible expense with borrowed money ordinarily does not negate a cash method taxpayer's right to deduct the expense currently.

9. To explain the deduction for interest on education loans.

10. To explain the rule regarding the deductibility of points.

IV. OVERVIEW

We Americans are borrowers. Purchasing everything from food to homes on credit, we are accustomed to paying substantial interest. Historically, interest was deductible regardless of whether incurred in connection with a trade, business or investment activity or with personal consumption. In 1986, Congress significantly limited the deduction for personal interest, leaving, however, almost intact the most significant personal interest deduction — that for mortgages on one's personal residence. This Chapter examines the interest deduction, focusing primarily on statutory limitations on the deduction as well as certain related timing rules. Some judicial limitations and additional statutory limitations of more general application are considered in Chapter 27.

A. What Is Interest?

A review of the case law and rulings reveals the question — What is interest? — is not always easily answered. Consider, for example, the additional fees known as "points" taxpayers are sometimes required to pay when borrowing money from a bank or savings and loan to purchase a home. (A "point" is equal to one percent of the amount of the loan, and is paid as a fee to the lender. Thus, for example, a charge of three points on a $100,000 loan would equal $3,000.) Do the points constitute prepaid interest, or are they instead a charge for specific services provided by the lender? In the typical situation involving a home loan they represent prepaid interest. Home loan agreements generally provide separate charges for all of the costs associated with the approval and processing of loans, *e.g.*, fees for the preliminary title report, the preparation of a deed and other documents; escrow fees; and title insurance. As the Service has noted, if, in addition to these fees, the loan agreement requires the borrower to pay points based on "economic factors that usually dictate an acceptable rate of interest," *e.g.*, the amount and duration of the loan and the kinds of risks undertaken by the lender, the points constitute interest. Revenue Ruling 69-188, 1969-1 C.B. 54.[1]

Revenue Ruling 69-188 provides the following instructive discussion on the nature of interest:

> For tax purposes, interest has been defined by the Supreme Court of the United States as the amount one has contracted to pay for the use of borrowed money, and as the compensation paid for the use or forbearance of money. A negotiated bonus or premium paid by a borrower to a lender in order to obtain a loan has been held to be interest for Federal income tax purposes. . . .
>
> The payment or accrual of interest for tax purposes must be incidental to an unconditional and legally enforceable obligation of the taxpayer claiming the deduction. . . . There need not, however, be a legally enforceable indebtedness already in existence when the payment of interest is

---

[1] According to the Service, the lender "considered the general availability of money, the character of the property offered as security, the degree of success that the borrower had enjoyed in his prior business activities, and the outcome of previous transactions between the borrower and his creditors." 1969-1 C.B. at 54.

made. It is sufficient that the payment be a "prerequisite to obtaining borrowed capital. . . . "

It is not necessary that the parties to a transaction label a payment made for the use of money as interest for it to be so treated. . . .

The method of computation also does not control its deductibility, so long as the amount in question is an ascertainable sum contracted for the use of borrowed money. . . . The fact that the amount paid . . . is a flat sum paid in addition to a stated annual interest rate does not preclude a deduction under section 163 of the Code.

To qualify as interest for tax purposes, the payment, by whatever name called, must be compensation for the use or forbearance of money per se and not a payment for specific services which the lender performs in connection with the borrower's account. For example, interest would not include separate charges made for investigating the prospective borrower and his security, closing costs of the loan and papers drawn in connection therewith or fees paid to a third party for servicing and collecting that particular loan. Also, even where service charges are not stated separately on the borrower's account, interest would not include amounts attributable to such services.

1969-1 C.B. at 55.

Interest expense incurred in a trade or business would be deductible under § 162 even if § 163 did not exist. Many of the characterization questions regarding interest arise in the business setting. For example, a common question is whether "loans" made by shareholders to their corporations are genuine debts or should be treated as shareholder contributions to capital. If treated as debts, the amounts repaid by the corporation to the shareholders with respect to the debt will constitute a combination of principal and interest, with the interest being deductible by the corporation. By contrast, if the "loan" is in substance a capital contribution, amounts paid to the shareholder are not interest but will likely be treated as dividends. Unlike interest, dividends paid to shareholders are not deductible by the corporation.

B.   Deduction of Personal Interest

Prior to 1986, taxpayers were entitled to deduct not only business and investment interest but also personal interest, *e.g.*, as interest on credit card balances. The allowance of a deduction for interest incurred in business and investment activities is appropriate in a system taxing only net income. The allowance of a deduction for personal interest, however, is an exception to the general rule that personal living expenses are not deductible.

In 1986, Congress significantly limited the deduction of "personal interest." § 163(h)(1). The Senate Report explained the reasoning as follows:

Present law excludes or mismeasures income arising from the ownership of housing and other consumer durables. Investment in such goods allows consumers to avoid the tax that would apply if funds were invested in assets producing taxable income and to avoid the cost of renting these items, a cost which would not be deductible in computing tax liability. Thus, the tax system provides an incentive to invest in consumer durables rather than assets which produce taxable income and, therefore, an incentive to consume rather than save.

Although the committee believes that it would not be advisable to subject to income tax imputed rental income with respect to consumer durables owned by the taxpayer, it does believe that it is appropriate and practical to address situations where consumer expenditures are financed by borrowing. By phasing out the present deductibility of consumer interest, the committee believes that it has eliminated from the present tax law significant disincentive to saving.

S. Rep. 99-313, 99th Cong. 2d Sess., p. 804. Note the general disallowance rule of § 163(h)(1) and the definition of "personal interest" in § 163(h)(2).

Section 163(h)(2) excludes various categories of interest from the definition of personal interest for purposes of the disallowance rule of § 163(h)(1). Among those excluded categories are: "interest paid or accrued on indebtedness properly allocable to a trade or business (other than the trade or business of performing services as an employee) . . . any investment interest within the meaning of [Section 163(d)] . . . any qualified residence interest (within the meaning of [Section 163(h)(3) and] any interest allowable as a deduction under section 221 (relating to interest of educational loans)." Qualified residence interest and investment interest are discussed below. With regard to "interest paid or accrued on indebtedness properly allocable to a trade or business," it is appropriate that such interest not be subject to the disallowance rule of § 163(h)(1). Again, in a system that seeks to tax only the net income generated by a business, those costs, including interest, incurred in producing business income ought to be deductible. Note, however, that Regulation § 1.163-9T(b)(2)(i)(A) defines personal interest to include interest "paid on underpayments of individual Federal, State, or local income taxes . . . regardless of the source of the income generating the tax liability." Thus, if a sole proprietor incurs interest expense to the Federal government for underpayment of federal income tax on her business income, the regulation will preclude the taxpayer from deducting the interest paid to the government.

1. Qualified Residence Interest

As previously noted, "qualified residence interest" is excepted from the rule disallowing deduction of "personal interest." § 163(h)(2)(D). Note also that § 67(b)(1) excepts the interest deduction from the 2% floor. Under § 163(h)(3), "qualified residence interest" is interest paid or accrued during the tax year on certain "acquisition indebtedness" and "home equity indebtedness" secured by the taxpayer's principal residence and on one other residence.[2] "Acquisition indebtedness" is

---

[2] Section 163(h)(4)(A)(i) defines a qualified residence as "the principal residence (within the meaning of § 121) of the taxpayer" and "1 other residence of the taxpayer which is selected by the taxpayer for purposes of this subsection for the taxable year and which is used by the taxpayer as a residence (within the meaning of § 280A(d)(1))." For a dwelling unit to qualify as a residence pursuant to § 280A(d)(1), the

indebtedness (not in excess of $1,000,000) incurred in "acquiring, constructing, or substantially improving any qualified residence of the taxpayer."[3] "Home equity indebtedness" is indebtedness (other than acquisition indebtedness) secured by a qualified residence, *e.g.*, a second mortgage. Home equity indebtedness, however, is limited to the excess of the fair market value of the qualified residence over the amount of acquisition indebtedness with respect to such residence. For purposes of the interest deduction, home equity indebtedness may not exceed $100,000. Thus, the overall limit of indebtedness on a principal and second residence, the interest on which will be deductible, is $1,100,000. The Service has recently ruled that, given the statutory definitions of "acquisition indebtedness" and "home equity indebtedness" and the dollar limitations on both, a loan used to purchase a qualified residence may constitute acquisition indebtedness in part and home equity indebtedness in part. Rev. Rul. 2010-25, included in the materials.

Note that, while a taxpayer must be "indebted" to claim an interest deduction, the regulations provide interest may be deducted as "interest on his indebtedness" where the taxpayer is "the legal or equitable owner" of the real estate, "even though the taxpayer is not directly liable" upon the mortgage note. Reg. § 1.163-1(b). However, when the taxpayer is not directly liable on the mortgage note, and does not establish legal or equitable ownership of the property, payment of interest on the mortgage does not give rise to a deduction even though the property is the taxpayer's principal residence at the time of payment. *Puentes v. Commissioner*, T.C. Memo. 2013-217.

Consider the following examples demonstrating the application of the qualified residence interest rules:

> **Example 1:** W purchased a home 10 years ago for $250,000. She borrowed $200,000 of the purchase price and gave the lender a mortgage on the home. The home is worth $500,000 today. W still owes $125,000 on the purchase money mortgage encumbering the home. W may deduct whatever interest she pays each year on the outstanding mortgage. The $125,000 represents acquisition indebtedness.

---

taxpayer must use it for the greater of 14 days or 10% of the number of days during the taxable year for which the unit is rented at a fair rental price. § 280A(d)(1). If the taxpayer, however, does not rent the dwelling unit at any time during a taxable year, the unit may be treated as a residence for the taxable year, notwithstanding § 280A(d)(1). § 163(h)(4)(A)(iii). A taxpayer may treat a residence that is "under construction" as a qualified residence for a period of up to 24 months if the residence becomes a qualified residence as of the time that the residence is ready for occupancy. Reg. § 1.163-10T(p)(5). *See Rose v. Commissioner*, T.C. Summ. Op. 2011-117. However, interest paid by a taxpayer with respect to a vacant lot which ohc and her husband owned and on which they camped yearly was not qualified residence interest within the meaning of § 163(h)(3) because the interest was not paid on a principal or second residence. *See Garrison v. Commissioner*, T.C. Memo. 1994-200, *aff'd without published opinion*, 1995 U.S. App. LEXIS 29726 (6th Cir. Sept. 28, 1995).

[3] Note that "acquisition indebtedness" also includes indebtedness resulting from the refinancing of acquisition indebtedness not in excess of the refinanced indebtedness. § 163(h)(3)(B). For example, if one borrows $100,000 to purchase a home and three years later refinances the $90,000 balance then owing on the home, the amount of the refinancing up to $90,000 will constitute acquisition indebtedness. By contrast, if the refinancing were for $100,000 instead of just $90,000, the additional $10,000 would not be considered acquisition indebtedness unless it were used to substantially improve the residence. If not used to improve the residence, it might nonetheless constitute "home equity indebtedness," the interest on which would be deductible. *See* § 163(h)(3)(C).

Example 2: Same facts as Example 1 except W borrows an additional $75,000 to add a room to her home and gives a second mortgage on the home to secure the loan. All $75,000 is used in the remodeling project. The additional $75,000 of debt will be considered acquisition indebtedness and W may deduct all interest paid with respect to that debt.

Example 3: Same facts as Example 1 except W borrows an additional $100,000, $75,000 of which is used to add a room to the home; the other $25,000 is used for matters unrelated to the home. The $75,000 borrowed to add the room will be considered acquisition indebtedness, the interest on which will be deductible. The other $25,000 will be considered home equity indebtedness and, since it is less than $100,000, W may deduct all of the interest paid on that amount.

Example 4: Same facts as Example 1, except W borrows an additional $130,000 and uses that amount to purchase a new Mercedes Benz convertible. $100,000 of the $130,000 borrowing will be considered home equity indebtedness; the other $30,000 will be personal indebtedness for which no interest deduction is allowed.

As the Staff of the Joint Committee noted in its explanation of the changes made to § 163 by the 1986 Act: "While Congress recognized that the imputed rental value of owner-occupied housing may be a significant source of untaxed income, the Congress nevertheless determined that encouraging home ownership is an important policy goal, achieved in part by providing a deduction for residential mortgage interest." General Explanation of the Tax Reform Act of 1986, p. 263–64. In view of the legislative rationale for the deduction of qualified residence interest, consider the following policy questions. Should the government use the tax code to encourage home ownership? To be equitable, should the government provide some corresponding tax break for individuals who cannot afford to own their own home and are forced to rent? Should the government allow a deduction for interest associated with the acquisition of a second home? Given the average housing price in this nation, is the $1,000,000 limitation on acquisition indebtedness too high? Is the allowance of a deduction for interest on home equity indebtedness consistent with the stated legislative purpose of limiting the incentive to invest in consumer durables?

Finally, note two aspects of the $1,000,000 acquisition indebtedness limitation and the $100,000 home equity indebtedness limitation. First, these limits are reduced by statute to $500,000 and $50,000, respectively, in the case of a married taxpayer filing a separate return. § 163(h)(3)(B)(ii), (C)(ii). Thus, married taxpayers cannot effectively double the $1,000,000 and $100,000 limits by filing separate returns. But are the limits still reduced to $500,000 and $50,000 for a married taxpayer filing a separate return, even where the spouse has no ownership interest in the residence, no liability on the mortgage note, pays no interest on the note, and thus claims no mortgage interest deduction? The Tax Court's answer in *Bronstein v. Commissioner*, included in the materials, was "Yes," the lower limits still apply.

A second aspect of the $1,000,000 and $100,000 limitations is whether they apply on a "per-taxpayer" or "per-residence" basis — that is, if two unmarried individuals own the same residence as their principal residence, is each of them entitled separately to the $1,000,000 and $100,000 limitations? In *Sophy v. Commissioner*, included in the materials, the Tax Court's answer was "No." The $1,000,000 and $100,000 limitations apply to the residence, and interest on debt in excess of these limits is not deductible.

2. Interest on Education Loans

In 1997, as part of a package of education tax incentives, Congress authorized the deduction of interest on education loans, a new category of deductible interest outside the confines of § 163. Section 221 authorizes a limited deduction for interest paid by an individual on any "qualified education loan." § 221(a). Qualified loans are essentially those incurred to pay higher education expenses — tuition, fees, room and board and related expenses — of the taxpayer, his or her spouse, or dependents. § 221(d). The term "qualified education loan," however, does not include any indebtedness owed to a person who is related to the taxpayer. § 221(d)(1). (See §§ 267(b) and 707(b)(1) for the definition of "related person.") For example, if taxpayer borrowed money from her parents to attend college, that indebtedness would not constitute a "qualified education loan." Among other restrictions, the deduction is limited to a maximum of $2,500, and is phased out for individuals with modified adjusted gross incomes from $50,000 to $65,000 ($100,000 to $130,000 on joint returns), amounts adjusted for inflation after 2002. § 221(b), (f). For example, as a result of the inflation adjustments, for taxable years beginning in 2015, the $2,500 maximum deduction for interest paid on qualified education loans under § 221 begins to phase out for taxpayers with modified adjusted gross income in excess of $65,000 ($130,000 for joint returns), and is completely phased out for taxpayers with modified adjusted gross income of $80,000 ($160,000 or more for joint returns).

C. Investment Interest

Taxpayers engaged in investment activity often borrow to purchase investment assets that, initially at least, are not income producing. As a result, the interest on such borrowing, rather than offsetting income from the investment activity, offsets income from nonrelated activities, *e.g.*, one's professional compensation. Concerned about this ability to insulate unrelated income from tax, Congress in 1969 enacted § 163(d), limiting the deduction of investment interest.

Until 1986, taxpayers were permitted under § 163(d) to deduct investment interest to the extent of net investment income plus some specified dollar amount. In 1986, Congress strengthened the limitation by providing that investment interest for any taxable year could not be deducted in an amount greater than the taxpayer's net investment income. Investment interest is defined as interest "paid or accrued on indebtedness properly allocable to property held for investment." § 163(d)(3)(A). Net investment income is the excess of investment income over investment expenses. § 163(d)(4)(A). Investment income includes gross income from "property held for investment" — for example, per § 163(d)(5)(A) and § 469(e)(1), interest, dividends, royalties, annuities not attributable to a trade or business — but generally investment income does not include net capital gain from the disposition of investment property. *See* § 163(d)(4)(B). (A taxpayer may, however, elect to include any amount of such net capital gain in computing investment income, but the price of such inclusion is an equivalent reduction in the net capital gain eligible for the maximum capital gain rates. *See* § 1(h)(2). As discussed below, "qualified dividend income" as defined in § 1(h)(11)(B) is treated in a manner similar to net capital gain.) Investment income does not include income subject to the passive activity rules of § 469. § 163(d)(4)(D).[4] Investment expenses are deductible expenses (other than interest and expenses taken into account under § 469) which are directly connected with the production of investment income. § 163(d)(4)(C) and (D).

For example, assume a taxpayer has interest income of $2,000 and dividend income of $3,000, for a total "investment income" of $5,000. Assume further the taxpayer has paid a fully-deductible $1,000 for investment advice related to dividend-producing stock, for a total of $1,000 in "investment expenses." The taxpayer's "net investment income" for the year is thus $4,000. If the taxpayer during the year has paid or incurred interest expenses on debt allocable to property held for investment — perhaps by borrowing money to purchase stock and paying interest on that borrowed money — such interest is deductible only to the extent of $4,000, the taxpayer's net investment income. § 163(d)(1).[5]

Congress in 2003 amended § 163(d)(4) to provide that net investment income will include "qualified dividend income" (as defined in § 1(h)(11)(B)) only to the extent the taxpayer agrees to forego the lower net capital gain rates applicable to these dividends under § 1(h)(11). §§ 1(h)(11)(D)(i), 163(d)(4)(B). Thus, in the preceding example, the taxpayer could include the $3,000 of dividends in the calculation of her total investment income only if she agreed to forego the benefit of having the dividends taxed under § 1(h)(11) at a maximum rate of 15% or 20%. If the taxpayer so agrees, her dividends will be subject to tax at ordinary income rates which are currently as high as 39.6% depending on the taxpayer's tax bracket.

Investment interest expense which, as a result of § 163(d)(1), cannot be deducted in one taxable year may be carried forward to the succeeding taxable year. § 163(d)(2). Reversing its position regarding the amount of disallowed investment interest which could be carried forward, the I.R.S. in Revenue Ruling 95-16, 1995-1 C.B. 9, ruled "the carryover of a taxpayer's disallowed investment interest to a succeeding taxable year under Section 163(d) is not limited by the taxpayer's taxable income for the taxable year in which the interest is paid or accrued." Thus, a taxpayer will be entitled to use the interest deduction if and when the investment becomes profitable. Presumably, the limitation on the deduction of investment interest will encourage taxpayers to consider the economic viability of investments and place less emphasis on tax advantages such as interest deductions. Taxpayers may not avoid the § 163(d) limitation by claiming the interest expense is deductible under § 212. As the Tax Court noted in *Malone v. Commissioner*, T.C. Memo. 1996-

---

[4] The passive activity rules are discussed in Chapter 44.

[5] Note that we must, of course, be able to allocate interest expenses in order to apply the rules of § 163(d). *See* Reg. § 1.163-8T, which provides for allocation to be accomplished by tracing interest expenses to specific debts, and by tracing the debts to specific expenditures based on use of the debt proceeds. An interest expense allocated to an "investment expenditure" would thus constitute investment interest subject to the § 163(d) limitation rule.

408, "the limitation of Section 163(d) would be undermined if taxpayers could deduct under Section 212 interest which is not deductible under Section 163(d)."

D. Timing Issues and Limitations

1. Section 461(g)

Some statutory limitations on interest deductions relate to timing. Section 461(g)(1), for example, generally prevents a cash method taxpayer from claiming a current deduction for interest payments which compensate a lender for the use or forbearance of money in future years.[6] Rather, the taxpayer is permitted to deduct only the interest expense related to the current year; the balance may be deducted in the year(s) to which it relates. In effect, § 461(g)(1) places the cash method taxpayer on the accrual method with respect to the deduction of prepaid interest.

Section 461(g)(2), however, provides an exception to this rule for qualifying "points" paid "in connection with the purchase or improvement of, and secured by, the [taxpayer's] principal residence." (Recall the discussion at the outset of this Overview characterizing points as "prepaid interest.") In *Huntsman v. Commissioner*, 91 T.C. 917 (1988), the Tax Court, interpreting and applying this phrase, held the taxpayers could not deduct currently points paid to refinance the debt on their personal residence. According to the Tax Court, the § 461(g)(2) exception is limited to points "paid in respect of financing the actual purchase of a principal residence or financing improvements to such residence." 91 T.C. at 920. The Tax Court emphasized that, in refinancing transactions, "the funds generated by the loans generally are used not to purchase or improve a principal residence but to pay off the loan that is already in existence and thereby lower the interest costs incurred or achieve some other financial goal not connected directly with home ownership." *Id.* In such refinancing circumstances, the exception in Section 461(g)(2) does not apply. If the points were otherwise deductible, they would be deductible ratably over the life of the loan.

The Eighth Circuit, however, reversed the Tax Court, concluding that § 461(g)(2) merely requires that indebtedness be incurred "in connection with" the purchase or improvement of a taxpayer's residence. According to the court, a fair reading of the statute requires only that the indebtedness have an "association" or "relation" with the purchase of taxpayer's residence. Contrary to the Tax Court, a direct relationship need not exist between the indebtedness and the actual acquisition or improvement of the principal residence. Responding to the Tax Court's concern that the refinancing generally occurs because taxpayers wish to reduce their rate of interest or achieve some other financial objective, the Eighth Circuit stressed those were not the circumstances in this case. Rather, the taxpayers refinanced their debt to obtain permanent financing for the purchase of their home. The indebtedness being refinanced was short term indebtedness. (The Huntsmans had financed the purchase of their home by obtaining a three year loan with a balloon payment due

---

[6] The cash method taxpayer may generally deduct amounts when paid. The accrual method taxpayer, by contrast, may deduct amounts only when the "all events test" has been satisfied. *See* Reg. § 1.461-1(a)(2); Chapters 28, 29.

at the end of three years.) According to the Eighth Circuit, this short term financing was merely an integrated step in the Huntsmans' efforts to secure permanent financing for the purchase of their home. Under these circumstances, the permanent mortgage obtained through the refinancing had sufficient connection with the purchase of the home to bring the Huntsmans' payment of points within the exception of § 461(g)(2). 905 F.2d 1182 (8th Cir. 1990).[7]

2. Section 263A

Section 263A disallows a current deduction for interest incurred during the production period[8] on indebtedness directly or indirectly attributable to a taxpayer's production of certain real or tangible personal property for use in a trade or business or activity conducted for profit. Such interest must be added to the basis of the property and will be recovered through depreciation deductions or when the taxpayer sells or otherwise disposes of the property.

3. Payment Issues

Aside from specific timing limitations, there are timing issues involving the application of general accounting rules. For example, a cash method taxpayer may claim a deduction only when payment has been made. Assume Ben, a cash method taxpayer, borrows $10,000 from a bank, repayable the following year. The borrowed funds are to be used for business purposes. Pursuant to the terms of the loan agreement, however, the bank gives Ben only $9,000. The $1,000 difference between the amount that Ben must repay and the amount he actually receives represents interest. Does the withholding of $1,000 by the bank constitute a payment by Ben enabling him to deduct the $1,000 in interest in the year he borrows the money?

To answer this question, one should begin with the general rule that the mere giving of a promissory note by a cash method taxpayer does not constitute a payment, even if the note is secured by collateral. *Helvering v. Price*, 309 U.S. 409 (1940). For example, had Ben borrowed $9,000 and given the lender two promissory notes due the following year — one for the principal amount of $9,000 and the other for interest in the amount of $1,000 — Ben's delivery of the $1,000 promissory note for interest would not constitute a payment of interest. That makes sense — the

---

[7] The Service has issued Rev. Proc. 94-27, 94-1 C.B. 613, "to minimize possible disputes regarding the deductibility of points." To satisfy the Revenue Procedure so that the Service will treat the points as deductible by a cash method taxpayer in the year paid, the points must (1) be appropriately designated on a Uniform Settlement Statement; (2) be computed as a percentage of the amount borrowed; (3) conform to local established business practice and not exceed the amount generally charged ("If amounts designated as points are paid in lieu of amounts ordinarily stated separately on the settlement statement (such as appraisal fees, inspection fees, title fees, attorneys fees, and property taxes), those amounts are not deductible as points."); (4) be paid to acquire the taxpayer's principal residence — the Revenue Procedure is not satisfied if the points are paid to improve the principal residence, to purchase a residence not the principal residence, or to refinance a loan —; and (5) be paid directly by the taxpayer out of funds not borrowed for this purpose as part of the overall transaction. (This may include points paid by the seller provided the taxpayer computes basis by subtracting seller-paid points from the purchase price of the residence.)

[8] The production period commences when production of property begins and ends when the property is ready to be placed in service or is ready to be held for sale. § 263A(f)(4)(B).

giving of the note is not a payment in cash or the equivalent of cash. In giving his own note, Ben has not reduced his funds; indeed, if Ben never paid the note he would have parted with nothing except his promise to pay. *See Cleaver v. Commissioner*, 158 F.2d 342 (7th Cir. 1946). Is this example substantively different from the initial hypothetical? The only differences are that there is one note in the initial example and the face amount of the loan was $10,000. In substance, however, Ben received only $9,000 of loan proceeds in each situation and agreed to pay $1,000 of interest. In both cases he would only be out of pocket the $1,000 interest in the year that he paid the note(s). Ben therefore is not entitled to an interest deduction in the year he borrowed the funds.

Consider a more complex example: Amy, a cash method taxpayer, owes the Last National Bank $5,000 interest on a business loan. Amy borrows $5,000 from that bank, immediately deposits it in her checking account at the First National Bank, and then delivers her check for $5,000 to the Last National Bank in "payment" of the interest owing. Has Amy actually "paid" the interest or should this be viewed as just a meaningless exchange of checks? Would your answer be different if Amy had borrowed the money from First National Bank and used it to pay the interest? Rather than providing the answers, we recommend that you carefully read the *Davison* case in the materials and draw your own conclusions. A threshold point is that generally, "when a deductible payment is made with borrowed money, the deduction is not postponed until the year in which the borrowed money is repaid. Such expenses must be deducted in the year they are paid and not when the loans are repaid." Rev. Rul. 78-38, 1978-1 C.B. 67; *Granan v. Comm'r*, 55 T.C. 753, 755 (1971).

REVENUE RULING 2010-25
2010-2 C.B. 571

ISSUE

Whether indebtedness that is incurred by a taxpayer to acquire, construct, or substantially improve a qualified residence can constitute "home equity indebtedness" (within the meaning of § 163 (h)(3)(C) of the Internal Revenue Code) to the extent it exceeds $1 million.

FACTS

In 2009, an unmarried individual (Taxpayer) purchased a principal residence for its fair market value of $1,500,000. Taxpayer paid $300,000 and financed the remainder by borrowing $1,200,000 through a loan that is secured by the residence. In 2009, Taxpayer paid interest that accrued on the indebtedness during that year. Taxpayer has no other debt secured by the residence.

LAW

Section 163(a) allows as a deduction all interest paid or accrued within the taxable year on indebtedness. However, for individuals § 163(h)(1) disallows a deduction for personal interest. Under § 163(h)(2)(D), qualified residence interest is not personal interest. Section 163 (h)(3)(A) defines qualified residence interest as interest paid or accrued during the taxable year on acquisition indebtedness or home equity indebtedness secured by any qualified residence of the taxpayer. Under § 163(h)(4)(A), "qualified residence" means a taxpayer's principal residence, within the meaning of § 121, and one other residence selected and used by the taxpayer as a residence.

Section 163 (h)(3)(B)(i) provides that acquisition indebtedness is any indebtedness that is incurred in acquiring, constructing, or substantially improving a qualified residence and is secured by the residence. However, § 163(h)(3)(B)(ii) limits the amount of indebtedness treated as acquisition indebtedness to $1,000,000 ($500,000 for a married individual filing separately). Accordingly, any indebtedness described in § 163(h)(3)(B)(i) in excess of $1,000,000 is, by definition, not acquisition indebtedness for purposes of § 163(h)(3).

Section 163(h)(3)(C)(i) provides that home equity indebtedness is any indebtedness secured by a qualified residence other than acquisition indebtedness, to the extent the fair market value of the qualified residence exceeds the amount of acquisition indebtedness on the residence. However, § 163(h)(3)(C)(ii) limits the amount of indebtedness treated as home equity indebtedness to $100,000 ($50,000 for a married individual filing separately). Accordingly, any indebtedness described in § 163(h)(3)(C)(i) in excess of $100,000 is, by definition, not home equity indebtedness for purposes of § 163(h)(3).

In *Pau v. Commissioner*, T.C. Memo. 1997-43, the Tax Court limited the taxpayers' deduction for qualified residence interest to the interest paid on $1 million of the $1.33 million indebtedness incurred to purchase their residence. The court stated that § 163(h) restricts home mortgage interest deductions to interest paid on $1 million of acquisition indebtedness and $100,000 of home equity indebtedness. Citing § 163(h)(3)(B), the court stated that acquisition indebtedness is defined as indebtedness that is incurred in acquiring, constructing, or substantially improving any qualified residence of the taxpayer, and is secured by the residence. Citing § 163(h)(3)(C), the court further stated that home equity indebtedness is defined as any indebtedness (other than acquisition indebtedness) secured by a qualified residence. The court concluded that the taxpayers failed to demonstrate that any of their debt was not incurred in acquiring, constructing, or substantially improving their residence and thus was not acquisition indebtedness. However, the court did not address the effect of the $1 million limitation in § 163 (h)(3)(B)(ii) on the definition of acquisition indebtedness for purposes of § 163(h)(3). The Tax Court followed *Pau* in *Catalano v. Commissioner*, T.C. Memo. 2000-82.

ANALYSIS

Taxpayer may deduct, as interest on acquisition indebtedness under § 163(h)(3)(B), interest paid in 2009 on $1,000,000 of the $1,200,000 indebtedness used to acquire the principal residence. The $1,200,000 indebtedness was incurred in acquiring a qualified residence of Taxpayer and was secured by the residence. Thus, indebtedness of $1,000,000 is treated as acquisition indebtedness under § 163(h)(3)(B).

Taxpayer also may deduct, as interest on home equity indebtedness under § 163(h)(3)(C), interest paid in 2009 on $100,000 of the remaining indebtedness of $200,000. The $200,000 is secured by the qualified residence, is not acquisition indebtedness under § 163(h)(3)(B), and does not exceed the fair market value of the residence reduced by the acquisition indebtedness secured by the residence. Thus, $100,000 of the $200,000 is treated as home equity indebtedness under § 163(h)(3)(C).

Under § 163(h)(3)(A), the interest on both acquisition indebtedness and home equity indebtedness is qualified residence interest. Therefore, for 2009 Taxpayer may deduct interest paid on indebtedness of $1,100,000 as qualified residence interest. Any interest Taxpayer paid on the remaining indebtedness of $100,000 is nondeductible personal interest under § 163(h).

The Internal Revenue Service will not follow the decisions in *Pau v. Commissioner* and *Catalano v. Commissioner*. The holding in *Pau* was based on the incorrect assertion that taxpayers must demonstrate that debt treated as home equity indebtedness "was not incurred in acquiring, constructing or substantially improving their residence." The definition of home equity indebtedness in § 163(h)(3)(C) contains no such restrictions, and accordingly the Service will determine home equity indebtedness consistent with the provisions of this revenue ruling, notwithstanding the decisions in *Pau* and *Catalano*.

HOLDING

Indebtedness incurred by a taxpayer to acquire, construct, or substantially improve a qualified residence can constitute home equity indebtedness to the extent it exceeds $1 million (subject to the applicable dollar and fair market value limitations imposed on home equity indebtedness by § 163(h)(3)(C)).

SOPHY v. COMMISSIONER
138 T.C. 204 (2012)

COHEN, JUDGE:

Background

In 2000 petitioner Charles J. Sophy and petitioner Bruce H. Voss purchased a house together in Rancho Mirage, California, and financed the purchase by obtaining a mortgage that was secured by the Rancho Mirage house. Petitioners acquired the Rancho Mirage house as joint tenants and held the property as joint tenants during the years in issue.

In 2002 petitioners refinanced the Rancho Mirage house with a new mortgage loan of $500,000. The proceeds of the new mortgage loan, which was secured by the Rancho Mirage house, were used to pay off the original mortgage loan. Petitioners were jointly and severally liable for the new mortgage on the Rancho Mirage house.

In 2002 petitioners purchased a house in Beverly Hills, California. Petitioners acquired the Beverly Hills house as joint tenants and held the property as joint tenants during the years in issue. To finance the purchase, petitioners obtained a mortgage secured by the Beverly Hills house. In 2003 petitioners refinanced the Beverly Hills house by obtaining a new mortgage loan of $2 million. The proceeds of this new mortgage loan, which was secured by the Beverly Hills house, were used to pay off the original mortgage loan. Petitioners were jointly and severally liable for the mortgage on the Beverly Hills house.

Also in 2003 petitioners obtained a home equity line of credit of $300,000 for the Beverly Hills house, on which petitioners were jointly and severally liable. For the years in issue, petitioners used the Beverly Hills house as their principal residence and the Rancho Mirage house as their second residence.

In 2006 Sophy paid mortgage interest of $94,698 for the two residences, and Voss paid $85,962. The total average balance in 2006 for the Beverly Hills house mortgage and home equity loan and the Rancho Mirage house mortgage was $2,703,568. In 2007 Sophy paid mortgage interest of $99,901, and Voss paid $76,635. The total average balance in 2007 for the two mortgages and the home equity loan was $2,669,136.

On their individual Federal income tax returns for 2006 and 2007, petitioners each claimed deductions for qualified residence interest. The Internal Revenue Service (IRS) audited petitioners' 2006 and 2007 individual income tax returns and disallowed portions of petitioners' deductions for qualified residence interest. . . .

These determinations followed the reasoning of advice issued in 2009 in which the IRS dealt with the question of how to apply the acquisition indebtedness limitation in a situation where the total acquisition indebtedness was more than $1 million and the taxpayer was one of two unmarried co-owners of the residence. See C.C.A. 200911007 (Mar. 13, 2009). This Chief Counsel Advice states:

> [T]he $1,000,000 limitation on acquisition indebtedness under § 163(h)(3)(B)(ii) is used to determine the portion [of] Taxpayer's interest payments that may be deducted. In particular, the amount of interest Taxpayer may deduct is determined by multiplying the amount of interest actually paid by Taxpayer on Taxpayer's qualified residence by a fraction the numerator of which is $1,000,000 and the denominator of which is * * * the average balance of the outstanding acquisition indebtedness during the years in question.

In these cases, the IRS computed the applicable limitation ratio as $1.1 million ($1 million for acquisition indebtedness plus $100,000 for home equity indebtedness) over the entire average balance of the qualifying loans. This limitation ratio was then multiplied by the amount of interest paid by each petitioner to arrive at the amount of deductible qualified residence interest that each petitioner could claim for each year in issue.

Discussion

Section 163(a) allows a deduction for all interest paid or accrued within the taxable year on indebtedness. As an exception, § 163(h) generally disallows a deduction for personal interest. Personal interest, however, does not include qualified residence interest. Sec. 163(h)(2)(D).

In general, a qualified residence is defined as a taxpayer's principal residence and one other home that is used as a residence by the taxpayer. Sec. 163(h)(4)(A)(i). Qualified residence interest means any interest paid or accrued during a tax year on acquisition indebtedness or home equity indebtedness with respect to the taxpayer's qualified residence. Sec. 163(h)(3)(A).

There is no dispute that petitioners' homes meet the definition of a qualified residence and that the mortgage interest paid by petitioners is qualified residence interest because it was paid on acquisition and home equity indebtedness secured by their homes.

Petitioners' sole contention is that the § 163(h)(3) limitations on indebtedness (indebtedness limitations) are properly applied on a per-taxpayer basis with respect to residence co-owners who are not married to each other. Petitioners argue that they should each be allowed a deduction for interest paid on up to $1.1 million of acquisition and home equity indebtedness with respect to the residences that they jointly own. Under their interpretation, because these cases involve two unmarried co-owners, together they should be able to deduct interest paid on up to $2.2 million of acquisition and home equity indebtedness.

Respondent's position, on the other hand, is that the indebtedness limitations are properly applied on a per-residence basis, regardless of the number of residence owners and whether co-owners are married to each other. Under respondent's interpretation, co-owners should collectively be limited to a deduction for interest paid on a maximum of $1.1 million of acquisition and home equity indebtedness.

We must decide whether the statutory limitations on the amount of acquisition and home equity indebtedness with respect to which interest is deductible under § 163(h)(3) are properly applied on a per-residence or per-taxpayer basis where residence co-owners are not married to each other.

When we interpret a statute, our purpose is to give effect to Congress' intent. To accomplish this we begin with the statutory language, which is the most persuasive evidence of the statutory purpose. . . .

We begin our analysis by looking closely at the definitions of acquisition indebtedness and home equity indebtedness in § 163(h)(3)(B)(i) and (C)(i). The acquisition indebtedness definition uses the phrase "any indebtedness which is incurred" in conjunction with "acquiring, constructing, or substantially improving any qualified residence of the taxpayer and is secured by such residence." We note that the word "taxpayer" in this context is used only in relation to the qualified residence, not the indebtedness. Similarly, the operative language in the definition of home equity indebtedness is "any indebtedness" that is secured by a qualified residence (other than acquisition indebtedness). Sec. 163(h)(3)(C)(i). Once again, the phrase "any indebtedness" is not qualified by language relating to an individual taxpayer.

Qualified residence interest is defined as "any interest which is paid or accrued during the taxable year on acquisition indebtedness with respect to any qualified residence of the taxpayer, or home equity indebtedness with respect to any qualified residence of the taxpayer." Sec. 163(h)(3)(A) (emphasis added). The definition of "home equity indebtedness" also includes the phrase "reduced by the amount of acquisition indebtedness with respect to such residence" (referring to a qualified residence). Sec. 163(h)(3)(C)(i)(II) (emphasis added). The definitions of the terms "acquisition indebtedness" and "home equity indebtedness" in § 163(h)(3)(B)(i) and (C)(i) establish that the indebtedness must be related to a qualified residence, and the repeated use of the phrases "with respect to a qualified residence" and "with respect to such residence" in the provisions discussed above focuses on the residence rather than the taxpayer.

From Congress' use of "any indebtedness" in the definition of acquisition indebtedness, which is not qualified by language regarding an individual taxpayer, it appears that this phrase refers to the total amount of indebtedness with respect to a qualified residence and which is secured by that residence. The focus is on the entire amount of indebtedness with respect to the residence itself. Thus when the statute limits the amount that may be treated as acquisition indebtedness, it appears that what is being limited is the total amount of acquisition debt that may be claimed in relation to the qualified residence, rather than the amount of acquisition debt that may be claimed in relation to an individual taxpayer.

Our analysis of the term "home equity indebtedness" is similar. The use of the phrase "any indebtedness", unqualified by language relating to an individual taxpayer, appears to limit the total amount of home equity indebtedness that may be claimed in relation to the qualified residence itself, rather than the amount of home equity indebtedness that may be claimed in relation to an individual taxpayer.

Because of references to an individual taxpayer in other provisions of § 163(h), petitioners would have us interpret the indebtedness limitations as applying on a per-taxpayer basis, rather than a per-residence basis. Such an interpretation, however, reads too much into the indebtedness limitations. While Congress references "a taxpayer" and "the taxpayer" several times in § 163(h), any reference to an individual taxpayer is conspicuously absent in the language of the indebtedness limitations. Moreover, as noted above, the "taxpayer" references in the definitions of acquisition indebtedness and home equity indebtedness are in relation to the qualified residence, rather than to the indebtedness.] "When 'Congress includes particular language in one section of a statute but omits it in another section of the same Act, it is generally presumed that Congress act[ed] intentionally and purposely' in so doing." . . .

With respect to Congress' repeated use of phrases such as "with respect to any qualified residence" and "with respect to such residence" in conjunction with terms that by their own definitions must already be in relation to a qualified residence, these phrases appear to be superfluous. However, " 'a statute ought, upon the whole, to be so construed that, if it can be prevented, no clause, sentence, or word shall be superfluous, void, or insignificant.' " . . . In addition, we must construe a provision not in isolation, but as part of the statutory scheme in which it is embedded. In the light of the language in § 163(h)(3) taken as a whole, it appears that Congress used these repeated references to emphasize the point that qualified residence interest and the related indebtedness limitations are residence focused rather than taxpayer focused.

Further support regarding application of the indebtedness limitations is found in the parenthetical language addressing married taxpayers filing separate returns. The parenthetical language in the acquisition indebtedness limitation in § 163(h)(3)(B)(ii) provides that married taxpayers who file separate returns are limited to acquisition indebtedness of $500,000 each, or one-half of the otherwise allowable amount of acquisition indebtedness. Similarly, the home equity indebtedness limitation in § 163(h)(3)(C)(ii) includes parenthetical language that provides that married taxpayers who file separate returns are limited to home equity indebtedness of $50,000 each, which is one-half of the otherwise allowable amount of home equity indebtedness. Thus the language used in these provisions suggests, without expressly stating, that co-owners who are married to each other and file a joint return are limited to a deduction of interest on $1 million of acquisition indebtedness and $100,000 on home equity indebtedness. Accordingly, in a case involving acquisition indebtedness of more than $1 million, this Court has limited a married couple's qualified residence interest deduction on a joint return to the interest paid on $1 million of acquisition indebtedness. . . .

Petitioners argue that Congress, in using this particular language in the indebtedness limitations, intended to create a special rule for married couples — a "marriage penalty" — that does not apply to co-owners who are not married to each other. However, in the light of the residence-focused language used throughout § 163(h)(3) and the absence of any reference to an individual taxpayer in the indebtedness limitations themselves, this argument is not persuasive. Rather than setting out a marriage penalty, this language simply appears to set out a specific allocation of the limitation amounts that must be used by married couples filing separate tax returns, thus implying that co-owners who are not married to one another may choose to allocate the limitation amounts among themselves in some other manner, such as according to percentage of ownership.

Although we have reached our conclusion by reviewing the language of the statute, nothing in the legislative history of the § 163(h)(3) indebtedness limitations suggests that Congress had any other intention than what we have determined from an examination of the language. We conclude that the limitations in § 163(h)(3)(B)(ii) and (C)(ii) on the amounts that may be treated as acquisition and home equity indebtedness with respect to a qualified residence are properly applied on a per-residence basis.

Decisions will be entered under Rule 155.

BRONSTEIN v. COMMISSIONER
138 T.C. 382 (2012)

GOEKE, JUDGE:

Petitioner was married throughout 2007. On February 12, 2007, petitioner and her father-in-law, Michael Bronstein (father-in-law), purchased real property in Brooklyn, New York (property), as joint tenants with right of survivorship. The price was $1.35 million. To obtain the necessary funds, petitioner and her father-in-law each signed and became liable on a mortgage for $1 million (mortgage) secured by the property. Petitioner paid $2,500 for a loan discount (points) at the time of closing.

From February through December 31, 2007, petitioner and her husband resided at the property, which was their principal residence for tax purposes. [During 2007 petitioner's husband did not have a legal ownership interest in the property and he did not have a legally enforceable obligation to pay the mortgage.] Petitioner's father-in-law never resided at the property. During 2007 petitioner used her own funds to make all payments on the mortgage; neither her husband nor her father-in-law made any payments on the mortgage. Petitioner paid $49,739 in interest on the mortgage during 2007.

Petitioner timely filed her 2007 Federal income tax return and elected "married filing separately" filing status. On her Schedule A, Itemized Deductions, she deducted $52,239 in home mortgage interest and points paid. [Neither petitioner's husband nor her father-in-law deducted any amounts resulting from her payment of the mortgage interest or points.] On August 2, 2010, respondent issued a notice of deficiency to petitioner for tax year 2007. Respondent's notice allowed petitioner only [part] of her claimed deduction for the home mortgage interest paid. . . .

Discussion

. . . .

II. Qualified Residence Interest Deduction and Indebtedness Limitations

Section 163(a) allows a deduction for all interest paid or accrued within the taxable year on indebtedness. As an exception, § 163(h) generally disallows a deduction for personal interest. Personal interest, however, does not include qualified residence interest. Sec. 163(h)(2)(D).

. . . .

There is no dispute that the property meets the definition of a qualified residence and that the mortgage interest petitioner paid is qualified residence interest because it was paid on acquisition indebtedness and home equity indebtedness secured by the property.

In his notice of deficiency respondent allowed petitioner to deduct home mortgage interest on a total of $550,000 of indebtedness ($500,000 in acquisition indebtedness under § 163(h)(3)(B)(ii) plus $50,000 of home equity indebtedness under § 163(h)(3)(C)(ii)). Petitioner claims that she should be allowed to deduct interest paid on the entire $1 million of indebtedness.

Petitioner correctly asserts that the parenthetical indebtedness limitations of § 163(h)(3)(B)(ii) and (C)(ii) are $550,000 for each spouse filing a separate return. However, petitioner further claims that these limitations were enacted so that, collectively, a married couple filing separately can claim $1.1 million of aggregate indebtedness across both of their returns and is not limited to claiming a maximum of $550,000 on any one return. We disagree. . . .

We believe § 163(h)(3)(B)(ii) clearly states that a married individual filing a separate return is limited to a deduction for interest paid on $500,000 of home acquisition indebtedness. Similarly, we believe § 163(h)(3)(C)(ii) clearly states that a married individual filing a separate return is limited to a deduction for interest paid on $50,000 of home equity indebtedness.

Petitioner has not offered any unequivocal evidence of legislative purpose which would allow us to override the plain language of § 163(h)(3)(B)(ii) and (C)(ii). As a result, we agree with respondent that petitioner is not entitled to a deduction for the interest paid on the entire $1 million of acquisition indebtedness incurred in purchasing the property. Rather, petitioner is entitled to deduct interest paid on only $550,000 of the mortgage indebtedness. . . .

***

DAVISON v. COMMISSIONER
United States Tax Court
107 T.C. 35 (1996)
aff'd per curiam, 141 F.3d 403 (2d Cir. 1998)

[Authors' summary of pertinent facts: The petitioner is a certified public accountant. During 1979, he was head partner of the accounting firm of Peat, Marwick & Mitchell, where he was associated with Samuel J. Esposito and John L. Vitale, who were also partners. Davison, Esposito and Vitale formed a general partnership (known as White Tail) for the purpose of entering into the business of acquiring, cultivating, and selling farm properties. White Tail reported its income on a calendar year basis using the cash method of accounting.

White Tail borrowed a substantial sum of money from the John Hancock Mutual Life Insurance Co. (John Hancock) The credit arrangement between White Tail and John Hancock required White Tail to make an interest payment on January 1, 1981. The amount of interest due was $1,587,310.46. The credit arrangement also called for a principal payment of $7,707.50 on the same date.

Because of financial difficulties, White Tail was not in a position to make the January 1, 1981 payments. White Tail negotiated an arrangement with John Hancock whereby John Hancock would lend White Tail the money to make the January 1981 payments.

On December 30, 1980, John Hancock made a wire transfer of $1,587,310.46 to

White Tail's account at the American National Bank and Trust Co. of Chicago (American National). This transfer increased the amount White Tail owed to John Hancock by $1,587,310.46. This amount was reflected as a deposit into the American National account on December 30, 1980. On December 31, 1980, White Tail made a wire transfer of $1,595,017.96 to John Hancock, representing $7,707.50 of principal and $1,587,310.46 in interest due under the 1980 credit arrangement.

The purpose of the $1,587,310.46 advance from John Hancock was to provide White Tail with sufficient funds to satisfy the interest due John Hancock on January 1, 1981, under the terms of the 1980 credit arrangement, as modified. White Tail's general ledger showed that its bank account at American National, as of December 31, 1980, was overdrawn with a negative balance of $138,931.80.

The IRS in its notice of deficiency disallowed the interest deduction which White Tail had claimed for the amount White Tail asserted it had "paid" to John Hancock on December 31, 1980, i.e., the $1,587,310.46. The issue in this case is whether White Tail was entitled to the interest deduction claimed.]

Discussion

Before we analyze the transactions in issue, it is appropriate to state some general principles with respect to interest deductions. Section 163(a) generally permits a deduction for "all interest paid or accrued within the taxable year on indebtedness." For cash basis taxpayers, payment must be made in cash or its equivalent. *Don E. Williams Co. v. Commissioner*, 429 U.S. 569, 577–578 (1977). . . . The delivery of a promissory note is not a cash equivalent but merely a promise to pay. *Helvering v. Price*, 309 U.S. 409, 413 (1940). . . . Where a lender withholds a borrower's interest payment from the loan proceeds, the borrower is considered to have paid interest with a note rather than with cash or its equivalent and, therefore, is not entitled to a deduction until the loan is repaid. . . . *Cleaver v. Commissioner*, 6 T.C. 452, 454, *aff'd*, 158 F.2d 342 (7th Cir. 1946). On the other hand, where a taxpayer discharges interest payable to one lender with funds obtained from a different lender, the interest on the first loan is considered paid when the funds are transferred to the first lender. . . . With these general principles in mind, we proceed to look at the specific transactions in issue. Because the December 30–31, 1980, transaction presents the more difficult issue, we address it first.

. . . .

On December 30, 1980, John Hancock wired $1,587,310.46 to White Tail's account at American National. This increased the amount White Tail owed John Hancock by $1,587,310.46. On December 31, 1980, White Tail wired John Hancock $1,595,017.96, which John Hancock reflected as a satisfaction of White Tail's January 1, 1981, interest obligation of $1,587,310.46 plus a principal payment of $7,707.50.

The purpose of John Hancock's $1,587,310.46 advance to White Tail on December 30, 1980, was to provide White Tail with sufficient funds to satisfy the interest due John Hancock on January 1, 1981. Petitioners argue that White Tail paid this interest when it made the wire transfer to John Hancock on December 31, 1980. Respondent contends that interest has not been paid but merely postponed, and, consequently, White Tail is not entitled to a deduction under section 163(a).

On brief, petitioners place particular reliance on prior decisions of this Court in which the deductibility of interest paid to a lender, with funds borrowed from the same lender, turns on whether the borrower exercised "unrestricted control" over the funds borrowed. Petitioners argue that they are entitled to a deduction pursuant to section 163(a), because White Tail possessed unrestricted control of the $1,587,310.46 wired from John Hancock to White Tail's account at American National on December 30, 1980. The concept of "unrestricted control" in cases of this nature had its origin in *Burgess v. Commissioner*, 8 T.C. 47 (1947). In *Burgess*, a cash basis taxpayer originally borrowed $203,988.90. On December 20, 1941, just prior to the due date of his interest payment, the taxpayer borrowed an additional $4,000 from the same lender, deposited the lender's check in the taxpayer's checking account, and commingled the $4,000 with other funds in the account. On December 26, 1941, the taxpayer drew a check on this account in the amount of $4,219.33 to cover $4,136.44 of interest due on the original loan plus $82.89 of prepaid interest on the $4,000 loan. At the time the taxpayer's check was drawn, the taxpayer had $3,180.79 in his account in addition to the $4,000 borrowed on December 20, 1941.

In a Court-reviewed opinion, we allowed the deduction. We rejected the Commissioner's argument that the taxpayer had simply substituted a note in place of the interest payable. We found that the taxpayer did not apply for the loan for the sole purpose of obtaining funds to pay interest, and the lender did not grant the loan for that exclusive purpose. We also found that the taxpayer had several bills that were due, needed sufficient funds to pay them as well as the interest, and commingled the loan proceeds with other funds in his account, causing them to lose their identity. As a result, we found that the loan proceeds could not be traced to the payment of interest.

Six judges dissented from the majority's holding. They believed that the facts demonstrated that the taxpayer borrowed the $4,000 for the purpose of paying interest. They believed that the substance of what occurred was no different than where a taxpayer simply executes a note to the lender in satisfaction of the current interest obligation.

In *Burgess v. Commissioner, supra*, the purpose of the second loan was obviously an important factor. However, our subsequent opinions relying on *Burgess* began to focus mostly on whether the borrower acquired possession or control over the proceeds of the second loan. This was later referred to as unrestricted control. See *Menz v. Commissioner*, 80 T.C. at 1187.

In *Burck v. Commissioner*, 63 T.C. 556 (1975), *aff'd on other grounds*, 533 F.2d 768 (2d Cir. 1976), a cash basis taxpayer borrowed $5,388,600 from a bank on December 29, 1969. Pursuant to negotiations that preceded the loan agreement, $1 million of these proceeds was deposited into the taxpayer's account at a second bank. Prior to this deposit, the taxpayer's other funds in the account totaled $42,009.02. On December 30, 1969, pursuant to the negotiated agreement between the lender and the taxpayer, $377,202 was transferred from the taxpayer's account back to the lender for 1 year's prepaid interest on the loan.

We concluded that the facts in *Burck* were within the scope of our decision in

Burgess v. Commissioner, supra, and allowed the interest deduction. In reaching this decision, we relied primarily on the fact that the loan proceeds were commingled with the other funds in the taxpayer's account. We also pointed out that the taxpayer owned other assets from which the interest could have, if need be, been prepaid, even though the taxpayer's bank account contained insufficient funds to pay the interest. We also considered the fact that prepayment of the $377,202 in interest was an "integral part" of the loan agreement because the bank would not have made the loan without it. It was clear that $377,202 of the loan proceeds was advanced for the purpose of paying interest to the lender.

Faced with essentially the same fact pattern in *Wilkerson v. Commissioner,* 70 T.C. 240 (1978), *revd. and remanded* 655 F.2d 980 (9th Cir. 1981), we followed the reasoning and result of *Burck v. Commissioner, supra.* Responding to the Commissioner's argument that the borrowers never had "unrestricted control" over the loan proceeds, we stated: "We have rejected that same argument where the lender gave up control of the borrowed funds, the funds were commingled with the taxpayer's own funds, and then the commingled funds were used to prepay interest. *Burgess v. Commissioner,* 8 T.C. 47 (1947); *Burck v. Commissioner,* 63 T.C. 556 (1975), aff'd, 533 F.2d 768 (2d Cir. 1976)."

In *Wilkerson,* without the loan, the borrowers did not have sufficient funds with which to satisfy their interest obligations. Prior to receipt of the loan proceeds used to satisfy their interest obligations, the borrowers had checking account balances of $2 and $1,873, respectively, while their respective interest payments were approximately $55,000. In response to the Commissioner's argument that there was insufficient commingling, we stated: "The partnerships here acquired control of the loan proceeds as evidenced by their deposit in the partnership checking accounts outside the lender's domain. That the partnerships exercised their control over the funds for only a brief period of time does not convert the transactions into discounted loans."

In *Wilkerson,* unrestricted control appears to mean unrestricted physical or mechanical control in the sense that there were no physical or mechanical restraints on the borrower's ability to withdraw borrowed funds for a purpose other than paying interest. Used in this sense, "unrestricted control" ignores the fact that the borrower may have obligated himself to use the loan proceeds to pay interest to the lender as a precondition to the loan, and also ignores the fact that failure to use loan proceeds for the purpose of satisfying a current interest obligation would result in a default and likely foreclosure proceedings.

Two Courts of Appeals have rejected this application of an "unrestricted control" rule. *Wilkerson v. Commissioner,* 655 F.2d 980 (9th Cir. 1981); *Battelstein v. IRS,* 631 F.2d 1182 (5th Cir. 1980) (en banc). In *Battelstein,* the lender agreed to make advances to cover the taxpayers' quarterly interest payments on a $3 million loan. The taxpayers never paid interest except by way of these advances. The lender notified the taxpayers each quarter of the amount of interest that was due; the taxpayers would then send a check for this amount, and the lender would send the taxpayers a check for an identical amount.

The Court of Appeals for the Fifth Circuit concluded that the check exchanges between the lender and borrower were plainly for no purpose other than to finance the taxpayers' current interest obligations and, therefore, denied the interest deduction. In rejecting the taxpayers' reliance on the fact that actual checks were exchanged, the Court of Appeals stated:

> In ignoring these exchanges, we merely follow a well-established principle of law, *viz.*, that in tax cases it is axiomatic that we look through the form in which the taxpayer has cloaked a transaction to the substance of the transaction. As the Supreme Court stated some years ago in *Minnesota Tea Co. v. Helvering*, 302 U.S. 609, 58 S.Ct. 393, 82 L.Ed. 474 (1938), "A given result at the end of a straight path is not made a different result because reached by following a devious path." . . . The check exchanges notwithstanding, the Battelsteins satisfied their interest obligations to Gibraltar by giving Gibraltar notes promising future payment. The law leaves no doubt that such a surrender of notes does not constitute payment for tax purposes entitling a taxpayer to a deduction.

The Court of Appeals rejected the taxpayers' reliance on *Burgess v. Commissioner*, 8 T.C. 47 (1947). The Court of Appeals determined that even if *Burgess* constituted good law, it was limited to cases where the purpose of a subsequent loan was not apparent (*i.e.*, whether it was to finance interest payments on a previous loan for which deductions are being claimed, or whether it was to fulfill some other unrelated objective). The Court of Appeals held that "If the second loan was for the purpose of financing the interest due on the first loan, then the taxpayer's interest obligation on the first loan has not been paid as Section 163(a) requires; it has merely been postponed." . . .

In *Wilkerson v. Commissioner*, 655 F.2d at 982, the Court of Appeals relied on *Battelstein v. IRS, supra*, and denied the interest deduction, because a portion of the loan proceeds was "specifically earmarked" for the purpose of paying the interest due. The Court of Appeals stated that "The fact that the loan proceeds were run through the taxpayers' bank account in a transaction intended to take not more than one business day, does not affect the substance of the transaction." . . . Moreover, the Court of Appeals explained that "A careful reading of *Burgess v. Commissioner*, 8 T.C. 47 (1947), indicates that it involved two separate loan transactions in which the proceeds of the second loan were not earmarked for the purpose of payment of interest on the first loan."

Shortly after the reversal in *Wilkerson v. Commissioner, supra*, we acknowledged the confusion in this area brought about by the disparity of results among cases of similar economic impact. *Menz v. Commissioner*, 80 T.C. at 1187. In *Menz*, we summarized this Court's previous application of the "unrestricted control" test as follows:

> Where a lender gives up control of borrowed funds, the funds are commingled with the taxpayer's other funds in an account at an institution separate from the lender, and the interest obligation is satisfied with funds from that separate account, there has been a payment of interest under section 163(a).

In *Menz*, we found that the taxpayer had not received unrestricted control over the funds borrowed for the purpose of paying interest. We based this conclusion on the following facts: (1) The loan to the borrower, the deposit into the borrower's checking account, and the retransfer of the funds to the lender were all simultaneous; (2) the remaining funds in the borrower's account with which it could have paid the interest in question were de minimis; (3) the loans were made solely for the purpose of paying the interest owed to the lender; (4) the borrowed funds were easily traceable through the borrower's account to the asserted interest payments; and (5) a wholly owned subsidiary of the lender was a 1-percent general partner of the borrower and possessed approval power over all the borrower's major transactions. The fifth factor is the only one that was not present in *Wilkerson*.

The 1-percent partner did not have signatory authority over the bank account into which the borrowed funds were deposited. *Menz v. Commissioner, supra* at 1190. Nevertheless, we found that the borrower lacked "unrestricted control," because the 1-percent general partner of the borrower was controlled by the lender and could have terminated the borrower's existence if it had failed to use the borrowed funds to satisfy interest obligations owed to the lender. We found that the 1-percent partner's control over the future of the partnership was too fundamental and significant to conclude that the partnership's control over the funds in its account was unrestricted. *Id.* at 1192.

We think that similar fundamental and significant factors restricted White Tail's control over the $1,587,310.46 that John Hancock wired to White Tail's account on December 30, 1980. White Tail had specifically agreed to borrow this amount to satisfy its interest obligation in order to prevent a default. Use of the funds for any other purpose would have breached the terms of its agreement with John Hancock and would have resulted in White Tail's default and a likely end to its business operations. In *Wilkerson*, we chose not to consider the impact of a default and its consequences on whether the borrower had unrestricted control over funds that it borrowed. However, in *Menz*, we expanded our analysis and considered factors beyond physical control over the borrowed funds. Similarly, in this case, we cannot ignore the reality that a borrower who borrows funds for the purpose of satisfying an interest obligation to the same lender in order to avoid a default does not have unrestricted control over the borrowed funds in any meaningful sense. In light of our expanded view of the considerations that must be taken into account in determining whether a borrower has unrestricted control over borrowed funds, our earlier opinions in *Burgess, Burck*, and *Wilkerson*, have been sapped of much of their vitality.

The issue before us arises when a borrower borrows funds from a lender and immediately satisfies an interest obligation to the same lender. In order to determine whether interest has been paid or merely deferred, it is first necessary to determine whether the borrowed funds were, in substance, the same funds used to satisfy the interest obligation. Whether the relevant transactions were simultaneous, whether the borrower had other funds in his account to pay interest, whether the funds are traceable, and whether the borrower had any realistic choice to use the borrowed funds for any other purpose would all be relevant to this issue. Once it is determined that the borrowed funds were the same funds used to satisfy the interest obligation, the purpose of the loan plays a decisive role.

In light of the foregoing analysis, we hold that a cash basis borrower is not entitled to an interest deduction where the funds used to satisfy the interest obligation were borrowed for that purpose from the same lender to whom the interest was owed. This test is consistent with our traditional approach of characterizing transactions on a substance-over-form basis by looking at the economic realities of the transaction. We agree with the Courts of Appeals in *Wilkerson* and *Battelstein* that there is no substantive difference between a situation where a borrower satisfies a current interest obligation by simply assuming a greater debt to the same lender and one where the borrower and lender exchange checks pursuant to a plan whose net result is identical to that in the first situation. In both situations, the borrower has simply increased his debt to the lender by the amount of interest. The effect of this is to postpone, rather than pay, the interest.

In the instant case, it is clear that the purpose of the $1,587,310.46 advance on December 30, 1980, from John Hancock to White Tail was to provide White Tail with funds to satisfy its interest obligation to John Hancock. White Tail's general partner had requested modification of the original 1980 credit arrangement so that the entire amount of interest could be borrowed from John Hancock, in order to prevent a default on the interest obligation. In the Letter Agreement between White Tail and John Hancock, both borrower and lender agreed that the $1,587,310.46 advance would increase White Tail's loan and that it would be used to satisfy the current interest obligation. Checks were exchanged within a 2-day period to effect the transaction. The effect was to increase the amount of White Tail's principal loan obligation to John Hancock by the amount of interest due. The fact that the loan proceeds were run through White Tail's bank account does not affect the substance of the transaction. *Wilkerson v. Commissioner*, 655 F.2d at 983. It follows that White Tail, a cash basis partnership, is not entitled to a deduction for interest paid.

AUTHOR'S NOTE:

Suppose Taxpayer owes $30,000 in past due interest on a home mortgage loan. If the loan is modified, and the past-due interest is added to the loan balance — that is, if the past-due interest is capitalized into the principal of the loan — has Taxpayer thereby "paid" the interest through its capitalization into the loan? The answer in *Copeland v. Commissioner*, T.C. Memo. 2014-226, citing *Davison* and other cases, was "No." The "economic reality," said the court, is that the borrower has postponed paying the interest, not paid it.

Chapter 23

THE DEDUCTION FOR TAXES

I. PROBLEMS

1. Identify which of the following taxes are deductible:

    (a) The state and city income tax paid on salaries.

    (b) State and city sales tax paid on clothing purchased for personal use.

    (c) State and local taxes paid on business property.

    (d) Social Security tax.

    (e) Federal income tax.

    (f) A special improvement district assessment for the installation of lighting in a residential area. Only landowners in the area are required to pay the assessment.

    (g) A hotel tax paid by a sole proprietor on a business trip away from home.

    (h) Highway tolls paid.

2. Laura sold a house to Patrick on an installment contract. Under the terms of the contract, Patrick was required to maintain insurance on the house and to pay the property taxes. When Laura learned Patrick had failed to pay the taxes, she paid the taxes herself to protect her interest in the property. May Laura deduct the taxes?

3. Joe sold Mary certain real property on May 15. The "real property tax year" is the calendar year. Under the law imposing the real property tax, the tax becomes a lien on January 1 of the "real property tax year" and is payable on April 1 of that year. There is no personal liability for the tax. Joe paid the entire amount of the tax on April 30. Joe and Mary agreed the taxes would be apportioned between them as of June 1; Mary would thus be required to reimburse Joe for 7/12 of the taxes which Joe paid. Assume the property taxes paid by Joe amounted to $1,200. How much may Joe and Mary each deduct?

Assignment for Chapter 23:

Complete the problems.

Read: Internal Revenue Code: §§ 164(a), (b)(1), (2), (5), (6), (c), (d)(1), (f); 275; Skim § 164(d)(2); 266.
   Treasury Regulations: §§ 1.164-1(a); 1.164-2(a), (g); 1.164-3(a), (b); 1.164-4(a), (b)(1); and 1.164-6(a). Skim §§ 1.164-6(b), (c), (d)(1)–(4), (d)(6).

Materials: Overview

Excerpts from President Reagan's "Tax Proposals to The Congress for Fairness, Growth and Simplicity"

II. VOCABULARY

tax
real property tax
state or local tax
real property tax year

III. OBJECTIVES

1. To identify taxes deductible as taxes for federal income tax purposes.

2. To recall that taxes are generally deductible only by the taxpayer on whom they are imposed.

3. To identify taxes deductible under §§ 162 or 212 as ordinary and necessary trade or business expenses or as expenses incurred in an income-producing activity.

4. To recall that § 164 provides for the apportionment of real property taxes between a buyer and seller.

5. To compute the amount of real property tax which may be deducted by a buyer and a seller of real property under the special apportionment rule in § 164.

6. To explain the circumstances under which state and local sales taxes may be deducted.

IV. OVERVIEW

We have all heard countless good news/bad news stories. We now add another. First the bad news: in addition to the federal individual income taxes you are studying, Americans are also subject to a variety of state and local taxes. The good news is that some of these taxes are deductible for federal income tax purposes. This Chapter considers this special federal tax deduction. Following the overview, an excerpt from a Presidential proposal questions the policy underpinnings of the deduction.

A. Historical Background

The deduction for taxes has been a part of the Internal Revenue Code since 1913. The 1913 Tax Act provided: "That in computing net income for the purpose of the normal tax, there shall be allowed as deductions . . . all national, State, county, school, and municipal taxes paid within the year, not including those assessed against local benefits." While the deduction for taxes has long been authorized, the specific content of the deduction provision has changed significantly over the years.

The most significant change in § 164 occurred in 1964 when the provision was amended to read essentially as it does today. Prior to its amendment in 1964, § 164, while generally allowing a deduction for taxes imposed by the United States, specifically disallowed a deduction for federal income taxes, FICA taxes on employees, federal estate and gift taxes and certain other federal taxes. In 1964, these disallowance provisions were removed from § 164 and became part of a new specific disallowance provision, § 275. Read § 275 and note the list of nondeductible taxes.

B. Taxes Deductible Under Section 164

Among the taxes § 164(a) specifically lists as deductible under current law are the following:

(1) State, local, and foreign real property taxes;

(2) State and local personal property taxes;

(3) State, local, and foreign income taxes; or, at the taxpayer's election, in lieu of state and local income taxes, state and local general sales taxes.[1]

---

[1] State and local sales taxes had been nondeductible since 1986 (unless attributable to a taxpayer's trade or business or § 212 activity). However, under § 164(b)(5), enacted in 2004, a taxpayer may elect to deduct state and local general taxes in lieu of state and local income taxes. This provision reflects the efforts of states that rely heavily on sales taxes to have those taxes treated under the Code the same as state and local income taxes. The legislative history notes that the election is intended to provide "more equitable Federal tax treatment across States" and to bring about a "more neutral [Federal] effect on the types of taxes" that state and local governments decide to adopt. H.R. Rep. 108-548, pt. 1, 108th Cong., 2nd Sess. (2004). As originally enacted, the provision was effective only for 2004 and 2005, but Congress has since extended it through 2014. § 165(b)(5)(I). Without further extension, sales taxes will again become nondeductible for 2015 and later years — but further extension would not be unexpected.

A taxpayer who makes the election can deduct either sales taxes actually paid or an amount determined under tables published by the Service. A taxpayer who uses the optional tables, that are

To the extent these taxes represent personal expenses (*e.g.*, state and local income taxes and real property taxes on one's personal residence), § 164 constitutes a significant exception to the general rule denying deductions for personal and family living expenses. *See* § 262. Note, if any of the taxes listed in § 164 represent trade or business expenses or expenses incurred in an income producing activity, they would presumably be deductible under §§ 162 or § 212 regardless of the existence of a specific reference to them in § 164.[2] The practical effect of § 164, therefore, is to allow taxpayers a deduction for certain taxes paid or accrued outside of a trade or business or other income-producing activity. Section 164 deductions are not subject to the 2% floor of § 67. § 67(b)(2).

C. Who May Claim the Deduction?

Taxes are generally deductible only by the person upon whom they are imposed. Reg. § 1.164-1. Thus, paying a tax deductible under § 164(a) does not assure the payor is entitled to a deduction. For example, a national bank, seeking to compete with state banks, elected to pay a state tax assessed against its depositors and requested no reimbursement from its depositors. The Service concluded the depositors received income in the amount of the taxes paid on their behalf and were also entitled to a deduction under § 164(a). The bank was not entitled to a tax deduction under § 164(a), but could deduct the tax payments paid as business expenses under § 162(a). Rev. Rul. 69-497, 1969-2 C.B. 162. Similarly, a taxpayer who gratuitously paid the tax liabilities of his partners and waived any right to contribution or reimbursement from them could not deduct his partners' share of the taxes which he paid. *Farnsworth v. Commissioner*, 270 F.2d 660 (3d Cir. 1959).

There are exceptions to the general rule that taxes are deductible only by the taxpayer on whom they are imposed. For example, as discussed *infra*, real property taxes must be apportioned between a buyer and a seller of real property regardless of which party is liable for the tax under state or local law. In some circumstances, moreover, it may not be entirely clear upon whom real property taxes are imposed. Suppose real property is owned by several co-owners. May one of the co-owners pay and deduct the entire real property tax? In *Powell v. Commissioner*, T.C. Memo. 1967-32, the Tax Court concluded the taxpayer, co-owner of an undivided one-sixth interest in real property, could deduct more than her one-sixth "share" of the property taxes she paid:

> Then what does give a taxpayer the right to deduct real property taxes? Certainly if the tax is imposed on the owner of the property, or if the tax can mature into a personal liability of the owner upon nonpayment, the answer is clear. It is no less clear that any owner of real property, regardless of the

---

based on the taxpayer's state of residence, filing status, adjusted gross income, and number of exemptions, can also deduct sales taxes paid on homes, motor vehicles, boats and certain other items. To be deductible, a sales tax must be a general one, imposed at one rate with respect to a broad range of items, although exception is made for special rates on food, clothing, medical supplies and motor vehicles. *See* § 164(b)(5)(B), (C), (H).

[2] As trade or business expenses, they would be deductible above the line in computing adjusted gross income. If they were expenses incurred in an income-producing activity, they would not be considered in computing adjusted gross income, unless allocable to rental or royalty income per § 62(a)(4), but would instead be deductions taken below the line as itemized deductions in computing taxable income.

fact or possibility of personal liability, has a legal right to protect his property interests by paying taxes justly due thereon. We see no reason why such a person should have any less right to the deduction of such taxes he pays.

It seems to us that the proper test of whether or not a real property tax is deductible by the person who paid such tax is whether that person satisfied some personal liability or protected some personal right or beneficial interest in property. Respondent agrees that petitioner was the owner of a one-sixth undivided interest in the properties in question but claims that she had no personal liability for any more than one-sixth of the taxes levied on the whole property. Therefore, respondent maintains that petitioner was a mere volunteer with respect to her payment of the other five-sixths of the taxes due. But in taking this position the respondent has not considered whether petitioner was protecting a personal right or beneficial interest in property by her payment of those taxes. We think she was. That tenants in common each must have the right to occupy the whole property in common with their co-tenants is universally accepted. This petitioner was not entitled merely to occupy one-sixth of the property held in common with her brothers and sisters, but she was entitled to occupy the whole in common with them.

D.   Special Problems Associated with the Deduction of Real Property Taxes and Assessments

1.   Are Real Property Assessments "Taxes" Under Section 164?

Local governments impose a variety of special assessments against property owners. Some of these assessments are for specific services rendered such as for the collection and disposal of refuse; others are for improvements to specific areas within the jurisdiction, for example, special assessments for sidewalks or sewers; and some are for maintenance of existing improvements, retirement of debt, or payment of interest. May a taxpayer paying these assessments treat them as real property taxes deductible under § 164? To answer that question, one must consider the meaning of the term "tax" in § 164 and the nature of the specific assessment.

A tax is an enforced contribution, exacted pursuant to legislative authority in the exercise of the taxing power, and imposed and collected for the purpose of raising revenue to be used for public or governmental purposes, and not as a payment for some special privilege granted or service rendered. Rev. Rul 79-180, 1979-1 C.B. 95. If a charge is levied by a local government for water and sewer services, by way of example, such charges are obviously not taxes at all, but simply fees paid for services. Rev. Rul. 79-201, 1979-1 C.B. 97. If a special assessment is levied to pay for local benefits which tend to increase the value of the property assessed, then, except to the extent it is allocable to maintenance or interest charges, it is not deductible as a "tax" under § 164. § 164(c)(1). For example, amounts imposed by a local government for benefits such as streets, sidewalks and other like improvements are not deductible when assessed only upon those properties that directly benefit from such improvements and when measured by the benefits each property receives. Reg. § 1.164-4(a). Such assessments are to be distinguished from deductible real property taxes levied for the general welfare at a like rate against all property under a taxing authority's jurisdiction.

The denial of a deduction for amounts assessed against local benefits, however, does not strip such payments of tax significance. Subject to the § 263 standard disallowing deductions for capital expenditures, such taxes are deductible under either §§ 162 or 212 if they are ordinary and necessary trade or business expenses or are incurred in an income producing activity. In the usual case where the assessment represents the cost of improvements in the nature of capital expenditures, the assessment may be added to the basis of the property subject to the assessment. § 1016(a)(1). *See National Lumber v. Commissioner*, 90 F.2d 216 (8th Cir. 1937).

2. Apportionment of Real Property Taxes Between Buyer and Seller

When real property is sold, § 164(d) provides that the portion of real property taxes allocable to that part of the "real property tax year" ending the day before the sale is treated as imposed on the seller; the portion allocable to that part of the real property tax year beginning on the day of the sale is treated as a tax imposed on the purchaser.[3] The "real property tax year" is determined under local law and is the period to which the tax imposed relates. Reg. § 1.164-6(c).

> **Example:** The real property tax year is a calendar year. Real property taxes for a given property for the real property tax year are $3,650. The real property is sold by Smith to Brown on March 1. $590 of the tax, *i.e.,* 59/365 is treated as imposed on Smith and the remaining $3,060, *i.e.,* 306/365 is treated as imposed on Brown.

The apportionment cannot be reallocated by an agreement between the buyer and the seller, because the Code does not allow a deduction for a real property tax treated as imposed on another taxpayer. § 164(c)(2). For deduction purposes, it makes no difference whether the purchaser was reimbursed by the seller for the seller's "share" of the tax. The "real property tax year" and the date of the sale control the apportionment. For example, in one case, the purchaser of certain real property, in addition to paying the current year's real property taxes, also paid the real property taxes owing on the property for years prior to the purchase. The Tax Court held the purchaser was entitled to deduct only that portion of the taxes allocable to the time the purchaser owned the property; the remainder of the taxes, attributable to the period prior to the purchase, was added to the purchaser's basis in the property. *Riordan v. Commissioner*, T.C. Memo 1978-194.

An aside: Special rules govern when the apportioned tax is deductible. As we shall see in subsequent chapters dealing with the timing of deductions, cash method accounting rules generally permit a deduction only upon actual payment of the

---

[3] The sale of real property is generally considered to occur at the earlier of the transfer of legal title or the assumption of the benefits and burdens of ownership. *Baird v. Comm'r*, 68 T.C. 115 (1977).

expense in question. However, if real property is sold and the *other party to the sale* is liable under local law for the tax for the real property tax year, a cash method buyer or seller is treated as having paid, on the sale date, the tax treated as imposed under the apportionment method described above. § 164(d)(2)(A). If neither party is liable for the tax under local law, the party holding the property when the tax becomes a lien is considered liable for the tax. § 164(d)(2)(A). The fact, however, that a taxpayer is considered liable for the tax does not mean that such a taxpayer can deduct more than the apportioned share of the tax.[4]

The regulations provide that a cash basis taxpayer who is not liable for the tax can elect to deduct the apportioned share either for the taxable year of the sale or, *if later*, for the year the tax is actually paid. Reg. § 1.164-6(d)(1),(2). The regulations also provide that a cash basis seller *who is liable* for a real property tax that is not payable until after the sale date can elect to treat the seller's portion of the tax as paid on the sale date or in a later year when the tax is actually paid. Reg. § 1.164-6(d)(1)(ii). The liberal approach of the regulations on the timing of deductions makes it unnecessary for a seller to determine when a tax is later paid, given the option of treating the tax imposed on the seller as paid on the sale date. Conversely, even when the seller is liable under local law for a tax due after the sale date, and the buyer pays the tax, the regulations nevertheless give the seller the option of treating such payment as payment by the seller and taking the deduction at that time.

An accrual basis taxpayer may elect to accrue any real property tax, which is related to a definite time period, ratably over that period. § 461(c). However, for accrual basis taxpayers who have not elected ratable accrual of their real property taxes and who would otherwise be unable to deduct the tax treated as imposed on them, the tax so imposed is treated as accruing on the date of the sale. § 164(d)(2)(B).

President Reagan's "Tax Proposals to the Congress for Fairness, Growth and Simplicity"
(1985)

PROPOSAL TO REPEAL DEDUCTION OF STATE AND LOCAL TAXES

General Explanation

Current Law [1985]

Individuals who itemize deductions are permitted to deduct certain state and local taxes without regard to whether they were incurred in carrying on a trade or business or an income-producing activity. The following such taxes are deductible:

• State and local real property taxes

---

[4] I.R.C. § 164(c)(2). *See Pederson v. Comm'r*, 46 T.C. 155 (1966).

- State and local personal property taxes. (In some states, payments for registration and licensing of an automobile are wholly or partially deductible as a personal property tax.)

  - State and local income taxes.

  - State and local general sales taxes.

Other state and local taxes are deductible by individuals only if they are incurred in carrying on a trade or business or income-producing activity. This category includes taxes on gasoline, cigarettes, tobacco, alcoholic beverages, admission taxes, occupancy taxes and other miscellaneous taxes. Taxes incurred in carrying on a trade or business or which are attributable to property held for the production of rents or royalties (but not other income-producing property) are deductible in determining adjusted gross income. Thus, these taxes are deductible by both itemizing and nonitemizing taxpayers. Taxes incurred in carrying on other income-producing activities are deductible only by individuals who itemize deductions. Examples of these taxes include real property taxes on vacant land held for investment and intangible personal property taxes on stocks and bonds. State and local income taxes are not treated as incurred in carrying on a trade or business or as attributable to property held for the production of rents or royalties, and therefore are deductible only by individuals who itemize deductions.

Reasons for Change

Fairness. The current deduction for state and local taxes disproportionately benefits high-income taxpayers residing in high-tax states. The two-thirds of taxpayers who do not itemize deductions are not entitled to deduct state and local taxes, and even itemizing taxpayers receive relatively little benefit from the deduction unless they reside in high-tax states. Although the deduction for state and local taxes thus benefits a small minority of U.S. taxpayers, the cost of the deduction is borne by all taxpayers in the form of significantly higher marginal tax rates.

The unfair distribution of benefits from the deduction for state and local taxes is illustrated by recent tax return data. For example, in 1982 itemizing taxpayers in New York received an average tax savings of $1,292 from the deduction, whereas itemizers in Wyoming on average saved only $257. In effect, the deduction requires taxpayers in certain communities to subsidize taxpayers in other communities. Moreover, the deduction effectively skews the burden of state and local taxes within particular communities. Consider the variation in effective sales tax rates for three persons facing a 6 percent state sales tax: a nonitemizer, an itemizer in the 50 percent tax bracket, and an itemizer in the 20 percent bracket. The nonitemizer pays the full 6 percent sales tax rate, whereas the two itemizers pay effective rates of 3 and 4.8 percent, respectively. The deduction thus causes effective sales tax rates to vary with a taxpayer's marginal income tax rate and with whether a taxpayer itemizes, and produces the lowest effective rate for high-bracket/high income taxpayers.

Erosion of the Tax Base. The deduction for state and local taxes is one of the most serious omissions from the Federal income tax base. Repeal of the deduction is projected to generate $33.8 billion in revenues for 1988. Recovery of those revenues will permit a substantial reduction in marginal tax rates. Indeed, unless those revenues are recovered, tax rates will almost certainly remain at the current unnecessarily high levels.

The Fallacy of the "Tax on a Tax" Argument. Some argue that the deductibility of state and local taxes is appropriate because individuals should not be "taxed on a tax." The argument is deficient for a number of reasons. First, it ignores the effect of state and local tax deductibility on the Federal income tax base. Deductibility not only reduces aggregate Federal income tax revenues, it shifts the burden of collecting those revenues from high-tax to low-tax states. High-tax states effectively shield a disproportionate share of their income from Federal taxation, leaving a relatively greater share of revenues to be collected from low-tax states. Absent the ability to impose Federal income tax on amounts paid in state and local taxes, the Federal government loses the ability to control its own tax base and to insist that the burden of Federal income taxes be distributed evenly among the states.

Second, the "tax on a tax" argument suggests that amounts paid in state or local taxes should be exempt from Federal taxation because they are involuntary and state or local taxpayers receive nothing in return for their payments. Neither suggestion is correct. State and local taxpayers have ultimate control over the taxes they pay through the electoral process and through their ability to locate in jurisdictions with amenable tax and fiscal policies. Moreover, state and local taxpayers receive important personal benefits in return for their taxes, such as public education, water and sewer services and municipal garbage removal. In this respect, the determination by state and local taxpayers of their levels of taxation and public service benefits is analogous to their individual decisions over how much to spend for the purchase of private goods.

It is, of course, true that not all benefits provided by state and local governments are directly analogous to privately purchased goods or services. Examples include police and fire protection, judicial and administrative services and public welfare. These services nevertheless provide substantial personal benefits to state and local taxpayers, whether directly or by enhancing the general quality of life in state and local communities.

Inefficient Subsidy. The deduction for state and local taxes may also be regarded as providing a subsidy to state and local governments, which are likely to find it somewhat easier to raise revenue because of the deduction. A general subsidy for spending by state and local governments can be justified only if the services which state and local governments provide have important spillover benefits to individuals in other communities. The existence of such benefits has not been documented.

Even if a subsidy for state and local government spending were desired, provision of the subsidy through a deduction for state and local taxes is neither cost effective nor fair. On average, state and local governments gain less than fifty cents for every dollar of Federal revenue lost because of the deduction. Moreover, a deduction for state and local taxes provides a greater level of subsidy to high-income states and communities than to low-income states and communities. In addition, a deduction for taxes does not distinguish spillover effects, but is as much a subsidy for spending on recreational facilities as for public welfare spending. Finally, the deduction distorts the revenue mix of state and local governments by creating a bias against the imposition of user charges in favor of more general taxes.

Proposal

The itemized deduction for state and local income taxes and for other state and local taxes that are not incurred in carrying on a trade or business or income-producing activity would be repealed. . . .

Analysis

The tax savings from deductibility vary widely among the states and provide the greatest benefits to individuals in high-income states. Because this tax expenditure requires tax rates for all individuals to be higher than they otherwise would be, those in the 15 states with above-average tax savings per capita currently gain at the expense of taxpayers in the other 35 states. Even within the high-tax states, less than one-half of all taxpayers itemize deductions.

Recent estimates indicate that the effect of tax deductibility on the level of state and local government spending is not large. A National League of Cities study found that total state and local spending is about 2% higher because of the existence of tax deductibility. This estimated effect is low in part because less than one-third of total state and local spending is financed by taxes potentially deductible from the Federal individual income tax. Because state and local spending has been growing by about 7% per year since 1980, the elimination of tax deductibility would not reduce the absolute level of state and local spending, but only reduce its rate of growth. However, because the proportion of taxpayers who itemize varies a great deal among the states as well as among local governments within a state, the effect on spending for a particular state or local government would be larger than 2 percent for a high-income community and may not affect spending at all in low-income communities where few residents itemize deductions.

The three most important sources of state and local tax revenue in the U.S. are general sales, personal income and property taxes. Some argue that itemized deductions should be eliminated for some of these taxes, but retained for others. . . . However, elimination of any one tax deduction would have an uneven effect on taxpayers among the states. In addition, since state and local governments would be likely to increase reliance on the remaining deductible taxes, disallowing deductions for particular taxes is likely to lead to sizeable distortions in state and local revenue mixes. For example, disallowing only the sales tax deduction might force a state, like Washington, that relies heavily on a general sales tax but does not have an individual income tax, to adopt one.

AUTHORS' NOTE

After considerable debate, Congress in the 1986 Tax Reform Act preserved the § 164 deduction for most state and local taxes but eliminated the deduction for state and local sales taxes. However, as noted in footnote 1, Congress in 2004 restored a deduction for state and local sales taxes for taxpayers who elect to deduct such taxes in lieu of deducting state and local income taxes. § 164(b)(5).

Although § 164(b)(5) is effective only through December 31, 2014, it is anticipated Congress will continue to extend the provision annually or make it permanent.

Chapter 24

CASUALTY LOSSES

I. PROBLEMS

1. Dennis paid $30,000 for a new car for his personal use.

   (a) Assume Dennis drives the car for three years and then sells it for its then fair market value of $10,000. What are the tax consequences, if any, to Dennis?

   (b) One year after purchasing the car, Dennis backed into a telephone pole and severely damaged the rear of the car. Repair of the car would necessitate replacing the entire back fender of the car and cost $6,000. Assume that, if the car were not repaired, its value would be reduced by $6,000. Dennis reported the accident to his insurance company and the company paid Dennis $6,000. Dennis chose not to repair the car. How should Dennis treat the $6,000 insurance recovery? If Dennis uses the proceeds to repair the car, how should Dennis treat the insurance recovery?

   (c) Assume the facts of (b) except that Dennis decided not to report the accident as he feared there would be an increase in his insurance premiums that would ultimately cost him far more than the $6,000 that the insurance company would have paid him. Assume Dennis' adjusted gross income for the year of the accident was $50,000. What casualty loss deduction, if any, may he claim?

   (d) Assume the facts of (a) except the car was not sold, but, instead, was stolen when Dennis parked the car outside a restaurant where he had stopped for lunch during a trip across the state. Assume the car, then worth $10,000, was not insured and was never recovered. Dennis' adjusted gross income for the year of the theft was $50,000. What casualty loss deduction, if any, may Dennis claim?

   (c) How would your answer to (d) change if Dennis had purchased and used the car solely for business purposes and the car was stolen when it was worth $10,000? Assume that Dennis' adjusted basis in the car was $12,000, reflecting the fact that Dennis had been allowed $18,000 in § 168 depreciation deductions with respect to the car.

   (f) Assume the facts of (e) except that six months before the car's theft Dennis had converted the car from use in his business to use solely for personal and family purposes. What casualty loss, if any, may Dennis deduct?

2. Read the following set of facts and identify any § 165(c)(3) losses. Assume in each set of facts that there is no insurance coverage for any loss.

    (a) Carlos paid $1,500,000 for a five-acre tract of land located on the northern coast of California. After purchasing the land, Carlos spent $1,000,000 for the home and $250,000 for the guest house he built on the western edge of the property quite near the bluffs overlooking the Pacific Ocean. In building the home and guest house in that location, Carlos ignored warnings from other landowners in the area that structures in that location would be particularly vulnerable to high winds and ocean waves during big storms that periodically buffet the coast.

        (i) Last month, a terrible storm struck and the resulting high waves destroyed the guest house. While the storm also caused severe erosion to the nearby bluffs, there was no erosion damage to Carlos' land nor was there any damage to Carlos' home.

        (ii) Because of the storm, however, the natural erosion processes are now expected to accelerate and will ultimately threaten Carlos' land and his home. In light of the more precarious situation of his home as a result of the storm, expert appraisers concluded that the home was worth $500,000 less than it was prior to the storm.

        (iii) Over the following three years, the ocean waves, rain, and winds eroded several feet of Carlos' land, reducing the value of his land by $250,000 and leading the local authorities, as a matter of public safety, to order the immediate uncompensated demolition of the home.

    (b) Gullible met Scam Artist through a personal ad Gullible placed in the newspaper. Gullible became romantically involved with Scam Artist and placed Scam Artist's name on Gullible's credit cards and bank accounts and also loaned Scam Artist substantial sums of money. After they dated for six months and just before they were to be married, Gullible discovered that Scam Artist had a rap sheet "a mile long." Scam Artist skipped town but only after running up huge credit card charges and emptying Gullible's bank accounts. Of course, Scam Artist never repaid any of the loans. Gullible can establish a loss of $300,000 as a result of Scam Artist's deceit.

    (c) Paula had a diamond brooch worth $5,000. Before going into a crowded restaurant one evening, she removed the brooch from her dress and placed it in the glove compartment of her car. She thought she had locked the car. When she returned to the car following the dinner, the car doors were unlocked and the brooch was missing. There was, however, no evidence of any forced entry into the car.

Assignment for Chapter 24:

Complete the problems.

Read: Internal Revenue Code: §§ 165(a), (b), (c)(3), (e), (h); 67(b)(3).
        Treasury Regulations: §§ 1.165-1(a), -1(b), -1(c)(1), -1(d)(2),

-1(d)(3), -7(a)(3), -7(b)(1), -7(b)(2), -8(a)(2), -8(c), -8(d).

Materials: Overview
             Revenue Ruling 72-592
             Popa v. Commissioner
             Chamales v. Commissioner

II.   VOCABULARY

casualty
personal casualty gain
personal casualty loss

III.   OBJECTIVES

1. To distinguish casualty losses from noncasualty losses.

2. To compute the amount of the § 165(c)(3) deduction, given a taxpayer's
    adjusted gross income and the losses and gains from casualties and thefts.

3. To identify the year in which a casualty loss is deductible, and the year in
    which a theft loss is deductible.

4. To recall and apply the "lesser of" rule for determining the amount of a
    casualty or theft loss.

5. To recall the requirement to file a timely insurance claim with respect to a
    loss.

IV. OVERVIEW

Section 165(c)(3) authorizes a deduction for an individual's uncompensated casualty and theft losses unconnected with a trade or business or with a transaction entered into for profit.[1] Each loss, however, is first subject to a $100 nondeductible floor; in addition, the net casualty loss for the year, determined after application of the $100 floor, is allowed only to the extent it exceeds 10% of the taxpayer's adjusted gross income. § 165(h)(1), (2).

As this text has observed in a (perhaps excessive) number of places, the general rule of § 262 bars a deduction for personal expenses. The allowance of a deduction on the loss of property is the functional equivalent, but for timing, of allowing a deduction on acquisition or for depreciation. Strict consistency with the general rule of § 262 would thus argue for the nondeductibility of losses on personal-use property whether the loss is occasioned by casualty or otherwise. However, § 165(c)(3), as limited by the rules of § 165(h), suggests Congress regards severe personal casualty losses as sufficiently different from life's ordinary losses and expenses, and as sufficiently related to one's wealth or ability to pay, so as to be taken into account in determining taxable income. Do you agree? Of course, given the 10% nondeductible threshold and the availability of insurance coverage for the more common significant risks, the average taxpayer will seldom be entitled to claim a casualty loss deduction.

A. Definitional Questions

Most of the § 165(c)(3) litigation has centered on the meaning of the words "other casualty" in the statutory listing of "fire, storm, shipwreck, or other casualty" and theft as occasions for deduction of loss. Revenue Ruling 72-592, included in the materials, notes that case law has limited qualifying casualties to those analogous to fire, storm, and shipwreck, and that the Service has insisted on an "identifiable event of a sudden, unexpected, and unusual nature." Such formulations are hardly free of ambiguity and elasticity, and differing interpretations of them can be expected.

In *White v. Commissioner*, 48 T.C. 430 (1967), a deduction was allowed for a diamond lost from a woman's diamond ring when a car door was accidentally slammed on her hand. As noted in Revenue Ruling 72-592, included in the materials, the Service has acquiesced in the Tax Court's decision in *White*. In *Keenan v. Bowers*, 91 F. Supp. 771 (E.D.S.C. 1950), a deduction was denied for the loss of two diamond rings that occurred when a woman, during an overnight stay in a hotel, took the rings off, wrapped them in tissue paper, and placed them on a table, all unbeknownst to her husband, who by mistake flushed them down the toilet the next morning. In another case, however, when a woman placed her diamond ring in a glass of ammonia to soak, and her husband, not knowing the ring was in the glass, poured the contents of the glass down the kitchen sink and turned on the disposal, thereby damaging the ring, a deduction was allowed. *Carpenter v. Commissioner*, T.C. Memo. 1966-228. Nonetheless, damage that results from the

---

[1] Individual casualty or theft losses that are business-or profit-related do not need any assistance from § 165(c)(3); they are properly deductible under § 165(c)(1) or (2). *See* Chapter 15.

taxpayer's "willful act or willful negligence" will not be allowed. *See, e.g.*, Reg. § 1.165-7(a)(3).

Forseeability or negligence will not take an occurrence outside the ambit of "other casualty." In *Heyn v. Comm'r*, 46 T.C. 302, 308 (1966), the Tax Court, in a case involving a loss caused by landslide, noted:

> Forseeability may be a circumstance to be taken into account in determining whether a particular event is a casualty. But forseeability alone is not conclusive. Meteorological forecasts may well forewarn a cautious property owner to take protective measures against an oncoming hurricane, but any ensuing losses may nevertheless be storm or casualty losses within the meaning of the law. Nor is negligence a decisive factor. Automobile accidents are perhaps the most familiar casualties today. Yet the owner of the damaged vehicle is not deprived of a casualty loss deduction merely because his negligence may have contributed to the mishap. . . .
>
> We are unable to perceive any distinction between a casualty loss arising from an automobile collision and one resulting from a landslide. Certainly, in the absence of gross negligence, the mere fact that the automobile owner negligently failed to have faulty brake linings replaced or that he negligently took a calculated risk in driving with smooth tires would not deprive him of a casualty loss if his vehicle were damaged in an accident occurring as a result of either of those conditions. The accident would nonetheless qualify as a casualty, notwithstanding the owner's negligence or that the accident was the consequence of his having taken a calculated risk in respect of known hazards. And it seems clear to us that petitioner's position in respect of the landslide is no weaker.

As noted in Revenue Ruling 72-592, "to be 'sudden' the event must be one that is swift and precipitous and not gradual or progressive." Consistent with that definition, the Service has ruled that, when a water heater bursts from rust and corrosion over a period of time, the damage to the water heater itself is not a casualty, but the resulting rust and water damage to rugs, carpet and drapes will qualify under § 165(c)(3). Rev. Rul. 70-91, 1970-1 C.B. 37.

Perhaps the most interesting and contentious cases regarding "suddenness" are those addressing the impact of insects or disease. The Service has ruled that damage caused by termites to property does not constitute a casualty loss because it lacks the requisite "suddenness" comparable to fire, storm and shipwreck. Rev. Rul. 63-232, 1963-2 C.B. 97. The ruling, reversing the Service's prior position that it would follow certain court decisions allowing a deductible casualty loss for damage caused by termites up to 15 months after infiltration, stated:

> [Termite] damage is the result of gradual deterioration through a steadily operating cause and is not the result of an identifiable event of a sudden, unusual or unexpected nature. Further, time elapsed between the incurrence of damage and its ultimate discovery is not a proper measure to determine whether the damage resulted from a casualty. Time of discovery of the damage, in some situations, may affect the extent of the damage, but

this does not change the form or the nature of the event, the mode of its operation, or the character of the result. These characteristics are determinative when applying § 165(c)(3) of the code.

Id.

By contrast, the Service has ruled the loss from the death of 40 ornamental pine trees over a 5–10 day period, caused by a mass attack of southern pine beetles, was a casualty loss. Rev. Rul. 79-174, 1979-1 C.B. 99. The ruling noted that, in addition to being sudden, the event was also "unusual and unexpected" since there had been no previous epidemic attacks in the area. Compare Revenue Ruling 79-174 with *Maher v. Commissioner*, 76 T.C. 593 (1981), *aff'd*, 680 F.2d 91 (11th Cir. 1982). *Maher* involved the death of ornamental palm trees following their infection by insects with lethal yellowing, a disease that kills palm trees in an average of nine to 10 months. When the palm trees were infected and the disease became apparent, there was no treatment for, or precautionary measures against, the disease. In denying a casualty loss deduction, the Tax Court reasoned that the suddenness of the loss itself, not the suddenness of its onset, determines whether the suddenness requirement is met. The lapse of time from infection to the death of the trees indicated not a sudden loss, but a loss resulting from gradual deterioration. In affirming the Tax Court decision, the U.S. Court of Appeals for the Eleventh Circuit noted that disease has not been treated as falling within the "other casualty" category of § 165(c)(3), acknowledging, however, that the line between diseases and other causes may be arbitrary.

Revenue Ruling 87-59, 1987-2 C.B. 59, relied upon *Maher* in addressing whether a taxpayer could claim a casualty loss associated with the worthlessness of pine trees killed by southern pine beetles. As noted by the Service in the ruling:

> The killing of the pine trees by the southern pine beetles had no immediate effect on the usefulness of the timber because the beetles do not appreciably damage wood. The death of the trees, however, rendered them vulnerable to wood-destroying organisms that gradually caused the deterioration of the wood in the uncut trees and eventually rendered the timber worthless. . . . The entire process occurred over a 9-month period. Applying the reasoning in *Maher* to a situation involving trees grown for timber rather than ornamental use, the period of time from the precipitating event, the beetle attack, to the identifiable event that fixes the loss, the bulldozing and burning of worthless timber, determines the suddenness of the timber loss, and the period of 9 months over which the damage occurred is not sufficiently sudden to indicate a casualty loss.

The Tax Court and other courts have required a showing of physical damage in order to establish a "casualty loss." Consider in this regard the Tax Court decision in *Chamales v. Commissioner*, included in the materials. Using this same rationale, a district court denied a casualty loss deduction to taxpayers who claimed that, as a result of avalanche risk, they not only were restricted in the use of their home during winter months but also suffered a loss in the appraised value of their home due to anticipated buyer resistance. *Lund v. U.S.*, 85 AFTR 2d 2000-1083, 2000-1 U.S. Tax Cas. (CCH) 50,234 (D. Utah 2000). Contrast these cases to the Eleventh Circuit's decision in *Finkbohner v. U.S.*, 788 F.2d 723 (1986). In *Finkbohner*, the taxpayer's home was in an area that had been flooded. To prevent damage from future floods, authorities demolished seven homes in the area in which taxpayer's home was located. In turn, the neighborhood became less desirable because there was greater likelihood of crime. Based on the regulations interpreting § 165(c)(3), the court held the loss is calculated as the difference between the fair market value before the casualty and the fair market value after the casualty. Where permanent buyer resistance exists (in this case, as a result of a change in the neighborhood) and impacts the fair market value of the property, the taxpayer is entitled to claim a casualty loss deduction, taking into account the impact of buyer resistance on the fair market value of the property. The regulations do not specifically require a physical injury and the court refused to impose such a requirement. Note the Tax Court's rejection of *Finkbohner* in *Chamales*.

With respect to theft losses, the regulations provide that "theft" includes, but is not necessarily limited to, larceny, embezzlement and robbery. Reg. § 1.165-8(d). The Service has ruled that the illegal taking of property, done with criminal intent, constitutes a theft loss for purposes of § 165(c)(3), even though the act may not fall within the technical statutory definition of "theft" under state law. Rev. Rul. 72-112, 1972-1 C.B. 60. According to Rev. Rul. 72-112, "to qualify as a 'theft' loss within the meaning of § 165(c)(3), the taxpayer needs only to prove that his loss resulted from a taking of property that is illegal under the law of the state where it occurred and that the taking was done with criminal intent. In *Kreiner v. Commissioner*, T.C. Memo 1990-587, the Tax Court held the taxpayer could deduct more than $19,000 in cash and property which he had given to two fortunetellers in New York, who had told him they could improve his health and solve his problems. The Commissioner argued that, even though fortunetelling is a crime in New York, it did not constitute theft. Specifically, the Commissioner emphasized that the taxpayer could not establish the elements of larceny. The Tax Court, rejecting this argument, noted the word "theft" in § 165(c)(3) is not like "larceny," a technical word with a narrowly defined meaning: "Theft covers a broad field of illegality including 'any criminal appropriation of another's property to the use of the taker, particularly including theft by swindling, false pretenses, and any other form of guile.' " *Id.*

In claiming a deduction for theft losses, however, the taxpayer must prove a theft has occurred; a mere mysterious disappearance of property does not suffice. *See, e.g., Allen v. Commissioner*, 16 T.C. 163 (1951). By contrast, the taxpayer need not prove who stole the property in question; it is sufficient that "the reasonable inferences from the evidence point to theft rather than mysterious disappearance." *Jacobson v. Commissioner*, 73 T.C. 610, 613 (1979). In that case, taxpayer was held to be entitled to a theft loss where property she stored in a home she no longer occupied and had previously shared with her estranged husband, was removed from the home without her knowledge or consent and never recovered.

B.   Timing of the Loss

A casualty loss is deductible in the year sustained, while a theft loss is deductible in the year discovered. § 165(a), (e). If there exists a claim for reimbursement with a "reasonable prospect" for recovery, allowance of the loss awaits the resolution of the claim with "reasonable certainty." *See* Reg. §§ 1.165-

1(d)(2), (3), 1.165-8(a)(2).

C. Amount of the Loss

The amount of a casualty loss under § 165(c)(3) is the lesser of (1) the adjusted basis of the property; and (2) the difference between the fair market value of the property beforehand and the fair market value afterwards — that is, the amount of the decline in value. Reg. § 1.165-7(b)(1).

For purposes of theft losses, the value afterwards is presumed to be zero, and the "lesser of" rule becomes simply the lesser of basis or value of the property beforehand. Reg. § 1.165-8(c). Thus, for example, if a diamond ring, purchased for $1,000, increases in value to $3,000 and is then stolen, the amount of the theft loss is only $1,000. Why should this be so? Conversely, if the family car is purchased for $10,000, declines in value to $4,000 and is then damaged beyond repair in an accident, the amount of the casualty loss cannot exceed $4,000. Is this result appropriate? The rule is different with respect to business or profit-related property; if the basis of such property exceeds the value, the "lesser of" rule does not apply. See the last sentence of Reg. § 1.165-7(b)(1). Why the difference?

The amount of the loss must, of course, be reduced by any reimbursements received and, pursuant to § 165(h)(1), further reduced by $100. (The $100 nondeductible floor is applied to each casualty or each theft, rather than to each item destroyed or stolen in a single casualty or theft. *See* Reg. § 1.165-7(b)(4)(ii).) Once the personal casualty and theft losses for the year have been determined, they will be deductible to the extent of any personal casualty gains for the year. § 165(h)(4)(A); § 1211(b). (A personal casualty gain would typically arise when the insurance proceeds received following a casualty or theft loss exceed the taxpayer's basis in the property in question. Assume some jewelry, purchased years previously for $1,000, is now worth $2,000, and is insured for that amount. An insurance payment of $2,000 following the theft of the jewelry would produce a $1,000 casualty gain for the taxpayer.) If personal casualty losses exceed personal casualty gains for the year, the net casualty loss is deductible only to the extent it exceeds 10% of the taxpayer's adjusted gross income. § 165(h)(2)(A). The following example demonstrates the limitations imposed by § 165(h)(1) and (2).

> **Example:** During a given year, as the result of separate incidents, a taxpayer sustains personal casualty losses in the amounts of $3,700 and $4,000 and a personal casualty gain of $1,500. Taxpayer's adjusted gross income for the year is $50,000. Taxpayer's § 165(c)(3) deduction is computed as follows. First, reduce the $7,700 of total casualty losses by $200 ($100 per casualty per § 165(h)(1)) to $7,500. Next, compute the amount of the excess of the taxpayer's personal casualty losses over the taxpayer's personal casualty gains. That excess is $6,000 (i.e., $7,500 [personal casualty losses after the § 165(h)(1) reduction] less $1,500 [the amount of the personal casualty gain]). Finally, compute the sum of (1) the taxpayer's personal casualty gains for the year ($1,500 in this example) and (2) so much of the $6,000 excess computed above that exceeds 10% of taxpayer's $50,000 adjusted gross income the taxpayer ($1,000 in this example, i.e., $6,000 less

$5,000 (10% of $50,000)). That sum — $2,500 — is the taxpayer's § 165(c)(3) deduction for the year.

Suffice it at this point simply to note that a casualty loss or gain is generally characterized as an "ordinary loss" or "ordinary gain" rather than as a "capital gain" or "capital loss." However, in the event personal casualty gains for the year exceed personal casualty losses, § 165(h)(2)(B) provides that all such gains and losses are treated as capital gains and losses. We study capital gains and losses beginning in Chapter 31, and in Chapter 32 we shall see that § 1231 establishes a special characterization rule somewhat similar to that of § 165(h)(2)(B). We will postpone development of the ordinary-versus-capital distinction to those later Chapters.

D. Insurance Coverage

Section 165(h)(5)(E) permits a casualty or theft loss, to the extent covered by insurance, to be taken into account only if a timely insurance claim is filed. This provision overruled prior case law that had permitted a deduction where the taxpayer suffered a loss covered by insurance, but declined to file a claim for fear the insurance would be cancelled. Is it appropriate that, to obtain a § 165(c)(3) deduction, a taxpayer is now required to file an insurance claim if he has obtained insurance coverage, but is not required to obtain the insurance coverage to begin with? Finally, recall that § 123, mentioned previously in the Note on Miscellaneous Exclusions following Chapter 11, excludes from income insurance compensation for increased living expenses occasioned by casualty to one's personal residence.

REVENUE RULING 72-592
1972-2 C.B. 101

In view of the decision of the Tax Court of the United States in *John P. White v. Commissioner*, 48 T.C. 430 (1967), reconsideration has been given to the meaning of the term "casualty" for purposes of § 165(c)(3) of the Internal Revenue Code of 1954. That section of the Code provides that an individual may deduct:

> (3) losses of property not connected with a trade or business, if such losses arise from fire, storm, shipwreck or other casualty . . . [but] only to the extent that the amount of loss to such individual arising from each casualty . . . exceeds $100. . . .

The provision allowing this deduction for losses from "other casualty" has been part of the Federal tax law since the enactment of the Revenue Act of 1916. However, there is neither statutory definition of the term "other casualty," nor legislative history expressing Congressional intent as to its meaning.

The courts have consistently upheld the Internal Revenue Service position that an "other casualty" is limited to casualties analogous to fire, storm or shipwreck. The Service position has been that a casualty is the complete or partial destruction of property resulting from an identifiable event of a sudden, unexpected and unusual nature.

In the *White* case, however, the Tax Court found that property that was accidentally and irretrievably lost could, under the circumstances described, be the basis for a casualty loss deduction under § 165(c)(3) of the Code. The Service has acquiesced in the decision of the Tax Court in the *White* case, C.B. 1969-1, 21.

In the *White* case, the taxpayer-husband accidentally slammed the car door on his wife's hand after helping her alight from the car. Her diamond engagement ring absorbed the full impact of the blow, which broke two flanges of the setting holding the diamond in place. His wife quickly withdrew her injured hand, shaking it vigorously, and the diamond dropped or flew out of the broken setting. The uninsured diamond was never found, and the taxpayer claimed a casualty loss deduction for its value in the year it was lost.

The Tax Court, convinced that the diamond was irrevocably and irretrievably lost, sustained the taxpayer's claim, indicating that the diamond was completely removed from the enjoyment of its owner and that it had no value to the owner after the loss. The Service, in acquiescing in the decision, agreed that property that is accidentally and irretrievably lost can be the basis for a casualty loss deduction under section 165(c)(3) of the Code if it otherwise qualifies as a casualty loss.

In other words, the Service position is altered only to the extent that the accidental loss of property can now qualify as a casualty. Such losses must, of course, qualify under the same rules as must any other casualty; namely, the loss must result from some event that is (1) identifiable, (2) damaging to property, and (3) sudden, unexpected, and unusual in nature. The meaning of the terms "sudden, unexpected, and unusual," as developed in court decisions, is set forth below.

To be "sudden" the event must be one that is swift and precipitous and not gradual or progressive.

To be "unexpected" the event must be one that is ordinarily unanticipated that occurs without the intent of the one who suffers the loss.

To be "unusual" the event must be one that is extraordinary and nonrecurring, one that does not commonly occur during the activity in which the taxpayer was engaged when the destruction or damage occurred, and one that does not commonly occur in the ordinary course of day-to-day living of the taxpayer.

POPA v. COMMISSIONER
United States Tax Court
73 T.C. 130 (1979)

STERRETT, JUDGE:

After concessions, the only issue for our decision is whether or not petitioner sustained a casualty loss within the meaning of section 165(c)(3), I.R.C. 1954, when various of his personal possessions, located in the Republic of Vietnam, were lost when the government of that nation fell to the North Vietnamese.

FINDINGS OF FACT

During the calendar year 1975, petitioner resided in the Republic of Vietnam, serving as the vice president and general manager of the Transworld Services Corp., a foreign subsidiary of the American Trading Co., Inc., a United States corporation. On April 26, 1975, petitioner left Vietnam on one of his frequent business trips to Bangkok, Thailand. He took with him only a suitcase and a briefcase. Everything else petitioner owned, such as furniture, clothing, appliances, books, and stored food stuffs, was left at his rented home in an affluent part of Saigon. Within a matter of days after Mr. Popa's departure from the Republic of Vietnam, that country's government collapsed. United States nationals were ordered evacuated by the President. Petitioner was never able to return to that country and has no reasonable hope of ever recovering his property or its value. None of the goods lost were insured.

. . . .

By contending that petitioner abandoned his property in Saigon, respondent concedes the fact that petitioner has suffered an economic loss. Further, we take it as implicit in respondent's memorandum brief that he also concedes that the loss took place when Saigon fell to enemy troops a day or two after petitioner left on a business trip to Bangkok. Nevertheless, respondent argues that petitioner's loss is nondeductible because it "does not constitute a casualty loss as is contemplated by I.R.C. section 165(c)(3)." Petitioner, on the other hand, argues that his loss in Vietnam was due to an "identifiable event of a sudden, unexpected and unusual nature" which event is ejusdem generis to the events specifically described in section 165(c)(3).

We believe that petitioner's loss of his goods is an "other casualty" within the meaning of Section 165(c)(3). We think that petitioner's loss in the fall of Saigon is ejusdem generis to losses due to "fire, storm [and], shipwreck." It was a sudden, cataclysmic, and devastating loss — just the sort of loss section 165(c)(3) was designed to address. We have previously noted that the application of the principle of ejusdem generis—

> [h]as been consistently broadened so that wherever unexpected, accidental force is exerted on property and the taxpayer is powerless to prevent application of the force because of the suddenness thereof or some disability, the resulting direct and proximate damage causes a loss which is like or similar to losses arising from the causes specifically enumerated in section 165(c)(3). [*White v. Commissioner*, 48 T.C. 430, 435 (1967)].

As "the events giving rise to the undisputed loss here were sudden, unexpected, violent and not due to deliberate or willful actions by petitioner," we conclude that these losses are deductible. See *White v. Commissioner, supra* at 433–434.

Our review of the cases convinces us that the only circumstance which could possibly have existed that would require us to deny petitioner his casualty loss would be that the property was confiscated under color of some hastily enacted local law. All the other possibilities (fire, theft, looting, etc.) are such that entitle him to a section 165(c)(3) casualty loss.

Respondent notes in his memorandum brief that, "It is extremely doubtful that petitioner knows or will ever know what became of his property, since he was precluded from returning to Vietnam after the U.S. military evacuation." We are, of course, well aware of the legion of cases that hold that the taxpayer must be put to his proof. However, in unusual circumstances such as this, we do not think it fair or reasonable to require that the taxpayer eliminate all possible noncasualty causes of his loss. We do not believe that we unduly stretch the bounds of judicial notice when we take into account the abruptness with which the United States abandoned Saigon and the stories with respect to the heavy damage to the city. A few days before the city fell, the United States Government was actively evacuating its citizens from the city. We can hardly fault petitioner for not remaining to determine whether his property was destroyed by gun fire, by looting, by fire, or some form of seizure by the remaining Saigon residents, the Vietcong, or the North Vietnamese. Certainly, petitioner's failure to return to the city was not a matter of personal choice. Nor can his inexactitude in this matter be held against him.

We note here that the difficulties in South Vietnam did not arise from a revolution from within such as occurred recently in Iran and Nicaragua, thus making less likely the possibility that even a despotic law authorized the taking at issue.

Accordingly, we believe that the most reasonable conclusion, on the particular facts of this case, is that the property at issue was either destroyed or pilfered with criminal intent.

Decision will be entered under Rule 155.

Reviewed by the Court.

Fay, J., dissenting.

In *Powers v. Commissioner*, 36 T.C. 1191 (1961), the taxpayer purchased an automobile in West Berlin, Germany. Three days later, while enroute from Berlin to Hamburg, the taxpayer's automobile was seized by the East German police and never returned to him. In holding that the taxpayer was not entitled to a deduction for the clear loss he sustained, we stated:

> Petitioner offers some suggestion that his loss was a "casualty" in any event. Assuming that that change of position is now open to him, it is of no assistance. What happened was not like a "fire, storm or shipwreck." Sec. 23(e)(3), I.R.C. 1939. It did not embody the requisite element of "chance, accident or contingency." *Alice P. Bachofen von Echt*, 21 B.T.A. 702, 709 (1930). The deduction was not permissible either as a theft or as a casualty. *Weinmann v. United States*, 278 F.2d 474 (C.A. 2, 1960). Petitioner's loss, though unfortunate, "was no more than a personal expense to petitioner, for the deduction of which the statute makes no provision." *Thomas F. Gurry*, 27 B.T.A. 1237, 1238 (1933). [36 T.C. at 1193].

In light of *Powers*, and cases which have followed it, it is clear that if petitioner's property was confiscated by the Communist government after the fall of Saigon, he would not be entitled to a casualty loss deduction under section 165(c)(3). However, based upon petitioner's complete lack of knowledge, the wartime circumstances, and judicially noticed "stories with respect to the heavy damage to the city," *supra* at 133, the majority infers that the property was most likely destroyed or criminally pilfered.

Admittedly, if petitioner's property were destroyed by ordnance or destroyed or pilfered before order was restored, he would be entitled to a casualty loss deduction. See *Davis v. Commissioner*, 34 T.C. 586 (1960) (vandalism). Unfortunately, under the circumstances, petitioner cannot prove the cause of his loss and for that reason, in my opinion, has failed to meet his burden of proof.

In *Allen v. Commissioner*, 16 T.C. 163 (1951), the taxpayer, Mary Allen, entered the Metropolitan Museum of Art in New York, wearing a diamond brooch on the left side of her dress. Before leaving the museum less than 2 hours later, Mary discovered that her brooch was missing. After carefully retracing her steps, she was unable to find the brooch. Although she testified that she didn't know whether the brooch was lost or stolen, she nevertheless argued that since the record showed that she was present only in well-lighted rooms that were so constructed that no article could have been lost, someone must have stolen her brooch and she was therefore entitled to a theft loss deduction. The trial judge felt this evidence was sufficient to substantiate her claim of a theft loss. *Allen v. Commissioner*, 16 T.C. at 167 (Judge Opper dissenting). However, in rejecting her claim, we stated:

> She does not, and cannot, prove that the pin was stolen. All we know is that the brooch disappeared and was never found by, or returned to, petitioner.
>
> Petitioner has the burden of proof. This includes presentation of proof which, absent positive proof, reasonably leads us to conclude that the article was stolen. If the reasonable inferences from the evidence point to theft, the proponent is entitled to prevail. If the contrary be true and reasonable inferences point to another conclusion, the proponent must fail. *If the evidence is in equipoise preponderating neither to the one nor the other conclusion, petitioner has not carried her burden.* [16 T.C. at 166, emphasis added].

In the present case, the record does not show whether petitioner's property was abandoned by him, confiscated by the North Vietnamese Government, pilfered, or destroyed. In my opinion, any of the above are reasonable inferences. That being so, based on *Allen*, I would hold that petitioner has not met his burden of proof by a preponderance of the evidence.

The majority would, however, relieve petitioner of his burden because his inability to determine what happened to his property was not his fault. This problem was addressed in *Burnet v. Houston*, 283 U.S. 223 (1931), wherein the taxpayer claimed it was impossible for him to prove his 1913 basis for stock which became worthless in 1920. The Supreme Court held:

> We cannot agree that the impossibility of establishing a specific fact, made essential by the statute as a prerequisite to the allowance of a loss, justifies a decision for the taxpayer based upon a consideration only of the remaining factors which the statute contemplates. . . . The impossibility of proving a material fact upon which the right to relief depends, simply leaves

the claimant upon whom the burden rests with an unenforceable claim, a misfortune to be borne by him, as it must be borne in other cases, as the result of a failure of proof. [283 U.S. at 228].

TANNENWALD, SIMPSON, and NIMS, J.J., agree with this dissenting opinion.

CHAMALES v. COMMISSIONER
United States Tax Court
T.C. Memo 2000-33

NIMMS, JUDGE:

MEMORANDUM FINDINGS OF FACT AND OPINION

Respondent determined a Federal income tax deficiency for petitioners' 1994 taxable year in the amount of $291,931.

The issue for decision [is] as follows: Whether petitioners are entitled to deduct a net casualty loss of $751,427 for the taxable year 1994. . . .

FINDINGS OF FACT

Gerald and Kathleen Chamales (petitioners) are married and resided in Los Angeles, California, at the time of filing their petition in this case. In the spring of 1994, petitioners became interested in purchasing a residence in Brentwood Park, an exclusive Los Angeles neighborhood. They were attracted to the beautiful, parklike setting and the quiet peacefulness of the area. Subsequently, on June 2, 1994, petitioners opened escrow on property located in Brentwood Park, at 359 North Bristol Avenue. They were represented in this transaction by Jay Solton, a real estate agent with more than 20 years of experience. Solton's work focused on sales of properties in the Westwood, Brentwood, Palisades, and Santa Monica areas of Los Angeles.

At the time petitioners opened escrow, O.J. Simpson owned and resided at the property located directly west of and adjacent to that being purchased by petitioners. Simpson's address was 360 North Rockingham Avenue. Both parcels were corner lots, bounded on the north by Ashford Street. The rear or westerly side of petitioners' land abutted the rear or easterly side of the Simpson property.

During the escrow period, on June 12, 1994, Nicole Brown Simpson and Ronald Goldman were murdered at Ms. Brown Simpson's condominium in West Los Angeles. Simpson was arrested for these murders shortly thereafter. Following the homicides and arrest, the Brentwood Park neighborhood surrounding the Simpson property became inundated with media personnel and equipment and with individuals drawn by the area's connection to the horrific events. The media and looky-loos[2] blocked streets, trespassed on neighboring residential property, and

---

[2] As explained by petitioners' counsel, "looky-loo" is a term developed in Hollywood to describe individuals who gather at places and events in hopes of glimpsing celebrities. The phrase is apparently

flew overhead in helicopters in their attempts to get close to the Simpson home. Police were summoned to the area for purposes of controlling the crowds, and barricades were installed at various Brentwood Park intersections to restrict traffic. This police presence, however, had little practical effect. Significant media and public attention continued throughout 1994 and 1995. Although Simpson was acquitted on October 4, 1995, civil proceedings in 1996 reignited public interest.

Petitioners closed escrow on June 29, 1994, purchasing the residence on North Bristol Avenue for $2,849,000. Petitioners had considered canceling the escrow and had discussed this possibility with their attorney, but upon being advised that liability would result from a cancellation, they decided to go through with the transaction. Later that summer, as the crowds and disruption persisted, Gerald Chamales (petitioner) inquired of his broker Solton whether the value of his property had declined. Solton indicated that she estimated a decrease in value of 20 to 30 percent.

Petitioners' 1994 tax return was prepared by Ruben Kitay, a certified public accountant. In the course of preparing this return, Kitay and petitioner discussed the possibility of claiming a deduction for casualty loss. After preliminary research in the regulations addressing casualty loss, Kitay spoke with two area real estate agents regarding the amount by which petitioners' property had decreased in value. The agents estimated the decline at 30 to 40 percent. Kitay and petitioner decided to use the more conservative 30 percent figure in calculating the deduction to be taken on petitioners' return. An expert appraisal was not obtained at this time, as Kitay felt that a typical appraisal based on values throughout the Brentwood Park area would be inconclusive as to the loss suffered by the few properties closest to the Simpson home.

Kitay and petitioner also recognized and discussed the fact that there existed a substantial likelihood of an audit focusing on petitioners' 1994 return. Hence, to clarify the position being taken and the reasons underlying petitioners' deduction, an explanatory supplemental statement labeled "Casualty Loss" was attached to the return. After indicating the location of petitioners' property in relation to that of Simpson, it stated that the casualty loss was premised on "the calamity of the murder & trial, which was sudden & unavoidable & which resulted in a permanent loss to value of property." A table enumerating instances of minor physical damage to petitioners' property, such as damage to lawn and sprinklers, was also attached to the return, but no valuation was placed upon the harm caused thereby.

At the time petitioners purchased their property, they were aware that the existing home required remodeling and repair. In the fall of 1994, petitioners demolished most of the house. Then, in March of 1995, they began a reconstruction project costing approximately $2 million. This reconstruction was completed in December of 1996, and petitioners moved into the residence. Petitioners continued to reside at 359 North Bristol Avenue up to and through the date of trial.

Other residents of Brentwood Park have undertaken similar reconstruction

---

used in California to denote those who frequent a location not because of its status as a conventional tourist sight but because of its association with a famous or notorious person. We adopt the terminology and spelling as used in petitioners' briefs and by the witnesses at trial.

projects in recent years. The Nebekers, who own the property across Ashford Street from the former Simpson residence, are proceeding with a $1 million remodeling of their home. Likewise, the property owned by Simpson was sold after he moved out in 1998, the existing house was demolished, and a new residence is currently being constructed.

As of early 1999, the area surrounding the former Simpson home was no longer inundated with media personnel or equipment. The police barricades restricting traffic in the immediate vicinity of petitioners' property had been removed. Looky-loos, however, continued to frequent the neighborhood, often advised of the location of Simpson's former residence by its inclusion on "star maps" published for the Los Angeles area. Anniversaries of the murders were also typically accompanied by periods of increased media and public attention.

OPINION

We must decide whether petitioners are entitled to a casualty loss deduction based upon a postulated decline in the value of their residential property and, if not, whether they are liable for the section 6662(a) accuracy-related penalty.

Petitioners contend that the media and onlooker attention following the murders and focusing on Simpson's home has decreased the value of their adjacent property. They argue that because the homicides were a sudden, unexpected, and unusual event, and because aspects of the public interest precipitated thereby continued at least to the time of trial in this case, they have suffered a permanent casualty loss. Petitioners further allege that the proximity of their residence to that of Simpson has stigmatized their property and rendered it subject to permanent buyer resistance.

Conversely, respondent asserts that public attention over the course of a lengthy murder trial is not the type of sudden and unexpected event that will qualify as a casualty within the meaning of the Code. Respondent additionally contends that the Court of Appeals for the Ninth Circuit, to which appeal in this case would normally lie, has limited the amount that may be claimed as a casualty loss deduction to the loss suffered as a result of physical damage to property. According to respondent, since petitioners have failed to substantiate any such damage, they are entitled to no deduction. In respondent's view, any decline in market value represents merely a temporary fluctuation and not a permanent, cognizable loss.

We agree with respondent that petitioners have not established their entitlement to a casualty loss deduction. The difficulties suffered by petitioners as a consequence of their proximity to the Simpson residence do not constitute the type of damage contemplated by section 165(c)(3). . . .

Section [165(c)(3)] governs the tax treatment of [casualty] losses. . . . As interpreted by case law, a casualty loss within the meaning of section 165(c)(3) arises when two circumstances are present. First, the nature of the occurrence precipitating the damage to property must qualify as a casualty. *See, e.g., White v. Commissioner*, 48 T.C. 430 (1967). . . . Second, the nature of the damage sustained must be such that it is deductible for purposes of section 165. At issue here then are whether the events surrounding the alleged Simpson murders and affecting petitioners' property can properly be termed a casualty and whether the type of loss suffered by petitioners as a consequence of these events is recognized as deductible. We conclude that both inquiries must be answered in the negative.

A. Nature of Occurrence Constituting a Casualty

The word "casualty" as used in section 165(c)(3) has been defined, through application of the principle of ejusdem generis, by analyzing the shared character-istics of the specifically enumerated casualties of fire, storm, and shipwreck. *See, e.g., White v. Commissioner, supra* at 433–435. . . . As explained by this Court:

> wherever unexpected, accidental force is exerted on property and the taxpayer is powerless to prevent application of the force because of the suddenness thereof or some disability, the resulting direct and proximate damage causes a loss which is like or similar to losses arising from the causes specifically enumerated in section 165(c)(3). [*White v. Commissioner, supra* at 435.]

Hence, casualty for purposes of the Code denotes "an undesigned, sudden and unexpected event" or "an event due to some sudden, unexpected or unusual cause." . . . Conversely, the term "excludes the progressive deterioration of property through a steadily operating cause." . . . The sudden and unexpected occurrence, however, is not limited to those events flowing from forces of nature and may be a product of human agency.

Here, we cannot conclude that the asserted devaluation of petitioners' property was the direct and proximate result of the type of casualty contemplated by section 165(c)(3). While the stabbing of Nicole Brown Simpson and Ronald Goldman was a sudden and unexpected exertion of force, this force was not exerted upon and did not damage petitioners' property. Similarly, the initial influx of onlookers, although perhaps sudden, was not a force exerted on petitioners' property and was not, in and of itself, the source of the asserted decrease in the home's market value. Rather, petitioners base their claim of loss on months, or even years, of ongoing public attention. If neither media personnel nor looky-loos had chosen to frequent the Brentwood Park area after the murders, or if the period of interest and visitation had been brief, petitioners would have lacked grounds for alleging a permanent and devaluing change in the character of their neighborhood. Hence, the source of their difficulties would appear to be more akin to a steadily operating cause than to a casualty. Press and media attention extending for months bears little similarity to a fire, storm, or shipwreck and is not properly classified therewith as an "other casualty."

B. Nature of Damage Recognized as Deductible

With respect to the requisite nature of the damage itself, this Court has traditionally held that only physical damage to or permanent abandonment of property will be recognized as deductible under section 165. . . . In contrast, the Court has refused to permit deductions based upon a temporary decline in market value. . . .

For example, in *Citizens Bank v. Commissioner* . . . the [Tax] Court stated that "physical damage or destruction of property is an inherent prerequisite in showing a casualty loss." When again faced with taxpayers seeking a deduction premised upon a decrease in market value, the Court further explained in *Pulvers v. Commissioner* . . . (quoting *Citizens Bank v. Commissioner*): "The scheme of our tax laws does not, however, contemplate such a series of adjustments to reflect the vicissitudes of the market, or the wavering values occasioned by a succession of adverse or favorable developments." Such a decline was termed "a hypothetical loss or a mere fluctuation in value." The Court likewise emphasized in *Squirt Co. v. Commissioner*, that "Not all reductions in market value resulting from casualty-type occurrences are deductible under section 165; only those losses are deductible which are the result of actual physical damage to the property." This rule was reiterated yet again in *Kamanski v. Commissioner*, when the Court observed:

> In the instant case there was likewise relatively small physical damage to petitioner's property and the primary drop in value was due to buyer resistance to purchasing property in an area which had suffered a landslide. If there had been no physical damage to the property, petitioner would be entitled to no casualty loss deduction because of the decrease in market value resulting from the slide. . . . [T]he only loss which petitioner is entitled to deduct is for the physical damage to his property.

Moreover, the Court of Appeals for the Ninth Circuit, to which appeal in the present case would normally lie, has adopted this rule requiring physical damage. *See, e.g., Kamanski v. Commissioner*, 477 F.2d at 452; *Pulvers v. Commissioner*, 407 F.2d 838, 839 (9th Cir.1969). In *Pulvers v. Commissioner*, the Court of Appeals reviewed the specific casualties enumerated in section 165(c)(3) and concluded: "Each of those surely involves physical damage or loss of the physical property. Thus, we read 'or other casualty,' in para materia, meaning 'something like those specifically mentioned.'" Even more explicitly, the Court of Appeals based affirmance in *Kamanski v. Commissioner*, on the following grounds:

> The Tax Court ruled that the loss sustained was a nondeductible personal loss in disposition of residential property and not a casualty loss; that the drop in market value was not due to physical damage caused by the [earth]slide, but to "buyer resistance"; that casualty loss is limited to damage directly caused by the casualty. We agree.

In *Caan v. United States*, 83 AFTR 2d 99-1640, 99-1 USTC par. 50,349 (C.D.Cal.1999), the District Court dismissed for failure to state a claim the complaint of taxpayers alleging facts nearly identical to those at issue here. The Caans, residents of Brentwood Park, argued that they were entitled to a section 165(c)(3) casualty loss deduction for the decline in market value and permanent buyer resistance to which they asserted their property became subject as a result of the O.J. Simpson double murders. The court, however, reiterated that "the Ninth Circuit only recognizes casualty losses arising from physical damage caused by enumerated or other similar casualties" and held that "Because the Caans have not alleged any physical damage to their property due to the murders and subsequent media frenzy, they have not alleged a casualty loss that is a proper basis for a deduction." . . .

Given the above decisions, we conclude that petitioners here have failed to establish that their claimed casualty loss is of a type recognized as deductible for purposes of section 165(c)(3). They have not proven the extent to which their property suffered physical damage, and their attempt to base a deduction on market devaluation is contrary to existing law.

With respect to physical damage and assuming arguendo that petitioners' loss stemmed from an occurrence that could properly be deemed a casualty, they would be entitled to a deduction for physical harm to their property. Nonetheless, although petitioners attached to their return a list of minor instances of physical damage and mentioned several other items at trial, they have neither offered evidence of the monetary value of nor provided any substantiation for such losses. We therefore have no basis for determining what, if any, portion of the claimed deduction might be allowable, and we cannot sustain a $751,427 deduction on the grounds of damage to a lawn or a sprinkler system.

As regards decrease in property value, petitioners' efforts to circumvent the established precedent repeatedly rejecting deductions premised on market fluctuation, through reliance on *Finkbohner v. United States*, 788 F.2d 723 (11th Cir.1986), are misplaced. In *Finkbohner v. United States*, the Court of Appeals for the Eleventh Circuit permitted a deduction based on permanent buyer resistance in absence of physical damage. The Finkbohners lived on a cul-de-sac with 12 homes, and after flooding damaged several of the houses, municipal authorities ordered 7 of the residences demolished and the lots maintained as permanent open space. Such irreversible changes in the character of the neighborhood were found to effect a permanent devaluation and to constitute a casualty within the meaning of section 165(c)(3).

However, as explicated above, this Court has long consistently held that an essential element of a deductible casualty loss is physical damage or, in some cases, physically necessitated abandonment. Furthermore, under the rule set forth in *Golsen v. Commissioner*, 54 T.C. 742, 756-757 (1970), *aff'd*, 445 F.2d 985 (10th Cir.1971), we are in any event constrained to apply the law of the court in which an appeal would normally lie. Since the Court of Appeals for the Ninth Circuit has adopted and has not diverged from a requirement of physical damage for a section 165(c)(3) deduction, to hold otherwise would contravene *Golsen*.

Moreover, we further note that petitioners' circumstances do not reflect the type of permanent devaluation or buyer resistance which would be analogous to that held deductible in *Finkbohner v. United States, supra*. The evidence in the instant case reveals that media and onlooker attention has in fact lessened significantly over the years following the murders. Access to petitioners' property is no longer restricted by media equipment or police barricades. Residents of Brentwood Park have continued to invest substantial funds in remodeling and upgrading their homes. Hence, petitioners' difficulties are more akin to a temporary fluctuation in value, which no court has found to support a deduction under section 165(c)(3). We therefore hold that petitioners have failed to establish their entitlement to a casualty loss deduction. Respondent's determination of a deficiency is sustained.

Chapter 25

MEDICAL EXPENSES

I. PROBLEM

Tom and Sue were married on June 1 of this year. Tom's former wife died two years ago, and Tom has a 12-year-old son, Junior, by that marriage. During the year, Tom paid the following amounts for which he received no reimbursement:

(1) $300 for a toupee for Tom.

(2) $5,000 for a vasectomy for Tom.

(3) $2,000 for joint counseling sessions to deal with the conflicting desires Tom and Sue have regarding children, and the anger and depression they each felt as a result.

(4) $300 for vitamin supplements for Junior.

(5) $30,000 for a swimming pool installed in their home on a doctor's recommendation that regular swimming exercise would be very beneficial for Sue's arthritis.

(6) $2,500 for special hand controls installed in Sue's car on account of her arthritis.

(7) $500 to a professed faith healer who promised that his laying on of hands would cure Sue's arthritis. (It did not.)

(8) $1,000 to a stop-smoking clinic to help Tom quit the habit. Tom has been unable to stop smoking to date, and Tom's employer has announced that employees smoking during working hours will be discharged.

(9) $1,000 in initiation fees and $500 in monthly dues for an exercise club Tom joined in order to lose, on doctor's orders, over 100 pounds of excess weight.

(10) $20,000 for tuition, room and board for Junior to attend a boarding school for two semesters (September 1 to May 31). Junior was experiencing serious learning disabilities and creating discipline problems in public high school, and a school psychologist strongly recommended boarding school to deal with these problems.

(11) Airfare of $300 for Junior (one way) and $600 for Tom (round trip) to take Junior to the boarding school. Tom stayed overnight and spent $75 on lodging and $25 on meals before returning home the next day.

(12) $2,500 for the services of a "nurse's aide" for two weeks when Sue was recovering from surgery on both feet and was unable to do household work and care for herself as she ordinarily would.

Tom's adjusted gross income for the year was $40,000. Sue's adjusted gross income (primarily from investments) was $60,000. Are they entitled to a § 213 deduction?

Assignment for Chapter 25:

Complete the problem.

Read: Internal Revenue Code: §§ 213(a), (b), (d)(1)–(5), (d)(9), (f); 67(b)(5). Skim §§ 213(d)(10), (11); 7702B(c); 62(a)(16); 220(a), (b)(1), (c)(1)(A), (f)(1), (2), (4), (6); 106(a), (b)(1).
Treasury Regulations: § 1.213-1(a)(1), (e), (g)(1).

Materials: Overview
Montgomery v. Commissioner
Revenue Ruling 78-266

II. VOCABULARY

qualifying medical expense
nondeductible floor

III. OBJECTIVES

1. To compute the § 213 deduction, given the amount of unreimbursed medical expenses paid during the year and the taxpayer's adjusted gross income for the year.

2. To recall that qualifying medical expenses must be actually paid, must be unreimbursed, and must be those of the taxpayer, spouse or dependent.

3. To distinguish a qualifying medical expense from a nondeductible personal expense related to medical care.

4. To provide examples of capital expenditures, institutional costs, and transportation costs that qualify for the § 213 deduction, and to provide examples of those that do not.

IV.   OVERVIEW

Section 213 provides a deduction for uncompensated medical expenses of the taxpayer and taxpayer's spouse and dependents to the extent the expenses exceed 7.5% of adjusted gross income for 2012 and prior years, and 10% of adjusted gross income beginning in 2013.[1] The deduction is allowed only for expenses "actually paid" during the year. Reg. § 1.213-1(a)(1). Section 213 is an exception to the general rule of § 262 prohibiting the deduction of personal expenses, but the exception is a limited one by virtue of the nondeductible floor amount. This nondeductible floor amount effectuates the congressional purpose of providing some relief to those individuals who sustain extraordinary unreimbursed medical expenses, but not to those whose medical expenses are judged to fall within more normal bounds. Compare, in this regard, the statutory exclusions from income for employer-provided medical insurance premiums and medical care expense reimbursement. §§ 106(a); 105(b). Is the policy expressed in § 213 consistent with these statutory exclusions?

The medical expense deduction has been part of the Code since 1942. As originally enacted, and for a number of years thereafter, the deduction was subject to varying maximum annual limitations, but these ceiling limitations have long since been removed. At one time, expenditures for drugs and medicine were taken into account for purposes of the § 213 deduction only to the extent such expenditures exceeded 1% of adjusted gross income. In 1984, this separate nondeductible amount for medicine and drugs was eliminated; at the same time, however, the category of qualifying medicine and drugs was considerably narrowed and now consists only of prescription drugs and insulin. § 213(b). Legislative history makes clear that only drugs that legally require a prescription constitute "prescribed" drugs. Pub. L. 97-248, 97th Cong., 2d Sess., Conf. Rep., p. 476. Thus, for example, the Service has held, in Revenue Ruling 2003-58, 2003-1 C.B. 959, that where an individual with an injured leg was taking aspirin, a nonprescription drug, on the recommendation of his doctor, the cost was nondeductible pursuant to § 213(b); however, the ruling also held that the costs of nonprescription equipment and supplies, such as crutches, were not subject to § 213(b) and would be deductible if they otherwise constituted medical care expenses.[2]

Section 213 has occasioned litigation, primarily over the issue of whether the expense in question was a medical expense or a nondeductible personal expense.

---

[1] The 7.5% floor remains in effect through 2016 if the taxpayer or the taxpayer's spouse is 65 or older. § 213(f). But for purposes of the alternative minimum tax, discussed in Chapter 45, the nondeductible floor is 10% of adjusted gross income. § 56(b)(1)(B).

[2] By way of contrast, Revenue Ruling 2003-102, 2003-2 C.B. 559, holds that, under § 105(b), discussed in Chapter 10, reimbursements by an employer of amounts paid by an employee for medicines and drugs (such as antacid, allergy medicine, pain relievers, and cold medicines) purchased without a physician's prescription are excludable from the employee's income. "Amounts, however, paid by an employee for dietary supplements that are merely beneficial to the general health of the employee or the employee's spouse or dependents, are not reimbursable or excludable from gross income under § 105(b)." Revenue Ruling 2003-102 distinguished Revenue Ruling 2003-58 by noting that "Section 105(b) specifically refers to 'expenses incurred by the taxpayer for . . . medical care' as defined in § 213(d). There is no requirement in § 105(b) that the expense be allowed as a deduction for medical care under § 213(a) or that only medicine or drugs that require a physician's prescription be taken into account."

The statutory definition of "medical care" is a broad one. The usual medical expenditures will clearly qualify as amounts paid for "diagnosis, cure, mitigation, treatment, or prevention of disease, or for the purpose of affecting any structure or function of the body" (§ 213(d)(1)(A)); the definition also extends to medically related transportation costs, qualified long-term care services, and medical insurance (§ 213(d)(1)(B), (C), (D)), and to certain lodging costs away from home for medical care (§ 213(d)(2)). It is nonetheless inevitable that some expenditures, arguably motivated by medical concerns, also appear to address nonmedical needs and thus raise questions of deductibility. The regulations, on this point, flesh out the statute to some degree by providing deductions shall be limited to expenses incurred "primarily" to prevent or alleviate physical or mental defects or illness, and will not extend to expenses that are "merely beneficial to . . . general health." Reg. § 1.213-1(e)(1)(ii). This guideline is useful, but it clearly leaves room for considerable debate. The Tax Court has interpreted the statute "as requiring a causal relationship in the form of a 'but for' test between a medical condition and the expenditures incurred in treating that condition. . . . The 'but for' test requires [a taxpayer] to prove (1) . . . the expenditures were an essential element of the treatment and (2) . . . they would not have otherwise been incurred for nonmedical reasons." *Magdalin v. Commissioner*, T.C. Memo 2008-293 (denying a § 213 deduction for certain expenses associated with fathering children through the use of unrelated gestational carriers).

Note § 213(d)(1)(A) is phrased disjunctively and also allows a deduction for amounts paid "for the purpose of affecting any structure or function of the body." How is this provision to be applied in view of the stricture of Reg. § 1.213-1(e)(1)(ii) that the deduction for "medical care" not extend to expenditures merely beneficial to an individual's general health? The Service, for example, historically interpreted "medical care" to include elective procedures such as cosmetic surgery, *e.g.*, face-lift operations, removal of hair by electrolysis, etc. on the theory the operation affected a structure or function of the body. *See, e.g.*, Rev. Rul. 76-332, 1976-2 C.B. 81. In 1990, Congress, however, added § 213(d)(9), which significantly limits the deductibility of expenses incurred for cosmetic surgery and other similar procedures. The legislative history indicates the amount expended for insurance to cover the costs of cosmetic surgery of the nature described in § 213(d)(9) will not be deductible, nor will reimbursement for such costs under a health plan provided by an employer be excludable. Thus, in Revenue Ruling 2003-57, 2003-1 C.B. 959, the Service held that amounts paid for breast reconstruction surgery following a mastectomy for cancer and for vision correction surgery (laser eye surgery to correct myopia) are medical care expenses under § 213(d) — such amounts, respectively, ameliorate a deformity directly related to a disease, and correct a bodily dysfunction — while amounts paid by individuals to whiten teeth discolored as a result of age are not medical care expenses under that section, but are instead expenses designed to improve appearance. In *O'Donnabhain v. Commissioner*, 134 T.C. 34 (2010), the Tax Court concluded that gender identity disorder is a disease for purposes of § 213(d). In that case, the court allowed a deduction for the costs of hormone therapy and sex reassignment surgery incurred by a taxpayer diagnosed with gender identity disorder. The court, however, refused to allow a deduction for the taxpayer's breast augmentation surgery.

The regulations further provide that capital expenditures, ordinarily nondeductible, may constitute a deductible medical expense where the primary purpose of the expenditure is medical care of the taxpayer, spouse or dependent. Reg. § 1.213-1(e)(1)(iii). The regulation embraces noncontroversial items such as wheelchairs, but it has also been the occasion of numerous taxpayer efforts, sometimes successful, to deduct the cost of such home improvements as swimming pools and various special equipment that seem to have nonmedical as well as medical uses. Note, however, that, where an improvement increases the value of property, the regulations limit the deduction to the amount by which the cost of the improvement exceeds the increase in value.

In *Henderson v. Commissioner*, T.C. Memo 2000-321, the Tax Court refused to allow as medical expenses under § 213(a) depreciation deductions on a van used to transport a disabled child. The van, which had been specially modified to accommodate the child, was necessary to transport the child to school and to the offices of medical providers. The Tax Court ruled that depreciation did not constitute an amount "paid" for medical care as required by § 213(a). The Service conceded in the case that amounts paid to modify the van would be deductible in the year the taxpayer paid for the modifications.

The cost of hospital care, including meals and lodging, constitutes a medical expense, and the regulations provide similar results obtain for other qualifying "institutions," including "special schools." Reg. § 1.213-1(e)(1)(v). Outside the institutional setting, the Service regards the cost of foods and beverage, including special diets, as a nondeductible personal expense, except when such special foods supplement, rather than substitute for, a normal diet, and are taken solely to alleviate or treat an illness. Rev. Rul. 55-261, 1955-1 C.B. 307. The Tax Court, however, has held that the cost of special foods taken as a substitute for a normal diet may be deductible to the extent it exceeds the cost of a normal diet. *Randolph v. Commissioner*, 67 T.C. 481 (1976).

Under the regulations, amounts expended for "illegal operations or treatment" are not deductible (Reg. § 1.213-1(e)(1)(ii)), and the term "medicine and drugs" includes only items "legally procured" (Reg. § 1.213-1(e)(2)). In *Halby v. Commissioner*, T.C. Memo 2009-204, the Tax Court applied this provision to deny a § 213 deduction for the cost of procuring prostitutes for therapy. Revenue Ruling 97-9, 1997-1 C.B. 77, relies on these provisions to deny a deduction for amounts paid to obtain and use marijuana for medical purposes — even with a physician's prescription, even when permitted under state law — where under federal laws the possession of marijuana is illegal. At the same time, however, the deductibility of medical care does not depend on licensing or other qualifications of the medical care provider. "Medical care" is determined by the nature of the services rendered, rather than the qualifications of the practitioner. Rev. Rul. 63-91, 1963-1 C.B. 54. Nursing services, for example, need not be rendered by licensed or trained nurses to be deductible, but they must nonetheless be medical in nature, within the meaning of § 213.

In general, services rendered must be medical in nature, rather than household or personal services, to constitute medical care. Note, however, in 1996 Congress provided that amounts paid for "qualified long-term care services" constitute medical care, although certain payments made to relatives for such services may not qualify. § 213(d)(1)(C), (d)(11). Qualified long- term care services include not only diagnostic, therapeutic, treating, etc. services, but maintenance and care services as well, required by a chronically ill individual under a plan of care prescribed by a physician or certain other licensed professionals. *See* § 7702B(c) and *Estate of Baral v. Commissioner*, 137 T.C. 1 (2011) (holding services of caregivers constituted qualified long-term care services within the meaning of § 7702B(c) where a physician determined 24-hour supervision was necessary to protect the health and safety of a patient suffering from severe dementia). While the payment of medical insurance premiums ordinarily constitutes medical care under § 213, only a limited amount of the premiums paid for long-term care insurance will qualify as medical care. § 213(d)(1)(D) (flush language), (d)(10).

Transportation expenses are deductible under § 213(d)(2), if incurred "primarily for and essential to" medical care. For example, car expenses, taxi fares, bus, railroad, and train fares incurred primarily for the rendition of medical services are allowable medical care expenses. As indicated in *Montgomery v. Commissioner*, reprinted below, food and lodging expenses incurred while away from home for medical care were initially deductible. However, in *Commissioner v. Bilder*, 369 U.S. 499 (1962), the Supreme Court interpreted the 1954 enactment of current § 213(d)(1)(B) to deny a deduction for meals and lodging expenses incurred in Florida by a taxpayer with a grave heart ailment whose doctor had advised him to spend the winter season in a warm climate. Section 213(d)(2), added in 1984, relaxes this rule of nondeductibility, to a limited extent, with respect to certain lodging costs. Read § 213(d)(2) carefully. This section was interpreted and applied in *Polyak v. Commissioner*, 94 T.C. 337 (1990), where the Tax Court denied a medical expense deduction to a taxpayer who had moved to Florida for the winter to alleviate her chronic heart and lung ailments. The Tax Court noted § 213(d)(2) was intended to equalize the tax treatment of inpatient and outpatient care for taxpayers required to seek medical care away from home. Because Ms. Polyak did not go to Florida to seek medical attention and did not receive medical treatment in a licensed hospital or its equivalent, the requirements of § 213(d)(2) were not met and no deduction was allowed.

The Service has ruled that the costs of transportation and registration to attend a medical conference relating to the chronic disease of a taxpayer's dependent child constituted medical expenses. On the facts of the ruling, the travel was found to be "primarily for and essential to" medical care within the meaning of § 213(d)(2). (Meals and lodging costs associated with attending the conference were nondeductible because the conference did not involve the receipt of medical care from a physician at a licensed hospital or similar institution, as required under § 213(d)(2).) Rev. Rul. 2000-24, 2000-1 C.B. 963.

Section 213(d)(2) does not specifically address the deductibility of the costs of meals and lodging incurred on the way to and from the site where the medical care is rendered; the deductibility of these items is open to question. *Montgomery* reflects the fact both the Tax Court and the Sixth Circuit have found such in-transit meals and lodging costs includable as "transportation" expenses. The Service has not accepted this view. Does the enactment of § 213(d)(2) call into question the viability of the *Montgomery* rule?

MONTGOMERY v. COMMISSIONER
United States Court of Appeals, Sixth Circuit
428 F.2d 243 (1970)

CELEBREZZE, CIRCUIT JUDGE:

During 1961, the Taxpayer and his wife made three round trips to the Mayo Clinic, Rochester, Minnesota, from their legal residence in Lawrenceburg, Kentucky. Each of these trips was for admittedly medical purposes and the Commissioner concedes that although the later two trips were for the medical treatment of Taxpayer's wife, the Taxpayer's accompaniment of his wife was required for medical reasons. . . . During these various trips, Taxpayer and his wife incurred a total expense for meals and lodging between Lawrenceburg and Rochester of $162.39.

The sole issue in the appeal is whether this $162.39 in expenses are deductible as expenses for "medical care" pursuant to Section 213 of the Internal Revenue Code of 1954.

The term "medical care" is defined under Section 213(c)(1) as amounts paid:

> (B) for transportation primarily for and essential to medical care referred to in subparagraph (A). . . .[3]

The Commissioner contends that moneys paid for food and lodging en route to a place of medication are "traveling" expenses in excess of the mere cost of "transporting" the person and baggage of the taxpayers to their place of destination. The Commissioner maintains that the use of the more narrow phrase "expenses for transportation," rather than "expenses . . . for traveling [to the place of medication]" indicates a plain intention to deny the deductibility of in-transit expenses for food and lodging. The Commissioner further contends that the cost of meals and lodging are "personal, living or family expenses" for which "no deduction shall be allowed, . . . [e]xcept as otherwise expressly provided." Internal Revenue Code, Section 262.

In response, the Taxpayer contends that "expenses . . . for transportation" includes, as the Tax Court held below, all expenses "required to bring the patient to the place of medication." 51 TC 410. Such expenses were deductible under the prior Internal Revenue Code of 1939, and the Tax Court found that the legislative history of the present Code, as well as the present Treasury Regulations, permit their continued deductibility. We agree.

Under the Internal Revenue Code of 1939, all food and lodging expenses of a patient on the way to the place of medication and at the place of medication were deductible. In *Commissioner of Internal Revenue v. Bilder*, 369 U.S. 499, 501, 82 S.Ct. 881, 8 L.Ed.2d 65 (1962), the United States Supreme Court denied the

---

[3] Subparagraph (A) reads: "for the diagnosis, cure, mitigation, treatment or prevention of disease, or for the purpose of affecting any structure or function of the body."

deductibility under the 1954 Code of lodging expenses at the place of medication. In doing so, it observed:

> The Commissioner concedes that prior to the enactment of the Internal Revenue Code of 1954 rental payments of the sort made by the taxpayer were recognized as deductible medical expenses. This was because § 23(x) of the Internal Revenue Code of 1939, 26 U.S.C.A. 23(x), though expressly authorizing deductions only for "amounts paid for the diagnosis, cure, mitigation, treatment, or prevention of disease," had been construed to include "travel primarily for and essential to . . . the prevention or alleviation of a physical or mental defect or illness," and the cost of meals and lodging during such travel.

Unfortunately, the liberal provisions of the 1939 Code for deductibility of "travel" expenses led to very significant abuses. Taxpayers would travel on doctors' orders to resort areas for the alleviation of a specific ailment and deduct all of the costs of their food and lodging while on such medical vacations. The legislative history of the Internal Revenue Code of 1954 indicates a specific intent to eliminate the resort area medication abuse. Both the House and Senate Committee Reports on the 1954 Code discuss the deductibility of medical care expenses. They state:

> The deduction permitted for "transportation primarily for and essential to medical care" clarifies existing law in that it specifically *excludes deduction of any meals and lodging while away from home receiving medical treatment*. For example, if a doctor prescribes that a patient must go to Florida in order to alleviate specific chronic ailments and to escape unfavorable climate conditions which have proven injurious to the health of the taxpayer, and the travel is prescribed for reasons other than the general improvement of a patient's health, *the cost of the patient's transportation to Florida would be deductible but not his living expenses while there.* (Emphasis added). H.R. Rep. No. 1337, 83d Cong. 2nd Sess. A 60 (1954); S. Rep. No. 1622, 83d Cong., 2nd Sess. 219–220 (1954), U.S. Code Cong. & Admin. News, p. 4856. The Treasury Department incorporated the substance of the above Reports in its Regulations interpreting Section 213. The Regulations provide:

> > [a] deduction for "transportation primarily for and essential to medical care" shall not include the cost of any meals and lodging *while away from home receiving medical treatment*. For example, if a doctor prescribes that a taxpayer go to a warm climate in order to alleviate a specific chronic ailment, the *cost of meals and lodging while there* would not be deductible.

Treasury Regulation § 1.213-1(e)(iv).

It is apparent that the concern of Congress and the Treasury was to eliminate the abuse of "resort area" medication. Thus Congress eliminated the deductibility of food and lodging expenses at the actual place of medication. Congress did not, however, eliminate the cost of transporting the patient to the place of medication.

We believe that the legislative history and the accompanying regulations indicate a Congressional intent to maintain "existing law" with regard to the deduction of all costs required to transport the patient to the critical place of medication.

The abuse Congress sought to eliminate — the taking of ordinary living expenses "while there" — did not occur until after the patient arrived at the place of care. The effect of regulations which deny deductibility for food and lodging expenses "while . . . receiving medical treatment" is to allow a deduction while traveling to the place of medical attention. If Congress had wished to exclude the costs for food and lodgings incurred in traveling to the place of medication, it could have so provided. The legislative history nowhere indicates an intention to exclude "all ordinary food and lodging expenses," nor does it limit transportation expenses "to the cost of transporting the patient and his baggage."

Food and lodging expenses incurred while traveling are likely to be substantially higher than the cost of living at home. We believe that Congress intended that these higher costs, required by the transportation of a patient to the place of medical care, are to be deductible expenses for medical care under Section 213 of the 1954 Code.

Finally, we are not unmindful of the opinions of the four dissenting judges on the Tax Court. They correctly indicate that the word "transportation" has historically been given a narrower meaning than "travel." The former word has generally been used to cover the costs of transporting the person and his baggage, while the latter has been used in conjunction with the allowance of such amenities as food and lodging. See Internal Revenue Code of 1954 §§ 62(2)(B), (C), 162(a)(2), 217(b)(1)(B) and 274(d)(1). Further, it is clear that in passing the 1954 Code, Congress intended to retreat somewhat from its prior liberal attitude towards medical expenses. This is indicated by the inclusion of Section 262 requiring that "personal, living or family expenses" shall not be deductible "except as otherwise expressly provided," and the present regulations which state "deductions for expenditures for medical care . . . will be confined strictly to expenses incurred primarily for the prevention or alleviation of a physical or mental defect or illness." Treasury Regulations § 1.213-1(e)(1)(ii).

These two factors would be of great influence, but for our belief that the legislative history of Section 213(e) is clear in its import. Food and lodging expenses while traveling to the place of medication and incurred prior to "receiving medical treatment" were to be maintained as deductible expenses. The use of the narrow term "transportation," rather than "travel" was indicative of Congress' intent to preclude food and lodging expenses after arrival at the place of medication. *Cf. Commissioner v. Bilder*, 369 U.S. 499, 82 S.Ct. 881 (1962). The phrase "expenses for traveling" might well have been construed to cover food and lodging expenses during periods of stay at the place of medical treatment; precisely the "abuse" Congress sought to eliminate by the 1954 Code.

We hold that the Taxpayer and his wife properly deducted under Section 213 food and lodging expenses required to bring them to the critical point of medical treatment. The judgment of the Tax Court is affirmed.

REVENUE RULING 78-266
1978-2 C.B. 123

Advice has been requested whether, under the circumstances described below, a medical expense deduction is allowable to a taxpayer for amounts paid for care of the taxpayer's children to enable the taxpayer to visit a physician for medical treatment.

The Taxpayer, B, has an ailment that requires treatment in a physician's office twice weekly on a regular basis. B is the parent of three normal, healthy children under six years of age. B hires a baby sitter to care for the children each time B goes to the physician's office and receives medical treatment.

. . . .

The courts have denied a medical expense deduction for expenses that are not directly for medical care, even though the expense may have some relation to medical care. For example, in *Ochs v. Commissioner*, 195 F.2d 692 (2d Cir. 1952), *cert. denied*, 344 U.S. 827 (1952), a deduction was denied for expenditures incurred to send the taxpayer's children to a boarding school on a physician's advice to alleviate the taxpayer's spouse's suffering from throat cancer that required her to rest her voice. In *McVicker v. United States*, 194 F. Supp. 607 (S.D. Cal. 1961), a deduction was denied for the taxpayers' payments to a domestic servant hired on a physician's advice that housework would cause a relapse of the taxpayer-wife's illness. In *Wendell v. Commissioner*, 12 T.C. 161 (1949), a medical expense deduction was denied for salaries paid to practical nurses employed to care for a child whose mother died at childbirth, the child being normal and having no unusual illness.

In *Gerstacker v. Commissioner*, 414 F.2d 448 (6th Cir. 1969), the court permitted a medical expense deduction for legal expenses necessary to establish guardianship for the taxpayer's wife, a mental patient, in order to keep her in a mental institution for care. Rev. Rul. 71-281, 1971-2 C.B. 165, announces that the Internal Revenue Service will follow *Gerstacker*. The facts in the instant case are distinguishable from *Gerstacker* and Rev. Rul. 71-281 because in *Gerstacker* the expense was essential to the medical treatment of the person for whom the expense was incurred in that the payment for legal services for the taxpayer's wife was made to obtain the medical treatment.

In the instant case, as in *Ochs, McVicker* and *Wendell*, the expenditures for the care of B's children are not expenses for medical care, even though the expenditures have some relation to medical care. Accordingly, a medical expense deduction is not allowable to B for amounts paid for the care of B's children to enable B to visit a physician for medical treatment. Such expenditures are personal expenses within the meaning of section 262 of the Code and, therefore, are nondeductible.

Rev. Rul. 73-597, 1973-2 C.B. 69, similarly denies a charitable contributions deduction under section 170 of the Code for amounts paid for a baby sitter to care for the taxpayers' children to enable the taxpayer to perform gratuitous services for a charitable organization to which contributions are deductible.

Rev. Rul. 71-281 is distinguished.

Chapter 26

CHARITABLE DEDUCTIONS

I. PROBLEMS

1. Maurice is very active in his church; he attends weekly service and takes advantage of its education programs for his children and its religious family counseling services. Maurice is expected to contribute at least 5% of his income to the church and to contribute to its overseas mission fund. Maurice does both. Contributors to the mission fund receive a mission T-shirt. May Maurice deduct the amounts he contributes?

2. Metropolitan High School, a private school, holds a fund-raising drive to raise money to send four students and a faculty supervisor to the Student World Conference held at the United Nations in New York City. Students are selected by a faculty committee in a competitive process. To the extent possible, travel, lodging, meals, and related expenses of the students are paid through the money raised; expenses beyond the amount raised are the responsibility of the four students and their parents. The faculty supervisor's expenses are paid in full. Many high schools throughout the country will send similar delegations to participate in the conference, meeting United Nations' officials, delegates, and agency heads; drafting, debating, and voting on mock resolutions; and, in general, learning how the United Nations operates.

    (a) Marcella, whose son Eric is one of the students selected, donates $1,000 to the fund-raising effort. May Marcella deduct the contribution?

    (b) Sean, the faculty supervisor who will accompany the students, contributes $1,000 to the fund-raising effort. May Sean deduct the contribution?

    (c) A local television station provides free advertising, worth $1,000, to assist in the fund-raising effort. May the station deduct the $1,000 value of the advertising?

    (d) After the conference was held, each student received a statement from the school noting that the fund-raising efforts did not raise enough money to cover all the expenses, and that each student would be required to contribute $500 to the school to satisfy the uncovered expenses. Marcella contributed $500 to the school in response to the statement. May Marcella deduct the $500 contribution?

3. Assume Peggy has a contribution base of $250,000. What are the tax consequences to Peggy if she gives $150,000 to a local college? Alterna-

tively, what are the tax consequences if Peggy gives $10,000 to a local college and $140,000 to Private Foundation (a foundation qualified under § 170(c)(2) but not within § 170(b)(1)(A)(vii))?

4. William, an attorney, makes the following donations to charity during the year. Assuming an adequate contribution base and adequate records to substantiate each donation, what deductions, if any, may he claim? What income, if any, does he have?

(a) William owns an office building in an excellent downtown location. A local charity is in need of an office. To assist the charity, William agrees to rent office space to the charity for $1,000 per month. The actual fair rental value of the office space is $3,000 per month.

(b) William serves as a member of an advisory board for the law school where he earned his law degree. The board meets four times a year. Board members receive free lodging in connection with the board meetings and also free football and basketball tickets for games played on the days of board meetings.

   (i) William incurs unreimbursed airfare expenses amounting to $4,000 per year for travel to and from the board meetings.

   (ii) In addition, he periodically handles legal matters for the school and never charges for his time.

(c) William owns a valuable 18th century painting. He executes a document transferring to the local art museum a remainder interest in the painting which the museum intends to retain as part of its permanent collection. William retains a life estate in the painting. The remainder interest is valued currently at $50,000. Would it make any difference if instead William gave the museum an undivided one-third interest in the painting and executed an instrument giving the museum the right to the use and possession of the painting for the months of June through September of each year — months when William is usually away from home on vacation? What implications does § 170(o) have on William's gift of a one-third interest in the painting?

(d) Assume the sale of the painting described in (c) would have generated long-term capital gain. What tax consequences to William if, in lieu of the transfers in (c), he gives the painting to his church as an item to be sold in the annual church auction? Would your answer change if the donated property were undeveloped land rather than a painting?

(e) William gives his alma mater a remainder interest in his personal residence. He retains a life estate in the residence.

(f) William sells $100,000 worth of XYZ stock to his church for $50,000. William's adjusted basis in the stock is $40,000.

(g) William contributes a parcel of land to the local hospital. The land has a value of $75,000 and is encumbered by a mortgage of $25,000, which the hospital agrees to assume. William's adjusted basis in the land is $15,000.

Assignment for Chapter 26:

Complete the problems.

Read: Internal Revenue Code: §§ 170(a), (b)(1)(A), (B), (G), (c), (d)(1)(A), (e)(1), (2), (f)(1)–(3), (f)(8)(A), (B), (f)(16), (17), (i), (j), (l), (o); 1011(b); 1221, 1222(3); 6115; skim § 170(b), (f).
Treasury Regulations: §§ 1.170A-1(a), (b), (c)(1)–(4), (e), (g), (h)(1)–(3); 1.170A-5; 1.170A-7(a); 1.170A-7(b)(1), (3), (4); 1.170A-7(d) Ex. 1-3; 1.170A-13(f)(1), (8)(i); 1.1011-2(a)(3); 1.1011-2(c) Ex. 1.

Materials: Overview
Davis v. United States
Revenue Ruling 67-246
Revenue Procedure 90-12
Revenue Ruling 2003-28
Sklar v. United States

II. VOCABULARY

charitable contribution
contribution base
primary benefit test

III. OBJECTIVES

1.   To identify contributions which qualify for a deduction under § 170.

2.   To recall that charitable contributions may only be deducted up to a percentage of a taxpayer's contribution base.

3.   To identify the tax year in which a charitable deduction may be claimed.

4.   To recall that while the value of services contributed to a charitable organization may not be deducted, the expenses incurred in providing services may be deducted.

5.   To evaluate whether sufficient donative intent exists to justify a charitable deduction.

6.   To compute the amount of the charitable deduction allowable to a taxpayer donating appreciated property to a charitable organization.

7.   To explain the deduction recapture rules of § 170(e)(7) and (o).

IV. OVERVIEW

A. In General

Charitable giving has tax-favored status. Although personal in nature, gifts to charities can be tax deductible. In allowing a deduction for charitable contributions, Congress seeks to encourage private support for a range of activities and organizations which "aid in the accomplishment of many social goals which our federal and local governments otherwise cannot or will not accomplish." *Brinley v. Commissioner*, 782 F.2d 1326, 1336 (5th Cir. 1986) (Hill, J., dissenting). Rather than the government deciding which causes are worthy of support, the government uses the tax laws to encourage the taxpayers to make that decision. In effect, because of the charitable deduction, the taxpayer contributing to a charity makes the government a partner in supporting the charitable enterprise. For example, a taxpayer in a 39.6% tax bracket who contributes $1,000 to an art museum will, as a result of the tax deduction, only be out-of-pocket $604, *i.e.*, the $1,000 charitable deduction will reduce the taxpayer's tax liability by $396.[1] The other $396 received by the museum may be viewed as the government's contribution in the nature of foregone tax revenue. By assuming part of the cost of a charitable gift, the government encourages charitable giving.

Is this indirect government support of charitable organizations justifiable? Would it be preferable to deny a deduction for charitable contributions and for the government to use the resulting increase in tax revenues to increase its support for activities and organizations it considers beneficial to the public welfare?

B. Requirements for Charitable Deductions

The charitable deduction made its initial appearance in the tax code in 1917 as a relatively simple provision. In its entirety, the original provision read as follows:

> [I]n computing net income in the case of a citizen or resident of the United States, . . . there shall be allowed as deductions . . . contributions or gifts actually made within the year to corporations or associations organized and operated exclusively for religious, charitable, scientific, or educational purposes, or to societies for the prevention of cruelty to children or animals, no part of the net income of which inures to the benefit of any private stockholder or individual, to an amount not in excess of fifteen per centum of the taxpayer's taxable net income as computed without the benefit of this paragraph. Such contributions or gifts shall be allowable as deductions only if verified under rules and regulations prescribed by the Commissioner of the Internal Revenue, with the approval of the Secretary of the Treasury.

---

[1] This example assumes that the taxpayer has itemized deductions in excess of the standard deduction. The charitable deduction is not available to taxpayers who compute their taxable income using the standard deduction. In view of the purpose of the charitable deduction, does limiting the charitable deduction to those taxpayers who itemize make sense?

By contrast, the charitable deduction in its current form in § 170 is a complex maze of rules limiting the deduction taxpayers may claim. The 1917 provision and the current provision, however, both impose similar requirements, *i.e.*, to be deductible a charitable transfer must:

(1)   be made to or for the use of a qualified recipient (§ 170(c));

(2)   constitute a transfer of money or property made with no expectation of a return benefit;

(3)   actually be *paid* to the recipient within the taxable year for which the deduction is claimed (§ 170(a)(1));

(4)   not exceed certain percentage limitations (§ 170(b)); and

(5)   be substantiated by a contemporaneous written acknowledgment prepared by the donee organization and provided to the donor for any contribution of $250 or more (§ 170(f)(8)) or otherwise verified as required by regulations (§ 170(a)(1)).

As discussed in this Overview, the determination of the amount of a charitable deduction depends on a variety of factors including: the nature of the contribution, *e.g.*, cash, tangible personal property, real property, intangible property, or services; the character of the property, *e.g.*, long or short-term capital gain property or ordinary income property; the recipient of the transfer, *e.g.*, a public charity or a private foundation; the use the recipient will make of the property, *e.g.*, immediate sale or use for tax exempt purposes; the form of the transfer (outright or in trust); and the nature of the interest given (undivided interest, future interest, etc.).

1.   Who Is a Qualified Recipient?

Section 170 allows a deduction for gifts or contributions to or for the use of a broad range of entities listed in § 170(c). Among the entities listed are the United States, the states and political subdivisions thereof, as well as religious, charitable, scientific, literary or educational organizations. The Internal Revenue Service publishes a "Cumulative List of Organizations Described in § 170(c)" to assist taxpayers in identifying organizations, contributions to which will be deductible.

The various requirements of § 170 which must be met before an entity will qualify as an appropriate recipient of contributions reflect congressional concern that deductible contributions be limited to those which will be used for genuinely charitable purposes. Thus, for an organization to qualify as a § 170(c) organization, it must be organized and operated exclusively for religious, charitable, or other specified purposes (§ 170(c)(2)(B)); its net earnings cannot inure to the benefit of any private shareholder or individual (§ 170(c)(2)(C)); and its lobbying and political activities must be limited (§ 170(c)(2)(D)).

A review of the qualified recipients listed in § 170(c) indicates that in no event will an individual be a qualified recipient. That limitation is appropriate since the charitable deduction is premised on the notion that amounts contributed to charity provide some societal benefit. A contribution benefiting only an individual is not a charitable contribution within the meaning of § 170(c). For example, in *Tripp v. Commissioner*, 337 F.2d 432 (5th Cir. 1964), the Fifth Circuit denied a charitable deduction to a donor who specified that amounts he "contributed" to a college's scholarship fund were to be used for a particular individual. The college had not awarded any scholarships or other assistance to the student, and it simply credited the payments to the student's account as directed by the donor. The fact that the college actually received the money from the donor was not itself enough to establish the gift as a charitable contribution to or for the use of a qualified recipient. Rather, the court held the college was merely a conduit for, and not the intended beneficiary of, the gift. If, by contrast, Tripp's donation had been intended for a common scholarship pool to be distributed as the college determined, and Tripp had merely expressed a desire that the money be used for a specific student, then a charitable deduction would have been appropriate. *Peace v. Commissioner*, 43 T.C. 1 (1964).

The *Davis* decision, included in the materials, presents an excellent example of the close questions courts have had to resolve with respect to the qualified recipient standard. The Supreme Court in *Davis* considered the appropriate interpretation of the statutory requirement that a gift purporting to be charitable in nature must be given "to or for the use of" a qualified recipient. Read the opinion carefully. What standard is established by the Court? Do you agree with the Court's decision?

Consistent with the "to or for the use of" requirement in § 170, a taxpayer who contributes cash or property to a trust for the benefit of a charitable organization is entitled to a charitable deduction.

2. What Is a "Contribution" or "Gift"?

In *Commissioner v. Duberstein*, 363 U.S. 278, 285 (1960), the Supreme Court, defining the term "gift" as used in § 102, noted that "[a] gift in the statutory sense . . . proceeds from a detached and disinterested generosity, . . . out of affection, respect, admiration, charity or like impulses. And in this regard, the most critical consideration . . . is the transferor's 'intention.' " The *Duberstein* gift standard has generally been applied in determining whether a charitable contribution has been made. *See, e.g., Allen v. U.S.*, 541 F.2d 786 (9th Cir. 1976). Given this standard, a donor who expects to benefit directly from the transfer will generally not satisfy the § 170 requirement of a "charitable contribution."

Consistent with the *Duberstein* analysis, Revenue Ruling 83-104, 1983-2 C.B. 46, provides: "A contribution for purposes of section 170 of the Code is a voluntary transfer of money or property that is made with no expectation of procuring a financial benefit commensurate with the amount of the transfer." That ruling examines six different situations in which parents contribute to an organization operating a private school attended by their child. According to the ruling, the determination of whether the contributions qualified as charitable contributions

> depends upon whether a reasonable person, taking all the facts and circumstances of the case into account, would conclude that enrollment in the school was in no manner contingent upon making the payment, that the payment was not made pursuant to a plan (whether express or implied) to convert nondeductible tuition into charitable contributions, and that receipt of the benefit was not otherwise dependent upon the making of the payment.

In determining this issue, the presence of one or more of the following factors creates a presumption that the payment is not a charitable contribution: the existence of a contract under which a taxpayer agrees to make a "contribution" and which contains provisions ensuring the admission of the taxpayer's child; a plan allowing taxpayers either to pay tuition or to make "contributions" in exchange for schooling; the earmarking of a contribution for the direct benefit of a particular individual; or the otherwise-unexplained denial of admission or readmission to a school of children of taxpayers who are financially able, but who do not contribute.

In other cases, although no single factor may be determinative, a combination of several factors may indicate that a payment is not a charitable contribution. In these cases, both economic and noneconomic pressures placed upon parents must be taken into account. The factors that the Service ordinarily will take into consideration, but will not limit itself to, are the following: (1) the absence of a significant tuition charge; (2) substantial or unusual pressure to contribute applied to parents of children attending a school; (3) contribution appeals made as part of the admission or enrollment process; (4) the absence of significant potential sources of revenue for operating the school other than contributions by parents of children attending the school; and (5) other factors suggesting that a contribution policy has been created as a means of avoiding the characterization of payments as tuition.

Id. Revenue Ruling 83-104 thus emphasizes the importance of the intention of the transferor and the circumstances surrounding the particular transfer.

In *Hernandez v. Commissioner*, 490 U.S. 680 (1989), the U.S. Supreme Court denied a § 170 charitable deduction for fees paid to the Church of Scientology for special auditing and training sessions. "The Church established fixed price schedules for auditing and training sessions in each branch church; it calibrated particular prices to auditing or training sessions of particular lengths and levels of sophistication; it returned a refund if auditing and training sessions went unperformed; it distributed 'account cards' on which persons who had paid money to the Church could monitor what prepaid services they had not yet claimed; and it categorically barred provision of auditing for training sessions for free." The Supreme Court noted "[t]he legislative history of the 'contribution or gift' limitation, though sparse, reveals that Congress intended to differentiate between unrequited payments to qualified recipients and payments made to such recipients in return for goods or services. Only the former were deemed deductible. . . . [T]hese payments were part of a quintessential quid pro quo exchange: in return for their money, [taxpayers] received an identified benefit, namely, auditing and training sessions." 490 U.S. at 691.

While the taxpayers in *Hernandez* conceded they expected to receive specific amounts of auditing and training for their payments, they argued that the quid pro quo analysis urged by the Service was inappropriate where the benefits received by the taxpayer are purely religious in nature. The Supreme Court rejected that argument, finding no support in § 170 for that position and warning that its adoption would "raise problems of entanglement between church and state." If the taxpayer's position were adopted, the Court speculated that similar claims might be made by other taxpayers regarding services provided by church-supported schools and hospitals. In this regard, see *Sklar v. Commissioner*, included in the materials.

Where a contribution is made to a charitable organization partly in consideration for goods or services, the regulations provide a two-part test, drawn from *United States v. American Bar Endowment*, 477 U.S. 105 (1986), for deductibility: the donor must both intend to make, and in fact make, a payment in excess of the fair market value of the goods or services. The charitable contribution is then limited to the amount of the payment that exceeds that value. Reg. § 1.170A-1(h)(1), (2). For this purpose, goods and services of insubstantial value may be disregarded. See Revenue Procedure 90-12 in the materials and Reg. § 1.170A-1(h)(3),-13(f)(8) and (9). Revenue Ruling 67-246, also included in the materials, provides examples of the application of a donor-benefit standard in connection with admission to or other participation in charitable fund raising activities such as charity balls, banquets, etc.

For an enforcement mechanism, note § 6115. It requires that most § 170(c) organizations, upon the receipt of a "quid pro quo contribution" in excess of $75, inform the donor that the deductible contribution is limited to the amount by which the donor's contribution to the charity exceeds the value of the goods or services provided to the donor by the charity. (Section 6115(b) defines "quid pro quo contribution" as a "payment made partly as a contribution and partly in consideration of goods or services provided by the payor to the donee organization." There is an exception for payments to religious organizations where the taxpayer receives religious benefits not sold in commercial transactions. *Id.*) See also § 170(l), restricting the amount of the deduction available for taxpayers who contribute to an institution of higher education and, as a result of their contributions, receive the right to purchase "tickets for seating at an athletic event in an athletic stadium of such institution." Only 80% of the amount contributed under that circumstance will be treated as a charitable contribution. Obviously, any amount given for actual payment of tickets to sporting events will not be deductible. Thus, for example, if the taxpayer contributes $2,000 to University X and, as a result is entitled to purchase two season tickets to University X's football games, the taxpayer will be entitled only to an $1,600 charitable deduction. If the $2,000 contribution resulted in the taxpayer receiving without charge two season tickets worth a total of $1,000, then the charitable contribution would be computed by first subtracting the value of the season tickets from the $2,000 contribution and multiplying the remainder by 80% — the taxpayer's charitable deduction under those circumstances would be limited to $800. In addition, note that § 170(f)(8) generally requires as a condition of deductibility that the taxpayer substantiate, by contemporaneous written acknowledgment from the donee, any contribution of $250 or more.

3. Actual Payment Required

Section 170(a)(1) allows a deduction for a contribution the "payment of which is made within the taxable year." Contrast that language with the "paid or incurred" language of § 162(a) or the "paid or accrued language" of § 163. Unlike those sections, § 170 imposes a specific timing rule with respect to charitable deductions. As noted in Reg. § 1.170A-1(a), "Any charitable contribution as defined in section 170(c), *actually paid* during the taxable year is allowable as a deduction in computing taxable income *irrespective of the method of accounting employed or of the date on which the contribution is pledged.*" (Emphasis added).

Regulation § 1.170A-1(b) provides that "a contribution is made at the time delivery is effected. The unconditional delivery or mailing of a check which subsequently clears in due course will constitute an effective contribution on the date of delivery or mailing." Consider the following example: Marcella, a calendar year taxpayer, pledges $500 to X Charity on June 15, Year 1; Marcella mails a check for $500 to X Charity on December 31, Year 1; X Charity receives the check January 3, Year 2 and the check is honored by Marcella's bank. Marcella's June 15 pledge does not entitle her to a charitable deduction. *Mann v. Commissioner*, 35 F.2d 873 (D.C. Cir. 1929). The mailing of the check on December 31 does. If Marcella had not mailed the check until January 3, Year 2, she would not be entitled to a deduction in Year 1 but would be entitled to a deduction in Year 2 when the check was mailed.

Revenue Ruling 78-38, 1978-1 C.B. 67, provides a taxpayer, who makes a contribution to a charity by means of a charge to the taxpayer's bank credit card, may claim a charitable deduction in the year the charge is made. The taxpayer may not postpone the deduction until the taxpayer actually pays the indebtedness resulting from the charge.

4.   Limitation on Charitable Deductions

The charitable deduction is not unlimited. Specifically, § 170(b) caps the amount which taxpayers may deduct in any one year. Note that the 1917 charitable deduction provision imposed a cap equal to 15% of the taxpayer's contribution base. Under our current Code, "contribution base" essentially means adjusted gross income. § 170(b)(1)(F). In 1969, Congress increased the cap to as much as 50% of a taxpayer's contribution base, thereby further encouraging charitable giving. Lower caps are imposed on contributions to organizations not listed in § 170(b)(1)(A). *See* § 170(b)(1)(B), (C), (D). In addition, lower caps are also applicable to so-called "capital gain property." § 170(b)(1)(C). Charitable contributions by corporations are limited to 10% of the corporation's taxable income. § 170(b)(2). The existence of a cap prevents a person from avoiding income tax by giving all income to charity. Charitable contributions which may not be currently deducted because of the percentage limitation may, however, be carried over for a five-year period. § 170(d)(1)(A). As these caps indicate, the amount of the charitable deduction depends on the type of taxpayer, the nature of the property contributed, and the nature of the donee organization. Detailed examination of these limitations is beyond the scope of this course.

C.   Contribution of Services

May one deduct the value of the services that one contributes to a charity? For example, assume that Terry, a musician, agrees to provide a benefit concert for his church. Although Terry would normally charge $1,000 for such a concert, he does not charge the church anything. May he deduct the $1,000? The answer is "No." *See* Reg. § 1.170A-1(g). Upon careful consideration, the rationale for this regulation becomes clear. Assume Terry was paid $1,000 for his services and later gave the church $1,000 as a contribution. Obviously, he would have $1,000 of gross income as a result of the compensation he received for his services and would be entitled to claim a $1,000 charitable deduction (assuming the percentage limitation discussed previously was not applicable). If Terry simply refuses payment in lieu of making a cash contribution, he should be in no better tax position than if he had received payment and later contributed that amount to the church. He should therefore either include $1,000 in income and claim a $1,000 charitable deduction or report no income and claim no deduction.

Reg. § 1.170A-1(g) provides that "unreimbursed expenditures made incident to the rendition of services to an organization contributions to which are deductible may constitute a deductible contribution." In its decision in the unusual case of *Van Dusen v. Commissioner*, 136 T.C. No. 25 (2011), the Tax Court concluded that many of the unreimbursed expenses incurred by a taxpayer in providing foster care for about 70 feral cats were deductible. The Tax Court found that, in taking care of the feral cats, the taxpayer was providing a service to a § 501(c)(3) organization specializing in the neutering of feral cats.

Problem 4 and, to some extent, the *Davis* case address the extent to which a taxpayer may deduct unreimbursed expenses incurred in providing services to a charitable organization. Note that while Reg. § 1.170A-1(g) authorizes a deduction for certain unreimbursed expenses incurred in providing services to charitable organizations, the Supreme Court in *Davis* held the regulation was not applicable to payments made to cover expenses incurred incident to *another* taxpayer's services to charity.

D. Contribution of Appreciated Property

Generally, if a taxpayer contributes property (other than cash) to a charitable organization, the amount of the contribution will be the fair market value of the property. Reg. § 1.170A-1(c)(1). Must the donor include in income the appreciation inherent in the donated property, *i.e.*, does donation of the property constitute a realization event? The answer is "No." The tax benefits to the donor should be obvious. Consider the following example: Charlotte owns stock valued at $10,000 and in which she has a $1,000 adjusted basis. Assume Charlotte wishes to make a $10,000 contribution to a charity. If she sells the stock for $10,000 and gives the proceeds to the charity, she will be entitled to a $10,000 charitable deduction but will have to report $9,000 of gain as a result of the sale. Assuming this gain is taxed at a maximum tax rate of 20%, Charlotte would be required to pay $1,800 in tax. By contrast, if she contributes the stock to the charity, she may claim a $10,000 charitable deduction, but will not be required to include anything in income. Charlotte thus will save $1,800 in taxes by donating the stock rather than first selling it and then donating the proceeds of the sale. Note the inconsistency between this result and the result in the example above involving contributed services.

Section 170(e) reflects a congressional effort "to put the heart back into giving," and place some limitations on the general rule allowing a charitable deduction for the fair market value of donated property. Under § 170(e), in the case of gifts of appreciated property, the charitable deduction will equal the difference between the fair market value of the property and the amount of the gain which would *not* have been so-called "long-term capital gain" if the property had been sold at its fair market value. § 170(e)(1)(A). In effect, this provision generally allows the taxpayer a deduction only in the amount of the taxpayer's adjusted basis in ordinary income property (*e.g.*, inventory, artistic works produced by the taxpayer) and taxpayer's adjusted basis in property that upon sale would produce so-called "short-term capital gain."

In the case of a charitable contribution of property that would have produced long-term capital gain if it had been sold, another § 170(e) limitation provides that the charitable deduction must be reduced by the amount of long-term capital gain that would have resulted had there been a sale of the property at fair market value if: (a) the property is tangible personal property and the use by the donee is unrelated to the donee's tax exempt purpose or function or, as discussed below, the property is disposed of within three years of the contribution; (b) the property is contributed to certain types of private foundations; or (c) the property is intellectual property or taxidermy property as specified by the statute. § 170(e)(1)(B). Again, with respect to contributions of the properties specified in the preceding sentence, the taxpayer is, in effect, allowed a charitable deduction equal only to the taxpayer's adjusted basis in the contributed property.

Although Chapter 31 addresses in detail the measuring of long-term and short-term capital gain and the distinction between capital gain and ordinary income, a brief discussion of capital gain is necessary here to understand the § 170(e) limitations. Preferential tax treatment is provided to certain gains known as long-term capital gains. Section 1222(3) defines "long-term capital gain" as "gain from the sale or exchange of a capital asset held for more than 1 year." Contrast this definition to that of "short-term capital gain" in § 1222(1). Section 1221 defines "capital asset" and provides that items such as inventory, literary and artistic compositions held by a taxpayer who created them, and accounts receivable for services performed are not capital assets. By contrast the shares of stock held by Charlotte in the example above constitute capital assets which, upon sale or exchange, will generate capital gain.

With that brief summary of capital gain, consider the following examples which demonstrate first the general rule authorizing a deduction for the fair market value of property and then address the application of the § 170(e) rules. (Assume the charity in each example is not a private foundation.)

> **Example 1:** Assume Laura contributes to her local art museum a painting worth $10,000 which she purchased several years ago for $1,000. Assume the painting is a capital asset and the museum will display the painting in its permanent collection. By giving the painting to charity rather than selling it, Laura avoids being taxed on the $9,000 of appreciation inherent in the painting and at the same time entitles herself to a $10,000 deduction. In other words, she is not subject to the § 170(e)(1)(A) or (B) limitations noted above.

> **Example 2:** Assume, instead, Laura is a well-known artist and contributes one of her own paintings valued at $10,000 to the local art museum. Pursuant to § 1221(a)(3)(A), the painting is not a capital asset. Disregarding any supplies used by Laura, her basis in the donated painting is $0. As a

result, under § 170(e)(1)(A), Laura will not be entitled to claim any charitable deduction (*i.e.*, she must reduce her charitable deduction ($10,000) by the amount of gain which would not have been long-term capital gain ($10,000) if she had sold the painting for $10,000).[2]

Example 3: Assume Mary contributed to her church a painting worth $10,000, which she had purchased five years ago for $1,000. Because it has no use for the painting, the church intends to sell it. Assume the painting was a capital asset.[3] Had Mary sold the painting for $10,000, she would have reported $9,000 of long-term capital gain.[4] Under § 170(e)(1)(B), because the painting is tangible personal property, the use of which by the donee is not related to the donee's tax exempt purpose or function, Mary's charitable deduction would be limited to $1,000, *i.e.*, her deduction (which, but for § 170(e)(1)(B), would have been equal to $10,000 or the fair market value of the painting) would be reduced by $9,000, the long-term capital gain inherent in the painting. Mary is thus limited to a deduction equal to her adjusted basis in the painting.

Example 4: Assume Mary contributes to her church appreciated stock she purchased for $1,000 five years ago. The stock is now worth $10,000. As was the case with the painting in Example 3, the church intends to sell the stock promptly. Since the stock is a capital asset, § 170(e)(1)(A) does not apply; since the stock is *intangible* personal property, § 170(e)(1)(B)(i) does not apply. Mary will be entitled to a $10,000 deduction.

Note § 170(e)(1)(B)(i)(II), added in 2006. That provision limits a taxpayer's deduction for a contribution of *tangible personal property* to the taxpayer's adjusted basis in the property if, before the end of the taxable year in which the contribution is made, the donee organization disposes of the property, the property was identified by the donee organization as being for a use related to its exempt function, and the property had a fair market value of more than $5,000. In addition, under § 170(e)(7), also added in 2006, if the disposition of the property described above occurs in a year subsequent to the year of contribution but within three years of the contribution, the donor must include in income (in the year of disposition by the donee organization) an amount equal to the excess (if any) of the amount of the deduction the donor was allowed over the donor's basis in the property at the time of the contribution. The deduction limitation rules of both §§ 170(e)(1)(B)(i)(II) and 170(e)(7) are inapplicable if the donee organization, pursuant to § 170(e)(7)(D),

---

[2] Section 170(e)(1)(A) was applied to deny a charitable deduction for an attorney's contribution of discovery material relating to his representation of Timothy McVeigh in the Oklahoma City bombing trial. *Jones v. Commissioner*, 560 F.3d 1196 (10th Cir. 2009). The court held that the discovery material (which the taxpayer's expert appraised at a value of almost $300,000) came within the plain language of § 1221(a)(3)(B) excluding from capital asset status a letter, memorandum, or similar property prepared or produced for the taxpayer and thereby limiting the charitable deduction under § 170(e)(1)(A) to the taxpayer's basis in the property. Since the taxpayer had no basis in the discovery material, the taxpayer was not entitled to a charitable deduction.

[3] Since Mary did not produce the painting herself, it does not lose "capital asset" status under § 1221(a)(3).

[4] The $9,000 gain is the difference between the selling price of $10,000 and Mary's adjusted basis in the painting of $1,000.

certifies that its use of the property furthered its exempt function, with a description of such use, or, alternatively, states the intended use of the property at the time of contribution and certifies that such use has become impossible or infeasible to implement. What is the purpose of these provisions?

E.   Contributions of Partial Interests in Property

In contributing property to charity, taxpayers often wish to retain an interest in the property for themselves or for some other individual or noncharitable entity. I.R.C. § 170(f)(3)(A) generally denies a charitable deduction for a contribution of any interest in property consisting of less than the donor's entire interest. (I.R.C. § 170(f)(2) provides special rules allowing certain transfers in trust to qualify for the charitable deduction. These complex rules are beyond the scope of this course.) Reg. § 1.170A-7(a)(1) notes "a contribution of the right to use property which the donor owns, *e.g.*, a rent-free lease, shall be treated as a contribution of less than the taxpayer's entire interest in such property." For example, if the owner of a commercial building were to give a charity the rent-free use of part of the building, the owner would not be entitled to a charitable deduction. The same result occurs if the owner rents the building to a charity at a below market rate of rent. See Revenue Ruling 2003-28, included in the materials, for a ruling interpreting and applying § 170(f)(3)(A) and Reg. § 1.170A-7(a)(1) and (b)(1).

If, however, a taxpayer's only interest in property is a partial interest, *e.g.*, the taxpayer owns only a remainder interest in a tract of land, the contribution of that partial interest to a qualifying charity will entitle the taxpayer to a charitable deduction. Reg. § 1.170A-7(a)(2)(i). Of course, the taxpayer may not purposely divide and transfer property in order to create such an interest and thereby avoid § 170(f)(3)(A). For example, assume a taxpayer desires to contribute to a charity an interest in certain rental property she owns in fee simple. If the taxpayer transfers the property to her son but retains a life estate and immediately contributes her life estate to a charity, the taxpayer will not be entitled to a charitable deduction for the contribution even though technically she transferred to the charity her entire interest in the property. Reg. § 1.170A-7(a)(2)(i).

I.R.C. § 170(f)(3)(B) provides a number of important exceptions to the general rule of § 170(f)(3)(A). A taxpayer will be entitled to a charitable deduction for (a) a contribution of a remainder interest in a personal residence or farm; (b) contributions of undivided portions of the taxpayer's entire interest in property; and (c) a contribution of a qualified conservation easement.[5]

---

[5] In two cases, charitable deductions were denied to taxpayers who each contributed a house to a local fire department on the condition that the house be burned as part of the fire department's training exercises. In *Rolfs v. Commissioner*, 668 F.3d 888 (7th Cir. 2012) and *Patel v. Commissioner*, 138 T.C. 395 (2012), the taxpayers had purchased property and determined they would demolish the house located on their respective properties to make room for the new house they intended to build. In *Rolfs*, the Seventh Circuit noted that "by deciding to destroy the house and then making that demolition a condition of their gift, the taxpayers themselves became responsible for [the] decrease in value, even if the fire department provided the mechanism to accomplish it. None of the value of the house, as a house, was actually given away. . . . The taxpayers [here] gave away only the right to come onto their property and demolish their house, a service for which they otherwise would have paid a substantial sum." *Rolfs*, at 895. In *Patel*, the Tax Court focused on § 170(f)(3) and noted that the taxpayers had given up only part of the "bundle of

An undivided portion of a donor's entire interest in property must consist of a fraction or percentage of each substantial interest or right owned by the donor in the property and must extend over the entire term of the donor's interest. Reg. § 1.170A-7(b)(1)(i).

> **Example 1:** Mike owns 100 acres of timber land in northwestern Montana. He contributes 50 acres to the University of Montana Foundation (a qualified charity). Mike will be entitled to a deduction based upon the fair market value of the 50 acres he transferred to the Foundation.

> **Example 2:** Same facts as Example 1 except Mike transfers title to the 100 acres to the University of Montana Foundation and himself as tenants in common. Mike will be entitled to a charitable deduction based on the fair market value of the undivided one-half interest in the land contributed to the Foundation.

Note that undivided gifts of a portion of a donor's entire interest are not subject to § 170(a)(3) which provides a charitable contribution consisting of a future interest in tangible personal property shall be treated as made only when all intervening interests in, and rights to actual possession or enjoyment of, the property have expired or are held by persons other than the taxpayer or related parties. Reg. § 1.170A-5(a)(2) provides "Section 170(a)(3) [has] no application in respect of a transfer of an undivided present interest in property. For example, a contribution of an undivided one-quarter interest in a painting with respect to which the donee is entitled to possession during three months of each year shall be treated as made upon the receipt by the donee of a formally executed and acknowledged deed of gift. However, the period of initial possession by the donee may not be deferred in time for more than one year." This regulation indicates, for example, that a taxpayer (other than the artist) owning a valuable painting could transfer an undivided one-quarter interest in the painting to an art museum, giving the museum the unrestricted right to the use and possession of the painting during July, August, and September of each year. Under these circumstances, the taxpayer should be entitled to a charitable deduction based upon the fair market value of the undivided one-quarter interest in the painting contributed to the museum.

The Pension Protection Act of 2006, however, added § 170(o), significantly changing the law with respect to gifts of undivided interests in *tangible personal property* such as the artwork in the above example. First, that section requires that, immediately before the contribution, all interests in the item are owned (1) by the donor or (2) by the donor and the donee organization. § 170(o)(1)(A).

Second, § 170(o)(2) provides that, for purposes of determining the deductible amount of each subsequent contribution of an interest in the same item (*e.g.*, the taxpayer in the above example gives another one-quarter interest in the painting to the same art museum the next year), the fair market value of the item for purposes of computing the charitable deduction will be the lesser of (1) the value used for purposes of determining the charitable deduction for the initial fractional contri-

---

sticks" associated with their ownership of the house — i.e., they had given the fire department only a license to destroy the house, not the right to use the house for other purposes. The Tax Court concluded the contribution of this license did not fall within any exception to the general rule of § 170(f)(3).

bution; or (2) the fair market value of the item at the time of the subsequent contribution. For example, assume the painting in our example had a fair market value of $100,000 at the time of the initial contribution and that the one-quarter interest was valued at $25,000. Assume that, when the owner made a second contribution of a one-quarter interest, the painting had a fair market value of $160,000. Under § 170(o), the painting would be considered to be worth only $100,000 for purposes of calculating the deduction allowable on the second contribution.

Third, § 170(o)(3) provides a recapture rule whereby the failure of a donor, who has made an initial fractional contribution, to contribute all of the donor's remaining interest in the item to the same donee before the earlier of 10 years from the initial fractional contribution or the donor's death results in the loss of all deductions the donor has taken with respect to contributions of that item (the deductions are "recaptured"). The effect of recapture is that the donor would be required to report income in the amount of the deductions claimed. Recapture will also be triggered if the donee fails to take substantial physical possession of the item or fails to use the item for an exempt purpose. Taken together, the changes made in § 170(o) make fractional contributions of tangible personal property far less attractive.

As noted above, § 170(f)(3)(B)(i) allows a charitable deduction for a non-trust transfer of a remainder interest in a personal residence or farm. The retained present interest may be either a life estate or a term of years. Reg. § 1.170A-7(b)(3) and (4). The term "personal residence" includes a vacation home or second home, *i.e.*, any home used a personal residence. Reg. § 1.170A-7(b)(3).

> **Example:** Ellen, who is single and has no children, transfers the remainder interest in her home to a local college, the campus of which is adjacent to Ellen's home. Ellen will be entitled to a charitable deduction for the fair market value of the remainder interest in Ellen's home.

Qualified conservation easements likewise qualify for a charitable deduction under § 170(f)(3)(B)(iii). Detailed rules regarding qualified conservation easements are to be found in § 170(h) and the regulations. These rules are beyond the scope of this course.

F.   Bargain Sale to Charity

If a taxpayer sells appreciated property to a charity at a bargain price, does the taxpayer recognize any gain? For example, assume a taxpayer sells property worth $100,000 to a charity for $25,000 and claims a charitable deduction for the difference. Assume also the taxpayer has a $28,000 basis in the property. Consistent with the part-gift/part-sale discussion in Chapter 4, the taxpayer will not be entitled to claim a loss deduction. Were this a transfer subject to the part-sale/part-gift rules, there would likewise be no gain recognition. In this hypothetical, however, the taxpayer is entitled to a charitable deduction. Under these circumstances Congress has provided a special rule in § 1011(b) requiring the apportionment of the basis between the charitable contribution and the sale. Here there is a $75,000 charitable contribution and a $25,000 sale. Read § 1011(b) carefully. Applying that section, the taxpayer's basis for purposes of the sale will equal $25,000/$100,000 × $28,000 = $7,000. The taxpayer will therefore recognize gain of $18,000. *See* Reg. § 1.1011-2(c), Ex. 1. Note that Reg. § 1.1011-2(a)(3) provides "[i]f property is transferred subject to an indebtedness, the amount of the indebtedness must be treated as an amount realized for purposes of determining whether there is a sale or exchange to which section 1011(b) and this section apply, even though the transferee does not agree to assume or pay the indebtedness."

G. Substantiation

A donor who claims a deduction for a charitable contribution must maintain reliable written records regarding the contribution, regardless of the value or amount of such contribution. For a contribution of money, applicable record keeping requirements are satisfied only if the donor maintains as a record of the contribution a bank record or a written communication from the donee showing the name of the donee organization, the date of the contribution, and the amount of the contribution. § 170(f)(17). Thus, if a taxpayer puts a $20 bill in the collection basket at a church service, the taxpayer will not be allowed to claim a charitable deduction for the $20 unless the donor satisfies the requirement of § 170(f)(17). The record-keeping requirements may not be satisfied by maintaining other written records. For a contribution of property other than money, the donor generally must maintain a receipt from the donee organization showing the name of the donee, the date and the location of the contribution, and a detailed description (but not the value) of the property. Reg. § 1.170A-13(b). A donor of property, other than money, need not obtain a receipt, however, if circumstances make obtaining a receipt impracticable. Under such circumstances, the donor must maintain reliable written records regarding the contribution. The required content of such a record varies depending upon factors such as the type and value of property contributed. Reg. § 1.170A-13(b).

In addition to the foregoing recordkeeping requirements, additional substantiation requirements apply in the case of charitable contributions with a value of $250 or more. As noted previously, no charitable deduction is allowed for any contribution of $250 or more unless the taxpayer substantiates the contribution by a contemporaneous written acknowledgment of the contribution by the donee organization. Such acknowledgment must include the amount of cash and a description (but not value) of any property other than cash contributed, whether the donee provided any goods or services in consideration for the contribution, and a good faith estimate of the value of any such goods or services. § 170(f)(8). In general, if the total charitable deduction claimed for non-cash property is more than $500, the taxpayer must attach a completed Form 8283 (Noncash Charitable Contributions) to the taxpayer's return or the deduction is not allowed. § 170(f)(11). Taxpayers are required to obtain a qualified appraisal for donated property with a value of more than $5,000 and to attach an appraisal summary to the tax return. § 170(f)(11)(C).

Note § 170(f)(16)(A), denying a deduction for contributions of clothing or household items unless the clothing or household items are in "good used condition or better." A deduction may be allowed for a charitable contribution of a single item of clothing or a household item not in "good used condition or better" if the amount claimed for the item is more than $500 and the taxpayer includes with the taxpayer's return a qualified appraisal with respect to the property. Household items include furniture, furnishings, electronics, appliances, linens, and other similar items. Food, paintings, antiques, and other objects of art, jewelry and gems, and collections are excluded from the provision. § 170(f)(16)(D).

DAVIS v. UNITED STATES
United States Supreme Court
495 U.S. 472 (1990)

JUSTICE O'CONNOR delivered the opinion of the Court.

We are called upon in this case to determine whether the funds petitioners transferred to their two sons while they served as full-time, unpaid missionaries for the Church of Jesus Christ of Latter-day Saints are deductible as charitable contributions "to or for the use of" the Church, pursuant to 26 U.S.C. § 170.

I.

Petitioners, Harold and Enid Davis, and their sons, Benjamin and Cecil, are members of the Church of Jesus Christ of Latter-day Saints. According to the stipulated facts, the Church operates a worldwide missionary program involving 25,000 persons each year. Most of these missionaries are young men between the ages of 19 and 22. If the Church determines that a candidate is qualified to become a missionary, the president of the Church sends a letter calling the candidate to missionary service in a specified geographical location. A follow-up letter from the Missionary Department lists the items of clothing the missionary will need, provides specific information relating to the mission, and sets forth the estimated amount of money needed to support the missionary service. This amount varies according to the location of the mission, and reflects an estimate of the amount the missionary will actually need.

The missionary's parents generally provide the necessary funds to support their son or daughter during the period of missionary service. If they are unable to do so, the Church will locate another donor from the local congregation or use money donated to the Church's general missionary funds. The Church believes that having individual donors send the necessary funds directly to the missionary benefits the Church in several important ways. Specifically, it "fosters the Church doctrine of sacrifice and consecration in the lives of its people" as well as reducing the administrative and bookkeeping requirements which would otherwise be imposed upon the Church.

After accepting the call, the missionary candidate receives priesthood ordinances to serve as an official missionary and minister of the Church. During the missionary service, the Mission President (leader of the mission) controls many aspects of the missionaries' lives, including the manner of dress and grooming. Missionaries are required to conform to a daily schedule which calls for at least 10 hours per day of actual missionary work in addition to study time, mealtime and planning time. Mission rules forbid dating, movies, plays, certain sports, and other activities; missionaries are not allowed to take vacations or travel for personal purposes.

Missionaries receive some supervision over their use of funds. The Missionary Handbook instructs missionaries that "[t]he money you receive for your support is sacred and should be spent wisely and only for missionary work. Keep expenses at a minimum. . . . Keep a financial record of all expenditures." The Mission Presidents give similar instructions to the missionaries under their supervision. Although missionaries are not required to obtain advance approval of each expenditure they make from their personal checking account, they do submit weekly reports to their group leader listing the amount of time spent in Church service, the type of missionary work accomplished, and a report of the total expenses for the week and month to date. If a missionary begins to accumulate surplus funds, he is expected to take action to reduce the amount of donations sent to him. The Mission President may alter his estimates of the amounts required each month to take into account changing circumstances.

Benjamin and Cecil Davis both applied to become missionaries. In 1979, the Church notified Benjamin by letter that he had been called to missionary service at the New York Mission. A second letter informed him of the estimated amount of money which would be needed to support his service. In 1980, Cecil Davis was notified that he had been called to missionary service at the New Zealand-Cook Island Mission. Cecil also received a second letter informing him about the mission and the amount of money he would need. Petitioners notified their bishop that they would provide the funds requested by the Church to meet their sons' mission expenses. According to petitioners, both sons made a commitment with them to use the money only in accordance with the Church's instructions.

Petitioners transferred to Benjamin's personal checking account, on which he was the sole authorized signatory, $3,480.89 in 1980 and $4,135 in 1981. During 1981, petitioners transferred $1,518 to Cecil's personal checking account, on which he was the sole authorized signatory. Benjamin and Cecil used this money primarily to pay for rent, food, transportation, and personal needs while on their missions. Benjamin also spent approximately $20 per month to purchase religious tracts and other materials used during his missionary work. Neither Benjamin nor Cecil was required to or sought specific approval of each expenditure made from his personal checking account. However, each week Benjamin and Cecil submitted a report of the total expenses for the week and month to date. At the end of their service, Cecil had no money remaining in his account; Benjamin had $150 which he used to purchase a camera. (Petitioners do not claim a deduction for this amount.)

In their joint tax returns filed in 1980 and 1981, petitioners claimed their sons as dependents, but did not claim a charitable contribution deduction under 26 U.S.C. § 170 for the funds sent their sons during their missionary service. On April 16, 1984, petitioners filed an amended income tax return for the years 1980 and 1981, claiming additional charitable contributions of the $3,480.89 and $4,882 paid to their sons during the missionary service. In January 1985, the Internal Revenue Service disallowed the refunds. Petitioners filed a refund suit in the United States District Court for the District of Idaho. In September 1986, petitioners filed a second set of amended returns, limiting their charitable deductions to the amounts indicated by the Church and correcting the number of dependents claimed for each year.

In District Court, petitioners and the United States both moved for summary judgment. . . . Petitioners argued that the payments they made to support their sons' missionary services were charitable contributions "for the use of" the Church. Alternatively, they claimed the payments were deductible under Treas. Reg. § 1.170A-1(g), 26 CFR § 1.170A-1(g) (1989), which allows the deduction of "unreimbursed expenditures made incident to the rendition of services to an organization contributions to which are deductible." The District Court ruled in favor of the United States. It rejected petitioners' claimed deduction for unreimbursed expenditures because petitioners were not themselves performing donated services and it held that petitioners' payments to their sons were not "for the use of" the Church because the Church lacked sufficient possession and control of the funds. 664 F. Supp., at 471–472.

The Court of Appeals for the Ninth Circuit affirmed. 861 F.2d 558 (1988). The Court of Appeals rejected petitioners' claim that the transferred funds were deductible contributions because they conferred a benefit on the Church. *Id.*, at 561. Instead, the Court of Appeals held that contributions are deductible only when the recipient charity exercises control over the donated funds. The Court of Appeals reasoned that the beneficiary of a charitable contribution must be indefinite, and that this requirement cannot be met when the taxpayer makes a contribution directly to the intended beneficiary. In this case, the Court of Appeals concluded that the Church lacked actual control over the disposition of the funds and thus they were not deductible. . . . The Court of Appeals agreed with the District Court that § 1.170A-1(g) did not apply to petitioners, as the regulation permits a deduction for unreimbursed expenses only by the taxpayer who performed the charitable service.

Because the Court of Appeals' decision conflicted with *White v. United States*, 725 F.2d 1269, 1270–1272 (CA10 1984), and *Brinley v. Commissioner*, 782 F.2d 1326, 1336 (CA5 1986), we granted certiorari, . . . and now affirm.

II.

Under § 170 of the Internal Revenue Code of 1954, . . . a taxpayer may claim a deduction for a charitable contribution only if the contribution is made "to or for the use of" a qualified organization. This section provides, in pertinent part:

(a) Allowance of deduction.

(1) General rule. — There shall be allowed as a deduction any charitable contribution (as defined in subsection (c)) payment of which is made within the taxable year. A charitable contribution shall be allowable as a deduction only if verified under regulations prescribed by the Secretary.

. . . .

(c) Charitable contribution defined. — For purposes of this section, the term "charitable contribution" means a contribution or gift to or for the use of—

. . . .

(2) A corporation, trust, or community chest, fund, or foundation—

. . . .

(B) organized and operated exclusively for religious, charitable, scientific, literary, or educational purposes. . . .

Petitioners contend that the funds they transferred to their sons' accounts are deductible as contributions "for the use of" the Church. Alternatively, petitioners claim these funds are unreimbursed expenditures under Treasury Regulation § 1.170A-1(g), and therefore are deductible as contributions "to" the Church. We first consider whether the payments at issue here are "for the use of" the Church within the meaning of § 170.

On its face, the phrase "for the use of" could support any number of different meanings. See, *e.g.*, Webster's New International Dictionary (2d ed. 1950) ("use" defined in general usage as "to convert to one's service"; "to employ"; or, in law, "use imports a trust" relationship). Petitioners contend that the phrase "for the use of" must be given its broadest meaning as describing "the entire array of fiduciary relationships in which one person conveys money or property to someone else to hold or employ in some manner for the benefit of a third person." Brief for Petitioners 17. Under this reading, no legally enforceable relationship need exist between the recipient of the donated funds and the qualified donee; in effect, any intermediary may handle the funds in any way that would arguably benefit a charitable organization, regardless of how indirect or tangential the benefit might be. Petitioners also advance a second, somewhat narrower interpretation, specifically that a contribution is "for the use of" a qualified organization within the meaning of § 170 so long as the donee has "a reasonable ability to ensure that the contribution primarily serves the organization's charitable purposes." Brief for Petitioners 26. In this case, petitioners argue that their payments at least meet this second interpretation. They point to the Church's role in requesting the funds, setting the amount to be donated, and requiring weekly expense sheets from the missionaries. The Service, on the other hand, has historically defined "for the use of" as conveying "a similar meaning as in trust for."

Although the language of § 170 would support the interpretation of either the Service or petitioners, the events leading to the enactment of the 1921 amendment adding the phrase "for the use of" to § 170 indicate that Congress had a specific meaning of "for the use of" in mind. The original version of § 170, promulgated in the War Revenue Act of 1917, did not allow deductions for gifts "for the use of" a qualified donee. Rather, it allowed individuals to deduct only "[c]ontributions or gifts . . . to corporations or associations organized and operated exclusively for religious, charitable, scientific, or educational purposes. . . . " In interpreting this provision in the Act (and in the subsequent Revenue Act of 1918, the Bureau of Internal Revenue stated that "[c]ontributions to a trust company (a corporation) in trust to invest and disburse them for a charitable purpose are not allowable deductions under [§ 170]." In hearings before the Senate Committee on Finance on the proposed Revenue Act of 1921, representatives of charitable foundations requested an amendment making gifts to trust companies and similar donees deductible even though a trustee, rather than a charitable organization, held legal title to the funds. Testimony before the Committee indicated that numerous communities had established charitable trusts, charitable foundations, or community chests so that individuals could donate money to a trustee who held, invested, and reinvested the principal, and then turned the principal over to a committee that distributed the funds for charitable purposes. Responding to these concerns, Congress overruled the Service's interpretation of § 170 [then § 214(a)(11)] by adding the phrase "for the use of . . . any corporation, or community chest, fund, or foundation. . . . " to the charitable deduction provision of the Revenue Act of 1921. In light of these events, it can be inferred that Congress' use of the phrase "for the use of" related to its purpose in amending § 170 of allowing taxpayers to deduct contributions made to trusts, foundations, and similar donees. An interpretation of "for the use of" as conveying a similar meaning as "in trust for" would be consistent with this goal.

It would have been quite natural for Congress to use the phrase "for the use of" to indicate its intent of allowing deductions for donations in trust, as this phrase would have suggested a trust relationship to the members of the 67th Congress. From the dawn of English common law through the present, the word "use" has been employed to refer to various forms of trust arrangements. See 1 G. Bogert, Trusts and Trustees § 2, p. 9 (1935); Black's Law Dictionary 1382 (5th ed. 1979) ("Use and trusts are not so much different things as different aspects of the same subject. A use regards principally the beneficial interest; a trust regards principally the nominal ownership"). In the early part of this century, the word "use" was technically employed to refer to a passive trust, but less formally used as a synonym for the word "trust." The phrases "to the use of" or "for the use of" were frequently used in describing trust arrangements. . . . Given that this meaning of the word "use" precisely corresponded with Congress' purpose for amending the statute, it appears likely that in choosing the phrase "for the use of" Congress was referring to donations made in trust or in a similar legal arrangement.

This understanding is confirmed by the Service's initial interpretation of the phrase. It is significant that almost immediately following the amendment of § 170, the Commissioner interpreted the phrase "for the use of" as "intended to convey a similar meaning as 'in trust for.' " I.T. 1867, II-2 Cum. Bull. 155 (1923). Rejecting a taxpayer's claim that a gift to a volunteer fire company was deductible as a contribution for the use of the municipality, the Service noted that "[i]t does not appear that the municipality in any way has any control over the property of the incorporated volunteer fire company or that it has any voice in the manner in which such property should be used. Upon dissolution of the company, the property would not escheat to the State. A right of appropriation or enjoyment of the property of the fire company does not rest in the municipality." The Service adhered to its interpretation that "for the use of" conveys "a similar meaning as 'in trust for' " in subsequent rulings permitting taxpayers to deduct the value of gifts irrevocably transferred to a trust for the benefit of qualified organizations. . . . Numerous judicial decisions have relied on this interpretation. . . . Congress' reenactment of the statute in 1954, using the same language, indicates its apparent satisfaction with the prevailing interpretation of the statute. . . .

The Commissioner's interpretation of "for the use of" thus appears to be entirely faithful to Congress' understanding and intent in using that phrase. Moreover, the Commissioner's interpretation is consistent with the purposes of § 170 as a whole. In enacting § 170, "Congress sought to provide tax benefits to charitable organizations, to encourage the development of private institutions that serve a useful public purpose or supplement or take the place of public institutions of the same kind." *Bob Jones University v. United States*, 461 U.S. 574, 588, 103 S.Ct. 2017, 2026, 76 L.Ed.2d 157 (1983). The Commissioner's interpretation of "for the use of" assures that contributions will in fact foster such development because it requires contributions to be made in trust or in some similar legal arrangement. A defining characteristic of a trust arrangement is that the beneficiary has the legal power to enforce the trustee's duty to comply with the terms of the trust. See, *e.g.*, 3 W. Fratcher, Scott on Trusts § 200 (4th ed. 1988); 1 Restatement of Trusts § 200 (1935). A qualified beneficiary of a bona fide trust for charitable purposes would have both the incentive and legal authority to ensure that donated funds are properly used. If the trust contributes funds to a range of charitable organizations so that no single beneficiary could enforce its terms, the trustee's duty can be enforced by the Attorney General under the laws of most States. . . . Although the Service's interpretation does not require that the qualified organization take actual possession of the contribution, it nevertheless reflects that the beneficiary must have significant legal rights with respect to the disposition of donated funds.

Petitioners argue that any interpretation of "for the use of" that requires a qualified donee to have the same degree of control over contributed funds as a beneficiary would have over a trust res, would make "for the use of" redundant, meaning no more than "to." We disagree. When Congress amended § 170, it was fully aware of the Service's ruling that the original statutory deduction for contributions "to" a qualified organization could not be claimed for contributions made in trust for the organization. Accordingly, Congress amended the statute specifically to overcome this interpretation. Moreover, a contribution made in trust for a charity does not give the charity immediate possession and control, as does a donation directly to a charity. Unlike a contribution that must go "to" a qualified organization, a contribution "for the use of" a donee may go to a trustee with the discretion to select among a number of qualified donees to whom the funds may be disbursed. Furthermore, a taxpayer may generally claim an immediate deduction for a gift to a trustee, even though receipt of the gift by the charity is delayed. Recognizing this characteristic of gifts in trust, Congress further amended § 170 in 1964 in order to encourage donations "to" a charity, because donations "in trust for" a charity "often do not find their way into operating philanthropic endeavors for extended periods of time."

Although the Service's interpretive rulings do not have the force and effect of regulations, we give an agency's interpretations and practices considerable weight where they involve the contemporaneous construction of a statute and where they have been in long use. Under the circumstances presented here, we think there is good reason to accept the Service's interpretation of "for the use of." The denial of deductions for donations in trust that prompted Congress to amend § 170, the accepted meaning of "use" as synonymous with the term "trust," and the Service's contemporaneous and longstanding construction of § 170 constitutes strong evidence in favor of this interpretation.

Although the language of the statute may also bear petitioners' interpretation, they have failed to establish that their interpretation is compelled by the statutory language. To the contrary, there is no evidence that Congress intended the phrase "for the use of" to be interpreted as referring to fiduciary relationships in general or as referring to a type of relationship that gives a qualified organization a reasonable ability to supervise the use of contributed funds. Rather, as noted above, there are strong indications that Congress intended a more specific meaning. Moreover, petitioners' interpretations would tend to undermine the purposes of § 170 by allowing taxpayers to claim deductions for funds transferred to children or other relatives for their own personal use. Because a recipient of donated funds need not have any legal relationship with a qualified organization, the Service would face virtually insurmountable administrative difficulties in verifying that any particular expenditure benefited a qualified donee. *Cf.* § 170(a)(1). Although there is no suggestion whatsoever in this case that the transferred funds were used for an improper purpose, it is clear that petitioners' interpretation would create an opportunity for tax evasion that others might be eager to exploit. . . . We need not determine whether petitioners' interpretation of "for the use of" would have been a permissible one had the Service decided to adopt it, though we note that the Service may retain some flexibility to adopt other interpretations in the future. It is sufficient to decide this case that the Service's longstanding interpretation is both consistent with the statutory language and fully implements Congress' apparent purpose in adopting it. Accordingly, we conclude that a gift or contribution is "for the use of" a qualified organization when it is held in a legally enforceable trust for the qualified organization or in a similar legal arrangement.

Viewing the record here in the light most favorable to petitioners, as we must after a grant of summary judgment for the United States, we discern no evidence that petitioners transferred funds to their sons "in trust for" the Church. It is undisputed that petitioners transferred the money to their sons' personal bank accounts on which the sons were the sole authorized signatories. Nothing in the record indicates that petitioners took any steps normally associated with creating a trust or similar legal arrangement. Although the sons may have promised to use the money "in accordance with Church guidelines," . . . they did not have any legal obligation to do so; there is no evidence that the guidelines have any legally binding effect. Nor does the record support the assertion . . . that the Church might have a legal entitlement to the money or a civil cause of action against missionaries who used their parents' money for purposes not approved by the Church. We conclude that, because petitioners did not donate the funds in trust for the Church, or in a similarly enforceable legal arrangement for the benefit of the Church, the funds were not donated "for the use of" the Church for purposes of § 170.

III.

Petitioners contend, in the alternative, that their transfer of funds into their sons' account was a contribution "to" the Church under Treas. Reg. § 1.170A-1(g), 26 CFR § 1.170A-1(g) (1989), which provides:

> Contributions of services. No deduction is allowable under section 170
> for a contribution of services. However, unreimbursed expenditures made

incident to the rendition of services to an organization contributions to which are deductible may constitute a deductible contribution. For example, the cost of a uniform without general utility which is required to be worn in performing donated services is deductible. Similarly, out-of-pocket transportation expenses necessarily incurred in performing donated services are deductible. Reasonable expenditures for meals and lodging necessarily incurred while away from home in the course of performing donated services are also deductible. For the purposes of this paragraph, the phrase "while away from home" has the same meaning as that phrase is used for purposes of section 162 and the regulations thereunder.

Petitioners assert that this regulation allows them to claim deductions for their sons' unreimbursed expenditures incident to their sons' contribution of services. We disagree. The plain language of § 1.170A-1(g) indicates that taxpayers may claim deductions only for expenditures made in connection with their own contributions of service to charities. Unless there is a specific statutory provision to the contrary, a taxpayer ordinarily reports his own income and takes his own deductions. . . . Section 1.170A-1(g) is thus most naturally read as referring to the individual taxpayer, who may deduct only those "unreimbursed expenditures" incurred in connection with the taxpayer's own "rendition of services to [a qualified] organization." This interpretation of the regulation is consistent with the Revenue Ruling that was the precursor to § 1.170A-1(g). See Rev. Rul. 55-4, 1955-1 Cum. Bull. 291 ("A taxpayer who gives his services gratuitously to an association, contributions to which are deductible under [§ 170] and who incurs unreimbursed traveling expenses . . . may deduct the amount of such unreimbursed expenses in computing his net income . . . "). It would strain the language of the regulation to read it, as petitioners suggest, as allowing a deduction for expenses made incident to a third party's rendition of services rather than to the taxpayer's own contribution of services. Similarly, the taxpayer is clearly intended to be the subject of the other provisions in the regulation. For example, it is most natural to read the regulation as referring to a taxpayer who incurs expenditures for meals and lodging while away from his home, not while a third party is away from his home.

Petitioners' interpretation not only strains the language of the statute, but would also allow manipulation of § 1.170A-1(g) for tax evasion purposes. . . . For example, parents might be tempted to transfer funds to their children in amounts greater than needed to reimburse reasonable expenses incurred in donating services to a charity. Parents and children might attempt to claim a deduction for the same expenditure. Controlling such abuses would place a heavy administrative burden on the Service, which would not only have to monitor the taxpayer's records, but also correlate them with the records of the third party. To the extent petitioners' interpretation lessens the likelihood that claimed charitable contributions actually served a charitable purpose, it is inconsistent with § 170.

We conclude that § 1.170A-1(g) does not allow taxpayers to claim a deduction for expenses not incurred in connection with the taxpayers' own rendition of services to a qualified organization. Therefore, petitioners are not entitled to a deduction under § 1.170A-1(g).

Accordingly, we hold that petitioners' transfer of funds into their sons' accounts was not a contribution "to or for the use of" the Church for purposes of § 170. The judgment of the Court of Appeals is Affirmed.

REVENUE RULING 67-246
1967-2 C.B. 104

Advice has been requested concerning certain fund-raising practices which are frequently employed by or on behalf of charitable organizations and which involve the deductibility, as charitable contributions under section 170 of the Internal Revenue Code of 1954, of payments in connection with admission to or other participation in fund-raising activities for charity such as charity balls, bazaars, banquets, shows, and athletic events.

To be deductible as a charitable contribution for Federal income tax purposes under section 170 of the Code, a payment to or for the use of a qualified charitable organization must be a gift. To be a gift for such purposes in the present context there must be, among other requirements, a payment of money or transfer of property without adequate consideration.

As a general rule, where a transaction involving a payment is in the form of a purchase of an item of value, the presumption arises that no gift has been made for charitable contribution purposes, the presumption being that the payment in such case is the purchase price.

Thus, where consideration in the form of admissions or other privileges or benefits is received in connection with payments by patrons of fund-raising affairs of the type in question, the presumption is that the payments are not gifts. In such case, therefore, if a charitable contribution deduction is claimed with respect to the payment, the burden is on the taxpayer to establish that the amount paid is not the purchase price of the privileges or benefits and that part of the payment, in fact, does qualify as a gift.

In showing that a gift has been made, an essential element is proof that the portion of the payment claimed as a gift represents the excess of the total amount paid over the value of the consideration received therefor. This may be established by evidence that the payment exceeds the fair market value of the privileges or other benefits received by the amount claimed to have been paid as a gift.

Another element which is important in establishing that a gift was made in such circumstances, is evidence that the payment in excess of the value received was made with the intention of making a gift. While proof of such intention may not be an essential requirement under all circumstances and may sometimes be inferred from surrounding circumstances, the intention to make a gift is, nevertheless, highly relevant in overcoming doubt in those cases in which there is a question whether an amount was in fact paid as a purchase price or as a gift.

The fact that the full amount or a portion of the payment made by the taxpayer is used by the organization exclusively for charitable purposes has no bearing upon the determination to be made as to the value of the admission or other privileges and the amount qualifying as a contribution.

Also, the mere fact that tickets or other privileges are not utilized does not entitle the patron to any greater charitable contribution deduction than would otherwise be allowable. The test of deductibility is not whether the right was accepted or rejected by the taxpayer. If a patron desires to support an affair, but does not intend to use the tickets or exercise the other privileges being offered with the event, he can make an outright gift of the amount he wishes to contribute in which event he would not accept or keep any ticket or other evidence of any of the privileges related to the event connected with the solicitation.

Example 1: The M Charity sponsors a symphony concert for the purpose of raising funds for M's charitable programs. M agrees to pay a fee which is calculated to reimburse the symphony for hall rental, musicians' salaries, advertising costs, and printing of tickets. Under the agreement, M is entitled to all receipts from ticket sales. M sells tickets to the concert charging $5 for balcony seats and $10 for orchestra circle seats. These prices approximate the established admission charges for concert performances by the symphony orchestra. The tickets to the concert and the advertising material promoting ticket sales emphasize that the concert is sponsored by, and is for the benefit of M Charity.

Notwithstanding the fact that taxpayers who acquire tickets to the concert may think they are making a charitable contribution to or for the benefit of M Charity, no part of the payments made is deductible as a charitable contribution for Federal income tax purposes. Since the payments approximate the established admission charge for similar events, there is no gift. . . .

Example 2: The facts are the same as in *Example 1*, except that the M Charity desires to use the concert as an occasion for the solicitation of gifts. It indicates that fact in its advertising material promoting the event, and fixes the payments solicited in connection with each class of admission of $30 for orchestra circle seats and $15 for balcony seats. The advertising and the tickets clearly reflect the fact that the established admission charges for comparable performances by the symphony orchestra are $10 for orchestra circle seats and $5 for the balcony seats, and that only the excess of the solicited amounts paid in connection with admission to the concert over the established prices is a contribution to M.

Under these circumstances a taxpayer who makes a payment of $60 and receives two orchestra circle seat tickets can show that his payment exceeds the established admission charge for similar tickets to comparable performances of the symphony orchestra by $40. The circumstances also confirm that that amount of the payment was solicited as, and intended to be, a gift to M Charity. The $40, therefore, is deductible as a charitable contribution.

Example 3: A taxpayer pays $5 for a balcony ticket to the concert described in *Example 1*. This taxpayer had no intention of using the ticket when he acquired it and he did not, in fact, attend the concert.

No part of the taxpayer's $5 payment to the M Charity is deductible as a charitable contribution. The mere fact that the ticket to the concert was not used does not entitle the taxpayer to any greater right to a deduction than if he did use it. The same result would follow if the taxpayer had made a gift of the ticket to another individual. If the taxpayer desired to support M, but did not intend to use the ticket to the concert, he could have made a qualifying charitable contribution by making a $5 payment to M and refusing to accept the ticket to the concert.

Example 4: A receives a brochure soliciting contributions for the support of the M Charity. The brochure states: "As a grateful token of appreciation for your help, the M Charity will send to you your choice of one of the several articles listed below, depending upon the amount of your donation." The remainder of the brochure is devoted to a catalog-type listing of articles of merchandise with the suggested amount of donation necessary to receive each particular article. There is no evidence of any significant difference between the suggested donation and the fair market value of any such article. The brochure contains the further notation that all donations to M Charity are tax deductible.

Payments of the suggested amounts solicited by M Charity are not deductible as a charitable contribution. Under the circumstances, the amounts solicited as "donations" are simply the purchase price of the articles listed in the brochure.

Example 5: A taxpayer paid $5 for a ticket which entitled him to a chance to win a new automobile. The raffle was conducted to raise funds for the X Charity. Although the payment for the ticket was solicited as a "contribution" to the X Charity and designated as such on the face of the ticket, no part of the payment is deductible as a charitable contribution. Amounts paid for chances to participate in raffles, lotteries, or similar drawings or to participate in puzzle or other contests for valuable prizes are not gifts in such circumstances, and therefore, do not qualify as deductible charitable contributions.

REVENUE PROCEDURE 90-12
1990-1 C.B. 471
(as amplified by Revenue Procedure 92-49, 1992-1 C.B. 987)

These guidelines are intended to provide charitable organizations with help in advising their patrons of the deductible amount of contributions under section 170 of the Code when the contributors are receiving something in return for their contributions. . . .

Rev. Rul. 67-246 [1967-2 C.B. 104] asks charities to determine the fair market value of the benefits offered for contributions in advance of a solicitation and to state in the solicitation and in tickets, receipts, or other documents issued in connection with a contribution how much is deductible under section 170 of the Code and how much is not. . . .

Many charities have suggested that this determination is difficult or burdensome particularly in the case of small items or other benefits that are of token value in relation to the amount contributed. The Service has determined that a benefit may be so inconsequential or insubstantial that the full amount of a contribution is deductible under section 170 of the Code. Under the following guidelines, charities offering certain small items or other benefits of token value may treat the benefits as having insubstantial value so that they may advise contributors that contributions are fully deductible under section 170.

SECTION 3. GUIDELINES

Benefits received in connection with a payment to a charity will be considered to have insubstantial fair market value for purposes of advising patrons if the requirements of paragraphs 1 and 2 are met:

1. The payment occurs in the context of a fund-raising campaign in which the charity informs patrons how much of their payment is a deductible contribution, and either

2.   (a) The fair market value of all of the benefits received in connection with the payment, is not more than 2 percent of the payment, or $50, whichever is less, or

    (b) The payment is $25 (adjusted for inflation as described below) or more and the only benefits received in connection with the payment are token items (bookmarks, calendars, key chains, mugs, posters, tee shirts, etc.) bearing the organization's name or logo. The cost (as opposed to fair market value) of all of the benefits received by a donor must, in the aggregate, be within the limits established for "low cost articles" under section 513(h)(2) of the Code . . . , [or]

    (c) The fund-raising campaign meets the following two requirements:

        (1) The charity mails or otherwise distributes free, unordered items to patrons. . . . Any item distributed must be accompanied by a request for a charitable contribution and by a statement that the patron may retain the item whether or not the patron makes a contribution, (2) The cost (as opposed to fair market value) of all such items, in the aggregate, distributed by or on behalf of the organization to a single patron in a calendar year is within the limits established for "low cost articles" in section 513(h)(2) of the Code.

For purposes of paragraph 2 of section [3], above, newsletters or program guides (other than commercial quality publications) will be treated as if they do not have a measurable fair market value or cost if their primary purpose is to inform members about the activities of an organization and if they are not available to nonmembers by paid subscription or through newsstand sales. . . .

In applying paragraph 2, the total amount of a pledge payable in installments will be considered to be the amount of the payment. Also, benefits provided by charities in the form of cash or its equivalent will never be considered insubstantial.

For purposes subparagraph (b) of paragraph 2, an item is a "low cost article" under section 513(h)(2) of the Code if its cost does not exceed $5, increased for years after 1987 by a cost-of-living adjustment under section 1(f)(3). The $25 payment required in subparagraph (b) of paragraph 2 must also be increased, in the same manner. . . .

These guidelines describe a safe harbor; depending on the facts in each case, benefits received in connection with contributions may be "insubstantial" even if they do not meet these guidelines.

REVENUE RULING 2003-28
2003-11 I.R.B. 594

ISSUES

(1) Is a taxpayer's contribution to a qualified charity of a license to use a patent deductible under § 170(a) of the Internal Revenue Code if the taxpayer retains any substantial right in the patent?

(2) Is a taxpayer's contribution to a qualified charity of a patent subject to a conditional reversion deductible under § 170(a)?

(3) Is a taxpayer's contribution to a qualified charity of a patent subject to a license or transfer restriction deductible under § 170(a)?

FACTS

Situation 1. X contributes to University, an organization described in § 170(c) (qualified charity), a license to use a patent, but retains the right to license the patent to others.

Situation 2. Y contributes a patent to University subject to the condition that A, a faculty member of University and an expert in the technology covered by the patent, continue to be a faculty member of University during the remaining life of the patent. If A ceases to be a member of University's faculty before the patent expires, the patent will revert to Y. The patent will expire 15 years after the date Y contributes it to University. On the date of the contribution, the likelihood that A will cease to be a member of the faculty before the patent expires is not so remote as to be negligible.

Situation 3. Z contributes to University all of Z's interests in a patent. The transfer agreement provides that University may not sell or license the patent for a period of 3 years after the transfer. This restriction does not result in any benefit to Z, and under no circumstances can the patent revert to Z.

LAW AND ANALYSIS

Issue (1)

Section 170(a) provides, subject to certain limitations, a deduction for any charitable contribution, as defined in § 170(c), payment of which is made within the taxable year.

Section 170(f)(3) denies a charitable contribution deduction for certain contributions of partial interests in property. Section 170(f)(3)(A) denies a charitable contribution deduction for a contribution of less than the taxpayer's entire interest in property unless the value of the interest contributed would be allowable as a deduction under § 170(f)(2) if the donor were to transfer the interest in trust.

Section 170(f)(2) allows a charitable contribution deduction, in the case of property that the donor transfers in trust, if the trust is a charitable remainder annuity trust, a charitable remainder unitrust, or a pooled income fund. Further, § 170(f)(2) allows a deduction for the value of an interest in property (other than a remainder interest) that the donor transfers in trust if the interest is in the form of a guaranteed annuity or the trust instrument specifies that the interest is a fixed percentage, distributed yearly, of the fair market value of the trust property (to be determined yearly) and the grantor is treated as the owner of such interest for purposes of applying § 671.

By its terms, § 170(f)(3)(A) does not apply to, and therefore does not disallow a deduction for, a contribution of an interest that, even though partial, is the taxpayer's entire interest in the property. If, however, the property in which such partial interest exists was divided in order to create such interest, and thus avoid § 170(f)(3)(A), a deduction is not allowed. Section 1.170A-7(a)(2)(i) of the Income Tax Regulations.

Sections 170(f)(3)(B)(ii) and 1.170A-7(b)(1) allow a deduction under § 170 for a contribution not in trust of a partial interest that is less than the donor's entire interest in property if the partial interest is an undivided portion of the donor's entire interest. An undivided portion of a donor's entire interest in property consists of a fraction or percentage of each and every substantial interest or right owned by the donor in such property and must extend over the entire term of the donor's interest in such property and in other property into which such property is converted. A charitable contribution in perpetuity of an interest in property not in trust does not constitute a contribution of an undivided portion of the donor's entire interest if the donor transfers some specific rights and retains other substantial rights.

In enacting § 170(f)(3), Congress was concerned with situations in which taxpayers might obtain a double benefit by taking a deduction for the present value of a contributed interest while also excluding from income subsequent receipts from the donated interest. In addition, Congress was concerned with situations in which, because the charity does not obtain all or an undivided portion of significant rights in the property, the amount of a charitable contribution deduction might not correspond to the value of the benefit ultimately received by the charity. The legislative solution was to guard against the possibility that such problems might arise by denying a deduction in situations involving partial interests, unless the contribution is cast in certain prescribed forms. *See* H.R. Rep. No. 91-413 at 57–58 (1969), 1969-3 C.B. 200, 237-239; S. Rep. No. 91-552 at 87 (1969), 1969-3 C.B. 423, 479. The scope of § 170(f)(3) thus extends beyond situations in which there is actual or probable manipulation of the non-charitable interest to the detriment of the charitable interest, or situations in which the donor has merely assigned the right to future income. Rev. Rul. 88-37, 1988-1 C.B. 97.

Section 170(f)(3)(A) and § 1.170A-7(a)(1) treat a contribution of the right to use property that the donor owns, such as a contribution of a rent-free lease, as a contribution of less than the taxpayer's entire interest in the property. Similarly, if a taxpayer contributes an interest in motion picture films, but retains the right to make reproductions of such films and exploit the reproductions commercially, § 1.170A-7(b)(1)(i) treats the contribution as one of less than the taxpayer's entire interest in the property. In both cases, the taxpayer has not contributed an undivided portion of its entire interest in the property. Accordingly, neither contribution is deductible under § 170(a).

In Situation 1, X contributes a license to use a patent, but retains a substantial right, i.e., the right to license the patent to others. The license granted to University is similar to the rent-free lease described in § 1.170A-7(a)(1) and the partial interest in motion picture films described in § 1.170A-7(b)(1)(i), in that it constitutes neither X's entire interest in the patent, nor a fraction or percentage of each and every substantial interest or right that X owns in the patent. As a result, the contribution in Situation 1 constitutes a transfer of a partial interest, and no deduction under § 170(a) is allowable. The result would be the same if X had retained any other substantial right in the patent. For example, no deduction would be allowable if X had contributed the patent (or license to use the patent) solely for use in a particular geographic area while retaining the right to use the patent (or license) in other geographic areas.

Issue (2)

Section 1.170A-1(e) provides that if, as of the date of a gift, a transfer of property for charitable purposes is dependent upon the performance of some act or the happening of a precedent event in order for it to become effective, no deduction is allowable unless the possibility that the charitable transfer will not become effective is so remote as to be negligible. Similarly, under § 1.170A-7(a)(3), if, as of the date of a gift, a transfer of property for charitable purposes may be defeated by the performance of some act or the happening of some event, no deduction is allowable unless the possibility that such act or event will occur is so remote as to be negligible.

In Situation 2, Y's contribution of the patent is contingent upon A continuing as a member of University's faculty for an additional 15 years, the remaining life of the patent. On the date of the contribution, the possibility that A will cease to be a member of the faculty before the expiration of the patent is not so remote as to be negligible. Therefore, no deduction is allowable under § 170(a).

Issue (3)

Section 1.170A-1(c)(1) provides that if a charitable contribution is made in property other than money, the amount of the contribution is the fair market value of the property at the time of the contribution, reduced as provided in § 170(e).

Section 1.170A-1(c)(2) provides that the fair market value is the price at which the property would change hands between a willing buyer and a willing seller, neither being under any compulsion to buy or sell and both having reasonable knowledge of relevant facts.

Rev. Rul. 85-99, 1985-2 C.B. 83, provides that when a donor places a restriction on the marketability or use of property, the amount of the charitable contribution is the fair market value of the property at the time of the contribution determined in light of the restriction. *See also Cooley v. Commissioner*, 33 T.C. 223, 225 (1959), *aff'd per curiam*, 283 F.2d 945 (2d Cir. 1960).

In Situation 3, Z transfers to University all of Z's interests in the patent with the restriction that University cannot transfer or license the patent for a period of 3 years after the transfer. Unlike the conditional reversion in Situation 2, the restriction on transfer or license is not a condition that can defeat the transfer. Thus, Z's contribution is deductible under § 170(a), assuming all other applicable requirements of § 170 are satisfied, and subject to the percentage limitations of § 170. *See* Publication 526, Charitable Contributions (describing other requirements for, and limitations on, the deductibility of charitable contributions). Under § 1.170A-1(c), however, the restriction reduces what would otherwise be the fair market value of the patent, and therefore reduces the amount of Z's charitable contribution. If Z had received a benefit in exchange for the contribution, the value of the benefit would further reduce the amount of Z's charitable contribution. *See* § 1.170A-1(h).

HOLDINGS

Under the facts of this revenue ruling:

(1) A taxpayer's contribution to a qualified charity of a license to use a patent is not deductible under § 170(a) if the taxpayer retains any substantial right in the patent.

(2) A taxpayer's contribution to a qualified charity of a patent subject to a conditional reversion is not deductible under § 170(a), unless the likelihood of the reversion is so remote as to be negligible.

(3) A taxpayer's contribution to a qualified charity of a patent subject to a license or transfer restriction is deductible under § 170(a), assuming all other applicable requirements of § 170 are satisfied, and subject to the percentage limitations of § 170, but the restriction reduces what would otherwise be the fair market value of the patent at the time of the contribution, and therefore reduces the amount of the charitable contribution for § 170 purposes.

SKLAR v. COMMISSIONER
United States Court of Appeals, Ninth Circuit
282 F.3d 610 (2002)

REINHARDT, CIRCUIT JUDGE

The taxpayer-petitioners in this action, Michael and Marla Sklar, challenge the Internal Revenue Service's ("IRS") disallowance of their deductions, as charitable contributions, of part of the tuition payments made to their children's religious schools. In the notice of deficiency sent to the Sklars, the IRS explained that "[s]ince these costs are personal tuition expenses, they are not deductible." Specifically, the Sklars sought to deduct 55% of the tuition, on the basis that this represented the proportion of the school day allocated to religious education. The Sklars contend that these costs are deductible under section 170 of the Internal Revenue Code, as payments for which they have received "solely intangible religious benefits." They also argue that they should receive this deduction because the IRS permits similar deductions to the Church of Scientology, and it is a violation of administrative consistency and of the Establishment Clause to deny them, as Orthodox Jews, the same deduction. The Tax Court found that tuition paid for the education of a taxpayer's children is a personal expense which is non-deductible under § 170. The Tax Court also rejected the administrative inconsistency argument and the Establishment Clause claim.

I. The Provisions of the Tax Code Governing Charitable Contribution Deductions Do Not Appear to Permit the Deduction Claimed by the Sklars

The Sklars assert that the deduction they claimed is allowable under section 170 of the Internal Revenue Code which permits taxpayers to deduct, as a charitable contribution, a "contribution or gift" to certain tax-exempt organizations. Not only has the Supreme Court held that, generally, a payment for which one receives consideration does not constitute a "contribution or gift" for purposes of § 170, see United States v. American Bar Endowment, 477 U.S. 105, 118 (1986) (stressing that "[t]he sine qua non of a charitable contribution is a transfer of money or property without adequate consideration"), but it has explicitly rejected the contention made here by the Sklars: that there is an exception in the Code for payments for which one receives only religious benefits in return. Hernandez v. Commissioner, 490 U.S. 680, 109 S. Ct. 2136, 104 L. Ed. 2d 766 (1989). The taxpayers in Hernandez, members of the Church of Scientology, sought to deduct, as charitable contributions under § 170(c), payments made by them to the Church of Scientology in exchange for the religious exercises of "auditing" and "training."[6] The Court affirmed the Tax Court's reading of the statute disallowing the deductions on the following three grounds: (1) Congress had shown no preference in the Internal Revenue Code for payments made in exchange for religious benefits as opposed to other benefits; (2) to permit the deductions the taxpayers demanded would begin a slippery slope of expansion of the charitable contribution deduction beyond what Congress intended; and (3) to permit these deductions could entangle the IRS and the government in the affairs and beliefs of various religious faiths and organizations in violation of the constitutional principle of the separation of church and state. Specifically, the Supreme Court stated that to permit these deductions might force the IRS to engage in a searching inquiry of whether a particular benefit received was "religious" or "secular" in order to determine its deductibility, a process which, the Court said, might violate the Establishment Clause.

Despite the clear statutory holding of Hernandez, the Sklars contend that recent changes to the Internal Revenue Code have clarified Congressional intent with respect to the deductibility of these payments. We seriously doubt the validity of this argument. The amendments to the Code appear not to have changed the substantive definition of a deductible charitable contribution, but only to have enacted additional documentation requirements for claimed deductions. Section

---

[6] The Supreme Court, in Hernandez, described "auditing" as the process by which, through a one-to-one encounter with a Church of Scientology official, one becomes aware of his spiritual dimension. The Court describes "training" as one of several "doctrinal courses" in which members study the tenets of the faith and train to become the leaders of auditing sessions.

170(f) of the Code adds a new requirement that taxpayers claiming a charitable contribution deduction obtain from the donee an estimate of the value of any goods and services received in return for the donation, and exempts from that new estimate requirement contributions for which solely intangible religious benefits are received. I.R.C. § 170(f)(8)(A) & (B)(ii). Similarly, § 6115 requires that tax-exempt organizations inform taxpayer-donors that they will receive a tax deduction only for the amount of their donation above the value of any goods or services received in return for the donation and requires donee organizations to give donors an estimate of this value, exempting from this estimate requirement contributions for which solely intangible religious benefits are received.

Given the clear holding of Hernandez and the absence of any direct evidence of Congressional intent to overrule the Supreme Court on this issue, we would be extremely reluctant to read an additional and significant substantive deduction into the statute based on what are clearly procedural provisions regarding the documentation of tax return information, particularly where the deduction would be of doubtful constitutional validity.

III. The Sklars' Tuition Payments Do Not Constitute Partially Deductible "Dual Payments" Under the Tax Code

A "dual payment" (or "quid pro quo payment") under the Tax Code is a payment made in part in consideration for goods and services, and in part as a charitable contribution. I.R.C. § 6115. For example, the purchase, for seventy-five dollars, of an item worth five dollars at a charity auction would constitute a dual payment: five dollars in consideration for goods, and seventy dollars as a charitable contribution. The IRS permits a deduction under § 170 for the portion of a dual payment that consists of a charitable contribution, but not for the portion for which the taxpayer receives a benefit in return. Although the Skiars concede that they received a benefit for their tuition payments, in that their children received a secular education, they claim that part of the payment — the part attributable to their children's religious education — should be regarded as a charitable contribution because they received only an "intangible religious benefit" in return. Leaving aside both the issue, discussed in section I, of whether the tax code does indeed treat payments for which a taxpayer receives an "intangible religious benefit" as a charitable contribution, as well as any constitutional considerations, we are left with the Sklars' contention that their tuition payment was a dual one: in part in consideration for secular education, and in part as a charitable contribution. The Sklars assert that because 45% of their children's school day was spent on secular education, and 55% on religious education, they should receive a deduction for 55% of their tuition payments.

On the record before this court, the Sklars failed to satisfy the requirements for deducting part of a "dual payment" under the Tax Code. The Supreme Court discussed the deductibility of such payments in United States v. American Bar Endowment, 477 U.S. 105 (1986), and held that the taxpayer must establish that the dual payment exceeds the market value of the goods received in return. The facts of that case were as follows: The American Bar Endowment ("ABE"), a tax-exempt corporation organized for charitable purposes and associated with the American

Bar Association ("ABA"), raised money for its charitable work by providing group insurance policies to its members, all of whom were also members of the ABA. ABE negotiated premium rates with insurers, collected premiums from its members and passed those premiums on to the insurers. Because the group policies purchased by ABE were "experience rated," the group members were entitled to receive, each year, a refund of the portion of their premiums paid above the actual cost to the insurer ofproviding insurance to the group. Although normally these refunds, called "dividends," would be distributed to individual policyholders, ABE required its members to agree to turn the dividends over to ABE for use in its charitable work. ABE members sought to deduct the dividends as charitable contributions to ABE, claiming that the premiums paid constituted partially deductible "dual payments." The Supreme Court held that the ABE members could not deduct the dividends as charitable contributions because they had not shown that the premiums they paid to ABE exceeded the market value of the insurance they purchased, or that the "excess payment," if any, was made with the intention of making a gift. Because the ABE insurance was no more costly to its members than other policies that were available to them, the taxpayers could not prove that they "purposely contributed money or property in excess of the value of any benefit [they] received in return."

Similarly, the Sklars have not shown that any dual tuition payments they may have made exceeded the market value of the secular education their children received. They urge that the market value of the secular portion of their children's education is the cost of a public school education. That cost, of course, is nothing. The Sklars are in error. The market value is the cost of a comparable secular education offered by private schools. The Sklars do not present any evidence even suggesting that their total payments exceeded that cost. There is no evidence in the record of the tuition private schools charge for a comparable secular education, and thus no evidence showing that the Sklars made an "excess payment" that might qualify for a tax deduction. This appears to be not simply an inadvertent evidentiary omission, but rather a reflection of the practical realities of the high costs of private education. The Sklars also failed to show that they intended to make a gift by contributing any such "excess payment." Therefore, under the clear holding of American Bar Endowment, the Sklars cannot prevail on this appeal.[7]

IV. Conclusion

We hold that because the Sklars have not shown that their "dual payment" tuition payments are partially deductible under the Tax Code, and, specifically, that the total payments they made for both the secular and religious private school education their children received exceeded the market value of other secular private school education available to those children, the IRS did not err in disallowing their

---

[7] Moreover, as the IRS argues in its brief, the Sklars' deduction was properly denied on the alternative ground that they failed to meet the contemporaneous substantiation requirement of § 170(f)(8)(A), (B) & (C). The Sklars did not present, prior to filing their tax return, a letter from the schools acknowledging their "contribution" and estimating the value of the benefit they received, as is required under the statute. As noted earlier, certain reporting requirements are not applicable where intangible religious benefits are received in exchange, but such exemptions apply only where the consideration consists solely of such benefits. See the discussion of § 170(0(8).

deductions, and the Tax Court did not err in affirming the IRS's decision. We affirm the decision of the Tax Court on that ground.

Affirmed.

AUTHORS' NOTE

In subsequent litigation (*"Sklar II"*) seeking a charitable deduction for tuition paid to the same private schools in a later year, the Sklars "made virtually identical arguments" as made in the case above (*"Sklar I"*) — with the same result: The Tax Court denied a deduction. 125 T.C. 281 (2005), *aff'd*, 549 F.3d 1252 (9th Cir. 2008).

Chapter 27

LIMITATIONS ON DEDUCTIONS

Part A:
Section 267 — Transactions Between Related Parties

I. PROBLEMS

1. Five years ago, Mary purchased a tract of undeveloped investment land for $350,000. Mary sold the land this year to her sister Margery for $300,000, the land's current fair market value.

   (a) May Mary deduct the loss she realized on the sale of the land?

   (b) What result if, instead, Mary sold the land to Fred, Margery's husband? Would it make any difference if Fred deeded the land to Margery two weeks later? Two years later?

   (c) What result if Mary sold the land to a corporation in which she owned all the stock? What difference would it make if, instead of Mary owning all the stock in the corporation, her sister Margery or Margery's husband Fred owned all the stock?

   (d) What result if Mary sold the land to a corporation in which her sister Margery owned a 51% interest? In answering this question, assume Mary and Margery had not spoken for years. Assume also that Mary needed the money and the corporation was the only party willing to purchase the land. Would your answer change if, instead of Margery owning a 51% interest in the corporation, Margery's husband Fred owned the 51% interest?

   (e) What result if the land had a fair market value of $400,000 and Mary sold the land to her sister Margery for $300,000?

2. Assume the facts of Problem 1(a). How much gain or loss, if any, will Margery recognize if she sells the land a year later for $275,000? For $325,000? For $425,000?

3. Dennis is a 60% shareholder in a corporation which provides tour guide and outfitting services in the Pacific Northwest. The corporation is a calendar year, accrual method taxpayer. Dennis' son, Michael, and Michael's wife, Meredith, are avid hikers and mountain climbers. Michael and Meredith, who are cash method, calendar year taxpayers, are employed full-time by the corporation. Michael owns 40% of the stock in the corporation. During the current year, the corporation fails to pay Michael and Meredith the

$25,000 salary owing to each for the services they performed. Payment of the salaries does not occur until February of the following year.

(a) When may the corporation deduct the salaries owed to Michael and Meredith? When must Michael and Meredith include the amounts owing to them?

(b) Would your answer to (a) change if it could be established that the corporation was willing and able to pay Michael and Meredith the salaries owed them but Michael and Meredith requested that the salaries not be paid until the following year?

Assignment for Chapter 27, Part A: Section 267

Complete the problems.

Read: Internal Revenue Code: §§ 267(a)–(d).
        Treasury Regulations: §§ 1.267(a)-1; 1.267(d)-1(a).

        Materials: Overview
                     McWilliams v. Commissioner
                     Miller v. Commissioner

II. VOCABULARY

related person
constructive ownership

III. OBJECTIVES

1. To recall that losses on sales or exchanges between related parties (as defined in § 267(b)) are disallowed by Code.

2. To explain the relief provided by § 267(d) with respect to losses disallowed by § 267(a)(1).

3. To apply § 267(a), (b) and (d) to a given set of facts.

4. To explain and apply the matching requirement of § 267(a)(2).

IV. OVERVIEW

Each of the prior chapters addressing specific deductions discussed both the requirements for and limitations on the deduction. As you have undoubtedly noted, the limitations imposed on the deductions often account for most of the complexity associated with a particular deduction section. These limitations serve the dual purposes of specifically defining the scope of the deduction and preventing abuse. This chapter addresses additional important limitations on deductions, beginning with § 267.

A. The Section 267(a)(1) Loss Rule

Assume Pete has an adjusted basis of $15,000 in certain stock having a fair market value of $10,000. If Pete sells the stock, he would realize and recognize $5,000 of loss, all of which he could use to offset gains he had realized earlier in the year on the sale of other stock. Because he believes the stock will increase in value during the coming year, Pete is not anxious to part with the stock. May Pete claim a $5,000 loss deduction if he sells the stock to his daughter for $10,000?

Initially, one must consider whether the specific requirements of § 165, the applicable loss deduction provision, are satisfied. A threshold requirement of that section is that a loss exist. The regulations indicate that, to be deductible, "a loss must be evidenced by closed and completed transactions, fixed by identifiable events, and . . . actually sustained during the taxable year." Reg. § 1.165-1(b). Furthermore, "only a bona fide loss is allowable. Substance and not mere form shall govern in determining a deductible loss." Reg. § 1.165-1(b). Does Pete's sale of stock to his daughter satisfy these requirements? The question is a close one. Certainly, it is possible Pete may still have considerable practical control over the stock, thus raising serious doubts as to whether any loss has actually occurred.

To prevent the deduction of artificial losses, Congress enacted § 267(a)(1), which denies a deduction for any loss incurred on the sale or exchange of property "directly or indirectly" between certain related persons. Note in § 267(b) the list of relationships which will trigger the disallowance rule. In the hypothetical presented above, the father-daughter relationship will negate the deduction of the loss incurred by the father on the sale of the stock. § 267(b)(1) and (c)(4).

Assume subsequent to purchasing the stock from her father, the daughter sold the stock to an unrelated person for $12,000. What gain, if any, would she report? Could her father then claim the previously disallowed loss? Ignoring § 267(d), one might answer these questions in a number of ways. First, one might conclude the daughter should have a § 1012 cost basis of $10,000 in the stock, and as a result realize and recognize $2,000 of gain on the sale of the stock for $12,000. As a corollary to the daughter's tax treatment, one might also conclude the father could now claim the $5,000 loss which had previously been disallowed. Another possibility would be to use the part-sale/part-gift standard for determining the daughter's basis. That would mean the daughter's basis would be $15,000, at least for purposes of computing gain. However, for purposes of computing loss, Reg. § 1.1015-4(a) provides that "the unadjusted basis of the property in the hands of the transferee shall not be greater than the fair market value of the property at the time of such transfer." Thus, if the part-sale/part-gift standard were to be used, the daughter would have neither a gain nor a loss.

Section 267(a)(1) does not provide that disallowed losses will be held in abeyance for future use of the seller; nor does it permit the purchaser to claim the seller's basis. In this example, therefore, the daughter's basis is a § 1012 cost basis of $10,000. Section 267, however, does provide some relief in the form of § 267(d), which provides that the daughter need recognize gain only to the extent that the gain exceeds the loss disallowed her father. Thus, while the daughter's realized gain on the sale is $2,000, none of that gain will be recognized because the gain does not exceed her father's loss of $5,000. In effect, § 267(d) treats the daughter and father as one taxpayer by giving the daughter the benefit (but only to a limited extent) of the father's loss. What happens to the other $3,000 of loss incurred by the father but disallowed under § 267(a)? It disappears.

Section 267(a)(1) will generally negate the need for courts to consider whether a loss has actually occurred. However, in cases which do not involve the relationship between buyer and seller required by § 267(a)(1), it will still be necessary for the courts, the Service and tax advisors to consider whether a loss has actually occurred. For example, in *Fender v. U.S.*, 577 F.2d 934 (5th Cir. 1978), the taxpayer-trusts realized substantial gain from the sale of certain stock. To offset this gain, the trustees sold some bonds which had declined substantially in value. The bonds were unrated and could not be sold in the public market. The purchaser of the bonds was a bank in which the trustee was a 40% shareholder. Forty-two days after the transfer of the bonds to the bank, the trusts repurchased the bonds for an amount even less than that which the bank had paid for the bonds. At the time of the repurchase, the trustee owned more than a 50% interest in the bank. Both the sale to the bank and the subsequent repurchase of the bonds were made at the fair market value of the bonds.

Agreeing with the Service's contention that no loss had been experienced by the trusts on the sale of the bonds to the bank, the court concluded the taxpayer-trusts had sufficient dominion over the bank through the stock ownership of the trustee to ensure that the apparent loss from the sale of the stock "could be recaptured through a repurchase of the bonds." Therefore, in selling the bonds, the trusts were not exposed to any real risk of loss. The court relied on *DuPont v. Commissioner*, 118 F.2d 544, *cert. den.*, 314 U.S. 623 (1941), in which the Third Circuit concluded no loss had occurred when two friends sold each other stock at a loss at the end of the year and repurchased the stock from one another at the start of the following year. Although both friends paid fair market value for the stock purchased and no legal obligation to repurchase existed, the court nonetheless concluded sufficient dominion existed to assure repurchase and thus negate a bona fide sale.

McWilliams v. Commissioner and *Miller v. Commissioner*, included in the materials, reflect some of the interpretation and application issues raised by taxpayers with reference to § 267(a)(1). These cases also provide helpful discussions regarding the purpose of § 267(a)(1).

B.   The Section 267(a)(2) Matching Requirement

Certain Code provisions condition the deduction of expenses on the inclusion of related income. One such provision, § 267(a)(2), is considered here. Other similar, more sophisticated provisions are considered in Chapter 43.

As discussed in greater detail in Chapters 28 and 29, a cash method taxpayer generally reports income when it is received, not when it is earned; an accrual method taxpayer generally deducts an expense when it is incurred, not when it is paid.[1] Assume a cash method taxpayer renders deductible services to an accrual method taxpayer. The cash method taxpayer has no income in all likelihood until payment is made, but the accrual method taxpayer may well become entitled to a deduction once the services are rendered, even though payment has not yet been made, and indeed may not be made for a substantial period of time. The concern underlying § 267(a)(2) is that the different accounting methods make arrangements possible under which related parties can generate current deductions without current income. The mismatching potential is clear.

Section 267(a)(2) responds to this concern essentially by placing an accrual method taxpayer on the cash method of accounting with respect to the deduction of amounts owed to related cash method taxpayers. Consider the following example: John is a cash method taxpayer, whose tax year is the calendar year. His father, Frank, operates a business on the accrual method and calendar year. At the end of Year 1, Frank owes John $50,000 for services rendered to the business in Year 1. Under the accrual method, Frank would normally claim a $50,000 § 162(a) deduction in Year 1. John, as a cash method taxpayer, would not be required to include anything in income until payment is actually (or constructively) received. However, because Frank and John are related parties under § 267(a)(2)(B), Frank may not claim a $50,000 deduction in Year 1 for the amount owed to John. Rather, Frank will claim a deduction in the year in which John includes the $50,000 in income, *i.e.*, presumably the year in which Frank pays John.[2]

---

[1] Strictly speaking, income is included under the cash method when it is actually or constructively received. Reg. § 1.451-1(a). A deduction is allowed under the accrual method when all events have occurred that establish the fact of liability, the amount can be determined with reasonable accuracy, and economic performance has occurred. Reg. § 1.461-1(a)(2).

[2] We merely note here two other statutory matching rules that tie the payor's deduction of compensation to the payee's inclusion of the compensation in income. With respect to "nonqualified" plans deferring the receipt of compensation — generally, per Reg. § 1.404(b)-1T, Q&A-2, this is any arrangement that defers the receipt of compensation by the payee more than 2.5 months after the close of the payor's tax year — § 404(a)(5) provides that the payor may not claim a deduction until the payee includes the compensation in income. This rule could certainly impact the example given above in the text. Note that § 404(a)(5), unlike § 267(a)(2), does not require that the parties be related. (So-called "qualified" deferred compensation plans are not subject to the rule of § 404(a)(5). *See generally* §§ 404(a)(1)–(3), § 401 *et seq.*. Qualified plans are subject to a set of extremely complex rules which authorize the deferral of compensation, a current deduction to employers for contributions to funded plans and also deferral of income generated on monies contributed to these plans. The tax advantages of qualified compensation deferral plans have made them one of the primary fringe benefits sought by employees today.)

Another matching rule, that of § 83(h), is concerned with compensatory transfers of property subject to restrictions. As noted by the Staff of the Joint Committee on Taxation in its General Explanation of the Tax Reform Act of 1969, 91st Cong. 2d Sess. 110–112 (1970), § 83 "provides that a person who receives

Consider another example. Under § 267(b)(2), an individual and a corporation in which the individual is a more than 50% owner are related parties. As a result, if the individual, a cash method taxpayer, makes a loan to the accrual method corporation, § 267(a)(2) denies an interest deduction to the corporation until the individual recognizes the corresponding interest income — that is, until the individual actually or constructively receives the interest from the corporation. Assume an interest deduction is thus barred for one or more years because it is not paid. If in a later year the individual sells his interest in the corporation and the parties are no longer related, may the corporation now deduct the accrued, but still unpaid, interest attributable to those earlier years? The answer was "No" in *Ronald Moran Cadillac v. United States*, 385 F.3d 1230 (9th Cir. 2004). The prior years' unpaid, accrued interest did not become deductible merely because the parties were no longer related. Rather, under § 267(a)(2), an interest deduction barred because of the relationship in the year it accrued becomes deductible only when the interest is includable in the income of the cash method individual — when it is paid. Interest that accrues after the parties are no longer related is, however, deductible upon accrual and is not subject to § 267(a)(2).

McWILLIAMS v. COMMISSIONER
United States Supreme Court
331 U.S. 695 (1947)

MR. CHIEF JUSTICE VINSON delivered the opinion of the Court.

The facts of these cases are not in dispute. John P. McWilliams had for a number of years managed the large independent estate of his wife, . . . as well as his own. On several occasions in 1940 and 1941 he ordered his broker to sell certain stock for the account of one of the two and to buy the same number of shares of the same stock for the other, at as nearly the same price as possible. He told the broker that

---

a beneficial interest in property, such as stock, by reason of his performance of services must report as income in the taxable period in which received, the value of the property unless his interest in the property is subject to a substantial risk of forfeiture and is nontransferable. . . . If the property is subject to a substantial risk of forfeiture and is nontransferable, the employee is not required to recognize any income with respect to the property until his interest in the property either becomes transferable or no longer is subject to such risk. A substantial risk of forfeiture is considered to exist where the recipient's rights to the full enjoyment of the property are conditioned upon his future performance of substantial services." Consider the following example: Kevin is employed by a publicly held corporation. As an incentive to keep Kevin in its employ, the company gives Kevin 100 shares of its common stock, but conditions the transfer on Kevin remaining in the service of the company for the next three years. When does Kevin include in income the value of the 100 restricted shares which he has received? Under § 83(a), Kevin is not required to include the shares upon receipt because there is a substantial risk of forfeiture encumbering his right to the stock. (Assume any transferee would also be subject to the risk of forfeiture and that therefore the stock is not transferable.) The risk of forfeiture will end after Kevin has worked for the company for three years, and Kevin will be required to include in income the value of the 100 shares *at that time.* Kevin's employer in this example is entitled to a deduction under § 162 for the value of the stock transferred to Kevin. Section 83(h) requires that there be a matching of income and deduction. Kevin's employer will be entitled to deduct the value of the stock when Kevin is required to include the value in income.

his purpose was to establish tax losses. On each occasion the sale and purchase were promptly negotiated through the Stock Exchange, and the identity of the persons selling to the buying spouse was never known. Invariably, however, the buying spouse received stock certificates different from those which the other had sold. Petitioners filed separate income tax returns for these years, and claimed the losses which he or she sustained on the sales as deductions from gross income.

The Commissioner disallowed these deductions on the authority of Sec. 24(b) [now § 267(a)(1)] of the Internal Revenue Code, which prohibits deductions for losses from "sales or exchanges of property, directly or indirectly . . . between members of a family," and between certain other closely related individuals and corporations.

On the taxpayer's application to the Tax Court, it held Sec. 24(b) inapplicable . . . and expunged the Commissioner's deficiency assessments. The Circuit Court of Appeals reversed the Tax Court and we granted certiorari. . . .

Petitioners contend that Congress could not have intended to disallow losses on transactions like those described above, which, having been made through a public market, were undoubtedly bona fide sales, both in the sense that title to property was actually transferred, and also in the sense that a fair consideration was paid in exchange. They contend that the disallowance of such losses would amount, *pro tanto*, to treating husband and wife as a single individual for tax purposes.

In support of this contention, they call our attention to the pre-1934 rule, which applied to all sales regardless of the relationship of seller and buyer, and made the deductibility of the resultant loss turn on the "good faith" of the sale, *i.e.*, whether the seller actually parted with title and control. They point out that in the case of the usual intra-family sale, the evidence material to this issue was peculiarly within the knowledge and even the control of the taxpayer and those amenable to his wishes, and inaccessible to the Government. They maintain that the only purpose of the provisions of the 1934 and 1937 Revenue Acts — the forerunners of Sec. 24(b) — was to overcome these evidentiary difficulties by disallowing losses on such sales irrespective of good faith. It seems to be petitioners' belief that the evidentiary difficulties so contemplated were only those relating to proof of the parties' observance of the formalities of a sale and of the fairness of the price, and consequently that the legislative remedy applied only to sales made immediately from one member of a family to another, or mediately through a controlled intermediary.

We are not persuaded that Congress had so limited an appreciation of this type of tax avoidance problem. Even assuming that the problem was thought to arise solely out of the taxpayer's inherent advantage in a contest concerning the good or bad faith of an intra-family sale, deception could obviously be practiced by a buying spouse's agreement or tacit readiness to hold the property sold at the disposal of a selling spouse, rather more easily than by a pretense of a sale where none actually occurred, or by an unfair price. The difficulty of determining the finality of an intra-family transfer was one with which the courts wrestled under the pre-1934 law, and which Congress undoubtedly meant to overcome by enacting the provisions of Sec. 24(b).

It is clear, however, that this difficulty is one which arises out of the close relationship of the parties, and would be met whenever, by prearrangement, one spouse sells and another buys the same property at a common price, regardless of the mechanics of the transaction. Indeed, if the property is fungible, the possibility that a sale and purchase may be rendered nugatory by the buying spouse's agreement to hold for the benefit of the selling spouse, and the difficulty of proving that fact against the taxpayer, are equally great when the units of the property which the one buys are not the identical units which the other sells.

Securities transactions have been the most common vehicle for the creation of intra-family losses. Even if we should accept petitioner's premise that the only purpose of Sec. 24(b) was to meet an evidentiary problem, we could agree that Congress did not mean to reach the transactions in this case only if we thought it completely indifferent to the effectuality of its solution.

Moreover, we think the evidentiary problem was not the only one which Congress intended to meet. Section 24(b) states an absolute prohibition — not a presumption — against the allowance of losses on any sales between the members of certain designated groups. The one common characteristic of these groups is that their members, although distinct legal entities, generally have a near-identity of economic interests. It is a fair inference that even legally genuine intra-group transfers were not thought to result usually in economically genuine realizations of loss, and accordingly that Congress did not deem them to be appropriate occasions for the allowance of deductions.

The pertinent legislative history lends support to this inference. The Congressional Committees, in reporting the provisions enacted in 1934, merely stated that "the practice of creating losses through transactions between members of a family and close corporations has been frequently utilized for avoiding the income tax," and that these provisions were proposed to "deny losses to be taken in the case of [such] sales" and "to close this loophole of tax avoidance." Similar language was used in reporting the 1937 provisions. Chairman Doughton of the Ways and Means Committee in explaining the 1937 provisions to the House, spoke of "the artificial taking and establishment of losses where property was shuffled back and forth between various legal entities owned by the same persons or person," and stated that "these transactions seem to occur at moments remarkably opportune to the real party in interest in reducing his taxability but, at the same time allowing him to keep substantial control of the assets being traded or exchanged."

We conclude that the purpose of Sec. 24(b) was to put an end to the right of taxpayers to choose, by intra-family transfers and other designated devices, their own time for realizing tax losses on investments which, for most practical purposes, are continued uninterrupted.

We are clear as to this purpose, too, that its effectuation obviously had to be made independent of the manner in which an intra-group transfer was accomplished. Congress, with such purpose in mind, could not have intended to include within the scope of Sec. 24(b) only simple transfers made directly or through a dummy or to exclude transfers of securities effected through the medium of the Stock Exchange, unless it wanted to leave a loop-hole almost as large as the one it had set out to close.

Petitioners suggest that Congress, if it truly intended to disallow losses on intra-family transactions through the market, would probably have done so by an amendment to the wash sales provisions, making them applicable where the seller and buyer were members of the same family, as well as where they were one and the same individual. This extension of the wash sales provisions, however, would bar only one particular means of accomplishing the evil at which Sec. 24(b) was aimed, and the necessity for a comprehensive remedy would have remained.

Nor can we agree that Congress' omission from Sec. 24(b) of any prescribed time interval, comparable in function to that in the wash sales provisions, indicates that Sec. 24(b) was not intended to apply to intra-family transfers through the Exchange. Petitioners' argument is predicated on the difficulty which courts may have in determining whether the elapse of certain periods of time between one spouse's sale and the other's purchase of like securities on the Exchange is of great enough importance in itself to break the continuity of the investment and make Sec. 24(b) inapplicable.

Precisely the same difficulty may arise, however, in the case of an intra-family transfer through an individual intermediary, who, by pre-arrangement, buys from one spouse at the market price and a short time later sells the identical certificates to the other at the price prevailing at the time of sale. The omission of a prescribed time interval negates the applicability of Sec. 24(b) to the former type of transfer no more than it does to the latter. But if we should hold that it negated both, we would have converted the section into a mere trap for the unwary.[3]

Petitioners also urge that, whatever may have been Congress' intent, its designation in Sec. 24(b) of sales "between" members of a family is not adequate to comprehend the transactions in this case, which consisted only of a sale of stock by one of the petitioners to an unknown stranger, and the purchase of different certificates of stock by the other petitioner, presumably from another stranger.

We can understand how this phraseology, if construed literally and out of context, might be thought to mean only direct intra-family transfers. But petitioners concede that the express statutory reference to sales made "directly or indirectly" precludes that construction. Moreover, we can discover in this language no implication whatsoever that an indirect intra-family sale of fungibles is outside the statute unless the units sold by one spouse and those bought by the other are identical. Indeed, if we accepted petitioners' construction of the statute, we think we would be reading into it a crippling exception which is not there.

Affirmed.

---

[3] We have noted petitioners' suggestion that a taxpayer is assured, under the wash sales provisions, of the right to deduct the loss incurred on a sale of securities, even though he himself buys similar securities thirty-one days later; and that he should certainly not be precluded by Sec. 24(b) from claiming a similar loss if the taxpayer's spouse, instead of the taxpayer, makes the purchase under the same circumstances. We do not feel impelled to comment on these propositions, however, in a case in which the sale and purchase were practically simultaneous and the net consideration received by one spouse and that paid by the other differed only in the amount of brokers' commissions and excise taxes.

MILLER v. COMMISSIONER
75 T.C. 182 (1980)

Dawson, Judge:

The principal issue for decision is whether the deductions for losses sustained from the sales of stock and real property by the petitioner to his brother, which were ordered by binding arbitration to separate the interests of the hostile brothers, were properly disallowed by respondent under the provisions of section 267. . . .

FINDINGS OF FACT

David L. Miller (petitioner) and I. Marvin Miller (Marvin) are the natural sons of Charles and Miriam Miller. Charles Miller died in 1954. Under his will, all of his shares of stock in Charles Miller, Inc., being 20 of 21 outstanding shares, were left in equal shares to the petitioner and Marvin. The remaining share was owned by Miriam Miller. The corporation was engaged in the real estate and insurance brokerage business. Also left in equal shares to petitioner and Marvin was certain real estate located at 2254 North Broad Street in Philadelphia, which was the location of the principal office of the corporation. After certain specific bequests to family members, the balance of Charles Miller's property was left in trust to his widow.

Petitioner and Marvin jointly purchased additional parcels of real estate in Philadelphia. This additional real estate, the stock in the corporation, and the real estate distributed under the Will of Charles Miller later became the subject of a dispute between the brothers. . . .

In January, 1971, a serious dispute arose between the brothers resulting from allegations by the petitioner that Marvin had improperly used funds collected on behalf of third parties in order to cover losses in the operation of the family business. By October 1971, the relationship between them became so strained that they could not mutually resolve their differences. They then retained arbitrators, who subsequently decided that the only way to end the dispute between the brothers was to enter into a binding award by the terms of which the petitioner would be required to sell to Marvin three parcels of real estate and his stock in the corporation. . . .

During the negotiation period, the brothers did not see each other socially and rarely spoke. Their strained relationship continued. They did not trust each other. Although petitioner is an attorney specializing in real estate and Marvin is in the real estate business, neither has referred any business to the other for several years.

. . . The brothers refused to abide by [the arbitrator's report] until December 29, 1976, when . . . the petitioner sold his stock in Charles Miller, Inc., to Marvin and his interests in the parcels of real estate at 2254 North Broad Street, 2222 North 15th Street, and 1248 W. Hazzard Street, all located in Philadelphia.

Petitioner has never reacquired an interest in the stock or properties he sold to Marvin. He has no control, directly or indirectly, over Marvin or the assets he sold to him.

On his Federal income tax return for 1976, the petitioner claimed a long-term capital loss of $4,999 and three ordinary losses of $331, $2,274, and $382, totaling $2,987, resulting from the sales of the stock and the properties to his brother, Marvin.

In his notice of deficiency for 1976, the respondent disallowed the claimed deductions for the losses on the ground that they were not allowable under the provisions of section 267.

OPINION

The issue here involves the application and interpretation of section 267, which disallows deductions for losses sustained from sales or exchanges of property between certain related parties.

Petitioner contends that section 267 does not prohibit the deductions for the losses he claimed on the sales to Marvin because the disallowed losses do not come within the intent or scope of section 267. He argues that (1) his relationship with Marvin was so hostile they were no longer "brothers"; (2) section 267(c)(4) refers not only to a connection established by birth, but also requires the presence of a "family relationship"; (3) section 267(c)(4) merely creates a rebuttable presumption that brothers by birth are within the ambit of section 267(a)(1); (4) the decision in *McWilliams v. Commissioner*, 331 U.S. 694 (1947), does not preclude a "family hostility" exception to section 267; and (5) some courts have created an exception to the family attribution rules of section 318 where the family members to the transactions were hostile. Respondent counters with arguments that (1) the plain language and intendment of section 267 precludes a "family hostility" exception; (2) there is an insufficient parallel between the provisions and legislative history of section 318 on the one hand and section 267, on the other; (3) all of the evidence, oral and documentary, relating to hostility between the petitioner and his brother should be treated as inadmissible because it is irrelevant in the application of section 267; and (4) no deduction for a loss sustained from a sale or exchange of property between brothers is allowable under these circumstances.

We agree with respondent. In construing the language of section 267, its plain and obvious meaning should be followed. The phrase "no deduction shall be allowed" is clear. It means that no exceptions, not expressly provided for in section 267, are allowed.

The forerunners of section 267(a)(1) were section 24(a)(6) of the Revenue Act of 1934, 48 Stat. 691, and its cognate section 24(b)(1)(A) of the Internal Revenue Code of 1939. Prior to 1934, there was a fertile field for phantom sales and exchanges with the sole purpose of creating tax losses in transactions between related individuals. The problems of proof in cases involving intimate family relations presented extraordinary difficulties. Accordingly, since the property remained within the same family group after sale, Congress decided to impose an absolute prohibition against deduction in respect of such transactions, irrespective of whether the sale was bona fide, voluntary or involuntary, or direct or indirect. In *Blum v. Commissioner*, 5 T.C. 702 (1945), this Court held that a loss from the sale of a partnership interest from one brother to another was not deductible. We concluded that it was irrelevant whether or not the sale was bona fide and characterized the prohibition as absolute in its reach. We said (5 T.C. at 711–712):

> It is true that a hardship may result in particular cases, as in this one, where the transaction is in entire good faith; and there is some indication in the history of the measure that the legislators were not unaware of that fact. However, it was the belief of the drafters that, on the whole, the measure would be fair to the great majority of taxpayers. Congress could have provided that no deduction should be allowed in respect of losses from intrafamily transactions unless they were bona fide. That it did not do. . . . We could not, without indulging in judicial legislation, graft an exception upon the broad measure adopted by Congress.

The scope of section 24(b)(1) of the 1939 Code was thoroughly considered by the Supreme Court in *McWilliams v. Commissioner*, 331 U.S. 694 (1947), which emphasized its broad sweep.

. . . .

Subsequently, the courts have rejected attempts to challenge the broad scope of section 267 by refusing to create an exception for "involuntary" sales.

The main thrust of petitioner's argument is that the hostile relationship between himself and Marvin disqualified them as "brothers" within the meaning of section 267(c)(4). He asserts that "the term family implies friendly, closeness and intimacy." This conclusory statement is unsupported in fact and law. He also asserts that section 267(c)(4), which defines the term "family," does not include the entire definition of that term, and therefore the Court must examine whether a "family relationship" existed between the brothers. This points out the flaw in petitioner's argument. After conceding that the Court should not investigate the underlying facts of the sale to determine whether it is bona fide, the petitioner argues that we should investigate those same facts to determine whether a "family relationship" exists between the brothers. Such an examination is neither necessary nor required. The parties have stipulated that the petitioner and Marvin are the natural children of Charles and Miriam Miller. That makes them "brothers," and the absolute prohibition of section 267(a)(1) denies the deductions of the losses sustained from the sales of the stock and real property between them. . . .

We reject the petitioner's argument that section 267(c)(4) establishes merely a rebuttable presumption that "brothers by birth" are within the reach of section 267(a)(1). This is contrary to the views expressed by the Supreme Court in *McWilliams v. Commissioner*, 331 U.S. 694 (1947), where it is stated that the forerunner of section 267 contains an "absolute prohibition" and not a presumption against the allowance of losses on any sales between members of certain designated groups. This by its terms includes brothers. . . .

The petitioner also argues that the term "brother" requires not only a blood relationship, "but a finding of social or economic affinity as well." He contends that the rationale behind the cases disallowing a deduction in similar situations is that the relationship between family members arises to some kind of unity of interest. He then argues that the record demonstrates "hostility" which in turn demonstrates that the unity of interest does not exist. Again we disagree. First, this interpretation of the term "brother" is an unsupported conclusion. Second, petitioner has failed to carry his burden of showing a lack of family unity throughout these transactions. The record shows that the dispute between the brothers was handled by and between members and close friends of the family and that, when available, resort to litigation was avoided in order to protect the family business. Third, although the petitioner recognizes the rationale of Congress in implementing section 267, he ignores the method which Congress chose to enforce that intent. Congress obviously did not want the courts to face the difficult task of looking behind the sales. Instead, Congress made its prohibition absolute in reach, believing that this would be fair to the great majority of taxpayers.

Accordingly, for the reasons previously stated, we hold that no deductions for losses sustained from sales or exchanges of property, directly or indirectly, between brothers are allowable, irrespective of the existence of hostility between them. . . .

Decisions will be entered under Rule 155.

Part B:
Section 265 — Expenses Related to Tax-Exempt Income

I. PROBLEMS

1. Assume Bill applies for Social Security disability benefits, and his claim is denied. Bill then pays a lawyer $5,000 to appeal the denial. The appeal is successful, and Bill collects $20,000 in Social Security disability payments. Assume that pursuant to § 86, $10,000 of the benefits are taxable. How much, if any, of his legal fees may Bill deduct?

2. During the current year, Christina paid interest on brokerage margin accounts through which only securities generating taxable income were bought and sold. She also paid interest on a bank loan she took out this year to make some improvements on her home. Throughout the year, Christina owned tax-exempt securities she purchased for cash; Christina has never pledged these securities as collateral. Furthermore, these tax-exempt securities have been held separately from her brokerage accounts. While Christina could have liquidated the tax-exempt securities and thereby negated the need for almost all of the borrowing she did through the margin accounts and the bank, Christina chose not to do so because of her desire to maintain a portfolio of taxable and tax-exempt securities. Christina intends to deduct all of the interest she paid on the margin accounts and on the bank loan. What would you advise her regarding the deductibility of interest she has paid?

Assignment for Chapter 27, Part B: Section 265:

Complete the problems.

Read: Internal Revenue Code: §§ 265(a)(1), (2). Skim § 265(a)(6).

           Materials: Overview
                          Revenue Procedure 72-18

II. VOCABULARY

tax-exempt income

III. OBJECTIVES

1. To recognize fact patterns in which § 265(a)(1) will disallow expenses related to the production of tax-exempt income.

2. To recall that only §§ 163 and 212 expenses related to tax-exempt interest income are disallowed by § 265(a)(1) and (2).

3. To identify circumstances in which indebtedness has been incurred "to purchase or to carry" obligations which produce tax-exempt interest income and to recall that § 265(a)(2) disallows an interest deduction on such indebtedness.

IV. OVERVIEW

Section 265 prevents taxpayers from claiming double tax benefits as a result of tax-exempt income. Specifically, it disallows certain deductions allocable to such income.

A. Section 265(a)(1)

Section 265(a)(1) disallows two categories of deductions: first, it disallows all deductions allocable to tax-exempt income, other than tax-exempt interest; second, it disallows § 212 expenses allocable to tax-exempt interest.

The first category of deductions disallowed by § 265(a)(1) includes deductions under § 162 (trade or business expenses); § 165 (losses); § 212 (investment expenses); §§ 167 and 168 (depreciation expenses), etc. For example, in *Jones v. Commissioner*, 231 F.2d 655 (3d Cir. 1956), the taxpayer purchased for investment certain contingent remainder interests in two estates. To protect his investment in case the contingent remaindermen whose interests he purchased failed to survive the life tenants, the taxpayer purchased policies of life insurance on the remaindermen. The taxpayer sought to deduct the premiums paid on the policy. Because the proceeds from the life insurance policies would have been excluded from tax under § 101, the court concluded that the deduction for the premiums (otherwise allowable under § 212) was disallowed under § 265(a)(1). Similarly, no deduction was allowed for home mortgage interest and real property taxes allocable to a tax-exempt housing allowance received by an employee of the U.S. Immigration and Naturalization Service stationed abroad. *Induni v. Comm.*, 990 F.2d 53 (2d Cir. 1993), *aff'g* 98 T.C. 618 (1992).[4] In another case, a physician, while a medical student, had received tax-exempt government scholarships that required her to perform future medical services in a "Health Manpower Shortage Area" to be designated by the government; the terms of the scholarships also provided that, in the event she failed to perform the services, she would repay three times the amount of the scholarships, plus interest. Some years after receiving the scholarships, the physician informed the government she would not perform the services agreement. She entered into a repayment agreement with the government, and sought to deduct the repayment amounts as business expenses or business losses from her income as a physician. The repayments were held to be directly allocable to the exempt scholarship income, and thus nondeductible under § 265(a)(1).[5]

In *Manocchio v. Commissioner*, 78 T.C. 989, *aff'd*, 710 F.2d 1400 (9th Cir. 1983), the Tax Court considered whether an otherwise-allowable § 162(a) deduction for expenses incurred in taking a flight training course would be disallowed by § 265(a)(1) because the taxpayer received reimbursement for 90% of the costs under a special federal law providing veteran benefits. The reimbursement

---

[4] The Second Circuit held that the effect of § 265(a)(6), exempting parsonage and military housing allowances from the operation of § 265, was to bring deductions allocable to other tax-exempt housing allowances within the general disallowance rule of § 265(a)(1).

[5] *Stroud v. U.S.*, 906 F. Supp. 990 (D.S.C. 1995), aff'd on this issue, but vacated in part and remanded on other grounds by the Fourth Circuit in an unpublished opinion. 96-2 U.S.T.C. (CCH) ¶ 50,446.

received by the taxpayer was tax-exempt under federal law. The taxpayer argued that the reimbursed expenses were instead properly allocable to the taxable income he derived from his employment as a pilot. He argued § 265(a)(1) "was intended to apply only to expenses incurred in the *production* of exempt income, and should not be construed to apply to expenses which were merely paid *out of* exempt income." 78 T.C. at 993. The Tax Court disagreed, stating "we think the proximate one-for-one relationship between the reimbursement and the deduction overrides the underlying relationship between the deduction and the employment income, leaving the deduction 'directly allocable,' as that term is used in section 1.265-1(c), Income Tax Regs., solely to the reimbursement and to no other class of income."[6]

With respect to tax-exempt interest, § 265(a)(1) disallows only § 212 deductions allocable to such interest. Thus, other deductions, *e.g.*, § 162 (trade or business) or § 164 (state and local taxes), are not subject to the disallowance rule. As discussed below, interest deductions allocable to indebtedness to purchase or carry tax-exempt obligations are disallowed by § 265(a)(2). Nevertheless, tax-exempt interest is accorded preferential treatment under § 265, since only §§ 163 and 212 deductions allocable to it are disallowed whereas *all* deductions allocable to other types of tax-exempt income are disallowed by § 265(a)(1). Classic examples of expenses subject to the disallowance rule are fees for safe-deposit boxes, investment advice and custodial care.

B.   Section 265(a)(2)

Section 265(a)(2) disallows interest expense deductions associated with the production of tax-exempt interest. Specifically, it disallows a deduction for "interest on indebtedness incurred to purchase or carry obligations the interest on which is wholly exempt from taxes. . . . " For example, while the interest generated by a municipal bond may be excludable under § 103(a),[7] a taxpayer may not deduct any interest paid on money borrowed to purchase the municipal bonds. It makes no difference that the taxpayer never realizes tax-exempt interest income from the obligations; it is only necessary that the obligations would produce interest wholly exempt from tax. Rev. Proc. 72-18, reprinted below.

The Supreme Court in *Denman v. Slayton*, 282 U.S. 514, 519–520 (1931), commented on the purpose of § 265(a)(2) as follows:

> The manifest purpose of [§ 265(a)(2)] was to prevent the escape from taxation of income properly subject thereto by the purchase of exempt securities with borrowed money.

> Under the theory of the respondent, "A," with an income of $10,000 arising from non-exempt securities, by the simple expedient of purchasing exempt ones with borrowed funds and paying $10,000 interest thereon,

---

[6] 78 T.C. at 995. The Ninth Circuit, in affirming the Tax Court decision, never reached the § 265(a)(1) issue. Rather, the appellate court concluded that the educational expenses were not deductible in any event under § 162(a) because they were reimbursed.

[7] See the discussion of § 103(a) in the Note following Chapter 11.

would escape all taxation upon receipts from both sources. It was proper to make provision to prevent such a possibility.

Application of § 265(a)(2) can be difficult in cases where a taxpayer has not borrowed money specifically for the purpose of purchasing obligations producing tax-exempt interest. For example, assume a taxpayer intends to invest in both tax-exempt bonds and real estate. The taxpayer uses $50,000 of her savings to purchase the tax-exempt bonds and borrows $75,000 to purchase a piece of commercial property. May the taxpayer deduct the interest incurred on the $75,000 indebtedness, or will the interest deduction be disallowed on the theory that the indebtedness is indirectly related to the production of the tax-exempt interest generated by the bond? Consider also the taxpayer who has a portfolio of tax-exempt bonds the taxpayer uses as collateral to borrow money for business or personal purposes. May the taxpayer deduct the interest paid on the loan?

With respect to the determination of whether indebtedness was incurred to purchase or carry obligations producing tax-exempt income, the courts will consider all of the facts and the circumstances. The mere fact the taxpayer has incurred or continued a debt while holding tax-exempt obligations will not trigger the § 265(a)(2) disallowance.[8] Revenue Procedure 72-18, included in the materials, provides important guidance for determining when the disallowance rule of § 265(a)(2) will be operative. After you have studied this Revenue Procedure, return to the prior paragraph and answer the questions raised.[9]

C. Allocation

In some circumstances, an expenditure may be indirectly allocable to both taxable and tax-exempt income. Only the portion of the expenditure allocable to the tax-exempt income is subject to § 265. The regulations require a "reasonable proportion" of the expenditure "in light of all the facts and circumstances" be allocated to the exempt income. Reg. § 1.265-1(c). In the absence of other bases for allocation, the expense will be allocated to the taxable and tax-exempt income in the same proportions as the taxable and tax-exempt income bear to the total income received. *See, e.g.,* Rev. Rul. 87-102, 1987-2 C.B. 78. Consider the tax pressure that may be brought to bear on this allocation. Suppose, for example, a taxpayer sustains a personal physical injury, retains a lawyer, and pursues and ultimately settles a claim for compensatory and punitive damages. An initial

---

[8] *See Wisconsin Cheesman, Inc. v. U.S.*, 388 F.2d 420 (7th Cir. 1968); *Illinois Terminal Railroad v. U.S.*, 375 F.2d 1016 (Ct. Cl. 1967); *Wynn v. U.S.* 288 F. Supp. 797 (E.D. Pa. 1968), *aff'd*, 411 F.2d 614 (3d Cir. 1969).

[9] In 1986, Congress added § 265(a)(6), which negates the application of § 265 to deductions for "interest on a mortgage on, or real property taxes on, the home of the taxpayer by reason of the receipt of an amount as (A) a military housing allowance, or (B) a parsonage allowance excludable from gross income under section 107." Consider the following example: A minister, in addition to receiving a salary, receives a rental allowance of $10,000 per year. The rental allowance is excludable under § 107. The minister uses this rental allowance to make the monthly payments on the mortgage on his home. These monthly payments include payments for taxes and interest. But for § 265(a)(6), the interest and tax deductions to the extent allocable to the rental allowance would be disallowed under § 265(a)(1). Rev. Rul. 83-3, 1983-1 C.B. 72, modified by Rev. Rul. 87-32, 1987-1 C.B. 131. Under § 265(a)(6), however, the tax and interest expense deductions are preserved.

allocation issue, previously noted in Chapter 10, may arise with respect to the settlement: To what extent is the settlement properly allocable to compensatory damages excludable under § 104(a)(2), and to what extent is it allocable to the taxable punitive damages? But a § 265 issue also arises with respect to any attorney's fees paid by the taxpayer: To what extent are these fees properly allocable to the punitive damages, and thus potentially deductible?[10] To what extent are they allocable to the excluded income, and thus nondeductible under § 265(a)(1)?

REVENUE PROCEDURE 72-18
1972-1 C.B. 740

Section 1. Purpose.

The purpose of this Revenue Procedure is to set forth guidelines for taxpayers and field offices of the Internal Revenue Service for the application of section 265(2) of the Internal Revenue Code of 1954 to certain taxpayers holding state and local obligations the interest on which is wholly exempt from Federal income tax. . . . This Revenue Procedure provides guidelines for the application of section 265(2) of the Code to individuals, to dealers in tax-exempt obligations, and to business enterprises that are not dealers in tax-exempt obligations. . . .

Sec. 2. Background.

.01 Section 265(2) of the Code provides, with two exceptions not here relevant, that no deductions shall be allowed for interest on indebtedness "incurred or continued to purchase or carry obligations . . . the interest on which is wholly exempt" from Federal income tax.

. . . .

.03 Where the required purposive relationship is established, section 265(2) of the Code will be applicable even though the taxpayer does not receive tax-exempt interest, as for example, where the taxpayer holds defaulted obligations . . . or where the taxpayer holds the obligation for a period before interest begins to accrue. . . . Similarly, section 265(2) of the Code may be applicable even though the taxpayer's purpose in purchasing or carrying the tax-exempt obligations is to produce a taxable profit rather than tax-exempt interest. See *Denman v. Slayton*, 282 U.S. 514 (1931).

Sec. 3. General Rules.

.01 Section 265(2) of the Code is only applicable where the indebtedness is incurred or continued for the purpose of purchasing or carrying tax-exempt

---

[10] However, see *Alexander v. IRS*, 72 F.3d 938 (1st. Cir. 1995), discussed in Chapter 45, barring a deduction for alternative minimum tax purposes.

securities. Accordingly, the application of section 265(2) of the Code requires a determination, based on all the facts and circumstances, as to the taxpayer's purpose in incurring or continuing each item of indebtedness. Such purpose may, however, be established either by direct evidence or by circumstantial evidence.

.02 Direct evidence of a purpose to *purchase* tax-exempt obligations exists where the proceeds of indebtedness are used for, and are directly traceable to, the purchase of tax-exempt obligations. *Wynn v. United States*, 411 F.2d 614 (1969), *certiorari denied* 396 U.S. 1008 (1970). . . .

.03 Direct evidence of a purpose to *carry* tax-exempt obligations exists where tax-exempt obligations are used as collateral for indebtedness. "[O]ne who borrows to buy tax-exempts and one who borrows against tax-exempts already owned are in virtually the same economic position. Section 265(2) makes no distinction between them." *Wisconsin Cheeseman v. United States*, 388 F.2d 420, at 422 (1968).

.04 In the absence of direct evidence linking indebtedness with the purchase or carrying of tax-exempt obligations as illustrated in paragraphs.02 and.03 above, section 265(2) of the Code will apply only if the totality of facts and circumstances supports a reasonable inference that the purpose to purchase or carry tax-exempt obligations exists. Stated alternatively, section 265(2) will apply only where the totality of facts and circumstances establishes a "sufficiently direct relationship" between the borrowing and the investment in tax-exempt obligations. . . . The guidelines set forth in sections 4, 5, and 6 shall be applied to determine whether such a relationship exists.

.05 Generally, where a taxpayer's investment in tax-exempt obligations is unsubstantial, the purpose to purchase or carry tax-exempt obligations will not ordinarily be inferred in the absence of direct evidence as set forth in sections 3.02 and 3.03. In the case of an individual, investment in tax-exempt obligations shall be presumed insubstantial only where during the taxable year the average amount of the tax-exempt obligations (valued at their adjusted basis) does not exceed 2 percent of the average adjusted basis of his portfolio investments (as defined in section 4.04) and any assets held in the active conduct of a trade or business. . . .

Sec. 4. Guidelines for Individuals.

.01 In the absence of direct evidence of the purpose to purchase or carry tax-exempt obligations (as set forth in sections 3.02 and 3.03), the rules set forth in this section shall apply.

.02 An individual taxpayer may incur a variety of indebtedness of a personal nature, ranging from short-term credit for purchases of goods and services for personal consumption to a mortgage incurred to purchase or improve a residence or other real property which is held for personal use. Generally, section 265(2) of the Code will not apply to indebtedness of this type, because the purpose to purchase or carry tax-exempt obligations cannot reasonably be inferred where a personal purpose unrelated to the tax-exempt obligations ordinarily dominates the transaction. For example, section 265(2) of the Code generally will not apply to an individual who holds salable municipal bonds and takes out a mortgage to buy a residence instead of selling his municipal bonds to finance the purchase price.

Under such circumstances the purpose of incurring the indebtedness is so directly related to the personal purpose of acquiring a residence that no sufficiently direct relationship between the borrowing and the investment in tax-exempt obligations may reasonably be inferred.

.03 The purpose to purchase or carry tax-exempt obligations generally does not exist with respect to indebtedness incurred or continued by an individual in connection with the active conduct of trade or business (other than a dealer in tax-exempt obligations) unless it is determined that the borrowing was in excess of business needs. However, there is a rebuttable presumption that the purpose to *carry* tax-exempt obligations exists where the taxpayer reasonably could have foreseen at the time of purchasing the tax-exempt obligations that indebtedness probably would have to be incurred to meet future economic needs of the business of an ordinary, recurrent variety. See *Wisconsin Cheeseman v. United States*, 388 F.2d 420, at 422. The presumption may be rebutted, however, if the taxpayer demonstrates that business reasons, unrelated to the purchase or carrying of tax-exempt obligations, dominated the transaction.

.04 Generally, a purpose to *carry* tax-exempt obligations will be inferred, unless rebutted by other evidence, wherever the taxpayer has outstanding indebtedness which is not directly connected with personal expenditures (see section 4.02) and is not incurred or continued in connection with the active conduct of a trade or business (see section 4.03) and the taxpayer owns tax-exempt obligations. This inference will be made even though the indebtedness is ostensibly incurred or continued to purchase or carry other portfolio investments.

A sufficiently direct relationship between the incurring or continuing of indebtedness and the purchasing or carrying of tax-exempt obligations will generally exist where indebtedness is incurred to finance portfolio investment because the choice of whether to finance a new portfolio investment through borrowing or through the liquidation of an existing investment in tax-exempt obligations typically involves a purpose either to maximize profit or to maintain a diversified portfolio. This purpose necessarily involves a decision, whether articulated by the taxpayer or not, to incur (or continue) the indebtedness, at least in part, to purchase or carry the existing investment in tax-exempt obligations.

A taxpayer may rebut the presumption that section 265(2) of the Code applies in the above circumstances by establishing that he could not have liquidated his holdings of tax-exempt obligations in order to avoid incurring indebtedness. The presumption may be overcome where, for example, liquidation is not possible because the tax-exempt obligations cannot be sold. The presumption would not be rebutted, however, by a showing that the tax-exempt obligations could only have been liquidated with difficulty or at a loss; or that the taxpayer owned other investment assets such as common stock that could have been liquidated; or that an investment advisor recommended that a prudent man should maintain a particular percentage of assets in tax-exempt obligations. Similarly, the presumption would not be rebutted by a showing that liquidating the holdings of tax-exempt obligations would not have produced sufficient cash to equal the amount borrowed.

The provisions of this paragraph may be illustrated by the following example:

Taxpayer A, an individual, owns common stock listed on a national securities exchange, having an adjusted basis of $200,000; he owns rental property having an adjusted basis of $200,000; he has cash of $10,000; and he owns readily marketable municipal bonds having an adjusted basis of $41,000. A borrows $100,000 to invest in a limited partnership interest in a real estate syndicate and pays $8,000 interest on the loan which he claims as an interest deduction for the taxable year. Under these facts and circumstances, there is a presumption that the $100,000 indebtedness which is incurred to finance A's portfolio investment is also incurred to carry A's existing investments in tax-exempt bonds since there are no additional facts or circumstances to rebut the presumption. Accordingly, a portion of the $8,000 interest payment will be disallowed under section 265(2) of the Code.

Sec. 7. Procedures.

.01 When there is direct evidence under sections 3.02 and 3.03 establishing a purpose to purchase or carry tax-exempt obligations (either because tax-exempt obligations were used as collateral for indebtedness or the proceeds of indebtedness were directly traceable to the holding of particular tax-exempt obligations) no part of the interest paid or incurred on such indebtedness may be deducted. However, if only a fractional part of the indebtedness is directly traceable to the holding of particular tax-exempt obligations, the same fractional part of the interest paid or incurred on such indebtedness will be disallowed. For example, if A borrows $100,000 from a bank and invests $75,000 of the proceeds in tax-exempt obligations, 75 percent of the interest paid on the bank borrowing would be disallowed as a deduction.

.02 In any other case where interest is to be disallowed in accordance with this Revenue Procedure, an allocable portion of the interest on such indebtedness will be disallowed. The amount of interest on such indebtedness to be disallowed shall be determined by multiplying the total interest on such indebtedness by a fraction, the numerator of which is the average amount during the taxable year of the taxpayer's tax-exempt obligations (valued at their adjusted basis) and the denominator of which is the average amount during the taxable year of the taxpayer's total assets (valued at their adjusted basis) minus the amount of any indebtedness the interest on which is not subject to disallowance to any extent under this Revenue Procedure.

Part C:
Section 1091 — Wash Sales

I. PROBLEM

The common stock of Silvertip, Inc., a publicly held corporation, dropped dramatically in value on June 1. Peggy had purchased 100 shares of Silvertip a year before for $200 per share. On June 1 her stock was worth only $125 per share. On June 15, Peggy entered into a contract with Michael giving her the right to buy 100 shares of Silvertip convertible preferred stock for $130 per share. On July 10, Peggy sold her 100 shares of Silvertip common stock for $120 per share. On December 15, when Silvertip common stock was worth $140 per share, Peggy exercised her rights under the June 15 contract and took delivery of the 100 shares of Silvertip convertible preferred stock, paying Michael $130 per share for that stock. (The Silvertip convertible preferred stock may be converted by the shareholder on a share-for-share basis into Silvertip common stock.) Peggy seeks to deduct the loss she incurred on the July 10 sale of her Silvertip common stock. What result?

Assignment for Chapter 27, Part C: Section 1091:

Complete the Problem.

Read: Internal Revenue Code: § 1091(a)–(d)
    Treasury Regulations: §§ 1.1091-1(a), (c), (d), (f), (h); 1.1091-2.
    Materials: Overview

II. VOCABULARY

wash sale

III. OBJECTIVES

1. To recall that § 1091 defers the loss generated by a wash sale.

2. In a wash sale situation, to compute the basis of the "substantially identical stock or securities" which triggered the loss deferral rule of § 1091.

3. To identify "substantially identical stock or securities" within the meaning of § 1091(a).

IV.　OVERVIEW

Another provision designed to prevent the deduction of artificial losses is § 1091, which disallows losses on the sale or other disposition of stock or securities if the seller has acquired "substantially identical stock or securities" within a specified period. Specifically, § 1091 disallows any loss realized on the sale of stock or securities if the seller acquires (or enters into a contract or option to acquire) substantially identical stock or securities within a period beginning thirty days before the date of the sale and ending thirty days after such a sale. There is thus a 61-day period during which acquisition of substantially identical stock or securities will result in disallowance of the loss realized on the sale.[11]

Unlike § 267(a)(1), § 1091 merely postpones, but does not permanently disallow, the loss realized. Deferral is accomplished through an adjustment to the basis of the stock or securities acquired during the 61-day period. The stock or securities will have a basis equal to the basis of the stock or securities sold, increased or decreased by the difference between the purchase price of the newly-acquired stock and the selling price of the stock disposed of. § 1091(d).

Consider the following example: Mary owns 100 shares of stock in Primo Corporation. Mary paid $100 per share for the stock which has recently fallen in value to $75 per share. Mary would like to claim the $2,500 loss inherent in the stock but is also convinced the Primo stock is currently selling at a bargain price. On December 5, Mary sells the stock on a stock exchange and on January 2 of the following year purchases an additional 100 shares of Primo stock for $80 per share. The $2,500 loss realized on the sale of the Primo stock will be disallowed by § 1091; the basis of the stock purchased on January 2 will be $105 per share (the basis of the Primo stock sold ($100) plus the difference between what the stock was sold for per share ($75) and what Mary paid per share for the Primo stock purchased ($80)). The $25 per share loss inherent in the stock sold on December 5 is thus preserved. Because Mary's investment position really has not changed — except in the sense that she has added $5 per share to her investment in Primo — deferral of the loss is appropriate.

Note § 1091 is applicable only to losses; it does not apply to the sale of stock or securities at a gain, even if like stock or securities are purchased shortly before or after the sale. In addition, the disallowance rule of § 1091 is triggered only if "substantially identical stock or securities" (or rights to acquire the same) are purchased within the 61-day period. The "substantially identical" standard significantly narrows the scope of § 1091. For example, in Revenue Ruling 60-195, 1960-1 C.B. 300, the Service concluded that certain bonds issued by the same governmental body and having the same maturity date were nonetheless not "substantially identical" because the bonds had different interest rates. As noted by the Service, "bonds are not 'substantially identical' if they are substantially different in any material feature, or because of differences in several material features considered together. Securities are substantially identical when the par value, interest yield, unit price and the security behind the obligation are the same."

---

[11] Except as otherwise provided in regulations, contracts or options to acquire or sell stock or securities are themselves "stock or securities" under § 1091. § 1091(a).

Part D:
Judicial Limitations on Interest Deductions

The interest deduction historically played a major role in tax-avoidance trans-actions. In combatting tax avoidance, the courts relied on a number of theories, including sham transaction, substance over form and lack of a proper purpose. In one of the leading cases, *Knetsch v. U.S.*, 364 U.S. 361 (1960), the taxpayer on December 11, 1953 purchased ten 30-year maturity deferred annuity savings bonds, each in the face amount of $400,000 and bearing interest at 2.5% compounded annually. The purchase price was $4,004,000. The taxpayer paid $4,000 in cash and for the balance gave a $4,000,000 nonrecourse note. "The notes bore 3.5% interest and were secured by the annuity bonds. The interest was payable in advance, and Knetsch on the same day prepaid the first year's interest, which was $140,000. Under the Table of Cash and Loan Values made part of the bonds, their cash or loan value at December 11, 1954, the end of the first contract year, was to be $4,100,000. The contract terms, however, permitted Knetsch to borrow any excess of this value above his indebtedness without waiting until December 11, 1954. Knetsch took advantage of this provision only five days after the purchase. On December 16, 1953, he received from the company $99,000 of the $100,000 excess over his $4,000,000 indebtedness, for which he gave his notes bearing 3.5% interest. This interest was also payable in advance and on the same day he prepaid the first year's interest of $3,465." 364 U.S. at 363. In his 1953 return, the taxpayer deducted $143,465 as interest paid on indebtedness. He followed this same pattern of prepaying interest, borrowing the cash value and deducting interest payments in each of the next two years. At the beginning of the fourth contract year, the taxpayer terminated the contract and received $1,000, the amount by which the cash value exceeded his indebtedness.

A review of the three years of the transaction indicated that the taxpayer had paid about $294,000 in interest and received back $203,000 in loans on the increase in cash surrender value. Thus, when the taxpayer terminated the insurance arrangement, he suffered an overall economic loss of $91,000 but the interest deductions claimed in 1953 and 1954 saved him approximately $233,000 in taxes.

The trial court concluded the transaction lacked commercial economic substance and was a sham. In its decision, the Supreme Court utilized the oft-quoted standard of *Gregory v. Helvering*, 293 U.S. 465, 469 (1935): "The legal right of a taxpayer to decrease the amount of what otherwise would be his taxes, or altogether avoid them, by means which the law permits, cannot be doubted. . . . But the question for determination is whether what was done, apart from the tax motive, was the thing which the statute intended."

The Court noted that, given the annual borrowing of cash values, Knetsch kept the cash value on which any annuity or insurance payments would be paid at the ridiculously low figure of $1,000; the monthly annuity of $90,171 which would be paid at the contract's maturity would therefore never occur. As stated by the Court: "Knetsch's transaction with the insurance company did 'not appreciably affect his beneficial interest except to reduce his tax' . . . for it is patent that there was nothing of substance to be realized by Knetsch from this transaction beyond a tax deduction. What he was ostensibly 'lent' back was in reality only the rebate of a substantial part of the so-called 'interest' payments." The Court viewed the $91,000 which was never returned to him as the insurance company's fee for "providing the facade of 'loans' whereby the taxpayer sought to reduce [his tax liability]." The Court characterized the transaction as a "sham." 363 U.S. at 366.

Knetsch does not provide much guidance for evaluating subsequent tax avoidance transactions. The above analysis of the Court establishes a broad economic substance test. Nonetheless, the case is regularly cited for the proposition that tax benefit alone is not enough to justify incurring of interest expense.

A factually interesting and instructive case that followed *Knetsch* is *Goldstein v. Commissioner*, 364 F.2d 734 (2d Cir.), *cert. den.*, 385 U.S. 1005 (1967). There, the taxpayer, a 70-year old housewife who lived with her husband on a meager pension, won over $140,000 in the Irish Sweepstakes. Her son, a C.P.A., together with an attorney, devised a scheme by which the taxpayer could shelter a significant amount of her winnings from tax. Pursuant to the plan, the taxpayer borrowed almost a million dollars from two banks, used the proceeds to purchase $500,000 of .5% U.S. Treasury notes and $500,000 1.5% U.S. Treasury notes, gave the Treasury notes to the banks as security, and prepaid over $81,000 in interest to the banks. The rate of interest on the bank loans exceeded the rate of interest paid on the Treasury notes. Although the taxpayer's son had projected a slight profit on the notes if they were held to maturity, the notes were sold before they matured and the taxpayer actually sustained an economic loss of over $25,000 because some notes were sold for less than the taxpayer had paid.

The Second Circuit rejected the Tax Court's holding that the transactions were a sham, finding instead that the loan arrangements were legitimate. The Second Circuit noted the loans were made by independent financial institutions which possessed significant control over the future of the loan arrangements, the loan transactions did not immediately return the parties to the same position they had been in when they had started, and the taxpayer's notes were recourse notes.

The court, however, agreed with the Tax Court holding that the taxpayer's purpose in entering the transaction "was not to derive any economic gain or to improve [her] beneficial interest; but was solely an attempt to obtain an interest deduction as an offset to her sweepstake winnings." 364 F.2d at 738.

Because the interest rate the taxpayer was required to pay on the loans from the banks was higher than the interest rate on the Treasury notes, and because the taxpayer had to pay her son and tax counsel $6,500 for their assistance, an economic loss was all but assured. The evidence indicated the taxpayer's son was aware of that fact and anticipated the economic loss would be more than offset by the tax savings from the interest deductions. The court therefore rejected the taxpayer's argument that she entered into the transaction intending to make a profit. Citing *Knetsch v. U.S.*, the court held that § 163(a) "does not permit a deduction for interest paid or accrued in loan arrangements [like the one before it] that can not with reason be said to have purpose, substance or utility apart from their anticipated tax consequences." 364 F.2d at 740. Discussing the § 163(a) deduction, the court stated:

[It] is fair to say that Section 163(a) is not entirely unlimited in its application and that such limits as there are stem from the Section's underlying notion that, if an individual or corporation desires to engage in purposive activity, there is no reason why a taxpayer who borrows for that purpose should fare worse from an income tax standpoint than one who finances the venture with capital that otherwise would have been yielding income.

In order fully to implement this Congressional policy of encouraging purposive activity to be financed through borrowing, Section 163(a) should be construed to permit the deductibility of interest when a taxpayer has borrowed funds and incurred an obligation to pay interest in order to engage in what with reason can be termed purposive activity, even though he decided to borrow in order to gain an interest deduction rather than to finance the activity in some other way. In other words, the interest deduction should be permitted whenever it can be said that the taxpayer's desire to secure an interest deduction is only one of mixed motives that prompts the taxpayer to borrow funds; or, put a third way, the deduction is proper if there is some substance to the loan arrangement beyond the taxpayer's desire to secure the deduction. . . . [T]o allow a deduction for interest paid on funds borrowed for no purposive reason, other than the securing of a deduction from income, would frustrate Section 163(a)'s purpose; allowing it would encourage transactions that have no economic utility and that would not be engaged in but for the system of taxes imposed by Congress. [364 F.2d at 741.]

In § 461(g), noted in Chapter 22, Congress has now prohibited a cash method taxpayer from claiming a deduction for prepayments of interest allocable to years subsequent to the year of payment. As a result, the schemes in both *Knetsch* and *Goldstein* have now largely been negated by statute. Nevertheless, the sham doctrine applied in *Knetsch* and the "purposive activity" standard of *Goldstein* remain important weapons which the Commissioner may use to attack unwarranted deductions.

Chapter 28

CASH METHOD ACCOUNTING

I. PROBLEMS

1. Mike, a cash method, calendar year taxpayer, provides legal services to a wide range of clients. On December 20 of Year 1, Mike sent Developer a bill for $50,000 for services Mike rendered in that year with respect to a complex suit filed against Developer. Developer mailed a check for $50,000 to Mike on December 30, Year 1. Mike, however, did not receive the check until January 2 of Year 2. When must Mike recognize the income? Would it make any difference if Developer's office were less than a block from Mike's office?

2. Assume the facts of Problem 1 except the U.S. Postal Service delivered Developer's check to Mike's office on December 31, Year 1. Mike's secretary received his mail, including Developer's check. Assume Mike was on a ski vacation at the time of the delivery and did not return to his office until January 15, Year 2. Mike deposited the check immediately upon his return. When must Mike recognize the income? Would your answer change if the U.S. Postal Service placed the mail in Mike's post office box on December 31?

3. Assume the facts of Problem 1, except that, on December 15, Developer called Mike and requested that Mike immediately send him a bill for all legal services rendered to date. Mike, who had not intended to send a bill to Developer until December 31, Year 1, agreed to send the bill that day but requested that Developer withhold making payment to Mike until January, Year 2. Developer sent Mike the check on January 5, Year 2. When must Mike recognize the income?

4. Assume the facts in Problem 1 except that, upon receiving the bill, Developer called Mike and explained that he was experiencing some cash flow problems. Developer indicated he could pay the bill on March 1 of Year 2. Mike agreed to the deferral of the payment and requested that Developer send Mike a signed promissory note for $50,000 payable on March 1, Year 2. Mike received the promissory note on December 30 of Year 1. Assume that Developer, consistent with the terms of the promissory note, paid Mike $50,000 on March 1, Year 2. When must Mike recognize the income?

5. Assume the legal fees owed to Mike by Developer, a cash method, calendar year taxpayer, are deductible by Developer under § 162. When may Developer claim a deduction in each of the foregoing Problems?

6. Angela, a popular graphic artist, owns her own graphic arts business. She is retained by a nursing home company to paint a mural in the dining room of each of its nursing homes. The contract between Angela and the company requires Angela to complete the murals during a fifteen month period extending from October of Year 1 through December of Year 2. The contract provides that Angela will be paid a total of $150,000 for her work with $5,000 being paid to her in advance on October 1, Year 1, $70,000 on July 1, Year 2 and the remaining $75,000 on March 1, Year 3. Assuming the company pays Angela, a cash method, calendar year taxpayer, on the dates provided in the contract, when must Angela recognize the income? Would it make any difference if the company had offered to pay Angela more at the outset of the contract and Angela had rejected that offer? In answering the above questions, assume that, under her contract with the nursing home, Angela is an independent contractor. Assume also that Angela has many other clients for whom she is doing substantial work.

7. Tom, a cash method taxpayer, restores vintage automobiles. Tom agrees to do specific restoration work on Carmen's Porsche for $10,000. As required by their agreement, Carmen deposits the $10,000 in an escrow account at a bank on November 1, Year 1, prior to Tom's commencement of work. The escrow instructions provide that the $10,000 be paid to Tom in all events on January 3, Year 2, even if Tom has completed the work earlier, and even if he has not completed the work by January 3. The bank will not pay interest on the escrowed amount. Neither Carmen not her creditors have any rights to the escrowed amount. Tom completes the work on December 15, Year 1. In accordance with the escrow instructions, the bank pays Tom $10,000 on January 3, Year 2. When must Tom recognize the income?

8. On December 30, Year 1, Hank, who needs additional land for use in his cattle business, enters into a year-to-year lease of Annie's land, agreeing to pay Annie $50,000 per year in rent. The lease commences January 1, Year 2 and requires Hank to pay Annie the annual rent in a lump sum on January 5 of each year. Each lease payment constitutes rent for a twelve month period extending from January 1 through December 31. In the following situations, when may Hank deduct the lease payments?

   (a) On December 30, Year 1, Hank pays Annie $50,000 to cover the lease payment for Year 2.

   (b) On December 30, Year 2, Hank pays Annie $50,000 to cover the lease payment for Year 3.

Assignment for Chapter 28:

Complete the problems.

Read: Internal Revenue Code: §§ 83(a), (c)(1), (c)(2), (h); 441(a)–(e), (g); 446(a)–(c); 451(a), (h); 461(a), (g). Skim §§ 404(a)(5); 409A(a)(1)(A), (2), (3), (4)(A)–(C), (c), (d)(1)–(4); 448.
Treasury Regulations: §§ 1.61-2(d)(4); 1.263(a)-4(d)(3), (f)(1) and (8) Exs. (1), (2), (5) and (6); 1.446-1(a), (b), (c)(1)(i); 1.451-1(a) (first sentence); 1.451-2; 1.461-1(a)(1).

Materials: Overview
             Revenue Ruling 60-31
             Ames v. Commissioner
             Cowden v. Commissioner
             Revenue Ruling 78-39

II. VOCABULARY

cash method
constructive receipt
cash equivalency doctrine
economic benefit doctrine
prepaid expense; prepayment
twelve month rule

III. OBJECTIVES

1. To explain when a cash method taxpayer must include items of income.

2. To explain when checks received at year end by a cash method taxpayer must be included in income.

3. To explain when a cash method taxpayer must include prepayments received for services to be rendered.

4. To identify arrangements to which the doctrine of constructive receipt is applicable.

5. To identify receipts which should be characterized as cash equivalents.

6. To identify arrangements to which the economic benefit doctrine is applicable.

7. To distinguish the constructive receipt, cash equivalency and economic benefit doctrines.

8. To apply the cash method accounting rules in determining the amount of gross income reportable in a given tax year by a cash method taxpayer.

9. To explain when expenses are deductible under the cash method.

10. To distinguish between issuance of a check and issuance of one's own note for deduction purposes under the cash method.

11. To describe the limitations on deductibility of prepayments under the cash method.

IV. OVERVIEW

Comedians and tax practitioners have at least one thing in common: an understanding of the importance of timing. For the tax lawyer, correctly identifying an item as income or a deduction is not enough; knowing when that item must be reported as income or taken as a deduction is equally important. Successful tax planning requires an intimate understanding of the tax timing rules.

As discussed in Chapter 1, ours is an annual tax accounting system. Section 441(a) confirms that. But knowing one must account to the government annually merely begins the fine tuning of the timing issue. Instead of "when is something income," the issue becomes "in what tax year is something income." The answer is not as simple as one might expect.

Congress has provided different methods for determining the tax year an item is reportable as income or is allowable as a deduction. The so-called "cash receipts and disbursements" method and "accrual" method are the most common. This chapter examines the rules of the cash receipts and disbursements method (hereinafter the cash method) of accounting.

A. Income Under the Cash Method

1. In General

Section 446(c)(1) authorizes the use of the cash method of accounting so long as it clearly reflects the taxpayer's income. *See* § 446(b). Because of its simplicity, most taxpayers, including almost all wage and salary earners, use the cash method. As suggested by its name, the cash method requires a taxpayer to report cash (and income in other forms) as received and to deduct expenses as they are paid. Receipt and disbursement or payment are thus the critical events. But don't let the apparent simplicity of the method deceive you. Complex issues arise, and your understanding of those issues is critical to your ability to advise cash method taxpayers.

The primary issues associated with cash accounting as applied to income are reflected in the three doctrines examined in this part of the chapter: constructive receipt, cash equivalency and economic benefit. As demonstrated in the case law, including the decision in *Cowden* included herein, the courts have sometimes confused these doctrines.

2. Constructive Receipt

As noted under the cash method, gains, profits, and other income are reported when received. May a cash method taxpayer delay receipt of income and thereby reduce his taxes for a given year? It depends. Regulation § 1.446-1(c)(1)(i) defines the cash method as follows: "Generally, under the cash receipts and disbursements method in the computation of taxable income, all items which constitute gross income (whether in the form of cash, property, or services) are to be included for the taxable year in which actually or *constructively* received." (Emphasis added)

Constructive receipt is explained in Reg. § 1.451-2(a):

> Income although not actually reduced to a taxpayer's possession is
> constructively received by him in the taxable year during which it is
> credited to his account, set apart for him, or otherwise made available so
> that he may draw upon it at any time, or so that he could have drawn upon
> it during the taxable year if notice of intention to withdraw had been given.
> However, income is not constructively received if the taxpayer's control of
> its receipt is subject to substantial limitations or restrictions.

In essence, the doctrine of constructive receipt means a taxpayer cannot turn his
back on income or, more accurately, the cash method taxpayer who has control over
his actual receipt of income must report it, regardless of whether he has actual
physical possession of it. Consider the following examples:

> **Example 1:** Employee picks up her paycheck each Friday from the firm's
> payroll office. At the end of December, Employee decides she will not pick
> up the paycheck that will be available to her on the last Friday in
> December. Instead, she plans to pick that check up on January 2 of the next
> year. She hopes her plan will enable her to defer reporting the paycheck in
> her income until the next year. Because of the constructive receipt doctrine,
> her plan will fail. She will be in constructive receipt of the paycheck on the
> last Friday in December and must include the paycheck in her gross
> income for that year.

> **Example 2:** On December 1, Tenant offers Landlord a rent check for the
> month of December. Even though the rent was then due, Landlord asks
> Tenant to wait until January of the following year to pay the December
> rent. Landlord is in constructive receipt of the rent on December 1 and
> must report it for that year.

Why is it important to prevent taxpayers from playing such deferral games? If all
income were taxed at a flat rate, would there still be need for the constructive
receipt doctrine?

a.   Specific Factors Affecting Application of
Constructive Receipt Doctrine

As indicated in Reg. § 1.451-2(a) above, two requirements must be satisfied
before the doctrine of constructive receipt is applicable: (1) the amount must be
available to the taxpayer; and (2) the taxpayer's control over receipt must not be
subject to substantial restrictions or limitations. Considering these two closely
related requirements together, the Tax Court noted in *Hornung v. Commissioner*,
47 T.C. 428, 434 (1967), that the "basis of constructive receipt is essentially
unfettered control by the recipient over the date of actual receipt." As stated in
Baxter v. Commissioner, 816 F.2d 493, 494 (9th Cir. 1987): "Although the notion of
constructive receipt blends a factual determination of what actually happened and
a legal assessment of its significance, we have held that a finding of constructive
receipt is a finding of fact. . . . As such, it can be set aside only if clearly
erroneous." *Ames v. Commissioner*, included in the materials, provides an
interesting example of the points made in both *Hornung* and *Baxter*.

Given the factual focus of a constructive receipt determination, it is helpful to review the kinds of factors courts consider relevant in evaluating whether a taxpayer had "unfettered control over the date of actual receipt" of income.

1. *Distance*: One factor is the taxpayer's geographic proximity to the location where an item of income is being made available to the taxpayer. For example, in *Hornung v. Commissioner*, Paul Hornung was informed by Sports Magazine on Sunday, December 31, that he had won a new Corvette for being named the most valuable player in the National Football League Championship game played that day in Green Bay, Wisconsin. The Corvette, however, was located at a New York dealership which was closed for the weekend. The court held that Hornung likely could not have taken possession of the car before January 1, and, therefore, did not have the kind of control necessary for constructive receipt.

The taxpayer in *Paul v. Commissioner*, T.C. Memo 1992-582, claimed he was in constructive receipt of lottery winnings in 1987, the year he won the New Jersey Lottery, and not in 1988, the year he received the check in payment of his lottery claim. Taxpayer mailed his lottery claim form to the New Jersey Lottery Commission in December 1987. He argued, however, that he could have driven 68 miles to Trenton, appeared in person before the Lottery Commission, and collected his winnings before the year end. The Tax Court, rejecting taxpayer's argument, stated: "The fact that [taxpayer] would like the doctrine to apply to this case and that traveling 68 miles would not have been a burden to him is irrelevant; if such travel is necessary in order to prove entitlement to and obtain funds in a current taxable year, we consider the requirement a substantial limitation affecting unfettered control. Accordingly, we conclude that petitioner should have reported the lottery winnings in taxable year 1988." Similarly, in *Baxter v. Commissioner*, *supra*, the Ninth Circuit held a taxpayer could not be confronted with the choice of either driving 40 miles at year end to pick up a commission check or facing application of the constructive receipt doctrine.

Generally, the date when a check is received and not the date it is mailed determines the year of taxation. In Revenue Ruling 73-99, 1973-1 C.B. 412, the Service confirmed this but noted that, if the taxpayer could have picked the check up before the year end, the taxpayer would be deemed in constructive receipt of the check. The Service in this ruling, however, failed to address the distance issue considered in both *Paul* and *Baxter*. When does distance become so significant that taxpayer's failure to pick up the check will not result in application of the constructive receipt doctrine? Across town? One mile? Five miles?

2. *Knowledge*: In *Davis v. Commissioner*, T.C. Memo 1978-12, the U.S. Postal Service attempted to deliver a certified letter containing a severance payment check to the taxpayer on December 31, 1974. The taxpayer was not home to sign the return receipt necessary to receive the letter. Taxpayer, who was not expecting the severance check until sometime in the new year, received notice of the attempted delivery on December 31, but only after the post office had closed. According to the Service, a taxpayer's absence from her home when delivery was attempted was not a limitation or restriction that would negate constructive receipt. *See* Rev. Rul. 76-3, 1976-1 C.B. 114. The Tax Court, in *Davis*, however, disagreed because the taxpayer did not know the check was available to her in 1974. In holding for the taxpayer, the court commented: "Implicit in availability is

notice to the taxpayer that the funds are subject to his will and control. Such notice is lacking here."

3. *Contractual arrangements*: Will a taxpayer be considered in constructive receipt upon refusing a payment not yet due? For example, assume a tenant on December 31 offers to pay rent not due until January 1, and the landlord refuses the payment. Is the landlord in constructive receipt of the rent? No. The Code does not require the landlord to forego contractual rights. If the rental payment is not due until January 1, the landlord should not be required to accept it before that time. See, for example, Revenue Ruling 60-31, reprinted in the materials.

4. *Forfeitures or other penalties*: Banks and savings and loan associations commonly impose a penalty if money is withdrawn from certain certificate accounts before maturity. Does the existence of a penalty for early withdrawal constitute a sufficient restriction to negate constructive receipt? Maybe. Regulation § 1.451-2(a)(1)–(4) provides examples of bank restrictions that will not be considered substantial enough to negate the application of the constructive receipt doctrine with respect to earnings on bank accounts. Read Reg. § 1.451-2 carefully. Regulation § 1.451-2(a)(2) provides there will be no constructive receipt of interest on a certificate of deposit or other deposit arrangement "if an amount equal to three months' interest must be forfeited upon withdrawal or redemption before maturity" of deposit arrangements of one year or less.

By contrast, Revenue Ruling 80-300, 1980-2 C.B. 167, provides an example of a restriction substantial enough to bar a finding of constructive receipt. In that ruling, key employees of a corporation received stock appreciation rights ("SARs") from the corporation. An employee could exercise — *i.e.*, cash in — SARs simply by giving written notification to the corporation. The employee would then receive a cash payment equal to the difference between the value of the corporation's stock on the date the SAR was exercised and the value of the stock on the date the SAR was granted. The issue was whether, prior to exercising the SAR, the employee would be in constructive receipt of income as the stock appreciated in value. The Service answered "No," holding that the "forfeiture of a valuable right" — in this case, "the right to benefit from further appreciation of stock . . . without risking any capital" — was "a substantial limitation that precludes constructive receipt of income." The ruling further held that the employee's stock appreciation rights would be lost and the limitation removed once the employee exercised the SAR, and at that point, the employee would recognize income.

5. *Relationship of the taxpayer to the payor*: Difficult constructive receipt questions often arise in the context of closely held corporations in which the owners are also the corporate employees and officers. If an officer-owner is not paid her salary during the year, will she nonetheless be deemed in constructive receipt of the salary because she has control over the corporation? The Second Circuit in *Hyland v. Commissioner*, 175 F.2d 422 (1979), rejected a taxpayer's effort to invoke the constructive receipt doctrine based on his 85% ownership interest in his corporation. The court noted that, if control of a corporation by an owner-officer were enough to establish constructive receipt of unpaid salaries, the distinction between shareholders and their corporation would be vitiated. "It would mean that in every close corporation, the corporate earnings are immediately constructively

received by the controlling stockholder provided their withdrawal would not make the corporation insolvent. But the law ordinarily treats a corporation and its controlling shareholder as separate juristic persons and they are separately taxable." 175 F.2d at 424.

Before a shareholder-employee will be considered in constructive receipt of the salary owed her by her corporation, there must be some corporate action to set aside or otherwise make the salary available to the shareholder-employee. In addition, the shareholder-employee must have some authority to draw a check payable to herself on the corporate accounts. In Revenue Ruling 72-317, 1972-1 C.B. 128, such facts, together with the fact the corporation was able to make the salary payment, were sufficient to justify a finding of constructive receipt.

Consider a situation where a corporation, by resolution or in an employment contract, postpones until a future year payment of the salary owed to a controlling shareholder/employee. Does the corporate resolution or contract constitute a "substantial limitation or restriction" within the meaning of Reg. § 1.451-2(a), thereby enabling the shareholder/employee to defer reporting income? Does it make a difference that, as controlling shareholder, the employee may modify the employment contract (or the corporate resolution) at will and has the power to withdraw corporate funds? If the answer to the latter question is "Yes," are closely held corporations barred from providing effective deferred compensation arrangements? In *Young Door Co. v. Commissioner*, 40 T.C. 890 (1963), the Tax Court held that a limitation in a corporate resolution with respect to bonus payments to controlling shareholders constituted a substantial restriction or limitation under Reg. § 1.451-2(a). In *Basila v. Commissioner*, 36 T.C. 111 (1961), the Tax Court similarly concluded a written employment contract specifying that a bonus would not be paid until the year following its computation prevented a controlling shareholder/employee from having an unrestricted right to demand payment of the bonus prior to the date set for payment. See the discussion of deferred compensation arrangements below.

What result if the shareholder-employee's salary is determined as a percentage of corporate profit and the corporate profit cannot be determined until after the close of the shareholder-employee's tax year? Assuming all other factors necessary for finding constructive receipt are present, would the inability to compute the actual salary during the tax year be a sufficient defense to a constructive receipt argument?

As a rule of law, the constructive receipt doctrine may be employed by either the taxpayer or the Service. Why would a taxpayer ever argue constructive receipt? Change in tax rates from one year to the next? Running of the statute of limitations?

b. Specific Exceptions to Constructive Receipt Rules

Various exceptions exist to the rule that one who has unfettered control over the receipt of income must report it. For example, although prizes are generally income, the Service has ruled that a taxpayer who refuses a prize is not required to report it as income. Rev. Rul. 57-374, 1957-2 C.B. 69. Unlike the examples above, the taxpayer refusing the prize is not merely deferring receipt of income but foregoing forever the right to receive it.

Another exception is found in § 125 with respect to "cafeteria plans" by which an employee may choose between receipt of cash or receipt of excludable fringe benefits. In effect, the employee who chooses to receive excludable benefits in lieu of cash from his employer has turned his back on income. But for § 125, which authorizes an exclusion under those circumstances, the employee arguably would be in constructive receipt of income.

3.   Cash Equivalency Doctrine

As established in Reg. § 1.61-1(a), "gross income includes income in any form, whether in money, property or services." Assume Tom, a cash method taxpayer, performs services for Mary, who, in lieu of cash, gives Tom one of the following:

    (a)   an automobile worth $5,000;

    (b)   I.B.M stock worth $5,000;

    (c)   an I.B.M. bearer bond worth $5,000;

    (d)   a promissory note in which Mary agrees to pay Tom $5,000;

    (e)   a letter acknowledging Mary owes Tom $5,000 for services rendered;

    (f)   an oral promise to pay Tom $5,000.

Which of the above must Tom include in gross income upon receipt? Considering Reg. § 1.61-1(a), if Tom received either the automobile or the stock, he would have reportable income in the year of receipt. Both are property with clear value and appear to be bargained-for consideration.

Although the I.B.M. bond merely represents I.B.M.'s promise to pay the bearer a sum certain on a specified date, it is also bargained-for consideration and should be included in income at its fair market value at the time of its receipt. *See* Reg. § 1.61-2(d)(4).

Are Mary's letter, promissory note or oral promise "property" within the meaning of Reg. § 1.61-1(a) and thus includible in income upon their receipt? As you will learn in the next chapter, a fundamental difference between cash accounting and accrual accounting is that an accrual method taxpayer must include income when it is earned even if the taxpayer has received nothing, while a cash method taxpayer includes income only upon receipt. If, upon receipt of an oral promise to pay, a cash method taxpayer were required to report income, the distinction between cash and accrual accounting would be significantly blurred, if not entirely negated. Appropriately, therefore, Tom need not include anything in income merely because of Mary's oral promise. Taxation of the amount owed to Tom will be deferred until he actually or constructively receives payment.

The same result should follow in the case of the letter acknowledging the debt. The letter merely evidences a debt; it doesn't constitute receipt of anything. Like the oral promise, the letter cannot be viewed as bargained-for consideration. It is not commonly traded and cannot be reduced to cash. Under these circumstances, deferral is appropriate. Both the oral promise and the letter establish Tom has an account receivable and nothing more. To the cash method taxpayer, an account receivable does not constitute income.

Mary's promissory note presents a more difficult question. If the receipt of the I.B.M. bond generated income, why shouldn't the receipt of Mary's promissory note? With respect to the tax treatment of the receipt of property other than cash, and in particular with reference to the receipt of intangibles such as the bond and Mary's note, courts have invoked what is known as the "cash equivalency doctrine." With reference to intangibles like Mary's note, the cash equivalency doctrine essentially embodies the notion certain intangibles have so clear a value and are so readily marketable that a cash method taxpayer receiving them should not be entitled to defer reporting income. By contrast, other intangibles have no market or even a clear "property" flavor. To take these intangibles into account as income would obliterate the distinction between cash and accrual accounting.

The *Cowden* decision, reprinted in the materials, provides an excellent discussion of the cash equivalency doctrine, emphasizing those qualities which will result in the characterization of a promise to pay as a cash equivalent. Specifically, the *Cowden* court states that a promise to pay will be considered a cash equivalent if it is made by a solvent obligor, "is unconditional and assignable, not subject to set-offs, and is of a kind that is frequently transferred to lenders or investors at a discount not substantially greater than the generally prevailing premium for money. . . . " Why should the size of the discount make any difference? Note the kind of instrument under consideration in *Cowden*. Note also the discussion of the difference between the cash equivalency doctrine and the constructive receipt doctrine. Can you describe a scenario in which both doctrines would be applicable?

In view of *Cowden*, is Mary's own note a cash equivalent? What additional information, if any, would you need to know about Mary and the note before you could determine whether Tom, upon receipt of the note, would be required to include it in gross income?

Jay Williams v. Commissioner, 28 T.C. 1000 (1957), which addresses the tax treatment of the receipt of a written promise, may be helpful in answering this question. In *Williams*, the taxpayer, an individual, performed services for a client, who gave the taxpayer a promissory note payable approximately 8 months later. The note was unsecured and bore no interest. At the time he gave the taxpayer the note, the client had no funds with which to pay it. On numerous occasions, the taxpayer tried unsuccessfully to sell the note to banks. The Service argued the taxpayer was required to include the note in income in the year received. The taxpayer contended he did not have to report the note until it was paid. The Tax Court held for the taxpayer, reasoning the note had been given only as security for or as evidence of the indebtedness and not as payment. The mere change in form from an account payable to a note payable was insufficient to cause the realization of income by the taxpayer. In addition, considering the note bore no interest and was not marketable, the court held it had no fair market value.

In light of *Williams*, one might qualify the *Cowden* definition of cash equivalent by stating that a promissory note is not a cash equivalent if it is merely intended as evidence of indebtedness and not the bargained-for consideration. What if the maker of the note is I.B.M., however, and a market rate of interest is provided?

The cash equivalency doctrine has generally been applied to negotiable notes and traditional securities; *Cowden* extends the doctrine beyond these usual limits applying it to deferred payment agreements. According to Revenue Ruling 68-606, 1968-2 C.B. 42, issued subsequent to *Cowden* and citing that case, a deferred-payment obligation which is "readily marketable and immediately convertible to cash" is properly includable on receipt under the cash method to the extent of its fair market value. The ruling held that the value of an installment bonus contract issued by an oil company was currently includable in the income of a cash method taxpayer since it was "freely transferable and readily saleable." (Unlike *Cowden* the ruling does not make the amount of discount a factor in determining cash equivalency status.) How far should *Cowden* be extended? If Taxpayer were to lease property to I.B.M. on a net, net, net basis (*i.e.*, I.B.M. is responsible for payment of property taxes, insurance and maintenance or repairs), would the lease constitute a cash equivalent to Taxpayer? As you formulate an answer for these questions, consider that the cash equivalency doctrine, like the constructive receipt doctrine, if extended too far, will blur the distinction between cash and accrual accounting.

Cash Equivalency and the Treatment of Checks. If a cash method taxpayer receives a check at year's end, how should that check be treated? In *Kahler v. Commissioner*, 18 T.C. 31 (1952), the taxpayer received a commission check for over $4,300 on December 31, 1946 after banking hours. The taxpayer cashed the check on January 2, 1947 at the drawee bank. The Tax Court concluded it made no difference that it was impossible to cash the check in 1946, noting "where services are paid for other than by money, the amount to be included as income is the fair market value of [the property] taken in payment." 18 T.C. at 34. Quoting from *Estate of Spiegel*, 12 T.C. 524, 529 (1949), the court stated: "It would seem to us unfortunate for the Tax Court to fail to recognize what has so frequently been suggested, that as a practical matter, in everyday personal and commercial usage, the transfer of funds by check is an accepted procedure. The parties almost without exception think and deal in terms of payment except in the unusual circumstance, not involved here, that the check is dishonored upon presentation, or that it was delivered in the first place subject to some condition or infirmity which intervenes between delivery and presentation." A concurring judge noted that merely because the taxpayer could not have cashed the check at a bank did not mean he couldn't make some other use of the check in 1946. Thus, assuming the check is honored in due course and is not subject to some condition, a check received at year's end by a cash method taxpayer must be included in income just as though cash had been received. *See Baxter v. Commissioner*, 816 F.2d 493 (9th Cir. 1987).

Assume on December 31 a taxpayer receives a check post-dated to January 2 for services rendered. Under these circumstances, the post-dated check may be viewed as nothing more than a promise to make funds available on January 2. Presumably, cash equivalency analysis is appropriate in this context. The likelihood, however, is that in most cases a post-dated check will not satisfy the cash equivalency requirements and therefore its receipt will not result in income.

4. The Economic Benefit Doctrine

The Supreme Court, in *Commissioner v. Smith*, 324 U.S. 177 (1945), recognized that an economic or financial benefit conferred upon an employee as compensation was included in the concept of income. The Tax Court relied upon the economic benefit doctrine in *Sproull v. Commissioner*, 16 T.C. 244, *aff'd*, 194 F.2d 541 (6th Cir. 1952), in finding that an amount irrevocably placed in trust for the benefit of an employee constituted income to the employee in that year, even though the money was not payable to the employee until subsequent years. The Tax Court emphasized the amount was fixed and was irrevocably paid out for the sole benefit of the employee.

The Service relied on *Sproull* in Example 4 of Revenue Ruling 60-31, included in the materials, in concluding that a football player had received a taxable economic benefit when the football club placed a bonus in escrow for him and required the escrowee to distribute the bonus to the player in installments over a five-year period.

The economic benefit doctrine has been applied most often in the employee compensation context and with respect to prizes and awards held in escrow or trust-type arrangements. As noted by the Ninth Circuit in *Minor v. U.S.*, 772 F.2d 1472, 1474 (1985), "Although taxation of deferred compensation plans is generally analyzed under the constructive receipt doctrine, . . . the economic benefit doctrine provides an alternate method of determining when a taxpayer receives taxable benefits. Under that doctrine, an employer's promise to pay deferred compensation in the future may itself constitute a taxable economic benefit if the current value of the employer's promise can be given an appraised value. . . . The economic benefit doctrine is applicable only if the employer's promise is capable of valuation. . . . A current economic benefit is capable of valuation where the employer makes a contribution to an employee's deferred compensation plan which is nonforfeitable, fully vested in the employee and secured against the employer's creditors by a trust arrangement."

In Revenue Ruling 62-74, 1962-1 C.B. 68, a cash method taxpayer was awarded a prize of $12x in a contest. Pursuant to the contest terms, the contest sponsor placed $12x in a noninterest-bearing escrow account with the amount to be paid to the taxpayer over a two-year period. The Service noted the only difference between this case and *Sproull* was that in *Sproull* the taxpayer was entitled to the interest accruing on the corpus of the trust; in the contest case the taxpayer was entitled to no interest. Given this difference, the Service ruled the taxpayer did not have to include the full $12x in income immediately, but only the discounted value of the payments. As the payments were received, the balance would be includible in income.

From authorities such as those noted above has emerged the economic benefit doctrine: gross income includes any economic benefit conferred upon a taxpayer to the extent the benefit has an ascertainable fair market value. As suggested by Revenue Ruling 60-31, Example 4, and Revenue Ruling 62-74, the use of an escrow to assure payment and yet at the same time to insulate a cash method taxpayer from receipt provides a classic context for application of the economic benefit doctrine.

If the doctrine of "cash equivalency" is broadly defined, it could render the economic benefit doctrine unnecessary. As indicated in *Cowden*, however, the cash equivalency doctrine has been defined rather narrowly, with its primary application being found in the treatment of promissory notes. The economic benefit doctrine, by contrast, has a much broader scope and should be treated as a doctrine separate from both the cash equivalency and constructive receipt doctrines.

As *Cowden* suggests, considerable confusion exists regarding the application of the constructive receipt, cash equivalency and economic benefit doctrines. As you read the cases in the materials addressing these doctrines, pay close attention to the differences between these doctrines and be prepared to explain those differences. In addition, ask yourself whether these doctrines are necessary to maintain the integrity of the cash accounting method and the annual accounting system.

Property Transfer Under Section 83. Section 83 provides, in general terms, that property transferred in connection with the performance of services is taxable to the extent that the fair market value of the property exceeds the amount (if any) paid for the property by the transferee. In many situations, the operation of § 83 is obvious and unremarkable: when property is transferred, with no strings attached, as compensation for services, it is perfectly obvious that the recipient has compensation income equal to the value of the property; § 83 is not needed to bring about this result — § 61 itself would be sufficient.

But suppose there are some strings attached to the transfer — suppose, for example, the recipient is the employee of the transferor, and the employee must return the property to the employer if the employee quits the job within the next three years. Section 83 was enacted to deal with this type of situation in particular: an employer-corporation's transfer to an employee of restricted corporate stock, requiring the employee to "earn out" the right to keep the stock by continuing to work for the employer for a certain length of time. If the employee remained for the requisite time, the stock became "nonforfeitable." If the employee quit before the requisite time had passed, the employee forfeited the stock back to the employer. Section 83, as noted, is far broader than this example, but the example does suggest a type of transfer § 83 was concerned with.

The general rule adopted by the statute addresses both the timing and the amount of the income of the service-provider (such as an employee). If the property transferred is not subject to a substantial risk of forfeiture, then compensation income is reported in the year of the transfer, and the amount of the compensation income is the fair market value of the property at the time of the transfer. If the property is subject to a substantial risk of forfeiture (and is not transferable), then the compensation income is reported at the time the restriction lapses (that is, when the property ceases to be subject to the substantial risk of forfeiture); and the amount of the compensation income is the value of the property at the time the restriction lapses. Section 83(a). Similarly, the amount and timing of the employer's deduction is based upon the amount and timing of the service-provider's income. § 83(h).

There are a number of special rules and complications that this brief overview of § 83 does not address. But at the core of § 83 is the notion of nonforfeitability. Income arises when the property transferred is nonforfeitable. In that sense, § 83 thus bears a close resemblance to the judicially-developed economic benefit doctrine, as explained in the excerpt from the I.R.S. Audit Guide noted above:

> Section 83 codifies the economic benefit doctrine in the employment context by providing that if property is transferred to a person as compensation for services, the service provider will be taxed at the time of receipt of the property if the property is either transferable or not subject to a substantial risk of forfeiture. If the property is not transferable and subject to a substantial risk of forfeiture, no income tax is incurred until the property is not subject to a substantial risk of forfeiture or becomes transferable.

> For purposes of § 83, the term "property" includes real and personal property other than money or an unfunded and unsecured promise to pay money in the future. However, the term also includes a beneficial interest in assets, including money, that are transferred or set aside from claims of the creditors of the transferor, for example, in a trust or escrow account.

> Property is subject to a substantial risk of forfeiture if the individual's right to the property is conditioned on the future performance of substantial services or on the nonperformance of services. In addition, a substantial risk of forfeiture exists if the right to the property is subject to a condition other than the performance of services and there is a substantial possibility that the property will be forfeited if the condition does not occur.

> Property is considered transferable if a person can transfer his or her interest in the property to anyone other than the transferor from whom the property was received. However, property is not considered transferable if the transferee's rights in the property are subject to a substantial risk of forfeiture.

5. Non-Qualified Deferred Compensation Arrangements

Because of the progressive tax rates, taxpayers have devised various methods for deferring compensation to years when the taxpayer expects her income to be subject to tax at lower rates. Some deferral arrangements are specifically authorized by the Internal Revenue Code, *e.g.*, qualified pension and profit sharing plans. In general, these plans enable a taxpayer to defer compensation until retirement when presumably most taxpayers are in a lower tax bracket and will therefore pay less tax when they receive the compensation they have deferred. Congressional authorization of these deferral arrangements serves a significant policy goal, *i.e.*, encouraging employees to save for their retirement years.

In addition to deferral arrangements specifically authorized by the Code, so-called "nonqualified" deferred compensation arrangements or plans have also been common as part of executive compensation packages. An Internal Revenue Service audit guide (April 13, 2005 Market Segment Specialization Program Audit Guide for Nonqualified Deferred Compensation Plans) summarized nonqualified deferred compensation arrangements under the doctrines of constructive receipt, cash equivalency, and economic benefit. Consider the following excerpt from that I.R.S. guide:

A nonqualified deferred compensation plan is any elective or nonelective plan, agreement, method, or arrangement between an employer and an employee (or service recipient and service provider) to pay the employee compensation some time in the future. Nonqualified deferred compensation plans do not afford employers and employees the tax benefits associated with qualified plans because they do not satisfy all of the requirements of [I.R.C. § 401(a)].

Nonqualified deferred compensation plans include, for example, arrangements such as salary or bonus deferral arrangements whereby an employee is permitted to defer receipt of a portion of his or her salary or bonus that would otherwise be currently includible in gross income. These plans are typically unfunded, *i.e.*, the employer has merely promised to pay the deferred compensation benefits in the future and the promise is not secured in any way. The employer may simply keep track of the benefit in a bookkeeping account, or it may voluntarily choose to invest in annuities, securities, or insurance arrangements to help fulfill its promise to pay the employee. Similarly, the employer may transfer amounts to a trust that remains a part of the employer's general assets, subject to the claims of the employer's creditors if the employer becomes insolvent, in order to help it keep its promise to the employee. To obtain the benefit of income tax deferral, it is important that the amounts are not set aside from the employer's creditors for the exclusive benefit of the employee. If amounts are set aside from the employer's creditors for the exclusive benefit of the employee, the employee may have currently includible compensation. [Authors' note: As discussed below, the economic benefit doctrine would likely be applicable under these circumstances.]

Nonqualified deferred compensation plans may be formal or informal, and they need not be in writing. While many plans are set forth in extensive detail, some are referenced by nothing more than a few provisions contained in an employment contract. In either event, the form of the arrangement is just as important as the way the plan is operated. That is, while the parties may have a valid nonqualified deferred compensation arrangement on paper, they may not operate the plan according to the plan's provisions. In such a circumstance, the efficacy of the arrangement is not dependent upon its form.

. . . .

Constructive Receipt Doctrine — Unfunded Plans

Establishing constructive receipt requires a determination that the taxpayer had control of the receipt of the deferred amounts and that such control was not subject to substantial limitations or restrictions. It is important to scrutinize all [deferred compensation] plan provisions relating to each type of distribution or access option. It also is imperative to consider how the plan has been operated regardless of the existence of provisions relating to types of distributions or other access options. Devices such as credit cards, debit cards, and check books may be used to grant employees unfettered control of the receipt of the deferred amounts. Similarly, permitting employees to borrow against their deferred amounts achieves the same result. [Authors' note: If an employee has unfettered control over deferred amounts, then, despite whatever the specific provisions of the deferred compensation plan might state, the doctrine of constructive receipt will operate to defeat the deferral objectives of employees possessing such control.]

Economic Benefit — Funded Plans

Under the economic benefit doctrine, if an individual receives any economic or financial benefit or property as compensation for services, the value of the benefit or property is currently includible in the individual's gross income. More specifically, the doctrine requires an employee to include in current gross income, the value of assets that have been unconditionally and irrevocably transferred as compensation into a fund for the employee's sole benefit, if the employee has a nonforfeitable interest in the fund.

[Cash Equivalency Doctrine]

The cash equivalency doctrine must also be considered when analyzing a nonqualified deferred compensation arrangement. Under the cash equivalency doctrine, if a promise to pay of a solvent obligor is unconditional and assignable, not subject to set-offs, and is of a kind that is frequently transferred to lenders or investors at a discount not substantially greater than the generally prevailing premium for the use of money, such promise is the equivalent of cash and taxable in like manner as cash would have been taxable had it been received by the taxpayer rather than the obligation. . . .

6.   Section 409A and Revenue Ruling 60-31

Revenue Ruling 60-31, included in the materials, has long been the Service's most significant pronouncement discussing compensation deferral techniques. Note that the ruling, while primarily focusing on the constructive receipt doctrine, also refers to the cash equivalency doctrine and, in Example 4, the economic benefit doctrine. More recently, in 2004, Congress enacted § 409A to provide comprehensive statutory treatment of nonqualified deferred compensation arrangements. Section 409A essentially requires that all amounts deferred under a nonqualified plan, unless subject to a substantial risk of forfeiture, are currently includible in income unless certain requirements are satisfied. Nonetheless, all pre-existing rules requiring inclusion of deferred amounts remain in effect.[1] Thus, Revenue Ruling

---

[1] "Taxpayers should note, that although the statute makes a number of fundamental changes, § 409A does not alter or affect the application of any other provision of the Code or common law tax doctrine. Accordingly, deferred compensation not required to be included in income under § 409A may nevertheless be required to be included in income under § 451, the constructive receipt doctrine, the cash equivalency doctrine, § 83, the economic benefit doctrine, the assignment of income doctrine or any other applicable provision of the Code or common law tax doctrine." Notice 2005-1, 2005-1 C.B. 274.

60-31 has continued viability after the enactment of § 409A and must be considered in conjunction with that provision. The ruling is particularly important with respect to deferred compensation arrangements of independent contractors who are engaged in their own trade or business. As noted below, § 409A does not apply to such independent contractors.

Between the issuance of Revenue Ruling 60-31 and the enactment of § 409A, sophisticated planners developed a range of deferred compensation arrangements, typically for company executives, that Congress believed should not qualify for tax deferral. Specifically, Congress was aware of creative deferral arrangements that gave employees considerable security with respect deferred amounts or provided employees with considerable control over deferred compensation. While, in general, such arrangements would negate deferral, planners devised methods that appeared to qualify for deferral when in fact they did not. For example, it was not uncommon for a nonqualified deferred compensation arrangement to be structured to allow an employee to change the terms of deferral or to receive a distribution of deferred amounts upon request subject to some minimal forfeiture provision (*i.e.*, a "haircut" provision). In sum, Congress was convinced greater policing of income deferral techniques was necessary and, for that purpose, enacted § 409A.

The specific details of § 409A are beyond the scope of this course, but as noted above, § 409A provides in general that all amounts deferred under a nonqualified deferred compensation plan are currently includible in gross income to the extent not subject to a substantial risk of forfeiture and not previously included in gross income, unless certain requirements are satisfied. § 409A(a)(1)(A). Among the requirements that must be satisfied if deferral is to be respected under § 409A are the following:

(1) distributions of deferred compensation must be allowed only upon separation from service, death, a time specified in the plan, change in ownership of a corporation, occurrence of an unforeseeable emergency, or disability [§ 409A(a)(2)];

(2) except as provided by regulations, acceleration of benefits is prohibited [§ 409A(a)(3)];

(3) the election to defer compensation earned during the year must be made no later than the close of the preceding taxable year or at such other time as provided in the regulations [§ 409A(a)(4)(B) — this requirement underscores congressional concern that deferral during or after the provision of services is generally inappropriate because the income has already been earned];

(4) certain requirements must be met if the plan permits a delay in a payment or a change in the form of payment, *e.g.*, the plan requires that such election may not take effect until at least 12 months after the date on which the election is made [§ 409A(a)(4)(C)].

Note that the above requirements greatly limit the service provider's control over the timing of distributions of deferred compensation and the actual deferral of compensation itself.

In Notice 2005-1, 2005-1 C.B. 274, noted above, the Service specified that § 409A would not apply to arrangements between taxpayers all of whom use the accrual method of accounting. (Chapter 29 addresses the accrual method.) In addition, § 409A also does not apply to arrangements between a service provider and a service recipient if (a) the service provider is actively engaged in the trade or business of providing substantial services, other than (I) as an employee or (II) as a director of a corporation; and (b) the service provider provides such services to two or more service recipients to which the service provider is not related and that are not related to one another. Reg. § 1.409A-1(f)(2). Thus, deferred compensation arrangements with independent contractors will generally not be subject to § 409A.

7. Lottery Prizes

Section 451(h) allows states to offer prize winners the option of receiving in a single cash payment any lottery prize that otherwise is payable over at least ten years, provided the option is exercised within sixty days of the date of the taxpayer's entitlement to the prize. For example, if a taxpayer wins a state lottery that provides an option consistent with § 451(h) and does not chose to receive the lottery prize in a single payment, the constructive receipt doctrine will not be applied to require inclusion of the entire prize in the year taxpayer wins. The economic benefit doctrine likewise will not be applicable because typically state lotteries do not provide an irrevocable set aside of funds for the benefit of the particular lottery winner. Rather, a state lottery typically purchases an annuity naming the lottery rather than the particular winner as the owner and beneficiary of the annuity. Likewise, the cash equivalence doctrine would not apply as it has not been established that prizes are frequently transferred to lenders or investors at a discount not substantially greater than the prevailing premium for the use of money. *See* Private Letter Ruling 200031031.

8. Prepayments

Receipt is the critical event under the cash method. If a taxpayer is prepaid for services to be rendered, the taxpayer must report the prepayment. For example, except as otherwise provided, Reg. § 1.61-8(b) specifically requires prepayments of rent to be included in the year of receipt "regardless of the period covered or the method of accounting employed by the taxpayer." As discussed below, although prepayments received by a cash method taxpayer must be included in income when received, prepayments of deductible expenses by cash method taxpayers may not be deductible in full.

B. Deductions Under the Cash Method

1. In General

Under the cash method, expenses are deductible when paid. Reg. §§ 1.446-1(c)(1)(i), 1.461-1(a)(1). The rule is ordinarily quite straightforward in operation and produces the expected results.[2] If, for example, Lawyer, a cash method, calendar

---

[2] However, several provisions of the Code delay deductibility of an item of expense until the item is

year taxpayer, pays her December 2012 office rent on December 31, 2012, she may deduct the rent payment on her 2012 tax return as a § 162 deduction. If, however, she failed to make the payment until January 2, 2013, she could not deduct the payment in 2012, but would deduct it on her 2013 return. Suppose, however, Lawyer tenders the rent to Landlord on December 31, 2012, but Landlord rejects the rent and tells Lawyer to return with the rent on January 1, 2013 instead. As we saw above, if Landlord is a cash method taxpayer, the rent will be includable in his 2012 income under the constructive receipt doctrine. Is Lawyer, who has clearly not yet paid the rent, therefore entitled to a 2012 deduction under a constructive payment doctrine? Review the regulations cited above. Deductions are allowed for payments only when "actually made," for expenditures only "when paid." There is thus no counterpart on the deduction side to the doctrine of constructive receipt. Should there be a constructive payment doctrine?

What constitutes "payment" of an expense? Clearly, payment has not occurred when the taxpayer transfers funds to his own agent. For example, a cash basis taxpayer may not deduct real estate taxes in the year paid into his mortgagee-bank's escrow account, but only when the mortgagee pays them to the taxing authority, since the mortgagee-bank is ordinarily treated as the agent of the taxpayer, not of the taxing authority. *Hradesky v. Commissioner*, 65 T.C. 87 (1975), *aff'd*, 540 F.2d 821 (5th Cir. 1976). Similarly, a cash method taxpayer's mere deposit of funds with a government agent as an offer in compromise of a disputed amount is not deductible when deposited, but instead the deduction awaits acceptance of the offer. *Standard Brewing Co. v. Commissioner*, 6 BTA 980 (1927).

It is, of course, not necessary that payment be made in cash; payment can be made in property other than money. A $100 business expense paid with property worth $100 entitles the taxpayer to a $100 deduction. This transfer of property in satisfaction of a business debt may in turn, however, generate a taxable gain (or a loss) to the taxpayer depending on the taxpayer's adjusted basis in the relinquished property and the nature of the property. §§ 1001, 165(c).

Suppose a taxpayer "pays" an expense with funds borrowed from a third party. Does the deduction wait upon taxpayer's repayment of the borrowed funds? As we saw in Chapter 22, it is clear that the answer is "No"; payment with borrowed funds constitutes payment for tax purposes. *Granan v. Commissioner*, 55 T.C. 753 (1971). (The answer might be different if the funds are borrowed from the person to whom the taxpayer makes payment. See *Davison v. Commissioner*, reprinted in Chapter 22.) Next, suppose a taxpayer pays an expense by check. Again, it is clear that for tax purposes payment takes place when the check is delivered, even though the

---

included in income by the recipient. Thus, for example, amounts deferred under so-called nonqualified deferred compensation arrangements cannot be deducted by the employer until the amount has been included in the employee's income. § 404(a)(5). Similarly, property transferred in connection with the performance of services by an employer or independent contractor cannot be deducted until included in the recipient's income. § 83(h). Sometimes, the major impact of a provision is to delay the deduction for an *accrual* method taxpayer (*see* Chapter 29) until the *cash* method recipient has actually been paid. *See, e.g.*, § 267(a)(2). Sometimes, there are circumstances where even a cash method taxpayer's payment may not be deductible — for example, where the payment is so restricted in the hands of the payee under § 83(a), regarding restricted transfers, that the payment is not currently taxable and is thus not deductible under § 83(h).

taxpayer has the power to stop payment on the check, provided the check is unconditional and subsequently clears in due course. *See Estate of Spiegel*, 12 T.C. 524 (1949) (quoted *supra*); *see also* Reg. § 1.170A-1(b). Also note the mailing of a check is regarded as the equivalent of delivery. Similarly, payment of an expense by a bank credit card is treated as payment at the time the charge is made, not when the taxpayer subsequently pays the bank. See Revenue Ruling 78-39, reprinted below. Suppose, however, the payee knows the payor has insufficient funds to cover the check at the time it is given to the payee, and, as a result, the payee waits to cash the check until there are sufficient funds to cover it. In this case, the "relation-back doctrine" — that is, the doctrine that provides a check is deemed paid when it is delivered — does not apply. Thus, when an employee received from an employer a year-end bonus check that could not have been paid due to insufficient funds, the employer's deduction for the year the check was delivered was disallowed. *Vanney Associates, Inc. v. Commissioner*, T.C. Memo. 2014-184.

The issuance of one's own promissory note, however, has been held not to constitute payment. The taxpayer in *Helvering v. Price*, 309 U.S. 409 (1939), executed a guaranty agreement and secured note in favor of a bank. Subsequently, when the guaranty was called upon, he gave the bank a second secured note, which it accepted as final payment of the original note given under the guaranty. The cash method taxpayer claimed a loss on the substitution of his note. The Supreme Court denied the loss, noting there was no cash payment and the giving of the taxpayer's own note did not constitute payment. Although the note was secured, the Court held that the giving of collateral was not payment and did not convert a promise to pay into payment. A subsequent case, *Don E. Williams Co. v. Commissioner*, 429 U.S. 569 (1977), involved an accrual method corporate taxpayer and § 404(a) of the Code, which allows a deduction for contributions "paid" by an employer to employee pension and profit-sharing plans. The Supreme Court held the employer's delivery of its fully secured promissory demand notes did not entitle the employer to a deduction. Citing *Helvering v. Price*, the Court said that its

> reasoning is apparent: the note may never be paid, and if it is not paid, "the taxpayer has parted with nothing more than his promise to pay. . . . "

> The taxpayer argues that because its notes are acknowledged to have had value, it is entitled to a deduction equal to that value. It is suggested that such a note would qualify as income to a seller-recipient. Whatever the situation might be with respect to the recipient, the note, for the maker, even though fully secured, is still only his promise to pay. It does not in itself constitute an outlay of cash or other property. A similar argument was made in *Helvering v. Price*, . . . and was not availing for the taxpayer there. . . .

> The taxpayer suggests that the transaction equates with a payment of cash to the trustees followed by a loan, evidenced by the note in return, in the amount of the cash advanced. But . . . [w]hat took place here is clear, and income tax consequences follow accordingly. We do not indulge in speculating how the transaction might have been recast with a different tax result.

Taxpayer heavily relies on the fact that three Courts of Appeals . . . have resolved the issue adversely to the Commissioner. . . .

The three Courts of Appeals seemed to equate a promissory note with a check. The line between the two may be thin at times, but it is distinct. The promissory note, even when payable on demand and fully secured, is still, as its name implies, only a promise to pay, and does not represent the paying out or reduction of assets. A check, on the other hand, is a direction to the bank for immediate payment, is a medium of exchange, and has come to be treated for federal tax purposes as a conditional payment of cash. . . . The factual difference is illustrated and revealed by taxpayer's own payment of each promissory note with a check within a year after issuance.

429 U.S. at 577, 583.

2.   Cash Method Prepayments

All else being equal, when given a choice between paying now and paying later, most people will opt to pay later. But the Code is one of the reasons why all else is rarely equal. If a cash method taxpayer pays a deductible expense now rather than later, he may take an immediate tax deduction. And, if the value of the earlier tax deduction exceeds the "cost" of making the prepayment, prepayment makes sense from an economic standpoint. Not surprisingly, the deductibility of prepayments is not unlimited. Suppose, for example, a cash method taxpayer purchases a building for use in trade or business. As we saw in Chapter 13, capital expenditures are not currently deductible. That the cash method taxpayer has actually paid for the building does not change this result; the deduction timing rules of § 461 are subject to the capital expenditure rules of § 263. Thus, when an expenditure "results in the creation of an asset having a useful life which extends substantially beyond the close of the taxable year," as was obviously the case with respect to the building, a current deduction may be denied in whole or in part. Reg. § 1.446-1(a)(1), (2).

Purchases of buildings and equipment, of course, present the easy cases. *See* Reg. § 1.263(a)-2(a). But how far does this capitalization requirement reach? Recall, for example, *Boylston Market* discussed in Chapter 13, where the court held that the prepayment of three years' premiums for fire insurance constituted a capital expenditure and required the taxpayer to deduct a pro-rata portion of the prepayment in each of the three years. What result if the taxpayer makes an insurance payment in Year 1 that provides insurance coverage that extends into Year 2? Similarly, what result if a taxpayer, pursuant to the terms of a lease agreement, prepays one year's rental which gives taxpayer the right to use the leased property for a period extending into the next year? In *Zaninovich v. Commissioner*, 616 F.2d 429 (9th Cir. 1980), the Ninth Circuit adopted a "one-year rule" allowing the taxpayer to deduct a rental payment made in December for a lease year that extended through November 30, eleven months into the following year. The court held the payment was fully deductible on December of the year of payment, finding that a one-year rule preserved the "simplicity" of the cash method without creating a distortion of income or allowing an evasion of taxes in these circumstances. Recall also that in *U.S. Freightways Corp. v. Commissioner*, discussed briefly in Chapter 13, the court adopted a similar one year rule with respect to payments for licenses and permits valid for a twelve month period extending across two tax years. In *Grynberg v. Commissioner*, 83 T.C. 255 (1984), the Tax Court ruled that a prepaid expense would be deductible if the taxpayer established actual payment (not just a deposit) had been made; there was a substantial business reason for the prepayment; and the prepayment did not cause a material distortion in taxable income for the year of prepayment.

In view of cases like *Grynberg*, *Zaninivoch* and *U.S. Freightways Corp.*, and in an effort to simplify administration both for the Service and the taxpayer, the Treasury decided to create its own one-year rule and, at the end of 2003, promulgated final regulations under § 263 superceding the prior case law and providing a "12-month rule" by which "a taxpayer is not required to capitalize amounts paid to create . . . any right or benefit for the taxpayer that does not extend beyond the earlier of (i) 12 months after the first date on which the taxpayer realizes the right or benefit; or (ii) the end of the taxable year following the taxable year in which the payment is made." Reg. § 1.263(a)-4(f)(1). This "12-month rule" represents an exception to the general rule requiring capitalization of prepaid expenses. Reg. § 1.263(a)-4(d)(3)(i). Regulation § 1.263(a)-4(d)(3)(ii) Ex. 1 posits a three year prepayment of insurance premiums and, applying the general rule, concludes, much as did the court in *Boylston Market*, that the prepaid expense must be capitalized. Similarly, Example 2 of the same regulation considers a situation where a cash method taxpayer enters into a 24-month lease of office space and prepays the rental for that period. The Example concludes the prepayment must be capitalized. Compare Example 2 to the 12-month lease in *Zaninovich* that extended 11 months into the next year.

By contrast to these examples requiring capitalization of prepaid expenses, Treasury has provided a series of examples demonstrating the application of the "12-month rule" defined above. Reg. § 1.263(a)-4(f)(8). In one example, the taxpayer, on December 1, 2005, pays a $10,000 insurance premium to obtain a property insurance policy with a one year term that begins on February 1, 2006. According to the regulation example, the "12-month rule" does not apply "because the right or benefit attributable to the $10,000 payment extends beyond the end of the taxable year following the taxable year in which the payment is made. The prepayment therefore must be capitalized. By contrast, if the one-year policy term had begun on December 15, 2005, the "12-month rule . . . applies to the $10,000 payment because the right or benefit attributable to the payment neither extends more than 12 months beyond December 15, 2005 (the first date the benefit is realized by the taxpayer) nor beyond the end of the taxable year in which the payment is made." Reg. § 1.263(a)-4(f)(8) Examples 1 and 2.

What if, on December 31, 2015, a cash method, calendar year taxpayer makes an insurance payment due on January 10, 2016? Assume the insurance payment provides casualty coverage on taxpayer's business property for a 12-month period beginning on January 10, 2016. May the taxpayer deduct the insurance payment in 2015? The "12-month rule" is not applicable here because the right or benefit attributable to the premium payment extends beyond the end of the taxable year following the taxable year in which the payment is made.

At one time, the prepayment of interest was so prominent a feature of many tax shelters, and such a source of taxpayer-Service disputes, that congressional intervention resulted. As discussed in Chapter 22, pursuant to § 461(g), enacted in 1976, cash method taxpayers must treat prepaid interest as having been paid in the period to which it is properly allocable. A cash method taxpayer, in effect, is put on the accrual method with respect to prepaid interest, with an exception allowed for "points" paid in connection with a principal residence. § 461(g)(2). Should the statutory treatment of prepaid interest be extended generally to encompass other categories of expenditures?

Prepaid expense questions are simply a manifestation of an inherent problem in cash method accounting. The chief virtue of the cash method is its simplicity, but the price of that simplicity is a certain tolerance of mismatching of income and expense. Income will not necessarily be received in the tax period earned, nor expenses paid in the tax period incurred, nor income and related expenses reported in the same tax period. Limiting the deductibility of certain prepaid expenses is one approach to fixing boundaries of tolerable mismatching. Another approach for addressing problems of cash method accounting is to forbid its use in certain circumstances. This approach is exemplified by § 448: Use of the cash method is prohibited for certain categories of taxpayers. Statutorily defined "tax shelters," as well as certain corporations and partnerships, simply may not compute taxable income under the cash method because the potential mismatching they may obtain is deemed unacceptable. In addition, as discussed in the Note following Chapter 29, the Regulations have long required that a taxpayer employ the accrual method for purchases and sales where use of an inventory is necessary. Reg. § 1.446-1(c)(2).

REVENUE RULING 60-31
1960-1 C.B. 174

Advice has been requested regarding the taxable year of inclusion in gross income of a taxpayer, using the cash receipts and disbursements method of accounting, of compensation for services received under the circumstances described below.

(1) On January 1, 1958, the taxpayer and corporation X executed an employment contract under which the taxpayer is to be employed by the corporation in an executive capacity for a period of five years. Under the contract, the taxpayer is entitled to a stated annual salary and to additional compensation of 10x dollars for each year. The additional compensation will be credited to a bookkeeping reserve account and will be deferred, accumulated, and paid in annual installments equal to one-fifth of the amount in the reserve as of the close of the year immediately preceding the year of first payment. The payments are to begin only upon (a) termination of the taxpayer's employment by the corporation; (b) the taxpayer's becoming a part-time employee of the corporation; or (c) the taxpayer's becoming partially or totally incapacitated. Under the terms of the agreement, corporation X is under a merely contractual obligation to make the payments when due, and the parties did not intend that the amounts in the reserve be held by the corporation in trust for the taxpayer.

The contract further provides that if the taxpayer should fail or refuse to perform his duties, the corporation will be relieved of any obligation to make further credits to the reserve (but not of the obligation to distribute amounts previously contributed); but, if the taxpayer should become incapacitated from performing his duties, then credits to the reserve will continue for one year from the date of the incapacity, but not beyond the expiration of the five-year term of the contract. There is no specific provision in the contract for forfeiture by the taxpayer of his right to distribution from the reserve; and, in the event he should die prior to his receipt in full of the balance in the account, the remaining balance is distributable to his personal representative at the rate of one-fifth per year for five years, beginning three months after his death.

(2) The taxpayer is an officer and director of corporation A, which has a plan for making further payments of additional compensation for current services to certain officers and key employees designated by its board of directors. This plan provides that a percentage of the annual net earnings (before Federal income taxes) in excess of 4,000x dollars is to be designated for division among the participants in proportion to their respective salaries. This amount is not currently paid to the participants; but, the corporation has set up on its books a separate account for each participant for the year, reduced by a proportionate part of the corporation's income taxes attributable to the additional compensation. Each account is also credited with the net amount, if any, realized from investing any portion of the amount in the account.

Distributions are to be made from these accounts annually beginning when the employee (1) reaches age 60, (2) is no longer employed by the company, including cessation of employment due to death, or (3) becomes totally disabled to perform his duties, whichever occurs first. The annual distribution will equal a stated percentage of the balance in the employee's account at the close of the year immediately preceding the year of first payment, and distributions will continue until the account is exhausted. However, the corporation's liability to make these distributions is contingent upon the employee's (1) refraining from engaging in any business competitive to that of the corporation, (2) making himself available to the corporation for consultation and advice after retirement or termination of his services, unless disabled, and (3) retaining unencumbered any interest or benefit under the plan. In the event of his death, either before or after the beginning of payments, amounts in an employee's account are distributable in installments computed in the same way to his designated beneficiaries or heir-at-law. Under the terms of the compensation plan, corporation A is under a merely contractual obligation to make the payments when due, and the parties did not intend that the amounts in each account be held by the corporation in trust for the participants.

(3) On October 1, 1957, the taxpayer, an author, and corporation Y, a publisher, executed an agreement under which the taxpayer granted to the publisher the exclusive right to print, publish and sell a book he had written. This agreement provides that the publisher will (1) pay the author specified royalties based on the actual cash received from the sale of the published work, (2) render semiannual statements of the sales, and (3) at the time of rendering each statement make settlement for the amount due. On the same day, another agreement was signed by the same parties, mutually agreeing that, in consideration of, and notwithstanding

any contrary provisions contained in the first contract, sums in excess of 100x dollars accruing in any one calendar year are to be carried over by the publisher into succeeding accounting periods; and the publisher shall not be required either to pay interest to the taxpayer on any such excess sums or to segregate any such sums in any manner.

(4) In June 1957, the taxpayer, a football player, entered into a two-year standard player's contract with a football club in which he agreed to play football and engage in activities related to football during the two-year term only for the club. In addition to a specified salary for the two-year term, it was mutually agreed that as an inducement for signing the contract the taxpayer would be paid a bonus of 150x dollars. The taxpayer could have demanded and received payment of this bonus at the time of signing the contract, but at his suggestion there was added to the standard contract form a paragraph providing substantially as follows:

> The player shall receive the sum of 150x dollars upon signing of this contract, contingent upon the payment of this 150x dollars to an escrow agent designated by him. The escrow agreement shall be subject to approval by the legal representatives of the player, the Club, and the escrow agent.

Pursuant to this added provision, an escrow agreement was executed on June 25, 1957, in which the club agreed to pay 150x dollars on that date to the Y bank, as escrow agent; the escrow agent agreed to pay this amount, plus interest, to the taxpayer in installments over a period of five years. The escrow agreement also provides that the account established by the escrow agent is to bear the taxpayer's name; that payments from such account may be made only in accordance with the terms of the agreement; that the agreement is binding upon the parties thereto and their successors or assigns; and that in the event of the taxpayer's death during the escrow period the balance due will become part of his estate.

As previously stated, the individual concerned in each of the situations described above employs the cash receipts and disbursements method of accounting. Under that method, . . . he is required to include the compensation concerned in gross income only for the taxable year in which it is actually or constructively received. Consequently, the question for resolution is whether in each of the situations described the income in question was constructively received in a taxable year prior to the taxable year of actual receipt.

A mere promise to pay, not represented by notes or secured in any way, is not regarded as a receipt of income within the intendment of the cash receipts and disbursements method. . . .

This should not be construed to mean that under the cash receipts and disbursements method income may be taxed only when realized in cash. For, under that method a taxpayer is required to include in income that which is received in cash or cash equivalent. *W.P. Henritze v. Commissioner*, 41 B.T.A. 505. And, as stated in the above-quoted provisions of the regulations, the "receipt" contemplated by the cash method may be actual or constructive.

With respect to the constructive receipt of income, section 1.451-2(a) of the Income Tax Regulations provides, in part, as follows:

Income although not actually reduced to a taxpayer's possession is constructively received by him in the taxable year during which it is credited to his account or set apart for him so that he may draw upon it at any time. However, income is not constructively received if the taxpayer's control of its receipt is subject to substantial limitations or restrictions. Thus, if a corporation credits its employees with bonus stock, but the stock is not available to such employees until some future date, the mere crediting on the books of the corporation does not constitute receipt.

Thus, under the doctrine of constructive receipt, a taxpayer may not deliberately turn his back upon income and thereby select the year for which he will report it. . . . Nor may a taxpayer, by a private agreement, postpone receipt of income from one taxable year to another. . . .

However, the statute cannot be administered by speculating whether the payor would have been willing to agree to an earlier payment. See, for example, *J.D. Amend, et ux., v. Commissioner*, 13 T.C. 178, *acquiescence*, C.B. 1950-1, 1; and *C.E. Gullett, et al., v. Commissioner*, 31 B.T.A. 1067, in which the court, citing a number of authorities for its holdings, stated:

It is clear that the doctrine of constructive receipt is to be sparingly used; that amounts due from a corporation but unpaid, are not to be included in the income of an individual reporting his income on a cash receipts basis unless it appears that the money was available to him, that the corporation was able and ready to pay him, that his right to receive was not restricted, and that his failure to receive resulted from exercise of his own choice.

Consequently, it seems clear that in each case involving a deferral of compensation, a determination of whether the doctrine of constructive receipt is applicable must be made upon the basis of the specific factual situation involved.

Applying the foregoing criteria to the situations described above, the following conclusions have been reached:

(1) The additional compensation to be received by the taxpayer under the employment contract concerned will be includable in his gross income only in the taxable years in which the taxpayer actually receives installment payments in cash or other property previously credited to his account. To hold otherwise would be contrary to the provisions of the regulations and the court decisions mentioned above.

(2) For the reasons in (1) above, it is held that the taxpayer here involved also will be required to include the deferred compensation concerned in his gross income only in the taxable years in which the taxpayer actually receives installment payments in cash or other property previously credited to his account.

(3) Here the principal agreement provided that the royalties were payable substantially as earned, and this agreement was supplemented by a further concurrent agreement which made the royalties payable over a period of years. This supplemental agreement, however, was made before the royalties were earned; in fact, it was made on the same day as the principal agreement and the two

agreements were a part of the same transaction. Thus, for all practical purposes, the arrangement from the beginning is similar to that in (1) above. Therefore, it is also held that the author concerned will be required to include the royalties in his gross income only in the taxable years in which they are actually received in cash or other property.

(4) In arriving at a determination as to the includability of the 150x dollars concerned in the gross income of the football player, under the circumstances described, in addition to the authorities cited above, consideration also has been given to Revenue Ruling 55-727, C.B. 1955-2, 25, and to the decision in *E.T. Sproull v. Commissioner*, 16 T.C. 244.

In Revenue Ruling 55-727, the taxpayer, a professional baseball player, entered into a contract in 1953 in which he agreed to render services for a baseball club and to refrain from playing baseball for any other club during the term of the contract. In addition to specified compensation, the contract provided for a bonus to the player or his estate, payable one-half in January 1954 and one-half in January 1955, whether or not he was able to render services. The primary question was whether the bonus was capital gain or ordinary income; and, in holding that the bonus payments constituted ordinary income, it was stated that they were taxable for the year in which received by the player. However, under the facts set forth in Revenue Ruling 55-727 there was no arrangement, as here, for placing the amount of the bonus in escrow. Consequently, the instant situation is distinguishable from that considered in Revenue Ruling 55-727.

In *E.T. Sproull v. Commissioner*, 16 T.C. 244, *aff'd*, 194 Fed. (2d) 541, the petitioner's employer in 1945 transferred in trust for the petitioner the amount of $10,500. The trustee was directed to pay out of principal to the petitioner the sum of $2,250 in 1946 and the balance, including income, in 1947. In the event of the petitioner's prior death, the amounts were to be paid to his administrator, executor, or heirs. The petitioner contended that the Commissioner erred in including the sum of $10,500 in his taxable income for 1945. In this connection, the court stated:

> . . . it is undoubtedly true that the amount which the Commissioner has included in petitioner's income for 1945 was used in that year for his benefit . . . in setting up the trust of which petitioner, or, in the event of his death then his estate, was the sole beneficiary. . . .

> The question then becomes . . . was "any economic or financial benefit conferred on the employee as compensation" in the taxable years. If so, it was taxable to him in that year. This question we must answer in the affirmative. The employer's part of the transaction terminated in 1945. It was then that the amount of the compensation was fixed at $10,500 and irrevocably paid out for petitioner's sole benefit. . . .

Applying the principles stated in the *Sproull* decision to the facts here, it is concluded that the 150x dollar bonus is includable in the gross income of the football player concerned in 1957, the year in which the club unconditionally paid such amount to the escrow agent.

AMES v. COMMISSIONER

United States Tax Court

112 T.C. 304 (1999)

GERBER, J.

Respondent determined deficiencies in petitioner's Federal income tax. . . . The issues for our consideration are: (1) Whether petitioner constructively received income from illegal espionage activities during 1985, when it was allegedly promised and/or set aside for him, or when it was received and/or deposited in his bank accounts during the taxable years 1989, 1990, 1991, and 1992 in the amounts of $745,000, $65,000, $91,000 and $187,000, respectively. . . .

FINDINGS OF FACT

Petitioner is incarcerated in a Federal penitentiary for turning over state secrets to a foreign government at a time when he held a position with the Central Intelligence Agency (CIA) of the United States. . . . Petitioner's employment with the CIA spanned the years 1962 to 1994, during which he was assigned to progressively more responsible positions involving the Union of Soviet Socialist Republics (Soviet Union) and Soviet Bloc Eastern European countries. Throughout that time, petitioner held a Top Secret security clearance, and he had access to information and documents classified Secret and Top Secret.

Petitioner timely filed joint Federal income tax returns with his wife, Rosario C. Ames, for the taxable years 1989, 1990, 1991, and 1992. Petitioner's returns were filed on the cash basis for reporting income and deductions. The returns primarily reflected income from petitioner's CIA employment in the amounts of $70,337, $60,340, $62,514, and $67,578 for 1989, 1990, 1991, and 1992, respectively.

In 1984, as part of his duties as a CIA Operations officer, petitioner began meeting with officials of the Soviet Union's Embassy in Washington, D.C. These meetings were authorized by the CIA and the Federal Bureau of Investigation (FBI) and were designed to allow petitioner access to Soviet officials as possible sources for intelligence information and recruitment.

Sometime during April 1985, petitioner entered into a relationship with Soviet officials under which he betrayed his country and sold classified CIA information and information sources in other branches of the U.S. Government to the KGB (the Soviet intelligence directorate) in return for large amounts of remuneration. Petitioner provided the KGB with classified Top Secret information relating to the penetration of the Soviet military and intelligence services by the CIA, including the identities of Soviet military and intelligence officers who were cooperating with the CIA and foreign intelligence services of governments friendly to the United States. Because of petitioner's disclosures, a number of these individuals were arrested and executed by the KGB.

In the fall of 1985, petitioner received a communication from a Soviet agent that $2 million had been set aside for him in an account that he would be able to draw upon. Petitioner was told that the money was being held by the Soviet Union, rather than in an independent or third-party bank or institution, on petitioner's behalf. Petitioner received $50,000 in cash for his initial disclosure to the KGB and additional cash payments, the specific dates of which have not been detailed in the record of this case.

Petitioner met with Soviet officials in Washington, D.C., and in 1989 he met with them in Rome. In the spring of 1989, as petitioner was preparing to return to CIA headquarters in Langley, Virginia, the KGB provided him with two written documents. The first was a financial accounting that indicated that as of May 1, 1989, approximately $1.8 million had been set aside for petitioner and that some $900,000 more had been designated for him. The second document was a nine- page letter containing a list of the types of classified U.S. Government information sought by the KGB. The second document also contained a discussion of arrangements for cash dropoff payments to petitioner upon his return to the United States, a warning to petitioner to avoid traps set by the CIA, and a detailed plan governing future communications between petitioner and the KGB.

After his return to Washington, D.C., in 1989, petitioner communicated with the Soviets primarily through a complex arrangement of signal sites (a prearranged location where an individual leaves an impersonal mark or item to convey a prearranged message) and dead drops (locations for secretly leaving packages for anonymous pickup). Petitioner personally met with the Soviets only about once a year. Throughout this period, it was typical for petitioner to make a delivery of information and receive cash by means of signal sites and dead drops. Petitioner continued his unlawful espionage activities until his arrest in 1994.

During the years 1989, 1990, 1991, and 1992, petitioner and his wife made deposits of cash received in connection with petitioner's unlawful espionage activities in the amounts of $745,000, $65,000, $91,000, and $187,000, respectively. These deposits did not represent transfers of funds from other accounts or redeposits of currency previously withdrawn from other accounts.

Petitioner did not report on his income tax returns for taxable years 1989, 1990, 1991, and 1992 any of the amounts received from the KGB in connection with his illegal espionage activities. Petitioner did not report on a Federal income tax return (including his 1985 return) any amount of unlawful income he received or that had been set aside for him.

On April 26, 1994, petitioner was indicted in the U.S. District Court for the Eastern District of Virginia on charges of conspiracy to commit espionage, under 18 U.S.C. sec. 794(c), and conspiracy to defraud the U.S. Internal Revenue Service, under 18 U.S.C. sec. 371. On April 28, 1994, petitioner pled guilty to both counts of the indictment. The indictment contained a criminal forfeiture count pursuant to 18 U.S.C. sec. 794(d). Petitioner was sentenced to life imprisonment on the espionage charge and to 27 months' imprisonment on the tax charge, the two sentences to run concurrently. In addition, the plea agreement provided for the criminal forfeiture of whatever interest petitioner had in espionage-related assets. At the time of trial, petitioner was serving a life sentence in a Federal penitentiary.

OPINION

II. WHEN SHOULD PETITIONER HAVE REPORTED THE INCOME FROM HIS ILLEGAL ESPIONAGE ACTIVITIES?

Petitioner contends that he constructively received most of the unlawful espionage income in 1985, and, accordingly, he was not required to report the income received and deposited during the taxable years 1989, 1990, 1991, and 1992. Respondent contends that the income was reportable in 1989 through 1992, the years petitioner actually received and deposited cash in his bank accounts. Petitioner concedes that the funds deposited during the years in issue represent cash received from the Soviet Union during the years of the deposits. Petitioner argues, however, that most of the amounts he received during the taxable years under consideration were constructively received in 1985.

A taxpayer reporting income on the cash method of accounting, such as petitioner, must include an item in income for the taxable year in which the item is actually or constructively received. See sec. 451(a). The concept of constructive receipt is well established in tax law. The courts have regularly looked to section 1.451-2(a), Income Tax Regs., for the following definition of the term "constructive receipt": (a) General rule. Income although not actually reduced to a taxpayer's possession is constructively received by him in the taxable year during which it is credited to his account, set apart for him, or otherwise made available so that he may draw upon it at any time, or so that he could have drawn upon it during the taxable year if notice of intention to withdraw had been given. However, income is not constructively received if the taxpayer's control of its receipt is subject to substantial limitations or restrictions. * * *

Following the regulatory definition, courts have held that income is recognized when a taxpayer has an unqualified, vested right to receive immediate payment. . . . Normally, the constructive receipt doctrine precludes the taxpayer from deliberately turning his back on income otherwise available. Here, however, petitioner relies on constructive receipt as a foil to respondent's determination that the unlawful income was reportable during the years before the Court. In any event, the essence of constructive receipt is the unfettered control over the date of actual receipt. See *Hornung v. Commissioner*, 47 T.C. 428, 434 (1967).

The determination of whether a taxpayer has constructively received income is to be made largely on a factual basis. Resolution of the controversy in petitioner's favor depends on whether he can show that he constructively received about $2 million in 1985, the year he was informed that an amount had been set aside for him. Under the circumstances here, petitioner did not possess "unfettered control" over the $2 million in 1985.

Assuming arguendo that some type of account was created and funds were segregated for petitioner, he did not have ready access to it, and certain conditions had to be met or had to occur before he could gain physical access to any funds. Petitioner had to contact the Soviets, using a complex arrangement of signal sites, to determine whether a "withdrawal" could be made. Next, the Soviets had to arrange to have the cash transferred into the United States and have it secretly left in a prearranged location for petitioner. There was no certainty that these conditions and steps could be accomplished under the existing circumstances, and the conditions represented substantial risks, limitations, and restrictions on petitioner's control of the funds, assuming they were even in existence and segregated for his exclusive benefit. See Paul v. Commissioner, T.C. Memo.1992-582 (no constructive receipt where taxpayer would have had to travel 68 miles in order to turn in winning lottery ticket). There is no constructive receipt of income where delivery of the cash is not dependent solely upon the volition of the taxpayer.

So long as the Soviets retained control over any funds or promised set-asides, there was no practical or legal way in which petitioner could compel payment. Constructive receipt of income has been found where a corporation offers payment or pays by check in one year, but the recipient refuses delivery or fails to cash the check until the following year. Here, no such proffer was made, and petitioner did not have a legally enforceable claim. If the KGB had questioned petitioner's loyalty at any time before payment, there is no assurance that petitioner would have continued to receive cash deliveries or payments. So long as the Soviet Union retained the ability to withhold or control the funds, there was no constructive receipt. Petitioner did not constructively receive the income before it was made physically and/or practically available to him. Accordingly, we hold that petitioner received and failed to report income in the amounts of $745,000, $65,000, $91,000, and $187,000 for the years 1989, 1990, 1991, and 1992, respectively.

COWDEN v. COMMISSIONER
United States Court of Appeals, Fifth Circuit
289 F.2d 20 (1961)

Jones, Circuit Judge:

We here review a decision of the Tax Court by which a determination was made of federal income tax liability of Frank Cowden, Sr., his wife and their children, for the years 1951 and 1952. In April 1951, Frank Cowden, Sr. and his wife made an oil, gas and mineral lease for themselves and their children upon described lands in Texas to Stanolind Oil and Gas Company. By related supplemental agreements, Stanolind agreed to make "bonus" or "advance royalty" payments in an aggregate amount of $511,192.50. On execution of the instruments $10,223.85 was payable, the sum of $250,484.31 was due "no earlier than" January 5, "no later than" January 10, 1952, and $250,484.34 was stipulated to be paid "no earlier than" January 5 "nor later than" January 10, 1953. One-half of the amounts was to be paid to Frank Cowden, Sr. and his wife, and one-sixth was payable to each of their children. In the deferred payments agreements it was provided that:

> This contract evidences the obligation of Stanolind Oil and Gas Company to make the deferred payments referred to in subparagraphs (b) and (c) of the preceding paragraph hereof, and it is understood and agreed that the obligation of Stanolind Oil and Gas Company to make such payments is a firm and absolute personal obligation of said Company, which is not in any manner conditioned upon the development or production from the demised premises, nor upon the continued ownership of the leasehold interest in

such premises by Stanolind Oil and Gas Company, but that such payments shall be made in all events.

On November 30, 1951, the taxpayer assigned the payments due from Stanolind in 1952 to the First National Bank of Midland, of which Frank Cowden, Sr. was a director. Assignments of the payments due in 1953 were made to the bank on November 20, 1952. For the assignment of the 1952 payments the bank paid the face value of the amounts assigned discounted by $257.43 in the case of Frank Cowden, Sr. and his wife, and $85.81 in the case of each of their children. For the amounts due in 1953 the discounts were $313.14 for Frank Cowden, Sr. and his wife, and $104.38 for each of their children. The taxpayers reported the amounts received by them from the assignments as long-term capital gains. The Commissioner made a determination that the contractual obligations of Stanolind to make payments in future years represented ordinary income, subject to depletion, to the extent of the fair market value of the obligations at the time they were created.

The Commissioner computed the fair market value of the Stanolind obligations, which were not interest bearing, by the deduction of the discount for four per cent on the deferred payments from the date of the agreements until the respective maturities. Such computation fixed a 1951 equivalent of cash value of $487,647.46 for the bonus payments, paid in 1951 and agreed to be paid thereafter, aggregating $511,192.50. The Commissioner determined that the taxpayers should be taxed in 1951 on $487,647.46, as ordinary income.

A majority of the Tax Court was convinced that, under the particular facts of this case, the bonus payments were not only readily but immediately convertible to cash and were the equivalent of cash, and had a fair market value equal to their face value. The Tax Court decided that the entire amounts of the bonus payments, $511,192.50, were taxable in 1951, as ordinary income. *Cowden v. Commissioner of Internal Revenue*, 32 T.C. 853. Two judges of the Tax Court dissented.

The Tax Court stated, as a general proposition, "that executory contracts to make future payments in money do not have a fair market value." The particular facts by which the Tax Court distinguishes this case from the authorities by which the general proposition is established, are as stated in the opinion of the majority

> that the bonus payors were perfectly willing and able at the time of execution of the leases and bonus agreements to pay such bonus in an immediate lump sum payment; to pay the bonus immediately in a lump sum at all times thereafter until the due dates under the agreements; that Cowden, Sr. believed the bonus agreements had a market value at the time of their execution; that a bank in which he was an officer and depositor was willing to and in fact did purchase such rights at a nominal discount; that the bank considered such rights to be bankable and to represent direct obligations of the payor; that the bank generally dealt in such contracts where it was satisfied with the financial responsibility of the payor and looked solely to it for payment without recourse to the lessor and, in short, that the sole reason why the bonuses were not immediately paid in cash upon execution of the leases involved was the refusal of the lessor to receive such payments.

The dissenting opinion of the Tax Court minority states that the conclusion reached by the majority "is in effect that the taxpayers are not free to make the bargain of their choice," and one of the taxpayers' specifications of error is that the Tax Court "erred in holding that taxpayers are not free to make the bargain of their choice."

The Tax Court majority distinguishes the authorities cited and relied upon by the taxpayers upon several grounds. The Tax Court seemingly lays stress upon the fact, found to be here present, that the bonus payor was willing and able to make the entire bonus payment upon the execution of the agreement. It is said by the taxpayers that the Tax Court has held that a constructive receipt, under the equivalent of cash doctrine, resulted from the willingness of the lessee to pay the entire bonus on execution of the leases and the unwillingness of the taxpayers, for reason of their own,[3] to receive the full amounts. If this be the effect of the Tax Court's decision there may be some justification for the criticism appearing in the opinion of the minority and the concern expressed elsewhere.

It was said in *Gregory v. Helvering*, 293 U.S. 465, 55 S.Ct. 266, 79 L.Ed. 596, 97 A.L.R. 1355, and recently repeated in *Knetsch v. United States*, 364 U.S. 361, 81 S.Ct. 132, 135, 5 L.Ed.2d 128, "The legal right of a taxpayer to decrease the amount of what otherwise would be his taxes, or altogether avoid them, by means which the law permits, cannot be doubted. . . . " As a general rule a tax avoidance motive is not to be considered in determining the tax liability resulting from a transaction. . . . The taxpayers had the right to decline to enter into a mineral lease of their lands except upon the condition that the lessee obligate itself for a bonus payable in part in installments in future years, and the doing so would not, of itself, subject the deferred payments to taxation. Nor would tax liability necessarily arise although the lease contract was made with a solvent lessee who had been willing and able to pay the entire bonus upon the execution of the lease.

While it is true that the parties may enter into any legal arrangement they see fit even though the particular form in which it was cast was selected with the hope of a reduction in taxes, it is also true that if a consideration for which one of the parties bargains is the equivalent of cash it will be subjected to taxation to the extent of its fair market value. Whether the undertaking of the lessee to make future bonus payments was, when made, the equivalent of cash and, as such, taxable as current income is the issue in this case. In a somewhat similar case, decided in 1941, the Board of Tax Appeals stated that "where no notes, bonds, or other evidences of indebtedness other than the contract were given, such contract had no fair market value." *Kleberg v. Commissioner*, 43 B.T.A. 277, quoting from *Titus v. Commissioner*, 33 B.T.A. 928. In 1959 the Tax Court held that where the deferred bonus payments were evidenced by promissory notes the equivalent of cash doctrine might be applicable. *Barnsley v. Commissioner*, 31 T.C. 1260 (1959).

The taxpayers urge that there can be no "equivalent of cash" obligation unless it is a negotiable instrument. [Authors' note: In general, for an instrument to be negotiable it must be in writing and signed by the maker; it must provide an

---

[3] It is not denied that a desire to save taxes was the sole purpose for that taxpayers' insistence that payment be postponed.

unconditional promise to pay a sum certain on demand or at a time certain; it must be payable to the bearer or to order; and it must not contain other promises or impose other obligations.] Such a test, to be determined by the form of the obligation, is as unrealistic as it is formalistic. The income tax law deals in economic realities, not legal abstractions, and the reach of the income tax law is not to be delimited by technical refinements or mere formalism.

A promissory note, negotiable in form, is not necessarily the equivalent of cash. Such an instrument may have been issued by a maker of doubtful solvency or for other reasons such paper might be denied a ready acceptance in the market place. We think the converse of this principle ought to be applicable. We are convinced that if a promise to pay of a solvent obligor is unconditional and assignable, not subject to set-offs, and is of a kind that is frequently transferred to lenders or investors at a discount not substantially greater than the generally prevailing premium for the use of money, such promise is the equivalent of cash and taxable in like manner as cash would have been taxable had it been received by the taxpayer rather than the obligation. The principle that negotiability is not the test of taxability in an equivalent of cash case such as is before us is consistent with the rule that men may, if they can, so order their affairs as to minimize taxes, and points up the doctrine that substance and not form should control in the application of income tax laws.

The Tax Court stressed in its findings that the provisions for deferring a part of the bonus were made solely at the request of and for the benefit of the taxpayers, and that the lessee was willing and able to make the bonus payments in cash upon execution of the agreements. It appears to us that the Tax Court, in reaching its decision that the taxpayers had received equivalent of cash bonuses in the year the leases were executed, gave as much and probably more weight to those findings than to the other facts found by it. We are persuaded of this not only by the language of its opinion but because, in its determination of the cash equivalent, it used the amounts which it determined the taxpayers could have received if they had made a different contract, rather than the fair market value cash equivalent of the obligation for which the taxpayers had bargained in the contracts which they had a lawful right to make. We are unable to say whether or not the Tax Court, if it disregarded, as we think it should have done, the facts as it found them as to the willingness of the lessee to pay and the unwillingness of the taxpayers to receive the full bonus on execution of the leases, would have determined that the deferred bonus obligations were taxable in the year of the agreements as the equivalent of cash. This question is primarily a fact issue. . . . There should be a remand to the Tax Court for a reconsideration of the questions submitted in the light of what has been said here.

Reversed and remanded.

AUTHORS' NOTE

On remand, the Tax Court found that the oil bonus agreements (which were not interest bearing and had an aggregate face amount of $511,192.50) were the equivalent of cash under the Fifth Circuit's formulation "in at least the total amount of $487,647.46 as determined by respondent." *Cowden v. Commissioner*, T.C. Memo 1961-229. As noted in the Fifth Circuit opinion, this calculation reflected a four percent discount from the non-interest-bearing face amount. In a subsequent case, the Tax Court, applying the *Cowden* formulation, held that an interest-bearing real estate contract, with a face value of $133,000, was not the equivalent of cash where its fair market value was only $76,980, a discount of approximately 42 percent. *Warren Jones Co. v. Commissioner*, 60 T.C. 663 (1973), *rev'd on other grounds*, 524 F.2d 788 (9th Cir. 1975).

REVENUE RULING 78-39
1978-1 C.B. 73

Advice has been requested whether the use of a credit card to pay an expense for medical care is "payment" sufficient to support a deduction of the amount of the charge as an expense for medical care "paid during the taxable year," for the year the credit card charge was made, under section 213 of the Internal Revenue Code of 1954.

An individual (cardholder), who files tax returns on a calendar year basis, uses credit cards issued by a bank to purchase goods and services. The contract between the cardholder and the bank includes a provision that the cardholder agrees to pay the bank the total amount on the charge statements (drafts) to participating vendors from whom the cardholder may make purchases by use of the bank credit card.

On November 15, 1976, the cardholder used the bank credit card to pay a hospital $500 for medical services rendered to the cardholder. The bank billed the cardholder for this charge in December 1976, but the cardholder made no payment until January 1977. The cardholder paid the full amount of the indebtedness to the bank during the course of calendar year 1977.

The specific question presented is whether the $500 payment to the hospital by the use of a bank credit card is includable in the medical expenses claimed on the cardholder's 1976 tax return.

Section 213(a) of the Code allows as a deduction expenses paid during the taxable year, not compensated for by insurance or otherwise, for medical care of the taxpayer, the taxpayer's spouse, or dependent, subject to certain limitations.

Section 1.213-1(a)(1) of the Income Tax Regulations provides, in pertinent part, that a deduction is allowable only to individuals and only with respect to medical expenses paid during the taxable year, regardless of when the incident or event that occasioned the expense occurred and regardless of the method of accounting employed by the taxpayer in making income tax returns. Thus, if the medical expenses are incurred but not paid during the taxable year, no deduction for such expenses shall be allowed for such year.

In the instant case, when the cardholder used the bank credit card to pay the hospital for the medical expenses, the cardholder became indebted to a third party (the bank) in such a way that the cardholder could not prevent the hospital from receiving payment. The credit card draft received by the hospital from the cardholder could be deposited in the bank and credited to the hospital's account as if it were a check.

Since the cardholder's use of the credit card created the cardholder's own debt to a third party, the use of the bank credit card to pay a hospital for medical services is equivalent to use of borrowed funds to pay a medical expense. The general rule is that when a deductible payment is made with borrowed money, the deduction is not postponed until the year in which the borrowed money is repaid. Such expenses must be deducted in the year they are paid and not when the loans are repaid. *William J. Granan*, 55 T.C. 753 (1971).

Accordingly, the $500 payment made by bank credit card to the hospital is includable in the medical expenses deductions claimed on the cardholder's 1976 tax return.

AUTHORS' NOTE

In a companion ruling, Revenue Ruling 78-38, 1978-1 C.B. 67, the Service held that a taxpayer who made a charitable contribution by means of a charge to a bank credit card was entitled to a deduction in the year the charge was made rather than in the year the debt was paid on the credit card.

Chapter 29

ACCRUAL METHOD ACCOUNTING

I. PROBLEMS

1. Mike, an accrual method taxpayer, owns a small service company he operates as a sole proprietor. Mike completed a three-month project for Developer on December 15 of last year and, within a week, sent Developer a bill for $50,000 for the services rendered. Developer, also an accrual method taxpayer, mailed a check to Mike on January 2 of this year. Mike received the check on January 4. Assume Developer will be allowed to deduct the cost of Mike's services.

   (a) When must Mike recognize the income from his work for Developer? When would Developer deduct the $50,000 he paid for Mike's services?

   (b) How would your answers to (a) change, if at all, if, on December 15 of last year, Developer offered to pay Mike the $50,000 immediately but Mike requested that Developer wait until this year to make the payment?

   (c) How would your answers to (a) change, if at all, if upon receiving Mike's bill, Developer informed Mike that he couldn't pay him until March 1 of this year and, at Mike's insistence, gave Mike a promissory note specifying that the $50,000 payment would be made on March 1 of this year?

   (d) Assume Developer is dissatisfied with Mike's work and, upon receipt of the bill for $50,000, informs Mike he will not pay him any more than $40,000. Early this year, Mike hired an attorney to sue Developer. In May of this year, however, Developer and Mike reached an agreement whereby Developer agreed to pay Mike $45,000 for the services Mike provided. Explain the tax consequences to Mike and Developer.

2. Connor, an accrual method taxpayer, is the sole proprietor of a residential and commercial painting business. In January of Year 1, Benjamin, who owns and operates a small hotel, contracted with Connor to repaint the outside of the hotel and 20 of the hotel's rooms. Three months later, Connor completed the requested painting services. Benjamin charged the entire $75,000 owing for those services to an account he had opened with Connor's business. Connor charges monthly interest on the unpaid balance of all accounts. Because of a recession, Benjamin's hotel business suffered and, as a result, he failed to make any payments to Connor. By December 1 of Year 1, Connor realized it was unlikely he would be able to collect the $75,000 and accrued interest Benjamin owed him. Benjamin declared

bankruptcy in February of Year 2. As a result, Connor never received payment for the painting services he provided Benjamin or the accrued interest on Benjamin's account.

(a) On his income return for Year 1, does Connor have to report either the income from the services he provided Benjamin or the interest that accrued through December of that year on Benjamin's account balance?

(b) What basis, if any, does Connor have in the $75,000 account receivable resulting from the services he provided Benjamin?

(c) Assuming Benjamin is also an accrual method taxpayer, may he deduct on his income tax return for Year 1 the cost of the services Connor rendered or the interest that had accrued through December of Year 1 on his account balance?

(d) What result to Connor when, as a result of Benjamin's bankruptcy, Connor never collects either the $75,000 owed him by Benjamin for the painting services or the accrued interest on Benjamin's account balance?

3. Clarita, an accrual method taxpayer, is in the business of compiling executive salary information for hospitals. On October 1, Year 1, Clarita entered into a contract with a large hospital system to provide executive salary information upon demand for a 24 month period beginning October 1 of Year 1. To take advantage of a prepayment discount Clarita offered, the hospital system prepays Clarita $24,000 for the two-year contract. Based on her experience with hospital systems, Clarita can demonstrate statistically that she will provide essentially the same amount of service to the system each month during the 24 month period of the contract.

(a) When must Clarita report the prepayment in her gross income if, in her applicable financial statements she recognized from the prepayment as follows: $4,000 in Year 1; $12,000 in Year 2; and $8,000 in Year 3? (See Rev. Proc. 2004-34, included in the materials.)

(b) How would your answer to (a) change if Clarita did not have any applicable financial statements?

4. Dennis, an accrual method calendar year taxpayer, owns and operates a restaurant in the city. A special, one-time, tax is assessed on all real property, including Dennis' restaurant, to fund the renovation of city hall. Dennis' share of this tax, in the amount of $10,000, is assessed on August 1 of Year 1 and becomes payable on February 1 of Year 2. Dennis pays the property tax on January 20, Year 2. When may he deduct it?

5. In an effort to increase patronage of his restaurant, Dennis enters into advertising agreements with several local businesses in neighboring towns. Under the agreements, Dennis will pay each business $1,500 if it displays, prominently and exclusively, certain promotional material for the restaurant throughout Year 2. The first $500 will be paid in December, Year 1, when the agreement is entered; the remaining $1,000 will be paid in January, Year 3, provided the business certifies in writing to Dennis that it

has displayed the promotional material in accordance with the agreement throughout Year 2. Assuming each business displays the promotional material as required by the agreement, when may Dennis deduct the $1,500 paid to each business?

Assignment for Chapter 29:

Complete the problems.

Read: Internal Revenue Code: §§ 446; 451(a); 461(a), (f), (g), (h); 448(d)(5). Skim § 448 generally.

Treasury Regulations: §§ 1.263(a)-4(f)(6), (8) Exs. 10 and 11; 1.446-1(a)(2), -1(c)(1)(i), (ii); 1.451-1(a); 1.461-1(a)(1), (2); 1.461-2(a)–(e)(1). Skim § 1.451-5 and the remainder of § 1.446-1(c). Also skim Reg. §§ 1.461-4(a)(1), (d)(1)–(6), (d)(7) Exs. 1 and 2, (e), (g)(1)–(g)(8).

Materials: Overview
Schlude v. Commissioner
Revenue Procedure 2004-34
United States v. General Dynamics
Revenue Ruling 2007-3

II. VOCABULARY

accrual method
all events test (with regard to income)
prepayments
deferral of prepaid income
prepaid expense; prepayment
all events test (with regard to expenses)
premature accrual
economic performance

III. OBJECTIVES

1. To explain the all events test for inclusion of income under the accrual method.

2. To contrast timing of income under the accrual method with timing of income under the cash method.

3. To recall that performance fixes the right to income under the accrual method.

4. To recall the treatment of uncollectible income under the accrual method.

5. To apply the rules relating to the treatment of contested items of income under the accrual method.

6. To distinguish the claim of right doctrine and the receipt of prepayments under the accrual method.

7. To explain and apply the "earliest of" rule and exceptions to that rule.

8. To describe how interest income is earned by performance.

9. To distinguish the tax treatment of prepayments and deposits.

10. To recall limitations on a taxpayer's choice of accounting methods.

11. To apply the accrual method accounting rules in determining the amount of gross income reportable in a given tax year by an accrual method taxpayer.

12. To explain and apply the all events test for deductions under the accrual method.

13. To describe limitations on deductions under the accrual method even when the fact of liability is established.

14. To recall the time when economic performance occurs for purposes of the all events test.

15. To distinguish fixed liabilities from contingent liabilities.

16. To recall the rules relating to the deduction of contested liabilities.

17. To explain whether the inability to pay an expense prevents accrual of a deduction for the expense.

IV. OVERVIEW

Nick, an accrual method taxpayer, owns a Florida landscaping service he operates as a sole proprietor. Nick provided landscaping services to XYZ Corporation in early December of last year and immediately sent XYZ a bill for $10,000. XYZ paid the bill in January of this year. For XYZ, the landscaping fees represent an ordinary and necessary expense of doing business. As discussed in the previous chapter, under the cash method of accounting, timing of income and deductions is determined by the actual or constructive receipt of income items and actual payment of deductible items. Assuming Nick and XYZ were both cash method taxpayers, Nick would have $10,000 of gross income in January of this year and XYZ would have a $10,000 deduction in January. If, however, Nick and XYZ are accrual method taxpayers, the results are different. In general, under the accrual method, the earning of income, rather than the receipt of it, is generally the critical event for inclusion purposes; and the fixing of the obligation to pay, not payment itself, is the critical event for deduction purposes. Accordingly, Nick must include the $10,000 in income in December and XYZ will be entitled to deduct the $10,000 fee in December.

A. The All Events Test

Section 451(a) provides that income is included in the year received, unless, under the taxpayer's accounting method, it is "properly accounted for as of a different period." Section 461 provides the amount of any allowable deduction "shall be taken for the taxable year which is the proper taxable year under the method of accounting used in computing taxable income." The regulations provide the following details regarding the accrual method:

(a) An item of income is includable in gross income "when all the events have occurred which fix the right to such income and the amount thereof can be determined with reasonable accuracy." Reg. §§ 1.451-1(a)(1); 1.446-1(c)(1)(ii).

(b) An expense is deductible when all the events occur which establish the fact of liability, the amount can be determined with reasonable accuracy, and economic performance has occurred with respect to the liability. Reg. §§ 1.461-1(a)(2), 1.446-1(c)(ii).

This formulation for accruing income and expense is commonly referred to as the "all events test." It originated in the Supreme Court decision in *United States v. Anderson*, 269 U.S. 422 (1926), where the court held that an accrual method taxpayer was required to deduct a tax on munitions profits in 1916, the year the munitions were sold and the tax was imposed, rather than in 1917, when the tax became due and was paid:

> Only a word need be said with reference to the contention that the tax upon munitions manufactured and sold in 1916 did not accrue until 1917. In a technical legal sense it may be argued that a tax does not accrue until it has been assessed and becomes due; but it is also true that in advance of the assessment of a tax, all the events may occur which fix the amount of the tax and determine the liability of the taxpayer to pay it. . . . In the economic

and bookkeeping sense with which the statute and Treasury decision were concerned, the taxes had accrued.

Id. at 440–41. As indicated, *Anderson* involved the proper timing of an expense. The Supreme Court extended the all events test to the income side of the ledger in *Spring City Foundry Co. v. Commissioner*, 292 U.S. 182 (1934). The accrual method taxpayer there sold some goods in 1920. Later that year, the purchaser filed a petition in bankruptcy and ultimately the taxpayer received only partial payment for the goods sold. The Supreme Court nonetheless held the taxpayer was required to accrue (*i.e.*, report as gross income) the entire sales price in the year of the sale:

> Keeping accounts and making returns on the accrual basis, as distinguished from the cash basis, import that it is the *right* to receive and not the actual receipt that determines the inclusion of the amount in gross income. When the right to receive an amount becomes fixed, the right accrues. When a merchandizing concern makes sales, . . . a claim for the purchase price arises.

Id. at 184–85. The taxpayer was relegated to the bad debt provisions of the Code to account for the purchaser's failure to pay the full purchase price.

B. Accrual of Income

1. General Rules

For purposes of computing income, the accrual method focuses on "fixing" a right to income, and determining its amount with reasonable accuracy. Nick, the landscaper, in the example at the beginning of this Overview, had a fixed right to the $10,000 landscaping fee in December because he had earned the fee by performance of the landscaping services. As a result, the $10,000 fee is includable in his gross income at that time. As discussed below, while the "all events" test under Reg. § 1.451-1(a)(1) historically focused on when income was earned, that test today is broader, *i.e.*, all the events fixing the right to income generally occur when (1) the payment is earned through performance, (2) payment is due, or (3) payment is received, whichever happens earliest. See Rev. Proc. 2004-34, in the materials.

The fixing of a right to income is not a process absolutely devoid of flexibility. The regulations state that a method in accord with generally accepted accounting principles, consistently used, and consistent with the regulations, will be acceptable. Reg. § 1.446-1(c)(1)(ii)(C). An example in the same regulation permits a manufacturer to account for a sale when an item is shipped, delivered, accepted, or when title passes. Thus, some flexibility exists in determining the time to accrue income on the sale of goods, if the determination is in accordance with the taxpayer's regular accounting method.

Suppose, however, in a case involving a casual sale rather than a sale from inventory, an accrual method taxpayer enters an executory contract for the sale of real estate in one year, but the transaction does not close and title does not pass until the following year. In *Lucas v. North Texas Lumber Co.*, 281 U.S. 11 (1930), the Supreme Court concluded the sales income was not properly accruable until the later year because no unconditional liability of the purchaser arose in the earlier year. *North Texas Lumber Co.*, however, should perhaps be viewed as addressing not only the issue of when a right to income is fixed under the all events test, but also the issue of when a sale is considered "closed" for tax purposes in order to compute gain or loss. More recently, in *Keith v. Commissioner*, 115 T.C. 605 (2000), the Tax Court held an accrual method taxpayer must include the gain realized on the sale of real estate under a contract for deed in the year the contract was executed. The taxpayers in *Keith* argued they were not required to include any of the gain on the sale of the property until the purchasers had made all payments required by the contract for deed. The court, rejecting the taxpayers' argument, noted that equitable title to the real estate had passed to the purchasers upon execution of the contract. For tax purposes, the transaction was closed at that time. The result would not be different even if the purchasers later defaulted on the contract and the taxpayers were never paid the full purchase price.

Income does not accrue until the amount can be determined with "reasonable accuracy." The regulations provide for accrual on the basis of a "reasonable estimate," with the difference between the estimate and the exact amount accounted for in the year the latter is determined. Reg. § 1.451-l(a)(l). As with much else in life, of course, reasonableness may lie in the eye of the beholder. See *Continental Tie & Lumber Co. v. United States*, 286 U.S. 290 (1932), a case where a taxpayer had a claim against the federal government for lost income, and Congress had passed a law authorizing awards in respect of such claims to be determined and made by a federal agency; the Court held that the right to the award was fixed by passage of the legislation, and the amount of the award could reasonably be estimated on the basis of information in the taxpayer's possession.

2.   Income Prior to Receipt: Accrual Issues

Suppose an accrual method taxpayer has grave doubts about its ability to collect for services provided or goods sold. The Supreme Court required accrual on sale in *Spring City Foundry*, but apparently no doubt regarding collectibility existed at the time of the sale. Other courts and the Service, however, have recognized a limited exception to the general rule regarding accrual of income when sufficient doubt exists as to the collectibility of the income at the time the right to the income arises. For example, interest income was not accruable while "reasonable doubt" existed as to collectibility, but, when collectibility was established, accrual was required. *Clifton Mfg. Co. v. Commissioner*, 137 F.2d 290 (4th Cir. 1943). According to Revenue Ruling 80-361, 1980-2 C.B. 164, interest income "uncollectible" at the time the right to it arose did not accrue; by contrast, where interest income was properly accrued, and subsequently became uncollectible, the taxpayer's remedy lay in the bad debt provisions of the Code rather than in the elimination of the proper accrual. The Tax Court held that a management fee was not accruable where the taxpayer was required to agree not to collect its fee as a condition for the debtor's obtaining a bank loan. *Commercial Solvents Corp. v. Commissioner*, 42 T.C. 455 (1964) (Acq). Accrual of income for services rendered to the Cuban Government was not required, where collection was "at the mercy" of future Cuban administrations, and there was "real doubt and uncertainty" as to whether any amount would ever be paid. *Cuba Railroad Co. v. Commissioner*, 9 T.C. 211 (1947) (Acq.). By contrast, a judgment creditor of the United States was required to accrue an "acknowledged liability" of the United States, even though a congressional appropriation to pay the judgment did not occur until a later year. Rev. Rul. 70-151, 1970-1 C.B. 116. In *Georgia School Book Depository v. Commissioner*, 1 T.C. 463 (1943), the taxpayer was required to accrue commissions earned, but not yet paid, on text books it had distributed, where "there was no serious doubt as to the ultimate collection of the accounts here involved." Similarly, a court required accrual of royalty income, despite the debtor's financial problems, where there was "no real doubt" about the "ultimate receipt" of the royalties. *Koehring Co. v. United States*, 421 F.2d 715 (Ct. Cl. 1970). Moreover, legal unenforceability of a claim does not necessarily bar accrual. In Revenue Ruling 83-106, 1983-2 C.B. 77, for example, the Service required the owner of a gambling casino to accrue gambling obligations owed by customers even though the obligations were not legally enforceable. According to the Service, the owner's collection experience indicated the owner had a reasonable expectancy of collecting on the obligations. In addition, see *Jones Lumber Co. v. Commissioner*, 404 F.2d 764 (6th Cir. 1968), where the receipt of unassignable notes, with no ascertainable value, did not prevent accrual of the sales price, since taxpayer did not establish reasonable doubt as to collectibility.

Finally, note the special rule of § 448(d)(5) providing that a taxpayer need not accrue any portion of amounts to be received for the performance of services that, on the basis of experience, will not be collected. The rule applies only if the taxpayer either (1) is performing services in one of several specified fields (health, law, engineering, architecture, accounting, actuarial science, performing arts, or consulting) or (2) does not exceed a $5,000,000 gross receipts test for any prior taxable year. The rule does not apply with respect to service income bearing interest or a late charge. The regulations establish several safe harbors taxpayers may use to establish their nonaccrual-experience. A taxpayer not using one of the safe harbors must test its chosen nonaccrual-experience method against actual experience. Reg. § 1.448-2(e), (f).

Suppose the validity of the claim itself is contested. As the language of the all events test suggests, an unconditional right to income is necessary before the income is accrued. If the claim is disputed, income accrual awaits resolution of the dispute. See, for example, Revenue Ruling 70-151, cited above, where accrual was required, not in the year taxpayer was awarded judgment against the United States, but in the following year when the government's petition for writ of certiorari was filed and denied. Consider at this point whether you are able to distinguish this accrual method rule from the claim of right doctrine. Review the facts of *North American Oil* in Chapter 3. Note, in that case, entitlement to the 1916 earnings was in dispute throughout 1916 and, regardless of accounting method, the taxpayer was not taxable then. The 1916 earnings, however, were held taxable as of 1917, even though the dispute continued until 1922, because they were received in 1917 under a claim of right.

Timing questions concerning amounts held in escrow should be analyzed under the foregoing accrual principles. If the escrowed amount is not to be released until the taxpayer has rendered performance, the taxpayer's right to the income is not yet fixed under the all events test, and accrual is not appropriate. Conversely, mere delay in ability to reach or apply amounts in escrow should not itself prevent accrual. Security or reserve accounts, often required by lenders or creditors, raise similar issues. In *Commissioner v. Hansen*, 360 U.S. 446 (1959), an automobile dealer on the accrual method sold the commercial installment paper received from his customers to a finance company. The finance company paid most of the purchase price to the dealer and credited the remainder to a "dealer's reserve account" as security for the dealer and guarantee of the installment paper. The dealer argued the withheld amount was not income until paid. The Supreme Court, however, held that the dealer had to accrue the withheld amounts when they were entered on the finance company's books at the time of the sale, reasoning the dealer's right to receive them was fixed at that time, *i.e.*, the amounts ultimately would either be paid to the dealer in cash, or would be used to satisfy his obligations to the finance company, and if the latter occurred, they would be as much "received" as if paid in cash.

The application of the "all events" test to certain kinds of income should be noted. Interest income is treated as accruing as it is earned over the life of the loan. Interest is earned one day at a time. Thus, when a lender allows a borrower to use his money for one day, performance has occurred and one day's interest has been earned or accrued. Accrual, however, is not required with respect to income, including interest, that cannot be collected at the time "performance" occurs. See *Clifton Manufacturing Co. v. Commissioner* and Rev. Rul 80-361, cited previously.

The regulations tax dividend income to shareholders when it is "unqualifiedly made subject to their demands" and make no distinction between cash and accrual method taxpayers. Reg. § 1.301-1(b). In effect, accrual method taxpayers are placed on the cash method with respect to dividend income, and ordinarily will be taxed on receipt of the dividend.

3. Receipt Prior to Earning: Prepayments and the "Earliest of" Test

As noted previously, the accrual method focuses on when all events have occurred that fix the right to income. Income thus typically accrues as it is earned, through performance, even though payment follows some time later. Where payment has not been earned, however, but is instead received in advance of performance, does the accrual method postpone income until performance is rendered? For financial accounting purposes, the income is not properly accruable. Does the same rule govern tax accounting? In a line of cases, culminating in *Schlude v. Commissioner*, reprinted in the materials, the Supreme Court held that accrual method taxpayers were required to include advance payments in income as well as payments that had not yet been received or earned but nonetheless were due. Consider, as you read *Schlude*, the basis on which the Court held for the Commissioner. Was the claim of right doctrine applied? What has emerged from *Schlude* and its progeny is the so-called "earliest of" test, which provides that "all the events that fix the right to receive income occur when (1) the payment is earned through performance, (2) payment is due the taxpayer, or (3) payment is received by the taxpayer, whichever happens earliest." Rev. Proc. 2004-34 (included in the materials).

Although *Schlude* might have appeared to slam the door on taxpayer efforts to defer the inclusion of prepayments in income, a few resourceful taxpayers and courts have occasionally found that a modest opening remains. *Artnell Co. v.*

Commissioner, 400 F.2d 981 (7th Cir. 1968), provides an excellent example. In *Artnell*, the taxpayer purchased all of the stock in Chicago White Sox, Inc. and immediately liquidated that corporation. At the time of the liquidation, the corporate balance sheets showed as "unearned income" proceeds from advance ticket sales for baseball games and revenues for related services such as season parking, broadcasting rights, etc. In filing an income tax return for Chicago White Sox, Inc. for the tax year ending with the date of the liquidation of the corporation, Artnell Co. did not include the deferred unearned income as gross income. Artnell argued that, since this income related to future scheduled games to be played by the White Sox, those revenues were reportable in the year the games were played and not in the year the revenues were received. The Commissioner, in refusing to allow this deferral of income, relied on the *Schlude* line of cases. The Seventh Circuit, however, noted the time and the extent of the performance of future services was uncertain in those cases. In *Artnell*, by contrast, the deferred income was allocable to White Sox games which were played on a fixed schedule. According to the Seventh Circuit, in cases such as *Artnell*, where the time and extent of performance are certain and where income can be properly allocated to performance, deferral of income until the year of performance will be found to reflect income clearly. Subsequently, the Tax Court, in *Tampa Bay Devil Rays, Ltd. v. Commissioner*, T.C. Memo. 2002-248 (2002), a case almost identical to *Artnell*, relied on *Artnell* in allowing the accrual taxpayer to defer prepaid income. *See also Boise Cascade Corp. v. United States*, 530 F.2d 1367 (Ct. Cl. 1976) (deferring until the following year prepaid income where services were to be performed at fixed dates or as expeditiously as possible); *Morgan Guaranty Trust Co. of New York v. United States*, 585 F.2d 988 (Ct. Cl. 1978) (deferring until the following tax year *de minimis* amounts of prepaid interest). Nonetheless, such cases are exceptions; the "earliest of" test of *Schlude* is the rule and it has been applied in numerous cases to hold prepaid income includable on receipt.

The most significant relief from the "earliest of" test has been provided by the Service, initially in Revenue Procedure 71-21, 1971-2 C.B. 549, and subsequently in Revenue Procedure 2004-34, which modified and superceded Revenue Procedure 71-21 and is included in the materials. Consider this common situation: An accrual method taxpayer provides services to a variety of clients, often over a period of many months. To assure payment, the taxpayer requires that all or a substantial portion of the total charges be paid before commencement of the services. Under the "earliest of" text, it is clear that the entire advance payment would be includible upon receipt. Revenue Procedure 2004-34, however, modifies the "earliest of" test and authorizes a one-year deferral for advance payments covered by its terms, except to the extent the taxpayer has included the advance payment in its revenues for financial accounting purposes — that is, by recognizing the payment in its "applicable financial statement."[1] To the extent of its inclusion in the taxpayer's

---

[1] An applicable financial statement is (1) a financial statement required to be filed with the Securities and Exchange Commission (SEC); (2) a certified audited financial statement by an independent CPA that is used for a "substantial non-tax purpose"; or (3) a financial statement, other than a tax return, required to be provided to the federal or state government or to a federal or state agency other than the SEC or IRS. See Rev. Proc. 2004-34, § 4.06, which also establishes a priority rule in the event there is more than one applicable financial statement.

applicable financial statement, the advance payment must be included in income in the year of receipt. If the taxpayer has no applicable financial statement, then the advance payment must be included in income to the extent earned.

The revenue procedure applies to prepayments for services and for other specified items.[2] Prepayments for rent or interest, and certain other prepayments, are explicitly excluded from the scope of the procedure.[3] In general terms, Revenue Procedure 2004-34 gives an option to the taxpayer receiving a covered advance payment: (1) include the full amount of the advance payment in income in the year of receipt (the "Full Inclusion Method"); or (2) include the advance payment in income in the year of receipt "to the extent recognized in revenues in its applicable financial statement," or if the taxpayer has no applicable financial statement, "to the extent earned" in that year (the "Deferral Method"). Any portion of the advance payment not included in income in the year of receipt must be included in income in the next tax year.

Thus, to draw upon an example given in Revenue Procedure 2004-34, assume the taxpayer receives an advance payment for services under a 24-month contract that extends from November, Year 1, through October, Year 3. Further assume that the taxpayer provides 1/12 of the services in Year 1, 6/12 of the services in Year 2, and 5/12 of the services in Year 3, and that the taxpayer recognizes the advance payment in those same proportions in its applicable financial statements for those years. Under the Full Inclusion Method, the taxpayer would include the entire advance payment in income in Year 1, the year of receipt. Under the Deferral Method (which the taxpayer is permitted to use at its option), the taxpayer would recognize 1/12 of the advance payment in income in Year 1, since that is the amount included in revenues in its applicable financial statement. (If the taxpayer had no applicable financial statement, then the taxpayer would include 1/12 of the payment in income in Year 1, since that is the amount earned in Year 1.) However, under the Deferral Method the remaining 11/12 of the advance payment must be included in income in Year 2, even though a lesser amount was both reflected in Year 2's applicable financial statement and earned in Year 2, because the deferral of an advance payment is not permitted to extend beyond the tax year following the year of receipt.

Schlude involved prepaid service income, but its principles have been applied to prepayments for goods. In *Hagen Advertising Displays, Inc. v. Commissioner*, 407 F.2d 1105 (6th Cir. 1969), unconditional advance payments for goods, received prior to delivery, were held includable in income on receipt, on the authority of the *Schlude* line of cases. As in the services area, however, the government has since provided some relief from the rule. The regulations at § 1.451-5 permit the deferral of those advance payments for goods that meet the requirements therein detailed. Is there a one-year limit on the deferral? Some legislative relief from the prepayment rule has also been extended. *See* §§ 455 (prepaid subscriptions), 456 (prepaid dues).

---

[2] Rev. Proc. 2004-34, § 4.01(3), lists the covered payments.

[3] Rev. Proc. 2004-34, § 4.02, lists the exclusions.

Two final points on prepayments. First, as discussed in Chapter 3, deposits do not constitute income; advance rentals are income on receipt regardless of the taxpayer's accounting method. Reg. § 1.61-8(b). An issue raised in Chapter 3 thus reappears here — the need to distinguish between a deposit and a prepayment. The more restricted the taxpayer's use of the funds received, the more likely they are to be in the nature of a deposit. Reconsider the security deposit cases. Are they consistent with *Schlude* and the "earliest of" test?

Finally, consider whether the "earliest of" test represents appropriate sound tax policy. Should the rules for financial accounting and tax accounting be different? Are the administrative exceptions to the prepayment rule sufficient to address the problems associated with the disparity between tax accounting and financial accounting? Section 452, enacted in 1954 and repealed retroactively in 1955, permitted prepaid income to be prorated, as earned, for up to five years following receipt. Is such a method preferable to the result in *Schlude*? Should an accrual method taxpayer be able to mitigate the impact of *Schlude* and the "earliest of" test by taking a current deduction for expenses to be incurred in the future and allocable to the includable prepaid income?

C. Deductions Under the Accrual Method

1. General Rules

As previously noted, under the accrual method an expense is deductible for the tax year in which "all the events have occurred which determine the fact of liability, the amount of the liability can be determined with reasonable accuracy, and economic performance has occurred with respect to the liability." Reg. §§ 1.461-1(a)(2); 1.446-1(c)(1)(ii). By contrast to the cash method under which payment of an expense is required for deductibility, deductions under the accrual method focus on establishing or "fixing" the "fact" of liability, determining its amount with reasonable accuracy, and establishing when economic performance has occurred. Thus, if Lawyer provides $1,000 worth of deductible legal services to Client, payment of the legal fee to Lawyer is not the critical event for deduction purposes. Rather, the completion of the legal work by Lawyer and the setting of the fee will determine the appropriate timing of the deduction. Under the accrual method, there tends to be a "matching" of income with the expenses incurred in producing that income; this matching concept is at the heart of accrual method accounting.

What events establish the fact of liability? It is sometimes stated that a liability must be "fixed and certain," "unconditional," or "absolute" to satisfy the all events test. A liability contingent upon the occurrence of future events is not "fixed" for tax purposes. Most typically, perhaps, a liability accrues when the taxpayer receives performance from another, *i.e.*, when the taxpayer receives services or property, or the use of property, and his obligation to make payment is thereby established. Thus, as the Service noted in Revenue Ruling 98-39, 1998-2 C.B. 198:

> Generally, in a transaction where one taxpayer is accruing a liability to pay another taxpayer, the last event necessary to establish the fact of liability under the all events test of § 1.461-1(a)(2)(1) is the same event that fixes the right to receive income under the all events test of § 1.451-

1(a). . . . In general, the event fixing the fact of liability pursuant to an agreement for the provision of services is performance of the services. . . .

More recently, in Revenue Ruling 2007-3, included in the materials, the Service stated that "Generally . . . all the events have occurred that establish the fact of the liability when (1) the event fixing the liability, whether that be the required performace or other event, occurs, or (2) payment therefore is due, whichever happens earliest."

But not all liabilities are readily encompassed by these formulas. In *United States v. Hughes Properties*, 476 U.S. 593 (1986), the Supreme Court held that an accrual basis taxpayer, a casino operator, was entitled to deduct the amounts guaranteed for payments on "progressive" slot machines, even though the amounts had not yet been won at year's end by playing patrons. As emphasized by the Court, state regulations prohibited reduction of the jackpot without paying it out, and no evidence of tax avoidance by the taxpayer existed. The possibility that the jackpot might not be won if the casino went out of business, lost its license, or went into bankruptcy was regarded as simply a risk inherent in the accrual method which should not prevent accrual.[4] By contrast, in *United States v. General Dynamics Corporation*, 481 U.S. 239 (1987), included in the materials, the Supreme Court distinguished *Hughes Properties* and held that an accrual basis taxpayer could not deduct the reserve account it established for unpaid claims under its self-insured employee medical care plan. According to the Court, the last event necessary to fix liability was not the receipt of medical services by covered individuals, but their filing of proper claim forms. Since such filing had not occurred, no liability had yet accrued. The Tax Court applied *General Dynamics* in *Chrysler Corporation v. Commissioner*, T.C. Memo. 2000-283, in holding that the last event fixing the liability of Chrysler Corporation under its automobile warranties occurred no sooner than the filing of a claim for warranty service by a customer who purchased a Chrysler product from a Chrysler dealer or a claim for reimbursement by one of its dealers. The court rejected Chrysler's argument that its liability under the warranty was fixed upon the sale of its vehicles to its dealer.

Recently in *Giant Eagle, Inc. v Commissioner*, T.C. Memo 2014-146, the court applied *United States v. Hughes Property* and *United States v. General Dynamics Corporation* in holding that a taxpayer operating a chain of supermarkets and gas stations could not deduct the estimated costs of redeeming so-called "fuelperks!" that were unexpired and unredeemed at the end of each year at issue in the case. "During the years at issue, petitioner offered a customer loyalty program by which customers making qualifying purchases at Giant Eagle could earn 'fuelperks!' redeemable for a discount against the purchase price of gas at [the taxpayer's gas stations]." Contrary to the taxpayer's contention that its liability for the fuelperks! became fixed when customers earned them, the Service argued the taxpayer's liability for fuelperks! became fixed only when they are redeemed. The court agreed

---

[4] Section 461(h), discussed *infra*, did not apply to this case because the tax year in question preceded the effective date of § 461(h). The Treasury, however, has issued a regulation, Reg. § 1.461-4(g)(4), which provides: "If the liability of a taxpayer is to provide an award, prize, jackpot, or other similar payment to another person, economic performance occurs as payment is made to the person to which the liability is owed. . . . "

with the Service, noting that, under "the fuelperks! promotion, the redemption of fuelperks! was structured as a discount on the purchase price of gas. Consequently, the purchase of gas was necessarily a condition precedent to the redemption of fuelperks!" The taxpayer's liability for outstanding fuelperks! thus became fixed upon their redemption, not when the customer earned the fuelperks!. As a result, the taxpayer did not satisfy the first prong of the three-pronged all events test as articulated in § 461(h)(4) and Reg. § 1.461-1(a)(2).

Accrual of a liability turns on the fixing, not the payment of the liability, and therefore the financial condition of the taxpayer at the time of accrual generally will not bar a deduction. For example, the Service in one ruling allowed the full amount of interest accrued during the year to be deducted, although there was "no reasonable expectancy" that the taxpayer would pay the accrued interest in full; the ruling, however, distinguished the "doubt as to the payment" from a contingency that postpones accrual pending resolution of the contingency. Rev. Rul. 70-367, 1970-2 C.B. 37. Similarly, the Tax Court held that a deduction was proper notwithstanding doubts as to the taxpayer's ultimate ability to pay. *Cohen v. Commissioner*, 21 T.C. 855 (1954) (Acq.). By contrast, where a taxpayer during the pendency of a bankruptcy proceeding entered into an agreement with the U.S. Department of Energy and admitted to $30,000,000.00 in overcharges, the court disallowed the deduction for the Government's claim against the taxpayer on the basis that the taxpayer was unable to pay even a fraction of the amount. According to the court, to allow a deduction under the circumstances would not result in an accurate reflection of the taxpayer's income. *In re Southwestern States Marketing Corporation*, 1994 U.S. Dist. LEXIS 19786 (N.D. Tex. Dec. 6, 1994), *aff'd*, 82 F.3d 413 (5th Cir. 1996).

2. Premature Accruals

Since deductions under the accrual method require the fixing of a liability, rather than the payment of the liability, an incentive is created for accrual basis taxpayers to exploit the distinction by attempting to fix a liability as soon as possible, while postponing its actual payment as long as possible. In these circumstances, a liability to be paid tomorrow produces tax savings today. Indeed, taken to extremes, the present value of the tax deduction gained from accruing the liability can exceed the present value of the future payment, *i.e.*, the *current* tax savings obtained by the fixing of the liability can be greater than the full cost of funding the liability today, if the liability need not actually be paid for a sufficiently long period of time. In any event, it is generally in the taxpayer's financial interest to assert that a particular liability has accrued for tax purposes at the earliest possible time.

Section 446(b) places an overarching, if ill-defined, limitation on any deductions that are part of an accrual method that "does not clearly reflect income." For example, assuming liability is otherwise fixed, should a current deduction be prohibited, on clear-reflection-of-income grounds, if the taxpayer will not be required to pay the liability for a considerable period of time? In *Mooney Aircraft, Inc. v. United States*, 420 F.2d 400 (5th Cir. 1969), which the court described as "yet another case in the continuing conflict between commercial accounting practice and the federal income tax," the accrual method taxpayer, an airplane manufacturer, issued with each airplane it manufactured and sold, an unconditional $1,000

"Mooney Bond", by which it promised to pay the bearer of the bond $1,000 when the corresponding airplane was permanently retired; 20 years or more could elapse between issuance of the bond and retirement of the airplane. The court agreed with the taxpayer that, upon issuance of the bond, the fact of liability was established, but it nonetheless upheld the Commissioner's refusal to allow a deduction upon issuance:

> The most salient feature in this case is the fact that many or possibly most of the expenses which taxpayer wishes to presently deduct will not actually be paid for 15, 20 or even 30 years (the taxpayer has not attempted to deny this). In no other case coming to our attention have we found anything even comparable to the time span involved in this case.

> In this case, the related expenditure is so distant from the time the money [from the sale of the plane] is received as to completely attenuate any relationship between the two. In what sense, is it an accurate reflection of income to regard it as an expense of doing business in the current year? We therefore find no difficulty in concluding that the Commissioner had a reasonable basis for disallowing the deduction as not clearly reflecting income.

> There is yet another reason why the time span is too long. The longer the time the less probable it becomes that the liability, though incurred, will ever in fact be paid.

> In the present case the taxpayer could in good faith use the monies it has received as capital to expand its business; if one day it became insolvent the expense might never be paid, yet the money would have been used as taxfree income. We repeat that because of the inordinate length of time involved in this case the Commissioner was clearly within his discretion in disallowing deduction of the "Mooney Bonds" as a *current* expense.

Id. at 409, 410.

Prior to the enactment of § 461(h) in 1984, there was considerable dispute as to whether the all events test permitted the taxpayer to deduct the estimated expenses of future performance. In *Schuessler v. Commissioner*, 230 F.2d 722 (5th Cir. 1956), for example, an accrual method taxpayer, engaged in the gas furnace business, sought to deduct a reserve account representing his estimated cost of carrying out a guarantee, given to purchasers, to turn their new furnace on and off for each of the next five years. According to the Fifth Circuit, the sale of the furnace established a legal liability to turn the furnaces on and off for the next five years, and the cost of doing so had been reasonably estimated and was therefore currently deductible. Following *Schlude*, however, some commentators argued that *Schuessler*-type decisions were of dubious validity, on the ground that allowing the deductions of future costs could frequently achieve for taxpayers much the same result as the prohibited deferrals of prepaid income. The Internal Revenue Service, in any event, argued that the all events test was not satisfied where the taxpayer had not yet rendered required performance.[5] For example, where an accrual method taxpayer installed oil and gas platforms pursuant to a lease with the federal government, and the taxpayer was contractually obligated to remove the platforms at the end of the lease, the Service held the cost of removal was not deductible until the removal services were actually performed. Rev. Rul. 80-182, 1980-2 C.B. 167.[6] By contrast, in *Ohio River Collieries Co. v. Commissioner*, 77 T.C. 1369 (1981), the Tax Court held that an accrual basis taxpayer was entitled to deduct the reasonably estimated cost of reclaiming strip-mined land in the year it engaged in the strip-mining and, under local law, thereby incurred an obligation to reclaim the land. The Tax Court rejected the Commissioner's position that reclamation costs would be deductible only when the reclamation was performed. Taxpayer victories in *Ohio River Collieries* and other cases led to the enactment of § 461(h), and the incorporation of the Service's economic performance standard into the Code.

3.   The Economic Performance Test — Section 461(h)

As part of the Tax Reform Act of 1984, Congress specifically adopted the Service's longstanding position that, for an amount to be deductible by an accrual method taxpayer, there must be current liability to pay that amount. In other words, that the liability is fixed and the amount of the liability can be determined with reasonable accuracy are not enough to justify a current deduction; economic performance must also occur. Section 461(h)(1) specifically adds this economic performance requirement to the all events test, providing "the all events test shall not be treated as met any earlier than when economic performance with respect to such item occurs." The legislative history for § 461(h) provides the following rationale for the economic performance test:

> Congress believed that the rules relating to the time of a deduction by a taxpayer using the accrual method of accounting should be changed to take into account the time value of money and the time the deduction is economically incurred. Recent court decisions in some cases permitted accrual method taxpayers to deduct currently expenses that were not yet economically incurred (*i.e.*, that were attributable to activities to be performed or amounts to be paid in the future). Allowing a taxpayer to take deductions currently for an amount to be paid in the future overstates the true cost of the expense to the extent that the time value of money is not taken into account; the deduction is overstated by the amount by which the face value exceeds the present value of the expenses. The longer the period of time involved, the greater is the overstatement.

General Explanation to the Tax Reform Act of 1984 prepared by the Staff of the Joint Committee on Taxation, p. 260.

Section 461(h)(2) establishes the following rules for determining when economic performance occurs:

---

[5] Section 461(h), discussed *infra*, adopts the economic performance requirement urged by the Service.

[6] Reg. § 1.461-4(d)(7) Example 1 addresses the same factual scenario presented in Revenue Ruling 80-182 and reaches the same conclusion on the authority of § 461(h).

(a) If the liability arises as a result of another person providing services to the taxpayer, economic performance occurs as the services are provided. § 461(h)(2)(A)((i). Thus, returning to the example on page 710 involving Lawyer's provision of deductible legal services to Client, economic performance occurred when Lawyer provided the legal services.

(b) If the liability results from the taxpayer's use of property, economic performance occurs "ratably over the period of time the taxpayer is entitled to the use of the property." § 461(h)(2)(A)(iii) and Reg. § 1.461-4(d)(3). For example, when an owner of equipment rents the equipment to a taxpayer, economic performance occurs each day the taxpayer uses or is entitled to use the equipment.

(c) If the liability results from the taxpayer providing services or property, economic performance occurs as the taxpayer provides the service or the property. § 461(h)(2)(B). For example, in *Ohio River Collieries*, discussed above, economic performance would occur as the strip-mined land was reclaimed.

Section 461(h)(2)(C), regarding workers compensation and tort liabilities, specifies that economic performance occurs when payment is made.

For recurring items, § 461(h)(3) provides a special exception under which a deduction is available even though economic performance has yet to occur. Note the four statutory requirements which must be satisfied for this exception to apply. See Regulation § 1.461-5(e) for examples of the application of the recurring items exception.

4. Capitalization

If an accrued liability creates an asset with a useful life extending substantially beyond the taxable year, the liability must be capitalized. Reg. § 1.461-1(a)(2). Deductions under the accrual method, as under the cash method, are subject to § 263.

As noted in prior chapters, in an effort to simplify administration of the capitalization requirement both for the Service and for the taxpayer, the Treasury issued regulations under § 263 which provide a "12-month rule" stating "a taxpayer is not required to capitalize amounts paid to create . . . any right or benefit for the taxpayer that does not extend beyond the earlier of (i) 12 months after the first date on which the taxpayer realizes the right or benefit; or (ii) the end of the taxable year following the taxable year in which the payment is made." Reg. § 1.263(a)-4(f)(1). This "12-month rule" represents an exception to the general rule specified in the regulations requiring the capitalization of prepaid expenses. Reg. § 1.263(a)-4(d)(3)(i).

If an accrual method taxpayer satisfies the "12-month rule," will the taxpayer be allowed a deduction if the economic performance requirement of § 461(h) has not been satisfied? The answer is "No." Regulation § 1.263(a)-4(f)(6) specifically provides the "12-month rule" will not affect "the determination of whether a liability is incurred during the taxable year, including the determination of whether economic performance has occurred with respect to the liability." For example, if, on

December 15, an accrual method taxpayer prepays rent for January through June of the following year, assuming the recurring item exception is inapplicable, no deduction would be available to the taxpayer because economic performance has not occurred, i.e., with regard to rent, economic performance occurs only as the taxpayer/renter is allowed to use the property. Reg. § 1.461-4(d)(3). The fact the payment might otherwise come within the "12-month rule" does not change this result. *See* Reg. § 1.263(a)-4(f)(8) Exs. 10 & 11.

5.   Contested Liabilities

In general, a contested liability cannot be deducted by an accrual method taxpayer because the contest, in effect, renders the liability contingent and prevents it from being "fixed" or "established." In *Dixie Pine Products Co. v. Commissioner*, 320 U.S. 516 (1944), the Supreme Court held that a taxpayer could not accrue a tax while contesting liability, and the Court suggested the proper date for accrual was when the liability was finally adjudicated. In *United States v. Consolidated Edison*, 366 U.S. 380 (1961), the Court extended the *Dixie Pine* rule to deny accrual of a contested tax that was actually paid; accrual instead was to wait until the contest was finally determined. Section 461(f) overturns the *Consolidated Edison* decision and provides, in general, that payment of a contested liability accrues the liability and provides a current deduction in the year of payment. To come within the provision, the taxpayer must contest a liability, transfer money or other property in satisfaction thereof, continue the contest after the transfer, and be entitled to a deduction but for the contest. If a contested liability is not paid, it will not accrue until the contest is resolved. It is not necessary to institute litigation to have a contest, but the regulations do require a bona fide dispute. Reg. § 1.461-2(b)(2). A contest is settled when the parties reach agreement or the matter is finally adjudicated. Reg. § 1.461-2(d).

As noted above, accrual during a contest requires the taxpayer to transfer money or other property in satisfaction of the liability. The regulation specifically requires the taxpayer to place the money or property beyond his control by transferring it to the person asserting the liability, to a court or public agency, or to a trustee or escrowee pursuant to written agreement between the taxpayer and the person asserting the liability, requiring delivery in accord with the outcome of the contest. Reg. § 1.461-2(c). For example, a unilateral transfer to a bank as trustee has been held not to qualify. *Poirier & McLane Corp. v. Commissioner*, 547 F.2d 161 (2d Cir. 1976); *Rosenthal v. United States*, 11 Cl. Ct. 165 (1986). In *Willamette Industries v. Commissioner*, 92 T.C. 1116 (1989), the court held that the transfer requirement of § 461(f)(2) was not satisfied by funding a settlement trust with a $20,000,000 letter of credit purchased from a bank for $85,000. The taxpayer was required to repay the bank for draws made on the letter of credit. Upon entry of final judgment against the taxpayer, the trust agreement directed the trustee to draw on the letter of credit for purposes of paying the plaintiffs. In rejecting the taxpayer's effort to deduct the $20,000,000 in the year when the trust was funded, the Tax Court concluded the taxpayer had merely "exchanged a contingent liability to the plaintiff for a contingent liability to the bank." *Id.* at 1182. This arrangement was a "type of legerdemain" that failed to satisfy the payment requirement of § 461(f)(2). Likewise, in *Trinity Industries, Inc. v. Commissioner*, 132 T.C. 6 (2009), the court held that the § 461(f) transfer requirement was not met where taxpayer's customers withheld certain amounts they owed taxpayer. As the court noted, to transfer money or property beyond its control, the taxpayer first had to have the money or property within its control.

Section 461(f) is applicable to cash method taxpayers as well as accrual method taxpayers, but its utility is essentially for the latter, since a cash method taxpayer may ordinarily deduct a liability upon payment even if the liability is contested.

D.   Choice of Accounting Methods

Section 446(c) provides a taxpayer generally has the right to select the cash or accrual method, any other permitted method, or any permitted combination of methods. As a practical matter, however, most businesses of substantial size select the accrual method. A taxpayer engaged in more than one business may select a different accounting method for each business. § 446(d). A taxpayer may use one method for a business and another method for personal purposes. Reg. § 1.446-1(c)(1)(iv)(b).

This freedom-of-choice is subject, however, to several general and specific limitations. The method of accounting chosen must be the one the taxpayer uses to compute income in keeping books. § 446(a). A taxpayer who keeps no books or records will be deemed to have selected the cash method. As discussed *supra*, the accounting method chosen is also subject to the overarching requirement of § 446(b) that it clearly reflect the taxpayer's income. Thus, for example, the regulations provide that, as a permitted combination of methods, a taxpayer may account for purchases and sales on the accrual method, and other items of income and expense on the cash method. But the same regulations also provide that a taxpayer using the cash method for gross income purposes must also use it for expenses, and use of the accrual method for business expenses requires use of the accrual method for gross income. Reg. § 1.446-1(c)(1)(iv)(a). The taxpayer's method must also provide consistent treatment of income and deduction items from year to year. Reg. § 1.446-1(c)(2)(ii). In addition, once an accounting method is employed, it may not be changed without the Commissioner's consent. § 446(e). Whether a change that is made constitutes a change in "the method of accounting" is often the threshold question. The Commissioner's consent to a change is typically conditioned on the taxpayer's agreeing to specified terms and adjustments.

Some specific limitations are applicable to certain taxpayers and activities. Section 448 prohibits use of the cash method by certain corporations and partnerships and by tax shelters. § 448(a), (b). In addition, the regulations provide that, in any case in which it is necessary to use an inventory, the accrual method is required with respect to purchases and sales. Reg. § 1.446-1(c)(2)(i). Inventories are necessary if the production, purchase or sale of merchandise is an income-producing factor. Reg. § 1.471-1.[7] Inventory accounting, and use of the accrual

---

[7] The Tax Court has held "where the inherent nature of the taxpayer's business is that of a service provider, and the taxpayer uses the materials that are an indispensable and inseparable part of the rendering of its services, the materials are not 'merchandise' . . . . " *RACMP Enterprises, Inc. v. Commissioner*, 114 T.C. 211, 222 (2000). Thus, where taxpayer used drugs and ancillary pharmaceuticals

method for purchases and sales, are thus required for many business operations. (In inventory accounting, gross profit or loss from sales in a given period is determined by subtracting the cost of goods sold from the gross sales proceeds. The cost of goods sold is, in turn, determined by adding together the cost of the opening inventory on hand at the commencement of the period and the cost of goods purchased during the period, and by then subtracting from that total the cost of the closing inventory on hand at the end of the period. For additional detail, see the Note on Inventory Accounting following this chapter.) Finally, a number of Code provisions mandate special treatment for certain income and expense items in given circumstances (see § 467 for an example).

SCHLUDE v. COMMISSIONER
United States Supreme Court
372 U.S. 128 (1963)

MR. JUSTICE WHITE delivered the opinion of the Court.

This is still another chapter in the protracted problem of the time certain items are to be recognized as income for the purposes of the federal income tax. The Commissioner of Internal Revenue increased in 1952, 1953 and 1954 ordinary income of the taxpayers by including in gross income for those years amounts received or receivable under contracts executed during those years despite the fact that the contracts obligated taxpayers to render performance in subsequent periods. These increases produced tax deficiencies which the taxpayers unsuccessfully challenged in the Tax Court on the ground that the amounts could be deferred under their accounting method. On appeal, the Court of Appeals for the Eighth Circuit agreed with the taxpayers and reversed the Tax Court, 283 F.2d 234, the decision having been rendered prior to ours in *American Automobile Assn. v. United States*, 367 U.S. 687. Following the *American Automobile Association* case, certiorari in this case was granted, the judgment of the lower court vacated, 367 U.S. 911, and the cause remanded for further consideration in light of *American Automobile Association*. 368 U.S. 873. In a *per curiam* opinion, the Court of Appeals held that in view of *American Automobile Association*, the taxpayers' accounting method "does not, for income tax purposes, clearly reflect income" and affirmed the judgment for the Commissioner, 296 F.2d 721. We brought the case back once again to consider whether the lower court misapprehended the scope of *American Automobile Association*. 370 U.S. 902.

Taxpayers, husband and wife, formed a partnership to operate ballroom dancing

---

as part of providing chemotherapy treatment to its patients, the drugs and ancillary pharmaceuticals were held not to be "merchandise," and taxpayer was permitted to use the cash method to expense its cost of the drugs. *Osteopathic Medial Oncology and Hematology, P.C. v. Commissioner*, 113 T.C. 376 (1999) (acq). Similarly, in *RACMP Enterprises*, a construction contractor who contracted to provide concrete foundations, driveways and walkways for real property developers, was held to be inherently a service provider using materials (liquid concrete, fill sand, etc.) that were an indispensable and inseparable part of its provision of services; the contractor was accordingly not required to use inventory accounting.

studios (collectively referred to as "studio") pursuant to Arthur Murray, Inc., franchise agreements. Dancing lessons were offered under either of two basic contracts. The cash plan contract required the student to pay the entire down payment in cash at the time the contract was executed with the balance due in installments thereafter. The deferred payment contract required only a portion of the down payment to be paid in cash. The remainder of the down payment was due in stated installments and the balance of the contract price was to be paid as designated in a negotiable note signed at the time the contract was executed.

Both types of contracts provided that (1) the student should pay tuition for lessons in a certain amount, (2) the student should not be relieved of his obligation to pay the tuition, (3) no refunds would be made, and (4) the contract was noncancelable.[8] The contracts prescribed a specific number of lesson hours ranging from five to 1,200 hours and some contracts provided lifetime courses entitling the student additionally to two hours of lessons per month plus two parties a year for life. Although the contracts designated the period during which the lessons had to be taken, there was no schedule of specific dates, which were arranged from time to time as lessons were given.

Cash payments received directly from students and amounts received when the negotiable notes were discounted at the bank or fully paid were deposited in the studio's general bank account without segregation from its other funds. The franchise agreements required the studio to pay to Arthur Murray, Inc., on a weekly basis, 10% of these cash receipts as royalty and 5% of the receipts in escrow, the latter to continue until a $20,000 indemnity fund was accumulated. Similarly, sales commissions for lessons sold were paid at the time the sales receipts were deposited in the studio's general bank account.

The studio, since its inception in 1946, has kept its books and reported income for tax purposes on an accrual system of accounting. In addition to the books, individual student record cards were maintained showing the number of hours taught and the number still remaining under the contract. The system, in substance, operated as follows. When a contract was entered into, a "deferred income" account was credited for the total contract price. At the close of each fiscal period, the student record cards were analyzed and the total number of taught hours was multiplied by the designated rate per hour of each contract. The resulting sum was deducted from the deferred income account and reported as earned income on the financial statements and the income tax return. In addition, if there had been no activity in a contract for over a year, or if a course were reduced in amount, an entry would be made canceling the untaught portion of the contract, removing that amount from the deferred income account, and recognizing gain to the extent that the deferred income exceeded the balance due on the contract, *i.e.*, the amounts received in advance. The amounts representing lessons taught and the gains from cancellations constituted the chief sources of the partnership's gross income. The balance of the deferred income account would be carried forward into the next fiscal year to be

---

[8] Although the contracts stated they were noncancelable, the studio frequently rewrote contracts reducing the number of lessons for a smaller sum of money. Also, despite the fact that the contracts provided that no refunds would be made, and despite the fact that the studio discouraged refunds, occasionally a refund would be made on a canceled contract.

increased or decreased in accordance with the number of new contracts, lessons taught and cancellations recognized.

Deductions were also reported on the accrual basis except that the royalty payments and the sales commissions were deducted when paid irrespective of the period in which the related receipts were taken into income. Three certified public accountants testified that in their opinion the accounting system employed truly reflected net income in accordance with commercial accrual accounting standards.

The Commissioner included in gross income for the years in question not only advance payments received in cash but the full face amounts of notes and contracts executed during the respective years. The Tax Court and the Court of Appeals upheld the Commissioner, but the United States in this Court has retreated somewhat and does not now claim the includability in gross income of future payments which were not evidenced by a note and which were neither due by the terms of the contract nor matured by performance of the related services. The question remaining for decision, then, is this: Was it proper for the Commissioner, exercising his discretion under § 41, 1939 Code, and § 446(b), 1954 Code, to reject the studio's accounting system as not clearly reflecting income and to include as income in a particular year advance payments by way of cash, negotiable notes and contract installments falling due but remaining unpaid during that year? We hold that it was since we believe the problem is squarely controlled by *American Automobile Association*, 367 U.S. 687.

The Court there had occasion to consider the entire legislative background of the treatment of prepaid income. The retroactive repeal of § 452 of the 1954 Code, "the only law incontestably permitting the practice upon which [the taxpayer] depends," was regarded as reinstating long-standing administrative and lower court rulings that accounting systems deferring prepaid income could be rejected by the Commissioner.

> [T]he fact is that § 452 for the first time specifically declared petitioner's system of accounting to be acceptable for income tax purposes, and overruled the long-standing position of the Commissioner and courts to the contrary. And the repeal of the section the following year, upon insistence by the Treasury that the proposed endorsement of such tax accounting would have a disastrous impact on the Government's revenue, was just as clearly a mandate from the Congress that petitioner's system was not acceptable for tax purposes. 367 U.S. at 695.

Confirming that view was the step-by-step approach of Congress in granting the deferral privilege to only limited groups of taxpayers while exploring more deeply the ramifications of the entire problem.

Plainly, the considerations expressed in *American Automobile Association* are apposite here. We need only add here that since the *American Automobile Association* decision, a specific provision extending the deferral practice to certain membership corporations was enacted, § 456, 1954 Code, added by § 1, Act of July 26, 1961, 74 Stat. 222, continuing, at least so far, the congressional policy of treating this problem by precise provisions of narrow applicability. Consequently, as in the *American Automobile Association* case, we invoke the "long-established policy of the Court in deferring, where possible, to congressional procedures in the tax field," and, as in that case, we cannot say that the Commissioner's rejection of the studio's deferral system was unsound.

The *American Automobile Association* case rested upon an additional ground which is also controlling here. Relying upon *Automobile Club of Michigan v. Commissioner*, 353 U.S. 180, the Court rejected the taxpayer's system as artificial since the advance payments related to services which were to be performed only upon customers' demands without relation to fixed dates in the future. The system employed here suffers from that very same vice, for the studio sought to defer its cash receipts on the basis of contracts which did not provide for lessons on fixed dates after the taxable year, but left such dates to be arranged from time to time by the instructor and his student. Under the contracts, the student could arrange for some or all of the additional lessons or could simply allow their rights under the contracts to lapse. But even though the student did not demand the remaining lessons, the contracts permitted the studio to insist upon payment in accordance with the obligations undertaken and to retain whatever prepayments were made without restriction as to use and without obligation of refund. At the end of each period, while the number of lessons taught had been meticulously reflected, the studio was uncertain whether none, some or all of the remaining lessons would be rendered. Clearly, services were rendered solely on demand in the fashion of the *American Automobile Association* and *Automobile Club of Michigan* cases.

Moreover, percentage royalties and sales commissions for lessons sold, which were paid as cash was received from students or from its note transactions with the bank, were deducted in the year paid even though the related items of income had been deferred, at least in part, to later periods. In view of all these circumstances, we hold the studio's accrual system vulnerable under § 41 and § 446(b) with respect to its deferral of prepaid income. Consequently, the Commissioner was fully justified in including payments in cash or by negotiable note[9] in gross income for the year in which such payments were received. If these payments are includable in the year of receipt because their allocation to a later year does not clearly reflect income, the contract installments are likewise includable in gross income, as the United States now claims, in the year they become due and payable. For an accrual basis taxpayer "it is the *right* to receive and not the actual receipt that determines the inclusion of the amount in gross income," *Spring City Co. v. Commissioner*, 292 U.S. 182, 184; *Commissioner v. Hansen*, 360 U.S. 446, and here the right to receive these installments had become fixed at least at the time they were due and payable.

We affirm the Court of Appeals insofar as that court held includable the amounts representing cash receipts, notes received and contract installments due and payable. Because of the Commissioner's concession, we reverse that part of the judgment which included amounts for which services had not yet been performed and which were not due and payable during the respective periods and we remand the case with directions to return the case to the Tax Court for a redetermination

---

[9] Negotiable notes are regarded as the equivalent of cash receipts, to the extent of their fair market value, for the purposes of recognition of income. § 39.22(a)-4, Treas. Reg. 118, 1939 Code; § 1.61-2(d)(4), Treas. Reg., 1954 Code; Mertens, *Federal Income Taxation* (1961), § 11.07. See *Pinellas Ice Co. v. Commissioner*, 287 U.S. 462.

of the proper income tax deficiencies now due in light of this opinion.

It is so ordered.

Mr. Justice Stewart, with whom Mr. Justice Douglas, Mr. Justice Harlan, and Mr. Justice Goldberg join, dissenting.

REVENUE PROCEDURE 2004-34
2004-1 C.B. 991

SECTION 1. PURPOSE

This revenue procedure allows taxpayers a limited deferral beyond the taxable year of receipt for certain advance payments. Qualifying taxpayers may defer to the next succeeding taxable year the inclusion in gross income for federal income tax purposes of advance payments (as defined in section 4 of this revenue procedure) to the extent the advance payments are not recognized in revenues (or, in certain cases, are not earned) in the taxable year of receipt. Except as [otherwise] provided . . . for certain short taxable years, this revenue procedure does not permit deferral to a taxable year later than the next succeeding taxable year. . . .

SECTION 2. BACKGROUND AND CHANGES

.01 In general, section 451 of the Internal Revenue Code provides that the amount of any item of gross income is included in gross income for the taxable year in which received by the taxpayer, unless, under the method of accounting used in computing taxable income, the amount is to be properly accounted for as of a different period. Section 1.451-1(a) provides that, under an accrual method of accounting, income is includible in gross income when all the events have occurred that fix the right to receive the income and the amount can be determined with reasonable accuracy. All the events that fix the right to receive the income generally occur when (1) the payment is earned through performance, (2) payment is due to the taxpayer, or (3) payment is received by the taxpayer, whichever happens earliest. *See* Rev. Rul. 84-31, 1984-1 C.B. 127. . . .

.03 Rev. Proc. 71-21, 1971-2 C.B. 549, was published to implement an administrative decision of the Commissioner in the exercise of his discretion under section 446 to allow accrual method taxpayers in certain specified and limited circumstances to defer the inclusion in gross income for federal income tax purposes of payments received (or amounts due and payable) in one taxable year for services to be performed by the end of the next succeeding taxable year. Rev. Proc. 71-21 was designed to reconcile the federal income tax and financial accounting treatment of payments received for services to be performed by the end of the next succeeding taxable year without permitting extended deferral of the inclusion of those payments in gross income for federal income tax purposes.

.04 . . . [T]he Service has determined that it is appropriate to expand the scope of Rev. Proc. 71-21 to include advance payments for certain non-services and combinations of services and non-services. Additionally, the Service has determined that it is appropriate to expand the scope of Rev. Proc. 71-21 to include advance payments received in connection with an agreement or series of agreements with a term or terms extending beyond the end of the next succeeding taxable year. The Service has determined, however, that for taxpayers deferring recognition of income under this revenue procedure it is appropriate to retain the limited one-year deferral of Rev. Proc. 71-21. . . .

. . . .

SECTION 4. DEFINITIONS

The following definitions apply solely for purposes of this revenue procedure —

.01 Advance Payment. Except as provided in section 4.02 of this revenue procedure, a payment received by a taxpayer is an "advance payment" if — (1) including the payment in gross income for the taxable year of receipt is a permissible method of accounting for federal income tax purposes (without regard to this revenue procedure); (2) the payment is recognized by the taxpayer (in whole or in part) in revenues in its applicable financial statement . . . for a subsequent taxable year (or, for taxpayers without an applicable financial statement . . . , the payment is earned by the taxpayer (in whole or in part) in a subsequent taxable year; and (3) the payment is for . . . services [or for specified other purposes]. . . .[10]

.02 Exclusions From Advance Payment. The term "advance payment" does not include: . . . rent; [or] payments with respect to financial instruments . . . , including purported prepayments of interest; [or other listed exclusions].[11] . . .

.04 Received. Income is "received" by the taxpayer if it is actually or constructively received, or if it is due and payable to the taxpayer.

.05 Next Succeeding Taxable Year. The term "next succeeding taxable year" means the taxable year immediately following the taxable year in which the advance payment is received by the taxpayer.

.06 Applicable Financial Statement. The taxpayer's applicable financial statement is the taxpayer's financial statement listed in paragraphs (1) through (3) . . . that has the highest priority (including within paragraph (2)). A taxpayer that does not have a financial statement described in paragraphs (1) through (3) . . . does not have an applicable financial statement for purposes of this revenue procedure. The financial statements are, in descending priority—

(1)   a financial statement required to be filed with the Securities and Exchange Commission ("SEC") (the 10-K or the Annual Statement to Shareholders);

---

[10] [Authors' Note: The revenue procedure also lists payments for the following purposes: the sale of goods, other than those deferred under section 1.451-5(b)(1)(ii); the use of intellectual property; the occupancy or use of property if that occupancy or use is ancillary to the provision of services; the sale, lease or license of computer software; certain guaranty or warranty contracts; subscriptions; memberships in an organization; or any combination of the foregoing items, including services.]

[11] [Authors' Note: Other listed exclusions include payments for certain insurance premiums; service warranty contracts; third party warranty and guaranty contracts; payments subject to sections 871(a), 881, 1441, or 1442: and payments in property to which section 83 applies.]

(2)   a certified audited financial statement that is accompanied by the report of an independent CPA . . . that is used for — (a) credit purposes, (b) reporting to shareholders, or (c) any other substantial non-tax purpose; or

(3)   a financial statement (other than a tax return) required to be provided to the federal or a state government or any federal or state agencies (other than the SEC or the Internal Revenue Service).

SECTION 5. PERMISSIBLE METHODS OF ACCOUNTING FOR ADVANCE PAYMENTS

.01 Full Inclusion Method. A taxpayer within the scope of this revenue procedure that includes the full amount of advance payments in gross income for federal income tax purposes in the taxable year of receipt is using a proper method of accounting under section 1.451-1, regardless of whether the taxpayer recognizes the full amount of advance payments in revenues for that taxable year for financial reporting purposes and regardless of whether the taxpayer earns the full amount of advance payments in that taxable year.

.02 Deferral Method.

(1)   In general.

    (a)   A taxpayer within the scope of this revenue procedure that chooses to use the Deferral Method . . . is using a proper method of accounting under section 1.451-1. Under the Deferral Method, for federal income tax purposes the taxpayer must — (i) include the advance payment in gross income for the taxable year of receipt, to the extent provided [in (3) below], and (ii) . . . include the remaining amount of the advance payment in gross income for the next succeeding taxable year. . . .

(3)   Inclusion of advance payments in gross income.

    (a)   Except as provided in paragraph (b) of this section 5.02(3), a taxpayer using the Deferral Method must — (i) include the advance payment in gross income for the taxable year of receipt . . . to the extent recognized in revenues in its applicable financial statement . . . for that taxable year, and (ii) include the remaining amount of the advance payment in gross income in [the next succeeding taxable year].

    (b)   If the taxpayer does not have an applicable financial statement . . . or if the taxpayer is unable to determine . . . the extent to which advance payments are recognized in revenues in its applicable financial statements . . . , a taxpayer using the Deferral Method must include the advance payment in gross income for the taxable year of receipt . . . to the extent earned in that taxable year and include the remaining amount of the advance payment in gross income in [the next succeeding taxable year].[12]

---

[12] [Authors' note: The revenue procedure indicates that the determination of an amount earned is made without regard to whether the taxpayer may be required to refund the advance payment on the occurrence of a condition subsequent. It also provides that where a taxpayer is unable to determine the extent to which a payment has been earned, as may be the case with a payment for contingent goods or

.03 Examples. In each example below, the taxpayer uses an accrual method of accounting for federal income tax purposes and files its return on a calendar year basis. Except as stated otherwise, the taxpayer in each example has an applicable financial statement as defined in section 4.06 of this revenue procedure.

Example 1. On November 1, 2004, A, in the business of giving dancing lessons, receives an advance payment for a 1-year contract commencing on that date and providing for up to 48 individual, 1-hour lessons. A provides 8 lessons in 2004 and another 35 lessons in 2005. In its applicable financial statement, A recognizes 1/6 of the payment in revenues for 2004, and 5/6 of the payment in revenues for 2005. A uses the Deferral Method. For federal income tax purposes, A must include 1/6 of the payment in gross income for 2004, and the remaining 5/6 of the payment in gross income for 2005.

Example 2. Assume the same facts as in Example 1, except that the advance payment is received for a 2-year contract under which up to 96 lessons are provided. A provides eight lessons in 2004, 48 lessons in 2005, and 40 lessons in 2006. In its applicable financial statement, A recognizes 1/12 of the payment in revenues for 2004, 6/12 of the payment in revenues for 2005, and 5/12 of the payment in gross income for 2006. For federal income tax purposes, A must include 1/12 of the payment in gross income for 2004, and the remaining 11/12 of the payment in gross income for 2005.

Example 3. On June 1, 2004, B, a landscape architecture firm, receives an advance payment for goods and services that, under the terms of the agreement, must be provided by December 2005. On December 31, 2004, B estimates that ¾ of the work under the agreement has been completed. In its applicable financial statement, B recognizes ¾ of the payment in revenues for 2004 and ¼ of the payment in revenues for 2005. B uses the Deferral Method. For federal income tax purposes, B must include ¾ of the payment in gross income for 2004, and the remaining ¼ of the payment in gross income for 2005, regardless of whether B completes the job in 2005.

Example 4. On July 1, 2004, C, in the business of selling and repairing television sets, receives an advance payment for a 2-year contract under which C agrees to repair or replace, or authorizes a representative to repair or replace, certain parts in the customer's television set if those parts fail to function properly. In its applicable financial statement, C recognizes ¼ of the payment in revenues for 2004, ½ of the payment in revenues for 2005, and ¼ of the payment in revenues for 2006. C uses the Deferral Method. For federal income tax purposes, C must include ¼ of the payment in gross income for 2004 and the remaining ¾ of the payment in gross income for 2005.

---

services, the taxpayer may determine the amount earned on a statistical basis if adequate data are available, on a straight line ratable basis if it is not unreasonable to anticipate the payment will be earned ratably over the term of the agreement, or by the use of any other method that clearly reflects income.]

UNITED STATES v. GENERAL DYNAMICS
United States Supreme Court
481 U.S. 239 (1987)

JUSTICE MARSHALL delivered the opinion of the Court.

The issue in this case is whether an accrual basis taxpayer providing medical benefits to its employees may deduct at the close of the taxable year an estimate of its obligation to pay for medical care obtained by employees or their qualified dependents during the final quarter of the year, claims for which have not been reported to the employer.

I.

Beginning in October, 1972, General Dynamics became a self-insurer with regard to its medical care plans. Instead of continuing to purchase insurance from outside carriers, it undertook to pay medical claims out of its own funds, while continuing to employ private carriers to administer the medical care plans.

To receive reimbursement of expenses for covered medical services, respondent's employees submit claim forms to employee benefits personnel, who verify that the treated persons were eligible under the applicable plan as of the time of treatment. Eligible claims are then forwarded to the plan's administrators. Claims processors review the claims and approve for payment those expenses that are covered under the plan.

Because the processing of claims takes time, and because employees do not always file their claims immediately, there is a delay between the provision of medical services and payment by General Dynamics. To account for this time lag, General Dynamics established reserve accounts to reflect its liability for medical care received, but still not paid for, as of December 31, 1972. It estimated the amount of those reserves with the assistance of its former insurance carriers.

Originally, General Dynamics did not deduct any portion of this reserve in computing its tax for 1972. In 1977, however, after the IRS began an audit of its 1972 tax return, General Dynamics filed an amended return, claiming it was entitled to deduct its reserve as an accrued expense, and seeking a refund. The IRS disallowed the deduction, and General Dynamics sought relief in the Claims Court.

The Claims Court sustained the deduction, holding that it satisfied the "all events" test embodied in Treas. Reg. 1.461-1(a)(2), 26 C.F.R. § 1.461-1(a)(2) (1986), since "all events" which determined the fact of liability had taken place when the employees received covered services, and the amount of liability could be determined with reasonable accuracy. Thus, the court held that General Dynamics was entitled to a refund. 6 Cl.Ct. 250 (1984). The Court of Appeals for the Federal Circuit affirmed, largely on the basis of the Claims Court opinion. 773 F.2d 1224, 1226 (1985).

The United States sought review of the question whether all the events necessary to fix liability had occurred.[13] We granted certiorari. . . . We reverse.

II.

As we noted in *United States v. Hughes Properties, Inc.*, 476 U.S. 593, 600, 106 S. Ct. 2092, 2096, 90 L.Ed.2d 569 (1986), whether a business expense has been "incurred" so as to entitle an accrual-basis taxpayer to deduct it under § 162(a) of the Internal Revenue Code, 26 U.S.C. § 162(a), is governed by the "all events" test that originated in *United States v. Anderson*, 269 U.S. 422, 441, 46 S.Ct. 131, 134, 70 L.Ed. 347 (1926). In *Anderson*, the Court held that a taxpayer was obliged to deduct from its 1916 income a tax on profits from munitions sales that took place in 1916. Although the tax would not be assessed and therefore would not formally be due until 1917, all the events which fixed the amount of the tax and determined the taxpayer's liability to pay it had occurred in 1916. The test is now embodied in Treas. Reg. 1.461-1(a)(2), 26 C.F.R. § 1.461-1(a)(2) (1986), which provides that "[u]nder an accrual method of accounting, an expense is deductible for the taxable year in which all the events have occurred which determine the fact of the liability and the amount thereof can be determined with reasonable accuracy." *Ibid.*[14]

It is fundamental to the "all events" test that, although expenses may be deductible before they have become due and payable, liability must first be firmly established. This is consistent with our prior holdings that a taxpayer may not deduct a liability that is contingent or contested. Nor may a taxpayer deduct an estimate of an anticipated expense, no matter how statistically certain, if it is based on events that have not occurred by the close of the taxable year.

We think that this case involves a mere estimate of liability based on events that had not occurred before the close of the taxable year, and therefore the proposed deduction does not pass the "all events" test. We disagree with the legal conclusion of the courts below that the last event necessary to fix the taxpayer's liability was the receipt of medical care by covered individuals.[15] A person covered by a plan could only obtain payment for medical services by filling out and submitting a health expense benefits claim form. Employees were informed that submission of satisfactory proof of the charges claimed would be necessary to obtain payment under the plans. General Dynamics was thus liable to pay for covered medical services *only* if properly documented claims forms were filed. Some covered individuals, through oversight, procrastination, confusion over the coverage provided, or fear of disclosure to the employer of the extent or nature of the services received, might not file claims for reimbursement to which they are plainly entitled. Such filing is not a

---

[13] The United States did not seek review of whether the amount of liability in this case could be determined with reasonable accuracy. See Pet. for Cert. 13, n. 2.

[14] [S]ection 461(h) does not apply in this case. It becomes effective as of July 8, 1984. . . . We do not address how this case would be decided under § 461(h), but note that the legislative history of the Act indicates that "[i]n the case of . . . employee benefit liabilities, which require a payment by the taxpayer to another person, economic performance occurs as the payments to such person are made."

[15] We do not challenge the Claims Court's final conclusion that the processing on the claims was "routine," "clerical," and "ministerial in nature," 6 Cl.Ct. 250, 254 (1984). The Claims Court did not, however, make any factual findings with respect to the *filing* of claims. We conclude that, as a matter of law, the filing of a claim was necessary to create liability.

mere technicality. It is crucial to the establishment of liability on the part of the taxpayer. Nor does the failure to file a claim represent the type of "extremely remote and speculative possibility" that we held in *Hughes*, 476 U.S., at 601, 106 S.Ct., at 2097, did not render an otherwise fixed liability contingent. . . . Mere receipt of services for which, in some instances, claims will not be submitted does not, in our judgment, constitute the last link in the chain of events creating liability for purposes of the "all events" test.

This is not to say that the taxpayer was unable to forecast how many claims would be filed for medical care received during this period, and estimate the liability that would arise from those claims. Based on actuarial data, General Dynamics may have been able to make a reasonable estimate of how many claims would be filed for the last quarter of 1972. In *Brown [v. Helvering]*, the taxpayer, a general agent for insurance companies, sought to take a deduction for a reserve representing estimated liability for premiums to be returned on the percentage of insurance policies it anticipated would be cancelled in future years. The agent may well have been capable of estimating with a reasonable degree of accuracy the ratio of cancellation refunds to premiums already paid and establishing its reserve accordingly. Despite the "strong probability that many of the policies written during the taxable year" would be cancelled. 291 U.S. at 201, 54 S.Ct., at 360, the Court held that "no liability accrues during the taxable year on account of cancellations which it is expected may occur in future years, since the events necessary to create the liability do not occur during the taxable year." 291 U.S., at 200, 54 S.Ct., at 359. A reserve based on the proposition that a particular set of events is likely to occur in the future may be an appropriate conservative accounting measure, but does not warrant a tax deduction. . . .

General Dynamics did not show that its liability as to any medical care claims was firmly established as of the close of the 1972 tax year, and is therefore entitled to no deduction. The judgment of the Court of Appeals is

Reversed.

REVENUE RULING 2007-3
2007-1 C.B. 350

ISSUES

(1) Under § 461 of the Internal Revenue Code, when does a taxpayer using an accrual method of accounting incur a liability for services?

(2) Under § 461, when does a taxpayer using an accrual method of accounting incur a liability for insurance?

FACTS

X is a corporation that uses an accrual method of accounting and files its federal income tax returns on a calendar year basis.

Situation 1. On December 15, 2006, X executes a contract with Y for the provision of services. The contract provides for services to begin on January 15, 2007, and *X* pays *Y* for the services on January 15, 2007. *X* uses the recurring item exception under § 1.461-5.

Situation 2. On December 15, 2006, *X* executes a contract with *W*, an insurance company regulated under state law, for the provision of insurance. The insurance contract covers the period from January 15, 2007, through December 31, 2007. Under the terms of the contract, payment of the insurance premium is due to *W* on January 15, 2007, and *X* pays the premium to *W* on January 15, 2007. *X* uses the recurring item exception under § 1.461-5.

LAW

Section 461(a) provides that the amount of any deduction or credit must be taken for the taxable year that is the proper taxable year under the method of accounting used by the taxpayer in computing taxable income.

Section 1.461-1(a)(2)(i) of the Income Tax Regulations provides that, under an accrual method of accounting, a liability is incurred, and is generally taken into account for federal income tax purposes, in the taxable year in which (1) all the events have occurred that establish the fact of the liability, (2) the amount of the liability can be determined with reasonable accuracy, and (3) economic performance has occurred with respect to the liability (the "all events test"). *See also* § 1.446-1(c)(1)(ii)(A).

The first prong of the all events test requires that all the events have occurred that establish the fact of the liability. Therefore, it is fundamental to the all events test that although expenses may be deductible before they become due and payable, liability first must be firmly established. *United States v. General Dynamics Corp.*, 481 U.S. 239, 243–4 (1987).

Generally, under § 1.461-1(a)(2), all the events have occurred that establish the fact of the liability when (1) the event fixing the liability, whether that be the required performance or other event, occurs or (2) payment therefore is due, whichever happens earliest. Rev. Rul. 80-230, 1980-2 C.B. 169; Rev. Rul. 79-410, 1972-2 C.B. 213, amplified by Rev Rul. 2003-90, 2003-2 C.B. 353. The terms of a contract are relevant in determining the events that establish the fact of a taxpayer's liability. *See, e.g., Decision, Inc. v. Commissioner*, 47 T.C. 58 (1966), *acq.*, 1967-2 C.B. 2.

Section 461(h) and § 1.461-4 provide that, for purposes of determining whether an accrual basis taxpayer can treat the amount of any liability as incurred, the all events test is not treated as met any earlier than the taxable year in which economic performance occurs with respect to the liability.

Section 1.461-4(d)(2) provides that if a liability of a taxpayer arises out of the providing of services or property to the taxpayer by another person, economic performance occurs as the services or property is provided.

Section 1.461-4(g)(5) provides that if a liability of a taxpayer arises out of the provision to the taxpayer of insurance, economic performance occurs as payment is made to the person to which the liability is owed.

Section 1.461-5(b)(1) provides a recurring item exception to the general rule of economic performance. Under the recurring item exception, a liability is treated as incurred for a taxable year if: (i) at the end of the taxable year, all events have occurred that establish the fact of the liability and the amount can be determined with reasonable accuracy; (ii) economic performance occurs on or before the earlier of (a) the date that the taxpayer files a return (including extensions) for the taxable year, or (b) the 15th day of the ninth calendar month after the close of the taxable year; (iii) the liability is recurring in nature; and (iv) either the amount of the liability is not material or accrual of the liability in the taxable year results in better matching of the liability against the income to which it relates than would result from accrual of the liability in the taxable year in which economic performance occurs.

ANALYSIS

Situation 1. In Situation 1, the first event that occurs to establish the fact of *X*'s liability for services is that payment is due under the contract on January 15, 2007. *See* Rev. Rul. 80-230; Rev. Rul. 79-410. Thus, for purposes of § 461, the fact of the liability is established on January 15, 2007. At that time, the amount can be determined with reasonable accuracy. Economic performance with respect to the liability occurs as the services are provided, from January 15, 2007 through January 31, 2007. *See* § 1.461-4(d)(2). Therefore, *X* incurs a liability for services in 2007.

The fact of the liability is not established in 2006, even though *X* executed the service contract on December 15, 2006. It is well established that an accrual basis obligor is not permitted to deduct an expense stemming from a bilateral contractual arrangement, that is, mutual promises, prior to the performance of the contracted for services by the obligee. Rev. Rul. 80-182, 1980-2 C.B. 167, citing *Levin v. Commissioner*, 21 T.C. 996 (1954), *aff'd*, 219 F.2d 588 (3d Cir. 1955) (an agreement for services to be performed in the next year did not establish the fact of the taxpayer's liability but was simply an agreement under which a liability would be incurred in the future) and *Amalgamated Housing Corp. v. Commissioner*, 37 B.T.A. 817 (1938), *aff'd per curiam*, 108 F.2d 1010 (2d Cir. 1940) (an agreement to renovate property in the future did not establish the fact of the taxpayer's liability; the accrual was for services in renovating, not the duty to renovate). Thus, the mere execution of the contract by *X* in 2006 is not sufficient, by itself, to establish the fact of liability. Further, the recurring item exception does not apply because the fact of liability is not established in 2006.

Situation 2. In Situation 2, the first event that occurs to establish the fact of *X*'s liability for insurance is that the premium is due under the contract. *See* Rev. Rul. 80-230; Rev. Rul. 79-410. Thus, for purposes of § 461, the fact of the liability is established on January 15, 2007. At that time, the amount can be determined with reasonable accuracy. Economic performance with respect to the liability occurs as payment is made, on January 15, 2007. *See* § 1.461-4(g)(5). Therefore, *X* incurs a liability for insurance in 2007.

The fact of the liability is not established in 2006, even though *X* executed the insurance contract on December 15, 2006. *See* Rev. Rul. 80-182. Although federal or state regulations may impose certain legal obligations on taxpayers, these obligations, without more, do not necessarily establish the fact of a taxpayer's liability under § 461. *See Chrysler Corp. v. Commissioner*, 436 F.3d 644 (6th Cir. 2006) (statutory obligation related to warranty obligation was not sufficient to establish the fact of the taxpayer's liability to provide warranty services). Further, the recurring item exception does not apply because the fact of the liability is not established in 2006.

HOLDINGS

(1) Under § 461, all the events have occurred that establish the fact of the liability for services provided to the taxpayer when (1) the event fixing the liability, whether that be the required performance or other event, occurs, or (2) payment is due, whichever happens earliest. The mere execution of a contract, without more, does not establish the fact of a taxpayer's liability for services.

(2) Under § 461, all the events have occurred that establish the fact of the liability for insurance when (1) the event fixing the liability, whether that be the required performance or other event, occurs, or (2) payment is due, whichever happens earliest. The mere execution of a contract, without more, does not establish the fact of a taxpayers's liability for insurance.

NOTE ON INVENTORY ACCOUNTING

Because a seller of property is entitled to subtract the adjusted basis of property from the amount realized in computing gain, the gross proceeds from the sale of property do not constitute gross income to the seller. Similarly, when a manufacturer or retailer sells goods from inventory, the sales proceeds are not gross income. Rather, to determine gross income, it is necessary to subtract from the sales price the "cost of goods sold." In the typical merchandising or manufacturing business, however, it is simply not possible or feasible to identify the specific cost attributable to each individual item sold from inventory. The rules of inventory accounting are designed to address this problem.

First, however, let us note some preliminary matters. The regulations provide that, where it is necessary to use an inventory, accrual method accounting must be used with respect to purchases and sales. Reg. § 1.446-1(c)(2). Elsewhere, the regulations provide that inventories must be used at the beginning and end of each tax year "in every case in which the production, purchase, or sale of merchandise is an income-producing factor." Reg. § 1.471-1. *See* § 471(a). It should thus be apparent that, with respect to purchases and sales, use of inventory accounting and the accrual method will be required of a great many businesses.

The gross income on sales from inventory is equal to total sales, minus the cost of goods sold. *See* Reg. § 1.61-3(a). Determining total sales, or gross receipts, is straightforward enough. Determining the cost of goods sold is somewhat more complex. The goods sold during the tax year, however, may be expressed as the sum of those on hand at the outset of the year ("opening inventory") plus those purchased during the year ("purchases"), minus the inventory on hand at the end of the year ("closing inventory"). In short, the total inventory on hand during the year consists of opening inventory and purchases. Once we subtract the closing inventory from that total, the balance is the inventory sold, the "goods sold," during the year. Assuming we know the cost of purchases during the year, we can determine the "cost of goods sold" by converting the opening inventory and closing inventory to dollar amounts. The cost of goods sold (CGS) may thus be expressed as opening inventory (OI) plus purchases (P) less closing inventory (CI).

To summarize:

$$\text{Gross Income} = \text{Sales} - \text{Cost of Goods Sold}$$

$$\text{Cost of Goods Sold} = \text{Opening Inventory} + \text{Purchases} - \text{Closing Inventory}$$

Thus:

$$\text{Gross Income} = \text{Sales} - (\text{Opening Inventory} + \text{Purchases} - \text{Closing Inventory})$$

or

Gross Income = Sales − Opening Inventory − Purchases + Closing Inventory

It should thus be apparent, for example, that gross income will decrease as opening inventory and purchases increase; but gross income will increase as closing inventory increases. Note, however, that since one year's closing inventory becomes the following year's opening inventory, the impact of closing inventory on the gross income of Year 1 is felt in the opposite direction in Year 2.

Inventory accounting requires a counting or measuring of inventory at the beginning and end of the tax year. As noted, it also requires that we be able to express the inventory count in dollar terms, *i.e.*, inventory must not only be identified, it must be valued. The valuation is commonly done in one of two ways. The inventory may be valued at cost. Reg. § 1.471-3. Alternatively, the inventory may be valued at cost or at market value, whichever is lower. Reg. §§ 1.471-2(c); 1.471-4. This latter approach, which reflects a decline in the market value of inventory in the current year's income, was originally developed for financial accounting purposes, but it may also generally be used for tax accounting purposes (except that it may not be used in conjunction with the so-called LIFO convention, discussed below). A change in the way inventory is valued cannot be made without the consent of the Commissioner. Reg. § 1.471-2(d).

Assume the taxpayer wishes to value inventory at cost, but inventory is extensive and the cost of acquiring inventory items changes frequently. The taxpayer can determine the closing inventory, but realistically there may be no way to know when each item in it was acquired and thus no way to know the cost to assign to each individual item. This problem is solved by the use of an accounting convention. The most common convention assumes that the inventory first acquired is also the inventory first sold — that is, "first in, first out" or "FIFO." Thus, the closing inventory under FIFO consists of the most recently acquired inventory. If the cost of inventory has been rising, the FIFO convention raises the dollar value assigned to closing inventory and thus also raises gross income. Under the "LIFO" convention, by contrast, the most recently acquired inventory is treated as the first sold — "last in, first out." The LIFO convention, in a time of rising prices, has the effect of reducing gross income since it assumes the closing inventory is comprised of the earliest (least expensive) items and thus puts a lower value on closing inventory than would the FIFO convention. Conversely, in a time of falling prices, FIFO would produce a lower-valued closing inventory, thus a lower gross income, than would LIFO. Over the life of the business, of course, the gross income totals are the same under both methods.

The authorization to elect the LIFO method is provided by § 472, and, once made, the election may not be revoked without the consent of the Commissioner. Reg. § 1.472-5. Valuation of inventory under LIFO must be made at cost. Reg. § 1.472-2(b). Under the FIFO convention, valuation may be made either at cost or under the lower-of-cost-or-market method.

The LIFO impact in a year of rising prices can be seen in the following example. Assume the taxpayer has an opening inventory of 50 widgets valued at a cost of $5 each, or $250. During the year, the taxpayer sells 110 widgets for $12 each, or $1,320. The taxpayer purchases 3 shipments of widgets during the year: an April shipment of 40 widgets at $6 each, or $240; an August shipment of 40 widgets at $7 each, or $280; and an October shipment of 40 widgets at $8 each, or $320. The taxpayer's closing inventory is thus 60 widgets.

(1) Under FIFO, those 60 widgets are deemed to consist of the October shipment of 40 ($320) and one-half the August shipment ($140) and are valued at $460. Thus, gross income equals sales ($1,320) less opening inventory ($250), less the three purchases ($240 + $280 + $320, or $840), plus the closing inventory ($460). The resulting gross income is $690.

(2) Under LIFO, the 60 widgets in closing inventory are the 50 in opening inventory ($250 value) plus 10 from the April shipment of 40 (at $6 each, a total of $60). Closing inventory under LIFO is thus $310, which is $150 less than the valuation of closing inventory under FIFO. The resulting gross income determined using LIFO will be $540, which is similarly $150 less than the $690 determined with FIFO. Recall, of course, that next year's opening inventory is this year's closing inventory, and the benefit of a relatively low value on closing inventory thus translates into next year's opening inventory burden. There is, nonetheless, a real deferral of income advantage to be gained from LIFO in a time of rising prices.

Inventory accounting, and the Treasury regulations that govern it, are considerably more complex and detailed than the foregoing overview suggests. See, for example, the regulations under § 472 dealing with LIFO accounting; see those at Reg. § 1.471-11 concerning manufacturing businesses (in contrast to retailers), which must allocate a variety of direct and indirect production costs among their inventory items. It should become apparent that this Note merely touches on some salient, general aspects of inventory accounting. Nonetheless, it should also be apparent that there is a direct relationship between accounting for inventory costs and the determination of gross income and a real potential for manipulation. The case that follows, *Thor Power Tool Co. v. Commissioner*, illustrates, among other things, the adverse interests that arise between taxpayers and the Commissioner in this field, and also permits the Supreme Court to highlight the differences between the purposes of tax accounting and financial accounting.

THOR POWER TOOL CO. v. COMMISSIONER
United States Supreme Court
439 U.S. 522 (1979)

Mr. Justice Blackmun delivered the opinion of the Court.

The Inventory Issue. In 1964, petitioner Thor Power Tool Co. . . . in accord with "generally accepted accounting principles," wrote down what it regarded as excess inventory to Thor's own estimate of the net realizable value of the excess goods. Despite this write-down, Thor continued to hold the goods for sale at original prices. It offset the write-down against 1964 sales and thereby produced a net operating loss for that year; it then asserted that loss as a carryback to 1963 under § 172 of the Internal Revenue Code of 1954, 26 U.S.C. § 172. The Commissioner of Internal Revenue, maintaining that the write-down did not serve to reflect income clearly for tax purposes, disallowed the offset and the carryback.

I

The Inventory Issue

A

Taxpayer is a Delaware corporation with principal place of business in Illinois. It manufactures hand-held power tools, parts and accessories, and rubber products. At its various plants and service branches, Thor maintains inventories of raw materials, work-in-process, finished parts and accessories, and completed tools. At all times relevant, Thor has used, both for financial accounting and for income tax purposes, the "lower of cost or market" method of valuing inventories.

In late 1964, new management took control and promptly concluded that Thor's inventory in general was overvalued.

Management concluded that many articles, mostly spare parts, were "excess" inventory, that is, that they were held in excess of any reasonably foreseeable future demand. It was decided that this inventory should be written down to its "net realizable value," which, in most cases, was scrap value.

Although Thor wrote down all its "excess" inventory at once, it did not immediately scrap the articles or sell them at reduced prices, as it had done with $3 million of obsolete and damaged inventory, the write-down of which the Commissioner permitted. Rather, Thor retained the "excess" items physically in inventory and continued to sell them at original prices. The company found that, owing to the peculiar nature of the articles involved, price reductions were of no avail in moving this "excess" inventory. . . .

Thor's total writedown of "excess" inventory in 1964 was . . . [$926,952]. Thor credited this sum to its inventory contraaccount, thereby decreasing closing inventory, increasing cost of goods sold, and decreasing taxable income for the year by that amount.[1] The company contended that, by writing down excess inventory to scrap value, and by thus carrying all inventory at "net realizable value," it had reduced its inventory to "market" in accord with its "lower of cost or market" method of accounting. On audit, the Commissioner disallowed the write-down in its entirety, asserting that it did not serve clearly to reflect Thor's 1964 income for tax purposes.

The Tax Court, in upholding the Commissioner's determination, found as a fact that Thor's write-down of excess inventory did conform to "generally accepted accounting principles"; indeed, the court was "thoroughly convinced . . . that such was the case." The court found that if Thor had failed to write down its inventory on some reasonable basis, its accountants would have been unable to give its financial statements the desired certification. The court held, however, that conformance

---

[1] For a manufacturing concern like Thor, Gross Profit basically equals Sales minus Cost of Goods Sold. Cost of Goods Sold equals Opening Inventory, plus Cost of Inventory Acquired, minus Closing Inventory. A reduction of Closing Inventory, therefore, increases Cost of Goods Sold and decreases Gross Profit accordingly.

with "generally accepted accounting principles" is not enough. § 446(b), and § 471 as well, of the 1954 Code, 26 U.S.C. §§ 446(b) and 471, prescribe, as an independent requirement, that inventory accounting methods must "clearly reflect income" The Tax Court . . . held that the Commissioner had not abused his discretion in determining that the write-down failed to reflect 1964 income clearly.

B

Inventory accounting is governed by §§ 446 and 471 of the Code, 26 U.S.C. §§ 446 and 471. Section 446(a) states the general rule for methods of accounting: "Taxable income shall be computed under the method of accounting on the basis of which the taxpayer regularly computes his income in keeping his books." Section 446(b) provides, however, that if the method used by the taxpayer "does not clearly reflect income, the computation of taxable income shall be made under such method as, in the opinion of the [Commissioner], does clearly reflect income." Regulations promulgated under § 446 and in effect for the taxable year 1964, state that "no method of accounting is acceptable unless, in the opinion of the Commissioner, it clearly reflects income." Treas. Reg. § 1.446-1(a)(2), 26 CFR § 1.446-1(a)(2) (1964).

Section 471 prescribes the general rule for inventories. It states:

> Whenever in the opinion of the [Commissioner] the use of inventories is necessary in order clearly to determine the income of any taxpayer, inventories shall be taken by such taxpayer on such basis as the [Commissioner] may prescribe as conforming as nearly as may be to the best accounting practice in the trade or business and as most clearly reflecting the income.

As the Regulations point out, § 471 obviously establishes two distinct tests to which an inventory must conform. First, it must conform "as nearly as may be" to the "best accounting practice," a phrase that is synonymous with "generally accepted accounting principles." Second, it "must clearly reflect the income." Treas. Reg. § 1.471-2(a)(2), 26 CFR § 1.471-2(a)(2) (1964).

It is obvious that on their face §§ 446 and 471, with their accompanying Regulations, vest the Commissioner with wide discretion in determining whether a particular method of inventory accounting should be disallowed as not clearly reflective of income.

The only question is whether the Commissioner abused his discretion in determining that the write-down did not satisfy the test's second prong in that it failed to reflect Thor's 1964 income clearly. Although the Commissioner's discretion is not unbridled and may be arbitrary we sustain his exercise of discretion here, for in this case the write-down was plainly inconsistent with the governing Regulations which the taxpayer, on its part, has not challenged.

It has been noted above that Thor at all pertinent times used the "lower of cost or market" method of inventory accounting. The rules governing this method are set out in Treas. Reg. § 1.471-4.

[T]he regulatory scheme is clear. The taxpayer must value inventory for tax purposes at cost unless the "market" is lower. "Market" is defined as "replacement cost," and the taxpayer is permitted to depart from replacement cost only in specified situations. When it makes any such departure, the taxpayer must substantiate its lower inventory valuation by providing evidence of actual offerings, actual sales, or actual contract cancellations. In the absence of objective evidence of this kind, a taxpayer's assertions as to the "market value" of its inventory are not cognizable in computing its income tax.

Thor's "excess" inventory was normal and unexceptional, and was indistinguishable from and intermingled with the inventory that was not written down.

More importantly, Thor failed to provide any objective evidence whatever that the "excess" inventory had the "market value" management ascribed to it. . . . Thor's management simply wrote down its closing inventory on the basis of a well-educated guess that some of it would never be sold. The formulae governing the write-down were derived from management's collective "business experience". . . . If a taxpayer could write down its inventories on the basis of management's subjective estimates of the goods' ultimate salability, the taxpayer would be able, as the Tax Court observed, "to determine how much tax it wanted to pay for a given year."

For these reasons, we agree with the Tax Court and with the Seventh Circuit that the Commissioner acted within his discretion in deciding that Thor's write-down of "excess" inventory failed to reflect income clearly. In the light of the well-known potential for tax avoidance that is inherent in inventory accounting, the Commissioner in his discretion may insist on a high evidentiary standard before allowing write-downs of inventory to "market." Because Thor provided no objective evidence of the reduced market value of its "excess" inventory, its write-down was plainly inconsistent with the Regulations, and the Commissioner properly disallowed it.

C

The taxpayer's major argument against this conclusion is based on the Tax Court's clear finding that the write-down conformed to "generally accepted accounting principles." Thor points to language in Treas. Reg. § 1.446-1(a)(2), 26 CFR § 1.446-1(a)(2) (1964), to the effect that "[a] method of accounting which reflects the consistent application of generally accepted accounting principles . . . *will ordinarily be regarded* as clearly reflecting income" (emphasis added). Section 1.471-2(b), 26 CFR § 1.471-2(b) (1964), of the Regulations likewise stated that an inventory taken in conformity with best accounting practice "can, *as a general rule*, be regarded as clearly reflecting . . . income" (emphasis added). These provisions, Thor contends, created a *presumption* that an inventory practice conformable to "generally accepted accounting principles" is valid for income tax purposes. Once a taxpayer has established this conformity, the argument runs, the burden shifts to the Commissioner affirmatively to demonstrate that the taxpayer's method does *not* reflect income clearly. . . . The Commissioner, Thor concludes, failed to rebut the presumption here.

If the Code and Regulations did embody the presumption petitioner postulates, it would be of little use to the taxpayer in this case. As we have noted, Thor's write-down of "excess" inventory was inconsistent with the Regulations; any general presumption obviously must yield in the face of such particular inconsistency. We believe, however, that no such presumption is present. Its existence is insupportable in light of the statute, the Court's past decisions, and the differing objectives of tax and financial accounting.

First, as has been stated above, the Code and Regulations establish two distinct tests to which an inventory must conform. . . . The Regulations embody no presumption; they say merely that, in most cases, generally accepted accounting practices will pass muster for tax purposes. And in most cases they will. But if the Commissioner, in the exercise of his discretion, determines that they do not, he may prescribe a different practice without having to rebut any presumption running against the Treasury.

Second, the presumption petitioner postulates finds no support in this Court's prior decisions. . . . By its president's concession, the company's write-down of "excess" inventory was founded on the belief that many of the articles inevitably would become useless due to breakage, technological change, fluctuations in market demand, and the like. Thor, in other words, sought a current "deduction" for an estimated future loss. Under the decided cases, a taxpayer so circumstanced finds no shelter beneath an accountancy presumption.

Third, the presumption petitioner postulates is insupportable in light of the vastly different objectives that financial and tax accounting have. The primary goal of financial accounting is to provide useful information to management, shareholders, creditors, and others properly interested; the major responsibility of the accountant is to protect these parties from being misled. The primary goal of the income tax system, in contrast, is the equitable collection of revenue; the major responsibility of the Internal Revenue Service is to protect the public fisc. Consistently with its goals and responsibilities, financial accounting has as its foundation the principle of conservatism, with its corollary that "possible error in measurement [should] be in the direction of understatement rather than overstatement of net income and net assets." In view of the Treasury's markedly different goals and responsibilities understatement of income is not destined to be its guiding light. Given this diversity, even contrariety, of objectives, any presumptive equivalency between tax and financial accounting would be unacceptable.

The difference in objectives is mirrored in numerous differences of treatment. Where the tax law requires that a deduction be deferred until "all the events" have occurred that will make it fixed and certain, *United States v. Anderson*, 269 U.S. 422, 441 (1926), accounting principles typically require that a liability be accrued as soon as it can reasonably be estimated. Conversely, where the tax law requires that income be recognized currently under "claim of right," "ability to pay," and "control" rationales, accounting principles may defer accrual until a later year so that revenues and expenses may be better matched. Financial accounting, in short, is hospitable to estimates, probabilities, and reasonable certainties; the tax law, with its mandate to preserve the revenue, can give no quarter to uncertainty. This is as it should be. Reasonable estimates may be useful, even essential, in giving shareholders and creditors an accurate picture of a firm's overall financial health; but the accountant's conservatism cannot bind the Commissioner in his efforts to collect taxes. . . .

Finally, a presumptive equivalency between tax and financial accounting would create insurmountable difficulties of tax administration. Accountants long have recognized that "generally accepted accounting principles" are far from being a canonical set of rules that will ensure identical accounting treatment of identical transactions. "Generally accepted accounting principles," rather, tolerate a range of "reasonable" treatments, leaving the choice among alternatives to management. Such, indeed, is precisely the case here. Variances of this sort may be tolerable in financial reporting, but they are questionable in a tax system designed to ensure as far as possible that similarly situated taxpayers pay the same tax. If management's election among "acceptable" options were dispositive for tax purposes, a firm, indeed, could decide unilaterally — within limits dictated only by its accountants — the tax it wished to pay. Such unilateral decisions would not just make the Code inequitable; they would make it unenforceable.

D

Thor complains that a decision adverse to it poses a dilemma. According to the taxpayer, it would be virtually impossible for it to offer objective evidence of its "excess" inventory's lower value, since the goods cannot be sold at reduced prices; even if they could be sold, says Thor, their reduced-price sale would just "pull the rug out" from under the identical "non-excess" inventory Thor is trying to sell simultaneously. The only way Thor could establish the inventory's value by a "closed transaction" would be to scrap the articles at once. Yet immediate scrapping would be undesirable for demand for the parts ultimately might prove greater than anticipated. The taxpayer thus sees itself presented with "an unattractive Hobson's choice: either the unsalable inventory must be carried for years at its cost instead of net realizable value, thereby overstating taxable income by such overvaluation until it is scrapped, or the excess inventory must be scrapped prematurely to the detriment or the manufacturer and its customers."

If this is indeed the dilemma that confronts Thor, it is in reality the same choice that every taxpayer who has a paper loss must face. It can realize its loss now and garner its tax benefit, or it can defer realization, and its deduction, hoping for better luck later. Thor, quite simply, has suffered no present loss. It deliberately manufactured its "excess" spare parts because it judged that the marginal cost of unsalable inventory would be lower than the cost of retooling machinery should demand surpass expectations. This was a rational business judgment and, not unpredictably, Thor now has inventory it believes it cannot sell. Thor, of course, is not so confident of its predication as to be willing to scrap the "excess" parts now; it wants to keep them on hand, just in case. This, too, is a rational judgment, but there is no reason why the Treasury should subsidize Thor's hedging of its bets. There is also no reason why Thor should be entitled, for tax purposes, to have its cake and to eat it too.

The judgment is affirmed.

Chapter 30

ANNUAL ACCOUNTING

I. PROBLEMS

1. In December of Year 1, Ellen, the CEO of ABC Industries (hereinafter ABC), received a performance-based bonus of $50,000 based on ABC's earnings for the year. The bonus was paid pursuant to ABC's Executive Incentive Compensation Program. As part of this program, ABC has a "clawback" policy requiring any executive who receives performance-based bonuses to return to ABC part or all of a bonus if it is subsequently determined that company earnings were erroneously overstated and, as a result, the bonus was excessive. Ellen's taxable income in Year 1 (taking into account the $50,000 bonus) was $300,000. Assume for ease of computation that all of the Year 1 taxable income was taxed at the rate of 30%. On March 1, Year 2, Ellen was informed by the chair of ABC's Board of Directors that ABC's accountants had made a major mistake in computing ABC's Year 1 earnings. ABC had actually earned considerably less than the earnings upon which Ellen's performance bonus had been calculated. As a result, Ellen, pursuant to ABC policy, was required to return $30,000 of the $50,000 bonus. On April 1, Year 2, Ellen returned the $30,000 excess bonus amount to ABC. Ellen's taxable income in Year 2 (after deducting the repayment) was $200,000. Assume a Year 2 tax rate of 20%. What tax consequences to Ellen in Year 2?

2. Assume the facts of Problem 1 except that, instead of having to return $30,000, Ellen only had to return $5,000. Rather than repaying the full $5,000 in Year 2, Ellen repaid $2,500 in Year 2 and $2,500 in Year 3. What result to Ellen? Would your answer change if Ellen were an accrual method taxpayer instead of a cash method taxpayer?

3. Assume the Year 1 bonus was not incorrectly computed. However, in Year 3, the Internal Revenue Service determines that Ellen's Year 1 compensation exceeded "reasonable" compensation by $50,000, and accordingly denied ABC a Year 1 deduction for the $50,000 bonus. In general, what result if Ellen and ABC thereupon enter an agreement requiring the return of any compensation determined excessive by the IRS, and Ellen then repays the excess $50,000 to ABC in Year 3? Would it matter if this agreement were entered in Year 2? Prior to the payment of the Year 1 bonus?

4. On her Year 1 tax return when she was in a 20% tax bracket, Terri correctly reported gross income of $30,000 and itemized deductions of $14,000 which included a deduction under § 170 of $10,000 for real estate given to charity.

Assume Terri's standard deduction is $5,000. Because the charity failed to comply with the terms of the gift, the real estate reverts to Terri in Year 4, when its value is still $10,000. Must Terri report any gross income in Year 4 (and if so, how much) as a result of recovering the property? Assume she is then in a 30% tax bracket. Suppose the value of the real estate in Year 4 were $5,000 or $15,000 instead of $10,000. Does your answer change?

5. George ran a mail-order plant business for several years. Last year he deducted $1,000 in cultivation expenses attributable to plants he gave away to a local garden club when he went out of business this year. Last year he also deducted $250 for stamps and $100 for stationery that remained on hand when he went out of business. He took the stamps home and discarded the stationery. What tax results this year?

6. In Year 1, ABC Corporation has taxable income of $10,000. In Years 2, 3 and 4, its taxable income is $10,000, $5,000 and $20,000, respectively. In Year 5, ABC's gross income is $40,000 and its allowable expenses are $100,000. In Year 6, its taxable income is $5,000. In Year 7, it has gross income of $30,000 and allowable expenses of $50,000. In Years 8 through 20, its taxable income is $10,000 per year. What tax results from the Years 5 and 7 operations?

Assignment for Chapter 30:

Complete the problems.

Read: Internal Revenue Code: §§ 67(b)(9); 111(a); 172(a); 172(b)(1)(A), (2), (3); 172(c); 441(a)–(e); 1341(a). Skim § 172(d)(1)–(4).

   Materials: Overview
   Burnet v. Sanford & Brooks Co.
   Alice Phelan Sullivan Corp. v. United States
   Hillsboro National Bank v. Commissioner

II. VOCABULARY

transactional accounting
annual accounting system
tax benefit rule — inclusionary aspect
tax benefit rule — exclusionary aspect
tax benefit rule — erroneous deduction exception
net operating loss
carryback
carryforward

III. OBJECTIVES

1. To distinguish between accounting on a transactional basis and on an annual accounting basis.

2. To recall that ours is an annual accounting system.

3. To determine whether § 1341 applies in a given set of facts, and to explain the tax consequences if it does and if it does not.

4. To apply the tax benefit rule to a set of facts in a manner that demonstrates both the inclusionary and exclusionary aspects of the rule.

5. To provide an example of a set of events that calls for application of the tax benefit rule and an example of a set of events that does not.

6. To calculate a net operating loss on a given set of facts, and apply it against the income of other years, in proper order, until fully absorbed.

IV. OVERVIEW

Section 441 establishes the general rule that taxpayers are to make an annual accounting of their taxable income. Taxpayers are thus required to report total income and expenses, gains and losses, on a yearly basis. In the main, such an annual accounting system seems administratively reasonable and also seems to produce tax results that fairly reflect one's ability-to-pay. Such, however, is not always the case. At times, the annual accounting system, in focusing on a twelve-month period of time, seems to produce distorted measurements of taxable income, since the economic transactions on which income is based do not necessarily fit within a single taxable year. Income and expenses can fluctuate measurably; income can be bunched in one year, expenses in another; a transaction seemingly done in one year may be undone in another. As a result, it often appears that a transactional approach to measuring taxable income would be more accurate and fair, *i.e.*, net profit or loss should be reported on a transaction by transaction basis rather than year by year. (Were it feasible, measuring taxable income on a lifetime basis would also be conceptually appealing.) The definitional and other administrative problems associated with transactional accounting could be daunting and, wholly apart from other concerns, these problems are probably enough to prevent the wholesale adoption of transactional accounting in lieu of the present system. Our focus in this chapter is on selected problems raised by the annual accounting system, and the responses to those problems. The case of *Burnet v. Sanford & Brooks Company*, reprinted below and illustrating one of the problems, also serves to emphasize the general annual accounting rule.

A. Restoring Amounts Received Under Claim of Right

As discussed in Chapter 3, amounts received under a claim of right, without restriction as to disposition, constitute income. As you will recall, in *North American Oil*, certain disputed funds, earned in 1916, were paid to the taxpayer in 1917. Although it was not until 1922 that the litigation involving the funds was finally terminated in the taxpayer's favor, the Supreme Court held that the funds were nonetheless reportable as income in 1917 under the claim of right doctrine. Imagine, however, that the taxpayer in *North American Oil* had ultimately not been victorious. What are the tax consequences when a taxpayer who is directed to include income under claim of right is subsequently required to restore the amount received? It seems clear that the tax system ought somehow to take account of that restoration, and, as was suggested in Chapter 3, it does. The question is how it should be taken into account. In *United States v. Lewis*, 340 U.S. 590 (1951), the taxpayer received an improperly computed bonus in 1944, which he properly reported as income in that year and repaid to his employer in 1946. The taxpayer sought a refund for overpayment of his 1944 taxes. Until repayment of the bonus in 1946, the taxpayer "had at all times claimed and used [the full bonus] unconditionally as his own, in the good faith though 'mistaken' belief that he was entitled [to the full bonus.]" The government's position was that, under the circumstances, the repayment should be taken as a deduction in 1946 rather than permit a recomputation of the 1944 tax. The Supreme Court agreed. The Supreme Court noted: "Income taxes must be paid on income received (or accrued) during an annual accounting period. The 'claim of right' interpretation of the tax laws has long been used to give finality to that period, and is now deeply rooted in the federal tax system. We see no reason why the Court should depart from this well-settled interpretation merely because it results in an advantage or disadvantage to a taxpayer."

What is at stake in the *Lewis*-type situation should be obvious. The *tax increase* that results from including in income an amount received under a claim of right will not always be the same as the *tax savings* resulting from deducting its repayment in a later year. A taxpayer's marginal tax bracket can vary from year to year. A taxpayer will quite naturally prefer to deduct the restored funds when the tax savings thus produced exceed the tax bite caused by inclusion in the earlier year. When the later year's tax savings are relatively small, a recomputation of the prior year's tax and a refund of the excess tax paid is preferable.

Congress responded to the *Lewis* decision by enacting § 1341. Note that, rather than choose between deduction and recomputation, Congress took an easy way out — the taxpayer who meets the requirements of § 1341(a)(1) through (3) is directed to compute tax liability under the approach that produces the more favorable tax result. Assume, for example, that in Year 1, when the taxpayers' marginal tax rate is 25%, $10,000 is properly included in income under a claim of right. The tax cost of inclusion is thus $2,500. Suppose the taxpayer is required to repay the $10,000 in Year 3. If the taxpayer's marginal tax rate in Year 3 is 30%, the $10,000 deduction saves $3,000 in taxes — the deduction, in other words, is worth more than the tax cost of the original inclusion, and § 1341(a) directs the taxpayer to deduct the repayment. Suppose, however, the taxpayer is in a 20% marginal tax bracket in Year 3. A $10,000 deduction is worth only $2,000, an amount less than the Year 1 tax cost. Section 1341(a) accordingly directs the taxpayer to forego the Year 3 deduction and instead to decrease his Year 3 tax liability by $2,500, the amount of the Year 1 tax increase. Section 1341 does not, it should be stressed, provide for reopening the earlier year's tax return or for filing an amended return. What § 1341(a)(5) provides instead (when it is more valuable than a deduction) is a tax decrease, in effect a tax credit, against the current year's tax liability in an amount equal to the added tax occasioned by the prior year's inclusion in income. Essentially, § 1341(a)(5) serves the function of an amended return without in fact authorizing one. This approach has a certain conceptual validity. Amended returns serve to correct errors and omissions in the original return, but the inclusion of income under a claim of right was in fact correct and appropriate, and not something rendered "erroneous" by virtue of subsequent events. Again, however, keep in mind that the tax decrease alternative in § 1341(a)(5) is only applied when it produces a bigger tax savings than the deduction alternative of § 1341(a)(4). Do you agree with this "best-of-both-worlds" approach of § 1341?

The requirements for applying § 1341 should be read with care. First, relatively minor amounts are barred from § 1341 treatment by the $3,000 threshold requirement of § 1341(a)(3). Secondly, it is necessary that the restored item have been included in income for a prior year because it "appeared" the taxpayer had an unrestricted right to the income. § 1341(a)(1). It has been held, for example, that there is no "appearance" of such a right with respect to embezzled funds, and repayment is thus outside § 1341. See, for example, Rev. Rul. 65-254, 1965-2 C.B. 50, relegating the individual taxpayer to a § 165(c)(2) deduction instead; also see

Kraft v. U.S., 991 F.2d 292 (6th Cir. 1993). The Service has also taken the position that the word "appeared" refers to "a semblance of an unrestricted right in the year received as distinguished from an unchallengeable right (which is more than an 'apparent' right) and from absolutely no right at all (which is less than an 'apparent' right). Whether the taxpayer had the semblance of an unrestricted right in the year of inclusion depends upon all the facts available at the end of such year." Rev. Rul. 68-153, 1968-1 C.B. 371, 373. The cited ruling thus holds that § 1341(a) does not apply to the repayment of funds received as the result of the taxpayer's "mere error," or to the repayment, "due to a subsequent event," of funds received under "absolute right." The ruling rather applies § 1341(a) in one situation where, in the year of inclusion, the facts available to the taxpayer did not enable it to determine the proper amount of income, and in another situation where a regulatory agency with jurisdiction over the taxpayer retroactively changed a billing rate applicable to the year of inclusion.

Suffice it to say that distinguishing among the appearance of a right, the lesser "no right" and the greater "unchallengeable right" may be problematic. Courts have certainly thought so. For example, in *Dominion Resources v. United States*, 219 F.3d 359 (4th Cir. 2000), the taxpayer, a public utility, successfully sought to apply § 1341 to customer refunds made in 1991, when tax rates were lower than they had been when the customers' payments were collected in prior years. The Fourth Circuit rejected the Service's construction of § 1341(a)(1), to the effect that the taxpayer must have an "apparent" right to income, but not an "actual" right to income, during the tax years at issue. The court commented:

> All that § 1341(a)(1) requires is that "an item be included in gross income for a prior taxable year (or years) because it appeared that the taxpayer had an unrestricted right to such item." Things very often "appear" to be what they "actually" are. As a matter of plain meaning, the word "appeared" generally does not, as the IRS urges, imply only false appearance, and generally does not exclude an appearance that happens to be true.

Id. at 364. The court went on to state that the only support for the Service's position was in its own dated revenue rulings — that the Tax Court had never adopted the "actual versus apparent" distinction, that two other circuit courts had rejected it, and that the Fourth Circuit would do so now. Rather, the court looked to the "same circumstances" rule that had been formulated by the Tax Court — namely, that the "requisite lack of an unrestricted right to an income item permitting deduction must arise out of the circumstances, terms, and conditions of the original payment of such item to the taxpayer." *Id.* at 367. Applying this test, the court concluded that the taxpayer was entitled to the application of § 1341.

Finally, § 1341(a)(2) requires the taxpayer to establish that he did not have an unrestricted right to the amount received in the prior year. Thus, for example, voluntary repayments do not come within § 1341. In *Pike v. Commissioner*, 44 T.C. 787 (1985) (acq.), the taxpayer, an attorney who represented life insurance companies, sold at a profit some stock in one of the companies. His right to retain the profits was disputed, and he subsequently paid the profits to the company, not because he admitted liability or was compelled to do so, but because he feared controversy over the matter would endanger his professional career. The Tax Court held that the taxpayer had failed to establish that he was not entitled to retain the profits, as required by § 1341(a)(2); but the court further held that the payment was allowable as a § 162 deduction.

In *Barrett v. Commissioner*, 96 T.C. 713 (1991) (nonacq.), the Tax Court held that the taxpayer, a stockbroker, was entitled to a credit under § 1341(a)(5) for amounts paid in 1984 to settle civil suits arising out of his purchase and sale of certain stock options in 1981. The 1981 sale of the options had generated a short-term capital gain of some $187,000, which the taxpayer reported, but had also led to the civil suits and the institution of civil proceedings by the Securities and Exchange Commission (SEC) to revoke taxpayer's brokerage license. The taxpayer maintained his innocence, but settled the suits by repaying part of the profits from the sale; the SEC administrative proceedings were then dropped as well. In applying § 1341(a)(5), the court rejected as "ludicrous" the Commissioner's argument that the repayment was voluntary, and held that the good faith, arm's length settlement of the dispute had the same effect as a judgment in establishing the fact and amount of taxpayer's legal obligation for repayment and establishing that he did not have an "unrestricted right" to that amount when he received it. *Pike* was held distinguishable on its facts.

The *Barrett* approach, however, was rejected by a district court in *Parks v. United States*, 945 F. Supp. 865 (W.D.Pa. 1996). In that case, the taxpayer sold his business at a profit and reported the income. He subsequently settled fraud-related litigation arising out of the sale, made repayment, and sought to apply § 1341 to the repayment. In denying the taxpayer's motion for summary judgment and reliance upon *Barrett*, the district court held the settlement did not eliminate the government's opportunity to demonstrate, if such were the case, that the previously-reported income had been obtained by fraud, and that § 1341 would therefore be inapplicable to the repayment on the grounds the taxpayer had not "appeared to have an unrestricted right" to the income, as required by § 1341(a)(1). According to *Parks*, to refuse to look behind the settlement agreement where there are allegations of intentional wrongdoing could effectively read § 1341(a)(1) out of the statute.

Barrett was distinguished in *Wang v. Commissioner*, T.C. Memo. 1998-389, where the taxpayer, an intern for a brokerage house, sold insider information. The Securities and Exchange Commission initiated civil and criminal proceedings against the taxpayer, who settled the civil action by payment of $125,000 to a restitution fund. The Tax Court rejected the taxpayer's effort to apply § 1341 to the payment, on the grounds the statute did not apply where, as here, there was no claim of right, or the appearance thereof, to the illegal funds the taxpayer received. *Barrett* was distinguished on the basis that its focus had been on whether the taxpayer's repayment was voluntary, not on whether the income had been received under claim of right or the appearance of an unrestricted right to income.

B.   The Tax Benefit Rule

The preceding section dealt with the repayment of amounts previously included in income. Suppose, conversely, the taxpayer instead recovers an amount that had been deducted in a prior year. To take a common example, suppose the taxpayer properly takes a bad debt deduction in one year, and in a later year receives payment on the supposed bad debt. The annual accounting system does not permit the reopening of a prior year's tax return to take account of events occurring in later years. The judicially-developed tax benefit rule, however, requires that the payment of the bad debt be included in income in the current year. There are, in fact, two aspects to the tax benefit rule when a taxpayer recovers a previously deducted amount. The "inclusionary aspect" of the tax benefit rule provides that the recovery constitutes gross income: the deduction gave rise to a tax benefit that, in light of later events, turned out to be unwarranted, and the taxpayer in effect gives back the tax benefit by including the recovered amount in income. It is likely, of course, the taxpayer's marginal tax brackets in the year of deduction and year of recovery will differ, and that the tax saved by the prior year's deduction will thus not be precisely equal to the tax increase caused by the subsequent inclusion. The tax benefit rule does not attempt to take account of such differences. It provides no "best-of-both-worlds" equivalent to § 1341. The recovered amount simply constitutes income in the year of recovery.

There is, however, a second aspect to the tax benefit rule, and this "exclusionary aspect" is what has been codified in § 111. To the extent a previously deducted amount did not produce a tax savings, its recovery will not constitute income. § 111(a). In effect, if the deduction produces no tax benefit, recovery of the deducted amount produces no income. Suppose, for example, the taxpayer in Year 1 properly takes a $10,000 business bad debt deduction, and in Year 3 the debt is paid in full. If, for ease of illustration, we assume that the taxpayer in Year 1 had $50,000 of taxable income prior to taking the bad debt deduction, then the entire $10,000 deduction produced a tax benefit, and all $10,000 recovered in Year 3 constitutes gross income under the inclusionary aspect of the tax benefit rule.[1] Suppose, however, the taxpayers' taxable income in Year 1, prior to taking the $10,000 bad debt deduction, had been zero. In these circumstances, the subsequent recovery is excluded from income under the exclusionary aspect of the tax benefit rule, since the deduction produced no tax savings. (A critical assumption in this example is that the net loss in Year 1 did not carryover to some other year and produce a tax savings in that year; see § 111(c) and the discussion below on net operating losses.) If the taxpayer's taxable income, prior to the deduction, had been $6,000 instead of zero, then $6,000 of the $10,000 deduction would have reduced tax liability in Year 1. The remaining $4,000 portion of the deduction that produced no tax savings in Year 1 (or in any other year, we are assuming) would be excluded from income on "recovery" of the $10,000 debt. The tax benefit rule, in its inclusionary and exclusionary aspects, thus represents an attempt to put the taxpayer in approximately (not exactly, given changes in marginal tax rates from year to year) the same position as if only the "proper" amount had been deducted originally.

Perhaps the most common context for application of the tax benefit rule involves the refund of previously deducted state income tax. Assume, for purposes of

---

[1] Since the tax tables most taxpayers use to compute tax liability move in $50 steps or brackets, it may be argued that some minor portion of the deduction — less than $50 — falls entirely within the final $50 bracket, produces no tax savings and is thus excludable. We will ignore this de minimis amount.

illustration, that in Year 1, Taxpayer's standard deduction is $5,000, the state income tax withheld and deducted is $3,000, and other itemized deductions are $2,400. (Also assume the § 68 overall limitation on itemized deductions does not apply.) Since allowable deductions thus total $5,400, Taxpayer itemizes rather than take the $5,000 standard deduction. Now, assume that in Year 2 Taxpayer receives a $500 state income tax refund on the Year 1 taxes. All $500 is income *unless* part of it is excluded by § 111(a). Taxpayer's itemized deductions would have totaled only $4,900 had the "extra" $500 in state income taxes not been deducted, but Taxpayer would nonetheless have effectively received $5,000 in deductions through the standard deduction. In effect, given the $5,000 standard deduction Taxpayer would receive at a minimum, part of the state income taxes paid produced no tax benefit. The part producing no tax benefit is the amount necessary to bring the itemized deductions up to the amount of standard deduction. In this example, with $2,400 in other itemized deductions, the first $2,600 in the state income taxes produced no tax benefit. The remaining $400 exceeded the standard deduction and did produce a tax benefit. Thus, the first $400 of the state income tax refund constitutes income; any refund in excess of $400 is excluded from income by § 111(a). Suppose, however, that Taxpayer's other itemized deductions had, by themselves, exceeded the standard deduction amount. Now the entire state income tax deduction of $3,000, not just a portion of it, would have produced a tax benefit. Accordingly, any refund would be included in income in its entirety.

Review the language of § 111(a). It excludes those recovered amounts that, when deducted, did not reduce tax. At one time, what § 111(a) excluded were those recovered amounts that had not reduced taxable income when deducted. The distinction is important in some instances because, by way of example, if a taxpayer is subject to the alternative minimum tax (*see* Chapter 45), a deduction may reduce taxable income but may not ultimately reduce tax liability. Thus, § 111(a) appropriately keys the exclusion to tax savings, not taxable income. Nonetheless, it is clear from the legislative history of the current version of § 111(a) that the simplified procedure described above may be followed for individual taxpayers receiving refunds of state and local income taxes. Such taxpayers may simply compare the amount of the refund with the amount by which the prior year's itemized deductions (determined after the application of § 68) exceeded the standard deduction. The lesser of these two amounts is included in income.[2] In Revenue Ruling 92-91, 1992-2 C.B. 49, a similar rule was applied with respect to a refund of a home mortgage interest overcharge. The taxpayer's deduction, upon payment in good faith of the amount erroneously asserted by the lender to be due, was held to be proper. The lender's refund of the interest overcharge in the following year was held includable in income under the tax benefit rule; and since the amount of the reimbursement was less than the amount by which the prior

---

[2] See the Explanation of Technical Corrections to the Tax Reform Act of 1984 and Other Recent Tax Legislation, Jt. Comm. on Taxation (1987), p. 74. See also Revenue Ruling 93-75, 1993-2 C.B. 63, which states the simplified procedure as follows: A refund of previously-deducted state income tax is included in income to the extent "the taxpayer's itemized deductions in the prior year (after the application of section 68 of the Code)" exceed "the deductions the taxpayer would have claimed ([*i.e.,*] the greater of (1) the itemized deductions after the application of section 68, or (2) the standard deduction) had the taxpayer paid the proper amount of state income tax in the prior year" and thus received no refund.

year's itemized deductions exceeded the standard deduction, the reimbursement was fully includable in income.

The tax benefit principle — that the restoration or refund of previously deducted amounts constitutes income — is pervasive in tax law. One sees it codified, for example, in § 104(a), where the general rule, excluding compensation for personal physical injuries or sickness from income, is not extended to amounts attributable to previously deducted medical expenses. As a further example, recall the rule of § 461(f) allowing a deduction for contested liabilities upon payment. Regulation § 1.461-2(a)(3), in an illustration of tax benefit principles, provides that the subsequent refund of a contested, deducted amount is includable in income, subject to the exclusionary rule of § 111. The cases that follow in the materials provide further illustrations of the contexts in which tax benefit questions arise, and also develop various underlying tax benefit issues. *Alice Phelan Sullivan Corporation*, for example, is a reminder that § 1341 does not have a tax benefit equivalent; income may be taxed more or less heavily in the year of deduction than the subsequent year of inclusion. The tax benefit rule makes no allowance for tax rate differentials between the years involved. Why is the § 1341 alternative not extended to the tax benefit situation? Next, read with care the Supreme Court's decision in *Hillsboro National Bank*. As you will see, the Court rejects the notion that some "recovery" of an item is required in order to apply the tax benefit rule. All that the rule requires is an event "fundamentally inconsistent" with the prior deduction. Does the Court's decision provide substantial guidance for future application of the rule?

Another issue may arise when the deduction the taxpayer takes is erroneous. Should the tax benefit rule apply to a subsequent refund, or should the Commissioner's remedy be limited to challenging the erroneous deduction within the time period of the statute of limitations? The Ninth Circuit in *Unvert v. Commissioner*, 656 F.2d 483 (9th Cir. 1981), rejected the so-called erroneous deduction exception to the tax benefit rule and instead held the refund was taxable under the tax benefit rule. The appellate court noted that the Tax Court had held that "Unvert had a duty of consistency and was estopped from contending that the deduction he had previously claimed was improper"; the Ninth Circuit, however, found it unnecessary to consider the estoppel theory and affirmed simply "on the basis that the erroneous deduction exception should be rejected." *Unvert*, 656 F.2d at 485. To the same effect in rejecting the erroneous deduction exception, and applying the tax benefit rule "regardless of the propriety of the original deduction," see *Hughes & Luce v. Commissioner*, 70 F.3d 16, 21 (5th Cir. 1995), holding that a law firm must include in income client reimbursements for expenses that it had previously paid and deducted, but which the firm later conceded should have been treated as nondeductible loans to the clients.

C. Net Operating Losses

The rather cursory treatment we give here to the topic of net operating losses belies its real-world significance. The harshness of the annual accounting rule is exemplified by the Supreme Court's decision in *Burnet v. Sanford & Brooks Co.*, reprinted below. Section 172 of the Code, the forerunner of which was first enacted in 1918, is the principal form of relief from that harshness. In broad outline, § 172 provides that a loss in one year may be used to offset income in another year so the loss is not wasted. Generally speaking, the loss is ordinarily carried back two years and carried forward twenty years until it has been fully absorbed, and thus it is very likely that a net business loss will be deducted by an ultimately profitable business. For example, assume a Year 3 loss of $100,000. The loss would first be applied against Year 1 taxable income. If there were insufficient Year 1 taxable income to absorb the loss, the unused portion of the loss would be carried to Year 2. If Year 2 income did not fully absorb the loss, the unused portion would be carried forward to Year 4, Year 5, etc., until fully absorbed. § 172(b)(1)(A), (2). A taxpayer, however, may elect, with respect to a given year's net operating loss, to dispense with the entire two-year carryback period, and carry the loss forward only. § 172(b)(3).

To illustrate the carryback and carryforward mechanics in simple form, assume a Year 3 loss of $100,000. Assume taxable income of $20,000 each in prior Years 1 and 2, and in subsequent Year 4. The $100,000 loss is first carried back to Year 1, where it fully offsets the $20,000 in income; Year 1 taxable income is thus reduced to zero, and the taxpayer will file an amended Year 1 tax return to this effect, and obtain a tax refund. $80,000 of loss is then carried to Year 2, where it fully absorbs the $20,000 of income and results in the filing of another amended tax return. The unused loss of $60,000 is carried forward to Year 4, where $20,000 more is absorbed. This leaves $40,000 of unused loss to carry forward to Year 5; if Year 5 income is $50,000 the $40,000 of loss is fully absorbed and effectively results in a Year 5 taxable income of $10,000.

This summary of § 172 has ignored its sometimes fearsome complexities. Section 172(c) defines net operating loss simply enough as the excess of deductions allowed over gross income. But the excess is to be computed as modified by § 172(d). In general, the losses that may be carried back and forward are business losses. (Capital losses, which will be studied in Chapter 31, have a separate carryover provision. § 1212; § 172(d)(2).) Unused personal exemptions may not be carried over to other years. § 172(d)(3). Nonbusiness deductions of individuals are allowable in computing a net operating loss only to the extent of nonbusiness income. § 172(d)(4). An individual thus, in general, computes a net operating loss as follows: Add together (1) business deductions and (2) nonbusiness deductions to the extent they do not exceed nonbusiness income. From this total, subtract the taxpayer's gross income. The balance is the individual taxpayer's net operating loss.

BURNET v. SANFORD & BROOKS COMPANY
United States Supreme Court
282 U.S. 359 (1931)

Mr. Justice Stone delivered the opinion of the Court.

In this case certiorari was granted . . . to review a judgment of the Court of Appeals for the Fourth Circuit . . . reversing an order of the Board of Tax Appeals . . . which had sustained the action of the Commissioner of Internal Revenue in making a deficiency assessment against respondent for income and profits taxes for the year 1920.

From 1913 to 1915, inclusive, respondent, a Delaware corporation engaged in business for profit, was acting for the Atlantic Dredging Company in carrying out a contract for dredging the Delaware River, entered into by that company with the United States. In making its income tax returns for the years 1913 to 1916, respondent added to gross income for each year the payments made under the contract that year, and deducted its expenses paid that year in performing the contract. The total expenses exceeded the payments received by $176,271.88. The tax returns for 1913, 1915 and 1916 showed net losses. That for 1914 showed net income.

In 1915 work under the contract was abandoned, and in 1916 suit was brought in the Court of Claims to recover for a breach of warranty of the character of the material to be dredged. Judgment for the claimant . . . was affirmed by this Court in 1920. . . . It held that the recovery was upon the contract and was "compensatory of the cost of the work, of which the government got the benefit." From the total recovery, petitioner received in that year the sum of $192,577.59, which included the $176,271.88 by which its expenses under the contract had exceeded receipts from it, and accrued interest amounting to $16,305.71. Respondent having failed to include these amounts as gross income in its tax returns for 1920, the Commissioner made the deficiency assessment here involved, based on the addition of both items to gross income for that year.

The Court of Appeals ruled that only the item of interest was properly included, holding, erroneously as the government contends, that the item of $176,271.88 was a return of losses suffered by respondent in earlier years and hence was wrongly assessed as income. Notwithstanding this conclusion, its judgment of reversal and the consequent elimination of this item from gross income for 1920 were made contingent upon the filing by respondent of amended returns for the years 1913 to 1916, from which were to be omitted the deductions of the related items of expenses paid in those years. Respondent insists that as the Sixteenth Amendment and the Revenue Act of 1918, which was in force in 1920, plainly contemplate a tax only on net income or profits, any application of the statute which operates to impose a tax with respect to the present transaction, from which respondent received no profit, cannot be upheld.

If respondent's contention that only gain or profit may be taxed under the Sixteenth Amendment be accepted without qualification . . . the question remains whether the gain or profit which is the subject of the tax may be ascertained, as here, on the basis of fixed accounting periods, or whether, as is pressed upon us, it can only be net profit ascertained on the basis of particular transactions of the taxpayer when they are brought to a conclusion.

All the revenue acts which have been enacted since the adoption of the Sixteenth Amendment have uniformly assessed the tax on the basis of annual returns showing the net result of all the taxpayer's transactions during a fixed accounting period, either the calendar year, or, at the option of the taxpayer, the particular fiscal year which he may adopt. Under Sections 230, 232 and 234 (a) of the Revenue Act of 1918, . . . respondent was subject to tax upon its annual net income, arrived at by deducting from gross income for each taxable year all the ordinary and necessary expenses paid during that year in carrying on any trade or business, interest and taxes paid, and losses sustained, during the year. By Sections 233(a) and 213(a) gross income "includes . . . income derived from . . . businesses . . . or the transaction of any business carried on for gain or profit, or gains or profits and income derived from any source whatever." The amount of all such items is required to be included in the gross income for the taxable year in which received by the taxpayer, unless they may be properly accounted for on the accrual basis under Sec. 212(b). . . .

That the recovery made by respondent in 1920 was gross income for that year within the meaning of these sections cannot, we think, be doubted. The money received was derived from a contract entered into in the course of respondent's business operations for profit. While it equalled, and in a loose sense was a return of, expenditures made in performing the contract, still, as the Board of Tax Appeals found, the expenditures were made in defraying the expenses incurred in the prosecution of the work under the contract, for the purpose of earning profits. They were not capital investments, the cost of which, if converted, must first be restored from the proceeds before there is a capital gain taxable as income. *See Doyle v. Mitchell Brothers Co.*, 247 U.S. 185.

That such receipts from the conduct of a business enterprise are to be included in the taxpayer's return as a part of gross income, regardless of whether the particular transaction results in net profit, sufficiently appears from the quoted words of Sec. 213 (a) and from the character of the deductions allowed. Only by including these items of gross income in the 1920 return would it have been possible to ascertain respondent's net income for the period covered by the return, which is what the statute taxes. The excess of gross income over deductions did not any the less constitute net income for the taxable period because respondent, in an earlier period, suffered net losses in the conduct of its business which were in some measure attributable to expenditures made to produce the net income of the later period.

But respondent insists that if the sum which it recovered is the income defined by the statute, still it is not income, taxation of which without apportionment is permitted by the Sixteenth Amendment, since the particular transaction from which it was derived did not result in any net gain or profit. But we do not think the amendment is to be so narrowly construed. A taxpayer may be in receipt of net income in one year and not in another. The net result of the two years, if combined in a single taxable period, might still be a loss; but it has never been supposed that

that fact would relieve him from a tax on the first, or that it affords any reason for postponing the assessment of the tax until the end of a lifetime, or for some other indefinite period, to ascertain more precisely whether the final outcome of the period, or of a given transaction, will be a gain or a loss.

The Sixteenth Amendment was adopted to enable the government to raise revenue by taxation. It is the essence of any system of taxation that it should produce revenue ascertainable, and payable to the government, at regular intervals. Only by such a system is it practicable to produce a regular flow of income and apply methods of accounting, assessment, and collection capable of practical operation. It is not suggested that there has ever been any general scheme for taxing income on any other basis. The computation of income annually as the net result of all transactions within the year was a familiar practice, and taxes upon income so arrived at were not unknown, before the Sixteenth Amendment. . . . It is not to be supposed that the amendment did not contemplate that Congress might make income so ascertained the basis of a scheme of taxation such as had been in actual operation within the United States before its adoption. While, conceivably, a different system might be devised by which the tax could be assessed, wholly or in part, on the basis of the finally ascertained results of particular transactions, Congress is not required by the amendment to adopt such a system in preference to the more familiar method, even if it were practicable. It would not necessarily obviate the kind of inequalities of which respondent complains. If losses from particular transactions were to be set off against gains in others, there would still be the practical necessity of computing the tax on the basis of annual or other fixed taxable periods, which might result in the taxpayer being required to pay a tax on income in one period exceeded by net losses in another.

The assessment was properly made under the statutes. Relief from their alleged burdensome operation which may not be secured under these provisions, can be afforded only by legislation, not by the courts.

Reversed

ALICE PHELAN SULLIVAN CORPORATION v. UNITED STATES
United States Court of Claims
381 F.2d 399 (1967)

COLLINS, JUDGE:

Plaintiff, a California corporation, brings this action to recover an alleged overpayment in its 1957 income tax. During that year, there was returned to taxpayer two parcels of realty, each of which it had previously donated and claimed as a charitable contribution deduction. . . . [T]he deductions claimed yielded plaintiff an aggregate tax benefit of $1,877.49.

Each conveyance had been made subject to the condition that the property be used either for a religious or for an educational purpose. In 1957, the donee decided not to use the gifts; they were therefore reconveyed to plaintiff. . . . The Commissioner . . . viewed the transaction as giving rise to taxable income and therefore adjusted plaintiff's income by adding to it $8,706.03 — the total of the charitable contribution deductions previously claimed and allowed. This addition to income, taxed at the 1957 corporate tax rate of 52%, resulted in a deficiency assessment of $4,527.60. After payment of the deficiency, plaintiff filed a claim for the refund of $2,650.11, asserting this amount as overpayment on the theory that a correct assessment could demand no more than the return of the tax benefit originally enjoyed, *i.e.*, $1,877.49. The claim was disallowed.

This court has had prior occasion to consider the question which the present suit presents. In *Perry v. United States*, 160 F. Supp. 270, 142 Ct.Cl. 7 (1958) (Judges Madden and Laramore dissenting), it was recognized that a return to the donor of a prior charitable contribution gave rise to income to the extent of the deduction previously allowed. The court's point of division — which is likewise the division between the instant parties — was whether the "gain" attributable to the recovery was to be taxed at the rate applicable at the time the deduction was first claimed or whether the proper rate was that in effect at the time of recovery. The majority, concluding that the Government should be entitled to recoup no more than that which it lost, held that the tax liability arising upon the return of a charitable gift should equal the tax benefit experienced at time of donation.

[T]he principle is well ingrained in our tax law that the return or recovery of property that was once the subject of an income tax deduction must be treated as income in the year of its recovery. *Rothensies v. Electric Storage Battery Co.*, 329 U.S. 296. . . . The only limitation upon that principle is the so-called "tax-benefit rule." This rule permits exclusion of the recovered item from income so long as its initial use as a deduction did not provide a tax saving. . . . But where full tax use of a deduction was made and a tax saving thereby obtained, then the extent of saving is considered immaterial. The recovery is viewed as income to the full extent of the deduction previously allowed.[3]

Formerly the exclusive province of judge-made law, the tax-benefit concept now finds expression both in statute and administrative regulations. Section 111 [prior to revision in 1984] of the Internal Revenue Code of 1954 accords tax-benefit treatment to the recovery of bad debts, prior taxes, and delinquency amounts. Treasury regulations have "broadened" the rule of exclusion by extending similar treatment to "all other losses, expenditures, and accruals made the bases of deductions from gross income for prior taxable years. . . . "

Drawing our attention to the broad language of this regulation, the Government insists that the present recovery must find its place within the scope of the regulation and, as such, should be taxed in a manner consistent with the treatment provided for like items of recovery, *i.e.*, that it be taxed at the rate prevailing in the year of recovery. We are compelled to agree.

Ever since *Burnet v. Sanford & Brooks Co.*, 282 U.S. 359 (1931), the concept of accounting for items of income and expense on an annual basis has been accepted

---

[3] The rationale which supports the principle, as well as its limitation, is that the property, having once served to offset taxable income (*i.e.*, as a tax deduction) should be treated, upon its recoupment, as the recovery of that which had been previously deducted. See Plumb, *The Tax Benefit Rule Today*, 57 Harv. L. Rev. 129, 131 n.10 (1943).

as the basic principle upon which our tax laws are structured. "It is the essence of any system of taxation that it should produce revenue ascertainable, and payable to the government, at regular intervals. Only by such a system is it practicable to produce a regular flow of income and apply methods of accounting, assessment, and collection capable of practical operation. . . . " To insure the vitality of the single-year concept, it is essential not only that annual income be ascertained without reference to losses experienced in an earlier accounting period, but also that income be taxed without reference to earlier tax rates. And absent specific statutory authority sanctioning a departure from this principle, it may only be said of *Perry* that it achieved a result which was more equitably just than legally correct.[4]

Since taxpayer in this case did obtain full tax benefit from its earlier deductions, those deductions were properly classified as income upon recoupment and must be taxed as such. This can mean nothing less than the application of that tax rate which is in effect during the year in which the recovered item is recognized as a factor of income. We therefore sustain the Government's position and grant its motion for summary judgment. *Perry v. United States, supra,* is hereby overruled, and plaintiff's petition is dismissed.

HILLSBORO NATIONAL BANK v. COMMISSIONER
United States Supreme Court
460 U.S. 370 (1983)

JUSTICE O'CONNOR delivered the opinion of the Court.

[This case presents] the question of the applicability of the tax benefit rule to . . . the repayment to the shareholders of taxes for which they were liable but that were originally paid by the corporation. . . . We conclude that, unless a nonrecognition provision of the Internal Revenue Code prevents it, the tax benefit rule ordinarily applies to require the inclusion of income when events occur that are fundamentally inconsistent with an earlier deduction. Our examination of the provisions granting the deductions . . . [in this case leads] us to hold that the rule [does not require] the recognition of income in case of the tax refund.

I.

In No. 81-485, *Hillsboro National Bank v. Commissioner,* the petitioner, Hillsboro National Bank, is an incorporated bank doing business in Illinois. Until

---

[4] This opinion represents the views of the majority and complies with existing law and decisions. However, in the writer's personal opinion, it produces a harsh and inequitable result. Perhaps, it exemplifies a situation "where the letter of the law killeth; the spirit giveth life." The tax benefit concept is an equitable doctrine which should be carried to an equitable conclusion. Since it is the declared public policy to encourage contributions to charitable and educational organizations, a donor, whose gift to such organizations is returned, should not be required to refund to the Government a greater amount than the tax benefit received when the deduction was made for the gift. Such a rule would avoid a penalty to the taxpayer and an unjust enrichment to the Government. However, the court cannot legislate and any change in the existing law rests within the wisdom and discretion of the Congress.

1970, Illinois imposed a property tax on shares held in incorporated banks. . . . Banks, required to retain earnings sufficient to cover the taxes, Sec. 558, customarily paid the taxes for the shareholders. Under Sec. 164(e) of the Internal Revenue Code of 1954, 26 U.S.C. Sec. 164(e), the bank was allowed a deduction for the amount of the tax, but the shareholders were not. In 1970, Illinois amended its constitution to prohibit ad valorem taxation of personal property owned by individuals, and the amendment was challenged as a violation of the Equal Protection Clause of the Federal Constitution. The Illinois courts held the amendment unconstitutional in *Lake Shore Auto Parts Co. v. Korzen*, 49 Ill. 2d 137, 273 N.E. 2d 592 (1971). We granted certiorari, and, pending disposition of the case here, Illinois enacted a statute providing for the collection of the disputed taxes and the placement of the receipts in escrow. . . . Hillsboro paid the taxes for its shareholders in 1972, taking the deduction permitted by Sec. 164(e), and the authorities placed the receipts in escrow. This Court upheld the state constitutional amendment in *Lehnhausen v. Lake Shore Auto Parts Co.*, 410 U.S. 356, 93 S.Ct. 1001, 35 L. Ed. 2d 351 (1973). Accordingly, in 1973 the County Treasurer refunded the amounts in escrow that were attributable to shares held by individuals, along with accrued interest. The Illinois courts held that the refunds belonged to the shareholders rather than to the banks. Without consulting Hillsboro, the Treasurer refunded the amounts directly to the individual shareholders. On its return for 1973, Hillsboro recognized no income from this sequence of events. The Commissioner assessed a deficiency against Hillsboro, requiring it to include as income the amount paid its shareholders from the escrow. Hillsboro sought a redetermination in the Tax Court, which held that the refund of the taxes, but not the payment of accrued interest, was includable in Hillsboro's income. On appeal, relying on its earlier decision in *First Trust and Savings Bank v. United States*, 614 F.2d 1142 (CA7 1980), the Court of Appeals for the Seventh Circuit affirmed. 641 F.2d 529, 531 (CA7 1981). . . .

II.

The Government relies solely on the tax benefit rule — a judicially developed principle[5] that allays some of the inflexibilities of the annual accounting system. An annual accounting system is a practical necessity if the federal income tax is to produce revenue ascertainable and payable at regular intervals. *Burnet v. Sanford & Brooks Co.*, 282 U.S. 359, 365 (1931). Nevertheless, strict adherence to an annual accounting system would create transactional inequities. Often an apparently completed transaction will reopen unexpectedly in a subsequent tax year, rendering the initial reporting improper. For instance, if a taxpayer held a note that became apparently uncollectible early in the taxable year, but the debtor made an unexpected financial recovery before the close of the year and paid the debt, the transaction would have no tax consequences for the taxpayer, for the repayment of the principal would be recovery of capital. If, however, the debtor's financial recovery and the resulting repayment took place after the close of the taxable year, the taxpayer would have a deduction for the apparently bad debt in the first year

---

[5] Although the rule originated in the courts, it has the implicit approval of Congress, which enacted Sec. 111 as a limitation on the rule. See note 12, *infra*.

under Sec. 166(a) of the Code, 26 U.S.C. Sec. 166(a). Without the tax benefit rule, the repayment in the second year, representing a return of capital, would not be taxable. The second transaction, then, although economically identical to the first, could, because of the differences in accounting, yield drastically different tax consequences. The Government, by allowing a deduction that it could not have known to be improper at the time, would be foreclosed[6] from recouping any of the tax saved because of the improper deduction.[7] Recognizing and seeking to avoid the possible distortions of income, the courts have long required the taxpayer to recognize the repayment in the second year as income.[8]

The [taxpayer] and the Government . . . propose different formulations of the tax benefit rule. The [taxpayer] contend[s] that the rule requires the inclusion of amounts *recovered* in later years, and [does] not view the [event in this case as a "recovery"]. The Government, on the other hand, urges that the tax benefit rule requires the inclusion of amounts previously deducted if later events are inconsistent with the deductions; it insists that no "recovery" is necessary to the application of the rule. Further, it asserts that the [event in this case is] inconsistent with the deductions taken by the [taxpayer]. We are not in complete agreement with either view.

An examination of the purpose and accepted applications of the tax benefit rule reveals that a "recovery" will not always be necessary to invoke the tax benefit rule. The purpose of the rule is not simply to tax "recoveries." On the contrary, it is to approximate the results produced by a tax system based on transactional rather than annual accounting. . . .

The basic purpose of the tax benefit rule is to achieve rough transactional parity in tax, see note 12, *supra*, and to protect the Government and the taxpayer from the adverse effects of reporting a transaction on the basis of assumptions that an event in a subsequent year proves to have been erroneous. Such an event, unforeseen at the time of an earlier deduction, may in many cases require the application of the tax benefit rule. We do not, however, agree that this consequence invariably follows.

---

[6] A rule analogous to the tax benefit rule protects the taxpayer who is required to report income received in one year under claim of right that he later ends up repaying. Under that rule, he is allowed a deduction in the subsequent year. See generally Sec. 1341, 26 U.S.C. Sec. 1341.

[7] When the event proving the deduction improper occurs after the close of the taxable year, even if the statute of limitations has not run, the Commissioner's proper remedy is to invoke the tax benefit rule and require inclusion in the later year rather than to re-open the earlier year.

[8] Even this rule did not create complete transactional equivalence. In the second version of the transaction discussed in the text, the taxpayer might have realized no benefit from the deduction, if for instance, he had no taxable income for that year. Application of the tax benefit rule as originally developed would require the taxpayer to recognize income on the repayment, so that the net result of the collection of the principal amount of the debt would be recognition of income. Similarly, the tax rates might change between the two years, so that a deduction and an inclusion, though equal in amount, would not produce exactly offsetting tax consequences. Congress enacted Sec. 111 to deal with part of this problem. Although a change in the rates may still lead to differences in taxes due, see *Alice Phelan Sullivan Corp. v. United States*, 381 F.2d 399, 180 Ct. Cl. 659 (Ct.Cl.1967), Sec. 111 provides that the taxpayer can exclude from income the amount that did not give rise to some tax benefit. See *Dobson v. Commissioner*, 320 U.S. 489, 505–506, 64 S.Ct. 239, 248–249, 88 L.Ed. 248 (1943). This exclusionary rule and the inclusionary rule described in the text are generally known together as the tax benefit rule. It is the inclusionary aspect of the rule with which we are currently concerned.

Not every unforeseen event will require the taxpayer to report income in the amount of his earlier deduction. On the contrary, the tax benefit rule will "cancel out" an earlier deduction only when a careful examination shows that the later event is indeed fundamentally inconsistent with the premise on which the deduction was initially based. That is, if that event had occurred within the same taxable year, it would have foreclosed the deduction. In some cases, a subsequent recovery by the taxpayer will be the only event that would be fundamentally inconsistent with the provision granting the deduction. In such a case, only actual recovery by the taxpayer would justify application of the tax benefit rule. For example, if a calendar-year taxpayer made a rental payment on December 15 for a 30-day lease deductible in the current year under Sec. 162(a)(3), see Treas. Reg. Sec. 1.461-1(a)(1), 26 CFR Sec. 1.461-1(a)(1) (1982); *e.g., Zaninovich v. Commissioner*, 616 F.2d 429 (CA9 1980), the tax benefit rule would not require the recognition of income if the leased premises were destroyed by fire on January 10. The resulting inability of the taxpayer to occupy the building would be an event not fundamentally inconsistent with his prior deduction as an ordinary and necessary business expense under Sec. 162(a). The loss is attributable to the business and therefore is consistent with the deduction of the rental payment as an ordinary and necessary business expense. On the other hand, had the premises not burned and, in January, the taxpayer decided to use them to house his family rather than to continue the operation of his business, he would have converted the leasehold to personal use. This would be an event fundamentally inconsistent with the business use on which the deduction was based. In the case of the fire, only if the lessor — by virtue of some provision in the lease — had refunded the rental payment would the taxpayer be required under the tax benefit rule to recognize income on the subsequent destruction of the building. In other words, the subsequent recovery of the previously deducted rental payment would be the only event inconsistent with the provision allowing the deduction. It therefore is evident that the tax benefit rule must be applied on a case-by-case basis. A court must consider the facts and circumstances of each case in the light of the purpose and function of the provisions granting the deductions.

. . . [The dissent] suggests that we err in recognizing transactional equity as the reason for the tax benefit rule. It is difficult to understand why even the clearest recovery should be taxed if not for the concern with transactional equity. . . . Nor does the concern with transactional equity entail a change in our approach to the annual accounting system. Although the tax system relies basically on annual accounting, see *Burnet v. Sanford & Brooks Co.*, 282 U.S. 359, 365, 51 S.Ct. 150, 152, 75 L.Ed. 383 (1931), the tax benefit rule eliminates some of the distortions that would otherwise arise from such a system. . . . The limited nature of the rule and its effect on the annual accounting principle bears repetition: *only* if the occurrence of the event in the earlier year would have resulted in the disallowance of the deduction can the Commissioner require a compensating recognition of income when the event occurs in the later year.

III.

In *Hillsboro* the key provision is Sec. 164(e). That section grants the corporation a deduction for taxes imposed on its shareholders but paid by the corporation. It also denies the shareholders any deduction for the tax. In this case, the Commissioner has argued that the refund of the taxes by the state to the shareholders is the equivalent of the payment of a dividend from Hillsboro to its shareholders. If Hillsboro does not recognize income in the amount of the earlier deduction, it will have deducted a dividend. Since the general structure of the corporate tax provisions does not permit deduction of dividends, the Commissioner concludes that the payment to the shareholders must be inconsistent with the original deduction and therefore requires the inclusion of the amount of the taxes as income under the tax benefit rule. . . .

Under Sec. 164(e), . . . the corporation is . . . satisfying a liability of the shareholder and is therefore paying a constructive dividend. . . . The transaction is . . . a wash for the shareholder; although Sec. 164(e) denies him the deduction to which he would otherwise be entitled, he need not recognize income on the constructive dividend, Treas. Reg. Sec. 1.164-7. . . . But the corporation is entitled to a deduction that would not otherwise be available. In other words, the only effect of Sec. 164(e) is to permit the corporation to deduct a dividend. Thus, we cannot agree with the Commissioner that, simply because the events here give rise to a deductible dividend, they cannot be consistent with the deduction. In at least some circumstances, a deductible dividend is within the contemplation of the Code. The question we must answer is whether Sec. 164(e) permits a deductible dividend in these circumstances — when, the money, though initially paid into the state treasury, ultimately reaches the shareholders — or whether the deductible dividend is available, as the Commissioner urges, only when the money remains in the state treasury, as properly assessed and collected tax revenue.

The *payment* by . . . corporations of a liability that Congress knew was not a tax imposed on them gave rise to the entitlement to a deduction; Congress was unconcerned that the corporations took a deduction for amounts that did not satisfy their tax liability. It apparently perceived the shareholders and the corporations as independent of one another, each "know[ing] nothing about" the payments by the other. In those circumstances, it is difficult to conclude that Congress intended that the corporation have no deduction if the state turned the tax revenues over to these independent parties. We conclude that the purpose of Sec. 164(e) was to provide relief for corporations making these payments, and the focus of Congress was on the act of payment rather than on the ultimate use of the funds by the state. As long as the payment itself was not negated by a refund to the corporation, the change in character of the funds in the hands of the state does not require the corporation to recognize income, and we reverse the judgment below.

Chapter 31

CAPITAL GAINS AND LOSSES

I. PROBLEMS

A. Definition of Capital Asset

1. Terry and Margaret, husband and wife, own all the stock of Friendly Car Dealership, Inc., a corporation engaged in the business of selling new cars to retail customers. Determine which of the following are capital assets:

    (a) The new sedan Friendly just received from the manufacturer and has placed in its sales showroom.

    (b) The van Friendly uses to transport customers to and from its service department.

    (c) The new station wagon Terry and Margaret have just purchased as their family car.

    (d) The land and building Friendly owns and uses in the car dealership.

    (e) The vacant land Terry and Margaret purchased as an investment several years ago.

    (f) The promissory note Friendly received on the sale of a new car.

    (g) Terry and Margaret's home.

    (h) A painting Margaret's mother painted and gave to Margaret shortly before the mother died; a second painting by Margaret's mother, which Margaret received as heir to her mother's estate.

    (i) The manuscript for a book Terry and Margaret wrote regarding the history of their car dealership.

    (j) Margaret's wedding ring.

    (k) Terry and Margaret's stock in Friendly Car Dealership.

    (l) The computer which Friendly formerly owned and used in the dealership, but which Terry and Margaret now own and use to manage their investments.

2. Three years ago, State University hired Steve as its head basketball coach. Under the five-year contract between Steve and State University, the University agreed to pay Steve $250,000 per year. After three losing seasons, the University bought out the remainder of Steve's five-year contract for $400,000. Steve believes he should report the $400,000 as long-term capital gain because he, in effect, is selling property, *i.e.*, his contract

rights, which he has held for more than 12 months. Assess Steve's position.

3. Four years ago, Dennis became aware of the rapid appreciation in the value of certain recreational properties located near a major national park. He purchased the properties anticipating they would appreciate in value and intending to resell them when he could make a satisfactory profit. Over a three-year period, Dennis purchased 15 tracts of the recreational property. He subdivided some of the tracts, made surveys, obtained some rights of way, installed some drainage facilities and extinguished easements on the land. He did not otherwise add any structures or facilities to the land purchased. The demand for large tracts of unimproved property like that owned by Dennis became so great that he did not have to advertise — prospective buyers using public records identified him as the owner and contacted him. Dennis sold 10 parcels of land this year. In each instance, the sale was initiated by the purchaser. Dennis never listed any properties with a real estate broker and realized a gain of $150,000 on the 10 parcels. What is the character of his gain?

B. Rate Preference for Long Term Capital Gains and Limitation on the Deduction of Capital Losses

1. During the current year, Henry and Nancy, who as husband and wife file a joint return, had the following transactions:

   (a) Henry and Nancy sold their summer home for $240,000. They had purchased the home 4 years ago for $170,000 and never used the home as their principal residence.

   (b) Henry sold a painting for $130,000. He had purchased the painting as an investment 6 years before for $50,000.

   (c) Nancy sold 100 shares of stock in Z corporation for $70,000. She had purchased the stock as an investment eight months before for $60,000.

   In addition to the three capital gain transactions above, assume Henry and Nancy earned total compensation of $275,000 from their employment during the year and received $10,000 in "qualified dividend" income within the meaning of § 1(h)(11)(B). Assume Henry and Nancy have no deductible expenses in the current year.

   (i) How much gross income will Henry and Nancy have?

   (ii) How much, net capital gain, if any, will Henry and Nancy have?

   (iii) How will the net capital gain be taxed?

   (iv) How will the gain on the sale of Nancy's shares in Z corporation be taxed?

2. How would their net capital gain be taxed if they had no compensation income and no dividend income and their taxable income consisted entirely of income from the three capital gain transactions listed in Problem 1? In answering this question, ignore the standard deduction and the deduction for personal exemptions and assume Henry and Nancy have no deductible expenses.

3. How would your answers to Problem 1 change, if at all, if the property in Problem 1(b) were "qualified small business stock" instead of a painting? Assume a 50% exclusion under § 1202.

4. How would your answers to Problem 1 change, if at all, if the property in Problem 1(b) were corporate stock that was not qualified small business stock?

5. Assume the same facts as in Problem 1 except that, in addition, Henry and Nancy sold some land which they had purchased 11 months previously and had held for investment. They paid $150,000 for the land and sold it for $90,000. How much loss may Henry and Nancy deduct currently? Compute Henry's and Nancy's net capital gain and explain how it will be taxed. What difference, if any, would it make if Henry and Nancy had held the land for 13 months before selling it?

6. Assume the facts of Problem 5 except Henry and Nancy had paid $250,000 for the land which they had held for 11 months. Assume also Henry and Nancy sold Y stock which they had held for 15 months at a $30,000 loss. Do Henry and Nancy have a net capital gain? How much loss may Henry and Nancy deduct this year? What will be the amount and character of any loss carryover?

C.   Miscellaneous Capital Gain/Loss Issues

1. Sharon, a newspaper publisher, purchased stock in the ABC Newsprint Company in order to assure a supply of paper. Sharon later sold the stock at a loss.

   (a) How would the loss be characterized?

   (b) What if, instead of purchasing stock, Sharon had entered into a ten-year contract with the newsprint company, under which she agreed to purchase a certain amount of newsprint each year. Assume that Sharon periodically assigns her right to some of the newsprint to other newspaper publishing companies. How should she characterize the payments received for these assignments?

2. Brian invests in the stock of newly-formed companies. Brian sold certain stock to a private party at a substantial gain, which he reported as long-term capital gain. The year following the stock sale, Brian was sued for failing to provide the purchaser with pertinent information regarding the stock sold. Brian denied the charges, but to avoid the costs of litigation and potential damage to his reputation as an investor, Brian settled the suit for $10,000. What tax consequences to Brian?

3. Late last year, Chris bought 100 shares of XYZ stock for $5,000. Early this year, he sold half the stock for $500. Shortly thereafter, the remaining XYZ stock became worthless. What tax consequences to Chris?

4. Middletown foreclosed upon certain land owned for many years by Jack for nonpayment of $175,000 in property taxes. Jack's basis in the land, which he held for investment purposes, was $200,000. What tax consequences to Jack?

Assignment for Chapter 31:

Complete the problems.

Read: Internal Revenue Code: §§ 1(h); 408(m); 1202(a)–(c), 1202(d)(1); 1211(b), 1212(b); 1221; 1222; 1223(1), (2) and (11); 165(a)–(c), 165(f); 1001(a)–(c); 1011(a); 1012; 62(a)(3); 64; 65, 165(g)(1), (2);
Treasury Regulations: §§ 1.1221-1(a)–(d).

Materials: Overview
Bynum v. Commissioner
Arkansas Best Corp. v. Commissioner
Hort v. Commissioner
Davis v. Commissioner
Kenan v. Commissioner

II. VOCABULARY

capital asset
capital gain
capital loss
long-term capital gain
short-term capital gain
long-term capital loss
short-term capital loss
net long-term capital gain
net long-term capital loss
net short-term capital gain
net short-term capital loss
net capital gain
adjusted net capital gain
unrecaptured section 1250 gain
28-percent rate gain
collectibles gain
qualified dividend income
Corn Products property
holding period
Arrowsmith rule
ordinary income
capital loss carryover
qualified small business stock

III. OBJECTIVES

1. To explain the significance of the character of gain and loss.
2. To identify capital assets.
3. To characterize gain or loss in any given situation.
4. To recognize ordinary income substitutes.
5. To recognize *Corn Products* property.

6. To compute a taxpayer's net capital gain and adjusted net capital gain.

7. To explain the operation of § 1(h) and in particular the varying maximum rates applicable to the various components of net capital gain.

8. To explain the tax preference afforded qualified small business stock held more than 5 years.

9. To compute the amount of capital loss which may be deducted by a taxpayer in a given taxable year.

10. To compute the amount of capital loss carryover and to determine the long or short-term character of the capital loss carryover.

11. To apply the *Arrowsmith* rule.

12. To recall that the deduction for capital losses is an "above the line" deduction under § 62.

13. To explain the impact of capital gains and losses on the taxable income of a taxpayer.

IV. OVERVIEW

A. Historical Overview

1. Preferential Treatment for Long Term Capital Gain

Taxpayer purchased stock in Year 1 and sold the stock five years later for $50,000 more than the original purchase price. Is the $50,000 "profit" realized on the sale of the stock income? While today the answer is clear, it required a Supreme Court decision to establish the principle that gains from the sale of assets like stock constitute income. In *Merchants' Loan and Trust Company v. Smietanka*, 255 U.S. 509 (1921), the taxpayer argued that the increase in value of stock when realized through a sale or other disposition did not constitute "income" within the meaning of the Sixteenth Amendment. According to the taxpayer, " 'income' as used in the Sixteenth Amendment . . . does not include the gain from capital realized by a single isolated sale of property but that only the profits realized from sales by one engaged in buying and selling as a business — a merchant, a real estate agent, or broker — constitute income which may be taxed." Rejecting that argument, the Court noted that the taxpayer's construction "would, in large measure, defeat the purpose of the [Sixteenth] Amendment." Contrary to the taxpayer's position, the appreciation on the stock was income subject to tax when the appreciation was realized through the sale of the stock. 255 U.S. at 520–21.

Congress, however, in the same year as the Court's decision in *Merchants Land and Trust Company*, acknowledged that special tax treatment for the gain recognized on the disposition of certain assets was justified. In the Revenue Act of 1921, Congress provided preferential tax treatment for the gains (referred to as "capital gains") from the sale or exchange of a class of assets Congress characterized as "capital assets." The Act defined a "capital asset" as "property acquired and held by the taxpayer for profit or investment for more than two years (whether or not connected with his trade or business), but does not include . . . stock in trade of the taxpayer or other property of a kind which would properly be included in the inventory of the taxpayer if on hand at the close of the taxable year." While tax rates on all other income ranged as high as 58%, the Act limited the tax which could be imposed on capital gains to 12.5%.[1]

Note that in the 1921 Revenue Act, Congress limited the preferential tax treatment to gains from assets which had been held "for more than two years." The length of the holding period required for capital asset designation suggests one of the major reasons justifying capital gain treatment, *i.e.*, to tax capital gains like all other income would be harsh, considering that the gain often represented appreciation accruing over a number of years. Recall that the gain inherent in an asset is

---

[1] Specifically, the Revenue Act of 1921 provided that in computing his tax, a taxpayer would segregate all capital gains (gains from the sale or exchange of capital assets), capital losses (losses from the sale or exchange of capital assets) and capital deductions (allowable deductions allocable to items of capital gain). The excess of the capital gains over the sum of the capital losses and capital deductions constituted "capital net gain." At the election of the taxpayer, the taxpayer's tax would be computed by adding the 12.5% of the capital net gain to the tax computed on the taxpayer's ordinary net income (*i.e.*, net income excluding all items of capital gain, capital loss and capital deduction).

not reportable as income until it has been "realized." Thus, even though an asset may appreciate at a steady rate over a number of years, the appreciation will generally not be taxed as income until the asset is sold or exchanged. As a result, gain accruing over the years is bunched into one tax year for purposes of taxation. By providing preferential treatment to such gains, Congress sought to mitigate this bunching problem.[2] The two-year holding period, included in the definition of "capital asset" in the 1921 Act, assured that gains generated over a short-term would not be tax-preferred. Beginning with the 1938 Revenue Act, tax-preferred capital gains were referred to as "long-term capital gains" while gains not tax-preferred were denominated "short-term capital gains."

Congressional concern regarding the bunching problem is best exemplified in the refinements made to the capital gain structure in the 1934 Revenue Act. The 1934 Act introduced a sliding scale approach to capital gain preferential treatment based on the holding period of capital assets. It provided that 100% of the gain or loss recognized upon the sale or exchange of a capital asset was to be taken into account in computing net income if the capital asset had been held for a year or less; the percentage of recognized gain or loss decreased in steps as the holding period lengthened, down to 30% if the asset was held more than 10 years. This sliding scale method, however, was shortlived. In the 1938 Revenue Act, Congress shortened the holding period required for preferential capital gains treatment to eighteen months. The 1942 Revenue Act further shortened the long-term holding period requirement to six months. The six-month holding period requirement for long-term capital gains existed from 1942 through 1976 and again from 1984 through 1987. For 1988 and following years, only the gains (and losses) from the sale or exchange of capital assets held for more than one year will be long-term and therefore eligible for preferential treatment.[3]

Congress not only varied the holding period necessary for preferential treatment, it also varied the nature and the amount of the preference itself. The Revenue Act of 1921 limited the tax on capital gain to 12.5%; by contrast, the Revenue Act of 1942 provided that only 50% of long-term gain (and long-term loss) would be taken into account in computing net income. Thus, under the 1942 Act, the rate of tax applicable to capital gains depended on the specific rate bracket of the taxpayer. Beginning with the Revenue Act of 1951, the preference for capital gains took the form of a deduction from gross income equal to 50% of the net capital gain, a term defined in § 1222(11) as "the excess of the net long-term capital gain for the taxable year over the net short-term capital loss for such year." The 50% deduction was increased in 1978 to 60% and remained at that level until the repeal of the preference in 1986 as part of a major tax act which reduced the top individual income tax rates from 50% to 28%.[4] With this significant reduction in tax rates, Congress concluded that there was no continuing need to provide a reduced rate of

---

[2] The bunching problem is a function of the rule that appreciation on property is not taxed as income until the appreciation is realized through an event like a sale or an exchange. If one were taxed each year on the increase in the value of one's property during the year, the bunching problem would not exist.

[3] The holding period for long-term capital gains was increased to nine months for 1977 and then to one year for the period 1978 through June 22, 1984.

[4] The deduction was an above-the-line deduction, *i.e.*, it was a deduction taken in computing adjusted gross income. *See* I.R.C. 1954 § 62(4) (repealed by the 1986 Tax Reform Act).

tax for net capital gains. The legislative history of the 1986 Tax Reform Act explained:

> The committee believes that as a result of the reduction of individual tax rates on such forms of capital income as business profits, interest, dividends, and short-term capital gains, the need to provide a reduced rate for net capital gain is eliminated. This will result in a tremendous amount of simplification for many taxpayers since their tax will no longer depend upon the characterization of income as ordinary or capital gain. In addition, this will eliminate any requirement that capital assets be held by the taxpayer for any extended period of time . . . in order to obtain favorable treatment. This will result in greater willingness to invest in assets that are freely traded (*e.g.*, stocks).

Tax Reform Act of 1986, Senate Finance Committee Report on H.R. 3838, 99th Cong. 2d Sess. 169 (1986).

The ink was not dry on the 1986 legislation, however, before many taxpayers and their advisors began complaining that the elimination of any preference for capital gains meant that Congress had in effect increased the tax on capital gains. Those taxpayers were correct. Prior to the 1986 Act there was a 60% above-the-line deduction for net capital gain and a maximum rate of tax of 50%, net capital gain was thus subject to a maximum tax rate of 20%. For example, if a taxpayer realized $1,000 of long-term capital gain on the sale of stock, only $400 of that gain would be taxable as a result of the 60% deduction and that $400 could not be taxed at a rate greater than 50%. The taxpayer in this scenario pre-1986 Act would not pay a tax greater than $200 on the sale of the stock. After the 1986 Act, however, the same taxpayer could be subject to a tax as high as $280 (28% of $1,000).

Since 1986, restoration of a preference for long-term capital gain has been a subject of continual debate within Congress. When it increased maximum individual rates from 28% to 31% in 1990 and from 31% to 39.6% in 1993, Congress retained the maximum rate (established in 1986) of 28% on net capital gain. By retaining the 28% maximum rate on net capital gain, Congress reintroduced into the Code a modest preference for long-term capital gains. That level of preference, however, did not satisfy the advocates of capital gain preferential treatment. In the 1997 Act, Congress established a new preferential treatment structure for net capital gain. The most prominent feature of that new structure was a 20% maximum rate on certain long-term capital gains, a rate that was initially retained when phased-in reductions in maximum individual rates were enacted in 2001 tax legislation, but was subsequently lowered to 15% in 2003. The American Taxpayer Relief Act of 2012, however, reimposed the 20% maximum rate for taxpayers in the highest income tax bracket, *i.e.*, 39.6%. As will be obvious in your review of current Section 1(h) and the discussion of it *infra*, the preference for long-term capital gains has introduced additional complexity into an already overly complex Code.

To encourage investors to fund new ventures and small businesses, Congress in 1993 added § 1202 allowing an exclusion from gross income of 50% of the gain from the sale or exchange of "qualified small business stock" held for more than 5 years. This provision was retained as a part of the new preferential rate structure for capital gains which emerged from the 1997 legislation. Congress subsequently raised the 50% exclusion to 100% on a temporary basis effective for qualifying small business stock acquired after September 10, 2010 and before January 1, 2015. § 1202(a)(4). (It would not be surprising if Congress extended the 100% exclusion beyond 2014 or even made it permanent.) Assuming a return to the original 50% exclusion under § 1202, the gain subject to tax would generally be taxed at a rate of 28%. Considering half of the gain is excluded from tax, the effective rate on the entire realized gain would thus be 14%, well below the 20% maximum rate applicable to the long-term stock gain of high income (39.6% bracket) taxpayers, but not significantly different from the 15% maximum rate otherwise generally imposed by § 1(h)(1)(c).

In general, gain eligible for the special benefit of § 1202 is limited to the greater of: (1) 10 times the taxpayer's basis in the stock or (2) $10,000,000 of gain from the disposition of the stock. § 1202(b)(1). "Qualified small business stock" is stock of a C corporation issued after August 10, 1993. § 1202(c)(1). The stock must be that of a qualified small business (in general, a corporation with gross assets not greater than $50 million at the time of the issuance of the stock); and must be acquired by the taxpayer at its original issuance. § 1202(d)(1). Section 1202 contains numerous requirements and limitations which significantly narrow the kind of stock eligible for this special preferential treatment. Detailed analysis of § 1202 is beyond the scope of this course.

2.   Limitation on the Deduction of Capital Losses

While providing preferential treatment for capital gain in the Revenue Act of 1921, Congress did not provide any corresponding limitation on the deduction of capital losses. In the Revenue Act of 1924, Congress rectified this situation. As noted by a member of the House Ways and Means Committee:

> the injustice to the Government is too obvious to require much comment. The taxpayer may refrain from taking his profits, or, if he does take them, pays but a 12.5 percent tax, whereas he is at liberty at any time to take advantage of any losses that may have been incurred and avail himself of a full deduction from his income. When we consider that the rate on the larger incomes runs as high as 58 percent, it can readily be realized how great the advantage is. The Government can collect but 12.5 percent of a gain, but it is compelled to lighten the burden of the taxpayer to the extent of 58 percent of his losses. Take, for example, the case of a man with an income of $350,000 a year. Assume that he bought in the year 1917 5,000 shares of stock X at $100 par, and that he sells those shares in 1922 for $600,000, showing a profit of $100,000. By reason of this transaction, he would pay, in addition to the tax on his regular income, $12,500 to the Government. But assume that instead of selling this stock at a profit, he sold it in 1922 at a loss of $100,000. He would then be entitled to deduct the $100,000 from his income of $350,000, and the loss to the government by reason of that deduction would be $58,000. Is there any further argument needed?

Report of the Committee on Ways and Means on H. R. 13770, H.Rep. No. 1388, 67th Cong. 4th Sess. (1923).

Just as the 1924 Revenue Act provided that the maximum tax on capital gains could not exceed 12.5%, the Act also provided that a taxpayer's tax liability (computed without considering capital gains and losses) could not be reduced by more than 12.5% of the "capital net loss" (the excess of the sum of the capital losses plus the capital deductions over the total amount of capital gain). Beginning with the Revenue Act of 1934, capital losses could only be deducted to the extent of capital gains; up to $2,000 of any excess of capital losses over gains could also be deducted. Any capital losses not deductible because of the limitation were carried over to the following year or years until used. As discussed in some detail *infra* similar limitations on the deductibility of capital losses continue to exist, except that the excess capital loss deduction has been raised to $3,000.

3.   Justification for Preferential Capital Gain Treatment

Before considering the current preferential treatment structure, it will be well to consider the kinds of arguments pro and con which have been made and continue to be made in the debates regarding the creation and retention of a capital gain preference. Proponents of preferential capital gain treatment justify such treatment on a number of theories in addition to the bunching theory described previously. First, some supporters contend the gain realized on the sale or exchange of a capital asset is often largely due to inflation and does not represent any real increase in the value of the asset. A reduced rate of tax on capital gains therefore negates, at least to some extent, imposition of tax on such illusory gains.

Second, proponents argue that the mobility of capital could be impaired if capital gains were taxed like any other income. Knowing the gain from the sale or exchange of a capital asset would be taxed like compensation or any other income, taxpayers might retain appreciated assets simply to avoid the tax burden. Indeed, taxpayers might continue to hold appreciated assets until death so as to take advantage of the stepped-up basis accorded property acquired from a decedent. § 1014(a). Many believe that this so-called "lock-in" effect could seriously harm the economy.

Third, proponents of preferential treatment argue that taxing capital gains at the same rate as other income is a disincentive to savings. By contrast, when capital gains are given preferential tax treatment, people are encouraged to save (by investing in stock, etc.), thus increasing the capital available for business investment. The availability of investment funds for capital formation is particularly critical to new and small businesses. Furthermore, additional business investment results in greater productivity and a correspondingly higher standard of living. Denial of preferential capital gain treatment would therefore significantly hinder economic growth.

While the arguments advanced for preferential capital gain treatment are many, there are strong arguments opposing preferential treatment. One of the primary arguments against preferential treatment is that such treatment creates the need for complex statutory provisions designed to prevent taxpayers from converting ordinary income into capital gain. Furthermore, the existence of preferential capital gain treatment requires the courts and the Service to determine whether in a particular case a gain is a capital gain or ordinary income. Indeed, a considerable body of case law and rulings has developed over time addressing the issue of what constitutes a capital gain.

In addition, critics of preferential capital gain treatment argue the problems identified by proponents of such treatment could be better addressed through other means. For example, inflation concerns could be addressed by periodically adjusting the basis of property to account for inflation; and bunching problems could be addressed through an income averaging mechanism. Indeed, with the shortening of the holding period for long-term capital gain treatment to one year, the argument that preferential capital gain treatment was justified because of bunching was rendered almost meaningless with respect to assets held for only the minimum period required for long-term capital gain treatment.

In this and the following chapters, you will gain some insight into the complexity created by preferential treatment for capital gain. As you consider the statutory, judicial and administrative rules in this area, ask yourself whether the reasons listed above supporting the existence of preferential capital gain treatment justify the complexity of the capital gain and loss structure.

B.   Current Law: Section 1(h)

1.   Maximum Rates on Long-Term Capital Gain Under the Current Law

The preferential rates of § 1(h) apply only when the taxpayer has net capital gain. As noted previously, "net capital gain" (NCG) is defined in § 1222(11) as "the excess of the net long-term capital gain [*i.e.*, the excess of long-term capital gains (LTCG) over long-term capital losses (LTCL)] over the net short-term capital loss [*i.e.*, the excess of short-term capital loss (STCL) over short-term capital gain (STCG)] for the year." Review the definitions in Section 1222 of long-term capital gain and loss and short-term capital gain and loss as well as the definitions of net long-term capital gain and net short-term capital loss. Careful consideration of the definition of "net capital gain" reveals that preferential treatment exists only for long-term capital gains. Technically, preferential treatment exists only when the taxpayer's long-term gains exceed the sum of taxpayer's long-term capital losses and net short-term capital loss. Short-term capital gains are accorded no preference and are therefore subject to tax at ordinary income rates as high as 35%.

> **Example 1 — Short-Term Capital Gain Only:** Assume that Betty sold stock for $50,000. Betty's basis in the stock was $40,000 and she had held the stock for 10 months. Betty thus had $10,000 of STCG. Assuming this was her only sale or exchange during the year, Betty had no net capital gain. (Applying the formula NLTCG − NSTCL = NCG, it is obvious there is $0 NLTCG and $0 NSTCL and therefore $0 NCG.) Therefore, Betty would not have been entitled to any preferential treatment on the gain from the stock sale. If Betty were in a 39.6% tax bracket, she would have been required to pay $3,960 in federal tax on the stock gain.

> **Example 2 — Long-Term Capital Gain Only:** Assume the same facts as Example 1 except Betty held the stock for 2 years. Under these circum-

stances, Betty would have had a net capital gain of $10,000 (NLTCG of $10,000 less NSTCL of $0 = $10,000). Under § 1(h), even if she were in the 39.6% bracket, her federal tax on the stock gain would be taxed at a preferential rate — in this case under current law at a rate of 20% for a tax of $2,000 on the stock gain. § 1(h)(1)(D).

Example 3 — Long-Term Capital Gain and Short-Term Capital Gain: Assume the facts of Example 2 except Betty also had a short-term capital gain of $10,000. Her net capital gain would still be $10,000 (NLTCG of $10,000 less NSTCL of $0 = $10,000). Assuming she were in the 39.6% bracket, Betty would pay a tax of $2,000 (.20 x $10,000) on the long-term capital gain and would pay a tax of $3,960 on the short-term capital gain.

Example 4 — Long-Term Capital Gain and Long-Term Capital Loss: Assume the facts of Example 2 except that Betty also had a long-term capital loss of $10,000. She would have no net capital gain (NLTCG of $0 less NSTCL of $0 = $0).

Prior to the enactment of the 1997 Act, net capital gain was taxed at a maximum rate of 28%. Under pre-1997 law, the only taxpayer who benefitted from the preferential capital gain treatment was a taxpayer in a rate bracket higher than 28%. Taxpayers in rate brackets of 28% or below would pay the same rate of tax on their net capital gain as they would on ordinary income. (Of course, it still made a difference to these taxpayers whether their gains were capital or ordinary gains. See, *e.g.*, the § 1211 limitation on capital losses.)

In adding § 1(h) in 1997 and thereafter amending it to provide increased preferential treatment for certain classes of long-term capital gain, Congress dramatically changed the rate structure applicable to net capital gains but did not change any of the definitions in § 1222. Thus, for example, "long-term capital gain" is still defined as the "gain from the sale or exchange of a capital asset held for more than 1 year. . . . "

2. The Components of Net Capital Gain: 28-Percent Rate Gain; Unrecaptured Section 1250 Gain; and Adjusted Net Capital Gain

Under current § 1(h), the maximum capital gain rate on net capital gain (or more to the point on long-term capital gains) will vary depending upon the nature of the assets giving rise to the long-term capital gains. In no event, however, will the maximum rate of tax on any long-term capital gains exceed 28%. To compute the tax on a taxpayer's net capital gain, one must first determine the extent, if any, to which net capital gain is made up of either "28-percent rate gain" (taxed at a maximum tax rate of 28%) or "unrecaptured section 1250 gain" (taxed at a maximum tax rate of 25%). Any net capital gain remaining after those two categories of gain have been determined is referred to as "adjusted net capital gain." Section 1(h)(3). Adjusted net capital gain is subject to the greatest preferential treatment, *i.e.*, a maximum tax rate of 15% unless the taxpayer is subject to the 39.6% marginal income tax rate in which case the maximum tax rate on adjusted net capital gain is 20%.

In the discussion that follows concerning the maximum rate of tax on the various groups or components of net capital gain, we will initially, for the sake of simplicity, assume there are no long-term or short-term capital losses to be taken into account in computing net capital gain. Thus, our focus will be solely on the long-term capital gains that are reflected in net capital gain.

a.   28-Percent Rate Gain: Collectibles Gain and Section 1202 Gain

As the name suggests, that part, *if any*, of a taxpayer's net capital gain which is characterized as 28-percent rate gain will be taxed at a maximum rate of 28%. This category of long-term capital gain provides preferential treatment only if the taxpayer is in a tax bracket higher than 28%. Thus, for example, if a taxpayer is in the 15% bracket, that taxpayer's 28-percent rate gain would be subject to tax at 15% just as in the case of the taxpayer's ordinary income. In general, 28-percent rate gain is the sum of "collectibles gain" and "section 1202 gain." Collectibles gain is defined in § 1(h)(5) as gain from the sale or exchange of any rug or antique, metal, gem stamp or coin or other collectible as defined by § 408(m), which is a capital asset held for more than one year. Section 1202 gain is defined in § 1(h)(7); in general, it is 50% of the gain from the sale or exchange of certain stock described in § 1202.[5]

> **Example — 28-Percent Rate Gain:** Mary is a taxpayer in the 35% tax bracket. During the current year, she realizes $5,000 long-term capital gain on the sale of some antique furniture which she had received as a wedding gift from her grandmother and $10,000 in long-term capital gain for a work of art Mary had held for three years. Assuming these are Mary's only capital gain/loss transactions during the year, Mary will have a net capital gain of $15,000. The gains from the sale of both the antique furniture and the work of art are 28-percent rate gain because they constitute collectibles gain as defined in § 1(h)(5). Mary will thus be subject to capital gains tax at a rate of 28% on the $15,000 of net capital gain. She will be subject to tax at a 35% rate on her other income. If Mary were in the 15% bracket, Mary would pay capital gains tax at a rate of 15% on the sale of the furniture and the art work. Mary thus will only get preferential treatment to the extent that she is in a bracket greater than 28% when she sells the art or the furniture.

---

[5] Technically, "section 1202 gain" is the gain that was not excluded from gross income under § 1202. See § 1(h)(7), defining § 1202 gain as the excess of the gain that would have been excluded under § 1202 but for the percentage limitations of § 1202, over the gain actually excluded. This excess will usually, but not always, be 50% of the total gain. As previously noted, the normal 50% exclusion provided by § 1202 for gain from the sale or exchange of "qualified small business stock" held for more than 5 years was temporarily increased to 100%. This temporary increase is effective only for qualified small business stock acquired after September 10, 2010 and before January 1, 2015.

b. Unrecaptured Section 1250 Gain — 25-Percent Rate

Net capital gain to the extent of so-called "unrecaptured section 1250 gain" is subject to a maximum rate of tax of 25%. Section 1(h)(1)(E). In general, unrecaptured § 1250 gain is the long-term capital gain attributable to depreciation allowed with respect to real estate (e.g., buildings) held for more than one year. Section 1(h)(6). We will not study the detail of unrecaptured § 1250 gain at this time, although Chapter 33 will address in some detail the concept of depreciation recapture. The following simple example will demonstrate the nature of this category of gain.

> **Example — Unrecaptured Section 1250 Gain:** Assume that during the current year Anna, a taxpayer in the 35% bracket, sold a commercial building for $100,000. Anna had paid $100,000 for the building 10 years ago and had been allowed straight-line depreciation deductions aggregating $25,000 on the building during the period in which she held the building for use in her business. Thus, Anna's adjusted basis in the building at the time of the sale was $75,000. Under § 1001, Anna's recognized gain on the sale of the building was therefore $25,000. Assume this was Anna's only disposition of property during the year and the $25,000 gain was characterized as long-term capital gain.[6] If one thinks about the circumstances presented, it should be clear the only reason that Anna had any gain on the property was because she had claimed $25,000 in depreciation over time and had to adjust her basis in the building down to reflect that depreciation. That downward adjustment in basis resulted in the $25,000 of gain on the sale of the property. Thus, all $25,000 of gain is the result of depreciation deductions claimed by Anna and all the gain is therefore characterized as unrecaptured section 1250 gain. (When we examine § 1250 and the concept of "recapture" in Chapter 33, this characterization will make more sense to you.) Given the assumption the sale of the building was Anna's only property disposition during the year, Anna's net capital gain would be $25,000. Because all of the net capital gain is unrecaptured 1250 gain, Anna would be subject to a maximum rate of tax on this gain of 25%.

c. Adjusted Net Capital Gain: 15-Percent and 0-Percent Rates

Net capital gain reduced by a taxpayer's 28% rate gain and unrecaptured section 1250 gain equals "adjusted net capital gain." § 1(h)(3). Adjusted net capital gain is subject to a maximum rate of 20% for taxpayers in the highest ordinary income tax bracket of 39.6%. For taxpayers in the 35%, 33%, 28%, or 25% ordinary income tax brackets, the maximum rate on adjusted net capital gain is 15%. The adjusted net capital gain tax rate is zero for taxpayers in the 10% or 15% brackets. (Note that, unlike 28% rate gain or unrecaptured section 1250 gain, adjusted net capital gain is accorded preferential treatment even if the taxpayer is in the 10% or 15% income tax rate brackets.) All three rates, *i.e.*, the 20%, 15%, and 0% rates

---

[6] This characterization rests on § 1231, studied in Chapter 32, and on § 1250, studied in Chapter 33.

were made permanent by the American Taxpayer Relief Act of 2012. Unlike 28% rate gain or unrecaptured section 1250 gain, adjusted net capital gain is accorded preferential treatment even if the taxpayer is in a 15% income tax bracket. In that case, the rate of tax on the adjusted net capital gain is zero.[7] A classic example of a transaction which will produce this category of gain would be the sale of corporate stock (*e.g.*, IBM stock) that does not constitute qualified small business stock under § 1202, and that was held by the taxpayer for more than one year.

Example 1 — Adjusted Net Capital Gain Taxed at 15-Percent Rate: Mark and Susan, married taxpayers filing jointly, are in the 35% tax bracket. During 2015, Mark and Susan realized $10,000 in long-term capital gain as a result of their sale of certain stock held for more than one year. They had no other capital gain/loss transactions during the year. The couple's net capital gain is thus $10,000. Since Mark and Susan had no 28% rate gain and no unrecaptured section 1250 gain as defined previously, their adjusted net capital gain is $10,000 (*i.e.*, adjusted net capital gain equals net capital gain in this example). Mark and Susan will therefore pay tax at the rate of 15% on their $10,000 of net capital gain and will be subject to a marginal tax rate of 35% on all of their other income. Note that, if Mark and Susan were in the 39.6% rate bracket, the tax rate on their stock gain would be 20%.

Example 2 — Adjusted Net Capital Gain Taxed in Part at Zero Percent and in Part at 15 Percent: In 2015, Carl and Diane, married taxpayers filing jointly, have $100,000 of taxable income made up of $66,000 of ordinary income and $34,000 of long-term capital gain from the sale of Microsoft stock held for more than one year. (Assume they have no deductions or exemptions.) To keep matters as simple as possible, assume that for taxpayers filing joint returns, the first $70,000 of taxable income is taxed in part at 10% and in part at 15% and amounts of taxable income in excess of $70,000 but less than $140,000 are taxed at 28%.

Carl and Diane have a net capital gain of $34,000. None of this gain constitutes either 28-percent rate gain or unrecaptured section 1250 gain. They thus have adjusted net capital gain of $34,000. Their tax liability will be computed as follows: First, the excess of the taxable income ($100,000) over the net capital gain ($34,000) or $66,000 (the ordinary income) will be taxed at the regular rates, *i.e.*, some at 10% (§ 1(i)) and some at 15% (§ 1(a)). Because the 15% income tax bracket covers taxable income up to $70,000, there will be $4,000 of the net capital gain which, but for the special rules of § 1(h), would be taxable at 15%. Since all of the net capital gain constitutes adjusted net capital gain, however, this $4,000 will be taxed, not at 15%, but at 0%. The remaining $30,000 of net capital gain (which here is the remaining amount of adjusted net capital gain) will be taxed at 15% instead of 28%. § 1(h)(1)(B), (C). Review the relevant language of amended

---

[7] § 1(h)(1)(B). Tax legislation in 2003 reduced the rate in question here from 10% to 5% (and to zero in 2008), and 2006 legislation extended the zero rate from 2008 to 2010. The rate was extended through 2012 by legislation in 2010. As noted above, the American Taxpayer Relief Act of 2012 made the zero rate permanent.

§ 1(h) to determine whether on your own you could reach this result. As noted above, § 1(h) is complex and its application to a rather simple problem such as this will require careful attention to detail.

While the above examples have addressed situations in which net capital gain was comprised solely of long-term capital gains characterized as 28% rate gain or solely of long-term capital gains constituting adjusted net capital gain, it is easy to imagine situations where taxpayer will have a net capital gain which includes a combination of the various components described above. Consider the following example:

> **Example — Mixture of Short-Term Capital Gain, 28-Percent Rate Gain and Adjusted Net Capital Gain:** Martin is in the 35% tax bracket. During 2015, he has short-term capital gain of $10,000 from the sale of ABC stock held for less than one year, $10,000 of long-term capital gain from the sale of a work of art held for a number of years, and $10,000 of long-term capital gain from the sale of XYZ stock held for two years. Martin has no other capital gain/loss transactions during the year. His net capital gain will be $20,000 (*i.e.*, NLTCG ($20,000) less NSTCL ($0) = $20,000). (Note that in this example, Martin's short-term capital gain has no impact on the determination of net capital gain.) His net capital gain will be taxed as follows: the $10,000 of 28% rate gain, *i.e.*, the gain on the sale of the work of art, will be taxed at 28% and the remaining net capital gain (*i.e.*, the adjusted net capital gain) which results from the sale of the XYZ stock will be taxed at 15%. Martin's remaining taxable income, including the short-term capital gain, will be subject to a marginal tax rate of 35%. Note that, if Martin were in the 39.6% income tax bracket, the analysis would be the same, except the adjusted net capital gain on the XYZ stock would be taxed at 20% and the remaining taxable income, including the short-term capital gain, would be subject to a marginal tax rate of 39.6%.[8]

d.   Adjusted Net Capital Gain: Qualified Dividend Income

Under 2003 tax legislation, "qualified dividend income" is treated as part of adjusted net capital gain and thus is taxed at the 20-percent, 15-percent or zero-percent rates currently applicable to such gain. This represents a major shift in the tax treatment of dividends, which were previously taxed at the rates applicable to ordinary income, rather than at capital gain rates. The change was justified by the claim that it would lower the cost of capital and lead to economic growth and job creation. (This treatment of dividend income was made permanent by the American Taxpayer Relief Act of 2012.)

Qualified dividend income consists of dividends from U.S. corporations (with

---

[8] If the taxpayer's marginal tax rate is 39.6%, but the amount of the taxable income in that bracket is less than the taxpayer's net capital gain, the adjusted net capital gain taxed at 20% will be the amount otherwise taxed at 39.6%. The remaining net capital gain will be taxed at 15%. By way of example, assume the 39.6% rate applies to taxable income over $450,000, the taxpayer has taxable income of $475,000, and $40,000 of the taxpayer's taxable income consists of adjusted net capital gain. In these circumstances, $25,000 of the adjusted net capital gain will be taxed at a 20% rate. ($475,000 minus $450,000 equals $25,000.) The remaining $15,000 of adjusted net capital gain will be taxed at 15%.

some exceptions) and from certain foreign corporations. § 1(h)(11)(B). The favorable tax treatment of this income is accomplished by including it in computing net capital gain, per § 1(h)(11)(A), and, more specifically, by including it in the computation of adjusted net capital gain. § 1(h)(3).

> **Example 1 — Qualified Dividend Income, With Additional Net Capital Gain:** Assume in 2015 Laura has $10,000 long-term capital gain from the sale of stock; $5,000 long-term capital gain from the sale of a collectible; and $3,000 of qualified dividend income. Net capital gain, as determined without regard to the dividend, is $15,000; the dividend income increases the net capital gain to $18,000. § 1(h)(11)(A). The adjusted net capital gain is determined by subtracting the 28-percent rate gain, here the collectibles gain, from the net capital gain (as determined without regard to the dividend income), and by adding the qualified dividend income. § 1(h)(3). Thus, the adjusted net capital gain in this example is $13,000 — that is, $15,000 net capital gain, excluding dividend income; less $5,000 28-percent rate gain; plus $3,000 dividend income. The dividend income is thus effectively taxed at the 20%, 15% or 0% rate applicable to adjusted net capital gain depending on the taxpayer's income tax bracket.

Why do § 1(h)(3) and § 1(h)(11) require that, as a preliminary matter, net capital gain and adjusted net capital gain be determined without regard to qualified dividend income? Why is the qualified dividend income added only after the preliminary determination has been made? Consider the following example.

> **Example 2 — Qualified Dividend Income, With No Additional Net Capital Gain:** Change the facts of Example 1 so that the stock sale produces a $10,000 long-term capital loss, rather than a gain, to go along with the $5,000 collectibles gain and the $3,000 dividend income. The capital loss here exceeds the total of the collectibles gain and the dividend income. If there were no preliminary determination of net capital gain under § 1(h)(11), there would be no net capital gain at all, and no adjusted net capital gain to be taxed at 20% or less. But, by first determining net capital gain without regard to dividend income, the special tax rate on dividend income is preserved. Thus, net capital gain, considering only the $10,000 stock loss and the $5,000 collectibles gain, is zero (not negative $5,000). Adding the dividend income to zero then produces net capital gain of $3,000. Similar calculations under § 1(h)(3) produce an adjusted net capital gain of $3,000, taxable at 20%, 15% or 0% depending on the taxpayer's income tax bracket. In this manner, the qualified dividend income is assured of taxation at these preferential rates even where there otherwise is no net capital gain (indeed, where there is otherwise a capital loss) for the taxpayer.

3. Attribution of Capital Losses Included in the Computation of Net Capital Gain

Now that we have considered the maximum tax rates applicable to various types of long-term gain included in a taxpayer's net capital gain, let us now focus briefly on the impact of capital losses which are taken into account in computing net capital gain. Because capital gains are offset by capital losses, and because long-term capital gains are subject to differing rates of tax, it is critically important to determine which long-term gains are offset by which losses. Therefore, let us consider how the Code attributes capital loss to the various components of net capital gain.

First, let us consider a situation where the taxpayer has a net short-term capital loss. Note, in computing capital gain, short-term capital losses are offset initially against short-term capital gain and it is only the excess, or net, short-term capital losses which must be attributed to one of the categories of long-term capital gain.

> **Example:** During the current year, Justin who is taxed in the 35% bracket has $5,000 of short-term capital gain from the sale of stock and $10,000 short-term capital loss from the sale of stock. In addition, Justin has $15,000 of long-term capital gain from the sale of stock held for more than one year. His net capital gain is $10,000. [Justin's NLTCG is $15,000; his NSTCL is 5,000 (*i.e.*, $10,000 STCL minus $5,000 STCG = $5,000). Therefore, NLTCG ($15,000) less NSTCL ($5,000) equals $10,000 NCG.] Since there is in this example only one category of long-term capital gain, the net short-term capital loss of $5,000 is of necessity attributed to that category.

Note in the above example, where a taxpayer has a short-term capital loss, the existence of short-term capital gain will have the effect of increasing the amount of net capital gain. Thus, in the above example, if there were no short-term capital gain, the net capital gain would have been $5,000 (*i.e.*, NLTCG ($15,000) less NSTCL ($10,000) = $5,000).

Let us now briefly consider how long-term capital losses and net short-term capital losses will be attributed among multiple categories of the long-term capital gains which are taken into account in computing net capital gain. As is demonstrated *infra*, that attribution will make a significant difference considering that the long-term capital gains included in net capital gain are subject to tax at varying rates. The applicable rules are very pro-taxpayer, and may be summarized as follows:

(1) *Short-term capital losses.* Short-term capital losses are first applied to reduce short-term capital gains. Any net short-term capital loss is then applied to reduce any net gain in the 28-percent rate category; then, to reduce any unrecaptured section 1250 gain; and finally, to reduce any adjusted net capital gain.

(2) *Long-term capital losses.* Long-term capital losses are first applied against long-term capital gains in the same category *e.g.*, collectibles losses are applied against collectibles gain; losses in the "20%/15%/0% group" — *i.e.*, losses on property not in the 28-percent rate gain category or the unrecaptured section 1250 gain category — are applied against gains from such property. Any net loss in the 28-percent rate gain category is applied to reduce unrecaptured section 1250 gain, and then to reduce the adjusted net capital gain category. Any net loss in the "20%/15%/0% group" first reduces gain in the 28-percent rate gain category, then reduces unrecaptured section 1250 gain.

Example 1 — Allocating a Net Short-Term Capital Loss Among Multiple Categories of Long-Term Capital Gain: Assume that a 35% bracket taxpayer has a total of $15,000 of long-term capital gain in 2015. That gain represents the aggregate of $9,000 of long-term capital gain from the sale of stock and $6,000 of long-term capital gain from the sale of antiques. Assume also the taxpayer has a $5,000 net short-term capital loss for the year. Taxpayer's net capital gain equals $10,000 (*i.e.*, NLTCG ($15,000) less NSTCL ($5,000) = $10,000). Note that included in the computation of net capital gain are some long-term capital gains which would be subject to a maximum tax of 15% and some long-term capital gains (collectibles gain) which would be subject to a maximum tax of 28%. To which of these gains will the $5,000 of net short-term capital loss be allocated? Section 1(h)(4) clearly provides that net short-term capital loss under these circumstances will be applied first to the 28-percent rate gain and only to the extent the 28-percent rate gain is less than the net short-term capital loss will the net short-term capital loss be attributable to the gain from the sale of stock. In other words, under § 1(h), the 28-percent rate gain will be $6,000 less the $5,000 net short-term capital loss or $1,000. In turn, the adjusted net capital gain will be $9,000 (*i.e.*, adjusted net capital gain equals net capital gain ($10,000) less 28-percent rate gain ($1,000)). This treatment of the net short-term capital loss, of course, is very favorable to the taxpayer as it maximizes the amount of long-term gain which will be taxed at the 15% rate.

Example 2 — Allocating Collectibles Loss Among Multiple Categories of Long-Term Capital Gain: Assume the same facts as Example 1 except that instead of a $5,000 net short-term capital loss, the taxpayer has a $5,000 long-term capital loss as a result of the sale of a work of art held for more than one year. Once again, the taxpayer's net capital gain will be $10,000 (*i.e.*, net long-term capital gain will be the excess of long-term capital gain ($15,000) over long-term capital loss ($5,000) or $10,000 and net short-term capital loss will be $0. Thus, net capital gain equals $10,000). The issue is to which category of long-term capital gain will the $5,000 of long-term capital loss be attributed. Not surprisingly, § 1(h)(4) requires that the $5,000 of long-term capital loss be allocated to the 28-percent rate gain since it is a collectibles loss, *i.e.*, a loss from the kind of property which would have given rise to 28-percent rate gain. § 1(h)(5). Thus, the 28-percent rate gain in this example will again be $1,000 (*i.e.*, $6,000 long-term capital gain from the sale of the antiques less $5,000 of long-term capital loss from the sale of the work of art.) In turn, the adjusted net capital gain will be $9,000 just as before ($10,000 net capital gain less $1,000 28-percent rate gain. So, the taxpayer will pay tax at the rate of 28% on $1,000 of net capital gain and 15% on the remaining $9,000 of the net capital gain.

Example 3 — Allocating Other Long-Term Capital Loss Among Multiple Categories of Long-Term Capital Gain: Assume the same facts as in Example 2 except that the $5,000 long-term capital loss is a result of the sale of stock held for more than one year. Again, net capital gain will be $10,000. Here, however, the $5,000 of long-term capital loss will not be attributed to the 28-percent rate gain since the loss in this case did not arise from the sale of assets which would have produced 28-percent rate gain. Thus, the 28-percent rate gain will equal $6,000. In turn, adjusted net capital gain will equal $4,000 (*i.e.*, net capital gain of $10,000 less $6,000 of 28-percent rate gain. Taxpayer will therefore be subject to a tax of 28% on $6,000 of the net capital gain and a tax of 15% on the remaining $4,000 of net capital gain.

As this brief overview of the attribution of capital losses suggests, the attribution rules are generally quite favorable to the taxpayers. Extended study of the capital loss attribution rules is beyond the scope of this course. Suffice it to say, the combination of the varying rates of tax on long-term capital gain and the attribution of capital losses to the various classes of long-term capital gain make § 1(h) unwieldy and adds significant complexity to this already complex characterization area.

C. Current Law: Application of the Section 1211(b) Limitation on the Deduction of Capital Losses

Throughout its tinkering in recent years with the preference for long-term capital gain, Congress has retained the limitation on the deduction of capital losses. Section 1211(b) specifically provides that capital losses may be deducted dollar for dollar to the extent of capital gains. For purposes of the § 1211 limitation, it makes no difference whether the capital gains and losses are long-term or short-term. For example, a dollar of short-term capital loss will offset one dollar of long-term capital gain. In addition, § 1211(b) provides that to the extent capital losses exceed capital gains, up to $3,000 of the excess may be deducted. In effect, a taxpayer may use capital losses (whether long-term or short-term) to offset on a dollar for dollar basis up to $3,000 of ordinary income in a given tax year. Capital losses which a taxpayer could not deduct because of the § 1211(b) limitation may be carried over to the next tax year. § 1212(b).

The following examples illustrate the application of §§ 1211(b) and 1212(b) while also demonstrating the overall mechanics of the capital gain and loss structure of the Code.

> **Example 1:** Assume in the current year Tanya has a salary of $75,000 and recognizes $5,000 of long-term capital gain from the sale of stock held for more than 1 year, $1,000 of short-term capital gain from the sale of stock held for six months, and $8,000 long-term capital loss from the sale of stock held for 15 months. Section 61(a)(3) specifies that gains derived from dealings in property constitute gross income. Therefore, Tanya's gross income for the current year is $81,000. Does Tanya have a net capital gain on these facts? The answer is "No." Review again the definition of net capital gain in § 1222(11). From the definition it should be clear to you that when a taxpayer's aggregate capital losses (both short-term and long-term) equal or exceed the taxpayers aggregate capital gains (both long-term and short-term), there is no possibility of net capital gain (apart from that arising from qualified dividend income, discussed *supra*).

With respect to the loss on the sale of the stock, it should be noted the loss is deductible under § 165(c)(2) as a loss on a transaction entered into for profit. Section 165(f), however, provides that capital losses may be deducted only to the extent provided in §§ 1211 and 1212. Read § 1211(b) carefully. There are two parts to the § 1211(b) limitation. Capital losses may be deducted to the extent of:

(1)   capital gains (this part of § 1211(b) will be referred to hereinafter as the capital gain offset rule);

PLUS

(2)   under § 1211(b)(1) and (2), up to $3,000 of any capital losses in excess of capital gains may be deducted against ordinary income (this part of § 1211 will be referred to hereinafter as the ordinary income offset rule).

Note § 1211 is not a deduction granting provision. Rather, § 1211 serves only to limit the deduction of losses which are deductible under other provisions of the Code. In this case, the loss on the stock is deductible under § 165(c)(2); Section 1211(b) represents only a potential limitation on the amount of the deduction which may be claimed in the current year. In Example 1, the total capital loss ($8,000) exceeds the total capital gains ($6,000) by $2,000. Under the capital gain offset rule of § 1211(b), Tanya may deduct capital losses of $6,000 (*i.e.*, an amount of loss equal to the capital gains); under the ordinary income offset rule of § 1211(b), she may deduct the $2,000 of excess capital loss as well since that amount is less than the $3,000 ceiling. Thus, Tanya, in this example, will be allowed to deduct all of her capital losses. Section 62(a)(3) provides that the $8,000 in deductible capital losses will be deducted in computing adjusted gross income. Assuming Tanya had no other above-the-line deductions, her adjusted gross income would be $73,000 (*i.e.*, $81,000 less $8,000).

As demonstrated by this Example, § 1211(b) permits long-term capital losses to offset dollar for dollar both short-term capital gains and long-term capital gains. Similarly, short-term capital losses will offset dollar for dollar short-term as well as long-term capital gains.

> **Example 2:** Assume the same facts as Example 1 except Tanya also recognized $3,000 of short-term capital loss from the sale of other investment property. Her gross income is still $81,000. She has a total of $11,000 in capital losses ($8,000 long-term capital loss and $3,000 short-term capital loss). Section 165(c)(2) authorizes a deduction for these losses subject to the § 1211(b) limitation. Based on Example 1, it should be clear that Tanya's § 165(c)(2) deduction for the capital losses recognized will be limited by § 1211(b) to $9,000: she may deduct (1) the capital losses to the extent of capital gains (thus, $6,000 of the capital losses are deductible under the capital gain offset portion of § 1211(b)) plus (2) up to $3,000 of the excess of the capital losses over capital gains (here, $3,000 of capital losses are deductible under the ordinary income offset portion of § 1211(b)). Her adjusted gross income will therefore be $72,000 ($81,000 less $9,000). Tanya has thus deducted a total of $9,000 of the $11,000 of capital losses. (As in Example 1, she has no net capital gain.)

Suppose Tanya had qualified dividend income. Would that permit her to deduct currently a greater amount of her capital losses? Is the dividend income, which is taxable at capital gain rates, treated as capital gain income for purposes of determining the dollar limitation on deductible capital losses? The answer to these questions is "No." Qualified dividend income is not a capital gain because it is not gain from the sale or exchange of a capital asset. § 1222(1), (3). Accordingly, it is not part of the § 1211(b) calculation on deducting capital losses. Thus, even if Tanya had qualified dividend income, the answer in Example 2 does not change. She can currently deduct only $9,000 of capital losses.

The $2,000 of capital loss in Example 2 which, because of § 1211, may not be deducted currently will be carried over to the next year pursuant to the rules of § 1212(b). Under § 1212(b), the capital losses carried over will retain their long-term or short-term status and will be deemed to have been incurred in the carryover year. For example, if the $11,000 of capital losses realized by Tanya in the current year had all been long-term capital losses, the $2,000 of carryover losses would be long-term capital losses. By contrast, had her losses all been short-term capital losses, the $2,000 carryover losses would retain their character as short-term capital losses. Losses disallowed under § 1211(b) will be carried over from year to year indefinitely until they are utilized to offset capital gains or ordinary income. Capital losses unused at a taxpayer's death simply disappear.

In Example 2, Tanya had a long-term capital loss of $8,000 and a short-term capital loss of $3,000, or a total of $11,000 in capital losses. Only $9,000 of these losses were deductible currently. Which of these losses were deducted and which were carried over? We know that, under the capital gain offset part of § 1211(b), she was allowed to deduct capital losses to the extent of capital gains. Because she had $6,000 of capital gain, she was entitled to deduct $6,000 of capital loss. Which capital losses were used to offset the $6,000 of capital gain? $6,000 of long-term capital loss? A combination of long-term and short-term capital losses? In addition, Tanya was permitted under the ordinary income offset part of § 1211(b)(1) and (2) to deduct an additional $3,000 of the capital losses. Which capital losses were used by her in claiming this deduction against ordinary income?

In addition to confirming the fact and amount of the capital loss carryover, § 1212(b) answers these character questions. Read § 1212(b) carefully. First, note it applies when the taxpayer (other than a corporation) has a "net capital loss," a term defined in § 1222(10) as capital losses in excess of those allowed under § 1211. Thus, in Example 2, Tanya has a net capital loss, and the § 1212(b) carryover rules will apply. Next, note that § 1212(b) in effect establishes two rules for determining which losses were deducted and therefore which losses remain to be carried over:

Rule 1: In applying the capital gain offset portion of § 1211(b), short-term capital losses will be netted first against short-term capital gains, and long-term losses will be netted first against long-term gains. If short-term losses exceed short-term capital gains, the excess (or net) short-term capital losses will then be netted against excess (or net) long-term capital gains, if any. Similarly, if long-term capital losses exceed long-term capital gains, the excess (or net) long-term capital losses will be netted against the excess (or net) short-term capital gains, if any.

Rule 2: Short-term capital losses, if any, will be deemed to have been deducted first in the ordinary income offset part of § 1211(b). That is accomplished by the "special rule" of § 1212(b)(2) which generally provides that the amount allowed under the ordinary income offset rule of § 1211(b) shall be treated as short-term capital gain in that year for purposes of applying Rule 1 above.[9] In other words, it is just as though the taxpayer, rather than offsetting ordinary income, were offsetting short-term capital gain. Thus, in this Example, since the ordinary income offset amounts to $3,000, it is as if Tanya had $4,000 of short-term capital gain, rather than only $1,000. For purposes of determining the capital loss carryover, we must assume that we have $5,000 of long-term capital gain and $4,000 of short-term capital gain.

Applying Rule 1, we would first use $5,000 of the long-term capital loss to offset the $5,000 long-term capital gain. We then have $3,000 net long-term capital loss, *i.e.*, the excess of the long-term capital loss over the long-term capital gain. Next, we must net the $3,000 of short-term capital loss against the $4,000 of deemed short-term capital gain. All $3,000 of the short-term capital loss is consumed and we are left with a net short-term capital gain of $1,000 (*i.e.*, excess of the short-term capital gain over the short-term capital losses). We now have $3,000 of net long-term capital loss and $1,000 of net short-term capital gain. These are netted against each other under § 1212(b)(1)(B) leaving $2,000 of long-term capital loss to be carried over to the following year.[10]

D. Definition of Capital Asset

As noted above, the Revenue Act of 1924 defined "capital asset" as "property acquired and held by the taxpayer for more than two years (whether or not connected with his trade or business)," but further provided that the term "does not include stock in trade of the taxpayer or other property of a kind which would properly be included in the inventory of the taxpayer if on hand at the close of the taxable year, or property held by the taxpayer primarily for sale in the course of his trade or business."[11] Under the 1924 Revenue Act, essentially all property, including personal use property, constituted capital assets unless the assets could be classified as inventory-type assets. Since then, Congress has added a number of other exceptions to the definition of capital asset. Read the current exceptions in § 1221 carefully. While the statutory definition of capital asset appears remarkably broad, it is clear that Congress intended capital gain treatment to be an exception and not the rule. The courts have tended to construe "capital asset" narrowly, thus

---

[9] However, where the taxpayer has a "negative taxable income," the amount treated as a short-term gain may be less than the amount allowed as a § 1211(b) offset. This has the effect of enhancing the amount of the carryover and preventing a "wasting" of the § 1211(b) offset in negative taxable income situations.

[10] For purposes of allocating long-term capital losses among multiple categories of long-term capital gain, note that long-term losses carried over by § 1212(b)(1)(B) will be allocated to the 28-percent rate gain category by § 1(h)(4)(B).

[11] The predecessor to the 1924 Revenue Act, the 1921 Revenue Act, denied capital asset status to "property held for the personal use or consumption of the taxpayer or his family" and specifically required that property be "acquired and held by the taxpayer for profit or investment." The 1924 Revenue Act and all subsequent tax laws, however, have accorded capital asset status to personal use property. *See* § 1221.

significantly limiting taxpayers' opportunities to claim preferential capital gain treatment.[12]

1. Section 1221(a)(1): Inventory, Stock in Trade, and Property Held Primarily for Sale to Customers in the Ordinary Course of the Taxpayer's Trade or Business

The denial of capital asset status (and therefore preferential capital gain treatment) to inventory-type items is consistent with the congressional purpose underlying preferential capital gain treatment. As the Supreme Court noted in *Corn Products Refining Co. v. Commissioner*:

> Congress intended that profits and losses arising from the everyday operation of business be considered as ordinary income or loss rather than capital gain or loss. The preferential treatment [historically provided gains from the sale or exchange of capital assets] applies to transactions in property which are not the normal source of business income. It was intended "to relieve the taxpayer from . . . excessive tax burdens on gains resulting from a conversion of capital investments, and to remove the deterrent effect of those burdens on such conversions. . . . "

350 U.S. 46, 52 (1955).

Because gains derived from the sale or exchange of inventory-type assets undoubtedly constitute ordinary business income, § 1221(a)(1) was drafted to encompass a wide range of everyday business income.[13] Clearly, there is consider-

---

[12] Note that § 1221(a) defines a capital asset as "property held by the taxpayer." The question of what constitutes "property" for § 1221 purposes was addressed recently by courts considering the character of amounts received from the United States by relators in a *qui tam* actions under the False Claims Act (FSA). (Recall that, in *Roco v. Commissioner*, a case included in Chapter 2, the Tax Court held the amount received by the taxpayer/relator in a *qui tam* action constituted gross income under § 61.) In *Alderson v. Commissioner*, 686 F.3d 791 (9th Cir. 2012), the court, in a case of first impression, held the amount received by a relator in a *qui tam* action under the FSA was ordinary income. The Ninth Circuit rejected the taxpayer's argument that the information supplied by the taxpayer to the government was a capital asset. In this regard, the court emphasized the information the taxpayer provided to the government was not his property and therefore no capital asset was involved.

> General principles of property law require that a property owner have the legal right to exclude others from use and enjoyment of that property. . . . Alderson had no legal right to exclude others from use of the information that he obtained through discovery and subsequently provided to the government. The information was known to other officials in the company, and Alderson had no right to prevent those officials from providing it to others. The FCA required Alderson to file his complaint and accompanying evidence under seal to allow the government to examine it, but that requirement does not alter the fact that Alderson could not prevent others who knew the information from revealing it to the government or to *The New York Times*.

Patrick v. Commissioner, 142 T.C. 124 (2014), followed the reasoning of the Ninth Circuit in concluding a *qui tam* award constituted ordinary income. (In addition to finding that the relators failed the capital asset requirement of § 1221, both the *Alderson* and *Patrick* courts concluded the relators in those cases did not engage in a sale or an exchange.)

[13] There is a special provision, discussed below under § 1221(a)(3), under which self-created musical works, otherwise classifiable as inventory, may be treated as capital assets at the taxpayer's election. § 1221(b)(3).

able overlap among the three categories of property listed in § 1221(a)(1). For example, "inventory" could be properly characterized as "property held by the taxpayer primarily for sale to customers in the ordinary course of his trade or business." At the same time each category includes property which may not be included in either of the other categories. For example, tracts of land held by a dealer in real property may not be viewed as either "inventory" or "stock in trade;" likewise raw materials used in the production of a product, while clearly inventory, may not be said to be "property held by the taxpayer primarily for sale to customers in the ordinary course of his trade or business."

Generally, few problems are encountered identifying the inventory or stock in trade of a taxpayer. The most troublesome questions involving § 1221(a)(1) have focused on the interpretation of the words "property held by the taxpayer primarily for sale to customers in the ordinary course of his trade or business." The interpretation of the words "primarily for sale" in § 1221(a)(1) was the focus of the Supreme Court's decision in *Malat v. Riddell*, 383 U.S. 569 (1966). There, the taxpayer was a member of a joint venture which had acquired property with the intent to develop it commercially or to sell it at a profit. Unable to secure the necessary financing for development, the joint venture sold the property. The taxpayer claimed capital gain treatment for his share of the gain, but the Service argued the gain was ordinary income. The Service reasoned the words "primarily for sale" in § 1221(a)(1) required only that the taxpayer's purpose to sell be "substantial." The Court rejected that interpretation, noting:

> The purpose of the statutory provision with which we deal is to differentiate between the "profits and losses arising from the everyday operation of a business" on the one hand . . . and "the realization of appreciation in value accrued over a substantial period of time" on the other. . . . A literal reading of the statute is consistent with this legislative purpose. We hold that, as used in Section [1221(a)(1)], "primarily" means "of first importance" or principally.

Id. at 572.

In a number of cases following *Malat v. Riddell*, the courts have found that, rather than having a dual purpose, the taxpayer's purpose had changed so that the taxpayer's sole purpose in holding the property was to sell it.

The gains from sales of subdivided real estate historically raised some of the more difficult and interesting questions regarding the interpretation of the § 1221(a)(1) language "primarily for sale to customers in the ordinary course of his trade or business." Consider the following scenario: The taxpayer, a farmer, owned a large tract of land bordering a town. As the town grew, the farmer's land became more valuable for subdivision purposes than for farming purposes. The farmer subdivided, improved and sold the land. What is the character of the farmer's gain on the sale of the subdivided land? Is the land property held for sale to customers in the ordinary course of the farmer's business? *Bynum v. Commissioner* included in the materials, is an excellent example of how courts have addressed this kind of case. Note the factors which the *Bynum* court emphasized as important. The Fifth Circuit, in *Biedenharn Realty Co., Inc. v. U.S.*, 526 F.2d 409 (5th Cir. 1976), while acknowledging "individual factors have varying weights and magnitudes, depending on the facts of the case," considered the following factors in determining the character of gains from the sale of subdivided land: frequency and substantiality of sales; improvements made to the land; taxpayer's solicitation and advertising efforts; and utilization of real estate brokers and agents. Of these factors, the frequency and substantiality of sales was the most important.[14] How do the *Biedenharn* factors compare to those used in *Bynum*?[15]

2. Section 1221(a)(2): Property Used in the Taxpayer's Trade or Business

Section 1221(a)(2) excludes from capital asset status property used in the taxpayer's trade or business that is either depreciable property or real property. Nonetheless, § 1221(a)(2) property held for more than a year is accorded special treatment by § 1231, which in effect provides quasi-capital asset status to such property. Sections 1231 and 1221(a)(2) are studied in detail in the next chapter, so at this point we shall do no more than note the § 1221(a)(2) exclusion for real or depreciable property used in the taxpayer's trade or business.

3. Section 1221(a)(3): Copyrights, Literary, Musical, or Artistic Compositions, Etc.

Prior to 1950, amateur composers, artists and authors who sold their works at a gain could characterize their gain as capital. Because their gain was comparable to personal service income, the capital gain characterization was viewed as inconsistent with the principle that ordinary business income was not eligible for preferential treatment. In the Revenue Act of 1950, Congress specifically provided that a "copyright, literary, musical, or artistic composition; or similar property" was not a capital asset if held by a taxpayer whose personal efforts created the property or by a taxpayer whose basis in the property was determined in whole or in part by reference to the basis of the property in the hands of a person whose efforts created the property. The provision, codified as § 1221(a)(3), was expanded in 1969 to include letters, memoranda and similar property.[16] However, in 2006 Congress provided a special tax break for the sale or exchange of self-created musical works. Section 1221(b)(3) provides that a taxpayer may elect to have § 1221(a)(1) and (a)(3) not apply to sales or exchanges of taxpayer-created musical compositions or copyrights in musical works. In effect, by providing that the inventory exclusion of § 1221(a)(1) and the copyright and musical composition exclusion of § 1221(a)(3) shall not apply, the sale of self-created musical works will receive capital gains treatment, rather

---

[14] *See also Suburban Realty v. U.S.*, 615 F.2d 171 (5th Cir. 1980), *cert. denied*, 449 U.S. 920 (1980).

[15] In an effort to reduce the volume of litigation regarding gains from subdivided land, Congress in 1954 enacted § 1237. This provision enables taxpayers to avoid the § 1221(a)(1) characterization if certain conditions are met. The provision, however, has proven in practice to be too narrow and complex to provide much solace to most taxpayers.

[16] The 1969 amendment provided that letters, memoranda or similar property would not constitute capital assets if held by (a) the author; (b) a taxpayer for whom such property was prepared or produced; or (c) a taxpayer whose basis was determined by reference to the basis of a taxpayer described in (a) or (b). The primary purpose for the 1969 amendment was to prevent taxpayers from claiming substantial charitable deductions when they donated their papers, etc. to a library or other charitable organization. See § 170(e), discussed in Chapter 26.

than ordinary income treatment, at the election of the taxpayer.[17]

4. Section 1221(a)(4): Accounts Receivable for Services Rendered or Inventory-Type Assets Sold

In some respects, in denying capital asset status to accounts receivable for services rendered or for inventory-type assets sold, § 1221(a)(4) states the obvious. Amounts received by a service provider or by one selling inventory-type assets are clearly normal business income and should be treated as ordinary income. Likewise, where a cash method taxpayer has an account receivable as a result of providing services or selling inventory, any gain recognized from the sale of that account receivable should be ordinary income. Section 1221(a)(4) insures that result by denying capital asset status to such accounts.

In contrast to a cash method taxpayer, an accrual method taxpayer has already included in income the amount represented by the account receivable. As a result, the accrual method taxpayer has a basis in the account receivable equal to the amount included in income. If the accrual method taxpayer sells her account receivable, she will often receive an amount less than her basis in the account and will therefore have a loss deductible under § 165(c)(1). What is the character of that loss? Capital? Ordinary? By denying capital asset status to the account receivable, § 1221(a)(4) insures the loss will be ordinary. Considering the limitation on the deductibility of capital losses, this result is favorable to the accrual method taxpayer. Of course, in the rare case where the account receivable is sold by the accrual method taxpayer for an amount in excess of basis, the taxpayer will have ordinary income.

5. Section 1221(a)(5): Certain Publications of the U.S. Government

The statutory exception to capital asset classification in § 1221(a)(5) is important primarily because of the limit it places on charitable deductions for gifts of government publications to public libraries, universities, etc. By denying capital asset status to U.S. Government publications (including the Congressional Record) when acquired other than by purchase at the price the publication is offered for sale to the public, § 1221(a)(5), in conjunction with § 170(e)(1), assures that the taxpayer contributing the publications will not be entitled to a charitable deduction in excess of the taxpayer's basis in the publications. Section 1221(a)(5) is only applicable if the publications described above are held by the taxpayer who received the publication or by a taxpayer whose basis in the publication is determined by reference to the basis of the publication in the hands of a taxpayer who received the publication. For example, government publications received by a member of Congress free of charge are not capital assets and, if sold, will generate ordinary income. More importantly, however, if these publications are contributed to a charitable organization, § 170(e)(1) will deny a charitable deduction. Likewise, if the publications are first

---

[17] Note that for charitable deduction purposes, however, a taxpayer will be limited to a deduction equal to the taxpayer's basis, rather than the fair market value of the self-created work. *See* § 170(e)(1)(A).

given to a family member, who then contributes them to charity, no charitable deduction will be allowed. *See* § 1221(a)(5)(B).

6. Section 1221(a)(8): Supplies Used or Consumed in the Taxpayer's Trade or Business

Section 1221(a)(8), enacted in 1999, excludes from capital asset status supplies of a type regularly used or consumed by the taxpayer in the ordinary course of trade or business. This type of asset can be thought of as so close to inventory (excluded from the definition of capital asset by § 1221(a)(1)) that capital asset characterization is likewise inappropriate for it as well.[18]

7. Judicially Established Limits on Capital Asset Characterization

Drawing the line between assets which should be characterized as capital assets and those which should not has on occasion proven difficult for the courts. Superficially at least, certain assets seem to be capital assets within the meaning of § 1221. On closer examination, however, courts have found that to accord those assets capital asset status would frustrate congressional purpose. For example, in the seminal case of *Corn Products Refining Co. v. Commissioner*, 350 U.S. 46 (1955), a manufacturer of products made from grain corn sought to protect itself from sharp increases in raw corn prices by buying "corn futures" — that is, by buying contracts for future delivery of raw corn at a set price — whenever the price of these futures was favorable. The taxpayer took delivery on the futures contracts when necessary to its operations, and it sold the remaining contracts if no shortages of raw corn developed. Over the two tax years in question, the taxpayer made a profit on the sales of the contracts; it contended that the futures were capital assets, generating capital gains and losses on their sales. The Supreme Court, noting the taxpayer's purchases of futures contracts had been found to "constitute an integral part of its manufacturing business," held to the contrary:

> Admittedly, petitioner's corn futures do not come within the literal language of the exclusions set out in section [1221]. They were not stock in trade, actual inventory, property held for sale to customers or depreciable property used in a trade or business. But the capital-asset provision of Section [1221] must not be so broadly applied as to defeat rather than further the purpose of Congress. Congress intended that profits and losses arising from the everyday operation of a business be considered as ordinary income or loss rather than capital gain or loss. The preferential treatment provided by Section [1221] applies to transactions in property which are not the normal source of business income. Since this section is an exception from the normal tax requirements of the Internal Revenue Code, the definition of a capital asset must be narrowly applied and its exclusions

[18] There are two additional categories of statutory exclusions from capital asset status. Section 1221(a)(7) provides that certain "hedging transactions" are not capital assets; hedging transactions are briefly discussed in footnote 21 below. Section 1221(a)(6) excludes from the definition of capital asset certain "commodities derivative financial instruments," a topic beyond the scope of this course.

interpreted broadly. This is necessary to effectuate the basic congressional purpose. This Court has always construed narrowly the term "capital assets" in Section [1221].

Id. at 51–52. The *Corn Products* decision thus added a gloss to § 1221 with which taxpayers and courts then had to struggle.

Following *Corn Products*, the courts decided numerous cases involving stock or securities, which, as in *Corn Products*, assured their holders of a source of supply. In many cases the stock or securities were also held for investment purposes. Where such dual purposes existed, a taxpayer realizing a gain on the sale of stock or securities found it advantageous to emphasize an investment purpose with respect to the stock or securities, thus hoping to assure capital gain treatment. By contrast, if a loss were realized on the sale of the stock or securities, the taxpayer, relying on *Corn Products*, would argue the primary purpose for holding the stock or securities had been for business reasons and that the loss, therefore, was an ordinary loss. Ironically, while the Service won in *Corn Products*, taxpayers subsequently used the doctrine established in that case to avoid the characterization of stock losses as capital losses. Partly to minimize the potential whipsawing of the government, the Tax Court eventually held in *W.W. Windle Company v. Commissioner*, 65 T.C. 694, 712 (1976), that "stock purchased with a substantial investment purpose is a capital asset even if there is a more substantial business motive for the purchase," and that a subsequent abandonment of the investment motive was irrelevant. The Service accepted this result in Revenue Ruling 78-94, 1978-1 C.B. 58,[19] and thus, prior to the Supreme Court's decision in *Arkansas Best Corp. v. Commissioner*, a case included in the materials, the taxpayer's motivation in purchasing an asset could be critical to the determination of whether it was a capital asset. Note the Supreme Court's rejection of the motivation test in *Arkansas Best* and its characterization now of *Corn Products* as simply "a broad reading of the inventory exclusion of § 1221."

In view of the Supreme Court's decision in *Arkansas Best*, may a taxpayer argue that stock is held to ensure a source of supply and that the loss upon the sale of stock is therefore ordinary?[20] In *Cenex, Inc. v. United States*, 156 F.3d 1377 (Fed.

<hr>

[19] The ruling was later suspended pending the Supreme Court decision in *Arkansas Best*. Notice 87-68, 1987-2 C.B. 378.

[20] As a result of questions which arose following the Supreme Court's decision in *Arkansas Best*, the Service issued regulations addressing the characterization of gains and losses from so-called hedging transactions. In these regulations, the Service abandoned its earlier position that gain or loss realized in the context of many common business hedging transactions was capital rather than ordinary in nature. Reg. § 1.1221-2(a)(1) provides that "the term capital asset does not include property that is part of a hedging transaction. . . . " Reg. § 1.1221-2(b)(1) defines a hedging transaction as a transaction entered by a taxpayer in the normal course of the taxpayer's business primarily to reduce the risk of price changes or currency fluctuations with respect to "ordinary property." The risk being reduced must relate to "ordinary property," *i.e.*, property the sale or exchange of which could not produce capital gain or capital loss regardless of the taxpayer's holding period when the sale or exchange occurs. Reg. § 1.1221-2(c)(5). The regulations are intended to negate claims that loss on corporate stock (*e.g.*, stock purportedly held to ensure a source of supply) are ordinary. The holding of stock will not be a hedging transaction even if the stock is held "to . . . ensure the availability of goods." T.D. 8555, 1994-33 I.R.B. 9, lll. Reg. § 1.1221-2(e)(1) imposes a requirement that the taxpayer identify a transaction as a hedging transaction "before the close of the day on which the taxpayer enters into the transaction." These

Cir. 1998), the court answered "No." The taxpayer in that case sold petroleum products and, to assure a source of supply of refined petroleum products, it acquired stock in a corporation that operated an oil refinery. That stock subsequently became worthless and the taxpayer claimed an ordinary loss, arguing that the stock qualified for the § 1221 inventory exclusion as an "inventory substitute . . . purchased in order to obtain a supply of petroleum products, which are actual inventory in its business." The Federal Circuit denied the claim, finding in the aftermath of *Arkansas Best* that surrogates or substitutes for inventory "must bear a close relationship to actual inventory and can do so if they are closely related to the taxpayer's inventory-purchase system." The corn futures in *Corn Products* satisfied this test because they were redeemable for corn and because the cost of inventory was directly related to the cost of the corn futures — gains and losses on futures were the same as gains and losses on actual inventory would have been. In contrast, the stock in *Cenex* was not redeemable for inventory, nor related in value to the value of the petroleum products — in sum, it was simply not closely related to its inventory-purchase system. The source of supply doctrine itself, according to the court, is "incompatible with *Arkansas Best*" and hence not a basis on which to treat the stock as an ordinary asset.

In a post — *Arkansas Best* case, the Fifth Circuit in *Azar Nut Company v. Commissioner*, 931 F.2d 314 (5th Cir. 1991), *aff'g* 94 T.C. 455, considered the meaning of the § 1221(a)(2) language "used in [the taxpayer's] trade or business." As part of the employment package it offered a high level executive, Azar Nut Company agreed to purchase the executive's residence at fair market value whenever the executive's employment with the taxpayer was terminated. Azar Nut subsequently fired the executive, purchased the residence pursuant to the agreement, and ultimately sold it at a substantial loss. The company claimed an ordinary loss deduction, arguing the residence was not a capital asset because it was "used in" its trade or business. The Fifth Circuit observed that "Azar argues that this 'used in' exception includes any asset acquired by a taxpayer under the terms of a contract or similar agreement that is an integral part of the taxpayer's business, even if the asset never plays a role in business operations after its acquisition." But the court rejected this reasoning:

> Azar's interpretations of the "used in" exception essentially excludes from capital asset treatment any asset purchased with a "business purpose," as that term was used under the *Corn Products* Doctrine. . . . The Supreme Court recently renounced the *Corn Products* Doctrine in *Arkansas Best Corporation v. Commissioner* . . . , holding that business purpose is irrelevant to determining whether an asset falls within the general definition of "capital asset." Azar urges us to consider business purpose in analyzing the "used in" exception. We conclude that the plain language of Section 1221[a](2) precludes consideration of business purpose in all but the most exceptional circumstances. The words "used in" clearly require ordinary asset treatment for properties that, once acquired, play a role in

---

regulations provide some certainty in an otherwise gray area and will benefit many taxpayers who realize losses as a result of hedging transactions. The regulations were issued in 1994. In 1999, Congress amended § 1221 to add certain hedging transactions as a statutory exclusion from capital asset treatment. Section 1221(a)(7).

the taxpayer's business operations. Those words do not suggest that an asset may be excepted from capital-asset treatment simply because the asset is acquired with a business purpose. To qualify under the "used in" exception, an asset must be "used in" the taxpayer's business, and an asset that has no meaningful association with the taxpayer's business operations after it is acquired cannot reasonably fall within the plain words of the statute.

Id. at 316–17.

Substitute for Ordinary Income Doctrine. Wholly apart from *Corn Products — Arkansas Best* issues, the courts have also been required to characterize payments received by taxpayers who have sold their right to collect future income. As a result of various court decisions, the "substitute for ordinary income doctrine" has emerged. The doctrine provides that, when a taxpayer receives a lump sum payment that is essentially a substitute for ordinary income that would have been received at a future time, the lump sum payment will be treated as ordinary income. This doctrine thus narrows "what a mechanical application of § 1221 would otherwise cause to be treated as a capital asset." *Long v. Commissioner*, 772 F.3d 670 (11th Cir. 2014). For example, consider the facts in *Estate of Stranahan v. Commissioner*, 472 F.2d 867 (6th Cir. 1973) (included in Chapter 34), where the taxpayer sold the right to collect future dividends on certain stock. The court there held the taxpayer had income in the year of receipt of the sale proceeds. What character should that income have had? If one considers that the taxpayer would have had ordinary income had he collected the dividends himself, it seems appropriate the amounts received for the right to collect such dividends likewise be treated as ordinary income. Applying the reasoning of *Hort v. Commissioner* and *Davis v. Commissioner*, included in the materials, the taxpayer in *Stranahan* should have been required to report the sale proceeds as ordinary income. The proceeds were a substitute for ordinary income and as such were not entitled to preferential capital gain treatment. Read *Hort* and *Davis* carefully. What ordinary income substitutes were addressed in those cases?[21]

E.   The Sale or Exchange Requirement

Pursuant to § 1222, only gains or losses resulting from the "sale or exchange" of capital assets will be treated as capital gains and losses. As noted in *Freeland v. Commissioner*, 74 T.C. 970, 980 (1980), "Congress intended the words 'sale or exchange' to have a broad meaning, not to be limited to the standard transfer of

---

[21] Congress added § 1258 in 1993 to prevent taxpayers from taking advantage of the increased differential between capital gain tax rates and ordinary income rates by treating certain financial transactions (referred to as "conversion transactions") as giving rise to capital gain. The rules of § 1258 provide that gain from these conversion transactions will be treated as ordinary income. A conversion transaction in general is a transaction where substantially all of the return is attributable to the time value of the taxpayer's net investment in the transaction. § 1258(c)(1). In other words, in a conversion transaction substantially all of the expected return stems from being in a position functionally equivalent to that of a lender. Although detailed discussion of § 1258 is beyond the scope of this course, the enactment of the section indicates Congress' continuing efforts to limit the scope of the preference for long-term capital gains.

property by one person to another in exchange for a stated consideration in money or money's worth."

In the common case, it will be easy to determine whether the sale or exchange requirement has been satisfied. Under certain circumstances, however, more difficult questions may arise. For example, in *Kenan v. Commissioner*, included in the materials, the court concluded the satisfaction of a bequest with appreciated property constituted a sale or exchange for purposes of § 1222. Similarly, in *Yarbro v. Commissioner*, 737 F.2d 479 (5th Cir. 1984), the issue before the court was "whether an individual taxpayer's loss resulting from the abandonment of unimproved real estate subject to a nonrecourse mortgage exceeding the market value is an ordinary loss or a capital loss." Concluding the loss was capital, the court relied upon a number of earlier decisions in rejecting the taxpayer's contention that the abandonment here did not constitute a sale or an exchange. *Yarbro* noted that in *Helvering v. Nebraska Bridge Supply & Lumber Co*, 312 U.S. 666 (1941), the Supreme Court held a tax forfeiture constituted a "sale or an exchange," and that in *Helvering v. Hammel*, 311 U.S. 504 (1941), the Supreme Court held an involuntary foreclosure sale of real estate satisfied the "sale or exchange" requirement. *Yarbro* also noted that in *Freeland v. Commissioner*,[22] an owner's conveyance of land to a mortgagee by a quitclaim deed constituted a "sale or exchange." According to the *Yarbro* court,

> [T]he abandonment followed by the mortgagee's foreclosure . . . is the functional equivalent of the foreclosure sale in *Hammel*, the tax forfeiture in *Nebraska Bridge Supply*, and the quitclaim in lieu of foreclosure in . . . *Freeland*. In all these transactions, the taxpayer-owner is relieved of his obligation to repay the debt and is relieved of title to the property. Because the mortgagee is legally entitled to recover the property in any of these cases, the fact that out of prudence he concludes he must go through foreclosure proceedings to formalize his interest in the land is not a rational basis for altering the character of the gain or loss realized by the taxpayer on the transaction. The differences in these transactions is not a difference in substance, but only in form. . . . [W]here the taxpayer would be eligible for capital gains treatment upon the sale of property had it appreciated in value, he should not be allowed to avoid the limitations on deductions for capital losses by using an artfully timed abandonment rather than a sale, voluntary reconveyance, or foreclosure.

737 F.2d at 485–86.

While technically § 1222 requires a particular type of disposition before there will be capital gain or capital loss, Congress has in many cases negated the need for a sale or an exchange. For example, § 165(g)(1) provides that if any security which is a capital asset becomes worthless, the loss resulting shall be treated as a loss from the sale or exchange of a capital asset. Another significant provision, § 1271(a), provides that amounts received on the retirement of a debt instruments shall be treated as received in exchange for that instrument. Similarly, § 1234A provides

---

[22] 74 T.C. 970 (1980). In *Freeland*, the nonrecourse indebtedness encumbering the property exceeded the fair market value of the property.

sale or exchange treatment on the cancellation, lapse, expiration or other termination of certain property rights or obligations. Also, in § 1231, which you will study in the next chapter, Congress has provided sale or exchange treatment in cases involving involuntary conversions which would traditionally not be considered sales or exchanges. See, *e.g.*, *Helvering v. William Flaccus Oak Leather Co.*, 313 U.S. 247 (1941), holding there was no sale or exchange when the taxpayer's fully-depreciated plant (including buildings, machinery, and equipment) was destroyed by fire and the taxpayer collected insurance proceeds. *See also* §§ 1235, 1241.

F.   The *Arrowsmith* Rule: Characterization of Certain Gains or Losses Dependent on Prior Tax Treatment of Related Gains or Losses

When a corporation liquidates, the shareholders are required to report the gain (or loss), if any, on the receipt of their share of liquidation proceeds. The gain or loss recognized by the shareholder is treated as gain or loss from an exchange of their stock. Thus, because the stock will generally be a capital asset in the hands of a shareholder, the gain or loss on receipt of the liquidation proceeds will be capital gain or capital loss. Subsequent to the liquidation, however, the shareholders may be held liable for unpaid debts of the corporation. A shareholder who is required to make payment to a creditor of the liquidated corporation is entitled to claim a loss deduction. The only question is the character of the loss — is it capital or ordinary? What if the payment occurs in a year subsequent to the year in which property of the corporation was distributed in complete liquidation of the corporation? Since the payment of the corporate debt does not constitute a sale or an exchange, can the payment generate a capital loss? In *Arrowsmith v. Commissioner*, 344 U.S. 6 (1952), the Supreme Court's answer was "Yes." The taxpayers in that case had received partial distributions in 1937–39 and a final liquidating distribution in 1940, which they properly reported as capital gains; in 1944, they were required to pay a judgment against the corporation, which they sought to classify as an ordinary business loss. The Supreme Court held that the loss was capital:

> It is not . . . denied that had this judgment been paid after liquidation, but during the year 1940, the losses would have been properly treated as capital ones. For payment during 1940 would simply have reduced the amount of capital gains taxpayers received during that year.

> It is contended, however, that this payment which would have been a capital transaction in 1940 was transformed into an ordinary business transaction in 1944 because of the well-established principle that each taxable year is a separate unit for tax accounting purposes. . . . But the principle is not breached by considering all the 1937–1944 liquidation transaction events in order properly to classify the nature of the 1944 loss for tax purposes. Such an examination is not an attempt to reopen and readjust the 1937 to 1940 tax returns, an action that would be inconsistent with the annual tax accounting principle.

Id. at 8–9.

The Supreme Court a number of years later relied on the so-called *Arrowsmith* rule in deciding *U.S. v. Skelly Oil Co*, 394 U.S. 678 (1969). As that case demonstrates, the *Arrowsmith* rule is much broader than just a gain/loss characterization rule. In *Skelly Oil*, the taxpayer refunded approximately $505,000 to certain customers for overcharges on the sale of natural gas in prior years. The taxpayer had included the refunded amount in gross income as part of its total receipts from the sale of natural gas. In the year when it refunded the $505,000, the taxpayer sought to deduct that amount on the theory that, when a taxpayer is required to restore amounts previously included in income under the claim-of-right doctrine, the taxpayer is entitled to a deduction. *See* Chapter 3; *North American Oil Consolidated v. Burnet*, 286 U.S. 417 (1932).

However, in the year the taxpayer had included the $505,000 overcharge in gross income, the taxpayer had also claimed a § 613 depletion deduction equal to 27.5% of the taxpayer's gross income from receipts from oil and gas wells. Thus, during the same year in which taxpayer included in gross income the $505,000 which taxpayer later refunded, the taxpayer was allowed to deduct 27.5% of that amount. The taxpayer's taxable income for that year was therefore increased by a net of only $366,000 as a result of the inclusion of the $505,000 in income. Given that fact, the Service argued that the refund of the half million dollars should generate only a $366,000 deduction. Agreeing with the Service, the Supreme Court noted that

> the annual accounting concept does not require us to close our eyes to what happened in prior years. For instance, it is well settled that the prior year may be examined to determine whether the repayment gives rise to a regular loss or a capital loss. *Arrowsmith v. Commissioner.* . . . The rationale for the *Arrowsmith* rule is easy to see; if money was taxed at a special lower rate when received, the taxpayer would be accorded an unfair tax windfall if repayments were generally deductible from receipts taxable at the higher rate applicable to ordinary income. The Court in *Arrowsmith* was unwilling to infer that Congress intended such a result.
>
> This case is really no different. . . . In essence, oil and gas producers are taxed on only 72.5% of their "gross income from the property" whenever they claim percentage depletion. The remainder of their oil and gas receipt is in reality tax exempt. We cannot believe that Congress intended to give taxpayers a deduction for refunding money that was not taxed when received. . . . Accordingly *Arrowsmith* teaches that the full amount of the repayment cannot, in the circumstances of this case, be allowed as a deduction.

394 U.S. at 684–85.

As *Skelly Oil* and the facts of *Arrowsmith* itself indicate, the *Arrowsmith* rule is one that should not be overlooked. For purposes of this Chapter, the import of *Arrowsmith* should be clear: gains or losses generated as a result of a transaction covering more than one year may be characterized as capital gains or losses even though technically the sale or exchange requirement does not appear to be met.

G. Holding Period

Under current law, property must be held for more than one year before its sale or exchange if there is to be long-term capital gain or loss. Recall, however, that the limitation on deductibility of capital losses does not depend on the long or short-term nature of the loss. The holding period of assets is also implicated in provisions like § 170(e) which limits the charitable deduction allowable on gifts of appreciated property.

In conclusion, Congress has enacted a complex preferential treatment structure for capital gains and has retained the limitation on capital losses. As a result, a clear understanding of characterization principles is necessary.

BYNUM v. COMMISSIONER
United States Tax Court
46 T.C. 295 (1966)

FORRESTER, JUDGE:

. . . The only issue now remaining for our decision is whether admitted gains from sales of real estate during the years in issue are taxable as ordinary income or as long-term capital gain. Requisite mathematical adjustments as to allowable medical expenses may be dependent upon our determination of such issue.

FINDINGS OF FACT

Some of the facts have been stipulated by the parties and are so found.

Petitioners S.O. Bynum and Fannie R. Bynum are husband and wife residing in Tuscaloosa, Ala. . . . In [their] return for 1960 they showed the sales of 12 subdivided lots in Morayshire Estates to 9 separate vendees for a total sales price of $40,075 (resulting in total gain of $28,749.78) and in their 1961 return they showed the sales of 8 similar lots to 7 separate vendees for a total sales price of $31,035 (resulting in total gain of $21,020.45). The amounts shown as the total gains in each year are not contested by respondent.

The subdivided lots sold in 1960 and 1961 were originally a part of the farm of about 113 acres which petitioners first leased in 1936. It is located on the Greensboro Road at the edge of the city of Tuscaloosa, Ala., and is approximately 30 miles from downtown Tuscaloosa. Petitioners have continuously used a portion of the tract for growing trees, plants, and shrubbery in connection with a nursery and landscaping business owned and operated by them and known as Southern Tree & Landscaping Co. Petitioners have also lived on this farm since about 1941 and have maintained an office separate from their residence on the farm since 1940 or 1941. From this office they have conducted all activities related to their nursery and landscaping business such as keeping records, preparing landscaping proposals, drawings, bids, etc.

Petitioners purchased this farm in January 1942, and although the record is not clear as to the price they paid, it indicates an allocated cost of $250 to each of the lots sold during the years in issue, and we so find.

By September 1960, 38 lots had been subdivided and improved as follows:

Item	Amount
Streets	$6,117.60
Water	4,278.13
Sewerage	5,449.10
Curb, gutter, drainage	3,708.98
Other	5,210.16
Total	$24,763.97

This amounted to about $650 for each of the 38 lots and to almost $1,100 per acre.

There was no further improvement or subdivision until 1962 when an additional 17 lots were similarly created at a development cost of $22,543.97, or about $1,300 for each of the 17 lots. The initial subdivision of 38 lots consumed between 20 and 25 acres of the 113-acre farm. Petitioners have purchased no additional land.

Petitioners had the formal opening of their subdivision which they called Morayshire Estates, on Sunday, September 11, 1960. It was announced by a full-page advertisement in the Graphic, a magazine-type newspaper circulated in Tuscaloosa, on September 8, 1960, and also by a full-page ad in the Sunday, Tuscaloosa News newspaper on September 11, 1960. Both of these ads advised the public to contact S.O. Bynum "or your favorite realtor." Petitioners also inserted a 2½ by 5-inch advertisement regarding the subdivision in the yellow pages of the 1961 Tuscaloosa telephone directory. In the newspaper and Graphic ads both daytime and nighttime telephone numbers were given for S.O. Bynum, and the newspaper ad purported to offer 73 lots (although only 38 had then been subdivided) and announced "160 Lots to Be Developed Later."

Petitioners listed their subdivided lots with all of the reputable realtors in and around Tuscaloosa, Ala., and neither of them sought or obtained a realtor's license; we conclude however, that all of the sales of lots during the years in issue were made by petitioner husband since no real estate commissions were paid.

OPINION

We are here concerned with the proper application of the language of two sections of the Code to the facts in this case. The sections are 1221(a)(1) and 1231(b)(1)(B). The statutory language in the two Code sections is identical. It is, "property held by the taxpayer primarily for sale to customers in the ordinary course of his trade or business." Section 1221 is the section which defines capital assets and the above-quoted language is an exclusion from the defined class. Section 1231 sets out special rules applicable to sales of property used in taxpayers' trade or business and again the above-quoted language is an exclusion from such special rules.

Petitioners have had varying acreages of the farm under cultivation in connection with the nursery and landscape business; the maximum so employed being about 50 acres and the amounts so employed during the years in issue being about 35 acres. Apparently none of this acreage was subdivided or sold. Also in connection with such business they maintained and used a small barn for the storage of equipment, etc., and a lattice shed of approximately 13,000 square feet for the growing of tender plants and shrubs.

Through the years and during the years in issue petitioners regularly employed 8 to 12 workmen in the nursery and landscaping business and petitioner husband personally supervised and participated in all phases of the planning and work for subject business, acting as his own foreman and superintendent and even working on Sundays a good portion of the time.

Petitioner wife apparently spent little or no time in connection with selling the subdivided lots during the years in issue and respondent does not contend otherwise. Petitioner husband spent 90 or 95 percent of his time during the years in issue in connection with the nursery and landscaping business and spent the other 5 or 10 percent in spasmodic intervals of subdividing and selling activities.

During 1960 sales of the shrubbery and landscaping business amounted to $27,435.43, which resulted in net income of $606.55. During 1961 such sales were $24,250.29, resulting in a loss of $4,321.74.

At some time prior to 1958 petitioners suffered losses in their landscaping and nursery business and began borrowing money from the City National Bank of Tuscaloosa, Ala. The record does not show how these loans were originally secured but by October 1958 they totaled $70,000 and had been questioned and partially charged off by national bank examiners. At about this same time such bank was acquired by new owners or acquired new management and the loans were combined and secured by a mortgage on the subject 113-acre farm. At the same time the bank put and continued heavy pressure upon petitioners to pay off or at least reduce such loan.

During 1959 the bank suggested that petitioners should sell the farm in order to pay off their loan and sent a prospective purchaser to talk with them. Such prospect made an offer of about $40,000 for the farm "as is" and petitioners discussed the matter with several realtors and concluded that they could not realize more than this without subdividing and improving activities, the farm would have had a fair market value of $450 per acre.

Late in 1959 petitioners finally decided to improve and subdivide a portion of their farm. In this connection they worked out an arrangement with the bank for partial releases from the mortgage on payments of about $2,750 for each lot sold, the average selling price of the lots, which were about six-tenths of an acre each in size, being a little under $4,000 each.

Petitioners in the instant case seek long-term capital gain treatment for the profits on the sales of lots subdivided out of their farm. The question or issue for our determination under each of the above-noted sections of the Code is singular; it is whether the taxpayers during the years in issue were in the real estate business and selling property held by them primarily for sale to customers in the ordinary course of such trade or business. The burden of proof, to establish the negative of this proposition, is on petitioners, and we recognize, as we must, that the capital gain provisions, being an exception to the normal-tax rates, are to be construed narrowly. *Corn Products Co. v. Commissioner*, 350 U.S. 46, 52 (1955).

The Supreme Court in the recent case of *Malat v. Riddell*, 383 U.S. 569 (1966), vacating and remanding 347 F.2d 23 (C.A. 9, 1965), has held that where the acquisition and holding of property was for a dual purpose (either to develop for rental, or to sell) that a "substantial" purpose is not necessarily the "primary" purpose, but that the statutory word "primarily" means "of first importance" or "principally" and that "The purpose of the statutory provision with which we deal is to differentiate between the 'profits and losses arising from the everyday operation of a business' on the one hand (*Corn Products Co. v. Commissioner*, 350 U.S. 46, 52) and 'the realization of appreciation in value accrued over a substantial period of time' on the other. (*Commissioner v. Gillette Motor Co.*, 364 U.S. 130, 134.)" Our considerations of the facts in the instant case have all been in the light of such teaching; however, we note at the outset that we are not dealing with such a dual purpose as concerned the Supreme Court in *Malat*, but with a change in purpose between the time the petitioners purchased this farm in 1942 and the sales at issue which occurred in 1960 and 1961.

The respondent contends only that the property here involved was being *"held"* by petitioners primarily for sale in the ordinary course of business at the times the sales occurred. The statutory word is *"held"* and the law is now well settled that no more is required. The taxpayers' purpose at the time of acquisition has evidentiary weight, but the end question is the purpose of the "holding" at the time of the sale or sales. As stated in *Mauldin v. Commissioner*, 195 F.2d 714, 717 (C.A. 10, 1952):

> While the purpose for which the property was acquired is of some weight, the ultimate question is the purpose for which it was held. . . .

> Admittedly, Mauldin originally purchased the property for purposes other than for sale in the ordinary course of trade or business. When, however, he subdivided and offered it for sale, he was undoubtedly engaged in the vocation of selling lots from this tract of land. . . .

Without any notable exceptions the many, many cases in this particular field have noted that each individual case must be considered and evaluated on its peculiar and particular facts, . . . For this reason we have endeavored to make our findings of fact in the instant case full and comprehensive.

Petitioners' position, of course, is that they were simply passive investors engaged in liquidating a portion of their farm to their best advantage in order to satisfy their mortgage, after having ascertained that on a single sale of the entire property they would have realized less than the existing mortgage. We cannot agree with petitioners' position since we believe it is not supported by the facts.

In 1959 petitioners were under pressure from the bank to pay off, or substantially reduce their $70,000 mortgage. They examined into their situation and concluded that an outright sale of the farm "as is" would still leave them in debt and that they would realize very much more if they improved and subdivided before selling.

To this end they spent over $1,000 per acre on the 20 or 25 acres which comprised the first subdivision of 38 lots. This amount was more than double either the allocated fair market value of such acreage or petitioners' original cost, and must be considered substantial. *Cf. Wellesley A. Ayling*, 32 T.C. 704.

Petitioners' position that they were trying to do just enough to get out of debt is not supported by the facts. Under their arrangement with the bank, $2,750 was paid on the mortgage for every lot sold; consequently the proceeds from 26 lots would have more than amortized the mortgage. But petitioners' efforts went far beyond this. Their initial subdivision was 38 lots, their advertising indicated that a total of 233 lots would eventually be offered, and 17 additional lots were in fact subdivided in 1962. This is not the posture of a passive investor who improved his property simply to make it more readily acceptable. . . .

Petitioners here personally conducted all phases of the considerable improving, subdividing, and promotional activities, and the record indicates that petitioner husband personally made each of the sales we are considering during the 2 years before us. The fact that the subdivided lots were "listed for sale" with various local realtors is of little moment when considered against this background. Petitioners urge that petitioner husband continued to spend 90 to 95 percent of his time on the nursery and landscaping business, only devoting the remaining 5 to 10 percent to all the above activities. We do not doubt that petitioner husband remained in the nursery and landscaping business during 1960 and 1961, but we are convinced, from all the facts of record, that during these years he had entered into, and was actively engaged in, a second business — that of selling the subdivided lots from petitioners' farm — and that such property was then held by petitioners primarily and principally for sale to customers in the ordinary course of that business, and that this purpose was of first importance to petitioners. See *Morris W. Zack*, 25 T.C. 676, 680–681, *affd.* 245 F.2d 235 (C.A. 7, 1957).

> The purchase and sale of the hoists was not a part of any other business regularly carried on by Zack, but it has long been recognized that a taxpayer may be engaged in several businesses. The question is whether Zack and his associates were selling the bomb hoists in the ordinary course of a business carried on by them. The only purpose in buying the bomb hoists was to resell them at a higher price. There was no "investment" such as might be made in other types of property, but on the contrary there was a general public offering and sales in such a manner that the exclusion of the statute cannot be denied.

> The activities amounted to the carrying on of a business of selling the bomb hoists and the sales were to customers in the ordinary course of that business. . . .

That this purpose had become of first importance to petitioners is confirmed by the more extensive (as to each individual lot) improvement activities engaged in in 1962 when the expenditures as to each of the 17 lots then subdivided amounted to $1,300 as against the $650 spent on each of the first 38 lots. In our view, petitioners were engaging in the business of adding extensive improvements to real estate, and then selling those improvements at a profit. *Cf. Morris W. Zack, supra.*

The record facts indicate that the value of the raw land of petitioners' farm had appreciated very little since 1942, such appreciation amounting to about $35 per acre, yet the gain on the approximately 13 acres sold during the years at issue amounted to almost $4,000 per acre. We cannot believe that gain of this character was contemplated by the Supreme Court in *Commissioner v. Gillette Motor Co.*, 364 U.S. 130 (1960), when it said at page 134:

> This Court has long held that the term "capital asset" is to be construed narrowly in accordance with the purpose of Congress to afford capital-gains treatment only in situations typically involving the realization of appreciation in value accrued over a substantial period of time, and thus to ameliorate the hardship of taxation of the entire gain in one year. *Burnet v. Harmel*, 287 U.S. 103, 106. . . .

We do believe that the gain here was generated by petitioners' actions and activities with regard to this property, . . . and as such, it is taxable as ordinary income.

Reviewed by the Court.

Decision will be entered for the respondent.

TANNENWALD, J., concurring: Since this is the first case reviewed by the Court after *Malat v. Riddell*, I think it extremely important that we be crystal clear as to the basis for our decision. Otherwise we will simply provide more fuel for the fires of further litigation in this area.

There are three elements in the identical language of sections 1221(a)(1) and 1231(b)(1)(B):

1. "Primarily" which, as the Supreme Court has mandated, means of "first importance." The element of substantiality is no longer enough. By the same token, the proscribed purpose does not, I believe, have to be capable of a quantitative measurement of more than 50 percent. It should be sufficient if such purpose is *primus inter pares*.

2. "For sale to customers." This is the least significant element. Unquestionably, any person who proposes to sell his property has "for sale" as his purpose. Equally clearly, anyone who buys the property is a "customer."

3. "In the ordinary course of business." This phrase is crucial. Thus, the taxpayer must be in a business of which the sale is a part. In addition, even though a sale is usually the "ordinary" way of disposing of property, it must also be in the "ordinary course" of the business. Thus, a decision by a manufacturer to sell an outmoded plant would not be within the proscribed purpose. These are the distinctions which I think the Supreme Court had in mind when it said in *Malat v. Riddell*:

> The purpose of the statutory provision with which we deal is to differentiate between the "profits and losses arising from the everyday operation of a business" on the one hand (*Corn Products Co. v. Commissioner*, 350 U.S. 46, 52) and "the realization of appreciation in value accrued over a substantial period of time" on the other. (*Commissioner v. Gillette Motor Co.*, 364 U.S. 130, 134.)

All of the foregoing are essential elements which must be satisfied when the witching hour of sale arrives.

Unquestionably in many cases involving change of purpose, the profit is realized in two parts. One part is properly attributable to the appreciation in value during the period when the property was held for investment. The other part represents the fruits of the business. To tax all of such appreciation as ordinary income where the activity is turned into a business may inflict hardship on the taxpayer, contrariwise, to tax all of such appreciation at long-term capital gains may give the taxpayer an unjustifiable windfall. Perhaps some method of allocation within an appropriate statutory framework is indicated. . . .

BRUCE, FAY and DAWSON, JJ., agree with this concurring opinion.

ARKANSAS BEST CORP. v. COMMISSIONER
United State Supreme Court
485 U.S. 212 (1988)

JUSTICE MARSHALL:

The issue presented in this case is whether capital stock held by petitioner Arkansas Best Corporation (Arkansas Best) is a "capital asset" as defined in § 1221 of the Internal Revenue Code regardless of whether the stock was purchased and held for a business purpose or for an investment purpose.

I

Arkansas Best is a diversified holding company. In 1968 it acquired approximately 65% of the stock of the National Bank of Commerce (Bank) in Dallas, Texas. Between 1969 and 1974, Arkansas Best more than tripled the number of shares it owned in the Bank, although its percentage interest in the Bank remained relatively stable. These acquisitions were prompted principally by the Bank's need for added capital. Until 1972, the Bank appeared to be prosperous and growing, and the added capital was necessary to accommodate this growth. As the Dallas real estate market declined, however, so too did the financial health of the Bank, which had a heavy concentration of loans in the local real estate industry. In 1972, federal examiners classified the Bank as a problem bank. The infusion of capital after 1972 was prompted by the loan portfolio problems of the bank.

Petitioner sold the bulk of its Bank stock on June 30, 1975, leaving it with only a 14.7% stake in the Bank. On its federal income tax return for 1975, petitioner claimed a deduction for an ordinary loss of $9,995,688 resulting from the sale of the stock. The Commissioner of Internal Revenue disallowed the deduction, finding that the loss from the sale of stock was a capital loss, rather than an ordinary loss, and that it therefore was subject to the capital loss limitations in the Internal Revenue Code.

Arkansas Best challenged the Commissioner's determination in the United States Tax Court. The Tax Court, relying on cases interpreting *Corn Products Refining Co. v. Commissioner*, 350 U.S. 46 (1955), held that stock purchased with a substantial investment purpose is a capital asset which, when sold, gives rise to a capital gain or loss, whereas stock purchased and held for a business purpose, without any substantial investment motive, is an ordinary asset whose sale gives rise to ordinary gains or losses. The court characterized Arkansas Best's acquisitions through 1972 as occurring during the Bank's " 'growth' phase," and found that these acquisitions "were motivated primarily by investment purpose and only incidentally by some business purpose." The stock acquired during this period therefore constituted a capital asset, which gave rise to a capital loss when sold in 1975. The court determined, however, that the acquisitions after 1972 occurred during the Bank's " 'problem' phase," and, except for certain minor exceptions, "were made exclusively for business purposes and subsequently held for the same reasons." These acquisitions, the court found, were designed to preserve petitioner's business reputation, because without the added capital the Bank probably would have failed. The loss realized on the sale of this stock was thus held to be an ordinary loss.

The Court of Appeals for the Eighth Circuit reversed the Tax Court's determination that the loss realized on stock purchased after 1972 was subject to ordinary-loss treatment, holding that all of the Bank stock sold in 1975 was subject to capital-loss treatment. The court reasoned that the Bank stock clearly fell within the general definition of "capital asset" in Internal Revenue Code § 1221, and that the stock did not fall within any of the specific statutory exceptions to this definition. The court concluded that Arkansas Best's purpose in acquiring and holding the stock was irrelevant to the determination whether the stock was a capital asset. We granted certiorari, 480 U.S. 930, and now affirm.

II

Section 1221 of the Internal Revenue Code defines "capital asset" broadly, as "property held by the taxpayer (whether or not connected with his trade or business)," and then excludes five specific classes of property from capital-asset status. . . . Arkansas Best acknowledges that the Bank stock falls within the literal definition of "capital asset" in § 1221, and is outside of the statutory exclusions. It asserts, however, that this determination does not end the inquiry. Petitioner argues that in *Corn Products Refining Co. v. Commissioner, supra,* this Court rejected a literal reading of § 1221, and concluded that assets acquired and sold for ordinary business purposes rather than for investment purposes should be given ordinary-asset treatment. Petitioner's reading of *Corn Products* finds much support in the academic literature and in the courts. Unfortunately for petitioner, this broad reading finds no support in the language of § 1221.

In essence, petitioner argues that "property held by the taxpayer (whether or not connected with his trade or business)" does not include property that is acquired and held for a business purpose. In petitioner's view an asset's status as "property" thus turns on the motivation behind its acquisition. This motive test, however, is not only nowhere mentioned in § 1221, but it is also in direct conflict with the parenthetical phrase "whether or not connected with his trade or business." The broad definition of the term "capital asset" explicitly makes irrelevant any consideration of the property's connection with the taxpayer's business, whereas petitioner's rule would make this factor dispositive.

In a related argument, petitioner contends that the five exceptions listed in § 1221 for certain kinds of property are illustrative, rather than exhaustive, and that courts are therefore free to fashion additional exceptions in order to further the general purposes of the capital-asset provisions. The language of the statute refutes petitioner's construction. Section 1221 provides that "capital asset" means "property held by the taxpayer[,] . . . but does not include" the five classes of property listed as exceptions. We believe this locution signifies that the listed exceptions are exclusive. The body of § 1221 establishes a general definition of the term "capital asset," and the phrase "does not include" takes out of that broad definition only the classes of property that are specifically mentioned. The legislative history of the capital-asset definition supports this interpretation, see H.R. Rep. No. 704, 73d Cong., 2d Sess., 31 (1934) ("[T]he definition includes all property, except as specifically excluded"); H.R. Rep. No. 1337, 83d Cong., 2d Sess., A273 (1954) ("A capital asset is property held by the taxpayer with certain exceptions"), as does the applicable Treasury regulation, see 26 CFR § 1.1221-1(a) (1987) ("The term 'capital assets' includes all classes of property not specifically excluded by section 1221").

Petitioner's reading of the statute is also in tension with the exceptions listed in § 1221. These exclusions would be largely superfluous if assets acquired primarily or exclusively for business purposes were not capital assets. Inventory, real or depreciable property used in the taxpayer's trade or business, and accounts or notes receivable acquired in the ordinary course of business, would undoubtedly satisfy such a business-motive test. Yet these exceptions were created by Congress in separate enactments spanning 30 years. Without any express direction from Congress, we are unwilling to read § 1221 in a manner that makes surplusage of these statutory exclusions.

In the end, petitioner places all reliance on its reading of *Corn Products Refining Co. v. Commissioner* — a reading we believe is too expansive. In *Corn Products*, the Court considered whether income arising from a taxpayer's dealings in corn futures was entitled to capital-gains treatment. The taxpayer was a company that converted corn into starches, sugars, and other products. After droughts in the 1930s caused sharp increases in corn prices, the company began a program of buying corn futures to assure itself an adequate supply of corn and protect against price increases. The company "would take delivery on such contracts as it found necessary to its manufacturing operations and sell the remainder in early summer if no shortage was imminent. If shortages appeared, however, it sold futures only as it bought spot corn for grinding." The Court characterized the company's dealing in corn futures as "hedging." *Id.*, at 51. As explained by the Court of Appeals in *Corn Products*, "[h]edging is a method of dealing in commodity futures whereby a person or business protects itself against price fluctuations at the time of delivery of the product which it sells or buys." 215 F.2d 513, 515 (CA2 1954). In evaluating the company's claim that the sales of corn futures resulted in capital gains and losses, this Court stated:

> Nor can we find support for petitioner's contention that hedging is not within the exclusions of [§ 1221]. Admittedly, petitioner's corn futures do not come within the literal language of the exclusions set out in that section.

They were not stock in trade, actual inventory, property held for sale to customers or depreciable property used in a trade or business. But the capital-asset provision of [§ 1221] must not be so broadly applied as to defeat rather than further the purpose of Congress. Congress intended that profits and losses arising from the everyday operation of a business be considered as ordinary income or loss rather than capital gain or loss. . . . Since this section is an exception from the normal tax requirements of the Internal Revenue Code, the definition of a capital asset must be narrowly applied and its exclusions interpreted broadly. [350 U.S. at 51–52 (citations omitted).]

The Court went on to note that hedging transactions consistently had been considered to give rise to ordinary gains and losses, and then concluded that the corn futures were subject to ordinary-asset treatment.

The Court in *Corn Products* proffered the oft-quoted rule of construction that the definition of capital asset must be narrowly applied and its exclusions interpreted broadly, but it did not state explicitly whether the holding was based on a narrow reading of the phrase "property held by the taxpayer," or on a broad reading of the inventory exclusion of § 1221. In light of the stark language of § 1221, however, we believe that *Corn Products* is properly interpreted as involving an application of § 1221's inventory exception. Such a reading is consistent both with the Court's reasoning in that case and with § 1221. The Court stated in *Corn Products* that the company's futures transactions were "an integral part of its business designed to protect its manufacturing operations against a price increase in its principal raw material and to assure a ready supply for future manufacturing requirements." 350 U.S., at 50. The company bought, sold, and took delivery under the futures contracts as required by the company's manufacturing needs. As Professor Bittker notes, under these circumstances the futures can "easily be viewed as surrogates for the raw material itself." 2 B. Bittker, Federal Taxation of Income, Estates and Gifts Para. 51.10.3, p. 51–62 (1981). The Court of Appeals for the Second Circuit in *Corn Products* clearly took this approach. That court stated that when commodity futures are "utilized solely for the purpose of stabilizing inventory cost[,] . . . [they] cannot reasonably be separated from the inventory items," and concluded that "property used in hedging transactions properly comes within the exclusions of [§ 1221]." 215 F.2d at 516. This Court indicated its acceptance of the Second Circuit's reasoning when it began the central paragraph of its opinion, "Nor can we find support for petitioner's contention that hedging is not within the exclusions of [§ 1221]." 350 U.S., at 51. In the following paragraph, the Court argued that the Treasury had consistently viewed such hedging transactions as a form of insurance to stabilize the cost of inventory, and cited a Treasury ruling which concluded that the value of a manufacturer's raw-material inventory should be adjusted to take into account hedging transactions in futures contracts. See *id.*, at 52–53 (citing G.C.M. 17322, XV-2 Cum. Bull. 151 (1936)). This discussion, read in light of the Second Circuit's holding and the plain language of § 1221, convinces us that although the corn futures were not "actual inventory," their use as an integral part of the taxpayer's inventory-purchase system led the Court to treat them as substitutes for the corn inventory such that they came within a broad reading of "property of a kind which would properly be included in the inventory of the taxpayer" in § 1221.

Petitioner argues that by focusing attention on whether the asset was acquired and sold as an integral part of the taxpayer's everyday business operations, the Court in *Corn Products* intended to create a general exemption from capital-asset status for assets acquired for business purposes. We believe petitioner misunderstands the relevance of the Court's inquiry. A business connection, although irrelevant to the initial determination of whether an item is a capital asset, is relevant in determining the applicability of certain of the statutory exceptions, including the inventory exception. The close connection between the futures transactions and the taxpayer's business in *Corn Products* was crucial to whether the corn futures could be considered surrogates for the stored inventory of raw corn. For if the futures dealings were not part of the company's inventory-purchase system, and instead amounted simply to speculation in corn futures, they could not be considered substitutes for the company's corn inventory, and would fall outside even a broad reading of the inventory exclusion. We conclude that *Corn Products* is properly interpreted as standing for the narrow proposition that hedging transactions that are an integral part of a business' inventory-purchase system fall within the inventory exclusion of § 1221. Arkansas Best, which is not a dealer in securities, has never suggested that the Bank stock falls within the inventory exclusion. *Corn Products* thus has no application to this case.

It is also important to note that the business-motive test advocated by petitioner is subject to the same kind of abuse that the Court condemned in *Corn Products*. The Court explained in *Corn Products* that unless hedging transactions were subject to ordinary gain and loss treatment, taxpayers engaged in such transactions could "transmute ordinary income into capital gain at will." 350 U.S., at 53–54. The hedger could garner capital-asset treatment by selling the future and purchasing the commodity on the spot market, or ordinary-asset treatment by taking delivery under the future contract. In a similar vein, if capital stock purchased and held for a business purpose is an ordinary asset, whereas the same stock purchased and held with an investment motive is a capital asset, a taxpayer such as Arkansas Best could have significant influence over whether the asset would receive capital or ordinary treatment. Because stock is most naturally viewed as a capital asset, the Internal Revenue Service would be hard pressed to challenge a taxpayer's claim that stock was acquired as an investment, and that a gain arising from the sale of such stock was therefore a capital gain. Indeed, we are unaware of a single decision that has applied the business-motive test so as to require a taxpayer to report a gain from the sale of stock as an ordinary gain. If the same stock is sold at a loss, however, the taxpayer may be able to garner ordinary-loss treatment by emphasizing the business purpose behind the stock's acquisition. The potential for such abuse was evidenced in this case by the fact that as late as 1974, when Arkansas Best still hoped to sell the Bank stock at a profit, Arkansas Best apparently expected to report the gain as a capital gain. See 83 T.C., at 647–48.

III

We conclude that a taxpayer's motivation in purchasing an asset is irrelevant to the question whether the asset is "property held by a taxpayer (whether or not connected with his business)" and is thus within § 1221's general definition of "capital asset." Because the capital stock held by petitioner falls within the broad definition of the term "capital asset" in § 1221 and is outside the classes of property excluded from capital-asset status, the loss arising from the sale of the stock is a capital loss. *Corn Products Refining Co. v. Commissioner, supra*, which we interpret as involving a broad reading of the inventory exclusion of § 1221, has no application in the present context.

It is so ordered.

HORT v. COMMISSIONER
United States Supreme Court
313 U.S. 28 (1941)

Mr. Justice Murphy delivered the opinion of the Court.

We must determine whether the amount petitioner received as consideration for cancellation of a lease of realty in New York City was ordinary gross income as defined in Section 22(a) of the Revenue Act of 1932 (47 Stat. 169, 178), and whether, in any event, petitioner sustained a loss through cancellation of the lease which is recognized in Section 23(3) of the same Act (47 Stat. 169, 180).

Petitioner acquired the property, a lot and ten-story office building, by devise from his father in 1928. At the time he became owner, the premises were leased to a firm which had sublet the main floor to the Irving Trust Co. In 1927, five years before the head lease expired, the Irving Trust Co. and petitioner's father executed a contract in which the latter agreed to lease the main floor and basement to the former for a term of fifteen years at an annual rental of $25,000, the term to commence at the expiration of the head lease.

In 1933, the Irving Trust Co. found it unprofitable to maintain a branch in petitioner's building. After some negotiations, petitioner and the Trust Co. agreed to cancel the lease in consideration of a payment to petitioner of $140,000. Petitioner did not include this amount in gross income in his income tax return for 1933. On the contrary, he reported a loss of $21,494.75 on the theory that the amount he received as consideration for the cancellation was $21,494.75 less than the difference between the present value of the unmatured rental payments and the fair rental value of the main floor and basement for the unexpired term of the lease. He did not deduct this figure, however, because he reported other losses in excess of gross income.

The Commissioner included the entire $140,000 in gross income, disallowed the asserted loss, made certain other adjustments not material here, and assessed a deficiency. The Board of Tax Appeals affirmed. 39 B.T.A. 922. The Circuit Court of Appeals affirmed per curiam on the authority of *Warren Service Corp. v. Commissioner*, 110 F.2d 723. 112 F.2d 167. Because of conflict with *Commissioner v.*

Langwell Real Estate Corp., 47 F.2d 841, we granted certiorari limited to the question whether, "in computing net gain or loss for income tax purposes, a taxpayer [can] offset the value of the lease canceled against the consideration received by him for the cancellation." 311 U.S. 641.

Petitioner apparently contends that the amount received for cancellation of the lease was capital rather than ordinary income. . . . Further, he argues that even if that amount must be reported as ordinary gross income he sustained a loss which Section 23(e) authorizes him to deduct. We cannot agree.

The amount received by petitioner for cancellation of the lease must be included in his gross income in its entirety. Section 22(a) . . . expressly defines gross income to include "gains, profits, and income derived from . . . rent, . . . or gains or profits and income derived from any source whatever." Plainly this definition reached the rent paid prior to cancellation just as it would have embraced subsequent payments if the lease had never been canceled. It would have included a prepayment of the discounted value of unmatured rental payments whether received at the inception of the lease or at any time thereafter. Similarly, it would have extended to the proceeds of a suit to recover damages had the Irving Trust Co. breached the lease instead of concluding a settlement. That the amount petitioner received resulted from negotiations ending in cancellation of the lease rather than from a suit to enforce it cannot alter the fact that basically the payment was merely a substitute for the rent reserved in the lease. So far as the application of Section 22(a) is concerned, it is immaterial that petitioner chose to accept an amount less than the strict present value of the unmatured rental payments rather than to engage in litigation, possibly uncertain and expensive.

The consideration received for cancellation of the lease was not a return of capital. We assume that the lease was "property," whatever that signifies abstractly. . . . Simply because the lease was "property" the amount received for its cancellation was not a return of capital, quite apart from the fact that "property" and "capital" are not necessarily synonymous in the Revenue Act of 1932 or in common usage. Where, as in this case, the disputed amount was essentially a substitute for rental payments which Section 22(a) expressly characterizes as gross income, it must be regarded as ordinary income, and it is immaterial that for some purposes the contract creating the right to such payments may be treated as "property" or "capital."

For the same reasons, that amount was not a return of capital because petitioner acquired the lease as an incident of the realty devised to him by his father. Theoretically, it might have been possible in such a case to value realty and lease separately and to label each a capital asset. . . . But that would not have converted into capital the amount petitioner received from the Trust Co., since Section 22(b)(3) of the 1932 Act (47 Stat. 169, 178) would have required him to include in gross income the rent derived from the property, and that section, like Section 22(a), does not distinguish rental payments and a payment which is clearly a substitute for rental payments.

We conclude that petitioner must report as gross income the entire amount received for cancellation of the lease, without regard to the claimed disparity between that amount and the difference between the present value of the unmatured rental payments and the fair rental value of the property for the unexpired period of the lease. The cancellation of the lease involved nothing more than relinquishment of the right to future rental payments in return for a present substitute payment and possession of the lease premises. Undoubtedly it diminished the amount of gross income petitioner expected to realize, but to that extent he was relieved of the duty to pay income tax. Nothing in Section 23(e) indicates that Congress intended to allow petitioner to reduce ordinary income actually received and reported by the amount of income he failed to realize. . . . We may assume that petitioner was injured insofar as the cancellation of the lease affected the value of the realty. But that would become a deductible loss only when its extent had been fixed by a closed transaction. . . .

The judgment of the Circuit Court of Appeals is

Affirmed.

DAVIS v. COMMISSIONER
United States Tax Court
119 T.C. 1 (2002)

CHIECHI, JUDGE:

Respondent determined a deficiency in petitioners' Federal income tax (tax) for 1997 in the amount of $210,166.

We must determine whether the amount that petitioners received in exchange for the assignment of their right to receive a portion of certain future annual lottery payments is ordinary income or capital gain. We hold that the amount is ordinary income.

Background

On July 10, 1991, petitioner James F. Davis (Mr. Davis) won $13,580,000 in the California State Lottery's On-Line LOTTO game (lottery). Pursuant to certain rules and regulations governing the California State Lottery (CSL) in effect during 1991, Mr. Davis became entitled upon winning the lottery to receive the $13,580,000 in 20 equal annual payments of $679,000 (annual lottery payments), less certain tax withholding. At the time that Mr. Davis won the lottery, CSL did not offer to any lottery winner the option to elect to receive a single lump sum payment of the lottery prize.

On December 13, 1991, CSL sent Mr. Davis a letter which stated, inter alia:

> This letter certifies that on July 10, 1991 you won $13,580,000 [sic] the California State Lottery's On-Line LOTTO game. You have already received your first payment of $679,000, less 20% for Federal Tax Withholding. In addition, you will receive nineteen (19) subsequent annual payments of $679,000 each, as near as possible to the anniversary of the day on which you won your prize, $13,580,000.

Please maintain this letter for your permanent record. In accordance with the Internal Revenue Service regulations, all payments are subject to appropriate Federal tax withholdings. Deductions authorized by California statutes, if such are appropriate, will also be made.

Your rights under this agreement cannot be assigned, but all remaining rights do become a part of your estate. This document is not negotiable.

On June 16, 1997, at a time when petitioners were entitled to receive 14 future annual lottery payments of $679,000 (less certain tax withholding) during the years 1997 through 2010, petitioners and Singer Asset Finance Company, LLC (Singer), entered into an agreement pursuant to which, in exchange for a lump-sum payment to petitioners by Singer of $1,040,000, petitioners assigned Singer their right to receive a portion (i.e., $165,000 less certain tax withholding) of each of 11 of the future annual lottery payments that they were entitled to receive during the years 1997 through 2007. (We shall refer to the foregoing assignment as petitioners' assignment.) Petitioners thus assigned to Singer the portions of those future annual lottery payments at a discount of $775,000 (i.e., $1,815,000 (total of 11 future annual payments of $165,000) less $1,040,000 (total of the amount that Singer paid to petitioners)). After petitioners' assignment, petitioners were entitled to receive from CSL for each of the years 1997 through 2007 only $514,000 (less certain tax withholding) to which they had been entitled prior to the assignment. After that assignment, CSL was to pay the balance of each of their future annual lottery payments (i.e., $165,000 (less certain tax withholding)) to Singer.

At all relevant times, the laws of the state of California precluded a lottery winner from assigning such person's right to receive future annual lottery payments without obtaining California Superior Court approval. On or about July 22, 1997, petitioners and Singer filed with the California Superior Court for the County of Sacramento (Sacramento County Superior Court) a joint petition "FOR AN ORDER APPROVING VOLUNTARY ASSIGNMENT OF LOTTERY WIN-NINGS." On August 1, 1997, Sacramento County Superior Court issued an order approving petitioners' assignment.

Singer issued to petitioners Form 1099-B, Proceeds From Broker and Barter Exchange Transactions (Form 1099-B), for 1997. That Form 1099-B showed gross proceeds from the sale of "Stocks, bonds, etc." in the amount of $1,040,000.

CSL issued to petitioners Form W-2G, Certain Gambling Winnings (Form W-2G), for 1997. That Form W-2G showed "Gross winnings" from "STATE LOTTERY" of $514,000 and tax withheld of $143,920.

On March 13, 1998, petitioners signed Form 1040, U.S. Individual Income Tax Return, for their taxable year 1997 (petitioners' 1997 joint return). In petitioners' 1997 joint return, they reported petitioners' assignment as a sale of a capital asset held for more than 1 year, a sale price of $1,040,000, a cost basis of $7,009, and long-term capital gain of $1,032,991. In that return, petitioners also reported as ordinary income the $514,000 payment that they received in 1997 from CSL.

In the notice that respondent issued to petitioners with respect to their taxable year 1997, respondent determined, inter alia, the following:

It is determined that you [petitioners] received the amount of $1,040,000.00 from Singer Asset Finance Company, for the tax year ended December 31, 1997, in payment of assignment of rights to future lottery payments from the State of California. This amount is determined to be ordinary income because rights to future annual lottery payments do not meet the definition of a capital asset according to the provisions of the Internal Revenue Code. Therefore, income is increased $1,040,000.00 for the year 1997.

Discussion

The parties agree that an amount received as a lottery prize constitutes ordinary income.

The parties' dispute is over whether the $1,040,000 that petitioners received in exchange for petitioners' assignment is ordinary income or capital gain. Resolution of that dispute depends on whether petitioners' right to receive future annual lottery payments constitutes property held by them and that such property meets the definition of the term "capital asset" in section 1221. Respondent acknowledges that petitioners' right to receive future annual lottery payments is property in the ordinary sense of the word. However, respondent contends that such right does not qualify as a capital asset within the meaning of section 1221. According to respondent, the $1,040,000 that petitioners received from Singer constitutes ordinary income, because petitioners received that amount in exchange for their future right to receive ordinary income.

In support of petitioners' position that the $1,040,000 that they received from Singer constitutes capital gain, petitioners rely on *Ark. Best Corp. v. Commissioner*, 485 U.S. 212, 108 S.Ct. 971, 99 L.Ed.2d 183 (1988). In support of respondent's position that that amount constitutes ordinary income, respondent relies on the principle established in the following cases: *Hort v. Commissioner*, 313 U.S. 28 (1941); *Commissioner v. P.G. Lake, Inc.*, 356 U.S. 260 (1958); *Commissioner v. Gillette Motor Transp.*, 364 U.S. 130 (1960); and *United States v. Midland-Ross Corp.*, 381 U.S. 54 (1965).

Petitioners concede that, before the Supreme Court of the United States (Supreme Court) decided *Ark. Best Corp. v. Commissioner, supra*, the line of cases on which respondent relies would have precluded characterizing petitioners' right to receive future annual lottery payments as a capital asset within the meaning of section 1221. However, according to petitioners, *Ark. Best Corp.* effectively overruled that line of cases and requires the result in the instant case that they advocate. Respondent disputes petitioners' reading of *Ark. Best Corp. v. Commissioner, supra*.

We agree with respondent's reading of *Ark. Best Corp. v. Commissioner, supra*. In fact, we have previously concluded that *Ark. Best Corp.* in no way affected the viability of the principle established in the line of cases on which respondent relies. *See Gladden v. Commissioner*, 112 T.C. 209, 221 (1999), *revd. on another issue* 262 F.3d 851 (9th Cir.2001); *FNMA v. Commissioner*, 100 T.C. 541, 573 n. 30 (1993). We based that conclusion on footnote 5 of the Supreme Court's opinion in *Ark. Best Corp.*, which states:

> Petitioner [Ark. Best Corp.] mistakenly relies on cases in which this Court, in narrowly applying the general definition of "capital assets" has "construed 'capital asset' to exclude property representing income items or accretions to the value of a capital asset themselves properly attributable to income," even though these items are property in the broad sense of the word. *United States v. Midland-Ross Corp.*, 381 U.S. 54, 57 (1965). *See, e.g., Commissioner v. Gillette Motor Co.*, 364 U.S. 130 (1960) ("capital asset" does not include proceeds from sale of oil payment rights); *Hort v. Commissioner*, 313 U.S. 28 (1941) ("capital asset" does not include payment to lessor for cancellation of unexpired portion of a lease). This line of cases, based on the premise that § 1221 "property" does not include claims or rights to ordinary income, has no application in the present context. Petitioner sold capital stock, not a claim to ordinary income. [*Ark. Best Corp. v. Commissioner, supra* at 217 n.5.]

We have reviewed *Hort v. Commissioner, supra*; *Commissioner v. P.G. Lake, Inc., supra*; *Commissioner v. Gillette Motor Trans., Inc., supra*; and *United States v. Midland-Ross Corp., supra*, and certain of their progeny on which respondent relies. As the Supreme Court stated in *Commissioner v. Gillette Motor Transp., Inc., supra* at 134:

> While a capital asset is defined in § 117(a)(1) [of the Internal Revenue Code of 1939] as "Property held by the taxpayer," it is evident that not everything which can be called property in the ordinary sense and which is outside the statutory exclusions qualifies as a capital asset. . . .

Petitioners assigned to Singer their right to receive a portion of certain future annual lottery payments. In exchange for petitioners' assignment, petitioners received the discounted value (i.e., $1,040,000) of certain ordinary income which they otherwise would have received during the years 1997 through 2007. We hold that Singer paid petitioners $1,040,000 for the right to receive such future ordinary income, and not for an increase in the value of income-producing property.[23]

We further hold that petitioners' right to receive future annual lottery payments does not constitute a capital asset within the meaning of section 1221 and that the $1,040,000 that petitioners received from Singer is ordinary income, and not capital gain. *See United States v. Midland-Ross Corp.*, 381 U.S. at 57–58; *Commissioner v. Gillette Motor Transp., Inc.*, 364 U.S. at 134–135; *Commissioner v. P.G. Lake, Inc.*, 356 U.S. at 265–267; *Hort v. Commissioner*, 313 U.S. at 31.

We have considered all of the petitioners' arguments and contentions that are not discussed herein, and we find them to be without merit and/or irrelevant.

---

[23] It is well established that the purpose for capital-gains treatment is to afford capital-gains treatment only in situations typically involving the realization of appreciation in value accrued over a substantial period of time, and thus to ameliorate the hardship of taxation of the entire gain in one year. . . . [*Commissioner v. Gillette Motor Transp., Inc.*, 364 U.S. 130, 134, 80 S.Ct. 1497, 4 L.Ed.2d 1617 (1960) (citing *Burnet v. Harmel*, 287 U.S. 103, 106, 53 S.Ct. 74, 77 L.Ed.199 (1932)).]

To reflect the foregoing,

Decision will be entered for respondent.

AUTHORS' NOTE

The Ninth Circuit in *U.S. v. Maginnis*, 356 F.3d 1179 (9th Cir. 2004), also concluded that the sale of lottery payments by a lottery winner results in ordinary income treatment. In reaching its decision, the Ninth Circuit relied on the substitute-for-ordinary-income doctrine originally enunciated in *Hort v. Commissioner*. The Ninth Circuit noted that there were two factors that were crucial to its conclusion that the lump sum received for the lottery payments was ordinary income, *i.e.*, "(1) Maginnis did not make any underlying investment of capital in return for the receipt of his lottery right, and (2) the sale of his right did not reflect an accretion in value over cost to any underlying asset Maginnis held." *Id.* at 1183.

The Third Circuit, in its decision in *Lattera v. Commissioner*, 437 F.3d 399 (3d Cir. 2006), regarding the sale of lottery payments, reached the same conclusion as the Tax Court in *Davis* and the Ninth Circuit in *Maginnis*. The Third Circuit noted the criticism that has been leveled against the Ninth Circuit's *Maginnis* decision:

> . . . [T]wo commentators have criticized the analysis in *Maginnis*, especially the two factors. The first factor — underlying investment of capital — would theoretically subject all inherited and gifted property (which involves no investment at all) to ordinary-income treatment. . . . The second factor also presents analytical problems. Not all capital assets experience an accretion in value over cost. For example, cars typically depreciate, but they are often capital assets. The *Maginnis* court held that there was no accretion of value over cost in lottery winnings because there was no cost as "Maginnis did not make any capital investment in exchange for his lottery right." . . . But if Maginnis' purchase of a lottery ticket had been a capital investment, would the second factor automatically have been satisfied? (That is, the "cost" in that scenario would have been $1, and the increase would have been $3,949,999.) Our first instinct is no. . . .

> Thus, while we agree with *Maginnis*' result, we do not simply adopt its reasoning. And it is both unsatisfying and unhelpful to future litigants to declare that we know this to be ordinary income when we see it.

Id. at 405.

The Third Circuit ultimately employed what it referred to as the "family resemblance" test whereby a court first tries to determine whether an asset is like either the "capital asset" category of assets (*e.g.*, stocks, bonds, or land) or like the "income items" category (*e.g.*, rental income or interest income). If the asset does not bear a family resemblance to items in either of those categories, the court looks to the nature of the sale.

> If the sale or assignment constitutes a horizontal carve-out [one in which temporal divisions are made in a property interest in which the person owning the interest disposes of part of his interest but also retains a portion

of it — exactly what happened in *Davis* where the taxpayer sold only some of the lottery payments and retained the remainder], then ordinary-income treatment presumably applies. If, on the other hand, it constitutes a vertical carve-out [one in which a complete disposition of a person's interest in property is made — exactly what happened in *Maginnis* where the lottery winners sold the rights to all of their remaining lottery payments], then we look to the character-of-the-asset factor. There, if the sale is a lump-sum payment for a future right to earned income [*e.g.*, a termination fee for a personal-services contract where the fee has already been "earned" and will simply be paid], we apply ordinary-income treatment, but if it is a lump-sum payment for a future right to earn income [*e.g.*, sale of a partnership interest where buyer must continue to work in order to generate income], we apply capital-gains treatment.

Id. at 409.

Applying the above test to the taxpayers in *Lattera*, the Third Circuit noted that

the right to receive annual lottery payments does not bear a strong family resemblance to either the 'capital assets' or the 'income items.' . . . The Latteras sold their right to all their remaining lottery payments, so this is a vertical carve-out, which could indicate either capital-gains or ordinary-income treatment. But because a right to lottery payments is a right to earned income (*i.e.*, the payment will keep arriving due simply to ownership of the asset), the lump-sum payment received by the Latteras should receive ordinary-income treatment. This result comports with *Davis* and *Maginnis*. It also ensures that the Latteras do not 'receive a tax advantage as compared to those taxpayers who would simply choose originally to accept their lottery winning in the form of a lump sum payment.' . . . "

Id. at 410.

The Second, Tenth, and Eleventh Circuits have recently agreed with the Third and Ninth Circuits and the Tax Court that the sale of lottery payments results in ordinary income. Prebola v. Commissioner, 482 F.3d 610 (2d Cir. 2007); *Watkins v. Commissioner*, 447 F.3d 1269 (10th Cir. 2006); Womack v. Commissioner, 510 F.3d 1295 (11th Cir. 2007).

KENAN v. COMMISSIONER
United States Court of Appeals, Second Circuit
114 F.2d 217 (1940)

AUGUSTUS N. HAND, CIRCUIT JUDGE:

The testatrix, Mrs. Bingham, died on July 27, 1917, leaving a will under which she placed her residuary estate in trust and provided in item "Seventh" that her trustees should pay a certain amount annually to her niece, Louise Clisby Wise, until the latter reached the age of forty, "at which time or as soon thereafter as compatible with the interests of my estate they shall pay to her the sum of Five Million ($5,000,000.00) Dollars." The will provided in item "Eleventh" that the trustees, in the case of certain payments including that of the $5,000,000 under item "Seventh," should have the right "to substitute for the payment in money, payment in marketable securities of a value equal to the sum to be paid, the selection of the securities to be substituted in any instance, and the valuation of such securities to be done by the Trustees and their selection and valuation to be final."

Louise Clisby Wise became forty years of age on July 28, 1935. The trustees decided to pay her the $5,000,000 partly in cash and partly in securities. The greater part of the securities had been owned by the testator and transferred as part of her estate to the trustees; others had been purchased by the trustees. All had appreciated in value during the period for which they were held by the trustees, and the Commissioner determined that the distribution of the securities to the niece resulted in capital gains which were taxable to the trustees under the rates specified in Section 117 of the Revenue Act of 1934, which limits the percentage of gain to be treated as taxable income on the "sale or exchange" of capital assets. On this basis, the Commissioner determined a deficiency of $367,687.12 in the income tax for the year 1935.

The Board overruled the objections of the trustees to the imposition of any tax and denied a motion of the Commissioner to amend his answer in order to claim the full amount of the appreciation in value as ordinary income rather than a percentage of it as a capital gain, and confirmed the original deficiency determination. The taxpayers contend that the decision of the Board was erroneous because they realized neither gain from the sale or exchange of capital assets nor income of any character by delivering the securities to the legatee pursuant to the permissive terms of the will. The Commissioner contends that gain was realized by the delivery of the securities but that such gain was ordinary income not derived from a sale or exchange and therefore taxable in its entirety. The trustees have filed a petition to review the order of the Board determining the deficiency of $365,687.12 and the Commissioner has filed a cross-petition claiming a deficiency of $1,238,841.99. . . .

The Taxpayer's Appeal

In support of their petition the taxpayers contend that the delivery of the securities of the trust estate to the legatee was a donative disposition of property pursuant to the terms of the will, and that no gain was thereby realized. They argue that when they determined that the legacy should be one of securities, it became for all purposes a bequest of property, just as if the cash alternative had not been provided, and not taxable for the reason that no gain is realized on the transfer by a testamentary trustee of specific securities or other property bequeathed by will to a legatee.

We do not think that the situation here is the same as that of a legacy of specific property. The legatee was never in the position occupied by the recipient of specific securities under a will. She had a claim against the estate for $5,000,000, payable either in cash or securities of that value, but had no title or right to the securities, legal or equitable, until they were delivered to her by the trustees after the exercise of their option. She took none of the chances of a legatee of specific securities or of a share of a residue that the securities might appreciate or decline in value between the time of the death of the testator and the transfer to her by the trustees, but instead had at all times a claim for an unvarying amount in money or its equivalent.

In the present case, the legatee had a claim which was a charge against the trust estate for $5,000,000 in cash or securities and the trustees had the power to determine whether the claim should be satisfied in one form or the other. The claim, though enforceable only in the alternative, was . . . a charge against the entire trust estate. If it were satisfied by a cash payment securities might have to be sold on which (if those actually delivered in specie were selected) a taxable gain would necessarily have been realized. Instead of making such a sale the trustees delivered the securities and exchanged them *pro tanto* for the general claim of the legatee, which was thereby satisfied.

The Board alluded to the fact that . . . the bequest was fixed at a definite amount in money, that . . . there was no bequest of specific securities (nor of a share in the residue which might vary in value), that the rights of the legatee . . . were a charge upon the corpus of the trust, and that the trustees had to part either with $5,000,000 in cash or with securities worth that amount at the time of the transfer. It added that the increase in value of the securities was realized by the trust and benefited it to the full extent, since, except for the increase, it would have had to part with other property. . . . Under circumstances like those here, where the legatee did not take securities designated by the will or an interest in the corpus which might be more or less at the time of the transfer than at the time of decedent's death, it seems to us that the trustees realized a gain by using these securities to settle a claim worth $5,000,000.

It seems reasonably clear that the property was not "transmitted at death" or "acquired by bequest . . . from the decedent." Section 113(a)(5). It follows that the fears of the taxpayers that double taxation of this appreciation will result because the legatee will take the basis of the decedent under *Brewster v. Gage*, 280 U.S. 327, 50 S.Ct. 115, 74 L.Ed. 457, are groundless. It is true that under Section 113(a)(5) the basis for property "acquired by bequest, devise, or inheritance" is "the fair market value of such property at the time of such acquisition" and that under *Brewster v. Gage, supra*, the date of acquisition has been defined as the date of death of the testator. But the holding of the present case is necessarily a determination that the property here acquired is acquired in an exchange and not "by bequest, devise or inheritance," since Sections 117 and 113(a)(5) seem to be mutually exclusive. The legatee's basis would seem to be the value of the claim surrendered in exchange for the securities. . . .

The Commissioner's Appeal

We have already held that a taxable gain was realized by the delivery of the securities. It follows from the reasons that support that conclusion that the appreciation was a capital gain, taxable at the rates specified in Section 117. Therefore, neither under Section 111(a) nor under Section 22(a), 26 U.S.C.A. Int.Rev.Acts, page 669, can the gain realized be taxed as ordinary income.

There can be no doubt that from an accounting standpoint the trustees realized a gain in the capital of their trust when they disposed of securities worth far more at the time of disposition than at the time of acquisition in order to settle (pro tanto) a claim of $5,000,000. It would seem to us a strange anomaly if a disposition of securities which were in fact a "capital asset" should not be taxed at the rates afforded by Section 117 to individuals who have sold or exchanged property which they had held for the specified periods.

The purpose of the capital gains provisions of the Revenue Act of 1934 is so to treat an appreciation in value, arising over a period of years but realized in one year, that the tax thereon will roughly approximate what it would have been had a tax been paid each year upon the appreciation in value for that year. The appreciation in value in the present case took place between 1917 and 1935, whereas the Commissioner's theory would tax it as though it had all taken place in 1935. If the trustees had sold the securities, they would be taxed at capital gain rates. Both the trustees and the Commissioner, in their arguments as respondent and cross-respondents, draw the analogy between the transaction here and a sale, and no injustice is done to either by taxing the gain at the rates which would apply had a sale actually been made and the proceeds delivered to the legatee. It seems to us extraordinary that the exercise by the trustees of the option to deliver to the legatee securities, rather than cash, should be thought to result in an increased deficiency of enormous proportions.

Orders affirmed.

Chapter 32

QUASI-CAPITAL ASSETS: SECTION 1231

I. PROBLEMS

1. George realizes all of the following gains and losses in Year 2. How would the gains and losses be characterized, and to what extent are any of the losses deductible by George?

   (a) George sold a parcel of land he had owned and used for a number of years in his truck rental business. George realized a gain of $150,000 on the sale.

   (b) George realized a loss of $60,000 on the sale of a summer cabin he had owned and used for personal purposes for many years.

   (c) George sustained an uninsured loss as a result of the theft of a truck he had owned and used in his business for more than a year. At the time of the theft, his adjusted basis in the truck was $25,000 and its value was $30,000.

   (d) George sold some corporate stock at a $30,000 loss. He had held the stock for two years.

   (e) George realized a $2,000 loss on the sale to his sister of a computer he had used in his business for more than one year.

2. In addition to the facts of Problem 1, assume George recognized a $25,000 gain from the collection of insurance proceeds on the destruction by earthquake of land he owned and used in his business for five years. How would George's gains and losses be characterized?

3. In addition to the facts of Problem 1, assume in Year 1 George recognized $45,000 in § 1231 losses from the sale of property he had owned and used in his business, and $15,000 of § 1231 gain from the involuntary conversion of property he had owned and used in his business. Explain how your answer to Problem 1 will change, if at all, in light of the assumption regarding Year 1.

Assignment for Chapter 32:

Complete the problems.

Read: Internal Revenue Code: §§ 1221(a)(2); 1231; 267(a)(1), (b)(1), (c)(4). Review §§ 1(h); 165(a), (b) and (c).
Treasury Regulations: §§ 1.1231-1(d), 1.1221-1(b).
Materials: Overview

II. VOCABULARY

quasi-capital asset
property used in the trade or business
hotchpot
preliminary hotchpot
net § 1231 gain (or loss)
non-recaptured net § 1231 loss

III. OBJECTIVES

1. To recall that certain gains and losses are characterized under § 1231, but must be recognized and allowed under other provisions of the Code.

2. To recall the types of property and types of dispositions to which § 1231 applies.

3. To demonstrate by example the operation of the hotchpot provisions of § 1231 and how they are favorable to the taxpayer.

4. To explain by example the operation of § 1231(c) relating to recapture of net ordinary losses.

5. To explain the relationship between § 1231 and § 1(h).

IV. OVERVIEW

At the risk of slighting important details and qualifications, one might summarize § 1231 by stating that its primary purpose is to provide special, favorable tax treatment to the sale or exchange (or involuntary conversion) of real or depreciable property used in the taxpayer's trade or business. Recall that under § 1221(a)(2) such property is excluded from the definition of "capital asset." But for § 1231, any gain or loss recognized on the disposition of such property would necessarily be ordinary gain or loss. Under § 1231, however, a recognized gain on the sale or exchange (or involuntary conversion) of such property may be characterized as capital gain (hence, the term "quasi-capital asset"), whereas a recognized loss may remain characterized as an ordinary loss. This capital-gain/ordinary-loss set of alternatives gives taxpayers the "best of both worlds." *See* Reg. § 1.1221-1(b).

While the enactment in 1938 of the predecessor of § 1221(a)(2) provided ordinary loss treatment to taxpayers holding depreciable trade or business property that had declined in value, it simultaneously eliminated capital gain treatment for those taxpayers holding depreciable property that had increased in value. (The reference to real property in § 1221(a)(2) was not added until 1942.) The enactment of the predecessor of § 1231 in 1942 drew its impetus from the wartime conditions then present. Congress concluded it was inappropriate to tax at high ordinary income rates the gains from sales to the government of vessels used in the taxpayer's business or gains resulting from the receipt of insurance proceeds in excess of the basis of property destroyed in the course of the on-going war. As enacted, however, the statute applied to dispositions well beyond those that were war-related. Section 1231 remains in the Code today long after the specific wartime conditions that prompted it had passed.

Now to those details and qualifications.

A. Definitions: Section 1231 Gains and Section 1231 Losses

The initial step in applying § 1231 is the identification of those gains and losses that are subject to its provisions. Section 1231 gains and losses are generated by two categories of transactions. First, as noted above, § 1231 gains and losses result from "the sale or exchange of property used in the trade or business." § 1231(a)(3)(A)(i). Read carefully the general definition in § 1231(b)(1) of the term "property used in the trade or business." Consider the following aspects of the general definition:

(1) The property must be depreciable or real property used in the trade or business. Thus, this definition embraces property excluded from capital asset classification under § 1221(a)(2).

(2) The property must have been held more than one year. In § 1231(a)(3)(A)(ii)(II), there is also a "more than one year" holding period requirement applicable to other property covered by § 1231. Thus, there is no such thing as a short-term § 1231 transaction.

(3) Property described in § 1221(a)(1), (3) or (5) is explicitly excluded from the definition in § 1231(b)(1). Property described in § 1221(a)(4) is

excluded from the definition by the requirement that such property be depreciable. Thus, by way of example, inventory will not constitute "property used in the trade or business," and will thus continue to generate ordinary income or loss on disposition.

Why are capital assets disposed of by sale or exchange not covered by § 1231? This question is answered below but you should be able to discern the answer now.

A second category of § 1231 gains and losses arises from the involuntary or compulsory conversion of two types of property: (1) the now-familiar "property used in the trade or business," and (2) capital assets held for more than one year in connection with a trade or business or a transaction entered into for profit. § 1231(a)(3)(A)(ii). (Note also that § 165(h)(2)(B), discussed in Chapter 24, addresses the characterization of gains and losses from the involuntary conversion of capital assets held for other than business or profit-seeking purposes and therefore § 1231 need not address those gains or losses.) By making the gains and losses from involuntary conversions subject to § 1231, Congress afforded the possibility of long-term capital gain (and long-term capital loss) treatment which otherwise would be unavailable since involuntary conversions generally do not constitute sales or exchanges as required by § 1222. (Condemnations, however, have historically been accorded sale or exchange treatment. Note that condemnation gains and losses do not enter the Preliminary Hotchpot, discussed below, but are instead considered only in the Principal Hotchpot analysis, also discussed below.)

As noted above, the phrase "property used in the trade or business" excludes property "held by the taxpayer primarily for sale to customers in the ordinary course of business." Definitional questions concerning this exclusion may arise under § 1231, as they have with the identical language in § 1221(a)(1). For example, in *International Shoe Machine Corp. v. United States*, 491 F.2d 157 (1st Cir. 1974), the taxpayer's main source of income was from the leasing of shoe machinery; only a small portion of the taxpayer's income resulted from sales of the machinery. The taxpayer argued that the gain recognized on the sale of the shoe machinery was § 1231 gain from the sale of "property used in the trade or business." Consequently, the taxpayer claimed capital gain treatment. Notwithstanding the taxpayer's argument, the Court concluded that, because the selling of the machinery was "an accepted and predictable, albeit small" part of the taxpayer's business, the machinery constituted property held primarily for sale to customers in the ordinary course of business and was not within § 1231. Any gain resulting from the sale was therefore ordinary income.

In sum, in determining whether a taxpayer's recognized gains or losses are § 1231 gains or losses and thus subject to the rules of § 1231, one must consider both the event that triggers the gain or loss and the nature of the property involved. For example, the gain or loss recognized on the sale or exchange of a piece of depreciable equipment held by the taxpayer for more than a year and used in the taxpayer's business will be § 1231 gain or loss as would the gain or loss from the involuntary conversion of that equipment. By contrast, the gain or loss from the sale or exchange of a capital asset held for more than one year, *e.g.*, stock, would not be a § 1231 gain or § 1231 loss. Of course, in the latter situation, there is no need for

§ 1231 — the taxpayer's gain or loss will be long-term capital gain or loss under the general definitions provided in § 1222.

B.   The Hotchpot Analysis

Once a taxpayer has identified all of her § 1231 gains and losses for the year, § 1231(a)(1) and (2) require that the taxpayer compare the total § 1231 gains to the total § 1231 losses. Under the general rules of § 1231(a)(1) and (2), if the taxpayer's § 1231 gains exceed her § 1231 losses, the § 1231 gains will be characterized as long-term capital gains and the § 1231 losses will be characterized as long-term capital losses. By contrast, if the taxpayer's § 1231 gains do not exceed the taxpayer's § 1231 losses, the gains and losses will not be treated as gains or losses from the sale of capital assets, *i.e.*, the gains or losses will be ordinary. This gain/loss comparison has been referred to as the "hotchpot" analysis, *i.e.*, all of the § 1231 gains and losses are combined in a hotchpot for purposes of characterization.

Section 1231(a)(1) and (2) as described above establishes the general rule which we will refer to as the "Principal Hotchpot Analysis." As a result of amendments made in 1969, a subset of the § 1231 gains and losses must first be analyzed pursuant to what we refer to as the "Preliminary Hotchpot Analysis." (The Preliminary Hotchpot is sometimes referred to in the literature as the "firepot" because § 1231 losses resulting from the destruction of property by fire are the most common § 1231 items subject to the Preliminary Hotchpot Analysis.)

Section 1231(a)(4)(C) provides the statutory base for the Preliminary Hotchpot Analysis. Note that it provides § 1231 gains and losses resulting from certain involuntary conversions will not be subject to characterization under § 1231, *i.e.*, they will not enter the Principal Hotchpot and will thus be ignored for § 1231 purposes, if the total of such losses exceeds the total of such gains. In that event, that subset of § 1231 gains and losses will be characterized outside of § 1231 and, as a result, will necessarily be ordinary gains and losses. If, however, the § 1231 losses included in the Preliminary Hotchpot do not exceed the § 1231 gains included in that hotchpot, this subset of § 1231 gains and losses is simply lumped with the other § 1231 gains and losses in the Principal Hotchpot and will be subject to the general rules of § 1231(a)(1) and (2).

With regard to the Principal Hotchpot, note that, while the Preliminary Hotchpot rules were applicable only to § 1231 gains and losses arising out of certain involuntary conversions, the Principal Hotchpot rules apply to all of a taxpayer's § 1231 gains and losses, except for those that are disregarded as a result of the operation of § 1231(a)(4)(C) (the Preliminary Hotchpot rules). As noted at the outset of this section of the Overview, once a taxpayer has determined the § 1231 gains and losses that enter the Principal Hotchpot, the taxpayer then compares the total § 1231 gains in the Principal Hotchpot to the total § 1231 losses in the Principal Hotchpot. (Note the special rule of § 1231(a)(4)(A) in this regard; among other things, we are told to disregard the capital loss limitation provisions of § 1211 in determining whether gains exceed losses.) A net positive number in the principal hotchpot renders all the gains and losses long-term capital gains and losses; a net negative number (or gains exactly equal to losses) renders all gains and losses ordinary.

Consider the following examples and the analysis of each:

Example 1: During the current year, Taxpayer realizes an uninsured $10,000 loss from a fire that destroyed depreciable personal property used in Taxpayer's trade or business for more than one year. Taxpayer also recognized a $5,000 gain from an insurance recovery resulting from the destruction by a hurricane of a garage used in Taxpayer's trade or business for the last few years. Assume Taxpayer has no other gains or losses for the year.

Analysis: First, determine whether the gain and the loss are described in § 1231(a)(3). They clearly are. Then determine whether they arise from transactions described in § 1231(a)(4)(C). The fire loss and the hurricane gain are both the result of involuntary conversions described in that provision and are related to the types of property referred to in the provision. Therefore, both the loss and the gain enter the Preliminary Hotchpot. Since the loss exceeds the gain, the § 1231(a)(1) and (2) or Principal Hotchpot analysis is inapplicable to them. As a result, the loss and the gain will not be characterized by § 1231. Instead, Taxpayer will deduct the loss as an ordinary loss under § 165(a), and will report the gain as ordinary income under § 61(a)(3). The loss is ordinary because depreciable personal property used in the trade or business is not a capital asset per § 1221(a)(2); the gain from the insurance recovery is not a capital gain because there is no sale or exchange and the asset is not a capital asset.

Example 2: Assume the same facts as in Example 1, except the gain from the insurance proceeds is $15,000 instead of $5,000.

Analysis: The insurance gain in the Preliminary Hotchpot now exceeds the fire loss. Remember that § 1231(a)(4)(C) (the Preliminary Hotchpot rule) only applies if the losses included in the Preliminary Hotchpot exceed the gains included in the Preliminary Hotchpot. As a result, § 1231(a)(4)(C) is inapplicable and therefore both the insurance gain and the fire loss will be characterized using the Principal Hotchpot analysis. Applying § 1231(a)(1), because the insurance gain exceeds the fire loss, the insurance gain will be characterized as a long-term capital gain and the fire loss will be a long-term capital loss.

Example 3: Same as Example 1, except, instead of Taxpayer realizing $5,000 gain from an insurance recovery, Taxpayer realized it from the sale of land used in the business and held for more than one year.

Analysis: As in Example 1, Taxpayer's $10,000 fire loss is included in the Preliminary Hotchpot. The gain from the sale of the land, however, would not be because a sale is not an event described in § 1231(a)(4)(C). Thus, the fire loss is the only § 1231 item included in the Preliminary Hotchpot and, as a result, the loss will be characterized outside of § 1231 and will be an ordinary loss. By contrast, the $5,000 gain is the only § 1231 item included in the Principal Hotchpot and will, therefore, be characterized as long-term capital gain under § 1231(a)(1). Is § 1231(a)(4)(C) pro-taxpayer? Note how the interaction between § 1231(a)(4)(C) and § 1231(a)(1) in this example provided Taxpayer with "the best of both worlds," *i.e.*, Taxpayer's fire loss was characterized as an ordinary loss and Taxpayer's gain on the sale of the land was characterized as long-term capital gain. Were § 1231(a)(4)(C) not in the Code, both the fire loss and the land sale gain would have been included in the Principal Hotchpot. Because the fire loss exceeded the land sale gain, § 1231(a)(2) would have applied and the fire loss would have been an ordinary loss and the land sale gain would have been an ordinary gain.

Example 4: Same as Example 1, except Taxpayer also realized a loss of $5,000 on the sale of her home.

Analysis: This loss is not allowed. Reg. § 1.165-9(a). Since it is not a "recognized" loss, it is not a § 1231 loss. Remember § 1231 is not a deduction-granting provision; rather it characterizes certain gains and losses otherwise recognized under the Code. (One could, of course, further note that the sale of a capital asset — the home — is not a transaction covered by § 1231.) Thus, the analysis of Example 1 is unchanged.

Example 5: Same as Example 1, except Taxpayer also has a recognized loss of $10,000 from the condemnation of a tract of land used in her business. The land was held more than one year.

Analysis: Since the Preliminary Hotchpot does not apply to condemnation gains and losses, the condemnation loss will be characterized pursuant to the Principal Hotchpot rules. The analysis of Example 1 remains unchanged with regard to the insurance gain and the fire loss — both will be ordinary. Since the condemnation loss is the only § 1231 item included in the Principal Hotchpot, § 1231(a)(2) provides it will not be treated as a loss from the sale or exchange of a capital asset. The condemnation loss will thus be an ordinary loss.

C.   Recapture of Net Ordinary Losses: Section 1231(c)

The preceding discussion has assumed § 1231(c) was not applicable. Section 1231(c) is described as a "recapture" provision, a term that will be more familiar following Chapter 33 on recapture. The problem § 1231(c) addresses can be illustrated with a simple example.

Example: Assume Taxpayer owns and is prepared to sell land and a truck, both of which have been used in Taxpayer's business and held for more than one year. The land is worth $25,000 and has an adjusted basis of $15,000; the truck is worth $5,000 and has an adjusted basis of $10,000. If Taxpayer sells the land and the truck in the same year, the $10,000 gain on the land will be long-term capital gain, and the $5,000 loss on the truck will be a long-term capital loss. § 1231(a)(1). However, if Taxpayer sells the land and the truck in *different* years, during which there are no other § 1231 transactions, the gain on the land will still be capital gain, but the loss on the truck will now be ordinary!

Section 1231(c) attempts to curtail the tax planning possibilities suggested by the above example. Assume the land and the truck in the example are Taxpayer's only § 1231 properties; further assume the respective gain and loss they will generate on sale remain constant. If in Year 1 only the truck is sold, the $5,000 loss is an ordinary one under the normal rules of § 1231(a)(2); but § 1231(c) denominates this loss a "net § 1231 loss." If, in any of the following five years, Taxpayer has a "net § 1231 gain," the first $5,000 of that gain (which would otherwise have been long-term capital gain under § 1231) is converted to ordinary income. Thus, if the land is sold in any of the next five years, producing in the year of sale a net § 1231 gain of $10,000, § 1231(c) will characterize $5,000 of that gain as ordinary income; the remaining $5,000 of the net § 1231 gain will remain long-term capital gain. In effect, § 1231(c) limits Taxpayer's long-term capital gain to $5,000, which equals the "net" long-term capital gain Taxpayer would have had on selling both the land and the truck in the same year.

In any year that § 1231(c) requires some of the § 1231 gains to be characterized as ordinary income, a question arises as to which § 1231 gains will be so characterized. For example, assume that this year Taxpayer entered into two transactions — the sale of a commercial building on which the taxpayer had claimed depreciation deductions and the sale of a tract of unimproved land used in taxpayer's business. Assume Taxpayer recognized a gain of $10,000 on each of these transactions and that, but for § 1231(c), both of the $10,000 gains would be characterized as long-term capital gains — with the $10,000 of gain from the sale of the commercial building taxable as unrecaptured § 1250 gain at a maximum rate of 25% and with the $10,000 of gain from the sale of the land taxable as adjusted net capital gain at a maximum rate of 15% or 20%, depending upon Taxpayer's taxable income. Assume also that, as a result of the application of § 1231(c), $10,000 of the § 1231 gain would be recharacterized as ordinary income. Which gain would be so characterized — the gain from the sale of the building or the gain from the sale of the land? Or would some part of the gain from each transaction be recharacterized as ordinary income? In Notice 97-59, 1997-2 C.B. 309, the Service stated:

> If a portion of the taxpayer's net section 1231 gain for the year is recharacterized as ordinary income under section 1231(c), the gain so recharacterized consists first of any net section 1231 gain [that is 28 percent rate gain], then any section 1231 gain [that is unrecaptured section 1250 gain], and finally any net section 1231 gain [that is adjusted net capital gain].

Thus, in this example, the $10,000 of gain which § 1231(c) treats as ordinary income will be the $10,000 of gain from the sale of the commercial property, i.e., the "unrecaptured section 1250 gain." None of the $10,000 of gain from the sale of the land will be recharacterized as ordinary income. Instead, the gain from the land sale will be taxed as adjusted net capital gain at a maximum rate of 15% or 20%.

Returning to the example provided at the outset of this discussion of § 1231(c) recapture, assume Taxpayer sells the land, instead of the truck, in Year 1. The result is a long-term capital gain of $10,000 under § 1231(a)(1). (It is also a net § 1231 gain under § 1231(c), but we are assuming this was Taxpayer's first § 1231 transaction, and thus there are no net § 1231 losses from any of the five prior years to worry about.) If Taxpayer sells the truck in a subsequent year, the result is a $5,000 ordinary loss under § 1231(a)(2). Section 1231(c) does not require that we re-open the Year 1 transaction and recharacterize the gain, nor does it require that the ordinary loss be converted to long-term capital loss to match long-term capital gain generated in Year 1. So, in a sense, the tax game can still be played, if one follows the right order. Congress apparently regarded it as sufficient that Taxpayer, as a result of the sale of the truck has $5,000 of "non-recaptured net § 1231 losses" that will cause $5,000 of any net § 1231 gain in the next five years to be converted into ordinary income.

Chapter 33

RECAPTURE OF DEPRECIATION

I. PROBLEMS

1. On January 1, Year 1, John purchased a boat for $200,000 for use in his charter fishing business. On June 1, Year 3, he sold the boat for $175,000. Assuming he claimed all proper depreciation deductions in Years 1, 2 and 3, how much is John's gain and how is it characterized? In answering this question, assume: (a) John elects a $100,000 § 179 deduction; (b) he does not make any election under § 168; (c) the boat is 5-year property; (d) the boat is used solely in John's business; and (e) § 168(d)(3) and (k) do not apply. What results if John sold the boat for $210,000?

2. Same facts as in Problem 1, except that on June 1, Year 3, John gave the boat to his brother Bob. The boat had a fair market value of $175,000 at the time. Bob used the boat solely for personal purposes. Bob sold the boat for $150,000 on July 1, Year 4. What are the tax consequences to John and Bob?

3. Same facts as Problem 1, except that on June 1, Year 3, when the boat was worth $175,000, John converted it to personal use. Three years later, John sold the boat for $100,000. What are the tax consequences to John?

4. On July 1, Year 1, John purchased an apartment building for $2,000,000 and placed it in service. (Assume that John purchased only the building and not the land.) He sold the building on January 2, Year 3 for $2,500,000. Assuming John takes the maximum allowable depreciation deductions, what is the amount and character of his gain on the sale?

5. How would your answer to Problem 4 change, if at all, if John sold the building to ABC Corporation, which is owned as follows: 15% by John; 30% by John's brother Bob; 15% by Bob's daughter Diane; and 40% by Mary-Belle Corporation. (Mary-Belle itself is owned 1/4 by John's wife Mary and 3/4 by Mary's sister Belle.)

Assignment for Chapter 33:

Complete the problems.

Read: Internal Revenue Code: §§ 1(h)(6); 64; 121(d)(6); 1245(a)(1), (2), (3)(A); 1245(b)(1), (2); 1245(c); 1245(d); 179(d)(10); 1250(a)(1)(A), (a)(1)(B)(v); 1250(b)(1), (3), (5); 1250(c); 1250(d)(1), (2); 1250(h); 1239(a), (b)(1), (c). Review §§ 1(h); 121; 267(b), (c); 1221; 1231; 168(d), (e), (g), (k); 1014(a)(1); 1015(a); 1016(a)(2). Treasury Regulations: §§ 1.1245-1(a)(1), (d); 1.1245-2(a)(1), (3), (4), (7); 1.1245-3(b); 1.1245-4(a)(1), (b)(1); 1.1245-6(a); 1.179-1(e); 1.1250-1(a)(1)(i),

(5); 1.1250-1(c)(1), (4); 1.1250-1(e)(1), (2), (3)(i); 1.1250-2(b)(1).
Materials: Overview

II. VOCABULARY

recapture of depreciation
Section 1245 property
Section 1250 property
recomputed basis
additional depreciation (under § 1250)
unrecaptured Section 1250 gain

III. OBJECTIVES

1. To explain the rationale for the depreciation recapture rules of § 1245.

2. To explain the interrelationship among §§ 1221(2), 1231, and 1245 and 1250.

3. Given a specific set of facts, to determine the amount and the character of gain recognized on the disposition of Section 1245 or Section 1250 property.

4. Given a specific set of facts, to determine the amount and character of gain recognized on the disposition of § 179 property.

5. To distinguish between § 1245 recapture and § 1250 recapture.

6. To recall that §§ 1245 and 1250 do not apply to losses.

7. To distinguish characterization under § 1239 from characterization under §§ 1245 and 1250.

8. To provide examples of dispositions to which §§ 1245 and 1250 apply and examples of dispositions excepted from these provisions.

9. To identify "unrecaptured section 1250 gain" and explain the significance of that characterization.

IV. OVERVIEW

Let us introduce the depreciation recapture provisions by means of an example involving personal property (as opposed to real property). Assume Taxpayer purchases some depreciable equipment for use in her business. The depreciation deductions Taxpayer is allowed on the equipment will, pursuant to § 1016(a)(2), reduce Taxpayer's adjusted basis in the equipment. For example, if Taxpayer purchased the equipment for $100 and properly took depreciation deductions of $30, her adjusted basis in the equipment would be $70. If Taxpayer sells the equipment for $80, she realizes and recognizes a gain of $10. [Amount realized of $80 less adjusted basis of $70 equals $10 of gain realized and recognized.] In substance, the gain of $10 results from Taxpayer's having taken depreciation deductions that proved to be $10 in excess of the $20 decline in the value of the equipment (from $100 to $80). This "excess" depreciation of $10 (excess only in that it exceeded the decline in value; we are assuming the depreciation taken was proper) is "recaptured" in the form of gain of $10 on the sale of the equipment. Taxpayer is, in effect, forced to give back the "excess" deduction of $10 by recognizing income of $10. This result is achieved through the basis adjustment mechanism of § 1016 and the amount-realized-minus-adjusted-basis formula of § 1001.

What is the character of the $10 of income? Under § 1221(a)(2), the equipment is not a capital asset, but, pursuant to § 1231, the gain might be characterized as long-term capital gain. This gain, however, resulted solely from the taking of depreciation deductions, not from any appreciation in the value of the equipment. The depreciation deductions reduced Taxpayer's ordinary income during the years depreciation was taken. Thus, as a result of the "excess" depreciation of $10, Taxpayer's ordinary income was $10 less than it otherwise would have been. True, Taxpayer recognized $10 of income on the sale, but § 1231 might result in that $10 being characterized as long-term capital gain. If ordinary income is taxed at a higher rate than capital gains, the "excess" depreciation saves more in taxes than is produced by its "recapture" in the year the equipment is sold if the recaptured amount is accorded long-term capital gain treatment. The perceived unfairness of that result prompted Congress in 1962 to enact the § 1245 recapture provisions. Section 1245 adopts a simple remedy: recognized recapture income is characterized as ordinary income. § 1245(a)(1). Stated another way, gain on the disposition of personal property that is attributable to depreciation deductions, rather than economic appreciation in value, is not eligible for capital gain treatment. To that extent, § 1245 overrides § 1231.

We thus come full circle as regards characterization. Under § 1221(a)(2), the $10 gain on the sale of the equipment in our example would be characterized as ordinary income. Under § 1231, the gain may be characterized as long-term capital gain. Section 1245, however, has the final word: to the extent § 1245 applies to the gain, the gain is ordinary income.

One additional aspect of the depreciation recapture provisions is worth noting at this point. They are primarily characterization provisions. They are also, however, recognition provisions — and in some circumstances they will require recognition of income at a time earlier than would otherwise be the case. See § 453(i) in Chapter 41.

A. Section 1245 Recapture

Section 1245 provides that recognized gain on the disposition of "Section 1245 property" shall be included in income as ordinary income to the extent of depreciation deductions taken with respect to the property. As a general proposition, § 1245 applies to depreciable personal property, while § 1250 (discussed below) applies to depreciable real property.[1] § 1245(a)(3)(A). Moreover, the term "personal property" encompasses both tangible and intangible personal property. Reg. § 1.1245-3(b). Note that the statutory definition of "Section 1245 property" includes property that "is or has been" of depreciable character. § 1245(a)(3). By way of illustration, the regulations point out that if father uses an automobile in his business — thus qualifying it as Section 1245 property — and then gives the automobile to his son as a gift for his son's personal use, the automobile is Section 1245 property in the hands of the son, even though the automobile is no longer depreciable given the son's personal use of it. Reg. § 1245-3(a)(3).

As noted above, § 1245 recaptures as ordinary income the gain on disposition attributable to depreciation deductions, as opposed to the gain resulting from an increase in the property's value. When Section 1245 property is disposed of at a gain, § 1245 accomplishes this result by labeling as "ordinary income" the difference between the taxpayer's adjusted basis and the lesser of (1) the "recomputed basis" or (2) the amount realized (or the fair market value, if the disposition is not a sale, exchange, or involuntary conversion). "Recomputed basis" is the basis that results from adding the adjusted basis and the depreciation or amortization previously taken with respect to the property; note that § 179 deductions are treated as amortization deductions for this purpose. § 1245(a)(2)(A), (C). As a practical matter, recomputed basis is generally the taxpayer's original basis in the property. Look closely, however, at § 1245(a)(2)(A): recomputed basis means the adjusted basis to which is added "all adjustments reflected in such adjusted basis on account of deductions (whether in respect of the same or other property)" on account of depreciation or amortization. For example, if the taxpayer acquired the property by gift, the taxpayer's basis under § 1015 may reflect depreciation deductions taken by the donor, which would enter into the computation of recomputed basis when the taxpayer disposed of the property. Thus, in this situation, the § 1245 ordinary income "taint" that attached to the property while in the hands of the donor continues to attach to the property in the hands of the donee. By way of contrast, the taint does not carry over to property acquired in an arm's length purchase. In this case, the purchaser's basis is based on the cost of the property, and does not reflect any adjustments on account of depreciation that may have been taken while in the hands of the previous owner.

Return to the example above of the equipment purchased for $100 and then sold for $80 after $30 in depreciation had been taken. The taxpayer's "recomputed basis" would be $100, i.e., the adjusted basis of $70 plus the $30 in depreciation deductions. § 1245(a)(2)(A). The amount realized, however, was only $80, which is

---

[1] Note that the definition of Section 1245 property encompasses limited categories of real property as well. § 1245(a)(3)(B)–(F).

less than the recomputed basis. As a result, § 1245(a)(1) characterizes as ordinary income "only" the $10 difference between the amount realized and the adjusted basis. Obviously, since the total realized gain in this example is $10, the § 1245(a)(1) formula cannot sensibly produce a result that treats more than $10 as ordinary income.

Suppose, however, the equipment were sold for $110 instead of $80. The recomputed basis remains the same — $100 — but it is now less than the amount realized. As a result, the amount § 1245(a)(1) treats as ordinary income is $30, the difference between recomputed basis ($100) and adjusted basis ($70). The total gain in this example, of course, was $40. What happens to the remaining $10 of gain? Section 1245 does not characterize it; only the first $30 of gain was subject to § 1245 characterization. The remaining $10 will presumably be characterized pursuant to §§ 1221(a)(2) and 1231, and, depending on the taxpayer's circumstances, may be characterized as long-term capital gain. Reg. § 1.1245-6(a). In overview, the property increased in value by $10 during the period when $30 in depreciation was taken. Section 1245 requires that the $30 of depreciation be recaptured as ordinary income, but permits the economic gain of $10 to enter the § 1231 hotchpot.

Note that § 1245 does not apply to losses. Reg. § 1.1245-1(d). The inapplicability of § 1245 to losses follows from the literal language of § 1245(a)(1) and is consistent with the rationale of the statute. Can you explain why?

Also note the striking scope of the statute. Section 1245 recapture may result whenever Section 1245 property is "disposed of," whether by sale, exchange, involuntary conversion or "other disposition." Moreover, if § 1245(a)(1) characterizes gain as ordinary income, the gain is recognized — and § 1245 applies — "notwithstanding any other provision of this subtitle." § 1245(a)(1), (d). Any escape from the recognition and characterization rule of § 1245(a)(1) must be found within § 1245 itself. Section 1245(b) in fact provides a number of exceptions. For the most part, the exceptions involve dispositions in which the basis of the property transferred carries over (in whole or in part) to the transferee. The "recapture potential" is thus preserved in the hands of the transferee — review § 1245(a)(2)(A) again on this point — and to the extent it is preserved, the application of § 1245(a)(1) may safely be postponed.

Section 179 Recapture. As noted, § 1245 is at least potentially applicable to any disposition of § 1245 property. The Service has ruled, however, that the conversion of an automobile from business use to personal use is not a "disposition" of the automobile. Rev. Rul. 69-487, 1969-2 C.B. 165. Does this mean a conversion to personal use entails no adverse tax consequences? Not necessarily. Recall § 179 expensing, discussed in Chapter 14 on depreciation. Section 179(d)(10) provides its own version of recapture. If property with respect to which a § 179 deduction was taken is converted to personal use — specifically, if such property is not used predominantly in a trade or business at any time during the recovery period — the taxpayer must give up the "benefit" of the § 179 deduction. The § 179 "benefit" is the difference between the deduction taken under § 179 and the deduction that would have been allowed under § 168 (with respect to the amount expensed under § 179, had § 179 not been elected) for the period of business use involved. *See* Reg.

§ 1.179-1(e)(1), (5) Ex. Note that, if § 179 recapture applies, the taxpayer appropriately adjusts her basis upward to reflect the fact the taxpaper has been forced to give up the benefit taxpayer had previously been allowed under § 179. Also note that § 179 recapture is inapplicable when § 1245 recapture applies. Reg. § 1.179-1(e)(3).

B. Section 1250 Recapture

The recapture rules of § 1250, first enacted in 1964, are considerably looser than those of its 1962 predecessor, § 1245. Section 1250 applies to depreciable real property, except for the limited categories of real property included within § 1245. § 1250(c). When Section 1250 property is disposed of at a gain, however, the depreciation subject to recapture and characterization as ordinary income is, in general, only the depreciation taken in excess of straight line depreciation. § 1250(a)(1)(A), (b)(1). Let us return again to the example used previously — property is purchased for $100 and sold for $80 after $30 in depreciation has been taken. Assume, however, the property in question is real property, such as a building. If the $30 in depreciation were taken on a straight line basis, the "additional depreciation" would be zero; none of the gain of $10 ($80 amount realized, $70 adjusted basis) would be characterized by § 1250; it would presumably all be characterized under §§ 1231 and 1221(a)(2). Suppose, however, the $30 of depreciation were computed using an accelerated method, and that only $25 in depreciation would have been allowed under a straight line method. The "additional depreciation" taken would equal $5, and that $5 would be characterized as ordinary income under § 1250(a)(1)(A). Since the taxpayer's total gain was $10, the remaining gain of $5 would be eligible for § 1231 treatment.

Under current law, in effect since 1986, depreciation on real property must be taken on a straight line basis. In general, therefore, there can be no "additional depreciation" on real property acquired after 1986, and § 1250 thus threatens to become mere surplusage. Note, however, that if Section 1250 property is not held more than a year, all depreciation taken is additional depreciation. § 1250(b)(1). Furthermore, "additional depreciation" may have been taken on property depreciated under pre-1986 law, and disposition of that property may trigger ordinary income under § 1250(a)(1)(A).

C. Unrecaptured Section 1250 Gain

As discussed in Chapter 31, long-term capital gain is accorded preferential treatment. Under § 1(h)(1)(E), that preferential treatment depends on the nature of the asset sold or exchanged and the holding period of that asset. Under § 1(h)(1)(E), the maximum rate of tax on "unrecaptured section 1250 gain" is 25%. Thus, unrecaptured § 1250 gain is accorded more favorable treatment than, for example, the long-term capital gain resulting from the sale of collectibles taxed at a maximum rate of 28%. By contrast, the tax treatment of unrecaptured § 1250 gain is not as favorable as, for example, the long-term capital gain resulting from the sale of stock held for more than 1 year, which is taxed at a maximum rate of 15% (or 20% in the case of certain high income taxpayers).

What is unrecaptured § 1250 gain? Section 1(h)(6) defines "unrecaptured section 1250 gain" as the long-term capital gain from Section 1250 property attributable to depreciation deductions allowed to the taxpayer and not otherwise recaptured as ordinary income. Consider carefully the following example:

> **Example:** Sam spent $500,000 on the construction of a commercial building on leased land. Sam used the property in his business for a number of years and then sold the property for $550,000. Using the straight line method, Sam properly claimed a total of $200,000 in depreciation deductions over the period during which he used the building. Sam's adjusted basis in the building was thus $300,000 at the time of the sale. He realized $250,000 in gain on the sale. § 1001.
>
> Considering the building was sold for only $50,000 more than Sam originally paid for it, only $50,000 of the $250,000 of realized gain is attributable to economic appreciation. The remaining $200,000 of the gain represents the depreciation deductions allowed to Sam. In effect, § 1001 requires Sam to include as part of his gain all of the depreciation deductions claimed since there was no actual economic depreciation on the property. (This analysis, of course, disregards inflation.)
>
> The character of the $250,000 gain would be determined under § 1231. (As explained below, none of the gain would be characterized under § 1250.) Assuming the sale of the building was Sam's only § 1231 transaction during the year, the $250,000 would constitute long-term capital gain. Were the property in this example "Section 1245 property" instead of "Section 1250 property," $200,000 of the $250,000 of gain would have been recaptured as ordinary income and Sam would have characterized only the remaining $50,000 of gain under § 1231. In other words, all of the depreciation would have been "recaptured" as ordinary income. Under § 1250, however, the gain on the Section 1250 property in this example would be recaptured as ordinary income only to the extent of the depreciation taken by Sam in excess of the depreciation allowable under the straight line method. Because Sam used the straight line method of depreciation with respect to the building, none of the gain would be characterized as ordinary income under § 1250.
>
> The $200,000 of gain attributable to the depreciation deductions claimed by Sam therefore constitutes unrecaptured section 1250 gain, *i.e.*, none of the gain would be characterized under § 1250. This $200,000 of gain would be subject to a maximum rate of tax of 25%. The other $50,000 of gain would be subject to a maximum rate of tax of 15% (or 20% if Sam's income tax bracket is 39.6%).

As the above example suggests, any time a taxpayer sells depreciable real property at a gain, the taxpayer must determine how much of the gain constitutes unrecaptured Section 1250 gain.

It may be well at this point to revisit the special exclusion rules under § 121 related to gain from the sale of a principal residence. (Chapter 6 provides a detailed discussion of § 121.) Note, under § 121(d)(6), gain attributable to depreciation allowed with respect to the residence is not excludable. A common context in which a taxpayer will claim depreciation deductions on a residence is in conjunction with a home office. (*See* Chapter 21.) The long-term gain attributable to depreciation allowed with respect to a principal residence will be characterized as unrecaptured Section 1250 gain and will be subject to tax at a maximum rate of 25%. For example, assume a single taxpayer realized a gain of $250,000 on the sale of her principal residence this year. Assume she had owned the residence since 2001 and had been allowed depreciation deductions amounting to $30,000 as a result of a business office she maintained in the home. As a result of § 121(d)(6), $30,000 of her $250,000 gain would not be excludable under § 121(a) but would be subject to a capital gains tax at a maximum rate of 25%. The remaining $220,000 of her gain on the sale would be excludable under § 121(a), assuming she met the requirements specified in § 121.

D. Section 1239 Ordinary Income

Section 1239 is a special characterization rule, not really a recapture-of-depreciation rule as in §§ 1245 and 1250. But it is worth noting here both to fill out the historical record and to point out the relationship of § 1239 to §§ 1245 and 1250. Section 1239, enacted in 1951, substantially predates §§ 1245 and 1250. It mandates that any gain recognized on a sale or exchange of depreciable property between certain related parties be characterized as ordinary income; none of the recognized gain, in other words, is eligible for capital gain treatment under § 1231. Section 1239 is thus at once narrower and broader than §§ 1245 and 1250. It is narrower in that it applies only with respect to related party transactions; §§ 1245 and 1250, of course, have no such limitation. It is broader in that it characterizes all recognized gain as ordinary income. Sections 1245 and 1250, by contrast, characterize ordinary income by reference to the depreciation (or additional depreciation) deductions taken; they do not characterize as ordinary income the gain that reflects actual appreciation in value.

See § 1239(b) and (c) for the principal related party transactions covered by the statute. Suppose, for example, an individual sells depreciable property to his wholly owned corporation. The parties are "related persons." § 1239(b)(1), (c)(1)(A). All gain recognized on the sale would thus be ordinary income.

The impetus for the enactment of § 1239 was the differential between the tax rates on ordinary income and capital gains. An individual could, for instance, depreciate high value business property to a point where its adjusted basis is very low, sell the property to her wholly owned corporation, and (prior to the enactment of § 1239) pay only capital gains tax on the sale. The purchasing corporation could then depreciate the property all over again, using as its basis the price paid for the property. In effect, the property is "redepreciated," offsetting the corporation's ordinary income, at the price of a capital gains tax to the individual taxpayer. Given sufficient rate differentials, the tax saved by the corporation could exceed the tax paid by the individual, although the parties are in essence a single economic unit. Section 1239 blocked this scheme by taxing the seller's gain at ordinary income rates.

Since §§ 1245 and 1250 apply to many more transactions than does § 1239, § 1239 declined in importance after the enactment of those provisions. It still, however, remains a trap for the unwary, since it can characterize as ordinary income gain that §§ 1245 and 1250 may not reach.

E.   Other Recapture Provisions

Perhaps at this point it would be useful to review § 1231(c), relating to recapture of net ordinary losses, in Chapter 32. Note that, as a result of § 1231(c), gain that may have escaped §§ 1245 and 1250 and was preliminarily classified as long-term capital gain under § 1231(a)(1), can nonetheless wind up as ordinary income.

In addition to the principle recapture provisions of §§ 1245 and 1250, the Code contains a number of other recapture provisions of limited applicability which are beyond the scope of this text. See, *e.g.*, §§ 1252, 1254, 1255.

Chapter 34

ASSIGNMENT OF INCOME

I. PROBLEMS

William is president and chairman of a small corporation. He is interested in equal measures in saving taxes and in providing financial help to his daughter Donna, who is also an employee of the corporation. William believes he already has all the income and assets he needs, so he is not concerned with accumulating more. He tells you of the following actions he plans to take this year and asks you to confirm that they are effective tax-saving steps for him.

(1) At the beginning of the year, William will ask the board of directors to reduce his compensation this year from $200,000 to zero. He will work this year for free. He will also ask the board to increase Donna's compensation this year by $200,000. The board is expected to approve both proposals.

(2) William has an accumulated balance of $500,000 in his account under the corporation's nonqualified deferred compensation plan. William has, appropriately, not yet been taxed on this amount because it has not been available to him. Assume the $500,000 is scheduled to be distributed to him on July 1 and will be taxable at that time. William plans to give the corporation's financial officer a directive on June 30 to pay the $500,000 to Donna instead of to him.

(3) William owns all of the stock in the corporation. A wealthy friend of his has for some time wanted to be a part owner of the corporation and has offered to pay $1,000 per share for any shares William wants to sell. William's adjusted basis in each of his shares is only $100. William plans to tell his friend that he is going to give 100 shares of corporate stock to Donna and that he will instruct Donna to sell the shares to the friend for $100,000.

(4) William will give all of his corporate stock to Donna for one year. William will retain all voting rights with respect to the stock. After one year, the stock will revert to William. During the year Donna has the stock, William estimates about $75,000 in corporate dividends will be paid to Donna.

(5) William owns the building that serves as the corporate headquarters. The corporation rents the building from William for $150,000 per year. William is thinking of selling to Donna for $150,000 the right to this year's rental income. In that case, Donna will pay William $150,000 plus interest at the beginning of next year.

(6) As an alternative to (5), William is thinking of giving the building to Donna as a gift. Donna can then lease the building to the corporation for $150,000 per year. In addition, because the building contains some vacant space that

is not rented to the corporation, Donna can generate additional rental income by renting the unused space to another tenant for about $25,000 per year.

Assignment for Chapter 34:

Complete the problems.

Read: Internal Revenue Code: §§ 61(a); 102; skim §§ 1(g); 66; 704(e); 482; 1366(e).

  Materials: Overview
  Lucas v. Earl
  Helvering v. Horst
  Helvering v. Eubank
  Salvatore v. Commissioner
  Stranahan v. Commissioner
  May v. Commissioner

II.   VOCABULARY

assignment of income
income-shifting or income-splitting
gift-leaseback
fruit/tree metaphor
"ripened fruit" theory or *Court Holding* doctrine

III.   OBJECTIVES

1.   To recall by name the cases of *Lucas v. Earl*, *Helvering v. Eubank*, and *Helvering v. Horst*, and the principles for which they stand.

2.   To recognize common situations in which assignment of income issues arise.

3.   To recall the two general rules of assignment of income: (1) income from services is taxable to the taxpayer controlling the earning of the income; and (2) income from property is taxed to the taxpayer who owns the property.

4.   To describe the common situations in which income-shifting is permissible.

5.   To distinguish between an effective and ineffective income-shifting arrangement.

6.   To predict the likely tax consequences of a given income-shifting arrangement.

7.   To distinguish relevant from irrelevant facts in income-shifting arrangements.

8.   To explain the arguments the taxpayer and the Internal Revenue Service are likely to make regarding a particular income-shifting arrangement.

IV. OVERVIEW

To this point in the course, our focus has been on the "what question," the "when question," and the "character question." We first considered what items are included in an individual's gross income, what expenditures should be reflected as deductions from income in arriving at the individual's taxable income, and when the items of income and deduction should be included or deducted. We then examined matters of characterization — capital gains and losses, ordinary income and loss, and their significance. Now, however, our focus shifts to assignment of income and a new question, the "who question" — who is the proper taxpayer to be charged with the income or expenditure at issue? As you might expect, the importance of our earlier questions is not diminished; we have simply added another ingredient to the mix.

In general, the taxpayer who receives income is the taxpayer taxed on it. In the usual case, there is simply no other taxpayer on the scene to whom the income could plausibly be attributed, and hence no real alternative exists in any event. On occasion, however, there are two or more candidates for taxation. A question this situation poses is whether the person receiving the income will be the person taxed on it. The assignment of income doctrine developed principally to answer this question in the numerous settings in which it arises.

A. The Progressive Rate Structure

The "who question" is significant because of the Code's progressive tax rate structure. *See* § 1. Because the "tax cost" of a dollar of income depends on the rate at which it is taxed, there is an obvious tax savings to taxpayers (and a corresponding tax loss to the Treasury) in shifting income from a higher-bracket taxpayer to a lower-bracket taxpayer. Thus, a worthwhile tax benefit may be achieved within a family unit if a family member whose income will be taxed at 35% can successfully shift some of her income to another family member whose income is taxed in the 15% bracket. If the taxpayers involved regard themselves as essentially a single economic unit, they may well be indifferent as to who actually receives the income, and concerned instead with who will be taxed on it.

The value of income-shifting is decreased as tax rates are compressed. To eliminate the value of income-shifting, one must assure that a dollar of income will be taxed identically, no matter which taxpayer bears the tax. One could accomplish this by adopting a system that taxed gross income — not net income, since the availability of deductions, and hence the effective rate of tax, could vary among taxpayers — and taxed the gross income at a flat rate, from the first dollar to the last. Alternatively, one could design a system that taxed the income of the group, not the individual, so that income shifts within the group would be meaningless. The joint return, of course, achieves precisely this result for husband and wife. When they file a joint return, they are taxed on their "group" income and, with certain exceptions, income-shifting between them is pointless. In general, however, our tax system taxes individuals, not groups, and taxes them at progressive rates on net income.

B.   Development of Rules Limiting Income-Shifting

Disparities in tax rates made it necessary to develop rules to answer the who-shall-be-taxed question. This "who" question is the most common issue in the assignment of income area. Assignment of income issues, however, can also arise with just one taxpayer. Because the tax rate disparity drives the planning where two or more taxpayers are involved, it becomes apparent that very similar issues can arise where rate disparity opportunities confront the individual taxpayer. The annual accounting principle provides one such set of opportunities. If, for whatever reason, the same income will be taxed at a higher rate next year than this year, there is an incentive to find a way to "accelerate" future income into the present tax period, and it may become necessary, for tax purposes, to determine whether and when the taxpayer has realized the income. *Estate of Stranahan*, included in the materials, provides an example of a successful taxpayer technique for accelerating income.

Another type of assignment of income issue arises with respect to a topic addressed in Chapter 31, the character of the income in question. As noted in that Chapter, capital gain income is subject to tax at a rate considerably lower than that of ordinary income. The rate disparity, of course, encourages creative taxpayers to try to convert ordinary income into capital gains. Taxpayers may seek to have income characterized as capital gains rather than ordinary income in order to take advantage of the preferential rate of tax on capital gain and also to increase the amount of capital losses they may deduct. As you will recall, under § 1211 the amount of capital losses that are currently deductible depends in part on the amount of capital gains currently reportable.

In answering the "who" question, two general rules should be kept in mind. First, income is taxed to the taxpayer who controls the earning of the income. For example, if a high-bracket employee directs his employer to pay his wages, or to pay other taxable benefits, directly to his low-bracket child, the income will nonetheless be taxed to the employee, the one who earned the income. The Supreme Court decisions in *Lucas v. Earl* and *Helvering v. Eubank*, included in the materials, provide the foundation for this rule. Second, as established in *Helvering v. Horst*, also included in the materials, income from property is taxed to the one who owns the property and thus controls the income generated from the property. For example, the landlord-parent directing that rent be paid to her child is still taxed on that rental income. Reflection on these examples would indicate that to use receipt as the criterion for determining who is the appropriate taxpayer would invite widespread manipulation of the progressive rate structure. The search is rather for the true earner of the income, and it is to that taxpayer that the income will be attributed.

Community property laws can impact the operation of the general rule discussed above attributing service income to the true earner of that income. Under such laws, earnings during marriage are deemed the property of the spousal community and not the property of the spouse performing the services generating the earnings. In *Poe v. Seaborn*, 282 U.S. 101 (1930), the Supreme Court held that, under the community property laws of the State of Washington, each of the spouses was taxable on half of his or her earnings and on half of the spouse's earnings. The effect of the Court's decision in *Poe v. Seaborn* is to permit spouses to split their income. As a result, a married couple's tax liability could vary significantly depending on whether the married couple lived in a community property jurisdiction or a common law jurisdiction. To negate this unfairness, Congress in 1948 authorized married couples to file joint returns.

Notwithstanding the congressional action in 1948, the rule of *Poe v. Seaborn* remains viable and the splitting of income in community property jurisdictions can still have some important tax consequences. For example, because, pursuant to *Poe v. Seaborn*, federal tax law generally respects state property law characterizations and definitions, the Service has taken the position that registered domestic partners and spouses in same-sex marriages in California must, for federal income tax purposes, each report one-half of his or her community income whether received in the form of compensation for personal services or income from property. Chief Counsel Advice 201021050 (May 5, 2010).

In *U.S. v. Windsor*, 133 S. Ct. 2675 (2013), the Supreme Court held Section 3 of the Defense of Marriage Act [110 Stat. 2419] unconstitutional as it deprived married same-sex couples the "equal liberty of person" protected by the Fifth Amendment. In the aftermath of that decision, the Service issued Revenue Ruling 2013-17, 2013-2 C.B. 201, reprinted in Chapter 37, which makes clear that for Federal income tax purposes same-sex married couples and opposite-sex married couples are treated the same.

Where pension benefits earned through the employment of one spouse during the marriage are community property, and where the employee-spouse is ordered, pursuant to a divorce decree, to pay half the monthly pension benefits to the nonemployee-spouse as her share of community property, the employee spouse and the nonemployee spouse will each be taxable on half the pension benefits. *Eatinger v. Commissioner*, T.C. Memo. 1990-310. The Ninth Circuit, however, has held that *Poe v. Seaborn* and *Eatinger* did not apply where an employee sought to reduce his gross income by the portion of his wages that funded monthly court-ordered payments to his ex-spouse. Even though the payments had been ordered, under state law, because the employee had postponed retirement and thus postponed commencement of monthly pension benefits, half of which would have been payable to his ex-spouse as community property, the wages that funded the court-ordered payments were separate property and were therefore fully taxable to the employee. *Commissioner v. Dunkin*, 500 F.3d 1065 (9th Cir. 2007)

C. Application of the Assignment of Income Rules

The Ninth Circuit decision in *Kochansky v. Commissioner*, 92 F.3d 957 (1996), provides a classic example of the application of the principles enunciated in *Lucas v. Earl* and *Helvering v. Eubank*. In *Kochansky*, the taxpayer, as part of a divorce settlement, agreed to pay to his wife a portion of any contingent fee to which he became entitled as a result of representing a client in a medical malpractice suit. After the divorce, the malpractice suit was favorably settled and the taxpayer received the contingent fee. Despite the fact the taxpayer, as required by the terms of the divorce settlement, distributed a portion of the fee to his ex-wife, the Commissioner argued that the taxpayer was taxable on the entire fee. Agreeing with the Commissioner and the Tax Court, the Ninth Circuit held the case was controlled by *Lucas v. Earl*. Income is taxable to the person who earns the income, and an anticipatory assignment of personal service income will not serve to shift the tax liability for that income. In *Kochansky*, the contingent fee represented compensation to the taxpayer for services he rendered. The taxpayer, after the divorce settlement, continued to render services to the client and controlled the personal services that produced the fee. Taxpayer transferred only a right to receive a portion of the income to his wife. Applying the tree-fruit metaphor of *Lucas v. Earl*, the Ninth Circuit noted that the taxpayer had transferred only the fruit. That the fee was contingent did not render the fee something other than compensation for taxpayer's professional services.

The shifting of income from services and property can occur in a variety of contexts that are anything but straight-forward. For example, in *Commissioner v. Giannini*, 129 F.2d 638 (9th Cir. 1942), the taxpayer, the president of a corporation, informed the corporation's board of directors that he would refuse to accept any income from the corporation for his services during the remainder of the year and suggested the corporation use the money for some worthwhile cause. The corporation contributed the compensation otherwise payable to the taxpayer to the Regents of the University of California. The Service argued that, even though the taxpayer had not actually received the income, the taxpayer had, in effect, directed the disposition of the income and therefore was taxable on it. Taxpayer argued, "A person has the right to refuse property proffered to him, and if he does so, absolutely and unconditionally, his refusal amounts to a renunciation of the proffered property, which, legally, is an abandonment of right to the property without a transfer of such right to another. Property which is renounced (*i.e.*, abandoned) cannot be 'diverted' or 'assigned' by the renouncer, and cannot be taxed upon the theory that it was received." The court held for the taxpayer, noting that the taxpayer did not direct the corporation to give the money to any specific organization. Indeed, "the corporation could have kept the money. All arrangements with the University of California regarding the donation . . . were made by the corporation, the taxpayer participating therein only as an officer of the corporation." 129 F.2d at 640–41.

Addressing a more common situation, the Service, in Revenue Ruling 66-167, 1966-1 C.B. 20, ruled that, because a taxpayer serving as the executor of an estate effectively communicated his intention to serve without compensation, he did not have to report as income the fees or commissions he would otherwise have had a right to receive under state law. According to the ruling, the requisite intention to serve on a gratuitous basis will ordinarily be deemed to have been adequately manifested if, within six months after his initial appointment, the executor or administrator of an estate supplies one or more of the decedent's principal devisees or heirs with a formal waiver of any right to compensation for his services.

In some instances, the incidence of taxation turns on agency law. For example, in Revenue Ruling 74-581, 1974-2 C.B. 25, law school faculty members who participated in the school's clinical programs and were appointed to represent indigent defendants through such programs, were required by the school to turn over to it any amounts they received for such representation. The Service ruled the faculty members were "working solely as agents of the law school" and were not taxable on the amounts thus received and paid over to the law school. By contrast, in Revenue Ruling 84-13, 1984-1 C.B. 21, a psychologist in private practice was required, pursuant to vows of poverty and obedience taken as a member of a religious order, to obtain the order's permission to establish the practice and to turn over to the order amounts received from the practice. The ruling held that based on all the facts and circumstances — the psychologist selected the clients, established the fees, maintained the records and paid the expenses; the order conducted an annual review of the psychologist's budget but did not engage in the provision of psychology services or control the details of the work or the means and method to accomplish it — the amounts received were earned in an individual capacity, not as an agent of the order, and were taxable to the psychologist despite the vow of poverty. See also *Fogarty v. United States*, 780 F.2d 1005 (Fed. Cir. 1986), holding that a Jesuit priest employed as a professor at the University of Virginia owed tax on the salary paid to him by the University and was not merely an agent for the Jesuit order. More recently, in *Commissioner v. Banks*, 543 U.S. 426 (2005), the Supreme Court concluded that a contingent-fee agreement amounted to "an anticipatory assignment to the attorney of a portion of the client's income from any litigation recovery." As in *Horst*, the client controls the income-generating asset, *i.e.*, the cause of action, and, because of the existence of a "quintessential principal-agent relationship," the gain realized by the attorney's-agent's efforts is income to the client-principal.

The distinction between services income and income from property is blurred when services result in the creation of property. For example, assume a professional author writes a short story and transfers the copyright on the story to her son. Given the author's reputation, numerous magazines are willing to purchase the story. Shortly after receiving the copyright, the son sells the story to a publisher. Who reports the income — the author or the author's son? One might argue that the income from the story represents personal service income, the tax liability for which the author could not shift to her son. By contrast, the son will surely argue the copyright represents property, the author's transfer of which effectively shifted the income. As the Ninth Circuit noted in *Siegel v. United States*, 464 F.2d 891 (1973), "the line between earned income and income from property is not always marked with dazzling clarity." In such a case, the copyright would be treated as property and the amounts received by the son upon the sale of the story to a publisher would constitute income to the son and not to the author. Rev. Rul. 54-599, 1954-2 C.B. 52.[1] How does this example differ from the situation presented in *Helvering v. Eubank*?

Assume the author in the preceding example had contracted with a publisher to write the short story. Upon completing the story, the author made a gift of the manuscript and copyright to her son, who, in turn, transferred the copyright to the publisher and collected the income. Who is taxed on the amounts paid by the publisher? Using the fruit-tree metaphor of *Lucas v. Earl*, the owner of the tree is taxed on the fruit of the tree. If, however, the fruit hanging on the tree at the time of the tree's transfer is ripe, the taxpayer, by transferring the tree, may not be able

---

[1] *Compare Wodehouse v. Comm'r*, 177 F.2d 881 (2d Cir. 1949), *with Wodehouse v. Comm'r*, 178 F.2d 987 (4th Cir. 1949).

to avoid being taxed on the income. For example, if a publicly held corporation declares a stock dividend payable to holders of stock on the record date, a gratuitous transfer of stock by a shareholder on the record date will not successfully deflect the dividend income to the donee. *Bishop v. Shaughnessy*, 195 F.2d 683 (2d Cir. 1962). By contrast, in *Caruth v. U.S.*, 865 F.2d 644 (5th Cir. 1989), where the controlling shareholder in a closely held corporation transferred preferred stock in the corporation to a charity after a dividend had been declared, but a few days before the record date, the Fifth Circuit held the dividend income was not taxable to the donor. The court cited Reg. § 1.61-9(c) in support of the distinction between declaration and record dates and found that neither the assignment of income doctrine nor the sham transaction doctrine was applicable to the transaction. With respect to the former doctrine, the court noted:

> When a taxpayer gives away earnings derived from an income-producing asset, the crucial question is whether the asset itself, or merely the income from it, has been transferred. If the taxpayer gives away the entire asset, with accrued earnings, the assignment of income doctrine does not apply. . . .

> The IRS, however, . . . urges that we hold [the donor] taxable upon the dividend because here the fruit was exceptionally ripe. . . . We fail to see why the ripeness of the fruit matters, so long as the entire tree is transplanted before the fruit is harvested. . . .

> We believe that, at bottom, the IRS mistakes the character of the asset donated. The IRS wishes to treat the [preferred stock] as a mere conduit for [the controlling shareholder's] earnings, rather than as a source of those earnings. . . .

> At the risk of mixing metaphors, the preferred stock was the tree that grew the fruit, rather than merely a crate for conveying the fruit.

Id. at 648–50.

In *Rauenhorst v. Commissioner*, 119 T.C. 157 (2002), a closely-held corporation (hereinafter the target corporation) received notice from an unrelated corporation (hereinafter the acquiring corporation) of the acquiring corporation's interest in purchasing all of the target corporation's stock. Taxpayers, who owned warrants to purchase stock in the target corporation, thereafter donated these warrants to four different charities. While the charities were under no obligation to sell to the acquiring corporation their warrants or the stock represented by the warrants, the charities ultimately did sell the warrants to that corporation. The Service, relying on anticipatory assignment of income principles, argued the taxpayers should be taxed on the gain inherent in the warrants. The Tax Court rejected the Service's argument, holding that under the Service's own ruling (Rev. Rul. 78-197, 1978-1 C.B. 83, addressing an analogous situation involving the redemption of stock given to a charity), the taxpayers would be taxable on the gain from the sale of the warrants only if the charities, at the time they received the gift of the warrants from the taxpayers, were bound to sell the warrants, or could be compelled by the target corporation to sell the warrants, to the acquiring corporation.

How does *Salvatore*, included in the materials, address this "ripened fruit" question? Note specifically the discussion of the *Court Holding* case in the *Salvatore* opinion.

D.   Income-Shifting Within Families and Between Related Parties

As you would expect, income-shifting is particularly tempting in family situations. When a parent shifts income to a child, the income remains in the family unit. If the income shift results in a lower tax payment, the family unit has more after-tax income than it otherwise would have had.

Intrafamily shifting of compensation income was largely controlled historically by cases like *Lucas v. Earl* and *Helvering v. Eubank*, included in the materials. However, Congress was concerned an unsatisfactory level of income deflection continued to exist as a result of intrafamily transfers of income-producing property. In 1986, Congress adopted a new mechanism for addressing intrafamily income shifting — the so-called "kiddie tax" of § 1(g). The kiddie tax has the effect of taxing the unearned income of certain children at the top marginal rate of their parents. The tax benefit normally associated with the shifting of income to a lower-bracket taxpayer is thus negated. The kiddie tax is discussed in greater detail in Chapter 35.

Income-shifting is a tactic that generally appeals to related parties. For example, a sole proprietor may create a corporation, or may enter into a partnership with a family member. The corporation or the family member partner may be in a lower tax bracket than the sole proprietor. If the latter transfers to the newly formed corporation or partnership accounts receivable for services performed as a sole proprietor, and it is the corporation or partnership that collects them, who should be taxed on the receivables? Suppose the same individual owns two separate corporations. If one corporation does work for the other, and undercharges or overcharges for the work, income has been artificially shifted between them. If the income shift is to the corporation in the lower tax bracket, the "related corporations" as a whole pay less tax.

Suppose an individual service-provider forms a corporation, which then hires the individual as its employee and contracts with third parties to provide the services. (Such arrangements were particularly attractive at one time due to certain corporate tax provisions, including marginal tax rates then lower than individual rates, and pension tax benefits not then available to sole proprietors or other self-employed persons.) Should the corporate formalities be respected or should payments made to the corporation be taxed directly to the individual under assignment of income principles? The answer seems clear in the ordinary case: the corporate form is respected and the payments it receives are taxable to the corporation; the individual service-provider is regarded simply as an employee of the corporation whom the corporation has the right to direct or control. However, in some circumstances, these arrangements generate tax controversies. For example, *Sargent v. Commissioner* involved a professional hockey player who formed a personal service corporation, which hired the player as its employee and then contracted with a professional hockey team to provide his services to the team. Given the nature of team sports and the resultant control the team and the coach were entitled to exercise over the player, a divided Tax Court held he was in fact an employee of the hockey team, not of his personal service corporation. Under assignment of income principles, payments to the corporation were therefore taxable to the player. 93 T.C. 572 (1989). On appeal, a divided Eighth Circuit reversed. 929 F.2d 1252 (8th Cir. 1991). In its view, the "'team' analysis of control" was an "arbitrary approach"; the bona fide contractual arrangements, under "traditional common law and tax code analysis," provided the necessary control to consider the player an employee of his corporation and to render the assignment of income doctrine inapplicable to the case. Subsequent to the Eighth Circuit's reversal of its decision, the Tax Court in *Leavell v. Commissioner*, 104 T.C. 140 (1995), on facts very similar to *Sargent*, concluded the taxpayer (a professional basketball player) and not the personal service corporation of the taxpayer was the employee of a professional basketball team. The basketball team and not the taxpayer's personal service corporation controlled the manner in which the taxpayer provided services. As a result, the taxpayer was required to report all payments made by the team to his personal service corporation.

As you will see, the law on assignment of income has been developed primarily by the courts, although there are some specific areas now controlled by statute and regulation. See, for example, § 704(e), directed at family partnerships; § 1366(e), dealing with a special type of corporation known as an "S corporation"; § 482, dealing with two or more businesses under common control, and § 1(g) above. In addition, there are also instances of congressional concessions in the assignment of income area. The joint return, as noted, taxes income to husband and wife as if each had earned half of it, regardless of who actually earned it.

LUCAS v. EARL
United States Supreme Court
281 U.S. 111 (1930)

MR. JUSTICE HOLMES delivered the opinion of the Court.

This case presents the question whether the respondent, Earl, could be taxed for the whole of the salary and attorney's fees earned by him in the years 1920 and 1921, or should be taxed for only a half of them in view of a contract with his wife which we shall mention. The Commissioner of Internal Revenue and the Board of Tax Appeals imposed a tax upon the whole, but their decision was reversed by the Circuit Court of Appeals, 30 F.2d 898. A writ of certiorari was granted by this Court.

By the contract, made in 1901, Earl and his wife agreed "that any property either of us now has or may hereafter acquire . . . in any way, either by earnings (including salaries, fees, etc.), or any rights by contract or otherwise, during the existence of our marriage, or which we or either of us may receive by gift, bequest, devise, or inheritance, and all the proceeds, issues, and profits of any and all such property shall be treated and considered and hereby is declared to be received, held, taken, and owned by us as joint tenants, and not otherwise, with the right of survivorship." The validity of the contract is not questioned, and we assume it to be unquestionable under the law of the State of California, in which the parties lived. Nevertheless we are of opinion that the Commissioner and Board of Tax appeals were right.

The Revenue Act of 1918 . . . imposes a tax upon the net income of every individual including "income derived from salaries, wages, or compensation for personal service . . . of whatever kind and in whatever form paid," Sec. 213(a). The provisions of the Revenue Act of 1921 . . . are similar. . . . A very forcible argument is presented to the effect that the statute seeks to tax only income beneficially received, and that taking the question more technically the salary and fees became the joint property of Earl and his wife on the very first instant on which they were received. We well might hesitate upon the latter proposition, because however the matter might stand between husband and wife he was the only party to the contracts by which the salary and fees were earned, and it is somewhat hard to say that the last step in the performance of those contracts could be taken by anyone but himself alone. But this case is not to be decided by attenuated subtleties. It turns on the import and reasonable construction of the taxing act. There is no doubt that the statute could tax salaries to those who earned them and provide that the tax could not be escaped by anticipatory arrangements and contracts however skillfully devised to prevent the salary when paid from vesting even for a second in the man who earned it. That seems to us the import of the statute before us and we think that no distinction can be taken according to the motives leading to the arrangement by which the fruits are attributed to a different tree from that on which they grew.

Judgment reversed.

HELVERING v. HORST
United States Supreme Court
311 U.S. 112 (1940)

Mr. Justice Stone delivered the opinion of the Court.

The sole question for decision is whether the gift, during the donor's taxable year, of interest coupons detached from the bonds, delivered to the donee and later in the year paid at maturity, is the realization of income taxable to the donor.

In 1934 and 1935 respondent, the owner of negotiable bonds, detached from them negotiable interest coupons shortly before their due date and delivered them as a gift to his son who in the same year collected them at maturity. The Commissioner ruled that . . . the interest payments were taxable, in the years when paid, to the respondent donor who reported his income on the cash receipts basis. The Circuit Court of Appeals reversed the order of the Board of Tax Appeals sustaining the tax. . . . We granted certiorari . . . because of the importance of the question in the administration of the revenue laws and because of an asserted conflict in principle of the decision below with that of *Lucas v. Earl*, 281 U.S. 111, and with that of decisions by other circuit courts of appeals. . . .

The court below thought that as the consideration for the coupons had passed to the obligor, the donor had, by the gift, parted with all control over them and their payments, and for that reason the case was distinguishable from *Lucas v. Earl*, *supra*, . . . where the assignment of compensation for services had preceded the rendition of the services, and where the income was held taxable to the donor.

The holder of a coupon bond is the owner of two independent and separable kinds of rights. One is the right to demand and receive at maturity the principal amount of the bond representing capital investment. The other is the right to demand and receive interim payments of interest on the investment in the amounts and on the dates specified by the coupons. Together they are an obligation to pay principal and interest given in exchange for money or property which was presumably the consideration for the obligation of the bond. Here respondent, as owner of the bonds, had acquired the legal right to demand payment at maturity of the interest specified by the coupons and the power to command its payment to others, which constituted an economic gain to him.

Admittedly not all economic gain of the taxpayer is taxable income. From the beginning the revenue laws have been interpreted as defining "realization" of income as the taxable event, rather than the acquisition of the right to receive it. And "realization" is not deemed to occur until the income is paid. But the decisions and regulations have consistently recognized that receipt in cash or property is not the only characteristic of realization of income to a taxpayer on the cash receipts basis. Where the taxpayer does not receive payment of income in money or property realization may occur when the last step is taken by which he obtains the fruition of the economic gain which has already accrued to him. . . .

In the ordinary case the taxpayer who acquires the right to receive income is taxed when he receives it, regardless of the time when his right to receive payment accrued. But the rule that income is not taxable until realized has never been taken to mean that the taxpayer, even on the cash receipts basis, who has fully enjoyed the benefit of the economic gain represented by his right to receive income, can escape taxation because he has not himself received payment of it from his obligor. The rule, founded on administrative convenience, is only one of postponement of the tax to the final event of enjoyment of the income, usually the receipt of it by the taxpayer, and not one of exemption from taxation where the enjoyment is consummated by some event other than the taxpayer's personal receipt of money or property. . . . This may occur when he has made such use or disposition of his power to receive or control the income as to procure in its place other satisfactions which are of economic worth. The question here is, whether because one who in fact receives payment for services or interest payments is taxable only on his receipt of the payments, he can escape all tax by giving away his right to income in advance of payment. If the taxpayer procures payment directly to his creditors of the items of interest or earnings due him, . . . or if he sets up a revocable trust with income payable to the objects of his bounty, . . . he does not escape taxation because he did not actually receive the money. . . .

Underlying the reasoning in these cases is the thought that income is "realized" by the assignor because he, who owns or controls the source of the income, also controls the disposition of that which he could have received himself and diverts the payment from himself to others as the means of procuring the satisfaction of his wants. The taxpayer has equally enjoyed the fruits of his labor or investment and obtained the satisfaction of his desires whether he collects and uses the income to procure those satisfactions, or whether he disposes of his right to collect it as the means of procuring them.

Although the donor here, by the transfer of the coupons, has precluded any possibility of his collecting them himself, he has nevertheless, by his act, procured payment of the interest as a valuable gift to a member of his family. Such a use of his economic gain, the right to receive income, to procure a satisfaction which can be obtained only by the expenditure of money or property, would seem to be the enjoyment of the income whether the satisfaction is the purchase of goods at the corner grocery, the payment of his debt there, or such nonmaterial satisfactions as may result from the payment of a campaign or community chest contribution, or a gift to his favorite son. Even though he never receives the money, he derives money's worth from the disposition of the coupons which he has used as money or money's worth in the procuring of a satisfaction which is procurable only by the expenditure of money or money's worth. The enjoyment of the economic benefit accruing to him by virtue of his acquisition of the coupons is realized as completely as it would have been if he had collected the interest in dollars and expended them for any of the purposes named.

In a real sense he has enjoyed compensation for money loaned or services rendered, and not any the less so because it is his only reward for them. To say that one who has made a gift thus derived from interest or earnings paid to his donee has never enjoyed or realized the fruits of his investment or labor, because he has assigned them instead of collecting them himself and then paying them over to the donee, is to affront common understanding and to deny the facts of common experience. Common understanding and experience are the touchstones for the interpretation of the revenue laws.

The power to dispose of income is the equivalent of ownership of it. The exercise of that power to procure the payment of income to another is the enjoyment, and hence the realization, of the income by him who exercises it. We have had no difficulty in applying that proposition where the assignment preceded the rendition of the services, *Lucas v. Earl, supra,* . . . for it was recognized that in such a case the rendition of the service by the assignor was the means by which the income was controlled by the donor and of making his assignment effective. But it is the assignment by which the disposition of income is controlled when the service precedes the assignments, and in both cases it is the exercise of the power of disposition of the interest or compensation, with the resulting payment to the donee, which is the enjoyment by the donor of income derived from them.

The dominant purpose of the revenue laws is the taxation of income to those who earn or otherwise create the right to receive it and enjoy the benefit of it when paid. . . . The tax laid by the 1934 Revenue Act upon income "derived from . . . wages, or compensation for personal service, of whatever kind and in whatever form paid, . . . [and] from interest . . . " therefore cannot fairly be interpreted as not applying to income derived from interest or compensation when he who is entitled to receive it makes use of his power to dispose of it in procuring satisfactions which he would otherwise procure only by the use of the money when received.

It is the statute which taxes the income to the donor although paid to his donee. *Lucas v. Earl, supra*. . . . True, in [that case] the service which created the right to income followed the assignment, and it was arguable that in point of legal theory the right to the compensation vested instantaneously in the assignor when paid, although he never received it; while here the right of the assignor to receive the income antedated the assignment which transferred the right and thus precluded such an instantaneous vesting. But the statute affords no basis for such "attenuated subtleties." The distinction was explicitly rejected as the basis of decision in *Lucas v. Earl*. It should be rejected here; for no more than in the *Earl* case can the purpose of the statute to tax the income to him who earns, or creates and enjoys it be escaped by "anticipatory arrangements however skillfully devised" to prevent the income from vesting even for a second in the donor.

Nor is it perceived that there is any adequate basis for distinguishing between the gift of interest coupons here and a gift of salary or commissions. The owner of a negotiable bond and of the investment which it represents, if not the lender, stands in the place of the lender. When, by the gift of the coupons, he has separated his right to interest payments from his investment and procured the payment of the interest to his donee, he has enjoyed the economic benefits of the income in the same manner and to the same extent as though the transfer were of earnings, and in both cases the import of the statute is that the fruit is not to be attributed to a different tree from that on which it grew.

Reversed.

HELVERING v. EUBANK
United States Supreme Court
311 U.S. 122 (1940)

Mr. Justice Stone delivered the opinion of the Court.

This is a companion case to *Helvering v. Horst*, and presents issues not distinguishable from those in that case.

Respondent, a general life insurance agent, after the termination of his agency contracts and services as agent, made assignments in 1924 and 1928 respectively of renewal commissions to become payable to him for services which had been rendered in writing policies of insurance under two of his agency contracts. The Commissioner assessed the renewal commissions paid by the companies to the assignees in 1933 as income taxable to the assignor in that year under the provisions of the 1932 Revenue Act, 47 Stat. 169, Sec. 22 which does not differ in any respect now material from Sec. 22 of the 1934 Revenue Act involved in the *Horst* case. The Court of Appeals for the Second Circuit reversed the order of the Board of Tax Appeals sustaining the assessment. 110 F.2d 737; 39 B.T.A. 583. We granted certiorari October 14, 1940.

No purpose of the assignments appears other than to confer on the assignees the power to collect the commissions, which they did in the taxable year. The Government and respondent have briefed and argued the case here on the assumption that the assignments were voluntary transfers to the assignees of the right to collect the commissions as and when they became payable, and the record affords no basis for any other.

For the reasons stated at length in the opinion in the *Horst* case, we hold that the commissions were taxable as income of the assignor in the year when paid. The judgment below is

Reversed.

MR. JUSTICE MCREYNOLDS, dissenting:

The cause was decided upon stipulated facts. The following statement taken from the court's opinion discloses the issues.

> The question presented is whether renewal commissions payable to a general agent of a life insurance company after the termination of his agency and by him assigned prior to the taxable year, must be included in his income despite the assignment.

> During part of the year 1924 the petitioner was employed by the Canada Life Assurance Company as its branch manager for the state of Michigan. His compensation consisted of a salary plus certain commissions. His employment terminated on September 1, 1924. Under the terms of his contract he was entitled to renewal commissions on premiums thereafter collected by the company on policies written prior to the termination of his agency, without the obligation to perform any further services. In November 1924 he assigned his right, title, and interest in the contract as well as the renewal commissions to a corporate trustee. From September 1, 1924 to June 30, 1927, the petitioner and another, constituting the firm of Hart & Eubank, were general agents in New York City for the Aetna Life Assurance Company, and from July 1, 1927 to August 31, 1927, the petitioner individually was general agent for said Aetna Company. The Aetna contracts likewise contained terms entitling the agent to commissions on renewal premiums paid after termination of the agency, without the performance of any further services. On March 28, 1928, the petitioner assigned to the corporate trustee all commissions to become due him under the Aetna contracts. During the year 1933 the trustee collected by virtue of the assignments renewal commissions payable under the three agency contracts above mentioned, amounting to some $15,600. These commissions were taxed to the petitioner by the Commissioner, and the Board has sustained the deficiency resulting therefrom.

The court below declared—

> In the case at bar the petitioner owned a right to receive money for past services; no further services were required. Such a right is assignable. At the time of assignment, there was nothing contingent in the petitioner's right, although the amount collectible in future years was still uncertain and contingent. But this may be equally true where the assignment transfers a right to income from investments, as in *Blair v. Commissioner*, 300 U.S. 5, and *Horst v. Commissioner*, 107 F.2d 906 (C.C.A.2), or a right

to patent royalties, as in *Nelson v. Ferguson*, 56 F.2d 121 (C.C.A.3), *certiorari denied*, 286 U.S. 565. By an assignment of future earnings a taxpayer may not escape taxation upon his compensation in the year when he earns it. But when a taxpayer who makes his income tax return on a cash basis assigns a right to money payable in the future for work already performed, we believe that he transfers a property right, and the money, when received by the assignee, is not income taxable to the assignor.

Accordingly, the Board of Tax Appeals was reversed; and this, I think, is in accord with the statute and our opinions.

The assignment in question denuded the assignor of all right to commissions thereafter to accrue under the contract with the insurance company. He could do nothing further in respect of them; they were entirely beyond his control. In no proper sense were they something either earned or received by him during the taxable year. The right to collect became the absolute property of the assignee without relation to future action by the assignor.

A mere right to collect future payments, for services already performed, is not presently taxable as "income derived" from such services. It is property which may be assigned. Whatever the assignor receives as consideration may be his income; but the statute does not undertake to impose liability upon him because of payments to another under a contract which he had transferred in good faith, under circumstances like those here disclosed.

SALVATORE v. COMMISSIONER
T.C. Memo. 1970-30

FEATHERSTON, JUDGE:

. . . The only issue presented for decision is whether petitioner is taxable on all or only one-half of the gain realized on the sale of certain real property in 1963.

Findings of Fact

Petitioner's husband operated an oil and gas service station in Greenwich, Connecticut, for a number of years prior to his death on October 7, 1948. His will, dated December 6, 1941, contained the following pertinent provisions:

SECOND: I give devise and bequeath all of my estate both real and personal of whatsoever the same may consist and wheresoever the same may be situated of which I may die possessed or be entitled to at the time of my decease, to my beloved wife, SUSIE SALVATORE, to be hers absolutely and forever.

I make no provision herein for my beloved children because I am confident that their needs and support will be provided for by my beloved wife.

For several years after her husband's death petitioner's three sons, Amedeo, Eugene, and Michael, continued operating the service station with the help of her daughter Irene, who kept the books of the business. Sometime prior to 1958, however, Michael left the service station to undertake other business endeavors; and in 1958 Eugene left to enter the real estate business, leaving Amedeo alone to manage and operate the service station.

During this period and until 1963, petitioner received $100 per week from the income of the service station. This sum was not based on the fair rental of the property, but was geared to petitioner's needs for her support. The remaining income was divided among the family members who worked in the business.

The land on which the service station was located became increasingly valuable. Several major oil companies from time to time made purchase proposals, which were considered by members of the family. Finally, in the early summer of 1963 representatives of Texaco, Inc. (hereinafter Texaco), approached Amedeo regarding the purchase of the service station property. Petitioner called a family conference and asked for advice on whether the property should be sold. Realizing that Amedeo alone could not operate the station at peak efficiency, petitioner and her children decided to sell the property if a reasonable offer could be obtained.

Amedeo continued his negotiations with Texaco and ultimately received an offer of $295,000. During the course of the negotiations Eugene discovered that tax liens in the amount of $8,000 were outstanding against the property. In addition, there was an outstanding mortgage, securing a note held by Texaco, on which approximately $50,000 remained unpaid. The family met again to consider Texaco's offer.

As a result of the family meeting (including consultation with petitioner's daughter Geraldine, who lived in Florida), it was decided that the proposal should be accepted and that the proceeds should be used, first to satisfy the tax liens and any other outstanding liabilities. Second, petitioner was to receive $100,000 the estimated amount needed to generate income for her life of about $5,000 per year — the approximate equivalent of the $100 per week she previously received out of the service station income. Third, the balance was to be divided equally among the five children. To effectuate this family understanding, it was agreed that petitioner would first convey a one-half interest in the property to the children and that deeds would then be executed by petitioner and the children conveying the property to Texaco.

On July 24, 1963, petitioner formally accepted Texaco's offer by executing an agreement to sell the property to Texaco for $295,000 the latter making a down payment of $29,500. Subsequently, on August 28, 1963, petitioner executed a warranty deed conveying an undivided one-half interest in the property to her five children. This deed was received for record on September 6, 1963. By warranty deeds dated August 28 and 30, 1963, and received for record on September 6, 1963, petitioner and her five children conveyed their interest in the property to Texaco; Texaco thereupon tendered $215,582.12, the remainder of the purchase price less the amount due on the outstanding mortgage.

Petitioner filed a Federal gift tax return for 1963, reporting gifts made to each of her five children on August 1, 1963, of a 1/10 interest in the property and disclosing a gift tax due in the amount of $10,744.35.

After discharge of the mortgage and the tax liens the remaining proceeds of the sale (including the down payment) amounted to $237,082, of which one-half, $118,541 was paid to petitioner. From the other half of the proceeds the gift tax of $10,744.35 was paid and the balance was distributed to the children.

In her income tax return for 1963 petitioner reported as her share of the gain from the sale of the service station property a long-term capital gain of $115,063 plus an ordinary gain of $665. Each of the children reported in his 1963 return a proportionate share of the balance of the gain.

In the notice of deficiency respondent determined that petitioner's gain on the sale of the service station property was $238,856, all of which was taxable as long-term capital gain. Thereafter each of petitioner's children filed protective claims for refund of the taxes which they had paid on their gains from the sale of the service station property.

Opinion

The only question is whether petitioner is taxable on all or only one-half of the gain realized from the sale of the service station property. This issue must be resolved in accordance with the following principle stated by the Supreme Court in *Commissioner v. Court Holding Co.*, 324 U.S. 331, 334 (1945):

> The incidence of taxation depends upon the substance of a transaction. The tax consequences which arise from gains from a sale of property are not finally to be determined solely by the means employed to transfer legal title. Rather, the transaction must be viewed as a whole, and each step, from the commencement of negotiations to the consummation of the sale, is relevant. *A sale by one person cannot be transformed for tax purposes into a sale by another by using the latter as a conduit through which to pass title.* To permit the true nature of a transaction to be disguised by mere formalisms, which exist solely to alter tax liabilities, would seriously impair the effective administration of the tax policies of Congress. [Emphasis added.]

The evidence is unmistakably clear that petitioner owned the service station property prior to July 24, 1963, when she contracted to sell it to Texaco. Her children doubtless expected ultimately to receive the property or its proceeds, either through gifts or inheritance, and petitioner may have felt morally obligated to pass it on to them. But at that time the children "held" no property interest there. Petitioner's subsequent conveyance, unsupported by consideration, of an undivided one-half interest in the property to her children — all of whom were fully aware of her prior agreement to sell the property — was merely an intermediate step in the transfer of legal title from petitioner to Texaco; petitioner's children were only "conduit[s] through which to pass title." That petitioner's conveyance to the children may have been a bona fide completed gift prior to the transfer of title to Texaco, as she contends, is immaterial in determining the income tax consequences of sale, for the form of a transaction cannot be permitted to prevail over its substance. In substance, petitioner made an anticipatory assignment to her children of one-half of the income from the sale of the property.

The artificiality of treating the transaction as a sale in part by the children is confirmed by the testimony by petitioner's witnesses that the sum retained by her from the sale was a computed amount — an amount sufficient to assure that she would receive income in the amount of approximately $5,000 annually. If the sales price had been less, petitioner would have retained a larger percentage of the proceeds; if more, we infer, she would have received a smaller percentage. While the children's desire to provide for their mother's care and petitioner's willingness to share the proceeds of her property with her children during her lifetime may be laudable, her tax liabilities cannot be altered by a rearrangement of the legal title after she had already contracted to sell the property to Texaco.

All the gain from the sale of the service station property was taxable to petitioner. . . .

Decision will be entered for the respondent.

STRANAHAN v. COMMISSIONER
United States Court of Appeals, Sixth Circuit
472 F.2d 867 (1973)

PECK, CIRCUIT JUDGE:

This appeal comes from the United States Tax Court, which partially denied appellant estate's petition for a redetermination of a deficiency in the decedent's income tax for the taxable period January 1, 1965 through November 10, 1965, the date of decedent's death.

The facts before us are briefly recounted as follows: On March 11, 1964, the decedent, Frank D. Stranahan, entered into a closing agreement with the Commissioner of Internal Revenue Service (IRS) under which it was agreed that decedent owed the IRS $754,815.72 for interest due to deficiencies in federal income, estate and gift taxes regarding several trusts created in 1932. Decedent, a cash-basis taxpayer, paid the amount during his 1964 tax year. Because his personal income for the 1964 tax year would not normally have been high enough to fully absorb the large interest deduction, decedent accelerated his future income to avoid losing the tax benefit of the interest deduction. To accelerate the income, decedent executed an agreement dated December 22, 1964, under which he assigned to his son, Duane Stranahan, $122,820 in anticipated stock dividends from decedent's Champion Spark Plug Company common stock (12,500 shares). At the time both decedent and his son were employees and shareholders of Champion. As consideration for this assignment of future stock dividends, decedent's son paid the decedent $115,000 by check dated December 22, 1964. The decedent thereafter directed the transfer agent for Champion to issue all future dividend checks to his son, Duane, until the aggregate amount of $122,820 had been paid to him. Decedent reported this $115,000 payment as ordinary income for the 1964 tax year and thus was able to deduct the full interest payment from the sum of this payment and his other income. During decedent's taxable year in question, dividends in the total amount of $40,050 were paid to and received by decedent's son. No part of the $40,050 was reported as income in the return filed by decedent's estate for this period. Decedent's son reported this dividend income on his own return as ordinary income subject to the offset of his basis of $115,000 resulting in a net amount of $7,282 of taxable income.

Subsequently, the Commissioner sent appellant (decedent's estate) a notice of deficiency claiming that the $40,050 received by the decedent's son was actually income attributable to the decedent. After making an adjustment which is not relevant here, the Tax Court upheld the deficiency in the amount of $50,916.78. The Tax Court concluded that decedent's assignment of future dividends in exchange for the present discounted cash value of those dividends "though conducted in the form of an assignment of a property right, was in reality a loan to [decedent] masquerading as a sale and so disguised lacked any business purpose; and, therefore, decedent realized taxable income in the year 1965 when the dividend was declared paid."

As pointed out by the Tax Court, several long-standing principles must be recognized. First, under Section 451(a) of the Internal Revenue Code of 1954, a cash basis taxpayer ordinarily realizes income in the year of receipt rather than the year when earned. Second, a taxpayer who assigns future income for consideration in a bona fide commercial transaction will ordinarily realize ordinary income in the year of receipt. . . . Third, a taxpayer is free to arrange his financial affairs to minimize his tax liability . . . thus, the presence of tax avoidance motives will not nullify an otherwise bona fide transaction. . . . We also note there are no claims that the transaction was a sham, the purchase price was inadequate or that decedent did not actually receive the full payment of $115,000 in tax year 1964. And it is agreed decedent had the right to enter into a binding contract to sell his right to future dividends.

The Commissioner's view regards the transaction as merely a temporary shift of funds, with an appropriate interest factor, within the family unit. He argues that no change in the beneficial ownership of the stock was effected and no real risks of ownership were assumed by the son. Therefore, the Commissioner concludes, taxable income was realized not on the formal assignment but rather on the actual payment of the dividends.

It is conceded by taxpayer that the sole aim of the assignment was the acceleration of income so as to fully utilize the interest deduction. [T]he substance of a transaction, and not the form, determines the taxable consequences of that transaction. . . . In the present transaction, however, it appears that both the form and the substance of the agreement assigned the right to receive future income. What was received by the decedent was the present value of that income the son could expect in the future. On the basis of the stock's past performance, the future income could have been (and was) estimated with reasonable accuracy. Essentially, decedent's son paid consideration to receive future income. Of course, the fact of a family transaction does not vitiate the transaction but merely subjects it to special scrutiny.

We recognize the oft-stated principle that a taxpayer cannot escape taxation by legally assigning or giving away a portion of the income derived from income producing property retained by the taxpayer. *Lucas v. Earl,* . . . Here, however, the acceleration of income was not designed to avoid or escape recognition of the dividends but rather to reduce taxation by fully utilizing a substantial interest deduction which was available. As stated previously, tax avoidance motives alone will not serve to obviate the tax benefits of a transaction. Further, the fact that this was a transaction for good and sufficient consideration, and not merely gratuitous, distinguishes the instant case from the line of authority beginning with *Helvering v. Horst* [311 U.S. 112 (1940)].

Hence the fact that valuable consideration was an integral part of the transaction distinguishes this case from those where the simple expedient of drawing up legal papers and assigning income to others is used. The Tax Court uses the celebrated metaphor of Justice Holmes regarding the "fruit" and the "tree" . . . and concludes there has been no effective separation of the fruit from the tree. Judge Cardozo's comment that "[m]etaphors in law are to be narrowly watched, for starting as devices to liberate thought, they end often by enslaving it" (*Berkey v. Third Avenue Railway Co.*, 244 N.Y. 84, 94, 155 N.E. 58, 61 (1926)) is appropriate here, as the genesis of the metaphor lies in a gratuitous transaction, while the instant situation concerns a transaction for a valuable consideration.

Accordingly, we conclude the transaction to be economically realistic, with substance, and therefore should be recognized for tax purposes even though the consequences may be unfavorable to the Commissioner. The facts establish decedent did in fact receive payment. Decedent deposited his son's check for $115,000 to his personal account on December 23, 1964, the day after the agreement was signed. The agreement is unquestionably a complete and valid assignment to decedent's son of all dividends up to $122,820. The son acquired an independent right against the corporation since the latter was notified of the private agreement. Decedent completely divested himself of any interest in the dividends and vested the interest on the day of execution of the agreement with his son.

The Commissioner cites *J. A. Martin*, 56 T.C. 1255 (1972), *aff'd*, No. 72-1416 (5th Cir., August 18, 1972), to show how similar attempts to accelerate income have been rejected by the courts. There taxpayer assigned future rents in return for a stated cash advance. Taxpayer agreed to repay the principal advanced plus a 7% per annum interest. These facts distinguish this situation from the instant case as there the premises were required to remain open for two years' full rental operation, suggesting a guarantee toward repayment. No such commitment is apparent here.

The judgment is reversed and the cause remanded for further proceedings consistent with this opinion.

MAY v. COMMISSIONER
United States Court of Appeals, Ninth Circuit
723 F.2d 1434 (1984)

PREGERSON, CIRCUIT JUDGE:

I. FACTS

This case presents a typical "gift-leaseback" situation. In 1971, the taxpayers, Dr. Lewis H.V. and Nancy C. May, deeded their entire title and interest in improved real property, located in Temple City, California, to an irrevocable trust for the benefit of their four children. The trust instrument appointed Dr. May and a friend, Harlos Gross, as co-trustees. Although executed and delivered in 1971, the deed was not recorded until 1973.

Dr. May, who conducted his medical practice at the property, rented it from the trust under an oral lease. Dr. May paid the trust rent of $1,000 per month. About four times a year, trustee Gross checked to see if the rent, which the government concedes was reasonable, had been paid. The Commissioner of Internal Revenue appeals the United States Tax Court's decision, reported at 76 T.C. 7 (1981), holding that Dr. May's rental payments in 1973 were ordinary and necessary business expenses under Internal Revenue Code (IRC) § 162(a). We affirm.

II. ANALYSIS

A. *Criteria to determine deductibility.*

In reviewing the Tax Court's decision, we first consider the statutory basis for the claimed deductions. I.R.C. § 162 provides, in pertinent part:

> (a) In general. — There shall be allowed as a deduction all the ordinary and necessary expenses paid or incurred during the taxable year in carrying on any trade or business, including—
>
>   . . . .
>
> (3) rentals or other payments required to be made as a condition to the continued use or possession of property to which the taxpayer has not taken or is not taking title or in which he has no equity.

If the requirements of the statute are met, the taxpayers are entitled to the deduction.

Whether rental payments in a gift-lease-back situation are deductible under § 162(a)(3) is a frequently litigated question. Although the Tax Court has developed standards to determine whether such rental payments are deductible,[2] the circuit courts are divided on the analysis to be used in determining whether a trustor's rental payments in a gift-leaseback situation are an allowable tax deduction.[3] Our

---

[2] In *Mathews v. Commissioner*, 61 T.C. 12, 18–20, (1973), *rev'd* 520 F.2d 323 (5th Cir. 1975), *cert. denied*, 424 U.S. 967 . . . (1976), the Tax Court set forth the criteria it uses to determine whether the deduction is to be allowed:

(1) The grantor must not retain substantially the same control over the property that he had before he made the gift.

(2) The leaseback should normally be in writing and must require payment of a reasonable rent.

(3) The leaseback (as distinguished from the gift) must have a bona fide business purpose.

(4) The grantor must not possess a disqualifying "equity" in the property within the meaning of Section 162(a)(3).

Since *Mathews*, the Tax Court has used these criteria to determine whether rental payments are deductible. . . .

[3] Some circuits allow the deduction only if there was a business purpose for the entire transaction, *i.e.*,

court in *Brooke v. United States*, 468 F.2d 1155 (9th Cir. 1972), established criteria by which we determine the deductibility of rental payments as a business expense in gift-leaseback cases.

In *Brooke*, the taxpayer/physician practiced medicine in Montana. As a gift, he conveyed to his children his interest in real estate improved by a pharmacy, a rental apartment, and the offices of his medical practice. The Montana State Probate Court appointed the taxpayer as guardian of the childrens' estate. As guardian, the taxpayer collected rents from the pharmacy and the apartment. In addition, he paid himself, as guardian of the children, the reasonable rental value of his medical offices. There was no written lease for the medical offices. The rents collected were used to pay the children's health care, educational, and insurance expenses beyond those required of a parent under Montana law.

In assessing the gift-leaseback situation in *Brooke* we stated:

> The fundamental issue presented involves the sufficiency of the property interest transferred. The transfer of a sufficient property interest justifies the taxation of the donees and the deduction of the rental payments under 26 U.S.C. § 162(a)(3) as ordinary and necessary business expenses by the donor.

468 F.2d at 1157. We then listed factors to be used in assessing the sufficiency of the property interest transferred:

(1)   the duration of the transfer;

(2)   the controls retained by the donor;

(3)   the use of the gift property for the benefit of the donor; and

(4)   the independence of the trustee.

Id.

In *Brooke*, we held that the property interest transferred was sufficient in light of the above listed factors: the transfer was irrevocable, the taxpayer retained few controls over the property, the trust benefits did not inure to the taxpayer, and the trustee as a court appointed guardian was considered independent. . . . In holding that the rental income was shifted to the trust, we concluded that "[n]either substance nor impact denies this [gift] transfer professional or economic reality. . . . " By requiring only that the transfer be grounded in professional or economic reality, we implicitly rejected application of the business purpose test to the gift portion of the gift-leaseback transaction.[4]

---

a business purpose for both the taxpayer's transfer of the property in trust and the subsequent leaseback. *See, e.g.*, *Mathews v. Commissioner*, 520 F.2d 323 (5th Cir. 1975), *cert. denied*, 424 U.S. 967 . . . (1976); *Perry v. United States*, 520 F.2d 235 (4th Cir. 1975), *cert. denied*, 423 U.S. 1052 . . . (1976); *Van Zandt v. Commissioner*, 341 F.2d 440 (5th Cir.), *cert. denied*, 382 U.S. 814 (1965). Other circuits follow a bifurcated approach — *i.e.*, initially determining the validity of the transfer of the property in trust and then examining the leaseback alone to determine if there was a business purpose for the rental payments. *See, e.g.*, *Quinlivan v. Commissioner*, 599 F.2d 269 (8th Cir.), *cert. denied*, 444 U.S. 996, 100 S. Ct. 531, 62 L. Ed. 2d 426 (1979). . . .

[4] Of course, the leaseback portion of the transaction must have a business purpose for the taxpayer to claim a business deduction under I.R.C. § 162(a)(3).

B. *Deductibility of Dr. May's rental payments under the Brooke Criteria.*

We conclude that the rental payments in the instant case are deductible under the *Brooke* criteria. The written trust instrument effectively transferred the property from the taxpayers to the trust in 1971. . . . We agree with the Tax Court's conclusions that the trust instrument effectively transferred title and that failure to record the deed until 1973 did not prevent the conveyance from being effective. . . .

In addition, we agree with the finding of the Tax Court that taxpayers did not retain substantially the same control over the property they had before making the irrevocable gift in trust to their children. We also concur with the Tax Court's finding that the trustees were sufficiently independent. As the Tax Court noted, Mr. Gross testified that he felt independent of Dr. May. . . . The Tax Court also noted that while Mr. Gross might have devoted more time to supervising the trust, because of its small size and lack of complexity, no more was required. The fourth factor of the *Brooke* test — that the gift property not be used for the benefit of the donor is also met. Dr. May's use of the property was strictly as a lessee pursuant to a lease agreement between himself and the trust.

As in *Brooke*, we conclude that none of the factors prevent the rental income from being shifted to the trust. The transfer in the instant case was not a "sham or a fraud. . . . " Rather, it was an irrevocable transfer of real property in trust to provide for the health, care, and educational needs of the taxpayers' children. The taxpayers did not retain the same control over the property as they had before the transfer, *i.e.*, the transfer was grounded in economic reality, and the leaseback of the medical property had a business purpose. Thus the rental payments were properly deductible under I.R.C. § 162(a)(3).

Affirmed.

Chapter 35

THE KIDDIE TAX

I. PROBLEMS

Assume in the following Problems that the § 63(c)(5)(A) limitation on the basic standard deduction, adjusted for inflation, is $1,050.

1. Junior, who is 15 years old and lives with both parents, is expert in computer programming and repair. During Year 1, he earned $4,000 from computer repairs and instruction. He deposited the money in a savings account where it earned $200 interest in Year 1. In addition, Junior had income of $1,500 in Year 1 from a trust established by his grandmother under which he is one of the beneficiaries. Assuming Junior has no itemized deductions, does the kiddie tax apply in Year 1?

2. Assume the same facts as Problem 1, except the trust income was $3,000 instead of $1,500. Does the kiddie tax apply?

3. How does the answer to Problem 2 change if Junior had $1,000 in deductions directly connected with the $4,000 earned from computer repairs and instruction, and another $1,150 in deductions directly connected with the trust income?

4. Assume Junior's parents, who are in a 35% tax bracket, establish separate trusts for Junior and his three siblings, Brother (age 17), Big Sister (age 25), and Little Sister (age 13), each of whom is in a 10% tax bracket. Each trust earns $3,600 of interest income, taxable to the child for whose benefit it was established. Junior's only other income is $2,000 from his computer work and $500 from winning the grand prize in a community raffle. Junior does not itemize deductions. His siblings have no income other than the trust income. What is the allocable parental tax and what is Junior's share of it? What election is available to Junior's parents and what are the consequences of it?

Assignment for Chapter 35:

Complete the problems.

Read: Internal Revenue Code §§ 1(g); 63(c)(4), (5); 151(d)(2).
Temporary Treasury Regulations: Skim § 1.1(i)-1T
Materials: Overview

II.   VOCABULARY

kiddie tax
earned income
unearned income
net unearned income
allocable parental tax

III.   OBJECTIVES

1.   To determine those individuals to whom the kiddie tax applies.

2.   To distinguish between earned and unearned income.

3.   To compute net unearned income on a given set of facts.

4.   To compute the allocable parental tax on a given set of facts.

5.   To compute the child's share of the allocable parental tax.

6.   To explain the rationale for the kiddie tax.

IV. OVERVIEW

As noted in the previous chapter, among the fundamental income tax principles are those directing that income from services be taxed to the service-performer and that income from property be taxed to the property owner. *Lucas v. Earl* and its progeny guard against assignment of service income, but it has long been recognized that income from property can be shifted by transferring ownership of the property. The tax benefits of such income-shifting, of course, are affected by changes in tax rates, but the practice retains utility as long as marginal rate differences are present.

The so-called "kiddie tax" of § 1(g) substantially eliminates the benefits of income-shifting to a child subject to the tax (hereinafter referred to as a "covered child"). Prior to the enactment of the kiddie tax in 1986, a favorite technique for reducing the aggregate tax liability of a family was to spread income-producing assets among the various members of the family. For example, since minor children were generally subject to the same income tax rules as adults, parental transfers of assets to those children — who were presumably in a lower tax bracket than the parents — effectively reduced the family tax bill. Disputes could arise about whether ownership had in fact been transferred, but if the transfer were properly carried out, the income from the property would be taxed to the child. Congress came to regard this income-splitting technique as a manipulation of the progressive rate structure, and a form of tax avoidance that should be restricted.

The approach taken by Congress in § 1(g) is to tax the "net unearned income" of a covered child at the top marginal tax rate of his or her parents (unless, of course, the child is in a higher bracket). The net unearned income is still taxed to the child, not to the parents, but it is taxed to the child as if it were additional parental taxable income. Subsection 1(g), however, casts a net that reaches far beyond the income-shifting technique just described, since it applies to all the net unearned income of a covered child, regardless of the source of the income. Temp. Reg. § 1.1(i)-1T, Q&A-8.[1] Earned income basically consists of personal services income. § 911(d)(2).[2] Unearned income includes not only the income attributable to property transferred from parents, but income attributable to property transferred from other relatives, friends or strangers as well. Moreover, as the regulations point out, § 1(g) applies to unearned income attributable to assets acquired with the child's own earned income, such as interest on bank deposits attributable to a child's newspaper route earnings. Temp. Reg. § 1.1(i)-1T, Q&A-8, Ex. (5). The decision to expand the reach of § 1(g) beyond parent-child or other intrafamily transfers was presumably based on the administrative difficulties that would have been encountered with a provision dependent on the source of the income-producing asset.

---

[1] The kiddie tax, originally designated § 1(i), was redesignated § 1(g) in 1990. The temporary regulations under § 1.1(i) were promulgated prior to the 1990 redesignation. Also note the regulations apply the kiddie tax to children under 14. The age 14 cutoff was established when the kiddie tax was enacted in 1986; Congress raised the cutoff to age 18 in 2006 and in 2007 raised the cutoff to age 24 in some circumstances.

[2] Income from a qualified disability trust is also treated as earned income. § 1(g)(4)(C).

At the same time, note the limitations on the scope of § 1(g). Section 1(g) applies to a child who is under the age of 18. § 1(g)(2)(A)(i). In addition, the kiddie tax also applies to a child if (1) the child has attained the age of 18 by the end of the tax year but is not yet 19 or the child is a full-time student under the age of 24 (§ 1(g)(2)(A)(ii)(I) and § 152(c)(3)); and (2) the child's earned income does not exceed one-half of the amount of the child's support (§ 1(g)(2)(A)(ii)(II)). Under no circumstance will the kiddie tax apply unless the child has at least one living parent, and it does not apply to a married child who files a joint return. § 1(g)(2)(B), (C). Given the above limitations regarding children covered by the kiddie tax, income shifting remains viable for a transferor's children, dependents and relatives whose age or circumstances negate the application of the kiddie tax to them. Moreover, the definition of net unearned income — the income subject to tax at the parental tax rate — permits a limited amount of unearned income of a covered child to be taxed at that child's tax rate instead of the parental rate.

The rules of § 1(g) are complemented by special provisions relating to the standard deduction and personal exemption. First, § 151(d)(2) provides that, if a dependency deduction with respect to an individual is allowable to another taxpayer, that individual may not claim a personal exemption on his or her own tax return. Second, that individual's standard deduction may not exceed the greater of an inflation-adjusted $500 or the sum of $250 and such individual's earned income. § 63(c)(5). Thus, a covered child who is allowable as a dependent on the return of one or both parents, will find that, on her own return, she may not claim the personal exemption or the basic standard deduction, but will instead take the limited standard deduction of § 63(c)(5).

Assuming § 1(g) applies, the tax imposed on the child is the greater of two amounts:

(1) The tax imposed without regard to § 1(g) (this would be the greater amount when the child is in a higher tax bracket than the parents); or

(2) The sum of: (a) the normal tax that would be imposed if the child's taxable income were reduced by net unearned income, and (b) the child's share of the "allocable parental tax." § 1(g)(1).[3]

"Net unearned income" is essentially unearned income, minus the sum of two amounts: (1) the limited standard deduction of § 63(c)(5)(A), as described above; and (2) a second § 63(c)(5)(A) deduction, or the allowable itemized deductions directly connected with the unearned income, whichever is greater. § 1(g)(4)(A). On the assumption that such itemized deductions will rarely exceed the § 63(c)(5)(A) amount, net unearned income will ordinarily equal the child's unearned income, minus twice the § 63(c)(5)(A) limited standard deduction. (For example, if the

---

[3] The Service has made clear not only the tax itself, but any penalties or interest imposed for failure to file the return or to pay the tax, are imposed on the child. Notice 89-7, Q&A-4 C.B. 627. "Generally, a child who can be claimed as a dependent on another taxpayer's return must file an income tax return if (i) all of the child's income is earned income (such as wages) totaling more than the basic standard deduction amount . . . or (ii) the child has unearned income (such as interest or dividends) and his other total income (earned and unearned) is more than $500 [inflation-adjusted]." Id., Q&A-1. See § 6013(a). The Service has promised to be aware of the "special communicative difficulties" involved in dealing with a child about tax liability. Id., Q&A-7.

limited standard deduction is $1,050, § 1(g) will not apply if the child's unearned income is $2,100.) Net unearned income, in any event, cannot exceed taxable income. § 1(g)(4)(B). For example, if a child under 18 has unearned income of $6,000 and if the limited standard deduction is $1,050, net unearned income will likely be $3,900, *i.e.*, $6,000 − 2($1,050) = $3,900. If, however, allowable itemized deductions directly connected with the unearned income were $1,250, then net unearned income would be $3,700 — that is, $6,000 minus the sum of $1,050 plus $1,250.

The "allocable parental tax" is the tax generated, by taxing, at the parental marginal rate, all of the net unearned income of all children of the parent to whom § 1(g) applies. § 1(g)(3)(A)(i). Assume, for example, Brother (under 18) has $4,000 of net unearned income and Sister (also under 18) has $2,000 of net unearned income. Assume this total net unearned income of $6,000, taxed at the marginal parental rate, generates tax liability of $2,100. Since Brother's net unearned income of $4,000 is 2/3 of the total net unearned income, his "share" of the allocable parental tax of $2,100 is equal to 2/3 of $2,100 or $1,400. § 1(g)(3)(B).

Where the parents of a covered child are not married, or if married, file separate returns, § 1(g)(5) provides special rules for determining which parent's taxable income is to be taken into account. If the child's parents file a joint return, or if the parent whose taxable income is to be taken into account files a joint return with a spouse not the child's parent, the total taxable income shown on the joint return is the parental income for kiddie tax purposes. Temp. Reg. § 1.1(i)-1T, Q&A-10, Q&A-13.

Finally, note the "parental election" provision of § 1(g)(7), under which parents in certain circumstances may elect to include unearned income of a covered child in the parental return. Note the child's gross income must be only from interest and dividends and, in addition, must be more than the limited standard deduction of § 63(c)(5)(A) but less than ten times that amount. § 1(g)(7)(A)(i), (ii). Review the flush language of § 1(g)(7)(A) and also § 1(g)(7)(B) for the impact of the election.

Chapter 36

INTEREST-FREE OR BELOW-MARKET LOANS

I. PROBLEMS

1. On January 1, Year 1, Bill makes a $100,000 loan to Maurice, payable on demand. Assume the loan is a bona fide loan evidenced by appropriate documentation. On the day Bill made the loan, and throughout the time the loan was outstanding, the applicable Federal rate was 10% compounded semi-annually. Under the terms of the loan, Maurice is required to pay only 5% simple interest annually. Explain the Year 1 consequences of this loan to Bill and Maurice under the following circumstances. Assume the loan remains outstanding throughout Year 1.

    (a) Bill is Maurice's employer and the loan is made for employment reasons.

    (b) Same as (a), except the loan is for $10,000 instead of $100,000.

    (c) Same as (a), except Bill is a corporation and Maurice is a shareholder of Bill, Inc. Alternatively, suppose Maurice is both an employee and the principal shareholder of Bill, Inc.

    (d) Same as (a), except Bill is Maurice's father and the loan was intended to assist Maurice in purchasing a tract of land Maurice intends to develop for business purposes. Maurice has no income from investments.

    (e) Same as (d), except Maurice received dividends amounting to $2,500 during the year.

2. Assume the same facts as in Problem 1(a) except, rather than being repayable on demand, the $100,000 loan is repayable January 1, Year 3. The applicable Federal rate remains 10% compounded semi-annually. Assume, however, that the loan is interest free and that the present value on January 1, Year 1, of $100,000 payable on January 1, Year 3, is $82,270. Explain the tax treatment of Bill and Maurice under these circumstances. If the loan were a gift loan and had a set term of two years, how would your answer change, if at all?

Assignment for Chapter 36:

Complete the problems.

Read: Internal Revenue Code: § 7872(a)–(f).
Treasury Regulations: Prop. Reg. §§ 1.7872-1(a), 1.7872-2(a)(1); 1.7872-4(d)(2), (e)(1); Temp. Reg. § 1.7872-5T(a), (b)(1), (5), (14), (c)(3).

Materials:　Overview

II.　VOCABULARY

interest-free loan
below-market loan
demand loan
term loan
gift loan
compensation-related loan
corporation-shareholder loan
applicable Federal rate
present value
original issue discount
forgone interest

III.　OBJECTIVES

1. To explain the holdings in *Dean* and *Dickman*.

2. To explain how § 7872 prevents taxpayers from shifting income and thereby avoiding tax.

3. To evaluate the income tax consequences to lender and to borrower in the case of a below-market demand loan or a below-market gift loan.

4. To evaluate the income tax consequences to lender and to borrower in the case of a below-market term loan other than a gift loan.

5. To apply the $10,000 *de minimis* exceptions and the $100,000 exception for gift loans.

IV. OVERVIEW

A. History: Pre-Section 7872

1. Early IRS Attempts

The history of taxation of interest-free or below-market loans is the story of IRS failure, persistence and ultimate success. That history begins in the Tax Court with *Dean v. Commissioner*, 35 T.C. 1083 (1961), *non acq.*, decided almost fifty years after the enactment of the first post-Sixteenth Amendment income tax legislation. In *Dean*, the Service claimed the taxpayers had understated their income by failing to report the economic benefit derived from over two million dollars of interest-free loans they had received from their family corporation. The Service argued the interest-free loans received by the Deans generated taxable income, just as a shareholder's rent-free use of corporate property does.[1] Rejecting the Service's argument, the court noted that, if instead of receiving the rent-free use of corporate property, the shareholders actually paid rent, they could not deduct the rent if their use of the property were personal. § 262. By contrast, if the shareholders borrowed *money* and agreed to pay interest, they could deduct the interest paid on the loan regardless of their use of the loan proceeds.[2] The Tax Court concluded: "We have heretofore given full force to interest-free loans for tax purposes, holding that they result in no interest deduction for the borrower . . . nor interest to the lender. We think it to be equally true that an interest-free loan results in no taxable gain to the borrower." 35 T.C. at 1090.

The Service's challenge to interest-free loans was not without merit. As both a concurring opinion and a dissenting opinion noted, the Tax Court's holding that interest-free loans did not generate taxable income was overly broad. According to the dissent, "[I]t is difficult to believe that the interest-free loan in excess of $2 million . . . by a personal holding company to its majority stockholder . . . did not result in any economic benefit to the borrower." Both the concurrence and dissent indicated that the majority's reliance on the § 163(a) deduction as a basis for distinguishing interest-free loans from rent-free use of corporate property was misplaced since, under certain circumstances, a § 163(a) deduction would be disallowed. For example, if the proceeds of a loan were used to purchase tax-exempt municipal bonds, a deduction for the loan interest would be disallowed under § 265(a)(2).[3]

---

[1] *See, e.g.*, *Frueauff v. Comm'r*, 30 B.T.A. 449 (1934).

[2] § 163(a). *Dean*, of course, was decided well before § 163(h) was enacted in 1986.

[3] In reaching its conclusion that an interest-free loan does not generate taxable income, the Tax Court appeared to suggest that interest-free loans could be ignored altogether for tax purposes. Thus, apparently, the economic benefit conferred by an interest-free loan would not have to be reflected in gross income. This distorted the computation of gross income, and in turn resulted in an understatement of adjusted gross income. Adjusted gross income is significant for various purposes, *e.g.*, determining the amount of deductible medical expenses and deductible charitable contributions. *See* §§ 213(a), 170(b)(1)(F).

In its most important income tax decision following *Dean*, the Tax Court, in *Greenspun v. Commissioner*,[4] explained its reasoning in *Dean* as follows:

> In holding that no income was realized . . . in *Dean* . . . we reasoned that had the taxpayers borrowed the funds on interest-bearing notes, their payment of interest would have been fully deductible under Section 163. Underlying this reasoning was the idea that, economically speaking, an interest-free loan from a corporation to its shareholder or employee is in substance no different from the making of a loan on which interest is charged accompanied by an increase in dividends or compensation in an amount equal to the interest charged. Consequently, to give effect to the economic reality of the situation, we attempted in Dean to equalize the tax treatment of the two loan transactions.

Id. at 948, 949. The court then provided the following example:

> [A]ssume that A, an employee of X Co., received as his only form of compensation an interest-free loan from X Co. in the amount of $20,000 for a period of 1 year. Further assume the prevailing interest rate at the time was 5 percent or $1,000 a year. The economic effect of this transaction is the same as if X Co. had charged A interest at 5 percent on the $20,000 loan, and, at the same time, paid him a salary of $1,000 which A in turn used to pay the interest. Assuming no other facts, in the second hypothetical, A would have gross income from his salary of $1,000 and an interest deduction of $1,000 or taxable income of $0. Consistent with this result, in the first hypothetical involving the interest-free loan, A's taxable income under our holding in *Dean* would be $0.

Id.

In *Greenspun*, the Tax Court, in effect, acknowledged that (1) an interest-free loan does generate *gross* income; and (2) the gross income generated is completely offset by an assumed interest deduction. Recognizing the *Dean* dissenters were correct in noting that under certain circumstances the interest deduction would not be available, the Tax Court in *Greenspun* stated "[w]hen and if we are confronted with such a case, we will decide at that time whether *Dean* is applicable, and if so, whether we shall continue to adhere to our decision in *Dean*." 72 T.C. at 950.

Judge Nims, dissenting in *Greenspun*, raised a cautionary note regarding the court's reasoning that the borrower would have a constructive interest deduction which would offset the gross income from the interest free loan. "If this approach is pursued, the Court may expect to be eventually confronted with a case in which the Commissioner asserts imputed interest income to the lender — a quid pro quo for the constructive deduction allowed the borrower. One can easily visualize this occurring, for example in the stockholder-controlled corporation context." 72 T.C. at 957–58. The Commissioner never did seek to charge the lender with income; as

---

[4] 72 T.C. 931 (1979) *aff'd*, 670 F.2d 123 (9th Cir. 1982), *Greenspun* involved a below-market loan, *i.e.*, interest at a rate less than the market rate was charged on the loan between Howard Hughes, the lender, and the editor and publisher of the Las Vegas Sun, a Las Vegas daily newspaper. The Service argued that the difference between a market rate of interest and the actual interest charged constituted gross income to the borrower.

discussed *infra*, the Congress in the 1984 Tax Reform Act did.

2.   Gift Tax Consequences of Interest-Free Loans

Shortly after its loss in *Dean*, the Service found itself again before a court challenging interest-free loans; in *Johnson v. United States*, 254 F. Supp. 73 (N.D. Tex. 1966), however, its attack changed. According to the Service, the taxpayers in *Johnson* had made a taxable gift to their children to whom they had made substantial interest-free loans repayable on demand. Rejecting the Service's imputation-of-interest argument, the *Johnson* court indicated that Congress was the proper body to change the long-standing position that interest-free loans were not taxable. *Johnson* represented the first time in the then 34-year history of the gift tax in which the Service had sought to tax interest-free loans as gifts.

3.   Post *Dean/Johnson* History

In addition to its failure to address the taxation of interest-free loans until the early 1960s, the Service also failed to respond timely to the decisions in *Dean* and *Johnson.* Indicative of an ambivalence regarding the taxation of interest-free loans, the Service waited 12 years before it announced its non-acquiescence in *Dean.* 1973-2 C.B. 4. The Service waited seven years to announce that it would not follow *Johnson.*[5]

Finally, more than a decade after the *Dean* decision, the Service began aggressively asserting the taxability of interest-free loans; and the Service consistently lost.[6] Prior to the Supreme Court decision in *Dickman v. Commissioner*, 465 U.S. 330 (1984), the only Service victory occurred in the Claims Court in *Hardee v. U.S.*, and that decision was reversed by the Court of Appeals for the Federal Circuit. 708 F.2d 661 (1983).

The Service's persistence, however, finally bore fruit in *Dickman v. Commissioner.* At issue in that case was whether taxable gifts resulted when a lender made interest-free demand loans to a relative and to a closely held corporation. The Eleventh Circuit rejected the Tax Court's view that such loans did not generate gift tax liability and held that interest-free loans are subject to the gift tax whether they are made for a fixed term or are made on a demand basis. 690 F.2d 812 (11th Cir. 1982). The appellate court reasoned that the use of money constitutes a property

---

[5] Rev. Rul. 73-61, 1973-1 C.B. 408. In this ruling, the Service provided means for determining the gift element of both demand and term loans. In the case of term loans, the Service provided that accepted actuarial methods should be used to compute the gift value of the loan at the time it was made. A term loan involves only one reportable gift, *i.e.*, the value of the interest-free use of the money for the term of the loan. By contrast, the value of the gift element of a demand loan is the value of the use of the money for such portion of the year as the donor permits the donee to use the money. Thus, at the end of each year that a demand loan is outstanding, the value of the gift for that year must be determined. If the demand loan is outstanding for five years, there would be a separate gift calculated for each of those years.

[6] *See, e.g., Suttle v. Comm'r*, T.C. Memo. 1978-393 (1978), *aff'd*, 625 F.2d 1127 (4th Cir. 1980); *Greenspun v. Comm'r*, 72 T.C. 931 (1979), *aff'd*, 670 F.2d 123 (9th Cir. 1982); *Creel v. Comm'r*, 72 T.C. 1173, *aff'd sub nom Martin v. Comm'r*, 649 F.2d 1133 (5th Cir. 1981); *Crown v. Comm'r*, 585 F.2d 234 (7th Cir. 1978) (gift tax decision).

interest, and whenever one transfers property for less than full consideration, a taxable gift has been made. The Eleventh Circuit noted that, for gift tax purposes, the lender had no deduction which would offset the gift comparable to the interest deduction a borrower could use to offset the income generated by an interest-free loan.

The Supreme Court agreed with the Eleventh Circuit, noting that "[t]he right to use money is plainly a valuable right, readily measurable by reference to current interest rates; the vast banking industry is positive evidence of this reality." 465 U.S. at 337–38. In holding that interest-free loans generated taxable gifts, the Court recognized the income-shifting potential of such loans: "A substantial no-interest loan from parent to child creates significant tax benefits for the lender quite apart from the economic advantages to the borrower. This is especially so when an individual in a high income tax bracket transfers income producing property to an individual in a lower income tax bracket, thereby reducing the taxable income of the high-bracket taxpayer at the expense, ultimately, of all other taxpayers and the Government." 465 U.S. at 339. The taxpayer argued unsuccessfully that to elevate interest-free loans to the status of taxable gifts would cause "a loan of the proverbial cup of sugar to a neighbor or a loan of lunch money to a colleague" or any number of intrafamily transfers to constitute taxable gifts. The Court rejected that argument, stating it did not believe the focus of the Service to be on such matters. "When the Government levies a gift tax on routine neighborly or familial gifts, there will be time enough to deal with such a case." 456 U.S. at 341.

The Service was quick to act on *Dickman* and issued Announcement 84-60, 1984-23 I.R.B. 58, providing guidelines for computing the gift value of interest free loans. According to the Announcement, the value of the gift element of demand loans was to be determined by multiplying the "average outstanding loan balance" for a period by the lesser of either the statutory interest rates on refunds and deficiencies or the annual average rate for three month Treasury bills. Consistent with the Court's analysis in *Dickman*, the Service in the Announcement limited the scope of interest-free loans to those to which the reasoning of *Dickman* would apply. Specifically, the Announcement provided that if the value of the gift were less than the annual gift exclusion (*see* § 2503(b)) no gift had to be reported.

B. 1984 Tax Reform Act — Rationale for Section 7872

In rejecting the Service's position regarding the income taxation of interest-free loans, many courts had stressed that the taxation of these loans was more appropriately a matter for congressional action. Congress finally addressed interest-free loans in the 1984 Tax Reform Act. As a review of § 7872 and the discussion which follows indicate, the tax treatment for interest-free loans fashioned by Congress reflects both gift and income tax notions developed in the case law. For example, recall that Judge Nims in *Greenspun* speculated that treating the borrower as having constructively paid interest might later result in the lender being deemed to have constructively received an interest payment. That is precisely how Congress chose to analyze interest-free loans. Likewise, § 7872 reflects the gift treatment accorded certain interest-free loans by the Supreme Court in *Dickman* and by the Service in Announcement 84-60.

The rationale for § 7872 provided by the Staff of the Joint Committee reflects this congressional reliance on various theories advanced in the pre-1984 income and gift cases. In particular, Congress was concerned about the income-shifting potential of interest-free loans the Supreme Court had identified in *Dickman.*

Under prior law, loans between family members (and other similar loans) were being used to avoid the assignment of income rules and the grantor trust rules. A below-market loan to a family member, for example, generally involves a gratuitous transfer of the right to use the proceeds of the borrowing until repayment is demanded (in the case of a demand loan) or until the end of the term of the loan (in the case of a term loan). If the lender had assigned the income from the proceeds to the borrower instead of lending the proceeds to the borrower, the assignment of income doctrine would have taxed the lender (and not the borrower) on the income. . . .

In addition, loans from corporations to shareholders were being used to avoid rules requiring the taxation of corporate income at the corporate level. A below-market loan from a corporation to a shareholder is the economic equivalent of a loan by the corporation to the shareholder requiring the payment of interest at a market rate, and a distribution by the corporation to the shareholder with respect to its stock equal to the amount of interest required to be paid under the terms of the loan. If a transaction were structured as a distribution and a loan, the borrower would have dividend income and an offsetting interest deduction. The lender would have interest income. Under prior law, if the transaction was structured as a below-market loan, the lender avoided including in income the interest that would have been paid by the borrower. As a result the lender was in the same economic position as it would have been if it had deducted amounts distributed as dividends to shareholders.

Finally, loans to persons providing services were being used to avoid rules requiring the payment of employment taxes and rules restricting the deductibility of interest in certain situations by the person providing the services. A below-market loan to a person providing services is the economic equivalent of a loan requiring the payment of interest at a market rate, and a payment in the nature of compensation equal to the amount of interest required to be paid under the terms of the loan. Under prior law, a transaction structured as a loan and a payment in the nature of compensation often did not result in any tax consequences for either the lender or the borrower because each would have offsetting income and deductions. However, there were a number of situations in which the payment of compensation and a loan requiring the payment of interest at a market rate did not offset. For example, if a taxpayer used the proceeds of an arm's-length loan to invest in tax-exempt obligations, the deduction for interest paid on the loan would be disallowed under section 265. Similarly, if a term loan extended beyond the taxable year in which it was made, income and deductions did not offset because the compensation income was includible in the year the loan was made. In such circumstances, substantial tax advantages could have been derived by structuring the transaction as a below-market loan.

General Explanation of the Revenue Provisions of the Deficit Reduction Act of 1984, Staff of the Joint Committee on Taxation, 98th Cong. at 527–28.

C. Operation of Section 7872

Section 7872 applies to "below-market loans," defined in § 7872(e)(1), as loans with respect to which either no interest, or an interest rate lower than the "applicable Federal rate" of interest, is charged. Note that the word "loan" is to be interpreted broadly for purposes of § 7872. Prop. Reg. § 1.7872-2(a)(1). Below-market loans are categorized according to their repayment requirements as either term loans or demand loans. A demand loan is payable in full at any time upon the demand of the lender. § 7872(f)(5). A term loan is any loan which is not a demand loan, *i.e.*, it is payable at a specified time. § 7872(f)(6). The "applicable Federal rate" refers to rates on marketable obligations of the United States, and depends on the maturity of the given obligation. Thus, the applicable Federal rate for term loans is the applicable Federal rate (compounded semiannually) as of the loan date for a government obligation having approximately the same maturity as the loan. § 7872(f)(2)(A). The applicable Federal rate for demand loans is the "Federal short-term rate in effect under section 1274(d) for the period of which the amount of [forgone] interest is being determined, compounded semiannually." § 7872(f)(2)(B).

Section 7872 applies to term or demand loans that fall into one of the following categories:

(a) Gift loans, *i.e.*, below-market loans in which the interest which is forgone is in the nature of a gift. § 7872(f)(3). The loans in *Johnson* and *Dickman* would have qualified as "gift loans."

(b) Corporation-shareholder loans, *i.e.*, below-market loans directly or indirectly between a corporation and its shareholders. § 7872(c)(1)(C). The loans in *Dean* would have been included in this category.

(c) Compensation-related loans, *i.e.*, below-market loans directly or indirectly between an employer (or party for whom an independent contractor provides services) and an employee (or independent contractor). § 7872(c)(1)(B). *Greenspun* involved this type of loan. In some instances, the recipient of a below-market corporate loan might be both a shareholder and an employee. See the special rule at Prop. Reg. § 1.7872-4(d)(2) for the circumstances in which such a loan will be presumed to be a corporate-shareholder loan, rather than compensation-related.

(d) Tax-avoidance loans, *i.e.*, a below-market loan which has as one of the principal purposes of the interest arrangements the avoidance of any Federal tax. § 7872(c)(1)(D). The proposed regulations state the forbidden purpose is present if a principal factor in structuring a transaction as a below-market loan, rather than a loan at market rates plus a payment by lender to borrower, is to reduce the tax liability of lender or borrower. Prop. Reg. § 1.7872-4(e)(1).

(e) "Significant-effect" loans, *i.e.*, certain below-market loans, to be determined by regulations,[7] where the interest arrangements have a significant effect on any Federal tax liability of the lender or borrower. § 7872(c)(1)(E). Note the potential scope of these latter two categories, a scope somewhat narrowed by regulatory exemptions.[8]

As explained by the Staff of the Joint Committee on Taxation, "[l]oans that are subject to [Section 7872] . . . are recharacterized as an arm's-length transaction in which the lender made a loan to the borrower in exchange for a note requiring the payment of interest at the applicable federal rate. This rule results in the parties being treated as if: (1) The borrower paid interest to the lender that may be deductible to the borrower and is included in income by the lender; and (2) the lender (a) made a gift subject to the gift tax (in the case of a gratuitous transaction), or (b) paid a dividend or made a capital contribution (in the case of a loan between a corporation and a shareholder), or (c) paid compensation (in the case of a loan to a person providing services). . . . " Deficit Reduction Act of 1984, Joint Committee Report, at 528. See also Prop. Reg. § 1.7872-1(a), characterizing below-market loans under the statute as "economically equivalent to loans bearing interest at the applicable Federal rate, coupled with a payment by the lender to the borrower sufficient to fund" the interest payment.

1.   Treatment of Term Loans Other than Term Gift Loans

The timing of the various deemed transfers and their amounts depend on whether the loan is characterized as (1) a term loan other than a term gift loan or (2) or a demand loan or a term gift loan. § 7872(a) and (b). In the case of a term loan other than a term gift loan, a two-step process must be followed in evaluating the tax consequences to the lender and the borrower. First, "the lender is treated as transferring to the borrower and the borrower is treated as receiving from the lender an amount equal to the excess of the amount of the loan over the present value of all principal and interest payments due under the loan. This transfer is treated as occurring on the date the loan is made." Deficit Reduction Act of 1984, Joint Committee Report at 532. As a result of this first step, the lender may have a deduction for payments deemed made to the borrower and the borrower may have income resulting from the deemed receipt. For our purposes in this Chapter, consider present value to be that amount which if placed in a bank at a given rate of interest and for a given period would increase to a specific dollar amount by the end of that period.

Consider the following example demonstrating the application of the first step in evaluating the tax consequences of term loans (other than term gift loans).

> **Example:** Assume an employer wishes to reward an employee for particu-
> larly good work during the year. Rather than giving that employee an
> outright bonus, the employer gives the employee an interest-free loan of
> $50,000, repayable in three years. Considering the time value of money, the

---

[7] The proposed regulations simply "reserve" significant-effect loans for future definition. Prop. Reg. § 1.7872-4(f).

[8] § 7872 also applies to loans to qualified continuing care facilities. § 7872(c)(1)(F).

employee has obviously received a significant benefit as a result of the receipt of the loan proceeds. Conceptually, one could quantify this benefit by determining the amount of money the employee would have to invest at a reasonable rate of interest to have a total of $50,000 in three years to repay the loan. The difference between that amount of money and the amount of the loan proceeds constitutes an immediate benefit to the employee in the nature of additional compensation. That is precisely how § 7872 measures the benefit to the employee. Under § 7872, one must determine the present value of a $50,000 payment required to be made three years hence. Let us assume the applicable Federal rate is 10% compounded annually. Using this rate, the present value of a $50,000 payment to be made in three years would be approximately $37,550. (*See* Appendix 2) In other words, were the employee to place $37,550 of the $50,000 loan proceeds in a bank account paying 10% interest compounded annually, the balance in the account would be $50,000 at the end of three years. Applying § 7872(b)(1), the employer would be treated as having given to the employee $12,450 in compensation at the time the loan was made (*i.e.*, the difference between the $50,000 currently received and the $37,550 *current* value of the $50,000 to be repaid). Therefore, assuming such additional compensation is reasonable, the employer will deduct the $12,450 under § 162 as an ordinary and necessary business expense. The employee is deemed to have received compensation valued at $12,450 and must include that amount in gross income in the year the loan was received.

Section 7872(b)(2) provides the second step of this two-step process, under which "an amount equal to the excess of the amount of the loan [$50,000, in our example] over the present value of the payments due under the loan [$37,750, in our example] is treated as original issue discount.[9] As a result, the borrower is treated as transferring to the lender, and the lender is treated as receiving from the borrower, interest income at a constant rate over the life of the loan. The interest which the borrower is treated as paying is [generally] deductible to the same extent as interest actually paid by the borrower." Deficit Reduction Act of 1984, Joint Committee Report, at 532. In the example above, the employee would be deemed to be paying interest of approximately $12,450 over 3 years to the lender. In Year 1, the employee would be deemed to pay $3,755 in interest (*i.e.*, $37,550 × 10%). In Year 2, the employee would be deemed to pay $4,131 (*i.e.*, $41,305 × 10%). [Note the $41,305 figure represents the original $37,550 amount to which is added the interest from Year 1 of $3,755. This is simply the effect of compounding the interest.] In Year 3, the employee will be deemed to pay $4,544 in interest (*i.e.*, $45,436 × 10%). [The amount of interest is slightly less than $12,450 because the present value table is carried only to the third decimal point.] The lender would thus have $12,450 interest

---

[9] Original issue discount is discussed in detail in Chapter 43. Essentially, "original issue discount" refers to the difference between the issue price of an obligation and the price to be paid at maturity. For example, assume a corporation issues a bond to evidence its indebtedness. Assume also the bond was issued in exchange for $9,000, and under the terms of the bond, $20,000 will be paid to the bearer at maturity. There is $11,000 of original issue discount inherent in the bond. Original issue discount represents interest which must be reported by the lender in the above example and which is generally deductible by the borrower-corporation. Rather than waiting until maturity of the loan, the lender and borrower must account for this interest element throughout the period of the loan.

income over 3 years, and the employee could deduct this deemed interest payment over the 3 years, subject to § 163(h) and any other provisions disallowing deduction of interest.

2.   Demand Loans and Term Gift Loans

The Joint Committee Report to the Deficit Reduction Act of 1984, at 532–33, explains the operation of § 7872(a) demand loans and gift loans as follows:

> In the case of a demand loan, the lender is treated as transferring to the borrower, and the borrower is treated as receiving from the lender, an amount equal to the [forgone] interest on an annual basis. . . . In the case of a term gift loan, the lender is treated as transferring to the borrower, and the borrower is treated as receiving from the lender, an amount equal to the excess of the amount of the loan over the present value of all principal and interest payments due under the loan.

> In addition, in the case of a demand loan or a term gift loan, the borrower is treated as transferring to the lender, and the lender is treated as receiving from the borrower, an amount equal to the [forgone] interest on an annual basis. This [forgone] interest is included in income by the lender and deductible by the borrower to the same extent as interest actually due on the loan from the borrower. . . . [U]nder the provisions generally applicable to term loans, an original issue discount analysis is required to determine the timing and amount of the deemed transfers by the borrower to the lender. By treating gift loans as demand loans for these purposes, such analysis is avoided.

The income tax effects of a term gift loan may be illustrated by an example based on the legislative history. Assume, on January 1, P, a calendar year taxpayer, makes a $200,000 gift loan to S, a calendar year taxpayer, for two years at 5 percent simple interest payable annually. S is thus required to pay P $10,000 interest each year. Assume that this is a below market loan because the applicable Federal rate is considerably higher than five percent; assume the present value of all payments to be made by S — the interest payments and the principal repayment — is $175,240. P is thus treated as making a transfer to S of $24,760 ($200,000 less $175,240) as a gift, excludable as such from S's income and nondeductible by P. [Note the deemed transfer of $24,760 is a gift by P for gift tax purposes as well, and may create gift tax liability for P; such transfer tax issues are beyond the scope of this course.] In addition, however, S is treated as re-transferring to P each year an amount equal to the difference between the interest actually paid by S (here, $10,000) and the interest that would be payable if interest were paid annually on $200,000 at the applicable Federal rate, compounded semiannually; assume that amount would be $24,720. Thus, the amount treated as re-transferred by S to P each year as interest is $14,720 (*i.e.*, the excess of interest computed at the applicable Federal rate (compounded semiannually) over interest actually payable on the loan). This amount, which would be included in income by the lender P and, subject to the rules governing the deductibility of interest, deductible by the borrower S, would be in addition to the $10,000 actually due each year under the terms of the loan.

Note that, for income tax purposes, a term gift loan is treated as though it were a demand loan except for purposes of the gift tax provisions of the Code. *See* § 7872(d)(2). Thus, as indicated by the example, the amount of the gift deemed made is determined under § 7872(b)(1), *i.e.*, it is the difference between the principal amount of the loan and the present value of all payments which must be made on the loan.[10] If, in the example above provided by the Staff of the Joint Committee, the loan had been a demand gift loan, there would have been no need to make a separate calculation of the gift amount. Rather, the amount of the gift deemed to be made by P to S would have equaled the forgone interest for the year. § 7872(a)(1)(A). For example, if applying the applicable Federal interest rate, the interest for one year on $200,000 would have amounted to $24,720 and S actually was only required to pay $10,000 interest that year, there would be $14,720 of forgone interest on the demand loan for the first loan year. That amount would have represented the amount of the gift from P to S for that year as well as the amount of the deemed transfer from S to P. The gift from P to S and the deemed transfer from S to P would both be presumed to have occurred on the last day of the taxable year. § 7872(a)(2). Assuming that the loan were outstanding for the next year, another gift in the same amount would be deemed made by P to S, and S would be deemed to have re-transferred as interest that same amount to P. P, of course, could not deduct the gift of $14,720 she is deemed to have made to S in each of the years the loan was outstanding; S would exclude the gifts from income. § 102(a). Assuming no disallowance rules (*e.g.*, §§ 163(h), 265(a)(2), 163(d)) were applicable, S would be entitled to deduct as interest the amounts deemed re-transferred to P on the last day of each calendar year.

Note that, if in the above demand loan example the relationship had been an employer/employee relationship rather than a donor/donee relationship, the $14,720 deemed transferred from P to S would have been characterized as compensation deductible by P and includible by S. The amount deemed re-transferred by S to P would have the same consequences to both parties as described in the gift demand loan case described above.

Finally, if P were a corporation and S a shareholder and this were a corporation-shareholder loan, P would be deemed to have paid a dividend of $14,720 to S in each year that the loan was outstanding. P would not be entitled to deduct the dividend and S would be required to include it in income. The tax consequences of the deemed retransfer of the forgone interest amount by S to P would be the same as in the gift demand loan example — *i.e.*, interest income to P and an interest expense to S, deductible subject to disallowance rules. For cases applying these rules in the corporate-shareholder setting, see *KTA Tator, Inc. v. Commissioner*, 108 T.C. 100 (1997) (interest income to corporation; no deduction for deemed distribution to

---

[10] Although § 7872 is ordinarily invoked with respect to below-market loans of money, it has been held that § 7872 is not so limited and that it may apply to sales of property in some circumstances. See *Frazee v. Commissioner*, 98 T.C. 554 (1992), involving the intra-family part-gift/part-sale of property, where the consideration for the part-sale was a below-market term promissory note. *Frazee* held that the below-market rate on the promissory note itself constituted an additional taxable gift, the value of which was to be determined under the rules of § 7872. Such property sales, however, introduce complexities beyond the scope of this Chapter and their analysis is best postponed to Chapter 43, in conjunction with the study of original issue discount.

shareholder) and *Mason v. Commissioner*, T.C. Memo. 1997-352 (imputed dividend income to shareholders). In *Roundtree Cotton Co. v. Commissioner*, 113 T.C. 422 (1999) (*aff'd per curiam* by the Tenth Circuit in an unpublished opinion), the Tax Court held § 7872 applies to interest-free loans made by a corporation to its shareholders even though none of the shareholders/borrowers owned a majority or controlling interest in the corporation. Likewise, the court held § 7872 applies to interest-free loans to partnerships, or other entities in which the corporation's shareholders have an interest.

3.   Exceptions to the Basic Operating Rules

Section 7872 provides exceptions to the general rules described above. Two "*de minimis*" exceptions exist: one relates to gift loans between individuals and the other relates not only to gift loans but also to compensation-related loans and corporation-shareholder loans. Essentially, so long as the outstanding amount of gift loans between borrower and lender does not exceed $10,000, § 7872 does not apply. This exception, however, will not apply to any gift loan directly attributable to the purchase or carrying of income-producing assets. § 7872(c)(2). This limit on the exception is consistent with the general purpose of § 7872 described previously, *i.e.*, to prevent avoidance of the assignment of income rules. This same $10,000 *de minimis* exception is also applicable to compensation-related loans and corporation-shareholder loans. This *de minimis* rule does not apply, however, if a principal purpose of the interest arrangement is avoidance of any Federal tax. § 7872(c)(3).

In the case of a gift loan directly between individuals, an additional exception is applicable: provided the aggregate outstanding loans from lender to borrower do not exceed $100,000, the amount considered as re-transferred by the borrower to the lender as of the close of any calendar year shall not exceed the borrower's net investment income. § 7872(d)(1). However, if a principal purpose of the arrangement is tax avoidance, the exception is inapplicable. § 7872(d)(1)(B). "Net investment income" has the same definition as under § 163(d). As the legislative history notes:

> Thus, the term [net investment income] generally means the excess of investment income over investment expense. The term "investment income" generally means (1) the gross income from interest, dividends, rents and royalties, (2) the net short-term capital gain attributable to the disposition of property held for investment, and (3) any amounts treated under section 1245 . . . but only to the extent such income, gain and amounts are not derived from the conduct of a trade or business. The term "investment expense" generally means the deductions allowable under sections 162, 164(a)(1) or (2), 166, 167, 171, 212 or 611 directly connected with the production of income.
>
> In addition, if a borrower has less than $1,000 of net investment income for the year, such borrower's net investment income for the year is deemed to be zero. Thus, if the aggregate outstanding amount of loans from the lender to the borrower does not exceed $100,000 on any day during a year, and the borrower has less than $1,000 of net investment income for the

year, no amount is treated as re-transferred by the borrower to the lender for such year.

General Explanation of the Provisions of the Deficit Reduction Act of 1984, Staff of the Joint Committee, 536. §§ 7872(d)(1)(D) and (E)(ii). For example, the $100,000 exception enables parents to provide large interest-free loans to their children to assist them in purchasing a home, or paying for education, travel, or other personal expenses. If the children have no investment income in excess of $1,000, there will be no tax consequences to the parent or child. Such interest-free arrangements were not the focus of congressional concern in enacting § 7872.[11]

---

[11] A number of other exemptions from § 7872 have been provided by regulation on the ground that "the interest arrangements do not have a significant effect" on tax liability. Temp. Reg. § 1.7872-5T(a)(1). The exemptions, however, are lost if the loan is a tax-avoidance loan. Among the exemptions are those for certain loans made available to the general public and for government-subsidized loans. Temp. Reg. § 1.7872-5T(b)(1), (5). Also exempt are loans which the taxpayer can show have no significant effect on tax liability, based on all the facts and circumstances, including "whether items of income and deduction generated by the loan offset each other . . . , the amount of such items . . . , the cost to the taxpayers of complying with . . . section 7872 . . . and any non-tax reasons for . . . [the] below-market loan. . . . " Temp. Reg. § 1.7872-5T(b)(14), (c)(3).

Chapter 37

TAX CONSEQUENCES OF DIVORCE

I. PROBLEMS

Frank and Maureen were married for fifteen years. On September 30, Year 1, they separated. Maureen remained in the family home which they had owned and used as their principal residence for ten years. Frank moved into an apartment.

1. In October, Year 1, immediately after the separation, Frank wrote a letter to Maureen in which he agreed to pay Maureen $2,000 per month starting October 1, Year 1. Maureen did not respond to the letter. Frank nonetheless made the promised payments. Do the payments constitute alimony?

2. They entered into a written separation agreement on January 1, Year 2, and a divorce decree, incorporating the terms of that agreement, was entered on July 1, Year 2. Which of the following payments, made pursuant to their January 1, Year 2 agreement, constitute alimony?

    (a) Throughout Year 2, Frank has been paying Maureen $2,000 per month.

    (b) On January 1, Year 2, Frank transferred to Maureen a parcel of land Frank purchased years before as an investment (value $100,000; basis $75,000).

    (c) As of January, Year 2, Frank has been paying Maureen's monthly rent of $1,000. Although not required to do so by the January 1, Year 2 agreement, Frank also has been paying Maureen's utility bills.

    (d) As an alternative to (c), assume Frank and Maureen owned their home as joint tenants with right of survivorship, subject to a mortgage they both signed when they acquired the home years ago. At the time of their separation, the home was put up for sale, but has not yet been sold. Until the sale occurs, Maureen will live in the home and Frank will make the monthly mortgage payments of $5,000 (which are allocated to both principal and interest). When the home is sold, the mortgage balance will be paid and the net sales proceeds will then be divided equally between Frank and Maureen. Do Frank's payments constitute alimony? What will the tax consequences to Frank and Maureen be under § 121 if there is $600,000 gain realized on the sale of the home?

3. Assume the January 1, Year 2 agreement requires Frank to pay Maureen the following amounts: $5,000 per month, commencing January 1, Year 2, and continuing until January 1, Year 3, at which time payments will

decrease to $4,000 per month; on January 1, Year 4, the payments will decrease again to $1,500 per month; on January 1, Year 5, payments will decrease to $1,000 per month and continue through December, Year 5, at which time they will cease. Assuming all payments are made as scheduled, what are the tax consequences to Maureen and Frank as a result of the payments?

4. Assume Frank and Maureen have one child, Donna, who was 12 years old on September 15, Year 1. Their written agreement provides that they will have joint custody of Donna, who will reside part of the year with each parent. The agreement provides:

   (a) Frank will pay Maureen $500 per month for child support, commencing January 1, Year 2, and continuing until Donna reaches age 18. What are the tax consequences to Frank and Maureen as a result of these payments?

   (b) In addition to the payments described in (a), Frank will pay Maureen $1,500 per month as alimony. What are the tax consequences to Frank and Maureen as a result of these payments, assuming, pursuant to the agreement, the alimony payments are reduced to $1,000 per month at the end of Year 4 and cease at the end of Year 7?

   (c) To assure payment of the child support and alimony, Frank will buy and maintain a term life insurance policy on his life, naming Maureen as beneficiary. Frank pays $2,500 per year to ABC Life Insurance Company for the policy. What are the tax consequences to Frank and Maureen as a result of these payments?

   (d) What additional facts would you need to determine who is entitled to the dependency exemption for Donna? Assuming Donna resides with Maureen for three-quarters of each year, what is the filing status of Frank and Maureen on the tax return each files?

5. What are the tax consequences to Frank and Maureen of the following property transactions?

   (a) Frank and Maureen jointly owned shares of ABC stock in which they had a basis totaling $50,000. The stock had a fair market value of $40,000. Frank and Maureen also owned a parcel of raw land valued at $120,000 and having an adjusted basis of $60,000. The land was encumbered by mortgage in the amount of $80,000. During Year 2, Frank transferred to Maureen his interest in the land and Maureen agreed to assume the $80,000 mortgage. In exchange, Maureen transferred to Frank her interest in the ABC stock. Frank subsequently sold the ABC stock for $40,000 and Maureen sold the land for $120,000 with the purchaser paying Maureen $40,000 in cash and assuming the $80,000 mortgage encumbering the land.

   (b) Instead of the exchange described in part (a) of this problem, assume Frank purchased for $20,000 Maureen's interest in the ABC stock and also purchased Maureen's interest in the land for $20,000 cash and assumed responsibility for the $80,000 mortgage on the land. Two years later, Frank sold the ABC stock for $60,000 and sold the land for

$130,000 with the purchaser paying Frank $70,000 in cash for the land and assuming the $60,000 then owing on the mortgage encumbering the land.

(c) Assume Maureen and Frank were the sole shareholders of DEF Corporation and that each of them owned 100 shares of DEF stock. Each of them paid $5,000 for the stock several years ago. Each block of 100 shares is now worth $50,000. Although their property settlement agreement required Frank to purchase Maureen's stock for $50,000, Frank, in Year 2, arranged for the purchase to be made by DEF as a redemption of Maureen's stock.

(d) On January 1, Year 2, Frank transferred to Maureen ownership of a car he had purchased for $30,000 a few years earlier and had been leasing to a local business. The lease term ended December 31, Year 1. Frank had claimed $18,000 in depreciation deductions with respect to the car. Maureen uses the car for personal purposes. At the time of transfer, the car was worth $15,000, and Frank was owed $1,000 in lease charges. In addition to transferring to Maureen the car, Frank assigned to her his right to collect the outstanding lease charges. During Year 2, Maureen collected the $1,000 and subsequently sold the car for $14,000.

(e) On January 1, Year 4, in lieu of a $1,500 cash alimony payment, Frank gave Maureen $1,500 worth of XYZ stock he had purchased for $1,000. Maureen later sold the stock for $1,300.

6. Are the following expenses deductible?

(a) Maureen paid her attorney fees of $5,000.

(b) Alternatively, pursuant to the divorce decree, Frank paid Maureen's attorney fees of $5,000.

(c) Frank paid his attorney fees of $5,000.

7. Would your answers to Problems 1–6 above be different if, instead of Frank and Maureen, the divorcing parties were Frank and David who had been legally married in Massachusetts and who had an adopted child named Donna?

Assignment for Chapter 37:

Complete the problems.

Read: Internal Revenue Code: §§ 61(a)(8); 71; 121(d)(3); 215; 62(a)(10); 151(a), (c); 152(a), (c), (d)(1)(D), (e), (f)(5); 1(a),(b), (c); 2(b), (c); 7703(b); 1015(e); 1041; 212. Glance at §§ 682; 152(d).
Treasury Regulations: §§ 1.71-1(b)(1)–(3); 1.71-1T, Q&A 1-10, 13–18, 22; 1.121-4(b); 1.152-4; 1.215-1T; 1.1041-1T, Q&A 1-12; 1.1041-2; 1.212-1(l); 1.262-1(b)(7).

Materials: Overview
Revenue Ruling 2002-22
United States v. Gilmore

Revenue Ruling 67-420
Revenue Ruling 2013-17

II.   VOCABULARY

alimony
divorce or separation instrument
front-loading of alimony
excess alimony payment
dependency exemption
custodial or noncustodial parent
head of household
incident to divorce

III.   OBJECTIVES

1. To recall the general requirements a payment must satisfy to constitute alimony.

2. To distinguish between third party payments on behalf of a spouse and third party payments not on behalf of a spouse.

3. To distinguish child support payments from alimony.

4. To compute the amount of an excess alimony payment under § 71(f) and describe its tax impact.

5. To determine, on a given set of facts, whether a divorced or separated parent is entitled to claim the dependency exemption for the child.

6. To determine the filing status of a divorced or separated parent.

7. To determine the tax consequences of property transfers between spouses or former spouses.

8. To distinguish between deductible and nondeductible legal expenses related to divorce or separation.

9. To explain the application of § 121(d)(3) in the divorce context.

IV. OVERVIEW

This chapter discusses the tax consequences of divorce and separation. These materials, however, could have been located elsewhere. Section 71 provides for the inclusion of alimony in income, and thus could have been considered among the early chapters in this book when our focus was on the question "What is gross income?" Section 215 allows a deduction for alimony paid, and might have been examined when we studied deductions. Property transfers between spouses and former spouses, incident to divorce, are nontaxable events under the special "nonrecognition" rule of § 1041; the study of such transfers could be postponed until later in this book when we examine in some detail the tax consequences of property dispositions, including other dispositions on which no gain or loss is recognized. Various special rules relating to the personal exemptions for dependent children of divorced parents, and to the proper filing status of parents following separation or divorce, could also be considered at other points. Our decision, however, was to deal with these various issues on a transactional basis, and thus to examine them as a unit. This chapter also follows close on the heels of our study of assignment of income. The timing is not coincidental. Many of the issues raised in this chapter are of the "who-is-the-proper-taxpayer" variety. The tax burden that was borne, prior to divorce, within a single economic unit, must now be allocated between taxpayers whose interests are often adverse. This chapter addresses the rules and rationales involved in the allocation.

As noted in Chapter 34, the Supreme Court in *Windsor v. United States*, 133 S. Ct 2675 (2013), held that Section 3 of the Defense of Marriage Act was unconstitutional because it violated the principles of equal protection. Subsequent to *Windsor*, the Service issued Revenue Ruling 2013-17, 2013-2 C.B. 201, included in the materials. Among other holdings, that ruling provides: "for Federal tax purposes, the terms 'spouse,' 'husband and wife,' 'husband,' and 'wife' include an individual married to a person of the same sex if the individuals are lawfully married under state law, and the term 'marriage' includes such a marriage between individuals of the same sex." In view of *Windsor* and Revenue Ruling 2013-17, the judicial decisions as well as the Code, regulations, and other administrative materials discussed in this chapter should be understood as applying to divorces between same-sex individuals who were lawfully married under state laws.

A. Alimony: General Requirements

In 1917, in the absence of any statute specifically addressing taxation of alimony, the Supreme Court held that alimony payments to a divorced wife did not constitute income. *Gould v. Gould*, 245 U.S. 151 (1917). For the next twenty-five years, alimony remained nontaxable to the recipient and nondeductible to the payor. In 1942, finding that the nondeductibility of alimony, in conjunction with high wartime tax rates, created an excessive tax burden on the payor, Congress reversed the rules and enacted the forerunners of present §§ 71 and 215. Under § 71(a) and § 61(a)(8), amounts received as "alimony or separate maintenance payments" are specifically includable in gross income. Section 215 provides an above-the-line deduction for such payments "actually paid," essentially mandating the cash method for deduction purposes. §§ 62(a)(10), 215(a); Reg. § 1.215-1(a).

In 1984, Congress revised and, in most respects, simplified the rules governing the tax consequences of divorce and separation. Alimony payments remained includable to the recipient and deductible by the payor, but the definition of alimony was changed substantially. The 1984 legislation (hereinafter the 1984 Act) eliminated prior law requirements that alimony payments be "periodic" and made in discharge of a legal obligation of support arising out of the marital or family relationship. Temp. Reg. § 1.71-1T(a), Q&A-3. Under current law, a payment must meet the following requirements to constitute alimony for federal tax purposes:[1]

(1) The payment must be in cash. § 71(b)(1). Payments in the form of property or services do not qualify as alimony, and a controversial matter under prior law — the proper characterization of a property transfer as either alimony or property settlement — is effectively neutralized by the cash-only requirement.

(2) The payment must be received by "or on behalf of" the spouse (or former spouse). § 71(b)(1)(A). Thus, cash payments to third parties may in some circumstances qualify as alimony. Temp. Reg. § 1.71-1T(a), Q&A-6. Consider, for example, whether mortgage payments, made by one spouse with respect to property occupied by the other spouse, may be deductible. See in this regard Revenue Ruling 67-420, in the materials, issued under pre-1984 law.

(3) The payment must be made "under a divorce or separation instrument." § 71(b)(1)(A), (2). When the alimony provisions were first enacted in 1942, the joint return was not part of the Code. To restrict income-splitting between spouses, the only payments qualifying as alimony were those made under a decree of divorce or separate maintenance, or a written instrument incident to such a decree — what is now § 71(b)(2)(A). The joint return, enacted in 1948, eliminated the incentive for income-shifting between spouses, and thus also eliminated the reason for so limiting the availability of the alimony deduction. In 1954, Congress accordingly broadened the alimony definition to encompass payments under a written separation agreement of the parties, whether or not divorce follows, and also payments under a support decree. See § 71(b)(2)(B), (C). The requirement for a "divorce or separation instrument" is thus easily satisfied in the ordinary case. Payments made under an oral agreement, not reduced to writing, however, do not qualify. Thus, in *Ewell v. Commissioner*, T.C. Memo. 1996-253, the Tax Court rejected the taxpayer's argument that an oral agreement with his former spouse constituted part of a written agreement. In addition, the court rejected the taxpayer's contention that "a written list of expenses his former spouse gave him, the letters exchanged by the attorneys, and notations [taxpayer] made on checks he issued, considered together, constitute[d] a written separation agreement." The court stressed "an agreement requires mutual assent or a meeting of the minds." As the court noted, "[l]etters which do not show that there was a meeting of the minds are not a written separation agreement under section 71(b)(2)." In some circumstances, an exchange of letters will amount to a written agreement. For example, in *Leventhal v. Commissioner*, T.C. Memo. 2000-92, letters signed by the attorneys representing each of the parties to a divorce were held to constitute a written separation agreement.

---

[1] Thus, a transfer qualifying as alimony under state law will not necessarily qualify as alimony for federal tax purposes.

(4) The divorce or separation instrument must not designate the cash payment as one that is excludable from the gross income of the recipient and nondeductible to the payor. § 71(b)(1)(B). This provision gives the parties the flexibility to deny § 71 and § 215 treatment to otherwise qualifying payments. See Temp. Reg. § 1.71-1T(b), Q&A-8, for the details of such designation. Absent such a provision, cash payments intended to be part of a property settlement could be taxed as alimony. Of course, even if the payments are in fact in the nature of spousal support, the parties have the ability to designate non-alimony treatment for them.

(5) If the spouses are legally separated under a decree of divorce or separate maintenance, they must not be members of the same household at the time the payment is made. § 71(b)(1)(C). If the parties are not legally separated, payments under a § 71(b)(2)(B) written separation agreement or a § 71(b)(2)(C) support decree may constitute alimony even though the parties are members of the same household. Temp. Reg. § 1.71-1T(b), Q&A-9. Presumably, the "same household" prohibition reflects a congressional concern that spouses who may go through "tax divorces" to avoid the so-called "marriage penalty" (*see Boyter v. Commissioner*, 74 T.C. 989 (1980)), but continue to live together, should be treated the same as never-married individuals living together, and should not be able to engage in income-shifting between themselves.

(6) The payor spouse must have no obligation to make payments for any period after the death of the payee spouse. § 71(b)(1)(D). Alimony is in the nature of spousal support, and, as a result, the alimony inclusion and deduction provisions are generally restricted to support-type payments. Payments continuing beyond the death of the payee spouse smack of property settlement arrangements, for which no deduction is allowed (and no inclusion required). Expressed another way, where the payor spouse is required to transfer a portion of her income to her spouse or former spouse, the transferred income is, in essence, ultimately taxed, through §§ 71 and 215, to the payee spouse, not the payor. By contrast, where the transfer is part of a property division, *i.e.*, a transfer of property as opposed to income, the rationale no longer exists for shifting the tax burden arising out of the payor's income. Sections 71 and 215, of course, do not impose any tracing requirement with respect to cash payments. Payments required to be made for periods after the payee's death are in effect deemed to lack the implicitly-required spousal support element or potential. Section 71(b)(1)(D) is satisfied if such post-death liability is barred pursuant to local law. In determining whether payments satisfy § 71(b)(1)(D), courts have conducted a two-part inquiry. First, courts have looked for an unambiguous condition terminating the payments; that condition may be found either in the plain language of the divorce decree itself or as imposed by operation of state law. Second, where there is no unambiguous termination condition in either the divorce decree or state law, courts have independently evaluated "the language of the decree" as a whole to determine whether the payments in question satisfy § 71(b)(1)(D).[2] If neither part is satisfied, the payments do not constitute alimony. *Hoover*, 102 F.3d at 848; *see also Johanson v.*

---

[2] Where "state family law is ambiguous as to the termination of payments upon the death of the payee, a federal court will not engage in complex, subjective inquiries under state law; rather the court will read the divorce instrument and make its own determination based on the language of the document." *Hoover v. Commissioner*, 102 F.3d 842, 846 (6th Cir. 1996).

Commissioner, 541 F.3d 973 (9th Cir. 2008).

In *Webb v. Commissioner*, T.C. Memo. 1990-540, the Tax Court applied § 71(b)(1)(D) to deny alimony characterization to a cash payment an ex-husband made to his ex-wife pursuant to the terms of their separation agreement. Under that agreement, he specifically agreed to pay her a lump-sum amount of $200,000 and an additional $15,000 to enable her to purchase an automobile. In another part of the agreement entitled "Maintenance," he agreed to pay her $40,000 per year for five years. These maintenance payments were to cease on the death of either party. Simultaneously with the execution of the agreement, he paid her the $215,000 and claimed it was a § 215 alimony deduction; she excluded the payment. The Tax Court concluded the $215,000 payment did not constitute alimony because it created a liability which would not have terminated with the ex-wife's death. According to the court, were she to have died before he paid her the $215,000, her estate could have enforced his obligation to pay, and such an obligation to pay does not comport with the requirements for alimony under § 71. That the payment was actually made simultaneously with the execution of the agreement did not change the result: "To conclude otherwise would cause any cash payment made simultaneously with the issuance of a decree or the execution of an agreement necessarily to be treated as alimony even though the provisions of the decree or agreement clearly reveal that the payments were lump sum payments for purposes other than support or maintenance." T.C. Memo. 1990-540.

While it seems clear from the separation agreement that the $215,000 payment in *Webb* was intended as a property settlement, could Mr. Webb have attained alimony status for that payment by merely adding language to the separation agreement providing that the $215,000 would not be payable after Mrs. Webb's death? Section 71(b)(1)(D), as originally enacted, required that, for a payment under a divorce or separation instrument to be treated as alimony, the divorce or separation instrument had to state that there was no liability to make the payment for any period after the death of the payee spouse. Concerned it had created a trap for the unwary, *i.e.*, an amount would not be treated as alimony and therefore would not deductible if the required statement were not included in the divorce instrument, Congress in 1986 eliminated the requirement that the divorce or separation instruments contain such a statement. Does *Webb*, in effect create a comparable trap?

Stedman v. Commissioner, T.C. Memo 2008-239, presents a situation much more common than that presented in *Webb*. In *Stedman*, the divorce court ordered the taxpayer to pay his ex-spouse's attorney fees which amounted to over $100,000. The court ordered that these fees be paid in monthly installments out of taxpayer's Civil Service Retirement System benefits. Taxpayer claimed a § 215 deduction for the monthly payments he made pursuant to this court order. The Tax Court concluded the payments were not deductible because they did not satisfy the requirement of § 71(b)(1)(D) and thus did not constitute alimony. The court reasoned that, because neither the court order nor applicable state law provided for the termination of the monthly payments upon the death of the ex-spouse, the taxpayer could be required to continue to make the attorney fee payments if his ex-spouse died before those payments had been made in full. Presumably, in view of *Webb*, the court would have reached the same conclusion if the taxpayer had been ordered to pay the attorney fees in a lump sum. As in *Webb*, the taxpayer's ex-spouse might die before the lump sum payment was made. Because, in that circumstance, the attorney fees would be payable even after the death of the ex-spouse, it could not satisfy the requirement of § 71(b)(1)(D).

In *Okerson v. Commissioner*, 123 T.C. 258 (2004), the taxpayer was ordered to pay alimony to his former wife over a period of approximately 10 years. Although the decree provided that the alimony payments would terminate upon her death, it also provided that any remaining installments were to be paid for the education of the children of the parties. Similarly, the taxpayer was ordered to make further alimony payments over several years to his former wife's lawyer, on behalf of his former wife and on account of her legal fees. These alimony payments would also terminate upon her death, but in that event any remaining installments were to be paid directly to the lawyer. The Tax Court held that both sets of alimony payments violated the "substitute payment" provision of § 71(b)(1)(D); that provision requires not only that there be no liability to make payments after the death of the payee spouse, but also that there be no liability to make any other payment as a substitute therefor. The potential obligations that arose in the event of the former wife's death — payments for the children's education and the payments to be made directly to the lawyer — were held to be prohibited substitute payments, and accordingly the payments in the decree designated as alimony failed to qualify as alimony.

B.   Child Support

In addition to satisfying the requirements described above, a cash payment must also avoid classification as child support in order to qualify as alimony. § 71(c). Child support payments, of course, merely reflect pre-existing parental support responsibilities for which the Code grants no deduction, except through the § 151 dependency exemption; the continuing parent-child relationship, unlike the marital relationship, is not terminated by the divorce decree. Thus, a payment "fixed" as child support by the divorce or separation instrument is not alimony. § 71(c)(1). Suppose, however, the parties' written separation agreement merely provides for specified reductions in the payments to the payee spouse as each of their children marries, dies or becomes emancipated. Does such a provision "fix" the amount of the specified reductions as child support? In *Commissioner v. Lester*, 366 U.S. 299 (1961), decided under pre-1984 law, the Supreme Court's answer was "no." A payment that clearly seemed to constitute child support might thus receive alimony treatment. Congress, in the 1984 Act, however, deliberately reversed the *Lester* decision by treating certain reductions in payments as amounts fixed for child support. § 71(c)(2). Thus, for example, where a divorce decree specified that a taxpayer's "alimony" payments of $150 per week to his ex-wife were to "continue to her death, remarriage, or until the youngest child reaches 18 years, whichever first occurs," and thereafter cease, the Tax Court held the payments did not constitute alimony, citing § 71(c)(2)(A). *Fosberg v. Commissioner*, T.C. Memo. 1992-713. The legislative reversal is consistent with the policy decision that spouses should be able to deny alimony status to otherwise qualifying payments — see § 71(b)(1)(B) again — but not create alimony out of payments manifesting too clearly a purpose other than spousal support. *See, e.g.,* § 71(b)(1)(D), (c), (f).

Assume, pursuant to a divorce decree, a taxpayer is required to pay his ex-spouse $1,000 per month child support and $500 per month alimony. During the year, the taxpayer, instead of making the child support and alimony payments totaling $18,000 (*i.e.*, $12,000 for child support and $6,000 for alimony), pays his ex-spouse only $13,000. May the taxpayer claim that he made full payment of the $6,000 alimony for the year and is therefore entitled to a $6,000 deduction under § 215? The answer is "No." Section 71(c)(3) will require that, for tax purposes, the $13,000 first be allocated to child support and only the remainder to alimony. The taxpayer, therefore, will only be able to claim payment of $1,000 of alimony for the year. *See Haubrich v. Commissioner*, T.C. Memo 2008-299.

The temporary regulations issued under § 71(c)(2)(B) identify limited specific circumstances under which reductions in payments can "clearly be associated" with a contingency related to a child, and thus constitute child support rather than alimony. For example, under Temp. Reg. § 1.71-1T(c), Q&A-18, payments otherwise qualifying as alimony are presumed to constitute child support if they are reduced within 6 months of the child turning 18, 21, or the local age of majority. In *Shepherd v. Commissioner*, T.C. Memo 2000-174, the taxpayer sought to treat certain "alimony payments" as child support. The taxpayer and her ex-husband, as part of a divorce settlement, agreed the ex-husband would pay taxpayer alimony for 10 years. As it turned out, the agreed-upon termination date for the alimony payments would occur within six months of the parties' younger child turning 18. Evidence suggested the taxpayer was aware of the tax significance of the agreed-upon termination date, but no evidence indicated the payor ex-husband was aware of it. The Tax Court held that the fixing of the termination date within six months of the younger child's 18th birthday was merely a coincidence; it was determined independently of the birthday; and the presumption that the amount of the reduction constituted child support was thus overcome.

C.   Excess Front-Loading

Cash payments which are not fixed as child support and which comply with the rules previously discussed thus constitute alimony, includable in the payee's income and deductible to the payor. These rules left open the possibility that several years' worth of alimony might be compressed into a single year or two, in order to obtain several years' tax deductions all at once. The rules also left open the prospect that cash payments could be taxed as alimony even when they were in substance part of a property settlement, *i.e.*, part of a division of marital assets, and bore no relationship to spousal support. (The spouses could elect non-alimony treatment under § 71(b)(1)(B) for such payments, but presumably would not do so where alimony treatment would result in a lower combined tax liability.) As a practical matter, property settlements tend to be characterized by relatively large payments over a relatively short period of time — perhaps simply a single lump-sum payment. To narrow these payment manipulations somewhat, the drafters of the 1984 Act created the excess front-loading rules of § 71(f) as part of their attempt "to define alimony in a way that would conform to general notions of what type of payments constitute alimony as distinguished from property settlements and to prevent the deduction of large, one-time lump-sum property settlements." General Explanation of the Revenue Provisions of the Tax Reform Act of 1984, Jt. Comm.

on Taxation, p. 714. As originally enacted, § 71(f) was particularly complex, and considerably at odds with the overall simplification the 1984 Act brought to the divorce tax area; many critics suggested that the potential abuse it curtailed was not worth the complexity. Congress in 1986 did not repeal the provision, but modified it considerably.

Section 71(f) is basically a recapture provision. Payments characterized as "excess alimony payments," having been included by the payee and deducted by the payor in a prior year, are "recaptured" in the subsequent year. The tax treatment is then reversed: the excess amount is deductible by the payee and includable by the payor. The payor, who is the real target of § 71(f), is forced to "give back" the excess deduction — excess in the sense that, retroactively, § 71(f) determines the prior alimony treatment was unwarranted at least in part. Rather than reopen and adjust the tax returns of the payor and payee for the year of payment, however, the give-back occurs in the year the determination of the excess is made. (The tax benefit rule operates in somewhat similar fashion; the payor spouse is giving back in a later year the tax benefit of a prior year. The payee spouse, by contrast, receives a later-year deduction on account of the prior-year excess included in income.)

Under § 71(f), recapture of excess alimony payments can take place in one year only — the "3rd post-separation year," a term defined in § 71(f)(6). Recapture cannot occur in any other year. § 71(f)(1). "Excess alimony payments," if any, are determined based on alimony payments in three years — the 1st, 2nd, and 3rd post-separation years. In other words, based on the alimony paid in these three years, it may be determined in year three that excess alimony was paid in years one and two. If so, that excess is recaptured in year three. The Joint Committee on Taxation summarized the rule as follows:

> The [1986] Act revises the front-loading alimony rules of Section 71(f) in order to better conform to the current trend of state divorce law to require short term support payments on a theory of "rehabilitative alimony." Under the Act, if the alimony payments in the first year exceed the average payments in the second and third year by more than $15,000, the excess amounts are recaptured in the third year by requiring the payor to include the excess in income and allowing the payee who previously included the alimony in income a deduction for that amount in computing adjusted gross income. A similar rule applies to the extent the payments in the second exceed the payments in the third year by more than $15,000. This rule is intended to prevent persons whose divorce occurs near the end of the year from making a deductible property settlement in the beginning of the next year. Recapture is not required if either party dies or if the payee spouse remarries by the end of the calendar year which is two years after the payments began and payments cease by reason of that event. Also the rule does not apply to temporary support payments (described in sec. 71(b)(2)(C)) or to payments which fluctuate as a result of a continuing liability to pay, for at least three years, a fixed portion or portions of income from the earnings of a business, property or services. The portions of the payor's income which are payable to the payee spouse under this exception

may vary as the payor's income varies, so long as the percentages are themselves fixed in the instrument.

Thus, for example, if the payor makes alimony payments of $50,000 in the first year and no payments in the second or third year, $35,000 will be recaptured (assuming none of the exceptions apply). If instead the payments are $50,000 in the first year, $20,000 in the second year and nothing in the third year, the recapture amount will consist of $5,000 from the second year (the excess over $15,000) plus $27,500 for the first year (the excess of $50,000 over the sum of $15,000 plus $7,500). (The $7,500 is the average payments for years two and three after reducing the payments by the $5,000 recaptured from year two.)

Explanation to the Technical Corrections Provisions of the Tax Reform Act of 1986, Jt. Comm. on Taxation, pp. 118–19.

D. Alimony Trusts

We shall note § 682 only in passing. Suppose a divorced or separated spouse (the husband, let us assume) establishes and funds a trust, the income from which is to be paid to the other spouse. Section 682 taxes to the wife, the trust beneficiary, the income from this so-called alimony trust, income which would otherwise be taxable to the husband under general rules relating to taxation of trust income. Under § 215(d), no deduction is allowed to the husband on account of the trust income taxed to the wife, an appropriate denial since the income in question was never taxable to the husband.

E. Dependency Exemption

In the case of a child of divorced or separated parents, the child will ordinarily be a dependent of the custodial parent, as a "qualifying child" of that parent, or in other words, the parent having custody of the child for the greater part of the year will ordinarily be entitled to the dependency exemption for the child. § 152(a)(1), (c)(1)(B), (c)(4)(B).[3] *See also* Reg. § 1.152-4(a). In 2008 the Treasury finalized regulations providing detailed guidance regarding determination of the "custodial parent" and "noncustodial parent." Thus, Reg. § 1.152-4(d) provides that, in general, the "custodial parent is the parent with whom the child resides for the greater number of nights during the calendar year, and the *noncustodial parent* is the parent who is not the custodial parent. . . . [A] child resides with a parent for a night if the child sleeps (i) at the residence of that parent (whether or not the parent is present); or (ii) in the company of the parent, when the child does not sleep at a parent's residence (for example, the parent and child are on vacation together)." The regulations address a number of special circumstances, including situations where a parent works at night. Reg. § 1.152-4(d)(5). The regulations also provide that, if a child is in the custody of one or both parents for more than one-half of the calendar year, and the child resides with each parent an equal number of nights during the calendar year, the parent "with the higher adjusted gross

---

[3] A "qualifying child" must also meet certain age limits, and must not have provided over one-half of his or her own support for the year. § 152(b)(1)(C), (D), (b)(3).

income for the calendar year is treated as the custodial parent." Reg. § 1.152-4(d)(4).

Prior to the amendment of § 152 in 1984, there was a special rule under which the noncustodial parent could be entitled to the exemption if he or she provided, or was treated as providing, more support to the child than was provided by the custodial parent. As a result of this special rule, it was not uncommon that both the custodial and noncustodial parent, based on support provided, claimed the dependency exemption. Prior law thus could foster uncertainty, put each parent to the test of measuring and documenting the support provided, and involve the Service in what was essentially a parental dispute. The aim of the 1984 amendments to § 152 was to put an end to these uncertainties and disputes.

Under the current version of § 152, the custodial parent receives the exemption even though the noncustodial parent may have provided more support than the custodial parent. The noncustodial parent is ordinarily allowed the exemption only if the custodial parent has released the claim to the exemption in writing. § 152(e)(2). The release can be permanent or cover one or more years, and a copy must be attached to the noncustodial parent's tax return for each year the exemption is sought. Reg. § 1.152-4(b).[4] Certain threshold requirements must be met for the release to be effective: the parents must be divorced or separated under a decree or written separation agreement, or live apart for the last six months of the year; they must provide more than half of the child's support, and they must have custody of the child for over half the year. § 152(e)(1). But as long as those requirements are met, the dependency exemption may thus be allocated to the noncustodial parent by agreement of the parents, which provides some additional tax flexibility to them. Other exceptions to the general rule awarding the dependency exemption to the custodial parent are provided for "multiple support agreements" and certain pre-1985 decrees or agreements. § 152(e)(3), (5). As a practical matter, of course, there is usually no question as to parental entitlement to the exemption, and § 152 provides the rules for determining which parent can claim it. It is, however, essential that the written declaration be obtained. A provision in the divorce decree awarding the dependency exemption to the noncustodial parent will not suffice. See, for example, *Curello v. Commissioner*, T.C. Summ. Op. 2005-23, noting that "State courts by their decisions cannot determine issues of Federal tax law," and the "language in a divorce decree purportedly giving a taxpayer the right to an exemption does not entitle the taxpayer to the exemption if the signature requirement of § 152(e) is not met."

In another case, the custodial parent had agreed to sign a document indicating she would not claim a child as a dependent provided the noncustodial parent paid all required child support. Nonetheless, where the custodial parent failed to sign such a document for the year in question, the Tax Court held the noncustodial parent was not entitled to claim a dependency exemption even though he was current in his child support payments. According to the court, the custodial parent's release of her claim must be unconditional to satisfy the statutory requirement; a release conditioned on the noncustodial parent's remaining current

---

[4] The same procedures apply for the custodial parent to release the claim to the child tax credit. § 24(a), (c)(1).

with child support payments is not sufficient. *Armstrong v. Commissioner*, 139 T.C. 468 (2012). Affirming the Tax Court, the Eighth Circuit "sympathize[d] with noncustodial parents who are entitled to receive documents necessary to support their claims for federal dependency exemptions and child tax credits and their former spouses violate contractual or court-ordered obligations to provide those documents. But Congress in the 1984 amendment to § 152(e)(2) precluded attempts to remedy such wrongs in federal income tax proceedings." *Armstrong v. Commissioner* 745 F.3d 890 (8th Cir. 2014).

F.   Filing Status

The filing status of divorced or separated parents has tax significance. For example, compare the tax rates for heads of household and unmarried individuals (other than surviving spouses and heads of household). § 1(b), (c). Review the definition of head of household under § 2(b), including the requirement that the individual claiming it be unmarried, not a surviving spouse, and maintain a home which satisfies a principal-place-of-abode test for a qualifying child of the individual or for certain other dependents or relatives. A custodial parent who has head of household status does not lose it, and the noncustodial parent does not achieve it, by virtue of the release of the claim to the dependency exemption under § 152(e). (Note also that a custodial parent who releases the claim may also remain eligible for the child and dependent care credit and earned income credit. §§ 21(e)(5), 32(c)(1)(A).) As to whether an individual is "not married" at the close of the tax year, as required for head of household purposes, see the provisions relating to marital status in §§ 2(b)(2), 2(c) and 7703(b).

G.   Property Transfers

In *United States v. Davis*, 370 U.S. 65 (1962), the Supreme Court held that a taxpayer's transfer of his appreciated property to his former wife, pursuant to their property settlement agreement, in return for her release of her marital rights, produced recognized taxable gain to the transferor-husband. The transferee-wife, in turn, took a fair market value basis in the property. (Moreover, subsequent to *Davis*, the Service ruled that the release of marital rights in return for property resulted in no realized gain or loss to the releasing spouse. Rev. Rul. 67-221, 1967-2 C.B. 63.)

In one sense, the *Davis* result was unremarkable. The transfer of appreciated property in satisfaction of an obligation ordinarily is a taxable event to the transferor, and *Davis* could be seen as an application of that principle. However, the *Davis* rule had its critics. For one thing, the tax treatment of the transferor often appeared harsh; the gain he or she was charged with seemed to be phantom gain. The tax consequences of the divorce, moreover, could vary according to the form in which the property was owned. For example, in contrast to the *Davis* result when appreciated property owned by one spouse was transferred to the other, no taxable gain resulted where the parties equally divided community property, or where jointly-held property was partitioned.

In addition, the *Davis* rule presented both a trap for taxpayers unaware of the tax consequence of their transfers, and also an enforcement problem for the government — transferors with recognized gain might overlook or decline to report the gain, where transferees could properly take a fair market value basis in the transferred property. The predictable consequences were confusion and litigation, followed by efforts by a number of states to tailor their divorce and property laws so as to make property transfers on divorce nontaxable. *See generally* H.R. Rep. 98-432, 98th Cong., 2d Sess., p. 1491. Essentially, divorce was simply regarded by many as an inappropriate occasion to tax the built-up gain in property that was, after all, not being transferred outside the two-spouse community.

One of the important changes wrought by the 1984 Act, therefore, was the legislative reversal of *Davis* by the enactment of § 1041. Under § 1041, no gain or loss is recognized on a property transfer between spouses or incident to divorce. The transfer instead is treated as a gift, with the transferee taking the transferor's basis. § 1041(a), (b); Temp. Treas. Reg. § 1.1041-1T(d), Q&A-10, -11. The significance of § 1041 thus extends well beyond the divorce tax area. It applies not only to transfers "incident to divorce" but to any transfer of property between spouses, whether in the form of a gift, or a sale or exchange at arm's length. Temp. Reg. § 1.1041-1T(a), Q&A-2. *See also* § 1015(e). (Special rules apply where the transferee spouse is a nonresident alien, or where there is a transfer in trust of property with liabilities in excess of basis. § 1041(d), (e).) Section 1041 reflects a Congressional policy that transfers between spouses are, in effect, transfers within a single economic unit, and accordingly, should not be taxed; this policy is then extended to encompass transfers incident to divorce as well, as part of an effort to keep tax laws "as unintrusive as possible with respect to relations between spouses." H.R. Rep. 98-432, 98th Cong., 2d Sess., p. 1491–2. Notwithstanding the effort, the tax laws, of course, do intrude on relations between divorcing spouses. Property transfers incident to divorce may be nontaxable, but they carry with them significant tax consequences. Since neither gain nor loss is recognized, and the transferor's basis carries over to the transferee, the parties effectively determine who bears the *future* tax burden in appreciated property, and who receives the *future* tax benefit on property with a value less than its basis, when they decide how their separately- owned and jointly-owned property is divided. For example, two items of property may each be worth $1,000, but if one has a basis of $100 and the other a basis of $2,000, their "values" are potentially quite different. Consider another example, drawn from the temporary regulations, involving liabilities: Taxpayer owns property with a basis of $1,000 and a value of $10,000. In contemplation of divorce, Taxpayer borrows $5,000, using the property as security. Incident to divorce, Taxpayer transfers the property to Spouse subject to the liability. Even though the liability relief exceeds Taxpayer's basis, Taxpayer recognizes no gain on the transfer under § 1041(a), and Spouse takes a basis in the property of only $1,000 under § 1041(b). Temp. Reg. § 1.1041-1T(d), Q&A-12.

Note that § 1041(c) defines transfers "incident to divorce" as those occurring within one year of the cessation of the marriage and those "related to the cessation of the marriage." The temporary regulations define transfers related to the cessation of the marriage as generally those provided for in the divorce or separation instrument and occurring within six years of the cessation of the marriage. A transfer that does not fall within this safe harbor is presumed not related to the cessation of the marriage, but the presumption may be rebutted in limited circumstances, such as where legal impediments prevented an earlier transfer that would have satisfied the requisite time period. Temp. Reg. § 1.1041-1T(b), Q&A-7.

The Temporary Regulations applying and interpreting § 1041 provide some helpful elaboration on the statute, and should be read with care. The statute, broad as it is, does have its limits. For example, it encompasses property transfers, but not transfers of services. Temp. Reg. § 1.1041-1T(a), Q&A-4.

Historically, there has been tension between § 1041 and assignment of income principles. For example, in Revenue Ruling 87-112, 1987-2 C.B. 207, the Service stated: "Although section 1041(a) . . . shields from recognition gain that would ordinarily be recognized on a sale or exchange of property, it does not shield from recognition income that is ordinarily recognized upon the assignment of that income to another taxpayer." In that ruling, the Service held that assignment of income principles combined with the specific rule of Reg. § 1.454-1(a) [dealing with dispositions of interest deferred obligations] required the deferred, accrued interest on United States savings bonds to be included in the transferor's gross income in the taxable year in which he transferred the bonds to his former spouse in a transfer described in § 1041. (As briefly noted below, Revenue Ruling 2002-22, included in the materials, while reaffirming the result in Revenue Ruling 87-112 on the basis of § 454, has clarified that ruling by eliminating references to assignment of income principles.) Compare *Kochansky v. Commissioner*, 92 F.3d 957 (9th Cir. 1996), discussed in Chapter 34.

Balding v. Commissioner, 98 T.C. 368 (1992), presents another example of the tension between § 1041 and assignment of income principles. In that case, subsequent to divorce, the taxpayer asserted a claim, based on California law, to a community property share of her ex-husband's military retirement pay. The parties reached an agreement under which taxpayer relinquished her claim to the retirement pay in return for three annual cash payments from her ex-husband. The Service did not argue that the payments were alimony nor did it argue that the payments were not "incident to divorce." Instead, the Service characterized the taxpayer's release of her community property share as an anticipatory assignment of income under which the annual payments were taxable to her as received. Agreeing such analysis would ordinarily be appropriate, the Tax Court found that § 1041 mandated a different result under the circumstances. The court held "whether we view petitioner's release as constituting (or equivalent to) a release of property, or simply a release of marital rights," the transaction was governed by § 1041, and the amounts received from the ex-husband were therefore nontaxable gifts under §§ 1041 and 102. *Balding*, at 373.[5] Revenue Ruling 2002-22, included in the materials, has largely resolved the tension between § 1041 and assignment of

---

[5] Footnote 8 of the opinion, interestingly, at least raised the possibility that the taxpayer's victory could be a pyrrhic one: "We do not here deal with the tax consequences to petitioner of retirement payments made by the Government on account of [her ex-husband's] retirement. . . . Accordingly, we have no occasion to consider whether the assignment of income doctrine would require petitioner's share of those retirement benefits to be taken into petitioner's income as paid by the Government to [her ex-husband] notwithstanding petitioner's lack of entitlement to such payments. . . . " *Balding*, at 373. Who should be taxed when the payments are made to the ex-husband?

income principles. Specifically, the ruling concludes that application of the assignment of income doctrine is generally inappropriate in the context of divorce.

The temporary regulations under § 1041 also provide that, in some circumstances, a transfer of property "on behalf of a spouse" to a third party may qualify under § 1041. The regulation identifies qualifying transfers to third parties as those where the transfer to a third party is required by the divorce or separation instrument or is made pursuant to written request of (or written consent or ratification by) the non-transferring spouse. *See* § 1.1041-1T(c), Q&A-9. When the regulation applies, the transfer of property on behalf of a spouse is treated as (1) a § 1041 transfer from the transferring spouse to the non-transferring spouse, followed by (2) a transfer not within § 1041 by the nontransferring spouse to the third party.

In addition, regulations under § 1041 address property transfers in the specialized context of corporate redemptions of stock. *See* Reg. § 1.1041-2. Under settled corporate tax law, if Shareholder A has a "primary and unconditional" obligation to purchase the stock of Shareholder B, and if in lieu of such purchase, the corporation redeems the stock of Shareholder B, then the corporation's redemption of B's stock will be treated as a "constructive distribution" — that is, typically a taxable dividend — to Shareholder A.[6] Suppose, however, Shareholder A and Shareholder B are husband and wife and own all of the stock of the corporation in question. Incident to their divorce, the corporation redeems the stock of Shareholder B. If the form of the transaction is respected, the redemption is a taxable event for Shareholder B. By contrast, if the corporation's redemption of the stock tendered by Shareholder B is treated as a transfer "on behalf of" Shareholder A, then Shareholder B will be deemed to have transferred the stock to Shareholder A in a nontaxable § 1041 transfer, and it will be Shareholder A who has a taxable event by way of a "constructive distribution" from the corporation. Reg. § 1.1041-2(a)(2), (b)(2). In turn, any property received by B from the corporation in respect of the redeemed stock will be deemed transferred by the corporation to A in redemption of A's stock, and then transferred from A to B. *Id.* The question that had arisen in several cases — and had produced inconsistent answers — was what standard should be applied to determine whether Shareholder B's transfer of stock to the corporation in redemption should be treated as a transfer on behalf of Shareholder A. The regulations essentially apply the "primary and unconditional obligation" standard ("the applicable tax law") from corporate tax law to resolve the issue; that is, if the corporation's redemption of Shareholder B's stock satisfies a primary and unconditional obligation of Shareholder A to purchase the stock from Shareholder B, then Shareholder B will be treated as engaging in a nontaxable § 1041 exchange, and Shareholder A will have a constructive distribution from the corporation. Indeed, the regulations, consistent with the policy of providing flexibility in the structuring of property transfers during marriage and incident to divorce, include a special rule allowing the parties by means of a written agreement or in the divorce or separation instrument, to designate whether the redemption will be taxable to the redeeming shareholder-spouse or the nonredeeming shareholder-spouse. In effect, the parties

---

[6] *See, e.g.*, Rev. Rul. 69-608, 1969-2 C.B. 42; Reg. § 1.1041-2(a)(2).

by agreement or decree may elect to apply or not apply the rule drawn from corporate tax law. But in the absence of agreement or decree, the corporate tax law standard of "primary and unconditional obligation" will govern. Reg. § 1.1041-2(c).

H. Special Rules Regarding Personal Residence — Section 121

As discussed in detail in Chapter 6, § 121 allows a taxpayer to exclude up to $250,000 of gain on the sale of a principal residence. A married couple filing a joint return may exclude up to $500,000 of gain. To qualify for the exclusion, a taxpayer, during the five year period ending on the date of the sale or exchange, must have owned and used the property as the taxpayer's principal residence for periods aggregating at least two years. Where spouses file a joint return and seek to take advantage of the $500,000 exclusion, only one spouse must meet the ownership requirement; both spouses, however, must meet the use requirement.

In enacting § 121, Congress provided two special rules applicable to circumstances commonly encountered in divorces. First, Congress provided that, where property is transferred to an individual in a transaction qualifying under § 1041, the period of ownership of that individual for purposes of § 121 will include the period the transferor owned the property. § 121(d)(3)(A). Consider the following example:

> **Example:** Assume A and B divorce and agree that, as part of their property settlement, A will transfer to B the title to the home in which they had lived for a number of years. Assume title to the home was in A's name alone. Assume B sells the home within one year of the divorce. But for § 121(d)(3)(A), B would not have owned the home long enough to satisfy the two year ownership requirement of § 121. Given § 121(d)(3)(A), however, B will be entitled to exclude up to $250,000 of gain from the sale so long as B satisfies the other requirements of § 121, including the use requirement. *See* Reg. § 1.121-4(b)(1).

The second special rule is specifically applicable to situations where a taxpayer continues to have an ownership interest in a residence but does not live in the residence because, pursuant to a divorce or separation instrument, the taxpayer's spouse or former spouse is granted the use of the residence. Under these circumstances, the taxpayer will be treated as using the residence while the residence is used by the taxpayer's spouse or former spouse. Read § 121(d)(3)(B) and Reg. § 1.121-4(b)(2) carefully and then consider the following example.

> **Example:** Assume X and Y divorce and, pursuant to their divorce decree, Y is entitled to live in the home (owned as tenants in common by X and Y) until their youngest child attains the age of 18. Assume six years later their youngest child attains the age of 18 and that Y used the home as Y's principal residence throughout the six year period. Consistent with the terms of the divorce decree, X and Y then sell the home and divide the proceeds. Given § 121(d)(3)(B), X will be deemed to have satisfied the use requirement of § 121. Assuming X meets all of the other requirements of

§ 121, X will be entitled to claim an exclusion of up to $250,000 for the gain attributable to X's share of the residence.

I. Legal Expenses

Review the case of *United States v. Gilmore*, reprinted in the materials, and review the brief discussion on deductibility of legal expenses in Chapter 19. Under the origin-of-the-claim test, legal expenses in connection with a divorce will generally be nondeductible; however, subject to the 2% floor rule of § 67, the cost of tax planning advice is generally regarded as deductible, as are the legal expenses attributable to amounts includable in income as alimony. *See* Reg. § 1.262-1(b)(7).

REVENUE RULING 2002-22
2002-1 C.B. 849

[Authors' Note: This Ruling addresses the application of the assignment of income doctrine to a taxpayer's transfer of nonstatutory stock options and nonqualified deferred compensation to the taxpayer's former spouse incident to divorce. Specifically, the Ruling considers whether the taxpayer is taxable on the transfer under assignment of income principles or, instead, whether the transfer would be governed by § 1041, and the taxpayer's former spouse would be required to include an amount in gross income when the former spouse exercised the stock options or when the deferred compensation was paid or made available to her. The Ruling concludes § 1041 is applicable and therefore the taxpayer does not have any income when the stock options and deferred compensation are transferred. Taxpayer's former spouse would instead be taxable upon the exercise of the stock options or receipt of the deferred compensation. We include only those parts of the Ruling related to the relationship between § 1041 and the assignment of income doctrine.]

LAW AND ANALYSIS

Section 1041 and the assignment of income doctrine

Section 1041 was enacted in part to reverse the effect of the Supreme Court's decision in *United States v. Davis*, 370 U.S. 65 (1962), which held that the transfer of appreciated property to a spouse (or former spouse) in exchange for the release of marital claims was a taxable event resulting in the recognition of gain or loss to the transferor. Section 1041 was intended to "make the tax laws as unintrusive as possible with respect to relations between spouses" and to provide "uniform Federal income tax consequences" for transfers of property between spouses incident to divorce, "notwithstanding that the property may be subject to differing state property laws." Congress thus intended that § 1041 would eliminate differing federal tax treatment of property transfers and divisions between divorcing taxpayers who reside in community property states and those who reside in non-community property states.

The term "property" is not defined in § 1041. However, there is no indication that Congress intended "property" to have a restricted meaning under § 1041. To the contrary, Congress indicated that § 1041 should apply broadly to transfers of many types of property, including those that involve a right to receive ordinary income that has accrued in an economic sense (such as interests in trusts and annuities). Accordingly, stock options and unfunded deferred compensation rights may constitute property within the meaning of § 1041.

Although § 1041 provides nonrecognition treatment to transfers between spouses and former spouses, whether income derived from the transferred property and paid to the transferee is taxed to the transferor or the transferee depends upon the applicability of the assignment of income doctrine. As first enunciated in *Lucas v. Earl*, 281 U.S. 111 (1930), the assignment of income doctrine provides that income is ordinarily taxed to the person who earns it, and that the incidence of income taxation may not be shifted by anticipatory assignments. However, the courts and the Service have long recognized that the assignment of income doctrine does not apply to every transfer of future income rights. *Hempt Bros., Inc. v. United States*, 490 F.2d 1172 (3d Cir. 1974), *cert. denied*, 419 U.S. 826 (1974). . . . Moreover, in cases arising before the effective date of § 1041, a number of courts had concluded that transfers of income rights between divorcing spouses were not voluntary assignments within the scope of the assignment of income doctrine. *See Meisner v. United States*, 133 F.3d 654 (8th Cir. 1998). . . .

In *Hempt Bros., Inc. v. United States*, the court concluded that the assignment of income doctrine should not apply to the transfer of accounts receivable by a cash basis partnership to a controlled corporation in a transaction described in § 351(a), where there was a valid business purpose for the transfer of the accounts receivable together with the other assets and liabilities of the partnership to effect the incorporation of an ongoing business. The court reasoned that application of the assignment of income doctrine to tax the transferor in such circumstances would frustrate the Congressional intent reflected in the nonrecognition rule of § 351(a). Accordingly, the transferee, not the transferor, was taxed as it received payment of the receivables. . . .

Similarly, applying the assignment of income doctrine in divorce cases to tax the transferor spouse when the transferee spouse ultimately receives income from the property transferred in the divorce would frustrate the purpose of § 1041 with respect to divorcing spouses. That tax treatment would impose substantial burdens on marital property settlements involving such property and thwart the purpose of allowing divorcing spouses to sever their ownership interests in property with as little tax intrusion as possible. Further, there is no indication that Congress intended § 1041 to alter the principle established in the pre-1041 cases such as *Meisner* that the application of the assignment of income doctrine generally is inappropriate in the context of divorce. . . .

Although a transfer of nonstatutory stock options in connection with a marital property settlement may, as a factual matter, involve an arm's length exchange for money, property, or other valuable consideration, it would contravene the gift treatment prescribed by § 1041 to include the value of the consideration in the transferor's income. . . . Accordingly, the transfer of nonstatutory stock options between divorcing spouses is entitled to nonrecognition treatment under § 1041.

When the transferee exercises the stock options, the transferee rather than the transferor realizes gross income to the extent determined by § 83(a). Since § 1041 was intended to eliminate differing federal tax treatment for property transferred or divided between spouses in connection with divorce in community property states and in non-community property states, § 83(a) is properly applied in the same manner in both contexts. Where compensation rights are earned through the performance of services by one spouse in a community property state, the portion of the compensation treated as owned by the non-earning spouse under state law is treated as the gross income of the non-earning spouse for federal income tax purposes. *Poe v. Seaborn*, 282 U.S. 101 (1930). Thus, even though the non-employee spouse in a non-community property state may not have state law ownership rights in nonstatutory stock options at the time of grant, § 1041 requires that the ownership rights acquired by such a spouse in a marital property settlement be given the same federal income tax effect as the ownership rights of a non-employee spouse in a community property state. Accordingly, upon the subsequent exercise of the nonstatutory stock options, the property transferred to the non-employee spouse has the same character and is includible in the gross income of the non-employee spouse under § 83(a) to the same extent as if the non-employee spouse were the person who actually performed the services.

CONCLUSION

Under the present facts, the interests in nonstatutory stock options and nonqualified deferred compensation . . . are property within the meaning of § 1041. Section 1041 confers nonrecognition treatment on any gain that [the taxpayer] might otherwise realize when taxpayer transfers these interests to [his former spouse]. . . . Further, the assignment of income doctrine does not apply to these transfers. Therefore, the taxpayer is not required to include in gross income any income resulting from [his former spouse's] exercise of the stock options or the [subsequent] payment of deferred compensation to [her]. When the former spouse exercises the stock options, [she] must include in income an amount determined under § 83(a) as if [she] were the person who performed the services. In addition, [she] must include the amount realized from payments of deferred compensation in income in the year such payments are paid or made available to her. The same conclusions would apply if [the taxpayer and his former spouse] resided in a community property state and all or some of these income rights constituted community property that was divided between [them] as part of their divorce.

This ruling does not apply to transfers of property between spouses other than in connection with divorce. This ruling also does not apply to . . . the extent that the transferor's rights to such income are subject to substantial contingencies at the time of the transfer. *See Kochansky v. Commissioner*, 92 F.3d 957 (9th Cir. 1996). . . .

UNITED STATES v. GILMORE
United States Supreme Court
372 U.S. 39 (1963)

MR. JUSTICE HARLAN delivered the opinion of the Court.

In 1955 the California Supreme Court confirmed the award to the respondent taxpayer of a decree of absolute divorce, without alimony, against his wife Dixie Gilmore. 45 Cal. 2d 142, 287 P.2d 769. The case before us involves the deductibility for federal income tax purposes of that part of the husband's legal expense incurred in such proceedings as is attributable to his successful resistance of his wife's claims to certain of his assets asserted by her to be community property under California law.

At the time of the divorce proceedings, instituted by the wife but in which the husband also cross-claimed for divorce, respondent's property consisted primarily of controlling stock interests in three corporations, each of which was a franchised General Motors automobile dealer. As president and principal managing officer of the three corporations, he received salaries from them aggregating about $66,800 annually, and in recent years his total annual dividends had averaged about $83,000. His total annual income derived from the corporations was thus approximately $150,000. His income from other sources was negligible.

As found by the Court of Claims, the husband's overriding concern in the divorce litigation was to protect these assets against the claims of his wife.

The respondent wished to defeat those claims for two important reasons. *First*, the loss of his controlling stock interests, particularly in the event of their transfer in substantial part to his hostile wife, might well cost him the loss of his corporate positions, his principal means of livelihood. *Second*, there was also danger that if he were found guilty of his wife's sensational and reputation-damaging charges of marital infidelity, General Motors Corporation might find it expedient to exercise its right to cancel these dealer franchises.

The end result of this bitterly fought divorce case was a complete victory for the husband. He, not the wife, was granted a divorce on his cross-claim; the wife's community property claims were denied in their entirety; and she was held entitled to no alimony.

Respondent's legal expenses in connection with this litigation amounted to $32,537.15 in 1953 and $8,074.21 in 1954 — a total of $40,611.36 for the two taxable years in question. The Commissioner of Internal Revenue found all of these expenditures "personal" or "family" expenses and as such none of them deductible. In the ensuing refund suit, however, the Court of Claims held that 80% of such expense (some $32,500) was attributable to respondent's defense against his wife's community property claims respecting his stockholdings and hence deductible as an expense "incurred . . . for the . . . conservation . . . of property held for the production of income." In so holding the Court of Claims stated:

> Of course it is true that in every divorce case a certain amount of the
> legal expenses are incurred for the purpose of obtaining the divorce and a

ccrtain amount are incurred in an effort to conserve the estate and are not necessarily deductible under section [212], but when the facts of a particular case clearly indicate [as here] that the property, around which the controversy evolves, is held for the production of income and without this property the litigant might be denied not only the property itself but the means of earning a livelihood, then it must come under the provisions of section [212]. . . . The only question then is the allocation of the expenses to this phase of the proceedings.

290 F.2d, at 947. The Government does not question the amount or formula for the expense allocation made by the Court of Claims. Its sole contention here is that the court below misconceived the test governing Section [212] deductions, in that the deductibility of these expenses turns, so it is argued, not upon the *consequences* to respondent of a failure to defeat his wife's community property claims but upon the *origin* and *nature* of the claims themselves. So viewing Dixie Gilmore's claims, whether relating to the existence or division of community property, it is contended that the expense of resisting them must be deemed nondeductible "personal" or "family" expense, not deductible expense. For reasons given hereafter we think the Government's position is sound and that it must be sustained.

I.

For income tax purposes Congress has seen fit to regard an individual as having two personalities: "one is [as] a seeker after profit who can deduct the expenses incurred in that search; the other is [as] a creature satisfying his needs as a human and those of his family but who cannot deduct such consumption and related expenditures."

A basic restriction upon the availability of a Section [162] deduction is that the expense item involved must be one that has a business origin. [I]t is clear that the "[p]ersonal . . . or family expenses" restriction of Section [262] must impose the same limitation upon the reach of Section [212] — in other words that the only kind of expenses deductible under Section [212] are those that relate to a "business," that is, profit-seeking, purpose. The pivotal issue in this case then becomes: was this part of respondent's litigation costs a "business" rather than a "personal" or "family" expense?

The answer to this question has already been indicated in prior cases. In *Lykes v. United States*, 343 U.S. 118, the Court rejected the contention that legal expenses incurred in contesting the assessment of a gift tax liability were deductible. The taxpayer argued that if he had been required to pay the original deficiency he would have been forced to liquidate his stockholdings, which were his main source of income, and that his legal expenses were therefore incurred in the "conservation" of income-producing property and hence deductible under [Section 212]. The Court first noted that the "deductibility [of the expenses] turns wholly upon the nature of the activities to which they relate" (343 U.S. at 123) and then stated:

Legal expenses do not become deductible merely because they are paid for services which relieve a taxpayer of a liability. That argument would carry us too far. It would mean that the expense of defending almost any claim would be deductible by a taxpayer on the ground that such defense was made to help him keep clear of liens whatever income-producing property he might have. For example, it suggests that the expense of defending an action based upon personal injuries caused by a taxpayer's negligence while driving an automobile for pleasure should be deductible. Section [212] never has been so interpreted by us. . . .

While the threatened deficiency assessment . . . added urgency to petitioner's resistance of it, neither its size nor its urgency determined its character. It related to the tax payable on petitioner's gifts. . . . The expense of contesting the amount of the deficiency was thus at all times attributable to the gifts, as such, and accordingly was not deductible.

If, as suggested, the relative size of each claim, in proportion to the income-producing resources of a defendant, were to be a touchstone of the deductibility of the expense of resisting the claim, substantial uncertainty and inequity would inhere in the rule. . . . It is not a ground for . . . [deduction] that the claim, if justified, will consume income-producing property of the defendant.

The principle we derive from these cases is that the characterization, as "business" or "personal," of the litigation costs of resisting a claim depends on whether or not the claim *arises in connection with* the taxpayer's profit-seeking activities. It does not depend on the *consequences* that might result to a taxpayer's income-producing property from a failure to defeat the claim, for, as *Lykes* teaches, that "would carry us too far" and would not be compatible with the basic lines of expense deductibility drawn by Congress.[7] Moreover, such a rule would lead to capricious results. If two taxpayers are each sued for an automobile accident while driving for pleasure, deductibility of their litigation costs would turn on the mere circumstance of the character of the assets each happened to possess, that is, whether the judgments against them stood to be satisfied out of income or nonincome-producing property. We should be slow to attribute to Congress a purpose producing such unequal treatment among taxpayers, resting on no rational foundation.

For these reasons, we resolve the conflict among the lower courts on the question before us in favor of the view that the origin and character of the claim with respect to which an expense was incurred, rather than its potential consequences upon the fortunes of the taxpayer, is the controlling basic test of whether the expense was "business" or "personal" and hence whether it is deductible or not under Section [212]. We find the reasoning underlying the cases taking the "consequences" view unpersuasive.

We turn then to the determinative question in this case: did the wife's claims respecting respondent's stockholdings arise in connection with his profit-seeking activities?

---

[7] Expenses of contesting tax liabilities are now deductible under Section 212(3) of the 1954 Code. This provision merely represents a policy judgment as to a particular class of expenditures otherwise nondeductible, like extraordinary medical expenses, and does not cast any doubt on the basic tax structure set up by Congress.

II.

It is enough to say that in both aspects the wife's claims stemmed entirely from the marital relationship, and not, under any tenable view of things, from income-producing activity. This is obviously so as regards the claim to more than an equal division on any community property found to exist. For any such right depended entirely on the wife's making good her charges of marital infidelity on the part of the husband. The same conclusion is not less true respecting the claim relating to the existence of community property. For no such property could have existed but for the marriage relationship. Thus none of respondent's expenditures in resisting these claims can be deemed "business" expenses, and they are therefore not deductible under Section [212].

In view of this conclusion it is unnecessary to consider the further question suggested by the Government: whether that portion of respondent's payments attributable to litigating the issue of the existence of community property was a capital expenditure or a personal expense. In neither event would these payments be deductible from gross income.

The judgment of the Court of Claims is reversed and the case is remanded to that court for further proceedings consistent with this opinion.

It is so ordered.

REVENUE RULING 67-420
1967-2 C.B. 63

Revenue Ruling 58-52, as modified by Revenue Ruling 62-38, holds, in part, that the portion of an alimony award paid by the husband and allocated by the decree of limited divorce for payment by the wife of installments of principal and interest due upon a note secured by a deed of trust, which is a first lien upon a residence acquired jointly by the divorced parties as tenants by the entirety, is not considered as a payment in the nature of alimony includable in the wife's gross income under section 71 of the Internal Revenue Code of 1954 and deductible by the husband under section 215 of the Code. The decree of limited divorce did not dissolve the tenancy by the entirety.

In [*Neely B. Taylor, Jr. v. Commissioner*, 45 T.C. 120 (1965)], the former husband and wife held property in "joint survivorship" and the parties agreed, in a written instrument incident to and incorporated in the divorce decree, that such ownership would continue and that the husband was to pay both his and his former wife's share of the mortgage obligation on the property. The court held that the payments on the mortgage made by the husband were not alimony. The court based this determination on the fact that the husband failed to produce any documents showing that the wife was personally liable on the mortgage and that any benefit she might receive by way of an increase in the value of her interest in the property was speculative since the mortgage was for the full value of the house.

However, the court expressed the view that the husband's mortgage payments on the property owned as joint tenants would be alimony only if they conferred a current economic benefit upon the wife. The court in its discussion implies that there are two instances where the mortgage payments confer a current economic benefit: (1) where the payment are a *pro tanto* discharge of the wife's personal obligation on the mortgage; and (2) where, though the wife is not personally liable on the mortgage, such payments ascertainably increased the value of the interest in the property she would receive in the event she became sole owner.

It is a general principle of property law that if one cotenant pays both his share and his fellow cotenant's share of a mortgage obligation on jointly held property, he has a right of contribution against his fellow cotenant. However, if his fellow cotenant is personally liable on the mortgage the paying cotenant can secure a personal judgment against his fellow cotenant. However, if the fellow cotenant is not personally liable the paying cotenant is merely subrogated or equitably assigned the mortgagee's interest against his fellow cotenant and he can enforce his rights only against the interest his fellow cotenant has in jointly owned property, that is, out of profits and rents or by a larger share of the property upon partition. . . .

If a former husband and wife hold property as joint tenants with a right of survivorship and the husband pays both his and his wife's share of the mortgage obligation on the jointly held property, the husband would, as a general rule, have a right of contribution against his wife for her share of the payment, if the wife is personally and equally liable on the mortgage. However, if the husband has agreed (in a written instrument incident to a divorce) to make the payments, the making of such payments relieves the wife of liability to the mortgagee for the payments. As the husband has waived his right to contribution under the divorce decree, the wife is completely relieved of any liability for the mortgage payments. The wife, under the circumstances, has received income under the general principles laid down in *Old Colony Trust Co. v. Commissioner*, 279 U.S. 716 (1929). . . .

Accordingly, regardless of the value of the wife's equity in property held by the wife and husband as co-owners with a right of survivorship, since the agreement between the parties, incorporated in the divorce decree, provides that from amounts the wife receives from the husband as support she is to make the principal and interest payments on the mortgage on the property, an indebtedness on which both parties are principal obligors, one-half of each principal and interest payment is includable in the wife's gross income under section 71 of the Code, provided such payments otherwise qualify as periodic payments under section 71 of the Code. To the extent such payments so qualify as alimony, they are deductible by the husband under section 215 of the Code.

Revenue Ruling 58-52, C.B. 1958-1, 29, and Revenue Ruling 62-38, C.B. 1962-1, 15, are modified to the extent they hold that a portion of such mortgage payments would not be alimony even though they discharged a personal liability of the wife on the mortgage.

REVENUE RULING 2013-17
2013-2 C.B. 201

ISSUES

1. Whether, for Federal tax purposes, the terms "spouse," "husband and wife," "husband," and "wife" include an individual married to a person of the same sex, if the individuals are lawfully married under state law, and whether, for those same purposes, the term "marriage" includes such a marriage between individuals of the same sex.

2. Whether, for Federal tax purposes, the Internal Revenue Service (Service) recognizes a marriage of same-sex individuals validly entered into in a state whose laws authorize the marriage of two individuals of the same sex even if the state in which they are domiciled does not recognize the validity of same-sex marriages.

3. Whether, for Federal tax purposes, the terms "spouse," "husband and wife," "husband," and "wife" include individuals (whether of the opposite sex or same sex) who have entered into a registered domestic partnership, civil union, or other similar formal relationship recognized under state law that is not denominated as a marriage under the laws of that state, and whether, for those same purposes, the term "marriage" includes such relationships.

LAW AND ANALYSIS

1. Background

In Revenue Ruling 58-66, 1958-1 C.B. 60, the Service determined the marital status for Federal income tax purposes of individuals who have entered into a common-law marriage in a state that recognizes common-law marriages. The Service acknowledged that it recognizes the marital status of individuals as determined under state law in the administration of the Federal income tax laws. In Revenue Ruling 58-66, the Service stated that a couple would be treated as married for purposes of Federal income tax filing status and personal exemptions if the couple entered into a common-law marriage in a state that recognizes that relationship as a valid marriage.

The Service further concluded in Revenue Ruling 58-66 that its position with respect to a common-law marriage also applies to a couple who entered into a common-law marriage in a state that recognized such relationships and who later moved to a state in which a ceremony is required to establish the marital relationship. The Service therefore held that a taxpayer who enters into a common-law marriage in a state that recognizes such marriages shall, for purposes of Federal income tax filing status and personal exemptions, be considered married notwithstanding that the taxpayer and the taxpayer's spouse are currently domiciled in a state that requires a ceremony to establish the marital relationship. Accordingly, the Service held in Revenue Ruling 58-66 that such individuals can file joint income tax returns under I.R.C. Section 6013.

The Service has applied this rule with respect to common-law marriages for over 50 years, despite the refusal of some states to give full faith and credit to common-law marriages established in other states. Although states have different rules of marriage recognition, uniform nationwide rules are essential for efficient and fair tax administration. A rule under which a couple's marital status could change simply by moving from one state to another state would be prohibitively difficult and costly for the Service to administer, and for many taxpayers to apply.

Many provisions of the Code make reference to the marital status of taxpayers. Until the recent decision of the Supreme Court in *United States v. Windsor*, 133 S. Ct. 2675 (2013), the Service interpreted section 3 of the Defense of Marriage Act (DOMA) as prohibiting it from recognizing same-sex marriages for purposes of these provisions. Section 3 of DOMA provided that:

> In determining the meaning of any Act of Congress, or of any ruling, regulation, or interpretation of the various administrative bureaus and agencies of the United States, the word 'marriage' means only a legal union between one man and one woman as husband and wife, and the word 'spouse' refers only to a person of the opposite sex who is a husband or a wife. [1 U.S.C. § 7.]

In *Windsor*, the Supreme Court held that section 3 of DOMA is unconstitutional because it violates the principles of equal protection. It concluded that this section "undermines both the public and private significance of state-sanctioned same-sex marriages" and found that "no legitimate purpose" overcomes section 3's "purpose and effect to disparage and to injure those whom the State, by its marriage laws, sought to protect[.]" . . . This ruling provides guidance on the effect of the *Windsor* decision on the Service's interpretation of the sections of the Code that refer to taxpayers' marital status.

2. Recognition of Same-Sex Marriages

There are more than two hundred Code provisions and Treasury regulations relating to the internal revenue laws that include the terms "spouse," "marriage" (and derivatives thereof, such as "marries" and "married"), "husband and wife," "husband," and "wife." The Service concludes that gender-neutral terms in the Code that refer to marital status, such as "spouse" and "marriage," include, respectively, (1) an individual married to a person of the same sex if the couple is lawfully married under state law, and (2) such a marriage between individuals of the same sex. This is the most natural reading of those terms; it is consistent with *Windsor*, in which the plaintiff was seeking tax benefits under a statute that used the term "spouse," and a narrower interpretation would not further the purposes of efficient tax administration.

In light of the *Windsor* decision and for the reasons discussed below, the Service also concludes that the terms "husband and wife," "husband," and "wife" should be interpreted to include same-sex spouses. This interpretation is consistent with the Supreme Court's statements about the Code in *Windsor*, avoids the serious constitutional questions that an alternate reading would create, and is permitted by the text and purposes of the Code.

First, the Supreme Court's opinion in *Windsor* suggests that it understood that its decision striking down section 3 of DOMA would affect tax administration in ways that extended beyond the estate tax refund at issue. . . . ("The particular case at hand concerns the estate tax, but DOMA is more than simply a determination of what should or should not be allowed as an estate tax refund. Among the over 1,000 statutes and numerous Federal regulations that DOMA controls are laws pertaining to . . . taxes."). The Court observed in particular that section 3 burdened same-sex couples by forcing "them to follow a complicated procedure to file their Federal and state taxes jointly" and that section 3 "raise[d] the cost of health care for families by taxing health benefits provided by employers to their workers' same-sex spouses."

Second, an interpretation of the gender-specific terms in the Code to exclude same-sex spouses would raise serious constitutional questions. A well-established principle of statutory interpretation holds that, "where an otherwise acceptable construction of a statute would raise serious constitutional problems," a court should "construe the statute to avoid such problems unless such construction is plainly contrary to the intent of Congress." . . . "This canon is followed out of respect for Congress, which [presumably] legislates in light of constitutional limitations" . . . and instructs courts, where possible, to avoid interpretations that "would raise serious constitutional doubts."

The Fifth Amendment analysis in *Windsor* raises serious doubts about the constitutionality of Federal laws that confer marriage benefits and burdens only on opposite-sex married couples. In *Windsor*, the Court stated that, "[b]y creating two contradictory marriage regimes within the same State, DOMA forces same-sex couples to live as married for the purpose of state law but unmarried for the purpose of Federal law, thus diminishing the stability and predictability of basic personal relations the State has found it proper to acknowledge and protect." . . . Interpreting the gender-specific terms in the Code to categorically exclude same-sex couples arguably would have the same effect of diminishing the stability and predictability of legally recognized same-sex marriages. Thus, the canon of constitutional avoidance counsels in favor of interpreting the gender-specific terms in the Code to refer to same-sex spouses and couples.

Third, the text of the Code permits a gender-neutral construction of the gender-specific terms. Section 7701 of the Code provides definitions of certain terms generally applicable for purposes of the Code when the terms are not defined otherwise in a specific Code provision and the definition in section 7701 is not manifestly incompatible with the intent of the specific Code provision. The terms "husband and wife," "husband," and "wife" are not specifically defined other than in section 7701 (a) (17), which provides, for purposes of sections 682 and 2516, that the terms "husband" and "wife" shall be read to include a former husband or a former wife, respectively, and that "husband" shall be read as "wife" and "wife" as "husband" in certain circumstances. Although Congress's specific instruction to read "husband" and "wife" interchangeably in those specific provisions could be taken as an indication that Congress did not intend the terms to be read interchangeably in other provisions, the Service believes that the better understanding is that the interpretive rule set forth in section 7701 (a) (17) makes it reasonable to adopt, in the circumstances presented here and in light of *Windsor* and the principle of constitutional avoidance, a more general rule that does not foreclose a gender-neutral reading of gender-specific terms elsewhere in the Code.

Section 7701 (p) provides a specific cross-reference to the Dictionary Act, 1 U.S.C. § 1, which provides, in part, that when "determining the meaning of any Act of Congress, unless the context indicates otherwise, . . . words importing the masculine gender include the feminine as well." The purpose of this provision was to avoid having to "specify males and females by using a great deal of unnecessary language when one word would express the whole." . . . This provision has been read to require construction of the phrase "husband and wife" to include same-sex married couples. The Dictionary Act thus supports interpreting the gender-specific terms in the Code in a gender-neutral manner "unless the context indicates otherwise." . . . "Context" for purposes of the Dictionary Act "means the text of the Act of Congress surrounding the word at issue, or the texts of other related congressional Acts." . . . Here, nothing in the surrounding text forecloses a gender-neutral reading of the gender-specific terms. Rather, the provisions of the Code that use the terms "husband and wife," "husband," and "wife" are inextricably interwoven with provisions that use gender-neutral terms like "spouse" and "marriage," indicating that Congress viewed them to be equivalent. For example, section 1 (a) sets forth the tax imposed on "every married individual (as defined in section 7703) who makes a single return jointly with his spouse under section 6013," even though section 6013 provides that a "husband and wife" make a single return jointly of income. Similarly, section 2513 of the Code is entitled "Gifts by Husband or Wife to Third Party," but uses no gender-specific terms in its text. See also, e.g., §§ 62 (b) (3), 1361 (c) (1).

This interpretation is also consistent with the legislative history. The legislative history of section 6013, for example, uses the term "married taxpayers" interchangeably with the terms "husband" and "wife" to describe those individuals who may elect to file a joint return, and there is no indication that Congress intended those terms to refer only to a subset of individuals who are legally married. Accordingly, the most logical reading is that the terms "husband and wife" were used because they were viewed, at the time of enactment, as equivalent to the term "persons married to each other." There is nothing in the Code to suggest that Congress intended to exclude from the meaning of these terms any couple otherwise legally married under state law.

Fourth, other considerations also strongly support this interpretation. A gender-neutral reading of the Code fosters fairness by ensuring that the Service treats same-sex couples in the same manner as similarly situated opposite-sex couples. A gender-neutral reading of the Code also fosters administrative efficiency because the Service does not collect or maintain information on the gender of taxpayers and would have great difficulty administering a scheme that differentiated between same-sex and opposite-sex married couples.

Therefore, consistent with the statutory context, the Supreme Court's decision in *Windsor*, Revenue Ruling 58-66, and effective tax administration generally, the Service concludes that, for Federal tax purposes, the terms "husband and wife," "husband," and "wife" include an individual married to a person of the same sex if they were lawfully married in a state whose laws authorize the marriage of two individuals of the same sex, and the term "marriage" includes such marriages of individuals of the same sex.

3. Marital Status Based on the Laws of the State Where a Marriage Is Initially Established

Consistent with the longstanding position expressed in Revenue Ruling 58-66, the Service has determined to interpret the Code as incorporating a general rule, for Federal tax purposes, that recognizes the validity of a same-sex marriage that was valid in the state where it was entered into, regardless of the married couple's place of domicile. The Service may provide additional guidance on this subject and on the application of *Windsor* with respect to Federal tax administration. Other agencies may provide guidance on other Federal programs that they administer that are affected by the Code.

Under this rule, individuals of the same sex will be considered to be lawfully married under the Code as long as they were married in a state whose laws authorize the marriage of two individuals of the same sex, even if they are domiciled in a state that does not recognize the validity of same-sex marriages. For over half a century, for Federal income tax purposes, the Service has recognized marriages based on the laws of the state in which they were entered into, without regard to subsequent changes in domicile, to achieve uniformity, stability, and efficiency in the application and administration of the Code. Given our increasingly mobile society, it is important to have a uniform rule of recognition that can be applied with certainty by the Service and taxpayers alike for all Federal tax purposes. Those overriding tax administration policy goals generally apply with equal force in the context of same-sex marriages.

In most Federal tax contexts, a state-of-domicile rule would present serious administrative concerns. For example, spouses are generally treated as related parties for Federal tax purposes, and one spouse's ownership interest in property may be attributed to the other spouse for purposes of numerous Code provisions. If the Service did not adopt a uniform rule of recognition, the attribution of property interests could change when a same-sex couple moves from one state to another with different marriage recognition rules. The potential adverse consequences could impact not only the married couple but also others involved in a transaction, entity, or arrangement. This would lead to uncertainty for both taxpayers and the Service.

A rule of recognition based on the state of a taxpayer's current domicile would also raise significant challenges for employers that operate in more than one state, or that have employees (or former employees) who live in more than one state, or move between states with different marriage recognition rules. Substantial financial and administrative burdens would be placed on those employers, as well as the administrators of employee benefit plans. . . . All of these problems are avoided by the adoption of the rule set forth herein, and the Service therefore has chosen to avoid the imposition of the additional burdens on itself, employers, plan administrators, and individual taxpayers. Accordingly, Revenue Ruling 58–66 is amplified to adopt a general rule, for Federal tax purposes, that recognizes the validity of a same-sex marriage that was valid in the state where it was entered into, regardless of the married couple's place of domicile.

4. Registered Domestic Partnerships, Civil Unions, or Other Similar Formal Relationships Not Denominated as Marriage

For Federal tax purposes, the term "marriage" does not include registered domestic partnerships, civil unions, or other similar formal relationships recognized under state law that are not denominated as a marriage under that state's law, and the terms "spouse," "husband and wife," "husband," and "wife" do not include individuals who have entered into such a formal relationship. This conclusion applies regardless of whether individuals who have entered into such relationships are of the opposite sex or the same sex.

HOLDINGS

1. For Federal tax purposes, the terms "spouse," "husband and wife," "husband," and "wife" include an individual married to a person of the same sex if the individuals are lawfully married under state law, and the term "marriage" includes such a marriage between individuals of the same sex.

2. For Federal tax purposes, the Service adopts a general rule recognizing a marriage of same-sex individuals that was validly entered into in a state whose laws authorize the marriage of two individuals of the same sex even if the married couple is domiciled in a state that does not recognize the validity of same-sex marriages.

3. For Federal tax purposes, the terms "spouse," "husband and wife," "husband," and "wife" do not include individuals (whether of the opposite sex or the same sex) who have entered into a registered domestic partnership, civil union, or other similar formal relationship recognized under state law that is not denominated as a marriage under the laws of that state, and the term "marriage" does not include such formal relationships.

Chapter 38

NONRECOURSE DEBT: BASIS AND AMOUNT REALIZED REVISITED

I. PROBLEMS

1. In Year 1, Amelia borrowed $400,000 from a bank on a nonrecourse basis and invested $100,000 of her own money to purchase an apartment complex at its fair market value of $500,000. In Year 6, when the balance owing the bank was $350,000, and the property had an adjusted basis of $440,000 and a fair market value of $800,000, Amelia refinanced the property to take advantage of lower interest rates and to borrow additional money to enable her to purchase a tract of land. The principal amount of the new loan was $600,000. Amelia used $350,000 of that amount to pay the balance owing on the original loan. She used the remaining $250,000 in loan proceeds to make the land purchase. The new loan, like the original loan, was nonrecourse and was secured by a mortgage on the apartment complex. In Year 9, because of a significant downturn in the economy, Amelia began experiencing difficulties in attracting and retaining tenants. As a result, she was forced to reduce rents. In turn, the fair market value of Amelia's apartment complex fell sharply. Unable to make the payments on the loan, Amelia transferred the apartment complex in Year 10 to Speculator who took it subject to the mortgage and paid Amelia $2,500. At the time of this transaction, Amelia's adjusted basis in the complex was $400,000 (she had claimed a total of $100,000 in depreciation during the time that she held the property). The complex had a value of $450,000. A balance of $550,000 was owing on the loan. Explain the tax consequences of the above transactions to Amelia.

2. What basis will Speculator take in the complex?

3. What are the tax consequences for Speculator if, after holding the apartment complex six months, he transfers it to New Owner subject to the mortgage? Assume the total balance owing remains $550,000, but the property's value has increased to $500,000.

4. What are the tax consequences to Amelia on the facts of Problem 1 if the bank agrees in Year 10 to reduce the nonrecourse debt to $450,000, and Amelia retains the apartment complex in lieu of transferring it to Speculator? Alternatively, what are the tax consequences to Speculator if the nonrecourse debt was reduced to $450,000 shortly after the Year 10 transfer from Amelia to Speculator?

5. Assume the facts of Problem 1 except all of the indebtedness is recourse and that the apartment complex was sold in Year 10 at a mortgage foreclosure sale for $450,000 instead of being sold by Amelia to Speculator. Assume also that a deficiency judgment in the amount of $100,000 was entered against Amelia. Explain the tax consequences to Amelia of the foreclosure sale. What tax consequences, if any, to Amelia when she subsequently pays the deficiency judgment?

Assignment for Chapter 38:

Complete the problems.

Read: Internal Revenue Code: §§ 1012, 7701(g).
Treasury Regulations: §§ 1.1001-2(a), (b), (c) Examples 1, 2, 7 and 8.

Materials: Overview
Crane v. Commissioner
Commissioner v. Tufts
Revenue Ruling 91-31
Estate of Franklin v. Commissioner
Aizawa v. Commissioner

II. VOCABULARY

recourse debt
nonrecourse debt
contingent debt

III. OBJECTIVES

1. To recall *Crane* and *Tufts* provide that recourse and nonrecourse liabilities are to be treated as equivalent for purposes of determining basis and amount realized.

2. To determine the taxpayer's basis when the taxpayer either (1) uses its own money to purchase property or (2) borrows money on a recourse or nonrecourse basis to purchase property.

3. To determine the taxpayer's amount realized on the sale of property (1) when there are no liabilities assumed or taken subject to and (2) when there are liabilities assumed or taken subject to by the purchaser.

4. To determine the amount of gain which a taxpayer realizes on the sale of property (1) when the property sold is not encumbered by liabilities; and (2) when it is encumbered by liabilities.

5. To recall the standard established in *Tufts* and to explain that standard in your own words.

6. To compute the taxpayer's amount realized when liabilities assumed or taken subject to by the purchaser exceed the fair market value of the property.

7. To identify debt that may be too contingent to justify recognition for tax purposes.

8. To explain the tax impact resulting from a finding that debt incurred in acquiring property is either not "true debt" or is contingent.

9. To explain the tax significance of nonrecourse borrowing, when the taxpayer's adjusted basis in the property securing the nonrecourse loan is less than the loan proceeds.

10. To explain the tax consequences to a taxpayer whose property is sold at a mortgage foreclosure sale and against whom a deficiency judgment is entered.

IV. OVERVIEW

In Chapter 4, we considered the meaning of "basis," "adjusted basis," and "amount realized" and the relationship of these concepts to one another, especially where recourse liabilities were involved. Subsequent chapters, *e.g.*, Chapter 14 on depreciation, addressed matters in which the above concepts played significant roles. This Chapter will further develop the relationship between debt, especially nonrecourse debt, and basis and amount realized.

A. *Crane v. Commissioner*

Crane v. Commissioner, included in this Chapter, is a seminal decision deserving very careful reading. In *Crane*, the taxpayer inherited property encumbered by considerable nonrecourse debt. The taxpayer claimed depreciation deductions based on the fair market value of the property at the time of the decedent's death. Later, she sold the property for a small amount of cash and the purchaser took the property subject to the outstanding debt. At issue was the amount of gain realized on the sale. The first question the Court addressed was the taxpayer's basis in the property when she inherited it. Section 1014(a) provides that the basis of inherited property shall be equal to the fair market value of the "property" at the date of the decedent's death. Taxpayer argued that the basis of the property should have been its fair market value at the decedent's death less the debt encumbering the property. The Commissioner argued, and the Supreme Court agreed, the fair market value of the property at a decedent's death was its value without any adjustment for outstanding liabilities, including nonrecourse liabilities.

The Court then considered the "amount realized" and concluded the nonrecourse debt taken subject to by the purchaser must be considered part of the amount realized. The Court reasoned that, if the debt encumbering the property had been recourse debt assumed by the purchaser, the taxpayer would have had to treat the relief from that debt as a benefit constituting part of the amount realized. The fact that the outstanding debt in *Crane* was nonrecourse made no difference. Based on *Crane*, two general rules could be stated:

> (1) liabilities, whether recourse or nonrecourse, assumed, taken subject to or otherwise incurred in the acquisition of property are included in a taxpayer's basis; and

> (2) the liabilities of a seller, whether recourse or nonrecourse, assumed or taken subject to by a purchaser, are included in the seller's amount realized.

In concluding a seller must include in the amount realized on a sale any nonrecourse liability taken subject to by a buyer, the *Crane* court reasoned "a mortgagor, not personally liable on [a] debt, who sells the property subject to the mortgage and for additional consideration, realizes a benefit in the amount of the mortgage as well as the boot." 331 U.S. at 14. This statement was qualified, however, by footnote 37, reading: "Obviously, if the value of property is less than the amount of the mortgage, a mortgagor who is not personally liable cannot realize a benefit equal to the mortgage. Consequently, a different problem might be encountered where a mortgagor abandoned the property or transferred it subject to the mortgage without receiving boot. That is not this case." Footnote 37, probably the most famous footnote in tax history, thus raised a question which was resolved by the Supreme Court in *Commissioner v. Tufts*, included in the materials.

B. *Commissioner v. Tufts*

Courts interpreted footnote 37 of *Crane* differently. According to the Third Circuit, in *Millar v. Commissioner*, 577 F.2d 212 (3d Cir.), *cert. denied*, 439 U.S. 1046 (1978), the *Crane* footnote did not allow a seller to exclude from the amount realized the nonrecourse indebtedness even if that indebtedness exceeded the fair market value of the property. The *Millar* court emphasized that allowing taxpayers to include nonrecourse indebtedness in the basis of property enabled taxpayers to claim large depreciation deductions. To prevent taxpayers from realizing, in effect, a double deduction, a seller had to include in the amount realized the entire amount of any nonrecourse indebtedness encumbering the property sold. With respect to footnote 37, the court noted:

> Footnote 37, if taken literally, might furnish support for the taxpayers' argument that the Supreme Court carved out an exception in the *Crane* holding in circumstances where the value of the property surrendered or exchanged is less than the value of the nonrecourse obligation which is satisfied. However, this Court declines to accept a literal reading of that footnote. . . . [I]t must be remembered that the footnote in *Crane* was *dictum*. Furthermore, the footnote was but a postulate or hypothetical set of facts not before the Court and, indeed, involving a clearly different time and clearly different legal circumstances. . . .

Id. at 215.

Judge Friendly echoed these same concerns in *Estate of Levine v. Commissioner*, 634 F.2d 12, 15 (2d Cir. 1980):

> If nonrecourse mortgages contribute to the basis of property, then they must be included in the amount realized on sale. Any other course would render the concept of basis nonsensical by permitting sellers of mortgaged property to register large tax losses, stemming from an inflated basis and a diminished realization of gain. It would also permit depreciation deductions in excess of a property holder's real investment which could never be subsequently recaptured.

The Fifth Circuit in its *Tufts* decision, 651 F.2d 1058 (1981), which was later reversed by the Supreme Court, rejected these concerns. The Fifth Circuit set forth its own theory as follows:

> There is an even more compelling reason why the fact that a taxpayer has previously enjoyed the benefit of large depreciation deductions is insufficient to justify an expansion of the definition of amount realized. We see, looking to the Internal Revenue Code, that Congress has already in fact accounted for those previous deductions. According to the Code, "gain" from the sale or other disposition of property is computed by subtracting

the "adjusted basis" from the "amount realized. . . . " The "adjusted basis" is the cost of the property adjusted to reflect the depreciation, depletion, and other costs chargeable against the property. . . . Thus, any tax benefits that the taxpayer may have received in the form of prior deductions have already been factored into the gain equation through adjustments to basis. Since those deductions have been accounted for through adjustments to basis, it follows logically that they cannot also support an expansion of the definition of amount realized. To account for those deductions twice in the same equation by expanding the definition of amount realized as well as adjusting basis downward would, we think, be taxing the taxpayer twice on the same component of gain. The Commissioner's reliance on a theory of tax benefit, then, is misplaced. The Code clearly provides for a "recapture" of the prior deductions, but not through its definition of amount realized.

Id. at 1060–61.

The Fifth Circuit also took exception to the *Crane* court's economic benefit theory:

> This economic benefit theory is, we think, seriously flawed in that it is premised on the notion that "an owner of property, mortgaged at a figure less than that at which the property will sell, must and will treat the conditions of the mortgage exactly as if they were his personal obligations." We admit that we initially succumbed to the facile appeal of that notion, but on reflection we are convinced that it rings true only so long as the taxpayer actually wants to keep the property. If the taxpayer decides, for any reason whatsoever, that he no longer wants the burdens and responsibilities that accompany ownership, he can transfer the property to a third party with absolutely no regard to that party's willingness or ability to meet the mortgage obligations, yet rest assured that his other assets cannot be reached. We agree with Professor Bittker:
>
> > Relief from a nonrecourse debt is not an economic benefit if it can be obtained only by giving up the mortgaged property. It is analogous to the relief one obtains from local real property taxes by disposing of the property. Like nonrecourse debt, the taxes must be paid to retain the property; but no one would suggest that the disposition of unprofitable property produces an economic benefit equal to the present value of the taxes that will not be paid in the future.
>
> Bittker, *Tax Shelters, Nonrecourse Debt, and the Crane Case*, 33 Tax L. Rev. 277, 282 (1978). We do not deny that Mrs. Crane received *some* benefit: a purchaser had to pay off the mortgage or at least be willing to take the property subject to the mortgage before Mrs. Crane could pocket her $2,500 in equity. We do, however, seriously question whether the full amount of nonrecourse debt is an accurate measure of that benefit.

Id. at 1062–63.

The conflicting views of the Fifth and Third Circuits were the focus of the Supreme Court's decision in *Tufts*. Reversing the Fifth Circuit, the Supreme Court held that the entire amount of nonrecourse indebtedness had to be included in the taxpayer's amount realized. As you read *Tufts*, consider carefully the different theories espoused by the Commissioner and the taxpayer. Be prepared to explain precisely the rationale used by the Court in reaching its conclusion. Note how § 7701(g) incorporates the *Tufts* holding. See also Reg. § 1.1001-2(b), cited by the Court in *Tufts*, in support of the proposition that the fair market value of the property is not relevant in determining the taxpayer's amount realized.

Cancellation of Nonrecourse Debt. An application of *Tufts* may be found in Revenue Ruling 91-31, 1991-1 C.B. 19, included in the materials. In that ruling, the principal amount of nonrecourse debt was reduced by the creditor (who was not the seller of the property securing the debt). On the authority of *Tufts*, the Service held the reduction gave rise to cancellation of debt income rather than a reduction in the property's basis. Review the ruling carefully. What result if the creditor was also the seller of the property? *See* § 108(e)(5).

Continuing Recourse Liability. In *Aizawa v. Commissioner*, included in the materials, the Tax Court considered the application of *Tufts* in a situation where the taxpayer continued to be liable on a recourse debt following a foreclosure sale of the property secured by the debt. Specifically, the taxpayer remained liable for that part of the recourse debt not satisfied by the proceeds of the foreclosure sale. For purposes of determining gain or loss on the foreclosure sale, the court concluded the amount realized equalled the proceeds of the foreclosure sale. Contrast the taxpayer's and Commissioner's positions regarding the calculation of the taxpayer's amount realized on the transaction. Why did the Tax Court reject both positions? Do you agree with the Tax Court's holding? In this regard, see Reg. § 1.1001-2(a)(1), including in the amount realized from a sale of property "the amount of liabilities from which the transferor is discharged" on account of the sale.

The Tax Court in *Webb v. Commissioner*, T.C. Memo 1995-486, applied the reasoning of *Aizawa* in concluding the taxpayer incurred a loss upon the foreclosure of a recourse mortgage. The court rejected the Commissioner's position that *Aizawa* was distinguishable because the fair market value of the property in *Webb* exceeded the foreclosure price. The taxpayer, like the taxpayer in *Aizawa*, was subject to a deficiency judgment after the foreclosure sale. As a result, the amount realized on the foreclosure sale was only the amount received at public auction. This amount was significantly less than the adjusted basis in the property, thus resulting in a realized and recognized loss.

C.   Nonrecourse Borrowing and the Section 108 Insolvency Exclusion

The Service in Revenue Ruling 92-53, 1992-2 C.B. 48, considered the impact of excess nonrecourse indebtedness, *i.e.*, nonrecourse debt in excess of the fair market value of property securing the debt, on the determination of insolvency for purposes of the § 108 insolvency exclusion. (For a detailed discussion of income from the discharge of indebtedness and the insolvency exclusion, see Chapter 9.) In that ruling, the Service concluded:

[t]he amount by which a nonrecourse debt exceeds the fair market value of the property securing the debt is taken into account in determining whether, and to what extent, a taxpayer is insolvent within the meaning of section 108(d)(3) of the Code, but only to the extent that the excess nonrecourse debt is discharged.

The Service reasoned that to ensure the fresh start intended by § 108,

the amount by which a nonrecourse debt exceeds the fair market value of the property securing the debt should be treated as a liability in determining insolvency for purposes of section 108 of the Code to the extent that the excess nonrecourse debt is discharged. Otherwise, the discharge could give rise to a current tax when the taxpayer lacks the ability to pay that tax. Nonrecourse debt should also be treated as a liability in determining insolvency under section 108 to the extent of the fair market value of the property securing the debt.

However, excess nonrecourse debt that is not discharged does not have a similar effect on a taxpayer's ability to pay a current tax resulting from the discharge of another debt (whether recourse or nonrecourse). That excess nonrecourse debt should not be treated as a liability in determining insolvency for purposes of section 108 of the Code.

Id. at 49.

Assume, for example, a taxpayer owed a local bank $500,000 on a nonrecourse loan secured by real property which had fallen in value to $400,000. The taxpayer's only other assets had an aggregate fair market value of $100,000 and the taxpayer was personally liable on other indebtedness in the amount of $50,000. The bank agreed to modify the terms of the nonrecourse loan by reducing the principal amount owing by $75,000. Pursuant to Revenue Ruling 92-53, the taxpayer's indebtedness for purposes of the § 108(a)(1)(B) exclusion will be the sum of:

a. $50,000 — the outstanding recourse indebtedness;

b. $400,000 — the portion of the nonrecourse debt equal to the fair market value of the property securing the debt; and

c. $75,000 — the amount of the excess nonrecourse indebtedness (the excess of the total nonrecourse debt of $500,000 over the $400,000 fair market value of the real estate or $100,000) which is discharged.

Thus, the taxpayer, prior to the discharge, is deemed for § 108 purposes to have total debt of $525,000. That debt exceeds the fair market value of the taxpayer's property ($400,000 + $100,000 = $500,000) by $25,000 and the taxpayer is considered insolvent to that extent. As a result, $25,000 of the $75,000 of discharged indebtedness will be excluded from gross income.

D. Nonrecourse Borrowing and Appreciated Property

Consider the following example: Bernie owns a commercial building which he purchased for $500,000 in 1990. Bernie used $100,000 of his own cash to purchase the building and borrowed the balance of the purchase price from a local bank on a nonrecourse basis. The current balance owing on this indebtedness, which is secured by a first mortgage on the building, is $75,000. Because of an upturn in business activity in the area in which the building is located, the building currently has a fair market value of $1,000,000. Given the large equity he has in the property, Bernie refinances and borrows $500,000 on a nonrecourse basis. $75,000 of the new borrowing is used to pay the balance owing on the old mortgage and the other $425,000 is used by Bernie to invest in a business venture unrelated to the commercial building. Assume Bernie's adjusted basis in the building is $225,000.[1] Does the new borrowing (a) generate additional basis for Bernie in the building or (b) represent a realization event resulting in gain recognition?

Because the new loan is not used to improve the building but rather is used in an unrelated venture, the loan does not result in any adjustment of the building's basis. *See* § 1016. Even that part of the loan used to repay the balance on the original indebtedness does not result in an upward adjustment of the basis. Consistent with the *Crane* teaching, Bernie's original basis of $500,000 in the property reflected not only the $100,000 of his own cash used to purchase the property but also the $400,000 which he had borrowed for that purpose. In other words, Bernie had already received credit for making the additional $400,000 investment.

Whether the new nonrecourse loan of $500,000 constitutes a realization event may appear to be a more difficult question. Bernie can do whatever he chooses to do with the loan proceeds and, because the loan is nonrecourse, he may never have to repay the loan. Unlike one who borrows on a recourse basis and is obligated to repay the borrowed funds, shouldn't Bernie, as a nonrecourse borrower, be deemed to have realized and recognized a gain to the extent of the difference between the amount of the loan ($500,000) and his adjusted basis in that mortgaged property ($225,000, disregarding any depreciation in the year of sale)? Certainly, if Bernie had sold the building for $500,000 (with the purchaser paying Bernie $425,000 in cash and taking subject to the $75,000 mortgage), Bernie would have had to report $275,000 in gain. Isn't nonrecourse borrowing in excess of the adjusted basis in property comparable to a sale?

The Second Circuit in *Woodsam Associates, Inc. v. Commissioner*, 198 F.2d 357 (2d Cir. 1952), considered this very issue. In *Woodsam Associates*, Mrs. Woods had purchased certain improved real property in New York City. Subsequent to the purchase, she borrowed on a nonrecourse basis an amount in excess of her adjusted basis in the property. She later contributed the property to a corporation, which in turn ultimately disposed of the property at a foreclosure sale. Because [under § 351] this exchange of the property for stock in the corporation was nontaxable, the corporation [under § 362] took the same basis in the property as that of Mrs. Woods. Woodsam Associates, Inc., however, contended that, when Mrs. Woods borrowed against the property on a nonrecourse basis, she recognized gain to the extent of the difference between the amount of the indebtedness and her adjusted basis in the property. If the corporation were correct in its analysis, Mrs. Woods' basis in the property would have been increased by the amount of gain she

---

[1] This example assumes that Bernie has claimed $275,000 in depreciation deductions since purchasing the property.

was required to report as a result of the borrowing. In turn, the corporation would have received the property with the increased basis, and ultimately realized a lesser gain on the foreclosure sale.

The Second Circuit rejected this argument, noting the mortgagee, even in the case of a nonrecourse loan, was in effect nothing more than a preferred creditor. Mrs. Woods, by borrowing against her equity, had not disposed of the property but rather had merely augmented the indebtedness outstanding against the property.

> Mrs. Woods was the owner of this property in the same sense after the execution of this mortgage that she was before. As pointed out in our decision in the *Crane* case . . . "the lien of a mortgage does not make the mortgagee a co-tenant; the mortgagor is the owner for all purposes. . . . He has all the income from the property; he manages it; he may sell it; any increase in its value goes to him; any decrease falls on him, until the value goes below the amount of the lien." Realization of gain was, therefore, postponed for taxation until there was a final disposition of the property at the time of the foreclosure sale. . . . Therefore, Mrs. Wood's borrowing did not change the basis for the computation of gain or loss.

Id. at 359.

Even though the taxpayer did not prevail in *Woodsam Associates*, the decision is obviously favorable to taxpayers who have considerable equity in property with a low adjusted basis. It enables them to withdraw (via nonrecourse borrowing) from the property an amount far greater than they invested and yet not be deemed to have "realized" gain. Nevertheless, the result is consistent with *Crane's* treatment of nonrecourse debt as recourse debt for purposes of computing basis and amount realized.

Given the preceding analysis, what would Bernie's amount realized be if he sold the building the following year for $1,100,000? Assume the purchaser paid Bernie $600,000 in cash and took the building subject to the nonrecourse debt encumbering the building. (For the sake of simplicity, assume the nonrecourse debt is still $500,000.) *Woodsam Associates* indicated the gain which the taxpayer sought to have triggered upon the borrowing by Mrs. Woods was "postponed for taxation until the time of the foreclosure sale." 198 F.2d at 359. Accordingly, Bernie's amount realized should be $1,100,000, *i.e.*, the sum of $600,000 in cash and the $500,000 in debt taken subject to by the purchaser. Disregarding depreciation deductions in the year of sale, Bernie's adjusted basis in the property is $225,000, and he will therefore recognize gain of $875,000. To check this result consider the following analysis:

> *Amount Contributed by Bernie:* $425,000 cash, *i.e.*, $100,000 downpayment plus $325,000 paid out of pocket to retire the initial mortgage.

> *Amount of Benefits Received by Bernie:* $275,000 in depreciation deductions; $425,000 net proceeds of the refinancing (*i.e.*, $500,000 less $75,000 withheld to pay the balance of the original indebtedness owing by Bernie); and $600,000, the amount paid to Bernie by the purchaser. Total benefits received by Bernie: $1,300,000.

Subtracting Bernie's total contribution ($425,000) from his total benefits ($1,300,000), Bernie has $875,000 of gain.

E.   Impact of Contingent Liabilities

The rule that nonrecourse liabilities incurred on the acquisition of property are includable in basis created an opportunity for abuse. At no risk to themselves, taxpayers could agree to pay inflated prices for depreciable property and finance their purchase by giving the seller a nonrecourse note. If respected, this arrangement would enable the taxpayer to claim a basis in the acquired property equal to the inflated purchase price. As a result, the taxpayer could claim greater depreciation deductions than would be available had the property been purchased at its fair market value. In addition, the taxpayer could claim an interest deduction with respect to the outstanding indebtedness. Likewise from the standpoint of the seller, little risk was entailed. The seller could report the sale of the property on an installment basis and thus report gain only if and when paid.[2]

In *Estate of Franklin v. Commissioner*, included in the materials, the Ninth Circuit addressed just such abuses. The court concluded that the purchase price for certain real property exceeded its fair market value and therefore the taxpayer could not be expected to make the investment in the property represented by the nonrecourse debt. As a result, the court ignored the nonrecourse debt for purposes of depreciation and interest deductions. Revenue Ruling 77-110, 1977-1 C.B. 58, issued in the aftermath of *Estate of Franklin*, also treats nonrecourse indebtedness under similar circumstances as too contingent to be considered for purposes of basis and the computation of interest and depreciation deductions, and allows inclusion in basis only that portion of the purchase price paid in cash.[3]

With respect to *Estate of Franklin*, one might argue that the Ninth Circuit erred in failing to hold the taxpayers had a basis at least equal to the fair market value of the property. However, the court apparently believed the liability was so great in relation to the fair market value of the property, it was unlikely any investment would ever be made. Indeed, unless the property substantially appreciated, the taxpayer almost assuredly would not make any further payments on the property. Where liability is so contingent and where the tax avoidance motive seems so clear, refusal to accord tax significance to the liability seems appropriate. Assume, however, in *Estate of Franklin*, that during the contract term the property increased in value making it advantageous for the doctors in that case to make the contract payments. Would the liability then be taken into account for basis purposes, *i.e.*, should the court have recognized the possibility of a "springing" basis?

With respect to this question of basis, the Third Circuit in *Pleasant Summit v. Commissioner*, 863 F.2d 263 (3d Cir. 1988), *cert. denied*, 493 U.S. 901 (1989), a case

---

[2] See Chapter 41 for discussion of the installment sales method. Essentially, this method of accounting permits a seller to report the gain realized on the sale when payments are actually received.

[3] As we shall see in Chapter 44, Congress has now directly addressed the problem of nonrecourse debt through the "at risk" rules of § 465, which place limits on the allowable deductions attributable to nonrecourse debt.

in which the nonrecourse debt exceeded the property's fair market value, permitted the nonrecourse debt itself to generate basis to the extent of the fair market value of the property. Subsequent to the Third Circuit decision in *Pleasant Summit*, the Second Circuit in *Lebowitz v. Commissioner*, 917 F.2d 1314, 1318 (2d Cir. 1990), held that, in determining the genuineness of nonrecourse debt for tax purposes, "the underlying question is whether the fair market value of the acquired asset approximates the amount of the nonrecourse note in question. . . . " The Second Circuit explicitly rejected the Third Circuit's decision in *Pleasant Summit* to the extent that case had held that, even if the value of the underlying asset was "substantially less" than the nonrecourse debt, the taxpayer was still entitled to a basis in the asset up to fair market value. The Fifth Circuit in *Lukens v. Commissioner*, 945 F.2d 92 (5th Cir. 1991) also refused to follow the reasoning of the Third Circuit in *Pleasant Summit*, finding instead that the proper inquiry in evaluating the genuineness of nonrecourse debt, as in *Estate of Franklin*, was whether "it would be reasonable for the buyer/debtor to make a capital investment in the unpaid purchase price." *Id.* at 99. Similarly, the U.S. Court of Federal Claims in its decision in *Bergstrom v. U.S.*, 37 Fed. Cl. 164 (1996), rejected the reasoning in *Pleasant Summit*, emphasizing "when nonrecourse purchase money debt exceeds a reasonable approximation of the property's fair market value, the debt is disregarded in its entirety for the purposes of determining depreciation and interest deductions."

What impact, if any, does the *Tufts* decision have on the standard announced in *Estate of Franklin*? Although *Tufts* requires nonrecourse debt to be included in the amount realized on the disposition of property even though the debt exceeds the fair market value of the property, *Tufts* is not inconsistent with *Estate of Franklin*. Because they are factually distinguishable, the two cases announce rules which may coexist. In *Estate of Franklin*, the debt incurred exceeded the fair market value of the property securing its payment, thus justifying the court's refusal to acknowledge it as a true debt for tax purposes. By contrast, in *Tufts*, the original debt did not exceed the value of the property; it was thus not contingent debt in the *Estate of Franklin* sense. Given the *Crane* rationale that nonrecourse debt is to be treated as recourse debt, the investors in *Tufts* appropriately claimed interest deductions with respect to the debt and included the debt in the basis of the property, thereby generating substantial depreciation deductions. In effect, for tax purposes, the taxpayers received advance credit for an investment they had not yet made. These tax benefits, as well as the exclusion of the loan proceeds from income, were justified, assuming the investors would make the investment represented by the nonrecourse debt, *i.e.*, they would repay the loan. Upon disposition, when there was no longer a possibility that the debt would be repaid (or the investment made), it was appropriate to require the balance of the indebtedness to be taken into income by including it in the amount realized.

In light of *Estate of Franklin*, what basis would you expect the purchaser of the property in *Tufts* to have in the property? Under the circumstances of *Tufts*, does *Estate of Franklin* require that the nonrecourse debt encumbering the property be ignored, thus resulting in a basis equal only to the actual cash payments made by the purchaser to the individual investors? Would that result be consistent with the *Crane* concern that depreciation deductions be computed with reference to the real value of property rather than the taxpayer's equity or investment in the property? Alternatively, assuming no tax avoidance motive on the part of the purchaser, should the basis equal the fair market value of the property?[4] To what extent should taxpayer motive determine whether nonrecourse liability is included in basis? As these questions suggest, the relationship between nonrecourse indebtedness and basis and amount realized is complex and, at times, uncertain.

CRANE v. COMMISSIONER
United States Supreme Court
331 U.S. 1 (1947)

Mr. Chief Justice Vinson delivered the opinion of the Court.

The question here is how a taxpayer who acquires depreciable property subject to an unassumed mortgage, holds it for a period, and finally sells it still so encumbered, must compute her taxable gain.

Petitioner was the sole beneficiary and the executrix of the will of her husband, who died January 11, 1932. He then owned an apartment building and lot subject to a mortgage, which secured a principal debt of $255,000.00 and interest in default of $7,042.50. As of that date, the property was appraised for federal estate tax purposes at a value exactly equal to the total amount of this encumbrance. Shortly after her husband's death, petitioner entered into an agreement with the mortgagee whereby she was to continue to operate the property — collecting the rents, paying for necessary repairs, labor, and other operating expenses, and reserving $200.00 monthly for taxes — and was to remit the net rentals to the mortgagee. This plan was followed for nearly seven years, during which period petitioner reported the gross rentals as income, and claimed and was allowed deductions for taxes and operating expenses paid on the property, for interest paid on the mortgage, and for the physical exhaustion of the building. Meanwhile, the arrearage of interest increased to $15,857.71. On November 29, 1938, with the mortgagee threatening foreclosure, petitioner sold to a third party for $3,000.00 cash, subject to the mortgage, and paid $500.00 expenses of sale.

Petitioner reported a taxable gain of $1,250.00. Her theory was that the "property" which she had acquired in 1932 and sold in 1938 was only the equity, or the excess in the value of the apartment building and lot over the amount of the mortgage. This equity was of zero value when she acquired it. No depreciation could be taken on a zero value. Neither she nor her vendee ever assumed the mortgage, so, when she sold the equity, the amount she realized on the sale was the net cash received, or $2,500.00. This sum less the zero basis constituted her gain, of which she reported half as taxable on the assumption that the entire property was a "capital asset."

The Commissioner, however, determined that petitioner realized a net taxable

---

[4] In the partnership context, § 752(c) provides authority for treating nonrecourse indebtedness as includable in basis to the extent of the fair market value of property.

gain of $23,767.03. His theory was that the "property" acquired and sold was not the equity, as petitioner claimed, but rather the physical property itself, or the owner's rights to possess, use, and dispose of it, undiminished by the mortgage. The original basis thereof was $262,042.50, its appraised value in 1932. Of this value $55,000.00 was allocable to land and $207,042.50 to building. During the period that petitioner held the property, there was an allowable depreciation of $28,045.10 on the building, so that the adjusted basis of the building at the time of sale was $178,997.40. The amount realized on the sale was said to include not only the $2,500.00 net cash receipts, but also the principal amount of the mortgage subject to which the property was sold, both totalling $257,500.00. The selling price was allocable in the proportion, $54,471.15 to the land and $203,028.85 to the building. The Commissioner agreed that the land was a "capital asset," but thought that the building was not. Thus, he determined that petitioner sustained a capital loss of $528.85 on the land, of which 50% or $264.42 was taken into account, and an ordinary gain of $24,031.45 on the building, or a net taxable gain as indicated.

The Tax Court agreed with the Commissioner that the building was not a "capital asset." In all other respects it adopted petitioner's contentions, and expunged the deficiency. Petitioner did not appeal from the part of the ruling adverse to her, and these questions are no longer at issue. On the Commissioner's appeal, the Circuit Court of Appeals reversed, one judge dissenting. We granted certiorari because of the importance of the questions raised as to the proper construction of the gain and loss provisions of the Internal Revenue Code.

The 1938 Act, Section 111(a), defines the gain from "the sale or other disposition of property" as "the excess of the amount realized therefrom over the adjusted basis provided in section 113(b). . . . " It proceeds, Section 111(b), to define "the amount realized from the sale or other disposition of property" as "the sum of any money received plus the fair market value of the property (other than money) received." Further, in Section 113(b), the "adjusted basis for determining the gain or loss from the sale or other disposition of property" is declared to be "the basis determined under subsection (a), adjusted . . . [(1)(B)] . . . for exhaustion, wear and tear, obsolescence, amortization . . . to the extent allowed (but not less than the amount allowable). . . . " The basis under subsection (a) "if the property was acquired by . . . devise . . . or by the decedent's estate from the decedent," Section 113(a)(5), is "the fair market value of such property at the time of such acquisition."

Logically, the first step under this scheme is to determine the unadjusted basis of property, under Section 113(a)(5), and the dispute in this case is as to the construction to be given the term "property." If "property," as used in that provision, means the same thing as "equity," it would necessarily follow that the basis of petitioner's property was zero, as she contends. If, on the contrary, it means the land and building themselves, or the owner's legal rights in them, undiminished by the mortgage, the basis was $262,042.50.

We think that the reasons for favoring one of the latter constructions are of overwhelming weight. In the first place, the words of statutes — including revenue acts — should be interpreted where possible in their ordinary, everyday senses. The only relevant definitions of "property" to be found in the principal standard dictionaries are the two favored by the Commissioner, i.e., either that "property" is the physical thing which is a subject of ownership, or that it is the aggregate of the owner's rights to control and dispose of that thing. "Equity" is not given as a synonym, nor do either of the foregoing definitions suggest that it could be correctly so used. Indeed, "equity" is defined as "the value of a property . . . above the total of the liens. . . . " The contradistinction could hardly be more pointed. Strong countervailing considerations would be required to support a contention that Congress, in using the word "property," meant "equity," or that we should impute to it the intent to convey that meaning.

In the second place, the Commissioner's position has the approval of the administrative construction of Section 113(a)(5). With respect to the valuation of property under that section, Reg. 101, Art. 113(a)(5)-1, promulgated under the 1938 Act, provided that "the value of property as of the date of the death of the decedent as appraised for the purpose of the Federal estate tax . . . shall be deemed to be its fair market value. . . . " The land and building here involved were so appraised in 1932, and their appraised value — $262,042.50 — was reported by petitioner as part of the gross estate. This was in accordance with the estate tax law and regulations, which had always required that the value of decedent's property, undiminished by liens, be so appraised and returned, and that mortgages be separately deducted in computing the net estate. As the quoted provision of the Regulations has been in effect since 1918, and as the relevant statutory provision has been repeatedly reenacted since then in substantially the same form, the former may itself now be considered to have the force of law.

Moreover, in the many instances in other parts of the Act in which Congress has used the word "property," or expressed the idea of "property" or "equity," we find no instances of a misuse of either word or of a confusion of the ideas. In some parts of the Act other than the gain and loss sections, we find "property" where it is unmistakably used in its ordinary sense. On the other hand, where either Congress or the Treasury intended to convey the meaning of "equity," it did so by the use of appropriate language.

A further reason why the word "property" in Section 113(a) should not be construed to mean "equity" is the bearing such construction would have on the allowance of deductions for depreciation and on the collateral adjustments of basis.

Section 23(1) permits deduction from gross income of "a reasonable allowance for the exhaustion, wear and tear of property. . . . " Sections 23(n) and 114(a) declare that the "basis upon which exhaustion, wear and tear . . . are to be allowed" is the basis "provided in section 113(b) for the purpose of determining the gain upon the sale" of the property, which is the Section 113(a) basis "adjusted . . . for exhaustion, wear and tear . . . to the extent allowed (but not less than the amount allowable). . . . "

Under these provisions, if the mortgagor's equity were the Section 113(a) basis, it would also be the original basis from which depreciation allowances are deducted. If it is, and if the amount of the annual allowances were to be computed on that value, as would then seem to be required, they will represent only a fraction of the cost of the corresponding physical exhaustion, and any recoupment by the mortgagor of the remainder of that cost can be effected only by the reduction of his taxable gain in the year of sale. If, however, the amount of the annual allowances were to be computed on the value of the property, and then deducted from an equity basis, we would in some instances have to accept deductions from a minus basis or deny deductions altogether. The Commissioner also argues that taking the mortgagor's equity as the Section 113(a) basis would require the basis to be changed with each payment on the mortgage, and that the attendant problem of repeatedly recomputing basis and annual allowances would be a tremendous accounting burden on both the Commissioner and the taxpayer. Moreover, the mortgagor would acquire control over the timing of his depreciation allowances.

Thus, it appears that the applicable provisions of the Act expressly preclude an equity basis, and the use of it is contrary to certain implicit principles of income tax depreciation, and entails very great administrative difficulties. It may be added that the Treasury has never furnished a guide through the maze of problems that arise in connection with depreciating an equity basis, but, on the contrary, has consistently permitted the amount of depreciation allowances to be computed on the full value of the property, and subtracted from it as a basis. Surely, Congress' long-continued acceptance of this situation gives it full legislative endorsement.

We conclude that the proper basis under Section 113(a)(5) is the value of the property, undiminished by mortgages thereon, and that the correct basis here was $262,042.50. The next step is to ascertain what adjustments are required under Section 113(b). As the depreciation rate was stipulated, the only question at this point is whether the Commissioner was warranted in making any depreciation adjustments whatsoever.

Section 113(b)(1)(B) provides that "proper adjustment in respect of the property *shall in all cases be made* . . . for exhaustion, wear and tear . . . to the extent allowed (but not less than the amount allowable). . . . " (Italics supplied.) The Tax Court found on adequate evidence that the apartment house was property of a kind subject to physical exhaustion, that it was used in taxpayer's trade or business, and consequently that the taxpayer would have been entitled to a depreciation allowance under Section 23(1), except that, in the opinion of that Court, the basis of the property was zero, and it was thought that depreciation could not be taken on a zero basis. As we have just decided that the correct basis of the property was not zero, but $262,042.50, we avoid this difficulty, and conclude that an adjustment should be made as the Commissioner determined.

Petitioner urges to the contrary that she was not entitled to depreciation deductions, whatever the basis of the property, because the law allows them only to one who actually bears the capital loss, and here the loss was not hers but the mortgagee's. We do not see, however, that she has established her factual premise. There was no finding of the Tax Court to that effect, nor to the effect that the value of the property was ever less than the amount of the lien. Nor was there evidence in the record, or any indication that petitioner could produce evidence, that this was so. The facts that the value of the property was only equal to the lien in 1932 and that during the next six and one-half years the physical condition of the building deteriorated and the amount of the lien increased, are entirely inconclusive, particularly in the light of the buyer's willingness in 1938 to take subject to the increased lien and pay a substantial amount of cash to boot. Whatever may be the rule as to allowing depreciation to a mortgagor on property in his possession which is subject to an unassumed mortgage and clearly worth less than the lien, we are not faced with that problem and see no reason to decide it now.

At last we come to the problem of determining the "amount realized" on the 1938 sale. Section 111(b), it will be recalled, defines the "amount realized" from "the sale . . . of property" as "the sum of any money received plus the fair market value of the property (other than money) received," and Section 111(a) defines the gain on "the sale . . . of property" as the excess of the amount realized over the basis. Quite obviously, the word "property," used here with reference to a sale, [has the same meaning as "property" with reference to] acquisition and depreciation in Section 113, both for certain of the reasons stated heretofore in discussing its meaning in Section 113, and also because the functional relation of the two sections requires that the word means the same in one section that it does in the other. If the "property" to be valued on the date of acquisition is the property free of liens, the "property" to be priced on a subsequent sale must be the same thing.

Starting from this point, we could not accept petitioner's contention that the $2,500.00 net cash was all she realized on the sale except on the absurdity that she sold a quarter-of-a-million dollar property for roughly one per cent of its value, and took a 99 per cent loss. Actually, petitioner does not urge this. She argues, conversely, that because only $2,500.00 was realized on the sale, the "property" sold must have been the equity only, and that consequently we are forced to accept her contention as to the meaning of "property" in Section 113. We adhere, however, to what we have already said on the meaning of "property," and we find that the absurdity is avoided by our conclusion that the amount of the mortgage is properly included in the "amount realized" on the sale.

Petitioner concedes that if she had been personally liable on the mortgage and the purchaser had either paid or assumed it, the amount so paid or assumed would be considered a part of the "amount realized" within the meaning of Section 111(b). The cases so deciding have already repudiated the notion that there must be an actual receipt by the seller himself of "money" or "other property," in their narrowest senses. It was thought to be decisive that one section of the Act must be construed so as not to defeat the intention of another or to frustrate the Act as a whole, and that the taxpayer was the "beneficiary" of the payment in "as real and substantial [a sense] as if the money had been paid it and then paid over by it to its creditors."

Both these points apply to this case. The first has been mentioned already. As for the second, we think that a mortgagor, not personally liable on the debt, who sells the property subject to the mortgage and for additional consideration, realizes a benefit in the amount of the mortgage as well as the boot.[5] If a purchaser pays boot, it is immaterial as to our problem whether the mortgagor is also to receive money from the purchaser to discharge the mortgage prior to sale, or whether he is merely to transfer subject to the mortgage — it may make a difference to the purchaser and to the mortgagee, but not to the mortgagor. Or, put in another way, we are no

---

[5] Obviously, if the value of property is less than the amount of the mortgage, a mortgagor who is not personally liable cannot realize a benefit equal to the mortgage. Consequently, a different problem might be encountered where a mortgagor abandoned the property or transferred it subject to the mortgage without receiving boot. That is not this case.

more concerned with whether the mortgagor is, strictly speaking, a debtor on the mortgage, than we are with whether the benefit to him is, strictly speaking, a receipt of money or property. We are rather concerned with the reality that an owner of property, mortgaged at a figure less than that at which the property will sell, must and will treat the conditions of the mortgage exactly as if they were his personal obligations. If he transfers subject to the mortgage, the benefit to him is as real and substantial as if the mortgage were discharged, or as if a personal debt in an equal amount had been assumed by another.

Therefore we conclude that the Commissioner was right in determining that petitioner realized $257,500.00 on the sale of property. . . .

Petitioner contends that the result we have reached taxes her on what is not income within the meaning of the Sixteenth Amendment. If this is because only the direct receipt of cash is thought to be income in the constitutional sense, her contention is wholly without merit. If it is because the entire transaction is thought to have been "by all dictates of common sense . . . a ruinous disaster," as it was termed in her brief, we disagree with her premise. She was entitled to depreciation deductions for a period of nearly seven years, and she actually took them in almost the allowable amount. The crux of this case, really, is whether the law permits her to exclude allowable deductions from consideration in computing gain. We have already showed that, if it does, the taxpayer can enjoy a double deduction, in effect, on the same loss of assets. The Sixteenth Amendment does not require that result any more than does the Act itself.

Affirmed.

COMMISSIONER v. TUFTS
United States Supreme Court
461 U.S. 300 (1983)

JUSTICE BLACKMUN delivered the opinion of the Court.

Over 35 years ago, in *Crane v. Commissioner*, 331 U.S. 1 (1947), this Court ruled that a taxpayer, who sold property encumbered by a nonrecourse mortgage (the amount of the mortgage being less than the property's value), must include the unpaid balance of the mortgage in the computation of the amount the taxpayer realized on the sale. The case now before us presents the question whether the same rule applies when the unpaid amount of the nonrecourse mortgage exceeds the fair market value of the property sold.

I

On August 1, 1970, respondent Clark Pelt, a builder, and his wholly owned corporation, respondent Clark, Inc., formed a general partnership. The purpose of the partnership was to construct a 120-unit apartment complex in Duncanville, Tex., a Dallas suburb. Neither Pelt nor Clark, Inc., made any capital contribution to the partnership. Six days later, the partnership entered into a mortgage loan agreement with the Farm & Home Savings Association (F&H). Under the agreement,

F&H was committed for a $1,851,500 loan for the complex. In return, the partnership executed a note and a deed of trust in favor of F&H. The partnership obtained the loan on a nonrecourse basis: neither the partnership nor its partners assumed any personal liability for repayment of the loan. Pelt later admitted four friends and relatives, respondents Tufts, Steger, Stephens, and Austin, as general partners. None of them contributed capital upon entering the partnership.

The construction of the complex was completed in August 1971. During 1971, each partner made small capital contributions to the partnership; in 1972, however, only Pelt made a contribution. The total of the partners' capital contributions was $44,212. In each tax year, all partners claimed as income tax deductions their allocable shares of ordinary losses and depreciation. The deductions taken by the partners in 1971 and 1972 totalled $439,972. Due to these contributions and deductions, the partnership's adjusted basis in the property in August 1972 was $1,455,740.

In 1971 and 1972, major employers in the Duncanville area laid off significant numbers of workers. As a result, the partnership's rental income was less than expected, and it was unable to make the payments due on the mortgage. Each partner, on August 28, 1972, sold his partnership interest to an unrelated third party, Fred Bayles. As consideration, Bayles agreed to reimburse each partner's sale expenses up to $250; he also assumed the nonrecourse mortgage.

On the date of transfer, the fair market value of the property did not exceed $1,400,000. Each partner reported the sale on his federal income tax return and indicated that a partnership loss of $55,740 had been sustained.[6] The Commissioner of Internal Revenue, on audit, determined that the sale resulted in a partnership capital gain of approximately $400,000. His theory was that the partnership had realized the full amount of the nonrecourse obligation.

Relying on *Millar v. Commissioner*, 577 F.2d 212, 215 (CA3), *cert. denied*, 439 U.S. 1046 (1978), the United States Tax Court, in an unreviewed decision, upheld the asserted deficiencies. 70 T.C. 756 (1978). The United States Court of Appeals for the Fifth Circuit reversed. 651 F.2d 1058 (1981). That court expressly disagreed with the *Millar* analysis, and, in limiting *Crane v. Commissioner, supra*, to its facts, questioned the theoretical underpinnings of the *Crane* decision. We granted certiorari to resolve the conflict. 456 U.S. 960 (1982).

II

Section 752(d) of the Internal Revenue Code . . . specifically provides that liabilities incurred in the sale or exchange of a partnership interest are to "be treated in the same manner as liabilities in connection with the sale or exchange of property not associated with partnerships." Section 1001 governs the determination of gains and losses on the disposition of property. Under Section 1001(a), the gain or loss from a sale or other disposition of property is defined as the difference

---

[6] The loss was the difference between the adjusted basis, $1,455,740, and the fair market value of the property, $1,400,000. On their individual tax returns, the partners did not claim deductions for their respective shares of this loss. In their petitions to the Tax Court, however, the partners did claim the loss.

between "the amount realized" on the disposition and the property's adjusted basis. Subsection (b) of Section 1001 defined "amount realized": "The amount realized from the sale or other disposition of property shall be the sum of any money received plus the fair market value of the property (other than money) received." At issue is the application of the latter provision to the disposition of property encumbered by a nonrecourse mortgage of an amount in excess of the property's fair market value.

A

In *Crane v. Commissioner*, this Court took the first and controlling step toward the resolution of this issue. Beulah B. Crane was the sole beneficiary under the will of her deceased husband. At his death in January 1932, he owned an apartment building that was then mortgaged for an amount which proved to be equal to its fair market value, as determined for federal estate tax purposes. The widow, of course, was not personally liable on the mortgage. She operated the building for nearly seven years, hoping to turn it into a profitable venture; during that period, she claimed income tax deductions for depreciation, property taxes, interest, and operating expenses, but did not make payments upon the mortgage principal. In computing her basis for the depreciation deductions, she included the full amount of the mortgage debt. In November 1938, with her hopes unfulfilled and the mortgage threatening foreclosure, Mrs. Crane sold the building. The purchaser took the property subject to the mortgage and paid Crane $3,000; of that amount, $500 went for the expenses of the sale.

Crane reported a gain of $2,500 on the transaction. She reasoned that her basis in the property was zero (despite her earlier depreciation deductions based on including the amount of the mortgage) and that the amount she realized from the sale was simply the cash she received. The Commissioner disputed this claim. He asserted that Crane's basis in the property [§ 1014] was the property's fair market value at the time of her husband's death, adjusted for depreciation in the interim, and that the amount realized was the net cash received plus the amount of the outstanding mortgage assumed by the purchaser.

In upholding the Commissioner's interpretation of [§ 1014], the Court observed that to regard merely the taxpayer's equity in the property as her basis, would lead to depreciation deductions less than the actual physical deterioration of the property, and would require the basis to be recomputed with each payment on the mortgage. . . . The Court rejected Crane's claim that any loss due to depreciation belonged to the mortgagee. The effect of the Court's ruling was that the taxpayer's basis was the value of the property undiminished by the mortgage. . . .

The Court next proceeded to determine the amount realized under [§ 1001(b)]. In order to avoid the "absurdity" of Crane's realizing only $2,500 on the sale of property worth over a quarter of a million dollars, the Court treated the amount realized as it had treated basis, that is, by including the outstanding value of the mortgage. To do otherwise would have permitted Crane to recognize a tax loss unconnected with any actual economic loss. The Court refused to construe one section of the Revenue Act so as "to frustrate the Act as a whole." . . .

Crane, however, insisted that the nonrecourse nature of the mortgage required different treatment. The Court, for two reasons, disagreed. First, excluding the nonrecourse debt from the amount realized would result in the same absurdity and frustration of the Code. . . . Second, the Court concluded that Crane obtained an economic benefit from the purchaser's assumption of the mortgage, identical to the benefit conferred by the cancellation of personal debt. Because the value of the property in that case exceeded the amount of the mortgage, it was in Crane's economic interest to treat the mortgage as a personal obligation; only by so doing could she realize upon sale the appreciation in her equity represented by the $2,500 boot. The purchaser's assumption of the liability thus resulted in a taxable economic benefit to her, just as if she had been given, in addition to the boot, a sum of cash sufficient to satisfy the mortgage.

In a footnote, pertinent to the present case, the Court observed:

> Obviously, if the value of the property is less than the amount of the mortgage, a mortgagor who is not personally liable cannot realize a benefit equal to the mortgage. Consequently, a different problem might be encountered where a mortgagor abandoned the property or transferred it subject to the mortgage without receiving boot. That is not this case.

Id., at 74, n. 37.

B

This case presents that unresolved issue. We are disinclined to overrule *Crane*, and we conclude that the same rule applies when the unpaid amount of the nonrecourse mortgage exceeds the value of the property transferred. *Crane* ultimately does not rest on its limited theory of economic benefit; instead, we read *Crane* to have approved the Commissioner's decision to treat a nonrecourse mortgage in this context as a true loan. This approval underlies *Crane's* holdings that the amount of the nonrecourse liability is to be included in calculating both the basis and the amount realized on disposition. That the amount of the loan exceeds the fair market value of the property thus becomes irrelevant.

When a taxpayer receives a loan, he incurs an obligation to repay that loan at some future date. Because of this obligation, the loan proceeds do not qualify as income to the taxpayer. When he fulfills the obligation, the repayment of the loan likewise has no effect on his tax liability.

Another consequence to the taxpayer from this obligation occurs when the taxpayer applies the loan proceeds to the purchase price of property used to secure the loan. Because of the obligation to repay, the taxpayer is entitled to include the amount of the loan in computing his basis in the property; the loan, under Section 1012, is part of the taxpayer's cost of the property. Although a different approach might have been taken with respect to a nonrecourse mortgage loan,[7] the

---

[7] The Commissioner might have adopted the theory, implicit in Crane's contentions, that a nonrecourse mortgage is not true debt, but, instead, is a form of joint investment by the mortgagor and the mortgagee. On this approach, nonrecourse debt would be considered a contingent liability, under which the mortgagor's payments on the debt gradually increase his interest in the property while

Commissioner has chosen to accord it the same treatment he gives to a recourse mortgage loan. The Court approved that choice in *Crane,* and the respondents do not challenge it here. The choice and its resultant benefits to the taxpayer are predicated on the assumption that the mortgage will be repaid in full.

When encumbered property is sold or otherwise disposed of and the purchaser assumes the mortgage, the associated extinguishment of the mortgagor's obligation to repay is accounted for in the computation of the amount realized. . . . Because no difference between recourse and nonrecourse obligations is recognized in calculating basis,[8] *Crane* teaches that the Commissioner may ignore the nonrecourse nature of the obligation in determining the amount realized upon disposition of the encumbered property. He thus may include in the amount realized the amount of the nonrecourse mortgage assumed by the purchaser. The rationale for this treatment is that the original inclusion of the amount of the mortgage in basis rested on the assumption that the mortgagor incurred an obligation to repay. Moreover, this treatment balances the fact that the mortgagor originally received the proceeds of the nonrecourse loan tax-free on the same assumption. Unless the outstanding amount of the mortgage is deemed to be realized, the mortgagor effectively will have received untaxed income at the time the loan was extended and will have received an unwarranted increase in the basis of his property.[9] The Commissioner's interpretation of Section 1001(b) in this fashion cannot be said to be unreasonable.

C

The Commissioner in fact has applied this rule even when the fair market value of the property falls below the amount of the nonrecourse obligation. Treas. Reg. Section 1.1001-2(b), Rev. Rul. 76-111, 1976-1 Cum. Bull. 214. Because the theory on which the rule is based applies equally in this situation, . . . we have no reason, after *Crane,* to question this treatment.[10]

---

decreasing that of the mortgagee. . . . Because the taxpayer's investment in their property would not include the nonrecourse debt, the taxpayer would not be permitted to include that debt in basis. . . .

We express no view as to whether such an approach would be consistent with the statutory structure and, if so, and *Crane* were not on the books, whether that approach would be preferred over *Crane's* analysis. We note only that the *Crane* Court's resolution of the basic issue presumed that when property is purchased with proceeds from a nonrecourse mortgage, the purchaser becomes the sole owner of the property. 331 U.S., at 6. Under the *Crane* approach, the mortgagee is entitled to no portion of the basis. *Id.*, at 10, no. 28. The nonrecourse mortgage is part of the mortgagor's investment in the property, and does not constitute a coinvestment by the mortgagee. . . .

[8] The Commissioner's choice in *Crane* "laid the foundation stone of most tax shelters," Bittker, *Tax Shelters, Nonrecourse Debt, and the Crane Case*, 33 Tax. L. Rev. 277, 283 (1978), by permitting taxpayers who bear no risk to take deductions on depreciable property.

[9] Although the *Crane* rule has some affinity with the tax benefit rule, . . . the analysis we adopt is different. Our analysis applies even in the situation in which no deductions are taken. It focuses on the obligation to repay and its subsequent extinguishment, not on the taking and recovery of deductions. *See generally* Note, 82 Colum. L. Rev., at 1526–1529.

[10] Professor Wayne G. Barnett, as *amicus* in the present case, argues that the liability and property portions of the transaction should be accounted for separately. Under his view, there was a transfer of the property for $1.4 million, and there was a cancellation of the $1.85 million obligation for a payment of $1.4 million. The former resulted in a capital loss of $50,000, and the latter in the realization of $450,000

Respondents received a mortgage loan with the concomitant obligation to repay by the year 2012. The only difference between that mortgage and one on which the borrower is personally liable is that the mortgagee's remedy is limited to foreclosing on the securing property. This difference does not alter the nature of the obligation; its only effect is to shift from the borrower to the lender any potential loss caused by devaluation of the property. If the fair market value of the property falls below the amount of the outstanding obligation, the mortgagee's ability to protect its interests is impaired, for the mortgagor is free to abandon the property to the mortgagee and be relieved of his obligation.

This, however, does not erase the fact that the mortgagor received the loan proceeds tax-free and included them in his basis on the understanding that he had an obligation to repay the full amount. *See Woodsam Associates, Inc. v. Commissioner*, 198 F.2d 357, 359 (CA2 1952); Bittker, 33 Tax. L. Rev., at 284. When the obligation is canceled, the mortgagor is relieved of his responsibility to repay the sum he originally received and thus realizes value to that extent within the meaning of Section 1001(b). From the mortgagor's point of view, when his obligation is assumed by a third party who purchases the encumbered property, it is as if the mortgagor first had been paid with cash borrowed by the third party from the mortgagee on a nonrecourse basis, and then had used the cash to satisfy his obligation to the mortgagee.

Moreover, this approach avoids the absurdity the Court recognized in *Crane*. Because of the remedy accompanying the mortgage in the nonrecourse situation, the depreciation in the fair market value of the property is relevant economically only to the mortgagee, who by lending on a nonrecourse basis remains at risk. To permit the taxpayer to limit his realization to the fair market value of the property

---

of ordinary income. Taxation of the ordinary income might be deferred under Section 108 by a reduction of respondents' bases in their partnership interests.

Although this indeed could be a profitable mode of analysis, it has not been adopted by the Commissioner. Nor is there anything to indicate that the Code requires the Commissioner to adopt it.

The Commissioner also has chosen not to characterize the transaction as cancellation of indebtedness. We are not presented with and do not decide the contours of the cancellation-of-indebtedness doctrine. We note only that our approach does not fall within certain prior interpretations of that doctrine. In one view, the doctrine rests on the same initial premise as our analysis here — an obligation to repay — but the doctrine relies on a freeing-of-assets theory to attribute ordinary income to the debtor upon cancellation. *See Commissioner v. Jacobson*, 336 U.S. 28, 38–40 (1949); *United States v. Kirby Lumber Co.*, 284 U.S. 1, 3 (1931). According to that view, when nonrecourse debt is forgiven, the debtor's basis in the securing property is reduced by the amount of debt canceled, and realization of income is deferred until the sale of the property. . . . Because that interpretation attributes income only when assets are freed, however, an insolvent debtor realizes income just to the extent his assets exceed his liabilities after the cancellation. *Lakeland Grocery Co. v. Commissioner*, 36 B.T.A. 289, 292 (1937). Similarly, if the nonrecourse indebtedness exceeds the value of the securing property, the taxpayer never realizes the full amount of the obligation canceled because the tax law has not recognized negative basis.

Although the economic benefit prong of *Crane* also relies on a freeing-of-assets theory, that theory is irrelevant to our broader approach. In the context of a sale or disposition of property under Section 1001, the extinguishment of the obligation to repay is not ordinary income; instead, the amount of the canceled debt is included in the amount realized, and enters into the computation of gain or loss on the disposition of property. According to *Crane*, this treatment is no different when the obligation is nonrecourse: the basis is not reduced as in the cancellation-of-indebtedness context, and the full value of the outstanding liability is included in the amount realized. Thus, the problem of negative basis is avoided.

would be to recognize a tax loss for which he has suffered no corresponding economic loss.[11] Such result would be to construe "one section of the Act . . . so as . . . to defeat the intention of another or to frustrate the Act as a whole." 331 U.S., at 13.

In the specific circumstances of *Crane*, the economic benefit theory did support the Commissioner's treatment of the nonrecourse mortgage as a personal obligation. The footnote in *Crane* acknowledged the limitations of that theory when applied to a different set of facts. *Crane* also stands for the broader proposition, however, that a nonrecourse loan should be treated as a true loan. We therefore hold that a taxpayer must account for the proceeds of obligations he has received tax-free and included in basis. Nothing in either Section 1001(b) or in the Court's prior decisions requires the Commissioner to permit a taxpayer to treat a sale of encumbered property asymmetrically, by including the proceeds of the nonrecourse obligation in basis but not accounting for the proceeds upon transfer of the encumbered property.

IV

When a taxpayer sells or disposes of property encumbered by a nonrecourse obligation, the Commissioner properly requires him to include among the assets realized the outstanding amount of the obligation. The fair market value of the property is irrelevant to this calculation. We find this interpretation to be consistent with *Crane v. Commissioner*, 331 U.S. 1 (1947), and to implement the statutory mandate in a reasonable manner.

The judgment of the Court of Appeals is therefore

Reversed.

REVENUE RULING 91-31
1991-1 C.B. 19

ISSUE

If the principal amount of an undersecured nonrecourse debt is reduced by the holder of the debt who was not the seller of the property securing the debt, does this debt reduction result in the realization of discharge of indebtedness income for the year of the reduction under section 61(a)(12) of the Internal Revenue Code or in the reduction of the basis in the property securing the debt?

---

[11] In the present case, the Government bore the ultimate loss. The nonrecourse mortgage was extended to respondents only after the planned complex was endorsed for mortgage insurance under Sections 221(b) and (d)(4) of the National Housing Act, 12 U.S.C. § 17151(b) and (d)(4) (1976 ed. and Supp. V). After acquiring the complex from respondents, Bayles operated it for a few years, but was unable to make it profitable. In 1974, F&H foreclosed, and the Department of Housing and Urban Development paid off the lender to obtain title. In 1976, the Department sold the complex to another developer for $1,502,000. The sale was financed by the Department's taking back a note for $1,314,800 and a nonrecourse mortgage. To fail to recognize the value of the nonrecourse loan in the amount realized, therefore, would permit respondents to compound the Government's loss by claiming the tax benefits of that loss for themselves.

FACTS

In 1988, individual A borrowed $1,000,000 from C and signed a note payable to C for $1,000,000 that bore interest at a fixed market rate payable annually. A had no personal liability with respect to the note, which was secured by an office building valued at $1,000,000 that A acquired from B with the proceeds of the nonrecourse financing. In 1989, when the value of the office building was $800,000 and the outstanding principal on the note was $1,000,000, C agreed to modify the terms of the note by reducing the note's principal amount to $800,000. The modified note bore adequate stated interest within the meaning of section 1274(c)(2).

The facts here do not involve the bankruptcy, insolvency, or qualified farm indebtedness of the taxpayer. Thus, the specific exclusions provided by section 108(a) do not apply.

LAW AND ANALYSIS

Section 61(a)(12) of the Code provides that gross income includes income from the discharge of indebtedness. Section 1.61-12(a) of the Income Tax Regulations provides that the discharge of indebtedness, in whole or in part, may result in the realization of income.

In Rev. Rul. 82-202, 1982-2 C.B. 35, a taxpayer prepaid the mortgage held by a third party lender on the taxpayer's residence for less than the principal balance of the mortgage. At the time of the prepayment, the fair market value of the residence was greater than the principal balance of the mortgage. The revenue ruling holds that the taxpayer realizes discharge of indebtedness income under section 61(a)(12) of the Code, whether the mortgage is recourse or nonrecourse and whether it is partially or fully prepaid. Rev. Rul 82-202 relies on *United States v. Kirby Lumber Co.*, 284 U.S. 1 (1931), X-2 C.B. 356 (1931), in which the United States Supreme Court held that a taxpayer realized ordinary income upon the purchase of its own bonds in an arm's length transaction at less than their face amount.

In *Commissioner v. Tufts*, 461 U.S. 300 (1983), 1983-1 C.B. 120, the Supreme Court held that when a taxpayer sold property encumbered by a nonrecourse obligation that exceeded the fair market value of the property sold, the amount realized included the amount of the obligation discharged. The Court reasoned that because a nonrecourse note is treated as a true debt upon inception (so that the loan proceeds are not taken into income at that time), a taxpayer is bound to treat the nonrecourse note as a true debt when the taxpayer is discharged from the liability upon disposition of the collateral, notwithstanding the lesser fair market value of the collateral. See section 1.1001-2(c), Example 7, of the Income Tax Regulations.

In *Gershkowitz v. Commissioner*, 88 T.C. 984 (1987), the Tax Court, in a reviewed opinion, concluded, in part, that the settlement of a nonrecourse debt of $250,000 for a $40,000 cash payment (rather than surrender of the $2,500 collateral) resulted in $210,000 of discharge of indebtedness income. The court, following the *Tufts* holding that income results when a taxpayer is discharged from liability for an undersecured nonrecourse obligation upon the disposition of the collateral, held that the discharge from a portion of the liability for an undersecured nonrecourse obligation through a cash settlement must also result in income.

The Service will follow the holding in *Gershkowitz* where a taxpayer is discharged from all or a portion of a nonrecourse liability when there is no disposition of the collateral. Thus, in the present case, A realizes $200,000 of discharge of indebtedness income in 1989 as a result of the modification of A's note payable to C.

In an earlier Board of Tax Appeals decision, *Fulton Gold Corp. v. Commissioner*, 31 B.T.A. 519 (1934), a taxpayer purchased property without assuming an outstanding mortgage and subsequently satisfied the mortgage for less than its face amount. In a decision based on unclear facts, the Board of Tax Appeals, for purposes of determining the taxpayer's gain or loss upon the sale of the property in a later year, held that the taxpayer's basis in the property should have been reduced by the amount of the mortgage debt forgiven in the earlier year.

The *Tufts* and *Gershkowitz* decisions implicitly reject any interpretation of *Fulton Gold* that a reduction in the amount of a nonrecourse liability by the holder of the debt who was not the seller of the property securing the liability results in a reduction of the basis in that property, rather than discharge of indebtedness income for the year of the reduction. *Fulton Gold*, interpreted in this manner, is inconsistent with *Tufts* and *Gershkowitz*. Therefore, that interpretation is rejected and will not be followed.

HOLDING

The reduction of the principal amount of an undersecured nonrecourse debt by the holder of a debt who was not the seller of the property securing the debt results in the realization of discharge of indebtedness income under section 61(a)(12) of the Code.

ESTATE OF FRANKLIN v. COMMISSIONER
United States Court of Appeals, Ninth Circuit
544 F.2d 1045 (1976)

SNEED, CIRCUIT JUDGE:

This case involves another effort on the part of the Commissioner to curb the use of real estate tax shelters. In this instance he seeks to disallow deductions for the taxpayers' distributive share of losses reported by a limited partnership with respect to its acquisition of a motel and related property. These deductions were disallowed by the Commissioner on the ground either that the acquisition was a sham or that the entire acquisition transaction was in substance the purchase by the partnership of an option to acquire the motel and related property on January 15, 1979. The Tax Court held that the transaction constituted an option exercisable in 1979 and disallowed the taxpayers' deductions. . . . We affirm this disallowance although our approach differs somewhat from that of the Tax Court.

The interest and depreciation deductions were taken by Twenty-Fourth Property Associates (hereinafter referred to as Associates), a California limited partnership of which Charles T. Franklin and seven other doctors were limited partners.

The deductions flowed from the purported "purchase" by Associates of the Thunderbird Inn, an Arizona motel, from Wayne L. Romney and Joan E. Romney (hereinafter referred to as the Romneys) on November 15, 1968.

Under a document entitled "Sales Agreement," the Romneys agreed to "sell" the Thunderbird Inn to Associates for $1,224,000. The property would be paid for over a period of ten years, with interest on any unpaid balance of seven and one-half percent per annum. "Prepaid interest" in the amount of $75,000 was payable immediately; monthly principal and interest installments of $9,045.36 would be paid for approximately the first ten years, with Associates required to make a balloon payment at the end of the ten years of the difference between the remaining purchase price, forecast as $975,000, and any mortgages then outstanding against the property.

The purchase obligation of Associates to the Romneys was nonrecourse; the Romneys' only remedy in the event of default would be forfeiture of the partnership's interest. The sales agreement was recorded in the local county. A warranty deed was placed in an escrow account, along with a quitclaim deed from Associates to the Romneys, both documents to be delivered either to Associates upon full payment of the purchase price, or to the Romneys upon default.

The sale was combined with a leaseback of the property by Associates to the Romneys; Associates therefore never took physical possession. The lease payments were designed to approximate closely the principal and interest payments with the consequence that with the exception of the $75,000 prepaid interest payment no cash would cross between Associates and Romneys until the balloon payment. The lease was on a net basis; thus, the Romneys were responsible for all of the typical expenses of owning the motel property including all utility costs, taxes, assessments, rents, charges, and levies of "every name, nature and kind whatsoever." The Romneys also were to continue to be responsible for the first and second mortgages until the final purchase installment was made; the Romneys could, and indeed did, place additional mortgages on the property without the permission of Associates. Finally, the Romneys were allowed to propose new capital improvements which Associates would be required to either build themselves or allow the Romneys to construct with compensating modifications in rent or purchase price.

In holding that the transaction between Associates and the Romneys more nearly resembled an option than a sale, the Tax Court emphasized that Associates had the power at the end of ten years to walk away from the transaction and merely lose its $75,000 "prepaid interest payment." It also pointed out that a deed was never recorded and that the "benefits and burdens of ownership" appeared to remain with the Romneys. Thus, the sale was combined with a leaseback in which no cash would pass; the Romneys remained responsible under the mortgages, which they could increase; and the Romneys could make capital improvements.

Our emphasis is different from that of the Tax Court. We believe the characteristics set out above can exist in a situation in which the sale imposes upon the purchaser a genuine indebtedness within the meaning of section 167(a), Internal Revenue Code of 1954, which will support both interest and depreciation deductions. They substantially so existed in *Hudspeth v. Commissioner*, 509 F.2d 1224 (9th Cir. 1975), in which parents entered into sale-leaseback transactions with their children. The children paid for the property by executing nonnegotiable notes and mortgages equal to the fair market value of the property; state law proscribed deficiency judgments in case of default, limiting the parents' remedy to foreclosure of the property. The children had no funds with which to make mortgage payments; instead, the payments were offset in part by the rental payments, with the difference met by gifts from the parents to their children. Despite these characteristics this court held that there was a bona fide indebtedness on which the children, to the extent of the rental payments, could base interest deductions.

In none of these cases, however, did the taxpayer fail to demonstrate that the purchase price was at least approximately equivalent to the fair market value of the property. Just such a failure occurred here. The Tax Court explicitly found that on the basis of the facts before it the value of the property could not be estimated.[12] . . . In our view this defect in the taxpayers' proof is fatal.

Reason supports our perception. An acquisition such as that of Associates if at a price approximately equal to the fair market value of the property under ordinary circumstances would rather quickly yield an equity in the property which the purchaser could not prudently abandon. This is the stuff of substance. It meshes with the form of the transaction and constitutes a sale.

No such meshing occurs when the purchase price exceeds a demonstrably reasonable estimate of the fair market value. Payments on the principal of the purchase price yield no equity so long as the unpaid balance of the purchase price exceeds the then existing fair market value. Under these circumstances the purchaser by abandoning the transaction can lose no more than a mere chance to acquire an equity in the future should the value of the acquired property increase. While this chance undoubtedly influenced the Tax Court's determination that the transaction before us constitutes an option, we need only point out that its existence fails to supply the substance necessary to justify treating the transaction as a sale *ab initio*. It is not necessary to the disposition of this case to decide the tax consequences of a transaction such as that before us if in a subsequent year the fair market value of the property increases to an extent that permits the purchaser to acquire an equity.

Authority also supports our perception. It is fundamental that "depreciation is not predicated upon ownership of property but rather upon an investment in property. . . . " No such investment exists when payments of the purchase price in accordance with the design of the parties yield no equity to the purchaser. . . . In the transaction before us and during the taxable years in question the purchase price payments by Associates have not been shown to constitute an investment in

---

[12] Such evidence of fair market value as was relied upon by the appellants, viz. two appraisals, one completed in 1968 and a second in 1971, even if fully admissible as evidence of the truth of the estimates of value appearing therein, does not require us to set aside the Tax Court's finding. As the Tax Court found, the 1968 appraisal was "error-filled, sketchy" and "obviously suspect." 64 T.C. at 767 n. 13. The 1971 appraisal had little relevancy as to 1968 values. On the other side, there existed cogent evidence indicating that the fair market value was substantially less than the purchase price. This evidence included (i) the Romneys' purchase of the stock of two corporations, one of which wholly-owned the motel, for approximately $800,000 in the year preceding the "sale" to Associates ($660,000 of which was allocable to the sale property, according to Mr. Romney's estimate), and (ii) insurance policies on the property from 1967 through 1974 of only $583,200, $700,000, and $614,000. 64 T.C. at 767–768.

the property. Depreciation was properly disallowed. Only the Romneys had an investment in the property.

Authority also supports disallowance of the interest deductions. This is said even though it has long been recognized that the absence of personal liability for the purchase money debt secured by a mortgage on the acquired property does not deprive the debt of its character as a bona fide debt obligation able to support an interest deduction. . . . However, this is no longer true when it appears that the debt has economic significance only if the property substantially appreciates in value prior to the date at which a very large portion of the purchase price is to be discharged. Under these circumstances the purchaser has not secured "the use or forbearance of money." Nor has the seller advanced money or forborne its use. . . . Prior to the date at which the balloon payment on the purchase price is required, and assuming no substantial increase in the fair market value of the property, the absence of personal liability on the debt reduces the transaction in economic terms to a mere chance that a genuine debt obligation may arise. This is not enough to justify an interest deduction. To justify the deduction the debt must exist; potential existence will not do. For debt to exist, the purchaser, in the absence of personal liability, must confront a situation in which it is presently reasonable from an economic point of view for him to make a capital investment in the amount of the unpaid purchase price. . . . Associates, during the taxable years in question, confronted no such situation. . . .

Our focus on the relationship of the fair market value of the property to the unpaid purchase price should not be read as premised upon the belief that a sale is not a sale if the purchaser pays too much. Bad bargains from the buyer's point of view — as well as sensible bargains from the buyer's, but exceptionally good from the seller's point of view — do not thereby cease to be sales. . . . We intend our holding and explanation thereof to be understood as limited to transactions substantially similar to that now before us.

Affirmed.

AIZAWA v. COMMISSIONER
United States Tax Court
99 T.C. 197 (1992), *aff'd*
without published opinion, 29 F.3d 630 (9th Cir. 1994)

TANNENWALD, JUDGE:

As a result of concessions of the parties, the only issue remaining for decision is the proper amount of petitioners' loss in 1987, resulting from a foreclosure sale.

Petitioners owned rental property which they purchased in 1981 for $120,000 plus $433 in closing costs. At the time of purchase, they gave the sellers a $90,000 recourse mortgage note with interest only payable at the rate of $750 monthly, and the entire principal due and payable in June 1985. They made their last payment of interest in February 1985. Petitioners did not make any payment on the principal when due.

In 1987, the sellers obtained a judgment of $133,506.91 against petitioners in a foreclosure action, consisting of $90,000.00 mortgage principal, $18,000.00 accrued and unpaid interest, $25,000.00 in attorney's fees and $500.00 in court costs. Also in 1987, the property was sold to the sellers at a foreclosure sale for $72,700.00 which was applied to petitioners' obligation under such judgment, leaving a deficiency judgment of $60,806.91.

There is no dispute between the parties that the foreclosure sale constituted a sale for tax purposes, that petitioners suffered a loss thereon in 1987, and that petitioners' basis in the property at the time of the foreclosure sale was $100,091.38. Their dispute is with respect to the calculation of the "amount realized" on the foreclosure sale which should be applied against petitioners' basis, under section 1001(a), in order to determine the amount of their loss.

Surprisingly, as far as we can determine, this is the first time a court has confronted this issue directly. Petitioners contend that the deficiency judgment should be deducted from the unpaid mortgage principal and that the difference of $29,193.09 ($90,000.00 minus $60,806.91) constitutes the amount realized on the foreclosure sale which, when deducted from their basis, produces a loss of $70,898.29 ($100,091.38 minus $29,193.09). Respondent counters that the $90,000.00 unpaid mortgage principal constitutes the amount realized on the foreclosure sale which, when deducted from petitioners' basis, produces a loss of $10,091.38 ($100,091.38 minus $90,000.00).

Petitioners' position suffers from the infirmity that it calculates the amount realized by offsetting against only the unpaid principal balance of the mortgage the total amount of the deficiency judgment, which includes not only such unpaid balance but also the amounts representing accrued interest, attorney's fees, and court costs, amounts which petitioners, who are cash-basis taxpayers, have not yet paid. A proper calculation along the lines of petitioners' position, at the very least, would have added such latter amounts to the unpaid mortgage principal before making the indicated subtraction or alternatively omitted them from the calculation of the deficiency judgment. Such equalizing would produce the result that the "amount realized" under section 1001(a) would be an amount represented by the proceeds of the foreclosure sale, a result we reach but by a different path.

Turning to respondent's position, we think it does not present an acceptable resolution of the issue before us. It requires petitioners to treat as money received an amount of their unpaid mortgage principal obligation from which they have not yet been discharged, leaving to the future the tax consequences of any subsequent payments or settlement of the deficiency judgment for less than the unpaid amount. Such treatment presents an obvious complication in that, if petitioners are thereafter relieved, either in whole or in part, of their obligation for the unpaid mortgage principal subsumed in the deficiency judgment, the usual rules as to income from discharge of an indebtedness will be difficult to apply. Those rules rest on the premise that taxpayers should not be permitted to retain the economic benefit of money received (or alternatively the freeing of assets which would otherwise have to be used to repay the indebtedness) in respect of which they have not previously paid a tax, see *Commissioner v. Tufts*, 461 U.S. 300, 311 n. 11 (1983). By hypothesis, this situation will not obtain because petitioners will have already in effect paid the tax on their obligation for the amount of the unpaid mortgage principal.

The key to the resolution of the issue before us lies in the recognition that, in this case, there is a clear separation between the foreclosure sale and the unpaid recourse liability for mortgage principal which survives as part of a deficiency judgment. In the decided cases, the courts concluded that such survival did not exist and that the discharge of the recourse liability was closely related to, and should be considered an integral part of, the foreclosure sale. Having so concluded, the courts reasoned that the same rationale as that of *Commissioner v. Tufts, supra* at 311–312, in respect of discharged recourse and nonrecourse mortgages, should be applied.

Where, as in this case, such separateness exists, the significance of the amount of the proceeds of the foreclosure sale becomes apparent. It cannot be gainsaid that the property was sold for $72,700 (an amount which we have no reason to conclude did not represent the fair market value of the property) and that petitioners received, by way of a reduction in the judgment of foreclosure, that amount and nothing more. That is the "amount realized" under section 1001(a) which is subtracted from petitioners' basis in order to determine the amount of their loss.

We are aware of the fact that this approach enables petitioners to increase their loss by $17,300 ($90,000 less $72,700) representing borrowed funds which they might not repay and on which they have not yet paid a tax. But this is nothing more than the logical consequence of *Crane v. Commissioner*, 331 U.S. 1 (1947), which has been treated as sanctioning the right of a cash-basis taxpayer to include the amount of an unpaid mortgage liability in his or her basis. To the extent that this presents a problem, it involves only a question of timing since subsequent events will eliminate any benefit petitioners may have obtained. They will not be entitled to deduct, as additional losses, any future payment against such unpaid principal, since the amount of such payment has already in effect been deducted. Additionally, they will be required to account for any benefit which they may obtain by way of a subsequent discharge, in whole or in part, of the amount of their indebtedness represented by the borrowed funds that have not been repaid.

Nothing in *Commissioner v. Tufts, supra*, requires the rejection of the proceeds of the foreclosure sale, which represent fair market value of the property, as the amount realized for the purpose of determining petitioners' loss. The language of the Supreme Court, which suggests that fair market value is irrelevant where that value is less than the amount of the unpaid mortgage principal, see *Commissioner v. Tufts*, 461 U.S. at 307, was directed to the situation where that mortgage obligation was discharged — a situation which does not obtain herein. In point of fact, the Supreme Court implied, *Id.* at 311 n. 11, that fair market value, and therefore the proceeds of the sale of the property for that amount, might indeed be relevant where the foreclosure sale and the treatment of the mortgage obligation were separate.

Our conclusion that the proceeds of the foreclosure sale is the "amount realized" under section 1001(a) is further supported by the following analogy. Assume that, prior to the foreclosure, petitioners had an opportunity to sell the property for $72,700 to a third party who wanted to acquire the property free and clear.

Petitioners asked their mortgagee to release the mortgage as security for their recourse obligation, and the mortgagee was willing to do so because petitioners were then persons of substantial means so that their unsecured obligation, which would continue, involved little or no risk. The mortgage was released (a nontaxable event, see *Lutz & Schramm Co. v. Commissioner*, 1 T.C. 682, 689 (1943)), and the property was then sold to the third party. There can be no doubt that, under these circumstances, petitioners' loss would be $27,391.38 ($100,091.38 basis minus $72,700.00). This scenario is, in substance, the same as exists herein; in both situations, the mortgage disappears as security and the personal obligation of the petitioners to pay the balance of their recourse obligation survives.

In sum, we conclude that the $72,700.00 proceeds of the foreclosure sale constitute the "amount realized" under section 1001(a) and that consequently petitioners' loss was $27,391.38 (petitioners' basis of $100,091.38 less the foreclosure sale proceeds of $72,700.00).

Chapter 39

LIKE KIND EXCHANGES

I. PROBLEMS

1. Kevin owns a tract of land which he has farmed for many years. The land has an adjusted basis of $300,000 and a value of $1,000,000. Kevin exchanges the land for improved commercial real estate owned by Ashley. Kevin intends to conduct a farm implement business on the property.

   (a) Assume Ashley's commercial real estate is worth exactly $1,000,000. Explain the tax consequences of this exchange to Kevin.

   (b) Assume Ashley's commercial real estate is worth $2,000,000. Ashley gives Kevin a one-half interest in that property in exchange for Kevin's land. One month following the exchange, Kevin and Ashley transfer their interests in the commercial real estate to a newly-created corporation in which they are the sole shareholders. The corporation will conduct the farm implement business on the property. Explain the tax consequences of the exchange to Kevin.

   (c) Assume the commercial real estate owned by Ashley has a fair market value of only $750,000. As a result, Ashley also gives Kevin $250,000 in cash in addition to the commercial real estate.

    (i) What are the tax consequences to Kevin?

    (ii) How would your answer change if Kevin's adjusted basis in his land were $800,000?

    (iii) How would your answer to (i) change if Kevin's adjusted basis in his land were $1,100,000?

    (iv) How would your answer to (i) change if Ashley, instead of giving Kevin $250,000 in cash, gave him $100,000 in cash and an undeveloped lakefront lot with a fair market value of $150,000? Assume Kevin plans to build a home for himself on the lakefront lot he receives from Ashley.

    (v) How would your answer to (iii) change if Kevin planned to hold the lakefront lot as an investment instead of using it for personal purposes?

   (d) Assume Kevin's land is worth only $900,000. He exchanges the land and a piece of business equipment worth $100,000 in which he has an adjusted basis of $125,000 for Ashley's commercial real estate worth $1,000,000. What are the tax consequences to Kevin?

(e) Assume Kevin's land is worth $1,000,000 and is subject to a mortgage of $100,000 and Ashley's commercial real estate is worth $900,000. Kevin and Ashley simply exchange properties, and Ashley takes Kevin's land subject to the mortgage. What are the tax consequences to Kevin?

(f) What difference in (e) if Ashley's commercial real estate is worth $1,500,000, but is subject to a $600,000 mortgage, and on the exchange Kevin takes Ashley's property subject to the mortgage?

(g) Assume the facts of (e) except Ashley's commercial real estate is worth $1,250,000, has an adjusted basis to Ashley of $500,000, and is encumbered by a $450,000 mortgage. Ashley transfers the commercial real estate plus $100,000 in cash to Kevin, and Kevin takes Ashley's property subject to the $450,000 mortgage. What tax consequences to Kevin and Ashley? In answering this question, assume Ashley used the commercial real estate in her business and plans to use the land she receives from Kevin in her business.

(h) Assume the facts of (a) except Ashley is Kevin's daughter. Assume Ashley had a $975,000 adjusted basis in the commercial real estate which she relinquished to Kevin in the exchange. Ashley also claimed § 1031 treatment on the exchange. What effect, if any, if Ashley sells the land for $1,000,000 during the year following the exchange?

2. Fifteen years ago Maureen bought some undeveloped lakefront land for $50,000 anticipating the lake would become a major year-round resort area and the land would greatly increase in value. Maureen's foresight was amply rewarded; the land is currently worth $500,000. Because she is not convinced that the property will appreciate much in the next few years, Maureen decided recently to sell the property and invest the proceeds in commercial real estate. In anticipation of selling the lake property, Maureen began looking at different commercial properties on the market and has identified a few parcels of commercial real estate which interest her. On June 1 of this year, Patrick offered to purchase Maureen's lake property for $500,000. Maureen accepted the offer and signed a buy/sell agreement requiring the parties to close the transaction on July 1. Prior to the closing, Maureen learns she could save significant taxes were she to exchange the lake property for commercial real estate. Patrick is insistent that Maureen abide by the terms of the buy/sell and transfer the lake property to him on July 1. Maureen consults you for advice. Explain how Maureen might fulfill her obligations under the buy/sell agreement and yet qualify for like kind exchange treatment under § 1031.

3. Carla, an entrepreneur with extensive real estate investments, learns Giovanni plans to sell a large tract of land adjacent to a national park. Carla, who has some highly appreciated real estate which she is willing to exchange, approaches Giovanni with an exchange proposal. Because he is interested in a cash sale, Giovanni rejects Carla's proposal. Knowing Giovanni's property will likely sell quickly, Carla seeks advice from you regarding a means of acquiring Giovanni's property but at the same time taking advantage of § 1031. Explain the advice you would give Carla.

4. In 2003, Fergus, who is single, paid $300,000 for a three-bedroom bungalow that served as his principal residence until January 1, 2013 when he moved and converted the bungalow to a rental. After renting the bungalow for two years, Fergus exchanged it on January 1, 2015 for a duplex worth $400,000 plus $350,000 in cash. He will hold the duplex as a rental. Assume that Fergus had appropriately claimed $50,000 in depreciation on the bungalow during the period he had rented it to tenants. Assuming he is otherwise eligible for the § 121 exclusion, explain the tax consequences to Fergus on the exchange. What basis will Fergus take in the duplex?

5. Assume the facts of problem 4 except that the bungalow was never Fergus' principal residence, but instead was, until 2013, used by Fergus solely as his vacation home. Because illness significantly limited his use of the vacation home, Fergus, on January 1, 2013, began to offer the bungalow for rent. He had never previously rented the bungalow or offered it for rent. During 2013, Fergus rented the bungalow at its fair market rental value for 240 days and used it for his own personal purposes on 12 days. During 2014, Fergus rented the bungalow at its fair market rental value for 280 days and used the bungalow for his own personal purposes on only 10 days. Assume, as in Problem 4, that, up to the time of the exchange in 2015, Fergus appropriately claimed $50,000 in depreciation deductions and, as a result, had a $250,000 adjusted basis in the bungalow. Explain the tax consequences of the exchange to Fergus.

Assignment for Chapter 39:

Complete the problems.

Read: Internal Revenue Code: §§ 121(d)(10); 267(a)(1), (b), (d); 1031(a)–(d), (f), (g); 1223(1); 1245(b)(4); 1250(d)(4) (skim).
Treasury Regulations: §§ 1.1002-1(c), (d); 1.1031(a)-1(a)-(c); 1.1031(a)-2; 1.1031(b)-1; 1.1031(b)-2; 1.1031(d)-1(a)–(e); 1.1031(d)-2 Examples (1) and (2); 1.1031(k)-1(a), (b), (c)(1)–(4), (d), (f)(1)–(3), (g)(1)–(5), (k), (m).

Materials: Overview
Revenue Ruling 77-297
Revenue Ruling 72-151
Bolker v. Commissioner
Bell Lines, Inc. v. United States
Revenue Ruling 90-34
Revenue Procedure 2008-16
Revenue Procedure 2000-37

II.   VOCABULARY

like kind property
exchange
holding requirements
continuity of investment
boot
three-way exchange

deferred exchange
anti-*Starker* rules

III.   OBJECTIVES

1. To evaluate whether particular properties are like kind.

2. To generalize as to when properties will be like kind.

3. To recall the policy underlying § 1031.

4. To explain the holding requirements.

5. To contrast real property and personal property in terms of the like kind rules.

6. To distinguish a sale of property from an exchange.

7. To recall that net liability relief, reduced by any cash paid, constitutes boot.

8. To recall that losses on like kind property are not recognized, even when boot is received.

9. To compute basis on property received in a like kind exchange.

10. To compute recognized gain on an exchange.

11. To identify exchanges on which losses are recognized.

12. To describe a three-way exchange.

13. To determine which parties in a three-way exchange are entitled to § 1031 treatment.

14. To identify the circumstances in which a three-way exchange will be used.

15. To compute gain recognized and adjusted basis in exchanges involving assumption of liabilities, or taking subject to liabilities, by both parties to the exchange, and the transfer of cash from one party to the other.

16. To explain the purpose of the anti-*Starker* (deferred exchange) rules.

17. To apply the anti-*Starker* rules.

18. To explain in how a "reverse *Starker*" exchange would be structured.

19. To explain how § 1031 is applied in an exchange to which § 121 is also applicable.

IV.   OVERVIEW

Gains or losses *realized* on the sale or exchange of property must generally be *recognized*. Section 1001(c). Under § 1031 of the Code, however, no gain or loss is recognized when property held for productive use in a trade or business or for investment is exchanged solely for property of "like kind" to be held for productive use in a trade or business or for investment. This *nonrecognition* rule has been part of the Code since its enactment in the Revenue Act of 1921.

Section 1031(a)(2) lists six exceptions to the rule. The exception for stock in trade or other property held primarily for sale was part of the original 1921 legislation. (Compare the wording of this exception with that of § 1221(a)(1), excluding certain property from the definition of a capital asset.) There are additional exceptions for exchanges of stocks, bonds, notes, choses in action, certificates of trust or beneficial interest, or other securities or evidences of indebtedness or interest. Congress added these exceptions in 1923, largely because the like kind provision was viewed as having been abused by brokers and investment houses that had established "exchange departments" to exchange appreciated securities for their customers without recognition of gain, while selling for cash and recognizing losses on those securities that had declined in value. Finally, the exception of § 1031(a)(2)(D) for interests in a partnership was added in response to several court decisions holding that, at least in certain circumstances, an exchange of an interest in one partnership for an interest in another partnership could qualify under § 1031. *Meyer v. Commissioner*, 58 T.C. 311 (1972), *aff'd per curiam*, 503 F.2d 556 (9th Cir. 1974). Congress, however, accepted the position of the Service that partnership interests were investment interests similar to those already excluded from § 1031 and thus not appropriate candidates for nonrecognition treatment.

A.   Continuity of Interest

For tax purposes, an exchange is typically equivalent to cashing in one's investment in the property exchanged. The nonrecognition rule of § 1031, however, assumes property received in an exchange is simply a continuation of that investment in a modified form. Since the investment is in substance a continuing one, the taxpayer has only technically, but not effectively, "realized" gain or loss, and the exchange is thus regarded as an inappropriate time to levy a tax or permit a deduction. In 1934, when Congress considered and rejected repeal of the predecessor of § 1031, it expressed concern that elimination of the nonrecognition rule would place a "severe handicap" on "legitimate exchanges," leaving taxpayers with paper gains on exchanges, but without cash to pay the tax on the gains. The courts have emphasized this congressional concern and the underlying continuity of investment principle in their application of § 1031. A secondary justification for § 1031 has been the supposed administrative difficulty in valuing the property received in like kind exchanges. The congressional justifications for nonrecognition, and for exclusions from nonrecognition, are reflected in the 1934 House Ways and Means Committee report rejecting repeal of the predecessor of § 1031:

> The law has provided for 12 years that gain or loss is recognized on exchanges of property having a fair market value, such as stocks, bonds, and negotiable instruments; on exchanges of property held primarily for

sale; or on exchanges of one kind of property for another kind of property; but not on other exchanges of property solely for property of like kind. In other words, profit or loss is recognized in the case of exchanges of notes or securities, which are essentially like money; or in the case of stock in trade; or in case the taxpayer exchanges the property comprising his original investment for a different kind of property; but, if the taxpayer's money is still tied up in the same kind of property as that in which it was originally invested, he is not allowed to compute and deduct his theoretical loss on the exchange, nor is he charged with a tax upon his theoretical profit. The calculation of the profit or loss is deferred until it is realized in cash, marketable securities, or other property not of the same kind having a fair market value.

The Treasury Department states that its experience indicates that this provision does not in fact result in tax avoidance. If all exchanges were made taxable, it would be necessary to evaluate the property received in exchange in thousands of horse trades and similar barter transactions each year, and for the time being, at least, claims for theoretical losses would probably exceed any profits which could be established. The committee does not believe that the net revenue which could thereby be collected, particularly in these years, would justify the additional administrative expense. Consequently, the exchange provisions have not been changed.

H. Rep. 704, 73d Cong., 2d Session, p. 13.

B.   The Like Kind Requirement

The regulations state that "like kind" refers to the nature or character of property, or its kind or class, not to its grade or quality. Reg. § 1.1031(a)-1(b). The regulations give a strikingly broad interpretation of "like kind" to real property, making it immaterial whether real estate is improved or unimproved for § 1031 purposes, and providing, as examples of qualifying transactions, an exchange of city real estate for a ranch or farm, an exchange of a 30-year leasehold in real estate for real estate, and an exchange of improved real estate for unimproved real estate. Reg. § 1.1031(a)-1(c). Provided the property interest in question constitutes an interest in real property, the cases and rulings have followed this liberal approach, applying § 1031 to such exchanges as the exchange of remainder interests in two parcels of farm land (Rev. Rul. 78-4, 1978-1 C.B. 256), a tenancy in common interest in land for 100% ownership of a portion thereof (Rev. Rul. 73-476, 1973-2 C.B. 300), a leasehold in a building for a sublease in another part of the building (Rev. Rul. 76-301, 1976-2 C.B. 241), the exchange of a leasehold interest (until exhaustion of the deposit) in a producing oil lease constituting real property for an improved ranch (Rev. Rul. 68-331, 1968-1 C.B. 352), an undivided interest in mineral rights in certain land for an undivided interest in improved realty (*Commissioner v. Crichton*, 122 F.2d 181 (5th Cir. 1941)), golf club property for property subject to 99-year condominium leases (*Koch v. Commissioner*, 71 T.C. 54 (1978)), and perpetual water rights recognized under local law as real property for a fee interest in land (Rev. Rul. 55-749, 1955-2 C.B. 295). In *Wiechens v. U.S.*, 228 F. Supp. 2d 1080 (D. Ariz. 2002), however, the court held the exchange of 50-year water rights limited in priority and quantity for a fee simple interest in farmland did not qualify as a like-kind transaction under § 1031, even though the water rights constituted an interest in real property. The court in *Wiechens* rejected as "inappropriate" the taxpayer's effort to analogize their nonperpetual water rights to a 30-year leasehold.

In *Peabody Natural Resources Company v. Commissioner*, 126 T.C. 261 (2006), the Tax Court concluded that, in the exchange of gold mines for coal mines, the supply contracts associated with the coal mines were like-kind property and not boot. While the IRS did not dispute that gold mines for coal mines met the like kind requirement, it argued the supply contracts were not real property and therefore constituted boot. The Tax Court concluded, however, that, even though under New Mexico law the contracts themselves were contracts to sell personal property, they were nonetheless servitudes on the property and therefore real property under New Mexico law.

As noted above, the regulations indicate a 30-year leasehold is like kind to a fee interest. The Service has ruled that optional lease renewal periods should be added to the initial term of a lease for purposes of determining whether the leasehold interest qualifies as like kind under the regulations. Rev. Rul. 78-72, 1978-1 C.B. 258. Will an exchange of a leasehold with less than 30 years to run for a fee simple interest in real estate qualify as an exchange of like-kind properties? The taxpayer in *VIP's Industries v. Commissioner*, T.C. Memo 2013-157 contended that Reg. § 1.1031(a)-1(c) noted above "does not exclude all exchanges of leasehold interests in real property with terms of less than 30 years for fee interests in real property from receiving like-kind exchange treatment but rather provides a safe harbor for exchanges of leaseholds with terms of 30 years or more for fee interests in real property." Based on that reasoning, the taxpayer argued its exchange of a leasehold interest (a nonextendable ground lease) with a term of 21 years and 4 months remaining for fee interests in certain real estate qualified for § 1031 treatment. The taxpayer argued the relinquished leasehold was of sufficient duration to be considered of like kind to the fee interests taxpayer received. Rejecting this argument, the Tax Court concluded the leasehold interest in question was closer in nature to leasehold interests the court had previously characterized as not equivalent to a fee interest. Specifically, the Tax Court noted that, in *May Dep't Stores Co. v. Commissioner*, 16 T.C. 547 (1951), it had held that a 20-year leasehold was not equivalent to a fee interest and, in *Standard Envelope Mfg. Co. v. Commissioner*, 15 T.C. 41 (1950), it had held a leasehold with a term of one year and an option to renew for a term of 24 years was not equivalent to a fee interest. The Tax Court noted, however, that, because it was deciding the case in accordance with its existing precedents, it did not need to decide whether Reg. §1.1031(a)-1(c) "mechanically excludes all exchanges of leaseholds with terms of less than 30 years for fee interests from receiving like-kind exchange treatment."[1]

---

[1] The Tax Court also rejected the taxpayer's argument the improvements taxpayer had built on the leased land were of like kind to the real estate taxpayer received in the exchange. The taxpayer had constructed a motel on the land at a cost of over $2.5 million. According to the taxpayer, the improvements represented 85% of the overall value of the property. Rejecting this argument, the Tax Court noted that, pursuant to the terms of the ground lease, the improvements made by taxpayer would belong to the lessor upon the expiration or sooner termination of the ground lease. As a result, the

Historically, a much narrower approach was taken with respect to exchanges of personal property. Prior to the promulgation of additional regulations in 1991, there were only two examples provided by the regulations of like kind exchanges of personal property — a business truck for a new business truck, and a passenger automobile used in business for a new passenger automobile to be used in business — and they hardly stretched the statutory language. In addition to these limited examples in the regulations, case law and Treasury rulings also provided examples of like kind exchanges of personal property. For example, like kind treatment has been extended to an exchange of gold bullion for "bullion-type" gold coins whose fair market value greatly exceeds the face amount (Rev. Rul. 82-96, 1982-1 C.B. 113), but gold bullion and silver bullion are not like kind (Rev. Rul. 82-166, 1982-2 C.B. 190), nor are U.S. currency and foreign currency (Rev. Rul. 74-7, 1974-1 C.B. 198), nor are Swiss francs and U.S. collector-type gold coins (*California Federal Life Ins. Co. v. Commissioner*, 76 T.C. 107 (1981), *aff'd*, 680 F.2d 85 (9th Cir. 1982)). Exchanges of football player contracts (Rev. Rul. 71-137, 1971-1 C.B. 104) are within § 1031.

Regulations issued in 1991 concerning exchanges of personal property provide considerably more guidance. *See* Reg. § 1.1031(a)-2. Under these regulations, the like kind requirement is satisfied if *depreciable tangible* personal property is exchanged for property that is *either* of a like kind *or* of a "like class." Depreciable tangible personal property is of like class to other depreciable tangible personal property if both properties are within the same "General Asset Class." Reg. § 1.1031(a)-2(b)(1). There are thirteen General Business Asset Classes, drawn from Revenue Procedure 87-56 (discussed in Chapter 14 on Depreciation), and described in the regulations. For example, office furniture, fixtures and equipment are all within the same General Business Asset Class. Reg. § 1.1031(a)-2(b)(2).

Depreciable tangible personal properties are also of like class if within the same "Product Class." Reg. § 1.1031(a)-2(b)(1). Property within a Product Class consists of depreciable tangible personal property listed in a 6-digit product class within certain sectors of the North American Industry Classification System described in Reg. § 1.1031(a)-2(b)(3).

Suppose the personal property in question is nondepreciable or intangible. Such personal property is eligible for like kind treatment based upon all the facts and circumstances. No like classes are provided for these properties. Thus, such personal properties qualify only if "like kind" to one another. Reg. § 1.1031(a)-2(c)(1). With respect to intangible personal property, the regulations state by way of example that an exchange of copyrights on two novels is a like kind exchange, but not an exchange of a copyright on a novel and a copyright on a song. Reg. § 1.1031(a)-2(c)(3) Exs. 1, 2. The goodwill or going concern value of one business is not like kind to the goodwill or going concern value of another business. Reg. § 1.1031(a)-2(c)(2).

The transfer of multiple assets creates special problems with respect to the like kind requirement. Revenue Ruling 72-151 in the materials addresses multiple asset

---

taxpayer's interest in the motel improvements represented a short-term interest comparable to taxpayer's leasehold interest.

exchanges. The Service in Revenue Ruling 57-365, 1957-2 C.B. 521, ruled the noninventory assets of two telephone companies, which included both real and personal property, were like kind. Hence, the exchange of all the assets (except inventory and securities) of one company for similar assets of another company was within § 1031. The Service subsequently clarified Revenue Ruling 57-365 and ruled that a transfer of assets of similar businesses cannot be treated as the transfer of a single property for another single property — that is, it is not to be analyzed as a "business for business" exchange, but must be analyzed in terms of the underlying assets. Rev. Rul. 89-121, 1989-2 C.B. 203. It is now essential to analyze multiple asset exchanges with reference to Reg. § 1.1031(j)-1 issued in 1991. Discussion of the multiple properties exchange regulations is beyond the scope of this course.

On occasion, an exchange may fail to qualify for nonrecognition because the property given up or received constitutes payment of income. For example, in one ruling the receipt of real estate in exchange for a lease on various properties was held to constitute advance rent to the taxpayer and not to be within § 1031. Rev. Rul. 66-209, 1966-2 C.B. 299.

C.   The Holding Requirements

Section 1031(a) requires the property relinguished in an exchange be property "held for productive use in a trade or business or for investment" and that the property acquired be property "to be held either for productive use in a trade or business or for investment." Compare those requirements with the "property used in a trade or business" language of §§ 1221(a)(2) and 1231.

The statutory language obviously excludes personal-use property from the scope of § 1031. Thus, the exchange of a piece of residential real estate used as a rental for another piece of residential real estate to be used as the taxpayer's personal residence does not satisfy the "to be held" requirement. Many taxpayers who have vacation homes and second homes have sought to treat those homes as investment property thereby affording them the possibility of a § 1031 exchange. Revenue Procedure 2008-16, included in the materials, provides a safe harbor under which the Service will not challenge whether a dwelling unit qualifies as property held for productive use in a trade or business or for investment for § 1031 purposes.

The applicability of § 1031 to one party to an exchange does not depend on its applicability to other parties. For example, if Smith exchanges rental real estate for Jones' personal residence, which Smith will hold for rental purposes, § 1031 is applicable to Smith even though on these facts it cannot apply to Jones.

The statute is phrased in the disjunctive, and the regulations make clear that an exchange of trade or business property for investment property, or vice versa, if the properties are otherwise like kind, may qualify for nonrecognition. Reg. § 1.1031(a)-1(a)(1). If, for example, land held for investment purposes is exchanged for business realty, the exchange falls within § 1031.

Section 1031 imposes two holding requirements, *i.e.*, the property given up in the exchange must be *"held"* for productive use in a trade or business or for

954   LIKE KIND EXCHANGES   CH. 39

investment, and the property received in the exchange is "to be held" for either productive use in a trade or business or for investment purposes. Assume, for example, a taxpayer purchases a residence that taxpayer holds for rental purposes. Six months later, the taxpayer exchanges the residence for another residence taxpayer also intends to hold for rental purposes. Alternatively, assume the residence given up had been held for a long period of time, but the residence acquired on the exchange is itself promptly sold. Does § 1031 apply in either case? In many instances, the answer may be academic. If property is acquired at a cost basis equal to its fair market value, and promptly exchanged, there is likely to be little or no gain or loss to recognize even if § 1031 does not apply to the exchange; conversely, if property acquired in an exchange is promptly sold for cash, it may not matter whether the exchange was itself a recognition event if the same total gain or loss is recognized on the exchange and sale combined.

The answer, however, is not always academic. Although the words of the statute may clearly disqualify many exchanges associated with brief holding periods, other exchanges may raise troublesome issues. Compare, for example, the facts and reasoning in Revenue Ruling 77-297 and the *Bolker* case in the materials. Section 1031 has been applied to a transaction in which the taxpayer exchanged real property and then promptly transferred the real property received to a two-person partnership in return for a general interest in the partnership; the property received was regarded as held for investment on the ground that its contribution to the partnership was a mere change in form, not a liquidation of the investment. *Magneson v. Commissioner*, 753 F.2d 1490 (9th Cir. 1985), *aff'g* 81 T.C. 767 (1983). An exchange may not qualify under § 1031 where the intent at the time of the exchange is to make a charitable contribution of the property received, *Lindsley v. Commissioner*, T.C. Memo. 1983-729, or to give the property received to one's children, *Click v. Commissioner*, 78 T.C. 225 (1982); but the absence of prearrangement or concrete plans at the time of the exchange may mean that a subsequent gift of the property received does not take the prior exchange out of § 1031. *Wagensen v. Commissioner*, 74 T.C. 653 (1980).

Section 1031 was amended in 1989 to impose a 2-year holding period on exchanges between related persons. § 1031(f), (g). As noted, specific holding periods are not otherwise provided in § 1031. The amendments are obviously aimed at restraining the taxpayer — for 2 years, at least — from effectively cashing out business or investment property through a related party, while using § 1031 to obtain nonrecognition. The holding period requirement applies with respect to both the property received by the taxpayer and the property transferred by the taxpayer to the related person. § 1031(f)(1)(C). A number of exceptions are provided including one for non-tax-avoidance transfers. § 1031(f)(2). If the holding requirements are not satisfied, the gain or loss that was not recognized on the exchange is reported in the year the subsequent, disqualifying transfer occurs. § 1031(f)(1).

> **Example:** In December of last year, Kurt exchanged an undeveloped lot in River City for a tract of land owed by his son, Mark. Kurt had held the lot for many years as an investment and also intends to hold the land acquired from Mark for investment purposes. Kurt's adjusted basis in the lot was $50,000 and the lot's fair market value was $250,000. Mark's land had a

value of $250,000 at the time of the exchange and Mark, who had recently purchased the land for investment purposes, had an adjusted basis in the land of $225,000. Mark intends to hold the lot received from Kurt for investment purposes. Both Kurt and his son will qualify for § 1031 nonrecognition on the exchange. In May of this year, Mark sells the lot for $250,000. What are the tax consequences of the exchange and the subsequent sale to Kurt and Mark?

Analysis: But for § 1031(a), Kurt would be required to report $200,000 gain on the exchange, *i.e.*, the difference between the value of the land he received from Mark ($250,000) and Kurt's adjusted basis in the lot ($50,000). In addition, if § 1031 were inapplicable, Kurt would have taken a fair market value basis of $250,000 in the land received from Mark. See *Philadelphia Park Amusement Co. v. U.S.*, discussed in Chapter 4. Instead, assuming § 1031 is applicable, Kurt will recognize no gain and, as discussed above, will take a $50,000 basis in the land received from Mark. § 1031(d).

If § 1031(a) applies, Mark likewise will not report any gain on the exchange and will take a basis of $225,000 in the lot received from Kurt. § 1031(d). Under those circumstances, when Mark sells the lot for $250,000, he will recognize the $25,000 of gain he had previously been allowed to defer under § 1031. But for § 1031(f), no other gain would have to be reported at the time. In effect, it was just as if Kurt had exchanged his basis in the lot ($50,000) for Mark's basis in the land ($225,000) thereby enabling the family unit of Kurt and Mark to sell Kurt's lot for $250,000 in cash and recognize only $25,000 of gain rather than the $200,000 of gain Kurt would have reported had Kurt, instead of exchanging the lot for Mark's land, simply sold the lot himself for $250,000 in cash.

Section 1031(f) prevents this swapping of basis between related parties. Under these circumstances, § 1031(f)(1) denies nonrecognition treatment to both Kurt and Mark on the exchange. In effect the exchange of properties between Kurt and Mark will be treated as a taxable exchange. Thus, on Kurt's exchange of his lot for Mark's land, Kurt will be required to report $200,000 of gain, *i.e.*, all the gain that inhered in his lot. Similarly, on his exchange of his land for Kurt's lot, Mark will be required to report the $25,000 of gain that inhered in Mark's land at the time. Both would then take a fair market value basis of $250,000 in the property each had acquired as a result of the exchange. *Philadelphia Park Amusement Co. v. U.S.* Thus, in May of this year, when Mark sold the lot he had received from Kurt, there would be no additional gain to report. In view of these consequences from the operation of § 1031(f), will Kurt and Mark have to amend their tax returns for last year to report their respective amounts of gain? No! Section 1031(f)(1) provides that the gain Kurt and Mark must recognize by reason of the application of that section will not be taken into account for tax purposes until the date on which the Mark's sale of the lot occurred. Since that sale occurred this year, Kurt and Mark would report their gain on their tax returns for this year.

To address more sophisticated arrangements, Congress enacted § 1031(f)(4) specifically making § 1031 inapplicable to any exchange which is part of a transaction (or series of transactions) structured to avoid the purposes of § 1031(f). The legislative history of the provision suggests Congress was concerned related persons might attempt to circumvent the purposes of § 1031(f) by using an unrelated third party. In Revenue Ruling 2002-83, 2002-2 C.B. 927, the Service applied § 1031(f)(4) to disallow the benefit of § 1031(a) nonrecognition treatment under the following circumstances:

> Individual A owns real property (Property 1) with a fair market value of $150x and an adjusted basis of $50x. Individual B owns real property (Property 2) with a fair market value of $150x and an adjusted basis of $150x. Both Property 1 and Property 2 are held for investment within the meaning of § 1031(a). A and B are related persons within the meaning of § 267(b). C, an individual unrelated to A and B, wishes to acquire Property 1 from A. A enters into an agreement for the transfer of Property 1 and Property 2 with B, C, and a qualified intermediary [a person or entity employed to help facilitate a like-kind exchange; see the discussion below in Subsection I]. The qualified intermediary is unrelated to A and B. Pursuant to their agreement, on January 6, 2003, A transfers Property 1 to the qualified intermediary who transfers Property 1 to C for $150x. On January 13, 2003, the qualified intermediary acquires Property 2 from B, pays B the $150x sales proceeds from the qualified intermediary's sale of Property 1, and transfers Property 2 to A.

According to the ruling, the above arrangement is comparable to a situation where A and B engaged in a like-kind exchange by which A transferred Property 1 to B in exchange for B's transfer of Property 2 to A. If B sold Property 1 to C within two years of the exchange, § 1031(f) would deny A nonrecognition treatment. Similarly, the ruling concludes that § 1031(f) will deny A nonrecognition treatment in the circumstances described in the ruling. In an analogous situation, the Tax Court, in *Teruya Brothers, Ltd. v. Commissioner*, 124 T.C. 45, *aff'd*, 580 F.3d 1038 (9th Cir. 2009), applied § 1031(f)(4) to deny nonrecognition treatment.

D. "Solely" for Like Kind Property: The Presence of "Boot"

Section 1031 would be of little utility if qualifying exchanges could consist only of like kind properties of equal value. The properties are almost invariably unequal in value and at least one of the parties will have to transfer cash or non-like kind property ("boot") to even up the exchange. The party giving, but not receiving, cash or other nonqualifying property, remains within the language of § 1031(a) since he receives solely like kind property for the property he gives up; the cash or other nonqualifying property he conveys will be reflected in the basis of the property acquired, a matter discussed below. By contrast, the party receiving cash or other nonqualifying property is not receiving "solely" like kind property. The statute, however, does not disqualify this exchange, but requires recognition of gain on the like kind property to the extent of the boot received (*but not in excess of gain realized*). Recognition of loss on like kind property, however, is prohibited. Assume, for example, an exchange of property worth $50,000, with an adjusted basis of

$20,000, for like kind property worth $40,000 and cash of $10,000. Gain of $10,000 is recognized under § 1031(b). If the property exchanged had an adjusted basis of $45,000 instead of only $20,000, only $5,000 of gain would be realized on the exchange. As a result, only $5,000 of gain would be recognized even though the taxpayer received $10,000 cash. If the property exchanged had an adjusted basis of $80,000 instead of $20,000, none of the $30,000 realized loss would be recognized.

The nonrecognition rules of § 1031 are addressed only to gain or loss inherent in the like kind property in the transaction. Gain or loss on non-like kind property is not governed by § 1031, and such gain or loss is recognized under the general rule of § 1001(c). Thus, the party giving nonqualifying property in an exchange recognizes gain or loss to the extent of the difference between the value and the adjusted basis of such property. For example, assume Taxpayer exchanges land worth $50,000 with an adjusted basis of $20,000 and a computer worth $5,000 with an adjusted basis of $12,000 for a parcel of real estate worth $55,000. While the gain inherent in Taxpayer's land will not be recognized, the loss of $7,000 incurred on the exchange of the nonqualifying property, *i.e.*, the computer, will be recognized (assuming the requirements of § 165 are satisfied).

E. Treatment of Liabilities

It is common for one or more of the properties in a like kind exchange to be transferred subject to a liability, or for one party to the exchange to assume a liability of another party. It will come as no surprise to learn that such liability relief is treated under § 1031 as money received by the taxpayer relieved of the liability. See the last sentence of § 1031(d). Liability relief is thus a form of boot. If Taxpayer A transfers land worth $50,000, but subject to a mortgage of $10,000, to Taxpayer B in return for land worth $40,000, Taxpayer A is treated as having received $10,000 in cash. (Taxpayer B, as we shall see, will be given credit in basis as if she had paid $10,000 in cash to A.)

To this point, the treatment of liabilities may seem a simple matter. A complication is therefore in order. Suppose both properties in a like kind exchange are transferred subject to liabilities. Assume taxpayer A transfers land worth $50,000, subject to a mortgage of $30,000; taxpayer B transfers land worth $30,000, subject to a mortgage of $10,000. According to the regulations, only the *net* liability relief constitutes money received. Reg. § 1.1031(b)-1(c). Thus, A is treated as receiving $20,000 in cash; B is treated as receiving none. Study carefully the two examples provided in Regulation § 1.1031(d)-2.

One further complication remains. Suppose in the above example that A's land was worth $40,000 instead of $50,000. A therefore pays B $10,000 in cash to equalize the transaction. The same regulation states "money received" is now present on both sides: B has $10,000 of money received in the form of the cash; A has $20,000 of net liability relief, which is treated as "money received." But in computing A's "money received," the net liability relief is offset by the $10,000 in cash money paid to B; A's "money received" is thus only $10,000. Reg. § 1.1031(d)-2 Example 2. Two rules therefore emerge: (1) Cash received always counts as "money received"; (2) *Net* liability relief, *reduced* by any cash paid, also constitutes "money received." Your understanding of these rules is tested in the problems.

F. Basis Calculations

Section 1031, in common with other nonrecognition provisions of the Code, defers the recognition of gain or loss rather than permanently excluding gain or disallowing loss. The unrecognized gain or loss is preserved, through the basis mechanism, in the like kind property received. Since non-like kind property constitutes boot, such property winds up with a fair market value basis in the recipient's hands. In effect, the taxpayer is treated as having purchased the non-like kind property. See the discussion of *Philadelphia Park Amusement Co. v. U.S.* in Chapter 4.

The mechanics of the basis calculation with respect to like kind property are set forth in the first sentence of § 1031(d). Unrecognized gain or loss is preserved by using as a starting point the total bases of all the properties given up. This "substituted basis" (*see* § 7701(a)(42)) is adjusted up or down for gain or loss recognized on the transaction (loss may be recognized when nonqualifying property is exchanged), and is also decreased by "money received." Although not specified in the statute, the examples in the regulations properly provide (a) liability relief is treated as money received, thus decreasing basis; (b) liabilities taken on are treated as money paid; and (c) money paid increases basis. (It may be somewhat confusing to see that, for basis computation purposes, the regulations increase basis by total liabilities taken on and by total cash paid, then decrease basis by total liability relief and by total cash received. By contrast, in determining "money received" for *gain recognition* purposes, it was only the *net* liability relief (reduced by any cash paid) not the total liability relief, that counted. It may ease the confusion to realize the basis answers remain precisely the same if the upward and downward adjustments are done based on a netting of liabilities.) Where non-like kind property (boot) is received, basis is first allocated to the non-like kind property to the extent of its fair market value, thus preserving in the like kind property, consistent with the general rule of § 1031(a), the unrecognized gain or loss.

Basis computations under § 1031 may seem difficult. A few reminders may be helpful. When money is received, or liability relief occurs, or loss is recognized, the taxpayer is in effect receiving a partial return of investment, and it is appropriate to reduce basis to reflect that fact. When money is paid, or liabilities are taken on, or gain is recognized, the taxpayer is in effect increasing investment, and it is appropriate to increase basis as a result. A single event may of course have offsetting effects. For example, $10 in cash received decreases basis since it is money received, but, if it also triggers $10 of recognized gain, it increases basis by the same amount, so the net effect is to leave basis unchanged. Finally, it may be helpful to try to see the basis rules in overview and to develop the habit of testing your basis answers. The non-like kind property received should have a fair market value basis. The like kind property received should have a basis that preserves the unrecognized gain or loss in the property given up. Section 1031(d) and the regulations thereunder provide the formula: the basis of the like kind property received equals (1) the *adjusted basis* of all like kind and non-like kind property given up; (2) *plus* any gain recognized, liability taken on, or cash paid; (3) *minus* any loss recognized, liability shed, or cash received; (4) with the resulting total basis *allocated* first to non-like kind property received to the extent of its fair market value; and (5) with the *remaining* basis constituting the basis of the like kind property.

G. The Relationship Between Sections 267(a)(1) and 1031

The preservation of unrecognized loss in cases where exchanges occur between related persons as defined in § 267(b) may result in what appears to be inconsistency between § 1031 and § 267(a)(1). Assume Taxpayer gives to his daughter a tract of land worth $100,000 and with an adjusted basis of $120,000 in exchange for $20,000 in cash and a piece of real estate worth $80,000. Assume also that, except with respect to the receipt of the cash, Taxpayer meets the holding and like kind requirements of § 1031. Under § 1031(c), even though Taxpayer is receiving boot, no loss can be recognized by Taxpayer. Section 1031(d), however, preserves Taxpayer's loss in the basis of the real estate received by Taxpayer from his daughter. Thus, under § 1031(d), Taxpayer in this example would take a basis of $100,000 in the real estate (*i.e.*, $120,000 basis in the land relinquished less $20,000 cash received). If Taxpayer later sold the real estate for $100,000, Taxpayer would recognize $20,000 of loss.

Compare those results to the results if § 1031 did not exist and the same exchange took place. Under those circumstances, § 267(a)(1) would disallow Taxpayer's $20,000 loss on the taxable exchange. Given *Philadelphia Park Amusement Co.*, Taxpayer would take a fair market value basis of $80,000 in the real estate received from his daughter. His daughter would likewise take a fair market basis in the tract of land received from her father. The $20,000 loss that inhered in Taxpayer's tract of land would simply disappear. Note, however, that § 267(d) might provide some relief to the Taxpayer/daughter family unit if the daughter were later to sell the tract of land at a gain.

Read Rev. Rul. 72-151, included in the materials, carefully. Note that it confirms that § 1031(d) controls in a situation like that presented in the example above.

H. Sale or Exchange?

Former Reg. § 1.1002-1(d) described an exchange as, ordinarily, "a reciprocal transfer of property, as distinguished from a transfer of property for a money consideration only." Suppose, for example, the taxpayer "sells" qualifying property for cash to a buyer, then by prearrangement immediately "purchases" qualifying like kind property from the same person. If the transaction is in substance an exchange rather than a sale and purchase, the provisions of § 1031 will govern. The Service has applied this principle to a situation in which a taxpayer sold used business equipment to a dealer under one contract, and purchased new like kind equipment from the same dealer under a separate contract; despite the separate contracts, the two transactions were "reciprocal and mutually dependent" and were treated as a trade-in exchange rather than a sale and purchase. Rev. Rul. 61-119, 1961-1 C.B. 395. The same exchange-in-substance rule has also been extended to cover a case where the sale of old trucks was made by the parent corporation and the purchase of the new trucks (from the same manufacturer) was made by the subsidiary corporation. *Redwing Carriers, Inc. v. Tomlinson*, 399 F.2d 652 (5th Cir.

1968). The *Bell Lines* case in the materials and the Problems consider variations on this issue. What result should obtain if a taxpayer initially contracts to exchange unimproved land for improved land, but when the other party fails to make certain improvements on time, the taxpayer sells his land for cash to the other party, and then three months later (when the improvements are complete) purchases the improved land? See *Swaim v. U.S.*, 651 F.2d 1066 (5th Cir. 1981), holding that a sale and purchase took place.

Another context in which the sale-or-exchange issue commonly arises involves the sale and leaseback of real estate. If the lease (with optional extensions) runs 30 years or more, the leasehold and a fee interest will be treated as like kind. Reg. § 1.1031(a)-1(c). Assume a taxpayer "sells" real property for cash but at a loss, and simultaneously enters into a 30-year lease of the property. Is the loss allowed, or does § 1031 apply? The view of the Service that § 1031 bars the loss was upheld in a case involving a sale of real property for cash and a 95-year leasehold in the property, where the lease had a capital value — that is, where the lease was worth more than the rent to be paid. *Century Electric Co. v. Commissioner*, 192 F.2d 155, (8th Cir. 1951). In other cases, where the sale was at full value and the lease at fair rental, and the lease had no capital value, the loss on the sale has been allowed. *See Jordan Marsh Co. v. Commissioner*, 269 F.2d 453 (2d Cir. 1959); *Leslie Co. v. Commissioner*, 64 T.C. 247 (1975) (non acq), *aff'd*, 539 F.2d 943 (3d Cir. 1976). Although the courts and the Service have treated sale-leasebacks under a sale-or-exchange analysis, consider whether mortgage analysis might be appropriate for these transactions. (For further discussion, see Chapter 42.)

I. Three-Way Exchanges and Deferred Exchanges

An exchange often cannot be effected with just two parties. Consider the following example: A is interested in disposing of her ranch and acquiring a farm owned by C. Because there is considerable gain inherent in A's property, she would prefer to exchange her ranch for C's farm. Unfortunately, C is not interested in an exchange but wants cash. Meanwhile, B offers to purchase A's ranch for cash. Instead of accepting B's offer, A proposes that B purchase C's farm and then exchange that farm for A's ranch. B agrees to accommodate A and the transaction proceeds pursuant to A's proposal. The *simultaneous* exchange of A's ranch for the farm acquired by B occurs. A three-way exchange such as this can qualify for § 1031 treatment, even though A could have sold the ranch for cash to B.[2] See, for example, Revenue Ruling 77-297 in the materials. Similarly, if A, B, and C had engaged in a round-robin exchange whereby A transferred her ranch to B, B transferred real property to C, and C transferred the farm to A, § 1031 would apply to each party satisfying the holding requirements, provided the properties are like kind. Rev. Rul. 57-244, 1957-1 C.B. 247. It is thus not necessary to receive the like kind property from the same person to whom one has transferred property. Revenue Ruling 90-34, included in the materials, extends a similar rule to "2-way" exchanges by, in effect, hypothesizing a 3-way exchange. *Cf.* Reg. § 1.1031(k)-1(g)(4)(iv).

---

[2] Because B fails to meet the holding requirements, only A, qualifies for § 1031 nonrecognition treatment in this example.

The receipt of cash in return for one's property, even if the proceeds are immediately invested in like kind property, is fatal to § 1031 treatment. For example, had A sold her ranch to B and five minutes later used the sale proceeds to purchase C's farm, A would not be entitled to § 1031 treatment. As originally described, the transaction resulted in A's securing § 1031 treatment as a result of B's willingness to purchase C's farm. Consider the problems that may be posed if B is unable or unwilling to take title to C's property. May A hire someone to serve as an accommodator, *i.e.*, to acquire C's farm using B's money and to transfer the farm to A and A's ranch to B? Regulation § 1.1031(b)-2 authorizes the use of a "qualified intermediary" in a *simultaneous* exchange such as that described in the example. See the discussion below regarding qualified intermediaries.

Unlike the simultaneous exchange described in the example above, taxpayers often are confronted with situations where they have a buyer for their property but would prefer to have the benefit of § 1031 treatment. Does § 1031 require that the exchange of properties be simultaneous? Assume, in the above example, A did not know of the availability of C's farm at the time that B offered to purchase A's ranch for cash. Would A be entitled to § 1031 treatment if A agreed to transfer the ranch immediately to B in exchange for B's promise to purchase and transfer to A properties to be designated by A within a given period of time?

In the first case to provide any detailed discussion of that issue, the court in *Starker v. U.S.*, 602 F.2d 1341 (9th Cir. 1979), held a taxpayer was entitled to § 1031 treatment on the ultimate receipt of like kind property even though the property to be received had not been identified at the time of the transfer of the property given up, and even though the taxpayer had reserved the right for up to 5 years to designate the property or properties to be received or to receive cash in whole or in part instead. Congress and the Treasury were not enamored with *Starker* or the indefinite deferral arrangements which it sanctioned. They viewed such arrangements as creating serious administrative problems for the Service, expanding § 1031 beyond congressional intent, and bearing sufficient resemblance to a sale to be taxed as one. In 1984, Congress responded to *Starker* by enacting § 1031(a)(3), requiring the taxpayer to identify replacement property within 45 days of the transfer of the relinquished property and to receive the replacement property no later than 180 days after the transfer or the due date (including extensions) of the taxpayer's tax return for the year of the transfer, whichever is earlier.

The regulations on deferred exchanges require a written, unambiguous designation of "replacement property" — that is, the property to be received on a deferred exchange — be made and delivered within the 45-day "identification period." Reg. § 1.1031(k)-1(b) and (c). Because of a number of contingencies which may render the replacement property unacceptable to the taxpayer, *e.g.*, zoning, title, or environmental problems, the regulations permit the taxpayer to identify alternate property under the "3-property rule," the "200-percent rule," or the "95-percent rule." Under these rules, a taxpayer may identify three replacement properties of any value (the 3-property rule), or alternatively, any number of replacement properties that in the aggregate do not exceed twice the value of the property relinquished (the 200-percent rule). *See* Reg. § 1.1031(k)-1(c)(4)(i). The receipt of incidental property, *e.g.*, furniture transferred with an apartment building, will not cause taxpayer to fail the 3-property rule. Reg. § 1.1031(k)-1(c)(5). As a general rule, if the taxpayer identifies too much property, the taxpayer will be treated as having identified *no* property and therefore will not be entitled to the benefit of § 1031 nonrecognition.

However, despite the failure to satisfy either the 3-property rule or the 200-percent rule, the taxpayer will nevertheless qualify for § 1031 treatment if the taxpayer actually receives "identified replacement property the fair market value of which is at least 95 percent of the aggregate fair market value of all identified replacement property (the '95-percent rule')." *See* Reg. § 1.1031(k)-1(c)(4)(ii)(B). The 95-percent rule may be helpful in situations where properties are subject to debt. Assume, for example, the taxpayer wishes to exchange property worth $100,000 that is not subject to debt. By the end of the identification period, the taxpayer has identified four replacement properties, each with a value of $100,000, and each subject to a $75,000 mortgage. In these circumstances, since the taxpayer identified four properties that in the aggregate have a fair market value that is 400 percent of the property relinquished, the taxpayer fails to satisfy either the 3-property rule or the 200-percent rule, and will ordinarily be deemed to have identified no replacement property. However, if prior to the end of the exchange period, the taxpayer receives all four of the identified properties (values and debts remaining constant for all properties), he will be deemed to have satisfied the identification requirements of the regulation, because the properties received will have a value at least 95 percent (in this case, 100 percent) of the properties identified. (Fair market value of identified property is determined on the earlier of the date received or the last day of the exchange period.)

The regulations provide that replacement property is received within the "exchange period" — the period designated in § 1031(a)(3)(B), not in excess of 180 days — if the replacement property received is "substantially the same property as identified." Reg. § 1.1031(k)-1(d)(1). Property being produced may qualify as like kind property. For example, real property may be exchanged for real property which is to be improved. For purposes of the "substantially the same property" test, real property to be produced need not be completed on or before the date the property is received. However, "the property received will be considered to be substantially the same property as identified only if, had production been completed on or before the date the taxpayer receives the replacement property, the property received would have been considered to be substantially the same property as identified." Reg. § 1.1031(k)-1(e)(3)(iii).

The regulations also provide several "safe harbors" that permit taxpayers to use security or guarantee arrangements, qualified escrow accounts, qualified intermediaries, and interest and growth factors as part of deferred exchanges. *See* Reg. § 1.1031(k)-1(g). The taxpayer who uses a safe harbor will not be in actual or constructive receipt of money or other property on account of such use. Actual or constructive receipt of money or other property, prior to completion of the exchange, can obviously trigger recognition of gain or loss, potentially to the full extent of the realized gain or loss. Reg. § 1.1031(k)-1(f)(2). A taxpayer thus ignores the safe harbors at its peril.

The most important of these safe harbors is the "qualified intermediary" safe harbor. Simply stated, this safe harbor authorizes a taxpayer to utilize the services of a person or entity (who is not a "disqualified person" within the meaning of § 1.1031(k)-1(k)) to acquire and transfer properties, thereby accommodating the exchange.[3] According to the regulations, the qualified intermediary will not be considered an agent of the taxpayer for purposes of § 1031. Consider again the example above involving A, B, and C. Assume B is unwilling to purchase and transfer to A property which A might identify. Under this safe harbor, A could hire an intermediary who would sell A's ranch to B, use the sale proceeds to acquire the property designated by A (in this case C's farm), and transfer C's farm to A. The fact the intermediary was technically an agent of A would not make any difference. The "qualified intermediary" safe harbor in effect allows an agent of A to sell A's ranch to B for cash without jeopardizing the availability of § 1031 treatment for A.

Regulation § 1.1031(k)-l(g)(4)(iii)(B) requires that the intermediary act as a true conduit, that is, that the intermediary acquire the relinquished property from the taxpayer and transfer it, and also acquire the replacement property and transfer it to the taxpayer. The regulations, however, permit direct deeding, thus enabling the intermediary to remain outside of the chain of title. *See* Reg. § 1.1031(k)-l(g)(4)(iv), (v). Compare Rev. Rul. 90-34, included in the materials. What benefits might be derived from direct deeding? The regulations impose a number of requirements that must be satisfied for the intermediary safe harbor and the other safe harbors to be operative. *See, e.g.,* Reg. § 1.1031(k)-1(g)(6). Review these regulations carefully.

J.   Reverse *Starker* Exchanges

So-called "reverse *Starker* exchanges" are exchanges where the replacement property is acquired before the relinquished property is transferred.

> **Example:** An undeveloped tract of commercial real estate located at a busy intersection of City X is advertised for sale. Dan, an entrepreneur, wants the property for his business. Instead of purchasing it, however, he would like to acquire the property through a § 1031 exchange. Fearing the commercial real estate will quickly sell, Dan arranges for an accommodating party to purchase it while Dan identifies which of his parcels of business or investment real estate he will relinquish in an exchange. (This arrangement with the accommodating party is commonly referred to as a "parking arrangement.") Once Dan has identified the property to be relinquished, he sets in motion a plan whereby he will ultimately exchange the relinquished property for the commercial real estate being held by the accommodating party. As part of the transaction, Dan's relinquished property will be sold

---

[3] Disqualified persons include ancestors and lineal descendants. Reg. § 1.1031(k)-1(k)(3). In *Blangiardo v. Commissioner*, T.C. Memo. 2014-14, the Tax Court denied § 1031 treatment to an exchange in which the taxpayer used his son, an attorney, as the intermediary. Although the son was serving as taxpayer's attorney in the transaction and all the documents referred to the transaction as a § 1031 exchange, the fact remained the son, as a lineal descendant of the taxpayer, was a disqualified person and therefore could not be a qualified intermediary.

by the accommodating party and the sale proceeds will be used to repay the accommodating party.

Regulation § 1.1031(k)-1 does not apply to reverse *Starker* arrangements. Revenue Procedure 2000-37, included in the materials, provides a safe harbor whereby reverse *Starker* arrangements such as that presented in the above example will qualify for § 1031 treatment if certain requirements are met. Review the Revenue Procedure carefully, noting specifically the requirement that the exchange accomodator must hold "qualified indicia of ownership" of the property. The application of Rev. Proc. 2000-37 is raised in Problem 3. What potential complications, if any, do you see with reverse *Starker* exchanges?

K. Interface of Sections 121 and 1031

1. Exchanges Qualifying for Both Section 121 and Section 1031 Treatment

As discussed in detail in Chapter 6, § 121 provides an exclusion for gain realized on the sale or exchange of a principal residence if, among other conditions, a taxpayer has owned and used the property as her principal residence for periods aggregating two years in the five year period preceding the date of the sale or the exchange. Thus, a taxpayer may qualify for the exclusion under § 121 even though, at the time of the disposition of the property, the taxpayer is holding the property for business or investment purposes. This, in turn, raises the possibility that § 1031 may also be applicable if there is an exchange of the property for other like kind property. Consider the following examples of situations where both § 121 and § 1031 would be applicable to an exchange:

> **Example 1:** John and Mary, husband and wife, purchased a home in River City in 2000. They used the home as their principal residence until 2013 when they moved into a senior residence. At the time of their move in 2013, they converted their River City home to rental use. In 2015, they exchanged the home for another rental unit. Under these circumstances, the exchange is potentially subject to both §§ 121 and 1031.

> **Example 2:** Assume the same facts as Example 1, except that John and Mary never converted the home to a rental but rather lived in it until the 2015 exchange. During the time of their ownership of the home, however, they used one-third of the home for business purposes and two-thirds of the home as their principal residence. Again, they should be entitled to use § 121 and, to a limited extent, § 1031 on the exchange.

With the exception of § 121(d)(10) (discussed below), neither §§ 121 nor 1031 addresses the application of both provisions to a single exchange of property. Revenue Procedure 2005-14, 2005-1 C.B. 528, acknowledges that both provisions may be applicable in a single exchange and provides important guidance as to how to apply the two provisions under those circumstances.

Utilizing as a model the rules of § 121(d)(5)(B), which addresses the interrelationship of §§ 121 and 1033 (discussed in the next chapter), Revenue Procedure

2005-14 spells out the following rules for applying §§ 121 and 1031 to the same transaction:

a. Section 121 must be applied to gain realized before applying § 1031.

b. Under § 121(d)(6), the § 121 exclusion does not apply to gain attributable to depreciation deductions for periods after May 6, 1997 claimed with respect to the business or investment portion of a residence. However, § 1031 may apply to such gain.

c. In applying § 1031, cash or other non-like kind property (boot) received in exchange for the property used in the taxpayer's trade or business or held for investment (the relinquished business property) is taken into account only to the extent the boot exceeds the gain excluded under § 121 with respect to the relinquished business property.

d. In determining the basis of the property received in the exchange to be used in taxpayer's trade or business or held for investment (the replacement property), any gain excluded under § 121 is treated as gain recognized by the taxpayer. Thus, under § 1031(d), the basis of the replacement business property is increased by any gain attributable to the relinquished business property that is excluded under § 121.

Consider the following example:

Example: John and Mary purchased a large older home near State University in 1990. They paid $150,000 for the home. The home was their principal residence until 2013 at which time they moved to a senior residence. Immediately prior to moving, John and Mary invested $50,000 to convert their University-area home into an executive rental. Early in 2015, when the home was worth $900,000, they exchanged it for a four-plex apartment building in River City (the four-plex had an appraised fair market value of $500,000) and $400,000 in cash. Assume John and Mary had claimed a total of $15,000 of depreciation on the University-area home and had an adjusted basis in the home at the time of the exchange of $185,000. John and Mary file a joint return for 2015.

Analysis: Because John and Mary had owned and used the University-area home as their principal residence for at least two of the five years preceding the sale of the property, they are entitled to exclude under § 121, up to $500,000 of the $715,000 gain realized on the exchange ($900,000 less $185,000 adjusted basis). (Technically, given § 121(d)(6), the § 121 exclusion would not apply to the first $15,000 of gain, *i.e.*, the gain in the amount of the depreciation claimed by John and Mary. The exclusion would apply to the remaining $700,000 of gain but not in excess of $500,000.)

John and Mary may defer the remaining $215,000 of gain, including the $15,000 of gain attributable to depreciation, under § 1031. Although John and Mary received $400,000 in cash (boot) on the exchange, they are not required to recognize gain because the boot is taken into account for purposes of § 1031(b) only to the extent the boot exceeds the amount of excluded gain. It does not.

Their basis in the River City four-plex will be their basis at the time of the exchange in their University-area property (the relinquished property) of $185,000 increased by the $500,000 (gain excluded under § 121) and reduced by the $400,000 cash they received. Thus, their basis in the four-plex will be $285,000. Note that this basis will preserve the $215,000 of unrecognized gain.

2. Section 121(d)(10) — Property Acquired in a Like Kind Exchange

The American Jobs Creation Act of 2004 amended § 121 to provide that, if property is acquired in a like-kind exchange, the property must be held for at least five years before gain on its sale or exchange may be excluded under § 121. § 121(d)(10).

The following example demonstrates the problem Congress sought to address with this new provision.

> **Example:** For many years, Katie and Patrick, a married couple, owned and used as rental property a duplex in Portland, Oregon. On March 1, 2001, they exchanged the Portland duplex for a large single family home on Lake Washington in Seattle. They intended to hold the Seattle home as rental property with the idea of renting it on a weekly or monthly basis to corporate executives, academics, or medical doctors whose work brought them to Seattle for short periods of time. At the time of the exchange, the Portland duplex had a fair market value of $800,000 and an adjusted basis of $300,000. The Seattle home they acquired in the exchange also had a fair market value of $800,000. Neither the Portland duplex nor the Seattle home was encumbered by any mortgage. As a result of § 1031, Katie and Patrick, although realizing a gain on the exchange of $500,000, did not recognize any gain. Instead, under § 1031, they took a $300,000 basis in the Seattle home, thus preserving the $500,000 of unrecognized gain associated with the duplex. In other words, the effect of § 1031 was to defer recognition of the $500,000 of gain inherent in the duplex.

> Katie and Patrick rented the Seattle home for six months. On September 1, 2001, they decided to move from Portland, where they had lived for a number of years, to Seattle. After looking for homes in Seattle, they finally decided that, instead of continuing to rent the home on Lake Washington, they would move into it themselves and establish it as their principal residence. During the period from October 1, 2001 through October 2003, the Lake Washington home served as their principal residence. On November 1, 2003, they sold that home for $800,000. Under § 121, they were able to exclude all $500,000 of the realized gain on the sale of the home. (Assume that their adjusted basis in the Lake Washington home had remained $300,000.)

> Note that § 121 combined with the deferral previously accorded them under § 1031, in effect enabled Katie and Patrick to exclude all of the gain ($500,000) that had been associated with the Portland duplex. Under § 121

as amended, if the exchange took place after the effective date of the American Jobs Creation Act, Katie and Patrick would not be eligible to exclude any portion of the realized gain from the sale of the Lake Washington home acquired in the exchange until they had owned that home for 5 years. (Note: Katie and Patrick still only need to use the Lake Washington home as their principal residence for periods aggregating 2 years.)

In 2005, Congress extended § 121(d)(10) so as to apply not only to the taxpayer who acquired property in a § 1031 exchange, but also to any person whose basis in the property is determined by reference to the taxpayer's basis. A prime target of this extension is presumably those who may receive the property from the taxpayer as a gift. Thus, in the above example, assume that Katie and Patrick, after living from October 2001 through October 2003 in the Lake Washington home (acquired March 1, 2001, in a § 1031 exchange), give the home to their daughter Donna. Under the 2005 Act, on a subsequent sale of the home, in order for Donna to be entitled to exclusion of gain under § 121, she would not only have to satisfy the two-year use and ownership requirements of § 121, but, as the donee of the home, would also have to satisfy the five-year rule of § 121(d)(10).

REVENUE RULING 77-297
1977-2 C.B. 304

Advice is requested whether the transaction described below is an exchange of property in which no gain or loss is recognized pursuant to section 1031(a) of the Internal Revenue Code of 1954.

A entered into a written agreement with B to sell B for 1,000x dollars a ranch (the "first ranch") consisting of land and certain buildings used by A in the business of raising livestock. Pursuant to the agreement, B placed 100x dollars into escrow and agreed to pay at closing an additional 200x dollars in cash, to assume a 160x dollar liability of A, and to execute a note for 540x dollars. The agreement also provided that B would cooperate with A to effectuate an exchange of properties should A locate suitable property. No personal property was involved in the transaction. A and B are not dealers in real estate.

A located another ranch (the "second ranch") consisting of land and certain buildings suitable for raising livestock. The second ranch was owned by C. B entered into an agreement with C to purchase the second ranch for 2,000x dollars. Pursuant to this agreement, B placed 40x dollars into escrow, agreed to pay at closing an additional 800x dollars, assume 400x dollars liability of C, and execute a note for 760x dollars. No personal property was involved in the transaction. C could not look to A for specific performance on the contract, thus, B was not acting as A's agent in the purchase of the second parcel of property.

At closing, B purchased the second ranch as agreed. After the purchase, B exchanged the second ranch with A for the first ranch and assumed A's liability of 160x dollars. With C's concurrence, A assumed C's 400x dollar liability and B's note for 760x dollars. C released B from liability on the note. The escrow agent returned the 100x dollars to B that B had initially placed in escrow. This sum had never been available to A, since the conditions of the escrow were never satisfied.

Section 1031(a) of the Code provides that no gain or loss shall be recognized if property held for productive use in trade or business or for investment (not including stock in trade or other property held primarily for sale, nor stocks, bonds, notes, choses in action, certificates of trust or beneficial interest, or other securities or evidence of indebtedness or interest) is exchanged solely for property of a like kind to be held either for productive use in trade or business or for investment.

Section 1031(b) of the Code states that if an exchange would be within the provisions of subsection (a) if it were not for the fact that the property received in exchange consists not only of property permitted by such provisions to be received without the recognition of gain, but also of other property or money, then the gain, if any, to the recipient shall be recognized, but in an amount not in excess of the sum of such money and the fair market value of such other property.

Section 1.1031(b)-1(c) of the Income Tax Regulations states that consideration received in the form of an assumption of liabilities is to be treated as "other property or money" for the purpose of section 1031(b) of the Code. However, if, on an exchange described in section 1031(b), each party to the exchange assumes a liability of the other party, then, in determining the amount of "other property or money" for purposes of section 1031(b), consideration given in the form of an assumption of liabilities shall be offset against consideration received in the form of an assumption of liabilities.

Ordinarily, to constitute an exchange, the transaction must be a reciprocal transfer of property, as distinguished from a transfer of property for a money consideration only.

In the instant case A and B entered into a sales agreement with an exchange option if suitable property were found. Before the sale was consummated, the parties effectuated an exchange. Thus, for purposes of section 1031 of the Code, the parties entered into an exchange of property. See *Alderson v. Commissioner*, 317 F.2d 790 (9th Cir. 1963), in which a similar transaction was treated as a like-kind exchange of property even though the original agreement called for a sale of the property. In addition, A's 160x dollar liability assumed by B was offset by B's liabilities assumed by A, pursuant to section 1.1031(b)-1(c) of the regulations.

Accordingly, as to A, the exchange of ranches qualifies for nonrecognition of gain or loss under section 1031 of the Code. As to B, the exchange of ranches does not qualify for nonrecognition of gain or loss under section 1031 because B did not hold the second ranch for productive use in a trade or business or for investment. See Rev. Rul. 75-291, 1975-2 C.B. 332, in which it is held that the nonrecognition provisions of section 1031 do not apply to a taxpayer who acquired property solely for the purpose of exchanging it for like-kind property.

However, in the instant case, B did not realize gain or loss as a result of the exchange since the total consideration received by B of 2,160x dollars (fair market value of first ranch of 1,000x dollars plus B's liabilities assumed by A of 1,160x dollars) is equal to B's basis in the property given up of 2,000x dollars plus A's liability assumed by B of 160x dollars. See section 1001 of the Code and the applicable regulations thereunder.

AUTHORS' NOTE

Note that Revenue Ruling 77-297 involves a simultaneous exchange as opposed to a deferred exchange arrangement. This kind of arrangement could be structured today using a qualified intermediary under Reg. § 1.1031(b)-2.

REVENUE RULING 72-151
1972-1 C.B. 224

Advice has been requested as to the application of the nonrecognition of gain or loss provisions of section 1031 of the Internal Revenue Code of 1954 under the circumstances described below.

The taxpayer is the sole stockholder of a corporation. In 1958, the taxpayer purchased real property consisting of land and a house, which has been used since that time as rental income producing property. In 1970, the taxpayer exchanged his rental property for farm properties that included real property (farm land and improvements) and personal property (farm machinery) owned by the corporation. The taxpayer will not live on the farm but intends to use the farm property to raise cattle for profit, and the corporation intends to hold the house and lot as rental income producing property. The fair market value of the rental property equalled the fair market value of the farm property at the time of the exchange.

Section 1031(b) of the Code provides, in part, that if an exchange would be within the provisions of section 1031(a) of the Code, if it were not for the fact that the property received in exchange consists not only of property permitted by such provisions to be received without the recognition of gain, but also of other property or money, then the gain, if any, to the recipient shall be recognized, but in an amount not in excess of the sum of such money and the fair market value of such other property.

Section 1031(c) of the Code provides, in part, that if an exchange would be within the provisions of section 1031(a) of the Code, if it were not for the fact that the property received in exchange consists not only of property permitted by such provisions to be received without the recognition of gain or loss, but also of other property or money, then no loss from the exchange shall be recognized.

Section 267 of the Code provides, in pertinent part, that no deduction shall be allowed in respect of losses from sales or exchanges of property (other than losses in cases of distributions in corporate liquidations), directly or indirectly, between persons specified within any one of the paragraphs of section 267(b) of the Code.

Section 267(b) of the Code provides at paragraph (2) that an individual and a corporation more than 50 percent in value of the outstanding stock of which is owned, directly or indirectly, by or for such individual represents a relationship referred to in section 267(a) of the Code.

Section 1031(d) of the Code provides, in part, that if property was acquired on an exchange described in that section, then the basis shall be the same as that of the property exchanged, decreased in the amount of any money received by the taxpayer and increased in the amount of gain or decreased in the amount of loss to the taxpayer that was recognized on such exchange. If property so acquired consisted in part of the type of property permitted by that section of the Code, to be received without the recognition of gain or loss, and in part of other property, the basis provided in that subsection shall be allocated between the properties (other than money) received, and for the purpose of the allocation there will be assigned to such other property an amount equivalent to its fair market value at the date of the exchange.

Where, as in the instant case, an exchange under section 1031 of the Code involves multiple assets, the fact that the assets in the aggregate comprise a business or an integrated economic investment does not result in treating the exchange as a disposition of a single piece of property. Rather, an analysis is required of the underlying property involved in the exchange.

Upon analysis of the property involved in the instant case, it is concluded that the rental real property (land and improvements) and the farm real property (land and improvements) are property of like kind for purposes of section 1031 of the Code. However, due to the inclusion of the farm machinery, the exchange does not solely involve property of "like kind" and thus does not come within the provisions of section 1031(a) of the Code.

If the taxpayer realized a gain on the exchange, such gain should be recognized under section 1031(b) of the Code in an amount not in excess of the fair market value of the farm machinery. The total basis of the farm land, improvements, and machinery received by the taxpayer is the adjusted basis of the land and house transferred increased by the amount of any gain recognized, such basis being allocated to the properties. For purposes of allocating such basis to the properties received, an amount equivalent to the fair market value of the farm machinery on the date of the exchange should be assigned as its basis.

If the exchange had resulted in a loss being realized by the taxpayer, sections 1031(c) and 267 of the Code each provide that such loss should not be recognized. In that event, the total basis of the farm land, improvements, and farm machinery received is the adjusted basis of the land and house transferred. This basis should be allocated to the properties received, and for this purpose, there must be allocated to the farm machinery an amount equivalent to its fair market value on the date of the exchange.

Accordingly, in the instant case, since the exchange includes property not of like kind (the farm machinery), the nonrecognition of gain or loss provisions of section 1031(a) of the Code are inapplicable. However, if the taxpayer realizes a gain from the exchange, such gain shall be recognized in accordance with section 1031(b) of the Code but only to the extent of the fair market value of the farm machinery. If the taxpayer realizes a loss from the exchange, such loss shall not be recognized in accordance with sections 1031(c) and 267 of the Code. The basis of the property received by the taxpayer in the exchange is governed by section 1031(d) of the Code.

BOLKER v. COMMISSIONER
United States Court of Appeals, Ninth Circuit
760 F.2d 1039 (1985)

BOOCHEVER, CIRCUIT JUDGE:

Bolker was the sole shareholder of the Crosby Corporation (Crosby) which owned the Montebello property. For tax purposes associated with the anticipated development of the property, Bolker decided to liquidate Crosby and distribute Montebello to himself. Before Crosby carried out the liquidation, problems in financing convinced Bolker to dispose of the Montebello property rather than developing it himself. On the day the Crosby liquidation actually occurred, Bolker contracted to exchange Montebello with Southern California Savings & Loan (SCS) for other like-kind investment property to be designated. This exchange took place three months later. Bolker asserted, and the Tax Court agreed, that the exchange qualified for nonrecognition treatment under I.R.C. § 1031(a). *Bolker v. Commissioner*, 81 T.C. 782 (1983). The Commissioner appeals. Because we believe that Bolker held the Montebello property for investment within the meaning of section 1031(a), we affirm.

The transaction was consummated as follows. In March 1972, Bolker commenced the liquidation of Crosby. On March 13, 1972, all of the following occurred:

(1)   Crosby transferred all its assets and liabilities to Bolker in redemption of all Crosby stock outstanding;

(2)   Bolker as president of Crosby executed the Internal Revenue Service liquidation forms;

(3)   A deed conveying Montebello from Crosby to Bolker was recorded;

(4)   Bolker and Parlex, a corporation formed by Bolker's attorneys to facilitate the exchange, executed a contract to exchange Montebello for properties to be designated by Bolker;

(5)   Parlex contracted to convey Montebello to SCS in coordination with the exchange by Bolker and Parlex; and

(6)   Bolker, Crosby, Parlex, and SCS entered into a settlement agreement dismissing a breach of contract suit pending by Crosby against SCS in the event that all the other transactions went as planned.

On June 30, 1972, all the transactions closed simultaneously, SCS receiving Montebello and Bolker receiving three parcels of real estate which he had previously designated.

Bolker reported no gain on the transaction, asserting that it qualified for nonrecognition under then-current I.R.C. § 1031(a).

The Commissioner sent Bolker statutory notices of deficiency on the ground that the transaction did not qualify under section 1031(a). In the Tax Court, the Commissioner argued two theories: that Crosby, not Bolker, exchanged Montebello with SCS, and in the alternative, that Bolker did not hold Montebello for productive use in trade or business or for investment.[4] The Tax Court rejected both arguments. The Commissioner does not appeal the decision that Bolker individually made the exchange. The Commissioner does not challenge any of the Tax Court's findings of fact; review of the Tax Court's decisions of law is de novo.

II. THE HOLDING REQUIREMENT

The Commissioner argued unsuccessfully in the Tax Court that because Bolker acquired the property with the intent, and almost immediate contractual obligation to exchange it, Bolker never held the property for productive use in trade or business or for investment as required by section 1031(a). Essentially, the Commissioner's position is that the holding requirement has two elements: that the taxpayer own the property to make money rather than for personal reasons, and that at some point before the taxpayer decides to exchange the property, he have intended to keep that property as an investment.

Bolker argues that the intent to exchange investment property for other investment property satisfies the holding requirement. Bolker's position also in essence posits two elements to the holding requirement: that the taxpayer own the property to make money, and that the taxpayer not intend to liquidate his investment.

Authority on this issue is scarce. This is not surprising, because in almost all fact situations in which property is acquired for immediate exchange, there is no gain or loss to the acquiring taxpayer on the exchange, as the property has not had time to change in value. Therefore, it is irrelevant to that taxpayer whether section 1031(a) applies. . . . The cases generally address the taxpayer's intent regarding the property *acquired* in an exchange, rather than the property *given up*. The rule of those cases, *e.g.*, *Regals Realty Co. v. Commissioner*, 127 F.2d 931, 933–34 (2d Cir. 1942), is that at the time of the exchange the taxpayer must intend to keep the property acquired, and intend to do so with an investment purpose. That rule would be nonsense as applied to the property given up, because at the time of the exchange the taxpayer's intent in every case is to give up the property. No exchange could qualify.

The Commissioner cites two revenue rulings to support his position, Rev. Rul. 77-337, 1977-2 C.B. 305, and Rev. Rul. 77-297. Revenue rulings, however, are not controlling. . . . Moreover, neither ruling is precisely on point here. In Revenue Ruling 77-337, A owned X corporation, which owned a shopping center. Pursuant to a prearranged plan, A liquidated X to acquire the shopping center so that he could immediately exchange it with B for like-kind property. A never held the shopping center, and therefore section 1031(a) did not apply. This case differs from 77-337 in two ways. First, the liquidation was planned before any intention to exchange the properties arose, not to facilitate an exchange. Second, Bolker did actually hold Montebello for three months.

In Revenue Ruling 77-297, B wanted to buy A's ranch, but A wanted to exchange

---

[4] The Commissioner concedes that the real estate received by Bolker was of like kind to the Montebello property.

rather than sell. A located a desirable ranch owned by C. Pursuant to a prearranged plan, B purchased C's ranch and immediately exchanged it with A for A's ranch. As to A, the exchange qualifies under section 1031(a). As to B, it does not, since B never held C's ranch, and acquired it solely to exchange. The same distinctions as in 77-337 apply between this ruling and the facts in *Bolker.* Neither ruling cites case authority for its holdings.

Bolker cites two cases that support his position. In each case, the Tax Court gave section 1031(a) nonrecognition to a transaction in which the property given up was acquired with the intention of exchange. However, neither case actually considered the holding issue, which diminishes the persuasiveness of the authority. [The court then reviewed *124 Front Street, Inc. v. Commissioner*, 65 T.C. 6 (1975), and noted that it provided some support for Bolker's theory . . . that an intent to exchange for like-kind property satisfies the holding requirement.]

Rutherford v. Commissioner, T.C.M., 1978-505, is an unusual case with a holding similar to *124 Front Street.* W, a cattle breeder, agreed with R, another breeder, to exchange W's twelve half-blood heifers for twelve three-quarter blood heifers to be bred from the half-blood heifers. W gave R the twelve half-blood heifers. R bred them to a registered bull and gave W the first twelve three-quarter blood heifers produced. At stake in the case were depreciation deductions. En route to determining R's basis in the half-blood heifers for depreciation purposes, the Tax Court held that the exchange of heifers qualified for nonrecognition under section 1031(a). Although the court did not even mention the point, the facts indicate that when by virtue of their birth R "acquired" the three-quarter blood heifers, the property he gave up, he had already contracted to exchange them. Thus, *Rutherford* also supports Bolker's position, albeit tacitly.

The Tax Court's holding in this case is based on its recent opinion in *Magneson v. Commissioner*, 81 T.C. 767 (1983) (court reviewed), *aff'd*, 753 F.2d 1490 (9th Cir. 1985). In *Magneson*, taxpayers exchanged property for like-kind property and then by prearrangement contributed the property they acquired to a partnership. Each transaction viewed separately was admittedly tax-free, but in combination raised the issue whether contribution to a partnership satisfies the holding requirement for the acquired property. The *Bolker* Tax Court interpreted *Magneson* as holding that an intent to continue the investment rather than selling it or converting it to personal use satisfied the holding requirement, even if the taxpayer never intended to keep the specific property acquired. In both *Bolker* and *Magneson*, the Tax Court emphasized the admitted nonrecognition treatment accorded each individual step in the transactions, and reasoned that if each step were tax-free, in combination they should also be tax-free, so long as the continuity of investment principle underlying section 1031(a) is respected.

We recently affirmed *Magneson* but our rationale differed from that of the Tax Court. While we recognized the importance of continuity of investment as the basic purpose underlying section 1031(a), see H.R.Rep. No. 704, 73d Cong., 2d Sess. 12, reprinted in 1939-1 C.B. (pt. 2) 554, 564, we did not hold that that principle justifies the failure to address the specific requirements of section 1031(a). Rather, we based affirmance on our holding that the Magnesons intended to and did continue to hold the acquired property, the contribution to the partnership being a change in the form of ownership rather than the relinquishment of ownership. Thus the Magnesons satisfied the specific requirements of section 1031(a). Nothing in *Magneson* relieves Bolker of his burden to satisfy the requirement that he have held the property given up, Montebello, for investment.

Finally, there is nothing in the legislative history which either supports or negates Bolker's or the Commissioner's position. In sum, the Commissioner is supported by two revenue rulings which are neither controlling nor precisely on point. Bolker is supported by two Tax Court decisions which did not explicitly address this issue. In the absence of controlling precedent, the plain language of the statute itself appears our most reliable guide.

The statute requires that the property be "held for productive use in trade or business or for investment." Giving these words their ordinary meaning, . . . a taxpayer may satisfy the "holding" requirement by owning the property, and the "for productive use in trade or business or for investment" requirement by lack of intent either to liquidate the investment or to use it for personal pursuits. These are essentially the two requirements courts have placed on the property *acquired* in a section 1031(a) exchange, see *e.g., Regals Realty*, 127 F.2d at 933–34 (intent to sell disqualifies exchange); *Click v. Commissioner*, 78 T.C. 225, 233–34 (1982) (intent to give as gift disqualifies exchange), so this interpretation would yield the symmetry the use of identical language seems to demand.

The Commissioner's position, in contrast, would require us to read an unexpressed additional requirement into the statute: that the taxpayer have, previous to forming the intent to exchange one piece of property for a second parcel, an intent to keep the first piece of property indefinitely. We decline to do so. . . . Rather, we hold that if a taxpayer owns property which he does not intend to liquidate or to use for personal pursuits, he is "holding" that property "for productive use in trade or business or for investment" within the meaning of section 1031(a). Under this formulation, the intent to exchange property for like-kind property satisfies the holding requirement, because it is *not* an intent to liquidate the investment or to use it for personal pursuits. Bolker acquired the Montebello property with the intent to exchange it for like-kind property, and thus he held Montebello for investment under section 1031(a). The decision of the Tax Court is therefore

Affirmed.

BELL LINES, INC. v. UNITED STATES
United States Court of Appeals, Fourth Circuit
480 F.2d 710 (1973)

CRAVEN, CIRCUIT JUDGE.

A corporation which trades in old trucks and pays boot in money for new trucks comes under Inter. Rev. Code of 1954, Section 1031; any gain on the trade-in is not recognized. There is, however, a capital gain, fully recognizable in the year of the transaction, where a corporation sells old trucks at a profit even though the proceeds are used to purchase new trucks. The two prior sentences are, obviously, simply different characterizations of the same economic event: replacement of property held for productive use in trade or business. If the transaction is said to be a sale and purchase rather than an exchange, the taxpayer's future basis for depreciation is the actual cost of the new trucks. In this case Bell Lines treated truck replacement in its tax returns as a sale of old trucks and a separate purchase of new ones, and depreciated the new ones at full purchase price. The Commissioner viewed the transaction as a nontaxable exchange of old trucks for new trucks and accordingly adjusted the basis of the new trucks downward, reducing claimed depreciation deductions. In this suit for refund of taxes paid, the taxpayer prevailed in the district court, and the government appeals. We affirm.

Details of the transaction are as follows. The taxpayer, Bell Lines, Inc. . . . operated an interstate trucking line during 1959, 1960, and 1961. During this period of time, taxpayer's stock was owned by its officers and directors: John Amos, President; Fred Sclavi, Vice-President and General Manager; Betty Winterholler, Secretary-Treasurer.

In the spring of 1959, taxpayer decided to replace the major portion of its truck tractors. Mack Trucks, Inc., and White Motor Corporation submitted competitive bids, and in the course of bargaining White urged the taxpayer that more could be obtained for the old trucks by selling them to a buyer White had found than by trading them to Mack. Mack immediately offered to buy the old trucks rather than take them as trades. The taxpayer refused Mack's offer and stated that taxpayer was only interested in purchasing new trucks from Mack. Mack, in order to be competitive with White, offered to help taxpayer find a buyer.

Subsequently Mack submitted a proposal for the new tractors with prices quoted without reference to any trade-ins. On June 24, 1959, the board of directors of taxpayer voted to accept the Mack proposal. At the same time the board authorized Sclavi to sell 143 old trucks.

Pursuant to the board's action, taxpayer submitted a purchase order to Mack on June 26, 1959, for 148 tractors, and pursuant to the purchase order taxpayer signed conditional sale agreements — on August 15, 1959, for 40 tractors; on September 15, 1959, for 65 tractors; and on October 15, 1959, for 43 new tractors.

To dispose of taxpayer's used tractors, Sclavi accepted an offer of $650,000 from the Horner Service Corporation, an independent used truck dealership in Vineland, New Jersey. Unknown to the taxpayer, the Horner offer was prompted by an agreement between Mack and Horner. Horner agreed that it would purchase taxpayer's trucks and attempt to resell them, Horner would keep any profit it made, and Mack guaranteed that Horner would not lose money on any truck. Pursuant to this agreement, Mack furnished funds to Horner with which to pay for the taxpayer's used trucks and subsequently took title from Horner of most of the used trucks. Mack on its books treated the transaction as a trade-in.

The taxpayer treated the acquisition of new tractors and the disposition of old tractors as a purchase and sale and reported it as such on its 1959 tax return, paying tax on the capital gain resulting from the disposition of the used tractors. For depreciation of the new trucks, taxpayer used actual cost as the basis for the tax years here in question, 1960 and 1961. The Commissioner determined that the transaction was an "exchange" of tractors for tractors. Under the Commissioner's view, the taxpayer could only use for depreciation purposes a transferred basis, computed under Section 1031(d). Since this was less than the basis used by taxpayer, a deficiency was assessed. Taxpayer paid the deficiency and brought this suit for a refund.

The district court found that taxpayer had entered into a contract with Mack for purchase of new trucks and had entered into a separate agreement with Horner for the sale of old trucks. The court further found that none of the officials or taxpayer knew of the arrangements between Mack and Horner. The government argues on appeal that the district court was clearly erroneous in finding: (1) that the transactions between taxpayer and Mack and between taxpayer and Horner were not mutually dependent; and, (2) that taxpayer did not have knowledge of the Mack-Horner arrangement.

The officers of taxpayer testified at the trial below. Winterholler stated that she would not have agreed to a trade-in and that taxpayer had never before traded-in tractors. Amos testified that he had no knowledge of the Horner-Mack arrangement and that the purchase by taxpayer of the 148 new trucks was not conditioned on the disposition of the old trucks. Sclavi also testified that the purchase from Mack was not conditioned on sale of the old trucks and that he had no knowledge of the Mack-Horner arrangement. The purchase order agreement of June 26, 1959, and the conditional sales agreements appear to have been fully enforceable against taxpayer regardless of whether it disposed of its used tractors.

We think the testimony of taxpayer's officials, if believed, and the evidence of the contracts with Mack are sufficient to support the district court's findings. The district court's findings (1) that taxpayer had a binding agreement with Mack to purchase 148 tractors, (2) that taxpayer had a separate agreement with Horner to buy its used trucks, and (3) that taxpayer was unaware of the side agreement between Mack and Horner are not clearly erroneous.

There remains for us to determine whether on these facts the district court erroneously characterized the transactions as a sale and purchase rather than an exchange. We think not.

In *Coastal Terminals, Inv. v. United States*, 320 F.2d 333 (4th Cir. 1963), we held:

> The purpose of Section 1031(a), as shown by its legislative history, is to defer recognition of gain or loss when a direct exchange of property between the taxpayer and another party takes place; *a sale for cash does not qualify as a nontaxable exchange even though the cash is immediately reinvested in like property.*

Id. at 337 (emphasis added).

The court in *Carlton v. United States*, 385 F.2d 238 (5th Cir. 1967), stated:

> The very essence of an exchange is the transfer of property between owners, while the mark of a sale is the receipt of cash for the property. . . . Where, as here, there is an immediate repurchase of other property with the proceeds of the sale, that distinction between a sale and exchange is crucial.

Id. at 242.

It is urged upon us that since Mack supplied funds to Horner to purchase the trucks and later took most of the trucks from Horner, the substance of the transaction is a trade-in or exchange between taxpayer and Mack. The question of sale or exchange often turns upon whether separate steps in a transaction are to be recognized or disregarded. This depends on whether the steps are mutually dependent or merely artificial transactions, as opposed to being steps with legal significance independent of the other steps and supported by legitimate business reasons. . . .

In the present case we cannot conclude that taxpayer had no legitimate business reasons for selling its old trucks and purchasing new ones. There was evidence it had always purchased without regard to trade-in value of old property, and it is doubtless possible to get a cheaper price where the dealer is not burdened with the necessity of disposing of old property. Moreover, as we have noted, the transactions were not mutually dependent as taxpayer was legally bound to purchase the 148 trucks from Mack whether it had sold the old ones or not. Thus the transaction between taxpayer and Horner may be reasonably viewed as one of substance to be treated separately from the taxpayer-Mack transaction.

That the two transactions were not mutually dependent also distinguishes this case from *Redwing Carriers, Inc. v. Tomlinson*, 399 F.2d 652 (5th Cir. 1968), and Rev. Rul. 61-119, 1961-1 Cum. Bull. 395. In *Redwing Carriers* the taxpayer had used its own wholly owned subsidiary to disguise an exchange as a sale and simultaneous purchase of property. The district court had specifically found that there would have been no purchase of the new equipment had there not been a concurrent and binding agreement for the sale of the old equipment. 399 F.2d at 655. The court thus held the transaction to be within Section 1031(a). In Rev. Rul. 61-119 the disposition of old equipment to and acquisition of new equipment from the same dealer where the transactions were reciprocal was held to be an exchange even though accomplished by separately executed contracts.

In distinguishing *Carlton*, the *Redwing Carriers* court stated:

> The most that could be said for the transactional relationship in *Carlton* was that the sale for cash between the taxpayer and a purchaser had been *complementary* with the later purchase of like property between the taxpayer and a seller.

Id. at 659.

Cases dealing with whether the replacement of property held for productive use in trade or business results in a sale or exchange have been termed "hopelessly conflicting." However, the result in a case such as this one is controlled by the district court's finding of facts, *i.e.*, whether the replacement transactions were "complementary" or "mutually dependent." The district court's finding below, not clearly erroneous, that the transactions in question were not mutually dependent, precludes our determining that an exchange occurred. Accordingly, the decision of the district court will be

Affirmed.

REVENUE RULING 90-34
1990-1 C.B. 154

ISSUE

If X transfers property to Y in exchange for property of a like kind, may the exchange as to X qualify for nonrecognition of gain or loss under section 1031 of the Internal Revenue Code even though legal title to the property received by X is never held by Y?

FACTS

X and Y are unrelated persons. X files its U.S. income tax return on a calendar year basis. On May 14, 1989, X and Y enter into a contract that requires X to transfer Blackacre to Y and Y to transfer to X property of a like kind with the same fair market value. Blackacre, unencumbered real property, has been held by X for productive use in its trade or business and has a fair market value of $1,000,000. Under the contract, X is required to locate and identify property with a fair market value of $1,000,000 that is of a like kind to Blackacre within 45 days of X's transfer of Blackacre to Y (the "identification period"), and Y is required to purchase and transfer the identified property to X before the earlier of 180 days from the transfer of Blackacre or the due date (including extensions) for X's U.S. income tax return for the taxable year in which X's transfer of Blackacre to Y occurs (the "exchange period"). If X fails to identify the property to be received in the transaction before the end of the identification period or Y fails to purchase and transfer such property to X before the end of the exchange period, Y is required to pay $1,000,000 to X. Neither X nor Y contracts to exchange Blackacre with any other party.

On May 23, 1989, X transfers Blackacre to Y. On June 1, 1989, X properly identifies Whiteacre as the property to be received. Whiteacre, owned by Z, a person unrelated to X, is unencumbered real property that has a fair market value of $1,000,000 and is of a like kind to Blackacre. On July 10, 1989, Y purchases Whiteacre from Z, and at Y's direction, Z transfers legal title to Whiteacre directly to X before the end of the exchange period. X thereafter holds Whiteacre for productive use in its trade or business.

LAW AND ANALYSIS

Under section 1031(a)(1) of the Code, no gain or loss is recognized on the exchange of property held for productive use in a trade or business or for investment if such property is exchanged solely for property of like kind that is to be held either for productive use in a trade or business or for investment.

Section 1031(a)(3) of the Code provides that any property received by a taxpayer will be treated as property which is not like-kind property if (A) such property is not identified as property to be received in the exchange on or before the day which is 45 days after the date on which the taxpayer transfers the property relinquished in the exchange or (B) such property is received after the earlier of (i) the day which is 180 days after the date on which the taxpayer transfers the property relinquished in the exchange, or (ii) the due date (including extensions) for the taxpayer's federal income tax return for the taxable year in which the transfer of the relinquished property occurs.

If Z had actually transferred legal title to Whiteacre to Y and Y had then transferred legal title to Whiteacre to X, the exchange of Whiteacre for Blackacre, as to X, would clearly qualify for nonrecognition of gain or loss under section 1031(a) of the Code. However, section 1031(a) does not require that Y hold legal title to Whiteacre, but merely that X receive solely property of a like kind to the property transferred in order for the exchange to qualify for nonrecognition of gain or loss. Therefore, the failure of Y to acquire legal title to Whiteacre does not disqualify X from nonrecognition of gain or loss under section 1031(a) on the transfer of Blackacre to Y in exchange for Whiteacre.

HOLDING

X's transfer of property to Y, in exchange for property of a like kind, qualifies as to X for nonrecognition of gain or loss on the exchange under section 1031 of the Code even though legal title to the property received by X is never held by Y.

REVENUE PROCEDURE 2008-16
2008-1 C.B. 547

SECTION 1. PURPOSE

This revenue procedure provides a safe harbor under which the Internal Revenue Service (the "Service") will not challenge whether a dwelling unit qualifies as property held for productive use in a trade or business or for investment for purposes of § 1031 of the Internal Revenue Code.

SECTION 2. BACKGROUND

.01 Section 1031 (a) provides that no gain or loss is recognized on the exchange of property held for productive use in a trade or business or for investment (relinquished property) if the property is exchanged solely for property of like kind that is to be held either for productive use in a trade or business or for investment (replacement property). Under § 1.1031 (a)-(1) (a) (1) of the Income Tax Regulations, property held for productive use in a trade or business may be exchanged for property held for investment, and property held for investment may be exchanged for property held for productive use in a trade or business.

.02 Rev. Rul. 59-229, 1959-2 C.B. 180, concludes that gain or loss from an exchange of personal residences may not be deferred under § 1031 because the residences are not property held for productive use in a trade or business or for investment.

.03 Section 2.05 of Rev. Proc. 2005-14, 2005-1 C.B. 528, states that § 1031 does not apply to property that is used solely as a personal residence.

.04 In *Moore v. Comm'r*, T.C. Memo. 2007-134, the taxpayers exchanged one lakeside vacation home for another. Neither home was ever rented. Both were used by the taxpayers only for personal purposes. The taxpayers claimed that the exchange of the homes was a like-kind exchange under § 1031 because the properties were expected to appreciate in value and thus were held for investment. The Tax Court held, however, that the properties were held for personal use and that the "mere hope or expectation that property may be sold at a gain cannot establish an investment intent if the taxpayer uses the property as a residence."

.05 In *Starker v. United States*, 602 F.2d 1341, 1350 (9th Cir. 1979), the Ninth Circuit held that a personal residence of a taxpayer was not eligible for exchange under § 1031, explaining that "[it] has long been the rule that use of property solely as a personal residence is antithetical to its being held for investment."

.06 The Service recognizes that many taxpayers hold dwelling units primarily for the production of current rental income, but also use the properties occasionally for personal purposes. In the interest of sound tax administration, this revenue procedure provides taxpayers with a safe harbor under which a dwelling unit will qualify as property held for productive use in a trade or business or for investment under § 1031 even though a taxpayer occasionally uses the dwelling unit for personal purposes.

SECTION 3. SCOPE

.01 In general. This revenue procedure applies to a dwelling unit, as defined in section 3.02 of this revenue procedure, that meets the qualifying use standards in section 4.02 of this revenue procedure.

.02 Dwelling unit. For purposes of this revenue procedure, a dwelling unit is real property improved with a house, apartment, condominium, or similar improvement that provides basic living accommodations including sleeping space, bathroom and cooking facilities.

SECTION 4. APPLICATION

.01 In general. The Service will not challenge whether a dwelling unit as defined in section 3.02 of this revenue procedure qualifies under § 1031 as property held for productive use in a trade or business or for investment if the qualifying use standards in section 4.02 of this revenue procedure are met for the dwelling unit.

.02 Qualifying use standards.

(1) Relinquished property. A dwelling unit that a taxpayer intends to be relinquished property in a § 1031 exchange qualifies as property held for productive use in a trade or business or for investment if:

(a) The dwelling unit is owned by the taxpayer for at least 24 months immediately before the exchange (the "qualifying use period"); and

(b) Within the qualifying use period, in each of the two 12-month periods immediately preceding the exchange,

(i) The taxpayer rents the dwelling unit to another person or persons at a fair rental for 14 days or more, and

(ii) The period of the taxpayer's personal use of the dwelling unit does not exceed the greater of 14 days or 10 percent of the number of days during the 12-month period that the dwelling unit is rented at a fair rental.

For this purpose, the first 12-month period immediately preceding the exchange ends on the day before the exchange takes place (and begins 12 months prior to that day) and the second 12-month period ends on the day before the first 12-month period begins (and begins 12 months prior to that day).

(2) Replacement property. A dwelling unit that a taxpayer intends to be replacement property in a § 1031 exchange qualifies as property held for productive use in a trade or business or for investment if:

(a) The dwelling unit is owned by the taxpayer for at least 24 months immediately after the exchange (the "qualifying use period"); and

(b) Within the qualifying use period, in each of the two 12-month periods immediately after the exchange,

(i) The taxpayer rents the dwelling unit to another person or persons at a fair rental for 14 days or more, and

(ii) The period of the taxpayer's personal use of the dwelling unit does not exceed the greater of 14 days or 10 percent of the number of days during the 12-month period that the dwelling unit is rented at a fair rental.

For this purpose, the first 12-month period immediately after the exchange begins on the day after the exchange takes place and the second 12-month period begins on the day after the first 12-month period ends.

.03 Personal use. For purposes of this revenue procedure, personal use of a dwelling unit occurs on any day on which a taxpayer is deemed to have used the dwelling unit for personal purposes under § 280A (d) (2) (taking into account § 280A(d)(3) but not § 280A(d)(4)).

.04 Fair rental. For purposes of this revenue procedure, whether a dwelling unit is rented at a fair rental is determined based on all of the facts and circumstances that exist when the rental agreement is entered into. All rights and obligations of the parties to the rental agreement are taken into account.

.05 Special rule for replacement property. If a taxpayer files a federal income tax return and reports a transaction as an exchange under § 1031, based on the expectation that a dwelling unit will meet the qualifying use standards in section 4.02 (2) of this revenue procedure for replacement property, and subsequently determines that the dwelling unit does not meet the qualifying use standards, the taxpayer, if necessary, should file an amended return and not report the transaction as an exchange under § 1031.

REVENUE PROCEDURE 2000-37
2000-2 C.B. 308

SECTION 1. PURPOSE

This revenue procedure provides a safe harbor under which the Internal Revenue Service will not challenge (a) the qualification of property as either "replacement property" or "relinquished property" (as defined in § 1.1031(k)-1(a) of the Income Tax Regulations) for purposes of § 1031 of the Internal Revenue Code and the regulations thereunder or (b) the treatment of the "exchange accommodation titleholder" as the beneficial owner of such property for federal income tax purposes, if the property is held in a "qualified exchange accommodation arrangement" (QEAA), as defined in section 4.02 of this revenue procedure.

SECTION 2. BACKGROUND

.01 Section 1031(a)(1) provides that no gain or loss is recognized on the exchange of property held for productive use in a trade or business or for investment if the property is exchanged solely for property of like kind that is to be held either for productive use in a trade or business or for investment.

.02 Section 1031(a)(3) provides that property received by the taxpayer is not treated as like-kind property if it: (a) is not identified as property to be received in the exchange on or before the day that is 45 days after the date on which the taxpayer transfers the relinquished property; or (b) is received after the earlier of the date that is 180 days after the date on which the taxpayer transfers the relinquished property, or the due date (determined with regard to extension) for the transferor's federal income tax return for the year in which the transfer of the relinquished property occurs.

.03 Determining the owner of property for federal income tax purposes requires an analysis of all of the facts and circumstances. As a general rule, the party that bears the economic burdens and benefits of ownership will be considered the owner of property for federal income tax purposes. See Rev. Rul. 82-144, 1982-2 C.B. 34.

.04 On April 25, 1991, the Treasury Department and the Service promulgated final regulations under § 1.1031(k)-1 providing rules for deferred like-kind exchanges under § 1031(a)(3). The preamble to the final regulations states that the deferred exchange rules under § 1031(a)(3) do not apply to reverse- *Starker* exchanges (*i.e.*, exchanges where the replacement property is acquired before the relinquished property is transferred) and consequently that the final regulations do not apply to such exchanges. T.D. 8346, 1991-1 C.B. 150, 151; see *Starker v. United States*, 602 F.2d 1341 (9th Cir. 1979). However, the preamble indicates that Treasury and the Service will continue to study the applicability of the general rule of § 1031(a)(1) to these transactions. T.D. 8346, 1991-1 C.B. 150, 151.

.05 Since the promulgation of the final regulations under § 1.1031(k)-1, taxpayers have engaged in a wide variety of transactions, including so-called "parking" transactions, to facilitate reverse like-kind exchanges. Parking transactions typically are designed to "park" the desired replacement property with an accommodation party until such time as the taxpayer arranges for the transfer of the relinquished property to the ultimate transferee in a simultaneous or deferred exchange. Once such a transfer is arranged, the taxpayer transfers the relinquished property to the accommodation party in exchange for the replacement property, and the accommodation party then transfers the relinquished property to the ultimate transferee. In other situations, an accommodation party may acquire the desired replacement property on behalf of the taxpayer and immediately exchange such property with the taxpayer for the relinquished property, thereafter holding the relinquished property until the taxpayer arranges for a transfer of such property to the ultimate transferee. In the parking arrangements, taxpayers attempt to arrange the transaction so that the accommodation party has enough of the benefits and burdens relating to the property so that the accommodation party will be treated as the owner for federal income tax purposes.

.06 Treasury and the Service have determined that it is in the best interest of sound tax administration to provide taxpayers with a workable means of qualifying their transactions under § 1031 in situations where the taxpayer has a genuine intent to accomplish a like-kind exchange at the time that it arranges for the acquisition of the replacement property and actually accomplishes the exchange within a short time thereafter. Accordingly, this revenue procedure provides a safe harbor that allows a taxpayer to treat the accommodation party as the owner of the property for federal income tax purposes, thereby enabling the taxpayer to accomplish a qualifying like-kind exchange.

SECTION 3. SCOPE

.01 Exclusivity. This revenue procedure provides a safe harbor for the qualification under § 1031 of certain arrangements between taxpayers and exchange accommodation titleholders and provides for the treatment of the exchange accommodation titleholder as the beneficial owner of the property for federal income tax purposes. These provisions apply only in the limited context described in this revenue procedure. The principles set forth in this revenue procedure have no application to any federal income tax determinations other than determinations that involve arrangements qualifying for the safe harbor.

.02 No inference. No inference is intended with respect to the federal income tax treatment of arrangements similar to those described in this revenue procedure that were entered into prior to the effective date of this revenue procedure. Further, the Service recognizes that "parking" transactions can be accomplished outside of the safe harbor provided in this revenue procedure. Accordingly, no inference is intended with respect to the federal income tax treatment of "parking" transactions that do not satisfy the terms of the safe harbor provided in this revenue procedure, whether entered into prior to or after the effective date of this revenue procedure.

.03 Other issues. Services for the taxpayer in connection with a person's role as the exchange accommodation titleholder in a QEAA shall not be taken into account in determining whether that person or a related person is a disqualified person (as defined in § 1.1031(k)-1(k)). Even though property will not fail to be treated as being held in a QEAA as a result of one or more arrangements described in section 4.03 of this revenue procedure, the Service still may recast an amount paid pursuant to such an arrangement as a fee paid to the exchange accommodation titleholder for acting as an exchange accommodation titleholder to the extent necessary to reflect the true economic substance of the arrangement. Other federal income tax issues implicated, but not addressed, in this revenue procedure include the treatment, for federal income tax purposes, of payments described in section 4.03(7) and whether an exchange accommodation titleholder may be precluded from claiming deprecia- tion deductions (e.g., as a dealer) with respect to the relinquished property or the replacement property.

.04 Effect of Noncompliance. If the requirements of this revenue procedure are not satisfied (for example, the property subject to a QEAA is not transferred within the time period provided), then this revenue procedure does not apply. Accordingly, the determination of whether the taxpayer or the exchange accommodation titleholder is the owner of the property for federal income tax purposes, and the proper treatment of any transactions entered into by or between the parties, will be made without regard to the provisions of this revenue procedure.

SECTION 4. QUALIFIED EXCHANGE ACCOMMODATION ARRANGE- MENTS

.01 Generally. The Service will not challenge the qualification of property as either "replacement property" or "relinquished property" (as defined in § 1.1031(k)- 1(a)) for purposes of § 1031 and the regulations thereunder, or the treatment of the exchange accommodation titleholder as the beneficial owner of such property for federal income tax purposes, if the property is held in a QEAA.

.02 Qualified Exchange Accommodation Arrangements. For purposes of this revenue procedure, property is held in a QEAA if all of the following requirements are met:

(1) Qualified indicia of ownership of the property is held by a person (the "exchange accommodation titleholder") who is not the taxpayer or a disqualified person and either such person is subject to federal income tax or, if such person is treated as a partnership or S corporation for federal income tax purposes, more than 90 percent of its interests or stock are owned by partners or shareholders who are subject to federal income tax. Such qualified indicia of ownership must be held by the exchange accom- modation titleholder at all times from the date of acquisition by the exchange accommodation titleholder until the property is transferred as described in section 4.02(5) of this revenue procedure. For this purpose, "qualified indicia of ownership" means legal title to the property, other indicia of ownership of the property that are treated as beneficial ownership of the property under applicable principles of commercial law (e.g., a contract for deed), or interests in an entity that is disregarded as an entity separate from its owner for federal income tax purposes (e.g., a single member limited liability company) and that holds either legal title to the property or such other indicia of ownership;

(2) At the time the qualified indicia of ownership of the property is transferred to the exchange accommodation titleholder, it is the taxpayer's

bona fide intent that the property held by the exchange accommodation titleholder represent either replacement property or relinquished property in an exchange that is intended to qualify for nonrecognition of gain (in whole or in part) or loss under § 1031;

(3) No later than five business days after the transfer of qualified indicia of ownership of the property to the exchange accommodation titleholder, the taxpayer and the exchange accommodation titleholder enter into a written agreement (the "qualified exchange accommodation agreement") that provides that the exchange accommodation titleholder is holding the property for the benefit of the taxpayer in order to facilitate an exchange under § 1031 and this revenue procedure and that the taxpayer and the exchange accommodation titleholder agree to report the acquisition, holding, and disposition of the property as provided in this revenue procedure. The agreement must specify that the exchange accommodation titleholder will be treated as the beneficial owner of the property for all federal income tax purposes. Both parties must report the federal income tax attributes of the property on their federal income tax returns in a manner consistent with this agreement;

(4) No later than 45 days after the transfer of qualified indicia of ownership of the replacement property to the exchange accommodation titleholder, the relinquished property is properly identified. Identification must be made in a manner consistent with the principles described in § 1.1031(k)-1(c). For purposes of this section, the taxpayer may properly identify alternative and multiple properties, as described in § 1.1031(k)-1(c)(4);

(5) No later than 180 days after the transfer of qualified indicia of ownership of the property to the exchange accommodation titleholder, (a) the property is transferred (either directly or indirectly through a qualified intermediary (as defined in § 1.1031(k)-1(g)(4))) to the taxpayer as replacement property; or (b) the property is transferred to a person who is not the taxpayer or a disqualified person as relinquished property; and

(6) The combined time period that the relinquished property and the replacement property are held in a QEAA does not exceed 180 days.

.03 Permissible Agreements. Property will not fail to be treated as being held in a QEAA as a result of any one or more of the following legal or contractual arrangements, regardless of whether such arrangements contain terms that typically would result from arm's length bargaining between unrelated parties with respect to such arrangements:

(1) An exchange accommodation titleholder that satisfies the requirements of the qualified intermediary safe harbor set forth in § 1.1031(k)-1(g)(4) may enter into an exchange agreement with the taxpayer to serve as the qualified intermediary in a simultaneous or deferred exchange of the property under § 1031;

(2) The taxpayer or a disqualified person guarantees some or all of the obligations of the exchange accommodation titleholder, including secured

or unsecured debt incurred to acquire the property, or indemnifies the exchange accommodation titleholder against costs and expenses;

(3) The taxpayer or a disqualified person loans or advances funds to the exchange accommodation titleholder or guarantees a loan or advance to the exchange accommodation titleholder;

(4) The property is leased by the exchange accommodation titleholder to the taxpayer or a disqualified person;

(5) The taxpayer or a disqualified person manages the property, supervises improvement of the property, acts as a contractor, or otherwise provides services to the exchange accommodation titleholder with respect to the property;

(6) The taxpayer and the exchange accommodation titleholder enter into agreements or arrangements relating to the purchase or sale of the property, including puts and calls at fixed or formula prices, effective for a period not in excess of 185 days from the date the property is acquired by the exchange accommodation titleholder; and

(7) The taxpayer and the exchange accommodation titleholder enter into agreements or arrangements providing that any variation in the value of a relinquished property from the estimated value on the date of the exchange accommodation titleholder's receipt of the property be taken into account upon the exchange accommodation titleholder's disposition of the relinquished property through the taxpayer's advance of funds to, or receipt of funds from, the exchange accommodation titleholder.

.04 Permissible Treatment. Property will not fail to be treated as being held in a QEAA merely because the accounting, regulatory, or state, local, or foreign tax treatment of the arrangement between the taxpayer and the exchange accommodation titleholder is different from the treatment required by section 4.02(3) of this revenue procedure.

AUTHORS' NOTE

Revenue Procedure 2004-51, 2004-2 C.B. 294 provides that Rev. Proc. 2000-37 does not apply if, prior to initiating a qualified exchange accommodation arrangement (QEAA), the taxpayer owned the property intended to qualify as replacement property. A taxpayer may not treat as a like-kind exchange a transaction in which the taxpayer transfers property to an exchange accommodation titleholder and receives that same property as replacement property in a purported exchange for other property they owned. As noted in Rev. Proc. 2004-51, "an exchange of real estate owned by a taxpayer for improvements on land owned by the same taxpayer does not meet the requirements of § 1031. . . . Moreover, Rev. Rul. 67-255, 1967-2 C.B. 270, holds that a building constructed on land owned by a taxpayer is not of a like kind to involuntarily converted land of the same taxpayer. Rev. Proc. 2000-37 does not abrogate the statutory requirement of § 1031 that the transaction be an exchange of like-kind properties." Rev. Proc. 2004-51 therefore provides that Rev. Proc. 2000-37 "does not apply to replacement property held in a QEAA if the property is owned by the taxpayer within the 180-day period ending on the date of transfer of qualified indicia of ownership of the property to an exchange accommodation titleholder."

Chapter 40

INVOLUNTARY CONVERSIONS

I. PROBLEMS

1. Patricia is in the business of selling pianos and other musical instruments. Her business is housed in a commercial building she owns on a tract of land located adjacent to a secondary highway on the outskirts of Anytown, U.S.A. The building was destroyed in an early morning fire of unknown origin. Within a month of the fire, Patricia collected $800,000 in insurance proceeds for the destruction of her building. Her adjusted basis in the building was $150,000. Immediately following the fire, Patricia hired an architect and a contractor to design and construct a new and larger building on the same site as the old building. The new building was completed twelve months later at a cost of $1,000,000. Patricia used all $800,000 of the insurance proceeds plus the proceeds of a bank loan to finance the construction. Upon completion of the building, Patricia immediately began to use it to conduct her musical instrument business albeit on a somewhat larger scale.

   (a) Will Patricia be entitled under § 1033 to defer recognition of her realized gain? If so, what basis will Patricia have in the new building?

   (b) How would your answers to (a) change, if at all, in each of the following alternative scenarios:

      (i) Because interest rates were low, Patricia decided to invest only $100,000 of the insurance proceeds in the new building and to borrow the other $900,000 needed for building construction. She used the remaining $700,000 of insurance proceeds to purchase stock in various technology companies.

      (ii) The new building cost Patricia only $600,000 and Patricia used the other $200,000 of insurance proceeds to purchase a lot on which she intends to build her new home.

      (iii) The newly constructed building was larger than Patricia needed for her musical instrument business and so Patricia leased one-half of the new building to an office supply chain. In evaluating this situation, assume that the part of the building she used for her musical instrument business was determined to have a value of $500,000.

      (iv) Patricia determined that she could no longer compete with the regional music stores and decided to use the newly constructed building for a retail carpet and flooring business which she will own and operate just as she did her musical instrument business.

(c)   Assume Patricia's building was significantly damaged by fire but not totally destroyed. The building, however, was no longer usable for Patricia's business. Assume Patricia collected $650,000 in fire insurance proceeds and promptly sold the building for its salvage value of $150,000. Within 12 months of the fire, Patricia constructed the new building on an adjacent tract of land she owned. The new building cost $1,000,000. Patricia immediately resumed her musical instrument business in the new building. How do your answers to (a) change, if at all?

(d)   Assume that, instead of fire destroying Patricia's building, the state had condemned the building as part of a highway expansion project. The state paid $800,000 for this taking. Assume also that Patricia decided to get out of the music instrument business. Instead of constructing a building to conduct her musical instrument business, she purchased a medical office building located near a local hospital. She paid $1,000,000 for the building. Patricia immediately began leasing office space to various health care professionals. Will Patricia be entitled to defer recognition of her gain under § 1033? If so, what basis will Patricia have in the new building?

2.   The home Aaron had owned and used as his principal residence for ten years was destroyed by fire. Aaron had a $300,000 adjusted basis in the residence, which had a fair market value of $750,000. Six months after the fire, Aaron received $750,000 in insurance proceeds and immediately purchased another residence for $600,000. Aaron had never previously taken advantage of § 121.

(a)   How much gain, if any, must Aaron report if he takes advantage of both §§ 121 and 1033? What basis will Aaron have in the new residence?

(b)   How would your answers to (a) change if Aaron's new residence cost $400,000?

(c)   How would your answers to (a) change if Aaron purchased the new residence from his sister?

(d)   What result in (a) if Aaron elects not to have § 121 apply?

(e)   How would your answer to (a) change if Aaron's adjusted basis in the destroyed home had been $800,000? Would it make any difference under these circumstances whether Aaron replaced the destroyed home with property that was "similar or related in service or use"?

Assignment for Chapter 40:

Complete the problems.

Read: Internal Revenue Code: §§ 121(d)(5); 1033(a)(1), (a)(2)(A), (a)(2)(B), (a)(2)(E)(ii), (b)(1), (b)(2), (g)(1), (g)(2), (g)(4), (h), (i)(1), (i)(2)(c), (i)(3); 1223(1). Review § 267(b)(1), (b)(2), (c).

Treasury Regulations: §§ 1.121-4(d); 1.1033(a)-1(a); 1.1033(a)-2(a), (b), (c)(1)–(c)(7), (c)(9), (c)(11), (c)(12); 1.1033(b)-1(b); 1.1033(g)-1(a).

Materials: Overview
             Liant Record, Inc. v. Commissioner
             Revenue Ruling 64-237
             Revenue Ruling 79-261
             Revenue Ruling 89-2
             Willamette Industries, Inc. v. Commissioner

II.   VOCABULARY

involuntary conversion
destruction
similar or related in service or use

III.   OBJECTIVES

1. To explain the policy underlying § 1033.

2. To evaluate whether properties are similar or related in service or use.

3. To contrast the "similar or related in service or use" standard of § 1033 to the "like kind" standard of § 1031.

4. To compare the basis provisions of §§ 1033 and 1031.

5. To compute the gain recognized upon an involuntary conversion.

6. To compute the basis of replacement property.

7. To recall § 1033, unlike § 1031, is not limited to investment property or property used in trade or business.

8. To recall § 1033 is elective when property is converted into money or other non-similar property and is mandatory in the event of direct replacement with qualified property.

9. To recall § 1033 is not applicable to losses.

10. To recall the time limit for acquiring replacement property.

11. To recall nonrecognition may not apply when replacement property is purchased from a related party.

12. To explain the application of § 1033 where § 121 is also applicable.

IV. OVERVIEW

A. General Policy

The Internal Revenue Code contains a number of relief provisions, some of which have been examined in prior Chapters of this text. Section 1033 is an important relief provision affording taxpayers the benefit of nonrecognition of gain in circumstances where recognition could create severe hardship.

Consider a common example: a state condemns farm land for highway use. The farmer's adjusted basis in the land is minimal relative to the value of the land. The farmer, who is compensated by the state for the taking, immediately uses the compensation to purchase replacement land. Technically, as a result of the condemnation, the farmer has realized gain in the amount of the difference between the condemnation award received and the farmer's adjusted basis in the condemned property. Will the realized gain be recognized? Will § 1031 negate recognition of the gain, given that the farmer immediately replaced the condemned land with other land of a like kind? The answer to both questions is "No." Gain will not be recognized; and the nonrecognition will not be attributable to § 1031. (Why?)

Section 1033 is the operative nonrecognition provision. Originally enacted in 1921, § 1033 provides taxpayers the opportunity to avoid the forced recognition of gain which, as the above hypothetical demonstrates, might otherwise result when the taxpayer's property is "compulsorily or involuntarily converted" as a result of destruction, theft, seizure, or requisition or condemnation or threat or imminence thereof. Congress understood the recognition of gain and the resulting imposition of tax liability might frustrate a taxpayer's efforts to replace condemned land.

Given § 1033, the farmer has the option of avoiding the recognition of gain by reinvesting the condemnation award in other property "similar or related in service or use" to the property condemned. To the extent that the farmer elects § 1033 treatment and completely invests the condemnation award in property meeting that standard (hereinafter *qualified replacement property*), the farmer will, in effect, be permitted to postpone the payment of tax upon the gain from the condemned farmland. Even if the farmer elects § 1033 treatment, gain will be recognized to the extent the proceeds from the condemnation are not completely reinvested in qualified replacement property.

While initially § 1033 applied also to losses, Congress in 1942 specifically exempted losses from the nonrecognition rule of § 1033. This is one of the significant differences between §§ 1033 and 1031. Another significant difference is that, unlike § 1031, § 1033 is applicable not only to property held for use in a trade or business or for investment purposes but also to property held for personal purposes, *e.g.*, one's residence.

B. The Mandatory and Elective Rules of Section 1033

Section 1033(a) actually provides two separate rules: § 1033(a)(l) applies to those relatively rare situations in which property is directly converted into qualified replacement property; § 1033(a)(2) applies to the more common situation in which property is first converted into money or nonqualified property and is subsequently replaced with qualified property. In the case of the direct conversion of property into qualified replacement property, nonrecognition of gain is mandatory. In the case of the conversion of property into nonqualified property or a combination of qualified and nonqualified property, nonrecognition is elective. The difference between the two rules is likely a function of the fact that a direct conversion of property into qualified replacement property seems so akin to a § 1031 exchange that Congress believed it should be treated as such for tax purposes. Thus, just as § 1031 nonrecognition treatment is mandatory in the case of like kind exchanges, nonrecognition treatment is mandatory in the case of a direct replacement under § 1033. Because cases and rulings involving direct replacement are rare, the focus of this chapter's Overview, Problems, and Materials will be on the elective nonrecognition rule of § 1033.

C. Involuntary Conversion Events

The involuntary conversion events listed in § 1033(a) have not created significant controversy. This is not to suggest, however, that in considering § 1033 problems, the attorney need not be concerned with the kind of event that has resulted in a conversion. See, for example, Revenue Ruling 89-2, in the materials, dealing with chemical contamination of property as an involuntary conversion. A few comments are therefore in order regarding involuntary conversion events. The term "destruction" in § 1033 has been analogized to the term "casualty" which has been discussed in Chapter 24. Thus, destruction as a result of fire, storm or shipwreck would be an involuntary conversion within the meaning of § 1033. The Service has issued numerous rulings finding that specific casualties such as the destruction of livestock by lightning (Rev. Rul. 53-195, 1953-2 C.B. 169) and the destruction of crops by hail (Rev. Rul. 59-8, 1959-1 C.B. 202) constitute involuntary conversion events. For § 165(c)(3) purposes, a casualty is defined as an event that is sudden, unusual and unexpected. However, the Service has ruled that destruction need not be sudden under § 1033. Rev. Rul. 59-102, 1959-1 C.B. 200. The Service has also ruled that, where a principal residence was destroyed by a tornado — clearly an involuntary conversion event — and the owner subsequently sold the land on which the residence was located, the sale of the land would be treated as part of a single involuntary conversion of the residence. Rev. Rul. 96-32, 1996-1 C.B. 177. Note the Service's argument in *Willamette Industries, Inc. v. Commissioner*, included in the materials, that, by processing damaged trees into end products which it then sold, a timber company was not entitled to claim that damages to its trees resulted in an involuntary conversion.

The term "seizure" in § 1033(a) is generally accorded the meaning of confiscation of property by a governmental entity without the payment of compensation. Presumably the seizure of a boat or car used in an illegal drug operation would be an example of a seizure contemplated by the language of § 1033. By contrast, the terms "requisition" and "condemnation" suggest a taking of property by a government agency for a public use. Involuntary conversions as a result of requisition or condemnation account for the majority of the reported § 1033 decisions and rulings. As the Court of Claims noted in *American Natural Gas Co. v. U.S.*, 279 F.2d 220, *cert. denied*, 364 U.S. 900 (1960), the words "requisition or condemnation" mean "the taking or the threat of taking property by some public or quasi-public corporation — by some instrumentality that has the power to do so against the will of the owner, and for the use of the taker. That is the common, well-recognized meaning of those words and there is nothing to indicate that Congress used them in any other sense." 279 F.2d at 225.

D. Similar or Related in Service or Use

Most of the litigation with respect to § 1033 addresses the issue of whether the property with which the taxpayer has replaced the converted property satisfies the "similar or related in service or use" standard of § 1033(a)(2). Just as the like kind standard and the holding requirements of § 1031 are intended to insure that nonrecognition is accorded only when there is continuity of investment, so too the "similar or related in service or use" standard limits the scope of § 1033 treatment. As the Tax Court noted in explaining the "similar or related in service or use" standard, "it is not necessary to acquire property which duplicates exactly that which was converted, [but] the fortuitous circumstance of involuntary conversion does not permit a taxpayer to change the character of his investment without tax consequences." *Maloof v. Commissioner*, 65 T.C. 263, 269–270 (1975).

Considering the central role that the "similar or related in service or use" standard plays in § 1033, it is surprising that, in enacting the predecessor to § 1033, Congress did not provide any guidance as to its application. Perhaps Congress believed the standard to be self-explanatory. Is it? Problem 1 is intended, among other things, to focus attention on this special standard. As the *Liant* decision and Revenue Ruling 64-237 in the materials indicate, there has been considerable disagreement regarding the meaning of the standard and its application. Due in large part to *Liant*, the Service has recognized that, in applying the "similar or related in service or use" standard, the analysis used with respect to owner-occupied property will differ from the analysis employed with respect to rental situations. Problem 1 suggests the difficulty inherent in this dual analysis. Does the distinction make sense?

Regulation § 1.1033(a)-2(c)(9) provides limited assistance in applying the "similar or related in service or use" standard, and at the same time suggests the narrowness of that standard. The regulation specifically identifies the following three circumstances as examples of when replacement property will not satisfy the "similar or related in service or use" standard:

> (i) The proceeds of unimproved real estate, taken upon condemnation proceedings, are invested in improved real estate. [Note that under § 1033(g), however, the replacement property could qualify under the "like kind" standard.]

> (ii) The proceeds of conversion of real property are applied in reduction of indebtedness previously incurred in the purchase of a leasehold.[1]

---

[1] Nonetheless, a leasehold interest may be similar or related in service or use to a fee interest. For example, a fee interest acquired to replace an involuntarily converted 15-year leasehold was held to be similar or related in service or use to the leasehold where the fee interest and the leasehold were used

(iii) The owner of a requisitioned tug uses the proceeds to buy barges.

In reading the assigned authority and applying it to Problem 1, consider the kind of evidence which would best aid a tax advisor in establishing that the replacement property qualifies the taxpayer for § 1033 nonrecognition.[2]

E. Condemnation of Real Property Used for Business or Investment — Availability of the Like Kind Standard

Having studied § 1031, you undoubtedly by this time have wondered what difference there is between the "like kind" standard of § 1031 and the "similar or related in service or use" standard of § 1033. That these standards are different is obvious from the fact that the Congress used different language. In 1958 Congress recognized the difference between the standards when it amended § 1033 by adding a new subsection — § 1033(g). Section 1033(g) provides, in part, that if real property "held for productive use in trade or business or for investment is, as the result of seizure, requisition, or condemnation, or threat or imminence thereof, compulsorily or involuntarily converted" after December 31, 1957, "property of like-kind to be held either for productive use in trade or business or for investment shall be treated as property similar or related in service or use to the property so converted." The enactment of this provision afforded Congress the opportunity to compare the "similar or related in service or use" standard of § 1033(a) with the "like kind" standard of § 1031. The legislative history of § 1033(g) provides the following instructive discussion:

> The Internal Revenue Service and courts have held that Section 1033 requires a relatively narrow construction of the words "property similar or related in service or use" with the result that the converted property must be substantially similar to that destroyed. It has been held not to include, for example, improved real estate which is converted into unimproved realty, nor a barge substituted for a tug. Similarly, it has been held not to include property used in the operation of a business which was substituted for rented property. Likewise, it has been held not to include city real estate exchanged for a farm or a ranch.

> Present law also provides for the nonrecognition of gain where property held for productive use in trade or business or for investment . . . is exchanged for property of a "like kind to be held either for productive use in trade or business or for investment." The phrase "like kind to be held either for productive use in trade or business or for investment" has been given a broader interpretation than the "similar or related" phrase. "Like kind," for example, has been held to include unimproved real estate which is exchanged for improved real estate, so long as both properties are held either for productive use in trade or business or for investment. Thus, the "like kind" phrase has been held to include the exchange of city real estate

---

for the same purposes in the same business. Rev. Rul. 83-70, 1983-1 C.B. 189.

[2] We simply note in passing that qualifying replacement property can consist of a controlling interest in the stock of a corporation that itself owns the property that is similar or related in service or use to the converted property. § 1033(a)(2)(A). Special basis rules apply in such cases. § 1033(b)(3).

(used in a trade or business) for a farm or ranch.

Both in the case of property involuntarily converted and in the case of the exchange of property held for productive use in trade or business or for investment, gain is not recognized because of the continuity of the investment. Your committee sees no reason why substantially similar rules should not be followed in determining what constitutes a continuity of investment in these two types of situations where there is a condemnation of real property. Moreover, it appears particularly unfortunate that present law requires a closer identity of the destroyed and converted property where the exchange is beyond the control of the taxpayer than that which is applied in the case of the voluntary exchange of business property.

S. Rep. No. 1983, 85th Cong. 2d Sess., 1958-3 C.B. 993–94.

As indicated in the legislative history of § 1033(g), the "like kind" standard of § 1031 generally affords taxpayers greater flexibility with regard to replacement property than does the "similar or related in service or use" standard of § 1033(a). Consider Problem 1(d) in this regard. (Given the benefits of § 1033(g), why did Congress limit the provision's relief to seizure, requisition, or condemnation, or threat or imminence thereof?)

Under certain circumstances, because of the replacement property acquired by taxpayer, the "similar or related in service or use" standard will prove broader than the "like kind" standard of § 1031. For example, in Revenue Ruling 83-70, 1983-1 C.B. 189, a city condemned land that a taxpayer used in its business of hauling, handling, and storing furniture. The taxpayer did not own the land but held a long-term lease on the land. There were 15 years remaining on the taxpayer's leasehold interest in the land at the time of the condemnation. As a result of the compensation the taxpayer received from the city for the taking of taxpayer's leasehold interest, the taxpayer realized a gain. Within the period specified in § 1033 (a)(2)(B) of the Code, the taxpayer acquired a fee simple interest in real property improved with a warehouse and an office building and used this replacement property in the same business and for the identical purposes the taxpayer had used the condemned leasehold. Revenue Ruling 83-70 first addressed the applicability of § 1033(g) and concluded that the "like kind" standard afforded by that provision was inapplicable. The ruling noted that, pursuant to Reg. § 1031(a)-1(b), "the leasehold interest must have a remaining term of at least 30 years in order to be of the same 'nature' as a fee interest in real property." Thus, the "like kind" standard of § 1031 would not be satisfied were a leasehold of less than thirty years exchanged for a fee simple interest. Under the facts of Rev. Rul. 83-70, the condemned leasehold had a remaining term of only 15 years and therefore the taxpayer could not rely on the "like kind" provisions of § 1033(g) to defer recognition of the gain realized on the condemnation. Revenue Ruling 83-70 then addressed the issue whether, under § 1033(a), a leasehold interest may be "similar or related in service or use" to a fee interest. The ruling noted that, in *Davis Regulator Company v. Commissioner*, 36 B.T.A. 437 (1937), *acq.*, 1937-2 C.B. 7, the United States Board of Tax Appeals held that "a taxpayer did not have to recognize gain on the receipt of proceeds received with respect to the condemnation of a leasehold interest to the extent the proceeds were invested in the construction of a building on land owned by the taxpayer. The new building was used for the identical purpose as the converted leasehold. The court's decision was based on the 'similar or related in service or use' standard currently found in section 1033(a)(2)(A) of the Code." Based on that decision, the Service in Revenue Ruling 83-70 concluded the taxpayer qualified for non-recognition of gain under § 1033(a) because the fee property acquired by the taxpayer with the proceeds from the involuntarily converted 15-year leasehold interest was to be used by the taxpayer in the same business and for the identical purposes as the condemned leasehold.

The replacement property acquired in some circumstances will qualify under neither the "similar or related in service" standard or the "like kind" standard. For example in Rev. Rul. 76-390, 1976-2 C.B. 243, a state condemned some of the land taxpayer owned and used for mobile home park. The taxpayer used the condemnation proceeds to build a motel on the remaining mobile home park land taxpayer owned. Citing the owner-user standard of Rev. Rul. 64-237, 1964-2 C.B. 319 (included in the materials), the Service concluded the motel to be constructed on land already owned by the taxpayer could not qualify under the § 1033(a) "similar or related in service or use" standard because the physical characteristics and end uses of a motel are not closely similar to those of a mobile home park. Similarly, the Service held the "like kind" standard of § 1033(g) was inapplicable. In regard to the latter standard, the Service relied on Rev. Rul. 67-255, 1967-2 C.B. 270 that concluded an office building taxpayer constructed upon land he already owned would not qualify as being of a like kind to land of the taxpayer that was involuntarily converted. "Although the term 'real estate' is often used to embrace land and improvements thereon, land and improvements are by nature not alike merely because one term is used to describe both. Land is not of the same nature or character as a building."

F. Property Damage in Federally Declared Disasters

Congress has provided special relief for taxpayers whose property is damaged in federally declared disasters. Thus, for example, § 1033(h)(1)(A)(i) provides that taxpayers will have no gain from insurance proceeds for personal property that was part of the contents of the taxpayer's principal residence[3] if the personal property was not "scheduled property" for purposes of insurance. ("Scheduled property" is an insurance term generally referring to property identified on an itemized list attached to an insurance policy. In addition to identifying each item of personal property specially covered by the policy, the "scheduled property" list typically reflects the value of each item of "scheduled property.") As a result of § 1033(h)(1)(A)(i), taxpayers can do anything they choose with the insurance proceeds attributable to unscheduled personal property. With respect to insurance proceeds for the residence itself and for any scheduled property, § 1033(h)(1)(A)(ii) treats the insurance proceeds for these properties as a common fund received for the conversion of a single item of property. Any replacement property that is "similar or related in service or use" to the residence or its contents will be treated

---

[3] "Principal residence" is defined for § 1033(h) purposes the same as it is for § 121 purposes except that the term includes a residence that would not be treated a principal residence solely because the taxpayer does not own the residence.

as "similar or related in service or use" to the deemed single item of property. Thus, if a taxpayer were to receive fire insurance proceeds of $500,000 for the destruction of taxpayer's residence and $150,000 for the destruction of the "scheduled property" contents of that residence, the taxpayer could avoid reporting any gain if the taxpayer spent at least a total of $650,000 on a replacement residence and contents for that residence. If, for example, the taxpayer spent $600,000 on the new residence and only $50,000 on contents for that residence, taxpayer would avoid reporting any gain. In other words, given the "single item" treatment of § 1033(h)(1)(A)(ii), the taxpayer need not replace the $150,000 of "scheduled property" with $150,000 of replacement contents for the replacement residence.

Section 1033(h)(2) provides that if a taxpayer's property held for productive use in a trade or business or for investment is located in a disaster area and is compulsorily or involuntarily converted as a result of a federally declared disaster, tangible property held for productive use in a trade or business is treated as property "similar or related in service or use" to the converted property. In explaining the reason for that provision, the legislative history of § 1033(h)(2) states:

> the property damage in a [federally] declared disaster may be so great that businesses may be forced to suspend operations for a substantial time. During that hiatus, valuable markets and customers may be lost. If this suspension causes the businesses to fail, and the owners of the business wish to reinvest their capital in a new business venture, the involuntary conversion rules will force them to recognize gain when they buy replacement property that is needed for the new business but not similar to that used in the failed business. This provision will offer relief to such businesses by allowing them to reinvest their funds in any tangible business property without being forced to recognize gain.

S. Rpt. 104-281, at 14.

G. Time for Replacement

As noted previously, the relief accorded by § 1033 is premised on the notion that where a taxpayer's investment in property continues, it is not appropriate to recognize gain that may have been involuntarily realized by the taxpayer. This continuity of investment rationale underlies the nonrecognition treatment accorded by § 1031 and accounts for the holding requirements imposed by § 1031. Unlike § 1031, however, § 1033 does not specifically impose any holding requirements. Instead, to assure that continuity of investment exists, § 1033(a)(2)(B) generally requires that converted property be replaced within a two-year period following the conversion of the property.[4]

Section 1033(a)(2)(A) specifically requires that the replacement property be purchased "for the purpose of replacing the property so converted." (Property

---

[4] A three-year replacement period is provided for § 1033(g) involuntary conversions, discussed above. § 1033(g)(4). A four-year replacement period is provided under § 1033(h)(1)(B) for personal residences and their contents damaged in Presidentially declared disasters.

acquired before the disposition of the converted property will not be deemed to have been acquired as replacement property unless it is held by the taxpayer on the date of the disposition of the converted property.) Furthermore, property will be considered "purchased" only if, but for the special basis rule of § 1033(b), discussed below, the unadjusted basis of such property would be its cost within the meaning of § 1012. Thus, for example, property received by gift will not satisfy the "purchased" requirement because the basis of that property will be determined under § 1015 and not § 1012. Reg. § 1.1033(a)-2(c)(4).

Finally, if the replacement property is acquired from a related person, nonrecognition treatment may be lost. § 1033(i). This rule applies to individual taxpayers if the aggregate realized gain for the year, on all involuntarily converted property on which there is realized gain, exceeds $100,000. The rule, however, does not apply if the related person acquired the replacement property from an unrelated person during the replacement period.

H. Partial Recognition of Gain Under Section 1033

Just as there may be partial recognition of gain in the case of a like kind exchange under § 1031, realized gain will be recognized under § 1033(a)(2) to the extent that the amount received upon the conversion exceeds the cost of the replacement property. For example, if the farmer in the hypothetical at the outset of this Chapter received a condemnation award in the amount of $50,000 and had replaced the converted property with property costing $40,000, a maximum of $10,000 of gain realized would be recognized. If the farmer's basis in the converted property had been $10,000, then $10,000 of the $40,000 of realized gain would be recognized. By contrast, if the farmer's basis in the converted property had been $45,000, then only $5,000 gain would have been realized and thus only $5,000 of gain would be recognized.

I. Basis

At first glance, the basis rules of § 1033(b) may seem quite confusing. Indeed, just as there are both mandatory and elective nonrecognition rules in § 1033(a), there are two separate basis rules contained in § 1033(b)(1) and (2). The rule provided in § 1033(b)(1) is applicable only to those rare cases in which property is directly converted into qualified replacement property. It is very similar to the § 1031 basis rule.

The more common basis rule of § 1033(b)(2) is applicable in cases where the taxpayer elects § 1033 nonrecognition, *i.e.*, it is applicable only when property is converted into nonqualified property, such as insurance proceeds, and qualified replacement property is subsequently purchased. Thus, for example, the farmer in the hypothetical at the outset of this Chapter would use this basis provision in computing the adjusted basis in the farm land which was purchased with the condemnation award. The basis rule is simple: the basis of the replacement property shall be the cost of such property decreased by the amount of gain realized on the conversion which as a result of § 1033 was not recognized.

Assume the farmer's adjusted basis in the condemned land was $10,000 and the amount of the condemnation award was $50,000. Further assume the farmer replaced the condemned farm land with farm land purchased for $60,000. If the farmer elects § 1033 treatment, none of the $40,000 in gain realized would be recognized. Applying § 1033(b), the farmer's basis in the replacement property would be $20,000, *i.e.*, the replacement land's cost of $60,000 less the $40,000 of unrecognized gain. The $40,000 gain is thus not permanently excluded, but is merely deferred.

J. Holding Period of Replacement Property

For purposes of characterizing gains or losses realized and recognized on the subsequent disposition of replacement property, the holding period of that property may be critical. Not surprisingly, § 1223(1) provides for the tacking of the holding period of the converted property onto the replacement property if the converted property was a capital asset under § 1221 or a § 1231 asset.

K. Involuntary Conversion of Principal Residence

As we studied in Chapter 6, § 121 excludes up to $250,000 ($500,000 in the case of a joint return) of the gain on the sale or exchange of a principal residence if certain requirements are met. Section 121(d)(5)(A) provides that the destruction, theft, seizure, requisition, or condemnation of property will be treated as a sale for purposes of § 121. Thus, the possibility exists that a taxpayer whose principal residence is involuntarily converted in this manner could take advantage of § 121 to exclude some or all of the realized gain; any realized gain not excluded under § 121 could be deferred under § 1033 if the requirements of that provisions were satisfied. Section 121(d)(5)(B) provides that for purposes of applying § 1033, the amount realized will be treated as equaling the difference between the proceeds of the involuntary conversion and the amount of gain excluded under § 121. In effect, § 121(d)(5)(B) requires that § 121 be applied before applying § 1033.

> **Example 1:** Aaron's principal residence is destroyed by fire. Aaron had an adjusted basis of $200,000 in the residence which had a fair market value of $800,000. Within six months of the fire, Aaron receives insurance proceeds of $800,000. Aaron uses the $800,000 plus an additional $100,000 of other money to construct a new principal residence on the same property. He completes and moves into the new residence exactly eighteen months after the fire. Assuming Aaron is eligible for the § 121 exclusion and does not make the election under § 121(f), Aaron will exclude $250,000 of the $600,000 gain realized on the involuntary conversion of the residence. For § 1033 purposes, Aaron's amount realized is $550,000 (*i.e.*, $800,000 insurance proceeds less the $250,000 of gain excluded under § 121). Therefore, after applying § 121, Aaron's gain realized for § 1033 purposes is only $350,000 ($550,000 amount realized less $200,000 basis). [Note that we could also arrive at this $350,000 figure by subtracting from the $600,000 gain realized on the conversion of the residence the $250,000 gain excluded under § 121.]

Since Aaron invested over $550,000 in the new principal residence (in this case he invested $900,000), he may elect to defer all $350,000 of the gain realized for § 1033 purposes. Assuming Aaron makes that election, Aaron's basis in the new residence will be $550,000, *i.e.*, the $900,000 cost of the residence less the $350,000 of unrecognized gain. [Note that if under § 121(f) Aaron elected to have § 121 not apply, Aaron could still defer all of his gain realized. In that case, Aaron's amount realized for § 1033 purposes would be the full $800,000 of insurance proceeds he received. Aaron's gain realized for § 1033 purposes would be $600,000 (*i.e.*, $800,000 less the $200,000 adjusted basis Aaron had in the destroyed residence). None of this gain realized would be recognized since Aaron invested more than $800,000 in the replacement residence. Aaron's basis therefore in the new residence would be $300,000, *i.e.*, the $900,000 cost of the new residence less the $600,000 of unrecognized gain. Note that, if Aaron subsequently sells this new residence, since its basis is determined under § 1033(b), Aaron's ownership and use of the old residence will be attributed to the new residence for purposes of applying § 121. *See* § 121(d)(5)(C).]

Example 2: Assume the same facts as Example 1 except that Aaron constructs a replacement home that costs him only $450,000. He uses the other $350,000 of insurance proceeds to invest in the stock market. Again, disregarding any application of § 121(f), $250,000 of the $600,000 gain realized by Aaron will be excluded under § 121. Just as in Example 1, for § 1033 purposes, Aaron's amount realized is $550,000 and his gain realized is $350,000. Since Aaron invested only $450,000 in qualifying replacement property, under § 1033 he must recognize $100,000 of this $350,000 of realized gain. Aaron's basis in the replacement home will be $200,000, *i.e.*, the cost of the new residence ($450,000) less the unrecognized gain ($250,000). [If Aaron elected not to have § 121 apply, his amount realized for § 1033 purposes would be the full $800,000 in insurance proceeds and his gain realized would be $600,000. Since he only invested $450,000 in the replacement residence, he would have to recognize $350,000 of gain. Thus there would be $250,000 of unrecognized gain. Under these circumstances, Aaron's basis in the new residence would be $200,000 (*i.e.*, $450,000 cost less the $250,000 of unrecognized gain.]

LIANT RECORD, INC. v. COMMISSIONER
United States Court of Appeals, Second Circuit
303 F.2d 326 (1962)

Lumbard, Chief Judge:

The sole question presented is whether the proceeds from the condemnation of an office building were reinvested in property which was "similar or related in service or use" within the meaning of § 1033 of the Internal Revenue Code of 1954 when the taxpayers purchased three apartment buildings. The Tax Court held that they were not, since the tenants of the office building used the property for a different purpose than the tenants of the apartment buildings. We reverse and remand.

The taxpayers and Norman Einstein owned a 25-story, steel-frame office building located on 1819 Broadway, Manhattan, New York. The building, which had been erected about 1913 was, on November 17, 1953, rented to 82 commercial tenants, including accountants, attorneys, real estate firms, a doctor, a dentist, and a bank, all of whom used it exclusively to conduct business. On November 17, 1953 the City of New York instituted condemnation proceedings against the taxpayers' office building and acquired title on the same date. Each of the taxpayers received payments in settlement for the condemned property during 1954 and 1955 which substantially exceeded their respective tax bases in the property.

Between July 12, 1955 and November 1, 1956 the taxpayers acquired three pieces of real estate each containing an apartment building. Each taxpayer's contribution to the total purchase prices of the three parcels exceeded his share of the proceeds from the condemnation. The 9-story building located at 55 West 11th Street, New York City, contained 77 apartments used for residential purposes and 6 commercial tenants. The 6-story brick building at 400 East 80th Street, New York City, contained 47 residential apartments and 4 stores. The 11-story, steel-frame building located at 35 East 84th Street, New York City, contained 40 residential apartments and 6 commercial tenants. The taxpayers held the properties for rental income and did not occupy any of the properties.

The taxpayers, contending that their gain on the involuntary conversion was nontaxable under § 1033 of the Internal Revenue Code of 1954, did not report any income from the disposition of the condemned office building. The Commissioner, on the other hand, took the view that the three apartment buildings were not "similar or related in service or use" to the condemned office building, and that therefore the taxpayers should have reported an aggregate capital gain on their 1955 income tax returns of $427,012.61. Consequently, the Commissioner asserted an aggregate deficiency of $107,716.51 against the taxpayers. The Tax Court upheld the deficiency on the ground that the actual physical end use of the original property by the lessees as offices, differed from the end use of the replacement properties by the lessees as apartments. The taxpayers appeal.

When a taxpayer's property is involuntarily converted into cash which the taxpayer immediately expends in replacing the converted property, Congress thought it fair to postpone any tax on the gain. . . . However, the fortuity of an involuntary conversion should not afford the taxpayer an opportunity to alter the nature of his investment tax-free. Therefore, under § 1033 and its predecessors, tax postponement turns on whether the replacement property is "similar or related in service or use" to the converted property.

Most of the early cases interpreting this phrase involved owners of property who themselves used the property in their businesses. In these cases the Tax Court adopted a so-called "functional test" to determine whether the replacement property was similar or related in service or use to the converted property, *i.e.*, the Tax Court compared the actual physical uses of both properties. In those cases where an owner of property, instead of being a user, held the property for rental to others and replaced it with rental property, the Commissioner, the Third Circuit and the Tax Court literally applied this "functional test" by holding that the tenants' actual physical use of the converted and replacement properties must be similar or related. Some courts, however, refusing to apply the "functional test" so strictly, have held that if the owner of rental property replaces it with rental property of "the same general class," he has maintained sufficient continuity of interest to deserve tax postponements.

Since in enacting this section Congress intended the taxpayer-owner to maintain continuity of interest and not to alter the nature of his investment tax-free, it is the service or use which the properties have to the taxpayer-owner that is relevant. Thus when the taxpayer-owner himself uses the converted property, the Tax Court is correct in comparing the actual physical service or use which the end user makes of the converted and the replacement properties. However, if the taxpayer-owner is an investor rather than a user, it is not the lessees' actual physical use but the nature of the lessor's relation to the land which must be examined. For example, if the taxpayer-owner himself operated a retail grocery business on the original land and operated an automobile sales room on the replacement land, it would be obvious that by changing his own end use he had so changed the nature of his relationship to the property as to be outside the nonrecognition provision. However, where the taxpayer is a lessor, renting the original land and building for a retail grocery store and renting the replacement land and building for an automobile sales room, the nature of the taxpayer-owner's service or use of the property remains similar although that of the end user changes. There is, therefore, a single test to be applied to both users and investors, *i.e.*, a comparison of the services or uses of the original and replacement properties *to the taxpayer-owner.* In applying such a test to a lessor, a court must compare, *inter alia*, the extent and type of the lessor's management activity, the amount and kind of services rendered by him to the tenants, and the nature of his business risks connected with the properties.

Section 1031 of the 1954 Code, 26 U.S.C.A. § 1031, has many similarities to § 1033, the provision here in question. While § 1033 postpones the taxation of gain on the involuntary conversion of any property into money which is then reinvested in property which is "similar or related in service or use," § 1031 postpones the taxation of gain when a narrower category, "property held for productive use in trade or business or for investment," is voluntarily exchanged directly for other property "of a like kind." "Like kind" has been interpreted as being much broader than "similar or related in service or use." In 1958 Congress, disapproving of the narrow manner in which the § 1033 standard had been applied, S. Rep. No. 1983, 85th Cong., 2d Sess., pp. 72–73, U.S. Code Cong. and Admin. News 1958, p. 4791, amended § 1033 and made the "like kind" standard applicable to the condemnation of real estate "held for productive use in trade or business or for investment." The government argues that because this amendment is specifically made prospective only, Congress meant to tax the gain on condemnations of real estate held for investment in transactions which antedated the amendment such as in the present case. However, the mere fact office buildings and apartment buildings are clearly of "like kind" does not mean that they are not also "similar or related in service or use."

Since the Tax Court examined only the actual physical end use of the properties in this case rather than comparing the properties' service or use to the taxpayer-lessor, we reverse and remand for further consideration in light of this opinion.

REVENUE RULING 64-237
1964-2 C.B. 319

The Internal Revenue Service has reconsidered its position with respect to replacement property that is "similar or related in service or use" to involuntarily converted property within the meaning of section 112(f) of the Internal Revenue Code of 1939 and section 1033(a) of the Internal Revenue Code of 1954 in light of the decision of the United States Court of Appeals for the Second Circuit in the case of *Liant Record, Inc. v. Commissioner*, 303 Fed. (2d) 326 (1962), and other appellate court decisions.

In previous litigation, the Service has taken the position that the statutory phrase, "similar or related in service or use," means that the property acquired must have a close "functional" similarity to the property converted. Under this test, property was not considered similar or related in service or use to the converted property unless the physical characteristics and end uses of the converted and replacement properties were closely similar. Although this "functional use test" has been upheld in the lower courts, it has not been sustained in the appellate courts with respect to investors in property, such as lessors.

In conformity with the appellate court decisions, in considering whether replacement property acquired by an investor is similar in service or use to the converted property, attention will be directed primarily to the similarity in the relationship of the services or use which the original and replacement properties have to the taxpayer-owner. In applying this test, a determination will be made as to whether the properties are of a similar service to the taxpayer, the nature of the business risks connected with the properties, and what such properties demand of the taxpayer in the way of management, services and relations to his tenants.

For example, where the taxpayer is a lessor, who rented out the converted property for a light manufacturing plant and then rents out the replacement property for a wholesale grocery warehouse, the nature of the taxpayer-owner's service or use of the properties may be similar although that of the end users change. The two properties will be considered as similar or related in service or use where, for example, both are rented and where there is a similarity in the extent and type of the taxpayer's management activities, the amount and kind of services rendered by him to his tenants, and the nature of his business risks connected with the properties.

In modifying its position with respect to the involuntary conversion of property held for investment, the Service will continue to adhere to the functional test in the case of owner-users of property. Thus, if the taxpayer-owner operates a light manufacturing plant on the converted property and then operates a wholesale grocery warehouse on the replacement property, by changing his end use he has so changed the nature of his relationship to the property as to be outside the nonrecognition of gain provisions.

REVENUE RULING 79-261
1979-2 C.B. 295

ISSUE

Does the reinvestment of proceeds from an involuntary conversion, under the circumstances set forth below, qualify as a replacement of the property converted with property similar or related in service or use to the property converted within the meaning of section 1033(a)(2)(A) of the Internal Revenue Code of 1954?

FACTS

The taxpayer, a corporation engaged in the banking business, owned an office building that it leased to tenants for the production of rental income. In 1977, the office building was destroyed by a tornado. The taxpayer received insurance proceeds in excess of its adjusted basis in the office building on the date the building was destroyed, and used these proceeds along with other funds to construct a new office building. The new office building is partially used by the taxpayer in conducting its banking business. The remainder of the building is tenant-occupied and used by the taxpayer for the production of rental income. The leases covering the tenant-occupied portion of the new building are substantially similar with respect to the extent and type of the taxpayer's management activities, services rendered, and the nature of the business risks, to the previous leases executed by the taxpayer in renting the converted building.

LAW

Rev. Rul. 64-237, 1964-2 C.B. 319, states that in considering whether replacement property acquired by an owner-lessor is similar or related in service or use to the converted property, attention will be directed primarily to the similarity in the relationship of the services or uses that the original and replacement properties have to the owner-lessor. In applying this test, a determination will be made as to whether the properties are of a similar service to the taxpayer, the nature of the business risks connected with the properties, and what such properties demand of the taxpayer in the way of management, services, and relations to tenants.

In Rev. Rul. 70-399, 1970-2, C.B. 164, the taxpayer owned a resort hotel that it leased to an operator under a net lease agreement. After the hotel was destroyed by fire, the taxpayer used the insurance proceeds to purchase another hotel that it operated itself. That Revenue Ruling holds that the taxpayer on becoming the owner-operator of the replacement hotel so changed the nature of its relationship to the property as to be outside the nonrecognition of gain provisions of section 1033 of the Code.

Rev. Rul. 70-466, 1970-2 C.B. 165, holds that a taxpayer who replaced a residence used for production of rental income with a residence used as the taxpayer's personal residence had so changed the nature of the taxpayer's relationship to the property as to be outside the nonrecognition of gain provisions of section 1033 of the Code.

ANALYSIS

In this case, the taxpayer used the proceeds from the involuntary conversion to construct a new office building used partly by the taxpayer in its banking business and partly for the production of rental income. The tenant-occupied part of the new building is similar or related in service or use to the converted property because under the respective leases the properties are of a similar service to the taxpayer, and place similar demands on the taxpayer in the way to management, service, and relations to tenants. The part of the new building that is owner-occupied is not similar or related in service or use to the converted property because the taxpayer, by utilizing the premises for its own use has, as in Rev. Rul. 70-399 and Rev. Rul. 70-466, so changed its relationship to the property as to be outside the nonrecognition of gain provisions of section 1033(a) of the Code.

The disallowance, however, of section 1033 of the Code treatment with respect to the owner-occupied part of the new building does not prevent the taxpayer from obtaining section 1033 treatment with respect to that part of the building that is tenant-occupied provided that the tenant-occupied part of the building can be clearly distinguished from the rest of the building and the taxpayer can establish an adequate method for ascertaining the cost of the tenant-occupied part of the building. There must be a clear division in terms of function and use between the part of the building that meets the similar in service or use test and that part of the building to qualify as replacement property under section 1033. If such conditions are met, the tenant-occupied and owner-used portions of the building will be treated as separate pieces of property in applying the provisions of section 1033.

The reinvestment of the proceeds from the involuntary conversion of the old office building into the construction of the new office building qualifies as a replacement of property with property similar or related in service or use to the property converted within the meaning of section 1033(a)(2)(A) of the Code only to the extent of the tenant-occupied part of the new building. The part of the new building that is owner-occupied is not property similar or related in service or use to the converted property within the meaning of section 1033(a)(2)(A).

The basis of the tenant-occupied part of the property will be its cost decreased by the amount of the gain not recognized on the involuntary conversion. This net amount would be added to the cost of the remainder of the building (the nonqualified replacement property) to determine the basis of the whole building.

The computation of basis can be illustrated by use of the following example. If the taxpayer had a basis of $50,000 in the converted property, and received $250,000 in insurance proceeds, the taxpayer could elect under section 1033 of the Code to have the $200,000 gain not recognized to the extent the proceeds are invested in qualifying replacement property which, in this case, would be the tenant-occupied part of the new building. If the tenant-occupied part is determined to have cost $225,000, then the taxpayer would recognize a gain of $25,000, as only $225,000 of the $250,000 proceeds would have been invested in qualifying replacement property. Under section 1033(b), the taxpayer would have a basis in the tenant-occupied part of the property of $50,000 ($225,000 cost minus $175,000, the amount of the gain or the involuntary conversion not recognized). This amount ($50,000) would be added to the cost of the remainder of the building (the owner-occupied part) to determine the basis of the whole building.

REVENUE RULING 89-2
1989-1 C.B. 259

ISSUES

(1) If chemical contamination renders property unsafe for its intended use, is the property destroyed for purposes of section 1033(a) of the Internal Revenue Code?

(2) Does the sale of the contaminated property to a governmental authority to protect the public health constitute a sale under the threat of condemnation for purposes of section 1033(a) and section 1033(g) of the Code?

FACTS

The taxpayer owned improved real estate that it used in its trade or business in city X. Through no fault of the taxpayer, dangerous chemicals were released in the city where the taxpayer's property was located. After sampling the soil in the area, a governmental agency found widespread chemical contamination in concentration levels greatly exceeding the level that is deemed safe for habitation. Responsible health authorities determined that prolonged contact with the chemically contaminated soil represents a serious health risk. The health hazard caused by the chemical contamination is expected to continue indefinitely.

Consequently, the governmental agency announced that the residents and businesses of the city should be relocated to protect the public health. Pursuant to an agreement among the federal, state, and city governments, all residents and businesses were asked to sell their contaminated property. The amount of compensation offered was based on the appraised value of the property undiminished by the contamination. City X also passed an ordinance authorizing eminent domain proceedings, if necessary, to acquire the affected properties. After passage of the ordinance, the taxpayer accepted an offer from city X to purchase its property. The taxpayer realized a gain from this sale.

LAW AND ANALYSIS

Section 1033(a) of the Code provides for the nonrecognition of gain realized upon the involuntary conversion of property into money as a result of its destruction in whole or in part, or condemnation or threat or imminence thereof. Under section 1033(a)(2), if the taxpayer purchases other property similar or related in service or use to the converted property within a period generally ending 2 years after the first tax year in which gain is realized, then at the election of the taxpayer the gain is recognized only to the extent that the amount realized exceeds the cost of the replacement property.

Involuntary conversion, within the meaning of section 1033(a) of the Code, means that the taxpayer's property, "through some outside force or agency beyond his control, is no longer useful or available to him for his purposes." *C.G. Willis, Inc. v. Commissioner*, 41 T.C. 468, 476 (1964), *aff'd, per curiam*, 342 F.2d 996 (3d Cir. 1965). Not all involuntary conversions fall within the scope of section 1033; to qualify, a conversion must result from one of the specified causes.

Physical damage that renders property unfit for its intended use is a "destruction" for purposes of section 1033(a) of the Code. Rev. Rul. 66-334, 1966-2 C.B. 320, concerns the gradual salt water contamination of an underground fresh water supply that was used for irrigation. The ruling holds that the contamination, which was caused by a fault in the earthen pit containing the salt water, is a destruction of property.

In the present case, chemically contaminated soil in city X poses an irremediable hazard to human health. The taxpayer's property is essentially uninhabitable for the foreseeable future, and, consequently, is unfit for the taxpayer's intended use. Thus, the taxpayer's property is destroyed for purposes of section 1033(a) of the Code.

For purposes of section 1033(a) of the Code, it does not matter whether the conversion stems from destruction, or the threat of condemnation, or both. To the extent that the conversion is attributable to the threat of condemnation, however, the taxpayer is eligible for the generally more liberal replacement requirements of section 1033(g).

Section 1033(g)(1) of the Code provides that if real property held for productive use in trade or business or for investment is, as the result of condemnation or threat or imminence thereof, compulsorily or involuntarily converted, property of a like kind to be held either for productive use in trade or business or for investment shall be treated as property similar or related in service or use to the converted property for purposes of section 1033(a). Section 1033(g)(4) provides that in such a case the replacement period is determined by substituting "3 years" for "2 years." Section 1.1033(g)-1(a) of the Income Tax Regulations provides explicitly that section 1033(g) does not apply to conversions attributable solely to destruction.

As used in section 1033(a) and section 1033(g) of the Code, the term "condemnation" refers to the process by which private property is taken for public use, without the consent of the property owner but upon the award and payment of just compensation. Rev. Rul. 57-314, 1957-2 C.B. 523. Public use includes a use intended to conserve the safety and health of the public, even though individual members of the public are unable to use the property taken. Normally, the measure of just compensation is the fair market value of the property taken by the government. *See* Uniform Eminent Domain Code § 1002 (1974).

Although a taking to protect the health of the public may qualify as a condemnation under section 1033 of the Code, the taxpayer must distinguish proceeds that are attributable to condemnation (that is, to the government's action in taking the property) from proceeds that compensate the taxpayer for destruction. In Rev. Rul. 74-206, 1974-1 C.B. 198, the taxpayer's property, which had been damaged by a flood, was condemned under a state eminent domain statute that disregarded flood damage in determining fair market value for purposes of establishing the amount of the condemnation award. Reasoning that the statute was designed to provide both fair compensation for the property and a reimbursement for loss resulting from the flood damage, Rev. Rul 74-206 concludes that the taxpayer's property was involuntarily converted in part as a result of condemnation and in part as a result of destruction.

Here, city X purchased the taxpayer's property after passing an ordinance authorizing eminent domain proceedings. The passage of the ordinance satisfies the requirement that there be a threat of condemnation. Rev. Rul. 71-567, 1971-2 C.B. 309. The amount paid by city X, however, was based on an appraised value that did not take into account the diminution in value caused by the chemical contamination. As in Rev. Rul. 74-206, the portion of the proceeds that compensates the taxpayer for the destruction of its property must be distinguished from the portion allocable to the condemnation only to the extent of the fair market value of the property, if any, after taking into account the contamination. The taxpayer may treat the portion of the gain attributable to compensation for the governmental taking under section 1033(a) or 1033(g) of the Code.

HOLDINGS

(1) Property that is rendered unsafe for its intended use as a result of chemical contamination is destroyed for purposes of section 1033(a) of the Code.

(2) In addition, for purposes of section 1033(a), which generally applies to all types of property, and for purposes of section 1033(g), which applies to real property held either for productive use in trade or business or for investment, if that property is sold to a governmental authority after the passage of an ordinance authorizing eminent domain proceedings to protect the public health, then the sale constitutes a sale under the threat of condemnation to the extent that the taxpayer can establish that the proceeds represent compensation for the taking of the property by the government, rather than compensation for the destruction caused by the contamination.

WILLAMETTE INDUSTRIES, INC. v. COMMISSIONER
United States Tax Court
118 T.C. 126 (2002)

GERBER, JUDGE:

The parties filed cross-motions for partial summary judgment. The controversy concerns whether petitioner is entitled to defer gain resulting from the salvage (processing and sale) of damaged trees under section 1033. The parties have agreed on the salient facts. The controverted issue involves a legal question that is ripe for summary judgment.

Background

Petitioner is an Oregon corporation with its principal office in Portland, Oregon. Petitioner operates a vertically integrated forest products manufacturing business, which includes the ownership and processing of trees (raw materials) at various types of manufacturing plants, including lumber mills, plywood plants, and paper mills. The raw materials used in the manufacturing process are derived from petitioner's trees and from trees grown by others. Approximately 40 percent of petitioner's timber needs is acquired from petitioner's timberland, which comprises 1,253,000 acres of forested land.

Petitioner suffered damage to some of its standing trees during each of the years in issue, 1992-95. The damage was caused by wind, ice storms, wildfires, or insect infestations. The damage left part of petitioner's damaged trees standing and part of them fallen. The intended use of the trees was continued growth and cultivation until maturity, at which time the trees would have been systematically and efficiently harvested. The damage occurred prior to the intended time for harvest.

Petitioner salvaged its damaged trees to avoid further loss (from decay, insects, etc.) by means of the following steps: (1) Taking down damaged trees that remained standing; (2) cutting damaged trees into standard length logs; (3) stripping the branches from the logs; (4) dragging the logs to a pickup point; (5) grading and sorting the logs; (6) stacking the logs at a landing point; and (7) loading the logs onto trucks for further use or processing.

Petitioner chose to take the seven steps described in the preceding paragraph, rather than attempting to sell the damaged trees in place to a third party. Once it performed the seven steps, its options were to (1) attempt to sell the partially processed damaged trees to a third party; or (2) complete the processing of the damaged trees in its own plants in the ordinary course of its business. Petitioner chose the latter and completed the processing itself.

Petitioner relies on section 1033 for involuntary conversion treatment (deferral of gain). Petitioner did not realize income from harvesting and processing the damaged trees until it sold the products it manufactured from the damaged trees. Petitioner is seeking to defer only that portion of the gain attributable to the difference between its basis and the fair market value of the damaged trees as of the time its salvage of them began; that is, the value petitioner contends would have been recognized if it had sold the damaged trees on the open market instead of further processing and/or milling the damaged trees into finished products. Petitioner further contends that it is not attempting to defer any portion of the gain attributable to the processing, milling, or finishing of products. Respondent determined that petitioner understated income by improperly deferring gain from the sale of the end product of the damaged trees, as follows: 1992 — $647,953; 1993 — $2,276,282; 1994 — $3,592,035; and 1995 — $4,831,462.

Discussion

The specific question we consider is whether petitioner is disqualified from electing deferral of gain under section 1033 because it processed damaged trees into end or finished products rather than being compelled simply to sell the damaged trees.

Respondent contends that under section 1033 the realization of gain must stem directly or solely from the damage and the involuntary conversion. More particularly, respondent asserts that petitioner's conversion was not "involuntary" because damaged trees were processed into end products in the ordinary course of its business. Respondent points out that section 1033 is a relief provision which does not or should not include petitioner's situation; i.e., where the damaged trees are processed in the same manner as undamaged trees. Finally, respondent contends that section 1033 was not intended for the long-term deferral of profits from petitioner's timber processing and manufacturing business.

Petitioner argues that its factual situation complies literally with the requirements of section 1033 allowing deferral of gain realized from salvaging its damaged trees. Specifically, petitioner contends that it was compelled (in order to avoid further damage or loss) to salvage (process) the damaged trees resulting in an involuntary conversion within the meaning of section 1033. Petitioner also points out that the conversion was "involuntary" because the damaged trees were not scheduled for harvest at the time of the damage. In response to respondent's argument, petitioner contends that its choices for salvaging the damaged trees should not preclude deferral of the portion of the gain that it was compelled to realize on account of the damage to its trees. Petitioner emphasizes that it is not attempting to defer gain from processing and/or milling the damaged trees. Petitioner seeks to defer only that portion of the gain attributable to the difference between its basis in the damaged trees and their fair market value at the time the process of salvaging the trees began.

Section 1033 provides, under certain prescribed circumstances, for relief from taxpayer's gains realized from involuntary conversion of property. The relief provided for under section 1033 is deferral of the gain from involuntary conversion, so long as the proceeds are used to acquire qualified replacement property.

The purpose of section 1033 was described, as follows:

> The purpose of the statute is to relieve the taxpayer of unanticipated tax liability arising from involuntary . . . [conversion] of his property, by freeing him from such liability to the extent that he re-establishes his prior commitment of capital within the period provided by the statute. The statute is to be liberally construed to accomplish this purpose. On the other hand, it was not intended to confer a gratuitous benefit upon the taxpayer by permitting him to utilize the involuntary interruption in the continuity of his investment to alter the nature of that investment tax free. . . .

Only a limited amount of legislative history has accompanied the enactment of the various involuntary conversion relief provisions since 1921.

From [the] limited legislative history, it can be gleaned that Congress intended relief from involuntary conversions only to the extent of the "proceeds of such conversion," and expected taxpayers to acquire replacement property within a reasonable time. Obviously, relief was intended only where the conversion was involuntary. Although Congress was concerned about the timeliness and "good faith" of efforts in seeking replacement property, there was no explanation or particular focus upon the use of damaged assets in the taxpayer's business.

Where the complete destruction or loss of property has occurred, there has been only a limited amount of litigation about whether a taxpayer should be allowed to defer the attendant gain. Where the destruction or loss to property is partial, however, additional questions have arisen.

In *C.G. Willis, Inc. v. Commissioner*, 41 T.C. 468 (1964), *affd.*, 342 F.2d 996 (3d Cir. 1965), the taxpayer's ship was damaged in a 1957 collision, and the insurance company paid $100,000 to the taxpayer. The insurance payment was approximately $9,000 less than the taxpayer's basis in the ship, and, accordingly, no gain was realized for 1957. In 1958, however, the taxpayer sold the damaged, but unrepaired, ship for an amount which exceeded the remaining basis by approximately $86,000. Under those circumstances, it was held that the 1958 sale was not an "involuntary conversion" within the meaning of section 1033 so that the gain had to be recognized and could not be deferred. In so holding, it was explained that the damage to the taxpayer's ship was insufficient to compel the taxpayer to sell and, accordingly, the sale was not involuntary. *Id.* 41. T.C. at 476. In that setting, "involuntary conversion" under section 1033 was defined to mean "that the taxpayer's property, through some outside force or agency beyond his control, is no longer useful or available to him for his purposes." *Id.*; *see also Wheeler v. Commissioner*, 58 T.C. 459, 462–463 (1972) (where it was held that the taxpayer's choice to destroy his building was not an involuntary conversion).

In *S.H. Kress & Co. v. Commissioner*, 40 T.C. 142, 153 (1963), we held that condemnation of the taxpayer's property was imminent and unavoidable, and that the only realistic alternatives were to either await condemnation or to sell to an appropriate buyer. We found that those circumstances met the "compulsorily or involuntarily converted" requirement of section 1033 (citing *Masser v. Commissioner*, 30 T.C. 741 (1958)). Accordingly, even though a taxpayer has choices or alternatives a disposition may be deemed involuntary so that section 1033 relief remains available.

Masser v. Commissioner, supra, involved section 112(f)(1) of the Internal Revenue Code of 1939 (another predecessor of section 1033). In *Masser*, the taxpayer operated an interstate trucking business from two proximately positioned pieces of business realty that were used as part of a single economic unit. One of the properties was subject to imminent condemnation, but the taxpayer sold both parcels. In that circumstance, we held that both pieces of realty were involuntarily converted and the gain from both could be deferred.

Those cases reveal two general elements as being necessary to qualify for deferral of gain under section 1033. First, a taxpayer's property must be involuntarily damaged, and second the property must no longer be available for the taxpayer's intended business purposes for the property.

The Commissioner issued a revenue ruling that specifically focused on whether gain from the sale of trees damaged by a hurricane qualified under section 1033. In that ruling it was held that the gain on sale of uprooted trees was "voluntary" and, in addition, that there was no direct conversion into money in the circumstances expressed in the ruling. *See* Rev. Rul. 72-372, 1972-2 C.B. 471. The principal rationale for the holding of Rev. Rul. 72-372, *supra*, was that the hurricane did not cause the conversion of the trees into cash or other property directly resulting in gain from the damage.

In a second ruling, however, the 1972 ruling was revoked. *See* Rev. Rul. 80-175, 1980-2 C.B. 230. The 1980 ruling permitted deferral of gain from the sale of damaged trees. The factual predicate for both rulings was as follows:

the taxpayer was the owner of timberland. As a result of a hurricane, a considerable number of trees were uprooted. The timber was not insured, and once downed, was subject to decay or being rendered totally worthless by insects within a relatively short period of time. The taxpayer was, however, able to sell the damaged timber and realized a gain from such sale. The proceeds of the sale were used to purchase other standing timber.

The rationale articulated in Rev. Rul. 80-175, *supra*, is that gain is "postponed on the theory that the taxpayer was compelled to dispose of property and had no economic choice in the matter" and that the taxpayer "was compelled by the destruction of the timber to sell it for whatever the taxpayer could or suffer a total loss." *Id.*, 1980-2 C.B. at 231. Accordingly, the taxpayer in the 1980 ruling was found to have met the two part test; i.e., that the damage was involuntary and the timber was no longer available for the taxpayer's intended business purpose. Most significantly, the 1980 ruling eliminated the requirement that the damage-causing event convert the property directly into cash or other property.

The 1980 ruling also contained a comparison with the holding in *C.G. Willis, Inc. v. Commissioner* as follows:

> In the present case, the downed timber was not repairable and was generally no longer useful to the taxpayer in the context of its original objective. The destruction caused by the hurricane forced the taxpayer to sell the downed timber for whatever price it could get. Unlike the situation in *Willis*, the sale of the downed timber was dictated by the damage caused by the hurricane. [Rev. Rul. 80-175, *supra*, 1980-2 C.B. at 232.]

The taxpayer in the 1980 ruling apparently intended to grow trees and/or hold timberland for sale at a particular maturity. The hurricane caused the taxpayer to involuntarily sell/use the trees prior to the time intended for harvest or sale. The taxpayer's intended purpose or use was only affected as to timing, and the sale was prior to the time the taxpayer intended to sell or harvest.

Returning to the disagreement here, petitioner contends that, at the time of the damage, it did not intend to harvest the damaged trees, so that the conversion was involuntary and within the meaning of the statute. Petitioner argues that a taxpayer may not have a choice as to whether to dispose of damaged property, but a taxpayer may have a choice as to how to dispose of damaged property.

Respondent contends that petitioner should not be entitled to such deferral because of its choice to further process the trees into logs or finished products, its original intention. Respondent's position in this case is a reversion to the requirement of the 1972 ruling that the sale (conversion to cash) be the direct result of the damage-causing event. For more than 21 years, the Commissioner's ruling position has permitted section 1033 deferral even though the conversion is not directly into cash.

Petitioner in this case is effectively no different from the taxpayer in the 1980 ruling. Petitioner's conversion was involuntary, and petitioner was forced to act or suffer complete loss of the damaged trees. Section 1033 could be interpreted to permit either a direct or an indirect conversion. The case law permits indirect conversion, but the Commissioner's 1972 ruling denied relief because the trees damaged by the hurricane were sold by the taxpayer. The Commissioner, in revoking the 1972 ruling has permitted, since 1980, section 1033 relief where there is a sale (a voluntary act) of the damaged property. Respondent has denied relief here because petitioner processed rather than sold the damaged trees.

The critical factor is that petitioner was compelled to harvest the damaged trees prior to the time it had intended. The possibility that the partial damage to petitioner's trees might have been relatively small or resulted in a nominal amount of reduction in gain is not a reason to deny relief. In addition, if petitioner's salvage efforts were more successful than other taxpayers that is not a reason for denial of relief under section 1033.

Petitioner's circumstances fulfill the statutory purpose and intent. There was unanticipated tax liability due to various casualties that damaged the trees. Petitioner seeks to defer the gain that was occasioned by the damage and which it had reinvested in like property. Petitioner had not planned to harvest the damaged trees. Identical to the taxpayer's situation in the 1980 ruling, petitioner's trees were damaged by forces without its control, and petitioner was compelled to salvage its damaged trees prior to the intended date for harvest, sale, and/or processing into end products. Unlike the taxpayer in *C.G. Willis v. Commissioner, supra*, petitioner was forced to salvage (process or sell) the damaged trees or suffer a total loss.

Respondent's attempt to distinguish petitioner's situation from the ruling does not reconcile with the rationale of the 1980 ruling, the underlying statute, and case law. The taxpayer in the ruling and petitioner were both forced to salvage the damaged trees or suffer the imminent and total loss of the damaged trees. The taxpayer in the ruling and petitioner were prematurely forced to salvage (sell or use) the damaged trees. The damaged trees were used in their businesses, but not in the same manner as they would normally have done. In the 1980 ruling, the taxpayer was forced to sell the trees under unintended business conditions. Likewise, petitioner was forced to use the damaged trees, albeit in its manufacturing process, under unintended business conditions; i.e. before maturity and/or before the time at which the trees would normally be ready for efficient harvest.

Respondent also argues that petitioner is not entitled to defer gain because "there were no actual sales of damaged timber." Respondent argues that section 1033 requires a sale or conversion of the damaged property into money or property similar in use to the damaged property. Section 1033 simply requires that property be involuntarily converted into money or property. There is no requirement, as argued by respondent, that the deferred gain be derived in a particular manner; i.e., only from a distress sale. Based on the holding of Rev. Rul. 80-175, 1980-2 C.B. 230, it is unlikely that respondent would have questioned the deferral of gain if petitioner had been forced to sell the damaged trees in place.

Finally, respondent contends that section 1033 was intended to provide relief for taxpayers who experience "destruction [of property] in whole or in part." Although respondent agrees that petitioner had a casualty, damage to the trees, and petitioner was compelled to salvage them, respondent infers that petitioner's situation is somehow not directly affected by the destruction. Respondent contends that petitioner's gain is voluntary or not caused by the damage because petitioner is able to process the logs into finished products.

Admittedly, petitioner's circumstances may appear more favorable than might have been expected after a "casualty," but the statute does not have a quantitative threshold. Petitioner is not seeking a windfall in the form of the deferral of gain from processing and/or making the finished products. Nor is petitioner attempting to "utilize the involuntary interruption in the continuity of his investment to alter the nature of that investment tax free." Petitioner is seeking to defer the unexpected gain that resided in trees that it had not, at the time of the damage, intended to harvest and to reinvest that gain in trees that will fulfill petitioner's intended purpose. Such deferral was the intended purpose for the enactment of section 1033.

Respondent argues that the purpose of section 1033 may be better served where a taxpayer is unable to process damaged property into the taxpayer's usual product(s). But that disability is not a threshold for relief or a requirement of the statute. Section 1033 is a relief provision, and we are to construe it liberally to effect its purpose.

Respondent would have this Court impose its own judgment as to which taxpayer deserves relief. So, for example, if a taxpayer, like the one in the 1980 ruling, was growing trees for eventual sale, relief is available even though the taxpayer sells the damaged trees to its usual customers. Under respondent's suggested approach, petitioner would not be entitled to relief because it had choices other than sale; i.e., to further process the damaged trees. Petitioner, under respondent's approach, would be deprived of relief from involuntarily generated gain merely because of happenstance. Under that type of reasoning, petitioner would be denied relief merely because it was a grower of trees and also a manufacturer of products using trees, whereas a similarly situated grower of trees without the ability to use the damaged trees to make products would be entitled to relief, even though its damaged trees might ultimately be manufactured into products by others. The line respondent asks us to draw would be illusive and a matter of conjecture.

Petitioner was growing its trees for harvest when they reached a certain maturity. The damage occurred outside of petitioner's control and forced petitioner to salvage its trees earlier than intended. That situation is indistinguishable from the circumstances set forth in Rev. Rul. 80-175, 1980-2 C.B. 230, where the taxpayer's trees were felled by a hurricane. The fact that the damage was sufficiently partial so as to result in a substantial amount of deferral is not a reason, under the statute, to deny relief.

We read the statute in light of respondent's Rev. Rul. 80-175, *supra*, which has been outstanding for 22 years.

In view of the foregoing,

Appropriate orders will be issued.

Chapter 41

INSTALLMENT SALES _____

I. PROBLEMS

Part A:

1. Bill purchased, as an investment, a tract of undeveloped land in Year 1 for $300,000. Bill sold the land to Betty in Year 8 for $1,000,000 on the following terms: $200,000 down, plus $100,000 payable in Year 9, $200,000 payable in Year 10, $100,000 payable in Year 11, and $400,000 payable in Year 12. Each of the Year 9 through Year 12 payment obligations is evidenced by a promissory note issued by Betty, in the appropriate face amount, and bearing adequate interest payable annually. (Assume § 453(f)(4) is inapplicable to Betty's notes.) Betty also gave Bill a mortgage on the land to secure the unpaid purchase price. Assume Bill is a cash method taxpayer and all notes are paid as scheduled. Ignoring interest income, what are the tax consequences to Bill from the sale, assuming he does not make an election under § 453(d)?

2. Assume Bill is an accrual method taxpayer. How does your answer to Problem 1 change?

3. Assume Bill makes a § 453(d) election. How do your answers to Problems 1 and 2 change? Would it make any difference if Bill could establish that the most he would receive on the sale of the notes is 70% of their face value?

4. Assume the facts of Problem 1, except Bill purchased the property for $1,200,000. What are the tax consequences of the sale?

5. Assume the facts of Problem 1, except the property is IBM stock instead of land. What are the tax consequences to Bill?

6. Assume the facts of Problem 1, except the property was subject to a $200,000 mortgage, which Betty assumed. Assume the Year 12 payment will be $200,000 instead of $400,000. What are the tax consequences to Bill of the sale?

7. Assume the facts of Problem 6, except a $150,000 second mortgage is also assumed by Betty and the downpayment was $50,000 instead of $200,000. What are the tax consequences to Bill of the sale?

8. Assume the facts of Problem 1, except the property in question is equipment purchased for $800,000 and used in Bill's business. At the time of the sale, the equipment had an adjusted basis of $300,000, reflecting $500,000 in depreciation deductions allowed. What are the tax results to Bill?

9. Assume the facts of Problem 1, except in Year 9, Bill sold the note payable in Year 10 to an unrelated third party for $175,000.

   (a) What are the Year 9 consequences to Bill?

   (b) Will the sale of the Year 10 note have any impact on the tax consequences to Bill when Betty pays Bill the amounts that become due under the notes for Years 11 and 12?

10. Assume the facts of Problem 1, except in Year 9, Bill gives the Year 10 note to Susan, his sister, who collects on the note. What are the tax consequences to Bill and Susan?

11. Assume the facts of Problem 10, except Susan is Bill's wife. What are the tax consequences to Bill and Susan?

12. Assume the facts of Problem 1, except the land is sold on the following terms: $200,000 down, plus 10% of the profits from Betty's business use of the land during Years 9 through 12, all subject to maximum aggregate payments (including the down payment) of $1,000,000. Under this agreement, Bill receives an additional $100,000 in Year 9, $200,000 in Year 10, $100,000 in Year 11, and $200,000 in Year 12. What are the tax consequences to Bill?

13. Assume the facts of Problem 12, except there is no maximum aggregate payment. What are the tax results? How would your answer to this problem change if Bill made a § 453(d) election?

14. Assume the facts of Problem 1, except Betty is Bill's spouse. How does your answer to Problem 1 change?

15. Assume the facts of Problem 1, except Betty is Bill's daughter. How does your answer to Problem 1 change?

Part B:

16. Assume the facts of Problem 15. In Year 9, Betty, before making the Year 9 payment to Bill, sells the property to a third party for $1,000,000 in cash. What tax consequences to Bill and Betty? How would your answer change, if at all, if Betty sold the property in Year 9 for $600,000 down and the balance of $400,000 payable in Year 10.

17. Assume the facts of Problem 8, except Bill sells the equipment to Betty's Corporation, which is equally owned by Bill, his sister Betty, and his partner Paul. What are the tax results?

18. Assume the facts of Problem 1, except in Year 9, Bill borrows $300,000 from Bank and pledges Betty's four promissory notes as security for the loan. How does your answer to Problem 1 change?

19. Assume the land in Problem 1 is used in Bill's business. Assume Bill bought the land for $7,500,000 and sold it for $30,000,000, including $2,000,000 down, with payments in the Years 9 through 12 of $8,000,000, $10,000,000, $6,000,000 and $4,000,000 respectively. What are the tax consequences to Bill from the sale? In answering this question, assume for purposes of § 453A(c)(3)(B) that the maximum rate of tax is 20%. (Assume a § 6621

underpayment rate of 10%.)

20. Assume the facts of Problem 1 except that Bill was using the land in his business. Assume also that, instead of the payment arrangements in Problem 1, Betty agreed to pay the $1,000,000 purchase price by (a) transferring to Bill in Year 8 another tract of land worth $600,000 and (b) paying Bill $100,000 each year for the next four years (together with a fair market rate of interest on the unpaid balance).

Assignment for Chapter 41:

Complete the problems.

Read:

Part A: Internal Revenue Code: §§ 453(a), (b), (c), (d), (f)(3)–(5), (f)(7) and (8), (i), (j), (k); 453B(a), (b), (f), (g); 1041(a); 1271(a)(1).
Treasury Regulations: § 15A.453-1(a), (b)(1)–(3)(i), (b)(5), (c)(1), (c)(2)(i)(A), (c)(3)(i), (c)(4), (d)(2); Prop. Reg. § 1.453-1(f)(1); Temp. Reg. § 1.1041-1T(a), Q&A-2.

Materials: Overview — Part A
Burnet v. Logan
Revenue Ruling 79-371

Part B: Internal Revenue Code: §§ 453(e), (f), (g), (l); 453A; 1239(a)–(c).
Teasury Regulations; Prop. Reg. § 1.453-1(f)(1).
Materials: Overview — Part B

II. VOCABULARY

Part A:

installment sale
installment method
payment
gross profit ratio
gross profit
total contract price
selling price
qualifying indebtedness
recapture income
election out
dealer dispositions
publicly traded property
contingent payment obligation
open transaction
closed transaction

Part B:

deferred tax liability
excess basis

III. OBJECTIVES

Part A:

1. To compute the gross profit ratio, and determine the income portion of an installment payment, given the necessary information on selling price, basis, and indebtedness assumed or taken subject to.

2. To determine the recapture income and the gross profit ratio on installment sales of depreciable property.

3. To determine the taxpayer's income in the year of sale when making an election out of installment reporting.

4. To recall that installment method reporting is not allowed with respect to publicly traded property and is generally not allowed on dealer dispositions.

5. To apply installment method reporting to contingent payment sales.

6. To determine gain or loss recognized on the disposition of an installment obligation, and the transferee's basis in the obligation.

Part B:

7. To determine the tax consequences for an installment method seller when a related purchaser disposes of the property acquired from the seller.

8. To recall that installment method reporting is not allowed on the sale of depreciable property to a controlled entity.

9. To recall that the net proceeds from the pledging of certain "nondealer installment obligations" are treated as payment.

10. To determine whether interest is payable on the deferred tax liability with respect to a nondealer installment obligation, and if so (given sufficient information), in what amount.

11. To determine, on a like kind exchange involving receipt of an installment obligation, the taxpayer's basis in the like kind property, and the gross profit ratio and income recognized with respect to any payments.

IV. OVERVIEW

Part A:

A. Statutory Framework

Under the ordinary rules of the Code, a taxpayer who sells property recognizes gain or loss at the time of the sale. § 1001(a), (c). Suppose, however, the property is sold at a gain on a deferred payment or installment basis, with all or part of the selling price to be paid following the year of sale. In these circumstances, it may seem harsh to apply the ordinary rules and tax all the gain currently since "possible liquidity problems . . . might arise from the bunching of gain in the year of sale when a portion of the selling price has not been actually received." S. Rep. No. 96-1000, p. 7, 96th Cong., 2d Sess. (1980). Accordingly, the installment sales rules of § 453 provide that the gain on the sale — and the tax liability it generates — is spread over the period during which the payments are received. In addition to spreading or deferring income, § 453 also addresses characterization of the income. Income recognized under the installment method, whether in the year of sale or thereafter, is income from a disposition of property, rather than income from the collection of an obligation. For example, if the property disposed of was a capital asset and the disposition was a sale, the gain recognized both in the year of sale and later years will be capital gain.

The basic statutory framework is as follows: First, income from an "installment sale" is to be reported under the "installment method." § 453(a). The statute does not apply to an installment sale at a loss. Second, § 453(b)(1) generally defines an "installment sale" as a disposition of property where at least one payment is to be received following the year of disposition. Thus, there is no requirement that any payment be received in the year of disposition. Similarly, there is no prohibition on the use of the installment method even where a substantial percentage of the total payments is received in the year of disposition. Third, the "installment method," defined in § 453(c), prorates the total gain on the sale over the total payments to be received. For example, assume taxpayer sells qualifying property, which has an adjusted basis of $40, for $100, payable at the rate of $20 per year, plus adequate interest on the unpaid balance. (Assume throughout this Chapter that adequate interest is charged and is paid annually. If such were not the case, a portion of the payment price could be recharacterized as interest. See §§ 1274 and 483, discussed in Chapter 43.) Taxpayer's total gain on the sale is $60, and the total payments to be received are $100. Pursuant to § 453(c), 60/100ths, or 60% of each $20 payment ($12 of each $20 payment) constitutes income from the sale. The remaining portion of each payment ($8) constitutes a tax-free return of basis. Over the five payments, taxpayer will recover the $40 basis tax-free ($8 × 5), and will report $60 of income ($12 × 5) at the rate of $12 per year.

In the language of the statute, income from an installment sale recognized in any year is "that proportion of the payments received in that year which the gross profit (realized or to be realized when payment is completed) bears to the total contract price." § 453(c). The regulations define the terms "gross profit" and "contract price," which are $60 and $100 respectively in the example just given. *See*

Reg. § 15A.453-1(b)(2). The ratio of gross profit to total contract price is known as the "gross profit ratio." Once the gross profit ratio is determined — 60% in our example — then the income portion of any payment is determined simply by multiplying the amount of the payment by the gross profit ratio. Returning to our example, suppose that the $100 "selling price" — a term defined in Reg. § 15A.453-1(b)(2)(ii) — were payable in four annual installments of $10, $20, $30, and $40. Since the total contract price and gross profit are still the same, so is the gross profit ratio: 60%. Applying that ratio to each payment, the income recognized on each payment is $6, $12, $18, and $24, respectively.

B. Payments and Liabilities

The above example involved the sale of property that was not subject to any mortgages or other liabilities. Assume the property — which is still worth $100 and has an adjusted basis of $40 — is subject to a mortgage of $20 the buyer agrees to assume. Since the equity in the property is only $80 now, the buyer will make four, rather than five, annual cash payments of $20 each. The seller's amount realized, of course, remains $100; the liability relief of $20 is as much a part of the amount realized as are the cash payments. The gross profit is therefore still $60. Is this liability relief treated as a "payment" for purposes of § 453(c)? The answer, in general, is "No." The mortgage presumably constitutes "qualifying indebtedness" — see the definition in Reg. § 15A.453-1(b)(2)(iv) — and qualifying indebtedness assumed, or taken subject to, by the buyer ordinarily is not a "payment" to the seller. Reg. § 15A.453-1(b)(3)(i). In effect, all of the mortgage relief is treated as tax-free return of basis, an approach favorable to the taxpayer and also in keeping with the underlying policy objective of alleviating potential liquidity problems on installment sales. Therefore, the "payments" total only $80. What is the gross profit ratio? The gross profit remains $60, but the "total contract price" now becomes $80, since it is determined by subtracting the qualifying indebtedness of $20 from the $100 selling price. Reg. § 15A.453-1(b)(2)(iii), (iv). The gross profit ratio is thus 75%. As a result, $15 of each $20 payment constitutes income. Total recognized gain will again be $60, as it should be.

Suppose, in the example, the mortgage in question secured a debt of $50 rather than $20. The purchaser, who is assuming the mortgage, agrees to make cash payments totaling only $50, the amount of the seller's equity in the property. Since the amount realized ($100) and adjusted basis ($40) are unchanged, so is the seller's gain of $60. However, that gain now exceeds the total cash payments to be received. Thus, even if the cash payments are fully taxed as income, the total gain will not be accounted for. Put another way, if the entire amount of mortgage relief is treated as return of basis, the taxpayer would recover too much basis. In these circumstances, the regulations treat the "excess" liability — that is, the amount by which the qualifying indebtedness exceeds the basis — as a payment; in this instance, $10. Reg. § 15A.453-1(b)(3)(i). Total payments will thus be $60. What is the gross profit ratio on this latest set of facts? Since the gross profit on the sale is also $60, a gross profit ratio of 100% is required. Compute the total contract price. Note that qualifying indebtedness offsets the selling price only to the extent of basis. Reg. § 15A.453-1(b)(2)(iii). Therefore, the total contract price is $60 — that is, the $100 selling price reduced by only $40 of qualifying debt — and the gross profit ratio is 100%. Thus, all $10 of the excess-liability "payment" and all $50 of the actual cash payments constitute income, and the total gain of $60 is properly accounted for.

To this point, "payments" have consisted either of cash or of liability relief in excess of basis. Suppose, at the time of the sale, the buyer issues a promissory note, or notes, to the seller in the amount of the unpaid purchase price. Do the buyer's own notes themselves constitute payment? In general, the answer is "No," even if such debt is guaranteed by a third party. § 453(f)(3). Note, however, the exceptions for debt instruments payable on demand and for readily tradable debt instruments. § 453(f)(4), (5). These exceptions reflect that, in some circumstances, a debt instrument is so close to cash that deferral of gain is inappropriate. Review carefully the general description of "payment" contained in the regulations. Reg. § 15A.453-1(b)(3)(i). Third-party notes will constitute payment, as will the "securing" of the buyer's own notes by cash or a cash equivalent. Review the discussion of constructive receipt and cash equivalency in Chapter 28.

The buyer's assumption of qualifying indebtedness, as we have noted, does not constitute payment (except to the extent the debt exceeds basis). What does this imply about the buyer's assumption of, or taking subject to, nonqualifying debt? The installment method changes the timing of income from a sale, not the total amount of income. Therefore, if the assumption of nonqualifying debt constitutes "payment," the gross profit ratio should be lower than would be the case with qualifying debt. Indeed, the definition of "contract price" in Reg. § 15A.453-1(b)(2)(iii) as, in part, "total contract price equal to selling price reduced by . . . qualifying indebtedness," accomplishes just this result. Only qualifying debt reduces contract price and total contract price (and thereby increases the gross profit ratio). Why this distinction between qualifying and nonqualifying debt? To classify debt a buyer assumes, or takes subject to, as qualifying indebtedness is to treat such debt relief as return of basis to the seller, rather than treating it as a "payment" which is in part a return of basis and in part income. Such favorable treatment may be appropriate for acquisition debt, but it is simply not appropriate for debt that reflects a partial cashing-out of one's interest in the property. For example, post-acquisition debt taken on in contemplation of disposition of the property may not constitute qualifying indebtedness. Likewise, debts incurred incident to disposition of the property or that are unrelated to the property will not qualify. Reg. § 15A.453-1(b)(2)(iv). The buyer's assumption of such debt will constitute payment.

C. Recapture Income

Section 453(i) is an exception to the normal rules of installment method reporting. Since the seller has already benefitted taxwise from the depreciation taken on the property prior to the sale, § 453(i) requires recognition in the year of sale of any "recapture income." "Recapture income" is defined as the amount that §§ 1245 or 1250 would classify as ordinary income if all payments to be received were received in the year of sale. Recall our example of property with a basis of $40 that is sold for $100, payable at the rate of $20 per year. Assume the property is subject to § 1245 depreciation recapture of $20. Under § 453(i)(1)(A), the recapture income of $20 is recognized currently, regardless of whether any payments are actually received in the year of sale.

Since recapture income is recognized regardless of any actual payments, the recaptured amount must be added to the seller's adjusted basis so as to avoid over-reporting income. The legislative history to § 453(i) recognizes the need for, and authorizes, such a basis adjustment. Thus, in our prior example, the $20 of recapture income would be added to the pre-sale basis of $40. Given a selling price of $100, the seller's gross profit would now be $40 rather than $60. The gross profit ratio applied to each $20 payment would therefore be 40%, resulting in $8 of installment method income each year. After all five annual payments had been made, the appropriate total gain — $60 — would have been reported: $20 of recapture income and $40 of gain on the five actual payments of $20 each.

D. Electing out of the Installment Method

Installment method reporting is not mandatory. Under § 453(d), a taxpayer may elect out of the installment method and report the gain on the sale in accordance with the taxpayer's normal method of accounting. The election must be made in a timely manner and may be revoked only with the consent of the Internal Revenue Service.[1] *See generally* Reg. § 15A.453-1(d)(3), (4). Prior to the Installment Sales Revision Act of 1980, a taxpayer seeking the benefit of § 453(a) had to make an affirmative election. Since a taxpayer would ordinarily prefer installment reporting, the 1980 Act reversed the pre-1980 rule and provided for the automatic application of § 453(a), subject to the election out.

How is income reported if the taxpayer elects out of § 453? The regulations treat the installment obligation as property valued at its fair market value, regardless of whether it is a cash equivalent. Reg. § 15A.453-1(d)(2)(i). In addition, if the election-out is made, a cash method taxpayer is directed to treat the fair market value of the obligation as having been realized in the year of sale, and to treat that value as not less than the fair market value of the property sold (less other consideration received); an accrual method taxpayer is directed to treat the total amount payable on the obligation as realized in the year of sale. Reg. § 15A.453-1(d)(2)(ii). The regulations clearly reject the election-out as a deferral of income technique, and instead make it, in effect, an occasion for acceleration of income.

E. Exclusions

The use of installment method reporting is not allowed for certain deferred payment sales. Section 453(k) denies installment reporting for sales of publicly traded property and for sales pursuant to a revolving credit plan. The legislative

---

[1] The Service has provided some guidance in Revenue Ruling 90-46, 1990-1 C.B. 107, on when it will grant permission to make a late election out of the installment method. A "subsequent change in circumstances or law" — such as a change in tax rates — or a taxpayer "change of mind" will not constitute good cause for a late election. However, where taxpayer's attempt to timely elect out is "thwarted by a mistake" — taxpayer's agent failed to follow written instructions to make the election out — and the taxpayer promptly tries to correct the mistake, the Service may find good cause and permit the late election.

history of § 453(k) provides the following reasons for these two limitations:

> First, the committee believes that sales under a revolving credit plan should not be permitted to be accounted for under the installment method. The committee believes that such sales more closely resemble the provision of a flexible line of credit accompanied by cash sales by the seller, and therefore is not appropriately afforded the use of the installment method. Second, the committee believes that the installment method should not be available for sales of certain publicly traded property. In general, publicly traded property is considered to be a sufficiently liquid asset to be treated the same as a payment of cash for purposes of applying the installment method. Moreover, since the taxpayer can easily sell such property for cash in the public market, the committee believes that such property does not present the same liquidity problem that the installment method is intended to alleviate.

S. Rep. No. 99-913, p. 124, 99th Cong. 2d Sess. (1986).

All payments to be received on such sales are treated as received in the year of disposition. The term "payment to be received" is defined as the aggregate amount of all payments not contingent as to amount, plus the fair market value of contingent-amount payments. § 453(f)(8).

In addition, installment reporting is generally not permitted for so-called "dealer dispositions." § 453(b)(2)(A). (Dispositions of personal property includable in inventory also do not qualify as installment sales. § 453(b)(2)(B).)

A "dealer disposition" is defined as any disposition of personal property by a person who regularly sells or otherwise disposes of personal property of the same type on the installment plan, or any disposition of real property held by the taxpayer for sale to customers in the ordinary course of business. § 453(l)(1). Exceptions are provided for dispositions of property used or produced in a farming business, and for dispositions of residential lots or timeshares if the taxpayer elects to pay interest on the tax deferred by reason of the use of installment method reporting. § 453(l)(2), (3). Consider the approach used with respect to these dealer dispositions of residential lots and timeshares: installment reporting is allowed only if interest is paid on the deferred tax. Should this approach be used with respect to installment sales generally? We will see in Part B that a similar approach is in fact taken on certain nondealer dispositions of property. § 453A.

F. Contingent Payment Sales

In some instances, a property's selling price is made contingent on future events, such as future profits or rents, and the aggregate selling price thus cannot be determined in the year of the sale. The question then arises as to how to account for the gain on such a contingent payment sale. One approach, given the uncertainty as to the ultimate amount to be realized, would be to hold the transaction "open" until all the payments had been made. Under this approach, no gain would arise and no tax liability would be imposed until the taxpayer had first fully recovered basis in the property. Once the basis had been recovered, remaining payments would constitute taxable gain. The taxpayer in *Burnet v. Logan*, reprinted below, successfully argued for open transaction treatment on a 1916 sale of stock for a price that was in part contingent on future mining operations. The Supreme Court concluded that the purchaser's promise of future money payments had no ascertainable fair market value. The Court rejected a second possible approach, advanced by the Commissioner, under which — despite valuation difficulties — a value would be placed on the purchaser's promise of future payments, and the transaction would thus be treated as "closed." (Note the reference in *Burnet v. Logan* to the fact that, for estate tax purposes, it was in fact possible to make such a valuation.)

Open transaction accounting is of limited applicability today. Section 453(j)(2) directs that regulations be provided for ratable basis recovery in a situation where gross profit or total contract price is not readily ascertainable. Thus, unless the taxpayer elects out of § 453, contingent payment sales are to be reported on the installment method. Reg. § 15A.453-1(c)(1). If the sale is subject to a "stated maximum selling price," this maximum selling price is generally treated as the "selling price" for purposes of computing the gross profit ratio and determining the income portion of each payment. Reg. § 15A.453-1(c)(2)(i). If a maximum selling price cannot be determined but there is a maximum period of time over which payments may be received, the taxpayer's basis is generally allocated over that "fixed period" in equal annual amounts. Reg. § 15A.453-1(c)(3)(i). Assume, for example, taxpayer sells property with a $10,000 basis for payments over a ten-year period, not subject to any maximum selling price. $1,000 of basis would be allocated to each of the ten years, and annual payments in excess of $1,000 would constitute income. No loss, however, is allowed ordinarily until the final payment year. Thus, if payments in any year were less than the basis allocated to that year, the unrecovered basis would carryover to the following year. Continuing with our example, if Year 1 payment were only $900, the Year 1 unrecovered basis would be $100, no loss would be allowed in Year 1, and the Year 2 basis allocation would become $1,100. Finally, when neither a maximum selling price nor a fixed period limits the payments, the transaction "will be closely scrutinized" to see whether a sale has in fact occurred, and if so, basis will ordinarily be allocated in equal amounts over a 15-year period. Reg. § 15A.453-1(c)(4). In this case, no loss is allowed unless the payment obligation has become worthless and all basis has not yet been recovered.

The foregoing discussion of contingent payment sales assumed the taxpayer had not elected out of § 453. If an election is made, gain or loss is computed on the sale under the ordinary rules of § 1001, and the "contingent payment obligation" is valued at its fair market value. Reg. § 15A.453-1(d)(2)(i). Pursuant to this regulation, however, the fair market value of a contingent payment obligation shall "in no event" be less than the fair market value of the property sold. Only in those "rare and extraordinary cases" where the fair market value of an obligation cannot be ascertained will the transaction be treated as "open," and even then the transaction will be scrutinized to see if it in fact constitutes a sale. Reg. § 15A.453-1(d)(2)(iii).

G. Dispositions of Installment Obligations

In general, when a taxpayer disposes of an installment obligation, the tax deferral authorized by § 453 with respect to that obligation ends. To determine the gain (or loss) recognized on this disposition, one must subtract the basis of the obligation from either the fair market value of the obligation or the amount realized on its disposition, depending on the type of disposition.

The basis of an obligation is the difference between its face value and the amount that would constitute income were the obligation satisfied in full. § 453B(b). Assume, for example, a taxpayer sells property with a basis of $10, for $50 in cash, plus the buyer's promissory note for $50 payable in a subsequent year. On these facts, the gross profit ratio is 90%. If the $50 note were paid in full, $45 of the payment would be reportable as income. Accordingly, the note's basis is $5.

If the taxpayer sells or exchanges the note, or it is satisfied at other than face value, gain or loss is recognized in an amount equal to the difference between the amount realized and the basis of the note. § 453B(a)(1). If the note is otherwise disposed of, such as by gift, the recognized gain or loss equals the difference between its fair market value and its basis. § 453B(a)(2). Cancellation of a note is treated as a disposition other than by sale or exchange, and if the parties are related, as described in § 453(f)(1), the fair market value will not be less than the face amount of the note. § 453B(f). The character of the recognized gain or loss will depend on the character of the underlying property. § 453B(a).

In the case of a transfer of an installment obligation between spouses or incident to a divorce, the rules of § 453B(a) do not apply, and no gain or loss is recognized. The transferee instead steps into the shoes of the transferor for purposes of reporting gain on the receipt of payments on the installment obligation. § 453B(g). Special rules, which we will not study, also apply with respect to installment obligations transferred at death. § 453B(c); § 691(a)(4).

Revenue Ruling 79-371, reprinted below, addresses the question of the transferee's basis in an installment obligation following a disposition by gift under § 453B(a)(2). The transferee's basis is augmented to reflect the income recognized by the transferor.

Part B:

Part B of this overview considers some additional selected issues that may arise with installment sales.

A. Second Dispositions by Related Persons

Assume Father sells property to Daughter at fair market value on an installment basis. Until payment is received, Father recognizes no income. Daughter, however, takes a cost basis in the property, equal to its fair market value. § 1012. If Daughter promptly sells the property for cash to a third party, at the same fair market value, consider the possible results: the Father-Daughter family unit has converted the property to cash; no gain is realized by Daughter; and no gain is recognized by Father until such time as Daughter makes payment to Father on the installment sale. This outcome seems too good to be true, and, thanks to § 453(e), it is. The Senate Finance Committee, explaining the Installment Sales Revision Act of 1980, summarized the operation of § 453(e) as follows:

> Under the bill, the amount realized upon certain resales by the related party installment purchaser will trigger recognition of gain by the initial seller, based on his gross profit ratio, only to the extent the amount realized from the second disposition exceeds actual payments made under the installment sale. Thus, acceleration of recognition of the installment gain from the first sale will generally result only to the extent additional cash and other property flows into the related group as a result of a second disposition of the property. In the case of a second disposition which is not a sale or exchange, the fair market value of the property disposed of is treated as the amount realized for this purpose. . . .

S. Rpt. No. 96-1000, p. 14–15, 96th Cong. 2d Sess. (1980).

Assume, for example, Father owns property with an adjusted basis of $10. He sells the property to Daughter for $100, payable twenty years later. Daughter promptly resells the property for $100 cash. Father is treated as receiving a payment of $100 under § 453(e)(1) — note that in this case the § 453(e)(3) limitation is also $100 — and since Father's gross profit ratio on these facts is 90%, Father will recognize $90 of income.

> The Senate Finance Committee report continued:

> > If . . . a resale results in the recognition of gain to the initial seller, subsequent payments actually received by the seller would be recovered tax-free until they have equaled the amount realized from the resale which resulted in the acceleration of recognition of gain.

S. Rpt. No. 96-1000, p. 15.

Thus, when Father actually receives the $100 payment from Daughter, no further gain is recognized since, for tax purposes, Father was treated as receiving the $100 payment at the time of Daughter's sale to the third party.

The Senate Finance Committee Report noted certain limitations on § 453(e):

In the case of property other than marketable securities, the resale rule will apply only with respect to second dispositions occurring within 2 years of the initial installment sale. . . .

The bill also contains several exceptions to the application of these rules. . . . [Under one exception] there would be no acceleration of recognition of gain as a result of a second disposition which is an involuntary conversion of the property if the first sale occurred before the threat or imminence of the conversion. . . . [F]inally the resale rules will not apply in any case where it is established to the satisfaction of the Internal Revenue Service that none of the dispositions had as one of its principal purposes the avoidance of Federal income taxes.

In the exceptional cases to which the nonavoidance exception may apply, it is anticipated that regulations would provide definitive rules so that complicated legislation is not necessary to prescribe substituted property or taxpayer rules which would not be of general application. In appropriate cases, it is anticipated that the regulations and rulings under the nontax avoidance exception will deal with certain tax-free transfers which normally would not be treated as a second disposition of the property, *e.g.*, charitable transfers, like kind exchanges, gift transfers, and transfers to a controlled corporation or a partnership. Generally it is intended that a second disposition will qualify under the nontax avoidance exception when it is of an involuntary nature, *e.g.*, foreclosure upon the property by a judgment lien creditor of the related purchaser or bankruptcy of the related purchaser. In addition it is intended that the exception will apply in the case of a second disposition which is also an installment sale if the terms of payment under the installment resale are substantially equivalent to, or longer than, those for the first installment sale. However, the exception would not apply if the resale terms would permit significant deferral of recognition of gain from the initial sale when proceeds from the resale are being collected sooner.

It is to be understood that the provisions governing the use of the installment method to report sales between related parties, and the definition of such relationships, are not intended to preclude the Internal Revenue Service from asserting the proper tax treatment of transactions that are shams.

S. Rep. No. 96-1000, p. 15–17.

B.   Sales of Depreciable Property to Related Persons

In general, the installment method is not available in the case of installment sales of depreciable property (as defined in § 453(f)(7)) between related persons. § 453(g)(1). Section 453(g)(2) provides that "related persons" shall have the meaning given that term by § 1239(b). Thus, the installment method cannot be used with respect to a sale between (a) a taxpayer and a controlled entity within the meaning of § 1239(c), (b) a taxpayer and a trust in which the taxpayer or her spouse is a beneficiary, or (c) an executor of an estate and a beneficiary of the estate. § 1239(b). The purpose of the rule is "to deter transactions which are structured in such a way as to give the related purchaser the benefit of depreciation deductions (measured from a stepped-up basis) prior to the time the seller is required to include in income the corresponding gain on the sale." S. Rep. No. 96-1000, p. 17. The rule does not apply where the sale does not have the avoidance of federal income tax as one of its principal purposes. § 453(g)(2). For example, the rule might not apply if the related purchaser were required to make all installment payments within five years of the sale but the nature if the property purchased was such that it was depreciable by the purchaser over a 39-year period. Where the rule applies, the seller is generally required to treat all payments to be received as received in the year of sale. Furthermore, § 1239(a), if applicable, will characterize the gain on the sale as ordinary income.

C. Special Rules for Nondealers

Section 453A provides two special rules for certain installment obligations (hereinafter, "§ 453A installment obligations") arising from nondealer dispositions of property. These specially-treated installment obligations are those arising from dispositions of property where the sales price of the property exceeds $150,000. § 453A(b)(1).[2]

Under one of the special rules, if a § 453A installment obligation is itself pledged as security for any debt, the net proceeds of the secured debt are treated as payment on the obligation. § 453A(d)(1).[3] Subsequent payments on the installment obligation are then disregarded up to the aggregate amount of the deemed payment. § 453A(d)(3). Consider whether similar treatment should apply on the pledging of any installment obligation, not just § 453A installment obligations, on the theory that pledging is tantamount to disposition, at least to the extent of the net proceeds.

The other rule provides that the taxpayer, in limited circumstances, must pay interest, at a rate prescribed in § 453A(c)(2)(B), on the deferred tax liability attributable to § 453A installment obligations. § 453A(a)(1). The sales price of property must exceed $150,000 before an installment obligation arising from such a sale is even potentially subject to § 453A. In addition, no interest is charged on the deferred tax liability attributable to such obligations unless the aggregate face amount of all such installment obligations, which arose during the taxable year in question and are outstanding at its close, exceeds $5,000,000. § 453A(b)(2). If this $5,000,000 threshold is not reached, no interest is payable.

The statute defines the "deferred tax liability" as the unrecognized gain on § 453A installment obligations, multiplied by the maximum tax rate in effect for the year in question. § 453A(c)(3). Interest is payable, however, not on the entire

---

[2] Installment obligations arising from the disposition of personal use property or the disposition of property used or produced in the farming business are excluded from the special rules of § 453A. § 453A(b)(3). Another exclusion is available under § 453A(b)(4) with respect to timeshares and residential lots.

[3] Similar rules apply to any arrangement that allows the taxpayer to satisfy an indebtedness with a § 453A installment obligation. § 453A(d)(4).

deferred tax liability attributable to such an obligation, but only on an "applicable percentage" of it; this percentage is determined in a manner that effectively incorporates the $5,000,000 no-interest threshold. § 453A(c)(4). If interest is payable with respect to a § 453A installment obligation that arises during any year, interest is payable in subsequent years as long as there remains an unpaid balance on the obligation. If interest is not payable with respect to such an installment obligation arising during a year, because the $5,000,000 threshold was not reached, interest on the obligation will not be payable in a subsequent year. § 453A(b)(2). Consider again whether the imposition of interest on the deferred tax liability inherent in an installment obligation should become the norm under § 453, not merely the object of a special rule under § 453A.

D.   Installment Obligations and Like Kind Exchanges

Suppose a taxpayer engages in an exchange of like kind property and, as part of the transaction, receives as "boot" an installment obligation issued by the other party. Conceptually, the policies of both §§ 1031 and 453 should be carried out; the taxpayer should receive nonrecognition treatment with respect to the like kind exchange and (assuming no exceptions apply) should receive deferral of tax liability with respect to the income inherent in the installment obligation, pending the receipt of payments on it. Accordingly, in a like kind exchange in which an installment obligation is part of the boot received, § 453(f)(6) provides (1) the like kind property is not treated as a "payment," and (2) the gross profit ratio is specially determined, with the total contract price reduced by the amount of like kind property received and the total gross profit reduced by the amount of gain not recognized under § 1031. The legislative history to this provision elaborates:

> The basis of the like kind property received (determined under section 1031(d)), will be determined as if the obligation had been satisfied at its face amount. Thus, the taxpayer's basis in the property transferred will first be allocated to the like kind property received (but not in excess of its fair market value) and any remaining basis will be used to determine the gross profit ratio. . . .

The legislative history illustrates this provision with an example under which property with a basis of $400,000 is exchanged for like kind property worth $200,000 and an installment obligation for $800,000. The like kind property takes a basis of $200,000, pursuant to the direction that basis allocations be made first to like kind property, but not in excess of fair market value. For § 453 purposes, the total contract price is only $800,000, since the value of the like kind property is not included. Because $200,000 of the $400,000 total basis has been allocated to the like kind property, the "remaining basis" for § 453 purposes is $200,000. With a total contract price of $800,000, and remaining basis of $200,000, the gross profit for § 453 purposes is $600,000, and the gross profit ratio is therefore 75%. Accordingly, 75% of each payment will constitute income, and a total of $600,000 of income will have been recognized when the note is fully paid. See also Prop. Reg. § 1.453-1(f)(1) which dictates the same approach as employed in this example from the legislative history.[4]

BURNET v. LOGAN
United States Supreme Court
283 U.S. 404 (1931)

Mr. Justice McReynolds delivered the opinion of the Court.

Prior to March, 1913, and until March 11, 1916, respondent, Mrs. Logan, owned 250 of the 4,000 capital shares issued by the Andrews & Hitchcock Iron Company. It held 12% of the stock of the Mahoning Ore. & Steel Company, an operating concern. In 1895 the latter corporation procured a lease for 97 years upon the "Mahoning" mine and since then has regularly taken therefrom large, but varying, quantities of iron ore — in 1913, 1,515,428 tons; in 1914, 1,212,287 tons; in 1915, 2,311,940 tons; in 1919, 1,217,167 tons; in 1921, 303,020 tons; in 1923, 3,029,865 tons. The lease contract did not require production of either maximum or minimum tonnage or any definite payments. Through an agreement of stockholders (steel manufacturers) the Mahoning Company is obligated to apportion extracted ore among them according to their holdings.

On March 11, 1916, the owners of all the shares in Andrews & Hitchcock Company sold them to Youngstown Sheet & Tube Company, which thus acquired, among other things, 12% of the Mahoning Company's stock and the right to receive the same percentage of ore thereafter taken from the leased mine.

For the shares so acquired, the Youngstown Company paid the holders $2,200,000 in money and agreed to pay annually thereafter for distribution among them 60 cents for each ton of ore apportioned to it. Of this cash Mrs. Logan received 250/4000ths — $137,500; and she became entitled to the same fraction of any annual payment thereafter made by the purchaser under the terms of sale.

Mrs. Logan's mother had long owned 1100 shares of the Andrews & Hitchcock Company. She died in 1917, leaving to the daughter one-half of her interest in payments thereafter made by the Youngstown Company. This bequest was appraised for federal estate tax purposes at $277,164.50.

During 1917, 1918, 1919 and 1920 the Youngstown Company paid large sums under the agreement. Out of these respondent received on account of her 250 shares $9,900.00 in 1917, $11,250.00 in 1918, $8,995.50 in 1919, $5,444.30 in 1920 — $35,589.80. By reason of the interest from her mother's estate she received $19,790.10 in 1919, and $11,977.49 in 1920.

Reports of income for 1918, 1919 and 1920 were made by Mrs. Logan upon the basis of cash receipts and disbursements. They included no part of what she had obtained from annual payments by the Youngstown Company. She maintains that until the total amount actually received by her from the sale of her shares equals

---

[4] Final regulations have been issued coordinating the deferred like kind exchange rules of § 1031 with the § 453 installment sales rules. Reg. §§ 1.1031(k)-1(j)(2), 1.1031(b)-2.

their value on March 1, 1913, no taxable income will arise from the transaction. Also, until she actually receives by reason of the right bequeathed to her, a sum equal to its appraised value, there will be no taxable income therefrom.

On March 1, 1913, the value of the 250 shares then held by Mrs. Logan exceeded $173,089.80 — the total of all sums actually received by her prior to 1921 from their sale ($137,500.00 cash in 1916 plus four annual payments amounting to $35,589.80). That value also exceeded original cost of the shares. The amount received on the interest devised by her mother was less than its valuation for estate taxation and also less than the value when acquired by Mrs. Logan.

The Commissioner ruled that the obligation of the Youngstown Company to pay 60 cents per ton had a fair market value of $1,942,111.46 on March 11, 1916; and that this value should be treated as so much cash and the sale of the stock regarded as a closed transaction with no profit in 1916. He also used this valuation as the basis for apportioning subsequent annual receipts between income and return of capital. His calculations, based upon estimates and assumptions, are too intricate for brief statement. He made deficiency assessments according to the view just stated and the Board of Tax Appeals approved the result.

The Circuit Court of Appeals held that, in the circumstances, it was impossible to determine with fair certainty the market value of the agreement by the Youngstown Company to pay 60 cents per ton. [The court also held] that respondent was entitled to the return of her capital — the value of 250 shares on March 1, 1913, and the assessed value of the interest derived from her mother — before she could be charged with any taxable income. As this had not in fact been returned, there was no taxable income.

We agree with the result reached by the Circuit Court of Appeals.

The 1916 transaction was a sale of stock — not an exchange of property. . . . Nor does the situation demand that an effort be made to place according to the best available data some approximate value upon the contract for future payments. This probably was necessary in order to assess the mother's estate. As annual payments on account of extracted ore coming in, they can be readily apportioned first as return of capital and later as profit. The liability for income tax ultimately can be fairly determined without resort to mere estimates, assumptions and speculation. When the profit, if any, is actually realized, the taxpayer will be required to respond. The consideration for the sale was $2,200,000.00 in cash and the promise of future money payments wholly contingent upon facts and circumstances not possible to foretell with anything like fair certainty. The promise was in no proper sense equivalent to cash. It had no ascertainable fair market value. The transaction was not a closed one. Respondent might never recoup her capital investment from payments only conditionally promised. Prior to 1921 all receipts from the sale of her shares amounted to less than their value on March 1, 1913. She properly demanded the return of her capital investment before assessment of any taxable profit based on conjecture.

In order to determine whether there has been gain or loss, and the amount of the gain, if any, we must withdraw from the gross proceeds an amount sufficient to restore the capital value that existed at the commencement of the period under consideration. *Doyle v. Mitchell Bros. Co.*, 247 U.S. 179, 184, 185. . . .

The judgments below are affirmed.

REVENUE RULING 79-371
1979-2 C.B. 294

ISSUE

What is the basis of an installment note in the hands of a transferee under the circumstances described below?

FACTS

In 1976, all of the common stock of corporation X owned by A, an individual, was redeemed by X for a cash downpayment of 20x dollars and a negotiable promissory note in the principal amount of 80x dollars. A had a basis of 10x dollars in the common stock, which A originally purchased in 1970.

The principal on the note was to be paid in eight annual installments of 10x dollars each, commencing in 1980. The note was to bear interest at the rate of 10 percent per annum from the date of redemption of the stock through 1979, and thereafter at the rate of seven percent per annum until the outstanding principal balance was paid.

A's initial basis in the note was 8x dollars. 18x dollars of the 20x dollars received by A from X in 1976 was reported as gain.

Under section 302 of the Internal Revenue Code the redemption qualifies for treatment as a distribution in full payment in exchange for A's stock. A elected in 1976 to report the gain from the redemption on the installment method of accounting under section 453(b).

In January 1978, A transferred the note by gift to A's child, B. The fair market value of the note at the time of transfer was its principal outstanding balance, the face amount of 80x dollars. At the time of the transfer all accrued interest had been paid to A.

LAW AND ANALYSIS

Section [453B(a)] of the Code provides that if an installment obligation is satisfied at other than its face value or distributed, transmitted, sold or otherwise disposed of, gain or loss results to the extent of the difference between the basis of the obligation and (A) the amount realized, in the case of a satisfaction at other than face value or a sale or exchange, or (B) the fair market value of the obligation at the time of distribution, transmission, or disposition otherwise than by sale or exchange. Any gain or loss so resulting shall be considered as resulting from the sale or exchange of the property in respect of which the installment obligation was received.

Section [453B(b)] of the Code provides that the basis of an installment obligation is the excess of the face value of the obligation over an amount equal to the income that would be returnable were the obligation satisfied in full.

Section 1015(a) of the Code provides that a transferee's basis for property acquired by gift is the same as it would be in the hands of the transferor.

Section 1015(d) of the Code provides that if property is acquired by gift, the basis is increased (but not above the fair market value of the property at the time of the gift) by the amount of gift taxes paid with respect to such gift.

A's transfer of the note to B was a disposition under section [453B(a)(2)] of the Code. Thus, upon such disposition, gain resulted in the amount of 72x dollars, the excess of the fair market value of the note at the time of the gift (80x dollars) over A's basis in the note determined under section [453B(b)] without regard to the gift (8x dollars).

Furthermore, if A were considered to hold the note at the time of transfer to B, A's basis in the note would be increased to include the gain resulting under section [453B(a)] of the Code. Thus, at the time of the gift, taking into account the gain resulting pursuant to section [453B(a)] of the Code, A's basis in the obligation under [453B(b)] would be 80x dollars, which is the excess of the face value of the obligation (80x dollars) over the amount of income that would be reportable were the obligation satisfied in full (zero).

HOLDING

Under section 1015(a) of the Code, the basis of the obligation in the hands of B is the same as it would be in the hands of A or 80x dollars. Because this amount equals the fair market value of the obligation at the time of the gift, no adjustment under section 1015(d) is made.

Chapter 42

SALE OF A BUSINESS AND SALE-LEASEBACKS

I. PROBLEMS

1. Liz owns and operates a retail specialty business featuring handmade Irish clothing, linens and crystal. She has operated the business as a sole proprietor for 20 years in a prime location in a large city with a sizeable Irish population. Over the years, Liz has also been deeply involved in music and has decided to sell her Irish specialty business to Sean and to open a music store in the same city. The following table lists the business assets to be sold and the adjusted basis (A/B) and fair market value of each asset.

Asset	A/B	FMV
Accounts Receivable	$100,000	$75,000
Building	50,000	750,000
Land	50,000	250,000
Inventory	250,000	500,000
Fixtures	0	100,000
Delivery Truck	0	25,000

Sean agrees to pay Liz $1,900,000 for the property. Under the terms of the agreement, Sean will be entitled to continue to use the name "Burke's Irish House" and Liz promises not to engage for five years in any similar Irish specialty business within a 100-mile radius of the current business location. The agreement between the parties specifically allocates the $1,900,000 purchase price to the above items in the amount of the fair market value indicated. In addition, their agreement allocates $100,000 to a covenant not to compete and $100,000 to goodwill.

(a) Explain the tax consequences to Liz of the sale of her business. Assume the gain inherent in the fixtures and the truck would be characterized entirely as § 1245 gain. Assume also Liz has an adjusted basis of $0 in the goodwill of her business. What is the tax significance to Sean of the allocations to goodwill and the covenant not to compete?

(b) Assume the agreement was silent as to allocations of the purchase price but that, for purposes of computing their taxes, the parties made the following allocations:

   (i) Liz treated the covenant not to compete as having no value and goodwill as having a value of $200,000. With respect to all of the other assets, she allocated the purchase price in a manner consistent with the fair market values set forth above.

(ii) Sean treated the covenant not to compete as having a value of $50,000 and goodwill as having a value of $40,000. He treated the fixtures (which are "7-year property" under § 168) as having a value of $150,000, the delivery truck (which is "5-year property" under § 168) as having a value of $35,000; and the inventory as having a value of $550,000. With respect to all of the other assets, he allocated the purchase price in a manner consistent with the fair market values set forth above.

Explain the likely rationale for the various allocations by the parties. Will the Service respect these allocations?

(c) Assume the allocation set forth in Problem (b)(i) above was specifically included in the agreement. Assume also that Liz insisted upon this allocation as a condition of the sale. Sean and Liz compute their taxes in accordance with this allocation. What result?

2. Becky recently purchased a tract of commercial land for $100,000 and had an office building constructed on it at a cost of $2,400,000. Becky owes $1,800,000 on a mortgage encumbering the property. Because she is in need of immediate cash to continue doing business on the property, Becky contracts to sell the land and building for $2,100,000 which is the highest price she can get for the property at this time. Becky simultaneously leases the property back from the buyer for a 40-year term at fair rental value. Assume Becky's adjusted basis in the property is $2,500,000.

(a) May Becky deduct the $400,000 loss she sustains on the sale?

(b) What if the building lease were for only 29 years?

(c) What tax consequences if Becky sells the property for $3,000,000, its fair market value, and has an option to repurchase the property at the end of the forty-year lease term for $10,000?

(d) What result in (c) if there were no option to repurchase the property because the parties assumed the building would have no salvage value at the end of the lease term?

Assignment for Chapter 42:

Complete the problems.

Read: Internal Revenue Code: §§ 197(a)–(d), (e)(2), (f)(1), (f)(3), (f)(7); 1060(a), (c); Review 1(h).
Treasury Regulations: §§ 1.197-2(b), (d)(1), (2); 1.1031(a)-1(c), 1.1060-1(a)–(b)(1)–(3), (c), (d).

Materials: Overview
Williams v. McGowan
Annabelle Candy Co. v. Commissioner
Frank Lyon Company v. United States
Leslie Company v. Commissioner

II. VOCABULARY

goodwill
going concern
covenant not to compete
sale-leaseback
strong proof rule
rule of *Danielson v. Commissioner*

III. OBJECTIVES

1. To recall that *Williams v. McGowan* requires that a sale of a business be fragmented and that a separate gain or loss analysis be made for each tangible and intangible asset of the business.

2. To explain how goodwill and going concern value should be valued.

3. To explain the tax consequences to sellers and buyers of purchase price allocations made to business intangibles such as goodwill, going concern value, and covenants not to compete.

4. To explain the possible strategies employed by sellers and buyers with respect to the allocation of the purchase price to business intangibles.

5. To evaluate the tax impact of a proposed sale on the buyer and the seller.

6. To recognize circumstances in which a sale-leaseback may be recharacterized as an exchange or a financing transaction.

7. To explain the tax differences to the parties if a sale-leaseback is respected rather than being recharacterized as either a tax-free exchange or a financing transaction.

IV. OVERVIEW

The face of Main Street, U.S.A. is constantly changing. Businesses come and go, and tax advisors are constantly called upon to structure the sale or purchase of a business so as to assure the accomplishment of their client's tax and other goals. This Chapter will address the major tax issues related to the sale (or purchase) of an unincorporated business, as well sale-leaseback arrangements.

A. Sale of a Sole Proprietorship — Sale of Single Asset or Sale of Separate Assets?

1. The Standard of *Williams v. McGowan*

Assume Steve decides to sell a bowling alley which he has owned and operated as a sole proprietor for a number of years. Housed in the same building as and associated with the bowling operation are a pro shop and a bar. Steve intends to sell the entire operation, including the building, equipment, receivables, liquor license, a long term lease on pinsetting equipment, inventory, etc. Should the sale of the business be deemed the sale of a single asset, or should the transaction be fragmented into separate sales of the building, fixtures, inventory, etc? Does it make a difference?

In *Williams v. McGowan*, included in the materials, the Second Circuit concluded that the sale of a hardware business could not be treated as the sale of a unified asset. Despite the functional interrelationship of a business' assets and the fact that the assets would not be as valuable if sold separately, the court held a separate tax analysis had to be made with respect to each business asset sold. Thus, one must determine the character of each business asset — *i.e.*, is it an ordinary asset, a capital asset, or a § 1231 asset — and must calculate the gain or loss recognized with respect to its disposition. To calculate the gain or loss, one must allocate a portion of the purchase price to each asset. Obviously, the Second Circuit's analysis complicates matters for the buyer, seller and their tax advisors. Do you agree with the Second Circuit's analysis?

The Service's concern in *Williams v. McGowan* was that to view the sale of a business as a sale of single asset would distort the operation of our tax system and enable taxpayers to avoid tax. If capital gains and losses are accorded special treatment, it may make a significant difference whether one's income is ordinary or long-term or short-term capital gain and whether one's losses are ordinary or long-term or short-term capital losses. Review § 1(h). To permit a taxpayer to treat a business sale as a sale of a single asset would negate in part these significant distinctions. For example, assume the sale of Steve's bowling business would generate a net loss. Considering the § 1211 limitation on the deduction of capital losses, Steve would benefit from the characterization of the overall loss as an ordinary loss. Such characterization would be possible if the sale of the business were treated as a sale of a single non-capital asset. By contrast, if Steve were required to fragment the sale, Steve might have ordinary income from the sale of inventory, capital gain and loss from the sale of investment property, and § 1231 gains and losses from the sale of business equipment. This fragmentation approach might result in capital losses that exceeded Steve's capital gains thereby triggering the § 1211 loss limitation rules.

2.   Goodwill, Going Concern Value, and Covenants Not to Compete

Valuable intangible items are often included in the sale of a business. Under the *Williams v. McGowan* analysis, part of the purchase price must be allocated to these items. For example, if Steve has a transferable lease on the pinsetting equipment used in his bowling operation, part of the purchase price of the business must be allocated to the transfer of that lease. In addition to intangibles such as leases, patents, and copyrights, there may also be goodwill, going concern value, and a covenant not to compete reflected in the purchase price of the business. See § 197(d) for an expanded list of intangibles commonly included in the sale of a business. Before considering the tax consequences of allocating the purchase price of a business to intangibles, let's first consider the nature of goodwill, going concern value, and covenants not to compete.

a.   Goodwill

Assume Steve had operated his bowling alley for many years and had a number of loyal patrons. Under these circumstances, Steve would likely charge more for the bowling alley than merely the fair market value of each of the assets being transferred. This premium might be deemed "goodwill." Goodwill has been defined in case law to mean "the expectancy that the old customers will resort to the old place. It is the sum total of all the imponderable qualities that attract customers and bring patronage to the business without contractual compulsion." *Richard Miller and Sons, Inc. v. Comm'r*, 537 F.2d 446, 451 (Ct. Cl. 1976). Regulation § 1.197-2(b)(1) defines goodwill as "the value of a trade or business attributable to the expectancy of continued customer patronage. This expectancy may be due to the name or reputation of a trade or business or any other factor." *See also* Reg. § 1.1060-1(b)(ii).

Not all businesses have goodwill. Typically, goodwill is associated with businesses which have an established reputation in an area, a good location, or a well-recognized trademark or tradename. For example, if a business is sold and the purchaser bargains for the right to continue using the tradename of the business, it is likely that goodwill has been transferred with the business. Similarly, in Steve's situation, the long and successful nature of his bowling business indicates that substantial goodwill will be transferred with the sale of the business. As suggested above, a purchase price in excess of the fair market value of the tangible and identifiable intangible items of a business indicates a payment for goodwill.

b.   Going Concern Value

In cases where the existence of goodwill was questionable, courts have held that a portion of the purchase price should be allocated to "going concern value." Regulation § 1.197-2(b)(2) provides, in part, that going concern value is "the additional value that attaches to property by reason of its existence as an integral part of an ongoing business activity" and "includes the value attributable to the ability of a trade or business to continue functioning or generating income without interruption notwithstanding a change in ownership." *See also* Reg. § 1.1060-1(b)(ii). For example, assume Steve owns a variety of fixtures and furniture used in conjunction with the bar he operates as part of his bowling business. When sold with his bowling business, these assets are likely to have more value than if they were sold separately from the business.

c.   **Covenant Not to Compete**

Before purchasing a business, a buyer may insist that the seller agree not to compete with the buyer in the same kind of business for a stated period of time. Such assurance is often necessary to insure the effective transfer of a business' goodwill the buyer has purchased. For example, if Steve's bowling business prospered because of Steve's expertise and reputation, a buyer of that business would want to be assured Steve would not open a competing bowling business in the same town.

Given the close relationship that may exist between goodwill and a covenant not to compete, should the covenant be viewed as a separately bargained-for asset to which part of the purchase price of a business must be allocated? Because the tax treatment of amounts allocated to a covenant not to compete differs from that of amounts allocated to goodwill (*i.e.*, a seller may claim capital gain treatment with respect to goodwill, where the seller must report as ordinary income amounts received for a covenant not to compete), courts have had to consider whether the facts justify a separate allocation of the purchase price to a covenant not to compete. In resolving this issue, some courts have applied a "severability test" focusing on the question of whether a covenant not to compete could be segregated and valued independently from other assets transferred, particularly goodwill. *Michaels v. Commissioner*, 12 T.C. 17 (1949). Under a "severability" analysis, if the covenant serves only to assure that the transferor will enjoy the benefit of the goodwill he has acquired, no part of the purchase price will be allocated to it. By contrast, if the covenant not to compete is understood by the parties to be a separate and distinct item, courts embracing the "severability analysis" will respect reasonable allocations to the covenant. 12 T.C. at 19; *Montesi v. Commissioner*, 340 F.2d 97 (6th Cir. 1965).

The test more commonly applied is the so-called "economic reality" test or "mutual intent" test. Under this test, courts seek to determine whether the buyer and seller intended that part of the purchase price be allocated to the covenant and whether the covenant has some independent basis in fact or some relationship to business reality. *Schulz v. Commissioner*, 294 F.2d 52, 55 (9th Cir. 1961). *Annabelle Candy Co. v. Commissioner*, included in the materials, provides an example of the application of the "economic reality" test. *See Becker v. Commissioner*, T.C. Memo 2006-264.

3. Tax Consequences of Allocations of Purchase Price to Goodwill, Covenants Not to Compete and Going Concern Value

The allocation of a part of the purchase price to goodwill, going concern value or a covenant not to compete has significantly different tax consequences to the buyer and the seller. From the seller's standpoint, the allocation will determine the amount realized with respect to each asset and, in turn, the amount and character of the gain or loss to be reported. From the buyer's standpoint, the allocation will determine the buyer's basis in the acquired assets, thus affecting the depreciation deductions the buyer claims and the amount and character of the buyer's gain or loss on any subsequent sale. With the enactment of § 197 in 1993, Congress radically changed the tax treatment of these and other business intangibles. As a result, the stakes associated with purchase price allocations have also changed. An understanding of the historic tax treatment of business intangibles and the strategies employed by sellers and buyers to enhance their tax positions is necessary for one to appreciate the significance of the changes wrought by § 197.

a.   Historic Allocation Strategies

Until 1993, goodwill and going concern value were considered assets without a determinable useful life and therefore not depreciable. Consequently, buyers of businesses sought to minimize the amount of the purchase price allocated to those assets. As part of their allocation strategy, they attempted to carve out of goodwill and going concern value items like customer subscription lists, insurance expirations lists, workforce in place, etc. By treating these items as separate intangible assets with limited useful lives, buyers could amortize the purchase price allocated to those items. *See Reg.* § 1.167(a)-3. From their standpoint, sellers were willing to accommodate the buyers' carve-out efforts because the sellers' gain from the sale of such carved-out items was still characterized as capital gain.

The most significant case testing such taxpayer carve-out efforts was *Newark Morning Ledger Co. v. U.S.*, 113 S. Ct. 1670 (1993), in which the Supreme Court concluded that a taxpayer could depreciate subscription lists acquired as a result of the purchase of other newspapers. While recognizing it is often difficult to separate depreciable intangible assets from goodwill, the Court nevertheless emphasized:

> [I]f a taxpayer can prove with reasonable accuracy that an asset used in the trade or business or held for the production of income has a value that wastes over an ascertainable period of time, that asset is depreciable under § 167, regardless of the fact that its value is related to the expectancy of continued patronage. The significant question for purposes of depreciation is not whether the asset falls "within the core of the concept of goodwill," . . . but whether the asset is capable of being valued and whether that value diminishes over time.

113 S. Ct. at 1680–81. The majority of the Court concluded that in this instance the taxpayer had carried its "substantial burden" of proving that the subscription lists had an ascertainable value and a limited, reasonably predictable useful life. Indicative, however, of the closeness of the question raised by the case, four justices

dissented. Justice Souter, writing for the dissenters, noted:

> Ledger would have us scrap the accepted and substantive definition of "goodwill" as an expectation of continued patronage, in favor of a concept of goodwill as a residual asset of ineffable quality, whose existence and value would be represented by any portion of a business's purchase price not attributable to identifiable assets with determinate lives. Goodwill would shrink to an accounting leftover.

Id. at 1684, 1685. Justice Souter's description of Ledger's effort was equally applicable to many other purchasers of businesses who had attempted to use similar carve-outs to limit the amount allocable to goodwill.

Goodwill and going concern value, however, were not the only business intangibles which generated allocation controversies. Buyers and sellers were often at odds regarding the allocation of the purchase price to covenants not to compete. Because covenants not to compete have a limited life (typically a few years), amounts allocated to the covenant are amortizable over that period. Buyers therefore sought to allocate as much of the purchase price as possible to such covenants. Because amounts received by sellers for their agreement not to compete constitute ordinary income, sellers preferred minimal allocation to covenants not to compete.

b. Section 197 — Amortization of Business Intangibles

In response to cases like *Newark Morning Ledger* and recurring issues regarding appropriateness of allocations to covenants not to compete and other business intangibles, Congress enacted § 197, authorizing the amortization over a 15-year period of goodwill, going concern value, covenants not to compete, and a broad range of other intangibles acquired in the purchase of a trade or business. See the definition of "amortizable Section 197 intangible" in § 197(c)(1) and the definition of "Section 197 intangible" in § 197(d). While negating the incentive for the kind of carve-outs made by taxpayers in cases like *Newark Morning Ledger*, however, § 197 creates new planning considerations for buyers and sellers.

Section 197 eliminates much of the historic tension between buyers and sellers regarding allocations to goodwill and going concern. To the extent amounts are allocated to those items, buyers benefit from the opportunity § 197 affords for amortization. Note that as amortizable items, goodwill and going concern value are § 1231 items in the hands of the buyers. Because the goodwill and going concern value were self-created items of the sellers, those items are capital assets with respect to the sellers. There sellers therefore are content with their continued right to claim capital gain treatment for amounts allocated to those items.

Nonetheless, buyers may view the 15-year amortization period as relatively long and prefer to allocate the purchase price to depreciable assets with shorter lives, thus accelerating the write-off of the purchase price of the business. For similar reasons, the buyer may not find allocations to covenants not to compete as attractive as such allocations might have been before the 1993 legislation. For example, while historically a 5-year covenant not to compete was amortized on a pro rata basis over a 5-year period, § 197 now requires that amortization to occur over a 15-year period.

Sellers, of course, welcome the diminished tax advantages to buyers of allocations to covenants not to compete. Presumably, it will be easier for sellers to negotiate what they believe is a more reasonable price (*i.e.*, a lower price) for their agreement not to compete. At the same time, sellers in some circumstances may be concerned about buyers' efforts to maximize allocations to depreciable assets with a short useful life, *e.g.*, 3-, 5-, or 7-year property. Because of recapture potential, increased allocation to such property might mean increased ordinary income. Review the § 1245 recapture rules discussed in Chapter 33.

Section 197 specifically excludes a number of intangibles from the 15-year amortization rule. Review § 197(e) carefully. For example, § 197(e)(4) excludes from § 197 treatment intangibles such as patents and copyrights which are not acquired as part of the acquisition of assets constituting a trade or business or substantial portion thereof. Section 197(e)(3) excludes certain computer software from the 15-year amortization rule. This exclusion of computer software must be read in conjunction with the very favorable depreciation treatment accorded software under § 167(f), which provides that computer software excluded from § 197 will be depreciated over a 36-month period using the straight line method of depreciation.

Section 197(c)(2) also excludes certain self-created § 197 intangibles from "amortizable § 197 intangible" status. Therefore, if self-created, goodwill and going concern value are not amortizable under § 197. Thus, for example, advertising expenditures, which may provide a benefit extending beyond the taxable year, will not be subject to the rules of § 197 but will generally continue to be deducted in the year incurred or paid. Likewise, the exception for self-created intangibles is inapplicable to a covenant not to compete. Review § 197(c)(2).

Assume a buyer, having appropriately allocated a portion of the purchase price to each § 197 intangible acquired in the purchase of a business, subsequently sells one of the intangibles at a loss. May the buyer claim a loss on the sale? Section 197(f)(1) denies loss recognition on the sale if the taxpayer still retains the other amortizable § 197 intangibles. Instead, the loss will be allocated among the remaining intangibles, thus increasing their basis.

Section 197(f)(7) treats amortizable § 197 intangibles as properties "of a character subject to the allowance for depreciation under § 167." Thus, for example, if the sale of a § 197 intangible results in a gain to the taxpayer, the gain may be subject to the recapture rules of § 1245 and/or characterization under § 1231.

B.   Valuing Goodwill, Going Concern Value, and Covenants Not to Compete

Generally, the Service will respect the values established by contracting parties in their sales agreement, particularly where the interests of the parties are adverse. As a result, the allocation of the purchase price to the various tangible and intangible items transferred in a sale of a business should generally be negotiated by the parties and should be specifically reflected in their agreement. The Service, of course, cannot be precluded from attacking allocations in an agreement that have no basis in economic reality. *Concord Control Inc. v. Commissioner*, 78 T.C. 742, 745 (1982).

In 1986, Congress added § 1060 to the Code. This provision requires that the "residual method" of valuation be used in valuing goodwill and going concern value in "applicable asset acquisitions." An applicable asset acquisition is, essentially, the purchase of the assets of a trade or business. *See* § 1060(c). As its name suggests, the residual method calculates goodwill and going concern value as the excess of the purchase price over the aggregate fair market value of the tangible and identifiable intangible assets (other than goodwill or going concern value). In the Senate Finance Committee report, the reason for requiring the residual method was explained as follows:

> The committee is aware that the allocation of purchase price among the assets of a going business has been a troublesome area of the tax law. Purchase price allocations have been an endless source of controversy between the Internal Revenue Service and taxpayers, principally because of the difficulty of establishing the value of goodwill and going concern value. The Service lacks the resources to challenge allocations to goodwill or going concern value in all or even a substantial portion of the cases in which it would otherwise assert that the value of those assets is misstated.

> The committee is also concerned about the potential for abuse inherent in the sale of a going business where there is no agreement between the parties as to the value of specific assets. In many instances, the parties' allocations for tax reporting purposes are inconsistent, resulting in a whipsaw of the government. The committee expects that requiring both parties to use the residual method for allocating amounts to nonamortizable goodwill and going concern value may diminish some of this "whipsaw" potential.

S. Rep. No. 99-313, 99th Cong. 2d Sess, 253–54 (1986).

Regulations § 1.1060-1(c)(2) requires the seller and the purchaser each to allocate the consideration paid or received in a sales transaction among seven classes of assets (specified in Reg. § 1.338-6(b)) in the following order:

Class I: Cash and general deposit accounts;

Class II: Actively traded personal property as defined in § 1092(d), certificates of deposit and foreign currency;

Class III: Assets the taxpayer marks to market at least annually for Federal income tax purposes and debt instruments (including accounts receivable, but excluding certain contingent or convertible debt instruments, and also excluding debt instruments issued by related persons);

Class IV: Stock in trade of the taxpayer or other property of a kind which would properly be included in the inventory of taxpayer if on hand at the close of the taxable year, property primarily held for sale to customers in the ordinary course of a trade or business;

Class V: All assets not included in I, II, III, IV, VI, or VII;

Class VI: All section 197 intangibles except goodwill or going concern value; and

Class VII: Goodwill and going concern value.

As the legislative history of § 1060 reflects, Congress was concerned the government might be whipsawed as a result of inconsistent reporting by taxpayers. This was often the case where parties did not allocate the purchase price to the various assets of the business. In such cases, it was not uncommon for a buyer to allocate less to goodwill than a seller. Even where the parties had made an allocation of the purchase price in the agreement, it was not uncommon for parties to report the transaction in a manner inconsistent with that allocation.

For example, in *Brams v. Commissioner*, T.C. Memo. 1980-584, the taxpayer sold his commercial salad-making business pursuant to an agreement which allocated $80,000 of the purchase price to the name "Salad House, Inc." and its accompanying goodwill, $150,000 to a ten-year covenant not to compete, and the remaining $130,000 of the purchase price to the other assets of the business. Instead of reporting the $150,000 as allocable to the covenant not to compete, the taxpayer reported it as allocable to business assets, primarily goodwill. The issue before the court was whether the taxpayer was bound by the allocations in the agreement. The court noted the two different standards that have evolved to resolve this issue. Under the rule of *Danielson v. Commissioner*, 378 F.2d 771, 775 (3d Cir. 1967), a taxpayer can avoid the tax consequences of his agreement if he can establish that its terms are unenforceable because of mistake, undue influence, fraud, duress, etc. The Tax Court refused to follow this rule, and instead applied the "strong proof" rule, which requires the taxpayer to establish that the allocation was not intended by the parties or that the allocation did not reflect economic reality. The court concluded that on the facts there was evidence establishing both intent and economic reality.

Section 1060(a), however, binds the parties to any written allocation of consideration or written agreement regarding fair market value of any asset, unless the Treasury determines the allocation or value is inappropriate. The legislative history of this provision indicates that while the Service is free to challenge any allocation or the valuation of any asset, particularly where the parties' interests are not adverse, the parties themselves are bound by their written agreement, unless they are "able to refute the allocation or valuation under the standards set forth in the *Danielson* case." House Ways and Means Comm. Rep., H.R. 5835, p. 103. *See* Reg. §§ 1.1060-1(c)(4), 1.1060-1(d) Ex. 2. Apparently, the "strong proof" test is no longer to be applied to written agreements in § 1060(a) acquisitions. Thus, while written allocation of the purchase price is recommended, the parties must consider carefully the tax consequences of their allocations. Notice the obligation imposed by § 1060(b) on the buyer and the seller to file information returns regarding allocations to various assets which are part of a sale. Query: what obligation, if any, does counsel for one party have to explain the tax implications of a proposed allocation to the other party? What if it is clear to counsel that the other party does not understand the tax significance of the allocation and is not represented by counsel who does?

As noted, the legislative history of § 1060 makes it clear that the Service may challenge the taxpayer's determination of the value of any asset. For example, a taxpayer may place an unduly high value on goodwill or another depreciable or amortizable asset, thus hoping to secure some tax advantage. The Service, however, may challenge that value using any appropriate means.

C. Sale-Leaseback

Chapter 13 briefly discussed whether a given transaction should be characterized as a sale or a lease. *See, e.g., Starr's Estate v. Commissioner*, 274 F.2d 294 (9th Cir. 1959). Casting a purchase as a lease could prove beneficial to a taxpayer, if as a "lessee" he would be entitled to claim rental deductions in excess of the depreciation and interest deductions available to a purchaser of the same property. Sale-leaseback arrangements raise comparable characterization questions. Will the sale of property to the purchaser, followed by the leaseback of the property to the seller, be respected as such? Or will the sale-leaseback be recharacterized as a tax-free exchange or as a mere financing arrangement? If respected, the sale-leaseback may provide a valuable mechanism for shifting tax benefits from one taxpayer to another. The seller-lessee in such a situation may claim a deduction for rent that may be greater than the tax deductions available to it as an owner of the property. Assume, for example, a tract of land, a nondepreciable asset, is the subject of a sale-leaseback. Assume also the seller-lessee has substantial net operating losses and cannot use other available deductions, *e.g.*, the deduction for real property taxes. The sale-leaseback in such circumstances may enable the seller-lessee to raise a substantial amount of cash, continue to possess and use the property, and pay "rent" lower than the interest expense that might be incurred if standard financing had been sought. Obviously, the Service is anxious to prevent the shifting of tax benefits and the resulting decrease in tax revenues which can result from such arrangements. The Service may recharacterize sale-leaseback transactions in various ways.

1. Sale-Leaseback Characterized as Financing Arrangement

A taxpayer owning business property may need substantial cash to finance business operations. She could, of course, borrow the funds, using the business property as security. This method of acquiring necessary financing may not be desirable for a variety of reasons, including local usury laws, adverse impact of debt on the borrower's financial statements, etc. Alternatively, she might sell the property to the would-be lender and then lease the property back with an option to purchase. This method enables the taxpayer to raise the cash necessary to continue its business while retaining possession of the property.

Assuming a sale-leaseback of depreciable property, who is entitled to claim the depreciation deductions? That question was considered by the Supreme Court in *Helvering v. Lazarus & Co.*, 308 U.S. 252 (1939), *aff'g* 101 F.2d 728 (6th Cir. 1939). There the taxpayer deeded developed real property to a bank and leased the property back from the bank under a 99-year renewable lease with an option to buy. The taxpayer sought to deduct the depreciation allowable on the leased property;

the Service argued the bank as title holder was entitled to the depreciation deductions. The Supreme Court affirmed the decision of the Sixth Circuit disregarding the sale-leaseback form of the transaction and recharacterizing it as merely a financing arrangement akin to a mortgage. The evidence established that the "sale" proceeds amounted to about half of the actual worth of the property and that the parties understood the arrangement to be a financing arrangement. The rental payments were viewed as simply constituting interest payments on a loan. Under these circumstances, the Court concluded that the taxpayer, and not the title holder, was entitled to the depreciation deductions.

In *Frank Lyon Co. v. U.S.*, included in the materials, the Supreme Court respected a sale-leaseback and allowed the taxpayer to claim both depreciation and interest deductions. What factors did the court emphasize as indicating the existence of a genuine sale followed by a leaseback? What guidance does the *Frank Lyon* decision provide for taxpayers contemplating sale-leaseback arrangements?

2. Sale-Leaseback Characterized as a Tax-Free Exchange

Assume a situation in which a corporate taxpayer owns real estate which it uses in its day-to-day operations. The real estate has a current fair market value which is less than its adjusted basis. The taxpayer seeks additional operating capital and decides to sell the property for its fair market value and then immediately lease the property back for a period in excess of thirty years. If this arrangement is respected, the taxpayer will have raised the desired amount of cash and will also be entitled to claim a loss deduction on the transfer of the property. As a result of the leaseback, taxpayer's possession and use of the property will continue uninterrupted. The Service, as discussed previously, could attack this arrangement, claiming it constitutes a mere financing arrangement. Another route of attack may also be available: treatment of the arrangement as a tax-free exchange under § 1031.

The Service first raised the § 1031 argument in a sale-leaseback situation in *Century Electric Co. v. Commissioner*, 192 F.2d 155 (8th Cir. 1951), *cert. denied*, 342 U.S. 954 (1952). There, Century Electric Company transferred its foundry building to William Jewell College. Under the sales agreement, William Jewell paid $150,000 cash and gave Century Electric a lease which enabled Century Electric to continue using the property for a 95-year period. The foundry building had an adjusted basis of approximately $532,000 and a fair market value considerably less than that. The taxpayer claimed a deductible loss of almost $382,000 on the transaction.

The Service, relying on Reg. § 1.1031(a)-1(c), argued that the transaction constituted a like kind exchange. That regulation provides that a lease with 30 or more years to run and a fee interest in real estate are like kind properties. The court agreed with the Service, noting that the purpose of § 1031 was to negate gain or loss in transactions where the taxpayer is in essentially the same economic position after the transaction as before. With respect to Century Electric's economic position, the court reasoned:

> It is undisputed that the foundry property before the transaction was held by petitioner for productive use in petitioner's business. After the transaction, the same property was held by the petitioner for the same use

in the same business. Both before and after the transaction the property was necessary to the continued operation of petitioner's business. The only change brought by the transaction was in the estate or interest of petitioner in the foundry property.

Id. at 159–60.

A more recent sale-leaseback case in which the Service argued § 1031 is *Leslie Co. v. Commissioner*, included in the materials. Unlike the taxpayer in *Century Electric*, the taxpayer in this case successfully overcame the Service's challenge. What were the critical factual differences in the two cases? Would you expect the Service to raise the § 1031 argument in a situation where gain was realized in the transaction?

WILLIAMS v. McGOWAN
United States Court of Appeals, Second Circuit
152 F.2d 570 (1945)

L. HAND, CIRCUIT JUDGE: . . .

Williams, the taxpayer, and one Reynolds, had for many years been engaged in the hardware business in the City of Corning, New York. On the 20th of January, 1926, they formed a partnership, of which Williams was entitled to two-thirds of the profits, and Reynolds, one-third. They agreed that on February 1, 1925, the capital invested in the business had been $118,082.05, of which Reynolds had a credit of $29,029.03, and Williams, the balance — $89,053.02. At the end of every business year, on February 1st, Reynolds was to pay to Williams interest upon the amount of the difference between his share of the capital and one-third of the total as shown by the Inventory; and upon withdrawal of one party the other was to have the privilege of buying the other's interest as it appeared on the books. The business was carried on through the firm's fiscal year, ending January 31, 1940, in accordance with this agreement, and thereafter until Reynolds' death on July 18th of that year. Williams settled with Reynolds' executrix on September 6th in an agreement by which he promised to pay her $12,187.90, and to assume all liabilities of the business; and he did pay her $2,187.98 in cash at once, and $10,000 on the 10th of the following October. On September 17th of the same year, Williams sold the business as a whole to the Corning Building Company for $63,926.28 — its agreed value as of February 1, 1940 — "plus an amount to be computed by multiplying the gross sales of the business from the first day of February, 1940 to the 28th day of September, 1940," by an agreed fraction. This value was made up of cash of about $8,100, receivables of about $7,000, fixtures of about $800, and a merchandise inventory of about $49,000, less some $1,000 for bills payable. To this was added about $6,000 credited to Williams for profits under the language just quoted, making a total of nearly $70,000. Upon this sale Williams suffered a loss upon his original two-thirds of the business, but he made a small gain upon the one-third which he had bought from Reynolds' executrix; and in his income tax return he entered both as items of "ordinary income," and not as transactions in "capital assets." This the Commissioner disallowed and recomputed the tax accordingly; Williams paid the deficiency and sued to recover it in this action. The only question is whether the business was "capital assets" under § 117(a)(1) [now § 1221] of the Internal Revenue Code.

When Williams bought out Reynolds' interest, he became the sole owner of the business, the firm had ended upon any theory, and the situation for tax purposes was no other than if Reynolds had never been a partner at all, except that to the extent of one-third of the "amount realized" on Williams' sale to the Corning Company, his "basis" was different. . . . We have to decide only whether upon the sale of a going business it is to be comminuted into its fragments, and these are to be separately matched against the definition in § 117(a)(1), or whether the whole business is to be treated as if it were a single piece of property.

Our law has been sparing in the creation of juristic entities; it has never, for example, taken over the Roman "universitas facti";[1] and indeed for many years it fumbled uncertainly with the concept of a corporation. One might have supposed that partnership would have been an especially promising field in which to raise up an entity, particularly since merchants have always kept their accounts upon that basis. Yet there too our law resisted at the price of great and continuing confusion; and, even when it might be thought that a statute admitted, if it did not demand, recognition of the firm as an entity, the old concepts prevailed. And so, even though we might agree that under the influence of the Uniform Partnership Act a partner's interest in the firm should be treated as indivisible, and for that reason a "capital asset" within § 117(a)(1), we should be chary about extending further so exotic a jural concept. Be that as it may, in this instance the section itself furnishes the answer. It starts in the broadest way by declaring that all "property" is "capital assets," and then makes three exceptions. The first is "stock in trade . . . or other property of a kind which would properly be included in the inventory"; next comes "property held . . . primarily for sale to customers"; and finally, property "used in the trade or business of a character which is subject to . . . allowance for depreciation." In the face of this language, although it may be true that a "stock in trade," taken by itself, should be treated as a "universitas facti," by no possibility can a whole business be so treated; and the same is true as to any property within the other exceptions. Congress plainly did mean to comminute the elements of a business; plainly it did not regard the whole as "capital assets."

As has already appeared, Williams transferred to the Corning Company "cash," "receivables," "fixtures" and a "merchandise inventory." "Fixtures" are not capital because they are subject to a depreciation allowance; the inventory, as we have just seen, is expressly excluded. So far as appears, no allowance was made for "good-will"; but, even if there had been, we held in *Haberle Crystal Springs Brewing Company v. Clarke, Collector*, 2 Cir., 30 F.2d 219, that "good-will" was a depreciable intangible. It is true that the Supreme Court reversed that judgment but it based its decision only upon the fact that there could be no allowance for the depreciation of "good-will" in a brewery, a business condemned by the Eighteenth Amendment. There can of course be no gain or loss in the transfer of cash; and,

---

[1] "By 'universitas facti' is meant a number of things of the same kind which are regarded as a whole; *e.g.*, a herd, a stock of wares." Mackeidey, Roman Law § 162.

although Williams does appear to have made a gain of $1072.71 upon the "receivables," the point has not been argued that they are not subject to a depreciation allowance. That we leave open for decision by the district court, if the parties cannot agree. The gain or loss upon every other item should be computed as an item in ordinary income.

Judgment reversed.

FRANK, CIRCUIT JUDGE (dissenting in part).

I agree that it is irrelevant that the business was once owned by a partnership. For when the sale to the Corning Company occurred, the partnership was dead, had become merely a memory, a ghost. To say that the sale was of the partnership's assets would, then, be to indulge in animism.

But I do not agree that we should ignore what the parties to the sale, Williams and the Corning Company, actually did. They did not arrange for a transfer to the buyer, as if in separate bundles, of the several ingredients of the business. They contracted for the sale of the entire business as a going concern. Here is what they said in their agreement: "The party of the first part agrees to sell and the party of the second part agrees to buy, *all of the right, title and interest of the said party of the first part in and to the hardware business* now being conducted by the said party of the first part, *including* cash on hand and on deposit in the First National Bank & Trust Company of Corning in the A.F. Williams Hardware Store account, in accounts receivable, bills receivable, notes receivable, merchandise and fixtures, including two G.M. Trucks, good will and all other assets of every kind and description used in and about said business. . . . Said party of the first part agrees not to engage in the hardware business within a radius of twenty-five miles from the City of Corning, New York, for a period of ten years from the 1st day of October, 1940."

To carve up this transaction into distinct sales — of cash, receivables, fixtures, trucks, merchandise, and good will — is to do violence to the realities. I do not think Congress intended any such artificial result. . . .

ANNABELLE CANDY CO. v. COMMISSIONER
United States Court of Appeals, Ninth Circuit
314 F.2d 1 (1962)

BARNES, CIRCUIT JUDGE:

Though other issues were before the Tax Court, the only question here presented is whether the Tax Court correctly held that petitioner-appellant was not entitled to deduct from its federal income taxes amounts represented as the amortized cost of a restrictive covenant.

The facts as found by the Tax Court (many of which were stipulated) which are here pertinent may be summarized as follows:

For several years prior to 1955, Sam Altshuler and Fred Sommers engaged in the business, as equal partners, of manufacturing and selling candy. They incorporated taxpayer under the laws of California in November 1954 and began doing business in corporate form on January 1, 1955. Each owned fifty per cent of taxpayer's outstanding common stock. Altshuler became president and Sommers became vice president, and both were directors and actively conducted taxpayer's business.

Virtually the entire volume of taxpayer's sales was dependent on one ten-cent candy bar marketed under the name of "Rocky Road." This name was taken from the type of marshmallow and chocolate candy which was well known in the candy industry and for years had been sold in bulk form in candy stores. The recipe or formula for manufacturing rocky road candy and the name "Rocky Road" are not subject to protection from competitors by registration in any manner, whether by patent, trade-mark, or trade name. There are, however, different methods of making rocky road candy which are not generally known or applied throughout the candy industry. Taxpayer employed unique production methods in manufacturing its candy bar which were valuable to taxpayer, and it marketed its candy bar in a distinctive red wrapper. Both Altshuler and Sommers had full knowledge of taxpayer's unique production methods.

Differences arose between Altshuler and Sommers and they finally decided, in the latter part of 1955, that they no longer could work together. Court action to dissolve taxpayer was a possibility. However, in December of 1955, attorneys for Altshuler and Sommers began negotiations for a method of eliminating one of the clients from participation in the business, but at the same time preserving the business. The attorneys mutually agreed that it would be best for their principals and for the business if a purchase and sale arrangement could be agreed upon without court action.

The agreement provided for a total consideration of $115,000 to be paid in installments to Sommers by taxpayer. Sommers agreed, *inter alia*, to transfer his fifty percent stock interest, to retire from active participation as an officer and director, and not to compete nor engage in any activities which might be prejudicial to taxpayer's business for a period of five years.

The restrictive covenants were first discussed by the parties and their counsel after the purchase price of $115,000 for the stock interest had been preliminarily agreed upon and when safeguards for the buyer and security for the seller were then considered. The agreement of May 15, 1956 made no allocation of any portion of the total consideration of $115,000 to the restrictive covenants. Prior to May 15, 1956, there were no discussions between Altshuler and Sommers or their respective attorneys concerning the subject of an allocation of the purchase price to be made to the covenants. Taxpayer's dollar allocation to the covenant not to compete was made subsequent to May 15, 1956, without the knowledge or consent of Sommers.

No separate or severable consideration was bargained for, or paid, for the covenant not to compete contained in the agreement of May 15, 1956.

In its 1956 income tax return, taxpayer allocated $80,554.67 of the $115,000 purchase price to the covenant not to compete and began amortization of the $80,554.67 over the covenant's five-year term at a rate of $16,110.93 per year, claiming $10,069.93 for the remainder of 1956, and the full $16,110.93 for 1957. The Commissioner disallowed these claimed deductions, determining that the entire $115,000 was paid for Sommers' stock interest, that no portion was allocable to the covenant not to compete, and that, accordingly, taxpayer was not entitled to amortization deductions for the taxable years.

The Tax Court sustained the Commissioner's deficiency determinations on the basis of its finding that no separate or severable consideration was bargained for or paid for the covenant not to compete.

. . . .

The Commissioner concedes that the depreciation deduction authorized by § 167(a)(1) of the Internal Revenue Code of 1954 for property used in trade or business applies to a covenant not to compete for a definite term. But, contends the Commissioner, the deduction, amortized over the term of the covenant, is "of the amount paid (or other basis) for the covenant. . . . [And,] if a contract contains such a covenant but nothing has been paid for it, there is nothing to be deducted." It is, therefore, the Commissioner's position that:

> [A] covenant not to compete contained in a contract has no tax effect as to either the vendor or the vendee unless (1) the parties *treat* the covenant as an item for which a *separate* amount is paid the vendee and (2) such treatment is in fact realistic. The first requirement — in effect, a showing that the parties intended separate payment for the covenant — will generally be satisfied if the contract allocates a part of the consideration to the covenant.

And, according to the Commissioner, "we are [here] primarily concerned with the *first* requirement, *i.e.*, that the parties treat the covenant as an item for which a separate amount is paid by the vendee."

The Commissioner's position, otherwise stated, is:

> We do not contend that the presence or absence of an express dollar allocation to the covenant not to compete is a *controlling* test *per se*. What we contend is that the *evidence* must show that the parties treated the covenant as a separate item for which consideration was paid. . . . (Italics the Commissioner's.)

The Tax Court's findings indicate that Sommers' covenant not to compete was contained in the contract dated May 15, 1956. But, according to the findings of the Tax Court, the parties had not discussed the covenant until *after* the purchase price had been *preliminarily* agreed upon and when safeguards to the parties were being discussed. The Tax Court therefore held there was no convincing proof the parties treated the covenant "in a separate and distinct manner," relying on *United Finance and Thrift Corporation of Tulsa*, 31 T.C. 278, 285, *affirmed* (4 Cir. 1960), 282 F.2d 919, *certiorari denied*, 366 U.S. 902, and,

> Thus, we were unable to find as petitioner contends that it was the intent of the agreement of May 15, 1956 that a portion of the $115,000 which petitioner agreed therein to pay Sommers was in consideration for Sommers' promise not to compete in the candy business. . . .

In the *United Finance* case, *supra*, cited by the Tax Court, the taxpayers claimed they were entitled to amortize the cost of covenants not to compete over their term; in the *United Finance* case the contracts, wherein the covenants were given, contained a specific allocation made to the cost of the covenants. Yet, there, the Fourth Circuit affirmed the Tax Court's decision that part of the cost allocated in the contract to the covenants should be attributed to the purchase of good will; the Fourth Circuit also affirmed the Tax Court's allocation between the cost attributable to the covenants and to the purchase of good will, which the Tax Court made according to its best judgment under the principles of *Cohan v. Commissioner*, 2 Cir. 1930, 39 F.2d 540.

Thus, we read the *United Finance* case as holding that the courts may look behind the contract. The form of the contract itself does not necessarily control. This interpretation of the *United Finance* case makes it entirely consistent with this court's recent decision in *Schulz v. C.I.R.*, 1961, 294 F.2d 52. In *Schulz*, this court said:

> The rules enunciated herein, namely, that in proper cases the commissioner can go beyond the formal dealings of the parties to see if these forms reflect meaningful substance — are elementary in the law of taxation and find support in the Supreme Court [Citations]. (294 F.2d at 56.)

In the *Schulz* case, the Tax Court also found a covenant not to compete nonseverable. There it was nonseverable from good will; here it was found nonseverable from Sommers' stock interest in taxpayer. The Tax Court apparently applied the same test for "severability" in both cases.

In *Schulz*, this court said:

> The determination of whether or not the covenant is "severable" or "nonseverable" has no probative value in determining whether or not it should be considered as a surrender of income — and hence a covenant — or a component of the business which was sold — and hence part of the assets.

> The difficulty may have arisen from confusion with a factual issue which is probative of the issue of whether or not there is a genuine covenant. If there is reason to believe that the business has prospered because of the character or the reputation of the proprietor or partner — the friendly bartender or the trusted stockbroker are examples — this would tend to show that a genuine business reason prompted the covenant. Such reputation or character would also form part of the good will. However, the question is one of fact and not one of classification as "severable" or "nonseverable." (294 F.2d at 56.)

In the case at bar (unlike the *Schulz* case), the Tax Court found that the covenant not to compete played a very real part in the negotiation of a final contract between the parties. The record also shows the uncontradicted testimony of taxpayer's president (Altshuler) that taxpayer "needed [the covenants] very badly." And, though the Commissioner urges facts by which he attempts to show that Sommers' covenant not to compete had little value, the evidence shows the contrary.

The taxpayer was a successful enterprise. As mentioned above, taxpayer employed unique methods in the production of its candy bar. And Sommers was generally in charge of the production of taxpayer's candy bar while he was associated with taxpayer. Furthermore, Altshuler testified that he himself had failed several times in the candy business, including twice in making Rocky Road candy bars. Thus, Altshuler's uncontradicted conclusion that he "needed [the covenants] very badly" has substantial basis in the record.

The fact that a preliminary purchase price had been agreed upon before the parties began discussing restrictive covenants does not necessarily preclude such covenants from being of value; nor does it preclude the court from allocating a value — to such covenants when no specific allocation is made by the parties in the contract. . . .

In the *Schulz* case this court also said:

> Of course, it is clear that we do not agree with the dicta found in *Hamlin's Trust* case regarding the covenant as severable or nonseverable. . . .

The *Hamlin Trust* case is one of the cases which the Commissioner here cites as announcing the correct "severability" rule. . . .

In the purchase agreement involved in the case before us, there is no allocation of consideration to the covenant not to compete. While this is pretty good evidence that no such allocation was intended it is not conclusive on the parties as would be the case if there had been an express affirmance or disavowal in the agreement. But the petitioner, which was asking for a redetermination of a tax deficiency, had the burden of proving that, notwithstanding the lack of any recital to that effect in the agreement, the parties intended to allocate consideration to the covenant. The Tax Court held that petitioner failed to sustain that burden of proof.

It is true, as the Tax Court found, that the covenant not to compete played a very real part in the negotiation of a final contract between the parties, and was a valuable benefit to the petitioner. But if the parties did not intend that a part of the purchase price be allocated to this important and valuable covenant, that intention must be respected. Unless respected, the tax consequences which they contemplated as incident to the benefits and burdens of the contract would be disturbed.

There was substantial evidence tending to show that no such allocation was intended. The desirability of a restrictive covenant was not discussed until the purchase price of $115,000 was settled by preliminary agreement. There was never any discussion of an allocation of part of that price as consideration for the covenant.

Before the agreement was executed Sam Altshuler was advised by petitioner's bookkeeper that an allocation should be made in the agreement or it would not be recognized for tax purposes, yet no allocation was therein made. After execution of the agreement petitioner made a unilateral allocation to its advantage and to the disadvantage of Sommers, without the latter's knowledge or consent. These circumstances warrant the inference that Altshuler purposely refrained from bringing up during the negotiations this matter concerning which he was fully informed because he was afraid Sommers would not agree.

We think that in this approach to the basic legal problem of the case the Commissioner admittedly was concerned "primarily" with whether there existed a separate sum to be paid for the covenant, and whether the covenant was "severable." Agreeing that a mere dollar designation is not controlling *per se*, we find the Commissioner applying again the weight of the evidence rule to determine if the parties agreed to the severability of the sum paid for the covenant not to compete, rather than the *intent* of the parties that *some* part of the contract, severable or unseverable, was paid for the covenant.

Did the parties, not preliminarily, but when they signed this agreement *intend* to allocate a portion of the purchase price to the covenant not to compete? If so, Altshuler should be allowed to obtain the tax benefits flowing therefrom. If not, Sommers should be allowed to obtain such tax benefits.

But that determination must be made from a consideration of conflicting facts, uninfluenced by the Tax Court's belief that "primarily" the question is whether or not the contract was "severable"; or whether the covenant was "treated in a separate and distinct manner."

We are left with the firm conviction that the Tax Court erred in placing too much emphasis on an erroneous theory of law. A mistake has been made, not in judging facts, but in applying law. . . . The parties are entitled to a clear cut decision as to what their intent was, as evidenced by the agreement and all the surrounding circumstances.

We remand the matter to the Tax Court. . . .

FRANK LYON CO. v. UNITED STATES
United States Supreme Court
435 U.S. 561 (1978)

Mr. Justice Blackmun delivered the opinion of the Court.

This case concerns the federal income tax consequences of a sale-and-leaseback in which petitioner Frank Lyon Company (Lyon) took title to a building under construction by Worthen Bank & Trust Company (Worthen) of Little Rock, Ark., and simultaneously leased the building back to Worthen for long-term use as its headquarters and principal banking facility.

Lyon is a closely held Arkansas corporation engaged in the distribution of home furnishings, primarily Whirlpool and RCA electrical products. Worthen in 1965 was an Arkansas-chartered bank and a member of the Federal Reserve System. Frank Lyon was Lyon's majority shareholder and board chairman; he also served on Worthen's board. Worthen at that time began to plan the construction of a multistory bank and office building to replace its existing facility in Little Rock. . . .

Worthen initially hoped to finance, to build, and to own the proposed facility at a total cost of $9 million for the site, building, and adjoining parking deck. . . . [Worthen was precluded by Arkansas and federal banking laws and regulations from building the building itself. Ed.]

Worthen therefore was forced to seek an alternative solution that would provide it with the use of the building, satisfy the state and federal regulators, and attract the necessary capital. In September 1967 it proposed a sale-and-leaseback arrangement. The State Bank Department and the Federal Reserve System approved this approach, but the Department required that Worthen possess an option to purchase the leased property at the end of the 15th year of the lease at a set price, and the federal regulator required that the building be owned by an independent third party.

Worthen then obtained a commitment from New York Life Insurance Company to provide $7,140,000 in permanent mortgage financing on the building, conditioned upon its approval of the titleholder. At this point Lyon entered the negotiations and it, too, made a proposal.

In the meantime, on September 15, before Lyon was selected, Worthen itself began construction.

In May 1968 Worthen, Lyon, City Bank, and New York Life executed complementary and interlocking agreements under which the building was sold by Worthen to Lyon as it was constructed, and Worthen leased the completed building back from Lyon.

1. Agreements between Worthen and Lyon. Worthen and Lyon executed a ground lease, a sales agreement, and a building lease.

Under the ground lease dated May 1, 1968, App. 366, Worthen leased the site to Lyon for 76 years and 7 months through November 30, 2044. The first 19 months were the estimated construction period. The ground rents payable by Lyon to Worthen were $50 for the first 26 years and 7 months and thereafter in quarterly payments:

         12/1/94 through 11/30/99 (5 years) — $100,000 annually

         12/1/99 through 11/30/04 (5 years) — $150,000 annually

         12/1/04 through 11/30/09 (5 years) — $200,000 annually

         12/1/09 through 11/30/34 (25 years) — $250,000 annually

         12/1/34 through 11/30/44 (10 years) — $10,000 annually

Under the sales agreement dated May 19, 1968, . . . Worthen agreed to sell the building to Lyon, and Lyon agreed to buy it, piece by piece as it was constructed, for a total price not to exceed $7,640,000, in reimbursements to Worthen for its expenditures for the construction of the building. [Lyon ultimately invested $500,000 of his money and New York Life financed the balance of the purchase price.]

Under the building lease dated May 1, 1968, . . . Lyon leased the building back to Worthen for a primary term of 25 years from December 1, 1969, with options in Worthen to extend the lease for eight additional 5-year terms, a total of 65 years. During the period between the expiration of the building lease (at the latest, November 30, 2034, if fully extended) and the end of the ground lease on November 30, 2044, full ownership, use, and control of the building were Lyon's, unless, of course, the building had been repurchased by Worthen. . . . Worthen was not obligated to pay rent under the building lease until completion of the building. For the first 11 years of the lease, that is, until November 30, 1980, the stated quarterly rent was $145,581.03 ($582,324.12 for the year). For the next 14 years, the quarterly rent was $153,289.32 ($613,157.28 for the year) and for the option periods the rent was $300,000 a year, payable quarterly. . . . The total rent for the building over the 25-year primary term of the lease thus was $14,989,767.24. That rent equaled the principal and interest payments that would amortize the $7,140,000 New York Life mortgage loan over the same period. When the mortgage was paid off at the end of the primary term, the annual building rent, if Worthen extended the lease, came down to the stated $300,000. Lyon's net rentals from the building would be further reduced by the increase in ground rent Worthen would receive from Lyon during the extension.

The building lease was a "net lease," under which Worthen was responsible for all expenses usually associated with the maintenance of an office building, including repairs, taxes, utility charges, and insurance, and was to keep the premises in good condition, excluding, however, reasonable wear and tear.

Finally, under the lease, Worthen had the option to repurchase the building at the following times and prices:

> 11/30/80 (after 11 years) — $6,325,169.85
>
> 11/30/84 (after 15 years) — $5,432,607.32
>
> 11/30/89 (after 20 years) — $4,187,328.04
>
> 11/30/94 (after 25 years) — $2,145,935.00

These repurchase option prices were the sum of the unpaid balance of the New York Life mortgage, Lyon's $500,000 investment, and 6% interest compounded on that investment.

2. Construction financing agreement. By agreement dated May 14, 1968, . . . City Bank agreed to lend Lyon $7,000,000 for the construction of the building. This loan was secured by a mortgage on the building and the parking deck, executed by Worthen as well as by Lyon, and an assignment by Lyon of its interests in the building lease and in the ground lease.

3. Permanent financing agreement. By Note Purchase Agreement dated May 1, 1968, New York Life agreed to purchase Lyon's $7,140,000 6 3/4% 25-year secured note to be issued upon completion of the building. Under this agreement Lyon warranted that it would lease the building to Worthen for a noncancelable term of at least 25 years under a net lease at a rent at least equal to the mortgage payments on the note. Lyon agreed to make quarterly payments of principal and interest equal to the rentals payable by Worthen during the corresponding primary term of the lease. . . . The security for the note was a first deed of trust and Lyon's assignment of its interests in the building lease and in the ground lease. . . . Worthen joined in the deed of trust as the owner of the fee and the parking deck.

In December 1969 the building was completed and Worthen took possession. At that time Lyon received the permanent loan from New York Life, and it discharged the interim loan from City Bank. The actual cost of constructing the office building and parking complex (excluding the cost of the land) exceeded $10,000,000.

C.

Lyon filed its federal income tax returns on the accrual and calendar year basis. On its 1969 return, Lyon accrued rent from Worthen for December. It asserted as deductions one month's interest to New York Life; one month's depreciation on the building; interest on the construction loan from City Bank; and sums for legal and other expenses incurred in connection with the transaction.

On audit of Lyon's 1969 return, the Commissioner of Internal Revenue determined that Lyon was "not the owner for tax purposes of any portion of the Worthen building," and ruled that "the income and expenses related to this building are not allowable . . . for Federal income tax purposes. . . . " He also added $2,298.15 to Lyon's 1969 income as "accrued interest income." This was the computed 1969 portion of a gain, considered the equivalent of interest income, the realization of which was based on the assumption that Worthen would exercise its option to buy the building after 11 years, on November 30, 1980, at the price stated in the lease, and on the additional determination that Lyon had "loaned" $500,000 to Worthen. In other words, the Commissioner determined that the sale-and-leaseback arrangement was a financing transaction in which Lyon loaned Worthen $500,000 and acted as a conduit for the transmission of principal and interest from Worthen to New York Life.

The United States Court of Appeals for the Eighth Circuit . . . held that the Commissioner correctly determined that Lyon was not the true owner of the building and therefore was not entitled to the claimed deductions. [536 F.2d 746 (1976)] It likened ownership for tax purposes to a "bundle of sticks" and undertook its own evaluation of the facts. It concluded, in agreement with the Government's contention, that Lyon "totes an empty bundle" of ownership sticks. *Id.*, at 751. It stressed the following: (a) The lease agreements circumscribed Lyon's right to profit from its investment in the building by giving Worthen the option to purchase for an amount equal to Lyon's $500,000 equity plus 6% compound interest and the assumption of the unpaid balance of the New York Life mortgage. (b) The option prices did not take into account possible appreciation of the value of the building or inflation. (c) Any award realized as a result of destruction or condemnation of the building in excess of the mortgage balance and the $500,000 would be paid to Worthen and not Lyon. (d) The building rental payments during the primary term were exactly equal to the mortgage payments. (e) Worthen retained control over the ultimate disposition of the building through its various options to repurchase and to renew the lease plus its ownership of the site. (f) Worthen enjoyed all benefits and bore all burdens incident to the operation and ownership of the building so that, in the Court of Appeals' view, the only economic advantages accruing to Lyon, in the event it were considered to be the true owner of the property, were income tax savings of approximately $1.5 million during the first 11 years of the arrangement. *Id.*, at 752–753. The court concluded, *id.*, at 753, that the transaction was "closely akin" to that in *Helvering v. Lazarus & Co.*, 308 U.S. 252 (1939). "In sum, the benefits, risks, and burdens which [Lyon] has incurred with respect to the Worthen building are simply too insubstantial to establish a claim to the status of owner for tax purposes. . . . The vice of the present lease is that all of [its] features have been employed in the same transaction with the cumulative effect of depriving [Lyon] of any significant ownership interest." 536 F.2d at 754. . . .

II.

This Court, almost 50 years ago, observed that "taxation is not so much concerned with the refinements of title as it is with actual command over the property taxed — the actual benefit for which the tax is paid." *Corliss v. Bowers*, 281 U.S. 376, 378 (1930). In a number of cases, the Court has refused to permit the transfer of formal legal title to shift the incidence of taxation attributable to ownership of property where the transferor continues to retain significant control over the property transferred. *E.g., Commissioner v. Sunnen*, 333 U.S. 591 (1948); *Helvering v. Clifford*, 309 U.S. 331 (1940). In applying this doctrine of substance over form, the Court has looked to the objective economic realities of a transaction rather than to the particular form the parties employed. The Court has never regarded "the simple expedient of drawing up papers," *Commissioner v. Tower*, 327 U.S. 280, 291 (1946), as controlling for tax purposes when the objective economic realities are to the contrary. "In the field of taxation, administrators of the laws, and the courts, are concerned with substance and realities, and formal written documents are not rigidly binding." *Helvering v. Lazarus & Co.*, 308 U.S. at 255. . . . Nor is the parties' desire to achieve a particular tax result necessarily relevant. *Commissioner v. Duberstein*, 363 U.S. 278, 286 (1960).

In the light of these general and established principles, the Government takes the position that the Worthen-Lyon transaction in its entirety should be regarded as a sham. The agreement as a whole, it is said, was only an elaborate financing scheme designed to provide economic benefits to Worthen and a guaranteed return to Lyon. The latter was but a conduit used to forward the mortgage payments, made under the guise of rent paid by Worthen to Lyon, on to New York Life as mortgagee. This, the Government claims, is the true substance of the transaction as viewed under the microscope of the tax laws. Although the arrangement was cast in sale-and-leaseback form, in substance it was only a financing transaction, and the terms of the repurchase options and lease renewals so indicate. It is said that Worthen could reacquire the building simply by satisfying the mortgage debt and paying Lyon its $500,000 advance plus interest, regardless of the fair market value of the building at the time; similarly, when the mortgage was paid off, Worthen could extend the lease at drastically reduced bargain rentals that likewise bore no relation to fair rental value but were simply calculated to pay Lyon its $500,000 plus interest over the extended term. Lyon's return on the arrangement in no event could exceed 6% compound interest. . . . Furthermore, the favorable option and lease renewal terms made it highly unlikely that Worthen would abandon the building after it in effect had "paid off" the mortgage. The Government implies that the arrangement was one of convenience which, if accepted on its face, would enable Worthen to deduct its payments to Lyon as rent and would allow Lyon to claim a deduction for depreciation, based on the cost of construction ultimately borne by Worthen, which Lyon could offset against other income, and to deduct mortgage interest that roughly would offset the inclusion of Worthen's rental payments in Lyon's income.

If, however, the Government argues, the arrangement was only a financing transaction under which Worthen was the owner of the building, Worthen's payments would be deductible only to the extent that they represented mortgage interest, and Worthen would be entitled to claim depreciation; Lyon would not be entitled to deductions for either mortgage interest or depreciation and it would not have to include Worthen's "rent" payments in its income because its function with respect to those payments was that of a conduit between Worthen and New York Life.

The Government places great reliance on *Helvering & Lazarus & Co., supra,* and claims it to be precedent that controls this case. The taxpayer there was a department store. The legal title of its three buildings was in a bank as trustee for land-trust certificate holders. When the transfer to the trustee was made, the trustee at the same time leased the buildings back to the taxpayer for 99 years, with option to renew and purchase. The Commissioner, in stark contrast to his posture in the present case, took the position that the statutory right to depreciation followed legal title. The Board of Tax Appeals, however, concluded that the transaction between the taxpayer and the bank in reality was a mortgage loan and allowed the taxpayer depreciation on the buildings. This Court, as had the Court of Appeals, agreed with that conclusion and affirmed. It regarded the "rent" stipulated in the leaseback as a promise to pay interest on the loan, and a "depreciation fund" required by the lease as an amortization fund designed to pay off the loan in the stated period. Thus, said the Court, the Board justifiably concluded that the transaction, although in written form a transfer of ownership with a leaseback, was actually a loan secured by the property involved.

The *Lazarus* case, we feel, is to be distinguished from the present one and is not controlling here. Its transaction was one involving only two (and not multiple) parties, the taxpayer-department store and the trustee-bank. The Court looked closely at the substance of the agreement between those two parties and rightly concluded that depreciation was deductible by the taxpayer despite the nomenclature of the instrument of conveyance and the leaseback. . . .

The present case, in contrast, involves three parties, Worthen, Lyon, and the finance agency. The usual simple two-party arrangement was legally unavailable to Worthen. Independent investors were interested in participating in the alternative available to Worthen, and Lyon itself (also independent from Worthen) won the privilege. Despite Frank Lyon's presence on Worthen's board of directors, the transaction, as it ultimately developed, was not a familial one arranged by Worthen, but one compelled by the realities of the restrictions imposed upon the bank. Had Lyon not appeared, another interested investor would have been selected. The ultimate solution would have been essentially the same. Thus, the presence of the third party, in our view, significantly distinguishes this case from *Lazarus* and removes the latter as controlling authority.

III.

There is no simple device available to peel away the form of this transaction and to reveal its substance. The effects of the transaction on all the parties were obviously different from those that would have resulted had Worthen been able simply to make a mortgage agreement with New York Life and to receive a $500,000 loan from Lyon. Then *Lazarus* would apply. Here, however, and most significantly, it was Lyon alone, and not Worthen, who was liable on the notes, first to City Bank, and then to New York Life. Despite the facts that Worthen had agreed to pay rent and that this rent equaled the amounts due from Lyon to New York Life, should anything go awry in the later years of the lease, Lyon was primarily liable. No matter how the transaction could have been devised otherwise, it remains a fact that as the agreements were placed in final form, the obligation on the notes fell squarely on Lyon. Lyon, an ongoing enterprise, exposed its very business well-being to this real and substantial risk.

The effect of this liability on Lyon is not just the abstract possibility that something will go wrong and that Worthen will not be able to make its payments. Lyon has disclosed this liability on its balance sheet for all the world to see. Its financial position was affected substantially by the presence of this long-term debt, despite the offsetting presence of the building as an asset. To the extent that Lyon has used its capital in this transaction it is less able to obtain financing for other business needs.

Other factors also reveal that the transaction cannot be viewed as anything more than a mortgage agreement between Worthen and New York Life and a loan from Lyon to Worthen. There is no legal obligation between Lyon and Worthen representing the $500,000 "loan" extended under the Government's theory. And the assumed 6% return on this putative loan — required by the audit to be recognized in the taxable year in question — will be realized only when and if Worthen exercises its options.

The Court of Appeals acknowledged that the rents alone, due after the primary term of the lease and after the mortgage has been paid, do not provide the simple 6% return which, the Government urges, Lyon is guaranteed, 536 F.2d at 752. Thus, if Worthen chooses not to exercise its options, Lyon is gambling that the rental value of the building during the last 10 years of the ground lease, during which the ground rent is minimal, will be sufficient to recoup its investment before it must negotiate again with Worthen regarding the ground lease. There are simply too many contingencies, including variations in the value of real estate, in the cost of money, and in the capital structure of Worthen, to permit the conclusion that the parties intended to enter into the transaction as structured in the audit and according to which the Government now urges they be taxed.

It is not inappropriate to note that the Government is likely to lose little revenue, if any, as a result of the shape given the transaction by the parties. No deduction was created that is not either matched by an item of income or that would not have been available to one of the parties if the transaction had been arranged differently. While it is true that Worthen paid Lyon less to induce it to enter into the transaction because Lyon anticipated the benefit of the depreciation deductions it would have as owner of the building, those deductions would have been equally available to Worthen had it retained title to the building. The Government so concedes. The fact that favorable tax consequences were taken into account by Lyon on entering into the transaction is no reason for disallowing those consequences. We cannot ignore the reality that the tax laws affect the shape of nearly every business transaction.

Lyon is not a corporation with no purpose other than to hold title to the bank building. It was not created by Worthen or even financed to any degree by Worthen.

The conclusion that the transaction is not a simple sham to be ignored does not, of course, automatically compel the further conclusion that Lyon is entitled to the items claimed as deductions. Nevertheless, on the facts, this readily follows. As has been noted, the obligations on which Lyon paid interest were its obligations alone, and it is entitled to claim deductions therefor under § 163(a) of the 1954 Code, 26 U.S.C. § 163(a).

As is clear from the facts, none of the parties to this sale-and-leaseback was the owner of the building in any simple sense. But it is equally clear that the facts focus upon Lyon as the one whose capital was committed to the building and as the party, therefore, that was entitled to claim depreciation for the compensation of that capital. The Government has based its contention that Worthen should be treated as the owner on the assumption that throughout the term of the lease Worthen was acquiring an equity in the property. In order to establish the presence of that growing equity, however, the Government is forced to speculate that one of the options will be exercised and that, if it is not, this is only because the rentals for the extended term are a bargain. We cannot indulge in such speculation. . . .

IV.

We recognize that the Government's position, and that taken by the Court of Appeals, is not without superficial appeal. One, indeed, may theorize that Frank Lyon's presence on the Worthen board of directors; Lyon's departure from its principal corporate activity into this unusual venture; the parallel between the payments under the building lease and the amounts due from Lyon on the New York Life mortgage; the provisions relating to condemnation or destruction of the property; the nature and presence of the several options available to Worthen; and the tax benefits, such as the use of double declining balance depreciation, that accrue to Lyon during the initial years of the arrangement, form the basis of an argument that Worthen should be regarded as the owner of the building and as the recipient of nothing more from Lyon that a $500,000 loan.

We, however, as did the District Court, find this theorizing incompatible with the substance and economic realities of the transaction: . . . Worthen's undercapitalization; Worthen's consequent inability, as a matter of legal restraint, to carry its building plans into effect by a conventional mortgage and other borrowing; the additional barriers imposed by the state and federal regulators; . . . the requirement, from the federal regulator, that the building be owned by an independent third party; the presence of several finance organizations seriously interested in participating in the transaction and in the resolution of Worthen's problem; . . . the three-party aspect of the transaction; Lyon's substantiality and its independence from Worthen; the fact that diversification was Lyon's principal motivation; Lyon's being liable alone on the successive notes to City Bank and New York Life; the reasonableness, as the District Court found, of the rentals and of the option prices; the substantiality of the purchase prices; Lyon's not being engaged generally in the business of financing; the presence of all building depreciation risks on Lyon; the risk, borne by Lyon, that Worthen might default or fail, as other banks have failed;

the facts that Worthen could "walk away" from the relationship at the end of the 25-year primary term, and probably would do so if the option price were more than the then-current worth of the building to Worthen; the inescapable fact that if the building lease were not extended, Lyon would be the full owner of the building, free to do with it as it chose; Lyon's liability for the substantial ground rent if Worthen decides not to exercise any of its options to extend; the absence of any understanding between Lyon and Worthen that Worthen would exercise any of the purchase options; the nonfamily and nonprivate nature of the entire transaction; and the absence of any differential in tax rates and of special tax circumstances for one of the parties — all convince us that Lyon has far the better of the case.

In so concluding, we emphasize that we are not condoning manipulation by a taxpayer through arbitrary labels and dealings that have no economic significance. Such, however, has not happened in this case.

In short, we hold that where, as here, there is a genuine multiple-party transaction with economic substance which is compelled or encouraged by business or regulatory realities, is imbued with tax-independent considerations, and is not shaped solely by tax-avoidance features that have meaningless labels attached, the Government should honor the allocation of rights and duties effectuated by the parties. Expressed another way, so long as the lessor retains significant and genuine attributes of the traditional lessor status, the form of the transaction adopted by the parties governs for tax purposes. What those attributes are in any particular case will necessarily depend upon its facts. It suffices to say that, as here, a sale-and-leaseback, in and of itself, does not necessarily operate to deny a taxpayer's claim for deductions.

The judgment of the Court of Appeals, accordingly, is reversed.

It is so ordered.

Mr. Justice Stevens, dissenting.

In my judgment the controlling issue in this case is the economic relationship between Worthen and petitioner, and matters such as the number of parties, their reasons for structuring the transaction in a particular way, and the tax benefits which may result, are largely irrelevant. The question whether a leasehold has been created should be answered by examining the character and value of the purported lessor's reversionary estate.

For a 25-year period Worthen has the power to acquire full ownership of the bank building by simply repaying the amounts, plus interest, advanced by the New York Life Insurance Company and petitioner. During that period, the economic relationship among the parties parallels exactly the normal relationship between an owner and two lenders, one secured by a first mortgage and the other by a second mortgage. If Worthen repays both loans, it will have unencumbered ownership of the property. What the character of this relationship suggests is confirmed by the economic value that the parties themselves have placed on the reversionary interest.

All rental payments made during the original 25-year term are credited against the option repurchase price, which is exactly equal to the unamortized cost of the financing. The value of the repurchase option is thus limited to the cost of the financing, and Worthen's power to exercise the option is cost free. Conversely, petitioner, the nominal owner of the reversionary estate, is not entitled to receive *any* value for the surrender of its supposed rights of ownership. Nor does it have any power to control Worthen's exercise of the option.

"It is fundamental that depreciation is not predicated upon ownership of property *but rather upon an investment in property.* No such investment exists when payments of the purchase price in accordance with the design of the parties yield no equity to the purchaser." *Estate of Franklin v. Commissioner*, 544 F.2d 1045, 1049 (CA9 1976) (citations omitted; emphasis in original). Here, the petitioner has, in effect, been guaranteed that it will receive its original $500,000 plus accrued interest. But that is all. It incurs neither the risk of depreciation, nor the benefit of possible appreciation. Under the terms of the sale-leaseback, it will stand in no better or worse position after the 11th year of the lease — when Worthen can first exercise its option to repurchase — whether the property has appreciated or depreciated. And this remains true throughout the rest of the 25-year period.

Petitioner has assumed only two significant risks. First, like any other lender, it assumed the risk of Worthen's insolvency. Second, it assumed the risk that Worthen might *not* exercise its option to purchase at or before the end of the original 25-year term. If Worthen should exercise that right *not* to repay, perhaps it would *then* be appropriate to characterize petitioner as the owner and Worthen as the lessee. But speculation as to what might happen in 25 years cannot justify the *present* characterization of petitioner as the owner of the building. Until Worthen has made a commitment either to exercise or not to exercise its option, I think the Government is correct in its view that petitioner is not the owner of the building for tax purposes. At present, since Worthen has the unrestricted right to control the residual value of the property for a price which does not exceed the cost of its unamortized financing, I would hold, as a matter of law, that it is the owner.

I therefore respectfully dissent.

LESLIE CO. v. COMMISSIONER
United States Court of Appeals, Third Circuit
539 F.2d 943 (1976)

GARTH, CIRCUIT JUDGE:

This appeal involves the tax consequences of a sale and leaseback arrangement. The question presented is whether the sale and leaseback arrangement constitutes an exchange of like-kind properties, on which no loss is recognized, or whether that transaction is governed by the general recognition provision of Int. Rev. Code [§ 1001(c)]. The Tax Court, on taxpayer's petition for a redetermination of deficiencies assessed against it by the Commissioner, held that the fee conveyance aspect of the transaction was a sale entitled to recognition, and that the leaseback was merely a condition precedent to that sale. The Tax Court thereby allowed the loss claimed by the taxpayer. For the reasons given below, we affirm.

I.

Leslie Company, the taxpayer, is a New Jersey corporation engaged in the manufacture and distribution of pressure and temperature regulators and instantaneous water heaters. Leslie, finding its Lyndhurst, New Jersey plant inadequate for its needs, decided to move to a new facility. To this end, in March 1967 Leslie purchased land in Parsippany, on which to construct a new manufacturing plant.

Leslie, however, was unable to acquire the necessary financing for the construction of its proposed $2,400,000 plant. Accordingly, on October 30, 1967, it entered into an agreement with the Prudential Life Insurance Company of America, whereby Leslie would erect a plant to specifications approved by Prudential and Prudential would then purchase the Parsippany property and building from Leslie. At the time of purchase Prudential would lease back the facility to Leslie. The property and improvements were to be conveyed to Prudential for $2,400,000 or the actual cost to Leslie, whichever amount was less.

The lease term was established at 30 years, at an annual net rental of $190,560, which was 7.94% of the purchase price. The lease agreement gave Leslie two 10-year options to renew. The annual net rental during each option period was $72,000, or 3% of the purchase price. The lease also provided that Leslie could offer to repurchase the property at five-year intervals, beginning with the 15th year of the lease, at specified prices as follows:

	(15th year	_____	$1,798,000
	(20th year	_____	$1,592,000
at the end of the	(25th year	_____	$1,386,000
	(30th year	_____	$1,180,000

Under the lease Prudential was entitled to all condemnation proceeds, net of any damages suffered by Leslie with respect to its trade fixtures and certain structural improvements, without any deduction for Leslie's leasehold interest.

Construction was completed in December, 1968, at a total cost to Leslie (including the purchase price of the land) of $3,187,414. On December 16, 1968 Leslie unconditionally conveyed the property to Prudential, as its contract required, for $2,400,000. At the same time, Leslie and Prudential executed a 30-year lease.

Leslie, on its 1968 corporate income tax return, reported and deducted a loss of $787,414 from the sale of the property. The Commissioner of Internal Revenue disallowed the claimed loss on the ground that the sale and leaseback transaction constituted an exchange of like-kind properties within the scope of Int. Rev. Code § 1031. That section of the Code, if applicable, provides for nonrecognition (and hence nondeductibility) of such losses. Rather than permitting Leslie to take the entire deduction of $787,414 in 1968, the Commissioner treated the $787,414 as Leslie's cost in obtaining the lease, and amortized that sum over the lease's 30-year term. Accordingly, Leslie was assessed deficiencies of $383,023.52 in its corporate income taxes for the years 1965, 1966 and 1968.

Leslie petitioned the Tax Court for a redetermination of the deficiencies assessed against it, contending that the conveyance of the Parsippany property constituted a sale, on which loss is recognized. The Tax Court agreed.

Although the Tax Court found as a fact that Leslie would not have entered into the sale transaction without a leaseback guarantee, 64 T.C. at 250, it concluded that this finding was not dispositive of the character of the transaction. Rather, it held that to constitute an exchange under Int. Rev. Code § 1031 there must be a reciprocal transfer of properties, as distinguished from a transfer of property for a money consideration only. 64 T.C. at 252, *citing* Treas. Reg. § 1.1002-1(d). Based on its findings that the fair market value of the Parsippany property at the time of sale was "in the neighborhood of" the $2,400,000 which Prudential paid, and that the annual net rental of $190,560 to be paid by Leslie was comparable to the fair rental value of similar types of property in the Northern New Jersey area, the Tax Court majority reasoned that Leslie's leasehold had no separate capital value which could be properly viewed as part of the consideration paid. Accordingly, Leslie having received $2,400,000 from Prudential as the sole consideration for the property conveyed, the Tax Court held that the transaction was not an exchange of like-kind properties within the purview of Int. Rev. Code § 1031, but was rather a sale, and so governed by the general recognition provision of Int. Rev. Code [§ 1001(c)].

Six judges of the Tax Court dissented from this holding. Judge Tannenwald, in an opinion in which Judges Raum, Drennen, Quealy and Hall joined, agreed with the Tax Court majority that the conveyance was a sale, but would have disallowed a loss deduction, reasoning that the leasehold had a premium value to Leslie equal to the $787,414 difference between cost and sales price. This dissent reasoned that since Leslie would not have willingly incurred the loss but for the guaranteed lease, this amount should be treated as a bonus paid for the leasehold, and should be amortized over the leasehold's 30-year term.

The Commissioner's appeal from the decision of the Tax Court followed.

II.

The threshold question in any dispute involving the applicability of Int. Rev. Code § 1031 is whether the transaction constitutes an exchange. This is so because § 1031 nonrecognition applies only to exchanges. Section 1031 does not apply where, for example, a taxpayer sells business property for cash and immediately reinvests that cash in other business property even if that property is "like-kind" property. *Bell Lines, Inc. v. United States*, 480 F.2d 710 (4th Cir. 1973). Hence, our inquiry must center on whether the Leslie-Prudential transaction was a sale, as Leslie contends, or an exchange, as the Commissioner argues. If a sale, then, as stated, § 1031 is inapplicable and we need not be concerned further with ascertaining whether the other requirements of that section have been met. *See Jordan Marsh Co. v. Commissioner*, 269 F.2d 453, 455 (2d Cir. 1959). If an exchange, then of course we would be obliged to continue our inquiry to determine if the properties involved were "like-kind."

The Tax Court's conclusion that the Leslie conveyance resulted in a sale was predicated almost totally on an analysis of the applicable Treasury Regulations. Noting that Treas. Reg. § 1.1001-1(b) requires a strict construction of § 1031, the

Tax Court tested the instant transaction against the definition of "exchange" contained in Treas. Reg. § 1.1002-1(d):

> (d) Exchange. Ordinarily, to constitute an exchange, the transaction must be a reciprocal transfer of property as distinguished from a transfer of property for a money consideration only.

Based on its conclusion that the leasehold had no capital value, the Tax Court held that it was not a part of the consideration received but was merely a condition precedent to the sale. Thus, the conveyance to Prudential was "solely for a money consideration" and therefore was not an "exchange." The Tax Court cited *Jordan Marsh Co. v. Commissioner, supra*, in support of its result. In light of its holding, it specifically declined to consider or resolve any possible conflict between *Jordan Marsh*, a decision of the Second Circuit, and the Eighth Circuit decision in *Century Electric Co. v. Commissioner*, 192 F.2d 155 (9th Cir. 1951), *cert. denied*, 342 U.S. 954, 72 S. Ct. 625, 96 L. Ed. 708 (1952).

The Commissioner, relying on *Century Electric*, argues that the Tax Court erred in holding the Leslie-Prudential conveyance to be a sale. He could not, and does not, dispute the Tax Court's findings as to the fair market value and fair rental value of the property. Rather, he argues that value in this context is irrelevant and that the only appropriate consideration is whether the conveyance of the fee and the conveyance of the leasehold were reciprocal. The Commissioner, without regard to his own regulations which define an "exchange," then seeks to support his position by reference to the legislative purpose giving rise to the enactment of the nonrecognition provision. He argues that this provision (§ 1031 and its predecessors) was adopted primarily to eliminate any requirement that the government value the property involved in such exchanges. Alternatively, the Commissioner argues that even if the conveyance is held to be a sale and thereby not within Int. Rev. Code § 1031, any expenditure incurred by Leslie over and above the selling price of $2,400,000 was not a loss as claimed, but rather a premium or bonus which Leslie paid to obtain the leasehold. Such an expenditure is a capital expenditure, the Commissioner argues, and therefore should be amortized over the 30-year lease term.

Leslie, on the other hand, urges affirmance of the Tax Court's holding, relying on *Jordan Marsh Co. v. Commissioner, supra*, and stresses, as does the Tax Court, that the initial issue to be resolved is the character of the transaction. . . .

In *Century Electric Co. v. Commissioner, supra*, the Eighth Circuit held a sale and leaseback arrangement to be a like-kind exchange governed by the nonrecognition provision of § 112 (the predecessor to § 1031). Its holding that no loss was to be recognized was based solely on its finding that the sale and leaseback transactions were reciprocal. The Eighth Circuit read the legislative history of § 112 as evidencing a Congressional purpose to relieve the government of the administrative burden of valuing properties received in like-kind exchanges. Thus the Court stated (192 F.2d at 159) that:

> the market value of the properties of like kind involved in the transfer does not enter into the equation.

By contrast, in *Jordan Marsh v. Commissioner, supra*, a case construing the same code provision as *Century Electric*, the Second Circuit held that a similar sale and leaseback transaction resulted in a sale, on which loss was recognized. The facts in *Jordan Marsh* were similar to the facts here. Jordan Marsh, the taxpayer, had sold two parcels of land for cash in the sum of $2.3 million, an amount which was stipulated to be equal to the fair market value of the property. Simultaneously, the premises were leased back to Jordan Marsh for a term of 30-plus years, with options to renew. The rentals to be paid by Jordan Marsh were "full and normal rentals," so that the Court found that the leasehold interest had no separate capital value.

The Court, in examining the legislative history of § 112 [current § 1031], took issue with the Eighth Circuit's interpretation of the Congressional purpose behind the nonrecognition provision. The Second Circuit said that:

> Congress was primarily concerned with the inequity, in the case of an exchange, of forcing a taxpayer to recognize a paper gain which was still tied up in a continuing investment of the same sort.

269 F.2d at 456. It reasoned further that, if gains were not to be recognized on the ground that they were theoretical, then neither should losses, which were equally theoretical, be recognized. Analyzing the Jordan Marsh transaction in the light of this interpretation of Congressional purpose, the Second Circuit, finding Jordan Marsh had liquidated its investment in realty for cash in an amount fully equal to the value of the fee, concluded that the taxpayer was not "still tied up in a continuing investment of the same sort." Accordingly, the Court held that there was no exchange within the purview of § 112(b), but rather a sale.

Thus we may interpret the essential difference between *Jordan Marsh* and *Century Electric* as centering on their respective views of the need to value property involved in a sale and leaseback.[2] *Jordan Marsh*, viewing the Congressional purpose behind the non-recognition provision as one of avoiding taxation of paper gains and losses, would value the properties involved in order to determine whether the requirements of an "exchange" have been met. *Century Electric*, on the other hand, viewing the legislative enactment as one to relieve the administrative burden of valuation, would regard the value of the properties involved as irrelevant.

We are persuaded that the *Jordan Marsh* approach is a more satisfactory one. First, it is supported by the Commissioner's own definition of "exchange" which distinguishes an exchange from a transfer of property *solely* for a money consideration. Treas. Reg. § 1.1002-1(d) (emphasis added). Second, if resort is to be had to legislative history, it appears to us that the view of Congressional purpose taken by the *Jordan Marsh* court is sounder than that of the Eighth Circuit in *Century*. As

---

[2] The Court in *Jordan Marsh* also distinguished *Century Electric* on its facts, since in that case there had been no finding that the cash received by the taxpayer was the full equivalent of the value of the fee which had been conveyed. Nor had there been a finding that the leaseback was at a rental which was a fair rental for the premises.

Indeed, as noted in *Jordan Marsh*, the record in *Century Electric* indicated that the sales price was substantially less than the fair market value. There was also evidence from which the Court could have found that the leasehold had a separate capital value, since the conveyance to a nonprofit college avoided considerable tax liabilities on the property.

the Court in Jordan Marsh said in discounting the purpose attributed to Congress by the Commissioner and by *Century Electric*:

> Indeed, if these sections had been intended to obviate the necessity of making difficult valuations, one would have expected them to provide for nonrecognition of gains and losses in all exchanges, whether the property received in exchanges were of a "like kind" or *not* of a like kind. And if such had been the legislative objective, § 112(c) providing for the recognition of gain from exchanges not wholly in kind, would never have been enacted. (Footnote omitted.)

It seems to us, therefore, that in order to determine whether money was the sole consideration of a transfer the fair market value of the properties involved must be ascertained. Here, the Tax Court found that Leslie had sold its property unconditionally for cash equal to its fair market value, and had acquired a leasehold for which it was obligated to pay fair rental value. These findings, not clearly erroneous, are binding on this Court. . . .

Nor do we think the Tax Court erred in concluding that the leasehold acquired by Leslie had no capital value. Among other considerations, the rental charged at fair market rates, the lack of compensation for the leasehold interest in the event of condemnation, and the absence of any substantial right of control over the property all support this conclusion. On this record, we agree with the Tax Court that the conveyance was not an exchange, "a reciprocal transfer of property," but was rather "a transfer of property for a money consideration only," and therefore a sale, see Treas. Reg. § 1.1002-1(d), governed by the general recognition provision of Int. Rev. Code § 1002.

The decision of the Tax Court will be affirmed.

Chapter 43

ORIGINAL ISSUE DISCOUNT

I. PROBLEMS

1. On January 1, Year 1, ABC Corporation issues a 10-year zero coupon bond with a face amount of $1,000,000. Tom purchases the bond for $377,000 and keeps it through Year 1. Tom is a cash method, calendar year individual. ABC Corporation is an accrual method, calendar year taxpayer. (Assume the bond is not an applicable high yield discount obligation under § 163(i).)

   (a) Does the bond have any original issue discount? How much? How would your answers change if Tom bought the bond for $980,000? How would your answers change if the bond bore 5% interest, payable twice a year? Payable at maturity?

   (b) Assuming the bond has a yield to maturity of 10% compounded semiannually, what tax consequences to Tom and ABC in Year 1?

   (c) If Tom sells the bond on July 1, Year 3 for $500,000, what tax consequences to Tom in Year 3? What result if the sales price were only $400,000?

   (d) If Tom holds the bond until maturity, what tax consequences for Tom on collection of the $1,000,000?

   (e) How would your answers to the previous questions change, if at all, if the debt instrument in question were a $10,000 note issued by A.B. Carter, an individual, instead of ABC Corporation?

2. On January 1, Year 1, Susan Seller sells to Paul Purchaser some investment land Susan bought several years ago for $1,000,000. Susan sells the property for $4,000,000, payable without interest on January 1, Year 6. Paul gives Susan his promissory note to that effect. Susan and Paul are cash method, calendar year taxpayers. (Assume no inflation adjustments have been made to the dollar limitations in § 1274A.)

   (a) Describe how the applicable Federal rate and the test rate will be determined; then for the remainder of the Problem, assume (except as otherwise noted) the test rate is 10%, compounded semiannually.

   (b) Describe how the imputed principal amount of the note will be determined; then assume the imputed principal amount is $2,456,000.

   (c) What are the tax consequences to Susan and Paul in Year 1? In Year 5?

   (d) What are the tax consequences to Susan when the note is paid on January 1, Year 6?

(e) Suppose the land is sold for $2,500,000 instead of $4,000,000. How would the imputed principal amount of the note be determined? Assuming the imputed principal amount is $1,610,000, what are the tax consequences to Susan and Paul in Year 1?

(f) Assume the land was sold for $400,000 instead of $4,000,000, and the imputed principal amount is $258,000. What tax consequences to Susan and Paul in Year 1? When the note is paid?

(g) Assume the land was sold for $200,000, payable five years later without interest. Assume Susan's basis was $45,000. Assume the present value of the future payment is $135,000, with a test rate of 8%, compounded semiannually. What tax consequences to Susan and Paul in Year 1? When the note is paid? Assume alternatively the land is sold for $193,000 with a $20,000 payment on January 1, Year 2, and a $173,000 payment on January 1, Year 6. If the test rate is 8%, compounded semiannually, and the two payments' aggregate present value is $135,000, what tax consequences to Susan and Paul when the $20,000 payment is made?

(h) Assume Susan sells the land for $4,000,000, with interest at 20%, compounded annually, all principal and interest payable on January 1, Year 4. Assume a test rate of 10%, compounded semiannually, and an imputed principal amount of $5,158,000. What tax consequences to Susan and Paul in Year 1? What Year 1 tax consequences if the 20% interest is paid annually? Assume, alternatively, that the interest rate is 5%, compounded annually. If the test rate is 10%, compounded semiannually, and the imputed principal amount is $3,455,000, what tax consequences in Year 1?

Assignment for Chapter 43:

Complete the problems. [Suggestions: For Problem 1, see Overview sections A and B, and the Code and regulation provisions therein cited. For Problems 2(a), (b), (c), (d), and (h), see Overview sections C through C(3), and the Code and regulation provisions therein cited. For Problems 2(e) and (f), see Overview sections C(6) and C(7) and the Code and regulation provisions therein cited. For Problem 2(g), see Overview sections C(4) and C(5), and the Code and regulation provisions therein cited.]

Read: Internal Revenue Code: §§ 163(e)(1), (e)(2); 483; 1271(a)(1), (b)(1); 1272(a), (c)(1), (d); 1273(a), (b); 1274(a), (b)(1), (b)(2), (c)(1), (c)(2), (c)(3), (d); 1274A; 1275(a)(1)(A), (a)(2), (b). [Skim 1275(c); 1276(a)(1), (b)(1), (b)(2); 1277(a), (c); 1278; 1287; 1288].

Treasury Regulations: §§ 1.163-7(a); 1.446-2(b), (c), (e)(1); 1.483-1(a)(2); 1.483-2(a); 1.483-3(a); 1.1272-1(a)(1), (b)(1); 1.1272-3(a); 1.1273-1(b), (c)(1)(i), (d)(1); 1.1273-2(a)(1); 1.1274-1(a), (b)(1); 1.1274-2(c); 1.1274-4(a)(1)(i), (ii).

Materials: Overview
             United States v. Midland-Ross Corp.

II. VOCABULARY

original issue discount
issue price
stated redemption price at maturity
zero coupon bond
ratable accrual
economic accrual
simple interest
compound interest
yield to maturity
market discount
applicable Federal rate
test rate
unstated interest
"cash method election" of § 1274A
personal use property

III. OBJECTIVES

1. To compute original issue discount, if any, on a debt instrument, and to determine the amount included in income (and allowed as a deduction) on a current basis.

2. To compute the original issue discount, if any, on a debt instrument issued on a sale or exchange of property, and to determine the amount included in income (and allowed as a deduction) on a current basis.

3. To compute the unstated interest, if any, on a contract for the sale or exchange of property, and to determine when, and in what amount, it is included in income (and allowed as a deduction).

IV. OVERVIEW

We study in this Chapter some selected provisions of the Code that address the issue of the time value of money. We have dealt with such provisions before — for example, in Chapter 36 with § 7872 and below market loans. The topics we deal with here are (1) the computation and treatment of "original issue discount" on debt instruments issued for cash or for property (§§ 1271–1275); and (2) the computation and treatment of "unstated interest" on certain deferred-payment sales of property (§ 483).

A. Original Issue Discount: Introduction

In general, the original issue discount Code provisions impute an interest equivalent — called "original issue discount" — to debt instruments that do not bear an adequate rate of interest, and require that this interest equivalent be included in income on a current basis. The original issue discount provisions are complex provisions, and their complexity is exacerbated by terminology that is unfamiliar to most beginning tax students. We shall not attempt to examine all the original issue discount rules in depth, but a grasp of the fundamentals is important.

Assume Corporation issues a 10-year, $1,000,000 noninterest bearing bond — that is, Corporation will pay the holder of the bond $1,000,000 ten years from now, but it will pay no interest on the bond (hence the term "zero coupon bond"). Obviously, no investor will pay $1,000,000 for such a bond on issuance. The value of the bond will move closer and closer to $1,000,000 as the maturity date draws nearer, but its value will be considerably less than $1,000,000 initially. Assume Investor purchases the bond on issuance for $385,000, and then holds the bond until it is redeemed at maturity, 10 years later, for $1,000,000. Although the bond nominally pays no interest, it is obvious that the $615,000 difference between the amount paid on issuance and the amount paid on redemption — that is, the "original issue discount" on the bond — serves the same purpose as interest.

How and when should the investor's gain of $615,000 be taxed? Assume the bond is a capital asset in the hands of our investor. Should the appreciation in the value of the bond be treated as capital gain? To the extent that appreciation is attributable to original issue discount — the economic equivalent of interest — the answer is "No." Such appreciation is treated as ordinary income. Moreover, this result obtains whether the investor simply collects the $1,000,000 proceeds on maturity or sells the bond for something less than $1,000,000 prior to maturity. A sale, in other words, does not convert the "earned" original issue discount to capital gain, even if the bond is a capital asset. Note the Supreme Court's rejection of a claim to the contrary in *United States v. Midland-Ross Corporation*, a case reprinted in the materials, on the notes sold there at a gain attributable to original issue discount. The *Midland-Ross* decision, based on the "application of general principles" of tax law, is confirmed in the statutory provisions discussed below.

The investor's gain of $615,000 is thus to be taxed as ordinary income — but when will it be so taxed? There are at least three potential answers. One possibility, for cash method taxpayers at least, is to tax the earned original issue discount (henceforth, OID) on receipt — that is, when the bond is redeemed, sold or otherwise disposed of. (An accrual method taxpayer would report interest income as it accrues.) Thus, one answer would be to charge our (presumably) cash method investor with $615,000 of ordinary income when the bond is redeemed at maturity. The OID rules now reject this approach, but it was the approach taken by Congress in 1954, when it first legislated in this area. The 1954 legislation essentially treated accrued OID as ordinary income, but permitted recognition to await the redemption, sale or exchange of the bond. Congress eventually decided that this approach presented too much opportunity for mismatching of income and deductions. The bond-issuing corporation, presumably on the accrual method, could deduct as interest the accrued, unpaid OID, while the cash method investor reported no income until payment was made. This deduction-now, income-later arrangement was satisfactory to the two taxpayers, of course, but not to the Treasury.

The second potential approach to the timing of the investor's income of $615,000 is exemplified by the second legislative effort, in 1969. Since the $615,000 of OID is earned over a ten-year period, one could treat one-tenth of the OID as earned each year. In other words, one could treat the OID as earned *ratably* over the ten years, at the rate of $61,500 per year. Then, in order to correct the mismatching of income and deductions permitted by the first approach, one could require current reporting of the OID by lender and borrower. Thus, the 1969 legislation required original issue discount income to be reported as earned, but it treated the income as earned in equal amounts throughout the period. This approach thus deals with the mismatching problems under the first approach by putting the parties on the accrual method. The investor would be required to report $61,500 of ordinary income each year; the corporation would have $61,500 of interest expense each year.

There is a major problem with the ratable accrual method, and the 1969 provisions that embodied it have been repealed. Economically speaking, it is unrealistic to treat the interest of $615,000 as accruing in equal amounts each year. Recall that the corporate obligor sold its $1,000,000 bond on issuance for $385,000. In effect, Investor loaned $385,000 to Corporation for 10 years. Whatever amount of interest is treated as earned in the first year of the loan, a greater amount should be treated as earned in the second year, and increasingly greater amounts should be treated as earned in subsequent years. The reason is obvious. From an economic standpoint, unpaid interest itself earns interest — that is, interest is "compounded" on some periodic basis. If we assume an annual compounding period, then at the end of Year 1, the unpaid Year 1 interest is added to the $385,000 principal amount; the interest earned in Year 2 is thus interest on the $385,000 principal and also interest on the unpaid Year 1 interest. Similarly, interest earned in Year 3 will be greater than interest earned in Year 2 because the Year 3 interest includes interest on the unpaid Year 2 interest. Because interest is not paid until the end of Year 10, the corporate obligor's real debt, consisting of principal and unpaid interest, increases each year; hence the interest on the debt also increases.

Let us illustrate this effect with the bond in our example, assuming an annual compounding period. We must first determine what interest rate, compounded annually, will result in a $1,000,000 payment on a 10-year loan of $385,000. It turns out the answer is about 10%. Now compare the annual interest amounts under the ratable accrual approach (column 1) and the annual compounding approach (column 2). The third column shows the total debt on which the column 2 interest is charged. For example, the Year 6 interest charge under annual compounding is $62,005. This is 10% of $620,047, which is the total of the combined unpaid principal ($385,000) and the unpaid interest earned in the five *prior* years ($235,047). (Ignore the slight difference between columns 1 and 2 in total interest accrued. It simply reflects the fact that the interest rate under annual compounding is actually a bit greater than 10%. The 10% figure is used here only for ease of computation. If the exact figure were used, column 2 would also total $615,000.) Thus, after 10 years, the same total amount is paid to the bond holder, but the interest portion accrues on quite different schedules.

		(1) Interest, ratably accrued	(2) Interest at 10% annually compounded	Unpaid Principal	+	Unpaid Interest	=	(3) Total Debt
Year	1	$61,500	$38,500	385,000	+	0	=	385,000
	2	61,500	42,350	385,000	+	38,500	=	423,500
	3	61,500	46,585	385,000	+	80,850	=	465,850
	4	61,500	51,244	385,000	+	127,435	=	512,435
	5	61,500	56,368	385,000	+	178,679	=	563,679
	6	61,500	62,005	385,000	+	235,047	=	620,047
	7	61,500	68,205	385,000	+	297,052	=	682,052
	8	61,500	75,026	385,000	+	365,257	=	750,257
	9	61,500	82,528	385,000	+	440,283	=	825,283
	10	61,500	90,781	385,000	+	522,811	=	907,811
Total		$615,000	$613,592					

The ratable accrual approach of the 1969 legislation thus did not seem to reflect an "economic accrual" of interest. To treat $61,500 of interest as accruing each year overstated the accrual in the early years and understated it in the later years. Such a distortion was quite satisfactory from the standpoint of the obligor — accelerating deductions into the early years increases their value by generating tax savings now rather than later. For the ordinary investor, on the other hand, the arrangement was unattractive; it accelerated income recognition, but without any cash payments. However, for tax-exempt investors, for other investors in low tax brackets, or for investors with sufficient deductions to offset the OID income, the income acceleration was acceptable. As a result, the practical effect of the ratable accrual method for OID was to accelerate corporate interest deductions, while the accelerated OID income (given the investors who purchased the OID bonds) would be taxed lightly or not at all.

The third potential approach to the timing of the investor's income of $615,000 — and not so incidentally, to the timing of the corporate obligor's interest expense of $615,000 — retains the matching concept of the 1969 legislation; it continues to place both parties on the accrual method for OID purposes, but it rejects ratable accrual in favor of "economic accrual" of OID. It is this third approach to OID, initially adopted by Congress in 1982, that is the law today.

Compounding of Interest. Before we turn to the technical aspects of OID under current law, however, some additional explanation is in order concerning the concepts of simple interest and compound interest, and the effect of compounding over different periods of time. Simple interest provides for payment of interest only on the principal amount of the loan; no interest is earned on the unpaid interest. For example, assume $100,000 is borrowed at 10% per annum, simple interest, with all principal and interest to be paid after three years. Each year, $10,000 of interest accrues. After three years, borrower pays lender $130,000 to retire the debt. Now assume, alternatively, the loan bears interest at the rate of 10%, compounded annually. The loan earns $10,000 in Year 1, as before. But in Year 2, the unpaid interest of $10,000 itself earns interest of 10%. The Year 2 debt is effectively $110,000, and the Year 2 interest is thus $11,000. The unpaid $11,000 is added to the prior debt of $110,000, and accordingly during Year 3, the total debt is now $121,000, which earns interest in Year 3 or $12,100. The amount borrower owes at the end of Year 3 is thus $133,100, rather than $130,000, as in the case of simple interest. Finally, to illustrate the effect of more rapid compounding, assume interest on the $100,000 is compounded semiannually instead of annually. The interest that accrues in the first six months of Year 1 is thus $5,000 — that is, 1/2 of 10% of $100,000. But in the second half of Year 1, 10% interest accrues on a total of $105,000; in other words, the interest earned in the latter six months is $5,250: 1/2 of 10% of $105,000. Semiannual compounding increases Year 1 interest from $10,000 to $10,250. The interest that accrues in Year 2 and 3 is determined as follows: in the first half of Year 2, accrued interest is $5,512.50 (1/2 × 10% × $110,250); in the second half of Year 2, the accrued interest is $5,788.13 (1/2 × 10% × $115,762.50); in the first half of Year 3, accrued interest is $6,077.53 (1/2 × 10% × $121,550.62); and in the second half of Year 3, accrued interest is $6,381.41 (1/2 × 10% × $127,628.15). Total interest earned over the three years under semiannual compounding is $34,009.55, and the amount owed to lender is thus $134,009.55. Note that this exceeds the total interest of $33,100 earned under annual compounding.

The point is simply this: the more rapidly interest is compounded, the greater the aggregate amount of interest earned. If interest is compounded daily, the interest earned today itself starts earning interest tomorrow. If interest is compounded annually, however, the interest earned on Day 1 earns nothing for the next 364 days, the interest earned on Day 2 waits 363 days before itself earning interest, etc. Put another way, as the frequency of compounding decreases, the interest rate must increase in order to earn the same total interest over the same time period.

Now to a summary of various technical aspects of the OID rules.

B. Original Issue Discount: Debt Instruments Issued for Cash

1. Determining the Amount of OID

Original issue discount on a debt instrument is defined as "the stated redemption price at maturity" over "the issue price." § 1273(a)(1). The stated redemption price at maturity is generally the total of all payments under the debt instrument, including interest payments, except for interest based on a fixed rate and unconditionally payable at fixed periods of one year or less. § 1273(a)(2). (Under the regulations to § 1273, the interest not included in the stated redemption price at maturity is called "qualified stated interest." Reg. § 1.1273-1(b), (c)(i).) The issue price is generally the amount paid on issuance. See § 1273(b)(2). If the issue of debt instruments is publicly offered, then the issue price is the initial public offering price at which a substantial amount of the debt instruments was sold. § 1273(b)(1).[1] This section deals with a debt instrument issued for cash, not one issued for property. Determining the issue price of debt instruments issued in connection with a sale of property is considered in Section C.

> **Example 1:** Assume on January 1, Year 1, Corporation issues a 10-year bond to Investor for $100,000. The bond bears no interest and will pay $265,330 at maturity. On these facts, the stated redemption price at maturity is $265,330, and the issue price is $100,000. Thus, the OID is $165,330.

> **Example 2:** Assume (unrealistically) the bond in Example 1 will pay $102,000 at maturity. Would the OID therefore be $2,000? Under a special *de minimus* rule, the answer is "No." OID is treated as zero if OID is less than 1/4% of the stated redemption price at maturity, multiplied by the number of years to maturity. § 1273(a)(3). Since 1/4% of $102,000 x 10 years equals $2,550, and since this amount exceeds the OID determined under the general rule of § 1273(a)(1), OID is treated as zero.[2]

> **Example 3:** A bond issued for cash can bear both stated and unstated interest. Corporation issues a 5-year bond for $80,000 that will pay $100,000 at maturity and that bears interest of 5% per year, compounded and paid semiannually. Since the stated interest is a fixed rate, unconditionally payable at least annually through the term of the debt, it is qualified stated interest. Thus, the stated redemption price at maturity is $100,000, and OID is $20,000.[3] § 1273(a)(1), (2). Assume, however, the stated interest is

---

[1] The regulations under § 1273 provide a common general rule for determining the issue price of debt instruments issued for money, whether publicly traded or not. The regulations provide that where a "substantial amount of the debt instruments in an issue is issued for money," the issue price will be "the first price at which a substantial amount of the debt instruments is sold for money." Reg. § 1.1273-2(a)(1).

[2] *De minimis* OID is generally included in income as principal payments are made. Reg. § 1.1273-1(d)(5)(i). The character of such income may be capital gain. Reg. § 1.1273-1(d)(5)(ii). *De minimis* OID, however, can also be characterized as qualified stated interest. See Reg. § 1.1273-1(d)(1).

[3] The regulations, however, permit both cash method and accrual method holders of debt instruments to elect to treat all interest as OID, including stated interest, *de minimis* OID, etc. Reg. § 1.1272-3(a).

not payable until maturity. The amount of the stated interest payment —
slightly more than $28,000 — is not qualified stated interest and it will
therefore be part of the stated redemption price at maturity, about
$128,000. OID will thus be $48,000.

2. Current Inclusion of OID

Return to the facts of Example 1. What is the consequence of this bond's having
$165,330 of OID? In general, the holder of any debt instrument having OID must
currently include the earned portion in income. Specifically, the holder must
currently include "the sum of the daily portions of the original issue discount for
each day during the taxable year on which such holder held such debt instrument."
§ 1272(a)(1).

Before deciphering the quoted language, however, note this current-inclusion-
in-income rule of § 1272(a)(1) does not apply to certain debt instruments, including
(1) tax-exempt obligations; (2) U.S. savings bonds; (3) debt instruments with fixed
terms of one year or less; (4) obligations issued by natural persons prior to March
2, 1984; and (5) in general, outstanding loans between natural persons not in excess
of $10,000 in the aggregate, not issued in the course of the lender's trade or
business, or for a tax avoidance purpose. § 1272(a)(2). Note also that § 1272 does not
apply to one who purchases a debt instrument at a premium — that is, for an
amount in excess of the principal amount. § 1272(c)(1). Generally, however, the
current-inclusion rule of § 1272(a)(1) applies to the holder of "any debt instrument"
having OID. The term "debt instrument" is defined very broadly to encompass, in
general, any "bond, debenture, note, or certificate or other evidence of indebtedness." § 1275(a)(1)(A).[4] Certain annuity contracts are excluded. § 1275(a)(1)(B).

What are the "daily portions of OID" that must be currently included in income?
See § 1272(a)(3). To answer the question, it is necessary to determine (with the help
of a calculator!) the debt instrument's "yield to maturity" — that is, the *constant
interest rate*, applied to the issue price and compounded at least annually, that will
produce the necessary OID over the period to maturity.[5] For consistency, the
examples we use throughout this Chapter will assume *semiannual compounding*.[6]

In that event, none of the interest will be treated as qualified stated interest.

   [4] The regulations define a debt instrument as, in general, any instrument or contractual arrangement
that constitutes indebtedness under general tax principles. Reg. § 1.1275-1(d).

   [5] The regulations define "yield to maturity" in terms of a "constant yield method." This yield is the
discount rate, constant over the term of the instrument, that when used to compute the present value of
all principal and interest payments under the debt instrument, produces a total equal to the issue price
of the instrument. Reg. § 1.1272-1(b)(1)(i). For ease of computation, we shall use the equivalent definition
expressed in terms of a constant interest rate applied to the issue price.

   [6] The statute contemplates semiannual compounding — that is, 6-month accrual periods — but
permits the regulations to provide other accrual periods. § 1272(a)(5). The regulations in turn authorize
accrual periods that vary and may be of any length up to one year. Reg. § 1.1272-1(b)(1)(ii). Accrual
periods chosen must be such that scheduled payments of principal or interest occur either on the first
or the last day of an accrual period. For the sake of simplicity, we shall assume accrual periods that are
always 6 months long. It might be noted, however, that if accrual periods vary in length, it will be
necessary to convert a yield based on one length into the equivalent yield based on a different length. *See,
e.g.*, Reg. § 1.1272-1(b)(1)(iii), -1(j) Ex. 1.

On the facts of Example 1, the yield to maturity, based on semiannual compounding, turns out to be 10% — in other words, $100,000, invested at 10%, compounded semiannually, will grow to $265,330 at the end of 10 years.

How much OID must Investor therefore include in income in the first year? The OID attributable to the first 6-month accrual period is $5,000 (1/2 × 10% × $100,000). Each day in that 6-month period is allocated a ratable portion of that $5,000 — or somewhat less than $27.50 per day. If Investor holds the bond for the entire 6-month period, Investor is charged with $5,000 of income. The OID attributable to the next 6-month period will be $5,250 (1/2 year × 10% × $105,000), and the daily portions of OID will accordingly be somewhat greater than they were in the first 6 months. If Investor holds the bond for one year, the OID inclusion is thus $10,250.

In the language of the statute, the daily portions of OID are determined by allocating to each day in the accrual period its ratable portion of the "increase in the adjusted issue price" during such period. § 1272(a)(3). The "adjusted issue price" is the issue price plus the adjustments in prior accrual periods. § 1272(a)(4). Consider our example. Recall that we will assume 6-month accrual periods. At the outset, the "adjusted issue price" is $100,000 — that is, the issue price ($100,000) plus adjustments thereto ($0). At the beginning of the second 6-month accrual period, the adjusted issue price is $105,000 — the issue price of $100,000 plus $5,000 of adjustments for the prior accrual period. The "increase" in the adjusted issue price for the first 6-month accrual period is thus $5,000. What is the increase in the adjusted issue price in the second 6-month accrual period? The increase is determined by multiplying the yield to maturity (here, 10%, compounded semiannually) by the adjusted issue price at the beginning of the period ($105,000 at the beginning of the second 6-month period); thus, as noted before, the increase in the second accrual period is $5,250, and it is ratably allocated to each day in the period. The adjusted issue price at the beginning of the third 6-month accrual period is therefore $110,250, and the increase in the adjusted issue price during that third period is $5,512.50 (1/2 × 10% × $110,250), allocated ratably to each day in that period and included in the holder's gross income. Similar computations are done for each succeeding accrual period. Assuming our investor holds the bond until maturity, all $165,330 of OID will have been included in income.[7]

3. Deduction of OID

Recall that the OID rules are designed to match interest income and expense by putting both parties on the accrual basis with respect to the interest. The issuer of a debt instrument having OID is thus treated as having an interest expense equal to the aggregate daily portions of OID for days during the issuer's tax year.

---

[7] The regulations describe the general rule for accrual of OID as a four-step process: (1) determine the yield to maturity; (2) determine the accrual periods; (3) determine the OID allocable to each accrual period; (4) determine the daily portions of OID. Reg. § 1.1273-1(b)(1).

§ 163(e)(1).[8] Its deductibility is subject to any other rules that may deny, limit or defer the deduction.[9]

4.   Gain or Loss on Sale, Exchange or Retirement

Assume that the bond in Example 1 is a capital asset and that OID is properly accounted for. The sale or exchange of the bond should generate capital gain or loss to the extent of the difference between the adjusted basis and the amount realized. Suppose the bond is held to maturity, however. Absent legislation to the contrary, the retirement of the bond would not constitute a sale or exchange and thus would not produce capital gain or loss. *See Fairbanks v. United States*, 306 U.S. 436 (1939). The *Fairbanks* result has, however, been legislatively reversed. In general, amounts received on retirement of a debt instrument are to be treated as amounts received on an exchange. § 1271(a)(1). Capital gain treatment on a retirement is thus made possible, and there is no need for a bond holder to sell a bond prior to maturity simply to avoid ordinary income treatment. Note that special rules apply where there is an intention to call a debt instrument before maturity. § 1271(a)(2).

Assume that our investor holds the bond in Example 1 until maturity. Is there any gain or loss at that point? To answer this question, it is necessary to determine the investor's basis in the bond. Pursuant to § 1272(d)(2), the original basis is appropriately increased by the OID included in income. Accordingly, the basis in the bond is now the $265,330 the corporation pays on maturity; the deemed exchange on retirement produces no gain or loss.

---

[8] See the general rule of deductibility, expressed by reference to the "constant yield method" for accrual of OID, at Reg. § 1.163-7(a). *De minimis* OID may be deducted using a straight line method over the term of the debt instrument, or in proportion to stated interest payments, or at maturity. Reg. § 1.163-7(b)(2).

[9] An exception to this general rule of deductibility should be noted. In 1989, Congress placed an added limitation on the deduction of OID on certain "high yield" obligations. We can give this limitation no more than a glancing acknowledgment in this course. The general rule of § 163(e)(1) provides that the issuer of a debt instrument having OID is (potentially, at least) entitled to an interest deduction equal to the OID accruing during that year's accrual periods. The enactment in 1989 of § 163(e)(5) and § 163(i), which limit the general rule, reflected the concern that developed about high yield, "junk bonds" that were issued with significant OID, and that thus provided significant interest deductions in advance of payment. The 1989 legislation thus provided that with respect to an "applicable high yield discount obligation" issued by a corporation (other than an S corporation), no deduction at all is allowed for the "disqualified portion" of OID, and a deduction for the remaining portion of OID is not allowed until the OID is paid. Section 163(e)(5)(A). An applicable high yield discount obligation is a debt instrument with statutorily-defined, "significant" OID, plus a maturity date more than five years from issuance and a yield to maturity at least five points greater than the applicable Federal rate at issuance. § 163(i)(1), (2). (Thus, our 10-year bond in Example 1 could be an applicable high yield discount obligation.) The theory underlying the harsh treatment given such instruments — which will obviously discourage their issuance — is expressed in the legislative history as follows:

> This . . . approach is adopted because . . . a portion of the return on certain high-yield OID obligations is similar to a distribution of corporate earnings with respect to equity. Thus, [the statute] bifurcates the yield on applicable instruments, creating an interest element that is deductible when paid and a return on equity element for which no deduction is granted. . . .

Conference Committee Report to the Revenue Reconciliation Act of 1989, p. 46.

The OID *inclusion* rules are not affected by these restrictions on the deduction of OID.

Assume, alternatively, that our investor sells the bond after 2 years for $125,000. At this point, the OID included in income would total $21,551 (based on $100,000 at 10% per annum, compounded semiannually). The bond's adjusted basis would be $121,551. Investor would thus recognize long term capital gain of $3,449.

This last example points up the obvious fact that debt instruments having OID can change hands. What are the tax consequences for the subsequent holder of a debt instrument having OID? We shall deal with this topic only in passing. In general, the subsequent holder must include OID in income pursuant to § 1272(a)(1). Note, however, the problem that would arise in this example if the subsequent holder purchased the bond 2 years after issuance for $125,000. If the original holder had retained the bond until maturity, the OID inclusion for Years 3 through 10 would have been $143,779 ($265,330 stated redemption price, less $121,551 basis at the end of Year 2). However, if the subsequent holder includes $143,779 of OID, the adjusted basis in the bond on retirement will be $268,779 ($125,000 of original basis plus $143,779 OID). If no adjustment is made, the subsequent holder's basis in the bond on retirement will exceed the redemption price by $3,449; a capital loss would be built into the bond. Accordingly, under § 1272(a)(7), the daily portions of OID are reduced to take this "premium" into account and eliminate the built-in loss and "excess" OID. As a result, if a subsequent holder holds the bond until retirement, the OID inclusion will total only $140,330, the difference between the basis of $125,000 and the stated redemption price of $265,330.[10]

5. Market Discount

Assume a 10-year bond has a face amount of $100,000, pays 10% interest semiannually, and has an issue price of $100,000. Since the issue price equals or exceeds the stated redemption price at maturity, the bond has no OID. Assume now that, subsequent to issuance, interest rates rise and the already-issued bond is now sold by the original holder for $90,000. The $10,000 decline in value constitutes "market discount." *See* § 1278(a)(2)(A). Alternatively, suppose this $100,000 bond was issued for $95,000, and thus had $5,000 of OID. Again, assume a subsequent rise in interest rates (or decline in the creditworthiness of the corporation issuing the bond) such that the sales price of the bond, on a sale to a subsequent holder, is only $90,000. The $5,000 decline in value again constitutes market discount. § 1278(a)(2)(B), (4). In this latter case, the bond has both OID and market discount. Assuming no exceptions apply, the subsequent holder must currently include the OID in income in accordance with § 1272(a). But how is market discount treated? From the standpoint of the subsequent holder, market discount, like OID, is the functional equivalent of interest. Thus, in general, to the extent any gain on disposition reflects market discount, it must be treated, like OID, as ordinary income. § 1276(a)(1). However, unlike OID, market discount accrues ratably, although an election may be made to accrue market discount in the same manner as OID accrues. § 1276(b). Moreover, again unlike OID, market discount is not

---

[10] *See generally* Reg. § 1.1272-2.

currently included in income as accrued by the subsequent holder.[11] (Consider whether the market discount rules should be conformed to OID rules.) In addition, note that interest incurred by the holder of the market discount bond, in order to purchase or carry the bond, may be subject to a special provision deferring the allowance of a deduction for such interest. § 1277.

C. Original Issue Discount and Unstated Interest: Debt Instruments Issued for Property

The preceding section dealt with OID with respect to debt instruments issued for cash. In this section we consider OID in connection with a debt instrument issued on a sale or exchange of property.[12]

Assume that Seller and Purchaser agree that certain property is worth $50,000; also assume the current interest rate is 10%, compounded annually. Among various possibilities, Seller and Purchaser could provide that the sales price is $55,000, payable one year later without interest; alternatively, they could provide that the sales price is $50,000, payable one year from now, plus $5,000 interest. From an economic standpoint, the choice hardly matters: either way, $55,000 will be paid one year from now. From a tax standpoint, however, the choices could have very different consequences. For example, for the seller, a $55,000 sales price might produce an extra $5,000 in capital gain in lieu of $5,000 of ordinary interest income. For the purchaser, if the property were depreciable, a $55,000 sales price would mean an additional $5,000 basis for depreciation, rather than $5,000 in interest expense. As you might expect, the parties will generally not be permitted to put whatever tax labels they wish on the dollar amounts paid. Instead, when property is sold on a deferred payment basis, the parties will generally be required to provide for adequate interest on the unpaid balance; if adequate stated interest is not provided, it will ordinarily be imputed, and the nominal selling price will be adjusted to take account of the unstated interest.[13]

---

[11] But note § 1.1272-3(a), generally permitting an election to treat all interest on a debt instrument, including market discount, as OID.

[12] There are a considerable number of OID topics that are beyond the scope of this chapter. Among the topics not covered, for example, are variable rate debt instruments (Reg. § 1.1275-5), contingent payment debt instruments (Reg. § 1.1275-4), inflation-indexed debt instruments (Reg. § 1.1275-7), assumptions of debt instruments (Reg. § 1.1274-5), and potentially abusive situations (Reg. § 1.1274-3). Special provisions exist relating to the current inclusion in income of "acquisition discount" on certain short-term obligations, and to the possible deferral of interest deductions on account of short-term obligations (§§ 1281–1283). Special treatment is also provided for "stripped bonds" — that is, debt instruments where the right to interest has been separated from the debt instrument (§ 1286). The failure to register a "registration-required obligation" may result in the loss of capital gain treatment otherwise available. § 1287. Finally, note that OID is treated as accruing on tax-exempt obligations for basis purposes (to avoid taxing the holder on this interest-equivalent on disposition) and for § 163 deduction purposes. § 1288.

[13] See Reg. §§ 1.1001-1(g) and 1.1012-1(g) for the determination of the seller's amount realized and the buyer's basis when a debt instrument is issued in exchange for property.

1. Determining Issue Price Under Section 1274: Inadequate Stated Interest

Example 4: Seller sells property to Purchaser for $10,000,000 payable 10 years from now. Purchaser issues a 10-year promissory note in that amount. Assume that neither the property nor the note is publicly traded. No interest is payable on the unpaid purchase price. Does the debt instrument have OID? In what amount?

As soon as we try to determine the OID on the note, a problem becomes apparent. In order to compute OID, we need to know the note's stated redemption price at maturity and its issue price. § 1273(a)(1). Here, the stated redemption price at maturity is $10,000,000, but what is the issue price? The issue price of a debt instrument essentially serves as a measurement of fair market value; to the extent the redemption price exceeds it, an economic equivalent to interest is present. The issue price is clear enough when the obligor issues the debt for cash — that is, the cash received essentially measures the value of the debt instrument. However, this cash measurement is not available when the debt is issued for property; we need some way to determine the "issue price" — the fair market value surrogate — so that OID can be determined. When the debt or property is publicly traded, it is easy enough to identify a fair market value, and thus to determine issue price and OID. *See* § 1273(b)(3). However, Example 4 assumes that neither the debt nor the property is publicly traded. In these circumstances, we turn (initially, at least) to § 1274 in order to determine issue price, which will in turn enable us to determine OID.

To determine issue price, we need a benchmark interest rate. If we knew that the benchmark rate was, for example, 9% per year, compounded annually, we could then determine what amount of money, invested at that rate, would grow to $10,000,000 in 10 years. That particular sum of money — which turns out to be about $4,220,000 — would then constitute the issue price of the property; and we could then compute the OID on the purchaser's note.

Section 1274 identifies such a benchmark rate, called the "applicable Federal rate." § 1274(d). Depending on the term of the debt instrument, the applicable Federal rate (henceforth, AFR) is the Federal short-term rate, mid-term rate, or long-term rate. (For the 10-year note in Example 4, the Federal long-term rate would apply.) These rates are determined each month by the Secretary of the Treasury, based on average yields of outstanding marketable obligations of the United States of comparable terms to maturity. § 1274(d)(1)(C). By using U.S. obligations to determine the benchmark interest rate, § 1274 winds up using an interest rate that is almost invariably lower than the interest rate the obligor would actually have paid. The issue price will thus be higher, and OID will be less, than would be the case if market interest rates served as the benchmark. Since applicable Federal rates change each month, which month's rates should be used to determine an issue price under § 1274? The rate to be used is known as the "test rate," and the regulations define the test rate as generally the "3-month rate" — that is, the lowest applicable Federal rate (based on the appropriate compounding period) during *either* the 3-month period ending with the month the sale or exchange occurs, *or* the 3-month period ending with the month in which there is a binding written contract for the sale or exchange. *See* § 1272(d)(2); *see also* Reg. § 1.1274-4(a)(1). Let us simply assume that the test rate for the 10-year note in Example 4, based on semiannual compounding, is 10%.

To summarize Example 4 to this point: The stated selling price for the property is $10,000,000, payable without interest in 10 years; the test rate is 10%, compounded semiannually. To determine OID, we need to know the stated redemption price at maturity (here, $10,000,000) and the issue price. Where there is "adequate stated interest," the issue price is the "stated principal amount" of the note. Where there is not "adequate stated interest" — and a zero interest rate must surely be inadequate — the issue price is the "imputed principal amount" of the note. § 1274(a).

The imputed principal amount of the note is the present value of *all payments* due under the note. § 1274(b)(1). To determine present value, the payments must be discounted to the date of the sale or exchange, using a compounding period and a test rate that is based on the same compounding period.[14] On the facts of Example 4, the question can be phrased as follows: What amount, invested at 10%, compounded semiannually, would grow to $10,000,000 in ten years? The answer — and thus the imputed principal amount — is $3,768,898. If there were multiple payments, equivalent calculations would be necessary for each payment to determine the total present value, or imputed principal amount.[15]

Section 1274(a) governs debt instruments "to which this section applies." Does this section apply? Yes. The debt instrument is given on the sale or exchange of property; the stated redemption price ($10,000,000) exceeds the imputed principal amount ($3,768,898) and some or all of the payments are due more than 6 months after the sale. § 1274(c)(1). We are now able to compute the OID. Here, we return to familiar (?) ground. OID equals stated redemption price at maturity, less issue price. § 1273(a)(1). OID on the note thus equals $6,231,102 — that is, $10,000,000, less $3,768,898.

This OID is currently included in Seller's income under the rules of § 1272(a). The "yield to maturity," however, has already been determined: it is the test rate of 10%, compounded semiannually, used to compute present values of payments under § 1274(b). If Seller holds the note throughout Year 1, the OID for the first 6 months would thus be $188,445 (1/2 × 10% × $3,768,898); for the next 6 months, $197,867 (1/2 × 10% × $3,957,343). Purchaser's imputed interest expense would equal the daily portions of the OID for the Purchaser's tax year. § 163(e).[16] The interest would be deductible subject to any limitations otherwise imposed.

---

[14] Reg. § 1.1274-2(c)(2). The statute directs that present value be determined using a discount rate equal to the applicable Federal rate, compounded semiannually. § 1274(b)(2)(B). The regulations, however, permit other compounding periods to be used, provided they are based on the applicable Federal rates appropriate for those compounding periods.

[15] We assume throughout this discussion that the "potentially abusive situation" rules of § 1274(b)(3) do not apply. The regulations at Reg. § 1.1274-3 add debt instruments with "clearly excessive interest" to the statutory list of potentially abusive situations.

[16] We here assume the § 163(e)(5) exception regarding "applicable high yield discount obligations" does not apply.

Example 5: Assume Purchaser's note for $10,000,000 bears interest, at the rate of 5% per annum, compounded annually, but not payable until maturity. Recall that the test rate is 10%, compounded semiannually. Is the 5% "stated interest" likely to be adequate interest?

The stated interest payable at maturity will be $6,288,942; the total payment due at maturity is thus $16,288,942. Its present value, and thus the imputed principal amount of the note, at the test rate of 10%, compounded semiannually, is $6,139,134. The stated interest of 5% is "adequate stated interest" only if the imputed principal amount of the note exceeds or equals the stated principal amount of the note (here, $10,000,000). § 1274(c)(2). Accordingly, this note does not bear adequate stated interest. Therefore, the issue price is the imputed principal amount — here, $6,139,134.

Is the stated redemption price at maturity still $10,000,000, as in Example 4? The answer is "No." The stated redemption price at maturity excludes "qualified stated interest," but since the interest in Example 5 was not unconditionally payable at fixed intervals of one year or less throughout the term of the instrument, it is not qualified stated interest. § 1273(a)(2). The stated redemption price at maturity will thus be $16,288,942. Subtracting the issue price of $6,139,134, OID on the note in Example 5 is $10,149,808. It will be currently includable in income pursuant to § 1272(a).

2. Determining Issue Price Under Section 1274: Adequate Stated Interest

Example 6: Assume Purchaser's note for $10,000,000 bears interest at 20%, compounded annually, payable at maturity. The test rate is 10%, compounded semiannually. Is the 20% stated interest adequate?[17]

Stated interest payable at maturity is $51,917,362. The total payment at maturity is thus $61,917,362. Its present value, and thus the imputed principal amount of the note, under our test rate, is $23,336.020. The stated principal amount ($10,000,000) is less than the imputed principal amount. Not surprisingly, "adequate stated interest" has been charged. § 1274(c)(2). As a result, the issue price is the stated principal amount of $10,000,000. There is, in other words, no need to recharacterize principal as interest, because sufficient interest is being charged.

The stated redemption price at maturity, which includes the $51,917,362 in nonqualified stated interest, is $61,917,362. Since the issue price is $10,000,000, OID is therefore $51,917,362. It will be includable in income pursuant to § 1272(a). In effect, what the parties labeled "interest" is indeed treated as interest, but it is also re-labeled "OID" and must be currently included in income under the rules of § 1272.

---

[17] Assume here and in Example 7 below that this interest rate does not trigger the potentially abusive situation rules of § 1274(b)(3); Reg. § 1.1274-3.

3. Adequate Interest Charged and Paid Currently: No OID

Example 7: Assume Purchaser's note bears interest at 20% per year, payable annually. The test rate is 10%, compounded semiannually. Since it appears that adequate interest is being charged *and paid currently*, will the OID rules come into play?

Here there are annual interest payments of $2,000,000 for 10 years, plus a principal payment of $10,000,000. The aggregate present value of all these payments, and thus the imputed principal amount of the note, is about $16,000,000. The stated principal amount remains $10,000,000, and is less than the imputed principal amount. As in Example 6, adequate stated interest was charged.

The stated redemption price at maturity however, now does *not* include the interest payable at maturity, since this interest meets the requirement of § 1273(a)(2) regarding payment at fixed periodic intervals and constitutes qualified stated interest. Therefore, the stated redemption price at maturity and the stated principal amount are the same — $10,000,000.

Re-read § 1274(c)(1). In general, § 1274 applies to a debt instrument, in cases where there is adequate stated interest, only if the stated redemption price at maturity *exceeds* the stated principal amount. Here they are the same. Accordingly, § 1274 does not apply. Now re-read § 1273(b)(4). Example 7 involves a note issued for property where neither the note nor the property is publicly traded. Section 1273(b)(1)–(3) thus does not apply, nor does § 1274. As a result, the issue price of the note is equal to the stated redemption price at maturity. § 1273(b)(4). Since issue price and redemption price are the same, there is no OID. § 1273(a)(1).

The message: When adequate interest is charged and paid currently, there is no need to introduce an OID interest-equivalent. And, indeed, the convoluted interaction of §§ 1273 and 1274 appropriately produces zero OID in Example 7.

4. Exceptions to Section 1274

Certain sales or exchanges of property are excepted from § 1274 even though adequate interest is not charged and paid at least annually. For example, sales of principal residences and certain farm sales are not subject to § 1274. *See* § 1274(c)(3)(A), (B). The following example considers another exception, based on the $250,000 threshold requirement of § 1274(c)(3)(C).

5. Unstated Interest: Section 483

Example 8: Assume Seller, a cash method taxpayer, sells property to Purchaser for $100,000, payable 5 years from now, with no interest on the unpaid principal. The test rate is 10%, compounded semiannually. The property and the debt instrument are not publicly traded. Does § 1274 apply?

The answer is "No." Since the total payments here do not exceed $250,000, § 1274 is inapplicable. § 1274(c)(3)(C). Note, however, that no interest is being charged. Presumably, therefore, interest should be imputed, even if § 1274 is inapplicable.

The imputed interest in this Example will be provided by § 483. The interest imputed by §§ 1273 and 1274 is called OID; the interest imputed by § 483 is called "unstated interest." There is a critical difference, however, between the general OID rule of § 1273 and the unstated interest rule of § 483. Under § 1273, OID is subject to current inclusion in income even where there are no current payments. Under § 483, on the other hand, unstated interest (and stated interest) is included in income under a taxpayer's regular method of accounting. Reg. § 1.483-1(a)(2)(ii). Thus, for example, a cash method holder would take such interest into income as payments were received or constructively received.

Section 483 was originally enacted in 1964, and was considerably revised when the OID rules of §§ 1273 and 1274 came into the Code in 1984. On the facts of Example 8, the applicability of § 483 and the amount of "unstated interest" would be determined as follows:

(1) Is there a deferred payment? Section 483 is potentially applicable to any payment on account of a sale or exchange of property, due more than 6 months after the sale, under a contract where at least one payment is due more than a year after the sale. § 483(c)(1)(A). The 5-years-from-now payment in Example 8 satisfies this initial requirement.

(2) Is there "total unstated interest" under this contract? § 483(c)(1)(B). There is not adequate stated interest if the sum of the deferred payments due under the contract (here, $100,000), exceeds the present values of such payments and of any interest payments due under the contract. The excess, if any, constitutes unstated interest. *See* § 483(b); Reg. § 1.483-2(a)(1)(i), (2). Present value is generally determined under the rule of § 1274(b)(2), using a discount rate equal to the test rate based on the "lowest 3-month" applicable Federal rates. *See* Reg. § 1.483-3(a). Here, we have a test rate of 10%, compounded semiannually.[18] Applying that test rate, the present value of the $100,000 payment at maturity is $61,391. (This present value is also the "issue price" of the contract. Reg. § 1.446-2(d)(1)(i).) Total unstated interest is thus $100,000 less $61,391, or $38,609.

(3) This unstated interest is "earned" in the same manner OID was earned under § 1272(a), that is, by applying the 10% test rate, compounded semiannually, to the issue price of $61,391, but the earned unstated interest is not taken into account and treated as income by our cash method taxpayer until payment is made. *See* § 483(a); Reg. § 1.446-2(a). On the facts of Example 8, when the payment of $100,000 is made at maturity, all of the unstated interest under the contract has been earned, and all of it is thus properly allocable to the payment.

(4) Therefore, under § 483(a), $38,609 of the payment at maturity is treated as interest received by Seller and paid by Purchaser. The remaining $61,391 will be treated as the sales price for purposes of determining gain or loss on the sale.

---

[18] Assume the property in question is new § 38 property, and the 9% limitation under § 1274A, discussed below, therefore does not apply.

Would § 483 have applied in our prior Examples where debt was issued in exchange for cash or where § 1274 was applicable? The answer is "No." See § 483(d)(1), which gives priority to § 1273(b)(1)–(3) and § 1274.

> **Example 9:** Assume the total unstated interest on a contract subject to § 483 is $40,000. Further assume the present value of all deferred payments due under the contract, and thus the issue price, is $100,000 and no stated interest payments are called for. Finally, assume the test rate is again 10%, compounded semiannually, and an initial payment of $20,000 is due one year after the sale. What portion of the $20,000 payment is treated as interest?

Under the method of § 1272(a), the unstated interest applicable to the first 6 months is $5,000 (1/2 × 10% × $100,000); the unstated interest for the next 6 months is $5,250 (1/2 × 10% × $105,000). $10,250 of unstated interest is thus properly allocable to the $20,000 payment and is treated as interest. The remaining $9,750 of the $20,000 payment is not treated as interest, but is instead treated as payment on the sales price of the property.

> **Example 10:** Suppose Seller sells property to Purchaser for $3,000 or less. If the sales price cannot exceed $3,000, § 483 does not apply. § 483(d)(2). Unstated interest will not be imputed to any payments. (Recall that § 1274 will not apply because of the $250,000 threshold exception. § 1274(c)(3)(C).)

6. Special Rules: The Cash Method Election of Section 1274A — The $2,000,000 Rule

> **Example 11:** Assume Seller sells property to Purchaser for $1,000,000, payable 10 years from now, with no interest on the unpaid balance. The test rate is 10%, compounded semiannually. Neither the property nor the debt instrument is publicly traded.

Based on our study to this point, it would seem (because the $250,000 threshold of § 1274(c)(3)(C) is exceeded) that § 1274 and the current-inclusion rules of § 1272(a) will apply.

However, pursuant to § 1274A(c), the parties may be able to make an election to apply cash method accounting principles to the transaction. The requirements are as follows: (a) Because the debt instrument must be a "qualified debt instrument" — a term explained below — the property sold or exchanged cannot be "new § 38 property";[19] typically, new section 38 property means tangible personal property, the original use of which commences with the taxpayer. (b) The stated principal amount cannot exceed $2,000,000 (adjusted for inflation after 1989);[20] (c) Seller must not use the accrual method; (d) The property sold must not be dealer property; (e) Section 1274 must be otherwise applicable; (f) Seller and Purchaser must jointly elect to take the interest on the debt into account under the cash method. § 1274A(c)(2).

---

[19] The term "new section 38 property" is defined in § 48(b), as in effect prior to the Revenue Reconciliation Act of 1990.

[20] For 2015, the inflation-adjusted limit is $4,033,800. Rev. Rul. 2014-30, 2014-49 I.R.B. 910.

Assuming the requirements are met, Seller takes the unstated interest computed under the rules of § 483 into account as income as payments are made. Purchaser, pursuant to the § 1274A(c) election, takes unstated interest into account as interest expense as payments are made.

7. Special Rules: Interest Rate Limitation on Qualifying Sales of $2,800,000 or Less

In the case of any "qualified debt instrument," the discount rate under §§ 1274 and 483 is limited to 9%, compounded semiannually. § 1274A(a). Of course, if the test rate is lower than 9%, compounded semiannually, the lower figure is used. A qualifying debt instrument is one given on a sale or exchange of property where the stated principal amount of the debt instrument does not exceed $2,800,000 and where the property in question is not new § 38 property. § 1274A(b). The $2,800,000 limit is adjusted for inflation after 1989. § 1274A(d)(2).[21]

> **Example 12:** Seller sells land to Purchaser for $2,500,000, payable 10 years from now, with no interest on the unpaid balance. The test rate is 10%, compounded semiannually.

The discount rate applied shall be 9%, compounded semiannually, pursuant to § 1274A(a). If the test rate were 8%, then the discount rate applied would be 8%.

If the property in question were, however, new depreciable tangible personal property, it might constitute new § 38 property, and the 9% limitation would not apply.

If the stated principal amount were an inflation-adjusted $2,000,000 or less, not only could the 9% limitation apply, but the "cash method election" described above would also be available, subject to the requirements of § 1274A(c).

8. Special Rules: Interest Rate Limitation on Certain Land Transfers Between Related Parties

In determining unstated interest on a sale of land between family members, the maximum discount rate applied is 6%, compounded semiannually. § 483(e)(1). When the test rate actually exceeds 6%, the effect of this special rule is to permit more of the amount paid under a deferred-payment sale to be characterized for tax purposes as principal, and to require less to be treated as interest than would otherwise be the case. To the extent that the aggregate sales price of qualifying sales between individuals for the calendar year exceeds $500,000, this special 6% rule does not apply. § 483(e)(3). Note that § 1274 will not apply to sales governed by § 483(e). § 1274(c)(3)(F).

9. Special Rules: Personal Use Property

Sections 1274 and 483 do not apply to the obligor on a deferred-payment sale of "personal use property," defined as property not used in a trade or business or for income-producing purposes. § 1275(b)(1), (3). The practical effect of the rule is to

---

[21] For 2015, the inflation-adjusted limit is $5,647,300. Rev. Rul. 2014-30, 2014-49 I.R.B. 910.

allow the cash method purchaser of personal use property to deduct OID (to the extent it is otherwise deductible) only when it is paid, not as it accrues. § 1275(b)(2). An accrual method seller, however, continues to report OID income as it accrues, not when it is paid. Section 1275(b)(2) thus operates mainly to postpone interest deductions without a concomitant postponement of income.

10.   Coordination with Section 7872

Section 7872 provides special rules governing the tax treatment of certain "below market loans." *See* Chapter 36. In order to avoid the potential application of differing sets of imputed-interest rules to the same sale or exchange of property, § 7872 provides that it shall not apply to any loan to which §§ 483 or 1274 applies. § 7872(f)(8).

11.   Ordering Between Sections 1274 and 483

Note that § 483 did not apply in the earlier examples where § 1274 was applicable. The unstated interest rules and the OID rules are coordinated by providing that § 483 does not apply where an issue price has been determined under § 1274 or § 1273(b)(1), (2), or (3). *See* § 483(d)(1).

AUTHORS' NOTE:
SECTION 467 RENTAL AGREEMENTS

In 1984, Congress extended the imputed interest concept to rentals with the enactment of § 467. As an illustration of some of the practices with which Congress was concerned, assume that a cash method landlord rents a commercial building to an accrual method tenant for 5 years for $500,000, with all the rent to be paid in a single lump sum payment at the end of the 5-year period. The accrual method tenant will claim annual rental deductions, each presumably equal to one-fifth of the lump sum payment, while the cash method landlord will report no income until payment is actually made at the end of the 5-year period. Do you recognize in this arrangement yet another version of the deduction-now, income-later mismatching game, played at the expense of the Treasury? Beyond the mismatching, one might also reasonably conclude the lump sum payment at the end of Year 5 is not entirely rent. Part of the rent payment could be characterized as compensation for the delayed payment of the rent attributable to the four prior years; part of the "rent," in other words, could be seen as interest on the unpaid rent of prior years. Accordingly, § 467 takes the following approach to the rental arrangements it covers: (1) it places both landlord and tenant on the accrual method with respect to their rental agreement; (2) it provides for the accrual and current reporting of rent each year; and (3) it provides for the accrual and reporting of interest on unpaid rent — as was done with deferred interest under the OID rules.

Section 467 applies to rental arrangements of tangible property involving total payments of more than $250,000, with either increases in rent over the lease term or the deferral of rent beyond the year after the year to which the rent relates. § 467(d). The complex rules governing section 467 arrangements are detailed in extensive regulations, and are beyond the scope of this chapter.

UNITED STATES v. MIDLAND-ROSS CORPORATION
United States Supreme Court
381 U.S. 54 (1965)

MR. JUSTICE BRENNAN delivered the opinion of the Court.

The question for decision is whether, under the Internal Revenue Code of 1939, certain gains realized by the taxpayer are taxable as capital gains or as ordinary income. The taxpayer bought noninterest-bearing promissory notes from the issuers at prices discounted below the face amounts. With one exception, each of the notes was held for more than six months, and, before maturity and in the year of purchase, was sold for less than its face amount but more than its issue price. It is conceded that the gain in each case was the economic equivalent of interest for the use of the money to the date of sale but the taxpayer reported the gains as capital gains. The Commissioner of Internal Revenue determined that the gains attributable to original issue discount were but interest in another form and therefore were taxable as ordinary income. Respondent paid the resulting deficiencies and in this suit for refund prevailed in the District Court for the Northern District of Ohio, 214 F. Supp. 631, and in the Court of Appeals for the Sixth Circuit, 335 F.2d 561. Because this treatment as capital gains conflicts with the result reached by other courts of appeals, we granted certiorari. We reverse.

The more favorable capital gains treatment applied only to gain on "the sale or exchange of a capital asset." [1221]. Although original issue discount becomes property when the obligation falls due or is liquidated prior to maturity and [1221] defined a capital asset as "property held by the taxpayer," we have held that "not everything which can be called property in the ordinary sense and which is outside the statutory exclusions qualifies as a capital asset. This Court has long held that the term 'capital asset' is to be construed narrowly in accordance with the purpose of Congress to afford capital-gains treatment only in situations typically involving the realization of appreciation in value accrued over a substantial period of time, and thus to ameliorate the hardship of taxation of the entire gain in one year." *Commissioner v. Gillette Motor Co.*, 364 U.S. 130, 134.

See also *Corn Products Co. v. Commissioner*, 350 U.S. 46, 52. In applying this principle, this Court has consistently construed "capital asset" to exclude property representing income items or accretions to the value of a capital asset themselves properly attributable to income. Thus the Court has held that "capital asset" does not include compensation awarded a taxpayer as representing the fair rental value of its facilities during the period of their operation under government control, *Commissioner v. Gillette Motor Co., supra*; the amount of the proceeds of the sale of an orange grove attributable to the value of an unmatured annual crop, *Watson v. Commissioner*, 345 U.S. 544; an unexpired lease, *Hort v. Commissioner*, 313 U.S. 28; and oil payment rights, *Commissioner v. P.G. Lake, Inc.*, 356 U.S. 260. Similarly, earned original issue discount cannot be regarded as "typically involving the realization of appreciation in value accrued over a substantial period of time . . .

[given capital gains treatment] to ameliorate the hardship of taxation of the entire gain in one year."

Earned original issue discount serves the same function as stated interest, concededly ordinary income and not a capital asset; it is simply "compensation for the use or forbearance of money." *Deputy v. du Pont*, 308 U.S. 488, 498. Unlike the typical case of capital appreciation, the earning of discount to maturity is predictable and measurable and is "essentially a substitute for . . . payments which [§ 61] expressly characterizes as gross income [; thus] it must be regarded as ordinary income, and it is immaterial that for some purposes the contract creating the right to such payments may be treated as 'property' or 'capital.' " *Hort v. Commissioner, supra*, at 31. The $6 earned on a one-year note for $106 issued for $100 is precisely like the $6 earned on a one-year loan of $100 at 6% stated interest. The application of general principles would indicate, therefore, that earned original issue discount, like stated interest, should be taxed under [§ 61] as ordinary income.[22]

The taxpayer argues, however, that administrative practice and congressional treatment of original issue discount under the 1939 Code establish that such discount is to be accounted for as capital gain when realized. [The Court proceeded to reject this argument.]

The concept of discount or premium as altering the effective rate of interest is not to be rejected as an "esoteric concept derived from subtle and theoretic analysis." *Old Colony R. Co. v. Commissioner*, 284 U.S. 552, 561, 52 S. Ct. 211, 214, 76 L. Ed. 484. For, despite some expressions indicating a contrary view, this Court has often recognized the economic function of discount as interest.

For these reasons we hold that earned original issue discount is not entitled to capital gains treatment under the 1939 Code.

Reversed.

---

[22] Our disposition makes it unnecessary to decide certain questions raised at argument, as to which we intimate no view:

(1) Since each note was sold in the year of purchase, we do not reach the question whether an accrual-basis taxpayer is required to report discount earned before the final disposition of an obligation;

(2) Since no argument is made that the gain on the sale of each note varied significantly from the portion of the original issue discount earned during the holding period, we do not reach the question of the tax treatment under the 1939 Code of "market discount" arising from post-issue purchases at prices varying from issue price plus a ratable portion of the original issue discount, or of the tax treatment of gains properly attributable to fluctuations in the interest rate and market price of obligations as distinguished from the anticipated increase resulting from mere passage of time.

Chapter 44

LIMITATIONS ON TAX SHELTERS — SECTIONS 465 AND 469

Part A:
Section 465 — The At Risk Rules

I. PROBLEMS

Raymond, a successful doctor, agreed to purchase an office complex from a business acquaintance, Noreen, who was having financial difficulties. Noreen had purchased the office building a few years before as an investment and still owed $990,000 to the seller under the terms of an assignable installment contract. Noreen was not personally liable on the contract. Noreen agreed to sell the office complex to Raymond for $1,000,000, with Raymond paying Noreen $10,000 and taking the property subject to the $990,000 installment indebtedness encumbering the property. The office complex had an appraised value of $1,050,000. Raymond, like Noreen, had no personal liability with respect to the $990,000 owing under the contract. The office complex was vacant at the time of Raymond's purchase and Raymond immediately leased the office complex on a net lease basis, requiring the lessee to pay the real property taxes and all other expenses in addition to the annual lease payments of $90,000.

(a) How much is Raymond at risk in the activity of holding and renting the office complex?

(b) Would your answer to (a) be different if Raymond had borrowed $990,000 cash on a nonrecourse basis from a bank and used this amount to pay the balance on Noreen's contract?

(c) What if in (b) Raymond borrowed the money from his sister instead of a bank?

(d) Assume in Year 1, Raymond's income from the building amounted to $90,000 and the total expenses (including interest and depreciation) amounted to $95,000. May Raymond deduct the $5,000 loss against the income which he generates from practicing medicine? How will the loss affect Raymond's amount at risk?

(e) Assume in Year 2 the deductions allowable on the complex exceeded the income by $7,000, how much could Raymond deduct? How much would he be at risk after Year 2?

(f)   Assume in Year 3 rental receipts equaled expenses and Raymond invested an additional $10,000 by making a principal payment on the installment indebtedness encumbering the property. How would that impact Raymond's amount at risk? What effect would that have on any losses which Raymond was not allowed to deduct in Year 2 because of the § 465 limitations?

(g)   Assume in Year 4 the rental receipts exceed Raymond's expenses by $15,000 so that Raymond is required to report that amount of net income from the activity. How will that affect Raymond's amount at risk? What impact on Raymond's amount at risk if Raymond uses the $15,000 excess to make a principal payment on the installment indebtedness?

(h)   Assuming the facts of (g), what consequences to Raymond under § 465 if he uses $25,000 of the Year 4 rental receipts for his own personal purposes?

Assignment for Chapter 44, Part A: Section 465:

Complete the problems.

Read: Internal Revenue Code: §§ 465(a)(1)–(2), (b), (c)(1)–(3), (d), (e); 49(a)(1)(D)(iv), (v)
Treasury Regulations: § 1.465-27(b)(1) and (3).

Materials: Overview

II.   VOCABULARY

at risk
qualified nonrecourse financing
loss (for § 465 purposes)
activity

III.   OBJECTIVES

1.   To explain the purpose of the at risk rules of § 465.

2.   To compute a taxpayer's initial amount at risk.

3.   To compute a taxpayer's amount at risk taking into consideration income, loss, and withdrawals from an activity.

4.   To explain and apply the recapture rule of § 465(e).

5.   To identify financing which will be characterized as qualified nonrecourse financing.

6.   To compute the taxpayer's amount at risk when qualified nonrecourse financing is involved.

IV. OVERVIEW

A. General Background

A taxpayer's basis in property generally limits the amount of deductions allowable with respect to that property. For example, a loss deduction under § 165 cannot exceed a taxpayer's adjusted basis in the property. § 165(b). Likewise, depreciation deductions are determined with reference to (and cannot exceed) a taxpayer's adjusted basis in the depreciable property. Thus, a direct correlation exists between the amount of one's basis in property and the amount potentially deductible with respect to that property.

In computing basis, we generally begin with the cost of the property. As you learned in Chapter 38, *Crane v. Commissioner* and its progeny established that the cost basis of acquired property includes that part of the purchase price financed by nonrecourse borrowing. In other words, a taxpayer's basis may reflect borrowed funds with respect to which the taxpayer has no personal liability. This treatment of nonrecourse liabilities set the stage for the modern tax shelter by enabling taxpayers to claim deductions far in excess of the dollars they actually had at risk. For example, assume a taxpayer purchases a piece of equipment for business use. The purchase price is $100,000, and the taxpayer finances the equipment entirely through a nonrecourse loan. Applying *Crane*, the taxpayer will have a $100,000 basis in the equipment. In turn, that basis will enable the taxpayer to claim substantial depreciation deductions under §§ 167 and 168, even though the taxpayer has not personally invested a single dollar in the equipment and cannot be forced to do so. The depreciation deductions generated by the equipment can be used by the taxpayer to offset income from other sources.

There is, of course, a downside to this arrangement. If the taxpayer never pays the nonrecourse loan, the taxpayer will ultimately be taxed on the loan proceeds when the taxpayer disposes of or abandons the property.[1] For example, if the taxpayer never paid any part of the principal of the loan, completely depreciated the equipment, and then sold the equipment for $100,000, the taxpayer's gain on the sale would be $100,000.[2] Thus, the taxpayer would have claimed $100,000 in depreciation (all of which is attributable to the basis provided by the nonrecourse financing) and upon the sale would report $100,000 of income. Note, however, that the taxpayer, as a result of the $100,000 in depreciation deductions, would have been allowed to defer tax on $100,000 of income (*i.e.*, the income offset by the depreciation deductions) until taxpayer finally disposed of the equipment.

---

[1] *Crane* and *Tufts*, as discussed in Chapter 38, require taxpayers to include in their amount realized any liabilities, recourse or nonrecourse, that a purchaser assumes or to which the purchaser takes the property subject. Note specifically, however, Reg. §. 1-1001-2(c) Example 8 illustrating the rule that the amount realized on a sale or other disposition of property securing a recourse liability does not include amounts that are income from the discharge of indebtedness under § 61(a)(12).

[2] Applying the *Crane* rule, the taxpayer's amount realized would be $100,000, *i.e.*, the amount of the nonrecourse liability taken subject to by the purchaser; the taxpayer's adjusted basis would be $0; and the taxpayer's § 1001(a) gain would be $100,000. All of the gain would be characterized as ordinary income under the § 1245 recapture rules.

The opportunity for tax deferral afforded by nonrecourse financing of investments encouraged taxpayers to invest in activities which were economically unsound. For example, in *Estate of Franklin*, included in Chapter 38, a group of doctors entered into a transaction to purchase a motel for a price far in excess of the fair market value of the property using nonrecourse financing. The doctors' out-of-pocket investment was minimal and they were not personally liable for the purchase price. They clearly had no interest in operating a motel. Rather, at very little cost to themselves, they sought to generate substantial interest and depreciation deductions computed with reference to an inflated purchase price. In turn, the doctors could use these deductions to offset the income from their medical practices. Simply stated, the doctors engaged in the transaction only because of the tax benefits available. *Estate of Franklin* provides a classic example of how tax shelters of that period were designed to exploit a tax system which (1) accorded taxpayers advance credit in basis for making the investment reflected by nonrecourse financing, and (2) permitted taxpayers to utilize deductions attributable to nonrecourse financing to offset income from other unrelated activities.

In 1976, Congress enacted the § 465 "at risk" limitations to prevent taxpayers from claiming artificial deductions of the type claimed by the doctors in *Estate of Franklin*. The legislative history of § 465 sets forth Congress' rationale: "[I]t was not equitable to allow individual investors to defer tax on income from other sources through losses generated by tax sheltering activities. One of the most significant problems in tax shelters was the use of nonrecourse financing and other risk-limiting devices [such as guarantees, stop-loss agreements, guaranteed repurchase agreements, etc.] which enabled investors in these activities to deduct losses from the activities in amounts which exceeded the total investment the investor actually placed at risk in the activity. The Act consequently provides an 'at risk' rule to deal directly with this abuse in tax shelters."[3]

B. Operation of the At Risk Rules

While quite complex, the at risk rules essentially prevent a taxpayer from deducting losses generated by certain business or income producing activities in excess of the aggregate amount with respect to which the taxpayer is at risk (*i.e.*, the amount the taxpayer could actually lose) in each activity. For § 465 purposes, a loss is the excess of the deductions attributable to the activity over the income from the activity. § 465(d). The rules are applicable to individuals, estates, trusts, and to most closely held corporations. § 465(a)(1).

1. Activities Subject to the At Risk Rules

Initially, the at risk rules were applicable only to a narrow range of activities. *See* § 465(c)(1). Today, any business or income producing activity, including real estate activity, engaged in by a taxpayer is covered. § 465(c)(3)(A). However, as explained herein, § 465 provides an important exception for real estate activity.

---

[3] Staff of the Joint Committee on Taxation, General Explanation of the Tax Reform Act of 1976, 94th Cong. 2d Sess., 1976-3 vol. 2 C.B. 47.

2.   Determination of the Initial Amount At Risk

A taxpayer's initial amount at risk is the sum of (1) the taxpayer's cash contributions to the activity; (2) the adjusted basis of other property contributed by the taxpayer to the activity; and (3) amounts borrowed for use in the activity for which the taxpayer is personally liable or has pledged property (other than property used in the activity) as security.[4] Amounts borrowed from any person who has an interest in the activity or from a person related to such person will not be considered amounts at risk. § 465(b)(3)(A).[5] Likewise, a taxpayer is not at risk with respect to amounts protected against loss through nonrecourse financing, guarantees or other similar arrangements. § 465(b)(4).

3.   Qualified Nonrecourse Financing

In extending the at risk rules to the activity of holding real property, Congress created a special exception, applicable only to that activity, which allows certain nonrecourse financing to be considered in computing a taxpayer's amount at risk. "Qualified nonrecourse financing" involves funds borrowed by the taxpayer with respect to the activity of holding real property and with respect to which no person is personally liable for repayment. It includes (1) amounts borrowed by the taxpayer from any Federal, State, or local government or instrumentality thereof; (2) borrowed amounts guaranteed by a Federal, State or local government; and (3) amounts borrowed from a "qualified person." § 465(b)(6); Reg. § 1.465-27(b)(1). As described by the Staff of the Joint Committee on Taxation, the term "qualified person" includes "any person actively and regularly engaged in the business of lending money. Such persons generally include, for example, a bank, savings and loan association, credit union, or insurance company regulated under Federal, State, or local law, or a pension trust. However, qualified persons do not include (1) any person from whom the taxpayer acquired the property (or a person related to such person)[6] or (2) any person who receives a fee (*e.g.*, a promoter) with respect to the taxpayer's investment in the property (or a person related to such person). For example, no portion of seller financing and promoter financing is qualified nonrecourse financing."[7] *See* § 49(a)(1)(D)(iv).

Nonrecourse financing obtained from a related person will constitute "qualified nonrecourse financing" if it is commercially reasonable and on substantially the same terms as loans involving unrelated persons. § 465(b)(6)(D)(ii). According to the Staff of the Joint Committee on Taxation, "Congress intends that terms of nonrecourse financing are commercially reasonable if the financing is a written unconditional promise to pay on demand or on a specified date or dates a sum or

---

[4] Section 465(b). Note that borrowing for which a taxpayer has pledged property is only taken into account to the extent of the net fair market value of the taxpayer's interest in such property. § 465(b)(2)(B).

[5] *See Alexander v. Commissioner*, 95 T.C. 467 (1990) (court applied § 465(c)(3)(D) and held that amounts borrowed from a party with an interest in the activity were not excluded from the taxpayer's amount at risk under § 465(b)(3)(A)).

[6] Related persons generally include family members, fiduciaries, and corporations or partnerships in which a person has at least a 10% interest. § 465(b)(3)(C).

[7] General Explanation of the Tax Reform Act of 1986, p. 258.

sums certain in money, and the interest rate is a reasonable market rate of interest (taking into account the maturity of the obligation). . . . The terms of the financing will also not be considered commercially reasonable if, for example, the term of the loan exceeds the useful life of the property, or if the right to foreclosure or collection with respect to the debt is limited (except to the extent provided under applicable local law)."[8]

4. Adjustments to the Amount At Risk

The amount a taxpayer has at risk in an activity is adjusted each year for income and losses generated by the activity and for withdrawals from the activity. Prop. Reg. § 1.465-22(b) and (c). The various adjustments which must be made to a taxpayer's amount at risk can be best explained by the use of an example.

Erik purchases property and uses it in a business activity (other than the activity of holding real property). The purchase price of the property is $100,000 and Erik makes a downpayment of $10,000 and borrows $90,000 of the purchase price on a nonrecourse basis. Applying § 465, Erik's initial amount at risk is $10,000. [Even though the property may in fact be worth $100,000 (or perhaps even more) and Erik will almost assuredly ultimately pay the nonrecourse debt, Erik nonetheless will not be treated as being at risk with respect to the nonrecourse debt.] Assume in its first year, the activity suffers a loss of $5,000.[9] The at risk rules will not prevent that loss from being fully deductible. Assuming the activity is not a passive activity (see discussion of the passive activity rules in Part B of this Chapter), the loss will be deductible against Erik's income from other sources.

Assume in Year 2, another $8,000 loss is generated. Assume also that $5,000 of the cash generated by the activity in Year 2 is used to make a payment on the nonrecourse indebtedness and Erik withdraws $2,000 of cash from the activity. Under § 465(b)(5), Erik is required to reduce his amount at risk from $10,000 to $5,000 as a result of the loss in Year 1. In addition, Erik must reduce his amount at risk from $5,000 to $3,000 by the $2,000 of cash which he has withdrawn.[10] Will the $5,000 payment made on the nonrecourse loan increase Erik's amount at risk? The answer is "No." The repayment of a nonrecourse loan from cash generated by the activity has no effect on the amount at risk.[11] That makes sense because the repayment does not represent any increase in Erik's investment in the business activity. (It is comparable to taking the money out of the activity, thus reducing the amount at risk and then reinvesting it in the activity by paying down the nonrecourse debt, thereby increasing the amount at risk.) Thus, in Year 2 there is only $3,000 at risk. Accordingly, § 465(a)(1) limits Erik's loss deduction in Year 2 to $3,000. The remaining $5,000 of loss is disallowed by the at risk rules and is treated

---

[8] General Explanation of the Tax Reform Act of 1986, pp. 258–259.

[9] For purposes of this example, assume all losses are a function of depreciation and interest deductions. Note that, under § 465(d), losses are the excess of deductions over income.

[10] Prop. Reg. § 1.465-22(b). The downward adjustment of the amount at risk is obviously appropriate since Erik now only has $8,000 of his own dollars in the activity.

[11] Prop. Reg. § 1.465-25(b)(2)(i). Obviously, if Erik were to use outside funds, *e.g.*, withdraws an amount from his bank account and pays down the nonrecourse debt, his amount at risk would increase accordingly. Read Prop. Reg. sect; 1.465-25(b)(3), Example 3.

as a deduction allocable to the activity in Year 3. § 465(a)(2).

Assume in Year 3 the income from the activity exactly equals the deductions available (other than the $5,000 deduction carried over from Year 2). Assume Erik also withdraws an additional $2,000 from the cash flow of the activity. As a result of the loss deduction of $3,000 allowed in Year 2, Erik's at risk amount was reduced to $0. Obviously, the $5,000 deduction carried over from Year 2 cannot be used and must be carried over to the following year. Furthermore, Erik's withdrawal of an additional $2,000 in cash from the activity creates a negative $2,000 balance in the at risk account. This withdrawal will trigger application of the § 465(e) recapture rule requiring Erik to include $2,000 in gross income. Section 465(e)(1) requires a taxpayer to include in income an amount equal to the deductions taken in excess of the taxpayer's amount at risk. Here, Erik in Years 1 and 2 had taken loss deductions totaling $8,000. Erik originally contributed and had at risk $10,000. In Years 2 and 3, he withdrew a total of $4,000. Thus, he had only $6,000 of his own money in the activity and yet had claimed a total of $8,000 in deductions. Section 465(e) requires a restoration of $2,000 of those deductions by means of a $2,000 inclusion in gross income. Section 465(e)(1)(B) allows Erik to treat this $2,000 amount as a deduction allocable to such activity in Year 4. Thus, there will be a total of $7,000 of deduction carried over to Year 4. With the inclusion of $2,000 in income, Erik's at risk amount will be returned to $0. Prop. Reg. § 1.465-3(b).

Assume in Year 4, the activity generates net income of $5,000 (not taking into account the $7,000 of loss deductions carried over from prior years under § 465(a)(2)). Erik may use $5,000 of the $7,000 loss deduction carryover to offset this $5,000 of net income in Year 4. § 465(a)(2), 465(e)(1)(B). Because Erik's amount at risk remains at $0, the other $2,000 of loss deduction carryover cannot be used and must be carried over to the following year.

Assume in Year 5, the activity generates income of $5,000 and there are no deductions other than the $2,000 of deductions carried over from Year 4. Erik will be entitled to offset the $5,000 of income by the $2,000 of carryover deductions and will have income from the activity of $3,000 to report. In turn, the inclusion of $3,000 in income will increase Erik's amount at risk by $3,000. Prop. Reg. § 1.465-22(c)(1). Thus, if Erik chose to withdraw $3,000 of the cash in the activity, he could do so without triggering the recapture rule of § 465(e), discussed previously.

Erik's amount at risk will be increased not only by income from the activity which he reports but also by (1) Erik's direct payment of the nonrecourse indebtedness; (2) additional cash contributions from Eric; and (3) additional property contributions by Erik. Prop. Reg. §§ 1.465-22(a), 1.465-23(a), and 1.465-25(a)(2). Proposed Regulation § 1.465-66 provides that, if a taxpayer transfers or otherwise disposes of part or all of an activity or an interest in an activity during the taxable year, the gain, if any, recognized on the transfer or disposition will be considered as income from the activity. This rule, in effect, will generally enable taxpayers to deduct losses suspended as a result of § 465 when the taxpayer disposes of the activity.

As this example demonstrates, Congress, by means of the at risk rules, successfully limited a taxpayer's ability to use losses in excess of the amounts the taxpayer actually could lose in an activity. The at risk rules thus reduced the use of the deferral benefits historically afforded by tax shelters. However, losses not disallowed by § 465 could, as noted, be used to offset income from other sources. As discussed in Part B of this Chapter, Congress in enacting § 469 sought to eliminate this additional benefit long associated with tax shelter activity.

Part B:

Section 469 — Limitation on Passive Activity
Losses and Credits

I. PROBLEMS

1. Jane, a practicing attorney, owns an interest in a limited partnership engaged in the business of producing an off-Broadway play. She spends an average of 5 hours per month assisting in the development of publicity campaigns. She also is a joint venturer with a friend in a cattle breeding operation. Jane has no knowledge of cattle and seldom visits the ranch where the cattle breeding activities occur. The ranch is owned by Jane's co-venturer and is located over 200 miles from Jane's home. Jane also has significant stock investments and a lucrative law practice. Assume, for § 469 purposes, the cattle breeding operation, the interest in the off-Broadway play, and the law practice are all separate activities.

   (a) Assume this year (Year 1) Jane's share of losses from the limited partnership is $5,000; her share of the losses from the cattle breeding operation is $10,000; her stock dividends amount to $15,000 and her income from her law practice is $125,000. May Jane deduct the losses from the limited partnership and the cattle breeding venture? How would your answer change if she spends approximately one week per month working on sales and marketing efforts in the cattle breeding operation?

   (b) Assume the following year (Year 2) Jane's share of losses from the limited partnership is $10,000; her share of the gain from the cattle breeding operation is $18,000; her stock dividends are $5,000 and her income from the law practice is $125,000. Explain the significance under § 469 of Jane's gain from the cattle breeding operation.

   (c) Assume, at the beginning of Year 3, Jane's limited partnership interest became worthless when the off-Broadway show was forced to close and the limited partnership dissolved. Assume Jane had a $15,000 basis in her limited partnership interest. In Year 3, her share of gain from the cattle breeding operation was $5,000; her stock dividends amounted to $5,000; and her income from her law practice equalled $100,000. Under § 469, what tax impact as a result of the worthlessness of the limited partnership interest?

2. Martha and Bill, husband and wife, own a single family residence they rent to college students. Bill and Martha have total income from wages of $95,000 per year. Assume Bill is employed as a mechanic and Martha as a nurse. Their wages and the rent from the residence constitute their only income. During the current year, the expenses (including interest and depreciation) related to the rental property exceed the total rent received from the property by $20,000. May Martha and Bill deduct the $20,000? What difference, if any, would it make if Martha and Bill had total income

of $110,000? In answering these questions, assume § 469(c)(7) is inapplicable to Martha and Bill.

Assignment for Chapter 44, Part B: Section 469:

Complete the problems.

Read: Internal Revenue Code: § 469(a),(b), (c)(1), (c)(2), (c)(4), (c)(6), (c)(7)[skim], (d)(1), (e)(1), (e)(3), (f)(1)[skim], (f)(3)[skim], (g)(1)(A), (h)(1)–(3), (h)(5), (i)(1)–(3)(A), (i)(3)(E), (i)(6)(A) and (D), (j)(6)–(7)[skim], (j)(8), (l).
Treasury Regulations: §§ 1.469-4; 1.469-5(f)(1); 1.469-5T(a)–(e)(2), (f).
Materials: Overview

II. VOCABULARY

activity
passive activity
passive activity loss
passive activity credit
material participation
active participation
portfolio income
suspended losses and credits

III. OBJECTIVES

1. To explain the purpose of the § 469 rules in limiting the deduction of passive activity losses and credits.

2. To identify passive activities.

3. To compute the amount of passive activity losses.

4. To evaluate whether a taxpayer is a material participant in an activity.

5. To evaluate whether a taxpayer is an active participant in a rental real estate activity.

6. To explain and apply the special $25,000 offset rule of § 469(i).

7. To determine the amount of deductions which a taxpayer may claim when a taxpayer disposes entirely of an interest in a passive activity.

8. To explain the consequences under § 469 of a taxpayer's death.

9. To explain the consequences under § 469 of a gift of a taxpayer's interest in a passive activity.

IV. OVERVIEW

A. Background

Prior to the 1986 Tax Reform Act, taxpayers were essentially free to offset income from one source with deductions (or credits) from tax shelter activities. For example, a taxpayer owning an interest in a real estate limited partnership could use the deductions generated by that tax shelter to offset the taxpayer's income from other sources, *e.g.*, salary, dividends, interest. Not only did such arrangements reduce federal tax revenues, they also contributed to a perception that the tax system was inequitable and benefitted the wealthy who could afford to invest in tax shelters. In turn, compliance suffered and tax shelters flourished. The various anti-tax shelter weapons available to the Service, *e.g.*, §§ 465 and 183, were not adequate to solve these problems. While measuring the maximum amount a taxpayer might lose in an activity, the at risk rules of § 465 (discussed in Part A of this Chapter) did not address whether and when deductions from one activity could be used to offset income from another activity. Section 183, limiting deductions attributable to activities not engaged in for profit (*see* Chapter 20), was likewise too narrow in focus and was also cumbersome administratively.[12]

In 1986, Congress enacted a new set of rules intended to address the problems associated with the burgeoning tax shelter industry. As noted by the Staff of the Joint Committee on Taxation:

> Congress determined that decisive action was needed to curb the expansion of tax sheltering and to restore to the tax system the degree of equity that was a necessary precondition to a beneficial and widely desired reduction in rates. So long as tax shelters were permitted to erode the Federal tax base, a low-rate system could provide neither sufficient revenues, nor sufficient progressivity, to satisfy the general public that tax liability bore a fair relationship to the ability to pay. In particular, a provision significantly limiting the use of tax shelter losses was viewed as unavoidable if substantial rate reductions were to be provided to high-income taxpayers without disproportionately reducing the share of total liability under the individual income tax borne by high-income taxpayers as a group.

> Congress viewed the question of how to prevent harmful and excessive tax sheltering as not a simple one. One way to address the problem would have been to eliminate substantially all tax preferences in the Internal Revenue Code. For two reasons, however, this course was determined by Congress to be inappropriate.

---

[12] The Commissioner used § 183 effectively in a number of tax shelter cases where taxpayers sought to use deductions from one activity to offset income from other activities. For example, in *Estate of Baron v. Commissioner*, 83 T.C. 542 (1984), the Commissioner successfully argued that the acquisition of rights in a master recording did not constitute an activity engaged in for profit. As a result, the taxpayer was not allowed to claim depreciation deductions which were far in excess of the income anticipated from the activity. *See also Soriano v. Commissioner*, 90 T.C. 44 (1988). As the decisions in these cases suggest, however, the application of § 183 requires complicated economic analysis to determine whether profit motivation exists.

First, while the Act reduces or eliminates some tax preference items that Congress decided did not provide social or economic benefits commensurate with their cost, there were many preferences that Congress concluded were socially or economically beneficial. It was determined that certain preferences were particularly beneficial when used primarily to advance the purposes upon which Congress relied in enacting them, rather than to avoid taxation of income from sources unrelated to the preferred activity.

Second, Congress viewed as prohibitively difficult, and perhaps impossible, the task of designing a tax system that measured income perfectly. For example, the statutory allowance for depreciation . . . reflects broad industry averages, as opposed to providing precise item-by-item measurements. Accordingly, taxpayers with assets that depreciate less rapidly than the average, or that appreciate over time (as may be the case with certain real estate), could engage in tax sheltering even under the minimum tax, in the absence of direct action regarding the tax shelter problem.

The question of what constituted a tax shelter that should be subject to limitations was viewed as closely related to the question of who Congress intends to benefit when it enacts a tax preference. For example in providing preferential depreciation for real estate or favorable accounting rules for farming, it was not Congress's primary intent to permit outside investors to avoid tax liability with respect to their salaries by investing in limited partnership syndications. Rather, Congress intended to benefit and provide incentives to taxpayers active in the businesses to which the preferences were directed.

Moreover, Congress concluded that restricting the use of losses from business activities in which the taxpayer did not materially participate against other sources of positive income (such as salary and portfolio income) would address a fundamental aspect of the tax shelter problem. Instances in which the tax system applies simple rules at the expense of economic accuracy encouraged the structuring of transactions to take advantage of the situations in which such rules gave rise to undermeasurement or deferral of income. Such transactions commonly were marketed to investors who did not intend to participate in the transactions, as devices for sheltering unrelated sources of positive income (*e.g.*, salary and portfolio income). Accordingly, by creating a bar against the use of losses from business activities in which the taxpayer does not materially participate to offset positive income sources such as salary and portfolio income, Congress believed that it was possible to significantly reduce the tax shelter problem.[13]

B.   Section 469 — In General

Section 469 represents the most significant anti-tax shelter legislation enacted by Congress. Section 469 is applicable to individuals, estates and trusts, and certain corporations. § 469(a)(2). Essentially, it requires taxpayers to classify their

---

[13] General Explanation of the Tax Reform Act of 1986, p. 210–213.

income, losses and credits as being generated either by so-called "passive activities" or "nonpassive activities." Passive activity deductions may only be used to offset income from passive activities; and tax credits related to passive activities may only offset tax liability of passive activities. § 469(a)(1), (d)(1), (2). Those passive activity losses which cannot be used currently because of the limitations imposed by § 469 will be carried forward to the next year and will be treated as passive activity losses in that year. § 469(b). There are no limits to the carryover of passive activity losses. As a general rule, suspended losses are allowed in full when the taxpayer disposes of the interest in the passive activity. § 469(g)(1)(A). Special rules govern the treatment of passive activity losses and credits when the taxpayer makes a gift of the passive activity or when the taxpayer dies. As this brief summary suggests, the passive activity rules result in the deferral and not the permanent disallowance of excess deductions and credits generated by passive activities.

C. Passive Activities

A passive activity involves the conduct of any trade or business in which the taxpayer does not materially participate. § 469(c)(1). The reference to "trade or business" includes those activities involving the conduct of a trade or business within the meaning of § 162.[14]

1. Material Participation

The rationale for limiting passive activities to those in which the taxpayer does not "materially participate" is explained by the Staff of the Joint Committee as follows:

> Congress determined that, in order for tax preferences to function as intended, their benefits should be directed primarily to taxpayers with a substantial and *bona fide* involvement in the activities to which the preference related. Congress also determined that it was appropriate to encourage nonparticipating investors to invest in particular activities, by permitting the use of preferences to reduce the rate of tax on income from those activities; however, such investors were viewed as not appropriately permitted to use tax benefits to shelter unrelated income.

> Congress believed that there were several reasons why it was appropriate to examine the materiality of a taxpayer's participation in an activity in determining the extent to which such taxpayer should be permitted to use tax benefits from the activity. A taxpayer who materially participated in an activity was viewed as more likely than a passive investor to approach the activity with a significant nontax economic profit motive, and to form a sound judgment as to whether the activity had genuine economic significance and value.

---

[14] Temp. Reg. § 1.469-1T(e)(1)(i). Section 469(c)(6) includes, to the extent provided by the regulations, any activity with respect to which expenses are allowable as a deduction under § 212.

A material participation standard identified an important distinction between different types of taxpayer activities. It was thought that, in general, the more passive investor seeks a return on capital invested, including returns in the form of reductions in the tax owed on unrelated income, rather than an ongoing source of livelihood. A material participation standard reduced the importance, for such investors, of the tax-reduction features of an investment, and thus increased the importance of the economic features in an investor's decision about where to invest his funds.[15]

For a taxpayer's participation to be considered material, it must be regular, continuous and substantial. § 469(h)(1). The temporary regulations provide seven alternative tests to satisfy this statutory requirement. For example, an individual materially participates in an activity for a given tax year if the individual's participation in the activity exceeds 500 hours during the year. Temp. Reg. § 1.469-5T(a)(1). Alternatively, material participation exists when the individual's participation for the year constitutes "substantially all of the participation" in that activity, or when the individual's participation for the year exceeds 100 hours and is also not less than the participation of any other individual. Temp. Reg. § 1.469-5T(a)(2), (3). Under yet another test, material participation in any activity for any five of the immediate past ten years constitutes material participation for the current year. Temp. Reg. § 1.469-5T(a)(5). Separate tests are also provided for "significant participation activities" and "personal service activities."[16] Finally, the temporary regulations also provide that material participation may be found based on "all the facts and circumstances." Temp. Reg. § 1.469-5T(a)(7), (b). Each of the tests must be examined before concluding that an individual did not materially participate in an activity in a given tax year.[17]

Special rules exist for limited partners. Except as provided by regulation, a limited partner does not materially participate with respect to his interest in the limited partnership. § 469(h)(2). Thus, as a general matter, a limited partnership interest generates passive income or passive loss. The temporary regulations, however, create significant exceptions to this general rule by providing a limited partner can materially participate by satisfying one of three material participation tests: the 500-hour test, the 5-years-out-of-10 test, or the personal-service-activity test. Temp. Reg. § 1.469-5T(e)(2). Despite the Service's arguments to the contrary, courts have ruled that for purposes of § 469(h)(2) an interest in a limited liability

---

[15] General Explanation of the Tax Reform Act of 1986, p. 212.

[16] Material participation exists if the activity is a significant participation activity — essentially a trade or business activity in which the individual participates for more than 100 hours during the year but not enough to achieve material participation under the other tests — and the individual's aggregate participation in all significant participation activities exceeds 500 hours. Temp. Reg. § 1.469-5T(a)(4), (c). Personal service activities are trades or businesses, such as law, in which capital is not a material income-producing factor. An individual materially participates in a personal service activity if the individual materially participated in the activity for any three prior years. Temp. Reg. § 1.469-5T(a)(6), (d).

[17] As a threshhold matter in satisfying the material participation requirement, the taxpayer's involvement with the activity must constitute "participation." Ordinarily, any work done in connection with the activity will suffice, but the temporary regulations define the term to exclude certain work not customarily done by owners and participation as an investor. Temp. Reg. § 1.469-5T(f)(2).

company will not be treated as an "interest in a limited partnership as a limited partner." *Newell v. Commissioner*, T.C. Memo 2010-23; *Garnett v. Commissioner*, 132 T.C. No. 19 (2009). In November 2011, Treasury issued proposed regulations to address this status issue. The proposed regulations eliminate the current regulation's reliance on limited liability for purposes of determining whether an interest is that of a limited partner and focus instead on the right to participate in the management of the entity. *See* Prop. Reg. § 1.469-5(a)(3).

2.   Rental Activities

Regardless of whether the taxpayer is a material participant, a rental activity is generally a passive activity subject to § 469. § 469(c) (2). A rental activity is any activity "where payments are principally for the use of tangible property." § 469(j)(8). If significant services are rendered in connection with the rental of property, however, the activity will not be treated as a rental activity. "For example, an activity consisting of the short-term leasing of motor vehicles, where the lessor furnishes services including maintenance of gas and oil, tire repair and changing, cleaning and polishing, oil changing and lubrication and engine and body repair, is not treated as a rental activity. . . . Based on similar considerations, renting hotel rooms or similar space used primarily for lodging of transients where significant services are provided generally is not a rental activity. . . . By contrast, renting apartments to tenants pursuant to leases (with, *e.g.*, month-to-month or yearly lease terms) is treated as a rental activity. Similarly, being the lessor of property subject to a net lease is a rental activity."[18]

In 1993, Congress amended § 469 to provide that rental real estate activities of a taxpayer would not be considered passive activities *per se* under § 469(c)(2) if the taxpayer met the following requirements:

> (1) more than half of the personal services the taxpayer performs in trades or businesses during the taxable year are performed in real property trades or businesses in which the taxpayer materially participates; and

> (2) the taxpayer performs more than 750 hours of service during the taxable year in real property trades or businesses in which the taxpayer materially participates.

§ 469(c)(7)(B). "Real property trade or business" is defined in § 469(c)(7)(C) to include "real property development, redevelopment, construction, reconstruction, acquisition, conversion, rental operation, management, leasing, or brokerage trade or business." Thus, a taxpayer meeting the above requirements who is engaged in rental real estate activities in which she materially participates may offset losses from those activities against nonpassive income including salary, portfolio income, etc.

---

[18] General Explanation of the Tax Reform Act of 1986, p. 249. Temp. Reg. § 1.469-1T(e)(3) discusses in detail what constitutes a rental activity and what services rendered in connection with the rental of property will be considered "significant."

D.   Scope of Passive Activities

Defining the scope of a passive activity is critical to the operation of § 469. The scope of an activity must be determined in order to assess whether a taxpayer is a material participant in the activity. Furthermore, the precise scope of the passive activity must be known before one can apply § 469(g), discussed herein, allowing the deduction of suspended losses of a passive activity when a taxpayer disposes of the entire interest in that activity.

As noted by the Staff of the Joint Committee, "[d]efining separate activities either too narrowly or too broadly could lead to evasion of the passive loss rule. For example, an overly narrow definition would permit taxpayers to claim losses against salary, portfolio, or active business income by selectively disposing of portions of their interests in activities with respect to which there has been depreciation or loss of value, while retaining any portion with respect to which there has been appreciation. An overly broad definition would permit taxpayers to amalgamate undertakings that in fact are separate, and thus to use material participation in one undertaking as a basis for claiming without limitation losses and credits from another undertaking."[19]

The Senate Finance Committee noted "[t]he determination of what constitutes a separate activity is intended to be made in a realistic economic sense. The question to be answered is what undertakings consist of an integrated and interrelated economic unit, conducted in coordination with or reliance upon each other, and constituting an appropriate unit for the measurement of gain or loss."[20] In determining the scope of an activity, one must consider the specific nature of the activity and identify an appropriate unit for determining gain and loss. For example, where different products or services are provided to customers, it is likely there is more than one activity. Of course, if it is customary that such products or services are provided together, there will only be one activity. Normal commercial practices will be relevant in determining the scope of an activity.[21]

The Treasury has issued Reg. § 1.469-4 providing a facts and circumstances test for determining what constitutes an activity and the scope of a given activity. The factors given the greatest weight "in determining whether activities constitute an appropriate economic unit for purposes of section 469" include: (i) similarities and differences in types of business; (ii) the extent of common control; (iii) geographical location; and (iv) interdependence between the activities. Reg. § 1.469-4(c)(2).

E.   Treatment of Losses and Credits

Section 469 requires a taxpayer to compute the gains and losses from each passive activity. The losses from an activity are first offset against the gains from that activity and any excess loss is then offset against excess gains from other passive activities. In other words, a taxpayer may deduct all the losses from passive activities from all the gains from passive activities. The excess of the aggregate

---

[19]   General Explanation of the Tax Reform Act of 1986, p. 245.

[20]   Sen. Rep. No. 99-313, 99th Cong. 2nd Sess., p. 739.

[21]   General Explanation of the Tax Reform Act of 1986, p. 246.

losses from one's passive activities over the aggregate gains from such activities, referred to as a "passive activity loss," cannot be used in the current taxable year. Rather, it may be carried forward and used in subsequent years. The disallowed passive activity loss must be apportioned among the various passive activities in which taxpayers realized a loss during the taxable year.

Temporary Regulation § 1.469-1T(f)(2)(i)(D) provides the following simple but instructive example:

Example 1. An individual holds interests in three passive activities, A, B, and C. The gross income and deductions from these activities for the taxable year are as follows:

	A	B	C	Total
Gross Income	$7,000	$4,000	$12,000	$23,000
Deductions	($16,000)	($20,000)	($8,000)	($44,000)
Net Income (Loss)	($9,000)	($16,000)	$4,000	($21,000)

The taxpayer's $21,000 passive activity loss for the taxable year is disallowed. Therefore, a ratable portion of the losses from activities A and B is disallowed. The disallowed portion of each loss is determined as follows:

A:	$21,000 × $9,000/$25,000	=	$7,560
B:	$21,000 × $16,000/$25,000	=	$13,440
	TOTAL		$21,000

Temporary Regulation § 1.469-1T(f)(2)(ii) provides specific rules for determining which part of each passive activity deduction for each loss activity is disallowed. Thus, in the example, the $7,560 of disallowed loss in activity A would in turn be allocated to the passive activity deductions claimed with respect to activity A. The detail of these allocations is beyond the scope of this course.

F. Portfolio Income and Expenses

A special rule found in § 469(e)(1) excludes from the determination of passive activity gains and losses portfolio income and expenses. As noted in the legislative history, "[p]ortfolio income generally includes interest, dividends, and royalties. Also included in portfolio income are gain or loss attribute to disposition of (1) property that is held for investment (and that is not a passive activity) and (2) property that normally produces interest, dividend, or royalty income."[22] Temporary Regulation § 1.469-2T(c)(3) defines "portfolio income" in some detail. The Senate Report on the Tax Reform Act explains the reason for excluding portfolio income as follows: "Portfolio investments ordinarily give rise to positive income, and are not likely to generate losses which could be applied to shelter other income. Therefore, for purposes of the passive loss rule, portfolio income generally is not treated as derived from a passive loss activity, but rather is treated

---

[22] Sen. Rep. No. 99-313, 99th Cong., 2d Sess. 728.

like other positive income sources such as salary. To permit portfolio income to be offset by passive losses or credits would create the inequitable result of restricting sheltering by individuals dependent for support on wages or active business income, while permitting sheltering by those whose income is derived from an investment portfolio."[23]

G. Exception for Active Participation in Rental Real Estate

As noted previously, under § 469(c)(2), all rental activity, except rental real estate activity that satisfies the special rule of § 469(c)(7), will be passive activity regardless of taxpayer's material participation. Congress nonetheless has provided a limited exception from the § 469 limitations for certain rental real estate activity, despite its status as passive activity. If a taxpayer, who is a natural person, *actively participates* in rental real estate activity, the taxpayer may apply the losses and credits from that activity against up to $25,000 of the taxpayer's nonpassive income. § 469(i)(1), (2). The relief is phased-out for taxpayers whose adjusted gross income exceeds $100,000. § 469(i)(3)(A).

As noted by the Staff of the Joint Committee on Taxation, this exception was created "because rental real estate is held, in many instances, to provide financial security to individuals with moderate incomes. In some cases, for example, an individual may hold for rental a residence that he uses part time, or that previously was and at some future time may be his primary residence. Even absent any such residential use of the property by the taxpayer, Congress believed that a rental real estate investment in which the taxpayer has significant responsibilities with respect to providing necessary services, and which serves significant nontax purposes of the taxpayer, is different in some respects from the activities that are meant to be fully subject to limitation under the passive loss provision."[24]

To be an *active participant* in a rental real estate activity, a taxpayer must own at least a 10 percent interest in it. § 469(i)(6). The "active participation" standard is more lenient than the "material participation" standard considered before. A taxpayer may be an active participant without regular, continuous, and substantial involvement in the operations. A taxpayer is an active participant if the taxpayer participates in a significant and bona fide sense in making management decisions or arranges for the provision of services such as repairs. Examples of management decisions that would establish a taxpayer as an active participant include selecting or approving new tenants, establishing rental terms, hiring a rental agent, hiring a person to provide repair services, and approving capital or repair expenditures.[25]

---

[23] *Id.* Income from a covenant not to compete is also passive income, per Temp. Reg. § 1.469-2T(c)(7)(iv), and that the validity of that regulation was upheld in *Schaefer v. Commissioner*, 105 T.C. 227 (1995).

[24] General Explanation of the Tax Reform Act of 1986, p. 243.

[25] Sen. Rep. No. 99-313, 99th Cong. 2nd Sess., p. 738.

H. Disposition of Taxpayer's Entire Interest in Passive Activity

If a taxpayer disposes of the entire interest in a passive activity, any suspended losses allocable to that activity (as well as any loss realized on the disposition of a passive activity) no longer are treated as passive activity losses. Instead, they are deductible against income (whether passive or nonpassive) as set forth in § 469(g)(1)(A). Under this provision, any net passive loss from the activity is first applied against passive income, with any remaining loss classified as nonpassive and available to offset nonpassive income. This release of suspended passive activity losses, however, is applicable only in the case of a fully taxable disposition of the taxpayer's interest in the activity to an unrelated party. § 469(g)(1)(A), (B).[26] An arm's length sale of the property for fair market value is the kind of fully taxable disposition envisioned by § 469(g)(1).[27]

The following excerpt from the legislative history explains the reason for releasing suspended losses upon the disposition of taxpayer's entire interest:

> When a taxpayer disposes of his entire interest in a passive activity, the actual economic gain or loss on his investment can be finally determined. . . . [P]rior to a disposition of the taxpayer's interest, it is difficult to determine whether there has actually been gain or loss with respect to the activity. For example, allowable deductions may exceed actual economic costs, or may be exceeded by untaxed appreciation. Upon a taxable disposition, net appreciation or depreciation with respect to the activity can be finally ascertained.

Sen. Rep. No. 99-313, 99th Cong. 2nd Sess., p. 725.

As noted previously, the determination of the scope of a passive activity is critical to the operation of this special rule regarding dispositions, since the taxpayer must establish she has disposed of her "entire" interest. To dispose of her "entire" interest, a sole proprietor must dispose of all assets created or used in the activity. *Id.*

If a passive activity is transferred as a result of taxpayer's death, the suspended losses are allowed only to the extent they exceed the amount, if any, by which the basis of such property in the hands of the transferee exceeds the adjusted basis of such property immediately before the death of the taxpayer. Any remaining suspended losses are forever disallowed. § 469(g)(2).

Because a gift is not a fully taxable disposition of property, a gift of part or all of a taxpayer's interest in an activity will not cause the release of the suspended losses

---

[26] If a taxpayer disposes of the entire interest in the property in a related party transaction (as defined in § 469(g)(1)(B)), the suspended losses allocable to such interest will not be released under the general rule of § 469(g)(1)(A) until the transferred interest is acquired in another fully taxable transaction by a person not related to the taxpayer. In the meantime, the taxpayer can continue to use these suspended passive losses against income from other passive activities.

[27] Sen. Rep. No. 99-313, 99th Cong. 2nd Sess., p. 725. By contrast, if a taxpayer were to transfer the interest in a passive activity to a corporation or a partnership in a nonrecognition transfer under § 351 or § 721, the suspended losses would not be released.

allocable to the activity. § 469(j)(6). However, the donor's basis in any gifted property will be increased by the suspended losses allocable to that property. Under § 1015, the donee's basis in the gifted property will reflect this increase, subject, of course, to the special rule in § 1015(a) limiting a donee's basis for purposes of the computation of loss. To the extent suspended losses are so used to increase the donor's basis in gifted property, they are eliminated. § 469(j)(6)(B).

Chapter 45

THE ALTERNATIVE MINIMUM TAX

I. PROBLEM

Laura is a physician. Her receipts and expenses this year include:

(1) Business gross income of $400,000;

(2) Section 162 deductions in connection with the medical practice (wages, insurance, supplies, etc.) of $200,000;

(3) Depreciation of $50,000 on $250,000 worth of used high technology medical equipment placed in service in January of this year;

(4) $25,000 of interest expense on the medical equipment;

(5) $60,000 in tax-exempt interest income, including $50,000 worth of "specified private activity bonds";

(6) Gain of $100,000 on the sale of land held for investment purposes for ten years;

(7) Income of $100,000 from the successful prosecution of a civil suit for defamation;

(8) Legal fees of $50,000 paid to her lawyer with respect to the defamation suit;

(9) $25,000 in taxable interest income;

(10) $10,000 for income tax preparation fees;

(11) Home mortgage interest of $20,000, reflecting a $200,000 mortgage on a home purchased for $250,000;

(12) $10,000 in local property taxes; and

(13) A contribution to State University of stock held for several years, worth $65,000 and having a basis of $5,000.

Assume the medical equipment in question constitutes qualified technological equipment under § 168(e)(3)(B)(iv), and the specified private activity bonds are described in § 57(a)(5)(C). Assume Laura is not married and has no children. Assume also that § 62(a)(20) does not apply to the legal expense Laura incurred in the defamation suit.

Based on the foregoing facts, what is the tax imposed on Laura this year? For simplicity sake, in making your calculations, assume the following: (a) the § 68(b) overall limitation on itemized deductions will result in a $2,000 reduction in the otherwise allowable itemized deductions Laura may claim; and (b) Laura's personal exemption, after taking into account the § 151(d)(3) phaseout, is $1,500.

Assignment for Chapter 45:

Complete the problem.

Reading: Internal Revenue Code: §§ 55; 56(a)(1)(A), (a)(6), (b)(1); 57(a)(5)(A),
(a)(7), 21(a); 26. Skim § 53. Merely glance at the remaining provisions of
§§ 56–59 and the credit provisions of §§ 21–53. Review Chapter 1 as
necessary to determine regular tax liability.

        Materials: Overview
                   Klaassen v. Commissioner

II. VOCABULARY

alternative minimum tax
tentative minimum tax
regular tax
exemption amount
alternative minimum taxable income
adjustments to alternative minimum taxable income
tax preference items
nonrefundable personal credits
minimum tax credit
taxable excess

III. OBJECTIVES

1. To be able to determine a taxpayer's alternative minimum taxable income
and tentative minimum tax.

2. To be able to determine the alternative minimum tax, if any, imposed on a
taxpayer.

IV. OVERVIEW

We have come full circle. Chapter 1, which introduced some fundamental aspects of the Federal income tax system, also included a detailed computation of the tax liability of Caroline Taxpayer. We now return in this Chapter to tax liability computations, but this time with an introduction to the concept and to some of the details of the alternative minimum tax of § 55.

The alternative minimum tax reflects a congressional determination that some provisions of the Code constitute tax preferences, apt to be utilized disproportionately by high income persons, and that a taxpayer's ability to reduce tax liability through the use of certain tax preferences should be restricted. When the alternative minimum tax was considerably revised in 1986, committee reports described its purpose as follows:

> The committee believes that the minimum tax should serve one overriding objective: to ensure that no taxpayer with substantial economic income can avoid significant tax liability by using exclusions, deductions, and credits. Although these provisions may provide incentives for worthy goals, they become counterproductive when taxpayers are allowed to use them to avoid virtually all tax liability. The ability of high-income taxpayers to pay little or no tax undermines respect for the entire tax system and, thus, for the incentive provisions themselves. In addition, even aside from public perceptions, the committee believes that it is inherently unfair for high-income taxpayers to pay little or no tax due to their ability to utilize tax preferences.

H. Rep. No. 99-426, 99th Cong. 1st Sess. p. 305–306; *see also* Sen. Rep. 99-313, 99th Cong. 2nd Sess., 518–519. Moreover, as the *Klaassen* case in the materials indicates, increasing numbers of middle-income taxpayers are now becoming subject to the alternative minimum tax. Accordingly, tax computations are not completed when a taxpayer's regular tax liability has been calculated; it still remains necessary to determine whether the type and amount of tax preferences render the taxpayer subject to the alternative minimum tax.

A. Mechanics

The alternative minimum tax is defined as the excess of the "tentative minimum tax" over the regular tax for the year. § 55(a). In effect, this simply means the taxpayer pays the regular tax or the tentative minimum tax, whichever is greater. For example, if the regular tax is $40,000 and the tentative minimum tax is $30,000, the alternative minimum tax is zero; the taxpayer would simply pay the regular tax of $40,000. However, if the tentative minimum tax is $50,000, the tax imposed consists of a regular tax of $40,000 and an alternative minimum tax of $10,000.

For 2015 the tentative minimum tax for individuals is generally equal to 26% of the first $185,400 in "taxable excess" plus 28% thereafter. (For married individuals filing separate returns, the 26% rate applies to the first $92,700.) § 55(b)(1)(A). There are separate lower maximum rates, drawn from § 1(h), on that portion of the taxable excess consisting of net capital gain. § 55(b)(3). "Taxable excess," in turn, is the excess of "alternative minimum taxable income" over the "exemption amount."

§ 55(b)(1)(A)(ii). For 2015, the exemption amount is $83,400 on joint returns (or for surviving spouses), $53,600 for an individual not married and not a surviving spouse, and $41,700 for married individuals filing separately. § 55(d)(1). For example, if a single taxpayer had alternative minimum taxable income of $89,600, none of which consisted of net capital gain, the tentative minimum tax would be 26% of a taxable excess of $36,000 ($89,600 less $53,600 exemption amount), or $9,360. (Technically, the tentative minimum tax is $9,360 less the "alternative minimum foreign tax credit." § 55(b)(1)(A). The foreign tax credit is a specialized topic not covered in this course, and we shall assume throughout this Chapter that the alternative minimum tax foreign tax credit is zero.) If the taxpayer's regular tax liability were less than $9,360, the alternative minimum tax would be applicable.

The exemption amount phases out when alternative minimum taxable income reaches sufficiently high levels. § 55(d)(3). For example, with respect to single taxpayers, the phase-out in 2015 begins when alternative minimum taxable income exceeds $119,200. Every $4 in excess of this amount reduces the exemption amount by $1 (but not below zero). Thus, given an alternative minimum taxable income of $159,200, the single taxpayer's exemption amount would be reduced by $10,000 (25% of $40,000, the excess of $159,200 over $119,200). For 2015, the exemption amount would thus be reduced from $53,600 to $43,600 and the tentative minimum tax rate of 26%, assuming no net capital gain, would be applied to a base of $115,600 ($159,200 less $43,600 exemption amount), resulting in a tentative minimum tax of $30,056.[1]

B. Determining Alternative Minimum Taxable Income

It should be clear from the previous section that the determination of "alternative minimum taxable income" (hereafter, AMTI) is central to the tentative minimum tax, and hence, to the alternative minimum tax. AMTI is defined as taxable income, adjusted as set forth in §§ 56 and 58, and increased by the items of tax preference in § 57. § 55(b)(2). Since the starting point in determining AMTI is taxable income, it might be helpful to review Chapter 1 to be sure you are familiar with the computation of taxable income. Recall the need to determine gross income and allowable deductions; to determine whether deductions are allowable above the line or below the line; to subject the "miscellaneous itemized deductions" to the 2% floor of § 67; to determine the standard deduction for nonitemizers; and to determine personal exemptions. Note, the § 68 overall limitation on itemized deductions does not apply in computing the alternative minimum tax. § 56(b)(1)(F).

Once the taxpayer's taxable income has been determined, the §§ 56 and 58 adjustments are made. Some of the required adjustments deal with corporate tax, including a special exemption for small corporations, and other matters beyond the scope of this course, and they are not discussed here at all. Among the other adjustments are the following:

---

[1] The "taxable excess" amounts to which the 26% and 28% minimum tax rates are applied, the exemption amounts, and the exemption phase-out amounts are indexed for inflation for taxable years beginning after 2012. § 55(d)(4). The 2015 inflation-adjusted figures are provided in Rev. Proc. 2014-61, 2014-47 I.R.B. 860.

(1) *Depreciation.* For purposes of determining AMTI, a depreciation adjustment will sometimes be required. Starting in 1999, the same recovery period is used for both regular tax and minimum tax purposes. However, except for § 1250 property (generally real property) and property otherwise depreciated under the straight line method, depreciation for minimum tax purposes must be calculated using the 150% declining balance method. The practical effect is that depreciation deductions will be the same under both the regular tax and alternative minimum tax for § 1250 real property, other straight line property, and property depreciated under the 150% declining balance method. However, tangible personal property depreciated under the 200% declining balance method for regular tax purposes, *i.e.*, 3-year, 5-year, 7-year and 10-year property, must use the less accelerated 150% declining balance method for alternative minimum tax purposes. Total depreciation deductions over the life of the property are of course the same under both the regular tax and the alternative minimum tax. This means that for some property the taxpayer must maintain two depreciation schedules — one for regular tax purposes, and one for alternative minimum tax purposes. (Since in these cases the property's AMTI basis will exceed its regular tax basis — assuming the basis has not been reduced to zero under both schedules — the gain on a sale of the property will be less (or the loss greater) when determining AMTI than when computing regular tax liability. § 56(a)(1).)

(2) *Limitation on Itemized Deductions, Standard Deductions and Personal Exemptions.* Miscellaneous itemized deductions, as defined in § 67(b), are not allowed in computing AMTI, nor are those state and local taxes that were deductible below the line for regular tax purposes. § 56(b)(1)(A). In some cases, disallowance of miscellaneous itemized deductions can have a substantial impact. Consider, for example, the situation where substantial attorney's fees are incurred to pursue a claim for taxable damages. The taxable damages are part of the tax base for regular tax and alternative minimum tax purposes, but if the attorney's fees are deductible under § 212, not § 162, and if the fees do not qualify for above-the-line treatment under provisions like § 62(a)(4) (expenses attributable to rents and royalties) or § 62(a)(20) (fees and costs attributable to claims of unlawful discrimination and certain other claims), the fees will be disallowed as miscellaneous itemized deductions in computing AMTI.[2] Taxpayers receiving

---

[2] *Alexander v. IRS*, 72 F.3d 938 (1st Cir. 1995), *aff'g* T.C. Memo. 1995-51, is a good illustration of the sometimes harsh impact of the disallowance of miscellaneous itemized deductions for AMT purposes. In *Alexander*, the taxpayer, after initiating a lawsuit against his former employer, received a settlement, most of which was taxable, and paid his own attorney's fees from the proceeds of the settlement. Although the attorney's fees allocable to the taxable portion of the settlement were deductible, the First Circuit held them to be allowable only as below-the-line deductions — thereby also categorizing them as miscellaneous itemized deductions under § 67(b). As such, they were subject to the 2% floor rule of § 67(a), but, much more importantly, as a miscellaneous itemized deduction, the allowable amount constituted an adjustment for AMT purposes under § 56(b)(1)(A)(i). The numbers show why the taxpayer resisted below-the-line classification: the taxable portion of the settlement was about $250,000; the legal fees allocable to this taxable portion were about $245,000 — that is, only about $5,000 less than the settlement. After application of the 2% floor rule, the allowable amount was about $240,000, a relatively minor cutback for regular tax purposes. But application of the § 56 adjustment rules, which inexorably followed, effectively disallowing the deduction in its entirety for AMT purposes, resulted in an additional tax liability of some $57,000! The *Alexander* case pre-dated the enactment of § 62(a)(20), which would now provide above-the-line treatment for the fees and avoid the AMT.

damages awards historically attempted to avoid this disallowance rule by arguing that a portion of their damage award or settlement belonged to the attorney representing them in contingent fee arrangements and was therefore excludable from the taxpayers' gross income. Had they been successful in this argument, of course, taxpayers would only have, in effect, had the benefit of a deduction for their attorney fees. The Supreme Court in *Commissioner v. Banks*, 543 U.S. 426 (2005), however, thwarted this strategy by holding held that, if a taxpayer's settlement or award constitutes gross income, the taxpayer must also include in gross income the portion of the settlement or award paid to the attorney as a contingent fee.

Medical expenses are allowed under AMTI only to the extent they exceed 10% of adjusted gross income (rather than 7.5% of adjusted gross income for taxpayers 65 or older in years before 2017). § 56(b)(1)(B). The interest deduction limitations of § 163(d) and (h) are modified. § 56(b)(1)(C). The standard deduction and personal exemptions are not allowed in computing AMTI. § 56(b)(1)(E). As noted above, the § 68 limitation on itemized deductions is not applicable to the alternative minimum tax.

Taxable income, as adjusted by these and other provisions of §§ 56 and 58, is then increased by the items of tax preference listed in § 57. These items include:

(1) *Certain Tax-Exempt Interest.* Certain otherwise tax-exempt interest must be included in income for AMTI purposes. Pursuant to § 57(a)(5), the interest on "specified private activity bonds" (reduced by deductions that were nondeductible in computing regular tax liability) is an item of tax preference taken into account in computing AMTI.

(2) *Qualified Small Business Stock.* In general, seven percent of the amount excluded under the qualified small business stock rules of § 1202 is an item of tax preference. As noted in Chapter 31, Congress has provided a 100% exclusion for qualified small business stock acquired after September 10, 2010 and before January 1, 2015. § 1202(a)(4). That code section specifically provides the excluded amount will not be an item of tax preference. § 1202 (a)(4)(C). Congress may extend § 1202(a)(4) beyond 2014 or even make it permanent.

Tax preference items may also include certain depletion deductions, intangible drilling costs, and a portion of the depreciation taken on certain property placed in service prior to 1987. *See* § 57(a). It is worth noting, however, that a charitable contribution of appreciated "capital gain property" does not generate an item of tax preference for AMTI purposes. As discussed in Chapter 26, a charitable contribution of such property may be deductible in an amount equal to its fair market value. *See* § 170(a), (e). In such cases, the taxpayer gets a deduction that takes into account the property's appreciation in value, but the taxpayer is not similarly required to take the appreciation into account for purposes of determining gross income. This asymmetrical treatment of appreciation in capital gain property was at one time altered, for AMTI purposes, by requiring that the § 170 deduction be reduced to the amount that would have been allowed had the capital gain property been taken into account at its adjusted basis. However, this provision was repealed in 1993, making such charitable contributions very attractive not only for regular tax purposes, but for minimum tax purposes as well.

C. Determining Tax Liability

Once the taxpayer's AMTI has been determined, the appropriate exemption amount is subtracted and the balance is the "taxable excess." § 55(b)(1)(A)(ii). Assuming no net capital gain, the tentative minimum tax is simply 26% of the first $175,000 of this taxable excess, plus 28% of the amount above $175,000 (less any alternative minimum tax foreign tax credit). § 55(b)(1)(A)(i). As noted above the "taxable excess" amounts are adjusted for inflation. To the extent of net capital gain, the special lower maximum rates of § 55(b)(3) must be applied in determining the tentative minimum tax. An alternative minimum tax is imposed only to the extent this tentative minimum tax exceeds the "regular tax."

Under § 55(c)(1), the regular tax is the taxpayer's specially-defined "regular tax liability," which in turn means "the tax imposed by this chapter" — that is, by Chapter 1, Code §§ 1-1399 — less certain specified taxes, including the alternative minimum tax. § 26(b). For our purposes, we shall assume that a taxpayer's regular tax liability, and the regular tax, consist simply of the tax imposed by § 1 of the Code. Therefore, upon determining the taxpayer's taxable income and filing status, and upon applying, if necessary, the maximum capital gains rate of § 1(h), the regular tax may be computed.

D. Credits Allowed

As we saw in Chapter 1 of this text, once the amount of the tax imposed has been calculated, it is then necessary to determine whether the taxpayer is entitled to claim any credits against it.

There are a number of credits allowed by the Code. The most familiar ones include the credit for tax withheld on wages (§ 31) and the earned income credit for low-income individuals (§ 32). The earned income credit is reduced by any alternative minimum tax imposed. § 32(h). Some other credits are subject to disallowance.

Finally, note the minimum tax credit of § 53.[3] Under this provision, a portion of the alternative minimum tax imposed in a prior year may be allowed as a credit against the current year's regular tax liability. The prior year's minimum tax portion that may be so credited is called the "adjusted net minimum tax" for the year; it consists of the actual alternative minimum tax for the year, less a specially-computed alternative minimum tax. § 53(d). The adjusted net minimum tax for all post-1986 prior years constitutes the "minimum tax credit" which may be applied

---

[3] The minimum tax credit addresses a potential whipsawing of the taxpayer between the regular tax and the alternative minimum tax. The whipsawing can occur because some minimum tax provisions essentially make only timing adjustments to regular tax "benefits" rather than disallow them permanently. For example, minimum tax depreciation cuts back on the front-loading of regular tax depreciation, but the total depreciation allowed under both schedules is the same. Thus, as a result of the front-loading differential, it is possible for the taxpayer to get the worst of both worlds — the minimum tax in the early years (when minimum tax depreciation is less than regular tax depreciation), and the regular tax in the later years (when minimum tax depreciation exceeds regular tax depreciation). In such circumstances, the minimum tax credit of § 53 may apply to eliminate the "overtaxation" of the taxpayer due to these (and other) timing differentials. The mechanics of the process are in the "adjusted net minimum tax" definition of § 53(d)(1)(B)(i) and (ii).

against the current year's regular tax liability. § 53(a). To the extent it is so applied, the minimum tax credit is reduced. § 53(b). In any event, the minimum tax credit is allowed only to the extent the taxpayer's regular tax liability, after having been reduced by most other allowable credits, still exceeds the taxpayer's tentative minimum tax for the year. § 53(c). The practical effect, in general, is that the minimum tax credit is not allowed in a year in which the alternative minimum tax is itself imposed.

KLAASSEN v. COMMISSIONER
United States Court of Appeals, Tenth Circuit
182 F.3d 932 (1999)

Before ANDERSON, KELLY, and BRISCOE, CIRCUIT JUDGES.

David R. and Margaret J. Klaassen appeal from the Tax Court's ruling that they are liable for an alternative minimum tax (AMT) in the amount of $1,085 for the 1994 tax year. The Klaassens contend that the tax court erred by applying the AMT provisions, I.R.C. §§ 55–59 (1988 & Supp. 1994), to them in violation of congressional intent. . . . We affirm.

BACKGROUND

The facts are undisputed. During the 1994 tax year, the Klaassens were the parents of ten dependent children. According to their 1994 joint tax return, they earned an adjusted gross income (AGI) of $83,056.42. On Schedule A, the Klaassens claimed deductions for medical expenses and for state and local taxes in the respective amounts of $4,767.13 and $3,263.56. Including their claimed deductions for interest and charitable contributions, their total Schedule A itemized deductions equaled $19,563.95. Therefore, they subtracted that amount from their AGI, and on line 35 of their Form 1040, they showed a balance of $63,492.47. On line 36, they entered a total of $29,400 for twelve personal exemptions — one each for themselves and their ten children. After subtracting that amount, they showed a taxable income of $34,092.47 on line 37 of their Form 1040, and a resulting regular tax of $5,111.00 on line 38. They did not provide any computations for AMT liability.

Following an audit, the IRS issued a notice of deficiency, advising the Klaassens that they were liable for a $1,085.43 AMT pursuant to I.R.C. §§ 55–59. n.1 Specifically, the IRS concluded that, in the Klaassens' case, I.R.C. §§ 55–56 required three specific adjustments, or increases, to the taxable income which they showed on line 37 of their Form 1040. According to the IRS's interpretation, subsection 56(b)(1)(A)(ii) required the entire $3,263.56 deduction for state and local taxes to be added back. Next, subsection 56(b)(1)(B) reduced the deduction allowable for medical expenses by setting a 10% floor in lieu of the 7.5% floor normally allowed under § 213(a) — resulting in a net adjustment of $2,076.41. Finally, § 56(b)(1)(E) deprived the Klaassens of the entire $29,400 deduction they claimed on line 36 of their Form 1040. After adjusting the taxable income by these three amounts, the IRS set the alternative minimum taxable income at $68,832.44. After deducting the

$45,000 exemption, the tentative minimum tax was computed on the excess: 26% x $23,832.44 = $6,196.43. The difference between that figure and the Klaassens' regular tax was $1,085.43. The Tax Court upheld the IRS's position and the Klaassens brought this appeal.

DISCUSSION

The Klaassens do not dispute the numbers or the mechanics used to calculate the AMT deficiency. Rather, they claim that, as a matter of law, the AMT provisions should not apply to them. We review the Tax Court's legal conclusions de novo.

I.R.C. § 56(b)(1)(E) plainly states that, in computing the alternative minimum taxable income, "the deduction for personal exemptions under section 151 . . . shall not be allowed." Nonetheless, the Klaassens argue that Congress intended the AMT to apply only to very wealthy persons who claim the types of tax preferences described in I.R.C. § 57. Essentially, the Klaassens contend that Congress did not intend to disallow personal exemptions for taxpayers at their income level when no § 57 preferences are involved. Although they cite no legislative history to support their contention, the Klaassens argue that their entitlement to their personal exemptions is mandated by I.R.C. §§ 151–153. In particular, they note that for 1994, I.R.C. § 151(d) allowed taxpayers filing joint returns to claim the full exemption so long as their AGI was less than $167,700. Appellant's Br. at 6. They then argue that the § 151(d) threshold amount should be interpolated as a threshold for the AMT provisions. We disagree.

In the absence of exceptional circumstances, where a statute is clear and unambiguous our inquiry is complete. The AMT framework establishes a precise method for taxing income which the regular tax does not reach. In creating this framework, Congress included several provisions, "marked by a high degree of specificity," by which deductions or advantages which are allowed in computing the regular tax are specifically disallowed for purposes of computing the AMT. Instead of permitting those separate "regular tax" deductions, Congress specifically substituted the $45,000 fixed exemption for purposes of AMT computations. I.R.C. § 55(d)(1). n.3. If, as the Klaassens claim, Congress had intended the AMT to apply only to taxpayers whose incomes reached a certain threshold, or only to taxpayers with § 57 tax preferences, it could have easily drafted the statute to achieve that result. Instead, as the tax court correctly held, the statute's plain language unequivocally reaches the Klaassens, and our inquiry is therefore complete. While the law may result in some unintended consequences, in the absence of any ambiguity, it must be applied as written. It is therefore from Congress that the Klaassens should seek relief. . . .

AFFIRMED.

KELLY, Circuit Judge, concurring.

Although I agree with the court that the taxpayers cannot prevail on the theories advanced, we are not precluded from examining the legislative history of the alternative minimum tax (AMT), despite the clarity of the statute. The legislative history supports an argument that the original purpose of the AMT, one of the more complex parts of the Internal Revenue Code, was to insure that taxpayers with substantial economic income pay a minimum amount of tax on it. The regular income tax may be insufficient to achieve that objective because it favors certain types of income and allows deductions, exclusions and credits for certain types of expenses.

For a variety of reasons, the number of moderate income taxpayers subject to the AMT has been steadily increasing. From a tax compliance and administration perspective, many of these taxpayers simply are unaware of their AMT obligations. If aware, they probably would need the assistance of a tax professional to comply with the separate rules and computations (apart from regular tax) and additional record keeping essential for the AMT. From a fairness perspective, many of these taxpayers have not utilized I.R.C. § 57 preferences (or other more arcane AMT adjustment items) to reduce regular taxable income but are caught up in the AMT's attempt to impose fairness. That certainly seems to be the case here. In the interest of progressivity, the regular tax already reduces or phases out itemized deductions and personal exemptions based upon income, see, *e.g.*, I.R.C. § 67(a) (miscellaneous itemized deductions), § 68 (overall reduction of itemized deductions), § 151(d)(3) (phaseout of personal exemptions); § 213(a) (medical and dental expenses deduction only for amounts beyond 7.5% floor); surely Congress never intended a family of twelve that still qualified for these items under the regular tax to partly forfeit them under the AMT.

That said, we must apply the law as it is plainly written, despite what appears to be the original intent behind the AMT. As the tax court has explained, neither the statutory language nor unequivocal legislative history support the argument that the AMT is limited to individuals with tax preferences. See *Huntsberry v. Commissioner*, 83 T.C. 742, 747–48 (1984). This is particularly true given the Congressional power to raise revenue. See *Okin v. Commissioner*, 808 F.2d 1338, 1341–42 (9th Cir. 1987). The solution to this inequity, whether it be (1) eliminating itemized deductions and personal exemptions as adjustments to regular taxable income in arriving at alternative minimum taxable income, (2) exempting low and moderate income taxpayers from the AMT, (3) raising and indexing the AMT exemption amount, or (4) some other measure, must come from Congress, as the tax court rightly concluded.

Appendix 1

RESEARCHING THE TAX LAW

A. THE INTERNAL REVENUE CODE

The primary source of the federal tax law is the Internal Revenue Code of 1986 *as amended* (and the Code is amended regularly). The 1986 Code replaced the 1954 Internal Revenue Code, which replaced the 1939 Internal Revenue Code. Prior to the 1939 Code, separate revenue acts were enacted every few years. The fact one code replaces another doesn't mean there is a wholesale revision of the tax law. Rather, most of the statutory provisions are carried over from one code to another. For example, the Internal Revenue Code of 1986 is comprised primarily of provisions from the Internal Revenue Code of 1954. Given the continuity found in code provisions, the researcher will find most tax cases decided under 1954 Code provisions may be relied on as authority for the interpretation and application of the Internal Revenue Code of 1986. The Code can be located in any of the major looseleaf services, *e.g.*, *United States Tax Reporter* (Research Institute of America), *Standard Federal Tax Reporter* (Commerce Clearing House), *CCH Federal Tax Service* (Commerce Clearing House), and *Federal Tax Coordinator 2d* (Research Institute of America), or on Lexis or Westlaw.

B. LEGISLATIVE HISTORY

Studying the language of the Internal Revenue Code, however, will not always provide an answer to a tax problem. Statutory language is often unclear and its application uncertain. Various sources are available to assist you in interpreting and applying Code provisions to particular fact patterns. The legislative history may illuminate congressional intent. For example, the committee reports discussing the various provisions of the American Taxpayer Relief Act of 2012 are "must" reading for any tax advisor probing the impact of the 2012 Act on a particular transaction. With the advent of each new tax act, the major tax services publish compilations of legislative histories as well as helpful explanations of the new provisions.

Volume 3 of the *United States Code Congressional and Administrative News* (1954) contains the legislative history for the Internal Revenue Code of 1954. Committee reports regarding new tax acts may also be found in the weekly Internal Revenue Bulletin or in the Cumulative Bulletin (discussed briefly *infra*). A reference guide to these legislative histories is contained in the "Finding Lists" of the M–Z Volume of the CCH Citator.

C. REGULATIONS

In addition to the legislative history, the regulations issued by the Treasury are critical to one's understanding of Code provisions. The regulations provide flesh to the skeletal structure of the Internal Revenue Code and have the force of law. They often provide a very helpful tool in understanding the meaning and application of complex statutory provisions. Unfortunately, the regulations are often not promulgated until years after a tax law has been enacted.

A taxpayer may challenge a regulation as being contrary to congressional intent. Courts, however, typically give particular deference to the Treasury and seldom find regulations to be invalid. The older the regulation is, the more likely the court is to uphold it on the theory that long-standing administrative interpretations and procedures apparently have the blessing of the Congress.

Tax regulations are promulgated by the Department of the Treasury of which the IRS is just a part. Section 7805(a) of the Internal Revenue Code gives the Secretary of the Treasury general authority to prescribe all necessary rules and regulations for the enforcement of the Code. Regulations are promulgated under the Administrative Procedure Act and are initially published in the Federal Register in proposed form to give the public ample opportunity to comment on the regulation. The proposed regulations may also be promulgated as temporary regulations effective immediately. After the comment period has expired and after any changes have been made, the Treasury publishes the regulations in final form as a Treasury Decision (T.D.).

Each regulation is identified by a prefix number and the particular code section which it interprets. The prefix for income tax regulations is "1." Thus, one will find the regulations interpreting § 61, the gross income definition, numbered "1.61-."

Regulations are published in numerous sources. While one can find tax regulations in the Federal Register or the Code of Federal Regulations, an attorney typically will rely on one of the major tax looseleaf services, *supra*, Lexis, or Westlaw, as a source for regulations, including proposed regulations.

D. REVENUE RULINGS AND PROCEDURES

Regulations, while the most important administrative interpretations of the statutory provisions, are not the only administrative interpretations. The Internal Revenue Service issues official rulings which are interpretative pronouncements designed to indicate the Service's position regarding the application of the tax law to a certain set of facts. Unlike the regulations, rulings are not published in proposed form; there is no opportunity for comment; and they are not approved by the Secretary of the Treasury.

Rulings are of two types: revenue rulings and letter rulings. Rulings which the IRS determines are of general interest are published as *revenue rulings* and will be found in the weekly *Internal Revenue Bulletin* and are consolidated semiannually in the *Cumulative Bulletin*. Revenue rulings are often the result of a taxpayer's request for advice on the position that the Service would take with respect to a proposed course of conduct, or may simply represent the Service's position on issues arising on audit of a taxpayer's return or on issues which have been decided by various federal courts. Unless superseded, modified or revoked, revenue rulings can be relied upon by any taxpayer whose circumstances are substantially the same as those set out in the ruling. While not having the force of a regulation, revenue rulings may be cited as precedent supporting a particular position. Revenue rulings are numbered chronologically. Each revenue ruling is identified by a prefix designating the year of issuance. For example, Revenue Ruling 2015-6 was the sixth revenue ruling issued in 2015.

Another valuable administrative pronouncement is known as a *revenue procedure*. Revenue procedures are statements of the Service regarding its internal management operations. Because they have a general effect upon taxpayers' rights and duties with respect to specific statutory provisions, revenue procedures to some extent represent interpretations of the statutory language and cannot be overlooked as one represents a client in a tax matter. Revenue procedures, like revenue rulings, appear initially in the *Internal Revenue Bulletin* and are later consolidated in the *Cumulative Bulletins*. They are numbered the same way as revenue rulings. For example, Revenue Procedure 2015-3 is the third revenue procedure issued in 2015.

While revenue rulings and revenue procedures appear initially in the *Internal Revenue Bulletin*, the most common source used in locating a revenue ruling or procedure is the *Cumulative Bulletin* (C.B.). Generally, the Government Printing Office publishes two cumulative bulletins each year. In years when there is major tax legislation, a third volume containing congressional committee reports on the legislation is published. With the exception of the first ten volumes of the series, the *Cumulative Bulletins* are denominated by year and part. For example, Revenue Procedure 2013-17 is found in 2013-2 C.B. 201, *i.e.*, the second volume of the *Cumulative Bulletin* issued in 2013. In addition to revenue rulings and procedures, the *Cumulative Bulletins* also contain other Treasury decisions and pronouncements as well as legislative histories of tax acts.

Revenue rulings and revenue procedures and other Treasury materials, of course, are available on both Lexis and Westlaw. One will also find revenue rulings and revenue procedures published in the various tax services. Mertens, *The Law of Federal Income Taxation*, has both a current rulings volume and volumes containing the major prior rulings.

Letter rulings are responsive to a particular taxpayer's request for advice on the tax consequences (from the Service's standpoint) of a specific transaction. Letter rulings have been made public under the Freedom of Information Act. While services like CCH make letter rulings available, Westlaw and Lexis are the easiest to access and are the most comprehensive sources of letter rulings. While the IRS does not consider itself bound by its letter rulings in dealings with other taxpayers, letter rulings nonetheless represent an important source of information regarding the Service's position on a given issue.

E. CASE LAW

Because the courts resolve many tax issues, court decisions have become a rich source for interpretations of the various sections and subsections of the Internal Revenue Code. This text contains edited versions of many of the leading tax cases, the holdings of which have often been codified by the Congress. The Tax Court, the United States Federal District Courts, the Federal Courts of Appeal and the United States Court of Federal Claims decide numerous tax cases each year. The decisions of these courts are found in a variety of official and unofficial sources. For example, as discussed *infra*, regular decisions of the Tax Court are officially published in the *Tax Court Reports* and both regular and memoranda decisions of the Tax Court are unofficially published by CCH, RIA and others. Decisions of federal courts *other than the Tax Court* can be found in the West National Reporter System, RIA's American Federal Tax Reports (AFTR), CCH's United States Tax Cases (U.S.T.C.) as well as other sources. Decisions of the Claims Court are published by West in its *United States Claims Court Reporter*. Lexis and Westlaw also provide easy access to the tax decisions of the various courts. Research on a tax issue is certainly not complete without determining whether any court has ruled on the issue.

There are two types of Tax Court decisions: regular decisions and memorandum decisions. Regular decisions are officially reported in the *Tax Court Reports* (T.C.) (1942 to date) and in the forty-seven volumes of its predecessor, the *United States Board of Tax Appeals Reports* (B.T.A.) (1924–1942). Regular decisions may also be found in two unofficial sources: *CCH Tax Court Reporter* and *RIA Tax Court Reported and Memorandum Decision*. Regular decisions of the Tax Court are distinguished from memorandum decisions in that regular decisions generally involve important issues in tax which may not have previously been resolved, while memorandum decisions generally involve the application of settled points of the tax law to particular facts. The line between the two types of decisions, however, is anything but bright, and one would be foolish to overlook the possible precedential value of a memorandum decision.

Memorandum decisions, unlike the regular decisions, are not officially published. Both RIA and Commerce Clearing House have series which report all memorandum decisions. Regular and memorandum decisions of the Tax Court can be accessed on both Westlaw and Lexis.

When the United States Tax Court, District Courts, Court of Federal Claims, or Circuit Courts of Appeal rule against the Internal Revenue Service in civil tax cases, the Service will often issue a notice of acquiescence or of nonacquiescence if the Service determines its guidance would be helpful.[1] An acquiescence indicates the Service accepts the conclusion of the court on the issue or issues decided adversely to the Government.[2] By contrast, a nonacquiescence indicates the Service does not accept the court's conclusion and intends to continue challenging taxpayers with respect to the issue or issues before the court. In evaluating a client's case, the success of which may be dependent on a particular decision of any of the courts noted above, one should determine whether the Service has issued a notice of acquiescence or of nonacquiescence. The Service's acquiescence or nonacquiescence in a decision is published in the *Internal Revenue Bulletin* and will appear in the bound *Cumulative Bulletins*. One may determine whether the Commissioner has acquiesced or nonacquiesced in a decision by using the RIA Citator, the CCH Standard Federal Tax Reporter Citator, or Lexis or Westlaw.

---

[1] Prior to 1991, the Service issued notices of acquiescence or nonacquiescence only in regular decisions of the Tax Court. The document announcing the Service's acquiescence or nonacquiescence is known as an Action on Decision.

[2] An acquiescence, however, should not be interpreted to mean the Service necessarily accepts the reasoning of the court underlying its conclusion.

F. UPDATING ONE'S RESEARCH

Having discovered a case or a ruling supporting a position, one's research is not complete without reference to a citator to determine the current status of that authority. For example, assume an attorney knows there is a revenue ruling authorizing a deduction for certain transportation expenses. Before relying on that ruling to advise a client regarding similar expenses, the attorney should use a citator to determine the current status of that ruling. Among other things, an attorney using the citator may find that the ruling has been superseded, modified or revoked by the Service. In addition, the citator would indicate whether any court had ever cited or discussed the ruling and may also provide a citation to law review articles citing or discussing the ruling. Needless to say, all of that information is critical if an accurate appraisal of a client's tax position is to be made.

In areas other than federal tax, Shepard's Citators are the most widely used citators and are used to locate all decisions and administrative materials as well as selected law reviews which have cited or discussed a given case. Shepard's Federal Tax Citations treats cases as well as rulings using the same symbol system for which it is known in non-tax areas to enable the researcher to determine quickly the issues in the cited material which are addressed in the citing material and whether the citing material approves, criticizes, etc. the holding in the cited case or ruling.

Both CCH and RIA, as part of their tax services, also provide citators. Both the CCH Standard Federal Tax Reporter Citator and the RIA Citator provide citator treatment of all federal tax cases as well as revenue rulings, revenue procedures, Treasury decisions and other internal memoranda of the IRS. Lexis and Westlaw also provide citator services.[3]

G. TAX SERVICES

As mentioned previously, a number of looseleaf tax services exist which provide enormous assistance to the tax advisor. In addition to those mentioned previously, *Tax Notes*, a weekly journal published by Tax Analysts, and the *Tax Management Portfolio* series published by BNA should be noted. Each of these services provide helpful explanations and planning pointers. Because the format and features of each service differ, we urge students to take the time to review each service available in your school's library. Note the various research techniques which may be used with respect to each service and the kinds of information provided by the services. The services are typically available on-line or by means of CD-ROM.

H. USEFUL TAX WEBSITES

The following list provides useful websites with which you may wish to familiarize yourself:

IRS Website: www.irs.gov

U.S. Tax Court: www.ustaxcourt.gov

---

[3] For an excellent discussion of tax research materials and techniques, see Richmond, *Federal Tax Research* (current edition), Foundation Press.

U.S. Senate Finance Committee: www.finance.senate.gov

U.S. House Ways and Means Committee: www.waysandmeans.house.gov

Tax and Accounting Sites Directory: www.taxsites.com

Appendix 2

ANNUAL COMPOUND INTEREST TABLES

Compounding of $1				Present Value of $1			

$1, when compounded annually at interest rate i, will equal $X after y number of years.

$$X = (1+i)^y$$

$1, to be paid in y years in the future, has a present value of $X, given an annual discount rate of i.

$$\frac{X+1}{(1+i)^y}$$

Year	5%	10%	15%	Year	5%	10%	15%
1	1.050	1.100	1.150	1	.952	.909	.870
2	1.103	1.210	1.323	2	.907	.826	.756
3	1.158	1.331	1.521	3	.864	.751	.658
4	1.216	1.464	1.749	4	.823	.683	.572
5	1.276	1.611	2.011	5	.784	.621	.497
6	1.340	1.772	2.313	6	.746	.564	.432
7	1.407	1.949	2.660	7	.711	.513	.376
8	1.477	2.144	3.059	8	.677	.467	.327
9	1.551	2.358	3.518	9	.645	.424	.284
10	1.629	2.594	4.046	10	.614	.386	.247
11	1.710	2.853	4.652	11	.585	.350	.215
12	1.796	3.138	5.350	12	.557	.319	.187
13	1.886	3.452	6.153	13	.530	.290	.163
14	1.980	3.797	7.076	14	.505	.263	.141
15	2.079	4.177	8.137	15	.481	.239	.123
16	2.183	4.595	9.358	16	.458	.218	.107
17	2.292	5.054	10.761	17	.436	.198	.093
18	2.407	5.560	12.375	18	.416	.180	.081
19	2.527	6.116	14.232	19	.396	.164	.070
20	2.653	6.727	16.367	20	.377	.149	.061
25	3.386	10.835	32.919	25	.295	.092	.030
30	4.322	17.449	66.212	30	.231	.057	.015

TABLE OF CASES

[References are to pages]

[References are to pages]

[References are to pages]

[References are to pages]

[References are to pages]

[References are to pages]

[References are to pages]

[References are to pages]

[References are to pages]

T

[References are to pages]

TABLE OF STATUTES

[References are to pages]

[References are to pages]

[References are to pages]

[References are to pages]

TAX SOURCES

Proposed Treasury Regulations

INDEX

[References are to pages.]

[References are to pages.]

BUSINESS MEALS (See ENTERTAINMENT AND BUSINESS MEALS)

C

CAPITAL EXPENDITURES
Advertising expenses . . . 306
Business downsizing cost . . . 305
Deductible expense . . . 288
Defined . . . 289
Employee training costs . . . 305
Expansion costs . . . 304
INDOPCO ruling . . . 289
Intangibles, amounts paid to acquire or create . . . 300
Lease . . . 307
Purchase . . . 307
Regulations
  Generally . . . 292
  Intangibles, amounts paid to acquire or create . . . 300
  Sale, removal, or retirement of asset, amounts paid with regard to . . . 303
  Tangible property (See subhead: Tangible property)
Sale, removal, or retirement of asset, amounts paid with regard to . . . 303
Tangible property
  Amounts paid to acquire or produce . . . 292
  Improvements, amounts paid to acquire or
    Final regulations . . . 296
    Historic rules . . . 294

CAPITAL GAINS AND LOSSES
Arrowsmith rule . . . 793
Deduction for capital losses, limitation on . . . 769
Definition of capital asset
  Generally . . . 783
  Accounts receivable for services rendered . . . 787
  Copyrights, literary, musical, or artistic compositions . . . 786
  Government publications . . . 787
  Inventory . . . 784
  Judicially established limits . . . 788
  Property held . . . 784
  Stock in trade . . . 784
  Supplied used or consumed in trade or business . . . 788
  Taxpayer's trade or business, property used in . . . 786
Holding period . . . 795
Limitation on deduction for capital losses . . . 769; 780
Long-term capital gain, maximum rates on . . . 766
Net capital gain components
  Adjusted net capital gain
    15-percent rate . . . 774
    Qualified dividend income . . . 776
    0-percent rates . . . 774
  28-percent rate gain . . . 773
  25-percent rate . . . 774

CAPITAL GAINS AND LOSSES—Cont.
Rate preferential treatment for long-term capital gains . . . 766
Sale or exchange requirement . . . 791
Section 1(h): current law
  Attribution of capital losses included in computation of net capital gain . . . 777
  Long-term capital gain, maximum rates on . . . 771
  Net capital gain components (See subhead: Net capital gain components)

CASH METHOD ACCOUNTING
Generally . . . 666
Deductions under
  Generally . . . 680
  Prepayments, cash method . . . 683
Income under
  Generally . . . 666
  Cash equivalency doctrine . . . 671
  Constructive receipt
    Generally . . . 666
    Doctrine, specific factors affecting application of . . . 667
    Rules, specific exceptions to . . . 670
  Economic benefit doctrine . . . 674
  Lottery prizes . . . 680
  Non-qualified deferred compensation arrangements . . . 676
  Prepayments . . . 680
  Revenue Ruling 60-31 . . . 678
  Section 409A . . . 678
Lottery prizes . . . 680
Prepayments . . . 680

CASUALTY LOSSES
Generally . . . 572
Amount of . . . 576
Definitional questions . . . 572
Insurance coverage . . . 577
Timing of . . . 575

CHARITABLE DEDUCTIONS
Generally . . . 602
Appreciated property, contribution of . . . 608
Bargain sale to charity . . . 613
Contribution
  Generally . . . 604
  Appreciated property, of . . . 608
  Partial interests in property, of . . . 611
  Services, of . . . 607
Gift . . . 604
Limitation on . . . 607
Partial interests in property, contribution of . . . 611
Qualified recipient . . . 603
Requirements for
  Generally . . . 602
  Contribution . . . 604
  Gift . . . 604
  Limitation on charitable deductions . . . 607
  Payment required, actual . . . 606
  Qualified recipient . . . 603
Services, contribution of . . . 607
Substantiation . . . 614

[References are to pages.]

CHILD CARE EXPENSES
Generally . . . 485

CLAIM OF RIGHT DOCTRINE
Generally . . . 58; 744

CONDEMNATION
Real property used for business or investment, of
. . . 995

CONTINGENT LIABILITIES
Impact of, nonrecourse debt . . . 923

COVENANT NOT TO COMPETE
Generally . . . 1042; 1045

D

DAMAGES
Allocation of awards . . . 199
Business . . . 188
Periodic payments . . . 200
Personal physical injuries . . . 189
Physical injury or sickness, restricting exclusion to
    Generally . . . 192
    Emotional distress . . . 195
    Personal physical injury or physical sickness
      . . . 193
    Recoveries by individuals . . . 196
Property . . . 188
Punitive damages . . . 198
Regulations and definition of damages, current
    . . . 197
Section 104(a)(2), Supreme Court limitations on
    . . . 191
Sickness . . . 189
Supreme Court limitations on Section 104(a)(2)
    . . . 191

DEBT
Depreciation and . . . 337
Discharge of indebtedness (See INDEBTEDNESS,
    DISCHARGE OF)
Losses and bad debts (See GAIN OR LOSS, sub-
    head: Losses and bad debts)
Nonrecourse debt (See NONRECOURSE DEBT)
Original issue discount
    Cash, debt instruments issued for (See ORIGI-
      NAL ISSUE DISCOUNT (OID), subhead:
      Cash, debt instruments issued for)
    Property, debt instruments issued for (See
      ORIGINAL ISSUE DISCOUNT (OID), sub-
      head: Property, debt instruments issued for)

DEDUCTIONS
Accrual method accounting (See ACCRUAL
    METHOD ACCOUNTING, subhead: Deductions
    under)
Business deductions, under Section 162 (See BUSI-
    NESS AND PROFIT SEEKING EXPENSES,
    subhead: Deduction, Section 162)
Capital losses, of
    Limitation on . . . 769
    Section 1211(b) limitation on . . . 780

DEDUCTIONS—Cont.
Cash method accounting
    Generally . . . 680
    Prepayments . . . 683
Charitable deductions (See CHARITABLE DEDUC-
    TIONS)
Depreciation, computing . . . 332
Home office . . . 512
Interest (See INTEREST DEDUCTION)
Limitations on
    Capital losses . . . 769
    Interest deductions, judicial limitations on
      . . . 659
    Related party transactions (See subhead: Related
      party transactions)
    Tax-exempt income (See subhead: Tax-exempt
      income)
    Wash sales under Section 1091 . . . 658
Losses . . . 372; 376
Original issue discount, of . . . 1082
Related party transactions
    Generally . . . 637
    Section 267(a)(1)
      Loss rule under . . . 637
      Matching requirement under . . . 639
Section 162, under
    Business deductions (See BUSINESS AND
      PROFIT SEEKING EXPENSES, subhead: De-
      duction, Section 162)
    Education expenses (See EDUCATION EX-
      PENSES, subhead: Deductions under Section
      162)
Section 183, deductions allowable under . . . 497
Section 212, under . . . 272
Taxes, for
    Generally . . . 559
    Real property taxes and assessments, problems
      associated with deduction of
      Buyer and seller, between . . . 562
      Section 164, under . . . 561
    Section 164, deduction under . . . 559
    Who may claim deduction . . . 560
Tax-exempt income
    Generally . . . 650
    Allocation . . . 652
    Section 265(a)(1) . . . 650
    Section 265(a)(2) . . . 651
Taxpayers' tax liability . . . 12
Vacation home . . . 518
Wash sales under Section 1091 . . . 658

DEMAND LOANS
Generally . . . 877

DEPOSITS
Generally . . . 61

DEPRECIATION
Generally . . . 324; 338
Basis and depreciation, relationship between
    . . . 335
Computing deduction . . . 332
Conventions . . . 330
Debt to depreciation, relationship of . . . 337

[References are to pages.]

[References are to pages.]

[References are to pages.]

[References are to pages.]